W9-BDV-564

Visit classzone.com and get connected

Online resources for students and parents

ClassZone resources are linked together and provide instruction, practice, and learning support.

eEdition Plus
ONLINE
This interactive version of the text encourages students to explore mathematics.

eWorkbook
Interactive practice, correlated to the text, provides support for key concepts and skills.

@HomeTutor
This interactive tutorial reinforces key skills and helps students prepare for tests.

Chapter–Based Support
State test practice, quizzes, vocabulary support, activities, and examples help students succeed.

Now it all clicks!™

CLASSZONE.COM

McDougal Littell

McDougal Littell

MATH

Course 1

Ron Larson
Laurie Boswell
Timothy D. Kanold
Lee Stiff

NEW YORK

Covers the

New York Grade 5
Performance Indicators

McDougal Littell
A DIVISION OF HOUGHTON MIFFLIN COMPANY

Evanston, Illinois • Boston • Dallas

McDougal Littell MATH

About Course 1

The focus of the early chapters in *McDougal Littell Math Course 1* is on numbers, their operations, and their algebraic representations. You will build your understanding of these concepts through a variety of models, such as base-ten pieces, rulers, and verbal models. You will also apply your skills to problem-solving situations and use estimation to check reasonableness. Topics from other math strands, such as measurement conversions, area, averages, and data displays, are introduced early in the course and then integrated and expanded upon throughout.

Later chapters in *McDougal Littell Math Course 1* include topics such as integers, functions, and probability. The number and variety of problems, ranging from basic to challenging, give you the practice you need to develop your math skills.

Every lesson in *McDougal Littell Math Course 1* has both skill practice and problem solving, including multi-step problems. These types of problems often appear on standardized tests and cover a wide variety of math topics. To help you prepare for standardized tests, *McDougal Littell Math Course 1* provides instruction and practice on standardized test questions in a variety of formats—multiple choice, short response, extended response, and so on. Technology support for course content and standardized test preparation is available at classzone.com.

ISBN-13: 978-0-618-80698-0
ISBN-10: 0-618-80698-9   123456789—DWO—09 08 07 06

Internet Web Site: http://www.mcdougallittell.com

About the Authors

Ron Larson is a professor of mathematics at Penn State University at Erie, where he has taught since receiving his Ph.D. in mathematics from the University of Colorado. Dr. Larson is well known as the author of a comprehensive program for mathematics that spans middle school, high school, and college courses. Dr. Larson's numerous professional activities keep him in constant touch with the needs of teachers and supervisors. He closely follows developments in mathematics standards and assessment.

Laurie Boswell is a mathematics teacher at The Riverside School in Lyndonville, Vermont, and has taught mathematics at all levels, elementary through college. A recipient of the Presidential Award for Excellence in Mathematics Teaching, she was also a Tandy Technology Scholar. She served on the NCTM Board of Directors (2002–2005), and she speaks frequently at regional and national conferences on topics related to instructional strategies and course content.

Timothy D. Kanold is the superintendent of Adlai E. Stevenson High School District 125 in Lincolnshire, Illinois. Dr. Kanold served as a teacher and director of mathematics for 17 years prior to becoming superintendent. He is the recipient of the Presidential Award for Excellence in Mathematics and Science Teaching, and a past president of the Council for Presidential Awardees in Mathematics. Dr. Kanold is a frequent speaker at national and international mathematics meetings.

Lee Stiff is a professor of mathematics education in the College of Education and Psychology of North Carolina State University at Raleigh and has taught mathematics at the high school and middle school levels. He served on the NCTM Board of Directors and was elected President of NCTM for the years 2000–2002. He is a recipient of the W. W. Rankin Award for Excellence in Mathematics Education presented by the North Carolina Council of Teachers of Mathematics.

Advisers and Reviewers

Curriculum Advisers and Reviewers

Donna Foley
Curriculum Specialist for Math
Chelmsford Middle School
Chelmsford, MA

Barbara Nunn
Secondary Mathematics Specialist
Broward County Schools
Fort Lauderdale, FL

Wendy Loeb
Mathematics Teacher
Twin Groves Junior High School
Buffalo Grove, IL

Tom Scott
Resource Teacher
Duval County Public Schools
Jacksonville, FL

New York Reviewers

Sharon Cichocki
Math Teacher Coordinator
Hamburg High School
Hanburg, NY

Joe Mahoney
Mathematics Teacher
Putnam Valley High School
Putnam Valley, NY

Nancy Smith
Mathematics Teacher
W. K. Doyle Middle School
Ballston Spa, NY

Heidi Christman
K–12 Administrator for Mathematics
Mohonasen Central School District
Schenectady, NY

Greg Massaroni
Mathematics Teacher
Draper Middle School
Schenectady, NY

Karin Snyder
Mathematics Teacher
Fredonia Middle School
Fredonia, NY

Amy Denault
Math Coach/Teacher
Peekskill Middle School
Peekskill, NY

Regina Newman
Mathematics Teacher
North Shore High School
Glen Head, NY

Heather Stotz
Mathematics Teacher
Alden Middle School
Alden, NY

Diane Fleming
Mathematics Teacher
Nathaniel Hawthorne Middle School
New York, NY

Scott E. Parker
Mathematics Teacher
Martha Brown Middle School
Fairport, NY

Steven Weiss
Mathematics Teacher
Roslyn High School
Roslyn Heights, NY

Ann Marie Hastings
Math Staff Developer 2–8
Felix V. Festa Middle School
West Nyack, NY

Carrie A. Peverly
6–8 Math Department Administrator
Shenendehowa Middle School
Clifton Park, NY

Patricia Winje
Mathematics Teacher
Eagle Hill Middle School
Manlius, NY

Teacher Panels

Kansas and Missouri Panel

Linda Cordes
Department Chair
Paul Robeson Middle School
Kansas City, MO

Rhonda Foote
Mathematics Department Chair
Maple Park Middle School
North Kansas City, MO

Jan Rase
Mathematics Teacher
Moreland Ridge Middle School
Blue Springs, MO

Linda Dodd
Mathematics Department Chair
Argentine Middle School
Kansas City, KS

Cas Kyle
District Math Curriculum Coordinator
Richard A. Warren Middle School
Leavenworth, KS

Dan Schoenemann
Mathematics Teacher
Raytown Middle School
Kansas City, MO

Melanie Dowell
Mathematics Teacher
Raytown South Middle School
Raytown, MO

Texas Panel

Judy Carlin
Mathematics Teacher
Brown Middle School
McAllen, TX

Judith Cody
Mathematics Teacher
Deady Middle School
Houston, TX

Lisa Hiracheta
Mathematics Teacher
Irons Junior High School
Lubbock, TX

Sally Legault
Mathematics Teacher
Garcia Middle School
Brownsville, TX

Kay Neuse
Mathematics Teacher
Wilson Middle School
Plano, TX

Louise Nutzman
Mathematics Teacher
Sugar Land Middle School
Sugar Land, TX

Clarice Orise
Mathematics Teacher
Tafolla Middle School
San Antonio, TX

Wonda Webb
Mathematics Teacher
William H. Atwell Middle School
 and Law Academy, Dallas, TX

Karen Young
Mathematics Teacher
Murchison Elementary School
Pflugerville, TX

Field Test Teachers

Kathryn Chamberlain
McCarthy Middle School
Chelmsford, MA

Sheree Daily
Canal Winchester Middle School
Canal Winchester, OH

Deborah Kebe
Canal Winchester Middle School
Canal Winchester, OH

Jill Leone
Twin Groves Junior High School
Buffalo Grove, IL

Wendy Loeb
Twin Groves Junior High School
Buffalo Grove, IL

Melissa McCarty
Canal Winchester Middle School
Canal Winchester, OH

Deb Mueth
St. Aloysius School
Springfield, IL

Gail Sigmund
Charles A. Mooney Middle School
Cleveland, OH

Teacher Reviewers

Susanne Artiñano
Bryn Mawr School
Baltimore, MD

Lisa Barnes
Bishop Spaugh Academy
Charlotte, NC

Beth Bryan
Sequoyah Middle School
Oklahoma City, OK

Jennifer Clark
Mayfield Middle School
Oklahoma City, OK

Lois Cole
Pickering Middle School
Lynn, MA

Louis Corbosiero
Pollard Middle School
Needham, MA

James Cussen
Candlewood Middle School
Dix Hills, NY

Kristen Dailey
Boardman Center Middle School
Boardman, OH

Shannon Galamore
Clay-Chalkville Middle School
Pinson, AL

Tricia Highland
Moon Area Middle School
Moon Township, PA

Myrna McNaboe
Immaculate Conception
East Aurora, NY

Angela Richardson
Sedgefield Middle School
Charlotte, NC

James Richardson
Booker T. Washington Middle School
Mobile, AL

Dianne Walker
Traverse City Central High School
Traverse City, MI

Stacey Wood
Cochrane Middle School
Charlotte, NC

New York Grade 5 Learning Standards for Mathematics

Number Sense and Operations

5.N.1	Read and write whole numbers to millions
5.N.2	Compare and order numbers to millions

5.N.3	Understand the place value structure of the base ten number system
	    10 ones = 1 ten
	    10 tens = 1 hundred
	    10 hundreds = 1 thousand
	    10 thousands = 1 ten thousand
	    10 ten thousands = 1 hundred thousand
	    10 hundred thousands = 1 million

5.N.4	Create equivalent fractions, given a fraction
5.N.5	Compare and order fractions including unlike denominators (with and without the use of a number line) *Note: Commonly used fractions such as those that might be indicated on ruler, measuring cup, etc.*
5.N.6	Understand the concept of ratio
5.N.7	Express ratios in different forms
5.N.8	Read, write, and order decimals to thousandths
5.N.9	Compare fractions using <, >, or =
5.N.10	Compare decimals using <, >, or =
5.N.11	Understand that percent means part of 100, and write percents as fractions and decimals
5.N.12	Recognize that some numbers are only divisible by one and themselves (prime) and others have multiple divisors (composite).
5.N.13	Calculate multiples of a whole number and the least common multiple of two numbers
5.N.14	Identify the factors of a given number
5.N.15	Find the common factors and the greatest common factor of two numbers
5.N.16	Use a variety of strategies to multiply three-digit by three-digit numbers *Note: Multiplication by anything greater than a three-digit multiplier/ multiplicand should be done using technology*
5.N.17	Use a variety of strategies to divide three-digit numbers by one- and two-digit numbers *Note: Division by anything greater than a two-digit divisor should be done using technology*
5.N.18	Evaluate an arithmetic expression using order of operations including multiplication, division, addition, subtraction and parentheses
5.N.19	Simplify fractions to lowest terms
5.N.20	Convert improper fractions to mixed numbers, and mixed numbers to improper fractions
5.N.21	Use a variety of strategies to add and subtract fractions with like denominators
5.N.22	Add and subtract mixed numbers with like denominators
5.N.23	Use a variety of strategies to add, subtract, multiply, and divide decimals to thousandths
5.N.24	Round numbers to the nearest hundredth and up to 10,000
5.N.25	Estimate sums and differences of fractions with like denominators
5.N.26	Estimate sums, differences, products, and quotients of decimals
5.N.27	Justify the reasonableness of answers using estimation

Algebra

5.A.1	Define and use appropriate terminology when referring to constants, variables, and algebraic expressions
5.A.2	Translate simple verbal expressions into algebraic expressions
5.A.3	Substitute assigned values into variable expressions and evaluate using order of operations
5.A.4	Solve simple one-step equations using basic whole-number facts

5.A.5	Solve and explain simple one-step equations using inverse operations involving whole numbers
5.A.6	Evaluate the perimeter formula for given input values
5.A.7	Create and explain patterns and algebraic relationships (e.g., 2,4,6,8...) algebraically: $2n$ (doubling)
5.A.8	Create algebraic or geometric patterns using concrete objects or visual drawings (e.g., rotate and shade geometric shapes)

Geometry

5.G.1	Calculate the perimeter of regular and irregular polygons
5.G.2	Identify pairs of similar triangles
5.G.3	Identify the ratio of corresponding sides of similar triangles
5.G.4	Classify quadrilaterals by properties of their angles and sides
5.G.5	Know that the sum of the interior angles of a quadrilateral is 360 degrees
5.G.6	Classify triangles by properties of their angles and sides
5.G.7	Know that the sum of the interior angles of a triangle is 180 degrees
5.G.8	Find a missing angle when given two angles of a triangle
5.G.9	Identify pairs of congruent triangles
5.G.10	Identify corresponding parts of congruent triangles
5.G.11	Identify and draw lines of symmetry of basic geometric shapes
5.G.12	Identify and plot points in the first quadrant
5.G.13	Plot points to form basic geometric shapes (identify and classify)
5.G.14	Calculate perimeter of basic geometric shapes drawn on a coordinate plane (rectangles and shapes composed of rectangles having sides with integer lengths and parallel to the axes)

Measurement

5.M.1	Use a ruler to measure to the nearest inch, 1/2, 1/4 and 1/8 inch
5.M.2	Identify customary equivalent units of length
5.M.3	Measure to the nearest centimeter
5.M.4	Identify equivalent metric units of length
5.M.5	Convert measurement within a given system
5.M.6	Determine the tool and technique to measure with an appropriate level of precision: lengths and angles
5.M.7	Calculate elapsed time in hours and minutes
5.M.8	Measure and draw angles using a protractor
5.M.9	Determine personal references for customary units of length (e.g., your pace is approximately 3 feet, your height is approximately 5 feet, etc.)
5.M.10	Determine personal references for metric units of length
5.M.11	Justify the reasonableness of estimates

Statistics and Probability

5.S.1	Collect and record data from a variety of sources (e.g., newspapers, magazines, polls, charts, and surveys)
5.S.2	Display data in a line graph to show an increase or decrease over time
5.S.3	Calculate the mean for a given set of data and use to describe a set of data
5.S.4	Formulate conclusions and make predictions from graphs
5.S.5	List the possible outcomes for a single-event experiment
5.S.6	Record experiment results using fractions/ratios
5.S.7	Create a sample space and determine the probability of a single event, given a simple experiment (e.g., rolling a number cube)

Course 1 Overview

Number and Operations

Algebra

Geometry and Measurement

Data Analysis and Probability

Problem Solving

Course 1 Content

Problem solving is integrated throughout the course with a section of problem solving exercises in every lesson. The following problem solving features also occur throughout. For examples see:

1

Number Sense and Algebraic Thinking

Getting Ready

Solving Equations, p. 38
$6t = 48$

Chapter 1 Highlights

STUDENT HELP

- Homework Help, 6, 13, 17, 23, 31, 36, 42
  At classzone.com: @HomeTutor, Online Quiz, eWorkbook, Hints and Homework
- Reading and Vocabulary, 2, 3, 11, 12, 15, 21, 29, 34, 35, 39, 47
- Notetaking, 2, 15, 21, 30, 35, 40
- Avoid Errors, 11, 16, 21, 40

★ ASSESSMENT

- Multiple Choice, 7, 8, 12, 13, 14, 17, 18, 19, 22, 23, 24, 25, 31, 32, 33, 37, 38, 42, 43, 45, 55
- Short Response, 7, 14, 19, 27, 32, 37, 38, 44, 46, 52, 54
- Extended Response, 8, 19, 25, 27, 33, 46, 55
- Writing, 7, 8, 10, 14, 18, 24, 28, 32, 38, 43
- Open-Ended, 10, 13, 24, 27, 42, 44, 46

PROBLEM SOLVING

- Real Life Examples, 4, 5, 12, 15, 16, 22, 30, 34, 36, 39, 40, 41
- Mixed Review of Problem Solving, 27, 46
- Multi-Step Problems, 5, 8, 14, 18, 22, 25, 27, 30, 33, 34, 38, 44, 46, 50
- Challenge, 8, 14, 19, 25, 26, 33, 38, 45

Measurement and Statistics

Estimating Height, p. 64

height of person × number of people

Chapter 2 Highlights

STUDENT HELP

- Homework Help, 62, 68, 74, 78, 85, 90, 95, 101
  At classzone.com: @HomeTutor, Online Quiz, eWorkbook, Hints and Homework
- Reading and Vocabulary, 58, 59, 60, 66, 72, 76, 83, 88, 89, 94, 95, 99, 106
- Notetaking, 58, 61, 66, 67, 84, 99, 100
- Avoid Errors, 67, 83, 88, 100

★ **ASSESSMENT**

- Multiple Choice, 63, 64, 65, 69, 70, 71, 73, 74, 75, 78, 79, 80, 85, 87, 91, 92, 95, 96, 101, 103, 104, 115
- Short Response, 64, 70, 71, 79, 81, 86, 92, 97, 102, 105, 115
- Extended Response, 64, 75, 81, 87, 102, 105, 112, 114
- Writing, 64, 70, 75, 79, 82, 86, 91, 96, 97, 102
- Open-Ended, 64, 71, 81, 87, 102, 103, 105

PROBLEM SOLVING

- Real Life Examples, 61, 66, 67, 73, 76, 77, 83, 84, 89, 90, 94, 95, 99, 100
- Mixed Review of Problem Solving, 81, 105
- Multi-Step Problems, 62, 65, 70, 73, 75, 79, 81, 87, 92, 97, 100, 103, 105, 115
- Challenge, 65, 71, 75, 80, 87, 92, 97, 103

Decimal Addition and Subtraction

Volcano Ages, p. 133
Order: 1.7, 0.375, 0.75, 1.32

Chapter 3 Highlights

STUDENT HELP

- Homework Help, 121, 127, 132, 139, 145, 151
  At classzone.com: @HomeTutor, Online Quiz, eWorkbook, Hints and Homework

- Reading and Vocabulary, 118, 119, 125, 126, 130, 137, 143, 148, 157

- Notetaking, 118, 119, 120, 126, 127, 131, 137, 149

- Avoid Errors, 138

★ ASSESSMENT

- Multiple Choice, 121, 122, 123, 127, 129, 130, 132, 133, 134, 140, 141, 145, 146, 147, 150, 151, 162, 164

- Short Response, 123, 129, 136, 141, 147, 153, 156, 165

- Extended Response, 136, 141, 147, 153, 156, 165

- Writing, 122, 124, 129, 133, 140, 142, 147, 152

- Open-Ended, 133, 136, 140, 145, 151, 154, 156

PROBLEM SOLVING

- Real Life Examples, 120, 125, 126, 130, 131, 138, 139, 143, 144, 149, 150

- Mixed Review of Problem Solving, 136, 156

- Multi-Step Problems, 123, 129, 134, 136, 141, 144, 147, 149, 153, 156, 162, 163

- Challenge, 123, 129, 134, 135, 141, 147, 153

Decimal Multiplication and Division

Dividing Numbers, p. 187
7 hits ÷ 23 at bats = batting average

Animated **Math**
classzone.com

Chapter 4 Highlights

STUDENT HELP

- Homework Help, 171, 177, 183, 188, 195, 200, 205, 209
  At classzone.com: @HomeTutor, Online Quiz, eWorkbook, Hints and Homework

- Reading and Vocabulary, 168, 169, 175, 176, 181, 186, 193, 198, 199, 203, 204, 207, 214

- Notetaking, 168, 171, 176, 181, 186, 193, 194, 198, 203

- Avoid Errors, 170, 176, 186, 187, 194, 208

★ ASSESSMENT

- Multiple Choice, 172, 173, 175, 177, 178, 179, 183, 185, 188, 189, 196, 197, 201, 202, 205, 206, 207, 209, 210, 220

- Short Response, 172, 179, 185, 191, 192, 196, 201, 206, 211, 213, 223

- Extended Response, 173, 185, 189, 190, 192, 202, 211, 213, 223

- Writing, 172, 179, 180, 184, 185, 190, 202, 206, 210

- Open-Ended, 172, 179, 189, 192, 213

PROBLEM SOLVING

- Real Life Examples, 170, 175, 176, 181, 183, 186, 187, 194, 199, 204, 208

- Mixed Review of Problem Solving, 192, 213

- Multi-Step Problems, 172, 179, 181, 185, 186, 187, 190, 192, 197, 202, 206, 207, 208, 210, 213

- Challenge, 173, 179, 185, 191, 197, 202, 206, 211, 212

Number Patterns and Fractions

Simplifying Fractions, p. 247

$$\frac{9 \text{ days of rain}}{30 \text{ days}} = \frac{3}{10}$$

Chapter 5 Highlights

STUDENT HELP

- Homework Help, 232, 238, 245, 252, 256, 263, 268, 273
  At classzone.com: @HomeTutor, Online Quiz, eWorkbook, Hints and Homework
- Reading and Vocabulary, 228, 230, 231, 236, 243, 250, 254, 260, 266, 271, 278
- Notetaking, 228, 230, 237, 243, 251, 271
- Avoid Errors, 244, 255, 261, 272

★ ASSESSMENT

- Multiple Choice, 232, 233, 235, 237, 238, 239, 240, 247, 248, 252, 253, 256, 257, 258, 262, 263, 264, 265, 268, 269, 270, 273, 274, 275, 287
- Short Response, 234, 239, 249, 253, 257, 264, 275, 277, 284, 286
- Extended Response, 234, 240, 249, 253, 257, 277, 287
- Writing, 235, 239, 242, 253, 258, 259, 264, 269, 275
- Open-Ended, 233, 234, 238, 247, 249, 252, 257, 258, 263, 264, 270, 273, 277

PROBLEM SOLVING

- Real Life Examples, 230, 231, 236, 237, 245, 250, 255, 260, 262, 267, 271
- Mixed Review of Problem Solving, 249, 277
- Multi-Step Problems, 234, 239, 247, 249, 253, 254, 255, 258, 262, 265, 269, 272, 274, 277
- Challenge, 235, 240, 248, 253, 258, 265, 270, 275

6

Addition and Subtraction of Fractions

Getting Ready

Adding Mixed Numbers, p. 309

$$2\frac{1}{3}\,\text{mi} + 4\frac{1}{3}\,\text{mi}$$

Chapter 6 Highlights

Multiplication and Division of Fractions

Changing Units, p. 382
$35{,}200 \text{ lbs} = x \text{ tons}$

Chapter 7 Highlights

STUDENT HELP

- Homework Help, 343, 351, 356, 364, 369, 375, 381
  At classzone.com: @HomeTutor, Online Quiz, eWorkbook, Hints and Homework
- Reading and Vocabulary, 340, 341, 348, 354, 362, 367, 373, 374, 378, 387
- Notetaking, 340, 341, 349, 362
- Avoid Errors, 350, 363, 368, 378

★ **ASSESSMENT**

- Multiple Choice, 343, 345, 351, 352, 353, 356, 357, 358, 364, 365, 366, 369, 370, 371, 375, 376, 377, 379, 381, 382, 384, 392
- Short Response, 344, 353, 357, 360, 366, 371, 372, 383, 386, 395
- Extended Response, 360, 372, 383, 386, 395
- Writing, 345, 352, 357, 358, 361, 383
- Open-Ended, 353, 360, 365, 372, 377, 386

PROBLEM SOLVING

- Real Life Examples, 342, 343, 348, 350, 355, 363, 368, 375, 379, 380
- Mixed Review of Problem Solving, 360, 386
- Multi-Step Problems, 345, 348, 353, 358, 360, 366, 368, 372, 377, 379, 383, 386, 393, 395
- Challenge, 345, 353, 358, 359, 366, 372, 377, 383

Ratio, Proportion, and Percent

Comparing Rates, p. 410

$$\frac{3000 \text{ beats}}{60 \text{ sec}} \overset{?}{=} \frac{180 \text{ beats}}{15 \text{ sec}}$$

Animated **Math**
classzone.com Activities **403, 408, 413, 414, 430, 431, 435**

Chapter 8 Highlights

STUDENT HELP

- Homework Help, 404, 409, 414, 419, 427, 431, 437
  At classzone.com: @HomeTutor, Online Quiz, eWorkbook, Hints and Homework
- Reading and Vocabulary, 400, 402, 407, 412, 417, 425, 429, 434, 436, 443
- Notetaking, 400, 412, 419, 425, 426, 431, 434, 436
- Avoid Errors, 418, 430, 435

★ ASSESSMENT

- Multiple Choice, 404, 405, 406, 409, 410, 415, 416, 420, 421, 427, 428, 432, 433, 436, 438, 439, 440, 448, 450
- Short Response, 405, 411, 416, 420, 423, 428, 433, 439, 442, 451
- Extended Response, 406, 422, 423, 442, 451
- Writing, 405, 411, 416, 421, 428, 432, 438
- Open-Ended, 411, 416, 422, 423, 427, 432, 433, 438, 442

PROBLEM SOLVING

- Real Life Examples, 402, 407, 408, 409, 413, 417, 426, 429, 430, 435, 436
- Mixed Review of Problem Solving, 423, 442
- Multi-Step Problems, 405, 409, 411, 416, 421, 423, 428, 433, 435, 436, 440, 442, 448, 449
- Challenge, 406, 411, 416, 422, 428, 433, 440

Geometric Figures

Corresponding Parts, p. 491
$m\angle A = m\angle D$

Animated Math classzone.com **Activities** 461, 465, 466, 481, 485, 495

Chapter 9 Highlights

STUDENT HELP

- Homework Help, 457, 462, 467, 473, 482, 487, 492, 496
  At classzone.com: @HomeTutor, Online Quiz, eWorkbook, Hints and Homework
- Reading and Vocabulary, 454, 455, 460, 465, 466, 471, 480, 485, 486, 490, 491, 494, 500
- Notetaking, 454, 466, 472, 480, 495
- Avoid Errors, 456, 462, 495

★ ASSESSMENT

- Multiple Choice, 457, 461, 463, 464, 467, 469, 473, 474, 475, 482, 483, 484, 487, 489, 492, 493, 496, 497, 498, 509
- Short Response, 458, 459, 464, 469, 476, 478, 484, 493, 497, 499, 506, 508
- Extended Response, 459, 469, 478, 484, 489, 499, 509
- Writing, 463, 469, 479, 484, 488, 489, 493, 498
- Open-Ended, 458, 459, 464, 474, 478, 483, 489, 493, 499

PROBLEM SOLVING

- Real Life Examples, 460, 467, 473, 482, 485
- Mixed Review of Problem Solving, 478, 499
- Multi-Step Problems, 459, 463, 467, 469, 475, 478, 484, 489, 493, 497, 499
- Challenge, 459, 464, 469, 476, 484, 489, 493, 498

Geometry and Measurement

Area of Triangles, p. 522

$\frac{1}{2}$ (base)(height) $= 16,848$

Chapter 10 Highlights

STUDENT HELP

- Homework Help, 516, 520, 527, 534, 543, 547, 552
   At classzone.com: @HomeTutor, Online Quiz, eWorkbook, Hints and Homework
- Reading and Vocabulary, 512, 514, 518, 525, 531, 532, 538, 541, 545, 550, 556, 559
- Notetaking, 512, 514, 518, 525, 531, 550
- Avoid Errors, 532, 542

★ ASSESSMENT

- Multiple Choice, 516, 517, 519, 521, 522, 526, 528, 529, 534, 537, 543, 544, 547, 549, 552, 553, 554, 567
- Short Response, 517, 522, 528, 535, 540, 544, 548, 553, 554, 558, 567
- Extended Response, 522, 536, 540, 554, 558, 564, 566
- Writing, 513, 517, 521, 523, 524, 529, 535, 544, 548, 554
- Open-Ended, 517, 522, 540, 544, 549, 558

PROBLEM SOLVING

- Real Life Examples, 515, 519, 527, 532, 546, 550, 551
- Mixed Review of Problem Solving, 540, 558
- Multi-Step Problems, 515, 517, 519, 522, 529, 532, 533, 536, 540, 544, 549, 553, 558, 566
- Challenge, 517, 522, 529, 537, 544, 549, 554, 555

Integers

Calculating Mean, p. 598

$$\text{Mean} = \frac{-6 + (-4) + (-2)}{3}$$

Chapter 11 Highlights

STUDENT HELP

- Homework Help, 575, 581, 588, 594, 599, 605, 610
  At classzone.com: @HomeTutor, Online Quiz, eWorkbook, Hints and Homework
- Reading and Vocabulary, 572, 573, 574, 579, 586, 592, 593, 597, 603, 608, 614, 617
- Notetaking, 572, 579, 580, 586, 592, 598
- Avoid Errors, 580, 598

★ ASSESSMENT

- Multiple Choice, 573, 575, 576, 577, 581, 582, 588, 589, 590, 594, 595, 596, 598, 599, 600, 601, 605, 606, 611, 613, 622, 624
- Short Response, 582, 583, 589, 591, 595, 596, 601, 607, 611, 616, 625
- Extended Response, 591, 601, 612, 616, 625
- Writing, 576, 577, 583, 589, 596, 601, 606
- Open-Ended, 576, 583, 588, 591, 596, 606, 607, 611, 616

PROBLEM SOLVING

- Real Life Examples, 573, 574, 579, 587, 593, 598
- Mixed Review of Problem Solving, 591, 616
- Multi-Step Problems, 576, 583, 587, 589, 591, 596, 601, 607, 612, 616, 622, 623, 625
- Challenge, 577, 583, 590, 596, 601, 607, 613

Equations and Functions

Evaluating Functions, p. 664

Number of riders $= 25 \times$ Number of trips

Chapter 12 Highlights

STUDENT HELP

- Homework Help, 631, 638, 642, 648, 656, 662
  At classzone.com: @HomeTutor, Online Quiz, eWorkbook, Hints and Homework

- Reading and Vocabulary, 628, 629, 633, 636, 640, 646, 649, 651, 654, 660, 669

- Notetaking, 628, 637, 641, 647, 661

- Avoid Errors, 629, 630, 637, 641, 652

★ ASSESSMENT

- Multiple Choice, 631, 638, 639, 642, 643, 644, 648, 650, 655, 657, 658, 659, 662, 663, 664, 666, 674, 675, 676

- Short Response, 632, 639, 643, 645, 649, 658, 664, 668, 678

- Extended Response, 632, 639, 645, 658, 665, 668, 678

- Writing, 632, 635, 643, 649, 558, 664

- Open-Ended, 632, 642, 645, 649, 658, 668

PROBLEM SOLVING

- Real Life Examples, 629, 630, 637, 641, 647, 651, 654, 660, 662

- Mixed Review of Problem Solving, 645, 668

- Multi-Step Problems, 632, 639, 643, 645, 649, 658, 660, 662, 664, 668

- Challenge, 632, 639, 643, 644, 650, 659, 665

Probability and Statistics

Finding Outcomes, p. 691

$$(\text{Number of sizes}) \times \left(\frac{\text{Number of items}}{\text{size}} \right)$$

Animated **Math**
classzone.com **Activities** 683, 684, 691, 696, 709, 714

Chapter 13 Highlights

STUDENT HELP
• Homework Help, 685, 693, 698, 706, 711, 716, 721   At classzone.com: @HomeTutor, Online Quiz, eWorkbook, Hints and Homework
• Reading and Vocabulary, 680, 682, 683, 684, 689, 691, 692, 696, 702, 704, 709, 714, 719, 725
• Notetaking, 680, 682, 689, 719, 720
• Avoid Errors, 683, 704, 709, 715

★ ASSESSMENT
• Multiple Choice, 684, 685, 686, 693, 695, 698, 699, 706, 708, 711, 712, 716, 721, 722, 723, 733
• Short Response, 687, 694, 699, 701, 707, 713, 723, 724, 730, 732
• Extended Response, 687, 695, 701, 707, 713, 724, 733
• Writing, 687, 695, 699, 707, 712, 713, 717, 722
• Open-Ended, 687, 694, 700, 701, 708, 716, 718, 724

PROBLEM SOLVING
• Real Life Examples, 682, 692, 696, 704, 705, 709, 715, 720
• Mixed Review of Problem Solving, 701, 724
• Multi-Step Problems, 687, 691, 695, 699, 701, 708, 712, 714, 717, 722, 724, 732, 733
• Challenge, 687, 695, 699, 700, 708, 713, 718, 723

Contents of Student Resources

McDougal Littell
MATH
Course 1

1 Number Sense and Algebraic Thinking

Before

In previous courses you've . . .

- Performed whole number operations
- Completed number fact families

Now

In Chapter 1 you'll study . . .

- 1.1 Whole number operations
- 1.2 Whole number estimation
- 1.3 Exponents
- 1.4 Order of operations
- 1.5 Variable expressions
- 1.6 Mental math equations
- 1.7 Problem solving

Why?

So you can solve real-world problems about . . .

- cheetahs, p. 7
- biking, p. 11
- weather, p. 32

Animated Math
at classzone.com

- Hitting the Target, p. 9
- Mountain Climbing Substitution Race, p. 28
- Problem Solving, p. 40

Get-Ready Games

Review Prerequisite Skills by playing *Whole Number Ride* and *Bumper Cars.*

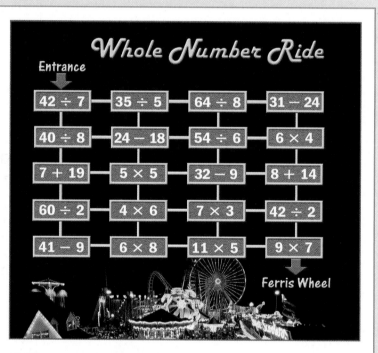

Skill Focus: Performing whole number operations

Find your way from the entrance to the Ferris wheel. Begin at the entrance. Find the sum, difference, product, or quotient. Then move one space along a path to a space that has a greater value.

Skill Focus: Number facts

Materials: One paper clip for each player

Place your paper clips on different numbers. Take turns following the directions below.

• Move one space in any direction to a new number. State one number fact using your old and new numbers. For example, if you move from 9 to 3, you could state these facts: $3 + 9$, $9 - 3$, 3×9, or $9 \div 3$.

• If the value of your number fact matches the number on which the other player is located, you may bump the player to any number except yours. Two players can never be on the same number at the same time. The first player to bump the other player 3 times wins.

Stop and Think

1. **WRITING** Suppose you wanted to move from the Ferris wheel to the entrance in *Whole Number Ride*. How would you rewrite the rules of the game?

2. **CRITICAL THINKING** List all the number facts you could make in *Bumper Cars* that would bump a player from the number 9.

1

Review Prerequisite Skills

REVIEW WORDS
- **whole number,** *p. 737*
- **place value,** *p. 737*
- **round,** *p. 739*
- **sum,** *p. 742*
- **difference,** *p. 742*
- **product,** *p. 743*
- **dividend,** *p. 744*
- **divisor,** *p. 744*
- **quotient,** *p. 744*

VOCABULARY CHECK

Copy and complete using a review word from the list at the left.

1. The result of adding two or more numbers is a __?__ .

2. The result of dividing one number by another is a __?__ .

3. The numbers 0, 1, 2, 3 … are called __?__ .

4. To __?__ means to approximate a number to a given place value.

SKILL CHECK

Identify the place value of the red digit. *(p. 737)*

5. 27	**6.** 56	**7.** 197	**8.** 813
9. 3460	**10.** 9601	**11.** 23,711	**12.** 10,872

Round the number to the place value of the red digit. *(p. 739)*

13. 16	**14.** 31	**15.** 257	**16.** 1909

Find the sum, difference, product, or quotient. *(pp. 742–744)*

17. $7 + 8$	**18.** $6 + 5$	**19.** $13 - 4$	**20.** $11 - 3$
21. 7×3	**22.** 9×5	**23.** $24 \div 4$	**24.** $16 \div 2$

@HomeTutor   Prerequisite skills practice at classzone.com

Notetaking Skills   Keeping a Notebook

In each chapter you will learn a new notetaking skill. In Chapter 1 you will apply the strategy of keeping a notebook to Example 3 on p. 30.

Useful items to put in your mathematics notebook are listed.

- vocabulary
- rules and properties
- worked-out examples
- symbols
- formulas

When you copy examples, include reminders about important details, as shown.

$$\begin{array}{r} \overset{1}{134} \\ + 49 \\ \hline 183 \end{array}$$

Remember to line up the ones, the tens, and so on.

$$\begin{array}{r} \overset{5\ 11\ 14}{\cancel{624}} \\ -259 \\ \hline 365 \end{array}$$

Remember to regroup so you can subtract.

1.1 Whole Number Operations

Before You learned basic number facts.

Now You'll add, subtract, multiply, and divide whole numbers.

Why? So you can solve problems, such as finding numbers of medals in Ex. 53.

KEY VOCABULARY
- **whole number,** *p. 737*
- **sum,** *p. 742*
- **difference,** *p. 742*
- **product,** *p. 743*
- **quotient,** *p. 744*

ACTIVITY

You can use addition skills to complete a magic square.

The numbers in each row, column, and diagonal add up to the same sum, and each consecutive number is used only once. Follow the steps below.

8	1	?
?	5	?
?	?	2

STEP 1 Which row, column, or diagonal shows three numbers? What is the sum for this magic square?

STEP 2 Which rows, columns, and diagonals have only one question mark? Copy the magic square and fill in the numbers for these marks.

STEP 3 Explain how you can complete your magic square.

Sums You find the sum of numbers with more than one digit by first lining up the ones. Then you add the ones, then the tens, then the hundreds, and so on. You may need to regroup.

EXAMPLE 1 Adding Whole Numbers

REVIEW PLACE VALUE
Need help with place value? See p. 737.

To find the sum $954 + 78$, you line up the numbers on the ones' place. Next you add the ones, then the tens, then the hundreds.

$$\begin{array}{r} \overset{1\,1}{954} \\ +\ 78 \\ \hline 1032 \end{array}$$

$\longleftarrow 4 + 8 = 12.$ Regroup the 12 ones as 1 ten and 2 ones.

$1 + 5 + 7 = 13.$ Regroup the 13 tens as 1 hundred and 3 tens.

✓ GUIDED PRACTICE for Example 1

Find the sum.

1. $95 + 37$ **2.** $44 + 87$ **3.** $406 + 95$ **4.** $614 + 196$

EXAMPLE 2 Subtracting Whole Numbers

To find the difference of 204 and 36, you line up the numbers on the ones' place. Next you subtract the ones, then the tens, and so on.

$$\begin{array}{r} {\scriptstyle 1\,9}\,{\scriptstyle 1}4 \\ 2\!\!\!/0\!\!\!/4 \\ -\ 36 \\ \hline 168 \end{array}$$

You need more ones to subtract 6, so regroup.

$204 = 100 + 90 + 14.$

EXAMPLE 3 Multiplying Whole Numbers

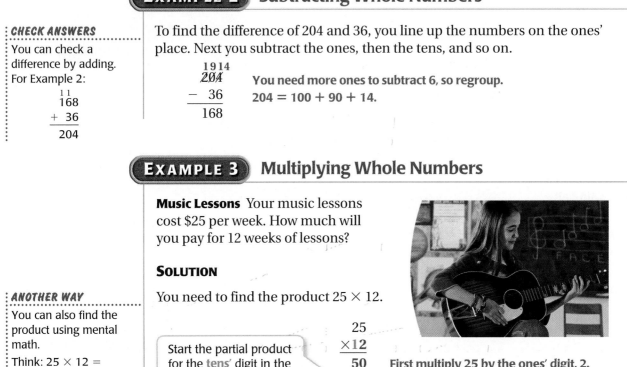

Music Lessons Your music lessons cost $25 per week. How much will you pay for 12 weeks of lessons?

SOLUTION

You need to find the product 25×12.

Start the partial product for the **tens'** digit in the **tens'** column.

$$\begin{array}{r} 25 \\ \times 12 \\ \hline 50 \\ 25 \\ \hline 300 \end{array}$$

First multiply 25 by the ones' digit, 2.
Then multiply 25 by the tens' digit, 1.
Add the partial products.

▶ **Answer** You will pay $300 for 12 weeks of music lessons.

EXAMPLE 4 Dividing Whole Numbers

To find the quotient of 592 and 7, you use long division. The dividend is 592 and the divisor is 7.

Align the 8 in the tens' column.

$$\begin{array}{r} 84\ \text{R}4 \\ 7\overline{)592} \\ 56 \\ \hline 32 \\ 28 \\ \hline 4 \end{array}$$

Divide 59 by 7, because 7 is more than 5.
Multiply: $8 \times 7 = 56$.
Subtract: $59 - 56 = 3$. Bring down the 2.
Repeat the process.
The remainder is 4.

✓ **GUIDED PRACTICE** for Examples 2, 3, and 4

Find the difference.

5. $95 - 37$ **6.** $82 - 49$ **7.** $406 - 95$ **8.** $500 - 315$

Find the product or quotient.

9. 29×31 **10.** 140×15 **11.** $721 \div 6$ **12.** $418 \div 21$

Interpreting Remainders

Framing You plan to construct wooden photo frames. You need 50 centimeters of wood for each frame. You have a total of 275 centimeters of wood. How many photo frames can you make?

SOLUTION

STEP 1 You need to divide to find the number of times 50 centimeters is contained in 275 centimeters.

$$
\begin{array}{r}
5\ \text{R}25 \\
50\overline{)275} \\
250 \\
\hline
25
\end{array}
$$

STEP 2 Interpret the remainder in the quotient 5 R25.

5 R25

5 whole photo frames   25 centimeters remain

▶ **Answer** You cannot make a complete photo frame from 25 centimeters of wood, so you need to round down to 5. You can make 5 photo frames.

EXAMPLE 6 Finding Patterns

Sports The Summer Olympics were held in 1992, 1996, 2000, and 2004. Describe the pattern. Then find the next two years in the pattern.

SOLUTION

Look to see how each number is related to the preceding number. Each year after 1992 is 4 more than the preceding year.

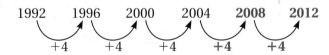

1992   1996   2000   2004   **2008**   **2012**
    +4   +4   +4   +4   +4

▶ **Answer** The next two years are 2008 and 2012.

Animated **Math**
at classzone.com

✓ **GUIDED PRACTICE**   for Examples 5 and 6

13. Banquet You are setting up tables for a banquet for 100 guests. Each table seats 8 people. What is the minimum number of tables you will need?

Describe the pattern. Then find the next two numbers.

14. 1, 4, 7, 10, __?__ , __?__   **15.** 55, 50, 45, 40, __?__ , __?__

16. 3, 6, 12, 24, __?__ , __?__   **17.** 320, 160, 80, 40, __?__ , __?__

1.1 EXERCISES

HOMEWORK KEY
★ = **STANDARDIZED TEST PRACTICE**
Exs. 44, 52, 54, 55, 58, 59, and 70

◯ = **HINTS AND HOMEWORK HELP**
for Exs. 7, 19, 25, 31, 53 at classzone.com

SKILL PRACTICE

VOCABULARY Match the word with its meaning.

1. difference   **A.** the result of adding two or more numbers

2. quotient   **B.** the result of dividing one number by another

3. sum   **C.** the result of subtracting one number from another

4. product   **D.** the result of multiplying two or more numbers

ADDING AND SUBTRACTING Find the sum or difference.

**SEE EXAMPLES
1 AND 2**
on pp. 3–4
for Exs. 5–16

5. $45 + 36$ 6. $76 - 39$ 7. $305 + 97$ 8. $802 - 19$

9. $54 - 38$ 10. $37 + 46$ 11. $281 - 72$ 12. $164 + 72$

13. $226 + 175$ 14. $812 - 125$ 15. $600 - 472$ 16. $399 + 214$

MULTIPLYING AND DIVIDING Find the product or quotient.

**SEE EXAMPLES
3 AND 4**
on p. 4
for Exs. 17–28

17. $78 \div 5$ 18. 24×18 19. 56×34 20. $58 \div 3$

21. 402×5 22. $607 \div 11$ 23. $725 \div 6$ 24. 15×40

25. $7296 \div 3$ 26. $634 \div 11$ 27. 630×25 28. 249×31

ALGEBRA *Describe* the pattern. Then find the next two numbers.

SEE EXAMPLE 6
on p. 5
for Exs. 29–34

29. 5, 10, 20, 40, __?__ , __?__   30. 54, 61, 68, 75, __?__ , __?__

31. 30, 28, 26, 24, __?__ , __?__   32. 60, 50, 40, 30, __?__ , __?__

33. 4, 12, 20, 28, __?__ , __?__   34. 2, 8, 32, 128, __?__ , __?__

REASONING Tell whether the statement is *true* or *false*. If it is false, change the underlined word to make the statement true.

35. The <u>sum</u> of 92 and 13 is 105.   36. The <u>difference</u> of 15 and 5 is 75.

37. The <u>product</u> of 26 and 3 is 23.   38. The <u>quotient</u> of 64 and 4 is 16.

39. **ERROR ANALYSIS** Describe and correct the error made at the right.

$$
\begin{array}{r}
27 \\
\times\ 15 \\
\hline
135 \\
27 \\
\hline
162
\end{array}
$$

MENTAL MATH Find the missing digit in the problem.

40.
$$
\begin{array}{r}
75 \\
+2\,? \\
\hline
102
\end{array}
$$

41.
$$
\begin{array}{r}
8\,? \\
-36 \\
\hline
45
\end{array}
$$

42.
$$
\begin{array}{r}
2\,?5 \\
\times\ \ 3 \\
\hline
645
\end{array}
$$

43.
$$
\begin{array}{r}
17 \\
?\,\overline{)102}
\end{array}
$$

44. ★ **MULTIPLE CHOICE** You have 28 boxes of apples. Each box has 26 apples. How can you find the total number of apples?

   (A) Add the number of boxes to the number of apples in a box.

   (B) Subtract the number of apples in a box from the number of boxes.

   (C) Multiply the number of boxes by the number of apples in a box.

   (D) Divide the number of boxes by the number of apples in a box.

LOOK FOR A PATTERN *Describe* the pattern. Then find the next two letters.

45. A, D, G, J, __?__, __?__   **46.** D, F, I, M, __?__, __?__   **47.** G, B, W, R, __?__, __?__

48. **CHALLENGE** Ten times the sum of 30 and 15 is the same as the sum of a number and 12. What is the number?

PROBLEM SOLVING

49. **BIOLOGY** A litter of cheetah cubs weighs about 3 pounds. One adult cheetah can weigh about 141 pounds. How many litters of cubs taken together would have the same weight as the adult cheetah?

50. **TEST SCORES** The scores on your first two math tests were 78 and 91. By how many points did your score improve?

51. **TICKET SALES** A ticket to the theater costs $26. Find the cost of 6 tickets.

52. ★ **MULTIPLE CHOICE** Two books cost $25 and $18. Find the total cost.

   (A) $7   (B) $13   (C) $33   (D) $43

SEE EXAMPLE 5
on p. 5
for Exs. 53–54

53. **AWARDS** You are putting ribbons on medals for a sports competition. Each medal needs 25 inches of ribbon. You have 192 inches of ribbon. How many medals can you complete with the ribbon you have? *Explain.*

54. ★ **SHORT RESPONSE** You are helping the science teacher plan a field trip to a natural history museum. There are 105 students signed up for the field trip. Each bus can hold 45 students. How many buses do you need? *Justify* your reasoning.

55. ★ **WRITING** You want to buy a T-shirt costing $19 and a pair of shorts costing $15. You have $45. Do you have enough money? *Explain.*

56. **LOOK FOR A PATTERN** A one-minute phone call costs 13 cents. A two-minute call costs 26 cents. A three-minute call costs 39 cents. *Describe* the pattern. If this pattern continues, what is the cost of a four-minute call? a five-minute call?

57. LOOK FOR A PATTERN In the magic square shown, the sum of the numbers in each row, column, and four-number diagonal is the same. Copy and complete the magic square.

58. ★ WRITING You find that the product of 67 and 5 is 335. How can you use addition to check if you are correct? How can you use division to check if you are correct?

59. ★ EXTENDED RESPONSE On a road trip, your family starts with a full tank of gas, which is 15 gallons. You stop at Gas Station 1 and buy 10 gallons of gas to refill the tank.

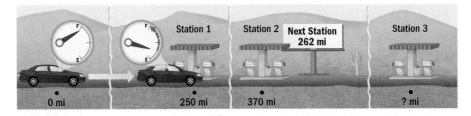

    a. Calculate How much gas did your car use to get to Gas Station 1? How many miles did your car travel for each gallon of gas?

    b. Predict Using your answer to part (a), predict how far your car can travel on one full tank before running out of gas.

    c. Apply Based on your answer to part (b), can your family reach Gas Station 3 without stopping at Gas Station 2 for more gas? *Explain.*

60. SHARING COSTS You have $14, one of your friends has $15, and two other friends each have $16. You combine your money to buy tickets for carnival rides. You pay your brother $1 for 2 tickets. The other tickets cost $2 each. If you and your friends split the tickets evenly, how many tickets do each of you get? *Justify* your answer.

61. CHALLENGE Create a 3 by 3 magic square using the whole numbers from 9 to 17 so the sum of the numbers in each row, column, and diagonal is 39.

MIXED REVIEW

Get-Ready

Prepare for
Lesson 1.2
in Exs. 62–69

Round the number to the place value of the red digit. *(p. 739)*

62. 32   **63.** 951   **64.** 988   **65.** 1384

In Exercises 66–69, find a low estimate. *(pp. 746–748)*

66. $311 - 178$ **67.** $1724 \div 8$ **68.** $4253 - 1877$ **69.** 902×343

70. ★ MULTIPLE CHOICE Which term describes the result of multiplying two or more numbers together? *(p. 743)*

    A division   **B** product   **C** quotient   **D** remainder

GOAL
Use estimation to find a sum, difference, product, or quotient close to a target number.

MATERIALS
• number cube

1.2 Hitting the Target

You can use estimation to solve problems in which you want to come close to some exact number.

EXPLORE Form a sum that is close to the target number 100.

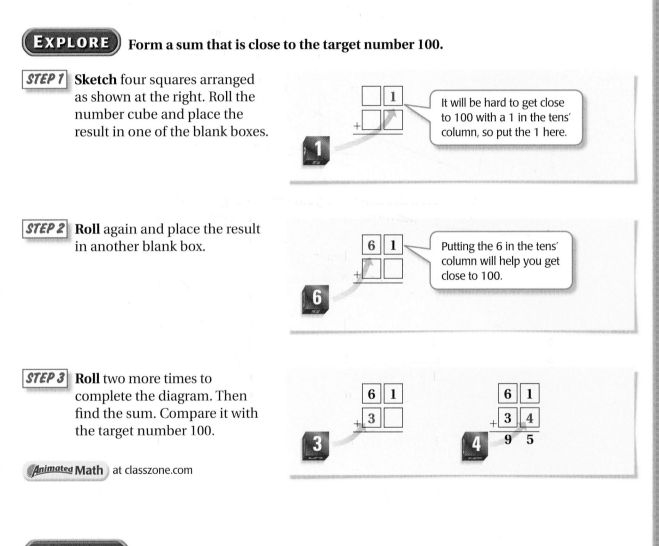

STEP 1 **Sketch** four squares arranged as shown at the right. Roll the number cube and place the result in one of the blank boxes.

It will be hard to get close to 100 with a 1 in the tens' column, so put the 1 here.

STEP 2 **Roll** again and place the result in another blank box.

Putting the 6 in the tens' column will help you get close to 100.

STEP 3 **Roll** two more times to complete the diagram. Then find the sum. Compare it with the target number 100.

Animated Math at classzone.com

PRACTICE Refer to the target game shown above.

1. Is it possible to rearrange the digits to get closer to the target sum? If so, how would you rearrange them?

2. Repeat Steps 1–3 above to form another sum that is close to the target sum. Is it possible to rearrange your digits to get closer to the target sum? If so, how would you rearrange them?

Continued on next page

INVESTIGATION

EXPLORE **Form a product that is close to the target number 200.**

STEP 1 **Copy** the diagram at the right. Think about some possible products that would get you close to 200.

□ □
× □

STEP 2 **Roll** the number cube and place the result in one of the blank boxes.

□ 2
× □

2

> Put the 2 in this box, or it will be hard to get close to 200.

STEP 3 **Roll** two more times to complete the diagram. Then find the product. Compare it with the target number 200.

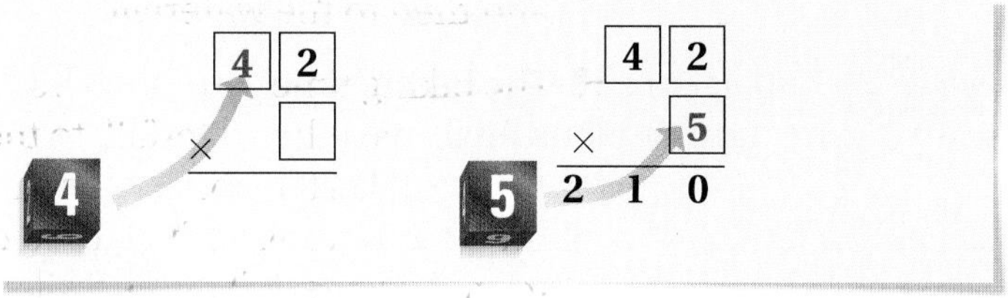

4 2
× □

4

4 2
× 5
2 1 0

5

PRACTICE **Refer to the target game shown above.**

3. Is it possible to rearrange the digits to get closer to the target product? If so, how would you rearrange them?

4. Repeat Steps 1–3 above to form another product close to the target product. Is it possible to rearrange your digits to get closer to the target product? If so, how would you rearrange them?

DRAW CONCLUSIONS

5. **REASONING** Use the diagram at the right to play "target difference." Use a target number of 50. How would you arrange the digits 5, 1, 6, and 3?

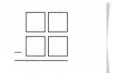

6. **WRITING** Write instructions telling how to play "target quotient" using the diagram at the right. What would be a good target number? *Explain* your answer.

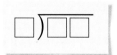

7. **OPEN-ENDED** Choose one of the target games that you played above. Tell how you used estimation to find numbers close to the target number.

1.2 Whole Number Estimation

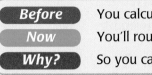

Before	You calculated using whole numbers.
Now	You'll round to estimate with whole numbers.
Why?	So you can estimate traveling time, as in Example 1.

KEY VOCABULARY
• **leading digit,** *p. 12*
• **compatible numbers,** *p. 12*

When you round to estimate a sum or difference, you should round the numbers to the same place value.

EXAMPLE 1 Estimating Sums and Differences

Biking The map shows biking times for a trail.

a. Estimate how long it takes to bike from the trailhead to the swinging bridge and then to the waterfall.

b. The biking time from the swinging bridge, past the waterfall, to the trailhead is 208 minutes. Estimate the number of minutes it takes to bike from the waterfall to the trailhead.

SOLUTION

AVOID ERRORS
Rounding numbers to different place values when adding or subtracting can cause your estimate to be less accurate.

a. Round the two times to the same place value. Then add.

$$\begin{array}{r} 28 \\ +114 \\ \hline \end{array}$$ **Round each number to the nearest ten.** → $\begin{array}{r} 30 \\ +110 \\ \hline 140 \end{array}$ **Round 28 up to 30. Round 114 down to 110.**

▸ **Answer** It takes about 140 minutes to bike from the trailhead to the swinging bridge and then to the waterfall.

b. $\begin{array}{r} 208 \\ -114 \\ \hline \end{array}$ **Round each number to the nearest hundred.** → $\begin{array}{r} 200 \\ -100 \\ \hline 100 \end{array}$ **Round 208 down to 200. Round 114 down to 100.**

▸ **Answer** It takes about 100 minutes to bike from the waterfall to the trailhead.

✓ GUIDED PRACTICE for Example 1

Estimate the sum or difference.

1. 27 + 64   **2.** 180 + 914   **3.** 91 − 49   **4.** 612 − 83

Using Leading Digits When you round to estimate a product, you should round the numbers to the place values of their *leading digits*. The **leading digit** of a whole number is the first digit at the left.

EXAMPLE 2 Estimating Products

Estimate to tell whether the given answer is reasonable.

a. $191 \times 11; 2101$

$200 \times 10 = 2000$ Round both numbers to the leading digit.

▸ **Answer** The answer is reasonable because 2000 is close to 2101.

b. $1127 \times 4; 6508$

$1000 \times 4 = 4000$ Round 1127 to its leading digit. Don't round the single digit.

▸ **Answer** The answer isn't reasonable because 4000 isn't close to 6508.

Quotients Look for **compatible numbers** when you estimate a quotient, which are numbers that will make the calculation easier.

★ EXAMPLE 3 Standardized Test Practice

Environment You are in a group of 59 volunteers who are planting 469 trees throughout a city. About how many trees will each volunteer plant if you all plant about the same number?

(A) 6   **(B)** 8   **(C)** 10   **(D)** 12

ELIMINATE CHOICES
If 59 volunteers each planted 10 trees, there would be 590 planted. So 10 is too many trees, and choices C and D can be eliminated.

READING
The symbol ≈ is read "is about equal to."

SOLUTION

The group of trees is divided among the volunteers. So use division to estimate the quotient $469 \div 59$.

$469 \div 59 \approx 469 \div 60$ Round the divisor to its leading digit.

$\approx 480 \div 60$ Replace the dividend with a number that is compatible with 60 and close to 469.

$= 8$ Divide. The quotient $469 \div 59$ is about 8.

▸ **Answer** Each volunteer will plant about 8 trees. The correct answer is B. (A) **(B)** (C) (D)

✓ GUIDED PRACTICE for Examples 2 and 3

Estimate the product or quotient.

5. 879×31 **6.** 193×4 **7.** $970 \div 4$ **8.** $213 \div 68$

1.2 EXERCISES

HOMEWORK
KEY

★ = **STANDARDIZED TEST PRACTICE**
Exs. 26, 34, 42, 43, 45, and 55

◯ = **HINTS** AND **HOMEWORK HELP**
for **Exs. 5, 9, 19, 23, 41** at classzone.com

SKILL PRACTICE

1. **VOCABULARY** Copy and complete: You should round numbers to the place values of their __?__ when rounding to estimate a product.

ESTIMATION **Estimate the sum, difference, product, or quotient.**

SEE EXAMPLE 1
on p. 11 for
Exs. 2–13, 26

2. $28 + 74$

3. $87 - 19$

4. $309 - 188$

5. $285 + 307$

6. $914 - 482$

7. $682 + 297$

8. $78 + 233$

9. $427 - 18$

10. $618 - 89$

11. $879 + 94$

12. $1129 + 403$

13. $2015 - 398$

SEE EXAMPLES 2 AND 3
on p. 12 for
Exs. 14–25

14. 38×2

15. $24 \div 5$

16. $39 \div 4$

17. 59×3

18. $702 \div 7$

19. 21×31

20. 12×89

21. $63 \div 19$

22. 123×41

23. $498 \div 11$

24. $597 \div 28$

25. 287×12

26. ★ **MULTIPLE CHOICE** For which sum or difference is 300 the best estimate?

(A) $68 + 277$ (B) $511 - 193$ (C) $214 + 39$ (D) $701 - 312$

CHECKING **Estimate to tell whether the given answer is reasonable.**

27. $9024 - 7182$; 1842

28. $1104 + 4018$; 6122

29. $2912 \div 52$; 560

30. 210×391; 82,110

31. 1982×35; 6937

32. $6104 - 3971$; 3133

33. **ERROR ANALYSIS** A student estimates the product as shown at the right. Describe and correct the error in the student's estimate.

$$\times \quad \begin{array}{l} 509 \times 86 \approx 400 \times 70 \\ \quad\quad\quad = 28{,}000 \end{array}$$

34. ★ **OPEN-ENDED MATH** Give two different products not equal to 6000 for which you could estimate that an answer of 6000 is reasonable.

CHALLENGE *Describe* the method used to estimate the sum, difference, product, or quotient. Then describe a better method and revise the estimate.

35. $19 \times 2 \approx 20 \times 0 = 0$

36. $148 + 138 \approx 100 + 100 = 200$

37. $362 - 118 \approx 400 - 100 = 300$

38. $305 \div 16 \approx 300 \div 20 = 15$

PROBLEM SOLVING

39. **GUIDED PROBLEM SOLVING** Hot dogs come in packages of 48. You buy 11 packages for a cookout. Estimate how many hot dogs you buy.

   a. What operation could you use to find the number of hot dogs?

   b. Round each number to an appropriate place value.

   c. Estimate the total number of hot dogs you buy.

SEE EXAMPLE 3
on p. 12
for Ex. 40

40. **GOLD PRICES** The McCulloch Gold Mill, a North Carolina historic site, was built in 1832. At that time, you could buy gold for $19 per ounce. Suppose gold is selling for $440 per ounce. About how many times the price in 1832 is this price?

41. **POPULATION** Colby has 1984 residents. Arletta has 1017 residents. About how many more people live in Colby than in Arletta?

42. ★ **SHORT RESPONSE** One document has a file size of 316 kilobytes and another has a file size of 1495 kilobytes. The total size of both files is about how many times the size of the smaller file? Show your steps.

43. ★ **WRITING** You want to know whether 5 hours is enough time to read a book for class. To be sure you finish, should your estimate of the number of pages you can read per hour be *high or low*? *Explain* your reasoning.

44. **MULTI-STEP PROBLEM** The map shows the direct distances, in miles, between 4 cities in Texas.

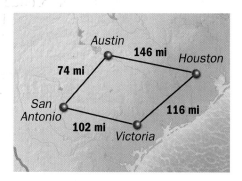

  a. Estimate the distance from San Antonio to Houston if you drive through Austin.

  b. Estimate the distance from San Antonio to Houston if you drive through Victoria.

  c. Can you use your estimates to decide which distance is shorter? *Explain* your answer. Then decide which distance is shorter.

45. ★ **SHORT RESPONSE** You are mailing 19 packages. It costs between $9 and $12 to mail each package. Estimate the total cost. *Explain* your method.

46. **CHALLENGE** Suppose you estimate the quotient 472 ÷ 58 using 500 ÷ 50 and using 420 ÷ 60. Which estimate should give a high estimate? Which estimate should give a low estimate? *Explain* your reasoning.

MIXED REVIEW

Get-Ready

Prepare for
Lesson 1.3
in Exs. 47–50

Find the product. *(p. 743)*

47. 9×9 **48.** 12×12 **49.** $6 \times 6 \times 6$ **50.** $11 \times 11 \times 11$

Find the sum or difference. *(p. 3)*

51. $429 - 52$ **52.** $3011 - 947$ **53.** $64 + 38$ **54.** $629 + 85$

55. ★ **MULTIPLE CHOICE** Two CDs cost $27 and $19. Find the total cost. *(p. 3)*

  (A) $30   **(B)** $36   **(C)** $46   **(D)** $50

1.3 Powers and Exponents

Before	You multiplied pairs of numbers.
Now	You'll find values of powers.
Why?	So you can express large distances, as in Example 1.

KEY VOCABULARY
- **factor,** *p. 15*
- **power,** *p. 15*
- **base,** *p. 15*
- **exponent,** *p. 15*

Astronomy A light-year is the distance light travels in one year. Astronomers estimate that the distance across the Virgo Spiral Galaxy is about 100,000 light-years. You can write 100,000 as a product.

$$100{,}000 = 10 \times 10 \times 10 \times 10 \times 10$$

This product has five *factors* of 10. When whole numbers other than zero are multiplied together, each number is a **factor** of the product. To write a product that has a repeated factor, you can use a **power**.

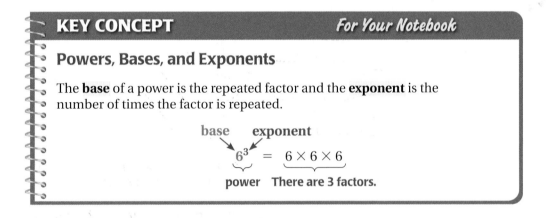

KEY CONCEPT *For Your Notebook*

Powers, Bases, and Exponents

The **base** of a power is the repeated factor and the **exponent** is the number of times the factor is repeated.

base exponent

$$6^3 = 6 \times 6 \times 6$$

power   There are 3 factors.

EXAMPLE 1 Writing a Power

Use the distance across the Virgo Spiral Galaxy given above. Write the distance as a power.

$$10 \times 10 \times 10 \times 10 \times 10 = 10^5$$

There are 5 factors.

▸ **Answer** The distance across the galaxy is about 10^5 light-years.

✓ **GUIDED PRACTICE** **for Example 1**

Write the product as a power.

1. $8 \times 8 \times 8$ **2.** $6 \times 6 \times 6 \times 6$ **3.** 20×20

4. $11 \times 11 \times 11 \times 11 \times 11$ **5.** $7 \times 7 \times 7 \times 7 \times 7$ **6.** $15 \times 15 \times 15$

Reading Powers When powers have an exponent of 2, the base is "squared." When powers have an exponent of 3, the base is "cubed."

3^2 is read "3 to the **second** power," or "3 **squared**."

4^3 is read "4 to the **third** power," or "4 **cubed**."

2^5 is read "2 to the **fifth** power."

EXAMPLE 2 Finding the Value of a Power

a. **Find the value of five cubed.**

$$5^3 = 5 \times 5 \times 5 \quad \text{Write 5 as a factor three times.}$$
$$= 125 \quad \text{Multiply.}$$

b. **Find the value of two to the sixth power.**

$$2^6 = 2 \times 2 \times 2 \times 2 \times 2 \times 2 \quad \text{Write 2 as a factor six times.}$$
$$= 64 \quad \text{Multiply.}$$

EXAMPLE 3 Powers in Real-World Problems

Telephone Calls You need to contact members of your softball league. You call 4 members in the morning. Those 4 people each call 4 more people in the afternoon. That evening, those additional people each call 4 others. How many people are called that evening?

AVOID ERRORS
Be sure to read the question carefully. In this case, you want just the number of people who were called in the evening.

SOLUTION

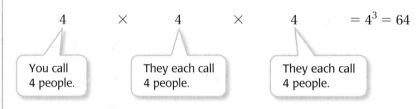

4   ×   4   ×   4 $= 4^3 = 64$

You call 4 people.   They each call 4 people.   They each call 4 people.

▶ **Answer** That evening, 64 people are called.

✓ **GUIDED PRACTICE** for Examples 2 and 3

Write the power as a product. Then find the value.

7. 11^2 **8.** 5^4 **9.** 3 to the sixth power   **10.** 6 squared

11. What If? Suppose each person in Example 3 (including you) calls 6 people instead of 4 people. How many people are called that evening?

1.3 EXERCISES

HOMEWORK KEY

★ = **STANDARDIZED TEST PRACTICE**
Exs. 12, 40, 47, 50, 52, 53, and 67

◯ = **HINTS** AND **HOMEWORK HELP**
for Exs. 9, 23, 29, 45 at classzone.com

SKILL PRACTICE

VOCABULARY Tell whether what is highlighted in red is a *power*, a *base*, or an *exponent*. Then find the value of the power.

1. 3^3 **2.** 9^2 **3.** 1^4

WRITING PRODUCTS Write the product as a power.

SEE EXAMPLE 1
on p. 15
for Exs. 4–12

4. 8×8 **5.** $12 \times 12 \times 12$ **6.** $9 \times 9 \times 9 \times 9$

7. $4 \times 4 \times 4 \times 4 \times 4$ **8.** $1 \times 1 \times 1 \times 1 \times 1 \times 1$ **9.** $3 \times 3 \times 3 \times 3$

ERROR ANALYSIS Describe and correct the error in the solution.

10.
$$4^3 = 4 \times 3$$
$$= 12$$

11.
$$5 \times 5 \times 5 \times 5 = 4^5$$
$$= 1024$$

12. ★ **MULTIPLE CHOICE** Which power is equal to $2 \times 2 \times 2$?

  A 2^2 **B** 2^3 **C** 3^2 **D** 3^3

SEE EXAMPLE 2
on p. 16
for Exs. 13–27

13. **WHICH ONE DOESN'T BELONG?** Which is *not* an example of a power?

  A. 3 cubed   **B.** 3 doubled   **C.** 5 squared   **D.** 5^4

EVALUATING POWERS Find the value of the power.

14. 7^2 **15.** 12^2 **16.** 6^3 **17.** 100^2

18. 3^5 **19.** 2^5 **20.** 10^4 **21.** 1^6

22. 4 squared   **23.** 8 squared   **24.** 2 cubed   **25.** 10 cubed

26. 2 to the seventh power   **27.** 10 to the first power

COMPARING POWERS Tell which power has a greater value.

28. 2^3 or 3^2 **29.** 4^3 or 6^2 **30.** 1^4 or 3^3 **31.** 10^3 or 13^2

32. 10^2 or 8^3 **33.** 5^3 or 1^5 **34.** 3^4 or 11^2 **35.** 2^{10} or 10^2

36. 16^2 or 8^4 **37.** 7^5 or 4^7 **38.** 24^5 or 25^5 **39.** 847^{12} or 833^{11}

Animated Math at classzone.com

40. ★ **MULTIPLE CHOICE** You stack boxes so that they are 7 boxes high, 7 boxes wide, and 7 boxes long. How many boxes do you stack?

  A 21 boxes   **B** 7^2 boxes   **C** 7^3 boxes   **D** 3^7 boxes

CHALLENGE Write each number as a power in three different ways.

41. 64   **42.** 256   **43.** 729   **44.** 15,625

SEE EXAMPLE 3
on p. 16
for Exs. 45, 48

45. CLASSROOM SEATING A large classroom has 12 rows of seats. Each row has 12 seats. How many seats are in the classroom? Write your answer as a power. Then find the value of the power.

46. ◆ **MULTIPLE REPRESENTATIONS** The figures below begin a pattern.

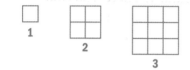

1

2

3

a. **Draw a Diagram** Copy each figure and draw the next two figures in the pattern.

b. **Make a Table** Copy and complete the table.

Small squares	1	4	9	?	?
Written as a power	1^2	2^2	?	?	?

47. ★ **WRITING** Find the value of 1^8, 1^9, and 1^{10}. What can you say about the value of any power of 1? *Explain* your reasoning.

48. SOLAR POWER A solar-powered water pump system in Desert Range, Utah, has two solar panels, each containing 6 rows of modules. Each row has 6 modules. How many modules are in each panel? Write your answer as a power. Then find the total number of modules in the system.

49. MULTI-STEP PROBLEM Your cousin, who washes high-rise windows, is assigned a section of 10 rows of windows. Each row contains 10 windows.

a. How many windows are in the section? Write your answer as a power.

b. Your cousin estimates that it takes 5 minutes to wash one window. How long will the entire job take?

c. Can your cousin complete the job in 8 hours? *Explain* your reasoning.

50. ★ **MULTIPLE CHOICE** You are enlarging a photo on your computer screen. The photo starts at 3 centimeters wide. Each time you enlarge the photo, its width is doubled. You enlarge the photo four times. What is the final width of the photo on your screen?

(A) 6 cm   (B) 12 cm   (C) 24 cm   (D) 48 cm

51. DISPLAYS A store display has 8 stacks of recycling bins. The bottom layer in each stack has 8 rows of bins, with 8 bins in each row. There are 7 identical layers on top of the bottom layer. How many bins are in the display? Write your answer as a power. Then evaluate the power.

52. ★ **SHORT RESPONSE** On Tuesday, you invited 2 friends to your party. On Wednesday, each of these friends invited 2 other friends. This pattern continued Thursday and Friday. How many people were invited on Friday? Write your answer as a power. How many people were invited in all? *Explain* your reasoning.

53. ★ **EXTENDED RESPONSE** An old legend tells of a poor man who created the game of chess. The king was so happy that he told the man he would grant him one request. The man asked for one grain of rice for the first square of the chessboard, two for the second, four for the third, and so on.

  a. Find the number of squares on the chessboard.

  b. Write as powers the numbers of grains of rice given for the fourth square and for the fifth square.

  c. Write as a power the number of grains given for the final square. *Explain* how you found your answer.

54. **CONSTRUCTION** You have 100 square tiles from a large square tabletop to make two smaller square tabletops. What dimensions can the smaller tabletops have so all the tiles are used? *Explain* your reasoning.

55. **CHALLENGE** Find a number between 1000 and 1500 that can be written as a power in three different ways.

56. **CHALLENGE** You start an e-mail chain by sending an e-mail to 3 friends. The next day, those 3 friends each forward the e-mail to 3 friends. The third day, these 9 friends each forward the e-mail to 3 friends, and so on.

  a. By the end of the fourth day, how many people besides you have seen the e-mail?

  b. After how many days has the e-mail been sent to at least 10,000 people? *Explain* how you found your answer.

MIXED REVIEW

Get-Ready

Prepare for Lesson 1.4 in Exs. 57–64

Find the sum or difference. *(p. 3)*

57. $939 + 16$ **58.** $2165 - 138$ **59.** $211 - 25$ **60.** $77 + 43$

Find the product or quotient. *(p. 3)*

61. 38×15 **62.** $306 \div 50$ **63.** $505 \div 16$ **64.** 252×12

Find the next two numbers in the pattern. *(p. 3)*

65. 20, 17, 14, 11, __?__ , __?__   **66.** 1, 2, 4, 8, __?__ , __?__

67. ★ **MULTIPLE CHOICE** For which sum or difference is 700 the best estimate? *(p. 11)*

   (A) $364 + 388$ **(B)** $212 + 559$ **(C)** $791 - 34$ **(D)** $812 - 118$

1.3 Finding Values of Powers

EXAMPLE You can use the power key 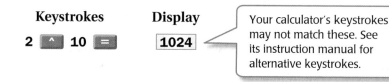 to evaluate powers.

A *byte* is a term used to describe a small unit of information stored in a computer's memory. For example, it takes one byte to store one character, such as a number or a letter. A *kilobyte* is defined as 2^{10} bytes. If a computer file is storing one kilobyte of data, how many characters can it be storing?

SOLUTION

To find the value of 2^{10}, use the power key ⌐^⌐.

Keystrokes

2 ⌐^⌐ 10 ⌐=⌐

Display

| 1024 |

Your calculator's keystrokes may not match these. See its instruction manual for alternative keystrokes.

▶ **Answer** One kilobyte is equal to 1024 bytes, so the file can be storing 1024 characters.

PRACTICE Use a calculator to find the value of the power.

1. 5^8
2. 3^{12}
3. 4^{10}
4. 7^7

5. 41^4
6. 15^3
7. 24^6
8. 96^5

9. 348^3
10. 832^2
11. 145^4
12. 627^2

13. twenty-seven cubed
14. eighty-four squared

15. nineteen to the fifth power
16. twenty-four to the third power

Recall from the example that a computer uses one byte of memory to store one character of data.

17. A megabyte is defined as 2^{20} bytes. If a disk can store one megabyte of data, how many characters can it store?

18. A gigabyte is defined as 2^{30} bytes. If a disk can store one gigabyte of data, how many characters can it store?

1.4 Order of Operations

Before   You found values using one operation.

Now   You'll evaluate expressions using the order of operations.

Why?   So you can calculate costs, such as ticket costs in Ex. 51.

KEY VOCABULARY
- numerical expression, *p. 21*
- grouping symbols, *p. 21*
- evaluate, *p. 21*
- order of operations, *p. 21*

A **numerical expression** represents a particular value. It consists of numbers and operations to be performed. An expression can also involve **grouping symbols**, as shown below.

$$7 + (11 - 2)$$

$$\frac{3 + 7}{9 - 4}$$

Operations in parentheses are done first.

A fraction bar groups the numerator separate from the denominator.

You **evaluate** an expression by finding its value. To make sure everyone gets the same result, mathematicians use the **order of operations**.

KEY CONCEPT   *For Your Notebook*

Order of Operations

1. Evaluate expressions inside grouping symbols.

2. Evaluate powers.

3. Multiply and divide from left to right.

4. Add and subtract from left to right.

EXAMPLE 1   Using the Order of Operations

AVOID ERRORS
Be sure to follow the order of operations. Don't automatically work from left to right.

a. $14 - 2 \times 5 = 14 - 10$ **First multiply 2 and 5.**

$\qquad\qquad\quad = 4$ **Then subtract 10 from 14.**

b. $11 - 8 + 2 = 3 + 2$ **First subtract 8 from 11.**

$\qquad\qquad\quad = 5$ **Then add 3 and 2.**

c. $16 + 4 \div 2 - 6 = 16 + 2 - 6$ **First divide 4 by 2.**

$\qquad\qquad\qquad\quad = 18 - 6$ **Next add 16 and 2.**

$\qquad\qquad\qquad\quad = 12$ **Then subtract 6 from 18.**

EXAMPLE 2 Powers and Grouping Symbols

a. $4 + 2^3 = 4 + 8$ First evaluate the power.

$\quad\quad\quad = 12$ Then add.

b. $(3 + 1) \times 5 = 4 \times 5$ First evaluate inside grouping symbols.

$\quad\quad\quad\quad = 20$ Then multiply.

c. $\dfrac{8 + 6}{5 - 3} = \dfrac{14}{2}$ Evaluate the numerator and the denominator.

$\quad\quad\quad = 7$ Then divide.

★ EXAMPLE 3 Standardized Test Practice

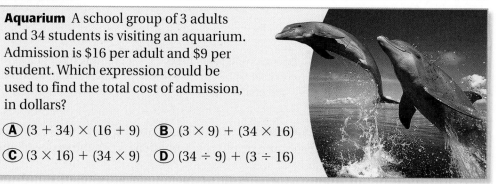

Aquarium A school group of 3 adults and 34 students is visiting an aquarium. Admission is $16 per adult and $9 per student. Which expression could be used to find the total cost of admission, in dollars?

(A) $(3 + 34) \times (16 + 9)$ **(B)** $(3 \times 9) + (34 \times 16)$

(C) $(3 \times 16) + (34 \times 9)$ **(D)** $(34 \div 9) + (3 \div 16)$

ELIMINATE CHOICES
You need to group as follows:
• number of adults with adult price
• number of students with student price.
So, choices A and B can be eliminated.

SOLUTION

STEP 1   **Multiply** to find the cost of admission for the **adults**.

$\quad\quad$ 3 adults $\times$ $16 per adult = **$48**

STEP 2   **Multiply** to find the cost of admission for the **students**.

$\quad\quad$ 34 students $\times$ $9 per student = **$306**

STEP 3   **Add** the **adult** cost and the **student** cost.

$\quad\quad$ **$48** + **$306** = $354

▶ **Answer** The total cost of admission is $(3 \times \$16) + (34 \times \$9)$, or $354. The correct answer is C. Ⓐ Ⓑ Ⓒ Ⓓ

✓ GUIDED PRACTICE   For Examples 1, 2, and 3

Evaluate the expression.

1. $9 - 7 + 3$ **2.** $8 + 4 \times 3$ **3.** $24 - 8 \times 2 + 9$ **4.** $21 - 4^2$

5. $12 \div (4 - 1)$ **6.** $4 \times (6 - 1)$ **7.** $6 + 1 \times 5^2$ **8.** $\dfrac{2 + 18}{9 - 4}$

9. What If? Suppose the adult admission price in Example 3 was $9. How would you find the new total cost of admission? Find the cost.

1.4 EXERCISES

SKILL PRACTICE

VOCABULARY **Copy and complete the statement.**

1. Parentheses and fraction bars are examples of __?__ .

2. To __?__ an expression means to find its value.

EVALUATING EXPRESSIONS **Evaluate the expression.**

SEE EXAMPLE 1
on p. 21 for
Exs. 3–11, 24

3. $9 - 8 + 5$

4. $10 - 4 \div 2$

5. $7 - 5 + 1$

6. $9 \times 2 \div 3$

7. $4 + 2 \times 3$

8. $9 - 2 \times 4$

9. $7 + 7 \div 7$

10. $10 - 4 \times 1 + 7$

11. $18 \div 3 - 1 \times 4$

SEE EXAMPLE 2
on p. 22 for
Exs. 12–23, 25

12. $6 \div 3 \times (3 + 1)$

13. $3 \times (7 - 5) + 4$

14. $(2 + 8) \times 3$

15. $8 + 4^2$

16. 5×10^3

17. $12 \div (11 - 5)$

18. $\dfrac{20}{2 + 8}$

19. $\dfrac{2^4}{13 - 5}$

20. $\dfrac{40 - 4}{6 + 3}$

21. $6 \times (7 - 5) \div 3$

22. $(6 + 4)^2 - 8$

23. $(12 \div 4)^3 + 5$

Animated Math at classzone.com

24. ★ **MULTIPLE CHOICE** What is the first step in evaluating $3 + 5 \times 8 - 7$?

(A) $3 + 5$ (B) 5×8 (C) $8 - 7$ (D) $3 + 7$

25. ★ **MULTIPLE CHOICE** Evaluate the expression $6 + 18 \div 3^2$.

(A) 8 (B) 31 (C) 42 (D) 64

*SEE EXAMPLES
1 AND 2*
on pp. 21–22
for Exs. 26–31

CHECKING REASONABLENESS **Tell whether the statement is *true* or *false*.**
If it is false, find the correct value for the expression.

26. $8 + 3 \times 4 = 44$

27. $18 - 15 \div 3 = 1$

28. $72 - 6 + 4 = 62$

29. $15 - 2 + 11 = 24$

30. $4 \times (12 + 4) = 64$

31. $3^2 \times 6 \div 3 = 18$

ESTIMATION **Match the expression with its closest estimate.**

32. $150 - 3 \times 21$ **A.** 100

33. $10 + 3 \times 29$ **B.** 20

34. $5 + 102 \div 4$ **C.** 90

35. $12 \times 8 \div 4$ **D.** 30

36. **ERROR ANALYSIS** Describe and correct the error in the solution.

$$6 + 12 \div 3 = 18 \div 3$$
$$= 6$$

CALCULATOR Use a calculator to evaluate the expression.

37. $190 - 16 \times 7 + 45$ **38.** $162 \div 18 + 14 \times 12$ **39.** $84 - 78 \div 6 + 5$

40. $378 \div 3^2 - 7 \times 4$ **41.** $11 \times 23 + 5 - 91$ **42.** $5^3 - 39 \div 3 + 2$

43. ★ **OPEN-ENDED MATH** Write an expression that should be evaluated in the order addition, evaluating a power, division, and then subtraction.

CHALLENGE Insert parentheses to make the statement true.

44. $12 + 4 \times 4 = 64$ **45.** $8 - 2 \times 6 \div 3^2 = 4$ **46.** $5 + 9 \div 4 - 1 = 8$

47. $2 \times 9 - 4 + 3 = 13$ **48.** $48 \div 8 - 2 + 6 = 4$ **49.** $3 \times 3 + 9 \div 9 = 4$

PROBLEM SOLVING

SEE EXAMPLE 3 on p. 22 for Exs. 50–55

50. GUIDED PROBLEM SOLVING A compact disc club charges $6 per CD for your first 5 CDs and $10 per CD for your next 4 CDs. If you complete the offer, how much money will you spend?

  a. What is the total cost for the first 5 CDs?

  b. What is the total cost for the next 4 CDs?

  c. How much money will you spend altogether?

51. ★ **MULTIPLE CHOICE** A group of 15 parents buys tickets to a fundraiser show and receives a group discount of $2 off the regular $25 ticket price. Which expression represents the total cost of the tickets, in dollars?

  (A) $15 \times 25 - 2$ **(B)** $15 \times (25 - 2)$ **(C)** $25 - 15 \times 2$ **(D)** $25 \times (15 - 2)$

52. ★ **MULTIPLE CHOICE** Small and large bags of grapefruit at a farmer's market cost $4 for a small bag and $6 for a large bag. You buy 5 of each size. Which procedure could you use to find the total cost?

  (A) Multiply 5 by the sum of the prices for a small and a large bag.

  (B) Add 5 to the sum of the prices for a small and a large bag.

  (C) Multiply 5 by the price of a small bag. Then add the price of a large bag.

  (D) Multiply the price of a small bag by the price of a large bag. Then add 5.

53. ★ **WRITING** You buy 3 pens for $4 each using a $30 gift card. Find the amount of money you have left on the gift card to spend. *Explain* how you found your answer.

54. THEATER CAPACITY One side of a movie theater has 20 rows with 4 seats per row. The other side has 18 rows with 6 seats per row. Find the total number of seats.

55. PURCHASING You buy 3 rolls of gift wrap for $7 each, 4 rolls of ribbon for $3 each, and 5 packs of gift cards for $4 each. What is the total cost?

56. MUSIC Your school band of 50 members is competing in a band competition. Each band member needs $10 for food. The band also rents 2 buses for $225 each. The cost of the buses will be split evenly among the band members. Write an expression for the total cost per student. Then find the total cost per student.

57. REASONING Are parentheses needed in the expression $(6 \times 7) - (5 \times 2)$? *Explain* your reasoning.

58. ★ **EXTENDED RESPONSE** You are tiling a wall with square tiles. The wall is exactly 9 tiles high and 20 tiles wide. You can use the expression 9×20 to find how many tiles you would need if there were no door in the wall.

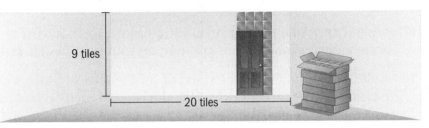

9 tiles

20 tiles

  a. Interpret Use the diagram to find the number of tiles you save by not tiling the space taken up by the door.

  b. Calculate Find how many *more* tiles you will need to cover the wall in addition to the tiles already shown on the wall.

  c. Predict Each box of tiles in the stack of boxes contains 24 tiles. Do you have enough tiles? *Explain* how you found your answer.

59. CHALLENGE Find an expression containing addition, subtraction, multiplication, and division, but no grouping symbols, whose value is the same when evaluated left to right and right to left.

60. CHALLENGE Using only the number 4 exactly three times, write an expression with a value of 2. Then repeat this exercise with values of 3, 4, and 5.

MIXED REVIEW

Get-Ready

Prepare for
Lesson 1.5
in Exs. 61–64

Write the power as a product. Then find the value. *(p. 15)*

61. 10^2 **62.** 4^4 **63.** 7^3 **64.** 1^5

Order the numbers from least to greatest. *(p. 738)*

65. 99, 19, 90, 9   **66.** 414, 41, 4, 404   **67.** 555, 50, 510, 505

68. ★ **MULTIPLE CHOICE** You pay $42 for 6 cases of fruit juice. How much does the juice cost per case? *(p. 3)*

  A $7   **B** $36   **C** $48   **D** $252

Find the sum, difference, product, or quotient. *(p. 3)*

1. $29 + 35$　　　**2.** $90 - 34$　　　**3.** 32×18　　　**4.** $124 \div 8$

Estimate the sum, difference, product, or quotient. *(p. 11)*

5. $284 - 48$　　　**6.** 147×5　　　**7.** $1004 + 678$　　　**8.** $163 \div 4$

Find the value of the power. *(p. 15)*

9. 10^2　　　**10.** 7^3　　　**11.** 2^6　　　**12.** 10^5

Evaluate the expression. *(p. 21)*

13. $9 + 7 \times 4$　　　**14.** $27 \div 3^2 + 5$　　　**15.** $3 \times (32 - 7)$　　　**16.** $48 \div 2^2 - 3$

17. PHONE CARD Your phone card has 404 minutes on it. You use 189 minutes. Estimate how many minutes your card has left. *(p. 11)*

18. DINING OUT Your family has a coupon for $1 off each value meal at a restaurant. Value meals are regularly priced at $5 each. Your family buys 5 value meals, 2 salads at $3 each, and 3 desserts at $2 each. Find the total cost of the order. *(p. 21)*

Brain Game

Solve the Riddle

Match each expression in the first column with the letter of the expression in the second column that has the same value. Then replace the number in each box with its matching letter to find the answer to the riddle.

Riddle: What goes around the world and stays in a corner?

1. $3 + 2 \div 1 - 4$　　　　　**R.** $(8 - 4 + 2) \div 2$

2. $4 - 2 + 9 \div 3$　　　　　**S.** $0 + (15 - 1) \div 2$

3. $8 \div (1 \times 2) - 2$　　　　**T.** $10 - (4 + 3) - 2$

4. $7 + (8 - 4 \times 2)$　　　　**E.** $2 \times (12 - 8) + 5$

5. $1 + 3 \times 4 - 3$　　　　　**P.** $(10 \div 5) \times 4 - 3$

　　　　　　　　　　　　　　M. $(7 - 4) \times 3 + 1$

　　　　　　　　　　　　　　A. $11 - 6 - 12 \div 4$

3		4	1	3	5	2

Lessons 1.1–1.4

1. **MULTI-STEP PROBLEM** A three month membership pass to a gym costs $15 per month. With this pass you can also use the swimming pool for $3 per visit for the first 5 visits, then $1 per visit after that.

   a. How much does the membership pass cost for the entire three month period?

   b. You visit the pool 23 times. How much do you pay to use the pool?

   c. How much money do you spend altogether in the three month period?

2. **MULTI-STEP PROBLEM** Your aunt asks you to pick all the ripe tomatoes in her vegetable garden. The garden has four rows, and each row contains four tomato plants.

   a. How many tomato plants are in the garden?

   b. It takes you about 2 minutes to pick all the tomatoes from one plant. About how long will it take to pick all the tomatoes?

   c. Your friend will be coming over a half hour after you start. Will you be done picking tomatoes by then? *Explain* how you found your answer.

3. **GRIDDED ANSWER** At Tony's pizza place, you get a free pizza for every 10 pizzas that you buy. Mr. Ridell got 60 pizzas for a party. A pizza costs $9. How many dollars did Mr. Ridell pay for the pizzas?

4. **OPEN-ENDED** Your class is purchasing sandwich rolls for a school picnic. You need 121 rolls. The rolls are sold in packages of 8 rolls and packages of 12 rolls. You do not want unopened packages left over. Give three examples of the numbers of packages you could purchase.

5. **EXTENDED RESPONSE** Use the expression $2^2 \cdot 2^3$ to solve this exercise.

   a. Rewrite the expression as a product of twos. Then rewrite this expression as a single power.

   b. How is the exponent in this new expression related to the exponents in the original expression?

   c. Write a rule for finding the product of two powers with the same base.

6. **SHORT RESPONSE** Helene and Andre both think of a number pattern. Each of them writes the first four numbers in the pattern as shown in the table below.

Helene	2	4	8	16
Andre	10	15	20	25

   a. Whose pattern is increasing faster? How can you tell?

   b. Will the next few numbers in Helene's pattern be greater than those in Andre's pattern? *Explain* your reasoning.

7. **GRIDDED ANSWER** The attendance at an indoor water park for one year is 54,976 people. Estimate the attendance for 9 weeks.

8. **GRIDDED ANSWER** This summer you worked 2 days a week and made $398 mowing lawns. Estimate how many dollars you could make if you mowed lawns 5 days a week.

INVESTIGATION
Use before Lesson 1.5

GOAL
Use symbols to represent quantities that may vary.

MATERIALS
• number cube

1.5 Representing Quantities

When an unknown number might have several different values, you can use a symbol to represent the quantity.

EXPLORE Roll a number cube to choose values for an unknown number.

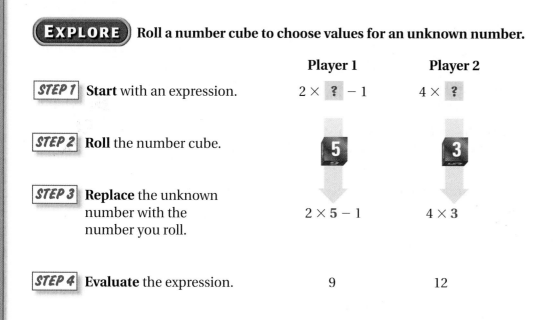

	Player 1	Player 2
STEP 1 **Start** with an expression.	$2 \times \boxed{?} - 1$	$4 \times \boxed{?}$
STEP 2 **Roll** the number cube.	**5**	**3**
STEP 3 **Replace** the unknown number with the number you roll.	$2 \times 5 - 1$	4×3
STEP 4 **Evaluate** the expression.	9	12

PRACTICE Work with a partner. Use each expression once.

1. Take turns choosing an expression below and evaluating it following Steps 2 through 4 above. Stop when each expression has been used once. Add the values from all your turns to get your score. The player with the higher score is the winner.

   A. $3 \times \boxed{?} - 2$ **B.** $3 + \boxed{?}$ **C.** $17 - 2 \times \boxed{?}$ **D.** $6 \times \boxed{?} \div 3$

   E. $60 \div \boxed{?}$ **F.** $5 \times \boxed{?} - 4$ **G.** $8 \times \boxed{?} - 5$ **H.** $180 \div (3 \times \boxed{?})$

   Animated Math at classzone.com

DRAW CONCLUSIONS

2. **REASONING** How many different values are possible for each expression above when you use a number cube to choose values for the unknown quantity? *Explain* your answer.

3. **WRITING** For any given expression, does rolling a high number like 5 always result in a greater value than rolling a low number like 2? *Explain*.

1.5 Variables and Expressions

Before You evaluated numerical expressions.

Now You'll evaluate expressions that involve variables.

Why? So you can budget costs, as for souvenirs in Ex. 51.

A **variable** is a symbol, usually a letter, that represents one or more numbers. A **variable expression** consists of numbers, variables, and the operations to be performed. To evaluate a variable expression, substitute a number for each variable and evaluate the resulting numerical expression.

To avoid confusion between the multiplication symbol $\times$ and the variable x, you should express multiplication with variables in one of the following ways.

multiplication dot	parentheses	no symbol
$3 \cdot x$	$3(x)$	$3x$

EXAMPLE 1 Evaluating Expressions

a. Evaluate $4 + t$, when $t = 2$.

$$4 + t = 4 + 2 \qquad \text{Substitute 2 for } t.$$
$$= 6 \qquad \text{Add.}$$

b. Evaluate $x \div 8$, when $x = 16$.

$$x \div 8 = 16 \div 8 \qquad \text{Substitute 16 for } x.$$
$$= 2 \qquad \text{Divide.}$$

c. Evaluate $3x$, when $x = 9$.

$$3x = 3(9) \qquad \text{Substitute 9 for } x.$$
$$= 27 \qquad \text{Multiply.}$$

✓ **GUIDED PRACTICE** for Example 1

Evaluate the expression.

1. $s + 9$, when $s = 7$
2. $13 - r$, when $r = 5$
3. $x - 3$, when $x = 8$
4. $m \div 4$, when $m = 32$
5. $6n$, when $n = 11$
6. $11 \cdot k$, when $k = 6$

EXAMPLE 2 Solve a Multi-Step Problem

Rules of Thumb The following rule of thumb is a useful way to compare the age of an adult dog with the age of a human. Call this the dog's age in "dog years."

Multiply the dog's age by 4 and then add 15.

How many dog years old is a dog that is 4 years old? 6 years old? 10 years old? To find out, evaluate the variable expression $4y + 15$ when $y = 4$, $y = 6$, and $y = 10$.

SOLUTION

STEP 1	*STEP 2*	*STEP 3*
Choose values for y (age in years).	**Substitute** for y in the expression $4y + 15$.	**Evaluate** the expression to find the age in dog years.
4	$4 \cdot 4 + 15$	31
6	$4 \cdot 6 + 15$	39
10	$4 \cdot 10 + 15$	55

▶ **Answer** A 4-year-old dog is 31 dog years old. A 6-year-old dog is 39 dog years old. A 10-year-old dog is 55 dog years old.

EXAMPLE 3 Expressions with Two Variables

xy **Evaluate the expression when $x = 8$ and $y = 2$.**

a. $x + y = 8 + 2$ Substitute 8 for *x* and 2 for *y*.

      $= 10$ Add.

b. $x - y^2 = 8 - 2^2$ Substitute 8 for *x* and 2 for *y*.

      $= 8 - 4$ Evaluate the power.

      $= 4$ Subtract.

TAKE NOTES
You may want to include Example 3(b) in your notebook as a reminder to use the order of operations when evaluating a variable expression.

✓ **GUIDED PRACTICE** for Examples 2 and 3

7. **Donations** Let b represent the number of books your friend is donating. She plans to donate 30 books to the library and split the rest evenly between two elementary schools. Use the expression $(b - 30) \div 2$ to find how many of her 150 books will go to each elementary school.

Evaluate the expression when $m = 10$ and $n = 5$.

8. mn 9. $3m \cdot n$ 10. $2n + 4$ 11. $25 - 2m$

12. $m - n$ 13. $m + 3n$ 14. $26 - n^2$ 15. $n + 9 - m$

1.5 EXERCISES

HOMEWORK KEY

★ = **STANDARDIZED TEST PRACTICE**
Exs. 36, 50, 52, 53, 55, and 70

◯ = **HINTS AND HOMEWORK HELP**
for Exs. 7, 13, 31, 53 at classzone.com

SKILL PRACTICE

1. **VOCABULARY** Identify the variable in the expression $5a - 2$.

2. **VOCABULARY** Is $10 + 7^2$ a variable expression? *Explain* why or why not.

EVALUATING EXPRESSIONS Evaluate the expression.

SEE EXAMPLE 1
on p. 29 for
Exs. 3–12, 19

3. $9 + x$, when $x = 7$

4. $t + 5$, when $t = 8$

5. $m + 8$, when $m = 3$

6. $y - 7$, when $y = 13$

7. $12 - n$, when $n = 3$

8. $w \div 4$, when $w = 20$

9. $18 \div s$, when $s = 3$

10. $r \cdot 9$, when $r = 5$

11. $6m$, when $m = 10$

12. $7n$, when $n = 9$

SEE EXAMPLE 2
on p. 30 for
Exs. 13–18

13. $16 - a^2$, when $a = 3$

14. $8 \div w + 5$, when $w = 2$

15. $5 + 12 \div u$, when $u = 6$

16. $d^3 - 8$, when $d = 5$

17. $2c - 5$, when $c = 4$

18. $13 + 4z$, when $z = 11$

ERROR ANALYSIS Describe and correct the error in evaluating the expression when $t = 2$, $x = 6$, and $y = 3$.

19.

$$3t = 3(2)$$
$$= 32$$

20.

$$6y + x = 6 \cdot 3 + 5$$
$$= 18 + 5$$
$$= 23$$

EVALUATING EXPRESSIONS Evaluate the expression when $x = 6$ and $y = 3$.

SEE EXAMPLE 3
on p. 30 for
Exs. 20–32

21. $x + y$

22. $x - y$

23. $x \div y$

24. xy

25. $4x - y$

26. $x^2 + 5y$

27. $y^3 + 2x$

28. $3y - x$

29. $2x \cdot y$

30. $y + 18 \div x$

31. $x - 18 \div y^2$

32. $y - 2 + x^2$

GEOMETRY The *perimeter* of a figure is the sum of the lengths of its sides. Find the perimeter of the triangle when $x = 3$ feet.

33.

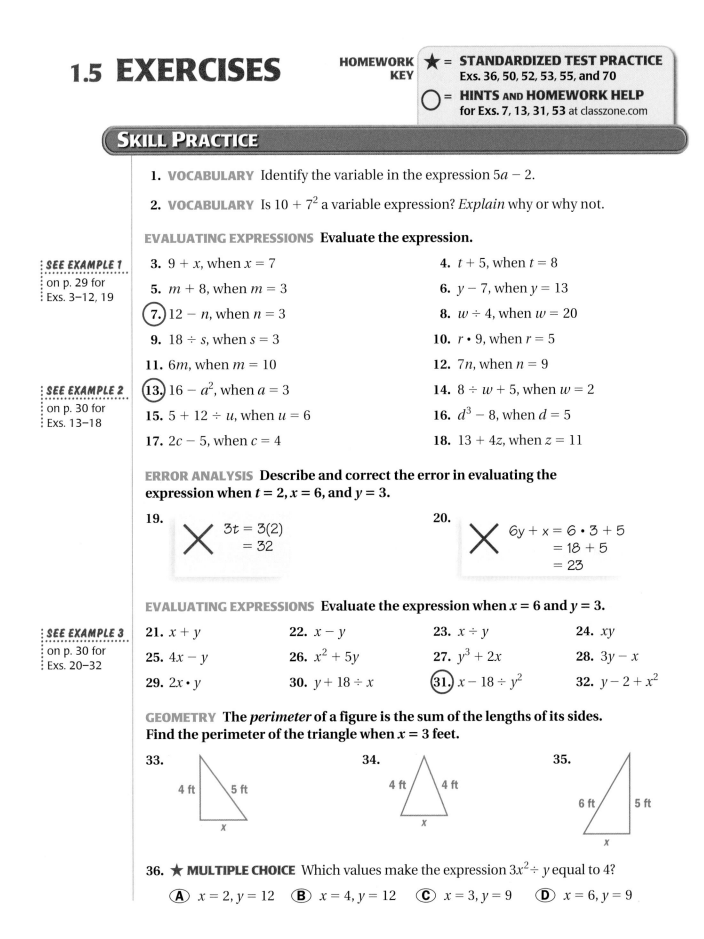

4 ft   5 ft

x

34.

4 ft   4 ft

x

35.

6 ft   5 ft

x

36. ★ **MULTIPLE CHOICE** Which values make the expression $3x^2 \div y$ equal to 4?

Ⓐ $x = 2$, $y = 12$ Ⓑ $x = 4$, $y = 12$ Ⓒ $x = 3$, $y = 9$ Ⓓ $x = 6$, $y = 9$

EVALUATING EXPRESSIONS Evaluate when $x = 6$, $y = 5$, and $z = 2$.

37. $x - z + y$ **38.** $x \div z + y$ **39.** $y \cdot (x - z)$ **40.** $x + 2y + z$

41. $x^2 + z - y$ **42.** $x + y^2 - z$ **43.** $xy - z$ **44.** $x + yz$

CHALLENGE Find a rule that relates each number and its result. Copy and complete the table, including a variable expression for the rule for n.

45.

Number	Result
1	6
2	7
3	8
4	?
n	?

46.

Number	Result
1	4
2	8
3	12
4	?
n	?

47.

Number	Result
2	5
3	7
4	9
5	?
n	?

PROBLEM SOLVING

48. COUPONS You receive a coupon for c dollars off a meal at a new restaurant. The expression $12 - c$ represents the cost of a $12 meal with a coupon. Use the expression to find how much you pay when $c = 5$.

49. WEATHER You can use the expression $n \div 5$ to estimate how many miles you are from lightning. The variable n represents the number of seconds from when you see the lightning to when you hear thunder. How far away is the lightning when $n = 20$?

50. ★ MULTIPLE CHOICE You can stuff 8 envelopes per minute. You can stuff $8x$ envelopes in x minutes. Which expression represents the number of envelopes you can stuff in 16 minutes?

   A $8 + 16$ **B** $16 - 8$ **C** $8 \cdot 16$ **D** $16 \div 8$

51. SOUVENIRS While visiting the Alamo, you buy a friend a souvenir costing c dollars. Use the expression $30 - c$ to find how much of $30 you will have left after you buy a pewter belt buckle costing $18.

52. ★ WRITING Write a series of steps explaining how to evaluate the expression $2u + 5w$ when $u = 7$ and $w = 9$. Then evaluate the expression.

SEE EXAMPLE 3 on p. 30 for Ex. 53

53. ★ SHORT RESPONSE You have some money saved, and you plan to save an additional $10 per week. You can model this situation with the expression $10w + x$, where w is the number of weeks and x is the amount of money you start with. How much money will you have after 14 weeks if you start with $32? *Explain* how you found your answer.

★ = STANDARDIZED TEST PRACTICE   ◯ = HINTS AND HOMEWORK HELP *at classzone.com*

54. MULTI-STEP PROBLEM The width of each rectangle in the quilt square is *x* inches. The perimeter of the quilt square is the sum of the lengths of its sides.

  a. Write a variable expression that represents the perimeter of the quilt square in terms of *x*.

  b. Use the expression to find the perimeter of the quilt square for *x* = 1 and for *x* = 2.

  c. Did the perimeter double when *x* doubled?

55. ★ EXTENDED RESPONSE Use the expression *r* • *t* to find how far you travel while rafting. The variable *r* is your speed, in miles per hour. The variable *t* is the number of hours traveled.

  a. Calculate How far do you travel if you raft at a speed of 4 miles per hour for 3 hours?

  b. Calculate How far would you travel if you rafted twice as fast for half the number of hours?

  c. Reasoning If your speed is doubled while your travel time is halved, will the distance you raft always be the same? *Justify* your answer.

56. CHALLENGE Write a series of four steps showing operations you can perform on the year you were born so that Step 4 results in your age. (Assume your birthday has already occurred this year.) How would you adjust your steps if your birthday has not occurred this year?

MIXED REVIEW

CHOOSE A STRATEGY Use a strategy from the list to solve the following problem. *Explain* your choice of strategy.

57. Copy the statement below. Use the symbols +, −, ×, or ÷ to make the statement true. You may use a symbol more than once.

  8 ? 2 ? 7 ? 4 = 44

Problem Solving Strategies
  ▪ Draw a Diagram *(p. 762)*
  ▪ Guess, Check, and Revise *(p. 763)*
  ▪ Work Backward *(p. 764)*
  ▪ Make a List *(p. 765)*

Get-Ready

Prepare for Lesson 1.6 in Exs. 58–69

Tell whether the statement is *true* or *false*. If it is false, find the correct answer. *(p. 740)*

58. $9 \times 5 = 54$ **59.** $7 + 4 = 11$ **60.** $10 \div 5 = 5$ **61.** $17 - 8 = 9$

62. $8 + 6 = 14$ **63.** $48 \div 8 = 7$ **64.** $13 - 5 = 6$ **65.** $3 \times 7 = 21$

66. $13 \times 0 = 13$ **67.** $6 - 0 = 0$ **68.** $16 + 0 = 16$ **69.** $1 \times 4 = 4$

70. ★ MULTIPLE CHOICE Evaluate the expression $8 + 6 \times 3$. *(p. 21)*

    (A) 10   **(B)** 17   **(C)** 26   **(D)** 42

1.6 Equations and Mental Math

Before	You evaluated numerical and variable expressions.
Now	You'll solve equations using mental math.
Why?	So you can find values, like team sizes in Ex. 52.

KEY VOCABULARY
- equation, *p. 34*
- solution, *p. 34*
- solve, *p. 35*

Camping You are going camping with friends. You fill your backpack until it weighs 13 pounds. Your friend adds another item from the list at the right, and then your backpack weighs 20 pounds. What item did your friend add?

clothes	3 pounds
food	6 pounds
sleeping bag	4 pounds
tent	7 pounds

EXAMPLE 1 Guess, Check, and Revise

To answer the question above about backpacking, you can use the problem solving strategy *guess, check, and revise*.

STEP 1
Try an item on the list.

$$13 + 4 = 17$$

This total weight is under 20 pounds.

STEP 2
Try the food, which is heavier.

$$13 + 6 = 19$$

This total weight is still one pound low.

STEP 3
Try the tent. It weighs 7 pounds.

$$13 + 7 = 20$$

This total weight equals 20 pounds.

▶ **Answer** Your friend added the tent to your backpack.

Equations You can use *equations* to answer questions like the one above. An **equation** is a mathematical sentence formed by placing an equal sign ($=$) between two expressions. A **solution** of an equation is a number that, when substituted for a variable, makes the equation true.

EXAMPLE 2 Checking a Possible Solution

Tell whether the given number is a solution of the equation.

READING

The symbol $\stackrel{?}{=}$ is read "is this equal to." The symbol $\neq$ is read "is not equal to."

a. $3y = 21; 6$

$3(6) \stackrel{?}{=} 21$

$18 \neq 21$

▶ **Answer** 6 is *not* a solution.

b. $x - 3 = 7; 10$

$10 - 3 \stackrel{?}{=} 7$

$7 = 7$

▶ **Answer** 10 is a solution.

Solving Equations To **solve** an equation, you find all the solutions of the equation. To solve simple equations using mental math, you can think of the equation as a question. Keep in mind the following rules that will help you to solve some equations that involve a 0 or a 1.

KEY CONCEPT   *For Your Notebook*

Properties of 0 and 1

Identity Property of Addition
The sum of any number and 0 is that number. $7 + 0 = 7$

Identity Property of Multiplication
The product of any number and 1 is that number. $5 \cdot 1 = 5$

Multiplication Property of 0
The product of any number and 0 is 0. $6 \cdot 0 = 0$

EXAMPLE 3   **Using Mental Math to Solve Equations**

Equation	Question	Solution	Check
a. $y - 8 = 4$	What number minus 8 equals 4?	12	$\mathbf{12} - 8 = 4$
b. $10x = 90$	10 times what number equals 90?	9	$10 \cdot \mathbf{9} = 90$
c. $n \div 4 = 7$	What number divided by 4 equals 7?	28	$\mathbf{28} \div 4 = 7$
d. $y + 2 = 2$	What number plus 2 equals 2?	0	$\mathbf{0} + 2 = 2$
e. $6 \cdot x = 6$	6 times what number equals 6?	1	$6 \cdot \mathbf{1} = 6$

Animated **Math** at classzone.com

✓ **GUIDED PRACTICE**   **for Examples 1, 2, and 3**

1. **What If?** Suppose your backpack weighed 17 pounds before your friend added an item from the list at the top of page 34, and 21 pounds afterward. What item did your friend add?

Tell whether the given number is a solution of the equation.

2. $9x = 36$; 4   3. $y - 6 = 11$; 16   4. $3x = 39$; 13

Solve the equation using mental math.

5. $x + 10 = 24$ 6. $13n = 13$ 7. $35y = 0$

8. $9x = 54$ 9. $y - 4 = 62$ 10. $18 \div n = 9$

◆ **EXAMPLE 4** Solving Problems Using Mental Math

Salmon Migration You are 100 miles upstream from the sea. Salmon migrating upstream have been spotted 41 miles from the sea. Use mental math to solve the equation $d + 41 = 100$ to find the distance d, in miles, between you and the salmon.

SOLUTION

ANOTHER WAY
You can also find the distance d using subtraction. Ask yourself what number results from $100 - 41$.

Think of the equation as a question.

Equation	d	+	41	=	100
	↓				
Question	**What number**	plus	41	equals	100?
	↓				
Solution	**59**	plus	41	equals	100.

▶ **Answer** The distance between you and the salmon is 59 miles.

Check Draw a diagram to visualize the equation.

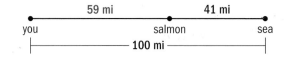

✓ **GUIDED PRACTICE** for Example 4

11. What If? Suppose the salmon in Example 4 are 29 miles from the sea, and you are 60 miles from the sea. How far are you from the salmon?

1.6 EXERCISES

HOMEWORK KEY

★ = **STANDARDIZED TEST PRACTICE**
Exs. 28, 47, 48, 49, 52, and 65

○ = **HINTS AND HOMEWORK HELP**
for Exs. 5, 15, 27, 47 at classzone.com

SKILL PRACTICE

1. **VOCABULARY** Copy and complete: The number 9 is the __?__ of the equation $x - 5 = 4$.

2. **VOCABULARY** *Describe* the difference between an equation and an expression.

CHECKING SOLUTIONS Tell whether the given number is a solution of the equation.

SEE EXAMPLE 2
on p. 34
for Exs. 3–11

3. $7 + x = 10; 3$

4. $y - 3 = 7; 4$

5. $9 - r = 8; 2$

6. $m + 2 = 6; 4$

7. $4c = 32; 9$

8. $4y = 4; 1$

9. $10s = 77; 7$

10. $30 \div x = 10; 10$

11. $72 \div r = 6; 12$

SOLVING EQUATIONS Solve the equation using mental math.

SEE EXAMPLE 3
on p. 35
for Exs. 12–28

12. $56 \div m = 7$
13. $3t = 27$
14. $8 + y = 10$
15. $s - 5 = 9$

16. $14 - z = 1$
17. $d + 3 = 11$
18. $2w = 16$
19. $27 \div r = 9$

20. $m \div 6 = 7$
21. $c + 6 = 13$
22. $23 - t = 10$
23. $22 - n = 17$

24. $x + 9 = 20$
25. $36h = 36$
26. $3f = 0$
27. $35 + a = 35$

28. ★ **MULTIPLE CHOICE** What is the solution of the equation $48 \div x = 8$?

(A) 6   (B) 8   (C) 16   (D) 40

29. **ERROR ANALYSIS** Describe and correct the error in solving the equation $5x = 5$.

$$5x = 5$$
$$5(0) = 5$$
So, 0 is the solution.

CHOOSE A METHOD Tell whether the given number is a solution of the equation. Then tell whether you used *mental math, paper and pencil, or a calculator* to get each answer.

30. $14t = 122; 8$
31. $10 + x = 25; 15$
32. $9r = 63; 7$

33. $16y + 6 = 300; 18$
34. $18 + 2k = 38; 10$
35. $3380 \div w = 13; 26$

WRITING EQUATIONS Rewrite the question as an equation and answer the question.

36. 2 times what number equals 12?
37. 8 times what number equals 24?

38. What number minus 12 equals 6?
39. 21 minus what number equals 12?

40. 121 divided by what number equals 11?
41. What number plus 39 equals 51?

CHALLENGE Tell whether the equation has *no solution, one solution,* or *many solutions.* Use examples to explain your answer.

42. $0 \cdot x = 0$
43. $x \cdot 0 = 8$
44. $1 \cdot x = x$
45. $0 + x = 0$

PROBLEM SOLVING

SEE EXAMPLE 4
on p. 36
for Exs. 46–48

46. **COMPUTER GAMES** You score 300 points playing a computer game. Your goal is to reach 500 points. Solve the equation $p + 300 = 500$ to find the number of additional points, p, you need to reach your goal.

47. ★ **MULTIPLE CHOICE** You earn $15 each time you mow your neighbor's lawn. Solve the equation $d \div 4 = 15$ to find the amount of money d, in dollars, you earn by mowing the lawn 4 times.

(A) 11   (B) 19   (C) 21   (D) 60

48. ★ **SHORT RESPONSE** Your friend makes $7 an hour baby-sitting. She earned $420 during one month. The equation $7x = 420$ represents this situation. Find the value of x. *Interpret* what it represents.

49. ★ **WRITING** The diagram at the right shows someone part way up a rock-climbing wall. *Interpret* what the equation $x + y = 40$ represents in this situation. What is the value of y when $x = 13$? when $x = 24$?

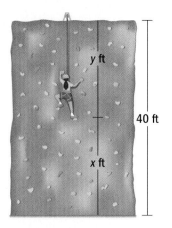

y ft

40 ft

x ft

SEE EXAMPLE 1 on p. 34 for Ex. 50

50. **GUESS, CHECK, AND REVISE** You are selling note cards and calendars for a school fundraiser. You have sold 15 items worth a total of $117. A box of note cards costs $10, and a calendar costs $7. How many of each item have you sold?

51. **REASONING** Your friend solved $2x - 3 = 45$ by thinking, "2 times what number equals 48?" *Explain* the reasoning behind this method.

52. ★ **SHORT RESPONSE** Your gym class is split up into teams of 6 students for a volleyball tournament. There are 48 students in the class. Solve the equation $6t = 48$ to find how many teams, t, you have. Suppose there are 46 students in your class. *Explain* how this could change the number of teams and the number of students on each team.

53. **CHALLENGE** Last year you spent a total of $480 racing go-carts at an indoor track twice each month. Each visit, you paid an admission fee and a $2 helmet rental fee.

  a. *Interpret* what n represents in the equation $(2 \times 12)(n + 2) = 480$.

  b. Find the value of n.

  c. You receive a helmet as a gift. How would you change the equation to represent your total cost for one year without helmet rental fees? *Justify* your answer.

54. **CHALLENGE** Suppose x is any number except 0. *Explain* why there is no number y such that $x \div 0 = y$.

MIXED REVIEW

Get-Ready Prepare for Lesson 1.7 in Exs. 55–56

55. **ATTENDANCE** You know that 717 children and 489 adults went to your school fair. Estimate the total number of people who went to the fair. *(p. 11)*

56. **PURCHASING** An online book seller charges a $2 shipping fee for each book. How much would you pay in shipping for 18 books? *(p. 3)*

Evaluate the expression when $y = 3$. *(p. 29)*

57. $15 - y$ **58.** $8 \cdot y$ **59.** $y + 9$ **60.** $18 \div y$

61. $10 \cdot y^3$ **62.** $y^2 - 4$ **63.** $5y + 6$ **64.** $25 - 7y$

65. ★ **MULTIPLE CHOICE** Which list is ordered from least to greatest? *(p. 738)*

  (A) 91, 90, 96   **(B)** 96, 91, 90   **(C)** 90, 91, 96   **(D)** 91, 96, 90

1.7 A Problem Solving Plan

Before	You used the strategy *guess, check, and revise.*
Now	You'll use a 4-step plan to solve many kinds of problems.
Why?	So you can apply strategies, such as models for expenses in Examples 1 and 2.

KEY VOCABULARY
• verbal model, *p. 39*

Shopping You went to the mall with $29 and came home with $3. Later, you made a list of how much you spent on each item, but you didn't have a receipt for the food. How much did you spend on food?

CD	$8
yo-yo	$3
sunglasses	$5
food	?

EXAMPLE 1 Understanding and Planning

To solve the problem about spending money, first make sure you understand the problem. Then make a plan for solving the problem.

READ AND UNDERSTAND

What do you know?

You started with $29. Now you have $3.

You bought a CD for $8, a yo-yo for $3, and sunglasses for $5.

What do you want to find out?

How much did you spend on food?

MAKE A PLAN

How can you relate what you know to what you want to find out?

Write a *verbal model* to describe how the values in this problem are related. A **verbal model** uses words to describe ideas and then uses math symbols to relate the words.

| Money spent on food | = | Money spent at the mall | − | Money spent on CD, yo-yo, and sunglasses |

✓ **GUIDED PRACTICE** for Example 1

Use the information at the top of the page.

1. How can you figure out how much you spent at the mall?

2. How can you figure out how much you spent for items besides food?

EXAMPLE 2 Solving and Looking Back

To solve the problem at the top of page 39 about spending money, you need to carry out the plan from Example 1 and then check the answer.

SOLVE THE PROBLEM

Write a verbal model to relate the amount of money spent on food to the dollar values you are given at the top of page 39.

Money spent on food	=	Money spent at the mall	−	Money spent on CD, yo-yo, and sunglasses
	=	$(29 - 3)$	−	$(8 + 3 + 5)$
	=	26	−	16
	=	10		

▶ **Answer** You spent $10 on food at the mall.

LOOK BACK

Make sure your answer is reasonable. Add the money you spent on each item to what you had left. This should be equal to the amount of money you had when you started.

$$8 + 3 + 5 + 10 + 3 = 29 ✔$$

 **Math** at classzone.com

AVOID ERRORS
Be sure to read the question carefully. $29 is how much you took to the mall, not how much you spent.

✓ **GUIDED PRACTICE** for Example 2

3. **What If?** In Example 2, suppose you came home with $5 instead of $3. How much did you spend on food at the mall?

4. **Studying** During one weekend, you spent 20 minutes on math homework, 30 minutes reading for English, and 2 hours 45 minutes on a social studies project. How much time did you spend on schoolwork that weekend?

KEY CONCEPT *For Your Notebook*

A Problem Solving Plan

1. **Read and Understand** Read the problem carefully. Identify the question and any important information.

2. **Make a Plan** Decide on a problem solving strategy.

3. **Solve the Problem** Use the problem solving strategy to answer the question.

4. **Look Back** Check that your answer is reasonable.

EXAMPLE 3 Draw a Diagram

Distances The mall is 12 miles from your home. Your school is one third of the way from your home to the mall. The library is one fourth of the way from the school to the mall. How far is the library from your home?

SOLUTION

REVIEW PROBLEM SOLVING STRATEGIES

Need help with problem solving strategies? See pages 761–770.

Read and Understand Your school and the library are between your home and the mall, which are 12 miles apart. You need to find the distance between your home and the library.

Make a Plan Use a diagram to show the relationships in the problem.

Solve the Problem Draw a line to show the 12 miles between your home and the mall. Then mark the locations of the school and library.

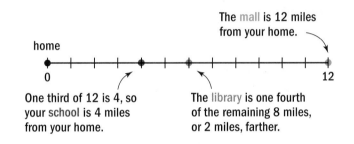

The mall is 12 miles from your home.

home

0   12

One third of 12 is 4, so your school is 4 miles from your home.

The library is one fourth of the remaining 8 miles, or 2 miles, farther.

▶ **Answer** From the diagram you can see that the library is 4 + 2 = 6 miles from your home.

Look Back The mall is 12 miles from your home and the library is between them. Because 6 is less than 12, the answer is reasonable.

✓ **GUIDED PRACTICE** for Example 3

5. **What If?** Suppose the library in Example 3 is one half of the way from the school to the mall. How far is the library from your home?

The map shows the distances between four cities.

6. How many different routes are possible from City A to City D without backtracking?

7. What is the longest route from City A to City D?

8. What is the longest route from City C to City B without backtracking?

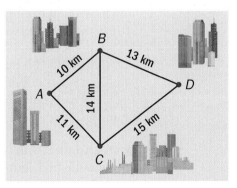

1.7 EXERCISES

HOMEWORK KEY

★ = STANDARDIZED TEST PRACTICE
Exs. 4, 5, 9, 14, 16, 21, and 44

○ = HINTS AND HOMEWORK HELP
for Exs. 3, 5, 13, 15 at classzone.com

SKILL PRACTICE

1. VOCABULARY *Explain* the four steps of the problem solving plan.

2. VOCABULARY Copy and complete: A verbal model uses __?__ to describe ideas and then uses __?__ to relate the words.

SEE EXAMPLE 1
on p. 39
for Exs. 3–4

3. **UNDERSTAND THE PROBLEM** You have saved $100 toward a DVD player that costs $160. You want to know when you will have exactly $160 if you save $20 more each month. Identify what you know and what you want to find out.

4. ★ **MULTIPLE CHOICE** Which expression represents Exercise 3?

(A) $(160 - 100) \div 20$

(B) $160 \div 20 + 100$

(C) $160 - 20 - 100$

(D) $160 - (100 \div 20)$

SEE EXAMPLE 2
on p. 40
for Exs. 5–6

5. ★ **MULTIPLE CHOICE** You went shopping with $25 and first spent $16. Then you bought a $1 pen, a $5 game, and a magazine. You calculate that you spent $3 on the magazine. Which is one way to look back and check whether your answer is reasonable?

(A) $1 + 5 + 3 \stackrel{?}{=} 25 + 16$

(B) $25 \stackrel{?}{=} 16 - (1 + 5)$

(C) $25 - (1 - 5 - 3) \stackrel{?}{=} 16$

(D) $16 + 1 + 5 + 3 \stackrel{?}{=} 25$

6. ERROR ANALYSIS Describe and correct the error in the solution at the right to the problem below.

Your school is sending 177 people on a field trip. Each bus can carry 40 people. How many buses are needed?

$$\begin{array}{r} 4\text{R}17 \\ 40\overline{)177} \\ \underline{160} \\ 17 \end{array}$$

So, 4 buses are needed.

SEE EXAMPLE 3
on p. 41
for Ex. 7

7. DRAW A DIAGRAM The mall is halfway from your house to a movie theater that is 8 miles from your house. There is a bus stop three quarters of the way from the theater to the mall. You want to find the distance from the bus stop to the mall. Draw a diagram to show the relationships.

8. MAKE A PLAN You need to measure a length of 1 centimeter by arranging the rods shown. What problem solving plan could you use?

|— 5 cm —|

|— 7 cm —|

|— 13 cm —|

9. ★ **OPEN-ENDED MATH** Give an example of a real-life problem that could be solved using the verbal model below.

Inches used = Total length − Inches remaining

10. MISSING INFORMATION A math quiz was worth 100 points. You scored a 92 on the quiz. Some problems on the quiz were worth 4 points; the rest were worth 8 points. Identify the missing information you need to find how many of each kind of problem were on the quiz.

11. CHALLENGE Find the missing number in the equation.

$$(\underline{\ ?\ } \div 11) \times 60 - 7 = 713$$

PROBLEM SOLVING

12. GUIDED PROBLEM SOLVING A conductor on a train has run out of quarters and has to make change using only dimes and nickels. What are all the ways that the conductor can make 40 cents in change?

Number of dimes	Number of nickels	Total value
?	?	?
?	?	?
?	?	?

   a. What are you trying to find?
   b. How can a table like the one above help you to solve the problem?
   c. Expand the table and solve the problem.
   d. How can you check whether your answer is reasonable?

13. DRAW A DIAGRAM A fence is 30 feet long. You need to place a fence post at both ends of the fence and every 5 feet along the fence. Draw a diagram to find how many posts you need.

14. ★ MULTIPLE CHOICE Four friends are standing in line for lunch. Tate is ahead of Anton in line. Beth is not first or last in line. Craig is directly in front of Tate. In what order from first to last are the four friends standing?

(A) Craig	**(B)** Tate	**(C)** Craig	**(D)** Craig
Beth	Craig	Tate	Tate
Tate	Beth	Beth	Anton
Anton	Anton	Anton	Beth

15. MAKE A TABLE The toll at a tollbooth is 45 cents for each car. Use a table to find all the different ways you can pay the toll exactly if you can use quarters, dimes, and nickels.

16. ★ WRITING Art museum tickets cost $12 for adults and $7 for children. Find the total cost for a group of 6 adults and 4 children to visit the museum. *Explain* how you could find the total cost by acting out the problem with a group of people using play money.

17. MAKE A LIST Alice, Omar, and Celine share the cost of buying a new video game. They want to decide the order in which they get to try the game. Make a list to show all the different possible orders.

18. NUMBER SENSE The product of two whole numbers is 24. Their sum is 10. Find the two numbers. Begin by making a list of pairs of whole numbers whose product is 24.

19. EXAMPLES AND NONEXAMPLES One puzzle in a computer game requires a number to advance. Your friends successfully used the numbers 42, 14, and 28. The numbers 63, 7, and 77 failed. Give 3 examples of numbers that will solve the puzzle and 3 numbers that will not. *Explain* how you tell if a number solves the puzzle.

20. REASONING John is second in a line of 11 people. There are 5 people between Lauren and Franco. There are 2 people between Franco and John. How many people are between Lauren and John? How many people are ahead of Lauren in line? *Explain* your reasoning.

21. ★ SHORT RESPONSE In a town of 30,000 residents, 10,000 subscribe to a morning newspaper, 6500 subscribe to an evening newspaper, and 1500 receive both.

   a. Draw a Venn diagram to represent the situation.

   b. An advertisement for the morning newspaper persuades one third of the residents who do not already subscribe to buy a newspaper subscription. How many new readers subscribe? *Explain* your steps.

READING *IN* MATH Read the passage below for Exercises 22–24.

Basketball The rules of basketball were written in 1892 and have been changing ever since. One change was the introduction of the 3-point line during the 1979–1980 professional basketball season. Before that, a player could score 1 point by making a free throw or 2 points by making a basket.

After 1979, a player could score 1 point for a free throw, 2 points for a basket made from inside the 3-point line, or 3 points for a basket made from outside the 3-point line.

3-point shot   2-point shot

Free throw

22. Calculate If Agatha made 5 free throws, 4 baskets from inside the 3-point line, and 2 baskets from outside the 3-point line, how many points did she score?

23. Open-Ended *Describe* one way a player could score 8 points in a basketball game before 1979.

24. Make a Plan Find all the different ways a player could score 8 points in a basketball game after 1979. Identify the steps in your problem solving plan.

★ = **STANDARDIZED TEST PRACTICE**   ◯ = **HINTS AND HOMEWORK HELP** *at classzone.com*

25. CHALLENGE You forgot the three-digit access code for your garage door. The first digit is 3 and the last two digits are odd numbers. How many different access codes are possible?

26. CHALLENGE Two numbers have a sum of 45. If you subtract one number from the other, the difference is 7. What are the two numbers?

MIXED REVIEW

Get-Ready

Prepare for Lesson 2.1 in Exs. 27–34

Round the number to the red digit. *(p. 739)*

27. 2562
28. 7439
29. 17,608
30. 32,098
31. 148,563
32. 552,140
33. 818,000
34. 924,375

Write the product as a power. *(p. 15)*

35. 17×17
36. $11 \times 11 \times 11$
37. $8 \times 8 \times 8 \times 8$

Evaluate the expression. *(p. 21)*

38. $12 \times 2 \div 3$
39. $8 + 2 \times 5$
40. $15 - 3 \times 4$
41. $5 + 5 \div 5$
42. $16 - 3 \times 2 + 9$
43. $80 \div 4 - 5 \times 3$

44. ★ **MULTIPLE CHOICE** Use mental math to solve $x + 32 = 96$. *(p. 34)*

(A) 44
(B) 64
(C) 66
(D) 128

QUIZ *for Lessons 1.5–1.7*

Evaluate the expression when $a = 12$ **and** $b = 3$**.** *(p. 29)*

1. $15 - a$
2. $a \div 6$
3. $7b$
4. $a + b$
5. $3 + 5b$
6. $(15 + a) \div b^2$

Tell whether the given number is a solution of the equation. *(p. 34)*

7. $m + 4 = 13$; 17
8. $31 - n = 11$; 20
9. $8 \div p = 2$; 16
10. $t \div 8 = 7$; 15
11. $6x = 36$; 6
12. $3 + y = 21$; 18

Solve the equation using mental math. *(p. 34)*

13. $r - 1 = 2$
14. $5 + z = 25$
15. $y \div 3 = 7$
16. $12m = 72$
17. $14x = 14$
18. $n - 10 = 41$
19. $3p = 0$
20. $q \div 6 = 7$

21. BASEBALL You swung the bat 15 times in a baseball game. Of those swings, 4 were strikes, 5 were foul balls, and the rest were hits. How many hits did you have? *(p. 39)*

22. FOOD You are ordering a pizza. You have a choice of three toppings: mushrooms, pepperoni, and peppers. How many different pizzas can you order if you select exactly two different toppings? *(p. 39)*

Lessons 1.5–1.7

1. **MULTI-STEP PROBLEM** The table shows the top three medal-winning countries of the 2004 Athens Summer Olympics and the number of each kind of medal won.

Country	Gold	Silver	Bronze	Total
United States	35	39	x	103
China	$x + 3$	17	14	?
Russia	27	$x - 2$	38	?

   a. Write an equation to find the number of bronze medals won by the United States.

   b. Solve the equation you wrote in part (a).

   c. Copy and complete the table using the solution from part (b).

2. **EXTENDED RESPONSE** Your family takes a road trip to visit a national park. Use the expression $r \cdot t$ to find how far you travel. The variable r is your average speed, in miles per hour. The variable t is the number of hours traveled.

   a. How far did you travel if you drove an average speed of 50 miles per hour for 11 hours?

   b. Suppose you had driven the same distance going an average speed of 55 miles per hour. Write an equation, using t, to find the hours traveled.

   c. How much time would you have saved by averaging 55 miles per hour? *Explain* your reasoning.

3. **SHORT RESPONSE** Two friends rake leaves for their neighbors. Together, they earn $12 per hour, and they divide the money at the end of the season. Each friend earns a total of $84. *Explain* why you cannot use the equation $12x = 84$ to find the number of hours x that the pair worked. Then find the number of hours that they worked.

4. **SHORT RESPONSE** Four friends are in a booth at a diner with two benches facing one another. Miguel is facing Andrea. Jordan is not beside Andrea. Who is facing Philip? *Explain* your reasoning.

5. **GRIDDED ANSWER** Your older brother plans to buy a computer for $980, plus a sales tax of $49. The first payment will be $150, and the rest of the cost will be paid in 3 equal payments. Find the amount, in dollars, of each equal payment.

6. **SHORT RESPONSE** A young woman spent $55 on tulips and daffodils. A pot of tulips costs $5, and a pot of daffodils costs $4. If she bought 12 pots, how many pots of each kind of flower did she buy? *Explain* how you found your answer.

7. **OPEN-ENDED** A rope is 36 feet long. You need to cut the rope into two pieces so that one piece is 3 times the length of the other, but you have nothing to measure with. *Describe* a problem solving plan that you could use to determine where to cut.

8. **GRIDDED ANSWER** A store sells a sweater in small, medium, and large. Each size is available in red, blue, black, and white. How many different varieties of the sweater does the store offer?

REVIEW KEY VOCABULARY

- whole number, *p. 737*
- sum, difference, *p. 742*
- product, *p. 743*
- dividend, divisor, quotient, remainder, *p. 744*
- leading digit, *p. 12*

- compatible numbers, *p. 12*
- factor, power, base, exponent, *p. 15*
- numerical expression, *p. 21*
- grouping symbols, *p. 21*
- evaluate, *p. 21*

- order of operations, *p. 21*
- variable, variable expression, *p. 29*
- equation, solution, *p. 34*
- solve, *p. 35*
- verbal model, *p. 39*

VOCABULARY EXERCISES

Copy and complete the statement.

1. You evaluate expressions with more than one operation using the __?__.

2. A(n) __?__ has a base and an exponent.

3. The __?__ in the expression $x + 2$ is x.

4. The mathematical sentence $3 \times 2 = 6$ is called a(n) __?__.

5. When a number is substituted for a variable, it is a(n) __?__ of the equation if it makes the equation true.

REVIEW EXAMPLES AND EXERCISES

1.1 Whole Number Operations

pp. 3–8

EXAMPLE

Find the sum, difference, product, or quotient.

a.
$$\begin{array}{r} \overset{1\,1}{986} \\ + 57 \\ \hline 1043 \end{array}$$

b.
$$\begin{array}{r} \overset{2\,9\,16}{\cancel{306}} \\ - 47 \\ \hline 259 \end{array}$$

c.
$$\begin{array}{r} 75 \\ \times 42 \\ \hline 150 \\ 300 \\ \hline 3150 \end{array}$$

d.
$$\begin{array}{r} 94\ \text{R1} \\ 8\overline{)753} \\ 72 \\ \hline 33 \\ 32 \\ \hline 1 \end{array}$$

EXERCISES

**SEE EXAMPLES
1, 2, 3, 4, AND 5**
on pp. 3–5
for Exs. 6–10

Find the sum, difference, product, or quotient.

6. $746 + 389$

7. $921 - 467$

8. 65×23

9. $451 \div 7$

10. **Labels** You are addressing labels to place on newsletters. Each sheet contains 15 labels. You need to make labels for 235 newsletters. How many sheets of labels will you use? *Explain.*

1.2 Whole Number Estimation

pp. 11–14

EXAMPLE

Use rounding or compatible numbers to estimate.

   a. $431 + 278 \approx 400 + 300 = 700$ **Round to the same place value.**

   b. $136 - 49 \approx 140 - 50 = 90$ **Round to the same place value.**

   c. $191 \times 43 \approx 200 \times 40 = 8000$ **Round to the leading digit.**

   d. $182 \div 21 \approx 180 \div 20 = 9$ **Round the divisor to the leading digit.**
                                                      Find a compatible dividend.

EXERCISES

Estimate the sum, difference, product, or quotient.

SEE EXAMPLES 1, 2, AND 3
on pp. 11–12
for Exs. 11–16

11. $123 + 68$ **12.** $882 - 407$ **13.** 87×13 **14.** $341 \div 52$

15. Population About how many people are living in a town with 3411 households if there are about 3 people per household?

16. Food Bank You are in a group of 26 volunteers loading 482 boxes of canned goods into a truck. About how many boxes will each volunteer load if you all carry about the same number?

1.3 Powers and Exponents

pp. 15–19

EXAMPLE

Find the value of two to the fourth power.

   $2^4 = 2 \times 2 \times 2 \times 2$ **Write 2 as a factor four times.**

        $= 16$ **Multiply.**

EXERCISES

Find the value of the power.

SEE EXAMPLES 2 AND 3
on p. 16
for Exs. 17–25

17. 5^2 **18.** 6 cubed   **19.** 1^{12} **20.** 11 squared

21. 13^1 **22.** 9^3 **23.** 50 squared   **24.** 8 cubed

25. E-mail You send an e-mail to 5 friends. The next day, each friend forwards the e-mail to 5 more friends. On the third day, each of those friends forwards the e-mail to 5 more friends. How many people are e-mailed on the third day?

1.4 Order of Operations

pp. 21–26

EXAMPLE

Evaluate the expression.

$$28 \div (9 - 5) + 3^2 = 28 \div 4 + 3^2 \qquad \text{Evaluate inside grouping symbols.}$$
$$= 28 \div 4 + 9 \qquad \text{Evaluate powers.}$$
$$= 7 + 9 \qquad \text{Multiply and divide from left to right.}$$
$$= 16 \qquad \text{Add and subtract from left to right.}$$

EXERCISES

Evaluate the expression.

**SEE EXAMPLES
1, 2, AND 3**
on pp. 21–22
for Exs. 26–35

26. $20 - 3 \times 5$

27. $2 \times (3 + 8) - 14$

28. 8×10^4

29. $\dfrac{6^2}{5 + 7}$

30. $4 \times (16 - 9) + 3$

31. $4^2 - 2^3$

32. $\dfrac{7 + 18}{5^2}$

33. $32 - 4 \times 6$

34. $15 + 5(8 - 3)$

35. Lifting Weights You are loading weights onto an exercise machine. You use four 20 pound weights, two 10 pound weights, and three 5 pound weights. What is the total weight?

1.5 Variables and Expressions

pp. 29–33

EXAMPLE

Evaluate $t + 17$ when $t = 4$.

$$t + 17 = 4 + 17 = 21 \qquad \text{Substitute 4 for } t. \text{ Then add.}$$

EXERCISES

Evaluate the expression.

**SEE EXAMPLES
1, 2, AND 3**
on pp. 29–30
for Exs. 36–43

36. $x + 4$, when $x = 6$

37. $22r$, when $r = 3$

38. $3n + 7$, when $n = 8$

Evaluate the expression when $x = 3$ and $y = 5$.

39. $9x - y$

40. $y - x$

41. $12 + xy$

42. $x + 4y$

43. Statues The total height of a statue standing on an 18 inch platform can be written as $18 + h$, where h is the statue's height in inches. What is the total height of the statue and the platform if the statue is 48 inches tall?

1.6 Equations and Mental Math

pp. 34–38

EXAMPLE

Solve $4n = 40$ using mental math.

Think of the equation as a question. Ask, "4 times what number equals 40?" The solution is 10, because $4 \cdot 10 = 40$.

EXERCISES

Solve the equation using mental math.

SEE EXAMPLES 3 AND 4
on pp. 35–36
for Exs. 44–48

44. $r - 1 = 15$ **45.** $7m = 7$ **46.** $40 \div c = 5$ **47.** $5d = 25$

48. Subway A subway train's total length is 540 feet. The train has 6 cars. Use mental math to solve the equation $6c = 540$ to find the length c, in feet, of one subway car.

1.7 A Problem Solving Plan

pp. 39–45

EXAMPLE

You pay $50 for a gym membership and $3 per visit. What is your total cost for 20 visits?

STEP 1   **Read and Understand**
You know the membership cost and the cost per visit.
You want to find the total cost for 20 visits.

STEP 2   **Make a Plan**
Find the total cost by using a verbal model.

STEP 3   **Solve the Problem**
Total cost = Membership cost + Cost for visits
$$= \$50 + \$3 \cdot 20$$
$$= \$110$$

STEP 4   **Look Back**
$\$110 - \$3 \cdot 20 = \$110 - \$60 = \$50$ ✓

EXERCISES

SEE EXAMPLES 1, 2, AND 3
on pp. 39–41
for Exs. 49–50

49. Phone Calls To make a phone call, you pay $2 for the first 20 minutes, then 10 cents per minute. What is the total cost of a 32 minute phone call?

50. Highways Exit 4 is 27 miles from Exit 1. Exit 2 is 12 miles from Exit 3 and 16 miles from Exit 4. How many miles is Exit 3 from Exit 1?

Find the sum, difference, product, or quotient.

1. $85 + 47$ **2.** $435 - 18$ **3.** 24×31

4. $527 \div 11$ **5.** $613 - 174$ **6.** 16×32

Estimate the sum, difference, product, or quotient.

7. $86 + 19$ **8.** 19×32 **9.** $272 \div 73$

10. $534 - 18$ **11.** $279 + 316$ **12.** 41×523

Find the value of the power.

13. 7^2 **14.** 4 cubed **15.** 2^5

Evaluate the expression.

16. $14 - 8 \div 2$ **17.** $4 + 3 \times 6$ **18.** $36 \div (2 + 7)$

19. $15 - 3^2$ **20.** $\dfrac{24}{4 \times 3}$ **21.** $2 + 5 \times 4 - 13$

Evaluate the variable expression when $x = 5$ and $y = 6$.

22. $9 + x$ **23.** $x - 3$ **24.** $x \cdot 7$

25. $23 - x$ **26.** $y - x$ **27.** $2x - y$

Solve the equation using mental math.

28. $9 + x = 15$ **29.** $11 - z = 7$ **30.** $10t = 90$

31. $n - 3 = 12$ **32.** $c + 21 = 21$ **33.** $y \div 5 = 35$

NUTRITION The table shows the protein content of several foods in a 160 gram serving.

34. How many more grams of protein are in one serving of roasted turkey than in one serving of fried chicken?

35. How does the amount of protein in one serving of roasted turkey compare with the amount of protein in two fish sandwiches?

Food	Protein content
fish sandwich	17 grams
roasted turkey	34 grams
tuna salad	26 grams
fried chicken	27 grams

36. ENVIRONMENT You are going to plant trees in your neighborhood. You can choose from apple, maple, oak, poplar, and spruce. Make a list to show how many ways you can choose a group of three different trees.

SHORT RESPONSE QUESTIONS

Scoring Rubric

Full Credit
- solution is complete and correct

Partial Credit
- solution is complete but errors are made, *or*
- solution is without error but incomplete

No Credit
- no solution is given, *or*
- solution makes no sense

PROBLEM

A banquet is being held for the 12 members of your basketball team. Each member needs to contribute $5 for food. Your team also plans to buy two gifts that cost $24 each, one for the coach and one for the assistant coach. The cost of the gifts will be split evenly among the team members. What is the total cost per team member? *Justify* your answer.

Below are sample solutions to the problem. Read each solution and the comments in blue to see why the sample represents full credit, partial credit, or no credit.

SAMPLE 1: Full Credit Solution

This reasoning is the key to choosing the correct problem solving plan.

The verbal model is written correctly.

You want to know the total cost per team member. You know the amount each member will pay for food, and you know the cost of the gifts and the number of members that will split this cost.

Total cost per team member	=	Contribution toward food	+	Contribution toward gifts
	=	5	+	$2 \times 24 \div 12$
	=	5	+	$48 \div 12$
	=	5	+	4
	=	9		

The answer is correct.

The total cost per team member is $9.

SAMPLE 2: Partial Credit Solution

The reasoning and process are correct.

The student interprets the cost of the gifts incorrectly.

Total cost per team member	=	Contribution toward food	+	Contribution toward gifts
	=	5	+	$24 \div 12$
	=	5	+	2
	=	7		

The answer is incorrect.

The total cost per team member is $7.

SAMPLE 3: Partial Credit Solution

The reasoning behind this calculation is unclear. ▸

$$5 + 24 \div 6 = 5 + 4$$
$$= 9$$

The answer is correct, but it is not justified. ▸

The total cost per team member is $9.

SAMPLE 4: No Credit Solution

No explanation is given. The expression is incorrect. ▸

$$(5 + 2 \times 24) \div 12 = (5 + 48) \div 12$$
$$= 53 \div 12$$
$$\approx 50 \div 10$$

The answer is incorrect. ▸

The total cost per team member is about $5.

PRACTICE   Apply the Scoring Rubric

Score the solution to the problem below as *full credit*, *partial credit*, or *no credit*. *Explain* your reasoning.

> **PROBLEM** You and three friends are throwing a party. You spend $40 for food. You buy 20 helium balloons for $2 each and 16 party favors for $1 each. The cost of the party will be split evenly among the four of you. What is the total cost per person? *Justify* your answer.

1. $$\text{Total cost per person} = \left(\text{Cost of food} + \text{Cost of balloons} + \text{Cost of favors}\right) \div 4$$
    $$= (40 + 20 \times 2 + 16 \times 1) \div 4$$
    $$= (40 + 40 + 16) \div 4$$
    $$= 96 \div 4$$
    $$= 24$$

    The total cost per person is $24.

2. Divide the cost of the party by 4.
    $$(40 + 20 \times 2 + 16) \div 4 = (60 \times 2 + 16) \div 4$$
    $$= (120 + 16) \div 4$$
    $$= 136 \div 4$$
    $$= 34$$

    The total cost per person is $34.

SHORT RESPONSE

1. Your family is driving from Ashville to Stockton using the map below, and you stop at a rest area. A sign there states that Stockton is 42 miles away. Let *m* represent the distance, in miles, from Ashville to the rest area. Write an expression for the number of miles from Ashville to Stockton. The total trip is 175 miles. Find the distance you have traveled so far. *Explain.*

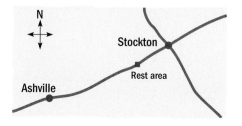

2. For a game show, 38 people were selected out of 8009 people who applied. About how many times the number of people selected was the number of people who applied? Give a high and low estimate. *Justify* your estimates.

3. Your neighbor pays you to clean her house for 2 hours after each school day for a week. After 5 days she paid you $40. The equation $5x = 40$ models this situation. What does the variable *x* represent in this equation? How much money do you earn per hour? per day? *Explain.*

4. The sixth grade is planning a field trip to a historical museum. Each bus can hold 48 people. Including parents and teachers, there are 185 people going on the trip. How many buses are needed? What is the least number of people that could ride on a single bus? *Explain.*

5. Steve, Joe, and Mai are golfing. Steve's ball is 150 yards away from the hole. Joe's ball is halfway between Steve's ball and the hole. Mai's ball is one third of the way between Joe's ball and the hole. Find the distance between Steve's ball and Mai's ball. *Explain* your reasoning.

6. There are 12 granola bars in a package. How many packages do you need to buy to give 2 granola bars to all 21 people in your class? Your friend says you need twice as many packages to give 4 granola bars to each person. Do you agree? *Explain.*

7. You can unload 6 boxes from a truck each minute. The expression $6x$ represents the number of boxes you can unload in *x* minutes. Find the number of boxes you can unload in 12 minutes. *Explain* how you used the expression to find your answer.

8. Damian is the second oldest of 5 friends. Layla is younger than Damian but older than Chris. Maria is the oldest. Scott is older than Layla. Order the friends from youngest to oldest. *Explain* how you know where to place Scott in the order.

9. Mark paid $70 for a shirt and two pairs of the same style of jeans. The shirt cost $18. What was the price of one pair of jeans? *Explain* how you found your answer.

10. An auditorium is divided into two sections. The first section contains 22 rows, and each row has 45 seats. The second section contains 18 rows, and each row has 34 seats. How many seats are in the auditorium? *Justify* your answer.

11. A cookbook has the guidelines shown for cooking slices of bacon in a microwave. For how long should 10 slices of bacon be cooked? *Explain.*

Slices	Cooking time
2	2 min
4	3 min 30 sec
6	5 min
8	6 min 30 sec

12. The student council treasurer tells 5 people about the upcoming school fundraiser. These 5 people each tell 5 more people. These additional people each tell 5 others. How many people were told about the fundraiser? *Explain* your reasoning.

MULTIPLE CHOICE

13. The attendance at a water park for a weekend is shown. What is the best estimate of the total attendance?

Day	Attendance
Friday	461
Saturday	925
Sunday	879

  Ⓐ 2100 people   **Ⓑ** 2200 people

  Ⓒ 2300 people   **Ⓓ** 2400 people

14. Marissa is putting decks of 52 cards into stacks of 5 cards each. How many decks does she need to have 4 cards left over?

  Ⓐ 1 deck   **Ⓑ** 2 decks

  Ⓒ 10 decks   **Ⓓ** 13 decks

15. A theater can hold 450 people. During one performance, an usher counts 17 empty seats. During another performance, an usher counts 12 empty seats. How many total seats are occupied for the two shows?

  Ⓐ 842 seats   **Ⓑ** 866 seats

  Ⓒ 871 seats   **Ⓓ** 876 seats

GRIDDED ANSWER

16. You have $25 and pay $8 to play laser tag. You can use the equation $x + 8 = 25$ to find the number of dollars, x, you have left after playing laser tag. What is the difference, in dollars, between the amount you have left and the amount you paid for laser tag?

17. Sarah buys movie tickets for 2 adults and 3 children for a total of $34. Each adult's ticket costs $8. What is the cost, in dollars, of one child's ticket?

18. During a basketball practice, a coach tells the team that the ball must be passed among three different players before anyone can shoot. As shown below, Amy has the ball. In how many different ways can the ball be passed from Amy to two other teammates?

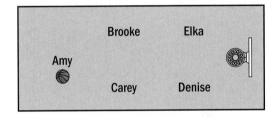

EXTENDED RESPONSE

19. At a restaurant, you can choose from four omelet fillings: cheese, peppers, tomatoes, and mushrooms. How many different omelets can you choose with no filling? with one filling? with two fillings? How many different omelets can you choose with anywhere from zero to four fillings? *Explain* how you got your answer.

20. The floor in the diagram is being tiled using the square pattern of tiles shown. An expression for the area of one green tile in the pattern is 2^2. An expression for the area of one purple tile is 2×4.

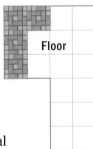

Floor

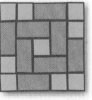

Square pattern of tiles

  a. Write and evaluate an expression for the area of one square pattern of tiles. *Explain* how you found your answer.

  b. Write and evaluate an expression that represents the total area of the floor. *Explain* how you found your answer.

  c. Find the difference between the area of the floor that will be covered by the purple tiles and the area that will be covered by the green tiles.

2 Measurement and Statistics

Review Prerequisite Skills by playing *Desert Math*.

Skill Focus: Interpreting data displays

DESERT MATH

HOW TO PLAY

 USE the data displays to answer each question. Then match each answer with a value and a letter from the table.

Match your Answer	
5 **A**	8 **N**
180,000 **Z**	200,000 **M**
120,000 **V**	50 **U**
86 **M**	36 **T**
160,000 **X**	120 **C**

• What is the average temperature in July in Saguaro National Park?

• Estimate the difference between the average July and January temperatures.

• What is the approximate area of the Sonoran Desert?

• The Chihuahuan Desert is about how many times as large as the Mojave Desert?

 FIND the least and greatest values among your answers. The letters associated with these values spell a two letter abbreviation for a state known for its beautiful deserts.

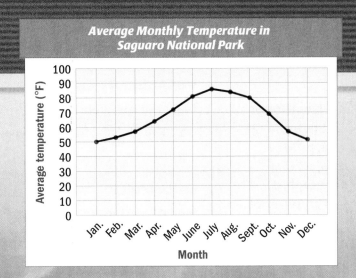

Average Monthly Temperature in Saguaro National Park

Average temperature (°F)

Month

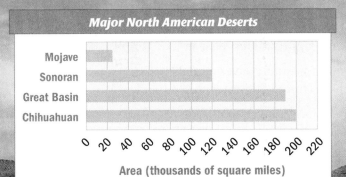

Major North American Deserts

Mojave
Sonoran
Great Basin
Chihuahuan

Area (thousands of square miles)

Stop and Think

1. **WRITING** What type of data display is used for the area data? Explain how you could use a pictograph for the area data.

2. **CRITICAL THINKING** Describe any patterns you see in the temperature graph. How might a graph showing the average monthly temperatures in the region where you live look different from this graph?

Review Prerequisite Skills

VOCABULARY CHECK

REVIEW WORDS
- **perimeter,** *p. 755*
- **area,** *p. 755*
- **data,** *p. 757*
- **bar graph,** *p. 757*
- **line graph,** *p. 758*

Copy and complete using a review word from the list at the left.

1. The __?__ of a figure is measured in square units.

2. In a __?__, you connect the data points with line segments.

SKILL CHECK

Find the perimeter of a triangle with the given side lengths. *(p. 755)*

3. 5 feet, 2 feet, 6 feet

4. 10 inches, 10 inches, 10 inches

The medal count for the United States in the 2004 Summer Olympics is shown in the bar graph. *(p. 757)*

5. About how many gold medals did the United States receive?

6. About how many silver medals did the United States receive?

7. About how many medals did the United States receive in all?

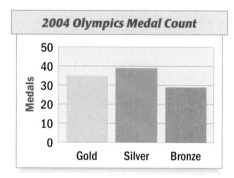

Evaluate the expression when $x = 8$ **and** $y = 2$. *(p. 29)*

8. $2x$ **9.** $4y$ **10.** xy **11.** $3xy$

12. $x + y$ **13.** $x - y$ **14.** $2x - y$ **15.** $3x + 2y$

@HomeTutor Prerequisite skills practice at classzone.com

Notetaking Skills   Taking Notes While Reading

In each chapter you will learn a new notetaking skill. In Chapter 2 you will apply the strategy of taking notes while reading Example 3 on p. 100.

Leave extra space while you take notes in class. Then review the lesson in your textbook to correct or add to your class notes. You may also want to copy the "Help" notes from the textbook in your own words, as shown below.

$$m = 3, n = 4$$

$$m + 2n = 3 + 2 \cdot 4 \longleftarrow \text{Follow the order of operations after substituting.}$$

$$= 3 + 8$$

$$= 11$$

2.1 Measuring Lengths

Before	You used a ruler to draw straight lines.
Now	You'll measure length using customary and metric units.
Why?	So you can find lengths, such as climbing distances in Ex. 47.

KEY VOCABULARY

- **inch,** *p. 59*
- **foot,** *p. 59*
- **yard,** *p. 59*
- **mile,** *p. 59*
- **millimeter,** *p. 60*
- **centimeter,** *p. 60*
- **meter,** *p. 60*
- **kilometer,** *p. 60*

ACTIVITY

You can use many different units to measure length.

STEP 1 **Look** at your math book and estimate the length of the spine in "paper clips."

STEP 2 **Measure** the length of your book using paper clips. How does the result compare to your estimate?

STEP 3 **Estimate** the width of your math book in "little fingers."

STEP 4 **Measure** the width using this unit. How does the result compare to your estimate?

Customary Units A small paper clip is about one inch long. An **inch** (in.) is a customary unit of length. Three other customary units of length are the **foot** (ft), the **yard** (yd), and the **mile** (mi). Inches, feet, yards, and miles are related to each other.

$$1 \text{ ft} = 12 \text{ in.} \qquad 1 \text{ yd} = 3 \text{ ft} = 36 \text{ in.} \qquad 1 \text{ mi} = 1760 \text{ yd} = 5280 \text{ ft}$$

EXAMPLE 1   Using Customary Units of Length

Find the length of the caterpillar to the nearest inch.

Line up one end of the caterpillar at the mark for 0.

The other end of the caterpillar is between the 1 inch and 2 inch marks and is closer to 2 inches.

▶**Answer** The caterpillar is about 2 inches long.

✓ GUIDED PRACTICE   for Example 1

1. Measure the length of your math book to the nearest inch.

The Latin prefixes *milli-* (thousand) and *centi-* (hundred) are used to form units less than a meter. The Greek prefix *kilo-* (thousand) is used to form a unit greater than a meter.

Metric Units Your little finger is about one centimeter wide. The commonly used metric units of length are the **millimeter** (mm), the **centimeter** (cm), the **meter** (m), and the **kilometer** (km). Here are some common metric unit relationships.

$$1 \text{ cm} = 10 \text{ mm} \qquad 1 \text{ m} = 100 \text{ cm} = 1000 \text{ mm} \qquad 1 \text{ km} = 1000 \text{ m}$$

EXAMPLE 2 **Using Metric Units of Length**

Find the length of the seashell to the nearest millimeter.

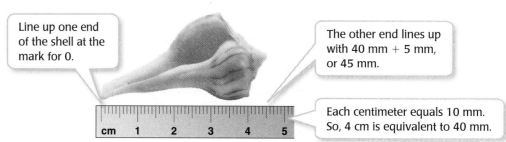

Line up one end of the shell at the mark for 0.

The other end lines up with 40 mm + 5 mm, or 45 mm.

Each centimeter equals 10 mm. So, 4 cm is equivalent to 40 mm.

▶**Answer** The seashell is about 45 millimeters long.

USE COMMON MEASURING TOOLS
foot ruler
centimeter ruler
yardstick
meterstick
tape measure

Measuring Tools To measure lengths accurately, use a tool that is closest in length to the object you want to measure. The most common measuring tools are listed at the left.

EXAMPLE 3 **Choosing Appropriate Tools**

Choose an appropriate measuring tool for the length. Explain your reasoning.

a. width of a calculator   b. length of a bus

SOLUTION

a. The width of a calculator is less than one foot and less than 30 centimeters. So, you should use a foot ruler or a centimeter ruler to measure the length.

b. The length of a bus is greater than one yard and greater than one meter. So, you should use a tape measure to measure the length.

✓ **GUIDED PRACTICE** for Examples 2 and 3

2. Measure the width of your math book to the nearest centimeter.

3. Measure the thickness of a quarter to the nearest millimeter.

Choose an appropriate measuring tool for the length. Explain your reasoning.

4. length of your pencil   5. height of a bookcase

EXAMPLE 4 **Choosing Appropriate Units**

Choose an appropriate customary unit and metric unit for the length. Explain your reasoning.

a. distance from Boston to Chicago   **b.** height of a full grown tree

SOLUTION

a. The distance from Boston to Chicago is much greater than one yard and much greater than one meter. So, use miles or kilometers.

b. The height of a tree is much greater than either one inch or one centimeter. The height is also much less than either one mile or one kilometer. So, use feet, yards, or meters.

 GUIDED PRACTICE for Example 4

Choose an appropriate customary unit and metric unit for the length. Explain your reasoning.

6. height of a two year old child   **7.** width of a baseball card

---

KEY CONCEPT *For Your Notebook*

Benchmarks for Units of Length

A *benchmark* approximates the size of a unit.

Customary Units

inch—length of a small paper clip

foot—distance from elbow to knuckle

yard—width of a door

Metric Units

millimeter—thickness of a dime

centimeter—width of your little finger

meter—height of a chair

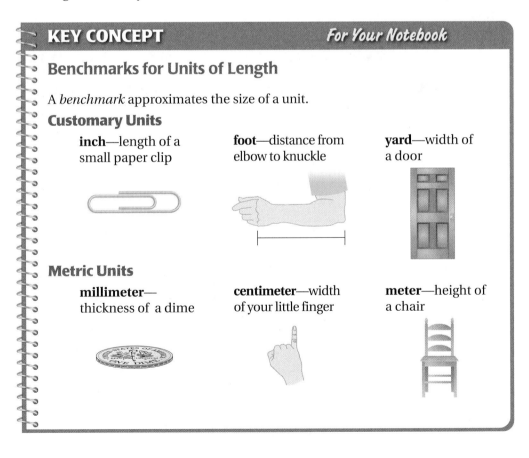

EXAMPLE 5 Estimating Length Using Benchmarks

Estimate the height, in meters, of the door below. Measure to check.

ANOTHER WAY
You can also use your own height as a benchmark when estimating height.

STEP 1 To estimate, imagine how high the door is in "chairs."

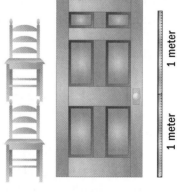

STEP 2 To check your estimate, measure the door with a meterstick.

▶ **Answer** The door is about 2 "chairs" high, which is about 2 meters. The height of the door is just over 2 meters.

✓ **GUIDED PRACTICE** for Example 5

8. **Window Length** Estimate the length of the nearest window in feet. Use the benchmarks on the previous page. Then measure to check.

2.1 EXERCISES

HOMEWORK KEY

★ = **STANDARDIZED TEST PRACTICE**
Exs. 9, 39, 45, 46, 48, 49, and 63

◯ = **HINTS AND HOMEWORK HELP**
for Exs. 5, 7, 13, 47 at classzone.com

SKILL PRACTICE

VOCABULARY Copy and complete the statement with the appropriate customary unit or metric unit.

1. 1 yd = 3 _?_   **2.** 1 cm = 10 _?_   **3.** 1 m = 100 _?_   **4.** 1 ft = 12 _?_

USING CUSTOMARY UNITS Find the length of the animal to the nearest inch.

SEE EXAMPLE 1
on p. 59
for Exs. 5–6, 10

USING METRIC UNITS Find the length of the line segment to the nearest millimeter and to the nearest centimeter.

SEE EXAMPLE 2
on p. 60
for Exs. 7–8

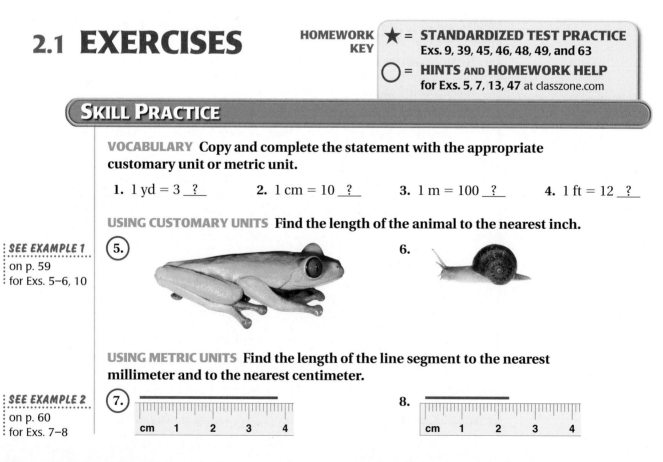

SEE EXAMPLE 2
on p. 60
for Ex. 9

9. ★ **MULTIPLE CHOICE** Which measure is closest to the length of the item?

OIL PASTEL

A 5 cm   **B** 53 mm   **C** 58 mm   **D** 6 cm

10. **ERROR ANALYSIS** Describe and correct the error made in measuring the length of the eraser.

The length of the eraser is about 3 inches.

CHOOSING MEASURING TOOLS Choose an appropriate measuring tool for the length. *Explain* your reasoning.

SEE EXAMPLE 3
on p. 60
for Exs. 11–16

11. height of your friend
12. length of a TV screen
13. diameter of a quarter
14. width of your classroom
15. length of a diving board
16. length of a porch railing

CHOOSING APPROPRIATE UNITS Choose an appropriate customary unit and metric unit for the length. *Explain* your reasoning.

SEE EXAMPLE 4
on p. 61
for Exs. 17–24

17. length of a marathon
18. thickness of a CD
19. length of a clarinet
20. distance to the moon
21. length of a bike
22. height of a building
23. height of a flagpole
24. length of a river

DRAWING SEGMENTS Draw a segment of the given length.

25. 12 centimeters
26. 48 millimeters
27. 5 inches
28. 8 inches

ESTIMATION Use a benchmark to estimate the length in the given unit. Tell which tool you would use to measure it. Then measure to check.

SEE EXAMPLE 5
on p. 62
for Exs. 29–34

29. height of a stove (feet)
30. length of a bed (feet)
31. width of a television (inches)
32. length of a spoon (inches)
33. height of a lamp (centimeters)
34. length of a shoe (centimeters)

Animated Math at classzone.com

REASONING Tell whether the statement is reasonable. If it is not, change the unit of measure so that it is reasonable.

35. A driveway is 14 *feet* wide.

36. A cat is 12 *inches* long.

37. A bike path is 8 *millimeters* long.

38. A book is 10 *meters* thick.

39. ★ **MULTIPLE CHOICE** Which could not be the length of a sofa?

    (A) 2 meters   **(B)** 6 feet   **(C)** 75 inches   **(D)** 90 centimeters

PRECISION The given length was measured to the nearest unit. Give one longer length and one shorter length that could be reported as the given length.

40. 6 centimeters   **41.** 40 centimeters   **42.** 7 feet   **43.** 12 feet

44. **CHALLENGE** Is there a shortest length that can be reported as a given measure? Is there a longest length? *Justify* your answers.

PROBLEM SOLVING

45. ★ **WRITING** Do you need an actual measurement or an estimate to decide whether a table will fit through a doorway? *Explain.*

46. ★ **OPEN-ENDED MATH** A line segment is 6 centimeters long, to the nearest centimeter. Give 5 possible lengths of the line segment in millimeters.

SEE EXAMPLE 5
on p. 62
for Exs. 47–48

47. ROCK CLIMBING The height of the person in the photo is 6 feet. *Estimate* the height of the rock that the person is climbing.

48. ★ **SHORT RESPONSE** Choose a benchmark that could be used for a mile. *Explain* how you would use that benchmark to measure a distance near where you live.

SEE EXAMPLES
3 AND 4
on p. 60–61
for Ex. 49

49. ★ **EXTENDED RESPONSE** The lights on a string are equally spaced over a length of 10 feet (or 120 inches). The diagram below shows the actual distance between each pair of light bulbs.

    a. Which measuring tool would you use to measure the distance between two lights? What customary unit would you use? *Explain* your choices.

    b. Estimate the distance between the lights. Then measure the distance.

    c. How many lights are on the 10 foot string of lights? *Explain.*

50. MEASUREMENT Measure the thickness of your math book to the nearest inch and then to the nearest millimeter. Which measurement is closer to the actual thickness? *Explain.*

51. REASONING You have bought a case that is 15 centimeters tall to store an electronic game. To the nearest centimeter, the game is also 15 centimeters tall. If the case is wide enough, can you be sure that the game will fit completely into the case? *Explain.*

CHALLENGE In Exercises 52 and 53 use the square at the right.

52. Measure the sides of the square in inches and in centimeters. What is the distance around the square in inches? in centimeters?

53. Draw one line representing the distance around the square in centimeters and draw another line representing the distance in inches. Place them side by side. Are they the same length? *Explain.*

MIXED REVIEW

Get-Ready

Prepare for Lesson 2.2 in Exs. 54–61

Evaluate the expression when $t = 4$ and $u = 6$. *(p. 29)*

54. $4t$ **55.** u^2 **56.** $t + u$ **57.** $u - t$

58. $u \div 3$ **59.** $u \times t$ **60.** $2t + u$ **61.** $2u - t$

CHOOSE A STRATEGY Use a strategy from the list to solve the problem. *Explain* your choice of strategy.

62. The distance around a triangle with two equal sides is 32 inches. The third side is 4 inches shorter than each of the other sides. Find the lengths of the sides.

> **Problem Solving Strategies**
> - Draw a Diagram *(p. 762)*
> - Guess, Check, and Revise *(p. 763)*
> - Make a List *(p. 765)*
> - Act It Out *(p. 770)*

63. ★ MULTIPLE CHOICE Which equation is related to $9 \times 2 = 18$? *(p. 740)*

     (A) $9 \div 2 = 18$ **(B)** $2 \div 18 = 9$ **(C)** $18 \div 2 = 9$ **(D)** $9 \div 18 = 2$

Brain Game

Optical Illusions

Which line segment is longer?   Which person is the tallest?

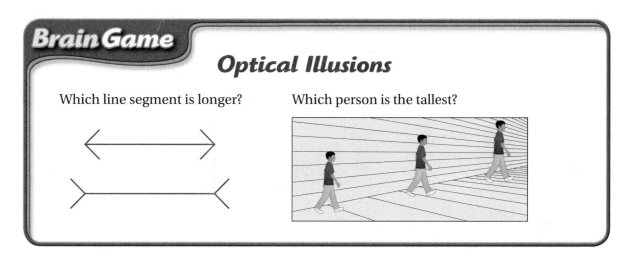

2.2 Perimeter and Area

Before	You found the square of a number.
Now	You'll use formulas to find perimeter and area.
Why?	So you can use measurements to solve problems, as in Example 3.

KEY VOCABULARY
- **perimeter,** *p. 66*
- **area,** *p. 67*

Carnival A carnival is going to be held in your school's parking lot. How much rope is needed to enclose the carnival? To answer this question, you can find the carnival's *perimeter*.

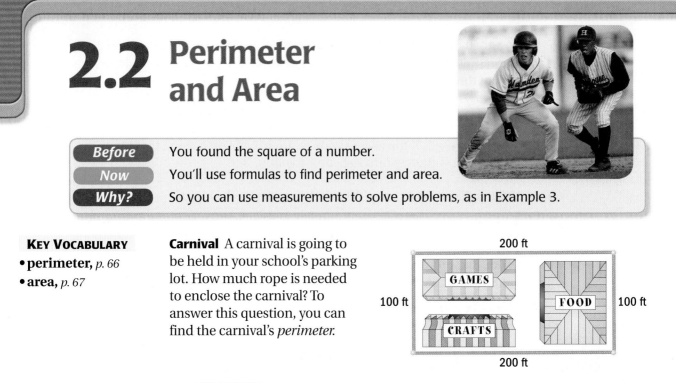

The **perimeter** of a figure is the distance around the figure. Perimeter is measured in linear units such as feet, inches, or meters.

KEY CONCEPT *For Your Notebook*

Perimeter of a Rectangle

Words   Perimeter = 2 · **length** + 2 · **width**

Algebra $P = 2l + 2w$

EXAMPLE 1 Finding the Perimeter of a Rectangle

ANOTHER WAY

You can also find the perimeter by adding all the lengths of the figure together.

```
  100
  200
  100
+ 200
  600
```

To answer the real-world question above, find the perimeter.

$P = 2l + 2w$	**Write the formula for perimeter of a rectangle.**
$= 2 \cdot 200 + 2 \cdot 100$	**Substitute 200 for *l* and 100 for *w*.**
$= 400 + 200$	**Multiply.**
$= 600$	**Add.**

▶ **Answer** The amount of rope needed to enclose the carnival is 600 feet.

✓ **GUIDED PRACTICE**   **for Example 1**

Find the perimeter of the rectangle with the given dimensions.

1. length = 9 m, width = 5 m

2. length = 20 in., width = 12 in.

Area The **area** of a figure is the amount of surface the figure covers. Area is measured in square units such as square feet (ft^2) or square meters (m^2).

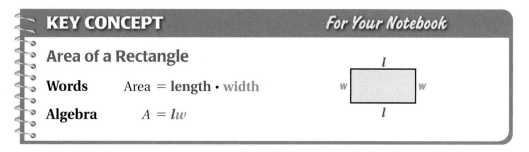

KEY CONCEPT   *For Your Notebook*

Area of a Rectangle

Words   Area $=$ **length** $\cdot$ **width**

Algebra $A = lw$

EXAMPLE 2   Finding the Area of a Rectangle

Find the area of the carnival lot shown at the top of page 66.

page 66

$A = lw$ Write the formula for area of a rectangle.

$= 200 \cdot 100$ Substitute 200 for *l* and 100 for *w*.

$= 20{,}000$ Multiply.

▶ **Answer** The area of the carnival is 20,000 square feet.

> **AVOID ERRORS**
> The units in this answer are square feet, not linear feet. To help you remember this, think of multiplying the units:
> $lw = \text{ft} \times \text{ft} = \text{ft}^2$.

Squares A square is a rectangle that has four sides with the same length. Use the following formulas for a square with side length *s*.

Perimeter $= 4 \cdot$ side length   Area $= (\text{side length})^2$

$P = 4s$ $A = s^2$

EXAMPLE 3   Perimeter and Area of a Square

Find the perimeter and the area of the softball diamond.

Perimeter $= 4s$ Area $= s^2$

$= 4 \cdot 60$ $= 60^2$

$= 240$ $= 3600$

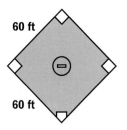

▶ **Answer** The perimeter is 240 feet. The area is 3600 square feet.

✓ **GUIDED PRACTICE**   for Examples 2 and 3

Tell whether to find the perimeter or the area to help you decide how much of the item to buy. Then find the measurement.

3. tiles to cover a 9 ft by 9 ft floor   **4.** fence for a 6 m by 7 m garden

5. tape around a 3 ft by 5 ft window   **6.** sod for a 12 ft by 15 ft lawn

EXAMPLE 4 Solving for an Unknown Dimension

(xy) Write and solve an equation to find the width of a rectangle.
Its area is 195 square meters and its length is 15 meters.

REVIEW
For help with writing
related equations, see
page 740.

$A = lw$	Write the formula for the area of a rectangle.
$195 = 15w$	Substitute the known values for A and l.
$w = 195 \div 15$	Write the related division equation.
$w = 13$	Divide.

▶**Answer** The width of the rectangle is 13 meters.

✓ **GUIDED PRACTICE**   for Example 4

Write and solve an equation to find the length.

7. Area of rectangle = 91 in.^{2}, width = 7 in., length = __?__

8. Perimeter of square = 132 cm, side length = __?__

2.2 EXERCISES

HOMEWORK
KEY

★ = **STANDARDIZED TEST PRACTICE**
   Exs. 16, 38, 39, 41, 43, 44, and 57

◯ = **HINTS AND HOMEWORK HELP**
   for Exs. 7, 13, 21, 37 at classzone.com

SKILL PRACTICE

1. **VOCABULARY** Copy and complete: The sum of twice the length and
   twice the width of a rectangle is the measure of its __?__.

2. **VOCABULARY** Copy and complete: The product of the length and the
   width of a rectangle is a measure of its __?__.

REASONING Does the measure represent a *perimeter* or an *area*? *Explain.*

3. 15 yd   4. 10 in.^{2} 5. 56 cm^2

**SEE EXAMPLES
1, 2, AND 3**
on pp. 66–67
for Exs. 3–14

GEOMETRY Find the perimeter and the area of the rectangle or square.
Use estimation to check your answers.

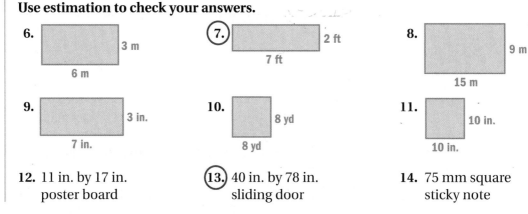

6. 3 m
    6 m

7. 2 ft
    7 ft

8. 9 m
    15 m

9. 3 in.
    7 in.

10. 8 yd
     8 yd

11. 10 in.
     10 in.

12. 11 in. by 17 in.
    poster board

13. 40 in. by 78 in.
    sliding door

14. 75 mm square
    sticky note

15. **ERROR ANALYSIS** Describe and correct the error made in finding the perimeter of the rectangle.

✗ Perimeter = 2 • 6 + 2 • 4
= 12 + 8
= 20 square feet

4 ft

6 ft

16. ★ **MULTIPLE CHOICE** A rectangle has an area of 40 square meters. Its width is 5 meters. What equation could you use to find its length?

$\textbf{A}$ $l = 40 \div 4$ $\textbf{B}$ $l = 40 \div 5$ $\textbf{C}$ $l = 4 \div 40$ $\textbf{D}$ $l = 5 \div 40$

SELECTING UNITS Tell whether you would use *perimeter* or *area* to help you decide how much of the item to buy. Tell which unit you would use.

17. fringe for the edges of a rug

18. paint for a ceiling

19. carpeting to cover a floor

20. lace to trim the edges of a pillow

(XY) **ALGEBRA** The perimeter or the area of the figure is given. Write and solve an equation to find the length.

21. Square: perimeter = 100 ft, side length = __?__

22. Rectangle: area = 42 in.^{2}, width = 3 in., length = __?__

23. Rectangle: area = 132 m^2, length = 12 m, width = __?__

SELECTING MEASURING TOOLS Use the tools listed on page 60. Choose the best tool for finding the perimeter of the object. *Explain* your choice.

24. greeting card

25. parking lot

SELECTING AND USING TOOLS In Exercises 26–28 use a wallet sized card, such as a driver's license, membership card, or library card.

26. *Estimate* the length, width, and perimeter of the card in centimeters.

27. Choose a tool for measuring the length and width in centimeters. *Explain* why you chose it.

28. Measure the length and width of the card to the nearest centimeter. Find its perimeter and area.

GEOMETRY The figure is made of rectangles and squares. Find its area.

29.
6 ft

6 ft

2 ft

12 ft

30.
36 m

8 m

8 m   4 m

12 m

12 m

CHALLENGE The area of a square is given. Estimate the length of a side to the nearest whole number.

31. $A = 50$ in.^{2} 32. $A = 22$ cm^2 33. $A = 10$ in.^{2} 34. $A = 120$ yd^2

SEE EXAMPLE 3
on p. 67
for Exs. 35–38

35. **GUIDED PROBLEM SOLVING** You plan to build a square dog run. You have 64 feet of fencing. How long will each side be?

   a. Decide whether 64 feet is the perimeter or the area of the dog run. *Explain* your reasoning.

   b. Write an equation to represent this situation.

   c. Solve the equation to find the length of each side of the dog run.

GYMNASTICS **The mat below is used for performing gymnastics floor routines. The gymnast must stay within the white lines.**

36. How much space does the gymnast have to perform in?

37. What is the length of tape needed to mark off the white lines?

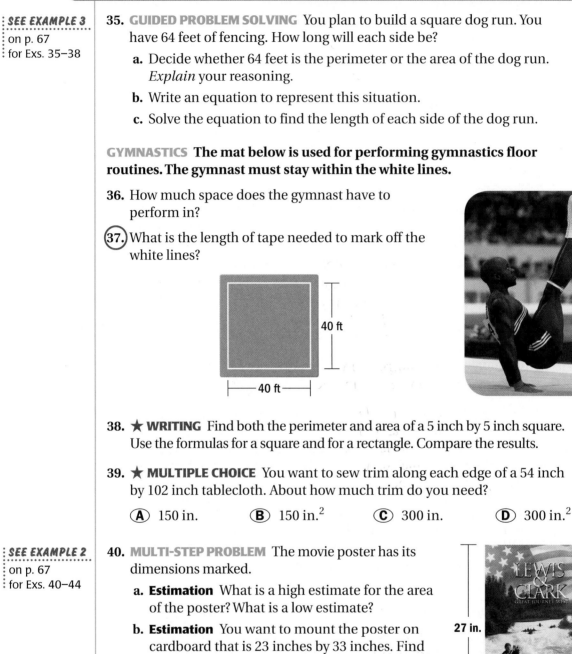

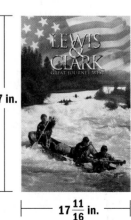

40 ft

40 ft

38. ★ **WRITING** Find both the perimeter and area of a 5 inch by 5 inch square. Use the formulas for a square and for a rectangle. Compare the results.

39. ★ **MULTIPLE CHOICE** You want to sew trim along each edge of a 54 inch by 102 inch tablecloth. About how much trim do you need?

   (A) 150 in.   **(B)** 150 in.^{2} **(C)** 300 in.   **(D)** 300 in.^{2}

SEE EXAMPLE 2
on p. 67
for Exs. 40–44

40. **MULTI-STEP PROBLEM** The movie poster has its dimensions marked.

   a. **Estimation** What is a high estimate for the area of the poster? What is a low estimate?

   b. **Estimation** You want to mount the poster on cardboard that is 23 inches by 33 inches. Find a high and low estimate of this area.

   c. **Reasoning** *Explain* how to use your estimates to find a high estimate of the area of the cardboard not covered by the poster. Then find a high and low estimate for this area.

27 in.

$17\frac{11}{16}$ in.

41. ★ **SHORT RESPONSE** A square has a side length of 8 inches. A rectangle has a length of 16 inches and a width of 8 inches. Without actually finding the areas, compare the two areas. How do the areas of the square and rectangle compare if the length of the rectangle is 24 inches? 32 inches? *Explain.*

42. ESTIMATION You are fertilizing a lawn that is 32 feet by 50 feet. Your bag of fertilizer covers 1500 square feet. Do you have enough fertilizer? *Explain.*

43. ★ SHORT RESPONSE Which figure has a greater area, a square that is 87 inches by 87 inches or a rectangle that is 198 inches by 61 inches? Use estimation to decide. *Explain* your reasoning.

44. ★ OPEN-ENDED MATH Give the dimensions of 3 different rectangles that each have a perimeter of 16 feet. Then find and compare the areas of the rectangles.

45. FLOOR PLANS The diagram at the right is a floor plan for a single story mini mall.

  a. What is the area of the building in square feet?

  b. A contractor is insulating the outer walls of the building. The walls are 9 feet high. How many square feet of insulation are needed?

  c. All the retail spaces have wood trim along the length of the walls where the walls meet the ceiling. How many feet of wood trim is needed for this purpose?

Animated Math at classzone.com

46. FENCING Your rectangular property covers 1302 square yards of land and is 42 yards long. How much fencing do you need to enclose it?

47. CHALLENGE You have 40 feet of fencing to enclose a rectangular garden. You want the length and width to be whole numbers. Make a table of values that shows the lengths, widths, and areas of all possible gardens you can make. Which dimensions form a garden with the greatest area? *Justify* your reasoning.

48. CHALLENGE You are tiling a room with 1 foot square tiles. The room is 11 feet 8 inches wide and 15 feet 8 inches long. How many whole tiles will you need? How many tiles will need to be cut? Each box of tiles covers 10 square feet. How many boxes of tiles will you need?

MIXED REVIEW

Get-Ready

Prepare for
Lesson 2.3 in
Exs. 49–52

Measure the length of the segment to the nearest centimeter. *(p. 59)*

49. _____

50. _____

51. _____

52. _____

Write the other three equations in the fact family. *(p. 740)*

53. $9 \times 8 = 72$ **54.** $6 \times 7 = 42$ **55.** $5 \times 8 = 40$ **56.** $11 \times 9 = 99$

57. ★ MULTIPLE CHOICE What is the value of 3^5? *(p. 15)*

  (A) 15   (B) 35   (C) 125   (D) 243

2.3 Scale Drawings

Before You used rulers to find the actual lengths of objects.

Now You'll use scale drawings to find actual lengths.

Why? So you can interpret maps and diagrams, as in Example 1.

KEY VOCABULARY
- scale drawing, *p. 72*
- scale, *p. 72*

ACTIVITY

You can use a map to find an actual distance.

Use the map to find the distance you will canoe.

STEP 1 Measure the distance, in centimeters, between the lodge and the dam.

STEP 2 The map indicates 1 cm : 2 km, so a distance of 1 cm on the map represents 2 km on the lake. What distance does your measurement represent?

The map in the activity is a *scale drawing*. A **scale drawing** is the same shape as the original object, but not the same size. The **scale** tells how the drawing's dimensions and the actual dimensions are related.

EXAMPLE 1 Interpreting Scale Drawings

READING

The standard way to write a scale is *scale model* to *actual object* or *scale : actual*.

Canoes Find the actual lengths that correspond to 1 inch, 2 inches, and 3 inches on the scale drawing. How long is the actual canoe?

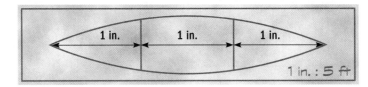

SOLUTION

Make a table. The scale on the drawing is 1 in.: 5 ft. Each inch on the drawing represents 5 feet on the canoe.

▸ **Answer** The actual canoe is 15 feet long.

Scale length	Length × 5	Actual length
1 in.	1 × 5	5 ft
2 in.	2 × 5	10 ft
3 in.	3 × 5	15 ft

EXAMPLE 2 Standardized Test Practice

Catalog Photos A catalog pictures a necklace smaller than its actual size. The scale is 3 cm : 8 cm. The length of the necklace in the catalog is 18 centimeters. How long is the actual necklace?

(A) 6 cm   **(B)** 20 cm   **(C)** 24 cm   **(D)** 48 cm

ELIMINATE CHOICES
The text in Example 2 indicates that the actual necklace will be larger than its picture. So you can eliminate choice A.

STEP 1 **Find** the relationship between the known length and the scale.

             picture : actual

              3 cm : 8 cm

× ?   **Ask, "3 times what number equals 18?"**

              18 cm : <u>?</u> cm

STEP 2 **Multiply** by 6 to find the actual length because $3 \times 6 = 18$.

              3 cm : 8 cm

                        × 6

            18 cm : 48 cm

▶ **Answer** The actual necklace is 48 centimeters long. The correct answer is D. (A) (B) (C) **(D)**

EXAMPLE 3 Using a Scale to Build a Model

Models You are building a model boat with a scale of 1 in. : 2 ft. The actual boat is 18 feet long. How long should you make your model?

SOLUTION

STEP 1 **Find** the relationship between the known length and the scale.

          model : actual

           1 in. : 2 ft

                    × ?   **Ask, "2 times what number equals 18?"**

         <u>?</u> in. : 18 ft

STEP 2 **Multiply** by 9, because $2 \times 9 = 18$.

     × 9   1 in. : 2 ft

            9 in. : 18 ft

▶ **Answer** You should make your model 9 inches long.

✓ **GUIDED PRACTICE** for Examples 1, 2, and 3

1. **What If?** Suppose the scale in Example 1 is 1 in. : 6 ft. How long is the actual canoe?

2. **What If?** Suppose the necklace described in Example 2 is pictured as 21 centimeters long. How long is the actual necklace?

3. **What If?** Suppose the scale in Example 3 is 1 in. : 3 ft. How long do you make your model?

2.3 EXERCISES

SKILL PRACTICE

1. **VOCABULARY** Copy and complete: A scale drawing is the same __?__ as the original object, but not the same __?__ .

INTERPRETING SCALES **Find the actual length for the length labeled in the photo.**

SEE EXAMPLE 1
on p. 72
for Exs. 2–4

2.   1 cm : 2 cm   3.   1 cm : 5 cm   4.   1 cm : 7 cm

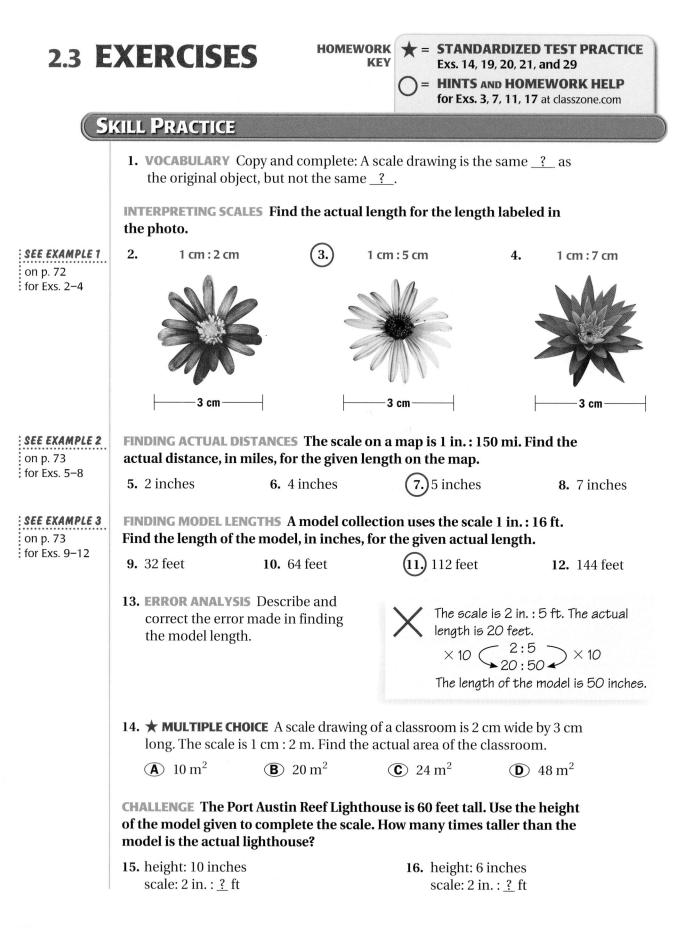

├── 3 cm ──┤   ├── 3 cm ──┤   ├── 3 cm ──┤

SEE EXAMPLE 2
on p. 73
for Exs. 5–8

FINDING ACTUAL DISTANCES **The scale on a map is 1 in. : 150 mi. Find the actual distance, in miles, for the given length on the map.**

5. 2 inches   6. 4 inches   7. 5 inches   8. 7 inches

SEE EXAMPLE 3
on p. 73
for Exs. 9–12

FINDING MODEL LENGTHS **A model collection uses the scale 1 in. : 16 ft. Find the length of the model, in inches, for the given actual length.**

9. 32 feet   10. 64 feet   11. 112 feet   12. 144 feet

13. **ERROR ANALYSIS** Describe and correct the error made in finding the model length.

> ╳ The scale is 2 in. : 5 ft. The actual length is 20 feet.
>
> × 10 ⌢ 2 : 5 ⌢ × 10
>   20 : 50
>
> The length of the model is 50 inches.

14. ★ **MULTIPLE CHOICE** A scale drawing of a classroom is 2 cm wide by 3 cm long. The scale is 1 cm : 2 m. Find the actual area of the classroom.

Ⓐ 10 m^2 Ⓑ 20 m^2 Ⓒ 24 m^2 Ⓓ 48 m^2

CHALLENGE **The Port Austin Reef Lighthouse is 60 feet tall. Use the height of the model given to complete the scale. How many times taller than the model is the actual lighthouse?**

15. height: 10 inches
    scale: 2 in. : __?__ ft

16. height: 6 inches
    scale: 2 in. : __?__ ft

SEE EXAMPLE 2
on p. 73
for Exs. 17–18

17. **MAPS** A map uses a scale of 1 in.: 200 mi. The distance between two cities on the map is 4 inches. What is the actual distance?

18. **EIFFEL TOWER** A model of the Eiffel Tower is 20 centimeters tall. Use the scale 5 cm : 80 m. Approximate the height of the actual Eiffel Tower.

19. ★ **MULTIPLE CHOICE** An architect constructs a model of a building that will be 120 feet tall. Every 2 inches on the model represents 5 feet on the building. How tall is the architect's model?

ⓐ 300 in.   ⓑ 60 in.   ⓒ 48 in.   ⓓ 24 in.

20. ★ **WRITING** *Explain* how you can use a scale drawing to find the area of an actual rectangle.

21. ★ **EXTENDED RESPONSE** The map shows part of Washington, D.C.

   a. **Measure** How many centimeters apart are the U.S. Capitol and the White House on the map?

   b. **Calculate** Find the actual distance between the landmarks in part (a).

   c. **Estimate** Estimate the shortest actual distance from Union Station to the Washington Monument by way of the other two red landmarks. *Justify* your estimate.

22. **DRAW A DIAGRAM** Using the scale 1 in. : 10 ft, make a scale drawing of a 30 feet by 40 feet dance floor. Use your drawing to find the distance between opposite corners of the floor.

23. **CHALLENGE** The actual distance across the fly's eye in the photo is 800 micrometers. (1000 micrometers = 1 mm). Measure the widest part of the eye and complete the scale for the photo: 1 mm : _?_ micrometers

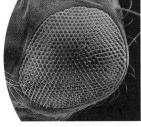

Get-Ready

Prepare for
Lesson 2.4 in
Exs. 24–26

Order the numbers from least to greatest. *(p. 738)*

24. 12, 3, 7, 6, 17, 21   **25.** 22, 25, 14, 11, 23   **26.** 206, 250, 262, 199, 260

Tell whether the unit is reasonable. If it is not, change it so that it is. *(p. 59)*

27. A bed is 7 *miles* long.   **28.** A computer keyboard is 18 *inches* long.

29. ★ **MULTIPLE CHOICE** Find the perimeter P and area A of a rectangle that is 4 feet by 6 feet. *(p. 66)*

ⓐ $P = 20 \text{ ft}^2$ ⓑ $P = 24 \text{ ft}^2$ ⓒ $P = 20 \text{ ft}$ ⓓ $P = 24 \text{ ft}$
    $A = 24 \text{ ft}$ $A = 20 \text{ ft}$ $A = 24 \text{ ft}^2$ $A = 20 \text{ ft}^2$

2.4 Frequency Tables and Line Plots

Before	You read data from a table and drew number lines.
Now	You'll create and interpret frequency tables and line plots.
Why?	So you can organize data, as in Exs. 10–12.

KEY VOCABULARY
- **data,** *p. 76*
- **frequency table,** *p. 76*
- **line plot,** *p. 77*

Art Projects Students in an art class chose one of three types of projects: painting, sculpture, or drawing. Which type of project was chosen most often?

You can organize **data**, or information, by using a **frequency table**. A frequency table lists the number of times each item occurs in a data set.

Student Choices for Art Projects	
painting	sculpture
painting	painting
painting	drawing
sculpture	sculpture
drawing	sculpture
painting	painting

EXAMPLE 1 Making a Frequency Table

To find which type of art project was chosen most often, you can make a frequency table.

Use a tally mark for each time a given project was chosen.

The frequency is the number of tally marks.

Art project	*Tally*	*Frequency*
painting	JHH I	6
sculpture	IIII	4
drawing	II	2

▶ **Answer** The students most often chose a painting project.

✓ **GUIDED PRACTICE**   for Example 1

1. The data at the top of the page could have been recorded in a frequency table as the information was gathered. *Explain* how this could be done and why this might be a better way to record the data.

2. **What If?** Suppose the choices for 5 more students were: sculpture, sculpture, drawing, drawing, sculpture. Make a new frequency table including these data. Which type of project was chosen most often?

Line Plots When the items or categories being tallied are numbers, you can display the data in a *line plot*. A **line plot** uses X marks above a number line to show the frequencies.

EXAMPLE 2 Making a Line Plot

Summer Reading The frequency table shows how many books the students in a class read during summer vacation.

a. Make a line plot of the data.

b. Use the line plot to find the total number of students.

c. Use the line plot to find how many students read four or more books.

Books read	Tally	Frequency
1	JHT	5
2	JHT	5
3	JHT I	6
4	II	2
5		0
6	IIII	4

SOLUTION

a. Make a line plot of the data.

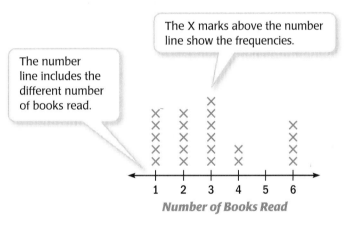

The X marks above the number line show the frequencies.

The number line includes the different number of books read.

REVIEW
To review number lines, see page 741.

Number of Books Read

b. There are 22 X marks in all, so the total number of students is 22.

c. The total number of X marks above the numbers 4, 5, and 6 is six, so six students read four or more books.

✓ **GUIDED PRACTICE** for Example 2

◆ **MULTIPLE REPRESENTATIONS** The following data show the numbers of letters in students' names. Use the data in Exercises 3–5.

6, 5, 4, 4, 5, 3, 9, 8, 6, 4, 3, 4, 7, 5, 4, 3, 8, 4, 9, 3

3. Make a frequency table of the data.

4. Make a line plot of the data.

5. Choose one of the displays. Use it to find out whether more students have names with 3 letters or names with 7 or more letters. *Describe* which display you choose and how you use it to answer the question.

2.4 EXERCISES

HOMEWORK KEY

★ = **STANDARDIZED TEST PRACTICE**
Exs. 7, 12, 15, 17, and 30

◯ = **HINTS** AND **HOMEWORK HELP**
for Exs. 3, 5, 11, 13 at classzone.com

SKILL PRACTICE

1. **VOCABULARY** Copy and complete: When creating a frequency table, you count the number of tally marks to find the ___?___ for each category.

2. **VOCABULARY** How are a frequency table and a line plot alike? How are they different?

◆ **MAKING DATA DISPLAYS** **Make a frequency table and a line plot of the data. Then tell which item(s) occur most often and which item(s) occur least often.**

SEE EXAMPLES 1 AND 2
on pp. 76–77
for Exs. 3–5

3. Point values of a team's shots during the first half of a basketball game:

   2, 2, 1, 3, 2, 2, 1, 3, 2, 2, 1, 2, 3, 2, 2, 1, 2, 1, 2, 1, 1

4. Number of weeks class members attended summer camp:

   4, 0, 1, 2, 8, 2, 4, 4, 8, 5, 6, 4, 6, 6, 4, 0, 6, 8, 4, 4, 8, 4, 4, 4, 8, 4

5. Ages of dancers in a ballet class:

   5, 6, 10, 8, 8, 10, 12, 8, 7, 10, 10, 6, 15, 15, 16, 5, 6, 5, 10, 12, 10, 8, 5

6. **COLLECTING DATA** Some of the first words you learned to read were *the*, *and*, *of*, *a*, and *an*. Make a frequency table of the number of times each word occurs on page 79. *Predict* which of these words occurs most often in the English language. *Justify* your reasoning.

INTERPRETING LINE PLOTS **The line plot below shows the heights, in inches, of players on a basketball team.**

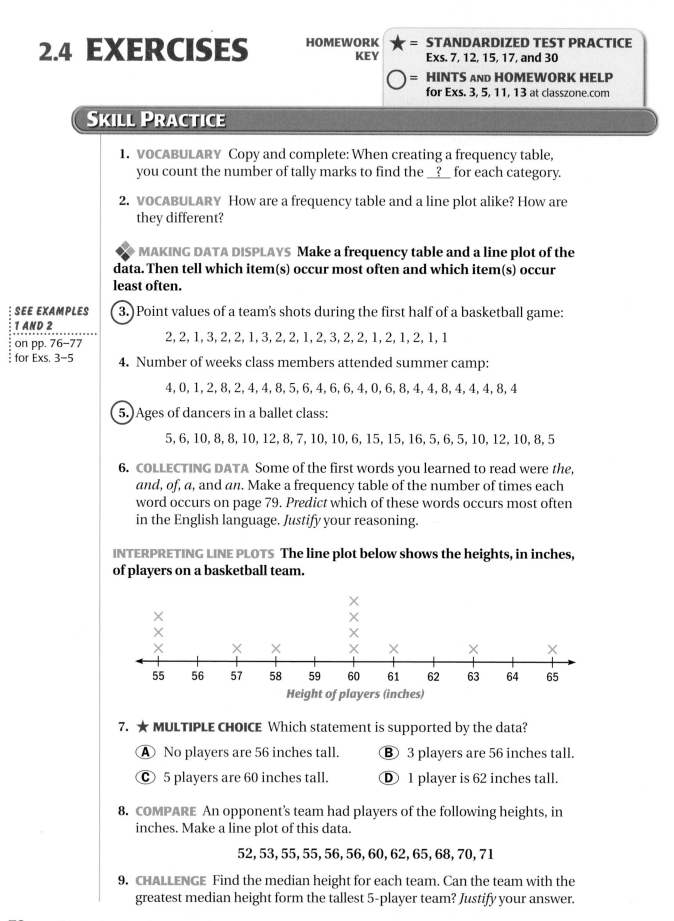

Height of players (inches)

7. ★ **MULTIPLE CHOICE** Which statement is supported by the data?

   A No players are 56 inches tall.   **B** 3 players are 56 inches tall.

   C 5 players are 60 inches tall.   **D** 1 player is 62 inches tall.

8. **COMPARE** An opponent's team had players of the following heights, in inches. Make a line plot of this data.

   52, 53, 55, 55, 56, 56, 60, 62, 65, 68, 70, 71

9. **CHALLENGE** Find the median height for each team. Can the team with the greatest median height form the tallest 5-player team? *Justify* your answer.

FIRE DEPARTMENT **The frequency table shows the number of calls a small volunteer fire department responded to in one year.**

Type of call	Tally	Frequency
building fires	JHT I	?
other fires	JHT JHT II	?
hazardous materials	JHT II	?
rescues	III	?
false alarms	JHT II	?
mutual aid	IIII	?

SEE EXAMPLE 1
on p. 76
for Exs. 10–13

10. Copy and complete the frequency table.

11. Which type of call occurred most often? least often?

12. ★ **MULTIPLE CHOICE** How many call responses were made that year?

　　Ⓐ 39　　　　　Ⓑ 40　　　　　Ⓒ 44　　　　　Ⓓ 49

13. **MUSIC** An orchestra has four sections: woodwinds (W), percussion (P), brass (B), and strings (S). The data below show the section each member of one school orchestra belongs to. Make a frequency table and use it to find the largest section of the orchestra.

　　P, S, B, W, S, S, S, B, S, W, S, S, W, S, S, B, S, W, S, B, S, W, S, W,
　　S, B, W, S, W, S, S, B, S, B, S, S, S, B, S, B, W, B, S, P, S, B, S

BICYCLES **In Exercises 14–15, use the list below showing the numbers of bicycles owned by families of class members.**

　　2, 3, 1, 0, 1, 1, 3, 1, 2, 1, 2, 3, 2, 1, 4, 0, 1, 4, 2, 6, 0

14. Make a frequency table and a line plot of the data.

15. ★ **SHORT RESPONSE** What number of bicycles is owned by exactly two families? How can you find this answer using the frequency table? the line plot?

16. **COLLECTING DATA** Gather data on the lengths of the last names of the U.S. presidents since 1950 and the current U.S. Supreme Court Justices. Make a line plot of each set of data. *Compare* the data sets.

17. ★ **WRITING** Compare the frequency table and the line plot you created in Exercise 5 on page 78. *Describe* one way in which each type of display is more helpful or easier to use than the other type.

WEATHER **Use the calendar and codes shown.**

18. Make a frequency table of the data.

19. How many more days were either cloudy or partly cloudy than were sunny?

20. **REASONING** How many days didn't have rain? *Describe* two ways to find the answer.

21. Can you make a line plot of the weather data? *Explain.*

22. ◆ **MULTIPLE REPRESENTATIONS** You have a bag containing nickels, dimes, and quarters. There are several ways you can make 60¢ using these coins. For instance, you can use one quarter, three dimes, and one nickel.

  a. **Make a List** List all the ways you can make 60¢ using these coins.

  b. **Make a Frequency Table** Count the number of coins needed to make 60¢ for each way described in your list. Then make a frequency table of the number of coins used for each possibility.

  c. **Draw a Line Plot** Use the frequency table from part (b) to make a line plot. What is the fewest number of coins necessary to make 60¢?

23. CHALLENGE The Venn diagram shows the school activities chosen by the seventh graders in one school. Make a frequency distribution of the data. Does the total in your frequency distribution match the total in the Venn diagram? *Explain.*

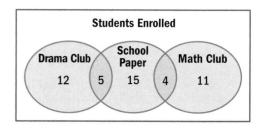

Students Enrolled

Drama Club 12 | 5 | School Paper 15 | 4 | Math Club 11

MIXED REVIEW

Get-Ready

Prepare for Lesson 2.5 in Exs. 24–27

List the first six numbers starting with zero and counting on. *(p. 743)*

24. count by 4s   **25.** count by 7s   **26.** count by 25s   **27.** count by 20s

Use the bar graph at the right. *(p. 757)*

28. How many more students chose a lake than a pool?

29. How many students in all were surveyed?

30. ★ **MULTIPLE CHOICE** Which value makes the expression $2x + 3x^2$ equal to 85? *(p. 29)*

  Ⓐ 5   Ⓑ 10
  Ⓒ 11   Ⓓ 15

Favorite Place to Swim

(bar graph: Ocean, Lake, Pool; Students axis 0–12)

QUIZ *for Lessons 2.1–2.4*

1. Estimate the length of the line segment in millimeters. Then measure to check. *(p. 59)*

Choose an appropriate customary unit and metric unit for the length. *(p. 59)*

2. height of a Ferris wheel   **3.** length of a calculator

Find the perimeter and the area of the rectangle described. *(p. 66)*

4. length = 4 ft, width = 2 ft   **5.** length = 7 m, width = 5 m

6. MODELS The scale for a model of the Titanic is 1 cm : 6 m. The model is 45 centimeters long. About how long was the actual Titanic? *(p. 72)*

7. Make a frequency table and a line plot of the data: 57, 58, 57, 55, 59, 59, 58. *(p. 76)*

Lessons 2.1–2.4

1. GRIDDED ANSWER Find the length of the grasshopper to the nearest inch.

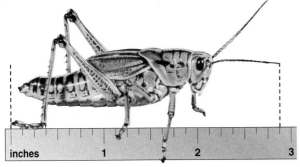

2. SHORT RESPONSE A student claims that the dimensions of a picture frame on the desk are 15 millimeters by 12 millimeters. Is the student's claim reasonable? *Explain* your reasoning.

3. GRIDDED ANSWER A map uses a scale of 1 in. : 150 mi. The distance between two cities on the map is 3 inches. How long will it take to drive the actual distance, if you drive at 50 miles per hour?

4. MULTI-STEP PROBLEM Use the key chain card below to complete the following.

  a. Measure the length and the width using a centimeter ruler.

  b. Find the perimeter and area of the card.

  c. Trace the card onto another sheet of paper. Divide the card in half with a vertical line. What is the perimeter and area of the right half of the card?

  d. Compare the perimeter and area of the right half of the card to the perimeter and area of the whole card.

5. EXTENDED RESPONSE The following data show the numbers of minutes it takes several students to get ready for school in the morning.

30, 35, 45, 75, 60, 60, 45, 30, 60, 75, 45, 60, 60, 45, 30, 50, 60, 50, 60, 35, 45, 70, 35, 40

  a. Make a frequency table of the data.

  b. Make a line plot of the data.

  c. Tell how you would use each display to find out how long it takes most students to get ready in the morning. *Decide* how long it takes most students.

  d. Do more students use less than an hour or an hour or more to get ready for school? *Justify* your answer.

6. EXTENDED RESPONSE The diagram is a scale drawing of a playground.

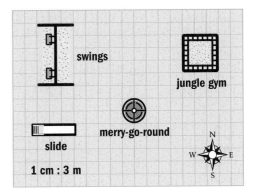

  a. Measure the distance between the swings and the slide using a centimeter ruler.

  b. Find the actual distance from the swings to the slide.

  c. Playground officials would like to add another slide. Can they place the slide 12 meters east of the swings? *Explain.*

7. OPEN-ENDED Describe a situation in your home when you would only need to estimate the length of an object rather than finding its actual length.

INVESTIGATION
Use before Lesson 2.5

GOAL
Collect and display data.

MATERIALS
• graph paper

2.5 Collecting and Organizing Data

You can make a modified frequency table to display data.

EXPLORE Display data you collect from a phone book in a modified frequency table.

STEP 1 **Look** at the last digit of 25 telephone numbers from a telephone book.

STEP 2 **List** the digits on graph paper. Beside each digit, shade one box for each telephone number that ends with that digit.

Kristine 34 Wrentham	555-0108
Kristine 16 Oakland	555-0198
L J 81 Ten Hills	555-0149
LaNell 515 Coolidge	555-0181
Lodish 64 Stetson	555-0190
Lois 36 Georgia	555-0120
Lucy 6 Lucerne	555-0185
M C 80 Highland	555-0189
M D 85 Melrose	555-0125
Mae 414 Bowdoin	555-0194
Mark 73 Winthrop	555-0191
Martin 7 Norcross	555-0144
Mary J 34 Foster	555-0134
Mary R,Dr 61 Franklin	555-0117
Melissa 652 Shawmut	555-0148
Mervyn 80 Park	555-0114
Mildred 54 Orleans	555-0132
Natalie 28 St Germain	555-0138
P 133 Marlborough	555-0153
Pamela 591 Fisher	555-0164
Pat 77 Moreland	555-0177
Patricia 25 Broadway	555-0173
Patrick 88 Liberty	555-0165
Patrick 84 Central	555-0109
Ruth 22 Haskell	555-0167

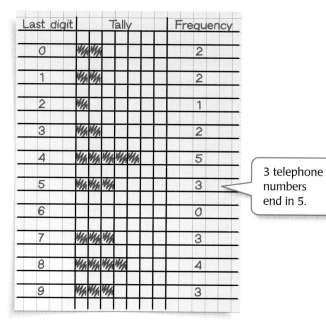

Last digit	Tally	Frequency
0		2
1		2
2		1
3		2
4		5
5		3
6		0
7		3
8		4
9		3

3 telephone numbers end in 5.

PRACTICE Use the data from Steps 1 and 2 above.

1. Which digit was the last digit most often? least often?

2. Make another modified frequency table using the sixth digit of the telephone number. Which digit is used most frequently? least frequently?

DRAW CONCLUSIONS

3. **WRITING** *Describe* how the display you made in Exercise 2 can help you compare frequencies.

2.5 Bar Graphs

Before	You organized and displayed data using frequency tables.
Now	You'll display data using bar graphs.
Why?	So you can visualize data, as in Example 1.

KEY VOCABULARY
• **bar graph,** *p. 83*
• **double bar graph,** *p. 84*

Wild Animals Two hundred sixth and seventh grade students were asked to name their favorite wild animal. The results are shown in the table. How can you represent these data visually?

A **bar graph** uses the lengths of the bars to represent and compare data. A numerical scale is used to find the lengths of the bars.

Favorite Wild Animal	
Animal	**Students**
lion	43
giraffe	19
monkey	55
elephant	49

EXAMPLE 1 Making a Bar Graph

You can display the data from the table above in a bar graph.

STEP 1 **Decide** how far to extend the scale.

Start the scale at 0. The greatest data value is 55, so end the scale at a value greater than 55, such as 60.

STEP 2 **Choose** the increments for the scale.

AVOID ERRORS
Make sure the marks on the scale are equally spaced, so that the bar graph accurately represents the data.

Use 3 to 10 equal increments for the scale. Choose an increment that is easy to work with and compatible with 60. The scale at the right uses increments of 10.

STEP 3 **Draw** and label the graph. Be sure to title your graph and label the scale.

Animated Math at classzone.com

✓ **GUIDED PRACTICE** for Example 1

1. **Make a graph of the data.**

Types of Books in a Home Library				
Type of book	children's	young adult	adult fiction	reference
Number of books	32	12	38	22

REVIEW

For help with reading bar graphs, see page 757.

Double Bar Graphs A **double bar graph** shows two sets of data on the same graph. The two bars for each category are drawn next to each other using two colors. A key tells which set of data belongs to each color.

EXAMPLE 2 Making a Double Bar Graph

Wild Animals Make a double bar graph of the wild animal data below.

Favorite Wild Animal	Sixth grade	Seventh grade
lion	19	24
giraffe	13	6
monkey	29	26
elephant	21	28

SOLUTION

TAKE NOTES

Write the steps needed to make a bar graph and a double bar graph in your notebook for reference.

STEP 1 **Draw** one set of bars using the sixth grade data, as shown below. The greatest data value in the table in both grades is 29, so end the scale at 30.

Leave room for the seventh grade bars.

STEP 2 **Draw** the seventh grade bars next to the sixth grade bars and shade them a different color. Add a title and a key.

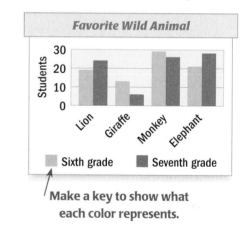

Make a key to show what each color represents.

✓ **GUIDED PRACTICE** for Example 2

2. **Favorite Sports** Make a double bar graph of the data.

Favorite Sports					
Sport	basketball	swimming	gymnastics	hockey	track
Watching	593	260	370	175	250
Participating	570	319	197	197	209

2.5 EXERCISES

HOMEWORK KEY

★ = **STANDARDIZED TEST PRACTICE**
Exs. 5, 14, 15, 16, 17, and 26

○ = **HINTS AND HOMEWORK HELP**
for Exs. 3, 5, 7, 13 at classzone.com

SKILL PRACTICE

1. VOCABULARY *Explain* how to choose a scale for a bar graph.

2. VOCABULARY How can you tell whether a set of data should be graphed as a single or a double bar graph?

BAR GRAPHS Make a bar graph of the data.

SEE EXAMPLE 1
on p. 83
for Exs. 3–6

3.

Mountain Ranges of the World	
Range	*Peaks (over 6000 m)*
Andes	102
Kunlun	228
St. Elias	1
Pamir	9

4.

Maximum Life Span of Animals in Captivity	
Animal	*Life Span (years)*
Asian elephant	77
giraffe	36
lion	30
monkey	37

5. ★ MULTIPLE CHOICE Choose the best increment for the numerical scale of a bar graph showing the data values 53, 31, 25, 13, and 46.

(A) 1   (B) 10   (C) 40   (D) 50

6. ERROR ANALYSIS A student is making a bar graph showing the amount of money raised by four students for a fundraiser. Describe and correct the error made in choosing the scale for this bar graph.

> ✗ Kaitlin: $120   Jose: $256
> Terrell: $234   Mia: $287
>
> 287 ÷ 7 = 41, which rounds to 40
> So, use 7 increments increasing by 40.

DOUBLE BAR GRAPHS Make a double bar graph of the data.

SEE EXAMPLE 2
on p. 84
for Exs. 7–8

7.

Cost of Food (cents per pound)		
Food	*1990*	*2000*
apples	77	82
chicken	86	108
eggs	100	96
ice cream	254	366
spaghetti	85	88

8.

Major Indoor Soccer League National Conference 2000–2001		
Team	*Wins*	*Losses*
Detroit	13	27
Kansas City	14	26
Milwaukee	24	16
Toronto	21	19
Wichita	18	21

9. Use your graph from Exercise 7. Which food had the greatest price increase between 1990 and 2000?

10. MULTIPLE BAR GRAPH The table at the right shows the records of the top three teams in the Eastern Conference of the National Hockey League during the 2003–2004 season.

a. How many bars for each team are needed to display the data?

b. Make a multiple bar graph of the data.

National Hockey League Eastern Conference 2003–2004			
Team	**Wins**	**Losses**	**Ties**
Boston	41	19	15
Philadelphia	40	21	15
Tampa Bay	46	22	8

11. CHALLENGE Which team in Exercise 10 scored about 6 times as many wins as ties? *Explain* how you can tell this from your graph.

PROBLEM SOLVING

SEE EXAMPLE 1
on p. 83
for Exs. 12–14

12. GUIDED PROBLEM SOLVING A survey asked the question, "What is the most important thing kids can do to protect the environment?" The results are shown below.

Activity	**Responses**
Buy environmentally friendly products	358
Plant trees	480
Raise money	401
Recycle	834
Write your elected representatives	221

a. Choose a scale for a bar graph of the data.

b. Draw and label the bar graph.

c. "Recycle" had about 4 times the number of responses as which other activity? *Justify* your answer.

13. MOVIE TICKET PRICES *Describe* how the appearance of the graph will change if the scale goes from 0 to 40 in increments of 10 or from 0 to 200 in increments of 50.

14. ★ WRITING How might the scale of a bar graph affect how the bar graph is interpreted?

SEE EXAMPLE 2
on p. 84 for
Exs. 15, 17–19

15. ★ SHORT RESPONSE *Explain* how to make a double bar graph of favorite recording artists from a graph showing favorites for sixth graders and a graph showing favorites for seventh graders.

16. ★ **OPEN-ENDED MATH** Ask your classmates what their favorite food is and record the responses in a frequency table. Then display the data in a bar graph.

17. ★ **EXTENDED RESPONSE** Several sixth and seventh graders were asked their favorite class. The results are shown in the table.

Favorite Classes				
Class	Math	Social Studies	Science	English
Sixth Grade	80	35	15	20
Seventh Grade	15	70	75	40

a. **Display** Make a double bar graph of the data.

b. **Interpret** Which class was most popular with sixth graders? Which class was most popular with seventh graders? *Justify* your answers.

c. **Reasoning** Which subject shows the greatest difference between sixth graders and seventh graders? the least difference? *Compare* how you would use the table to answer the question with how you would use the graph.

IN-LINE SKATING The stacked bar graph at the right shows the results of a survey about how people use in-line skates.

18. **COMPARE AND CONTRAST** What are the advantages and disadvantages of a stacked bar graph?

19. **CHALLENGE** Draw the stacked bar graph as a double bar graph.

20. **CHALLENGE** Draw the data in Exercise 10 in a stacked bar graph. Why are the stacked bars all about the same height?

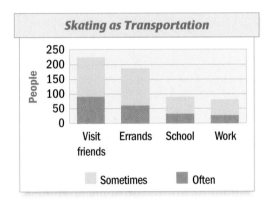

MIXED REVIEW

Get-Ready

Prepare for Lesson 2.6 in Ex. 21

21. Make a frequency table and a line plot of the following scores for a 10 point quiz: 9, 10, 6, 7, 7, 8, 9, 8, 9, 6, 7, 9, 8, 7, 7, 9. *(p. 76)*

Solve the equation using mental math. *(p. 34)*

22. $x + 2 = 15$ 23. $10 - x = 6$ 24. $3x = 24$ 25. $72 \div x = 9$

26. ★ **MULTIPLE CHOICE** What is the perimeter of the baseball diamond shown at the right? *(p. 66)*

    A 180 ft   **B** 360 ft

    C 4050 ft   **D** 8100 ft^2

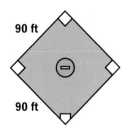

2.6 Coordinates and Line Graphs

Before	You plotted points on number lines and made bar graphs.
Now	You'll plot points on coordinate grids and make line graphs.
Why?	So you can visualize how data change, as in Ex. 31.

KEY VOCABULARY
- **axes,** *p. 88*
- **coordinates,** *p. 88*
- **ordered pair,** *p. 88*
- **origin,** *p. 88*
- **line graph,** *p. 89*

The graph below shows a point on a coordinate grid. Each point is described by an **ordered pair** of numbers. The numbers are the **coordinates** of the point. The grid is formed by two number lines, one vertical and one horizontal, called *axes*. The axes intersect at the *origin*.

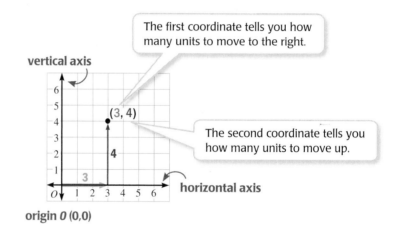

The first coordinate tells you how many units to move to the right.

The second coordinate tells you how many units to move up.

EXAMPLE 1 Graphing Points

AVOID ERRORS
Remember, the first coordinate in an ordered pair indicates a horizontal move, and the second coordinate indicates a vertical move.

a. Graph the point (4, 3) on a coordinate grid.

Start at (0, 0). Move **4** units to the right and **3** units up.

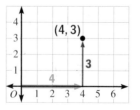

b. Graph the point (0, 2) on a coordinate grid.

Start at (0, 0). Move **0** units to the right and **2** units up.

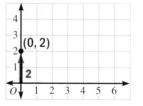

✓ **GUIDED PRACTICE** for Example 1

Graph the point on a coordinate grid. Label the coordinates.

1. (1, 0)   **2.** (1, 4)   **3.** (3, 2)   **4.** (5, 5)

Line Graphs A **line graph** represents data using points connected by line segments. Line graphs are often used to show change over time. You can make a break at the beginning of the scale to focus on the interval where the data fall.

EXAMPLE 2 Making a Line Graph

Population The table below shows the population of Austin County in southeast Texas from 1920 to 1990. Make a line graph of the data.

Population of Austin County, Texas								
Year	1920	1930	1940	1950	1960	1970	1980	1990
Population	18,874	18,860	17,384	14,663	13,777	13,831	17,726	19,832

STEP 1 **Make** a list of ordered pairs. Think of each column in the table as an ordered pair: (**year**, **population**)

(1920, 18,874), (1930, 18,860), (1940, 17,384), (1950, 14,663), (1960, 13,777), (1970, 13,831), (1980, 17,726), (1990, 19,832)

READING
The symbol ⥮ on the vertical scale indicates that the scale is broken.

STEP 2 **Choose** a scale that includes all the population values in your table.

STEP 3 **Graph** each point.

STEP 4 **Draw** line segments to connect the points.

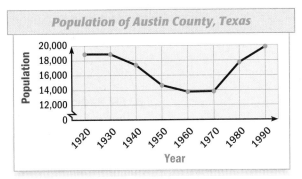

GUIDED PRACTICE for Example 2

In Exercises 5 and 6, use the graph above.

5. In which year was Austin County's population the greatest?

6. Over which decades did the population have its greatest increase? How can you tell from the graph?

7. **Pet Cats** The table below shows the number of pet cats in the United States from 1993 to 2003. Make a line graph of the data.

Pet Cats in the United States						
Year	1993	1995	1997	1999	2001	2003
Cats (millions)	64	66	70	73	76	78

EXAMPLE 3 Comparing Graphs

Radio Stations The two graphs below both show the number of AM radio stations in the United States. The first uses a full scale. The second uses a broken scale, deleting values between 0 and 4500. Compare the graphs.

MISLEADING GRAPHS
Certain graphs with broken axes can be misleading. See Lesson 13.4 for a full discussion of misleading graphs.

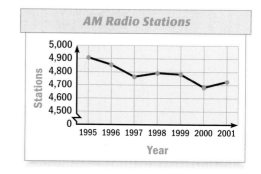

SOLUTION

Both graphs are accurate displays.

The number of AM radio stations is declining. The full scale shows that the decline is very slow.

The broken scale makes the data easy to read, but makes the decline seem sharper than it is.

✓ **GUIDED PRACTICE** for Example 3

8. FM Radio Stations Make two line graphs of the data, with and without a break in the scale. Then compare how you would use each graph.

Year	1995	1996	1997	1998	1999	2000	2001
FM stations	5296	5419	5542	5662	5766	5892	6051

2.6 EXERCISES

HOMEWORK KEY

★ = **STANDARDIZED TEST PRACTICE**
Exs. 19, 20, 25, 28, and 37

◯ = **HINTS** AND **HOMEWORK HELP**
for Exs. 7, 13, 15, 27 at classzone.com

SKILL PRACTICE

VOCABULARY Choose the letter that shows the location of the item on the coordinate grid.

1. point (2, 1) **2.** origin **3.** point (0, 3)

4. vertical axis **5.** point (1, 2) **6.** point (3, 0)

GRAPHING Graph and label the point on a coordinate grid.

SEE EXAMPLE 1
on p. 88
for Exs. 7–14

7. (6, 3) **8.** (2, 7) **9.** (0, 0) **10.** (4, 0)

11. (1, 8) **12.** (0, 6) **13.** (9, 0) **14.** (5, 5)

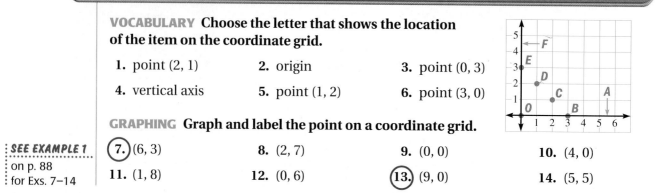

MAKING LINE GRAPHS Decide whether or not to use a broken scale to make a line graph of the data. Then make a line graph of the data.

SEE EXAMPLES 2 AND 3
on pp. 89–90
for Exs. 15–18

15.

Hour (A.M.)	7	8	9	10
Cars in lot	1	4	15	17

16.

Hour (P.M.)	1	2	3	4
Tickets sold	81	90	103	120

17.

Year	1998	2000	2002
Students	1253	1425	1310

18.

Snow (in.)	8	16	24	32
Rain (in.)	1	2	3	4

INTERPRETING LINE GRAPHS Use the line graph below.

19. ★ **MULTIPLE CHOICE** Which measurement is the best estimate of the puppy's weight on Day 6?

Ⓐ 11 oz   Ⓑ 12 oz

Ⓒ 13 oz   Ⓓ 14 oz

20. ★ **MULTIPLE CHOICE** Which ordered pair represents point *Z*?

Ⓐ (1, 10)   Ⓑ (10, 2)

Ⓒ (2, 10)   Ⓓ (10, 1)

Growth of Puppy

GRAPHING POINTS Draw a coordinate grid using intervals of $\frac{1}{2}$. Plot and label each point.

21. $(3, 1\frac{1}{2})$ **22.** $(\frac{1}{2}, 2\frac{1}{2})$ **23.** $(1\frac{1}{4}, 3)$ **24.** $(\frac{3}{4}, 1\frac{1}{4})$

PROBLEM SOLVING

SEE EXAMPLE 1
on p. 88
for Ex. 25

25. ★ **WRITING** The first coordinate is the number of minutes since the start of a race. The second coordinate is the total distance in kilometers. Interpret each point.

a. (0, 0)   **b.** (5, 1)   **c.** (15, 3)

SEE EXAMPLES 2 AND 3
on pp. 89–90
for Ex. 26

26. ◆ **MULTIPLE REPRESENTATIONS** The table below shows the number of students enrolled at a college.

a. Make a Bar Graph Make a double bar graph of the data.

b. Make a Line Graph Make a double line graph of the data using a full scale.

c. Make a Double Line Graph Make a double line graph of the data using a broken scale. Start the scale at 800 and use increments of 100.

d. Compare For each graph give one use for which it is better suited.

College Enrollment		
Year	Female	Male
1998	900	800
2000	1100	850
2002	1150	860
2004	1200	850

Animated Math at classzone.com

27. **INTERNET** Make a line graph of the data below. Use it to estimate the number of countries connected to the Internet in 1995.

Year	1988	1990	1992	1994	1996	1998	2000
Countries connected	8	22	43	81	165	200	214

28. ★ **SHORT RESPONSE** The table below shows the number of endangered or threatened bird species in the United States. Make two line graphs of the data, one with a broken scale and one without. *Compare* the graphs.

Year	1992	1993	1994	1995	1996	1997	1998	1999	2000
Species	84	88	90	91	90	93	93	89	93

TELEVISION **The table at the right shows the average number of minutes a teenager watches TV each day.**

29. Make a line graph of the data using a broken scale. *Explain* how you chose your scale.

30. How did the amount of time teenagers spent watching TV change between 1992 and 2000? *Explain.*

Year	Minutes each day
1992	190
1994	185
1996	169
1998	178
2000	184

CHALLENGE **During exercise, most people's heart rate should be between the minimum and maximum recommended rates shown.**

31. Make a double line graph. Use a different color for the minimum rates and the maximum rates. Include a key.

32. What rates would be the minimum and maximum for a 24 year old? Estimate the rate for the middle of this range.

Recommended Heart Rate (beats per minute)		
Age	Minimum	Maximum
20	130	160
30	124	152
40	117	144
50	111	136
60	104	128

MIXED REVIEW

Get-Ready

Prepare for Lesson 2.7 in Exs. 33–35

Find the sum or difference. *(p. 742)*

33. $3 + 8 + 7$

34. $2 + 13 + 8 + 7$

35. $200 - 125$

36. The table shows the mast heights of sailboats in a regatta. Make a bar graph of the data. *(p. 83)*

37. ★ **MULTIPLE CHOICE** You are drawing a map to your house for friends who live 75 miles away. Which scale would give the largest map that would fit into a 4 inch by 4 inch square? *(p. 72)*

    (A) 1 in. : 2 mi   **(B)** 1 in. : 10 mi

    (C) 1 in. : 25 mi   **(D)** 1 in. : 50 mi

Mast Height	Number of Boats
31 ft	2
34 ft	6
36 ft	3
41 ft	6

2.6 Creating Data Displays

EXAMPLE You can create bar graphs, line graphs, and other data displays using a spreadsheet program.

The table shows the population of the United States from 2000 to 2004. Make a bar graph of the data.

	A	B
1	Year	Population (thousands)
2	2000	282,178
3	2001	285,094
4	2002	287,974
5	2003	290,810
6	2004	292,801

> A2:B6 in Step 1 refers to the rectangle of cells whose opposite corners are A2 and B6.

SOLUTION

STEP 1 **Enter** the data in the first two columns of the spreadsheet. Use an apostrophe in front of each year ('2000). Highlight the data in cells A2:B6 and insert a chart. Select *column* chart as the chart type.

STEP 2 **Choose** chart options, such as the title, grid lines, and a legend (key).

STEP 3 **Double-click** on a feature to change its formatting. For example, use a population scale from 0 to 300,000 in increments of 50,000.

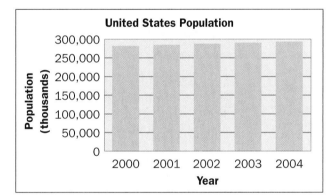

PRACTICE Use the data below.

1. Make a double bar graph of the data. Follow Steps 1–3 above, but highlight three columns of data.

2. Make a double line graph of the data. Follow Steps 1–3 above, but enter the years without apostrophes, and select a scatter plot that connects points with lines as the type of chart. Show major grid lines for both axes. The population scale doesn't have to start at 0.

	A	B	C
1	Year	Male population (thousands)	Female population (thousands)
2	2000	138,456	143,721
3	2001	140,009	145,085
4	2002	141,533	146,441
5	2003	143,037	147,773

2.7 Circle Graphs

Before You made and interpreted bar graphs and line graphs.

Now You'll interpret circle graphs and make predictions.

Why? So you can visualize data about a whole group, as in Example 1.

KEY VOCABULARY
• circle graph, p. 94

Roller Coasters A group of teenagers are asked what they think about roller coasters. Their answers are shown in the circle graph at the right. How many of them think roller coasters are great?

A **circle graph** is a graph that represents data as parts of a circle. The entire circle represents all of the data. You can make conclusions about the data in a circle graph based on the size of each section.

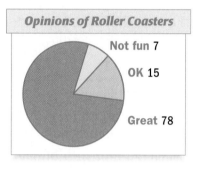

Opinions of Roller Coasters

Not fun 7
OK 15
Great 78

EXAMPLE 1 Interpreting a Circle Graph

Use the circle graph above.

a. To find out how many of the teenagers think roller coasters are great, find the data value in the section labeled "Great."

▶ **Answer** The number who think roller coasters are great is 78.

b. To find out how many of the teenagers do not think roller coasters are great, add the values in the "OK" and the "Not fun" sections: 15 + 7 = 22.

▶ **Answer** The number who do not think roller coasters are great is 22.

✓ GUIDED PRACTICE for Example 1

The circle graph shows how many people out of 100 prefer each of four types of shoes.

1. Which type of shoe is least popular?

2. How many of the people do not prefer loafers?

3. Is it reasonable to say that "sneakers" is the most popular choice? *Explain.*

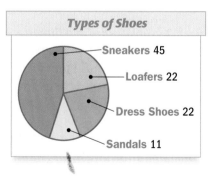

Types of Shoes

Sneakers 45
Loafers 22
Dress Shoes 22
Sandals 11

EXAMPLE 2 Using a Graph

Frozen Yogurt The circle graph shows the favorite frozen yogurt flavors of 100 students. About 300 students will attend a party. Predict how many students will ask for vanilla frozen yogurt.

Favorite Flavors

SOLUTION

Find the relationship between the number of students surveyed and the number of students at the party: $100 \times 3 = 300$.

Multiply the number of students who prefer vanilla by 3 to predict the number of students who will ask for vanilla at the party: $38 \times 3 = 114$.

▶ **Answer** About 114 students will ask for vanilla frozen yogurt at the party.

✓ **GUIDED PRACTICE** for Example 2

4. **What If?** Use the graph above. Suppose only 200 students attend the party. Predict how many students will ask for strawberry frozen yogurt.

2.7 EXERCISES

HOMEWORK KEY

★ = **STANDARDIZED TEST PRACTICE**
Exs. 7, 14, 15, 21, 27, 29, and 37

◯ = **HINTS AND HOMEWORK HELP**
for Exs. 5, 9, 11, 19 at classzone.com

SKILL PRACTICE

VOCABULARY **Which type of graph is best suited for the purpose?**

1. comparing separate categories

2. comparing part of a data set to the entire set

3. showing change over time

A. circle graph

B. line graph

C. bar graph

READING CIRCLE GRAPHS **Tell which section of the circle graph below fits the description.**

4. It represents about half the data.

5. It represents the least data value.

6. It represents the greatest data value.

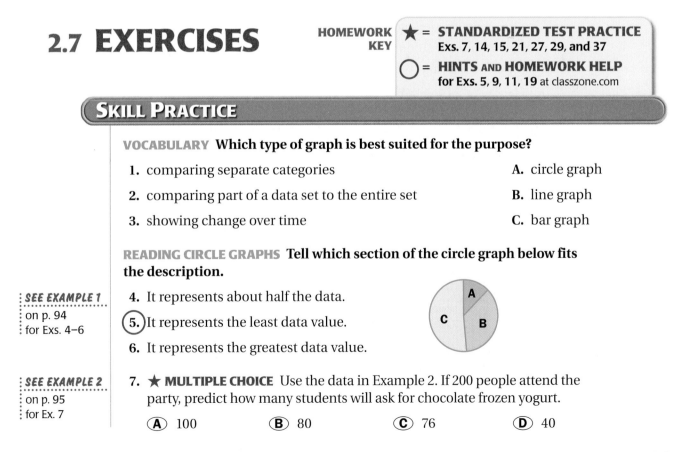

7. ★ **MULTIPLE CHOICE** Use the data in Example 2. If 200 people attend the party, predict how many students will ask for chocolate frozen yogurt.

(**A**) 100 (**B**) 80 (**C**) 76 (**D**) 40

READING CIRCLE GRAPHS The circle graph at the right shows the population of the United States, in millions, in 2003.

SEE EXAMPLE 1
on p. 94
for Exs. 8–13

8. Which age group was the smallest?

9. How can you tell from the graph that about half the population was under 35 years old?

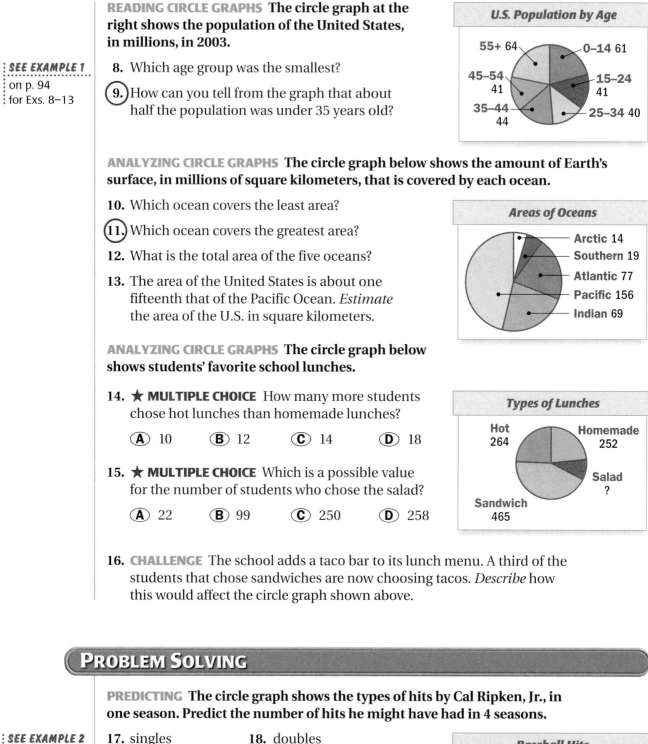

U.S. Population by Age

55+ 64   0–14 61
45–54 41   15–24 41
35–44 44   25–34 40

ANALYZING CIRCLE GRAPHS The circle graph below shows the amount of Earth's surface, in millions of square kilometers, that is covered by each ocean.

10. Which ocean covers the least area?

11. Which ocean covers the greatest area?

12. What is the total area of the five oceans?

13. The area of the United States is about one fifteenth that of the Pacific Ocean. *Estimate* the area of the U.S. in square kilometers.

Areas of Oceans

Arctic 14
Southern 19
Atlantic 77
Pacific 156
Indian 69

ANALYZING CIRCLE GRAPHS The circle graph below shows students' favorite school lunches.

14. ★ **MULTIPLE CHOICE** How many more students chose hot lunches than homemade lunches?

A 10   **B** 12   **C** 14   **D** 18

15. ★ **MULTIPLE CHOICE** Which is a possible value for the number of students who chose the salad?

A 22   **B** 99   **C** 250   **D** 258

Types of Lunches

Hot 264   Homemade 252
Salad ?
Sandwich 465

16. **CHALLENGE** The school adds a taco bar to its lunch menu. A third of the students that chose sandwiches are now choosing tacos. *Describe* how this would affect the circle graph shown above.

PROBLEM SOLVING

PREDICTING The circle graph shows the types of hits by Cal Ripken, Jr., in one season. Predict the number of hits he might have had in 4 seasons.

SEE EXAMPLE 2
on p. 95
for Exs. 17–21

17. singles   18. doubles

19. triples   20. home runs

21. ★ **WRITING** Explain how you can use the data to predict the total number of hits Cal Ripken, Jr., might have gotten in 3 seasons. Then make the prediction.

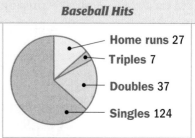

Baseball Hits

Home runs 27
Triples 7
Doubles 37
Singles 124

★ = **STANDARDIZED TEST PRACTICE**   ○ = **HINTS AND HOMEWORK HELP** at *classzone.com*

MARINE MAMMALS The circle graph shows the total amount of money spent to feed the three types of mammals at an aquarium for one year.

22. Predict how much money will be spent to feed the sea otters for four years.

23. There are 4 sea lions. About how much does it cost to feed one sea lion for one year?

24. There are 7 harbor seals. About how much does it cost to feed one harbor seal for one year?

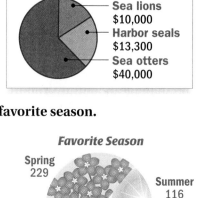

Yearly Feeding Costs

Sea lions $10,000
Harbor seals $13,300
Sea otters $40,000

COMPARING GRAPHS A group of people voted for their favorite season. The results are shown in the circle graph.

25. Use the data to make a bar graph.

26. Which season got the most votes? Which graph did you use to decide?

27. ★ **SHORT RESPONSE** On which graph can you more easily see that spring and summer combined got slightly more than half the votes? *Justify* your choice.

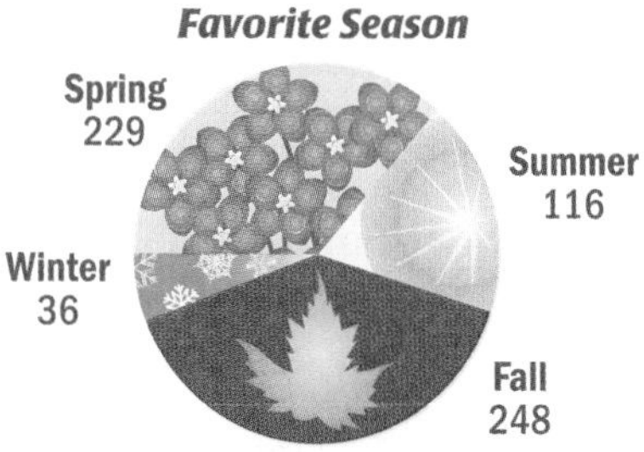

Favorite Season

Spring 229
Summer 116
Winter 36
Fall 248

MOVIES The graph shows the amounts 100 people paid to rent a movie.

28. How many people out of 300 would you expect to pay $4 or less?

29. ★ **WRITING** *Explain* how a bar graph of the data would be similar to the circle graph.

30. **CHALLENGE** Is a line graph a good choice to represent the data? Why or why not?

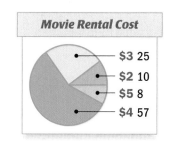

Movie Rental Cost

$3 25
$2 10
$5 8
$4 57

MIXED REVIEW

Get-Ready

Prepare for Lesson 2.8 in Exs. 31–36

Find the quotient. *(p. 3)*

31. $255 \div 5$

32. $1250 \div 25$

33. $4725 \div 21$

Evaluate the expression. *(p. 21)*

34. $\dfrac{2 + 8}{5}$

35. $\dfrac{14 + 13 + 8}{7}$

36. $\dfrac{5 + 11 + 8 + 12}{4}$

37. ★ **SHORT RESPONSE** The table shows the number of pencils four students have in their book bags. *Explain* how to choose a scale for a bar graph of the data. Then make a bar graph. *(p. 83)*

Student	Number of Pencils
John	10
Olivia	25
Parker	18
Camille	3

38. Describe how to graph the point (0, 8) on a coordinate grid. *(p. 82)*

INVESTIGATION
Use before Lesson 2.8

GOAL
Use numbers to describe
a set of data.

MATERIALS
• counters or coins

2.8 Finding Typical Data Values

EXPLORE Use counters to find values to describe a set of data.

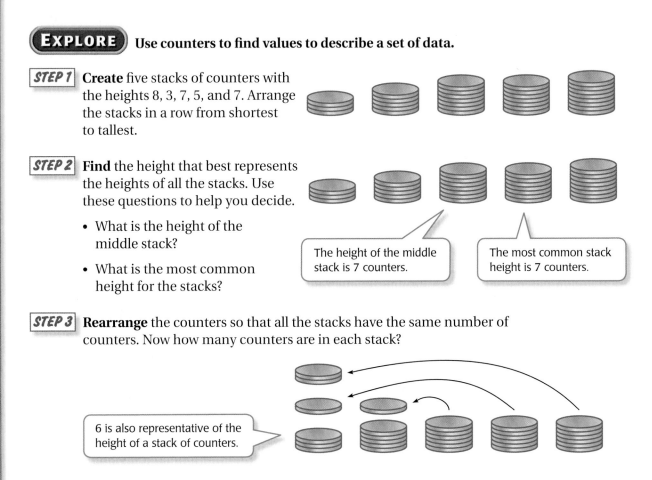

STEP 1 **Create** five stacks of counters with the heights 8, 3, 7, 5, and 7. Arrange the stacks in a row from shortest to tallest.

STEP 2 **Find** the height that best represents the heights of all the stacks. Use these questions to help you decide.

- What is the height of the middle stack?

- What is the most common height for the stacks?

The height of the middle stack is 7 counters.

The most common stack height is 7 counters.

STEP 3 **Rearrange** the counters so that all the stacks have the same number of counters. Now how many counters are in each stack?

6 is also representative of the height of a stack of counters.

You can use either 6 or 7 to describe about how tall each stack is.

PRACTICE Repeat Steps 1–3 to find three values to describe the data set.

1. stack heights: 2, 7, 5, 9, 9, 5, 5

2. stack heights: 2, 8, 6, 2, 7

DRAW CONCLUSIONS

3. **REASONING** Do you think all three values you found to describe the data are representative of the data in Exercise 1? of the data in Exercise 2? Why or why not?

2.8 Mean, Median, and Mode

Before	You represented data using graphs.
Now	You'll describe data using mean, median, mode, and range.
Why?	So you can find averages, as in Example 1.

KEY VOCABULARY
- **mean,** *p. 99*
- **median,** *p. 99*
- **mode,** *p. 99*
- **range,** *p. 100*

Astronauts In the Apollo space program, each lunar landing mission had one lunar module pilot. What is the average age of these pilots? Use the data below.

Apollo mission	11	12	13	14	15	16	17
Pilot's age	39	37	36	40	41	36	37

You can use three types of averages to describe a data set.

KEY CONCEPT *For Your Notebook*

Averages

The **mean** of a data set is the sum of the values divided by the number of values.

The **median** of a data set is the middle value when the values are written in numerical order. If a data set has an even number of values, the median is the mean of the two middle values.

The **mode** of a data set is the value that occurs most often. A data set can have one mode, more than one mode, or no mode.

EXAMPLE 1 Finding a Mean

ANOTHER WAY
To find the mean, you can redistribute the years among the 7 pilots until they all have an equal number of years.

To find the mean of the ages for the Apollo pilots given above, add their ages. Then divide by 7, the number of pilots.

$$\text{Mean} = \frac{39 + 37 + 36 + 40 + 41 + 36 + 37}{7} = \frac{266}{7} = 38$$

▶ **Answer** The mean of the Apollo pilots' ages is 38 years.

✓ **GUIDED PRACTICE** for Example 1

Find the mean of the data.

1. 20, 25, 25, 20, 25
2. 14, 17, 9, 2, 4, 10, 5, 3
3. 91, 150, 80, 71, 74, 81, 83
4. 44, 23, 69, 36, 50, 48

Range The **range** of a data set is the difference between the greatest value and the least value. It describes how spread out the data are.

EXAMPLE 2 Finding Median, Mode, and Range

Astronauts Find the median, mode(s), and range of the pilots' ages from the data on page 99.

Put the ages in order from least to greatest.

$$36 \quad 36 \quad 37 \quad 37 \quad 39 \quad 40 \quad 41$$

AVOID ERRORS
Always write the data values in numerical order before determining the median.

Median: The middle number is 37, so the median is 37 years.

Mode: Both 36 and 37 occur twice. The two modes are 36 and 37 years.

Range: Range = Oldest age − Youngest age

= 41 years − 36 years

= 5 years

EXAMPLE 3 Solving a Multi-Step Problem

TAKE NOTES
Be sure your notes include an example that has an even number of data values, as in Example 3. Note that the median is the mean of the two middle numbers.

Music The minutes that students practice a musical instrument each week are listed at the right. Which average(s) are representative of the data set?

Students' Practice Times			
30	30	50	90
100	120	150	630

SOLUTION

STEP 1 **Find the mean:** $1200 \div 8 = 150$ minutes
Most of the students practiced less than this, some much less. It is not representative.

STEP 2 **Find the median:** $(90 + 100) \div 2 = 95$ minutes
The median is the middle value of all the data. Half the data are greater than it and half are less than it. It is representative of this data set.

STEP 3 **Find the mode:** 30 minutes, because 30 appears twice in the data set. The mode is the least value in this data set. Most of the students practiced much more than this. It is not representative.

▶**Answer** The median is the only average that represents this data set well.

✔ **GUIDED PRACTICE** for Examples 2 and 3

Find the median, mode(s), and range of the data.

5. 8, 13, 8, 4, 11, 4, 2, 6   **6.** 91, 150, 80, 71, 74, 81, 80, 77

7. Choose the best average(s) to represent the data in Exercise 6.

2.8 EXERCISES

HOMEWORK KEY

★ = **STANDARDIZED TEST PRACTICE**
Exs. 14, 33, 38, 39, 40, 46, and 53

◯ = **HINTS** AND **HOMEWORK HELP**
for Exs. 7, 11, 17, 37 at classzone.com

SKILL PRACTICE

1. **VOCABULARY** Copy and complete: The difference between the greatest and the least values of a data set is its __?__.

2. **VOCABULARY** Copy and complete: The middle value of a data set when the values are written in numerical order is its __?__.

AVERAGES AND RANGE Find the mean, median, mode(s), and range.

SEE EXAMPLES
1 AND 2
on pp. 99–100
for Exs. 3–13

3. 2, 3, 1, 1, 3

4. 10, 8, 9, 8, 5

5. 7, 1, 2, 6, 1, 7

6. 13, 8, 11, 7, 5, 10

7. 7, 9, 12, 5, 12

8. 5, 11, 9, 5, 25

9. 14, 10, 9, 7, 14, 16, 14

10. 42, 37, 25, 33, 25, 18, 37

11. 26, 22, 10, 12, 16, 28

12. 30, 60, 10, 30, 30, 50, 80, 30

13. **ERROR ANALYSIS** Your friend found the median and the mode of a data set. Describe and correct your friend's error(s).

$\times$ Median ⌐→
36, 32, 35, 42, 38, 32, 34
⌐ Mode →

SEE EXAMPLE 3
on p. 100
for Exs. 14–17

14. ★ **MULTIPLE CHOICE** Which number is *not* the mean, median, or mode of the data set 4, 3, 15, 11, 3, 8, 7, 5?

ⓐ 3   ⓑ 5   ⓒ 6   ⓓ 7

FINDING THE BEST AVERAGE Find the mean, median, and mode(s). Then tell which average(s) best represents the data set. *Explain* your choice.

15. Bowling scores: 180, 170, 190, 200, 130, 30, 180, 160

16. Math test scores: 70, 71, 97, 71, 62, 94, 95

17. Video game scores: 575, 575, 400, 890, 625, 670, 520, 675, 720, 1550

CALCULATOR Find the mean of the data.

18. 142, 131, 135, 148, 139

19. 796, 849, 833, 840, 827, 836, 843

20. 2064, 2870, 4610, 8640, 5009, 3003

21. 9440, 4571, 5456, 7673, 1705, 2235

FINDING MODES Find the mode(s) of the data.

22. green, red, green, blue, blue, green, green, red, red, blue, green, red

23. left, right, straight, right, left, right, straight, left, right, left, straight

24. **REASONING** For Exercises 22 and 23, is there a mean? a median? *Explain* your reasoning.

NUMBER SENSE Tell whether the mean is reasonable. If it is not reasonable, suggest a more reasonable mean. *Justify* your choice.

25. 13, 16, 9, 21, 25, 30; Mean: 32

26. 5, 11, 4, 11, 7, 7, 10, 8, 9; Mean: 5

27. 6, 4, 3, 8, 9, 12, 13, 9; Mean: 8

28. 9, 12, 13, 8, 33, 15, 22; Mean: 30

REASONING Tell whether the statement is *true* or *false*. *Explain.*

29. The mode is always one of the numbers in a data set.

30. The mean can be one of the numbers in a data set.

31. The median is always one of the numbers in a data set.

32. A data set always has a mode.

33. ★ **OPEN-ENDED MATH** Make up a data set for a situation where the best average is the mean. Repeat this exercise for the median and the mode(s).

CHALLENGE Use the given mean or median to find the missing data value.

34. 14, 24, __?__, 18, 30;
Mean: 23

35. 40, 28, 16, 18, 37, 20, __?__, 35;
Median: 26

Animated Math at classzone.com

PROBLEM SOLVING

BASKETBALL Use the data showing the heights, in inches, of the players on a basketball team to answer Exercises 36–37.

77, 76, 67, 77, 76, 68, 73, 77, 70, 72, 70

SEE EXAMPLE 3
on p. 100
for Exs. 36–37

36. **CALCULATE** Find the mean, median, mode(s), and range of the data. Which average(s) best represents the data set?

37. **COMPARE** If the 67 inch player is replaced with a 78 inch player, how is the range affected? How are the mean, median, and mode affected?

38. ★ **SHORT RESPONSE** Paint for your garage should be applied when the temperature is at or above 60°F. The average temperature for a week is 65°F. Can you paint every day of that week? *Explain.*

39. ★ **WRITING** The average of the temperatures at noon on Inauguration Day from 1957 to 1997 was 36°F. Do you think the temperature was near freezing (32°F) for every inauguration from 1957 to 1997? *Explain.*

40. ★ **EXTENDED RESPONSE** A student has scored 90, 93, 65, and 92 on the first four quizzes in her history class.

  a. **Calculate** Find the mean, median, and mode(s) of the quiz scores.

  b. **Interpret** Which average(s) best represents the quiz scores? *Explain* your reasoning.

  c. **Reasoning** The student scores a 100 on her next quiz. *Explain* how this will affect the mean, median, and mode(s) of her scores.

★ = STANDARDIZED TEST PRACTICE   ◯ = HINTS AND HOMEWORK HELP *at classzone.com*

Sea Turtles Sea turtles come in many sizes, as the table at the right shows. Sea turtles hatch from eggs that are laid in nests buried in the sands of beaches. The hatchlings spend a very short time in the nest before making a run for the sea. Some types of sea turtles migrate only a few miles in search of food. Others travel thousands of miles. Their diets consist of seaweed, or a mixture of seaweed and sea animals.

Adult Sea Turtle Lengths (inches)			
Type of turtle	*Length*	*Type of turtle*	*Length*
Kemps Ridley	30	Loggerhead	48
Olive Ridley	30	Black	39
Leatherback	96	Flatback	39
Green	48	Hawksbill	30

Green Sea Turtle

41. **Calculate** Find the mean, median, and mode(s) of the data.

42. **Compare** Which average(s) is/are the greatest?

43. **Reasoning** Remove the Leatherback turtle from the data set and find the mean length of the remaining turtles. *Explain* why this value is different from the mean length of all 8 turtles.

44. **Compare** Does the median or the mode(s) change when these measures are computed for the 7 turtles not including the Leatherback?

45. **Open-Ended** Which average(s) best represents the entire data set? *Justify* your choice.

46. ★ **MULTIPLE CHOICE** A survey reported that the number of pets owned by 11 students were 0, 1, 2, 2, 4, 4, 5, 6, 6, 6, 8. Which measures of these data are the same?

Ⓐ mean and median   Ⓑ median and range

Ⓒ mode and mean   Ⓓ mode and median

47. **CHALLENGE** The line plot shows the ages of all but two runners in a three-legged race. Suppose the mean, median, mode(s), and range are the same with or without the data for the other two runners. If the runners have different ages, what could these ages be?

Ages of runners

48. **CHALLENGE** A pair of runners, both the same age, joins the 18 runners in Exercise 47. The mean age is now 13 years. How old are the two new runners? How does adding these two runners to the data change the median, mode, and range?

Get-Ready

Prepare for
Lesson 3.1
in Exs. 49–52

Write the number in words. *(p. 737)*

49. 35   **50.** 126   **51.** 607   **52.** 1578

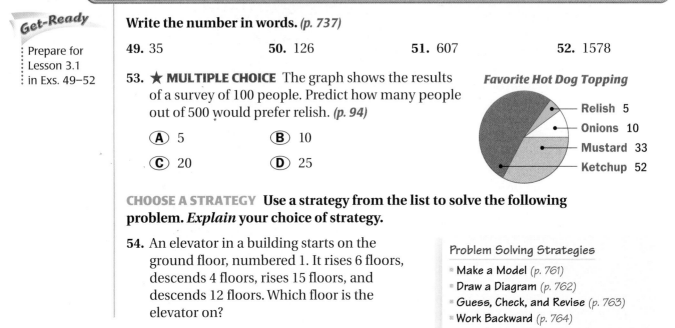

53. ★ **MULTIPLE CHOICE** The graph shows the results of a survey of 100 people. Predict how many people out of 500 would prefer relish. *(p. 94)*

(A) 5   (B) 10

(C) 20   (D) 25

Favorite Hot Dog Topping

Relish 5
Onions 10
Mustard 33
Ketchup 52

CHOOSE A STRATEGY Use a strategy from the list to solve the following problem. *Explain* your choice of strategy.

54. An elevator in a building starts on the ground floor, numbered 1. It rises 6 floors, descends 4 floors, rises 15 floors, and descends 12 floors. Which floor is the elevator on?

Problem Solving Strategies

▪ Make a Model *(p. 761)*
▪ Draw a Diagram *(p. 762)*
▪ Guess, Check, and Revise *(p. 763)*
▪ Work Backward *(p. 764)*

QUIZ *for Lessons 2.5–2.8*

RAINFALL The table shows the average daily rainfall in millimeters recorded at a local airport for five months. *(p. 83)*

1. Make a bar graph of the data.

2. Make a line graph of the data.

Graph the points on one coordinate grid. Label the coordinates. *(p. 88)*

3. (4, 2)   **4.** (0, 3)   **5.** (1, 0)

Average Daily Rainfall (millimeters)	
Month	*Rainfall*
January	11
February	12
March	12
April	19
May	4

FISHING The circle graph below shows the results of a survey of 100 people who like fishing. *(p. 94)*

6. How many more people prefer freshwater fishing to deep-sea fishing?

7. Predict the number of people who would prefer deep-sea fishing in a group of 400 people who like fishing.

8. Find the mean, median, mode(s), and range of the data. Choose the best average(s) to represent these data: 11, 17, 5, 7, 11, 3.

Favorite Type of Fishing

Freshwater 52
Fly 29
Deep-sea 17
Ice 2

Lessons 2.5–2.8

1. **SHORT RESPONSE** The data give the total number of points scored in a season for six players on a team. Make a bar graph of the data. *Explain* how you chose your scale and the intervals for it.

   Justin: 85   Mike: 120   Tyler: 75

   Aidan: 250   Ryan: 110   Ethan: 50

2. **EXTENDED RESPONSE** The table shows the distances you traveled on your bike.

Day of the week	Distance (in miles)	
	Week 1	Week 2
Monday	2	5
Tuesday	0	2
Wednesday	5	0
Thursday	3	3
Friday	2	1

   a. *Describe* the steps in making a double bar graph of the data.
   b. Make a double bar graph of the data.
   c. *Explain* how to use your graph to find which days you increased your miles from the previous week.

3. **SHORT RESPONSE** The table shows the number of students enrolled in a high school. Make a line graph of the data using a break in the scale. *Explain* how you chose your scale. Then use the graph to estimate the number of students enrolled in 2003.

Year	1998	2000	2002	2004
Students	2020	2115	2285	2315

4. **OPEN-ENDED** *Describe* information about your city or town that could be displayed by using a line graph.

5. **EXTENDED RESPONSE** The circle graph below shows the number of wins, losses, and ties for a hockey team in one season.

   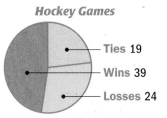

   Hockey Games

   Ties 19
   Wins 39
   Losses 24

   a. How many games were played that season?
   b. *Compare* the number of wins to the number of ties and losses.
   c. A third of the losses occurred in overtime. How many losses was this?
   d. *Explain* how you can use the circle graph to predict the number of wins for two seasons.

6. **GRIDDED ANSWER** The average age of a group of 8 college professors is 50 years. A new professor, age 32, joins the group. What is the average age of the group now?

7. **MULTI-STEP PROBLEM** The test scores on a recent science exam are given below.

   84, 90, 91, 50, 84, 90, 100, 96, 88,
   88, 50, 91, 86, 92, 50, 98, 100, 48

   a. List the data values in increasing order.
   b. Find the mean, median, mode, and range of the data set.
   c. Which average best represents the data set? How well did the class do overall on the exam? *Explain* your reasoning.

8. **OPEN-ENDED** Make up a data set with at least three different data values in which the mean, median, and the mode are equal.

2 CHAPTER REVIEW

@HomeTutor
classzone.com
Vocabulary Practice

REVIEW KEY VOCABULARY

- inch, foot, yard, mile, *p. 59*
- millimeter, centimeter, meter, kilometer, *p. 60*
- perimeter, *p. 66*
- area, *p. 67*
- scale drawing, scale, *p. 72*
- data, frequency table, *p. 76*
- line plot, *p. 77*
- bar graph, *p. 83*
- double bar graph, *p. 84*
- axes, coordinates, ordered pair, origin, *p. 88*
- line graph, *p. 89*
- circle graph, *p. 94*
- mean, median, mode, *p. 99*
- range, *p. 100*

VOCABULARY EXERCISES

Tell whether the statement is *true* or *false*. If it is false, change one word and rewrite it as a true statement.

1. The perimeter of a figure is a measure of how much surface the figure covers.
2. A line graph is often used to represent data that change over time.

Copy and complete the statement.

3. In the ordered pair (3, 5) the first __?__ is 3.
4. In a data set the sum of the values divided by the number of values is the __?__.
5. In a data set the value or values that occur most often is the __?__.

REVIEW EXAMPLES AND EXERCISES

2.1 Measuring Lengths

pp. 59–65

EXAMPLE

Using the "width of a little finger" as a benchmark, you can see that the length of the line segment is about 4 centimeters. Using the centimeter ruler, you can see that the length of the line segment is exactly 42 millimeters.

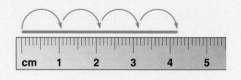

EXERCISES

SEE EXAMPLES 2 AND 5 on pp. 60–62 for Exs. 6–7

Use a benchmark to estimate the length of the line segment in centimeters. Then find the length of the line segment to the nearest millimeter and to the nearest centimeter.

6. ____________________

7. ________________

2.2 Perimeter and Area

pp. 66–71

EXAMPLE

Find the perimeter and the area of the rectangle or square.

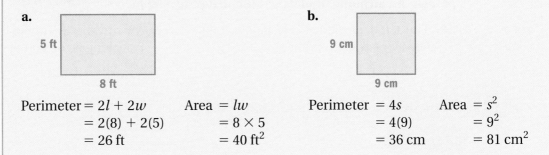

a.

5 ft

8 ft

$$\text{Perimeter} = 2l + 2w \qquad \text{Area} = lw$$
$$= 2(8) + 2(5) \qquad = 8 \times 5$$
$$= 26 \text{ ft} \qquad = 40 \text{ ft}^2$$

b.

9 cm

9 cm

$$\text{Perimeter} = 4s \qquad \text{Area} = s^2$$
$$= 4(9) \qquad = 9^2$$
$$= 36 \text{ cm} \qquad = 81 \text{ cm}^2$$

EXERCISES

Find the perimeter and the area of the rectangle or square.

SEE EXAMPLES 1, 2, 3, AND 4
on pp. 66–68
for Exs. 8–11

8.

11 yd

11 yd

9.

12 m

4 m

10.

11 km

20 km

11. **Field Hockey** A rectangular field hockey playing field has an area of 6000 square yards. The length of the field is 100 yards. What is the width of the field?

2.3 Scale Drawings

pp. 72–75

EXAMPLE

The length of a wall on a scale drawing is 192 millimeters. The scale on the drawing is 8 mm : 2 m. Find the actual length.

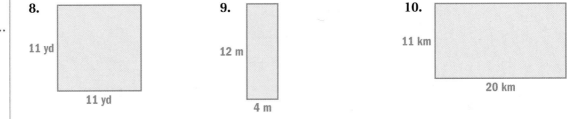

drawing : actual

× ? ⟨ 8 mm : 2 m   **Ask "8 times what number equals 192?"**
      192 mm : ____ m

Multiply by 24, because 8 × 24 = 192

8 mm : 2 m
192 mm : 48 m

The actual length of the wall is 2 × 24 = 48 meters.

EXERCISES

Find the actual length of the wall in the Example using the given scale.

SEE EXAMPLES 2 AND 3

on p. 73
for Exs. 12–17

12. 3 mm : 1 m   **13.** 4 mm : 2 m   **14.** 6 mm : 1 m   **15.** 6 mm : 6 m

Models An airplane model uses the scale 1 in. : 32 in.

16. The actual airplane is 512 inches long. How long is the model?

17. A stripe on the model is 8 inches long. How long is the actual stripe?

2.4 Frequency Tables and Line Plots

pp. 76–80

EXAMPLE

The list below shows the numbers of pets that students in a class have. Make a frequency table and a line plot of the data.

2, 0, 1, 3, 0, 2, 1, 1, 0, 3, 3, 1, 4, 0, 1, 1, 0, 0, 2, 1, 0

Pets Owned	Tally	Frequency
0	ЖΙΙ	7
1	ЖΙΙ	7
2	ΙΙΙ	3
3	ΙΙΙ	3
4	Ι	1

Number of Pets

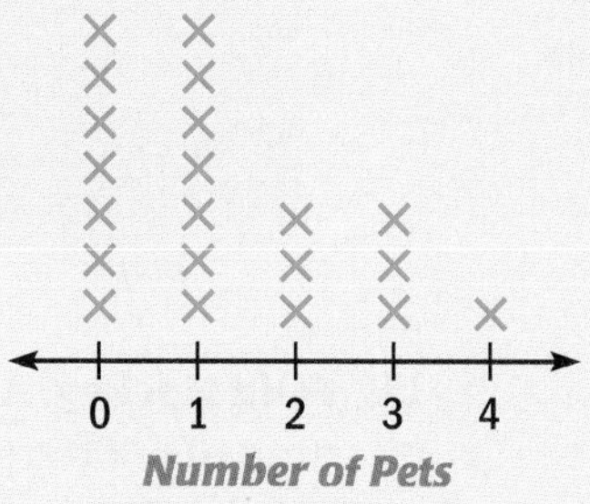

EXERCISES

SEE EXAMPLES 1 AND 2

on pp. 76–77
for Exs. 18–20

18. **Yearbook Committee** The data below list the ages of students on a yearbook committee. Make a frequency table and a line plot of the data.

12, 11, 10, 15, 14, 12, 13, 10, 11, 13, 15, 15, 13, 11, 12

19. **Marching Band** The data below show the scores for a band competition. Make a frequency table and a line plot of the data.

71, 81, 72, 81, 72, 80, 78, 75, 71, 78, 80, 73, 76, 78, 81, 72, 75, 79, 80, 79, 72, 71, 80, 81, 71

20. **Fishing Tournament** The data below are the weights in ounces of fish caught. Make a frequency table and a line plot of the data.

23, 19, 24, 33, 20, 25, 23, 23, 26, 21, 31, 20, 20, 21, 22, 21, 25, 24, 25, 17, 19, 15, 19, 36, 31, 21, 29, 26, 27

Bar Graphs   *pp. 83–87*

EXAMPLE

Choose an appropriate scale and make a bar graph of the data.

Team	Games Won
Bears	14
Cardinals	11
Otters	9
Eagles	13

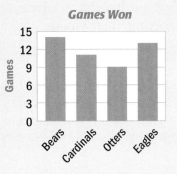

EXERCISES

SEE EXAMPLES
1 AND 2
on pp. 83–84
for Exs. 21–22

21. Make a bar graph of the data at the right showing the number of shots made by each player.

22. Make a double bar graph of the data. Include a key.

Player	Shots made	Shots attempted
Kaye	14	15
Teva	8	13
Olivia	16	22

2.6 **Coordinates and Line Graphs**   *pp. 88–92*

EXAMPLE

Choose an appropriate scale and make a line graph of the data.

Year	Male Soccer Players
1995	7,691,000
1996	8,626,000
1997	8,303,000
1998	8,232,000

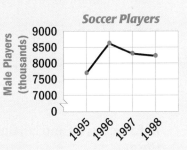

EXERCISES

SEE EXAMPLES
1 AND 2
on pp. 88–89
for Exs. 23–24

23. Graph and label the points (7, 1) and (0, 8) on a coordinate grid.

24. Butter Prices The table shows prices of butter, in cents per pound. Make a line graph of the data.

Year	1996	1997	1998	1999
Price	217	246	318	227

2.7 Circle Graphs

pp. 94–97

EXAMPLE

Great Lakes The circle graph shows the shoreline lengths, in kilometers, of the Great Lakes and their islands. Which lake has the greatest amount of shoreline? How long is its shoreline?

The largest section of the circle graph is labeled "Lake Huron" and has a data value of 6157. So, Lake Huron has the greatest amount of shoreline. It is 6157 kilometers long.

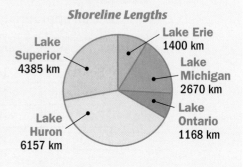

Shoreline Lengths

Lake Superior 4385 km
Lake Erie 1400 km
Lake Michigan 2670 km
Lake Ontario 1168 km
Lake Huron 6157 km

EXERCISES

In Exercises 25–27, use the circle graph above.

SEE EXAMPLE 1
on p. 94
for Exs. 25–27

25. Which lake has the least amount of shoreline?

26. What is the total shoreline of all five Great Lakes?

27. Which lake has about one quarter of the shoreline? Is it easier to identify this lake from the data or from the graph?

2.8 Mean, Median, and Mode

pp. 99–104

EXAMPLE

The prices of several pairs of shoes are: $35, $45, $55, $55, $60, $140. Find the mean, median, mode(s), and range of the data set.

Mean: $\frac{35 + 45 + 55 + 55 + 60 + 140}{6} = 65$ **Median:** $\frac{55 + 55}{2} = 55$

Mode: The mode is 55. **Range:** $140 - 35 = 105$

EXERCISES

In Exercises 28 and 29, find the mean, median, mode(s), and range of the data.

SEE EXAMPLES 1, 2, AND 3
on pp. 99–100
for Exs. 28–30

28. Prices of portable CD players (dollars): 70, 180, 110, 100, 200, 100, 80

29. Ages of houses in a neighborhood (years): 28, 20, 28, 26, 20, 63, 23, 24

30. Choose the best average(s) to represent the data in Exercise 29. *Explain.*

Choose an appropriate customary unit and metric unit for the length.

1. distance between Earth and the sun

2. height of a waterfall

3. Use a ruler to draw a line segment that is 4 inches long.

4. Measure to find the length, in centimeters, of one side of the square at the right. Then find its perimeter and area.

5. A scale drawing uses a scale of 1 in. : 3 yd. A distance on the drawing is 12 inches. What is the actual distance?

6. The rolls of a number cube are given. Make a frequency table and a line plot of the data.
2, 3, 6, 4, 5, 4, 4, 4, 3, 2, 5, 3, 6, 6, 4, 1, 1, 2, 3, 2, 4, 2, 1, 4, 2

Graph the points on the same coordinate grid. Label each point with its coordinates.

7. (10, 4)   8. (4, 5)   9. (0, 7)   10. (2, 7)

11. **GEOMETRY** Two of a rectangle's sides measure 1 and 5 meters. Find the perimeter and area of the rectangle.

12. **ASTRONOMY** The table shows the number of moons that are thought to orbit the planets in our solar system that are beyond Earth as of 2005. Make a bar graph of the data.

Planet	Mars	Jupiter	Saturn	Uranus	Neptune	Pluto
Number of Moons	2	63	34	27	13	1

THEATER SEATS The circle graph shows the number of seats available in a theater.

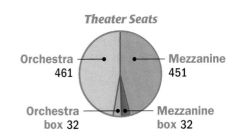

Theater Seats

13. How many seats are in the theater?

14. How many more orchestra seats than mezzanine seats are there?

15. How many mezzanine box tickets will be sold if a show sells out for 5 performances?

In Exercises 16 and 17, find the mean, median, mode(s), and range.

16. Monthly allowances: 40, 20, 32, 80, 28, 20, 20, 28, 20

17. Ages of grandchildren: 2, 3, 4, 6, 7, 2, 9, 7

18. In Exercise 17, which average best represents the data? *Explain* your choice.

EXTENDED RESPONSE QUESTIONS

Scoring Rubric

Full Credit
- solution is complete and correct

Partial Credit
- solution is complete but errors are made, *or*
- solution is without error but is incomplete

No Credit
- no solution is given, *or*
- solution makes no sense

> **PROBLEM**
>
> The table at the right shows the weekly grocery bills for 5 consecutive weeks. Find the mean, median, and mode(s) of the weekly grocery bills. Estimate the amount of money that would be spent on groceries in one year. *Explain* your reasoning.

Grocery Bills	
Week	**Amount**
1	$155
2	$150
3	$60
4	$158
5	$162

Below are sample solutions to the problem. Read each solution and the comments in blue to see why the sample represents *full credit, partial credit,* or *no credit*.

SAMPLE 1: Full Credit Solution

The steps of the solution are clearly written, and the calculations are correct.

Write the weekly grocery bills in order from least to greatest.

$60 $150 $155 $158 $162

Mean: (60 + 150 + 155 + 158 + 162) ÷ 5 = 137

Median: The middle number is 155, so the median is 155.

Mode: No data values occur more than once, so there is no mode.

The answer is correct. The explanation is clear and reflects correct mathematical thinking.

The mean is lower than all of the grocery bills but one. There is no mode. So, the mean and the mode are not typical of the data. The median, $155, best represents the weekly grocery bill. $155 × 52 weeks = $8060. About $8000 would be spent on groceries in one year.

SAMPLE 2: Partial Credit Solution

Write the weekly grocery bills in order from least to greatest.

$60 $150 $155 $158 $162

Mean: (60 + 150 + 155 + 158 + 162) ÷ 5 = 137   **Median:** 155

The calculations are incomplete; no mode.

The answer is correct, but lacks justification.

The median best represents the grocery bills. $155 × 52 weeks = $8060 in a year.

SAMPLE 3: No Credit Solution

......................➤ No explanation is given, and the median and the mode are incorrect.

Mean: 137

Median: 60

Mode: 0

......................➤ The answer is incorrect and incomplete.

The mean best represents the grocery bills.

PRACTICE Apply the Scoring Rubric

Score each of the following solutions to the problem on the previous page as *full credit*, *partial credit*, or *no credit*. *Explain* your reasoning. If you choose partial credit or no credit, explain how you would change the solution so that it earns a score of full credit.

1. **Mean:**   (155 + 150 + 60 + 158 + 162) ÷ 5 = 137

    Median: The middle number is 155, so the median is 155.

    Mode: No mode

    The mean, $137, best represents the grocery bills.

    $137 × 52 weeks = $7124. About $7000 would be spent on groceries.

2. **Mean:**   (155 + 150 + 60 + 158 + 162) ÷ 5 = 137

    Median: $60 $150   **$155** $158 $162
    The median is 155.

    Mode: No mode

    The mean and the mode are not typical of the data. The median, $155, best represents the grocery bills. $155 × 52 weeks = $8060. $8060 would be spent on groceries in one year.

3. **Mean:**   137

    Median: $155 $150   **$60** $158 $162
    The middle number is 60, so the median is 60.

    Mode: No data values occur more than once, so there is no mode.

    The median is lower than all of the other grocery bills. There is no mode. So, neither the median nor the mode represent the data well.

EXTENDED RESPONSE

1. The dimensions of two rectangles are 4 centimeters by 9 centimeters and 3 centimeters by 12 centimeters. Use a centimeter ruler to draw each figure. What is the area of each figure? Which figure has the greater perimeter? Draw the rectangle with the least perimeter that has the same area as the rectangles above. What are its dimensions? *Explain* your reasoning.

2. A survey was sent to families asking how many times anyone in the family went to an amusement park in the past two years. Completed surveys were returned by 18 families and the results are shown below.

   Make a frequency table and a line plot of the data. *Describe* the similarities and differences of the displays. *Explain* how to use each display to find the number of families whose members went to an amusement park fewer than 2 times.

   SURVEY
   How many times has anyone in your family gone to an amusement park in the past two years?

   RESULTS
   0 4 1 1 2 5 2 2 2
   2 4 0 1 1 1 4 2 2

3. The students in Mr. Hanson's science class planted tree seedlings and are monitoring their growth. The table at the right shows the height of each tree in inches.

Tree	Height (inches)
Apple	7
Maple	15
Cedar	20
Oak	29

   a. Make a bar graph of the heights.

   b. Find the difference in height between the tallest and shortest trees. Is it easier to use the *table* or the *bar graph* to answer this question?

   c. Which two trees are closest in height? Is it easier to use the *table* or the *bar graph* to answer this question? *Explain* your reasoning.

4. A television show gets the following ratings over a period of 9 weeks. Make a line plot and a bar graph of the data. Choose one of the displays and use it to find which rating is most common. Which display did you use? *Describe* how you used the display to find your answer.

Week	1	2	3	4	5	6	7	8	9
Rating	18	20	19	18	21	22	18	20	18

5. The lowest daily temperatures for one week are given below. Find the mean, median, and mode(s) of the data. Which average does *not* represent the data well? *Explain* your reasoning.

   5°F   12°F   18°F   16°F   13°F   15°F   5°F

MULTIPLE CHOICE

6. Which item is *least* likely to be measured in centimeters?

  (A) a lima bean   **(B)** a pencil

  (C) a soccer field   **(D)** height of a dog

7. Gary mows a field that is 120 yards by 75 yards. He can mow 3000 square yards in 2 hours. How many hours will it take Gary to mow the field?

  (A) 2 hours   **(B)** 3 hours

  (C) 4 hours   **(D)** 6 hours

8. Which is the best increment for the scale of a bar graph showing the data values 23, 24, 28, 33, 30, and 32?

  (A) 1   **(B)** 5   **(C)** 20   **(D)** 30

9. Which two points have an *x*-coordinate of 5?

  (A) *W* and *Z*

  (B) *X* and *W*

  (C) *X* and *Y*

  (D) *Y* and *Z*

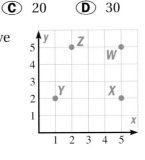

GRIDDED ANSWER

10. The length of the Nile River on a map is 33 inches. The map has the scale 1 in. : 125 mi. About how long is the actual river in miles?

11. The circle graph shows how often 100 students exercise. Predict how many out of 300 students will exercise less frequently than once a week.

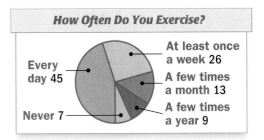

How Often Do You Exercise?

Every day 45

Never 7

At least once a week 26

A few times a month 13

A few times a year 9

12. Ann evenly distributes 2 pounds of fertilizer over the garden on one side of her house. It is 23 feet by 20 feet. She also wants to fertilize the garden on the other side of her house. It is 46 feet by 30 feet. Ann wants to use the same amount of fertilizer per square foot for both gardens. How many pounds of fertilizer will Ann need for the larger garden?

SHORT RESPONSE

13. Paula is selling 12 flower wreaths at a craft fair. The line plot at the right shows the prices of the wreaths. For which price group did Paula make the most money? the least money? *Explain* your reasoning.

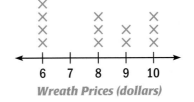

Wreath Prices (dollars)

14. Chang buys a 5 meter long board to make some shelving. He cuts 15 pieces of wood, each 240 millimeters long, from the board. Is the remaining length of wood greater than or less than a meter? How many more 240 millimeter pieces could be cut? *Justify* your answer.

15. The median height of the students in your class is 65 inches. The heights have a range of 6 inches. Is it possible that a student in the class has a height of 71 inches? *Explain* your reasoning.

3

Decimal Addition and Subtraction

Before

In previous chapters you've ...

- Rounded whole numbers
- Added and subtracted whole numbers

Now

In Chapter 3 you'll study ...

- 3.1 Decimal place value
- 3.2 Metric lengths
- 3.3 Ordering decimals
- 3.4 Rounding decimals
- 3.5 Decimal estimation
- 3.6 Adding decimals

Why?

So you can solve real-world problems about ...

- fossils, p. 125
- volcanoes, p. 133
- skateboarding, p. 140
- mountains, p. 147

 **Math**

at classzone.com

- Writing Decimals, p. 121
- Comparing Decimals, p. 131
- Adding Decimals, p. 148

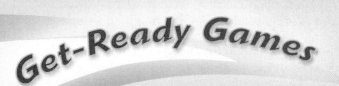

Review Prerequisite Skills by playing *Three-Putt Golf* and *Windmill Challenge.*

Three-Putt Golf

Total Distance

236
623
362

Skill Focus: Rounding whole numbers

- The numbers above represent distances in centimeters.

- Choose one of the numbers to be your first putt. Choose another number and round it to the nearest 10. The result is your second putt. Round the remaining number to the nearest 100 for your third putt.

- Add your three putts to find your total distance. Then use the same numbers but pick a different order of putts. Try to raise your total distance.

Windmill Challenge

900–1000   650–800

100–250   400–500

I
583
−176

E
474
+389

M
873
−379

O
159
+456

F
823
−479

T
565
+145

L
725
−271

R
209
+612

Skill Focus: Adding and subtracting whole numbers

• Find the sum or difference associated with each golf ball. A golf ball passes through the windmill only if its sum or difference does not fall into any of the ranges on the spokes of the windmill.

• Once you know which golf balls can pass through the windmill, order their sums and differences from least to greatest. The corresponding letters spell out a cry that you might hear on a miniature golf course.

Stop and Think

1. **WRITING** What is the greatest distance you can get in *Three-Putt Golf*? What is the least? Explain how you know.

2. **CRITICAL THINKING** In *Windmill Challenge*, are there any sums or differences for which you could use estimation rather than an exact calculation? Explain.

Review Prerequisite Skills

REVIEW WORDS
• **millimeter (mm),** *p. 60*
• **centimeter (cm),** *p. 60*
• **meter (m),** *p. 60*
• **number line,** *p. 738*
• **round,** *p. 739*
• **sum,** *p. 3*
• **difference,** *p. 4*

VOCABULARY CHECK

Copy and complete using a review word from the list at the left.

1. A __?__ is a metric unit of length longer than a centimeter.

2. A __?__ is a metric unit of length shorter than a centimeter.

3. When you __?__ the number 125 to the nearest ten, the answer is 130.

4. The __?__ of 17 and 9 is 8.

SKILL CHECK

Round the number to the place value of the red digit. *(p. 739)*

5. 7149   **6.** 4512   **7.** 13,387   **8.** 25,500

Graph the numbers on a number line to order them from least to greatest. *(p. 738)*

9. 5, 19, 16, 9, 12, 6, 13   **10.** 10, 7, 3, 2, 15, 11, 17

11. 24, 21, 20, 27, 19, 30, 25   **12.** 40, 37, 41, 39, 44, 35, 42

Estimate the sum or difference. *(p. 11)*

13. $16 + 27$ **14.** $34 + 79$ **15.** $82 + 59$ **16.** $123 + 85$

17. $81 - 42$ **18.** $65 - 17$ **19.** $91 - 83$ **20.** $107 - 36$

Find the length of the line segment to the nearest centimeter. *(p. 59)*

21. ————   **22.** ————   **23.** ——

@HomeTutor Prerequisite skills practice at classzone.com

Notetaking Skills **Write Down Your Questions**

In each chapter you will learn a new notetaking skill. In Chapter 3 you will apply the strategy of writing questions about homework to Exercises on pp. 127–129.

As you complete your homework assignments, write down in your notebook any questions you want to ask the teacher. An example is shown below.

$$1. \quad \begin{array}{r} 39 \rightarrow 40 \\ +160 \rightarrow +160 \\ \hline 200 \end{array}$$

$$2. \quad \begin{array}{r} 345 \rightarrow 350 \\ -171 \rightarrow -170 \\ \hline 180 \end{array}$$

Am I right to round up? Ask in class tomorrow.

3.1 Decimals and Place Value

Before	You learned how to read and write whole numbers.
Now	You'll read and write decimals.
Why?	So you can interpret decimals such as scores, as in Ex. 58.

KEY VOCABULARY
• **decimal,** *p. 120*

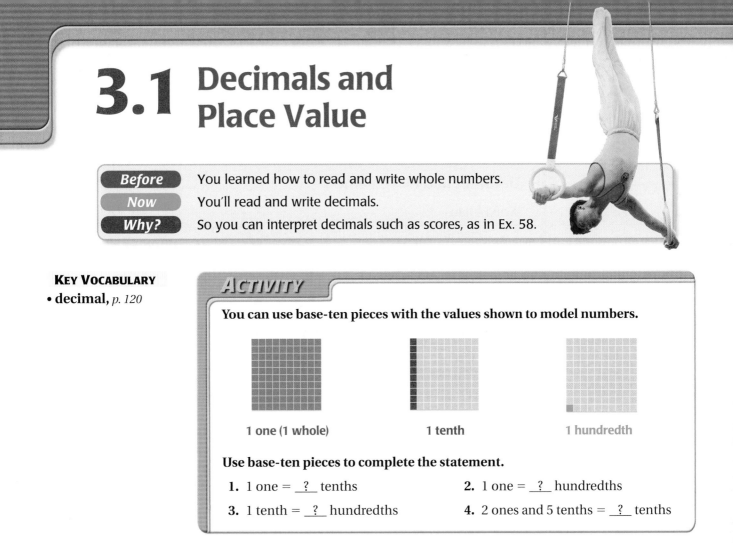

ACTIVITY

You can use base-ten pieces with the values shown to model numbers.

1 one (1 whole)   1 tenth   1 hundredth

Use base-ten pieces to complete the statement.

1. 1 one = _?_ tenths

2. 1 one = _?_ hundredths

3. 1 tenth = _?_ hundredths

4. 2 ones and 5 tenths = _?_ tenths

EXAMPLE 1 · Expressing a Number in Different Ways

a. Write 20 hundredths using only tenths.

20 hundredths

2 × 10 hundredths

2 × 1 tenth

2 tenths

> Think of **10 hundredths** as **1 tenth**.

TAKE NOTES
You might want to record relationships between base-ten pieces in your notebook, such as 1 one = 10 tenths.

b. Write 1 one and 4 tenths using only tenths.

1 one and 4 tenths

10 tenths and 4 tenths

14 tenths

> Use the fact that **1 one** equals **10 tenths.**

✓ **GUIDED PRACTICE**   **for Example 1**

Copy and complete the statement.

1. 500 hundredths = _?_ tenths

2. 4 ones and 9 tenths = _?_ tenths

Decimals A **decimal** is a number that is written using the base-ten place-value system. Each place value is ten times the place value to its right.

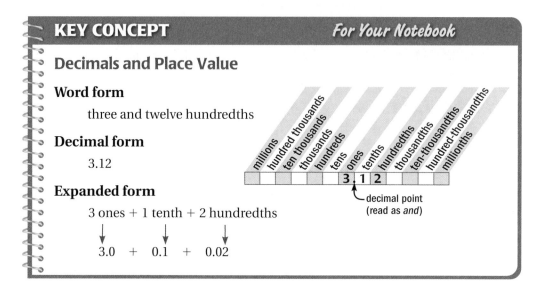

KEY CONCEPT   *For Your Notebook*

Decimals and Place Value

Word form

three and twelve hundredths

Decimal form

3.12

Expanded form

3 ones + 1 tenth + 2 hundredths

3.0   +   0.1   +   0.02

3 . 1 2

decimal point
(read as *and*)

EXAMPLE 2   **Writing Decimals**

Swimming A person timing your swim meet says your time was twenty-eight and six tenths seconds. Write your time as a decimal.

The word *and* indicates the decimal point.

twenty-eight and six tenths

28 . 6 seconds

EXAMPLE 3   **Reading Decimals**

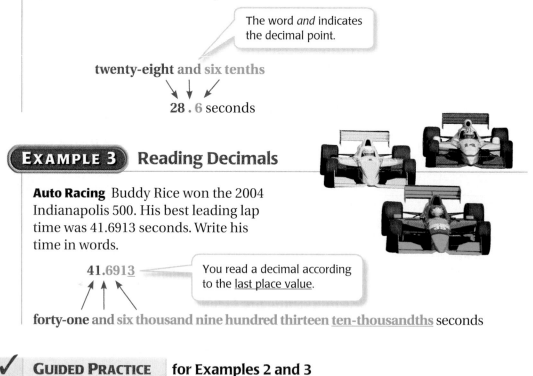

Auto Racing Buddy Rice won the 2004 Indianapolis 500. His best leading lap time was 41.6913 seconds. Write his time in words.

41.6913

You read a decimal according to the <u>last place value</u>.

forty-one and six thousand nine hundred thirteen <u>ten-thousandths</u> seconds

---

✓ **GUIDED PRACTICE**   **for Examples 2 and 3**

3. Write *twenty-five and seven hundred-thousandths* as a decimal.

4. Write 5.029 in words.   **5.** Write 5.068 in words.   **6.** Write 76.25 in words.

3.1 EXERCISES

HOMEWORK KEY

★ = STANDARDIZED TEST PRACTICE
Exs. 27, 52, 53, 54, 57, and 65

○ = HINTS and HOMEWORK HELP
for Exs. 7, 9, 17, 21, 47 at classzone.com

SKILL PRACTICE

VOCABULARY Name the place value of the 3 in the decimal.

1. 1.038   **2.** 16.329   **3.** 4.61093   **4.** 564.0732

EXPRESSING NUMBERS Copy and complete the statement.

SEE EXAMPLE 1
on p. 119
for Exs. 5–7

5. 4 tenths = __?__ hundredths

6. 200 hundredths = __?__ tenths = __?__ ones

7. 1 one and 5 tenths = __?__ tenths = __?__ hundredths

WRITING DECIMALS Write the number as a decimal.

SEE EXAMPLE 2
on p. 120
for Exs. 8–14

8. five and eighteen hundredths   **9.** six and nine thousandths

10. thirty and fifteen hundredths   **11.** fifty-eight and twenty-seven thousandths

12. seven hundred five thousandths   **13.** two hundred seventy-eight ten-thousandths

Animated Math at classzone.com

14. ERROR ANALYSIS Describe and correct the error in the solution.

> ✗ four hundred twelve thousandths = 400.012

READING DECIMALS Write the decimal in words.

SEE EXAMPLE 3
on p. 120
for Exs. 15–27

15. 0.45   **16.** 0.99   **17.** 4.16   **18.** 0.367

19. 17.022   **20.** 24.006   **21.** 0.0005   **22.** 7.0009

23. 8.0014   **24.** 2.0093   **25.** 10.0255   **26.** 46.1003

27. ★ MULTIPLE CHOICE How do you write the number thirty-four and seventy-one thousandths as a decimal?

  A 34.0071   **B** 34.071   **C** 34.701   **D** 34.71

WRITING EXPANDED FORMS Copy and complete the expanded form of the decimal.

28. $8.6 = 8.0 + \underline{\ ?\ }$ **29.** $5.392 = 5.0 + 0.3 + \underline{\ ?\ } + \underline{\ ?\ }$

30. $4.25 = 4.0 + \underline{\ ?\ } + \underline{\ ?\ }$ **31.** $0.1472 = 0.1 + 0.04 + \underline{\ ?\ } + \underline{\ ?\ }$

WRITING DOLLAR AMOUNTS Write the amount as a decimal part of a dollar.

32. 1 quarter   **33.** 4 nickels   **34.** 89 pennies   **35.** 7 dimes

36. 6 quarters   **37.** 32 nickels   **38.** 121 pennies   **39.** 14 dimes

MODELING DECIMALS Write the decimal number. Model your answer with base ten pieces.

40. one tenth more than 2.8

41. one hundredth less than 1.77

42. one tenth more than 0.31

43. one hundredth more than 2.06

44. one tenth less than 4.7

45. one hundredth more than 3.29

46. CHALLENGE Sketch a model of 1 ten using ones' pieces. How many ones' pieces did you need? How many tenths' pieces would you need to make the model? How many hundredths' pieces? Do you notice a pattern in the number of pieces you need? *Explain* your reasoning.

PROBLEM SOLVING

GEMSTONES The table shows the weights of several gemstones at a jewelry store.

Gemstone	Weight (carats)
amethyst	0.48
diamond	1.29
emerald	1.05
topaz	1.98
sapphire	0.50

SEE EXAMPLE 1
on p. 119
for Exs. 47–49

47. Write the weight of the topaz in words.

48. Write the weight of the emerald in words.

49. Sketch a base-ten model to represent the weight of the diamond.

50. Which gems weigh less than 1 carat?

SEE EXAMPLES
2 AND 3
on p. 120
for Ex. 51

51. ◆ **MULTIPLE REPRESENTATIONS** The main section of the Akashi-Kaikyo bridge in Japan is about one and ninety-nine hundredths kilometers long.

   a. Make a Model Sketch a base-ten model to represent the length of the main section.

   b. Write an Expression Write the decimal in expanded form.

   c. Write a Decimal Write the length as a decimal.

52. ★ **WRITING** Write the numbers modeled in words and as decimals. Do the models represent the same amount? *Explain*.

Model A ▓▓▓   Model B ▪▪▪▪▪▪
                              ▪▪▪▪▪▪
                              ▪▪▪▪▪▪
                              ▪▪▪▪▪▪
                              ▪▪▪▪▪▪

53. ★ **MULTIPLE CHOICE** The moon revolves around Earth once every twenty seven and three thousand two hundred seventeen ten-thousandths days. How do you write this number in decimal form?

   A 27.307   **B** 27.2317   **C** 27.3217   **D** 273.217

54. ★ **MULTIPLE CHOICE** A runner has completed 26 miles of a marathon and has about two tenths of a mile to go. Which decimal equals the distance of the marathon?

   A 26.002 mi   **B** 26.02 mi   **C** 26.10 mi   **D** 26.2 mi

55. REASONING A number is between 0 and 1. Its right most place value is the thousandths place. The number contains each of the digits 0, 2, and 5. What is the number, if it is the least number formed by these digits? *Explain.*

56. TURBOJETS The Spirit of Australia set a record for the fastest water vehicle. This turbojet was timed at 511.11 kilometers per hour.

  a. **Speed** Write the turbojet's speed in words.

  b. **Estimation** The maximum speed of some cruise ships is about 42 kilometers per hour. Estimate how many times the speed of this turbojet is the speed of a cruise ship.

57. ★ SHORT RESPONSE Your friend added 50 cents to $110.39. He said the amount was one hundred and ten and eighty-nine hundredths dollars. *Explain* what is wrong with his answer.

GYMNASTICS The table shows the scores for men's gymnastics teams at the 2000 Olympics.

58. CHALLENGE Which team's score is between 230 and 230.1? *Explain* your reasoning.

59. REASONING Which team's score is closest to 229? *Explain* your reasoning.

Team	Score
China	231.919
Ukraine	230.306
Russia	230.019
Japan	229.857
United States	228.983

MIXED REVIEW

Get-Ready

Prepare for Lesson 3.2 in Exs. 60–62

Draw a segment of the given length. *(p. 59)*

60. 7 centimeters   **61.** 3 inches   **62.** 35 millimeters

CHOOSE A STRATEGY Use a strategy from the list to solve the problem in Exercise 63. *Explain* your choice of strategy.

63. The booths at a carnival are 6 feet wide and spaced 4 feet apart. Find the maximum number of booths you can fit in a row that is 50 feet long. *Explain* which strategy you used.

Problem Solving Strategies
- Guess, Check, and Revise (p. 763)
- Draw a Diagram (p. 762)
- Make a List (p. 765)

64. Out of 40 students, 4 said they check their e-mail less than once a week, 10 said once a week, 8 said twice a week, 12 said once a day, and 6 said several times a day. Make a bar graph of the data. *(p. 83)*

65. ★ MULTIPLE CHOICE You are constructing a model of an historic building that is 360 feet tall. Every 3 inches on the model represents 40 feet on the building. How tall will your model be? *(p. 72)*

   (A) 18 in.   **(B)** 27 in.   **(C)** 48 in.   **(D)** 120 in.

INVESTIGATION

Use before Lesson 3.2

GOAL
Express lengths in different metric units.

MATERIALS
• metric ruler
• meter stick

3.2 Using Different Metric Units

You can express the same length using different metric units.

EXPLORE Measure the pencil in different units.

STEP 1 **Find** the length of the pencil in centimeters and millimeters. Write your answer as a sum.

> Line up one end of the pencil with the zero mark on the ruler.

> Look at where the tip of the pencil lines up with the tick marks on the ruler.

cm 1 2 3 4 5 6 7 8 9 10

The length of the pencil is 9 centimeters + 4 millimeters.

STEP 2 **Find** the length of the pencil in millimeters. Use the fact that 10 millimeters equal 1 centimeter.

$$9 \text{ cm} + 4 \text{ mm} = (10 \times 9) \text{ mm} + 4 \text{ mm} = 94 \text{ mm}$$

PRACTICE

1. Copy and complete the table by measuring the objects in your classroom.

Object	Measurement 1	Measurement 2
length of a pencil	9 cm + 4 mm	94 mm
length of a notebook	_?_ cm + _?_ mm	_?_ mm
height of a desk	_?_ m + _?_ cm	_?_ cm
width of a door	_?_ m + _?_ cm	_?_ cm

DRAW CONCLUSIONS

2. **WRITING** The length of a pen is 112 millimeters. *Explain* how you can find the length in centimeters and millimeters without measuring.

3. **REASONING** A height is given in centimeters. How can you find the height in meters and centimeters without measuring?

3.2 Measuring Metric Lengths

Before You measured lengths to the nearest whole metric unit.

Now You'll use decimals to express metric measurements.

Why? So you can measure lengths precisely, as in Ex. 36.

KEY VOCABULARY
• **millimeter (mm)**, *p. 60*
• **centimeter (cm)**, *p. 60*
• **meter (m)**, *p. 60*

Fossils Scientists study fossils to learn about plants and animals that lived in prehistoric times. The size of a fossil can help a scientist figure out what type of plant or animal it came from. A scientist finds a dinosaur tooth that is about 3 centimeters long. What is a more precise measurement for the tooth? You can use decimal parts of a centimeter to find out.

EXAMPLE 1 Writing Measurements as Decimals

To answer the question above about dinosaur teeth, use a metric ruler and write your answer as a decimal number of centimeters.

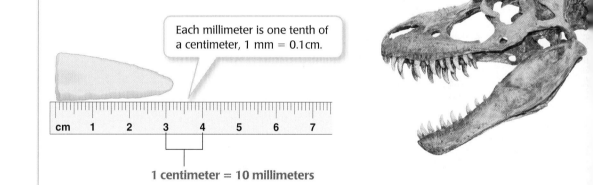

Each millimeter is one tenth of a centimeter, 1 mm = 0.1 cm.

1 centimeter = 10 millimeters

From the metric ruler you can see that 2 millimeters is 2 tenths centimeter. The length is about 3 and 2 tenths centimeters.

▶ **Answer** The length of the dinosaur tooth is about 3.2 centimeters.

✓ **GUIDED PRACTICE** for Example 1

Write the length of the line segment as a decimal number of centimeters.

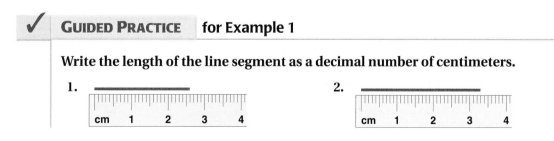

1.

2.

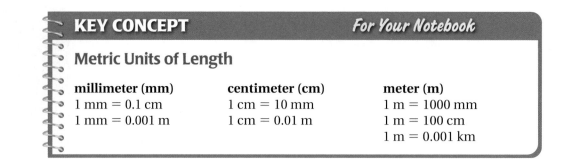

KEY CONCEPT

For Your Notebook

Metric Units of Length

millimeter (mm)
1 mm = 0.1 cm
1 mm = 0.001 m

centimeter (cm)
1 cm = 10 mm
1 cm = 0.01 m

meter (m)
1 m = 1000 mm
1 m = 100 cm
1 m = 0.001 km

EXAMPLE 2 Measuring in Centimeters

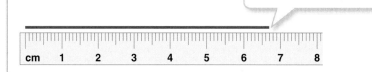

USING METRIC UNITS
Need help with metric units of length? See p. 59.

Find the length of the line segment to the nearest tenth of a centimeter.

6 and 7 tenths centimeters

cm 1 2 3 4 5 6 7 8

▶ **Answer** The length of the line segment is about 6.7 centimeters.

EXAMPLE 3 Measuring in Meters

Dinosaurs Find the length of the triceratops horn to the nearest hundredth of a meter.

SOLUTION

The length of the horn is about 25 centimeters. Because 1 centimeter is 1 hundredth of a meter, 25 centimeters is 25 hundredths of a meter.

▶ **Answer** The length of the triceratops' horn is about 0.25 meter.

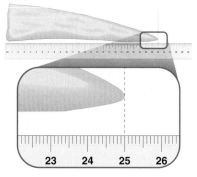

READING
It takes more of a smaller unit of length to equal a measurement written in a larger unit of length. For example, it takes 300 cm to equal 3 m.

✓ **GUIDED PRACTICE** for Examples 2 and 3

Find the length of the line segment to the given unit.

3. to the nearest tenth of a centimeter

cm 1 2 3 4

4. to the nearest hundredth of a meter

cm 1 2 3 4

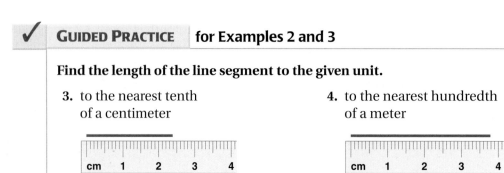

3.2 EXERCISES

HOMEWORK KEY

★ = **STANDARDIZED TEST PRACTICE**
Exs. 12, 16, 33, 34, 35, and 42

◯ = **HINTS AND HOMEWORK HELP**
for Exs. 5, 9, 11, 13, 33 at classzone.com

SKILL PRACTICE

VOCABULARY Copy and complete the statement.

1. 1 centimeter = ___?___ meter

2. 1 millimeter = ___?___ centimeter

3. 1 meter = ___?___ centimeters

4. 1 centimeter = ___?___ millimeters

WRITING MEASUREMENTS Copy and complete the statement.

SEE EXAMPLE 1
on p. 125
for Exs. 5–11

5. 3 and 8 tenths centimeters = ___?___ centimeters

6. 5 and 2 hundredths meters = ___?___ meters

7. 6 and 7 tenths meters = ___?___ meters

8. 12 and 4 thousandths meters = ___?___ meters

9. The height of a stack of pancakes is nine and one tenth centimeters. The stack is ___?___ centimeter(s) high.

10. The width of a library desk is eighty-eight hundredths of a meter. The desk is ___?___ meter(s) wide.

11. A trail is 1 and 4 tenths kilometers long. The trail is ___?___ kilometer(s) long.

SEE EXAMPLE 2
on p. 126
for Exs. 12–16

12. ★ **MULTIPLE CHOICE** What is the length of the goldfish?

A 4.6 meters

B 4.6 centimeters

C 4.4 centimeters

D 44 millimeters

13. **MEASUREMENT** Write the measurement for each letter to the nearest tenth of a centimeter.

MEASUREMENT Measure the bead to the nearest tenth of a centimeter.

14.

15.

TAKE NOTES
As you work on the exercises, write down any questions you want to ask your teacher.

16. ★ **MULTIPLE CHOICE** What is the length of the line segment?

A 0.027 km

B 0.27 m

C 2.7 cm

D 2.7 mm

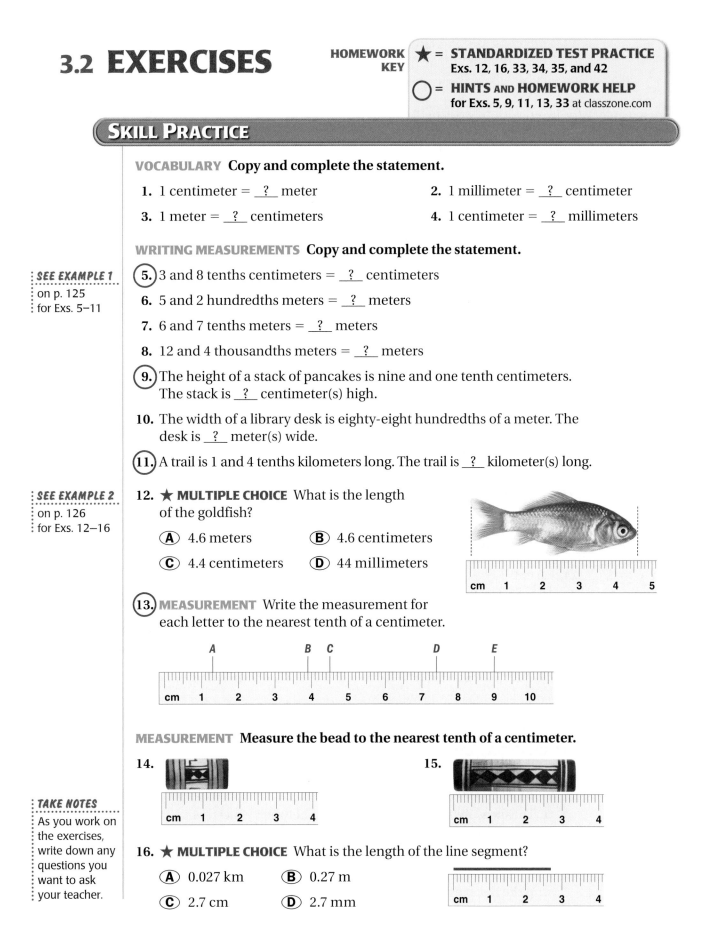

17. ERROR ANALYSIS Describe and correct the error in the measurement.

The length of the line segment is 22 cm.

SEE EXAMPLE 3
on p. 126
for Ex. 18

18. MEASURING IN METERS Use the meter sticks to give the measure of the snowboard to the nearest thousandth of a meter.

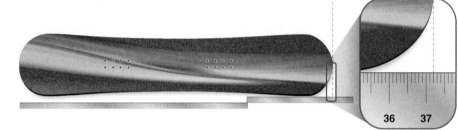

WRITING MEASUREMENTS Write the length to the nearest hundredth of a meter.

19. The length of an electronic keyboard is 85 centimeters.

20. A guitar case is 8 centimeters longer than a meter.

21. A poster is 20 millimeters shorter than a meter.

22. A bookshelf is 10 centimeters longer than a meter.

23. CHECKING REASONABLENESS Is it reasonable to give the length of the objects in Exercises 19–22 in kilometers? *Explain* your reasoning.

ESTIMATION Sketch a line segment of the given length without using a ruler. Then use a ruler to check your estimate. How close was your estimate?

24. 6.5 cm   **25.** 45 mm   **26.** 0.01 m   **27.** 0.15 m

CHALLENGE Which measurement in each group is the smallest distance? *Explain* your reasoning.

28. 300 m, 0.035 km, 3.5 mm, 35 cm   **29.** 0.005 km, 1 m, 5 cm, 1500 mm

30. 240 mm, 0.24 km, 24 m, 0.024 m   **31.** 7.7 m, 0.07 km, 770 m, 77 mm

---

PROBLEM SOLVING

SEE EXAMPLE 1
on p. 125
for Ex. 32

32. GUIDED PROBLEM SOLVING The wingspan of the Blue Metalmark butterfly is more than 2 centimeters.

   a. The measurement of the wingspan is between which two centimeter marks?

   b. How many millimeters greater is the wingspan than the smaller number in part (a)?

   c. Write the wingspan of the butterfly as a decimal number of centimeters.

★ = **STANDARDIZED TEST PRACTICE**   ◯ = **HINTS AND HOMEWORK HELP** *at classzone.com*

33. ★ **MULTIPLE CHOICE** In the 2004 Summer Olympics, Laverne Eve threw a javelin 77 centimeters more than 62 meters. Which choice represents the distance she threw the javelin as a decimal number of meters?

(**A**) 77.62 cm   (**B**) 62.077 m   (**C**) 62.77 m   (**D**) 77.62 m

34. ★ **WRITING** Is measuring to the nearest meter the same as measuring to the nearest thousandth of a kilometer? *Explain* your reasoning.

35. ★ **SHORT RESPONSE** Susie's height is 470 thousandths of a meter more than one meter. Shirley's height is 4.7 centimeters more than one meter. Who is taller? *Explain* your reasoning.

36. **SEA OTTERS** Use the meter stick to find the length of the sea otter to the nearest hundredth of a meter.

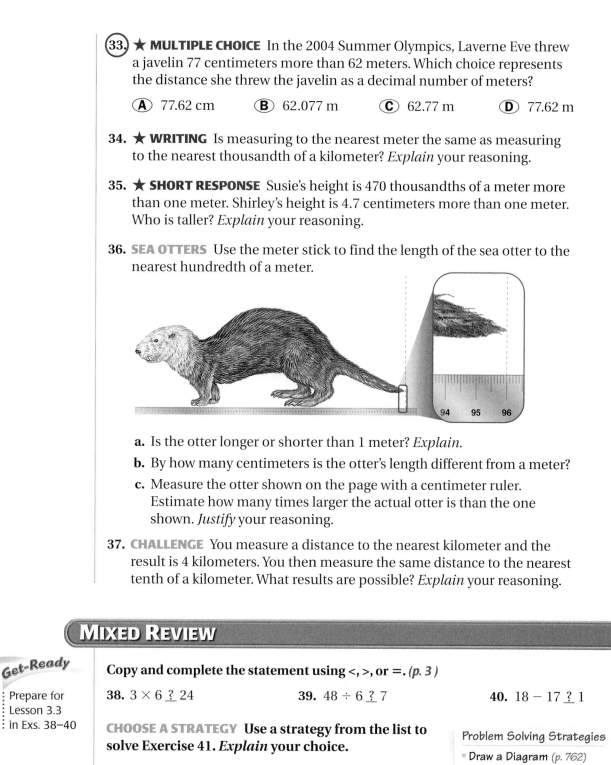

  a. Is the otter longer or shorter than 1 meter? *Explain.*

  b. By how many centimeters is the otter's length different from a meter?

  c. Measure the otter shown on the page with a centimeter ruler. Estimate how many times larger the actual otter is than the one shown. *Justify* your reasoning.

37. **CHALLENGE** You measure a distance to the nearest kilometer and the result is 4 kilometers. You then measure the same distance to the nearest tenth of a kilometer. What results are possible? *Explain* your reasoning.

MIXED REVIEW

Get-Ready

Prepare for
Lesson 3.3
in Exs. 38–40

Copy and complete the statement using <, >, or =. *(p. 3)*

38. $3 \times 6 \underline{\ ?\ } 24$ **39.** $48 \div 6 \underline{\ ?\ } 7$ **40.** $18 - 17 \underline{\ ?\ } 1$

CHOOSE A STRATEGY **Use a strategy from the list to solve Exercise 41.** *Explain* **your choice.**

41. Your friend is thinking of a number between 1 and 10. This number raised to the fourth power is 81. What is your friend's number?

Problem Solving Strategies

■ Draw a Diagram *(p. 762)*
■ Guess, Check, and Revise *(p. 763)*
■ Look for a Pattern *(p. 766)*
■ Solve a Simpler Problem *(p. 768)*

42. ★ **SHORT RESPONSE** You are making a scale drawing of a room you are redecorating. The room is 10 meters long. Give an example of a scale that you might use. *Explain* how you found your answer. *(p. 72)*

3.3 Ordering Decimals

Before	You compared and ordered whole numbers.
Now	You'll compare and order decimals.
Why?	So you can order data, as in Ex. 48.

KEY VOCABULARY
• **number line,** *p. 738*

Gerbils A Mongolian gerbil's tail is about the same length as its body. A gerbil has a body length of 11 centimeters and a tail length of 10.6 centimeters. Which is longer, the body or the tail?

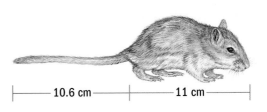

	10.6 cm	11 cm

EXAMPLE 1 Comparing Metric Lengths

To answer the question above, picture the metric ruler below. The tail length, 10.6 centimeters, is to the left of the body length, 11 centimeters.

READING

Less than and *greater than* symbols always point to the lesser number.

You can say: 10.6 < 11   or   11 > 10.6

↑   ↑

is less than   ***is greater than***

▶ **Answer** The gerbil's body is longer than its tail.

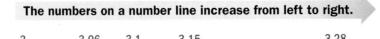

tail   body
length length
↓   ↓

10   11   12

★ EXAMPLE 2 Standardized Test Practice

> **Order the numbers 3.1, 3.28, 3.06, 3, and 3.15 from least to greatest.**
>
> **Ⓐ** 3, 3.06, 3.15, 3.1, 3.28   **Ⓑ** 3, 3.06, 3.1, 3.15, 3.28
>
> **Ⓒ** 3.06, 3, 3.1, 3.15, 3.28   **Ⓓ** 3.28, 3.15, 3.1, 3.06, 3

ELIMINATE CHOICES

From the number line, you know 3 should be the first number in the ordered list. So, choices C and D can be eliminated.

SOLUTION

Graph each number on a number line. Begin by marking tenths from 3.0 to 3.3. Then mark hundredths by dividing each tenth into ten sections.

The numbers on a number line increase from left to right.

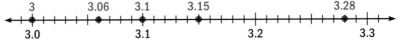

3	3.06	3.1	3.15		3.28

3.0   3.1   3.2   3.3

▶ **Answer** An ordered list of the numbers is 3, 3.06, 3.1, 3.15, and 3.28. The answer is B. Ⓐ **Ⓑ** Ⓒ Ⓓ

Comparing Decimals When you graph decimals on a number line to compare them, the greater number is farther to the right. You can also compare decimals by looking at their place values.

> **KEY CONCEPT** *For Your Notebook*
>
> ## Comparing Decimals
>
> 1. Write the decimals in a column, lining up the decimal points.
>
> 2. If necessary, write zeros to the right of the decimals so that all decimals have the same number of decimal places.
>
> 3. Compare place values from left to right.

EXAMPLE 3 Comparing Decimals

Copy and complete the statement with <, >, or =.

a. 5.796 ? 5.802

The ones' digits are the same.

5.796
5.802

The tenths' digits are different: 7 < 8.

▸ **Answer** 5.796 < 5.802

b. 2.94 ? 2.9

The ones' and tenths' digits are the same.

2.94
2.90 ← Write a zero.

The hundredths' digits are different: 4 > 0.

▸ **Answer** 2.94 > 2.9

EXAMPLE 4 Ordering Decimals

Order the gerbils from heaviest to lightest.

SOLUTION

The digits are the same through the tenths' place. Compare **hundredths** and then **thousandths** if necessary: 77.0250, 77.0212, 77.0113, and 77.0033.

▸ **Answer** The gerbils, from heaviest to lightest, are Alexi, Donald, Edgar, and Herbie.

Gerbil	Mass (grams)
Edgar	77.0113
Donald	77.0212
Herbie	77.0033
Alexi	77.0250

Animated **Math** at classzone.com

✓ **GUIDED PRACTICE** for Examples 1, 2, 3, and 4

Copy and complete the statement with <, >, or =.

1. 7.54 ? 7.45　　　**2.** 8.5 ? 8.50　　　**3.** 0.409 ? 0.411

4. Order the lengths from longest to shortest: 0.6445 m, 0.6544 m, 0.6545 m, and 0.6454 m.

3.3 EXERCISES

HOMEWORK KEY

★ = STANDARDIZED TEST PRACTICE
Exs. 26, 46, 47, 49, and 60

◯ = HINTS AND HOMEWORK HELP
for Exs. 5, 13, 25, 31, 45 at classzone.com

SKILL PRACTICE

VOCABULARY Copy and complete the statement using the number line.

1. 7.41 is __?__ 7.55.

2. 7.33 is __?__ 7.24.

3. __?__ is between 7.33 and 7.41.

4. 7.41 is between 7.33 and __?__ .

SEE EXAMPLE 1
on p. 130
for Exs. 5–10

COMPARING DECIMALS Copy and complete the statement with <, >, or =.

⑤ 7 cm __?__ 7.2 cm

6. 12.0 cm __?__ 12 cm

7. 3.4 cm __?__ 3.9 cm

8. 2.8 cm __?__ 2.6 cm

9. 7.1 cm __?__ 6.9 cm

10. 8.5 cm __?__ 9.4 cm

SEE EXAMPLE 3
on p. 131
for Exs. 11–19

11. 1.21 __?__ 1.12

12. 9.50 __?__ 9.05

⑬ 8.7 __?__ 8.70

14. 4.40 __?__ 4.4

15. 2.746 __?__ 2.76

16. 0.4 __?__ 0.038

17. 5 __?__ 5.00

18. 6.203 __?__ 6

19. 8.113 __?__ 8.1139

ORDERING DECIMALS Order the decimals from least to greatest.

SEE EXAMPLE 2
on p. 130
for Exs. 20–26

20. 5.34, 5.12, 5.43

21. 9.07, 9.06, 9.1

22. 4.3, 4.25, 4.31

23. 0.9, 1.1, 0.1, 1.5

24. 7.4, 7.9, 7, 6.9

㉕ 1.2, 1.05, 1.15, 0.98

26. ★ **MULTIPLE CHOICE** Use a number line to order the decimals from least to greatest: 0.3454, 0.4345, 0.3354, and 0.3345.

Ⓐ 0.4345, 0.3454, 0.3354, 0.3345

Ⓑ 0.3354, 0.3345, 0.4345, 0.3454

Ⓒ 0.3345, 0.3354, 0.3454, 0.4345

Ⓓ 0.3354, 0.3454, 0.3345, 0.4345

ORDERING DECIMALS Order the decimals from greatest to least.

SEE EXAMPLE 4
on p. 131
for Exs. 27–32

27. 2.94, 2.90, 2.93, 2.99, 2.97

28. 0.5, 0.9, 0.1, 0.06, 0.4

29. 1.009, 1.003, 1.008, 1.002

30. 7.033, 7.034, 7.031, 7.039

㉛ 8.010, 8.011, 8.101, 8.001

32. 0.461, 0.416, 0.466, 0.411

33. **ERROR ANALYSIS** Describe and correct the error in the statement.

✗ Four and three hundred twenty thousandths is *greater than* four and thirty-two hundredths.

xy **ALGEBRA** Find a value of *k* that makes the statement true.

34. 8.3 < *k* and *k* < 9

35. 0.5 < *k* and *k* < 1

36. 3.6 < *k* and *k* < 3.7

37. 0.451 < *k* and *k* < 0.452

38. 9.036 < *k* and *k* < 9.0365

39. 5.009 < *k* and *k* < 5.01

COMPARING LENGTHS Copy and complete the statement with <, >, or =.

40. 0.1 cm ? 1.1 mm

41. 0.001 km ? 100.5 cm

42. 0.5 m ? 50.5 cm

CHALLENGE In Exercise 43, use only the digits 0 and 1.

43. Write all the different decimals of the form ? . ? ? .

44. Order the decimals you wrote in Exercise 43 from least to greatest.

PROBLEM SOLVING

SEE EXAMPLE 4
on p. 131
for Exs. 45–46

45. **MILK PRICES** The average cost of a gallon of milk in various cities in 2001 is given below. Order the costs from least to greatest.

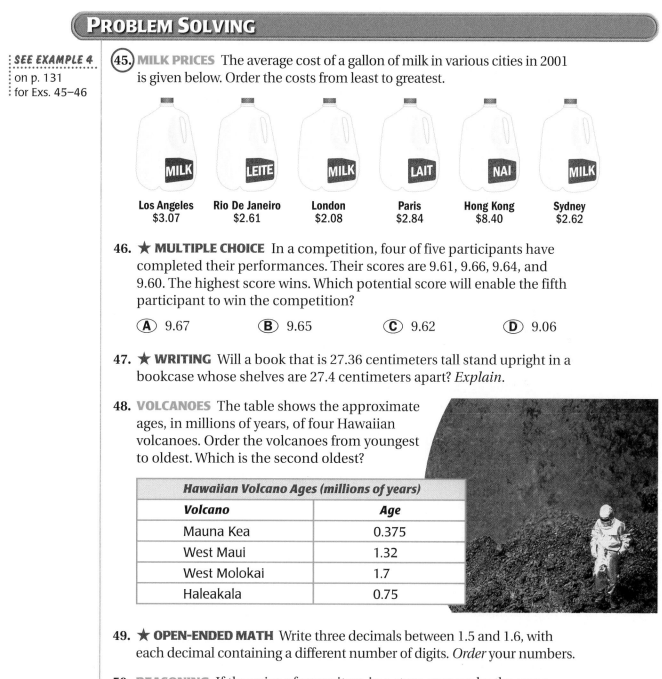

| Los Angeles | Rio De Janeiro | London | Paris | Hong Kong | Sydney |
| $3.07 | $2.61 | $2.08 | $2.84 | $8.40 | $2.62 |

46. ★ **MULTIPLE CHOICE** In a competition, four of five participants have completed their performances. Their scores are 9.61, 9.66, 9.64, and 9.60. The highest score wins. Which potential score will enable the fifth participant to win the competition?

(A) 9.67

(B) 9.65

(C) 9.62

(D) 9.06

47. ★ **WRITING** Will a book that is 27.36 centimeters tall stand upright in a bookcase whose shelves are 27.4 centimeters apart? *Explain.*

48. **VOLCANOES** The table shows the approximate ages, in millions of years, of four Hawaiian volcanoes. Order the volcanoes from youngest to oldest. Which is the second oldest?

Hawaiian Volcano Ages (millions of years)	
Volcano	**Age**
Mauna Kea	0.375
West Maui	1.32
West Molokai	1.7
Haleakala	0.75

49. ★ **OPEN-ENDED MATH** Write three decimals between 1.5 and 1.6, with each decimal containing a different number of digits. *Order* your numbers.

50. **REASONING** If the price of every item in a store goes up by the same amount, does the order of least expensive item to most expensive item change? *Explain* your reasoning.

51. MULTI-STEP PROBLEM Use the chart of long distance telephone calls.

	Aruba	*India*	*Mongolia*	*Poland*	*Thailand*
Cost	$11.40	$11.60	$11.90	$11.65	$11.05
Call Time (min)	15.75	6.55	4.5	9.44	6.53

Order the calls by cost from least to greatest. Then order the calls by length of call from least to greatest. Does ordering the calls by cost result in the same order as ordering the calls by length of call? *Explain* your reasoning.

52. CHALLENGE The tables show the top five finishers for the men's pommel horse finals for the 2000 and 2004 Olympics games.

2000	
Athlete	**Score**
Nemov	9.800
Kil-Su	9.762
Poujade	9.825
Urzica	9.862
Jang-Hyung	9.775

2004	
Athlete	**Score**
Kashima	9.787
Urzica	9.825
Cano	9.762
Huang	9.775
Teng	9.837

a. **Compare** A gold medal is awarded for first place, a silver medal for second, and a bronze medal for third. Who won medals in 2004 and which medals did they win?

b. **Analyze** Which medals, if any, did Urzica win in 2000 and 2004? *Explain* your reasoning.

c. **Reasoning** If Kashima's 2004 performance had occurred in 2000, would he still have won a bronze? *Explain* your reasoning.

d. **Interpret** A friend concludes that a score of 9.825 guarantees a silver medal. Do you agree? *Justify* your answer.

MIXED REVIEW

Get-Ready

Prepare for
Lesson 3.4 in
Exs. 53–55

Round the number to the place value of the red digit. *(p. 739)*

53. 2713   **54.** 106,503   **55.** 1,970,241

Evaluate the expression. *(p. 21)*

56. $16 - 4 \div 2$ **57.** $15 + 10 \div 5 - 3$ **58.** $24 - 3 \times 8 + 10$

59. TREES The heights, in feet, of newly planted trees are given below. Find the mean, median, mode(s), and range of the data. *(p. 99)*

    4, 5, 7, 5, 3, 4, 6, 5, 4, 5, 6, 4, 7

60. ★ **MULTIPLE CHOICE** What is the number *twenty-eight and sixteen ten-thousandths* written as a decimal? *(p. 119)*

(A) 28.000016   **(B)** 28.00016   **(C)** 28.0016   **(D)** 28.016

Write the decimal in words. *(p. 119)*

1. 6.52

2. 17.017

3. 0.1234

Write the number as a decimal. *(p. 119)*

4. ten and nineteen hundredths

5. eight and seven hundred fifty-two thousandths

6. thirteen and seventy-three ten-thousandths

Copy and complete the statement with <, >, or =. *(p. 130)*

7. 6.81 ? 6.8

8. 12 ? 12.0

9. 5.02 ? 5.21

10. 38.90 ? 38.9

11. 24.632 ? 24.236

12. 17.585 ? 17.508

13. MEASUREMENT Find the length of the line segment to the nearest tenth of a centimeter. *(p. 125)*

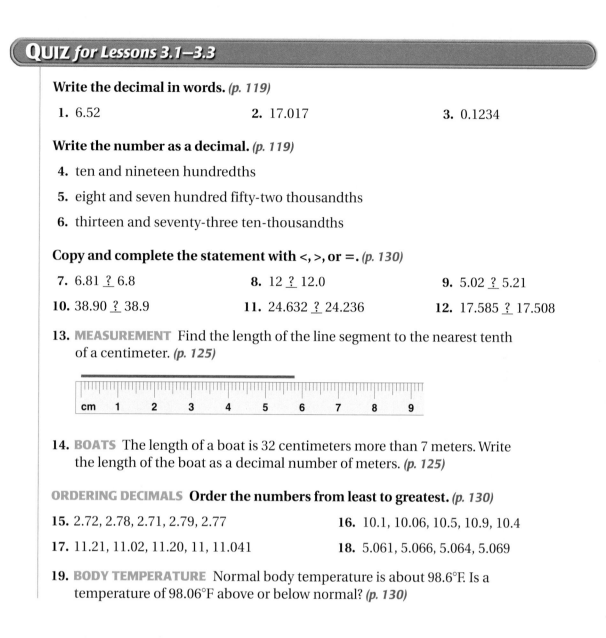

14. BOATS The length of a boat is 32 centimeters more than 7 meters. Write the length of the boat as a decimal number of meters. *(p. 125)*

ORDERING DECIMALS **Order the numbers from least to greatest.** *(p. 130)*

15. 2.72, 2.78, 2.71, 2.79, 2.77

16. 10.1, 10.06, 10.5, 10.9, 10.4

17. 11.21, 11.02, 11.20, 11, 11.041

18. 5.061, 5.066, 5.064, 5.069

19. BODY TEMPERATURE Normal body temperature is about 98.6°F. Is a temperature of 98.06°F above or below normal? *(p. 130)*

Brain Game

What Number Am I?

I have two digits to the left of my decimal point and two digits to the right of my decimal point. My hundredths' digit is two times my tenths' digit. When 1 is subtracted from my tens' digit, the answer is 5. I have a 2 as my tenths' digit. My ones' digit is greater than 0 and less than my tenths' digit. What number am I?

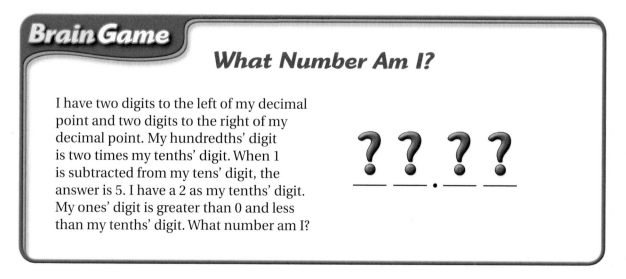

Lessons 3.1–3.3

1. **MULTI-STEP PROBLEM** The table shows the qualifying speeds in miles per hour of five competitors in the 2004 Indianapolis 500.

Name	Speed (mi/h)
Adrian Fernandez	220.999
Buddy Rice	222.024
Dan Wheldon	221.524
Tony Kanaan	221.200
Vitor Meira	220.958

   a. Of the competitors listed above, who had the fastest qualifying speed?

   b. Write his speed in words.

   c. What does the zero represent in his speed?

2. **SHORT RESPONSE** The diameter of a lead pipe is two and twenty-five hundredths inches. What is the diameter of a pipe that is one hundredth of an inch larger than the lead pipe? Write your answer in words and as a decimal. *Explain* your reasoning.

3. **EXTENDED RESPONSE** Use the diagram below.

   a. Find the length of the insect to the nearest millimeter.

   b. Find the length of the insect to the nearest tenth of a centimeter.

   c. Which measurement is more accurate? *Explain* your reasoning.

   d. *Describe* how you could use the length of the insect in millimeters to write the length in meters.

4. **GRIDDED ANSWER** To the nearest centimeter, a piece of chalk is 6 centimeters long. To the nearest millimeter, the chalk is 62 millimeters long. What is the length of the chalk to the nearest thousandth meter?

5. **SHORT RESPONSE** Mark is sixty and one hundred twenty-five thousandths inches tall. Hannah is sixty and fifteen hundredths inches tall.

   a. Write their heights as decimals.

   b. Who is taller? *Explain* your reasoning.

6. **EXTENDED RESPONSE** The table shows the scores of five contestants after one round of a competition.

Name	Score
Sean	35.8
Adrianna	35.75
LaDainian	35.3
T.J.	36.1
Chrystal	32.5

   a. Order the scores from least to greatest.

   b. The contestants with the three highest scores move on to Round 2. Which contestants will move on to Round 2?

   c. The scores of every contestant in Round 2 increase by 50 points. How does this affect the order of the scores? Which contestant is winning the contest after 2 rounds? *Explain* your reasoning.

7. **OPEN-ENDED** Give three different real-world objects whose measurements are between 10 inches and 13.5 inches.

8. **SHORT RESPONSE** Elroy finds a toadstool 0.08 meters across. Phil finds one 75 millimeters across. Whose toadstool is wider? *Explain.*

3.4 Rounding Decimals

Before	You rounded whole numbers.
Now	You'll round decimals.
Why?	So you can use small measurements, as in Ex. 49.

KEY VOCABULARY
• **leading digit,** *p. 12*
• **place value,** *p. 737*
• **round,** *p. 739*

A number line can help you picture how to round a decimal.

The decimal 2.2 is closer to 2 than to 3, so 2.2 rounds down to 2.

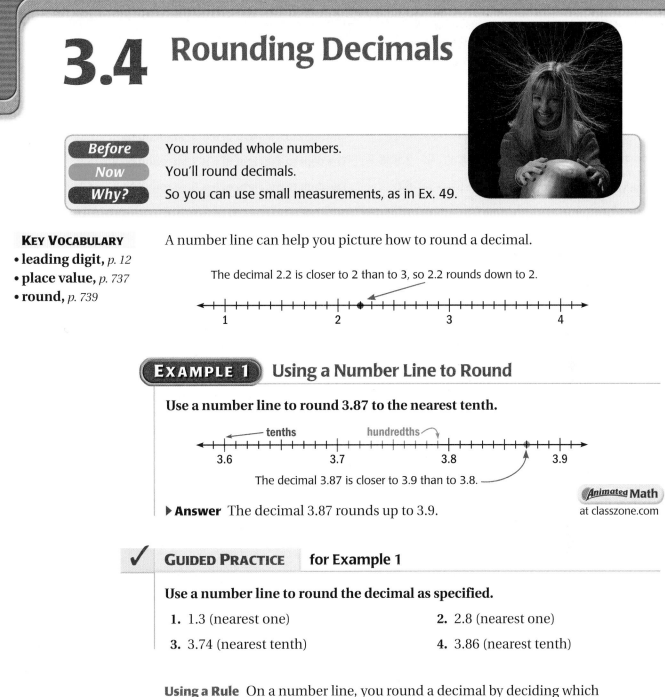

EXAMPLE 1 Using a Number Line to Round

Use a number line to round 3.87 to the nearest tenth.

tenths   hundredths

3.6   3.7   3.8   3.9

The decimal 3.87 is closer to 3.9 than to 3.8.

▶ **Answer** The decimal 3.87 rounds up to 3.9.

Animated **Math**
at classzone.com

✓ **GUIDED PRACTICE** for Example 1

Use a number line to round the decimal as specified.

1. 1.3 (nearest one)

2. 2.8 (nearest one)

3. 3.74 (nearest tenth)

4. 3.86 (nearest tenth)

Using a Rule On a number line, you round a decimal by deciding which number it is closer to. The same idea applies when you use the rule below.

KEY CONCEPT   *For Your Notebook*

Rounding Decimals

To round a decimal to a given place value, look at the digit in the place to the right.

• If the digit is 4 or less, round down.

• If the digit is 5 or greater, round up.

EXAMPLE 2   Rounding Decimals

Round the decimal to the place value of the red digit.

a. 3.23 ⟶ 3.2   The digit to the right of 2 is 3, so round down.

b. 6.485 ⟶ 6.49   The digit to the right of 8 is 5, so round up.

c. 2.83619 ⟶ 2.836   The digit to the right of 6 is 1, so round down.

d. 5.961 ⟶ 6.0   The digit to the right of 9 is 6, so round up.

✓ **GUIDED PRACTICE**   **for Example 2**

Round the decimal as specified.

5. 5.29 (nearest tenth)

6. 7.096 (nearest hundredth)

7. 6.48 (nearest one)

8. 3.9876 (nearest thousandth)

Rounding Small Numbers You can round a very small number to the place value of its leading digit to help make it easier to understand. In a decimal, the leading digit is the first nonzero digit as you read from left to right.

EXAMPLE 3   Rounding to the Leading Digit

Music A guitar was created that is 0.0003937 inch long. Round the length of the guitar to the place value of the leading digit.

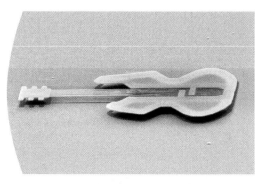

SOLUTION

The first nonzero digit as you read 0.0003937 from left to right is 3 and it is in the ten-thousandths' place. You should round the length to the nearest ten-thousandth.

    0.0003937   3 is in the ten-thousandths' place.

Because 9 is to the right of the ten-thousandths' place, round 3 up to 4.

▶ **Answer** The length of the guitar rounded to the place value of the leading digit is 0.0004 inch.

✓ **GUIDED PRACTICE**   **for Example 3**

Round the decimal to the leading digit.

9. 0.058   **10.** 0.0091   **11.** 0.0952   **12.** 0.006192

◆ **EXAMPLE 4** Using Decimals for Large Numbers

Baseball Salaries Round the annual salaries shown to the nearest hundred thousand. Then write each rounded salary as a decimal number in millions. Display your results in a bar graph.

Position	Average Salary	Rounded Salary	Salary in Millions
First Base	$4,996,933	$5,000,000	$5.0 million
Outfield	$3,480,792	$3,500,000	$3.5 million
Pitcher	$3,064,021	$3,100,000	$3.1 million
Catcher	$2,767,726	$2,800,000	$2.8 million

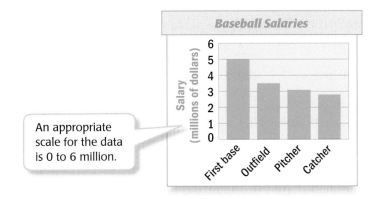

An appropriate scale for the data is 0 to 6 million.

✓ **GUIDED PRACTICE** for Example 4

13. **Sports** Shortstops averaged $2,504,993 and relief pitchers averaged $1,220,412. Round and write each salary as a decimal number in millions, as in Example 4. Add your results to a copy of the bar graph.

3.4 EXERCISES

HOMEWORK KEY

★ = **STANDARDIZED TEST PRACTICE**
Exs. 14, 38–41, 47, 49, 50, and 60

◯ = **HINTS AND HOMEWORK HELP**
for Exs. 7, 17, 29, 47 at classzone.com

SKILL PRACTICE

VOCABULARY Identify the place value of the leading digit.

1. 0.024　　　**2.** 0.0078　　　**3.** 0.00149　　　**4.** 0.000485

SEE EXAMPLE 1
on p. 137
for Exs. 5–13

USING NUMBER LINES Use a number line to round as specified.

5. 5.3 (nearest one)　　　**6.** 9.5 (nearest one)　　　**7.** 3.76 (nearest tenth)

8. 1.41 (nearest tenth)　　　**9.** 0.2 (nearest one)　　　**10.** 6.46 (nearest tenth)

11. 2.0 (nearest one)　　　**12.** 4.95 (nearest tenth)　　　**13.** 9.99 (nearest tenth)

14. ★ **MULTIPLE CHOICE** You record the weight of a package weighing 14.57 pounds to the nearest pound. What weight do you record?

(A) 10 pounds   **(B)** 14 pounds   **(C)** 14.5 pounds   **(D)** 15 pounds

ROUNDING DECIMALS **Round the decimal as specified.**

15. 9.41 (nearest one)

16. 2.59 (nearest one)

17. 8.087 (nearest tenth)

18. 8.981 (nearest tenth)

19. 1.159 (nearest hundredth)

20. 3.902 (nearest hundredth)

21. 2.5634 (nearest thousandth)

22. 7.2961 (nearest thousandth)

23. 0.35575 (nearest ten-thousandth)

24. 14.05099 (nearest ten-thousandth)

LEADING DIGITS **Round to the place value of the leading digit.**

25. 0.0263   **26.** 0.0588   **27.** 0.0092   **28.** 0.006178

29. 0.00019   **30.** 0.000231   **31.** 0.00009888   **32.** 0.0000177

33. **ERROR ANALYSIS** Describe and correct the error in the solution.

> ✗ Round to the nearest tenth.
> 9.95 ⟶ 10

NUMBERS IN MILLIONS **Round to the nearest hundred thousand. Then write the rounded number as a decimal number of millions.**

34. 15,925,000   **35.** 6,549,000   **36.** 9,987,260   **37.** 14,962,000

★ **OPEN-ENDED MATH** **Find three decimals that round to the number.**

38. 4   **39.** 15.00   **40.** 3.4   **41.** 8.7

ROUNDING **Find the maximum and minimum 6-digit decimal that rounds to the given number.**

42. 2 m   **43.** 350 cm   **44.** 1.08 km   **45.** 0.0040 m

46. **CHALLENGE** In Exercise 38, you are asked to find three decimals that round to 4. How many answers are possible? *Explain.*

PROBLEM SOLVING

47. ★ **WRITING** Why is it not reasonable to round the scores from the skateboarding competition to the nearest one? *Explain.*

		Round		
		1	**2**	**3**
Name	**Carlos**	80.7	84.4	80.8
	Ruth	83.3	78.6	81.1
	Gunnar	81.2	83.6	80.6
	Jessica	82.7	79.2	80.9

48. SHARING COSTS After sharing a pizza, you and two friends divide the cost by three. You each owe $2.66. *Explain* how to round this to the nearest dime.

49. ★ SHORT RESPONSE The width of a human hair is about 0.00389763 inch.

   a. *Explain* why it is not reasonable to round the width to the nearest hundredth.

   b. Round the width to the place value of the leading digit.

   c. How does your answer in part (b) compare to the rounded length of the guitar in Example 3?

50. ★ EXTENDED RESPONSE The table below shows the scores of 5 divers in a competition. To find each diver's rank, you could first round the scores to the nearest one and then order them from greatest to least. Or you could rank the divers without rounding the scores. Which method is better? *Explain* what is wrong with the other method.

Diver	Dionne	Ashley	Ellie	Alina	Julie
Score	136.35	137.5	136.7	137.45	137.35

51. ◆◆ MULTIPLE REPRESENTATIONS The table shows the total visitors to state parks of five states in one year.

   a. Round Data Round each number to the nearest hundred thousand.

   b. Draw a Graph Display your results in a bar graph. Compare and contrast the uses of the graph and the table.

   c. Analyze A display of state park visitors shows the numbers of visitors for New York and Ohio being identical. To what place value had the numbers of visitors been rounded?

State	Visitors
Michigan	25,297,000
Illinois	43,623,000
New York	56,864,000
Ohio	57,246,000
Pennsylvania	36,627,000

52. CHALLENGE When estimating the sum of two decimals, how is your answer affected if you round each number and then add? What if you add first and then round the answer? *Explain*.

MIXED REVIEW

Get-Ready

Prepare for
Lesson 3.5
in Exs. 53–56

Estimate the sum or difference. *(p. 11)*

53. $136 + 75$ **54.** $418 + 397$ **55.** $572 - 269$ **56.** $343 - 27$

Copy and complete the statement with <, >, or =. *(p. 130)*

57. $0.79 \underline{\ ?\ } 0.9$ **58.** $0.05 \underline{\ ?\ } 0.05000$ **59.** $3.037 \underline{\ ?\ } 3.073$

60. ★ MULTIPLE CHOICE What is the value of $126 \div 3 + 4 \times 10$? *(p. 21)*

   (A) 28   **(B)** 82   **(C)** 116   **(D)** 460

GOAL
Develop number
sense skills for adding
decimals.

MATERIALS
• metric ruler
• number cube
• colored pencils or markers

3.5 Targeting a Sum of 10

You can use number sense skills to choose values that come close to a target without going over. When these values are ones and tenths, you can use a metric ruler to help you.

EXPLORE **Use a metric ruler to come close to 10 centimeters without going over.**

STEP 1 **Draw** a line segment that is 10 centimeters long.

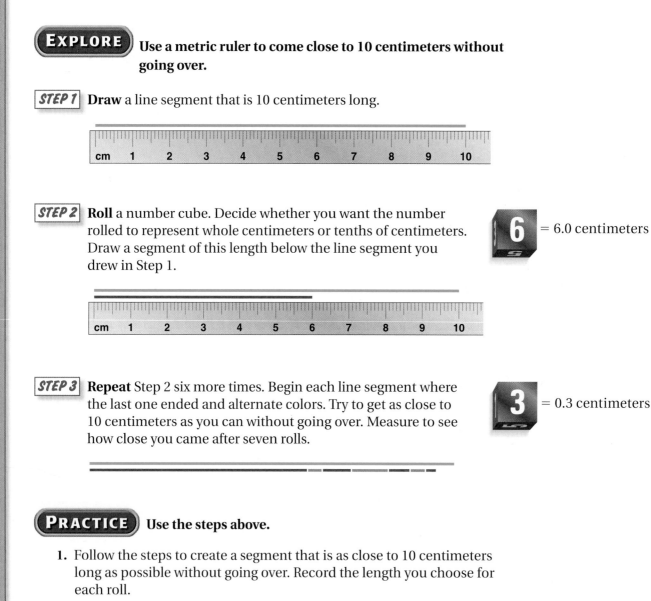

STEP 2 **Roll** a number cube. Decide whether you want the number rolled to represent whole centimeters or tenths of centimeters. Draw a segment of this length below the line segment you drew in Step 1.

= 6.0 centimeters

STEP 3 **Repeat** Step 2 six more times. Begin each line segment where the last one ended and alternate colors. Try to get as close to 10 centimeters as you can without going over. Measure to see how close you came after seven rolls.

= 0.3 centimeters

PRACTICE **Use the steps above.**

1. Follow the steps to create a segment that is as close to 10 centimeters long as possible without going over. Record the length you choose for each roll.

DRAW CONCLUSIONS

2. **WRITING** In Exercise 1, *explain* what strategies you could use to come as close as possible to 10 centimeters in 7 rolls without going over.

3.5 Decimal Estimation

Before	You estimated sums and differences of whole numbers.
Now	You'll estimate sums and differences of decimals.
Why?	So you can estimate sports participation, as in Example 1.

KEY VOCABULARY
- front-end estimation, *p. 144*

Sports The table shows the number of people, in millions, who participated in five sports in a recent year. About how many people played golf? About how many more females bicycled than played soccer?

One way to estimate a sum or a difference is to use rounding.

Sports Participation (millions)		
Activity	*Males*	*Females*
Bicycling	22.5	18.9
Golf	22.4	5.8
Hiking	15.4	15.2
Soccer	9.0	5.5
Swimming	25.4	29.2

EXAMPLE 1 Estimating Sums and Differences

Use the table above.

a. Estimate how many people played golf. Round each decimal to the nearest whole number. Then add.

$$
\begin{array}{r}
22.4 \\
+ \ 5.8 \\
\end{array}
\longrightarrow
\begin{array}{r}
22 \\
+ \ 6 \\
\hline
28 \\
\end{array}
$$

Round 22.4 down to 22.
Round 5.8 up to 6.

▶ **Answer** About 28 million people played golf.

b. Estimate how many more females bicycled than played soccer. Round each decimal to the nearest whole number. Then subtract.

$$
\begin{array}{r}
18.9 \\
- \ 5.5 \\
\end{array}
\longrightarrow
\begin{array}{r}
19 \\
- \ 6 \\
\hline
13 \\
\end{array}
$$

Round 18.9 up to 19.
Round 5.5 up to 6.

▶ **Answer** About 13 million more females bicycled than played soccer.

✓ GUIDED PRACTICE for Example 1

Use the information provided at the top of the page.

1. Estimate the total number of people who participated in hiking.

2. Estimate how many more males participated in swimming than in bicycling.

EXAMPLE 2 Predicting Results

Shopping You buy a T-shirt that costs $9.21. You give the clerk $20.00. Estimate your change. Is this estimate high or low?

$$\begin{array}{r} \$20.00 \\ - \quad \$9.21 \end{array} \longrightarrow \begin{array}{r} \$20 \\ - \quad \$9 \end{array}$$ **Round 9.21 down to 9.**

▶ **Answer** Your change is about $11. This estimate is high because you subtracted too little by rounding $9.21 down to $9.

Front-End Estimation You can also estimate sums using **front-end estimation**. You add the front-end digits to get a low estimate. Then you use the remaining digits to adjust the sum and get a closer estimate.

EXAMPLE 3 Solve a Multi-Step Problem

Grocery List	
bread	$1.79
milk	$2.18
cereal	$3.34
popcorn	$3.65

Groceries You have $10 to buy bread, milk, and cereal. If you have enough money, you would like to buy popcorn. The prices of these items are shown. Do you have enough money to buy popcorn?

SOLUTION

Estimate the sum of all the prices, including the price of the popcorn.

ANOTHER WAY
You could round then add:

$$\begin{array}{r} 1.79 \\ 2.18 \\ 3.34 \\ + 3.65 \end{array} \longrightarrow \begin{array}{r} 2 \\ 2 \\ 3 \\ + 4 \\ \hline 11 \end{array}$$

STEP 1 Add the front-end digits: the dollars.

$$\begin{array}{r} \$\mathbf{1}.79 \\ \$\mathbf{2}.18 \\ \$\mathbf{3}.34 \\ + \$\mathbf{3}.65 \\ \hline \$9.00 \end{array}$$

STEP 2 Estimate the sum of the remaining digits: the cents.

$$\begin{array}{r} \$1.\mathbf{79} \\ \$2.\mathbf{18} \longrightarrow \$1 \\ \$3.\mathbf{34} \\ + \$3.\mathbf{65} \longrightarrow \$1 \\ \hline \$2 \end{array}$$

STEP 3 Add your results.

$$\begin{array}{r} \$9 \\ + \$2 \\ \hline \$11 \end{array}$$

▶ **Answer** Because 11 > 10 you do not have enough money to buy popcorn.

✓ **GUIDED PRACTICE**   for Examples 2 and 3

Use front-end estimation to estimate the sum.

3. 6.42 + 7.64 + 3.94 + 2.21   **4.** 8.59 + 1.37 + 2 + 6.12

5. How can you estimate the difference in Example 2 so that your answer is a low estimate?

3.5 EXERCISES

HOMEWORK KEY

★ = **STANDARDIZED TEST PRACTICE**
Exs. 23, 31, 43, 47, 48, 49, and 62

○ = **HINTS AND HOMEWORK HELP**
for Exs. 5, 15, 21, 25, 45 at classzone.com

SKILL PRACTICE

VOCABULARY Identify the front-end digit of the number.

1. $1.12   **2.** $2.55   **3.** $5.86   **4.** $9.97

ROUNDING TO ESTIMATE Use rounding to estimate the sum or difference.

SEE EXAMPLE 1
on p. 143
for Exs. 5–19

5. $2.6 + 8.9$ **6.** $9.7 + 5.4$ **7.** $8.3 - 3.8$

8. $9.3 - 6.9$ **9.** $7.2 - 4.6$ **10.** $15.5 - 14.7$

11. $12.43 + 5.8$ **12.** $10.64 + 7.49$ **13.** $2.25 + 0.93$

14. $12.81 - 1.92$ **15.** $10.72 - 2.85$ **16.** $15.99 + 3.4$

17. $12.385 + 12.84$ **18.** $20.28 - 10.301$ **19.** $9.1 - 8.988$

ESTIMATING CHANGE Estimate the change you will receive and tell whether the estimate is *high* or *low. Explain.*

SEE EXAMPLE 2
on p. 144
for Exs. 20–23

20. You buy a gallon of milk for $2.75. You give the cashier $5.00.

21. You buy several postcards totaling $3.82. You give the clerk $10.00.

22. You buy a bag of pretzels for $1.15. You give the cashier $5.00.

23. ★ **MULTIPLE CHOICE** What is the best estimate of the sum
$5.80 + 1.22 + 8.93$?

(A) 14   (B) 15   (C) 16   (D) 17

USING FRONT-END ESTIMATION Use front-end estimation to estimate the sum.

SEE EXAMPLE 3
on p. 144
for Exs. 24–29

24. $4.79 + 5.16 + 8.08$ **25.** $6.23 + 4.75 + 3.91$ **26.** $4.5 + 8.92 + 9.21$

27. $6.46 + 3.22 + 2.58$ **28.** $5.55 + 7.19 + 4.49$ **29.** $6.31 + 2.5 + 1.93$

30. ERROR ANALYSIS Describe and correct the error in the estimate.

$$\times \quad \begin{array}{r} \$4.\boxed{79} \rightarrow \$1 \\ + \$1.\boxed{22} \\ \hline \$6 \end{array} \quad \longrightarrow \quad \begin{array}{r} \$6 \\ + \$1 \\ \hline \$7 \end{array}$$

31. ★ **OPEN-ENDED MATH** Describe two different examples in which it is useful to use estimation.

GEOMETRY Estimate the perimeter of the triangle or rectangle by rounding.

32.
4.8 cm   7.1 cm
7.9 cm

33.
6.5 km   8.4 km
10.9km

34.
6.7 km
3.3 km

CHOOSE A METHOD Identify whether *front-end estimation, rounding,* or *either method* was used for each estimate.

35. $3.72 + $5.15 is about $9

36. $8.89 + $10.70 is about $20

37. $2.49 + $10.42 is about $12

38. $9.79 + $20.78 is about $31

39. CHALLENGE You estimate the sum $4.79 + $2.47 + $5.44 to the nearest dollar. If you use front-end estimation, how much does your estimate differ from the actual sum of $12.70? What if you round to the nearest dollar?

40. REASONING Three friends each estimate the sum $104.89 + $22.48 + $.39. *Explain* why their estimates could differ. Is there a best estimate?

PROBLEM SOLVING

41. GUIDED PROBLEM SOLVING A table is 73.66 centimeters tall. An iguana tank on the table is 76.2 centimeters tall. Estimate to decide whether they will fit beneath a shelf that is 157.16 centimeters off the floor.

   a. Draw a diagram of the situation.

   b. Estimate the height of the table and the tank combined.

   c. Will the table and tank fit beneath the shelf?

42. FINANCE In 2004, a company had a profit of $18.7 million. The following year, the company's profit was $11.9 million.

   a. Estimate the total profit for the two years.

   b. About how much more did the company make in 2004?

43. ★ MULTIPLE CHOICE At a fishing competition, the competitors enter the weights of their three biggest fish. For which three weights is 9 pounds a reasonable estimate?

   (A) 2.6 pounds, 2.25 pounds, 3 pounds

   (B) 2.75 pounds, 2.8 pounds, 3.2 pounds

   (C) 2.1 pounds, 2.45 pounds, 2.68 pounds

   (D) 1.95 pounds, 2.3 pounds, 3.3 pounds

SPORTS You take $20 to a baseball game. Estimate whether you have enough money to purchase the given items. Then estimate your change, if any. Is the estimate *high* or *low*?

Hat: $12.99
T-shirt: $9.99
Pennant: $2.25
Hot dog: $3.50
Nachos: $4.00
Peanuts: $4.75
Soda: $4.50

SEE EXAMPLES
2 AND 3
on p. 144
for Exs. 44–46

44. Hat and peanuts

45. Hat, pennant, and hot dog

46. Pennant, peanuts, soda, and a T-shirt

47. ★ **WRITING** The sale price for a DVD boxed set is $42.99. The sale price for a compact disk boxed set is $25.75. About how much more is the cost of the DVD boxed set? You purchase the DVDs and the compact disks. *Estimate* the total cost. Is the estimate *high* or *low*? *Explain.*

48. ★ **SHORT RESPONSE** You have $25 to buy prizes for a game. The table shows the prizes and their prices. Use rounding to estimate the total cost and decide if this estimate is *high* or *low.* Then use front-end estimation to find the total cost. Which method is better when you have a fixed amount of money to spend? *Explain.*

Prize	Price
Yo-yo	$1.48
Bear	$9.46
Sunglasses	$1.07
Magic tricks	$5.91
Set of books	$8.00

49. ★ **EXTENDED RESPONSE** The Seven Summits are the highest mountain peaks on each of the seven continents. The heights above sea level of the summits are shown in the table.

   a. Compare Order the heights of the mountains from shortest to tallest. Find the median height.

   b. Estimation Estimate the mean of the heights. Is your estimate *high* or *low*? *Explain.*

   c. Reasoning Which of your answers in parts (a) and (b) is more representative of the heights? *Explain.*

50. CHALLENGE How can you use rounding to overestimate the sum of two numbers? the difference of two numbers? How can you use rounding to underestimate the sum of two numbers? the difference of two numbers? *Explain* and show examples.

Mountain	Height (miles)
Elbrus (Europe)	3.5
Kosciusko (Australia)	1.38
Aconcagua (South America)	4.33
Everest (Asia)	5.50
Kilimanjaro (Africa)	3.7
McKinley (North America)	3.85
Vinson Massif (Antarctica)	3.04

MIXED REVIEW

Get-Ready

Prepare for Lesson 3.6 in Exs. 51–53

Find the sum or difference. *(p. 751)*

51. $10.75 + $1.25   **52.** $9.80 + $4.20   **53.** $2.85 − $1.35

Evaluate the expression when $x = 2$ and $y = 3$. *(p. 29)*

54. $x + 14$ **55.** $9y$ **56.** $x + y$ **57.** $y + x \cdot y$

Write the decimal in words. *(p. 119)*

58. 0.91   **59.** 9.54   **60.** 0.023   **61.** 12.786

62. ★ **MULTIPLE CHOICE** What is 4.79663 rounded to the nearest hundredth? *(p. 137)*

   (A) 4.79   **(B)** 4.7966   **(C)** 4.797   **(D)** 4.80

3.6 Adding and Subtracting Decimals

Before	You added and subtracted whole numbers.
Now	You'll add and subtract decimals.
Why?	So you can analyze times, as in Ex. 57.

KEY VOCABULARY
- commutative property of addition, *p. 149*
- associative property of addition, *p. 149*

ACTIVITY

You can use base-ten pieces to model sums, such as 1.15 + 0.95.

STEP 1 **Model** the numbers.

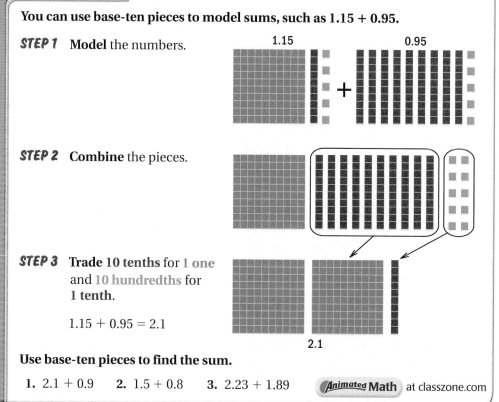

1.15   0.95

STEP 2 **Combine** the pieces.

STEP 3 **Trade 10 tenths for 1 one** and **10 hundredths for 1 tenth.**

1.15 + 0.95 = 2.1

2.1

Use base-ten pieces to find the sum.

1. 2.1 + 0.9   **2.** 1.5 + 0.8   **3.** 2.23 + 1.89

Animated **Math** at classzone.com

Decimal Operations To add and subtract decimals, line up the decimal points. Then add or subtract as with whole numbers and bring down the decimal point.

EXAMPLE 1   Adding and Subtracting Decimals

ADDING ZEROS
You can write zeros after the last digit of a decimal number to help you line up the decimal points.

a. 9.8 + 2.12

$$\begin{array}{r} 9.80 \\ + 2.12 \\ \hline 11.92 \end{array}$$

b. 8 − 1.65

$$\begin{array}{r} 8.00 \\ - 1.65 \\ \hline 6.35 \end{array}$$

c. 8.75 + 6.394

$$\begin{array}{r} 8.750 \\ + 6.394 \\ \hline 15.144 \end{array}$$

EXAMPLE 2 **Evaluating Algebraic Expressions**

Evaluate $20 - x$ when $x = 4.71$.

$$20 - x = 20 - 4.71 \qquad \text{Substitute 4.71 for } x.$$
$$= 15.29 \qquad \text{Subtract.}$$

EXAMPLE 3 **Using Mental Math to Add Decimals**

Bakery Costs Find the total cost for a sweet roll that costs $1.30, two hard rolls that cost $1.20 each, and a coffee cake that costs $3.70.

STEP 1 **List** the prices.

$1.30
$1.20
$1.20
$3.70

STEP 2 **Rearrange** and group pairs of prices.

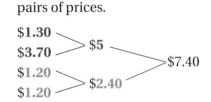

▶ **Answer** The bakery goods will cost $7.40.

✓ **GUIDED PRACTICE** for Examples 1, 2, and 3

Evaluate the expression when $x = 5.82$ and $y = 9.1$.

1. $4.7 + x$ **2.** $12.56 - y$ **3.** $y - x$

4. **Electronics Costs** Find the total cost for a pair of headphones that costs $19.75, two compact disks that cost $11.50 each, and a pack of batteries that costs $4.25.

Mental Math In Example 3, you rearranged numbers and grouped them. The properties that allow you to do this are shown below.

KEY CONCEPT *For Your Notebook*

Properties of Addition

Commutative Property You can add numbers in any order.

    Numbers $2 + 5 = 5 + 2$
    Algebra $a + b = b + a$

Associative Property The value of a sum does not depend on how the numbers are grouped.

    Numbers $(2 + 5) + 4 = 2 + (5 + 4)$
    Algebra $(a + b) + c = a + (b + c)$

EXAMPLE 4 Using Properties of Addition

Tell whether the *commutative* or *associative* property of addition allows you to rewrite the problem as shown. *Explain* **your choice.**

a. $4 + 2.75 + 11 = 2.75 + 4 + 11$

The order of the numbers has changed. This is allowed by the commutative property of addition.

b. $(3.5 + 10) + 7 = 3.5 + (10 + 7)$

The grouping of the numbers has changed. This is allowed by the associative property of addition.

EXAMPLE 5 Standardized Test Practice

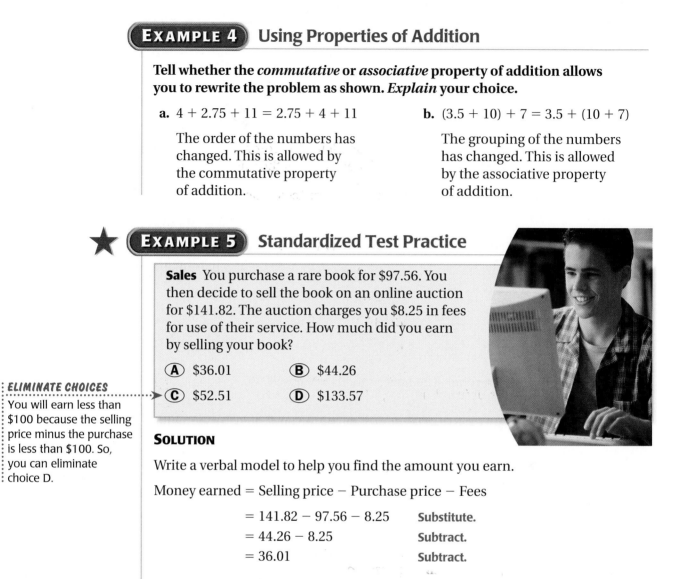

Sales You purchase a rare book for $97.56. You then decide to sell the book on an online auction for $141.82. The auction charges you $8.25 in fees for use of their service. How much did you earn by selling your book?

(**A**) $36.01 (**B**) $44.26

(**C**) $52.51 (**D**) $133.57

ELIMINATE CHOICES
You will earn less than $100 because the selling price minus the purchase is less than $100. So, you can eliminate choice D.

SOLUTION

Write a verbal model to help you find the amount you earn.

Money earned = Selling price − Purchase price − Fees

$= 141.82 - 97.56 - 8.25$ **Substitute.**

$= 44.26 - 8.25$ **Subtract.**

$= 36.01$ **Subtract.**

▶ **Answer** Your sale earns you $36.01.
The correct answer is A. (**A**) (**B**) (**C**) (**D**)

Check Use estimation to check that your answer is reasonable. Round $141.82 to $142, $97.56 to $98, and $8.25 to $8. Because $142 - 98 - 8 = 36$, the answer is reasonable.

✓ GUIDED PRACTICE for Examples 4 and 5

Tell whether the *commutative* or *associative* property allows you to rewrite the problem as shown. *Explain* **your choice. Then find the sum.**

5. $(6.4 + 4.8) + 5.2 = 6.4 + (4.8 + 5.2)$ **6.** $9.3 + 2.9 = 2.9 + 9.3$

7. What If? Suppose you bought the book in Example 5 for $78.45, you sold the book for $126.78, and the auction fees were the same. How much would you earn selling the book?

3.6 EXERCISES

HOMEWORK KEY

★ = **STANDARDIZED TEST PRACTICE**
Exs. 32, 33, 52, 59, and 67

○ = **HINTS AND HOMEWORK HELP**
for Exs. 9, 21, 29, 51 at classzone.com

SKILL PRACTICE

1. **VOCABULARY** Copy and complete: According to the _?_ property, the value of a sum does not depend on how the numbers are grouped.

2. **VOCABULARY** Copy and complete: According to the _?_ property, you can add numbers in any order.

FINDING SUMS AND DIFFERENCES Find the sum or difference.

SEE EXAMPLE 1
on p. 148
for Exs. 3–19

3. $3.6 + 1.89$
4. $6.54 + 12.1$
5. $9.8 - 7.96$
6. $4 - 0.25$

7. $5.56 + 3.7$
8. $2.88 + 6.7$
9. $16.2 + 8.34$
10. $18.4 + 1.6$

11. $4.091 + 5.87$
12. $3.781 + 4.19$
13. $5.56 - 2.3$
14. $7.42 - 3.2$

15. $6.180 - 1.731$
16. $9.147 - 6.641$
17. $4.6 - 1.242$
18. $8.5 - 6.684$

19. **ERROR ANALYSIS** Describe and correct the error in subtracting 3.06 from 8.4.

$$\times \quad \begin{array}{r} 8.4 \\ - 3.06 \\ \hline 5.46 \end{array}$$

XY ALGEBRA Evaluate the expression when $x = 2.4$ and $y = 8.75$.

SEE EXAMPLE 2
on p. 149
for Exs. 20–27

20. $4.52 + x$
21. $y + 7.5$
22. $y - 3.01$
23. $6.48 - x$

24. $x + y$
25. $y - x$
26. $y - 7.9$
27. $7 - x$

MENTAL MATH Tell which property is being illustrated. Then use mental math to evaluate the expression in red.

SEE EXAMPLES
3 AND 4
on pp. 149–150
for Exs. 28–32

28. $(9.5 + 4.9) + 5.1 = \mathbf{9.5 + (4.9 + 5.1)}$

29. $4.2 + (2.8 + 11.95) = \mathbf{(4.2 + 2.8) + 11.95}$

30. $1.5 + (1.74 + 3.5) = \mathbf{1.5 + (3.5 + 1.74)}$

31. $(3.7 + 8.9) + 6.3 = \mathbf{(8.9 + 3.7) + 6.3}$

32. ★ **MULTIPLE CHOICE** Evaluate the expression $(12.4 - 2.35) + 24.6$.

(A) 34.65
(B) 34.75
(C) 39.35
(D) 44.65

33. ★ **OPEN-ENDED MATH** Write an expression with two decimal numbers whose sum is 3.

FINDING SUMS AND DIFFERENCES Evaluate the expression.

34. $3.6 + 4.25 + 1.8$
35. $9.17 + 2.3 + 8.3$

36. $7 - 2.96 + 0.22$
37. $8 + 3.17 - 5.83$

38. $2.7 + 5.167 + 0.29$
39. $14.2 + 21.87 - 11.235$

USING PROPERTIES Rewrite each expression using the given addition property.

40. 7.2 + (3.8 + 4.8); commutative property

41. (5.3 + 4.6) + 1.9; associative property

GEOMETRY Find the perimeter of the triangle. Use estimation to check.

42.

6 cm
7.5 cm
7.5 cm

43.

9.1 mm
6.5 mm
5.85 mm

44.

3.075 m
4.1 m
5.125 m

NUMBER SENSE Copy and complete the statement with <, >, or =.

45. 3.8 + 4.1 + 5.2 ? 4.6 + 3.3 + 4.4

46. 3.1 + 2.1 + 13.9 ? 2.6 + 2.5 + 13.5

47. (6.5 + 7.2) + 9.8 ? 8.5 + (7.9 + 7.5)

48. (6.2 − 2.9) + 1.3 ? 6.1 − (2.8 + 1.3)

49. CHALLENGE For the expression 3.2 + 2.32 + 5.68, show all the possible groupings using parentheses that result in the same sum. Show all the ways to order the numbers in the expression, with no grouping symbols, that result in the same sum.

PROBLEM SOLVING

SEE EXAMPLE 5
on p. 150 for
Exs. 50–52

50. GUIDED PROBLEM SOLVING The number of miles of track in three Metro rail systems is shown. How many more miles of track does Washington, D.C. have than the Metros of Cleveland and Boston combined?

Cleveland, 38.2 mi

Boston, 76.3 mi

Washington, D.C., 206.6 mi

  a. Write a verbal model of the problem.

  b. Use the model to solve the problem.

  c. Check your answer using estimation.

CHECKING REASONABLENESS In Exercises 51 and 52, solve the problem. Use estimation to check that your answer is reasonable.

51. MEAL COSTS Your meal at a diner costs $5.29. Your guest's meal costs $4.95. You give the cashier $15 for the two meals. How much change should you get?

52. ★ WRITING The bank charges a fee if the minimum balance in your account drops below $250. You have $298 in your savings account. During one month, you deposit $22.75 and withdraw $68.75. Should you expect to pay a bank fee? *Explain.*

Space Shuttle On a space shuttle mission, astronauts are allowed 1.5 pounds of personal items. The table shows the weights of some possible items. A penny from space is a popular collectible.

Astronauts' Personal Items	
Item	**Weight (pounds)**
2 Rolls of pennies	0.55
5 Golf balls	0.506
Watch	0.09
College sweatshirt	0.750
Whistle	0.125
Camera	0.625

53. **Calculate** An astronaut decides to bring two rolls of pennies, a watch, and a college sweatshirt on the mission. What is the total weight?

54. **Calculate** Another astronaut brings five golf balls and a camera. How much weight allowance is left for a third item?

55. **Compare** List the items in this table in order from lightest to heaviest.

56. **Open-Ended** A third astronaut wants to bring four different items from this table. Find four items that the astronaut could choose.

ORIENTEERS In Exercises 57 and 58, use the table.

In the sport of orienteering, people use maps and compasses to find their way from point to point along an unfamiliar outdoor course in the least time. For each of five top women orienteers, the table shows their times in a championship.

Orienteer	Time (min.)
Jenny Johansson	25.4
Anu Annus	27.75
Hanne Staff	28.7
Karin Schmalfeld	29.05
Sara Gemperle	29.32

57. Which two women have the closest times? How close are they?

58. What is the greatest difference between any two consecutive times?

59. ★ **SHORT RESPONSE** For $19.95 a month, you can rent an unlimited number of videos. Otherwise, renting a video costs $3.67 per rental. Using addition, *explain* how to find how many videos you could rent per month before the monthly rate became the better deal.

60. **REASONING** Your friend is buying one DVD for $14.95 and renting one for $4.31. Your friend hands the cashier a $20 bill and 1 penny. *Explain* how the penny affects the number of coins your friend receives in change.

61. **CHALLENGE** When estimating the sum of two decimals, should you round each decimal before adding or should you find the sum and then round? How will these two methods affect the estimate? *Explain* which method gives a better estimate.

Get-Ready

Prepare for
Lesson 4.1 in
Exs. 62–65

Find the product. *(p. 3)*

62. 120×4 **63.** 30×15 **64.** 504×12 **65.** 237×43

66. Make a frequency table of the data. *(p. 76)*

2, 3, 5, 9, 4, 1, 0, 2, 3, 4, 5, 6, 7, 8, 1, 3, 5, 9, 1, 3, 5, 6, 4, 5, 1

67. ★ **OPEN-ENDED MATH** Give three conclusions about the information shown in the circle graph. *(p. 94)*

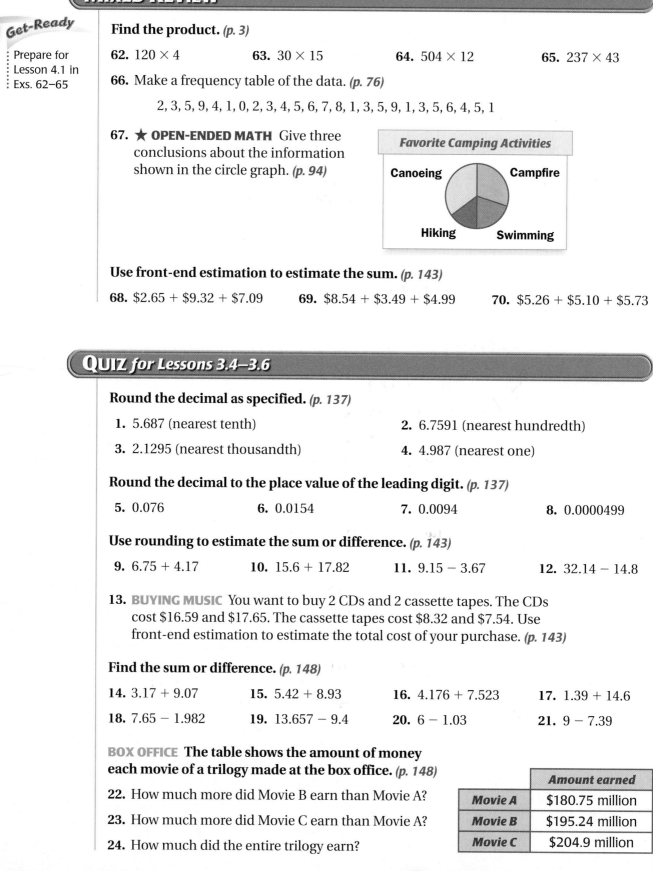

Favorite Camping Activities

Canoeing   Campfire

Hiking   Swimming

Use front-end estimation to estimate the sum. *(p. 143)*

68. $2.65 + 9.32 + 7.09$ **69.** $8.54 + 3.49 + 4.99$ **70.** $5.26 + 5.10 + 5.73$

QUIZ *for Lessons 3.4–3.6*

Round the decimal as specified. *(p. 137)*

1. 5.687 (nearest tenth)   **2.** 6.7591 (nearest hundredth)

3. 2.1295 (nearest thousandth)   **4.** 4.987 (nearest one)

Round the decimal to the place value of the leading digit. *(p. 137)*

5. 0.076   **6.** 0.0154   **7.** 0.0094   **8.** 0.0000499

Use rounding to estimate the sum or difference. *(p. 143)*

9. $6.75 + 4.17$ **10.** $15.6 + 17.82$ **11.** $9.15 - 3.67$ **12.** $32.14 - 14.8$

13. **BUYING MUSIC** You want to buy 2 CDs and 2 cassette tapes. The CDs cost $16.59 and $17.65. The cassette tapes cost $8.32 and $7.54. Use front-end estimation to estimate the total cost of your purchase. *(p. 143)*

Find the sum or difference. *(p. 148)*

14. $3.17 + 9.07$ **15.** $5.42 + 8.93$ **16.** $4.176 + 7.523$ **17.** $1.39 + 14.6$

18. $7.65 - 1.982$ **19.** $13.657 - 9.4$ **20.** $6 - 1.03$ **21.** $9 - 7.39$

BOX OFFICE The table shows the amount of money each movie of a trilogy made at the box office. *(p. 148)*

22. How much more did Movie B earn than Movie A?

23. How much more did Movie C earn than Movie A?

24. How much did the entire trilogy earn?

	Amount earned
Movie A	$180.75 million
Movie B	$195.24 million
Movie C	$204.9 million

GOAL
Use a calculator to add and subtract decimals.

3.6 Adding and Subtracting Decimals

EXAMPLE **You can add and subtract decimals using the [+] and [−] keys.**

A national collegiate triathlon championship consists of a 0.932 mile swim, a 24.9 mile bike ride, and a 6.21 mile run. What is the total length of the triathlon?

SOLUTION

When using a calculator to add and subtract decimals, you do not have to worry about lining up the decimal points.

Keystrokes	**Display**
0 [.] 932 [+] 24 [.] 9 [+] 6 [.] 21 [=]	32.042

▸ **Answer** The triathlon is 32.042 miles long.

Check Round each number to the nearest whole number.

$0.932 + 24.9 + 6.21 \longrightarrow 1 + 25 + 6$

Because $1 + 25 + 6 = 32$, the answer is reasonable.

PRACTICE **Use a calculator to evaluate the expression.**

1. $6.705 + 0.68$
2. $9.83 - 5.846$
3. $12.753 - 4.1$
4. $6.14 - 0.09$
5. $12.74 + 3.06$
6. $17.19 - 9.8$
7. $9.32 - 7.3 - 0.02$
8. $6.942 + 3.3 - 5.39$
9. $20.87 - 9.7 + 3.42$
10. **GEOMETRY** A triangle has side lengths of 4.5 inches, 6.2 inches, and 9.4 inches. What is the perimeter of the triangle?
11. **BODY TEMPERATURE** To convert a temperature in kelvins (K) to degrees Celsius (°C), you subtract 273.15. Normal body temperature is 310.15 K. What is normal body temperature in degrees Celsius?
12. **TRIATHLON** A national triathlon championship for athletes who are 11 to 14 years old consists of a 0.114 mile swim, a 6.2 mile bike ride, and a 1.2 mile run. What is the total length of the triathlon?
13. **BUDGET** How much of \$437.26 will you have after paying bills for \$23.55, \$132.50, and \$217.42?

MIXED REVIEW *of Problem Solving*

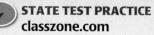

Lessons 3.4–3.6

1. **GRIDDED ANSWER** The batting average of a softball player is 0.34375. What is her batting average rounded to the nearest thousandth?

2. **EXTENDED RESPONSE** The population of Los Angeles has grown rapidly in the last 40 years. The table shows the population of Los Angeles in several years.

Year	Population
1960	2,479,015
1970	2,816,061
1980	2,966,850
1990	3,485,398
2000	3,694,820

   a. Round the data to the nearest hundred thousand.

   b. Write each rounded number as a decimal number of millions.

   c. Display your results in a line graph.

   d. About how much did the population grow, in millions, between the years 1960 and 2000? *Explain.*

3. **OPEN-ENDED** Give examples of three different prices that round to $3.50.

4. **SHORT RESPONSE** The dimensions of a dresser and its mirror are given in the diagram below. Will the dresser and mirror fit in a room with a ceiling that is 84 inches high? *Explain* how you can use estimation to decide.

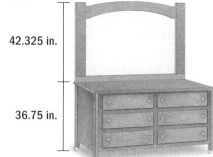

42.325 in.

36.75 in.

5. **SHORT RESPONSE** At a department store, you buy a sweater for $29.99, a notebook for $3.79, and a CD for $11.99. You give the cashier $50. About how much change should you expect? *Explain* your reasoning.

6. **MULTI-STEP PROBLEM** The heights, in inches, of six players on your hockey team are given below.

   52.5, 52.8, 63.2, 52.5, 60, 62

   a. Find the median and mode of the data set.

   b. Estimate the mean of the heights. Is your estimate *high* or *low*? *Explain.*

   c. Which average best represents the data set? *Explain* your reasoning.

7. **EXTENDED RESPONSE** The table below shows the prices of some sale items.

Item	Price
Cordless phone	$32.99
CD player	$14.49
DVD	$15.99
Table lamp	$18.29
Phone card	$15.69
Radio controlled car	$17.78

   a. Marta bought a phone card and a DVD. Andre bought a cordless phone. Who spent more money?

   b. Jordan paid for 2 lamps with a $50 bill. How much change did she receive?

   c. Estimate how many dollars you would spend to buy one of each item.

   d. Is your estimate in part (c) lower or higher than the actual total?

   e. When estimating if you have enough cash for purchases, is it better to have a low or a high estimate? *Justify* your reasoning.

3 CHAPTER REVIEW

REVIEW KEY VOCABULARY

- decimal, *p. 120*
- front-end estimation, *p. 144*
- commutative property of addition, *p. 149*
- associative property of addition, *p. 149*

VOCABULARY EXERCISES

1. Copy and complete: When you add the front-end digits and estimate the sum of the remaining digits, you are using __?__ .

Tell whether the statement is *true* or *false*. Correct any false statements.

2. One millimeter is one hundredth of a centimeter.

3. One centimeter is one hundredth of a meter.

4. One millimeter is one hundredth of a meter.

Tell which property is illustrated.

5. $6.51 + 7.21 = 7.21 + 6.51$

6. $(4.3 + 6.2) + 9.8 = 4.3 + (6.2 + 9.8)$

REVIEW EXAMPLES AND EXERCISES

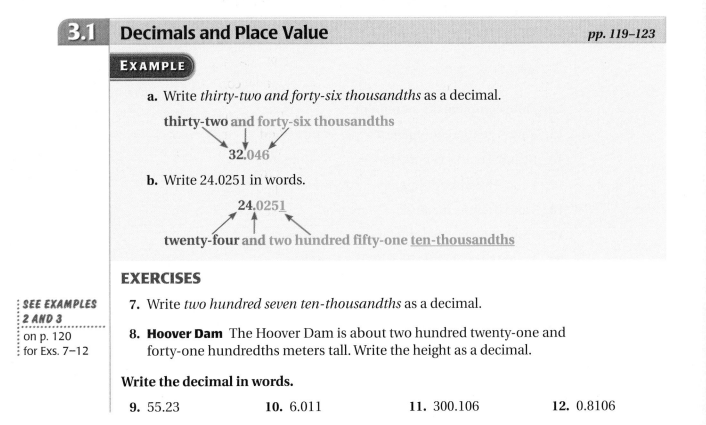

3.1 Decimals and Place Value
pp. 119–123

EXAMPLE

a. Write *thirty-two and forty-six thousandths* as a decimal.

thirty-two and **forty-six thousandths**

32.046

b. Write 24.0251 in words.

24.0251

twenty-four and **two hundred fifty-one ten-thousandths**

EXERCISES

SEE EXAMPLES 2 AND 3
on p. 120
for Exs. 7–12

7. Write *two hundred seven ten-thousandths* as a decimal.

8. **Hoover Dam** The Hoover Dam is about two hundred twenty-one and forty-one hundredths meters tall. Write the height as a decimal.

Write the decimal in words.

9. 55.23　　　10. 6.011　　　11. 300.106　　　12. 0.8106

3.2 Measuring Metric Lengths

pp. 125–129

EXAMPLE

Find the length of the line segment. Write the length of the line segment in centimeters and meters.

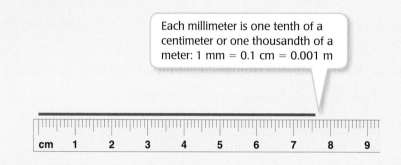

> Each millimeter is one tenth of a centimeter or one thousandth of a meter: 1 mm = 0.1 cm = 0.001 m

The length of the line segment is about 7.6 centimeters or 0.076 meter.

EXERCISES

Find the length of the line segment to the given unit.

SEE EXAMPLES 1, 2, AND 3 on pp. 125–126 for Exs. 13–25

13. to the nearest tenth of a centimeter

14. to the nearest thousandth of a meter

Copy and complete the statement.

15. 2 and 1 tenths centimeters = __?__ centimeters

16. 10 and 5 tenths centimeters = __?__ centimeters

17. 4 and 9 hundredths meters = __?__ meters

18. 3 and 8 tenths meters = __?__ meters

19. 5 and 5 thousandths meters = __?__ meters

20. 7 and 16 hundredths meters = __?__ meters

Draw a line segment of the given length using a ruler.

21. 3.5 cm   **22.** 28 mm   **23.** 0.07 m   **24.** 0.11 m

25. Measurement Use a centimeter ruler to measure the height of the rulers on this page in centimeters and in meters.

3.3 Ordering Decimals

EXAMPLE

Compare the decimals.

a. 3.604 ? 3.592

The ones' digits are the same.

3.604
3.592

The tenths' digits are different: 6 > 5.

3.604 > 3.592

b. 7.8 ? 7.85

The ones' and tenths' digits are the same.

7.80 ← Write a zero.
7.85

The hundredths' digits are different: 0 < 5.

7.8 < 7.85

EXERCISES

Copy and complete the statement with <, >, or =.

SEE EXAMPLES 3 AND 4
on p. 131
for Exs. 26–30

26. 6.54 ? 6.45

27. 2.536 ? 2.541

28. 9.7 ? 9.70

29. Baseball The batting averages of four players on a baseball team are: 0.298, 0.336, 0.283, 0.332. Write the batting averages in order from least to greatest.

30. Rainfall The average annual rainfall of five cities are: 45.03 in., 70.23 in., 39.12 in., 45.79 in., and 54.29 in. Write the rainfall amounts in order from greatest to least.

3.4 Rounding Decimals

pp. 137–141

EXAMPLE

Round the decimal to the place value of the red digit.

a. 6.247 ⟶ 6.25   The digit to the right of 4 is 7, so round up.

b. 2.839 ⟶ 2.8   The digit to the right of 8 is 3, so round down.

EXERCISES

Round the decimal as specified.

SEE EXAMPLES 2 AND 3
on p. 138
for Exs. 31–35

31. 0.0068 (leading digit)

32. 10.226 (nearest tenth)

33. 1.606 (nearest hundredth)

34. 4.8873 (nearest thousandth)

35. Printer Paper A piece of printer paper is about 0.00409 inch thick. Round the thickness of the paper to the place value of the leading digit.

3.5 Decimal Estimation

pp. 143–147

EXAMPLE

Estimate the sum or difference.

a. Round to estimate the difference.

$$16.7 \longrightarrow 17 \quad \text{Round up.}$$
$$-\ 6.2 \longrightarrow -\ 6 \quad \text{Round down.}$$
$$\overline{\hphantom{-\ 6.2 \longrightarrow}\ 11}$$

b. Use front-end estimation to estimate the sum.

$$\begin{array}{r} 9.67 \\ 8.39 \\ +\ 4.2 \\ \hline 21 \end{array} \searrow 1 \qquad \begin{array}{r} 21 \\ +\ 1 \\ \hline 22 \end{array}$$

EXERCISES

Use rounding to estimate the sum or difference.

SEE EXAMPLES 1 AND 3
on pp. 143–144
for Exs. 36–43

36. $7.5 + 3.8$ **37.** $5.38 + 6.65$ **38.** $12.71 - 3.54$ **39.** $9.2 - 5.81$

Use front-end estimation to estimate the sum.

40. $5.6 + 7.2 + 9.3 + 4.8$ **41.** $1.02 + 3.7 + 0.8 + 6.4$

42. $3.61 + 1.5 + 7.3 + 5.34$ **43.** $3.51 + 6.30 + 9.49 + 4.72$

3.6 Adding and Subtracting Decimals

pp. 148–154

EXAMPLE

Find the sum or difference.

a. $2.8 + 4.63$

$$\begin{array}{r} 2.80 \\ +\ 4.63 \\ \hline 7.43 \end{array} \quad \text{Line up the decimal points.}$$

b. $7.61 - 5.438$

$$\begin{array}{r} 7.610 \\ -\ 5.438 \\ \hline 2.172 \end{array} \quad \begin{array}{l}\text{Write a zero after}\\ \text{the last digit.}\end{array}$$

EXERCISES

Find the sum or difference.

SEE EXAMPLE 1 AND 6
on p. 148 and
p. 150 for
Exs. 44–52

44. $3.9 + 2.08$ **45.** $4.61 + 1.015$ **46.** $0.8 + 6.47$ **47.** $5.372 + 3.87$

48. $9.173 - 1.03$ **49.** $8.32 - 2.161$ **50.** $7 - 2.195$ **51.** $7.62 - 4.7$

52. Exercise You are exercising on a treadmill. You walk for 1.2 miles, jog for 3.7 miles, and then walk for another 0.9 mile. Your goal is to walk or jog for a total of 6 miles. How much farther must you walk or jog?

1. Write the number eighteen and six thousandths as a decimal.

2. Write 0.12 in words.

3. Write 220.0022 in words.

Copy and complete the statement.

4. 6 and 4 tenths centimeters = __?__ centimeters

5. 5 and 28 hundredths meters = __?__ meters

Copy and complete the statement with < , >, or =.

6. 3.07 _?_ 3.009

7. 13.76 _?_ 13.760

8. 25.853 _?_ 25.883

9. 5.5912 _?_ 5.5921

Order the numbers from least to greatest.

10. 6.2, 6.04, 6.16, 6.02, 6.1, 6.056

11. 0.056, 0.49, 0.509, 0.0487, 0.005

Round the decimal as specified.

12. 10.0962 (nearest tenth)

13. 14.925 (nearest hundredth)

14. 0.5691 (nearest thousandth)

15. 0.00291 (leading digit)

Use rounding to estimate the sum or difference.

16. 6.9 + 0.8

17. 12.4 + 10.7

18. 15.2 − 9.9

19. 5.7 − 2.8

Use front-end estimation to estimate the sum.

20. 4.39 + 1.84 + 5.62 + 9.1

21. 2.07 + 1.74 + 1.24 + 2.88

Find the sum or difference.

22. 18.79 + 3.6

23. 10.29 + 19.71

24. 6.073 − 5.02

25. 7.5 − 1.54

Tell which property is illustrated.

26. (10 + 2.9) + 7.1 = 10 + (2.9 + 7.1)

27. 3.4 + 19.2 = 19.2 + 3.4

28. **ASTRONOMY** The diameter of the sun is about 1,392,000 kilometers. Round the diameter to the nearest hundred thousand. Then write the rounded diameter as a decimal number of millions.

29. **COMPUTERS** Your computer's hard drive stores 120 gigabytes of data and you are currently using 35.93 gigabytes. How much data storage is available on your computer?

MULTIPLE CHOICE QUESTIONS

If you have difficulty solving a multiple choice problem directly, you can try another approach. You may want to eliminate incorrect answer choices to obtain the correct answer.

PROBLEM 1

A helideck is a takeoff and landing area for helicopters on ships. A rectangular helideck has a length of 16.76 meters and a width of 12.19 meters. What is the best estimate for the perimeter of the helideck?

(A) 29 meters   **(B)** 58 meters   **(C)** 80 meters   **(D)** 204 meters

METHOD 1

SOLVE DIRECTLY Round the length and width of the helideck to the nearest whole number. Then use the perimeter formula.

STEP 1 **Identify** the length l and width w.

$l = 16.76$ m $w = 12.19$ m

STEP 2 **Round** the length and width to the nearest whole number.

16.76 m ⟶ 17 m

12.19 m ⟶ 12 m

STEP 3 **Write** the formula for perimeter. Substitute 17 for l and 12 for w.

Perimeter $= 2l + 2w$

$= 2(\mathbf{17}) + 2(\mathbf{12})$

$= 34 + 24$

$= 58$

The correct answer is B. (A) (B) (C) (D)

METHOD 2

ELIMINATE CHOICES In some cases, you can identify choices of a multiple choice question that can be eliminated.

STEP 1 **Make** a low estimate. Two sides of the helideck have a length of about 17 meters. So, because $17 + 17 = 34$, you can eliminate choice A.

STEP 2 **Make** a high estimate. The length and width of the helideck are both less than 20 meters. So, because $4 \times 20 = 80$, you can eliminate choices C and D. These perimeters are too long.

The correct answer is B. (A) (B) (C) (D)

PROBLEM 2

The data set shows the altitudes, in miles, of seven airplanes. How far above the median altitude is an eighth airplane that has an altitude of 7.12 miles?

6.51, 6.63, 6.53, 7.01, 6.61, 6.82, 6.42

A 0.11   **B** 0.51   **C** 0.7   **D** 1.1

METHOD 1

SOLVE DIRECTLY Find the median. Then find the difference between the median and the altitude.

STEP 1 **Write** the altitudes from least to greatest.
6.42, 6.51, 6.53, 6.61, 6.63, 6.82, 7.01

STEP 2 The middle number is 6.61, so the median is 6.61.

STEP 3 **Find** the difference between the median altitude and the altitude of the eighth airplane.

$$\begin{array}{r} 7.12 \\ -\ 6.61 \\ \hline 0.51 \end{array}$$

The correct answer is B. Ⓐ Ⓑ Ⓒ Ⓓ

METHOD 2

ELIMINATE CHOICES In some cases, you can identify choices of a multiple choice question that can be eliminated.

The value 0.11 represents the difference in altitude between the highest altitude, 7.01 miles, and 7.12 miles. The difference must be greater than this for the median altitude, so you can eliminate choice A.

The value 0.7 represents the difference in altitude between the lowest altitude, 6.42 miles, and 7.12 miles. The difference must be less than this for the median altitude, so you can eliminate choice C.

None of the other airplanes are more than a mile in altitude lower than the eighth plane at its altitude of 7.12 miles, so you can eliminate choice D.

The correct answer is B. Ⓐ Ⓑ Ⓒ Ⓓ

PRACTICE

Explain why you can eliminate the highlighted answer choice.

1. A portion of a sidewalk has a length of 9.8 feet and a width of 4.1 feet. What is the best estimate for the perimeter of the sidewalk?

    A 14 ft   **B** 26 ft   **C** 28 ft   ✗**D** 40 ft

2. The data set shows the lengths, in meters, of six blue whales.

    28.75, 28.7, 26.57, 27.87, 30.15, 26.75

    What is the range of the lengths?

    A 3.4   **B** 3.58   **C** 4.57   ✗**D** 5.76

MULTIPLE CHOICE

1. Two runners in a 400 meter race cross the finish line in a photo finish. From the photo, officials find that the second runner was 80 centimeters behind the winner. How many meters had the second runner completed when the winner crossed the finish line?

  (A) 0.8 m   **(B)** 320 m

  (C) 399.2 m   **(D)** 399.92 m

2. You measure the lengths of three worms for a biology experiment. The shortest worm is 1.28 inches and the longest worm is 1.285 inches. Which of the following could *not* be the length of the third worm?

  (A) 1.2809 in.   **(B)** 1.281 in.

  (C) 1.284 in.   **(D)** 1.286 in.

3. In 1980, colleges enrolled 12,086,800 students. In 2000, colleges enrolled 15,312,300 students. About how many more students, in millions, enrolled in 2000 than in 1980?

  (A) 2.8 million   **(B)** 3.0 million

  (C) 3.2 million   **(D)** 4.5 million

4. You are standing in line at a grocery store with the items shown. Your best estimate of your total bill is $6. Which of the following could *not* be the price of the eggs?

  (A) $1   **(B)** $1.39

  (C) $1.49   **(D)** $1.89

5. An archer competes by shooting six arrows at a target. The first 5 arrows strike at distances (in centimeters) of 1.785, 0.6844, 0.549, 0.995, and 1.314 away from the center of the target. Which of the answer choices is the *farthest* distance the sixth archer's arrow can be from the center such that it is at least the third closest arrow shot?

  (A) 0.6839 cm   **(B)** 0.6843 cm

  (C) 0.6845 cm   **(D)** 0.9951 cm

6. What is the best estimate of the perimeter of the bowling lane shown below?

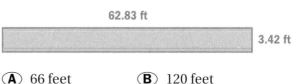

62.83 ft

3.42 ft

  (A) 66 feet   **(B)** 120 feet

  (C) 126 feet   **(D)** 132 feet

7. The table below shows the final scores from a 2004 Olympic diving competition. Which diver's score is closest to 0.87 away from the median score?

Name	Score
Alexandre Despatie	707.46
Peter Waterfield	669.24
Liang Tian	729.66
Jia Hu	748.08
Mathew Helm	730.56

  (A) Despatie   **(B)** Helm

  (C) Hu   **(D)** Tian

8. Your uncle buys a new television on sale for $449.99. The regular price for the television is $724.99. What is the best estimate of the total amount he saved?

  (A) $275   **(B)** $300

  (C) $375   **(D)** $500

GRIDDED ANSWER

9. If the boxes in the expression below are filled with the digits 0, 0, 8, 5, 9, and 3, what is the greatest value the expression can have?

$$\boxed{?}.\boxed{?}\;\boxed{?} - \boxed{?}.\boxed{?}\;\boxed{?}$$

10. Beth's hourly pay during 4 years is shown in the table. If the pattern continues, in what year will Beth make $10.50 per hour?

Year	Hourly pay
2001	$8.05
2002	$8.40
2003	$8.75
2004	$9.10

11. What decimal is halfway between 0.99 and 1.00 on a number line?

12. Your subway fare card has $8 in credit. Each ride on the subway costs $1.25. You take 3 rides and then add another $1.50 to your fare card. How many rides are left on the card?

SHORT RESPONSE

13. A scale drawing of a lake is shown below. What is a reasonable estimate of the area of the lake? *Explain* your reasoning.

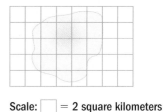

Scale: ☐ = 2 square kilometers

14. You have a piece of paper that measures 8.5 inches by 11 inches. *Explain* how could you use only the paper and a pencil (no ruler) to draw a length of 5 inches.

15. Derek and Reggie measure each other's height to the nearest inch. Derek is 70 inches tall and Reggie is 68 inches tall. Can Derek actually be 3 inches taller than Reggie? *Explain*.

EXTENDED RESPONSE

16. The boys' track team at Kennedy Middle School has enough runners to enter two teams of 4 runners each in the 4×100 meter relay. The runners' best individual times, in seconds, are shown in the table. Assume that all 8 runners will match their best times in the race.

Team 1	Team 2
10.99	10.90
11.50	11.15
11.54	11.25
11.09	11.05

a. Without performing any calculations, determine which relay team will win. *Explain* your reasoning.

b. If the fastest 4 runners all ran on the same relay team, by how many seconds would they beat the relay team made up of the 4 remaining runners? Show your work.

c. The track coach decides that the fastest person on a relay team should always run last. In how many different ways can the other 3 fastest runners be ordered? *Explain*.

4 Decimal Multiplication and Division

Before

In previous chapters you've ...

- Multiplied whole numbers
- Added and subtracted decimals

Now

In Chapter 4 you'll study ...

- 4.1 Decimals and whole numbers
- 4.2 The distributive property
- 4.3 Multiplying decimals
- 4.4 Dividing by whole numbers
- 4.5 Powers of ten
- 4.6 Dividing by decimals
- 4.7 Mass and capacity
- 4.8 Metric units

Why?

So you can solve real-world problems about ...

- car washes, p. 175
- sports cards, p. 186
- mountain climbing, p. 206

 **Math**

at classzone.com

- The Distributive Property, p. 177
- Multiplying Decimals, p. 183
- Multiplying a Number by a Power of Ten, p. 195

Get-Ready Games

Review Prerequisite Skills by playing *Operation Cover-Up.*

Skill Focus:

- Multiplying and dividing whole numbers
- Estimating products and quotients

OPERATION COVER-UP

MATERIALS

- 1 deck of *Operation Cover-Up* cards

- 2 *Operation Cover-Up* game boards

HOW TO PLAY Each player uses his or her own game board. Players share the deck of cards. First shuffle the deck, then place it face down between the two players. On each turn, each player should follow the steps on the next page. Wait until both players are done before beginning the next turn.

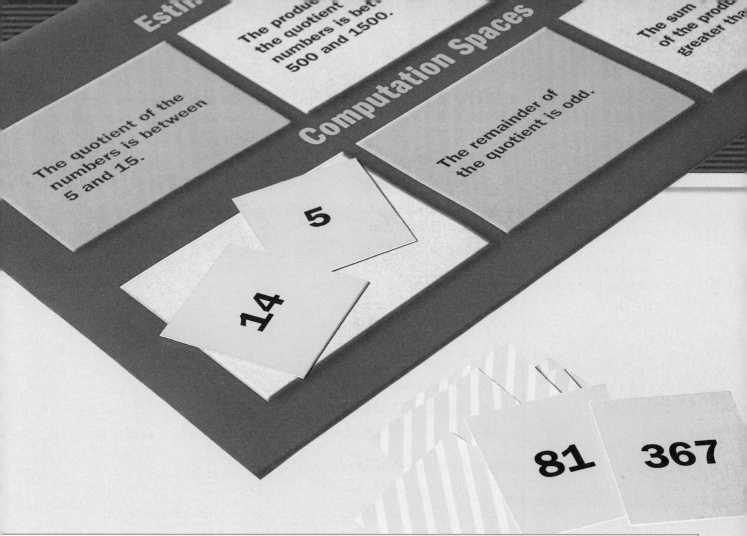

Esti...

The product...
the quotient...
numbers is bet...
500 and 1500.

Computation Spaces

The sum
of the prod...
greater tha...

The quotient of the
numbers is between
5 and 15.

The remainder of
the quotient is odd.

5

14

81   367

---

1 **DRAW** 2 cards. Each card has a number.

14   5

2 **DECIDE** whether the numbers form a product or a quotient that satisfies one of the conditions on a space on your game board.

14   5

3 **COVER** the space with your cards. If your numbers do not satisfy any of the conditions that are uncovered, discard them.

HOW TO WIN Be the first player to cover all 6 spaces on your game board, or be the player with the most spaces covered when you run out of cards.

Review Prerequisite Skills

VOCABULARY CHECK

Tell whether the number is the *divisor*, *quotient*, or *dividend* in the problem shown.

$$\begin{array}{r} 13 \\ 4\overline{)52} \end{array}$$

1. 52 **2.** 13 **3.** 4

SKILL CHECK

Find the product or quotient. *(p. 3)*

4. 71×100 **5.** 6×1000 **6.** 95×1000 **7.** 138×100

8. $150 \div 10$ **9.** $1640 \div 10$ **10.** $2300 \div 100$ **11.** $500 \div 100$

Estimate the product or quotient. *(p. 11)*

12. 32×46 **13.** 119×11 **14.** 315×4 **15.** 78×62

16. $25 \div 8$ **17.** $36 \div 5$ **18.** $158 \div 83$ **19.** $211 \div 67$

Round the decimal as specified. *(p. 137)*

20. 1.068 (nearest hundredth) **21.** 28.556 (nearest tenth)

22. 5.21354 (nearest thousandth) **23.** 14.997 (nearest tenth)

Find the sum or difference. *(p. 148)*

24. $4.68 + 1.9$ **25.** $7.05 + 9.2$ **26.** $13.4 + 4.6$ **27.** $10.7 + 5.12$

28. $3.47 - 1.4$ **29.** $9.62 - 5.3$ **30.** $4 - 1.6$ **31.** $6 - 1.08$

@HomeTutor Prerequisite skills practice at classzone.com

Notetaking Skills Previewing the Chapter

In each chapter you will learn a new notetaking skill. In Chapter 4 you will apply the strategy of previewing the chapter to Lesson 4.7 beginning on p. 203.

Before you start a lesson or chapter, look at what you are about to learn. Find familiar words and write them down. Then list what you already know about the words and topics you see.

Multiply Whole Numbers

$$\begin{array}{r} 25 \\ \times\ 12 \\ \hline 50 \\ 25 \\ \hline 300 \end{array}$$

← Line up the partial products correctly.

Decimal

$$8\ .\ 2\ 5\ 6$$

tenths → ← thousandths
hundredths

4.1 Multiplying Decimals and Whole Numbers

Before	You multiplied whole numbers by whole numbers.
Now	You'll multiply decimals and whole numbers.
Why?	So you can convert distances and heights as in Ex. 35.

KEY VOCABULARY

- commutative property of multiplication, *p. 171*
- associative property of multiplication, *p. 171*

ACTIVITY

You can use base-ten pieces to multiply.

With base-ten pieces, *one hundredth* is represented by ■ = 0.01, and *one tenth* is represented by ▬▬▬▬▬▬▬▬▬▬ = 0.1.

STEP 1 Model 1×0.04.

$$1 \times 0.04 = 0.04$$

STEP 2 Model 2×0.04.

$$2 \times 0.04 = 0.08$$

STEP 3 Model 3×0.04.

$$3 \times 0.04 = 0.12$$

Use a model to find the product.

1. 3×0.02 **2.** 3×0.2 **3.** 4×0.03 **4.** 4×0.3

5. How do the number of decimal places in your answers to Exercises 1–4 compare to the number of decimal places in the factors?

Multiplying with Decimals When you multiply a decimal and a whole number, the number of decimal places in the product is the same as the number of decimal places in the decimal factor.

EXAMPLE 1   Multiplying Decimals by Whole Numbers

ANOTHER WAY

You may want to think of Example 1 in words: *7 times 6 thousandths is 42 thousandths*. Then you can see why a zero is needed as a placeholder in the product.

Find the product 7×0.006.

Because 0.006 has 3 decimal places, the answer will have 3 decimal places.

$$\begin{array}{r} 0.006 \\ \times 7 \\ \hline 0.042 \end{array}$$

Write a zero as a placeholder so that the answer has 3 decimal places.

✓ GUIDED PRACTICE   for Example 1

Find the product. Then write the product in words.

1. 3×0.005 **2.** 4×0.024 **3.** 1.2×7 **4.** 2.36×6

Including Zeros You need to include the zeros at the *end* of a product in order to count the decimal places correctly. Once you place the decimal point, however, you can drop any zeros that occur at the end of the answer.

EXAMPLE 2 Solving a Problem

Junior Iditarod Race In the 2001 Junior Iditarod race, one team completed the race in about 18 hours over two days. The team's average rate was 8.325 miles per hour. About how long was the race? Round to the nearest mile.

SOLUTION

Use the formula *Distance = Rate × Time.*

$$
\begin{array}{r}
8.325 \\
\times\ \ \ \ 18 \\
\hline
66600 \\
8325\ \ \ \\
\hline
149.850 \\
\end{array}
$$

Place the decimal point before dropping any zeros.

▶**Answer** The race was about 150 miles long.

EXAMPLE 3 Checking for Reasonableness

Use estimation to check that the answer to Example 2 is reasonable.

$$
\begin{aligned}
\text{Distance} &= 8.325 \times 18 \\
&\approx 8 \times 18 \qquad \textbf{Round 8.325 to its leading digit.} \\
&= 144
\end{aligned}
$$

▶**Answer** Because 150 is close to 144, the distance is reasonable.

✓ GUIDED PRACTICE for Examples 2 and 3

Find the product.

5. 0.9 × 50

6. 1.505 × 8

7. 3.14 × 75

8. Bicycle Race You complete the first leg of a bike race in about 12 hours over two days. Your cyclometer shows that your average speed for this leg was 15.95 miles per hour. About how long was this leg of the race?

Use estimation to check whether the answer is reasonable.

9. 3.254 × 18; 58.572

10. 12.706 × 3; 381.18

11. 15.312 × 4; 61.248

12. *Explain* why the answer 84 is *not* reasonable for the product 3 × 2.8.

Properties of Multiplication You used properties of addition in Lesson 3.6. There are similar properties for multiplication.

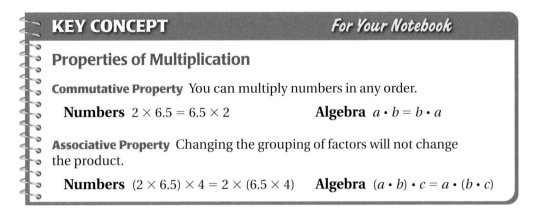

KEY CONCEPT   *For Your Notebook*

Properties of Multiplication

Commutative Property You can multiply numbers in any order.

    Numbers $2 \times 6.5 = 6.5 \times 2$ **Algebra** $a \cdot b = b \cdot a$

Associative Property Changing the grouping of factors will not change the product.

    Numbers $(2 \times 6.5) \times 4 = 2 \times (6.5 \times 4)$ **Algebra** $(a \cdot b) \cdot c = a \cdot (b \cdot c)$

EXAMPLE 4   **Using Properties of Multiplication**

Tell whether the *commutative* or *associative* property of multiplication allows you to rewrite the problem as shown. Explain your choice.

    $5 \times 3.25 \times 2 = 3.25 \times 5 \times 2$ The commutative property of multiplication allows you to change the order of the numbers.

✓   **GUIDED PRACTICE**   **for Example 4**

Tell which property of multiplication is shown. Explain your choice.

13. $(3.25 \times 5) \times 2 = 3.25 \times (5 \times 2)$ **14.** $0.4 \times 32 \times 5 = 32 \times 0.4 \times 5$

4.1 EXERCISES

HOMEWORK KEY

★ = **STANDARDIZED TEST PRACTICE**
Exs. 11, 22, 33, 34, 36, 37, 38, and 43

◯ = **HINTS AND HOMEWORK HELP**
for Exs. 5, 7, 11, 13, 35 at classzone.com

SKILL PRACTICE

1. VOCABULARY Which property does $(2 \cdot 8) \cdot 9 = 2 \cdot (8 \cdot 9)$ illustrate?

WRITING PRODUCTS Find the product. Then write the product in words.

SEE EXAMPLE 1
on p. 169
for Exs. 2–10

2. 3×0.2 **3.** 6×0.9 **4.** 5.06×8 **5.** 1.22×6

6. 9.03×10 **7.** 215×0.1 **8.** 3.164×5 **9.** 2.78×45

10. ERROR ANALYSIS Describe and correct the error in the solution.

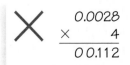

$$\begin{array}{r} 0.0028 \\ \times \quad\quad 4 \\ \hline 0\,0.112 \end{array}$$

SEE EXAMPLES 2 AND 3
on p. 170
for Exs. 11–19

11. ★ **MULTIPLE CHOICE** Which product can *not* be used to represent the model?

   (**A**) 2×0.012 (**B**) 3×0.08

   (**C**) 4×0.06 (**D**) 6×0.04

FINDING PRODUCTS Find the product. Use estimation to check.

12. 0.29×82 **13.** 0.32×55 **14.** 7.25×34 **15.** 3.072×8

16. 9.426×3 **17.** 2.125×15 **18.** 52×0.088 **19.** 18×0.005

SEE EXAMPLE 4
on p. 171
for Exs. 20–21

USING PROPERTIES Copy and complete each statement. Tell whether you used the *commutative* or *associative* property of multiplication.

20. $2 \times 79 \times 0.5 = 79 \times \underline{\ ?\ } \times 0.5$ **21.** $(0.4 \times 83) \times 5 = 0.4 \times (\underline{\ ?\ } \times 5)$

22. ★ **OPEN-ENDED MATH** Use estimation to find a decimal that, when multiplied by 18, gives a product between 24 and 30.

XY **ALGEBRA** Evaluate the expression.

23. $120x + 3$, when $x = 0.1$ **24.** $7 + 16x$, when $x = 4.2$

25. $1.57x + 5$, when $x = 2$ **26.** $100 - 9.21x$, when $x = 10$

27. $8 \times (4.37 + 15.011) - 90.93$ **28.** $(6.43 - 5.044) \times 10.5 + 7$

29. **CHALLENGE** For what values of a that are greater than 0 is the expression $10a$ less than 5? equal to 5? greater than 5? between 5 and 10? *Explain* your reasoning.

PROBLEM SOLVING

PURCHASING Find the amount you would spend in the situation.

SEE EXAMPLE 2
on p. 170
for Exs. 30–33

30. You buy 6 balloons for a friend's birthday. The balloons cost $1.50 each.

31. Each ticket for a rock concert costs $48.35. You buy 7 tickets.

32. It costs $.12 to make a photocopy. You make 84 copies.

33. ★ **SHORT RESPONSE** A company sells spring water in 0.375 quart bottles. Make a table showing how many quarts are in 1 to 6 bottles of water. Use your table to estimate the number of bottles needed to fill a 5 quart picnic jug. *Explain* your reasoning.

34. ★ **WRITING** *Explain* why you can drop the zero at the end of the products in your answers to Exercise 33. Why might you need to keep the final zero in the product for a situation involving money?

35. **HISTORY** The diagram at the right shows the heights of three suits of armor. Change the heights from centimeters to inches. Use the fact that 1 cm ≈ 0.3937 in.

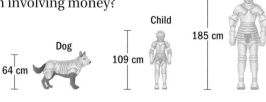

Dog 64 cm   Child 109 cm   Adult 185 cm

36. ★ **SHORT RESPONSE** Kari earns $9.75 per hour with an extra $5 per hour on Saturdays and Sundays. Will she make more money if she works Monday through Friday for 4 hours each day or if she works only Friday, Saturday and Sunday for 5 hours each day? *Justify* your answer.

37. ★ **EXTENDED RESPONSE** You and three friends have dinner at a restaurant. Each person orders dinner for $7.30 and a beverage for $1.05.

   a. Find the total cost of the meal.

   b. Multiply your answer from part (a) by 0.06 to calculate the tax. Then find the total cost of the meal, including the tax.

   c. Round the total cost from part (a) to a whole number. Multiply your answer from part (a) by 0.17 to calculate the tip.

   d. If you have only $40, can you afford to pay the entire bill without the tip? with the tip? Is an estimate sufficient to answer these questions? *Explain* your reasoning.

38. ★ **MULTIPLE CHOICE** To his best customers, Lyle gives away 26 basketball tickets and 22 symphony tickets. The basketball tickets cost $19.25 each and the symphony tickets cost $23.25 each. By how much did Lyle exceed his $1000 budget?

   (A) $12   (B) $15   (C) $2.50   (D) $34.50

39. **CHALLENGE** Kasey writes down her race times in the 50 meter freestyle for each of her 6 swim meets. The times, in seconds, are shown at the right. However, one of the times got wet and can no longer be read. Kasey knows that her mean time is 26.86 seconds. What is the missing race time, in seconds?

25.95	26.58
28.03	27.19
27.24	

MIXED REVIEW

Get-Ready

Prepare for Lesson 4.2 in Exs. 40–42

Evaluate the expression. *(p. 21)*

40. $104 \times (25 - 2 \times 7)$ **41.** $5 \times (36 \div 3)$ **42.** $(8 - 2) \times 3^2$

43. ★ **MULTIPLE CHOICE** What is the perimeter of a rectangle that is 12 feet by 9 feet? *(p. 66)*

   (A) 18 feet   (B) 33 feet   (C) 42 feet   (D) 108 feet

CHOOSE A STRATEGY Use a strategy from the list to solve the problem. *Explain* your choice of strategy.

44. You are at an awards dinner and have a choice of 3 dinner entrees, 2 side dishes, and 2 desserts. You can choose only one of each. How many different meals can you select?

Problem Solving Strategies

- Draw a Diagram *(p. 762)*
- Make a List *(p. 765)*
- Make a Table *(p. 765)*
- Look for a Pattern *(p. 766)*

4.1 Multiplying Decimals by Whole Numbers

EXAMPLE You can enter formulas in a spreadsheet to multiply numbers.

A biologist works 40 hours each week and earns $22.18 per hour. How much does the biologist earn in one week? How much does the biologist earn in one year?

SOLUTION

Create a spreadsheet like the one shown.

STEP 1 **Enter** the number of hours worked in cell B1.

STEP 2 **Enter** the hourly wage in cell B3.

	A	B
1	Hours per week:	40
2		
3	Dollars per hour:	$22.18
4		
5	Weekly earnings:	$887.20
6		
7	Yearly earnings:	$46,134.40

In cell B5, enter the formula = B1 * B3.

In cell B7, enter the formula = B5 * 52.

STEP 3 **Find** the biologist's weekly earnings. Use a formula to multiply the number of hours worked by the hourly wage.

STEP 4 **Find** the biologist's yearly earnings. Use a formula to multiply the weekly earnings by the number of weeks in a year.

▶ **Answer** The biologist earns $887.20 per week and $46,134.40 per year.

PRACTICE Use a spreadsheet to find the person's weekly and yearly earnings.

1. A programmer works 56 hours each week and earns $26.33 per hour.

2. A hairdresser works 50 hours each week and earns $10.81 per hour.

3. A doctor works 40 hours each week and earns $63.21 per hour.

4. A babysitter works 12 hours each week and earns $9.50 per hour.

4.2 The Distributive Property

Before	You used order of operations to evaluate expressions.
Now	You'll use the distributive property to evaluate expressions.
Why?	So you can calculate values more efficiently, as in Ex. 48.

KEY VOCABULARY
• distributive property, *p. 175*

Example 1 shows two expressions that can be used to solve for *t*. These two expressions illustrate the *distributive property*, stated on the next page.

★ **EXAMPLE 1** Standardized Test Practice

Car Wash Your class held a two-day car wash. The class washed 40 cars on the first day and 30 cars on the second day. The class charged $5 for each car. Which equation can be used to find *t*, the total amount of money raised by the class?

ELIMINATE CHOICES
You need to multiply the number of cars by the amount of money charged per car. So, choices A and C can be eliminated.

Ⓐ $t = 5(40) + 30$ **Ⓑ** $t = 5(40) - 5(30)$

Ⓒ $t = 40 + 30$ **Ⓓ** $t = 5(40 + 30)$

SOLUTION

METHOD 1 Write an expression for the total number of cars washed. Then multiply by the charge per car.

$$t = \textbf{Charge per car} \times \textbf{Total number of cars washed}$$
$$= \mathbf{5(40 + 30)}$$
$$= 5(70)$$
$$= 350$$

METHOD 2 First write expressions for the amount raised each day. Then find their sum.

$$t = \textbf{First day amount} + \textbf{Second day amount}$$
$$= \mathbf{5 \times 40 + 5 \times 30}$$
$$= 200 + 150$$
$$= 350$$

▶ **Answer** Your class raised $350. An equation for the money raised is $t = 5(40 + 30)$. The correct answer is D. Ⓐ Ⓑ Ⓒ **Ⓓ**

✓ **GUIDED PRACTICE** for Example 1

1. **What If?** In Example 1, how much money would you raise by charging $4 per car?

KEY CONCEPT *For Your Notebook*

The Distributive Property

Words You can multiply a number and a sum by multiplying the number by each part of the sum and then adding these products. The same property applies with subtraction.

Numbers $3(4 + 6) = 3(4) + 3(6)$ $\quad$ $2(8 - 5) = 2(8) - 2(5)$

Algebra $a(b + c) = ab + ac$ $\quad$ $a(b - c) = ab - ac$

EXAMPLE 2 Using the Distributive Property

VOCABULARY

To help remember the distributive property, you can think of it as *distributing* the number to each part of the sum.

a. $2(50 + 6) = 2(50) + 2(6)$

$= 100 + 12$

$= 112$

b. $10(8.6 - 2.4) = 10(8.6) - 10(2.4)$

$= 86 - 24$

$= 62$

EXAMPLE 3 Evaluating Using Mental Math

AVOID ERRORS

Remember that both numbers inside the parentheses must be multiplied by the factor on the outside.

a. To find 6(87), rewrite 87.

$6(87) = 6(90 - 3)$

$= 6(90) - 6(3)$

$= 540 - 18$

$= 522$

b. To find 8(6.1), rewrite 6.1.

$8(6.1) = 8(6 + 0.1)$

$= 8(6) + 8(0.1)$

$= 48 + 0.8$

$= 48.8$

EXAMPLE 4 Using a Formula

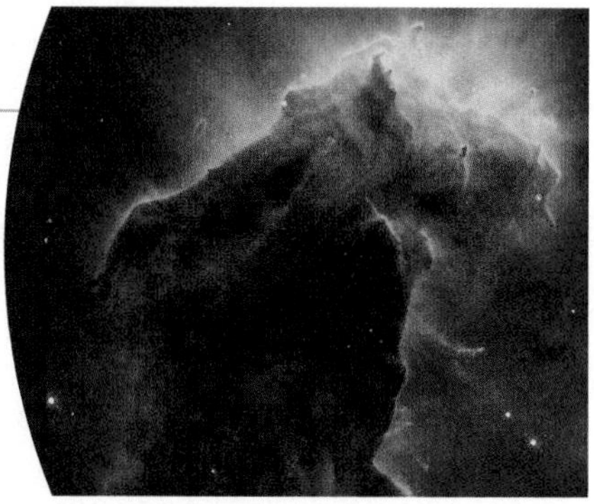

Astronomy The Hubble Telescope orbited Earth at a rate of about 4.78 miles per second. How far did the telescope travel in 3 seconds?

SOLUTION

Use the formula *Distance* = *Rate* × *Time.*

Distance $= (4.78)3$	**Use 4.78 for the rate and 3 for the time.**
$= (5 - 0.22)3$	**Rewrite 4.78 as 5 − 0.22.**
$= (5)3 - (0.22)3$	**Use the distributive property.**
$= 15 - 0.66$	**Multiply.**
$= 14.34$	**Subtract.**

▶ **Answer** The telescope traveled about 14.34 miles in 3 seconds.

Use the distributive property and mental math to evaluate.

2. $7(20 - 3)$ **3.** $0.5(24 + 18)$ **4.** $8(53)$ **5.** $7(1.4)$

6. What If? In Example 4, find the distance the Hubble Telescope traveled in 4 seconds.

4.2 EXERCISES

HOMEWORK KEY

★ = **STANDARDIZED TEST PRACTICE**
Exs. 15, 41, 45, 46, 47, and 55

○ = **HINTS** AND **HOMEWORK HELP**
for Exs. 5, 11, 17, 23, 43 at classzone.com

SKILL PRACTICE

1. VOCABULARY Rewrite $2(3.1 + 7.4)$ using the distributive property.

2. VOCABULARY Copy and complete: You can use the distributive property when you are multiplying a number by a __?__ or a __?__ .

EVALUATING EXPRESSIONS Use the distributive property to evaluate.

SEE EXAMPLE 2
on p. 176
for Exs. 3–16

3. $4(80 + 3)$ **4.** $6(7 + 50)$ **5.** $2(39 - 10)$ **6.** $15(2 + 9)$

7. $6(8.2 + 3)$ **8.** $8(3.1 + 5.7)$ **9.** $10(4.8 + 2.7)$ **10.** $14(8.1 - 6)$

11. $3(90 + 0.6)$ **12.** $9(7 - 0.11)$ **13.** $7(13 - 0.02)$ **14.** $12(3 + 0.4)$

15. ★ **MULTIPLE CHOICE** Which expression is equivalent to $4(5) - 4(3)$?

A $4(4 - 3)$ **B** $12(5 - 4)$ **C** $3(5 - 4)$ **D** $4(5 - 3)$

16. ERROR ANALYSIS Describe and correct the error in the solution.

$$\times \quad \begin{aligned} 2(32 + 6) &= 2(32) + 6 \\ &= 64 + 6 \\ &= 70 \end{aligned}$$

MENTAL MATH Use the distributive property and mental math to multiply.

SEE EXAMPLE 3
on p. 176
for Exs. 17–24

17. $6(37)$ **18.** $3(85)$ **19.** $9(41)$ **20.** $8(5.7)$

21. $5(9.2)$ **22.** $7(6.9)$ **23.** $2(4.4)$ **24.** $4(7.6)$

Animated Math at classzone.com

MATCHING Match the statement with the property that is illustrated.

25. $63 + (8 + 10.1) = (63 + 8) + 10.1$ **A.** commutative property of addition

26. $4 \times 55.2 \times 11 = 55.2 \times 4 \times 11$ **B.** associative property of addition

27. $(0.9 \times 17) \times 15 = 0.9 \times (17 \times 15)$ **C.** commutative property of multiplication

28. $2(15.3 + 4) = 2(15.3) + 2(4)$ **D.** associative property of multiplication

29. $5.1 + 790 + 0.13 = 5.1 + 0.13 + 790$ **E.** distributive property

SEE EXAMPLE 4
on p. 176 for
Exs. 30 and 31

30. GEOMETRY Use the distributive property and the formula $P = 2(l + w)$. Find the perimeter of a flower box with length 27 inches and width 6 inches.

31. GEOMETRY Use the distributive property and the formula $A = l \cdot w$. Find the area of a rectangular floor with length 8 feet and width 6.25 feet.

32. APPLYING PROPERTIES Alyssa simplified the expression as shown. Which property or method did she use for each step?

1. $15 + 4(5.8) + 5$	1. Given expression
2. $= 4(5.8) + 15 + 5$	2. ___?___ property
3. $= 4(5.8) + (15 + 5)$	3. ___?___ property
4. $= 20 + 3.2 + (15 + 5)$	4. ___?___ property
5. $= 43.2$	5. Simplify.

XV ALGEBRA Use the distributive property to rewrite the expression. For example, $2(x + 4) = 2x + 8$.

33. $3(x + 7)$ **34.** $5(x + 5.2)$ **35.** $6(4 - x)$ **36.** $10(8 + x)$

XV CHALLENGE Rewrite the expression as a product.

37. $4x + 7x$ **38.** $0.5m - 0.9m$ **39.** $5.5x - 5.5y + 5.5$ **40.** $3a + 3b + 3c$

PROBLEM SOLVING

SEE EXAMPLE 1
on p. 175
for Exs. 41, 43

41. ★ MULTIPLE CHOICE During a soccer game, three of your teammates drank three 8-ounce glasses of water and three 16-ounce bottles of sports drink. Which equation can be used to find x, the total number of ounces of fluids they drank?

(A) $x = 3(8 + 16)$ **(B)** $x = 8(3 + 16)$ **(C)** $x = 3(8) + 16$ **(D)** $x = 8 + 3(16)$

42. LUNCH COSTS Each day, you pay $2.50 for lunch and $.45 for milk. Write two expressions for the amount of money you spend in d days. Evaluate the expressions for $d = 5$.

43. FIELD TRIP Thirty students are visiting an art museum. The cost for each student is $9 for admission plus $5 for a special exhibit. What is the cost for all the students to see the museum and the special exhibit?

44. CHECKING REASONABLENESS Your brother burns an average of 5.8 calories per minute on a stair-step machine and 7.3 calories per minute on a treadmill. Use the distributive property to find how many calories he burned after 20 minutes on each machine. Use estimation to check the reasonableness of your answer. *Explain* your method.

45. ★ **SHORT RESPONSE** A song on your favorite CD lasts 5.25 minutes. How long does it take to play the song three times in a row? *Explain* how you can use the distributive property to find the answer.

46. ★ **OPEN-ENDED MATH** Describe a situation that can be modeled by the equation $x = 5(3.25 + 0.39)$. Then solve the problem and interpret the solution.

47. ★ **WRITING** You eat 2 ounces of sunflower seeds. Each ounce contains 5.48 grams of protein. *Explain* how to use mental math and the distributive property to find the total amount of protein that you eat.

U.S. MINT **In Exercises 48–49, use the coin data. They show what it costs to produce four U.S. coins in two years.**

2000 – 5.0¢   2000 – 3.0¢   2000 – 0.8¢   2000 – 2.0¢
2003 – 7.7¢   2003 – 3.8¢   2003 – 1.0¢   2003 – 3.2¢

48. *Explain* how to use the distributive property to find the increase in production costs in cents for 50 dimes from 2000 to 2003.

49. Write an expression to find how much more it cost to produce 50 nickels in 2003 than in 2000. Then evaluate the expression.

50. **CHALLENGE** You and three friends go to a movie theater. Together you have $40. Admission is $8 per person, and each of you buys a small fountain drink. When you leave the theater, you have $3 left altogether. How much did each drink cost?

51. **CHALLENGE** Multiply 52 and 26 using paper and pencil. Compare it to evaluating the expression $26(50 + 2)$. *Explain* why the process of multiplying whole numbers with two or more digits works.

MIXED REVIEW

Get-Ready

Prepare for
Lesson 4.3 in
Exs. 52–54

Find the product. *(p. 169)*

52. 8×0.15 **53.** 3×2.25 **54.** 13×1.6

55. ★ **MULTIPLE CHOICE** Order the numbers 7.63, 7.06, 7.61, and 7.6 from least to greatest. *(p. 130)*

  (A) 7.63, 7.61, 7.06, 7.6   **(B)** 7.6, 7.06, 7.61, 7.63

  (C) 7.06, 7.6, 7.61, 7.63   **(D)** 7.06, 7.61, 7.63, 7.6

Evaluate the expression when $x = 3.1$ and $y = 5.62$. *(p. 148)*

56. $x + 2.83$ **57.** $x + y$ **58.** $y - 3.092$

GOAL
Use an area model to find the product of two decimals.

MATERIALS
• graph paper
• colored pencils

4.3 Multiplying Decimals Using Models

In this Investigation, you'll draw base-ten pieces on graph paper and use their dimensions and areas shown below to explore decimal multiplication.

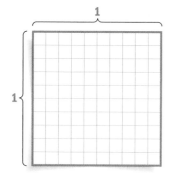

Area = 1 whole = 1

Area = 1 tenth = 0.1

Area = 1 hundredth = 0.01

EXPLORE Model 0.8 × 0.7 using an area model.

STEP 1 **Draw** a 10 ×10 square on graph paper. Let the length of each side be 1. Use a colored pencil to shade a 0.8 × 0.7 rectangle.

STEP 2 **Use** the diagram and the fact that each small square has an area of 1 hundredth (0.01) to copy and complete the following:

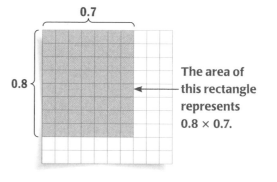

The area of this rectangle represents 0.8 × 0.7.

Shaded Area = _?_ × _?_ small squares

0.8 × 0.7 = _?_ hundredths

0.8 × 0.7 = _?_ ◄—— decimal

PRACTICE Use a model to find the product.

1. 0.3 × 0.9   **2.** 0.4 × 0.4   **3.** 0.5 × 0.6   **4.** 0.7 × 0.3

DRAW CONCLUSIONS

5. REASONING *Describe* the relationship between the factors 0.8 and 0.7 and the decimal product you found in Step 2 above. Does the same relationship hold for the products in Exercises 1–4? *Explain* how to find the product 0.9 × 0.5 without using a model.

4.3 Multiplying Decimals

Before You multiplied decimals by whole numbers.

Now You'll multiply decimals by decimals.

Why? So you can find distance traveled, as in Example 1.

KEY VOCABULARY
• factor, *p. 15*

EXAMPLE 1 ◆ Using a Model to Multiply Decimals

Sloths The sloth is commonly referred to as the "slowest mammal on Earth." Its top speed on the ground is about 0.2 mile per hour. To find the farthest a sloth might go in 0.6 hour, use a model to find 0.2 × 0.6.

SOLUTION

STEP 1 **Draw** a 10 × 10 square. The whole square represents 1. The width of each row or column is 1 tenth, or 0.1.

STEP 2 **Shade** a 0.2 × 0.6 rectangle. Each small square represents 1 hundredth, or 0.01. The shaded area consists of 12 squares, or 12 hundredths. So, 0.2 × 0.6 = 0.12.

▶ **Answer** The farthest a sloth might go in 0.6 hour is 0.12 mile.

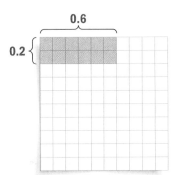

 GUIDED PRACTICE   **for Example 1**

Draw a model to find the product.

1. 0.1 × 0.7   **2.** 0.3 × 0.8   **3.** 0.9 × 0.7

Multiplying Decimals In the Investigation on page 180 and in Example 1, you explored the relationship between decimal factors and products outlined below.

KEY CONCEPT   *For Your Notebook*

Multiplying Decimals

Words   Multiply decimals as you do whole numbers. Then place the decimal point. The number of decimal places in the product is the total number of decimal places in the factors.

Numbers   3.14   ×   15.6   =   48.984
               └┘   └┘   └─┘
            2 places   1 place   3 places

EXAMPLE 2 Placing a Decimal Point in a Product

Place the decimal point in the correct location.

$$252.64 \quad \times \quad 0.842 \quad = \quad 212.72288$$

2 places   **3 places**   **5 places**

The first factor has 2 decimal places. The second factor has 3 decimal places. Because $2 + 3 = 5$, the answer has 5 decimal places.

▶ **Answer** $252.64 \times 0.842 = 212.72288$

Check Estimate using compatible numbers.

$$252.64 \times 0.842 \approx 250 \times 1 = 250.$$

So, the product 212.72288 is reasonable.

ANOTHER WAY
To check this decimal product, you can also round each decimal to its leading digit:
$300 \times 0.8 = 240.$

EXAMPLE 3 Multiplying Decimals

Find the product.

a. 5.08×2.1 **b.** 1.159×0.03 **c.** 7.215×4.8

SOLUTION

a.
$$\begin{array}{r} 5.08 \\ \times\ 2.1 \\ \hline 508 \\ 1016 \\ \hline 10.668 \end{array}$$

2 decimal places
+ 1 decimal place

3 decimal places

Check Use leading digits.
$5.08 \times 2.1 \approx 5 \times 2 = 10$

b.
$$\begin{array}{r} 1.159 \\ \times\ 0.03 \\ \hline 0.03477 \end{array}$$

3 decimal places
+ 2 decimal places
5 decimal places

Check Use leading digits.
$1.159 \times 0.03 \approx 1 \times 0.03 = 0.03$

USE ZEROS
You may need to write zeros in the product as placeholders to place the decimal point correctly.

c.
$$\begin{array}{r} 7.215 \\ \times\ 4.8 \\ \hline 57720 \\ 28860 \\ \hline 34.6320 \end{array}$$

3 decimal places
+ 1 decimal place

4 decimal places

Check Use rounding.
$7.215 \times 4.8 \approx 7 \times 5 = 35$

> Once you place the decimal point, drop the zero at the end of the final answer. You write the product as 34.632.

✓ **GUIDED PRACTICE**   for Examples 2 and 3

Multiply. Use estimation to check your answer.

4. 2.15×5.4 **5.** 12.7×2.9 **6.** 6.289×0.2 **7.** 0.86×0.04

EXAMPLE 4 Finding the Area of a Rectangle

American Flag One of the largest flags ever made is about 153.9 meters long and 77.7 meters wide. Find the area of the flag to the nearest hundred square meters.

Remember that area is measured in square units such as square feet (ft^2) or square meters (m^2).

SOLUTION

$A = lw$	Write the formula for the area of a rectangle.
$= (153.9)(77.7)$	Substitute 153.9 for l and 77.7 for w.
$= 11{,}958.03$	Multiply.

▶ **Answer** The area of the flag is about 12,000 square meters.

Check Estimate: $(153.9)(77.7) \approx 150 \times 80 = 12{,}000$. The product of about 12,000 is reasonable.

Animated **Math**
at classzone.com

✓ **GUIDED PRACTICE**   for Example 4

8. What If? A flag is 16.15 feet long and 8.5 feet wide. Find the area of the flag to the nearest ten square feet.

4.3 EXERCISES

HOMEWORK KEY

★ = **STANDARDIZED TEST PRACTICE**
Exs. 12, 41, 42, 43, 44, and 58

◯ = **HINTS AND HOMEWORK HELP**
for Exs. 5, 7, 15, 21, 39 at classzone.com

SKILL PRACTICE

1. **VOCABULARY** How many decimal places are in the first factor of the product $305.02 \times 0.495 = 150.9849$?

2. **VOCABULARY** Copy and complete: The number of decimal places in a product is equal to the __?__ of the number of decimal places in the factors.

SEE EXAMPLE 1
on p. 181
for Exs. 3–5

USING A MODEL Draw a 10-by-10 square to model the product.

3. 0.4×0.5 4. 0.3×0.9 5. 0.1×0.6

PLACING A DECIMAL POINT Copy the answer and place the decimal point in the correct location.

SEE EXAMPLES 2 AND 3
on p. 182
for Exs. 6–12

6. $0.17 \times 0.6 = \mathbf{0102}$ 7. $16.36 \times 3.7 = \mathbf{60532}$ 8. $4.7 \times 6.1 = \mathbf{02867}$

9. $0.09 \times 18 = \mathbf{0162}$ 10. $518.3 \times 0.09 = \mathbf{46647}$ 11. $1.74 \times 0.003 = \mathbf{000522}$

12. ★ **MULTIPLE CHOICE** Find the product: 0.205×0.4.

Ⓐ 8.2   Ⓑ 0.82   Ⓒ 0.082   Ⓓ 0.0082

MULTIPLYING DECIMALS Find the product. Use estimation to check.

SEE EXAMPLE 3
on p. 182
for Exs. 13–20

13. 0.3×0.6 **14.** 1.1×0.4 **15.** 3.052×4.7 **16.** 3.25×4.6

17. 1.08×0.45 **18.** 1.126×0.08 **19.** 9.817×8.6 **20.** 6.87×9.61

GEOMETRY Find the area of the rectangle. Use estimation to check.

SEE EXAMPLE 4
on p. 183
for Exs. 21–22

21.

2.75 ft

6.3 ft

22.

8.1 cm

10.36 cm

NUMBER SENSE Copy and complete the statement with <, >, or =.

23. $64.2 \times 1.12 \; \underline{?} \; 64$ **24.** $2.2 \times 0.12 \; \underline{?} \; 2.64$

25. $32.5 \times 0.01 \; \underline{?} \; 3.25$ **26.** $0.505 \times 10.1 \; \underline{?} \; 5.1005$

ESTIMATION Check that the location of the decimal point in the product is reasonable. Correct the answer if necessary.

27. $4.2 \times 0.9; \; 37.8$ **28.** $32.06 \times 11.94; \; 3.827964$

29. $109.452 \times 5.7; \; 623.8764$ **30.** $48.005 \times 17.3; \; 83{,}0486.5$

EVALUATING POWERS Find the value of y^3 for the given value of y.

31. $y = 0.01$ **32.** $y = 0.002$ **33.** $y = 0.5$ **34.** $y = 1.01$

(xy) ALGEBRA Write a related multiplication sentence to solve.

35. $x \div 7.25 = 80.4$ **36.** $x \div 5.4 = 110.02$ **37.** $x \div 26.125 = 0.13$

38. CHALLENGE Write an addition expression for the area of the figure using the given lengths. Then write a subtraction expression for the area. Choose one expression and calculate the area.

0.56 m

0.54 m

0.46 m

0.14 m

PROBLEM SOLVING

39. ANIMAL SPEED A turtle travels 4.015 meters per minute. How far does the turtle travel in 8.5 minutes, to the nearest meter?

40. GROWTH RATE Sophia's hair grows at a rate of about 0.5 inch per month. How much does Sophia's hair grow in 4.5 months?

41. ★ WRITING The rectangular floor of a tent is 11.25 feet long and 8.5 feet wide. Find the area of the tent floor to the nearest square foot. Did you round before or after you multiplied? *Explain* your reasoning.

42. ★ **SHORT RESPONSE** Oranges cost $3.29 per pound. Apples cost $2.89 per pound. You buy 1.8 pounds of oranges and 2.3 pounds of apples. Which costs you more, the oranges or the apples? *Explain.*

43. ★ **EXTENDED RESPONSE** The figure shows several items at a deli counter.

Ham
$5.49
per lb

Cheese
$4.79
per lb

Turkey
$6.29
per lb

0.75 lb   0.50 lb   1.25 lb

a. You use 0.15 lb of ham and 0.08 lb of cheese to make a sandwich. Is there enough ham and cheese to make 5 sandwiches? *Explain.*

b. You use 0.24 lb of turkey for a turkey sandwich. Is there enough turkey to make 5 turkey sandwiches? *Explain.*

c. Find the total amount you pay for the items at the deli counter. Can you stay within a budget of $1.50 per sandwich? *Explain.*

44. ★ **WRITING** *Explain* when you need to include a zero as a placeholder in a product. Give an example.

LOOK FOR A PATTERN Find the next two numbers in each pattern.

45. 1, 0.8, 0.64, 0.512, _?_ , _?_   46. 4, 1, 0.25, 0.0625, _?_ , _?_

REASONING Choose the correct response. *Explain* your choice.

47. When you multiply a number greater than 1 by a number between 0 and 1, is the product *less than* or *greater than* the first number?

48. When you multiply two decimals between 0 and 1, is the product *less than* or *greater than* both factors?

49. **CHALLENGE** A square table top is 18 inches wide. You have 1800 square tiles that are each 1 centimeter wide. Do you have enough to cover the table? (*Hint:* 1 inch = 2.54 centimeters.)

MIXED REVIEW

Get-Ready

Prepare for Lesson 4.4 in Exs. 50–53

Find the quotient. *(p. 3)*

50. 798 ÷ 3   51. 1340 ÷ 4   52. 208 ÷ 13   53. 315 ÷ 3

Graph the points on a coordinate grid. *(p. 88)*

54. (2, 1)   55. (1, 4)   56. (0, 8)   57. (3, 0)

58. ★ **MULTIPLE CHOICE** In 1989, a distance record of ninety-five and four tenths miles was set for walking backward in a 24 hour period. Which answer gives the length, in miles, of the distance? *(p. 148)*

(**A**) 95.410   (**B**) 95.4   (**C**) 95.04   (**D**) 95.004

4.4 Dividing by Whole Numbers

Before	You multiplied decimals and whole numbers.
Now	You'll divide decimals by whole numbers.
Why?	So you can find unit costs, as in Example 1.

KEY VOCABULARY
- **dividend,** *p. 4*
- **divisor,** *p. 4*
- **quotient,** *p. 4*

Soccer Your soccer team orders sports cards for each player. You buy a set of 8 cards for $9.92. How much do you pay for each card? You can use the rule below to find how much you paid for each card.

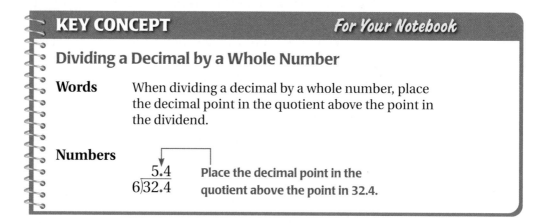

KEY CONCEPT *For Your Notebook*

Dividing a Decimal by a Whole Number

Words When dividing a decimal by a whole number, place the decimal point in the quotient above the point in the dividend.

Numbers
$$\frac{5.4}{6)32.4}$$
Place the decimal point in the quotient above the point in 32.4.

EXAMPLE 1 Dividing a Decimal by a Whole Number

To answer the question above about sports cards, find $9.92 \div 8$.

STEP 1 Place the decimal point.

$$8)\overset{.}{9.92}$$

STEP 2 Then divide.

$$
\begin{array}{r}
1.24 \\
8)\overline{9.92} \\
8 \\
\hline
1\,9 \\
1\,6 \\
\hline
32 \\
32 \\
\hline
0
\end{array}
$$

AVOID ERRORS
Remember, it is important to keep both digits and decimal points lined up when dividing.

▶ **Answer** You pay $1.24 for each sports card.

✓ **GUIDED PRACTICE** for Example 1

Find the quotient.

1. $5)\overline{13.5}$ **2.** $4)\overline{24.8}$ **3.** $7)\overline{4.48}$

EXAMPLE 2 Writing Additional Zeros

Find the quotient 14 ÷ 8.

STEP 1 Place the decimal point and begin dividing.

$$\begin{array}{r} 1. \\ 8\overline{)14.} \\ \underline{8} \\ 6 \end{array}$$

STEP 2 Write additional zeros in the dividend as needed.

$$\begin{array}{r} 1.75 \\ 8\overline{)14.00} \\ \underline{8}\downarrow \\ 6\,0 \\ \underline{5\,6}\downarrow \\ 40 \\ \underline{40} \\ 0 \end{array}$$

▸**Answer** $14 \div 8 = 1.75$.

EXAMPLE 3 Using Zeros as Placeholders

Baseball A batting average is the number of hits divided by the number of times at bat. Find the batting average of a player who made 7 hits in 23 times at bat. Round your answer to the nearest thousandth.

SOLUTION

$$\begin{array}{r} .3043 \\ 23\overline{)7.0000} \\ \underline{6\,9}\downarrow \\ 10 \\ \underline{0}\downarrow \\ 100 \\ \underline{92}\downarrow \\ 80 \\ \underline{69} \\ 11 \end{array}$$

Write zeros in the dividend as needed.

> You cannot divide 10 by 23, so put a **zero** in the quotient as a placeholder.

Stop when the quotient reaches the ten-thousandths' place.

AVOID ERRORS
Don't stop after the quotient has only three decimal places. If you do, you won't know whether to round your answer up or down.

▸**Answer** The player's batting average is 0.304.

✓ **GUIDED PRACTICE** for Examples 2 and 3

Divide. Round to the nearest thousandth if necessary.

4. $26 \div 4$ **5.** $15.2 \div 30$ **6.** $49.92 \div 8$ **7.** $29.37 \div 12$

8. What If? Suppose the player in Example 3 makes 10 hits in 33 times at bat. What is the player's batting average? Round your answer to the nearest thousandth.

4.4 EXERCISES

HOMEWORK KEY

★ = **STANDARDIZED TEST PRACTICE**
Exs. 12, 13, 38, 51, 53, 59, 60, and 71

◯ = **HINTS AND HOMEWORK HELP**
for Exs. 5, 15, 23, 25, 47 at classzone.com

SKILL PRACTICE

VOCABULARY Tell whether the number is the *divisor*, *quotient*, or *dividend* in the problem shown at the right.

$$2\overline{)5.8}^{\,2.9}$$

1. 2.9

2. 5.8

3. 2

PLACING A DECIMAL POINT Copy the answer and place the decimal point correctly.

SEE EXAMPLE 1
on p. 186
for Exs. 4–13

4. $49.5 \div 6 = $ **825**

5. $2.98 \div 4 = $ **745**

6. $110.16 \div 9 = $ **1224**

7. $7 \div 4 = $ **175**

8. $731 \div 5 = $ **1462**

9. $9 \div 8 = $ **1125**

10. $891.8 \div 7 = $ **1274**

11. $379.62 \div 6 = $ **6327**

12. ★ **MULTIPLE CHOICE** Find the quotient $34.5 \div 5$.

(A) 0.069

(B) 0.69

(C) 6.9

(D) 69

13. ★ **MULTIPLE CHOICE** Find the quotient $2.72 \div 8$.

(A) 0.034

(B) 0.34

(C) 3.4

(D) 34

DIVIDING DECIMALS Divide. Round to the nearest tenth if necessary.

SEE EXAMPLES
1, 2, AND 3
on p. 187
for Exs. 14–29

14. $6\overline{)32.4}$

15. $5\overline{)22}$

16. $7\overline{)51}$

17. $6\overline{)7.42}$

18. $11.6 \div 4$

19. $21 \div 6$

20. $7.86 \div 6$

21. $33.6 \div 7$

22. $43.2 \div 6$

23. $31.75 \div 8$

24. $44.16 \div 5$

25. $20 \div 3$

26. $37 \div 12$

27. $28.46 \div 3$

28. $34.92 \div 20$

29. $24.61 \div 13$

ALGEBRA Evaluate the variable expression. Round the answer to the nearest tenth.

30. $5 \div x$, when $x = 3$

31. $6 \div x$, when $x = 14$

32. $23.51 \div x$, when $x = 7$

33. $89.34 \div x$, when $x = 25$

NUMBER SENSE Copy and complete the statement using <, >, or =.

34. $1.9 \div 2 \; \underline{?} \; 1$

35. $0.36 \div 1 \; \underline{?} \; 0.36$

36. $3 \div 9 \; \underline{?} \; 0.3$

37. **ERROR ANALYSIS** Describe and correct the error made in the long division. Round the answer to the nearest hundredth.

$$
\begin{array}{r}
4.83 \\
12\overline{)49.000} \\
48 \\
\hline
100 \\
96 \\
\hline
40 \\
36 \\
\hline
4
\end{array}
$$

38. ★ OPEN-ENDED MATH Give three examples of quotients that require you to write additional zeros in the dividend when dividing.

POWERS Evaluate the expression to the thousandth's place.

39. $(9.9 \div 7)^2$ **40.** $(8.66 \div 5)^2$ **41.** $(25 \div 11)^2$

42. CHALLENGE Divide 8 by 7 until the quotient has nine decimal places. *Describe* what you observe about the quotient. *Predict* what digit will appear in the thirteenth decimal place. Divide to confirm this.

PROBLEM SOLVING

RESTAURANT BILLS The number of people who eat together at a restaurant and the total bill are given. The bill is divided equally. Find the amount each person pays.

SEE EXAMPLES
1 AND 2
on pp. 186–187
for Exs. 43–46

43. 6 people; bill is $47.10   **44.** 4 people; bill is $39.20

45. 8 people; bill is $102   **46.** 7 people; bill is $80.50

BATTING AVERAGES Find the batting average of the player described. Round your answer to the nearest thousandth.

SEE EXAMPLE 3
on p. 187
for Exs. 47–50

47. 13 hits in 45 times at bat   **48.** 8 hits in 26 times at bat

49. 11 hits in 36 times at bat   **50.** 9 hits in 29 times at bat

51. ★ EXTENDED RESPONSE Speed skater Hiroyasu Shimizu of Japan recorded the times shown in the table for three 500 meter races in the 2000–2001 season. His time for a 500 meter race at the 2002 Winter Olympic Games was 34.65 seconds.

a. Write an expression to find the mean of the times in the table. Then find the mean.

b. How does his time at the 2002 Games compare to his times in the 2000–2001 season?

c. Is he getting faster? *Justify* your conclusion.

Time (sec)
34.32
34.83
35.22

52. SCHOOL FAIR You are organizing volunteers to work at an exhibit at a science fair. You have 6 volunteers to cover a total of 27 hours. How many hours will each volunteer have to work?

53. ★ MULTIPLE CHOICE An advertisement for a shoe sale states that when you buy 2 pairs of shoes for $24.95 each, you will get a third pair for free. What is the mean cost for a pair of shoes?

A $8.32   **B** $12.48   **C** $16.63   **D** $24.95

54. CHEMISTRY A chemical formula requires dividing 90 milliliters of a solution equally into 8 test tubes. How much should go into each test tube?

Mackinac Bridge Upon its completion in 1957, Michigan's Mackinac Bridge was the longest suspension bridge in the world. The total length of "Big Mac" is 26,372 ft. The bridge connects the upper and lower peninsulas of Michigan where Lake Michigan and Lake Huron meet.

In 1996, a new project was established to repaint the bridge. The cost of the project is estimated at $80 million and will require over 60,000 gallons of paint. It will take 21 years to complete this project.

55. Calculate There are 5,280 feet in a mile. How many miles long is the Mackinac Bridge? Round your answer to the nearest mile.

56. Calculate How many gallons of paint will be applied to the bridge per year?

57. Analyze It costs $2.50 to cross the bridge. However, you can buy a roll of 24 tokens for $36.00. How much is this for each crossing? How much do you save if you cross the bridge 24 times?

MEASURE LENGTHS
Need help measuring lengths? See p. 59.

58. MEASUREMENT You measure a board using a measuring tape whose units are meters, as shown at the right. You cut the board into 4 equal pieces. How long is each piece?

59. ★ WRITING You agree to paint a fence behind three houses for $6.50 per hour. The job takes you 7.25 hours. Three homeowners agree to split the payment evenly among themselves, rounding each contribution to the nearest quarter. *Explain* how to find how much each homeowner pays.

60. ★ EXTENDED RESPONSE Sometimes items at a grocery store are priced in groups of items. For lunch, you only want one of each item.

APPLES	RAISINS	JUICE	Bagels
$1.80	$1.10	$3.40	$2.88

a. **Model** Write an expression to find the cost of one box of raisins; one box of juice.

b. **Calculate** Evaluate the expressions you wrote in part (a). *Explain* why it is necessary to round your answers to the nearest hundredth.

c. **Apply** Find the total cost of your lunch.

61. PEOPLE MOVER There are 123 students waiting in line to take a tram to the city's hilltop historic district. Each tram can take 40 people at a time. After carrying all 123 students from the bottom to the top, it traveled a total of 10.5 kilometers. What is the length of a one-way trip up the hill?

62. CHALLENGE You buy 5 yards of fabric for $12.40 and 5 bags of stuffing for $17.44. You make two pillows. Each pillow uses 0.75 yard of fabric and 1.5 bags of stuffing. What is the total cost of materials for these pillows? *Justify* your answer.

MIXED REVIEW

Get-Ready

Prepare for
Lesson 4.5 in
Exs. 63–66

Find the value of the power.

63. 10^1 *(p. 15)*   **64.** 10^2 *(p. 15)*   **65.** $(0.1)^2$ *(p. 181)*   **66.** $(0.01)^2$ *(p. 181)*

Solve the equation using mental math. *(p. 34)*

67. $x - 4 = 5$ **68.** $1 + x = 8$ **69.** $24 \div x = 12$ **70.** $3x = 0$

71. ★ SHORT RESPONSE The following list shows the number of animals a rescue shelter placed in homes each day: 2, 8, 3, 5, 3, 2, 1, 4, 3, 3, 2, 6, 4, 3, 5, 2, 5, 6, 1, 2. Make a line plot of the data. *Explain* how to use the line plot to find the median. *(pp. 76, 99)*

Find the product. *(p. 181)*

72. 5.42×6.3 **73.** 1.8×0.04 **74.** 3.107×2.7 **75.** 2.56×4.1

QUIZ *for Lessons 4.1–4.4*

Multiply. Use estimation to check your answer.

1. 4.7×6 *(p. 169)*   **2.** 4×2.083 *(p. 169)*   **3.** 1.45×0.03 *(p. 181)*   **4.** 6.08×3.7 *(p. 181)*

5. TRAVEL A car can travel about 27.5 miles on a gallon of gas. About how far can the car travel on 8 gallons of gas? *(p. 169)*

Use the distributive property to evaluate the expression. *(p. 175)*

6. $8(20 + 7)$ **7.** $10(7.6 - 3)$ **8.** $4(9 + 1.5)$ **9.** $7(5 + 11)$

10. TELEVISION SCREEN One of the largest television sets in the world is in Tokyo, Japan. The screen has a length of 24.3 meters and a width of 45.7 meters. Find the area of the screen. *(p. 181)*

Divide. Round to the nearest tenth if necessary. *(p. 186)*

11. $6\overline{)31.78}$ **12.** $5\overline{)44.21}$ **13.** $9\overline{)4}$ **14.** $8\overline{)15}$

Lessons 4.1–4.4

1. **MULTI-STEP PROBLEM** At a deli counter, the items are priced per pound. You select a salad and a container of fruit as shown below.

Salad
$5.99
per lb

Fruit
$7.00
per lb

1.78 lb

0.95 lb

   a. Find the cost of the salad.
   b. Find the cost of the fruit.
   c. You have a total of $20. After buying the salad and fruit, how much money do you have left over?
   d. You want to buy three bananas with the remaining money. How much can you spend per banana?

2. **MULTI-STEP PROBLEM** Your coach buys goggles for the swim team. The goggles are sold in packages of 4 for $12.96.

   a. Write an expression to find the cost of one pair of goggles. Then find the cost.
   b. The team uses 18 pairs of goggles. Find the total value of the goggles used.

3. **OPEN-ENDED** *Describe* a real world situation that can be solved by finding a decimal divided by a whole number.

4. **SHORT RESPONSE** Tennis balls are sold in cans of 3 balls or in cases of 24 cans. A can of one brand of tennis balls costs $2.58 while a case of the same brand costs $64.48. Which has the lower cost per ball, the *can* or the *case*? *Explain* how you found your answer.

5. **SHORT RESPONSE** You make $6.50 per hour mowing lawns. You mow for 5 hours the first day, and 3 hours the next day. Write and evaluate two expressions to find the total amount you earn after two days. Which expression was easier to evaluate? *Explain.*

6. **SHORT RESPONSE** When will the product of a whole number and a positive decimal be greater than the whole number? When will it be less than the whole number? Give examples to support your answers.

7. **EXTENDED RESPONSE** Irene is designing a rectangular flower bed. The length of the flower bed will be three times the width.

   a. The width of the flower bed is 8.2 feet. Estimate the length of the flower bed and its perimeter.
   b. Irene wants to spread bark mulch on the flower bed. Estimate the area, in square yards, of the flower bed. *Explain* your answer.
   c. Irene needs mulch for the flower bed, and a fence to surround it. Fencing material costs 20¢ a foot, and mulch costs $1.25 per square yard. Irene has $42 to spend. Does she have enough money for her project? *Explain.*

8. **GRIDDED ANSWER** A toy racecar crosses the starting line of a racetrack traveling at a constant speed of 20 feet per second. The car completes 3 laps in 9.75 seconds. How many feet long is the racetrack?

9. **GRIDDED ANSWER** At lunch, three friends each give you $7.00. You hand this plus $10 to the cashier. You receive change of $4.12. What was the total bill in dollars and cents?

4.5 Multiplying and Dividing by Powers of Ten

Before	You multiplied and divided decimals.
Now	You'll use mental math to help multiply and divide.
Why?	So you can interpret sports data, as in Ex. 48.

KEY VOCABULARY
- **power,** *p. 15*
- **exponent,** *p. 15*

ACTIVITY

What happens when you multiply by a power of ten?

STEP 1
Complete the table.

STEP 2
How does the position of the decimal point change when you multiply by whole number powers of 10? by decimal powers of 10?

Whole Number Powers of Ten	Decimal Powers of Ten
$10 \times 8.3 = $ __?__	$0.1 \times 8.3 = $ __?__
$100 \times 8.3 = $ __?__	$0.01 \times 8.3 = $ __?__
$1000 \times 8.3 = $ __?__	$0.001 \times 8.3 = $ __?__
$10{,}000 \times 8.3 = $ __?__	$0.0001 \times 8.3 = $ __?__

You can multiply by a power of ten by simply moving the decimal point. Use the following rules to find how many places to move it.

KEY CONCEPT
For Your Notebook

Multiplying by Powers of Ten

Multiplying by Whole Number Powers of 10 Move the decimal point one place *to the right* for each zero in the whole number power of 10.

Numbers $3.995 \times 100 = 399.5$

Multiplying by Decimal Powers of 10 Move the decimal point one place *to the left* for each decimal place in the decimal power of 10.

Numbers $399.5 \times 0.001 = 0.3995$

EXAMPLE 1 Multiply Decimals Using Mental Math

WRITE ZEROS
When you move a decimal point to the right or left, you may need to write zeros as placeholders.

a. $0.05 \times 1000 = 0050. = 50$ **Move 3 places to the right.**

b. $95.38 \times 0.0001 = .0095338 = 0.009538$ **Move 4 places to the left.**

EXAMPLE 2 Multiply Decimals by Powers of Ten

Bridges The graph shows the number of vehicles that crossed bridges during 2000. How many vehicles crossed the Golden Gate Bridge?

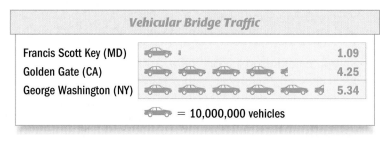

Vehicular Bridge Traffic		
Francis Scott Key (MD)		1.09
Golden Gate (CA)		4.25
George Washington (NY)		5.34

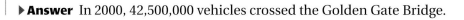 = 10,000,000 vehicles

$4.25 \times 10{,}000{,}000 = 4\,2\,5\,0\,0\,0\,0\,0.$ **Move 7 places to the right.**

$= 42{,}500{,}000$

▶**Answer** In 2000, 42,500,000 vehicles crossed the Golden Gate Bridge.

KEY CONCEPT   *For Your Notebook*

Dividing by Powers of Ten

Dividing by Whole Number Powers of 10 Move the decimal point one place *to the left* for each zero in the whole number power of 10.

Numbers $35 \div 100 = 0.3\,5$

Dividing by Decimal Powers of 10 Move the decimal point one place *to the right* for each decimal place in the decimal power of 10.

Numbers $35 \div 0.001 = 3\,5\,0\,0\,0.$

TAKE NOTES

In your notes, include a summary of the rules for multiplying and dividing by powers of ten. You may want to note the similarities and differences in your own words.

EXAMPLE 3 Divide Decimals Using Mental Math

AVOID ERRORS

For division problems, you move the decimal point in the *opposite* of the direction used for multiplication.

a. $508.3 \div 10 = 5\,0.8\,3 = 50.83$ **Move 1 place to the left.**

b. $508.3 \div 0.01 = 5\,0\,8\,3\,0. = 50{,}830$ **Move 2 places to the right.**

✓ **GUIDED PRACTICE**   **for Examples 1, 2, and 3**

Find the product or quotient using mental math.

1. 6.07×1000 **2.** 153.6×0.01 **3.** $42.6 \div 100$

4. $509 \div 1000$ **5.** $5 \div 0.1$ **6.** $3.2 \div 0.001$

7. Bridges Use the graph in Example 2 to estimate the number of vehicles that crossed the George Washington Bridge in 2000.

4.5 EXERCISES

HOMEWORK KEY

★ = **STANDARDIZED TEST PRACTICE**
Exs. 15, 46, 47, 50, and 67

◯ = **HINTS** AND **HOMEWORK HELP**
for Exs. 5, 7, 13, 17, 45 at classzone.com

SKILL PRACTICE

VOCABULARY Of the numbers 10, 0.01, 100, and 0.1, tell which fit the description.

1. Whole number powers of 10

2. Decimal powers of 10

MENTAL MATH Find the product or quotient using mental math.

SEE EXAMPLES 1, 2, AND 3
on pp. 193–194
for Exs. 3–15

3. 7.58×10

4. 24.831×0.1

5. 16.35×0.01

6. 0.7×1000

7. $0.502 \times 10,000$

8. 4.9×0.1

9. $3.108 \div 0.1$

10. $726.9 \div 1000$

11. $82.93 \div 10$

12. $12.57 \div 0.01$

13. $0.9813 \div 0.1$

14. $0.31725 \div 0.001$

Animated Math at classzone.com

15. ★ **MULTIPLE CHOICE** What is the product 43.64×0.1?

A 0.4364

B 4.364

C 43.64

D 436.4

MATCHING Match the expression with its quotient.

SEE EXAMPLE 3
on p. 194
for Exs. 16–20

16. $320.7 \div 100$

17. $320.7 \div 10$

18. $320.7 \div 0.01$

19. $320.7 \div 0.1$

A. 32.07

B. 3207

C. 3.207

D. 32,070

20. ERROR ANALYSIS Describe and correct the error in the solution.

✗ $631.17 \div 0.00001 = 0.0063117$

NUMBER SENSE Copy and complete the statement using <, >, or =.

21. $532.4 \times 0.001 \ \underline{?} \ 5.32$

22. $12.22 \div 0.01 \ \underline{?} \ 0.12$

23. $99.99 \div 0.001 \ \underline{?} \ 10,000$

24. $12.22 \times 0.01 \ \underline{?} \ 0.12$

ⓧ ALGEBRA Evaluate the expression.

25. $8.3x$, when $x = 1000$

26. $3.06x - 1.5$, when $x = 10$

27. $5 \div x + 0.2$, when $x = 100$

28. $50 - 8x$, when $x = 0.001$

29. $3(6 \div x)$, when $x = 0.01$

30. $3.75 \div x$, when $x = 0.01$

REASONING Tell whether the statement is *true* or *false*. *Justify* your answer.

31. When you divide a whole number by a whole number power of 10, the quotient is less than or equal to the dividend.

32. When you divide a whole number by a decimal power of 10, the quotient is less than the dividend.

ⓧ CHALLENGE Use mental math to solve the equation.

33. $a \times 1000 = 16.9$

34. $b \div 0.001 = 16.9$

35. $c \div 10,000 = 4.65$

SCIENTIFIC NOTATION In Exercises 36–39, write the number in scientific notation.

> **EXTENSION** Writing Numbers in Scientific Notation
>
> A number written in *scientific notation* has two factors. The first factor is greater than or equal to 1 and less than 10. The second is a power of ten.
>
> | Standard form | Product form | Scientific notation |
> |:---:|:---:|:---:|
> | 120,000 | $1.2 \times 100{,}000$ | 1.2×10^5 |
> | 5 decimal places | 5 zeros | Exponent is 5. |
>
> ▸**Answer** The scientific notation for 120,000 is 1.2×10^5.

36. 7,000,000,000   **37.** 49,200   **38.** 500   **39.** 93,000,000

STANDARD FORM Write the number in standard form.

40. 3.2×10^{14} **41.** 2.1×10^{18} **42.** 6.4×10^{15} **43.** 1.7×10^{10}

PROBLEM SOLVING

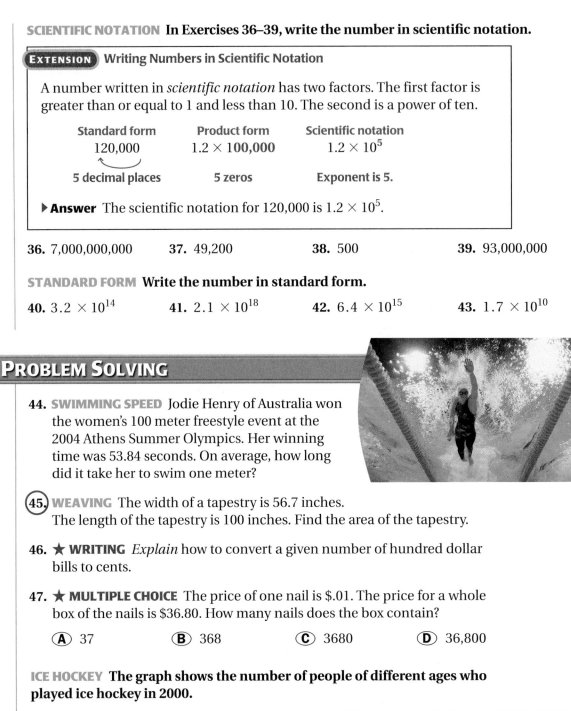

44. SWIMMING SPEED Jodie Henry of Australia won the women's 100 meter freestyle event at the 2004 Athens Summer Olympics. Her winning time was 53.84 seconds. On average, how long did it take her to swim one meter?

45. WEAVING The width of a tapestry is 56.7 inches. The length of the tapestry is 100 inches. Find the area of the tapestry.

46. ★ WRITING *Explain* how to convert a given number of hundred dollar bills to cents.

47. ★ MULTIPLE CHOICE The price of one nail is $.01. The price for a whole box of the nails is $36.80. How many nails does the box contain?

(A) 37   **(B)** 368   **(C)** 3680   **(D)** 36,800

ICE HOCKEY The graph shows the number of people of different ages who played ice hockey in 2000.

SEE EXAMPLE 2
on p. 194
for Exs. 48–49

48. How many more 7–11 year olds played ice hockey in 2000 than 18–24 year olds?

49. In 2000, about 43,000 players in the U.S. were ages 6 and under. How would you represent 43,000 on this graph?

Ice Hockey Players in 2000	
7–11 year olds	3.74
12–17 year olds	4.41
18–24 year olds	2.93
⬭ = 100,000 people	

50. ★ SHORT RESPONSE A micrometer is a distance of 0.001 millimeter. A leaf has a length of 87.2 millimeters. Find its length in micrometers. *Write* a procedure for converting between millimeters and micrometers.

SEE EXAMPLE 1
on p. 193
for Ex. 51

51. MULTI-STEP PROBLEM About 14 million 10–14 year olds use a computer at home. About one tenth of them do not use it to play games.

    a. Write the number of 10–14 year olds who use a computer at home in standard form.

    b. Multiply your answer from part (a) by 0.1 to find the number of 10–14 year olds who do *not* use the computer to play games.

    c. How many 10–14 year olds use the computer to play games? *Explain.*

52. ◆ MULTIPLE REPRESENTATIONS The table shows the top five ranked golfers of the 2004 PGA Tour, and their winnings for that year.

    a. Calculate Find each player's winnings in millions by dividing each number by 1,000,000. Round to the nearest tenth.

    b. Draw a Graph Make a pictograph.

    c. Compare and Contrast Use your pictograph to estimate whether Vijay Singh earned twice as much money as Tiger Woods.

Player	Winnings
1. Vijay Singh	$10,905,166
2. Tiger Woods	$ 5,365,472
3. Ernie Els	$ 5,787,225
4. Retief Goosen	$ 3,885,573
5. Phil Mickelson	$ 5,784,823

53. METRIC CONVERSION How many millimeters are in one mile? (*Hint:* 1 mile ≈ 1.609 kilometer.) *Justify* your answer.

CONVERTING LENGTHS The angstrom (Å) was a unit of length that measured atoms. Nanometers (nm) are now used. There are 10 angstrom in each nanometer. Convert the angstrom measure to nanometers.

54. 120 Å   **55.** 0.17 Å   **56.** 13.6 Å   **57.** 4 Å

58. CHALLENGE The width across a dime is about 18 millimeters. For a fundraiser, you line up dimes end-to-end in the hallway of your school. You raise $180. How long is the trail of dimes, in meters?

MIXED REVIEW

Get-Ready

Prepare for
Lesson 4.6 in
Exs. 59–62

Find the quotient. *(p. 186)*

59. $6.79 \div 7$ **60.** $42 \div 12$ **61.** $0.38 \div 19$ **62.** $39.1 \div 34$

Find the sum or difference. *(p. 148)*

63. $5.5 + 4.8$ **64.** $18.7 + 2.19$ **65.** $6 - 3.4$ **66.** $7.21 - 5.94$

67. ★ MULTIPLE CHOICE What is the length of the pencil? *(p. 125)*

    A 9.6 millimeters   **B** 90.6 millimeters   **C** 9.6 centimeters   **D** 96 centimeters

4.6 Dividing by Decimals

Before	You divided by whole numbers.
Now	You'll divide by decimals.
Why?	So you can find average weight, as in Ex. 48.

KEY VOCABULARY
- **dividend,** *p. 4*
- **divisor,** *p. 4*
- **quotient,** *p. 4*

Cost per Pound At a pumpkin patch you choose a pumpkin weighing 9.5 pounds and pay $4.75. What is the cost per pound of the pumpkin?

You will answer this question in Example 3. You will need to divide by a decimal.

KEY CONCEPT *For Your Notebook*

Dividing by a Decimal

Words   When you divide by a decimal, multiply both the divisor and the dividend by a power of ten that will make the divisor a whole number.

Numbers

$$2.5)\overline{3.75} \xrightarrow{\text{Multiply 2.5 and 3.75 by 10.}} 25)\overline{37.5} = 1.5$$

EXAMPLE 1   Writing Divisors as Whole Numbers

Rewrite the division problem so that the divisor is a whole number.

COUNT DECIMAL PLACES
When you divide by a decimal with one decimal place, multiply the divisor and the dividend by 10. For a divisor with two decimal places, multiply by 100, and so on.

a. $1.83 \div 2.5$

$2.5)\overline{1.83}$ ← Multiply the divisor and dividend by 10.

▶ **Answer** $18.3 \div 25$

b. $3 \div 0.15$

$0.15)\overline{300}$ ← Write zeros as placeholders

Multiply the divisor and dividend by 100.

▶ **Answer** $300 \div 15$

✓ GUIDED PRACTICE   for Example 1

Rewrite the division problem so that the divisor is a whole number.

1. $0.7)\overline{5.6}$ **2.** $3.8)\overline{4.56}$ **3.** $0.14)\overline{0.84}$

4. $0.25)\overline{62.5}$ **5.** $0.133)\overline{0.0665}$ **6.** $0.038)\overline{171}$

EXAMPLE 2 Using Zeros While Dividing

Find the quotient.

a. $0.88 \div 1.6$

$$1.6\overline{)0.88}$$

$$\begin{array}{r} .55 \\ 16\overline{)8.80} \\ \underline{8\ 0}\downarrow \\ 80 \\ \underline{80} \\ 0 \end{array}$$

▶ **Answer** $0.88 \div 1.6 = 0.55$

Animated **Math** at classzone.com

b. $30 \div 0.02$

$$0.02\overline{)30.00}$$

$$\begin{array}{r} 1500 \\ 2\overline{)3000} \\ \underline{2}\downarrow \\ 10 \\ \underline{10} \\ 0 \end{array}$$

> Sometimes you need to write zeros as placeholders in the quotient.

▶ **Answer** $30 \div 0.02 = 1500$

EXAMPLE 3 Solving Problems Involving Decimals

Find the cost per pound of the pumpkin discussed at the top of page 198.

SOLUTION

Divide the total cost of the pumpkin by the number of pounds.

$9.5\overline{)4.75}$ **Multiply the divisor and dividend by 10.**

$$\begin{array}{r} .5 \\ 95\overline{)47.5} \\ \underline{475} \\ 0 \end{array}$$

READING
When the units are dollars, you can read decimals as whole numbers of cents. The answer $.50 can be read as "fifty cents" instead of "fifty hundredths of a dollar."

▶ **Answer** Because money is represented with two decimal places, the pumpkin costs $.50 per pound.

Check Estimate: $4.75 \div 9.5 \approx 5 \div 10 = 0.5$. So, the answer of $.50 per pound is reasonable.

✓ **GUIDED PRACTICE** for Examples 2 and 3

Divide. Round to the nearest tenth.

7. $0.2\overline{)0.99}$ **8.** $1.3\overline{)7.69}$ **9.** $0.28\overline{)25.5}$ **10.** $9.5\overline{)63}$

11. Cost of Fruit You paid $10.17 for 3.4 pounds of dried fruit. What was the cost per pound?

12. Cost of Fabric You pay $5.21 for 0.75 yard of fabric. What is the cost per yard?

4.6 EXERCISES

HOMEWORK KEY

★ = **STANDARDIZED TEST PRACTICE**
Exs. 22, 50, 51, 53, 55, and 63

◯ = **HINTS AND HOMEWORK HELP**
for Exs. 5, 11, 15, 19, 47 at classzone.com

SKILL PRACTICE

VOCABULARY Identify the given number in the equation $8.49 \div 0.3 = 28.3$.

1. dividend

2. divisor

REWRITING Rewrite each problem so that the divisor is a whole number.

SEE EXAMPLE 1
on p. 198
for Exs. 3–9

3. $3.1)\overline{12.8}$

4. $0.28)\overline{4.76}$

5. $0.93)\overline{14.88}$

6. $1.32 \div 0.55$

7. $8.1 \div 0.614$

8. $32.32 \div 0.08$

9. ERROR ANALYSIS Describe and correct the error made in rewriting the problem.

$\times \quad 0.38)\overline{17} \longrightarrow 38)\overline{170}$

DIVIDING DECIMALS Divide. Round to the nearest tenth if necessary.

SEE EXAMPLE 2
on p. 199
for Exs. 10–23

10. $0.09 \div 3$

11. $8.69 \div 4.1$

12. $40 \div 0.05$

13. $48 \div 0.6$

14. $1.18 \div 0.2$

15. $4.96 \div 1.6$

16. $97.2 \div 0.9$

17. $2.16 \div 0.02$

18. $21.3 \div 0.07$

19. $23.5 \div 0.008$

20. $8.93 \div 0.016$

21. $5.72 \div 0.098$

22. ★ MULTIPLE CHOICE What is the quotient $6.56 \div 0.4$?

(A) 1.64

(B) 16.4

(C) 164

(D) 1640

23. WHICH ONE DOESN'T BELONG? Which quotient does *not* equal 10.2?

(A) $0.0306 \div 0.003$

(B) $0.306 \div 0.03$

(C) $3.06 \div 0.3$

(D) $30.6 \div 30$

⊗ ALGEBRA Evaluate the expression when $x = 4.54$ and $y = 7.5$. Round to the nearest hundredth if necessary.

24. $(8.5 - x) \div y$

25. $y \div (x - 4)$

26. $x + 3.15 \div y$

27. $y + x \div 0.8$

28. $y \div 0.82 - x$

29. $(y - x) \div 2.96$

30. $x - 9.54 \div y$

31. $x - y \div 2.8$

WRITING RECIPROCALS A number is a reciprocal of a given number if the product of the two numbers is 1. Write the reciprocal of the number. Round to the hundredth's place.

32. 8.12

33. 0.031

34. 2.17

35. 0.0049

NUMBER SENSE Copy and complete the statement using <, >, or =.

36. $13.42 \div 1.18 \ \underline{?} \ 134.2 \div 118$

37. $6.857 \div 2.56 \ \underline{?} \ 685.7 \div 256$

38. $43.75 \div 2.28 \ \underline{?} \ 43.75 \div 22.8$

39. $21.74 \div 1.02 \ \underline{?} \ 21.74 \div 0.102$

40. $15.28 \div 1.01 \ \underline{?} \ 150.28 \div 10.1$

41. $1.576 \div 0.02 \ \underline{?} \ 157.6 \div 0.002$

REASONING Tell whether the statement is *always, sometimes,* or *never* true. Assume all numbers are greater than zero. *Justify* your answer.

42. If the divisor is less than the dividend, the quotient is greater than 1.

43. If the divisor is greater than the dividend, the quotient is less than 1.

44. CHALLENGE The diagonal, *d*, of a square is about 1.4 times the length of a side. How does the length of the side change if the length of the diagonal is doubled? tripled? *Justify* your reasoning.

PROBLEM SOLVING

45. GUIDED PROBLEM SOLVING A stack of books is 1.35 meters tall. Each book is about 0.09 meter thick. How many books are in the stack?

   a. Do you need to *multiply* or *divide* to solve the problem? *Explain.*

   b. Write an expression to find the number of books in the stack.

   c. Evaluate your expression. How many books are in the stack?

SEE EXAMPLE 3
on p. 199
for Exs. 46–50

46. GAS MILEAGE Juan drives his car the number of miles shown on the trip odometer and uses 14.5 gallons of gasoline. Find the gas mileage (miles divided by gallons) of Juan's car. Round to the nearest tenth.

`0 0 4 7 0 . 8`

CHOOSE AN OPERATION In Exercises 47–49, explain your choice of operation.

47. PHOTOS You have a roll of 24 pictures developed and each picture is 15.24 centimeters long. How long will the pictures be if placed end-to-end?

48. AVERAGE WEIGHT Only 3 pumpkin boats competed in the world's first pumpkin boat race. The boats weighed 814 pounds, 787 pounds, and 752.6 pounds. What was the mean of the weights of these 3 boats?

49. GEOMETRY A rectangle has an area of 43.7 square centimeters. The length of the rectangle is 9.5 centimeters. Find the width.

50. ★ SHORT RESPONSE A chain of paper clips that are linked together is 387.5 centimeters long. The length of each paper clip is 3.3 centimeters. About how many paper clips are in the chain? *Explain* why knowing the thickness of the paper clips' wire could help you to make a better estimate.

51. ★ MULTIPLE CHOICE List the fruits in the grocery receipt from least to greatest cost per pound.

   (A) k, p, a, b   **(B)** a, b, p, k

   (C) b, a, k, p   **(D)** b, a, p, k

Apples (a)	7.1 lb	$7.85
Bananas (b)	4.8 lb	$4.93
Peaches (p)	4.5 lb	$6.75
Kiwis (k)	3.2 lb	$8.28

POPULATION In Exercises 52–53, use the table. **Round to the nearest tenth.**

World Population (billions)								
Year	1650	1700	1750	1800	1850	1900	1950	2000
Population	0.51	0.63	0.79	0.97	1.26	1.66	2.56	6.08
Quotient	—	?	?	?	?	?	?	?

52. Divide the population in 1700 by the population in 1650. Continue to divide the population in each column by the population in the previous column to complete the table.

53. ★ **WRITING** Describe the pattern. Is it consistent? *Explain.*

54. **AMUSEMENT PARKS** The entry price for a theme park is $18.50. The park operates 200 days per year and collects about $6.29 million from entry fees each year. About how many people visit the park on an average day?

55. ★ **EXTENDED RESPONSE** The school cafeteria sells a 1.5 ounce bag of pretzels for $.45. A store sells a pack of six 1.75 ounce bags of pretzels for $3.45.

   a. Calculate Find the price per ounce of each type of pretzel. Which is the better buy? *Explain.*

   b. Compare and Contrast You find a 14.5 ounce bag of pretzels for $3.99. How does the cost of buying this bag and taking individual servings to school compare with the cost per ounce of the 1.5 ounce bag? with the cost of the 1.75 ounce bags?

   c. Evaluate If you buy and divide a large bag of pretzels into single servings, then you will pay about $0.03 more per serving for individual sandwich bags. *Describe* how this affects your purchasing choice.

56. **CHALLENGE** Each page of a 1534 page dictionary has two columns that are 10 inches tall. Each definition uses an average of 0.375 inch of vertical space in a column. About how many definitions does the dictionary have?

MIXED REVIEW

Get-Ready

Prepare for
Lesson 4.7
in Exs. 57–59

Choose an appropriate customary unit and metric unit to measure the height of the object. *(p. 59)*

57. movie screen   **58.** housefly   **59.** Mount Everest

Divide. Round to the nearest tenth if necessary. *(p. 186)*

60. $12.7 \div 3$ **61.** $9.45 \div 6$ **62.** $73.9 \div 11$

63. ★ **MULTIPLE CHOICE** Which product equals 0.04? *(p. 169)*

   A 0.02×0.2 **B** 0.2×2 **C** 0.02×2 **D** 2×0.002

4.7 Mass and Capacity

Before	You measured length using customary and metric units.
Now	You'll use metric units of mass and capacity.
Why?	So you can choose units, as for mass in Ex. 25.

KEY VOCABULARY
- **gram,** *p. 203*
- **milligram,** *p. 203*
- **kilogram,** *p. 203*
- **liter,** *p. 204*
- **milliliter,** *p. 204*
- **kiloliter,** *p. 204*

ACTIVITY

Perform an experiment to measure *mass.*

STEP 1 One person in the group holds a pen in one hand and a paper clip in the other hand.

STEP 2 Another person adds paper clips until the first person feels that both hands hold the same amount. Record the number of paper clips.

STEP 3 Each person in the group makes an estimate of the pen's mass. Find the mean of the group's results.

STEP 4 Based on the mean you found in Step 3, how many paper clips would you have in your hand for 10 pens? for 100 pens?

TAKE NOTES

As you preview this lesson, you may want to review what you learned about benchmarks for metric units of length in Lesson 2.1.

Units of Mass The *mass* of an object is the amount of matter it has. The **gram** (g) is a metric unit of mass. Two other metric units of mass are the **milligram** (mg) and the **kilogram** (kg).

milligram about the mass of a grain of sugar

gram about the mass of a small paper clip

kilogram about the mass of a book

Grams, milligrams, and kilograms are related to each other.

$$1 \text{ g} = 1000 \text{ mg} \qquad 1 \text{ mg} = 0.001 \text{ g} \qquad 1 \text{ kg} = 1000 \text{ g}$$

EXAMPLE 1 Choosing Units of Mass

An item has a mass of 10.3 kilograms. Is it a *dog* or a *pencil*? Explain.

The mass of a book is about 1 kg, so 10.3 kg is the mass of about 10 books. The mass of a *dog* is closer to the mass of 10 books, so the item is a dog.

Units of Capacity *Capacity* measures the amount that a container can hold. The **liter** (L) is a metric unit of capacity. Two other metric units of capacity are the **milliliter** (mL) and the **kiloliter** (kL).

milliliter about the capacity of an eyedropper

liter about the capacity of a large bottle of water

kiloliter about the capacity of 5 bathtubs

VOCABULARY
Notice that the prefixes are the same for units of length, units of mass, and units of capacity.

Liters, milliliters, and kiloliters are related to each other.

1 L = 1000 mL   1 mL = 0.001 L   1 kL = 1000 L

EXAMPLE 2 Choosing Units of Capacity

Tell whether the most appropriate unit to measure the capacity of the item is *milliliters, liters,* or *kiloliters.*

a. bucket   **b.** teaspoon

SOLUTION

a. The capacity of a bucket is closest to the capacity of a large bottle of water. You should use liters.

b. The capacity of a teaspoon is closest to the capacity of an eyedropper. You should use milliliters.

EXAMPLE 3 Choosing Metric Units

Choose an appropriate metric unit to measure the item.

a. mass of an eraser   **b.** capacity of a bottle of nail polish

SOLUTION

a. The mass of an eraser is much greater than one milligram and much less than one kilogram. So, you should use grams.

b. The capacity of a bottle of nail polish is much less than one liter or one kiloliter. So, you should use milliliters.

✓ **GUIDED PRACTICE**   for Examples 1, 2, and 3

1. Mass An animal has a mass of 56 grams. Is it a *cat* or a *mouse*? *Explain.*

Choose an appropriate metric unit to measure the item.

2. capacity of a wheelbarrow   **3.** mass of a test tube

4. mass of a car   **5.** capacity of a thermos

4.7 EXERCISES

HOMEWORK KEY

★ = **STANDARDIZED TEST PRACTICE**
Exs. 27, 34, 35, and 46

◯ = **HINTS** AND **HOMEWORK HELP**
for Exs. 3, 5, 9, 13, 33 at classzone.com

SKILL PRACTICE

VOCABULARY Copy and complete the statement.

1. Liters, milliliters, and kiloliters are examples of metric units of __?__.

2. The __?__ of an object is the amount of matter it has.

RECOGNIZING A MASS Choose the object that best fits the description.

SEE EXAMPLE 1
on p. 203
for Exs. 3–5

3. The mass of an item is 5 kg. Is the item a *shoelace*, a *plate*, or a *chair*?

4. Isaac picks up an object with a mass of 5 grams. Is the object a *book* or a *nickel*?

5. Gail is describing an object that has a capacity of 1.9 liters. Is she describing a *washing machine*, a *water pitcher*, or a *cereal bowl*?

CHOOSING UNITS OF CAPACITY Tell whether the most appropriate unit to measure the capacity of the item is *milliliters*, *liters*, or *kiloliters*.

SEE EXAMPLE 2
on p. 204
for Exs. 6–11

6. town water tower
7. contact lens case
8. portable cooler
9. bird bath
10. tanker truck
11. hot sauce bottle

IDENTIFYING UNITS Tell whether the measurement is a *mass*, a *capacity*, or a *length*.

SEE EXAMPLES 1 AND 2
on p. 203
for Exs. 12–17

12. 10 L
13. 0.68 kg
14. 7.5 mm
15. 9.2 mL
16. 5.5 g
17. 2 m

CHOOSING UNITS Choose an appropriate metric unit to measure the item.

SEE EXAMPLE 3
on p. 204
for Exs. 18–27

18. mass of a leaf
19. capacity of a sink
20. mass of a kick ball
21. capacity of a pool
22. capacity of a lake
23. mass of a bubble
24. capacity of a glass
25. mass of a bicycle
26. ink capacity of a pen

27. ★ **MULTIPLE CHOICE** The mass of a piece of paper would most likely be expressed with which unit of measurement?

Ⓐ liters
Ⓑ milligrams
Ⓒ grams
Ⓓ kilograms

CHOOSING A TOOL Tell whether an appropriate measurement tool for the item would be a *bathroom scale*, a *truck stop scale*, or an *eyedropper*.

28. juice in a lemon
29. laptop computer
30. load of bricks

31. **CHALLENGE** A cube one centimeter on a side can hold one milliliter of water. How many such cubes fit in a bigger cube that is one meter on each side? How many liters would the big cube hold?

MOUNTAIN CLIMBING A mountain climber uses a piece of equipment called a *carabiner*. A carabiner is a small metal ring that attaches to the climber's ropes.

SEE EXAMPLE 1 on p. 203 for Exs. 32–33

32. Do you think the mass of a carabiner should be measured in *milligrams, grams,* or *kilograms*? *Explain* your choice.

33. Do you think the mass of the climber should be measured in *milligrams, grams,* or *kilograms*? *Explain* your choice.

34. ★ **WRITING** Using metric units, approximate the mass or capacity of the items in Exercises 28–30. *Explain* your reasoning.

35. ★ **SHORT RESPONSE** To determine how much iced tea will fit into a pitcher, do you need to know the mass or the capacity of the pitcher? Would an appropriate measuring tool be a *scale*, a *measuring cup*, or a *tablespoon*? *Explain.*

36. **MULTI-STEP PROBLEM** The table shows the amounts of water a person usually uses for certain activities.

Activity	Water used
Showering	75.7
Brushing teeth	3.8
Washing hands	3.2

  a. **Conjecture** Are the amounts measured in liters or milliliters? *Explain* your choice.

  b. **Calculate** In one day, each person in a family of four takes 1 shower, brushes his or her teeth 3 times, and washes his or her hands 5 times. How much water do they use?

  c. **Extend** How much water is used in a week by the family in part (b)? Express this amount in kiloliters. *Explain* how you found your answer.

37. **CHALLENGE** Your 20-by-25 foot basement floods with 1 inch of water. Is there enough water to fill a bathtub 5 times? (*Hint:* A 1-inch cube of water contains about 0.02 liter.) *Explain* your reasoning.

Get-Ready

Prepare for Lesson 4.8 in Exs. 38–41

Evaluate the expression. *(p. 193)*

38. 1.26×1000 **39.** $5.7 \div 100$ **40.** $6.3 \div 0.1$ **41.** 37.4×0.01

Estimate the quotient. *(p. 11)*

42. $10\overline{)98}$ **43.** $19\overline{)105}$ **44.** $32\overline{)305}$ **45.** $102\overline{)9982}$

46. ★ **MULTIPLE CHOICE** Round the number 34.49 to the ones' place. *(p. 137)*

  (A) 34.4   **(B)** 34.5   **(C)** 34   **(D)** 35

4.8 Changing Metric Units

Before	You learned metric units for length, mass, and capacity.
Now	You'll change from one metric unit of measure to another.
Why?	So you can compare masses of objects, as in Ex. 45.

KEY VOCABULARY
• **meter,** *p. 60*
• **gram,** *p. 203*
• **liter,** *p. 204*

You can change from one unit to another in the metric system by multiplying or dividing by a power of 10. The chart shows meters, but the same method also works for grams and liters.

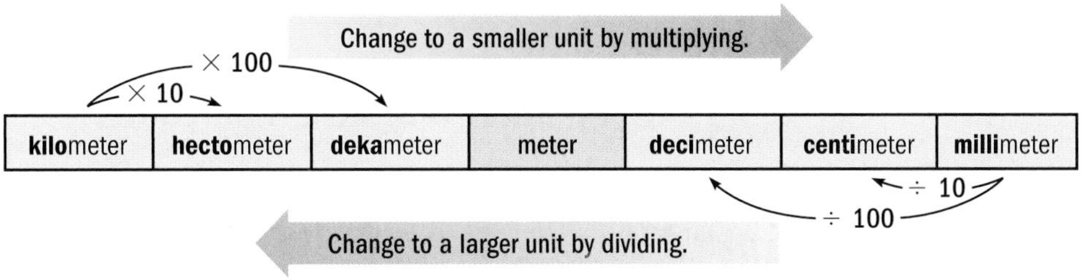

Change to a smaller unit by multiplying.

× 100
× 10

kilo**meter**	hecto**meter**	deka**meter**	**meter**	**deci**meter	**centi**meter	**milli**meter

÷ 10
÷ 100

Change to a larger unit by dividing.

EXAMPLE 1 Changing Units Using Multiplication

Change 0.64 liters to milliliters.

STEP 1 **Decide** whether to multiply or divide. Because you are changing to a smaller unit, you will need more of those units. So, you need to multiply.

STEP 2 **Select** the power of 10 and multiply.   L ———— × 1000 ————▶ mL

▶**Answer** 0.64 L = 640 mL   **0.64 × 1000 = 640.**

★ EXAMPLE 2 Standardized Test Practice

A notepad has a mass of 23.6 grams. What is its mass in kilograms?

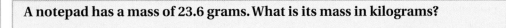

(A) 0.0236 kg   **(B)** 0.236 kg   **(C)** 2.36 kg   **(D)** 23,600 kg

ELIMINATE CHOICES
Because a kilogram is three steps away from a gram, you divide by 10^3, or 1000. So, choice D can be eliminated.

SOLUTION

STEP 1 **Decide** whether to multiply or divide. Because you are changing to a larger unit, you will need fewer of those units. So, you need to divide.

STEP 2 **Select** the power of 10 and divide.   kg ◀——— ÷ 1000 ——— g

▶**Answer** The mass of the notepad is   **23.6 ÷ 1000 = 0.0236**
0.0236 kg. The answer is A. **(A) (B) (C) (D)**

Comparing Measures To compare measures that have different units, change one of them so that both measures have the *same* units.

EXAMPLE 3 Comparing Measures

Which is longer, 170 cm or 1.6 m?

Change 170 cm to meters so the units are the same for both measures.

$$170 \text{ cm} = (170 \div 100) \text{ m} \qquad \textbf{100 cm} = \textbf{1 m}$$
$$= 1.7 \text{ m}$$

Then compare the measures. Because 1.7 m > 1.6 m, you know that 170 cm > 1.6 m.

▶ **Answer** 170 cm is longer than 1.6 m.

ANOTHER WAY
You could change
1.6 meters to centimeters
instead:
1.6 m = (1.6 × 100) cm
      = 160 cm
Then compare:
170 cm > 160 cm

EXAMPLE 4 Solve a Multi-Step Problem

State Quarters A jar filled with state quarters has a mass of 2.3 kilograms. The jar's mass is 0.9 kilograms when empty. Each quarter has a mass of about 5.6 grams. About how many quarters are in the jar?

SOLUTION

STEP 1 **Write** a verbal model to find the mass of the quarters in the jar.

Mass of quarters	=	**Mass of full jar**	−	Mass of empty jar
	=	**2.3 kg**	−	0.9 kg
	=	1.4 kg		

AVOID ERRORS
Ask yourself, "Are grams larger or smaller than kilograms?" Because they are smaller, you need *more* of those units to measure the mass of the quarters. So, you *multiply*.

STEP 2 **Change** the mass of the quarters to grams.

$$1.4 \text{ kg} = (1.4 \times 1000) \text{ g}$$
$$= 1400 \text{ g}$$

STEP 3 **Find** the number of quarters by dividing the mass of the quarters by the mass of one quarter.

$$\begin{array}{r} 250. \\ 56\overline{)14000.} \\ 112 \\ \hline 280 \\ 280 \\ \hline 0 \end{array}$$

▶ **Answer** There are about 250 state quarters in the jar.

✓ **GUIDED PRACTICE** for Examples 1–4

1. Change 230 g to kilograms.
2. Change 2.5 mL to liters.
3. Compare 50 mm and 3.5 cm.
4. Compare 0.01 kg and 8 g.
5. **What If?** About how many quarters are in the jar in Example 4 if the mass of the filled jar is 2.58 kg?

4.8 EXERCISES

HOMEWORK KEY

★ = **STANDARDIZED TEST PRACTICE**
Exs. 25, 41, 42, 44, 45, and 60

◯ = **HINTS** AND **HOMEWORK HELP**
for Exs. 5, 11, 13, 17, 35 at classzone.com

SKILL PRACTICE

1. **VOCABULARY** Name the three base units for length, mass, and capacity in the metric system.

2. **VOCABULARY** Is a dekameter *longer* or *shorter* than a decimeter?

SELECTING A POWER OF TEN **Copy and complete the statement.**

**SEE EXAMPLES
1 AND 2**
on p. 207
for Exs. 3–14

3. To change from millimeters to centimeters, you divide by __?__ .

4. To change from meters to kilometers, you divide by __?__ .

5. To change from liters to milliliters, you multiply by __?__ .

CHANGING UNITS **Copy and complete the statement.**

6. $520 \text{ mg} = \underline{\ ?\ } \text{ g}$

7. $360 \text{ cm} = \underline{\ ?\ } \text{ m}$

8. $0.8 \text{ L} = \underline{\ ?\ } \text{ mL}$

9. $8 \text{ mm} = \underline{\ ?\ } \text{ cm}$

10. $0.04 \text{ L} = \underline{\ ?\ } \text{ mL}$

11. $468 \text{ mL} = \underline{\ ?\ } \text{ L}$

12. $0.8 \text{ kg} = \underline{\ ?\ } \text{ g}$

13. $7.4 \text{ cm} = \underline{\ ?\ } \text{ mm}$

14. $8.1 \text{ kL} = \underline{\ ?\ } \text{ L}$

COMPARING MEASURES **Copy and complete the statement with <, >, or =.**

SEE EXAMPLE 3
on p. 208
for Exs. 15–25

15. $308 \text{ g} \ \underline{\ ?\ } \ 0.4 \text{ kg}$

16. $1.2 \text{ km} \ \underline{\ ?\ } \ 1300 \text{ m}$

17. $1.3 \text{ kL} \ \underline{\ ?\ } \ 1300 \text{ L}$

18. $70 \text{ mL} \ \underline{\ ?\ } \ 0.7 \text{ L}$

19. $34.8 \text{ kg} \ \underline{\ ?\ } \ 3480 \text{ g}$

20. $452 \text{ L} \ \underline{\ ?\ } \ 4600 \text{ mL}$

21. $31 \text{ mg} \ \underline{\ ?\ } \ 0.03 \text{ g}$

22. $1.94 \text{ m} \ \underline{\ ?\ } \ 0.0194 \text{ km}$

23. $75 \text{ kg} \ \underline{\ ?\ } \ 0.075 \text{ g}$

24. **ERROR ANALYSIS** Describe and correct the error made in comparing the measures 0.3 L and 31.3 mL.

$$\times \quad \begin{array}{l} 0.3 \text{ L} = (0.3 \div 1000) \text{ mL} \\ \quad\quad = 0.0003 \text{ mL} \\ 0.0003 \text{ mL} < 0.3 \text{ L, so } 0.3 \text{ L} < 31.3 \text{ mL.} \end{array}$$

25. ★ **MULTIPLE CHOICE** Which statement shows why 0.09 km > 89 cm?

Ⓐ $900 \text{ cm} > 89 \text{ cm}$

Ⓑ $0.09 \text{ km} > 0.00089 \text{ km}$

Ⓒ $0.09 \text{ km} > 0.089 \text{ km}$

Ⓓ $9000 \text{ cm} > 89 \text{ cm}$

COMPARING MEASURES **List the measures in order from least to greatest.**

26. 24 hectometers, 0.24 kilometer, 3 kilometers, 30,000 centimeters

27. 5000 grams, 5 centigrams, 1.19 decigram, 0.119 dekagram

ⓧⓥ ALGEBRA **Tell whether the statement is *true* or *false*. If it is false, write the correct statement for the given units.**

28. x meters $= 100x$ centimeters

29. x meters $= x \div 100$ kilometers

30. x meters $= x \div 1000$ millimeters

31. x meters $= 1000x$ kilometers

32. PIXEL WIDTH A computer pixel is 0.264 mm long. How many pixels would it take to display a thin line one decimeter long? Assume the line has a width of one pixel. Round to the nearest pixel.

33. CHALLENGE In a race, you drink 0.8 liter of water every mile. How many milliliters do you drink per kilometer to the nearest milliliter? (*Hint:* 1 mi ≈ 1.61 km)

PROBLEM SOLVING

34. GUIDED PROBLEM SOLVING You are comparing lemonade mixes. Mix A will make four 2 liter pitchers of lemonade. Mix B will make twenty 500 milliliter glasses of lemonade. Which mix will make more lemonade?

   a. Find the total number of liters of lemonade Mix A makes. Find the total number of milliliters of lemonade Mix B makes.

   b. Change the amount of lemonade Mix B makes to liters.

   c. Compare the two amounts. Which mix will make more lemonade?

MEASURING DIMENSIONS A sunflower has the dimensions shown. Use the picture to answer Questions 35–37.

35. What is the sunflower's height in centimeters?

36. What is the width of the sunflower's head in meters?

37. What is the length of one of the sunflower's leaves in millimeters?

50 cm

2.75 m

48 cm

38. CHANGING UNITS A grown male lion has a mass of about 180,000 grams. What is the mass of the lion in kilograms?

39. WINGSPAN A butterfly has a wingspan of 77 millimeters and a height of 7 centimeters. Which is greater, its *wingspan* or *height*?

40. ARM SPAN An orangutan has an arm span of 2.1 meters and a height of 140 centimeters. Which is greater, its *arm span* or *height*?

41. ★ WRITING *Explain* why you need to divide when changing from a smaller unit to a larger unit.

SEE EXAMPLE 4 on p. 208 for Ex. 42

42. ★ MULTIPLE CHOICE A beaker contains 62 milliliters of a solution. A chemist fills the rest of the beaker with ammonium chloride. The beaker's capacity when full is 1.5 liters. Which expression can be used to find c, the amount of ammonium chloride that is poured into the beaker?

   A $(0.0015 - 62)$ mL   **B** $(1500 - 62)$ mL

   C $(1.5 \text{ L} - 0.62)$ L   **D** $(1.5 - 62000)$ L

43. GEOGRAPHY On a map, 1 centimeter represents an actual distance of 200 meters. The distance between two cities on the map is 8.5 centimeters. How many kilometers apart are the actual cities?

44. ★ SHORT RESPONSE A 591 milliliter container of juice costs $1.25. A 1.89-liter container of the same juice costs $3.29. Which container is the better buy? *Explain* how you found your answer.

45. ★ EXTENDED RESPONSE You and your friend go bowling. The chart shows the masses of 6 bowling balls that are available.

Bowling Balls
2.72 kg
7260 g
5,980,000 mg
2,720,000 mg
4.52 kg
6790 g

   a. Choose a Unit What common unit of mass could you use so that each mass is in the same unit?

   b. Convert Change the masses to the unit you chose in part (a).

   c. Compare List the masses in order from least to greatest. Which two balls are closest in mass?

   d. Reasoning You want to use a ball whose mass is slightly above average. Which ball would you use? *Justify* your choice.

GEOMETRY **Use a square with side length 1.2 kilometers.**

46. Find the area of the square in square kilometers.

47. Find the side length of the square in meters and its area in square meters.

48. Compare square kilometers to square meters based on your answers above.

49. By what number should you multiply the number of square meters to find the number of square centimeters? *Explain* your reasoning.

50. ADVERTISING A tub of pretzels has a label stating "Guaranteed to contain over 350 pretzels!" The full tub has a mass of 2.15 kg. The mass of one pretzel is 5.7 g. The mass of the empty tub is 0.43 kg. *Describe* how you could verify the statement without counting the pretzels.

51. 🔵 CHALLENGE A football field, including the end zones, is 120 yards long. Use the fact that 1 inch = 2.54 centimeters to find a rule for converting x yards to y meters. Find the length of the field in meters.

52. CHALLENGE The speed of light is 3×10^8 m/sec. Write this speed in miles per hour. If the Sun is about 150 million kilometers away, then how long (in seconds) does it take light from the Sun to reach Earth? (*Hint:* 1 mile ≈ 1609 meters)

Get-Ready

Prepare for
Lesson 5.1 in
Exs. 53–56

Find the value of the power. *(p. 15)*

53. 3^3 **54.** 2^6 **55.** 10 squared   **56.** 4 cubed

Multiply. Use estimation to check that the product is reasonable.

57. 2.8×0.9 *(p. 181)*   **58.** 7.318×5.1 *(p. 181)*   **59.** 1000×3.492 *(p. 193)*

60. ★ **MULTIPLE CHOICE** Which expression is equivalent to $3(9) - 9(2)$? *(p. 175)*

    Ⓐ $9(3 - 2)$ **Ⓑ** $3(9 - 2)$ **Ⓒ** $27(9 - 2)$ **Ⓓ** $9(18 - 3)$

QUIZ *for Lessons 4.5–4.8*

Find the product or quotient using mental math. *(p. 193)*

1. 4.56×100 **2.** 9.75×0.01 **3.** 0.18×10

4. $29.5 \div 0.001$ **5.** $100 \div 1000$ **6.** 988.1×0.1

Find the quotient. Round to the nearest tenth if necessary. *(p. 198)*

7. $27.9 \div 0.09$ **8.** $50.8 \div 0.5$ **9.** $0.748 \div 0.22$

10. $0.435 \div 0.18$ **11.** $65.5 \div 1.25$ **12.** $12.04 \div 2.3$

13. Is the capacity of a picnic jug measured in *liters* or *milliliters*? *(p. 203)*

14. Is the mass of a CD measured in *kilograms* or *grams*? *(p. 203)*

Copy and complete the statement. *(p. 207)*

15. $10 \text{ L} = \underline{\ ?\ } \text{ mL}$ **16.** $\underline{\ ?\ } \text{ mm} = 2 \text{ km}$ **17.** $\underline{\ ?\ } \text{ kL} = 5.1 \text{ L}$

18. $\underline{\ ?\ } \text{ mg} = 0.215 \text{ g}$ **19.** $887 \text{ mg} = \underline{\ ?\ } \text{ kg}$ **20.** $26.5 \text{ m} = \underline{\ ?\ } \text{ km}$

Brain Game

Chemistry Experiment

You want to make a solution for a chemistry experiment, but the graduated cylinder that you need has been broken. You need to measure out 500 mL of water for the solution.

You have a container for the solution, an unmarked 300 mL container, and an unmarked 1 L container. How can you measure out the right amount of water for the solution?

Lessons 4.5–4.8

1. **MULTI-STEP PROBLEM** You are comparing two frozen fruit smoothie kits. Kit A makes two 2-liter batches of smoothies. Kit B makes twelve 350-milliliter glasses of smoothies.

   a. Find the total amount of fruit smoothies, in liters, that Kit A makes. Find the total amount of fruit smoothies, in milliliters, that Kit B makes.

   b. Change the amount that Kit A makes to milliliters.

   c. Compare the two amounts. Which mix will make more smoothies?

2. **MULTI-STEP PROBLEM** A deck of 54 playing cards (including jokers) is 1.8 cm thick. Each card is 5.5 cm × 8.5 cm. A 900 page book has 450 leaves and is 3 cm thick.

   a. How thick is each playing card? Round your answer to the nearest hundredth.

   b. How thick is each leaf of the book? Round your answer to the nearest thousandth.

   c. How many times thicker is a playing card than a book leaf? Round to the nearest tenth.

3. **OPEN-ENDED** You baby-sit on Fridays and Saturdays for $5.25 per hour. You want to save enough money to buy a $73.50 jacket. Find a combination of days and hours to work that will enable you to buy the jacket in 4 weeks.

4. **SHORT RESPONSE** The fish actually measures 16 millimeters in length. In a poster-sized photo, the fish appears to be 1.6 meters long.

   Rewrite the enlarged length in millimeters. Then use a power of 10 to describe how the two sizes are related.

5. **GRIDDED ANSWER** Chang buys 5.25 liters of punch for a party. Fifteen glasses of punch are poured, with 300 mL in each glass. How many more 300 mL glasses can be poured?

6. **EXTENDED RESPONSE** The table shows the average salaries for professional baseball players in selected years.

Year	Average salary (millions of $)
1967	0.019
1980	0.1
1990	0.6
2000	1.9
2001	2.1
2002	2.3
2003	2.4

   a. About how many times greater was the average salary in 2003 than in 1967?

   b. Between which two years did the average salary increase by a power of 10? In how many years did this happen?

   c. Suppose from 2003 to 2036 the average salary increases by the same power of ten you found in part (b). What would be the 2036 salary, written as a whole number?

   d. Do you think this is likely? *Explain* your reasoning.

7. **OPEN-ENDED** Write a real-world division problem that has a quotient of 2.6. Explain how you found the divisor and the dividend.

REVIEW KEY VOCABULARY

- commutative property of multiplication, *p. 171*
- associative property of multiplication, *p. 171*
- distributive property, *p. 175*

- mass, *p. 203*
- gram, *p. 203*
- milligram, *p. 203*
- kilogram, *p. 203*

- capacity, *p. 204*
- liter, *p. 204*
- milliliter, *p. 204*
- kiloliter, *p. 204*

VOCABULARY EXERCISES

1. Which property is illustrated by $3.1 \times 24 \times 3 = 3.1 \times 3 \times 24$?

2. Copy and complete: The __?__ property of multiplication states that the value of a product does not depend on how the numbers are grouped.

3. Which property allows you to write $3(70 + 0.8)$ as $3(70) + 3(0.8)$?

4. Explain the first step needed to find the quotient $31.97 \div 2.78$.

5. Give three examples of metric units used to measure mass.

6. Give three examples of metric units used to measure capacity.

7. Copy and complete: To change from milliliters to liters, you divide by __?__.

8. Copy and complete: To change from kilograms to grams, you __?__ by 1000.

9. Copy and complete: Any question dealing with the volume of a container involves measuring its __?__.

REVIEW EXAMPLES AND EXERCISES

4.1 Multiplying Decimals and Whole Numbers
pp. 169–173

EXAMPLE

Find the product 9×0.008.

Because 0.008 has 3 decimal places, the answer will have 3 decimal places.

$$
\begin{array}{r}
0.008 \\
\times \quad 9 \\
\hline
0.072
\end{array}
$$

3 decimal places

Write zero as a placeholder so that the answer has 3 decimal places.

▶ **Answer** The product $9 \times 0.008 = 0.072$.

EXERCISES

Find the product.

**SEE EXAMPLES
1 AND 4**
on pp. 169–171
for Exs. 10–15

10. 1.742×3 **11.** 0.05×12 **12.** 16×0.78 **13.** 0.004×23

Tell whether the *commutative* or *associative* property of multiplication allows you to rewrite the problem as shown.

14. $(2 \times 5.4) \times 6.3 = 2 \times (5.4 \times 6.3)$ **15.** $7 \times 3.76 \times 15 = 3.76 \times 7 \times 15$

4.2 The Distributive Property
pp. 175–179

EXAMPLE

$$4(70 + 9) = 4(70) + 4(9) \qquad \text{Use the distributive property.}$$
$$= 280 + 36 \qquad \text{Multiply.}$$
$$= 316 \qquad \text{Add.}$$

EXERCISES

**SEE EXAMPLES
2 AND 3**
on p. 176
for Exs. 16–23

Use the distributive property to evaluate the expression.

16. $5(50 + 8)$ **17.** $8(30 - 7)$ **18.** $6(70 - 0.5)$ **19.** $10(9.7 + 5.6)$

Use the distributive property and mental math to find the product.

20. $2(98)$ **21.** $9(71)$ **22.** $4(93)$ **23.** $11(43)$

4.3 Multiplying Decimals
pp. 181–185

EXAMPLE

$$\begin{array}{r} 2.47 \\ \times\, 1.3 \\ \hline 741 \\ 247 \\ \hline 3.211 \end{array}$$

2 decimal places
+ 1 decimal place

3 decimal places

Check Estimate:
$2.47 \times 1.3 \approx 2.5 \times 1 = 2.5$
2.5 is close to 3.2, so the answer is reasonable.

EXERCISES

Find the product. Check that your answer is reasonable.

SEE EXAMPLE 3
on p. 182
for Exs. 24–31

24. 1.4×0.3 **25.** 5.61×7.2 **26.** 0.213×0.4 **27.** 21.1×0.005

28. 4.57×0.799 **29.** 25.27×8.02 **30.** 294.7×5.0025 **31.** 0.0019×1.05

4.4 Dividing by Whole Numbers

pp. 186–191

EXAMPLE

Find the quotient 40 ÷ 13. Round to the nearest hundredth.

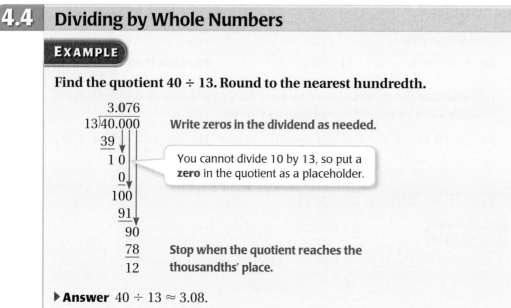

Write zeros in the dividend as needed.

You cannot divide 10 by 13, so put a **zero** in the quotient as a placeholder.

Stop when the quotient reaches the thousandths' place.

▶ **Answer** $40 \div 13 \approx 3.08$.

EXERCISES

Divide. Round to the nearest tenth if necessary.

SEE EXAMPLES 2 AND 3 on p. 187 for Exs. 32–41

32. $3\overline{)21.9}$ **33.** $5\overline{)32.64}$ **34.** $4\overline{)13}$ **35.** $105\overline{)22}$

36. $25\overline{)1102.5}$ **37.** $33\overline{)2153.25}$ **38.** $12\overline{)9.84}$ **39.** $2\overline{)2.012}$

40. Shopping You buy 11 identical paintbrushes for a total of $25.19. How much does each paintbrush cost?

41. Dining If five people go out for dinner and their bill is $40.25, how much does each person pay if the bill is divided evenly?

4.5 Multiplying and Dividing by Powers of Ten

pp. 193–197

EXAMPLE

Find the product or quotient using mental math.

a. $1357.25 \times 0.001 = 1.35725$ Move decimal point 3 places to the left.

$= 1.35725$

b. $46.9 \div 0.01 = 4690.$ Move decimal point 2 places to the right.

$= 4690$

EXERCISES

Find the product or quotient using mental math.

**SEE EXAMPLES
1, 2, AND 3**
on pp. 193–194
for Exs. 42–50

42. 38.06×10

43. 459.1×0.01

44. $621.37 \div 10$

45. $97.8 \div 0.001$

46. 63.65×0.1

47. 123.4×100

48. $221.4 \div 100$

49. $15.7 \div 0.01$

50. Entertainment The pictograph shows the numbers of adults who attended certain events in 2002. How many adults went to an amusement park?

Entertainment		
Movies	☺☺☺☺☺☺☺☺☺☺☺(	12.35
Sporting events	☺☺☺☺☺☺(	7.21
Amusement parks	☺☺☺☺☺☺☺☺(	8.65

☺ = 10,000,000 people

4.6 Dividing by Decimals

pp. 198–202

> **EXAMPLE**

Find the quotient $34 \div 0.02$.

SOLUTION

First multiply the divisor and dividend by 100.

Then divide.

$$\begin{array}{r} 1700. \\ 2\overline{)3400} \\ \underline{2} \\ 14 \\ \underline{14} \\ 0 \end{array}$$

Sometimes you need to write zeros as placeholders in the quotient.

▸ **Answer** $34 \div 0.02 = 1700$.

EXERCISES

Divide. Round to the nearest tenth if necessary.

**SEE EXAMPLES
1, 2, AND 3**
on pp. 198–199
for Exs. 51–64

51. $620 \div 0.58$

52. $11.8 \div 0.27$

53. $38 \div 1.6$

54. $303.2 \div 0.5$

55. $331 \div 0.93$

56. $1.52 \div 15.6$

57. $19 \div 6.4$

58. $18.2 \div 3.2$

59. $723 \div 0.48$

60. $3.69 \div 12.3$

61. $62 \div 3.2$

62. $3.24 \div 2$

63. Cost per Pound You pay \$11.06 for 2.8 pounds of beads at a craft store. What is the cost per pound of beads?

64. Gas Mileage Daniel drives his truck 254.25 miles and uses 22.5 gallons of gas. What is Daniel's car's gas mileage?

4.7 Mass and Capacity

pp. 203–206

EXAMPLE

Choose an appropriate metric unit to measure the mass of a bucket of sand.

SOLUTION

A kilogram is about the mass of this book and the mass of a bucket of sand would be at least the same as this book. So, kilograms is an appropriate unit of measure for the mass of a bucket of sand.

EXERCISES

Choose an appropriate metric unit to measure the item.

SEE EXAMPLES 1 AND 3 on pp. 203–204 for Exs. 65–68

65. mass of a toad

66. capacity of a coffee cup

67. Choosing Units An item has a capacity of 378 liters. Is it an *aquarium,* a *silo,* or a *scuba tank*? *Explain.*

68. Choosing Units Choose an appropriate unit to measure the mass of a pencil.

4.8 Changing Metric Units

pp. 207–212

EXAMPLE

Copy and complete the statement.

   a. $52 \text{ g} = \underline{\ ?\ } \text{ mg}$

      $52 \times 1000 = 52{,}000$

    ▶ **Answer** $52 \text{ g} = 52{,}000 \text{ mg}$

   b. $36.8 \text{ mL} = \underline{\ ?\ } \text{ L}$

      $36.8 \div 1000 = 0.0368$

    ▶ **Answer** $36.8 \text{ mL} = 0.0368 \text{ L}$

EXERCISES

Copy and complete the statement.

SEE EXAMPLES 1 AND 2 on p. 207 for Exs. 69–76

69. $24.5 \text{ L} = \underline{\ ?\ } \text{ kL}$

70. $21.2 \text{ kg} = \underline{\ ?\ } \text{ g}$

71. $20 \text{ mm} = \underline{\ ?\ } \text{ cm}$

72. $26 \text{ g} = \underline{\ ?\ } \text{ kg}$

73. $12.3 \text{ kL} = \underline{\ ?\ } \text{ L}$

74. $17 \text{ m} = \underline{\ ?\ } \text{ mm}$

75. Marine Biology Newborn blue whales are about 762 centimeters long. What is their length in meters?

76. Reptiles An Anaconda snake weighs 148,500 grams. What is the snake's weight in kilograms?

CHAPTER TEST

Multiply. Use estimation to check that the answer is reasonable.

1. 5.8×3 **2.** 9.2×17 **3.** 2.692×100 **4.** 3.115×8

5. 7.25×4.6 **6.** 12.46×3.2 **7.** 8.51×6.3 **8.** 13.77×0.04

Tell whether the commutative or associative property of multiplication allows you to rewrite the problem as shown.

9. $(3 \times 7.2) \times 2.1 = 3 \times (7.2 \times 2.1)$ **10.** $2 \times 6.82 \times 25 = 6.82 \times 2 \times 25$

11. Use the distributive property and mental math to find the product $9(4.8)$.

Divide. Round to the nearest tenth if necessary.

12. $28.95 \div 2$ **13.** $13.72 \div 4$ **14.** $9.4 \div 52$ **15.** $6 \div 16$

16. $10 \div 0.8$ **17.** $3.24 \div 0.6$ **18.** $109.2 \div 0.15$ **19.** $22.54 \div 0.23$

Find the product or quotient using mental math.

20. 13.77×1000 **21.** 12.46×0.01 **22.** $1.5 \div 100$ **23.** $6.25 \div 0.1$

Copy and complete the statement.

24. $0.9 \text{ g} = \underline{\ ?\ } \text{ mg}$ **25.** $98 \text{ m} = \underline{\ ?\ } \text{ km}$ **26.** $3200 \text{ L} = \underline{\ ?\ } \text{ kL}$

Copy and complete the statement with <, >, or =.

27. $4300 \text{ L} \underline{\ ?\ } 4.39 \text{ kL}$ **28.** $215 \text{ kg} \underline{\ ?\ } 2150 \text{ g}$ **29.** $321 \text{ mm} \underline{\ ?\ } 3.21 \text{ cm}$

30. **AUTO RACING** The distance around the racetrack at Talladega Superspeedway in Alabama is about 2.66 miles. What is the total distance for 16 laps? 100 laps?

31. **WHALES** Eight whales have been born at an aquarium. Their total mass is 1300 kilograms. Find the mean mass of the whales.

32. **CHOOSING UNITS** Do you think the mass of a desk lamp should be measured in *milligrams*, *grams*, or *kilograms*? *Explain.*

33. **SOUP** A can of soup contains 710 milligrams of sodium. How many grams of sodium are in the can?

CONTEXT-BASED MULTIPLE CHOICE QUESTIONS

Some of the information you need to solve a context-based multiple choice question may appear in a table, a diagram, or a graph.

PROBLEM 1

STEP 1
Read the problem carefully. Decide how you can use the information in the diagram to solve the problem.

The rectangular floor in the diagram is to be painted in the checkerboard pattern shown. What is the area of the portion of floor that is to be painted blue?

Ⓐ 6.3 square feet

Ⓑ 11.8 square feet

Ⓒ 48.4 square feet

Ⓓ 50.4 square feet

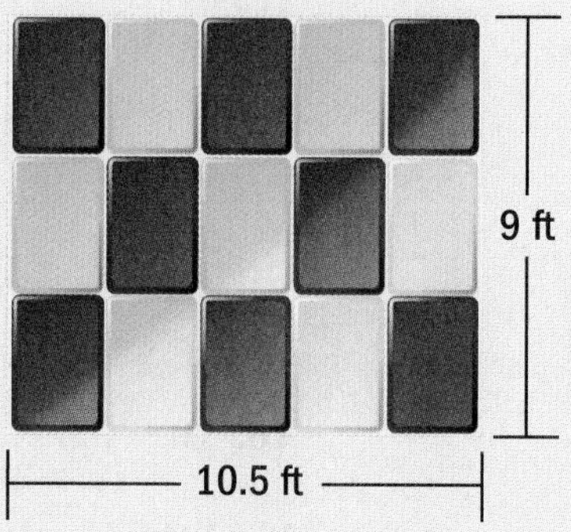

9 ft

10.5 ft

Plan

INTERPRET THE DIAGRAM From the diagram, you can see that the floor is divided into 15 rectangles of equal size, 8 blue and 7 green. The diagram also shows that the floor is 10.5 feet long and 9 feet wide. You can use this information to calculate the area of the blue portion of the floor.

Solution

STEP 2
Find the area of the entire floor.

The area of the entire floor is *length* · *width* = 10.5×9.

$$\begin{array}{r} 10.5 \\ \times\ \ \ 9 \\ \hline 94.5 \end{array}$$

STEP 3
Find the area of one rectangle in the pattern.

Divide the total area by 15 to find the area of one rectangle in the pattern.

$$\begin{array}{r} 6.3 \\ 15\overline{)94.5} \\ \underline{90} \\ 45 \\ \underline{45} \\ 0 \end{array}$$

STEP 4
Multiply by 8 to find the area of the blue portion of the floor.

There are 8 blue rectangles, each with an area of 6.3 square feet. So the area of the blue portion of the floor is $6.3 \times 8 =$ 50.4 square feet.

The correct answer is D. Ⓐ Ⓑ Ⓒ Ⓓ

PROBLEM 2

You are hiking at Glacier National Park using the trail map shown. You hike from the Avalanche Creek Campground to McDonald Falls. About how many miles do you hike?

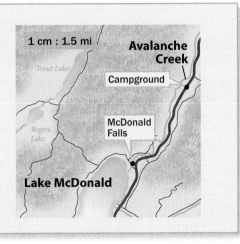

STEP 1
Decide how to read the map to solve the problem.

Ⓐ 3.71 miles   Ⓑ 3.75 miles

Ⓒ 4.1 miles   Ⓓ 31 miles

Plan

INTERPRET THE MAP The scale on the map is 1 cm : 1.5 miles. Each centimeter on the map represents 1.5 miles on the trail. Measure the distance between the Avalanche Creek Campground and McDonald Falls. Then multiply this distance by 1.5 to find the actual distance.

Solution

STEP 2
Use a ruler.

Using a ruler, you can find that the distance between the two points on the map is about 2.5 centimeters.

STEP 3
Multiply by 1.5 to find the actual distance.

Because each centimeter represents 1.5 miles, multiply 2.5 by 1.5 to find the actual distance: $2.5 \times 1.5 = 3.75$.

So, the actual distance that you hike is about 3.75 miles.
The correct answer is C. Ⓐ Ⓑ ● Ⓓ

EXERCISES

Use the table of scores for the winning pie in a baking competition. Six judges scored the pie on a scale of 1 to 10 in two categories.

1. What was the winning pie's mean score in the taste category?

   Ⓐ 9.0   Ⓑ 9.5   Ⓒ 10   Ⓓ 57

2. Which judge gave the *highest* combined mean score?

   Ⓐ Judge A   Ⓑ Judge B

   Ⓒ Judge C   Ⓓ Judge D

Judge	Taste	Appearance
A	9.5	7.5
B	9.8	8.2
C	10	9.8
D	9.5	9.2
E	9.0	8.8
F	9.2	8.1

CONTEXT-BASED MULTIPLE CHOICE

1. The table shows the amount of different kinds of shellfish caught in 2000, and the value of each, in millions of dollars. What was the value, in dollars, of one pound of lobsters?

Type of shellfish	Millions of pounds caught	Value ($millions)
Clams	118	154
Crabs	299	405
Lobsters	83	301
Shrimp	332	690

(A) 3.63　　　　(B) 3.01

(C) 217　　　　(D) 301,000,000

2. You complete the first two segments of the bike race below in 4.5 hours. What is your average speed in miles per hour?

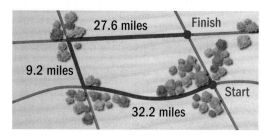

(A) 7.2　　　　(B) 8.2

(C) 9.2　　　　(D) 15.3

3. You have a punch recipe that calls for 1.5 liters of pineapple juice. A store only sells small bottles labeled as shown at the right. How many bottles do you need to buy?

(A) 1　　　　(B) 2

(C) 3　　　　(D) 4

4. Below is a scale drawing of a caterpillar. How long is the actual caterpillar?

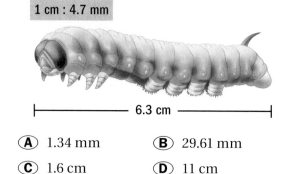

1 cm : 4.7 mm

6.3 cm

(A) 1.34 mm　　　　(B) 29.61 mm

(C) 1.6 cm　　　　(D) 11 cm

5. In a bulk foods store, peanuts cost $1.89 per pound. You fill a bag with peanuts and place it on the scale shown. What is the total cost of the peanuts?

(A) $5.09　　　　(B) $5.67

(C) $6.05　　　　(D) $60.48

6. Every year the Department of Transportation checks the condition of the roads. The graph shows the number of miles of urban interstates that were in various conditions in 2003. How many miles of roads were in better than fair condition?

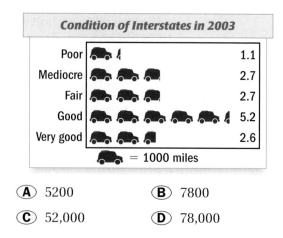

Condition of Interstates in 2003		
Poor		1.1
Mediocre		2.7
Fair		2.7
Good		5.2
Very good		2.6

= 1000 miles

(A) 5200　　　　(B) 7800

(C) 52,000　　　　(D) 78,000

GRIDDED ANSWER

7. A tornado typically moves about 48,000 meters in an hour. How many kilometers will it move in 3 hours?

8. There were six events in the men's finals of the 2003 World Gymnastics Championships. The table shows the top score in each event. What was the mean top score, rounded to three decimal places?

Event	Score
Floor	9.762
Pommel horse	9.762
Still rings	9.787
Vault	9.818
Parallel bars	9.825
High bar	9.775

9. Peaches cost $1.38 per pound, but you have a coupon for $.50 off per pound. You buy 3.5 pounds of peaches. How much, in dollars, do you pay?

10. You are putting up wallpaper on a wall that is 15 feet wide and 8.5 feet high. A single roll of wallpaper contains 32 square feet of wallpaper. How many rolls do you need?

SHORT RESPONSE

11. Which item below has the greater capacity? What would be an appropriate unit to measure the capacity of each item? *Explain.*

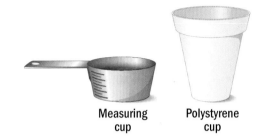

Measuring cup   Polystyrene cup

12. Michelle buys 5 yards of fabric for $13.45 and 7 yards of another fabric for $17.08. Which fabric is a better buy? *Explain.*

13. About 20,000 of the earthquakes that occur each year are recorded by the U.S. National Earthquake Information Center. The portion of these earthquakes that have no magnitude is 0.15. Find the number of earthquakes that have no magnitude. Will the number of earthquakes with no magnitude be more or less if the portion is 0.2? *Explain* without doing calculations.

EXTENDED RESPONSE

14. A dish filled with marbles has a mass of 1.916 kilograms. The dish's mass is 0.32 kilograms when empty. The mass of one marble is about 4.2 grams.

  a. About how many marbles are in the dish?

  b. You place the dish filled with marbles onto a balance scale that has a 2 kilogram weight on the other side. How many more marbles do you need to add to the dish to make the scale balance? *Justify* your answer.

15. The diagram shows the standard proportions of the American flag. You are painting a flag that is 13 centimeters wide using this model.

  a. What should the length of your flag be?

  b. Find the dimensions of the blue rectangle on your flag. *Explain* your reasoning.

  c. You find a miniature flag that measures 9.88 centimeters by 5.2 centimeters. Does this flag have the same measure relationships as your painted flag? *Explain.*

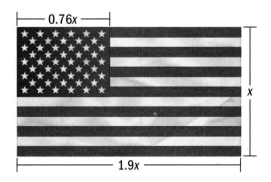

Find the sum, difference, product, or quotient.

1. $129 - 62$ *(p. 3)*

2. $125 + 416$ *(p. 3)*

3. $671 - 98$ *(p. 3)*

4. 36×18 *(p. 3)*

5. $312 \div 6$ *(p. 3)*

6. $3.8 + 7.2$ *(p. 148)*

7. $12.8 - 5.5$ *(p. 148)*

8. 8.3×3 *(p. 169)*

9. 5×4.7 *(p. 169)*

10. 7.04×0.3 *(p. 181)*

11. $10.2 \div 6$ *(p. 186)*

12. 3.75×1000 *(p. 193)*

13. $6.24 \div 0.01$ *(p. 193)*

14. $3.36 \div 0.14$ *(p. 198)*

15. $7.9 \div 0.4$ *(p. 198)*

Evaluate the expression. *(p. 21)*

16. $17 - 2 \times 7$

17. $12 - 8 + 3$

18. 5×42

19. $8 \times (4 - 1) \div 6$

20. $\dfrac{6^2}{5 + 7}$

21. $\dfrac{55 - 6}{1 + 2 \times 3}$

Make a frequency table and a line plot of the data. *(p. 76)*

22. Number of siblings in friends' families: 2, 0, 1, 2, 3, 4, 5, 3, 1, 1, 0, 2

23. Number of miles driven: 400, 400, 450, 500, 475, 420, 400, 426, 475

Graph the point on a coordinate grid. *(p. 88)*

24. $(6, 1)$

25. $(0, 4)$

26. $(2, 8)$

27. $(5, 0)$

Find the mean, median, mode(s), and range of the data. *(p. 99)*

28. 2, 3, 4, 6, 7, 2, 9, 7, 1, 8

29. 22, 32, 26, 22, 44, 160, 28, 48, 22, 36

Order the numbers from least to greatest. *(p. 130)*

30. 3.2, 3.04, 3.16, 3.02, 3.056, 3.1

31. 0.039, 0.3, 0.309, 0.0386, 0.003

Round the decimal as specified. *(p. 137)*

32. 7.0851 (nearest tenth)

33. 0.00297 (leading digit)

34. 0.1043 (nearest hundredth)

35. 8.00662 (nearest thousandth)

Use the distributive property to evaluate the expression. *(p. 175)*

36. $5(30 + 7)$

37. $100(8.2 - 4)$

38. $6(11 + 1.5)$

Choose an appropriate metric unit to measure the item. *(p. 203)*

39. mass of a turkey

40. length of a nail

41. capacity of a car fuel tank

Copy and complete the statement. *(p. 207)*

42. $0.8 \text{ g} = \underline{\ ?\ } \text{ mg}$

43. $82 \text{ m} = \underline{\ ?\ } \text{ km}$

44. $4600 \text{ L} = \underline{\ ?\ } \text{ kL}$

45. $8.2 \text{ L} = \underline{\ ?\ } \text{ mL}$

46. $9 \text{ mm} = \underline{\ ?\ } \text{ cm}$

47. $9.01 \text{ kg} = \underline{\ ?\ } \text{ g}$

48. **TRAINS** The length of a train with an engine and three cars can be represented by the expression $n + 3c$, where n is the length, in feet, of the engine and c is the length, in feet, of a car. An engine is 64 feet long and a car is 90 feet long. What is the train's total length? *(p. 29)*

49. Measure to find the length and width, in centimeters, of the rectangle. Then find its perimeter and its area. *(pp. 59, 66)*

HOMEWORK **The double bar graph shows the total numbers of hours the students in Mr. Frank's and Ms. McCarty's classes spent doing homework each week for four weeks.** *(p. 83)*

50. About how many hours did Mr. Frank's class spend studying in Week 2?

51. Which class spent more hours doing homework in Week 3?

52. During which week was the difference in homework hours between the two classes the greatest? *Explain* your reasoning.

53. Which class spent more time doing homework? *Explain.*

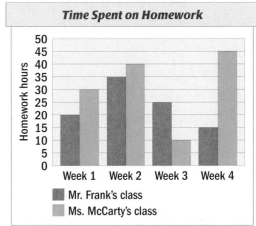

54. **HOUSES** The ages, in years, of 8 houses in a neighborhood are 28, 20, 28, 26, 20, 63, 23, and 24. Find the mean, median, mode(s), and range of the data. Which average best represents the data? *Explain.* *(p. 99)*

FOOD **The table shows the costs of a 2 kilogram sack of potatoes in five cities.**

City	Cost
Dublin	$3.31
London	$3.54
New York	$1.82
Tokyo	$6.06
Paris	$3.19

55. Round each cost to the nearest dime. *(p. 137)*

56. Order the costs from least to greatest. In which city are potatoes most expensive? least expensive? *(p. 130)*

57. How much less does a sack of potatoes cost in Paris than in London? *(p. 148)*

58. **EMPLOYMENT** You earn $7.50 an hour. How much will you be paid for 18 hours of work? *(p. 169)*

59. **STATE POPULATION** In 2003, the population of California was about 35.5 million. Write the population as a whole number. *(p. 193)*

60. **MAP READING** On a map, 1 centimeter represents an actual distance of 300 meters. You measure 5.5 centimeters on the map. How many kilometers does it represent? *(p. 207)*

5 Number Patterns and Fractions

Animated Math
at classzone.com

Get-Ready Games

Review Prerequisite Skills by playing *Follow the Clues* and *Mystery Numbers*.

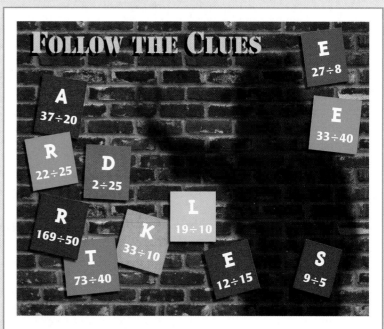

FOLLOW THE CLUES

E	$27 \div 8$
E	$33 \div 40$
A	$37 \div 20$
R	$22 \div 25$
D	$2 \div 25$
L	$19 \div 10$
R	$169 \div 50$
K	$33 \div 10$
T	$73 \div 40$
E	$12 \div 15$
S	$9 \div 5$

Skill Focus: Dividing whole numbers and ordering decimals

- Each clue shown above contains an expression and a letter. Evaluate the expression on each clue.

- Order your answers from least to greatest. Write the letters associated with the answers in the same order. These letters spell out the name of the type of hat Sherlock Holmes wears.

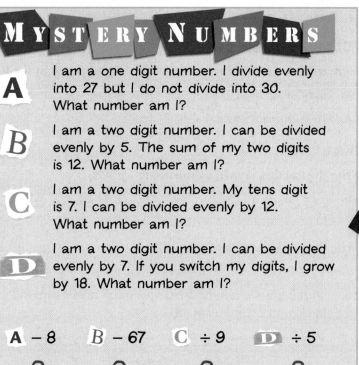

MYSTERY NUMBERS

A I am a one digit number. I divide evenly into 27 but I do not divide into 30. What number am I?

B I am a two digit number. I can be divided evenly by 5. The sum of my two digits is 12. What number am I?

C I am a two digit number. My tens digit is 7. I can be divided evenly by 12. What number am I?

D I am a two digit number. I can be divided evenly by 7. If you switch my digits, I grow by 18. What number am I?

A – 8   **B** – 67   **C** ÷ 9   **D** ÷ 5

?   ?   ?   ?

Skill Focus: Understanding place value and dividing whole numbers

- Use the clues to find the mystery numbers.

- Use the mystery numbers to evaluate the expressions above.

- The values of the expressions, written in the order shown, give the year in which Sir Arthur Conan Doyle published the first Sherlock Holmes story.

Stop and Think

1. **CRITICAL THINKING** In *Follow the Clues*, could you figure out the hidden word by using estimation rather than exact division? Why or why not?

2. **WRITING** Pick a two digit number. Write a few clues about it like the ones in *Mystery Numbers*. Then see if someone else can guess the number.

Review Prerequisite Skills

REVIEW WORDS
- **factor,** *p. 15*
- **inch,** *p. 59*
- **foot,** *p. 59*
- **yard,** *p. 59*
- **fraction,** *p. 753*
- **numerator,** *p. 753*
- **denominator,** *p. 753*

VOCABULARY CHECK

Copy and complete using a review word from the list at the left.

1. 12 inches = 1 __?__   **2.** 3 feet = 1 __?__   **3.** 36 __?__ = 1 yard

4. The numbers 6 and 4 are __?__ of 24.

SKILL CHECK

Write the fraction shown by the model. *(p. 753)*

5. 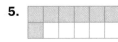   **6.**

Write the product as a power. *(p. 15)*

7. $5 \times 5 \times 5 \times 5$ **8.** $10 \times 10 \times 10$ **9.** 11×11

10. Estimate the length of the straw to the nearest inch. Then measure to check your estimate. *(p. 59)*

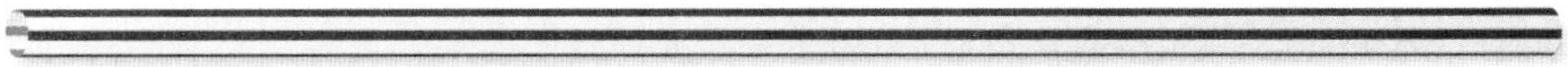

Use a number line to order the decimals from least to greatest. *(p. 130)*

11. 1.4, 1.8, 1.5, 1.6, 1.7, 2   **12.** 2.7, 2.07, 2.77, 2.71, 2.17

13. 3.28, 2.83, 3.82, 8.23, 2.38   **14.** 7.24, 7.31, 7.03, 7.26, 7.17

@HomeTutor   Prerequisite skills practice at classzone.com

Notetaking Skills   Learning Vocabulary

In each chapter you will learn a new notetaking skill. In Chapter 5 you will apply the strategy of learning vocabulary to Example 1 on p. 243.

You need to learn the complete and accurate meanings of vocabulary words. Copy the words from each lesson's Key Vocabulary in your notebook with a definition and an example as shown below.

Factor   a whole number other than zero that is multiplied by another whole number to give a product

Example

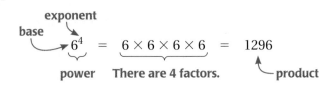

exponent

base

6^4 = $6 \times 6 \times 6 \times 6$ = 1296

power   There are 4 factors.   product

INVESTIGATION
Use before Lesson 5.1

GOAL
Use number sense to test whether 2, 3, 6, and 9 are factors of a number.

MATERIALS
• paper
• pencil

5.1 Divisibility Rules

You can use rules to decide whether certain numbers are factors of another number. For example, 2 is a factor of a number if the number is even.

EXPLORE Copy and complete the table to decide if 3 is a factor of each number.

STEP 1 **Decide** whether 3 is a factor of 18. Because $18 = 6 \times 3$, you know 3 is a factor of 18.

Number	Is 3 a factor?	Sum of digits	Is 3 a factor of the sum?
18	Yes	9	Yes
60	?	?	?
80	?	?	?
99	?	?	?
315	?	?	?
329	?	?	?

STEP 2 **Add** the digits in the number 18: $1 + 8 = 9$.

STEP 3 **Decide** whether 3 is a factor of the sum from Step 2.

Because $9 = 3 \times 3$, you know 3 is a factor of 9.

STEP 4 **Repeat** Steps 1–3 for all the numbers in the first column of the table.

PRACTICE Use the table above.

1. Decide whether 2 is a factor of each number in the first column.

2. Follow the steps above to create another table that shows which of the numbers have 9 as a factor.

DRAW CONCLUSIONS

3. **WRITING** Look back at the tables you made. Write a rule that tells you whether 3 is a factor of a given number. Write a similar rule for 9.

4. **REASONING** If 2 and 3 are factors of a number, is 6 always a factor of the number? *Explain.*

5.1 Prime Factorization

Before	You found products of whole numbers.
Now	You'll write whole numbers as the product of prime factors.
Why?	So you can form groups, as with dancers in Example 1.

KEY VOCABULARY

- **divisible,** *p. 230*
- **prime number,** *p. 231*
- **composite number,** *p. 231*
- **prime factorization,** *p. 232*
- **factor tree,** *p. 232*

Dancers A dance teacher is planning a dance for a show. The dancers will be in rows with the same number of dancers in each row. Does a group of 12 dancers or a group of 14 dancers offer more possibilities?

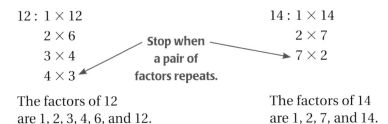

EXAMPLE 1 Finding Factors

To answer the question above, list all the factors of 12 and 14 by writing each number as a product of two numbers in as many ways as possible.

$$12 : 1 \times 12 \qquad\qquad 14 : 1 \times 14$$
$$2 \times 6 \qquad\qquad\qquad 2 \times 7$$
$$3 \times 4 \qquad\qquad\qquad 7 \times 2$$
$$4 \times 3$$

Stop when a pair of factors repeats.

The factors of 12 are 1, 2, 3, 4, 6, and 12.

The factors of 14 are 1, 2, 7, and 14.

▶ **Answer** A group of 12 dancers offers more possibilities than a group of 14 dancers, because 12 has more factors than 14.

Divisibility A number is **divisible** by another number if that other number is a factor of the first. Divisibility rules such as those given below can help you find factors.

KEY CONCEPT *For Your Notebook*

Divisibility Rules for 2, 3, 5, 6, 9, and 10

A whole number is divisible by:

- 2 if the number is even.
- 3 if the sum of its digits is divisible by 3.
- 5 if it ends with 5 or 0.

- 6 if it is even and divisible by 3.
- 9 if the sum of its digits is divisible by 9.
- 10 if it ends with 0.

EXAMPLE 2 Using Divisibility Rules

READING
You can think of Example 2 as asking if 60 is divisible by 2, 3, 5, 6, 9, and 10. Then you can use divisibility rules to solve the problem.

Food Production Bagels are cooked in batches of 60. Can the batches be divided into groups that contain 2 bagels each? 3 bagels? 5 bagels? 6 bagels? 9 bagels? 10 bagels?

SOLUTION

60 is even, so it is divisible by 2.

$6 + 0 = 6$, and 6 is divisible by 3, but not by 9. So, 60 is divisible by 3, but it is not divisible by 9.

60 ends with 0, so it is divisible by 5 and by 10.

60 is even and divisible by 3, so it is divisible by 6.

▶ **Answer** The bagels can be divided into equal groups containing 2, 3, 5, 6, and 10 bagels, but not 9 bagels.

Primes and Composites A **prime number** is a whole number greater than 1 whose only factors are 1 and itself. A **composite number** is a whole number greater than 1 that has factors other than 1 and itself. The number 1 is neither prime nor composite.

EXAMPLE 3 Classifying as Prime or Composite

ANOTHER WAY
You can also tell if a number is composite by using divisibility rules. For example, 51 is divisible by 3. So, 3 is a factor of 51, and 51 is composite.

Tell whether the number is *prime* or *composite*.

a. 51

List the factors of 51: 1, 3, 17, 51

▶ **Answer** 51 has factors other than 1 and itself, so 51 is composite.

b. 59

List the factors of 59: 1, 59

▶ **Answer** 59 is prime, because its only factors are 1 and itself.

✓ **GUIDED PRACTICE** for Examples 1, 2, and 3

List all the factors of the number.

1. 8   **2.** 9   **3.** 15   **4.** 18

Test the number for divisibility by 2, 3, 5, 6, 9, and 10.

5. 100   **6.** 456   **7.** 783   **8.** 1584

Tell whether the number is *prime* or *composite*.

9. 11   **10.** 13   **11.** 14   **12.** 35

13. 29   **14.** 16   **15.** 10   **16.** 31

Prime Factorization Writing the **prime factorization** of a number means writing the number as the product of prime numbers. You can use a diagram called a **factor tree** to write a factorization of a number. You must continue factoring until only prime factors appear in the product.

⭐ **EXAMPLE 4** Standardized Test Practice

What is the prime factorization of 180?

A $2 \times 3 \times 5$ **B** $2 \times 3^2 \times 5$ **C** $4 \times 5 \times 9$ **D** $2^2 \times 3^2 \times 5$

ELIMINATE CHOICES
The prime factorization must consist of prime numbers, so choice C can be eliminated.

SOLUTION

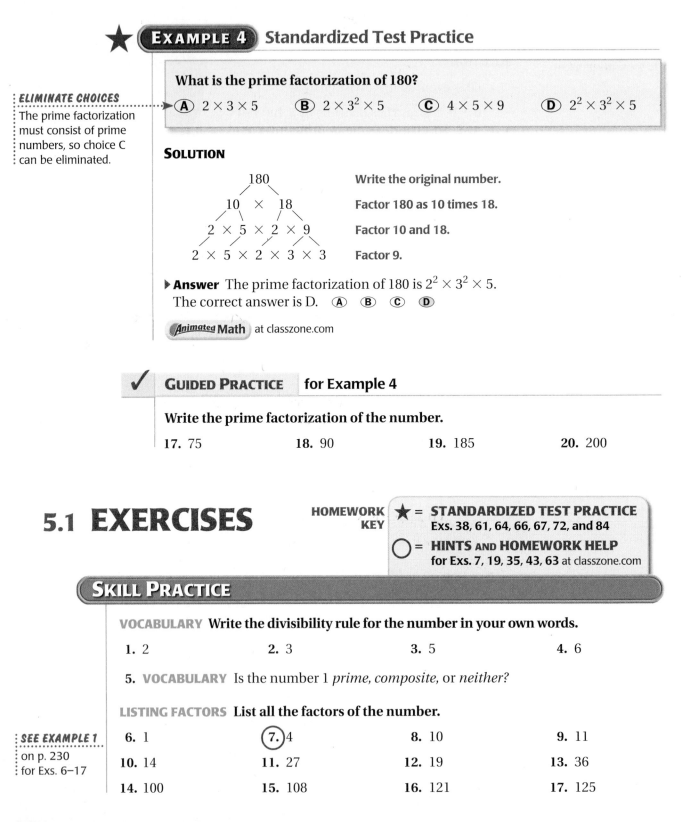

180 — Write the original number.

10×18 — Factor 180 as 10 times 18.

$2 \times 5 \times 2 \times 9$ — Factor 10 and 18.

$2 \times 5 \times 2 \times 3 \times 3$ — Factor 9.

▶ **Answer** The prime factorization of 180 is $2^2 \times 3^2 \times 5$.
The correct answer is D.   ⓐ Ⓑ Ⓒ **Ⓓ**

Animated **Math** at classzone.com

✓ **GUIDED PRACTICE** for Example 4

Write the prime factorization of the number.

17. 75   **18.** 90   **19.** 185   **20.** 200

5.1 EXERCISES

HOMEWORK KEY

⭐ = **STANDARDIZED TEST PRACTICE**
Exs. 38, 61, 64, 66, 67, 72, and 84

◯ = **HINTS AND HOMEWORK HELP**
for Exs. 7, 19, 35, 43, 63 at classzone.com

SKILL PRACTICE

VOCABULARY Write the divisibility rule for the number in your own words.

1. 2   **2.** 3   **3.** 5   **4.** 6

5. VOCABULARY Is the number 1 *prime*, *composite*, or *neither*?

LISTING FACTORS List all the factors of the number.

SEE EXAMPLE 1
on p. 230
for Exs. 6–17

6. 1   **7.** 4   **8.** 10   **9.** 11

10. 14   **11.** 27   **12.** 19   **13.** 36

14. 100   **15.** 108   **16.** 121   **17.** 125

SEE EXAMPLE 2
on p. 231
for Exs. 18–25

DIVISIBILITY Test the number for divisibility by 2, 3, 5, 6, 9, and 10.

18. 140   **19.** 144   **20.** 282   **21.** 315

22. 1578   **23.** 4860   **24.** 8745   **25.** 9990

CLASSIFYING NUMBERS Tell whether the number is *prime* or *composite*.

SEE EXAMPLE 3
on p. 231
for Exs. 26–38

26. 4   **27.** 17   **28.** 5   **29.** 6

30. 7   **31.** 19   **32.** 28   **33.** 37

34. 49   **35.** 43   **36.** 107   **37.** 144

38. ★ **MULTIPLE CHOICE** Which of the following numbers is composite?

    A 11   **B** 17   **C** 20   **D** 23

MAKING FACTOR TREES Copy and complete the factor tree. Then write the prime factorization.

SEE EXAMPLE 4
on p. 232
for Exs. 39–50

39.
```
      42
     /  \
   ? × ?
  /    / \
 2 × ? × 7
```

40.
```
      68
     /  \
    2 × ?
   /    / \
  ? × 2 × ?
```

41.
```
         81
        /  \
      ? × 9
     /    / \
  ? × 3 × ? × 3
```

PRIME FACTORIZATIONS Write the prime factorization of the number.

42. 39   **43.** 55   **44.** 63   **45.** 48

46. 105   **47.** 121   **48.** 150   **49.** 165

50. **ERROR ANALYSIS** Describe and correct the error made in the prime factorization.

```
        18
       /  \
      2 × 9
      |   / \
  1 × 2 × 3 × 3
```
$$18 = 1 \times 2 \times 3^2$$

NUMBER SENSE Tell whether the statement is *true* or *false*. Explain.

51. Any number that is divisible by 6 is divisible by 2.

52. Any number that is divisible by 5 is divisible by 10.

53. All prime numbers are odd.

54. All multiples of 3 are composite.

USING DIVISIBILITY RULES Find the least number that is divisible by the given numbers.

55. 2, 6, and 9   **56.** 2, 3, and 5   **57.** 2, 5, and 7

58. 3, 5, and 9   **59.** 6, 9, and 10   **60.** 5, 6, and 7

61. ★ **OPEN-ENDED MATH** List 10 prime numbers between 100 and 200.

62. **CHALLENGE** Find all the numbers between 30 and 40 that are composite and have prime factors that add up to 12.

63. **FITNESS** A fitness instructor needs to arrange 80 people in equal rows. Can the instructor arrange them in rows of 6? Why or why not?

64. ★ **SHORT RESPONSE** *Explain* why the factor tree at the right is not complete. Copy and complete the factor tree in two different ways to write the prime factorization of 450. Compare the results.

450
25 × 18

65. **MARCHING BAND** You are planning a half-time show for your school's marching band. There are 75 musicians in the band, and you want to divide them into groups of equal size to make different formations. Which of the following group sizes are possible? *Justify* your answer.

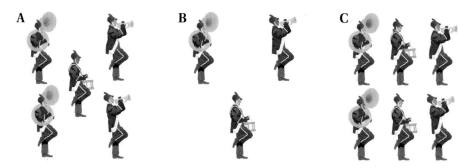

A   B   C

66. ★ **OPEN-ENDED MATH** A teacher divides the class into 6 equal groups containing 10 students each. Find two other ways that the teacher can divide the class into equal groups. *Explain.*

67. ★ **EXTENDED RESPONSE** You are planning a relay race for 48 students. Teams of equal size must be formed with at most 6 students per team.

   a. **Mental Math** What are the possible team sizes? How many teams would there be for each team size?

   b. **Decide** The race will be divided into heats with exactly 6 teams in each heat. Which team sizes from part (a) are still possible? How many heats will be run?

   c. **Explain** You want to have a runoff among the winning teams. What team size from part (a) should you use if you want 4 teams in the runoff? *Explain.*

GROUP PHOTOGRAPHS A photographer needs to arrange each group of people in rows with the same number of people for a photograph. List all the possible numbers of rows.

68. 15 people   **69.** 18 people   **70.** 56 people   **71.** 60 people

72. ★ **WRITING** A student made the factor tree at the right by looking for a prime factor at each step. Make a different factor tree for 140. *Compare and contrast* the methods and the results.

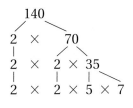

73. **CRYPTOGRAPHY** To keep electronic information private, cryptographers use large numbers that are difficult to factor. Use a calculator to find the prime factorization of 3551.

74. **REASONING** Why is a number that is divisible by 3 and 5 always divisible by 15, when a number that is divisible by 2 and 6 isn't always divisible by 12?

75. **CHALLENGE** *Twin primes* are pairs of prime numbers whose difference is 2. An example is 3 and 5. Find the next 4 pairs of twin primes.

MIXED REVIEW

Get-Ready

Prepare for Lesson 5.2 in Exs. 76–83

Complete the number fact family. *(p. 740)*

76. $9 \times 8 = \underline{\ ?\ }$
77. $72 \div \underline{\ ?\ } = 9$
78. $\underline{\ ?\ } \times 8 = 72$
79. $72 \div \underline{\ ?\ } = 8$

80. $13 \times 7 = \underline{\ ?\ }$
81. $91 \div \underline{\ ?\ } = 7$
82. $\underline{\ ?\ } \times 13 = 91$
83. $91 \div \underline{\ ?\ } = 13$

84. ★ **MULTIPLE CHOICE** You would like to buy a pair of jeans for $35. You have $23. How much more money do you need? *(p. 3)*

ⓐ $12   ⓑ $23   ⓒ $35   ⓓ $58

85. **MONEY** Your sister has 87 pennies. Her friend gives her 16 more pennies. How many pennies does she have? *(p. 3)*

Use the distributive property to evaluate the expression. *(p.175)*

86. $7(40 + 8)$
87. $8(30 + 7)$
88. $5(50 - 8)$
89. $4(60 - 6)$

Brain Game

Which Telephone Number?

Joey has a list of five telephone numbers on a slip of paper, but his hamster ate a part of this paper that had all the names next to the numbers. Now he wants to call Paul, and he does not know which of the five numbers to dial. He does remember the following facts about Paul's number:

1. It is divisible by 9.
2. It is divisible by 2.
3. It is not divisible by 10.
4. It is not divisible by 4.

Ignoring the hyphens, which telephone number could be Paul's?

835-6257
555-6902
903-1248
420-2730
642-3174

5.2 Greatest Common Factor

Before	You found all the factors of a number.
Now	You'll find the greatest common factor of two or more numbers.
Why?	So you can find arrangements, as for a garden in Example 1.

KEY VOCABULARY
- common factor, *p. 236*
- greatest common factor (GCF), *p. 236*

A whole number that is a factor of two or more nonzero whole numbers is a **common factor** of the numbers. The largest of the common factors is the **greatest common factor (GCF)**.

EXAMPLE 1 Multiple Representations

Gardening You are dividing a garden into sections. You have 64 marigolds and 120 petunias. You want each section to have the same number of each type of flower and use all the flowers. At most, how many sections can you have?

SOLUTION

The greatest number of sections that you can have in the garden described above is the GCF of 64 and 120. Two methods for finding the GCF are shown.

METHOD 1 List all the factors of 64 and 120.

Factors of 64: **1**, **2**, **4**, **8**, 16, 32, 64

Factors of 120: **1**, **2**, 3, **4**, 5, 6, **8**, 10, 12, 15, 20, 24, 30, 40, 60, 120

The common factors are **1**, **2**, **4**, and **8**. The GCF is **8**.

METHOD 2 Write the prime factorization of 64 and 120. Then find the product of the common prime factors.

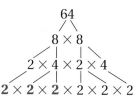

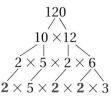

The common prime factors are **2**, **2**, and **2**. The GCF is 2^3, or 8.

▶ **Answer** The greatest number of sections that you can have is 8.

✓ **GUIDED PRACTICE** for Example 1

1. **What If?** What is the greatest number of sections you can have in Example 1 if you have 72 marigolds and 144 petunias?

KEY CONCEPT
For Your Notebook

Finding the Greatest Common Factor (GCF)

Method 1: List all the factors of each number. Then find the greatest factor that is common to all numbers.

Method 2: Write the prime factorization of each number. Then find the product of the common prime factors.

⭐ **EXAMPLE 2** **Standardized Test Practice**

> **What is the greatest common factor of 16, 24, and 36?**
>
> (A) 4   (B) 6   (C) 12   (D) 24

ELIMINATE CHOICES
A number cannot be a factor of a smaller number. Because 24 cannot be a factor of 16, choice D can be eliminated.

SOLUTION

Factors of 16: 1, 2, **4**, 8, 16

Factors of 24: 1, 2, 3, **4**, 6, 8, 12, 24

Factors of 36: 1, 2, 3, **4**, 6, 9, 12, 18, 36

▶ **Answer** The GCF of 16, 24, and 36 is 4.
The correct answer is A. (A) (B) (C) (D)

EXAMPLE 3 **Making a List**

Ticket Prices Three groups will pay $27, $45, and $72 to take the Cave of the Winds tour of Niagara Falls. Each ticket is the same price. What is the most a ticket could cost?

SOLUTION

Find the GCF of the amounts spent by listing the factors.

Factors of 27: **1**, **3**, **9**, 27

Factors of 45: **1**, **3**, 5, **9**, 15, 45

Factors of 72: **1**, 2, **3**, 4, 6, 8, **9**, 12, 18, 24, 36, 72

▶ **Answer** The GCF is 9. The most a ticket could cost is $9.

✓ **GUIDED PRACTICE** for Examples 2 and 3

Find the GCF of the numbers.

2. 14, 35   **3.** 12, 20, 30   **4.** 24, 48, 72

5.2 EXERCISES

SKILL PRACTICE

VOCABULARY **Copy and complete the statement using the factors of 18 and 32.**

Factors of 18: 1, 2, 3, 6, 9, 18   Factors of 32: 1, 2, 4, 8, 16, 32

1. The common factors of 18 and 32 are __?__ .

2. The greatest common factor of 18 and 32 is __?__ .

LISTING FACTORS **List all the common factors of the numbers. Then find the GCF.**

SEE EXAMPLE 1
on p. 236
for Exs. 3–14

3. 10, 28   **4.** 24, 84   **5.** 16, 48   **6.** 11, 44

CREATING FACTOR TREES **Find the GCF of the numbers using factor trees.**

7. 12, 54   **8.** 32, 40   **9.** 20, 75   **10.** 36, 90

CHOOSE A METHOD **Find the GCF of the numbers using either method.**

11. 9, 42   **12.** 15, 52   **13.** 12, 21, 30   **14.** 16, 40, 88

SEE EXAMPLE 2
on p. 237
for Exs. 15–21

15. ★ **MULTIPLE CHOICE** What is the greatest common factor of 14, 26, and 42?

(A) 2   (B) 7   (C) 14   (D) 182

ERROR ANALYSIS **Describe and correct the error.**

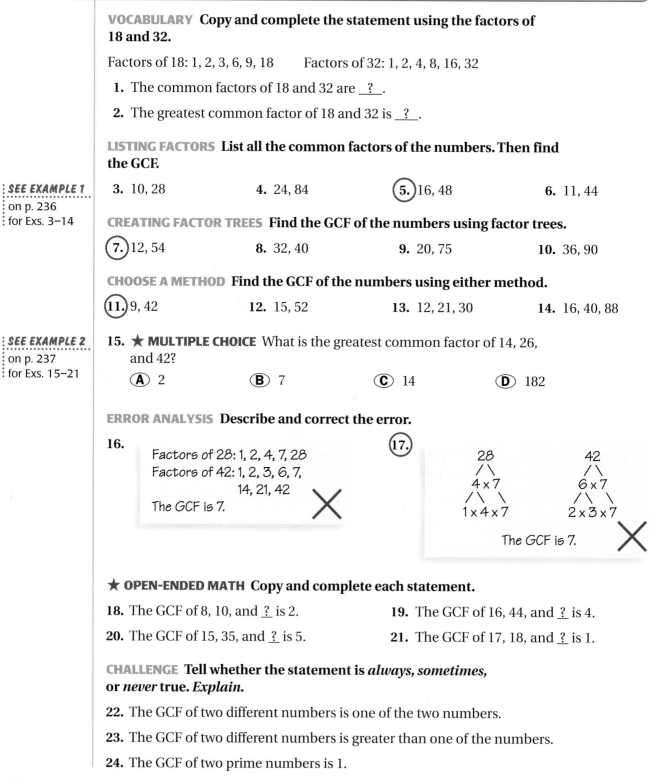

16.
Factors of 28: 1, 2, 4, 7, 28
Factors of 42: 1, 2, 3, 6, 7,
          14, 21, 42
The GCF is 7.   ✗

17.
28   42
/ \   / \
4 × 7   6 × 7
/ \ \   / \ \
1 × 4 × 7   2 × 3 × 7

The GCF is 7.   ✗

★ **OPEN-ENDED MATH** **Copy and complete each statement.**

18. The GCF of 8, 10, and __?__ is 2.   **19.** The GCF of 16, 44, and __?__ is 4.

20. The GCF of 15, 35, and __?__ is 5.   **21.** The GCF of 17, 18, and __?__ is 1.

CHALLENGE **Tell whether the statement is *always, sometimes,* or *never* true. *Explain.***

22. The GCF of two different numbers is one of the two numbers.

23. The GCF of two different numbers is greater than one of the numbers.

24. The GCF of two prime numbers is 1.

25. CHALLENGE Write all the numbers from 2 to 50. Circle the number 2 and cross out all other even numbers. Circle the number 3 and cross out all other numbers divisible by 3. Do the same for the numbers 5 and 7. What can you say about the numbers you circled? about the numbers that are not crossed out? *Justify* your reasoning.

PROBLEM SOLVING

SEE EXAMPLE 3
on p. 237
for Exs. 26–29

26. GUIDED PROBLEM SOLVING For your school's fair, you make 42 magnets and 36 key chains with your school's mascot on them. You want to display them in rows of equal size, but you do not want to mix the items.

  a. Find the GCF of 42 and 36.

  b. What is the greatest number of items you can have in a row?

  c. How many rows of each item will there be?

27. ★ MULTIPLE CHOICE A halftime show uses 96 dancers and 144 singers. The coordinator wants to arrange dancers and singers in rows with the same number in each row, without mixing the groups. What is the greatest number of people there can be in each row?

  A 12   **B** 16   **C** 24   **D** 48

28. MULTI-STEP PROBLEM A grocery store is making identical fruit baskets. The store has 120 bananas, 60 oranges, and 144 apples. Find the greatest number of fruit baskets the store can make if each basket has to have the same number of each kind of fruit.

  a. Write the prime factorizations of 120, 60, and 144.

  b. What is the greatest number of fruit baskets the store can make?

  c. How many pieces of each type of fruit are in each basket?

29. PARADES A group of 45 singers will march behind a group of 30 clowns in a parade. You want to arrange the two groups in rows with the same number of people in each row, but without mixing the groups in each row.

  a. How many rows of clowns will you have in the parade? *Explain* your reasoning.

  b. How many rows of singers will you have in the parade? *Explain* your reasoning.

30. ★ WRITING *Describe* two methods for finding the GCF of 50 and 75.

31. ★ SHORT RESPONSE Ashley has 27 violet marbles, 54 blue marbles, and 72 white marbles. She wants to divide the marbles into groups so that each group has the same number of each color. How many of each color are in each group? *Explain.*

★ **EXTENDED RESPONSE** In Exercises 32–34, use the information below.

A museum has groups of 48, 112, and 144 people scheduled for tours. Tour guides divide the groups into smaller groups of equal size, without mixing any of the groups.

32. What is the greatest number in each group?

33. How many groups of people will there be?

34. Tours begin every 15 minutes and last an hour. How many hours will it take to complete all tours? *Explain.*

35. ◆ **MULTIPLE REPRESENTATIONS** You want to cut fencing into pieces of the same length and make the fewest cuts.

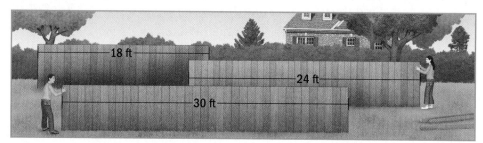

VISUALIZE INFORMATION
For help with Venn diagrams, See p. 756.

a. Make a Factor Tree Make a factor tree for the measures.

b. Make a Venn Diagram Create a Venn diagram showing the prime factors of the measures.

c. Conclude Can you fence a square area with your pieces? *Explain.*

36. **CHALLENGE** Which composite number from 6 to 20 is closest in value to the sum of its prime factors?

37. **CHALLENGE** For which composite number between 1 and 100 is the sum of its prime factors greatest?

MIXED REVIEW

Get-Ready

Prepare for Lesson 5.3 in Exs. 38–40

What fraction is shown by the model? *(p. 753)*

38.

39.

40.

Evaluate the expression using mental math. *(p. 193)*

41. $0.05 \div 100$ **42.** $3.46 \div 0.01$ **43.** $0.9 \div 0.001$

44. ★ **MULTIPLE CHOICE** Which list is from least to greatest? *(p. 130)*

Ⓐ 1.6 m, 1.26 m, 1.216 m, 0.96 m   Ⓑ 0.96 m, 1.6 m, 1.216 m, 1.26 m

Ⓒ 0.96 m, 1.216 m, 1.26 m, 1.6 m   Ⓓ 0.96 m, 1.26 m, 1.216 m, 1.6 m

GOAL
Use models to find
equivalent fractions.

MATERIALS
• paper
• pencil

5.3 Modeling Equivalent Fractions

You can use paper models to represent fractions in more than one way.

EXPLORE 1 Model the fraction $\frac{1}{2}$ in different ways.

STEP 1 **Fold** a piece of paper in half. Then unfold the paper and draw a line along the fold. Shade one half as shown.

STEP 2 **Refold** the paper. Then fold it in half again in the same direction. Unfold the paper and draw a line along each new fold.

Copy and complete the statement: $\frac{1}{2} = \frac{?}{4}$.

STEP 3 **Fold** the paper in half in the other direction. Then unfold the paper and draw a line along the new fold.

Copy and complete the statement: $\frac{1}{2} = \frac{?}{8}$.

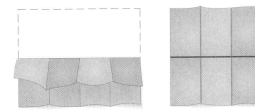

PRACTICE Use the fractions in Steps 1–3 above.

1. *Describe* a pattern in the numerators of the fractions above. Do you see the same pattern in the denominators?

2. Use your answers to Exercise 1 to help you copy and complete the following fractions.

$$\frac{1}{2} = \frac{2}{4} = \frac{4}{8} = \frac{?}{16}$$

Continued on next page

INVESTIGATION

Continued from page 241

EXPLORE 2 Model the fraction $\frac{1}{3}$ in different ways.

STEP 1 **Fold** a piece of paper in thirds. Then unfold the paper and draw a line along each fold. Shade one third as shown.

STEP 2 **Refold** the paper. Then fold it in thirds again in the same direction. Unfold the paper and draw a line along each new fold.

Copy and complete the statement: $\frac{1}{3} = \frac{?}{9}$.

STEP 3 **Fold** the paper in thirds in the other direction. Then unfold the paper and draw a line along each new fold.

Copy and complete the statement: $\frac{1}{3} = \frac{?}{27}$.

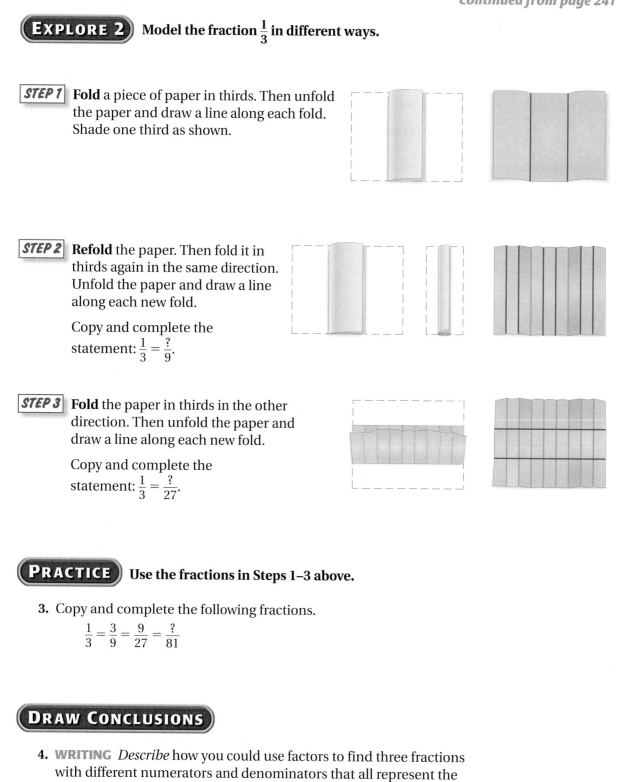

PRACTICE Use the fractions in Steps 1–3 above.

3. Copy and complete the following fractions.

$$\frac{1}{3} = \frac{3}{9} = \frac{9}{27} = \frac{?}{81}$$

DRAW CONCLUSIONS

4. **WRITING** *Describe* how you could use factors to find three fractions with different numerators and denominators that all represent the same fraction.

5.3 Equivalent Fractions

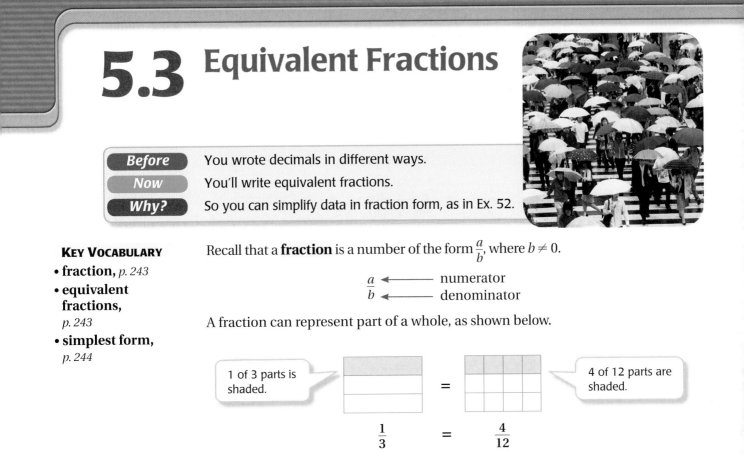

Before	You wrote decimals in different ways.
Now	You'll write equivalent fractions.
Why?	So you can simplify data in fraction form, as in Ex. 52.

KEY VOCABULARY

• **fraction,** *p. 243*
• **equivalent fractions,** *p. 243*
• **simplest form,** *p. 244*

Recall that a **fraction** is a number of the form $\frac{a}{b}$, where $b \neq 0$.

$$\frac{a}{b} \quad \begin{matrix} \longleftarrow \text{numerator} \\ \longleftarrow \text{denominator} \end{matrix}$$

A fraction can represent part of a whole, as shown below.

1 of 3 parts is shaded.   =   4 of 12 parts are shaded.

$$\frac{1}{3} \quad = \quad \frac{4}{12}$$

The fractions above are **equivalent** because they represent the same number. In the activity, you may have seen how you can write equivalent fractions. You can multiply or divide the numerator and denominator by the *same* nonzero number.

EXAMPLE 1   Writing Equivalent Fractions

TAKE NOTES

In your notebook, you may want to record models of the equivalent fractions shown in Example 1.

Write two fractions that are equivalent to $\frac{1}{3}$.

$\frac{1}{3} = \frac{1 \times 2}{3 \times 2} = \frac{2}{6}$ **Multiply the numerator and denominator by 2.**

$\frac{1}{3} = \frac{1 \times 3}{1 \times 3} = \frac{3}{9}$ **Multiply the numerator and denominator by 3.**

▸ **Answer** The fractions $\frac{2}{6}$ and $\frac{3}{9}$ are equivalent to $\frac{1}{3}$.

✓ **GUIDED PRACTICE**   for Example 1

Write two fractions that are equivalent to the given fraction.

1. $\frac{1}{2}$ **2.** $\frac{1}{4}$ **3.** $\frac{3}{5}$ **4.** $\frac{2}{3}$

Animated **Math** at classzone.com

EXAMPLE 2 Completing Equivalent Fractions

Complete the equivalent fraction.

a. $\dfrac{3}{5} = \dfrac{12}{?}$

$\dfrac{3}{5} = \dfrac{12}{20}$

3×4

5×4

You multiply 3 by 4 to get 12, so multiply the denominator by 4.

b. $\dfrac{16}{24} = \dfrac{?}{12}$

$16 \div 2$

$\dfrac{16}{24} = \dfrac{8}{12}$

$24 \div 2$

You divide 24 by 2 to get 12, so divide the numerator by 2.

Simplifying A fraction is in **simplest form** if its numerator and denominator have a greatest common factor of 1. To *simplify* a fraction, divide its numerator and denominator by their greatest common factor.

EXAMPLE 3 Simplifying Fractions

Surveys In a survey of 16 middle school students, 12 said that comedy was their favorite type of movie. Write this as a fraction in simplest form.

AVOID ERRORS

When simplifying a fraction, be sure that you use the greatest common factor, rather than just any factor. Otherwise, the result may not be in simplest form.

SOLUTION

Write "12 out of 16" as a fraction. Then simplify.

$\dfrac{12}{16} = \dfrac{3 \times 4}{4 \times 4}$ Use the GCF to write the numerator and denominator as products.

$= \dfrac{3 \times \overset{1}{\cancel{4}}}{4 \times \underset{1}{\cancel{4}}}$ Divide the numerator and denominator by the GCF.

$= \dfrac{3}{4}$ Simplest form

▶ **Answer** In simplest form, the fraction of students who said comedy was their favorite type of movie is $\dfrac{3}{4}$.

✓ **GUIDED PRACTICE** for Examples 2 and 3

Copy and complete the statement.

5. $\dfrac{2}{5} = \dfrac{6}{?}$ **6.** $\dfrac{4}{7} = \dfrac{?}{21}$ **7.** $\dfrac{15}{20} = \dfrac{3}{?}$ **8.** $\dfrac{18}{27} = \dfrac{?}{3}$

9. What If? In Example 3, 14 of the 16 students surveyed said that adventure was one of their top three favorite types of movies. Write this as a fraction in simplest form.

244   Chapter 5   Number Patterns and Fractions

EXAMPLE 4 **Simplifying Fractions**

Homework You spent an hour on homework last night. Write a fraction in simplest form to describe the amount of time you spent on each subject.

a. You spent 15 minutes on literature. $\dfrac{15}{60} = \dfrac{1 \times \overset{1}{\cancel{15}}}{4 \times \cancel{15}} = \dfrac{1}{4}$ hour

b. You spent 25 minutes on math. $\dfrac{25}{60} = \dfrac{5 \times \overset{1}{\cancel{5}}}{12 \times \cancel{5}} = \dfrac{5}{12}$ hour

c. You spent 20 minutes on science. $\dfrac{20}{60} = \dfrac{1 \times \overset{1}{\cancel{20}}}{3 \times \cancel{20}} = \dfrac{1}{3}$ hour

✓ **GUIDED PRACTICE** **for Example 4**

School Supplies You spent \$32 on supplies. Write a fraction in simplest form to describe the portion of \$32 that you spent on each item.

10. notebooks costing \$24   **11.** pencils costing \$6   **12.** a ruler costing \$2

5.3 EXERCISES

HOMEWORK KEY

★ = **STANDARDIZED TEST PRACTICE**
Exs. 49, 53, 54, and 63

◯ = **HINTS** AND **HOMEWORK HELP**
for Exs. 7, 15, 23, 51 at classzone.com

SKILL PRACTICE

1. VOCABULARY Is $\dfrac{4}{10}$ in simplest form? *Explain.*

2. VOCABULARY Copy and complete: Fractions that represent the same number are called __?__ fractions.

SEE EXAMPLE 1
on p. 243
for Exs. 3–13

3. MODELS Write two fractions that can be modeled by the shaded area in the diagram.

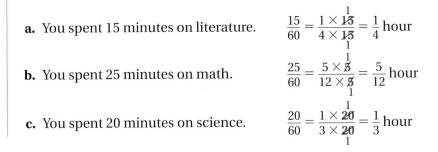

WRITING EQUIVALENT FRACTIONS Write two fractions that are equivalent to the given fraction.

4. $\dfrac{1}{5}$ **5.** $\dfrac{1}{10}$ **6.** $\dfrac{3}{7}$ **⑦.** $\dfrac{3}{5}$

8. $\dfrac{3}{11}$ **9.** $\dfrac{9}{20}$ **10.** $\dfrac{4}{25}$ **11.** $\dfrac{3}{100}$

WHICH ONE DOESN'T BELONG? Which fraction is *not* equivalent to the given fraction?

12. $\dfrac{1}{8}$ **A.** $\dfrac{2}{9}$ **B.** $\dfrac{2}{16}$ **C.** $\dfrac{3}{24}$ **D.** $\dfrac{5}{40}$

13. $\dfrac{12}{36}$ **A.** $\dfrac{1}{24}$ **B.** $\dfrac{1}{3}$ **C.** $\dfrac{2}{6}$ **D.** $\dfrac{4}{12}$

COMPLETING FRACTIONS Copy and complete the statement.

SEE EXAMPLE 2
on p. 244
for Exs. 14–22

14. $\dfrac{4}{5} = \dfrac{?}{20}$

15. $\dfrac{7}{9} = \dfrac{35}{?}$

16. $\dfrac{18}{30} = \dfrac{6}{?}$

17. $\dfrac{20}{25} = \dfrac{?}{5}$

18. $\dfrac{6}{7} = \dfrac{18}{?}$

19. $\dfrac{9}{11} = \dfrac{?}{66}$

20. $\dfrac{44}{52} = \dfrac{?}{13}$

21. $\dfrac{28}{49} = \dfrac{4}{?}$

22. ERROR ANALYSIS Describe and correct the error made in completing the equivalent fraction.

$$\times \quad \dfrac{15}{20} \overset{\div 5}{=} \dfrac{?}{100}$$

$$\dfrac{15}{20} = \dfrac{3}{100}$$

SIMPLIFYING FRACTIONS Tell whether the fraction is in simplest form. If it is not, simplify it.

SEE EXAMPLE 3
on p. 244
for Exs. 23–34

23. $\dfrac{7}{14}$

24. $\dfrac{9}{27}$

25. $\dfrac{9}{32}$

26. $\dfrac{13}{64}$

27. $\dfrac{15}{48}$

28. $\dfrac{40}{45}$

29. $\dfrac{24}{77}$

30. $\dfrac{50}{175}$

31. $\dfrac{76}{104}$

32. $\dfrac{180}{222}$

33. $\dfrac{95}{245}$

34. $\dfrac{207}{270}$

ALGEBRA Find the value of x.

35. $\dfrac{x}{8} = \dfrac{2.5}{4}$

36. $\dfrac{x}{420} = \dfrac{0.1}{6}$

37. $\dfrac{12}{x} = \dfrac{0.2}{0.9}$

38. $\dfrac{0.7}{0.1x} = \dfrac{4.9}{7}$

GEOMETRY What fraction of the large rectangle's area is shaded red? Write the answer in simplest form.

39.

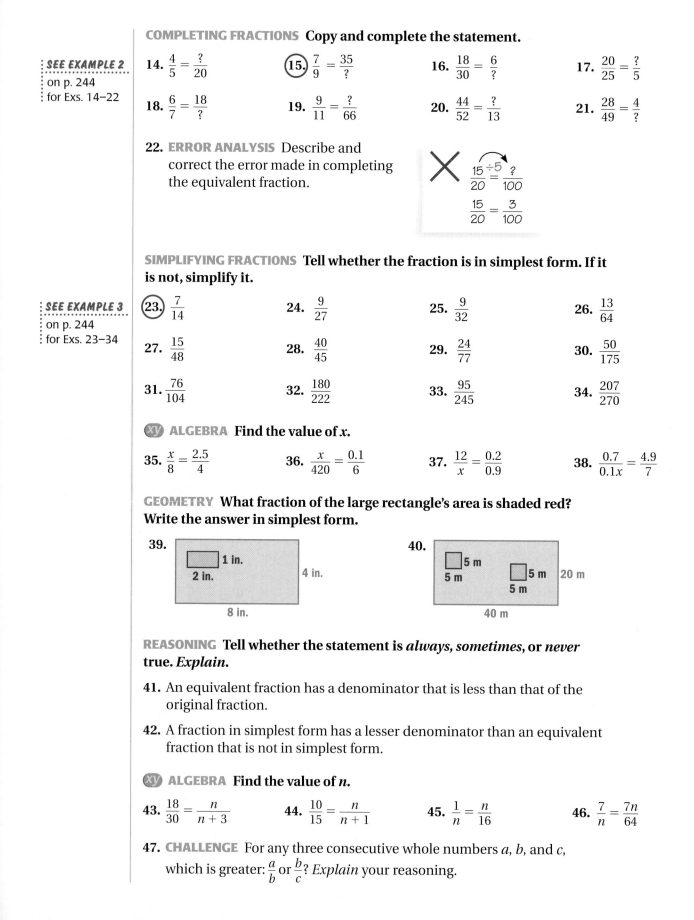

40.

REASONING Tell whether the statement is *always, sometimes,* or *never* true. *Explain.*

41. An equivalent fraction has a denominator that is less than that of the original fraction.

42. A fraction in simplest form has a lesser denominator than an equivalent fraction that is not in simplest form.

ALGEBRA Find the value of n.

43. $\dfrac{18}{30} = \dfrac{n}{n+3}$

44. $\dfrac{10}{15} = \dfrac{n}{n+1}$

45. $\dfrac{1}{n} = \dfrac{n}{16}$

46. $\dfrac{7}{n} = \dfrac{7n}{64}$

47. CHALLENGE For any three consecutive whole numbers a, b, and c, which is greater: $\dfrac{a}{b}$ or $\dfrac{b}{c}$? *Explain* your reasoning.

SEE EXAMPLE 4
on p. 244
for Exs. 48–51

48. MAKING BRACELETS You are using the beads below to make a bracelet. Write fractions in simplest form to describe the portion of beads that are each color.

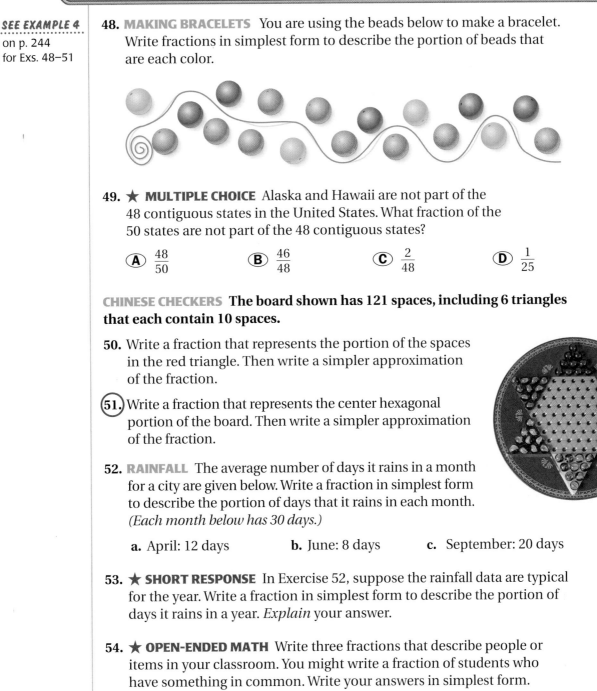

49. ★ MULTIPLE CHOICE Alaska and Hawaii are not part of the 48 contiguous states in the United States. What fraction of the 50 states are not part of the 48 contiguous states?

(A) $\frac{48}{50}$ (B) $\frac{46}{48}$ (C) $\frac{2}{48}$ (D) $\frac{1}{25}$

CHINESE CHECKERS The board shown has 121 spaces, including 6 triangles that each contain 10 spaces.

50. Write a fraction that represents the portion of the spaces in the red triangle. Then write a simpler approximation of the fraction.

51. Write a fraction that represents the center hexagonal portion of the board. Then write a simpler approximation of the fraction.

52. RAINFALL The average number of days it rains in a month for a city are given below. Write a fraction in simplest form to describe the portion of days that it rains in each month. *(Each month below has 30 days.)*

   a. April: 12 days   **b.** June: 8 days   **c.** September: 20 days

53. ★ SHORT RESPONSE In Exercise 52, suppose the rainfall data are typical for the year. Write a fraction in simplest form to describe the portion of days it rains in a year. *Explain* your answer.

54. ★ OPEN-ENDED MATH Write three fractions that describe people or items in your classroom. You might write a fraction of students who have something in common. Write your answers in simplest form.

55. TIME MANAGEMENT Choose an activity you spend between 1 and 3 hours on each day. Write and simplify a fraction that represents the portion of each day on that activity. About how many days in one year do you spend on this activity?

56. REASONING Write a rule to tell when you can simplify a fraction that has a prime number in its numerator. Is it possible to write a rule to tell when you can simplify a fraction that has prime numbers in its numerator and denominator? *Explain.*

57. CHALLENGE One ancient calendar used 28 days as a lunar month and 365 days for a solar year. What fraction of a solar year is 1 lunar month? 5 lunar months? Write your answers in simplest form. Then list the factors of 365 and use the list to *explain* why it is so difficult to create a calendar consisting of equal size periods of time.

MIXED REVIEW

Get-Ready

Prepare for
Lesson 5.4 in
Exs. 58–61

Find the GCF of the numbers using factor trees. *(p. 236)*

58. 12, 34   **59.** 14, 42   **60.** 36, 40   **61.** 27, 63

CHOOSE A STRATEGY Use a strategy from the list to solve the following problem. *Explain* your choice of strategy.

62. The denominator of a fraction is 8 more than the numerator. The denominator is also 3 times the numerator. Find the fraction.

> *Problem Solving Strategies*
> ▪ Guess, Check, and Revise *(p. 763)*
> ▪ Make a Table *(p. 765)*
> ▪ Solve a Simpler Problem *(p. 768)*
> ▪ Look for a Pattern *(p. 766)*

63. ★ **MULTIPLE CHOICE** What is the product 1000×12? *(p. 3)*

    (A) 120   **(B)** 1012   **(C)** 1200   **(D)** 12,000

QUIZ *for Lessons 5.1–5.3*

Test the number for divisibility by 2, 3, 5, 6, 9, and 10. Then tell whether the number is *prime* or *composite*. *(p. 230)*

1. 54   **2.** 77   **3.** 405   **4.** 1270

Write the prime factorization of the number. *(p. 230)*

5. 34   **6.** 48   **7.** 164   **8.** 840

Find the GCF of the numbers. *(p. 236)*

9. 7, 56   **10.** 10, 21   **11.** 42, 90   **12.** 8, 40, 54

13. FIELD TRIP Three science classes go on a field trip to an observatory. The classes spend \$75, \$54, and \$96 for student admission. Find the greatest possible student admission price for the observatory. *(p. 236)*

14. Copy and complete: $\dfrac{6}{11} = \dfrac{?}{55}$. *(p. 243)*

Write the fraction in simplest form. *(p. 243)*

15. $\dfrac{6}{45}$ **16.** $\dfrac{10}{110}$ **17.** $\dfrac{14}{50}$ **18.** $\dfrac{39}{130}$

Lessons 5.1–5.3

1. SHORT RESPONSE Use the following table.

Inner Planets	Mercury, Venus, Earth, Mars
Outer Planets	Jupiter, Saturn, Uranus, Neptune, Pluto

a. Write a fraction in simplest form for the portion of the planets that are classified as inner planets.

b. *Explain* how you can tell that the fraction in part (a) is in simplest form.

2. MULTI-STEP PROBLEM There are 68 students going on a field trip. The teacher organizing the trip wants the students to be divided into groups of equal size.

a. Can the students be divided into groups of equal size with 3 students per group?

b. Can the students be divided into groups of equal size each with at least 15 students?

c. There are a total of 4 adults to supervise the students. Can the teacher break the students into groups of equal size so that there is 1 adult per group?

3. SHORT RESPONSE You have entered the school science fair with an experiment. The guidelines allocate 40 square feet per participant. Find possible dimensions for a rectangular space with whole-number dimensions. *Explain* your method.

4. EXTENDED RESPONSE An animal shelter has 24 large dogs, 48 small dogs, and 60 medium sized dogs. The manager wants to divide the animals into groups so that each group has the same number of each size of dog.

a. List all of the possibilities for group sizes.

b. What is the greatest number of groups that the manager can make? How many dogs are in each group?

c. *Explain* the relationship between the answers in part (b).

5. MULTI-STEP PROBLEM Copy and extend the table to find all the ways you can combine change to get 25 cents.

Pennies	Nickels	Dimes	Quarters
25	0	0	0
20	1	0	0
15	2	0	0

a. What fraction of the ways has at least 10 coins?

b. What fraction of the ways has at most 3 dimes?

6. OPEN-ENDED You divide 100 senators into 2 groups each containing 50 senators. Find two other ways that you can divide the senators into equal groups.

7. GRIDDED ANSWER You want to arrange a group of 50 quarters and a group of 80 nickels in rows with the same number of coins in each row, but without mixing the groups. What is the greatest number of coins you can have in each row?

8. SHORT RESPONSE Paper plates come in packages of 75 and 100. Forks come in packages of 25 and 50. You want to buy an equal number of forks and plates. Is there a way to do this buying eight packages? *Explain* your reasoning.

5.4 Least Common Multiple

Before	You found greatest common factors.
Now	You'll find least common multiples.
Why?	So you can plan schedules, as for soccer in Ex. 40.

KEY VOCABULARY
- **multiple,** *p. 250*
- **common multiple,** *p. 250*
- **least common multiple (LCM),** *p. 251*

Ferry Boats Two ferry boats leave a loading platform at the same time. One of the ferry boats returns to the loading platform every 25 minutes. The other returns every 30 minutes. In the next 300 minutes, when will they return at the same time?

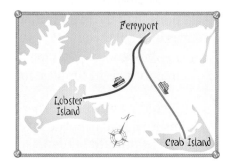

You can use *multiples* to answer the question above. A **multiple** of a number is the product of the number and any nonzero whole number.

— The three dots show that the pattern continues forever.

Multiples of 2: 2, 4, 6, 8, 10, 12, 14, . . .

A multiple shared by two or more numbers is a **common multiple.**

EXAMPLE 1 Finding a Common Multiple

You can use common multiples to answer the question above about ferry boats. Begin by writing the multiples of 25 and 30. Then identify common multiples through 300.

Multiples of 25: 25, 50, 75, 100, 125, **150**, 175, 200, 225, 250, 275, **300**

Multiples of 30: 30, 60, 90, 120, **150**, 180, 210, 240, 270, **300**

The common multiples of 25 and 30 are 150 and 300.

▸ **Answer** The ferry boats will return to the loading platform at the same time in 150 minutes and in 300 minutes.

✓ **GUIDED PRACTICE** for Example 1

Find two common multiples of the numbers.

1. 2, 3   **2.** 3, 5   **3.** 8, 10   **4.** 6, 18

5. Clocks A cuckoo clock has birds that pop out of their nests every 6 minutes and dancers that pop out every 15 minutes. The birds and dancers have just popped out at the same time. When will this happen again in the next 60 minutes?

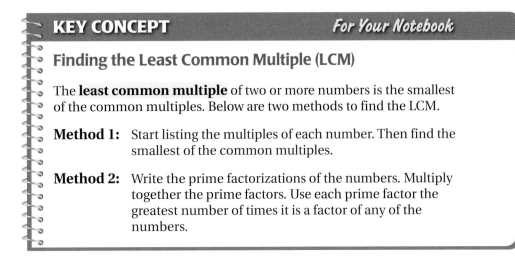

KEY CONCEPT   *For Your Notebook*

Finding the Least Common Multiple (LCM)

The **least common multiple** of two or more numbers is the smallest of the common multiples. Below are two methods to find the LCM.

Method 1:   Start listing the multiples of each number. Then find the smallest of the common multiples.

Method 2:   Write the prime factorizations of the numbers. Multiply together the prime factors. Use each prime factor the greatest number of times it is a factor of any of the numbers.

EXAMPLE 2   **Using Multiples**

Find the LCM of 9 and 12.

Multiples of 9: 9, 18, 27, **36**, 45, 54, . . .

Multiples of 12: 12, 24, **36**, 48, . . .

▶**Answer** The LCM of 9 and 12 is 36.

EXAMPLE 3   **Using Prime Factorization**

COMPARE FACTORS
If the only common factor of two numbers is 1, then their least common multiple is the product of the two numbers.

Find the LCM of 42 and 60 using prime factorization.

STEP 1 **Write** the prime factorizations. Circle any common factors.

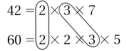
$$42 = 2 \times 3 \times 7$$
$$60 = 2 \times 2 \times 3 \times 5$$

STEP 2 **Multiply** together the prime factors, using each circled factor the greatest number of times it occurs in either factorization.

$$2 \times 2 \times 3 \times 5 \times 7 = 420$$

▶**Answer** The LCM of 42 and 60 is 420.

Animated **Math**
at classzone.com

✓ **GUIDED PRACTICE**   **for Examples 2 and 3**

Find the LCM of the numbers by listing multiples.

6. 6, 8   **7.** 5, 9   **8.** 9, 15

Find the LCM of the numbers using prime factorization.

9. 8, 12   **10.** 8, 14   **11.** 50, 90

5.4 EXERCISES

HOMEWORK
KEY

★ = **STANDARDIZED TEST PRACTICE**
Exs. 27, 29–32, 39, 41–43, and 49

◯ = **HINTS** AND **HOMEWORK HELP**
for Exs. 3, 7, 13, 19, 41 at classzone.com

SKILL PRACTICE

VOCABULARY Copy and complete using the given multiples.

Multiples of 3: 3, 6, 9, 12, 15, 18 . . .   Multiples of 6: 6, 12, 18, 24, 30, 36 . . .

1. Common multiples of 3 and 6 are __?__.   **2.** The LCM of 3 and 6 is __?__.

SEE EXAMPLE 1
on p. 250
for Exs. 3–10

LISTING MULTIPLES Find all common multiples less than 100 for each pair of numbers by listing multiples.

3. 7, 8   **4.** 4, 5   **5.** 6, 8   **6.** 9, 12

7. 6, 9   **8.** 8, 18   **9.** 20, 30   **10.** 10, 14

SEE EXAMPLE 2
on p. 251
for Exs. 11–18

USING MULTIPLES Find the LCM of the numbers by listing multiples.

11. 3, 7   **12.** 5, 8   **13.** 6, 10   **14.** 10, 12

15. 3, 6, 9   **16.** 4, 8, 16   **17.** 2, 3, 5   **18.** 4, 9, 24

SEE EXAMPLE 3
on p. 251
for Exs. 19–27

PRIME FACTORIZATION Find the LCM of the numbers using prime factorization.

19. 21, 28   **20.** 30, 42   **21.** 22, 36   **22.** 32, 40

23. 27, 45   **24.** 56, 64   **25.** 24, 60, 72   **26.** 30, 50, 75

27. ★ **MULTIPLE CHOICE** What is the least common multiple of 10 and 3?

A 1   **B** 13   **C** 30   **D** 60

28. ERROR ANALYSIS Describe and correct the error made in finding the LCM of 24 and 36.

$24 = 2 \times 2 \times 2 \times 3$
$36 = 2 \times 2 \times 3 \times 3$
The LCM of 24 and 36 is $2 \times 2 \times 3 = 12$.

★ **OPEN-ENDED MATH** Use factors to complete each statement.

29. The LCM of 8 and __?__ is 120.   **30.** The LCM of 7 and __?__ is 119.

31. The LCM of 12 and __?__ is 132.   **32.** The LCM of 32 and __?__ is 960.

NUMBER SENSE Find a pair of numbers that matches the description.

33. The LCM of two prime numbers is 51.

34. The LCM of two numbers is 48. Their sum is 19.

35. The LCM of two numbers is 16. Their product is 64.

CHALLENGE Find two numbers with the given GCF and LCM.

36. GCF: 6; LCM: 36   **37.** GCF: 3; LCM: 84   **38.** GCF: 5; LCM: 90

39. ★ **WRITING** A store gives every 20th customer a $20 gift certificate. Every 75th customer gets a $75 gift certificate. Which customer will be the first to receive both types of gift certificates? *Explain* how you found your answer.

40. **SCHEDULING** You bring water for your soccer team every sixth game. Every third game is a home game. When will you first bring the drinks to a home game? There are 20 games in a season. How many times will you bring water to a home game this season?

41. ★ **MULTIPLE CHOICE** A timer is set to beep every 14 minutes. At the same time, another timer is set to beep every 30 minutes. After how many hours will the timers first beep at the same time?

 A 1.5 hours **B** 2 hours **C** 3.5 hours **D** 7 hours

42. ★ **SHORT RESPONSE** Pencils come in packages of 10. Rulers come in packages of 8. Hannah wants exactly one pencil for every ruler. What is the smallest number of packages of each she needs to buy? *Explain* how you found your answer.

43. ★ **EXTENDED RESPONSE** A cricket and a grasshopper are at the starting line of a jumping contest. Name four points where the cricket and the grasshopper will both land. How many jumps will it take each of them to land at these points? *Explain.*

44. **CHALLENGE** Find the GCF and the LCM of 6 and 12. How does the product of the GCF and the LCM compare to the product of 6 and 12? Try several pairs of numbers. What does this suggest about the product of two whole numbers and the product of their GCF and LCM?

MIXED REVIEW

Get-Ready

Prepare for Lesson 5.5 in Exs. 45–48

Write two fractions that are equivalent to the given fraction. *(p. 243)*

45. $\frac{1}{8}$ **46.** $\frac{3}{10}$ **47.** $\frac{5}{12}$ **48.** $\frac{12}{17}$

49. ★ **MULTIPLE CHOICE** What is *two and fifty-six thousandths* written as a decimal? *(p. 119)*

 A 0.0256 **B** 0.256 **C** 2.056 **D** 2.56

Copy and complete the statement with <, >, or =. *(p. 738)*

50. 416 ? 419 **51.** 680 ? 68 **52.** 32 ? 352 **53.** 36 ? 390

5.5 Ordering Fractions

Before You compared and ordered decimals.

Now You'll compare and order fractions.

Why? So you can compare sizes, as in Example 3.

KEY VOCABULARY
- **least common denominator (LCD),** *p. 254*

ACTIVITY

You can use models to compare $\frac{3}{4}$ and $\frac{7}{8}$.

STEP 1 **Fold** one piece of paper into fourths and shade three of the fourths.

STEP 2 **Fold** a second piece of paper into eighths and shade seven of the eight eighths.

STEP 3 **Compare** the shaded regions. You can see that $\frac{3}{4} < \frac{7}{8}$.

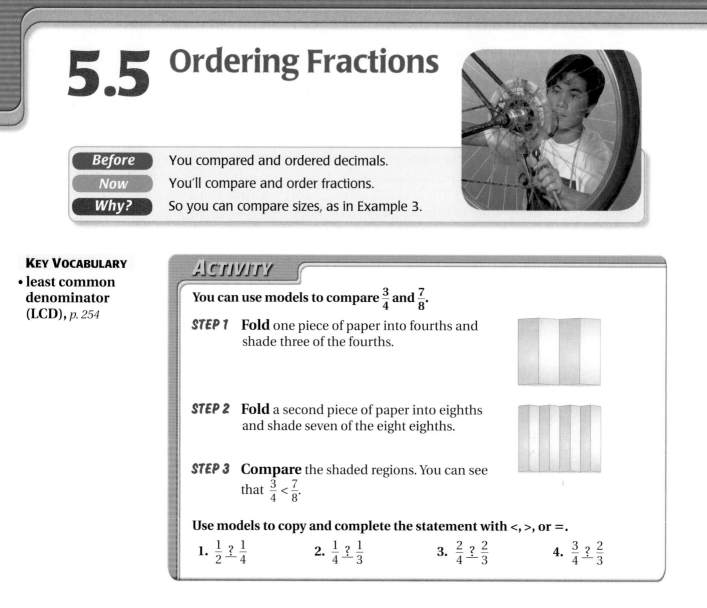

Use models to copy and complete the statement with <, >, or =.

1. $\frac{1}{2} \, ? \, \frac{1}{4}$ 2. $\frac{1}{4} \, ? \, \frac{1}{3}$ 3. $\frac{2}{4} \, ? \, \frac{2}{3}$ 4. $\frac{3}{4} \, ? \, \frac{2}{3}$

Least Common Denominator You can use models to compare fractions, or you can use the *least common denominator* to write equivalent fractions. The **least common denominator (LCD)** of two or more fractions is the least common multiple of the denominators.

EXAMPLE 1 Comparing Fractions Using the LCD

Compare $\frac{5}{6}$ and $\frac{7}{9}$.

USE THE LCD

You can use any common denominator to compare two fractions, but it is usually easiest to use the LCD.

STEP 1 **Find** the LCD: Because the LCM of 6 and 9 is 18, the LCD is 18.

STEP 2 **Use** the LCD to write equivalent fractions.

$$\frac{5}{6} = \frac{5 \times 3}{6 \times 3} = \frac{15}{18} \qquad\qquad \frac{7}{9} = \frac{7 \times 2}{9 \times 2} = \frac{14}{18}$$

STEP 3 **Compare:** Because 15 > 14, you know that $\frac{15}{18} > \frac{14}{18}$. So, $\frac{5}{6} > \frac{7}{9}$.

EXAMPLE 2 Ordering Fractions

Order the fractions $\frac{3}{10}$, $\frac{2}{5}$, and $\frac{1}{4}$ from least to greatest.

STEP 1 **Find** the LCD: Because the LCM of 10, 5, and 4 is 20, the LCD is 20.

STEP 2 **Use** the LCD to write equivalent fractions.

$$\frac{3}{10} = \frac{3 \times 2}{10 \times 2} = \frac{6}{20} \qquad \frac{2}{5} = \frac{2 \times 4}{5 \times 4} = \frac{8}{20} \qquad \frac{1}{4} = \frac{1 \times 5}{4 \times 5} = \frac{5}{20}$$

STEP 3 **Compare:** Because $\frac{5}{20} < \frac{6}{20}$, you know that $\frac{1}{4} < \frac{3}{10}$.

Because $\frac{6}{20} < \frac{8}{20}$, you know that $\frac{3}{10} < \frac{2}{5}$.

▶ **Answer** The fractions, from least to greatest, are $\frac{1}{4}$, $\frac{3}{10}$, and $\frac{2}{5}$.

AVOID ERRORS
The fractions with common denominators are used only for comparison. The correct answer is an ordering of the original fractions.

EXAMPLE 3 Ordering Fractions to Solve a Problem

Wrench Sizes You are making repairs to your bicycle. You grab a $\frac{1}{2}$ inch wrench from the toolbox and find it is too small. Should you try a $\frac{5}{8}$ inch wrench or a $\frac{7}{16}$ inch wrench?

SOLUTION

Order the fractions from least to greatest.

STEP 1 **Find** the LCD: Because the LCM of 2, 8, and 16 is 16, the LCD is 16.

STEP 2 **Use** the LCD to write equivalent fractions.

$$\frac{1}{2} = \frac{1 \times 8}{2 \times 8} = \frac{8}{16} \qquad \frac{5}{8} = \frac{5 \times 2}{8 \times 2} = \frac{10}{16} \qquad \frac{7}{16}$$

STEP 3 **Order** the fractions from least to greatest.

$$\frac{7}{16}, \frac{1}{2}, \text{ and } \frac{5}{8}$$

▶ **Answer** You should try the $\frac{5}{8}$ inch wrench.

✓ **GUIDED PRACTICE** for Examples 1, 2, and 3

1. Copy and complete the statement with <, >, or =: $\frac{3}{7} \underline{?} \frac{2}{5}$.

2. Order the fractions from least to greatest: $\frac{7}{12}, \frac{5}{9}, \frac{2}{3}$

3. **What If?** If you needed a wrench slightly smaller than $\frac{3}{4}$ inch, would you choose a $\frac{5}{8}$ inch wrench or a $\frac{13}{16}$ inch wrench?

5.5 EXERCISES

HOMEWORK KEY

★ = STANDARDIZED TEST PRACTICE
Exs. 15, 30–42, 49, 51–54, and 71

◯ = HINTS AND HOMEWORK HELP
for Exs. 5, 7, 19, 21, 47 at classzone.com

SKILL PRACTICE

1. **VOCABULARY** What is a *least common denominator*?

2. **VOCABULARY** Copy and complete: Two fractions are __?__ if they represent the same number.

COMPARING FRACTIONS Copy and complete the statement with <, >, or =.

SEE EXAMPLE 1
on p. 254
for Exs. 3–15

3. $\frac{5}{7} \, ? \, \frac{6}{7}$

4. $\frac{1}{3} \, ? \, \frac{1}{6}$

5. $\frac{9}{21} \, ? \, \frac{3}{7}$

6. $\frac{3}{7} \, ? \, \frac{4}{11}$

7. $\frac{1}{6} \, ? \, \frac{1}{8}$

8. $\frac{2}{3} \, ? \, \frac{5}{7}$

9. $\frac{5}{8} \, ? \, \frac{2}{3}$

10. $\frac{11}{15} \, ? \, \frac{7}{9}$

11. $\frac{3}{4} \, ? \, \frac{5}{7}$

12. $\frac{5}{18} \, ? \, \frac{4}{15}$

13. $\frac{18}{35} \, ? \, \frac{11}{27}$

14. $\frac{15}{38} \, ? \, \frac{41}{98}$

15. ★ **MULTIPLE CHOICE** Which fraction is greater than $\frac{11}{16}$?

Ⓐ $\frac{5}{8}$　　Ⓑ $\frac{6}{8}$　　Ⓒ $\frac{1}{2}$　　Ⓓ $\frac{9}{16}$

16. **ERROR ANALYSIS** Describe and correct the error made in comparing the fractions.

✗ $\frac{7}{100} < \frac{7}{150}$ *because 100 < 150.*

17. **WHICH ONE DOESN'T BELONG?** Which fraction doesn't belong?

A. $\frac{4}{5}$　　B. $\frac{8}{10}$　　C. $\frac{28}{35}$　　D. $\frac{36}{60}$

ORDERING FRACTIONS Order the fractions from least to greatest.

SEE EXAMPLE 2
on p. 255
for Exs. 18–30

18. $\frac{6}{11}, \frac{8}{11}, \frac{5}{11}$

19. $\frac{3}{4}, \frac{2}{3}, \frac{5}{8}$

20. $\frac{7}{9}, \frac{5}{6}, \frac{13}{18}$

21. $\frac{9}{10}, \frac{17}{20}, \frac{4}{5}$

22. $\frac{8}{14}, \frac{11}{28}, \frac{3}{7}$

23. $\frac{5}{9}, \frac{3}{4}, \frac{7}{12}$

24. $\frac{7}{10}, \frac{14}{25}, \frac{1}{2}$

25. $\frac{3}{8}, \frac{11}{24}, \frac{4}{9}$

26. $\frac{37}{50}, \frac{61}{75}, \frac{11}{15}$

27. $\frac{17}{150}, \frac{13}{100}, \frac{4}{30}$

28. $\frac{63}{120}, \frac{41}{80}, \frac{1}{2}$

29. $\frac{105}{225}, \frac{22}{50}, \frac{71}{150}$

30. ★ **MULTIPLE CHOICE** Which list of fractions is in order from least to greatest?

Ⓐ $\frac{3}{7}, \frac{1}{2}, \frac{4}{7}$　　Ⓑ $\frac{1}{2}, \frac{1}{3}, \frac{2}{3}$　　Ⓒ $\frac{1}{3}, \frac{1}{7}, \frac{2}{7}$　　Ⓓ $\frac{1}{2}, \frac{2}{3}, \frac{3}{7}$

★ **OPEN-ENDED MATH** Find a fraction between each pair of fractions.

31. $\frac{3}{7}, \frac{1}{2}$

32. $\frac{7}{12}, \frac{3}{4}$

33. $\frac{7}{10}, \frac{5}{6}$

34. $\frac{3}{8}, \frac{5}{9}$

35. $\frac{2}{13}, \frac{5}{11}$

36. $\frac{1}{3}, \frac{5}{8}$

37. $\frac{11}{16}, \frac{13}{18}$

38. $\frac{9}{10}, \frac{29}{30}$

★ **OPEN-ENDED MATH** Find three fractions between each pair of fractions.

39. $\frac{9}{14}, \frac{11}{14}$

40. $\frac{4}{9}, \frac{7}{9}$

41. $\frac{17}{19}, \frac{18}{19}$

42. $\frac{13}{25}, \frac{14}{25}$

43. CHALLENGE *Explain* how you could compare two fractions whose numerators are the same, such as $\frac{2}{7}$ and $\frac{2}{5}$, without changing them to equivalent fractions with the same denominator.

CHALLENGE Suppose x and y are whole numbers and $x < y$. Copy and complete the statement with <, >, or =.

44. $\frac{1}{x} \; ? \; \frac{1}{y}$

45. $\frac{x}{3} \; ? \; \frac{x}{4}$

46. $\frac{x}{x+1} \; ? \; \frac{y}{y+1}$

PROBLEM SOLVING

on p. 255
for Exs. 47–52

SEE EXAMPLE 3
on p. 255
for Exs. 47–52

47. HEEL HEIGHTS The heel heights on three pairs of shoes in a catalog are $\frac{1}{2}$ inch, $\frac{3}{8}$ inch, and $\frac{3}{4}$ inch. Order the heights from least to greatest.

48. PHOTO ALBUMS You have two photo albums. One is $\frac{13}{16}$ inch thick, and the other is $\frac{7}{8}$ inch thick. Which one is thicker?

49. ★ **SHORT RESPONSE** Jewelry made of 14 carat gold is 14 parts gold and 10 parts other metals, or $\frac{14}{24}$ gold. You are looking at three bracelets that are $\frac{1}{2}, \frac{5}{12}$, and $\frac{2}{3}$ gold. Which bracelet contains the most gold? Are any of the bracelets made of 14 carat gold? Explain.

50. ELECTION RESULTS In a school election, John won $\frac{1}{3}$ of the votes, Ella won $\frac{4}{15}$ of the votes, and Jen won $\frac{2}{5}$ of the votes. Who won the election?

51. ★ **MULTIPLE CHOICE** You need wood for a shelf with a thickness between $\frac{7}{16}$ inch and $\frac{1}{2}$ inch. Which thickness of wood can you use?

(A) $\frac{4}{9}$ in.
(B) $\frac{3}{5}$ in.
(C) $\frac{2}{5}$ in.
(D) $\frac{3}{8}$ in.

52. ★ **EXTENDED RESPONSE** Jeff is purchasing paint brushes. He looks at a set of three paintbrushes with widths $\frac{7}{16}$ inch, $\frac{3}{8}$ inch, and $\frac{1}{4}$ inch. Should he buy the set if he wants a paintbrush with a width of at least $\frac{1}{2}$ inch? with a width less than $\frac{5}{16}$ inch? Should he buy the set if he wants all the brushes to have widths between $\frac{3}{16}$ and $\frac{5}{8}$ inch? *Justify* your answers.

5.5 Ordering Fractions **257**

53. ★ WRITING Jamila says that you can compare fractions by rewriting them with any common denominator. You don't need to use the least common denominator. Is she correct? *Explain.*

54. ★ OPEN-ENDED MATH Write and solve a real-world problem that involves ordering three fractions.

CONTINENTS In Exercises 55–58, use the diagram that shows the fraction of Earth's total land area covered by five of the seven continents. For each given pair of continents, which has the greater land area?

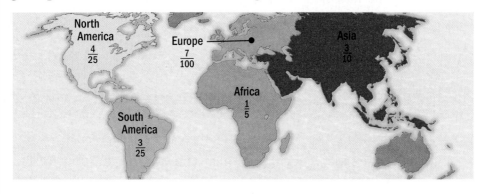

55. Asia or Africa

56. North America or Africa

57. Europe or South America

58. South America or Asia

59. CHALLENGE The continents of Australia and Antarctica (not shown) are the smallest continents. Which continent's area is the median of the seven continents? *Explain* how you found your answer.

60. CHALLENGE Colby, Halle, Joshua, Miguel, and Ruby live on Main Street Colby lives $\frac{3}{8}$ mile from Halle and $\frac{5}{12}$ mile from Miguel. Ruby lives $\frac{1}{9}$ mile from Joshua and $\frac{17}{36}$ mile from Miguel. Miguel lives $\frac{19}{24}$ mile from Halle. If Joshua lives 1 mile west of Colby, what is the order of the houses from west to east?

MIXED REVIEW

Get-Ready

Prepare for Lesson 5.6 in Exs. 61–63

Draw a line segment that has the given length. *(p. 59)*

61. 9.5 centimeters

62. 23 millimeters

63. 7 inches

Copy and complete the statement. *(p. 207)*

64. 10 mg = __?__ g

65. 12 kg = __?__ g

66. 15 L = __?__ kL

Write the fraction in simplest form. *(p. 243)*

67. $\frac{7}{28}$

68. $\frac{12}{20}$

69. $\frac{16}{40}$

70. $\frac{10}{42}$

71. ★ MULTIPLE CHOICE What is the quotient $12.4 \div 4$? *(p. 186)*

Ⓐ 3.1 Ⓑ 8.4 Ⓒ 16.4 Ⓓ 49.6

ONLINE QUIZ at classzone.com

INVESTIGATION

Use before Lesson 5.6

GOAL
Read fractions of an inch on a ruler and express them numerically.

MATERIALS
• ruler

5.6 Measuring Fractions of an Inch

The marks on a ruler represent different fractions of an inch.

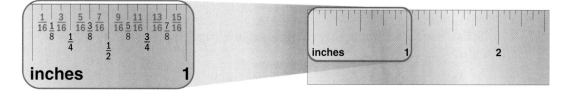

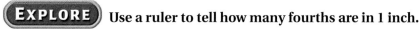

EXPLORE Use a ruler to tell how many fourths are in 1 inch.

STEP 1 **Count** the number of fourths in 1 inch.

STEP 2 **Write** the result of Step 1 as a fraction:

$$1 \text{ inch} = \frac{4}{4} \text{ inch}$$

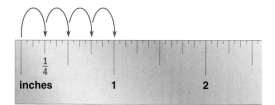

PRACTICE Follow Steps 1 and 2 above to copy and complete the table.

1.

Measure	Whole	Halves	Fourths	Eighths	Sixteenths
1 in.	$\frac{1}{1}$	$\frac{?}{2}$	$\frac{4}{4}$	$\frac{?}{8}$	$\frac{?}{16}$
2 in.	$\frac{2}{1}$	$\frac{?}{2}$	$\frac{?}{4}$	$\frac{?}{8}$	$\frac{?}{16}$
$2\frac{1}{4}$ in.	——	——	$\frac{?}{4}$	$\frac{?}{8}$	$\frac{?}{16}$

DRAW CONCLUSIONS

2. **WRITING** How many eighths are in $2\frac{3}{8}$ inches? *Explain* how you can answer this without using a ruler.

5.6 Mixed Numbers and Improper Fractions **259**

5.6 Mixed Numbers and Improper Fractions

Before	You wrote equivalent fractions.
Now	You'll rewrite mixed numbers and improper fractions.
Why?	So you can express measurements, as in Example 1.

KEY VOCABULARY
- mixed number, *p. 260*
- improper fraction, *p. 260*
- proper fraction, *p. 261*

You can use a ruler to measure lengths to the nearest half, fourth, eighth, or sixteenth of an inch.

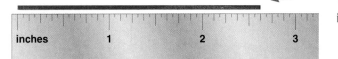

The length of the segment is $2\frac{5}{8}$ inches, or $\frac{21}{8}$ inches.

The number $2\frac{5}{8}$, read as "two and five eighths," is a *mixed number*.

A **mixed number** is the sum of a whole number part and a fraction part.

An **improper fraction**, such as $\frac{21}{8}$, is any fraction in which the numerator is greater than or equal to the denominator. Note that every whole number can be written as an improper fraction with a denominator of 1.

EXAMPLE 1 Measuring to a Fraction of an Inch

VOCABULARY
To help remember the definition of a mixed number, you can think of it as a *mix* involving a whole number and a fraction.

Industrial Arts You are building a birdhouse. You need to measure a piece of wood and then hammer it to the roof. Write the length as a mixed number and as an improper fraction.

SOLUTION

Measure the piece of wood and write the length as a mixed number: $3\frac{3}{4}$ inches.

Then count fourths to write the length as an improper fraction: $\frac{15}{4}$ inches.

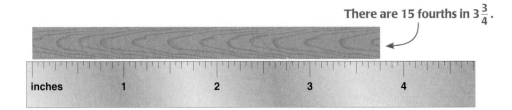

There are 15 fourths in $3\frac{3}{4}$.

✓ **GUIDED PRACTICE** for Example 1

1. Draw a line segment that has a length of $6\frac{1}{4}$ inches.

Rewriting Mixed Numbers One whole can be written in different forms. You can use these and other forms of 1 to write mixed numbers as improper fractions.

$$1 = \frac{1}{1} \qquad 1 = \frac{2}{2} \qquad 1 = \frac{3}{3} \qquad 1 = \frac{4}{4} \qquad 1 = \frac{5}{5}$$

EXAMPLE 2 Rewriting Mixed Numbers

Hat Size A hat has a size of $6\frac{7}{8}$. Write the size as an improper fraction.

SOLUTION

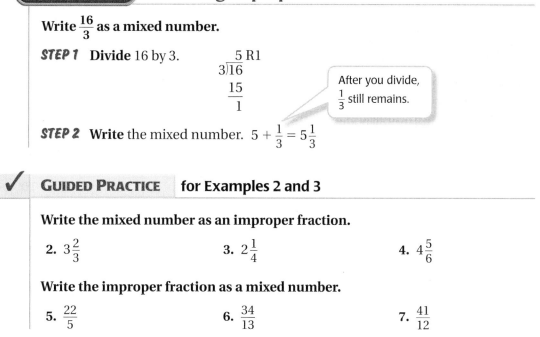

$$6\frac{7}{8} = \frac{48 + 7}{8} \qquad \text{1 whole} = \frac{8}{8}, \text{ so}$$

$$\text{6 wholes} = \frac{6 \times 8}{8}, \text{ or } \frac{48}{8}.$$

$$= \frac{55}{8} \qquad \text{Simplify the numerator.}$$

▶ **Answer** The size of the hat is $\frac{55}{8}$.

Animated **Math** at classzone.com

Rewriting Fractions You can write an improper fraction as a mixed number. First divide the numerator by the denominator. Then write the remainder over the denominator. Make sure that the fraction part is a **proper fraction**, or a fraction in which the numerator is less than the denominator.

EXAMPLE 3 Rewriting Improper Fractions

Write $\frac{16}{3}$ as a mixed number.

STEP 1 Divide 16 by 3.

$$\begin{array}{r} 5\ \text{R1} \\ 3\overline{)16} \\ \underline{15} \\ 1 \end{array}$$

After you divide, $\frac{1}{3}$ still remains.

STEP 2 Write the mixed number. $5 + \frac{1}{3} = 5\frac{1}{3}$

✓ **GUIDED PRACTICE** for Examples 2 and 3

Write the mixed number as an improper fraction.

2. $3\frac{2}{3}$ **3.** $2\frac{1}{4}$ **4.** $4\frac{5}{6}$

Write the improper fraction as a mixed number.

5. $\frac{22}{5}$ **6.** $\frac{34}{13}$ **7.** $\frac{41}{12}$

Comparing Numbers To compare and order mixed numbers and improper fractions, begin by writing them all in the same form. You can use the symbols < and > to replace words when you compare.

⭐ **EXAMPLE 4** Standardized Test Practice

Baseball Bats The widths of three baseball bats at their widest part are $2\frac{5}{8}$, $2\frac{3}{4}$, and $\frac{9}{4}$ inches. What is the order of the widths from least to greatest?

Ⓐ $2\frac{3}{4}, 2\frac{5}{8}, \frac{9}{4}$

Ⓑ $\frac{9}{4}, 2\frac{5}{8}, 2\frac{3}{4}$

Ⓒ $\frac{9}{4}, 2\frac{3}{4}, 2\frac{5}{8}$

Ⓓ $2\frac{5}{8}, \frac{9}{4}, 2\frac{3}{4}$

SOLUTION

STEP 1 **Write** all of the widths as improper fractions.

$$2\frac{5}{8} = \frac{16+5}{8} = \frac{21}{8} \qquad 2\frac{3}{4} = \frac{8+3}{4} = \frac{11}{4} \qquad \frac{9}{4}$$

STEP 2 **Rewrite** all of the widths using the LCD, 8.

$$\frac{21}{8} \qquad \frac{11}{4} = \frac{11 \times 2}{4 \times 2} = \frac{22}{8} \qquad \frac{9}{4} = \frac{9 \times 2}{4 \times 2} = \frac{18}{8}$$

STEP 3 **Compare** the fractions.

Because $\frac{18}{8} < \frac{21}{8}$ and $\frac{21}{8} < \frac{22}{8}$, you know $\frac{9}{4} < 2\frac{5}{8}$ and $2\frac{5}{8} < 2\frac{3}{4}$.

▶ **Answer** The widths, from least to greatest, are $\frac{9}{4}$, $2\frac{5}{8}$, and $2\frac{3}{4}$ inches. The correct answer is B. Ⓐ ⬤ Ⓒ Ⓓ

✓ **GUIDED PRACTICE** for Example 4

Order the numbers from least to greatest.

8. $\frac{15}{4}, 3\frac{1}{4}, 3\frac{1}{2}$

9. $\frac{13}{6}, \frac{7}{3}, 2\frac{2}{9}$

10. $1\frac{1}{2}, \frac{13}{9}, 1\frac{5}{6}$

11. **What If?** Suppose the width of a fourth bat in Example 4 is $2\frac{1}{2}$ inches. Order the four bat widths from least to greatest.

12. **Knitting** Sue, Leann, and Charlie were each knitting a scarf in a knitting class. After the first week Sue had $6\frac{7}{8}$ inches, Leann had $\frac{27}{4}$ inches, and Charlie had $6\frac{4}{9}$ inches. Order the three scarf lengths from greatest to least.

5.6 EXERCISES

HOMEWORK KEY

★ = **STANDARDIZED TEST PRACTICE**
Exs. 14, 19, 34–37, 45, 46, 48, and 60

○ = **HINTS** AND **HOMEWORK HELP**
for Exs. 7, 15, 17, 45 at classzone.com

SKILL PRACTICE

VOCABULARY Define the term and give an example.

1. improper fraction

2. mixed number

MEASUREMENT Use a ruler to measure the candle to the end of its wick. Write the answer as a mixed number and as an improper fraction.

SEE EXAMPLE 1
on p. 260
for Exs. 3–5

3.

4.

5. Draw a line segment that has a length of $\frac{11}{4}$ inches.

REWRITING NUMBERS Write the mixed number as an improper fraction.

SEE EXAMPLE 2
on p. 261
for Exs. 6–14

6. $6\frac{1}{2}$

7. $3\frac{1}{4}$

8. $5\frac{2}{3}$

9. $2\frac{3}{4}$

10. $1\frac{5}{8}$

11. $5\frac{3}{4}$

12. $10\frac{1}{2}$

13. $12\frac{1}{4}$

14. ★ **OPEN-ENDED MATH** Write three fractions equivalent to 1.

SEE EXAMPLE 3
on p. 261
for Exs. 15–19

REWRITING FRACTIONS Write the improper fraction as a mixed number.

15. $\frac{25}{6}$

16. $\frac{15}{4}$

17. $\frac{22}{3}$

18. $\frac{33}{4}$

19. ★ **MULTIPLE CHOICE** Which mixed number is equivalent to $\frac{19}{5}$?

A $3\frac{3}{5}$

B $3\frac{4}{5}$

C $4\frac{1}{5}$

D $4\frac{3}{5}$

20. **ERROR ANALYSIS** Describe and correct the error made in writing the improper fraction as a mixed number.

$$\times \quad \frac{51}{14} \implies 14\overline{)51}^{\;3}_{\;\underline{42}}_{\;\;9} \implies 9\frac{3}{14}$$

SEE EXAMPLE 4
on p. 262
for Exs. 21–37

COMPARING NUMBERS Copy and complete the statement with <, >, or =.

21. $\frac{7}{4}$? $1\frac{1}{4}$

22. $3\frac{2}{3}$? $\frac{11}{3}$

23. $5\frac{2}{5}$? $\frac{28}{5}$

24. $2\frac{4}{7}$? $\frac{20}{7}$

ORDERING NUMBERS Order the numbers from least to greatest.

25. $\frac{7}{2}, 2\frac{3}{4}, 3$

26. $\frac{23}{5}, \frac{19}{4}, 4\frac{1}{2}$

27. $5, \frac{41}{8}, \frac{17}{3}, 5\frac{1}{6}$

28. $1\frac{4}{5}, \frac{15}{8}, \frac{7}{4}, 1\frac{5}{6}$

29. $6\frac{2}{3}, \frac{13}{2}, 6\frac{5}{6}, \frac{33}{5}$

30. $\frac{27}{10}, 2\frac{3}{5}, 2\frac{7}{12}, \frac{11}{4}$

31. $8\frac{3}{8}, \frac{25}{3}, \frac{76}{9}, 8\frac{1}{4}$

32. $\frac{89}{9}, 9\frac{4}{5}, \frac{59}{6}, \frac{119}{12}$

33. $\frac{36}{5}, 7\frac{4}{9}, \frac{43}{6}, 7\frac{3}{8}$

★ **OPEN-ENDED MATH** Find a mixed number that is between the numbers.

34. $1\frac{3}{5}$, $\frac{11}{5}$ **35.** $\frac{9}{2}$, 5   **36.** 3, $\frac{27}{8}$ **37.** $5\frac{4}{9}$, $\frac{29}{5}$

DRAWING You are drawing a branch for an art class. Find the distance to each point along the branch to the nearest inch, half inch, quarter inch, eighth inch, and sixteenth inch. Write the distance as either a fraction or as a mixed number and improper fraction.

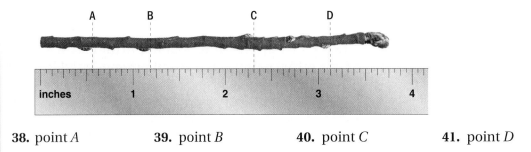

38. point A **39.** point B **40.** point C **41.** point D

42. **CHALLENGE** In Exercises 38–41, you read a ruler marked in sixteenths of inches. *Explain* how you would measure a length to the nearest sixteenth if your ruler was marked only in eighth inches.

43. **CHALLENGE** Can you write any whole number as a proper fraction? Can you write any whole number as an improper fraction? If so, is it unique? *Explain.*

PROBLEM SOLVING

44. **REPAIRS** A cracked decorative window in a front door is $\frac{13}{4}$ inches wide. Write the improper fraction as a mixed number.

45. ★ **MULTIPLE CHOICE** A jewelry box is $4\frac{5}{8}$ inches wide. Which choice shows $4\frac{5}{8}$ written as an improper fraction?

Ⓐ $\frac{20}{8}$ inches   Ⓑ $\frac{32}{8}$ inches   Ⓒ $\frac{37}{8}$ inches   Ⓓ $\frac{37}{5}$ inches

46. ★ **SHORT RESPONSE** You have $3\frac{1}{3}$ bags of peanuts and you want to give $\frac{1}{3}$ bag each to 15 people. Do you have enough peanuts? *Explain.*

47. **MULTI-STEP PROBLEM** In a swimming competition, three swimmers finished $2\frac{19}{20}$, $\frac{16}{5}$, and $3\frac{11}{15}$ seconds behind the winning swimmer.

  a. Write the three numbers as improper fractions with a common denominator.

  b. How far behind the winner was the second place swimmer? the third place swimmer? the fourth place swimmer?

48. ★ **WRITING** *Explain* how to rewrite a mixed number as an improper fraction and how to rewrite an improper fraction as a mixed number.

Read the pattern information below for Exercises 49–50.

Sewing The amount of material you need to make a garment is shown in a chart on the pattern. The amount depends on the width of the fabric (generally 45 inches or 60 inches), the style of the garment, and the size.

	Sizes	small (6–8)	medium (10–12)	large (14–16)
	Top (Long Sleeved)			
	45 in.	$1\frac{1}{2}$ yards	$1\frac{1}{2}$ yards	$1\frac{5}{8}$ yards
	60 in.	$1\frac{1}{2}$ yards	$1\frac{1}{2}$ yards	$1\frac{1}{2}$ yards
	Top (Short Sleeved)			
	45 in.	$1\frac{1}{8}$ yards	$1\frac{1}{4}$ yards	$1\frac{5}{8}$ yards
	60 in.	$\frac{7}{8}$ yard	1 yard	$1\frac{1}{4}$ yards

49. **Calculate** Write an improper fraction for the yards of fabric needed to make a small short sleeved top, using material that is 45 inches wide. Is this more than $\frac{5}{4}$ yards? *Explain.*

50. **Decide** With $1\frac{1}{3}$ yards of 45-inch wide material left over from another project, which medium-sized garment can you sew? *Explain.*

51. **POLE VAULTING** The pole vault records for four schools are shown in the table. Which school's record is the highest?

School	Oakmont	Chester	Central	Perry
Pole vault height (feet)	$\frac{49}{3}$	$16\frac{3}{8}$	$\frac{33}{2}$	$16\frac{9}{16}$

52. **CHALLENGE** An improper fraction is more than 2 and less than $2\frac{1}{4}$. The sum of the numerator and the denominator is 19. What is the number?

MIXED REVIEW

Get-Ready
Prepare for Lesson 5.7 in Exs. 53–56

Write the decimal in words. *(p. 119)*

53. 14.1   54. 23.5   55. 64.92   56. 78.15

Evaluate the expression. *(p. 29)*

57. $20 \div x$, when $x = 2$ 58. $x - 2$, when $x = 21$ 59. $15 - x + 4$, when $x = 3$

60. ★ **MULTIPLE CHOICE** What is $\frac{48}{80}$ in simplest form? *(p. 243)*

Ⓐ $\frac{24}{40}$ Ⓑ $\frac{12}{20}$ Ⓒ $\frac{6}{10}$ Ⓓ $\frac{3}{5}$

5.7 Changing Decimals to Fractions

Before	You wrote decimals and fractions.
Now	You'll write a decimal as a fraction.
Why?	So you can write numbers multiple ways, such as planet data in Example 2.

KEY VOCABULARY

- **simplest form,** *p. 244*
- **mixed number,** *p. 260*

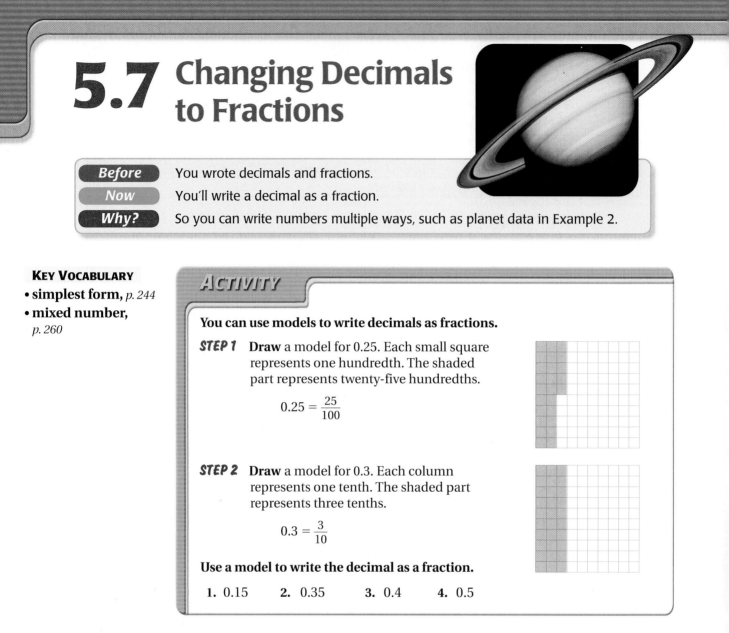

ACTIVITY

You can use models to write decimals as fractions.

STEP 1 Draw a model for 0.25. Each small square represents one hundredth. The shaded part represents twenty-five hundredths.

$$0.25 = \frac{25}{100}$$

STEP 2 Draw a model for 0.3. Each column represents one tenth. The shaded part represents three tenths.

$$0.3 = \frac{3}{10}$$

Use a model to write the decimal as a fraction.

1. 0.15　　**2.** 0.35　　**3.** 0.4　　**4.** 0.5

You can use decimal place value to help you write a decimal as a fraction in simplest form.

one tenth	one hundredth	one thousandth
$0.1 = \frac{1}{10}$	$0.01 = \frac{1}{100}$	$0.001 = \frac{1}{1000}$

EXAMPLE 1　Writing Decimals as Fractions

COMMON DECIMALS

Learn the fraction form of these common decimals:

$0.5 = \frac{1}{2}$　　$0.125 = \frac{1}{8}$

$0.25 = \frac{1}{4}$　　$0.75 = \frac{3}{4}$

$0.2 = \frac{1}{5}$　　$0.4 = \frac{2}{5}$

Write the decimal as a fraction in simplest form.

a. $0.8 = \frac{8}{10} = \frac{4}{5}$　　Write eight tenths as a fraction. Simplify.

b. $0.36 = \frac{36}{100} = \frac{9}{25}$　　Write thirty-six hundredths as a fraction. Simplify.

EXAMPLE 2 Writing Decimals as Mixed Numbers

Planets The length of a planet's day is the time it takes the planet to rotate once about its axis. Write each length as a mixed number in simplest form.

a. Length of day on Saturn: 10.5 hours

b. Length of day on Jupiter: 9.92 hours

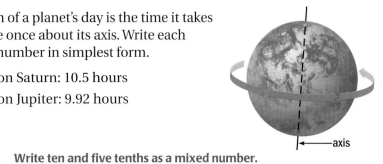

←—axis

SOLUTION

ANOTHER WAY

You may have written the decimal as a mixed number in one step by recognizing the common decimal 0.5, which equals $\frac{1}{2}$.

a. $10.5 = 10\frac{5}{10}$ Write ten and five tenths as a mixed number.

$ = 10\frac{1}{2}$ Simplify.

▶ **Answer** The length of a day on Saturn is $10\frac{1}{2}$ hours.

b. $9.92 = 9\frac{92}{100}$ Write nine and ninety-two hundredths as a mixed number.

$ = 9\frac{23}{25}$ Simplify.

▶ **Answer** The length of a day on Jupiter is $9\frac{23}{25}$ hours.

EXAMPLE 3 Decimals with Zeros

Write the decimal as a fraction or mixed number in simplest form.

a. $2.04 = 2\frac{4}{100}$ Write two and four hundredths as a mixed number.

$ = 2\frac{1}{25}$ Simplify.

b. $4.005 = 4\frac{5}{1000}$ Write four and five thousandths as a mixed number.

$ = 4\frac{1}{200}$ Simplify.

c. $0.608 = \frac{608}{1000}$ Write six hundred eight thousandths as a fraction.

$ = \frac{76}{125}$ Simplify.

✓ **GUIDED PRACTICE**   for Examples 1, 2, and 3

Write the decimal as a fraction or mixed number in simplest form.

1. 0.4   **2.** 0.18   **3.** 1.7   **4.** 1.82

5. 0.03   **6.** 2.005   **7.** 1.025   **8.** 0.405

9. What If? The length of a day on Mars is 24.62 hours. Write the length as a mixed number in simplest form.

5.7 EXERCISES

HOMEWORK KEY

★ = **STANDARDIZED TEST PRACTICE**
Exs. 11, 49, 51, 54, and 57

◯ = **HINTS** AND **HOMEWORK HELP**
for Exs. 3, 9, 13, 23, 47 at classzone.com

SKILL PRACTICE

1. **VOCABULARY** Explain how you know a fraction is in simplest form.

2. **VOCABULARY** Which number below is a mixed number? *Explain.*

$$2\frac{1}{8}, \frac{17}{4}, 6.8, 0.25$$

WRITING FRACTIONS Write the decimal as a fraction in simplest form.

SEE EXAMPLE 1
on p. 266
for Exs. 3–12

3. 0.5   **4.** 0.1   **5.** 0.7   **6.** 0.95

7. 0.02   **8.** 0.23   **9.** 0.005   **10.** 0.039

11. ★ **MULTIPLE CHOICE** Which fraction is equivalent to the decimal 0.24?

   A $\frac{1}{24}$ **B** $\frac{3}{25}$ **C** $\frac{6}{25}$ **D** $\frac{12}{25}$

12. **ERROR ANALYSIS** Describe and correct the error made in the solution.

$$\bcancel{\quad} \; 0.7 = \frac{7}{100}$$

COMPLETING FRACTIONS Copy and complete the statement.

SEE EXAMPLE 2
on p. 267
for Exs. 13–20

13. $3.27 = ?\frac{27}{100}$ **14.** $2.3 = 2\frac{3}{?}$ **15.** $6.2 = 6\frac{?}{10}$ **16.** $5.23 = 5\frac{23}{?}$

WRITING FRACTIONS Write the decimal as a fraction or mixed number in simplest form.

17. 5.9   **18.** 9.3   **19.** 1.24   **20.** 12.32

SEE EXAMPLE 3
on p. 267
for Exs. 21–28

21. 4.06   **22.** 3.01   **23.** 9.02   **24.** 1.09

25. 0.039   **26.** 0.102   **27.** 6.306   **28.** 9.005

ALGEBRA Solve the equation.

29. $0.6 = \frac{x}{5}$ **30.** $0.25 = \frac{3}{k}$ **31.** $0.375 = \frac{a}{8}$ **32.** $1.5 = \frac{3}{y}$

33. $0.9 = \frac{27}{d}$ **34.** $11.5 = \frac{23}{g}$ **35.** $2.125 = \frac{b}{16}$ **36.** $1.32 = \frac{n}{25}$

WRITING IMPROPER FRACTIONS Write the decimal as an improper fraction in simplest form.

37. 2.37   **38.** 6.95   **39.** 9.86   **40.** 5.34

WRITING FRACTIONS Write each decimal as two fractions, one with a denominator of 16 and the other with a denominator of 40.

41. 0.25   **42.** 0.5   **43.** 0.75   **44.** 0.875

45. CHALLENGE *Explain* how you can write a decimal as an improper fraction without first writing the decimal as a mixed number.

46. CHALLENGE Find the sum of 0.03 and 0.7 by writing both decimals as fractions, adding the fractions, and writing the sum as a decimal.

PROBLEM SOLVING

SEE EXAMPLE 2
on p. 267
for Ex. 47

47. MILEAGE A bus driver records the distance traveled during a week as 398.4 miles. Write this distance as a mixed number in simplest form.

48. CAR RENTAL Some friends rent a car for a weekend trip. At the end of the trip, the car's dashboard computer reports that the gas tank is 0.05 full. Write the gas they used as a fraction in simplest form.

49. ★ MULTIPLE CHOICE A survey at a middle school found that 0.65 of the sixth grade students named basketball as their favorite sport. Which fraction represents the decimal 0.65?

Ⓐ $\frac{3}{5}$ Ⓑ $\frac{13}{20}$ Ⓒ $\frac{7}{10}$ Ⓓ $\frac{3}{4}$

50. PRECIPITATION The normal monthly precipitation for Tucson, Arizona, is 0.20 inches in May and 1.65 inches in September. Write the difference of these amounts as a mixed number in simplest form.

51. ★ WRITING Yesterday's midday temperature was 42.3°F. The low and high temperatures for the day were each 11.8°F from the midday temperature. Find the high and low temperatures for the day written as mixed numbers. *Explain* how you found your answers.

52. MULTI-STEP PROBLEM The graph shows the portion of space in a mall occupied by each type of store. The portions are written as decimals.

a. Which type of store occupies the least amount of space in the mall? the most?

b. Use the circle graph to order the types of stores by the portion of space they occupy, from least to greatest.

c. Write the decimals from part (b) as fractions in simplest form, in order from least to greatest.

d. The mall has an area of about 200,000 square feet. Estimate the square feet occupied by each of the store types.

Mall Space by Store Type

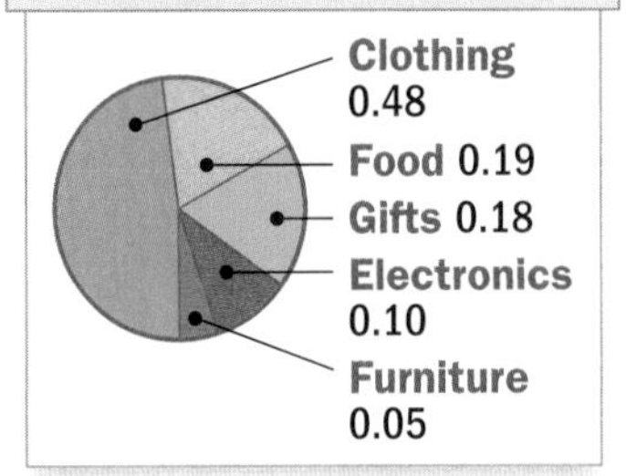

Clothing 0.48
Food 0.19
Gifts 0.18
Electronics 0.10
Furniture 0.05

53. BEE LENGTH A bee has a length of approximately 0.4708 inch.

   a. Write the bee's length as a fraction in simplest form.

   b. Write the bee's length as a decimal rounded to the nearest tenth.

   c. Write the rounded length as a fraction in simplest form.

   d. Compare the fractions from parts (a) and (c). Which is greater? *Explain* your reasoning.

54. ★ OPEN-ENDED MATH *Describe* a real-life situation where it would be easier to have a quantity in the form of a fraction or a mixed number rather than a decimal.

55. CHALLENGE The number of free throws a basketball player made in a season divided by the number of attempted free throws was 0.82. The player attempted 400 free throws. How many free throws did the player make?

56. CHALLENGE Mark says that 60.08 is 10 times 6.08. Rewrite both numbers as mixed numbers to tell whether you agree or not. If you disagree, find the improper fraction that is 10 times 6.08.

MIXED REVIEW

57. ★ MULTIPLE CHOICE Which is equivalent to 367 minutes? *(p. 754)*

   (A) 3 hours 67 minutes   **(B)** 6 hours 7 minutes

   (C) 6 hours 17 minutes   **(D)** 7 hours 17 minutes

Get-Ready

Prepare for Lesson 5.8 in Exs. 58–65

Divide. Round your answer to the nearest tenth, if necessary. *(p. 186)*

58. $8 \div 11$ **59.** $6 \div 12$ **60.** $3 \div 5$ **61.** $5 \div 9$

62. $3.5 \div 5$ **63.** $7.2 \div 9$ **64.** $4.5 \div 6$ **65.** $2.2 \div 9$

CHOOSE A STRATEGY Use a strategy from the list to solve the following problem. *Explain* your choice of strategy.

66. You have 2 photographs that are the same size. How many ways can you arrange them (face up and right-side up) next to each other to form a rectangle with twice the area of one photo?

67. Order the fractions $\frac{5}{6}$, $\frac{1}{2}$, and $\frac{13}{18}$ from least to greatest. *(p. 254)*

Problem Solving Strategies

- Draw a Diagram *(p. 762)*
- Guess, Check, and Revise *(p. 763)*
- Work Backward *(p. 764)*
- Act It Out *(p. 770)*

5.8 Changing Fractions to Decimals

Before	You wrote decimals as fractions.
Now	You'll write fractions as decimals.
Why?	So you can rewrite lengths, as in Example 2.

KEY VOCABULARY
- terminating decimal, *p. 272*
- repeating decimal, *p. 272*

Lighthouses At one time, 31 out of the 50 states in the United States had lighthouses. This can be written as the fraction $\frac{31}{50}$. How can you write this fraction as a decimal?

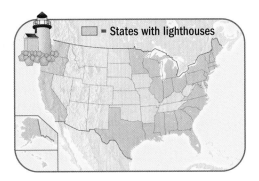

= States with lighthouses

EXAMPLE 1 Writing a Fraction as a Decimal

ANOTHER WAY

If the denominator can easily be divided into 10, 100, or 1000, use equivalent fractions.

$\frac{31}{50} = \frac{62}{100}$, or 0.62

To answer the question above about lighthouses, write the fraction $\frac{31}{50}$ as a decimal by dividing 31 by 50.

$$
\begin{array}{r}
0.62 \\
50\overline{)31.00} \\
\underline{30\ 0} \\
1\ 00 \\
\underline{1\ 00} \\
0
\end{array}
$$

The remainder is 0.

▸ **Answer** The quotient is 0.62, so 0.62 of the states had lighthouses.

KEY CONCEPT　　　　　　　　　　　*For Your Notebook*

Writing a Fraction as a Decimal

Words　To write a fraction as a decimal, divide the numerator by the denominator.

Numbers　$\frac{1}{4}$ means $1 \div 4$　**Algebra**　$\frac{a}{b}$ means $a \div b$ ($b \neq 0$)

✓ **GUIDED PRACTICE**　for Example 1

Write the fraction as a decimal.

1. $\frac{1}{2}$　　　　**2.** $\frac{4}{5}$　　　　**3.** $\frac{1}{4}$　　　　**4.** $\frac{3}{8}$

EXAMPLE 2 Writing a Mixed Number as a Decimal

Deer A deer has an antler spread of $15\frac{2}{5}$ inches. Write this as a decimal.

SOLUTION

STEP 1 **Divide** 2 by 5.

$$\begin{array}{r} 0.4 \\ 5\overline{)2.0} \\ \underline{2\ 0} \\ 0 \end{array}$$

STEP 2 **Add** the whole number and the decimal.

$$15 + 0.4 = 15.4$$

▶ **Answer** Written as a decimal, the spread of the antlers is 15.4 inches.

Types of Decimals A decimal is called a **terminating decimal** when it has a final digit, such as 15.4 in Example 2. A decimal is called a **repeating decimal** when one or more nonzero digits repeat forever. A repeating decimal can be written with a bar over the digits that repeat.

One digit repeats: $0.3333\ldots = 0.\overline{3}$

Two digits repeat: $2.010101\ldots = 2.\overline{01}$

Three digits repeat: $0.4205205\ldots = 0.4\overline{205}$

EXAMPLE 3 Repeating Decimals

a. Write $\frac{7}{6}$ as a decimal.

$$\begin{array}{r} 1.166\ldots \\ 6\overline{)7.000} \\ \underline{6} \\ 1\ 0 \\ \underline{6} \\ 40 \\ \underline{36} \\ 40 \\ \underline{36} \\ 4 \end{array}$$

The digit 6 repeats.

▶ **Answer** $\frac{7}{6} = 1.1\overline{6}$

b. Write $1\frac{5}{33}$ as a decimal.

$$\begin{array}{r} 0.1515\ldots \\ 33\overline{)5.0000} \\ \underline{3\ 3} \\ 170 \\ \underline{165} \\ 50 \\ \underline{33} \\ 170 \\ \underline{165} \\ 5 \end{array}$$

The digits 1 and 5 repeat.

▶ **Answer** $1\frac{5}{33} = 1.\overline{15}$

Animated Math at classzone.com

✓ **GUIDED PRACTICE** for Examples 2 and 3

Write the fraction or mixed number as a decimal.

5. $5\frac{2}{5}$ **6.** $3\frac{5}{8}$ **7.** $\frac{2}{3}$ **8.** $3\frac{2}{11}$

9. $7\frac{3}{8}$ **10.** $\frac{9}{11}$ **11.** $4\frac{11}{12}$ **12.** $2\frac{5}{16}$

5.8 EXERCISES

HOMEWORK
KEY

★ = **STANDARDIZED TEST PRACTICE**
Exs. 13, 39–42, 52, 55, 56, and 67

◯ = **HINTS AND HOMEWORK HELP**
for Exs. 5, 11, 19, 25, 49 at classzone.com

SKILL PRACTICE

VOCABULARY Is the decimal *repeating* or *terminating*?

1. 0.875

2. 0.2$\overline{3}$

3. 4.2$\overline{27}$

4. 0.700

SEE EXAMPLE 1
on p. 271
for Exs. 5–8,
13, 26

WRITING DECIMALS Write the fraction or mixed number as a decimal.

5. $\dfrac{3}{10}$

6. $\dfrac{2}{5}$

7. $\dfrac{3}{5}$

8. $\dfrac{9}{20}$

SEE EXAMPLE 2
on p. 272
for Exs. 9–12

9. $1\dfrac{1}{8}$

10. $2\dfrac{3}{4}$

11. $3\dfrac{1}{4}$

12. $2\dfrac{21}{25}$

13. ★ **MULTIPLE CHOICE** Andre read $\dfrac{21}{40}$ of a history chapter to prepare for his presentation. What decimal represents the portion he read?

(A) 0.053

(B) 0.525

(C) 1.905

(D) 5.25

SEE EXAMPLE 3
on p. 272
for Exs. 14–25

USING BAR NOTATION Rewrite the repeating decimal using bar notation.

14. 0.111111 . . .

15. 3.727272 . . .

16. 8.040404 . . .

17. 0.466666 . . .

REPEATING DECIMALS Write the number as a repeating decimal.

18. $\dfrac{8}{15}$

19. $4\dfrac{5}{22}$

20. $\dfrac{1}{6}$

21. $\dfrac{5}{18}$

22. $\dfrac{8}{3}$

23. $5\dfrac{8}{9}$

24. $1\dfrac{6}{11}$

25. $\dfrac{7}{12}$

26. **ERROR ANALYSIS** Describe and correct the error made in writing the fraction as a decimal.

$$\frac{7}{33} \longrightarrow 33\overline{)7.00} \quad \begin{array}{r} 0.21 \ldots \\ \underline{6\,6} \\ 40 \\ \underline{33} \\ 7 \end{array} \longrightarrow 0.2\overline{1}$$

COMPARING NUMBERS Copy and complete the statement with <, >, or =.

27. $4\dfrac{1}{11}$ $\underline{?}$ 4.1

28. $\dfrac{11}{16}$ $\underline{?}$ 0.6875

29. $\dfrac{7}{9}$ $\underline{?}$ 0.$\overline{7}$

30. $\dfrac{22}{3}$ $\underline{?}$ 7.0$\overline{3}$

31. 0.45 $\underline{?}$ $\dfrac{8}{20}$

32. 2.1 $\underline{?}$ $\dfrac{23}{10}$

33. $5\dfrac{7}{10}$ $\underline{?}$ 5.65

34. 0.56 $\underline{?}$ $\dfrac{14}{25}$

35. 5.15 $\underline{?}$ $\dfrac{103}{20}$

36. $1\dfrac{7}{20}$ $\underline{?}$ 1.85

37. $2\dfrac{41}{200}$ $\underline{?}$ 2.255

38. 6.625 $\underline{?}$ $6\dfrac{5}{8}$

★ **OPEN-ENDED MATH** Find a decimal that is between the two numbers.

39. $\dfrac{9}{16}, \dfrac{5}{8}$

40. $2\dfrac{12}{13}, 3\dfrac{1}{8}$

41. $\dfrac{22}{5}, 1$

42. $7\dfrac{6}{7}, 8$

ORDERING NUMBERS **Order the numbers from least to greatest.**

43. $\frac{7}{11}$, 0.56, $\frac{11}{16}$, $0.\overline{5}$

44. $3.\overline{45}$, $3\frac{7}{13}$, 3.482, $3\frac{12}{25}$

45. $2\frac{13}{19}$, $2.6\overline{81}$, $2\frac{17}{25}$, $2.\overline{68}$

46. $0.\overline{259}$, $\frac{11}{41}$, $\frac{5}{19}$, $0.25\overline{7}$

47. CHALLENGE Write $\frac{1}{7}$ as a decimal. How many digits repeat?

48. CHALLENGE Classify each of the fractions $\frac{5}{6}$, $\frac{3}{11}$, $\frac{1}{2}$, $\frac{12}{25}$, $\frac{2}{3}$, and $\frac{3}{5}$ as *repeating* or *terminating*. For each fraction, list the prime factors of the denominator. Using the list of prime factors, *explain* how you can tell if a fraction will be repeating or terminating.

PROBLEM SOLVING

TEXAS LIZARDS **The three species of Texas horned lizards and their maximum lengths are shown. Use the diagram for Exercises 49–51.**

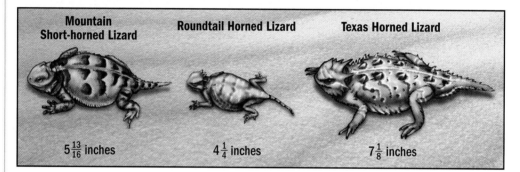

Mountain Short-horned Lizard $5\frac{13}{16}$ inches

Roundtail Horned Lizard $4\frac{1}{4}$ inches

Texas Horned Lizard $7\frac{1}{8}$ inches

49. Write each length as a decimal.

50. Write as a decimal the difference between the lengths of the shortest and longest lizards.

51. Write the difference you calculated in Exercise 50 as an improper fraction.

52. ★ **MULTIPLE CHOICE** Janet got a hit $\frac{7}{27}$ of her times at bat. What is the fraction written as a decimal rounded to the nearest thousandth?

(**A**) 0.258   (**B**) 0.259   (**C**) 0.260   (**D**) 0.369

53. FISHING On a fishing trip, you catch five fish. The lengths, in inches, of the fish are given below. Order the lengths from least to greatest.

$13\frac{3}{16}$ 13.25 $\frac{55}{4}$ $13\frac{3}{8}$ 13.1

54. WATER CONTENT About $\frac{23}{25}$ of a watermelon is water. Write this fraction as a decimal. Then write the part of a watermelon that is *not* water as a decimal.

★ = **STANDARDIZED TEST PRACTICE**   ◯ = **HINTS AND HOMEWORK HELP** *at classzone.com*

55. ★ SHORT RESPONSE Write $\frac{1}{11}$, $\frac{2}{11}$, and $\frac{3}{11}$ as decimals. Predict what the decimal equivalents of $\frac{4}{11}$ and $\frac{5}{11}$ will be. *Explain.*

56. ★ WRITING Describe the procedure for rewriting a mixed number as a decimal.

57. CHALLENGE Based on the following examples, write a rule for writing as a fraction any decimal in which all digits repeat.

$$0.\overline{2} = \frac{2}{9} \qquad 0.\overline{5} = \frac{5}{9} \qquad 0.\overline{16} = \frac{16}{99} \qquad 0.\overline{412} = \frac{412}{999}$$

58. CHALLENGE Based on the following examples, write a rule for writing as a fraction any decimal in which some digits repeat.

$$0.\overline{1} = \frac{1}{9} \qquad 0.0\overline{1} = \frac{1}{90} \qquad 0.01\overline{45} = \frac{145 - 1}{9900} \qquad 0.12\overline{51} = \frac{1251 - 12}{9900}$$

MIXED REVIEW

Get-Ready

Prepare for Lesson 6.1 in Exs. 59–66

Round the decimal as specified. *(p. 137)*

59. 0.45 (nearest tenth)

60. 0.689 (nearest hundredth)

61. 1.9999 (nearest thousandth)

62. 6.9135 (nearest one)

Estimate the sum.

63. $488 + 310 + 845$ *(p. 11)*

64. $1987 + 5006 + 2640$ *(p. 11)*

65. $8.62 + 1.75$ *(p. 143)*

66. $3.8 + 10.55 + 1.81$ *(p. 143)*

67. ★ MULTIPLE CHOICE What is the prime factorization of 504? *(p. 230)*

Ⓐ $2^3 \times 63$ Ⓑ $2^3 \times 7 \times 9$ Ⓒ $2^3 \times 3^2 \times 7$ Ⓓ $2^2 \times 3^3 \times 7$

QUIZ *for Lessons 5.4–5.8*

Find the LCM of the numbers. *(p. 250)*

1. 4, 11   **2.** 4, 14   **3.** 21, 72   **4.** 4, 6, 10

5. Order the fractions $\frac{9}{28}$, $\frac{3}{14}$, $\frac{1}{4}$ from least to greatest. *(p. 254)*

Copy and complete the statement with <, >, or =. *(p. 260)*

6. $3\frac{2}{5}\ \underline{?}\ \frac{16}{5}$ **7.** $1\frac{17}{28}\ \underline{?}\ \frac{13}{7}$ **8.** $\frac{28}{15}\ \underline{?}\ 1\frac{4}{5}$ **9.** $2\frac{1}{11}\ \underline{?}\ \frac{45}{22}$

10. Write $\frac{31}{8}$ as a mixed number. *(p. 260)*   **11.** Write $2\frac{3}{14}$ as an improper fraction. *(p. 260)*

12. Write $3\frac{4}{15}$ as a decimal. Does it terminate or repeat? *(p. 271)*

Write the decimal as a fraction or mixed number in simplest form. *(p. 266)*

13. 0.56   **14.** 0.409   **15.** 1.03   **16.** 1.88

5.8 Decimals and Fractions

EXAMPLE You can write fractions as decimals using a calculator.

On January 29, 2001, the New York Stock Exchange began reporting all stock prices as decimals instead of fractions and mixed numbers. The value of a stock was listed as \$$34\frac{5}{8}$ before the conversion. How would this value be listed after the conversion?

SOLUTION

To convert a mixed number to a decimal, divide the numerator of the fraction by the denominator and add the whole number part.

Keystrokes	Display
5 ÷ 8 + 34 =	**34.625**

Since dollar amounts are given in cents, round your answer to the nearest hundredth.

▶ **Answer** After the conversion, the value of this stock would be listed as \$34.63.

PRACTICE Write the fraction or mixed number as a decimal. Round to the nearest hundredth, if necessary.

1. $\frac{5}{6}$ 2. $\frac{1}{8}$ 3. $\frac{5}{16}$ 4. $\frac{99}{160}$

5. $5\frac{3}{8}$ 6. $4\frac{11}{20}$ 7. $13\frac{7}{18}$ 8. $18\frac{9}{40}$

9. $29\frac{3}{16}$ 10. $45\frac{9}{32}$ 11. $50\frac{41}{50}$ 12. $67\frac{23}{125}$

13. $36\frac{7}{20}$ 14. $61\frac{11}{35}$ 15. $48\frac{7}{12}$ 16. $27\frac{15}{23}$

17. **ORDER OF OPERATIONS** A calculator that follows the order of operations will get 34.625 from the keystrokes 34 **+** 5 **÷** 8. Determine whether your calculator observes the order of operations.

18. **STOCKS** The value of a stock was listed as \$$13\frac{3}{8}$ before the conversion to decimals. How was this value listed after the conversion?

Lessons 5.4–5.8

1. **SHORT RESPONSE** The table shows the annual average wind speed for various cities.

City	Wind Speed (miles per hour)
Omaha	$10\frac{1}{2}$
Chicago	$10\frac{3}{10}$
Honolulu	$\frac{113}{10}$

   a. Order the wind speeds from least to greatest.

   b. Cleveland has an annual average wind speed of $\frac{21}{2}$ miles per hour. How does this compare with each of the cities in the table? *Explain.*

2. **SHORT RESPONSE** Nitrogen makes up $\frac{39}{50}$ of Earth's atmosphere.

   a. Write the fraction as a decimal.

   b. Write the portion of the Earth's atmosphere that is *not* nitrogen as a decimal.

3. **OPEN-ENDED** Sara wants to find a repeating decimal between 4 and 4.1. Describe a strategy she could use, and name a decimal that fits the description.

4. **GRIDDED ANSWER** A baseball player pitches every fifth day. An opposing player pitches every fourth day. The two pitchers just pitched on the same day. In how many days will they pitch on the same day again?

5. **MULTI-STEP PROBLEM** A penny is $\frac{3}{4}$ inch across and a dime is $\frac{141}{200}$ inch across.

   a. Which is wider, a penny or a dime?

   b. The Euro, a currency used in Europe, has a 10 cent piece that is about $\frac{7}{9}$ inch across. Is this coin wider than a dime? Is it wider than a penny?

   c. You have each of the three coins in front of you and want to stack them with the widest on the bottom. In what order would you stack them? *Explain.*

6. **EXTENDED RESPONSE** Visitors to a redesigned website were asked their opinion on the new design. The graph shows the portion of participants who chose each response. The portions are written as decimals.

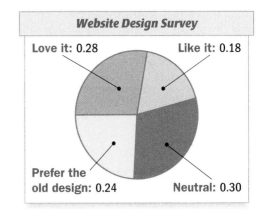

Website Design Survey

Love it: 0.28
Like it: 0.18
Prefer the old design: 0.24
Neutral: 0.30

   a. Write the decimals from the graph as fractions in simplest form.

   b. Order the fractions from part (a) from least to greatest.

   c. Of the 10,000 visitors who participated in the survey, how many chose the most common response?

   d. What was the difference between the number of people who chose the most common response and the number who chose the least common response? *Explain* your reasoning.

REVIEW KEY VOCABULARY

- divisible, *p. 230*
- prime number, *p. 231*
- composite number, *p. 231*
- prime factorization, *p. 232*
- factor tree, *p. 232*
- common factor, *p. 236*
- greatest common factor (GCF), *p. 236*

- fraction, *p. 243*
- equivalent fractions, *p. 243*
- simplest form, *p. 244*
- multiple, *p. 250*
- common multiple, *p. 250*
- least common multiple (LCM), *p. 251*

- least common denominator (LCD), *p. 254*
- mixed number, *p. 260*
- improper fraction, *p. 260*
- proper fraction, *p. 261*
- terminating decimal, *p. 272*
- repeating decimal, *p. 272*

VOCABULARY EXERCISES

1. What is a *common multiple*?

2. What does it mean when one number is divisible by another number?

3. Give three examples of a prime number. What makes them prime?

4. Give three examples of a composite number. What makes them composite?

Copy and complete the statement.

5. Two fractions are __?__ if they represent the same number.

6. A fraction is in __?__ if its numerator and denominator have a GCF of 1.

7. The numerator of a __?__ is less than the denominator.

REVIEW EXAMPLES AND EXERCISES

5.1 Prime Factorization
pp. 230–235

EXAMPLE

Test 574 for divisibility by 2, 3, 5, 6, 9, and 10.

574 is even, so it is divisible by 2.

$5 + 7 + 4 = 16$, which is not divisible by 3 or 9, so 574 is not either.

574 does not end with 0 or 5, so it is not divisible by 5 or 10.

574 is not divisible by 6 because it is not divisible by 3.

▶ **Answer** 574 is divisible by 2.

EXERCISES

Test the number for divisibility by 2, 3, 5, 6, 9, and 10.

SEE EXAMPLES
1, 2, AND 4
on pp. 230–232
for Exs. 8–24

8. 49   **9.** 252   **10.** 396   **11.** 1402

12. 720   **13.** 105   **14.** 597   **15.** 295

Write the prime factorization of the number.

16. 32   **17.** 70   **18.** 72   **19.** 441

20. 54   **21.** 120   **22.** 625   **23.** 96

24. Teams A coach is dividing his 45 players into teams. Can the coach divide the players evenly into 2 groups? 3 groups? 5 groups? 6 groups?

5.2 Greatest Common Factor

pp. 236–240

EXAMPLE

Find the GCF of 90 and 126.

$$
\begin{array}{cc}
90 & 126 \\
9 \times 10 & 2 \times 63 \\
3 \times 3 \times 2 \times 5 & 2 \times 9 \times 7 \\
& 2 \times 3 \times 3 \times 7
\end{array}
$$

▶ **Answer** The GCF of 90 and 126 is $2 \times 3 \times 3$, or 18.

EXERCISES

Find the GCF of the numbers.

SEE EXAMPLES
1, 2, AND 3
on pp. 236–237
for Exs. 25–34

25. 48, 84   **26.** 21, 75   **27.** 25, 70   **28.** 54, 81

29. 16, 192   **30.** 18, 405   **31.** 24, 60, 72   **32.** 13, 78, 104

33. Movie Theater You go to the movies with a different group of friends three weekends in a row. The amount the whole group spent on tickets each weekend is given at the right. Each ticket is the same price. What is the most a ticket could cost?

	Amount
Weekend 1	$30
Weekend 2	$18
Weekend 3	$42

34. Seating A group of 60 parents will sit behind a group of 84 students in a school auditorium. You want to arrange the groups in rows with the same number of people in each row, but without mixing the groups. What is the greatest number of people you can have in each row?

5.3 Equivalent Fractions

pp. 243–248

EXAMPLE

Write (a) $\frac{6}{24}$ and (b) $\frac{15}{33}$ in simplest form.

Rewrite the numerator and denominator as products using the GCF. Then divide the numerator and denominator by the GCF.

a. $\frac{6}{24} = \frac{1 \times \cancel{6}^{1}}{4 \times \cancel{6}_{1}} = \frac{1}{4}$

b. $\frac{15}{33} = \frac{5 \times \cancel{3}^{1}}{11 \times \cancel{3}_{1}} = \frac{5}{11}$

EXERCISES

Write the fraction in simplest form.

SEE EXAMPLE 3
on p. 244
for Exs. 35–43

35. $\frac{3}{21}$ **36.** $\frac{20}{45}$ **37.** $\frac{14}{98}$ **38.** $\frac{36}{96}$

39. $\frac{15}{24}$ **40.** $\frac{18}{63}$ **41.** $\frac{24}{36}$ **42.** $\frac{11}{44}$

43. Groceries Your friend has a carton of one dozen eggs. The carton falls to the ground and three eggs break. What fraction of the eggs do not break? Write your answer in simplest form.

5.4 Least Common Multiple

pp. 250–253

EXAMPLE

Find the LCM of 8 and 52.

Prime factorization of 8: $2 \times 2 \times 2$

Prime factorization of 52: $2 \times 2 \times 13$

▸ **Answer** The LCM of 8 and 52 is $2 \times 2 \times 2 \times 13 = 104$.

EXERCISES

Find the LCM of the numbers.

SEE EXAMPLES
2 AND 3
on p. 251
for Exs. 44–48

44. 4, 10   **45.** 35, 45   **46.** 10, 100   **47.** 6, 9, 24

48. Watches Ana sets her watch to beep every 15 minutes. Sam sets his watch to beep every 20 minutes. They just set their watches. After how many minutes will the watches beep at the same time?

5.5 Ordering Fractions

pp. 254–258

EXAMPLE

Order the fractions $\frac{2}{3}$, $\frac{2}{9}$, and $\frac{3}{5}$ from least to greatest.

STEP 1 **Use** the LCD to write equivalent fractions. The LCM of 3, 9, and 5 is 45.

$$\frac{2}{3} = \frac{30}{45} \qquad \frac{2}{9} = \frac{10}{45} \qquad \frac{3}{5} = \frac{27}{45} \longrightarrow \frac{10}{45} < \frac{27}{45} \text{ and } \frac{27}{45} < \frac{30}{45}$$

STEP 2 **Compare:** Because $\frac{10}{45} < \frac{27}{45}$, you know that $\frac{2}{9} < \frac{3}{5}$.

Because $\frac{27}{45} < \frac{30}{45}$, you know that $\frac{3}{5} < \frac{2}{3}$.

STEP 3 **Order** the fractions from least to greatest: $\frac{2}{9}$, $\frac{3}{5}$, and $\frac{2}{3}$.

EXERCISES

Order the fractions from least to greatest.

SEE EXAMPLE 2
on p. 255
for Exs. 49–51

49. $\frac{1}{7}, \frac{9}{56}, \frac{1}{8}$

50. $\frac{5}{28}, \frac{1}{4}, \frac{3}{14}$

51. $\frac{7}{25}, \frac{2}{5}, \frac{3}{10}$

5.6 Mixed Numbers and Improper Fractions

pp. 260–265

EXAMPLE

Write the number as an improper fraction or mixed number.

a. $2\frac{5}{8} = \frac{16 + 5}{8}$ **Rewrite using** $2 = \frac{16}{8}$.

$\qquad = \frac{21}{8}$ **Simplify numerator.**

▶ **Answer** $2\frac{5}{8} = \frac{21}{8}$

b. $\frac{19}{8} \longrightarrow$ $\begin{array}{r} 2 \text{ R3} \\ 8\overline{)19} \\ \underline{16} \\ 3 \end{array}$

▶ **Answer** $\frac{19}{8} = 2 + \frac{3}{8} = 2\frac{3}{8}$

EXERCISES

Write the number as an improper fraction or mixed number.

**SEE EXAMPLES
2 AND 3**
on p. 261
for Exs. 52–55

52. $\frac{15}{7}$

53. $4\frac{1}{5}$

54. $3\frac{4}{7}$

55. $\frac{23}{9}$

5.7 Changing Decimals to Fractions

pp. 266–270

EXAMPLE

Write the decimal as a fraction or mixed number in simplest form.

a. $0.54 = \dfrac{54}{100}$ Write fifty-four hundredths as a fraction.

$= \dfrac{27}{50}$ Simplify.

b. $1.8 = 1\dfrac{8}{10}$ Write one and eight tenths as a mixed number.

$= 1\dfrac{4}{5}$ Simplify.

EXERCISES

Write the decimal as a fraction or mixed number in simplest form.

SEE EXAMPLES 1, 2, AND 3 on pp. 266–267 for Exs. 56–64

56. 0.34 **57.** 4.8 **58.** 2.05 **59.** 0.605

60. 9.2 **61.** 0.125 **62.** 0.72 **63.** 3.64

64. Height Your friend's dog is 2.35 feet high. Write the dog's height as a mixed number in simplest form.

5.8 Changing Fractions to Decimals

pp. 271–275

EXAMPLE

Write the fraction or mixed number as a decimal.

a. $2\dfrac{13}{20} \longrightarrow$

$$\begin{array}{r} 0.65 \\ 20\overline{)13.00} \\ \underline{12\ 0} \\ 1\ 00 \\ \underline{1\ 00} \\ 0 \end{array}$$

▶ **Answer** $2\dfrac{13}{20} = 2 + 0.65 = 2.65$

b. $\dfrac{7}{9} \longrightarrow$

$$\begin{array}{r} 0.77\ldots \\ 9\overline{)7.00} \\ \underline{6\ 3} \\ 70 \\ \underline{63} \\ 7 \end{array}$$

▶ **Answer** $\dfrac{7}{9} = 0.\overline{7}$

EXERCISES

Write the fraction or mixed number as a decimal.

SEE EXAMPLES 1, 2, AND 3 on pp. 271–272 for Exs. 65–76

65. $\dfrac{7}{8}$ **66.** $3\dfrac{2}{5}$ **67.** $5\dfrac{4}{9}$ **68.** $\dfrac{17}{6}$

69. $6\dfrac{1}{4}$ **70.** $\dfrac{27}{25}$ **71.** $\dfrac{11}{12}$ **72.** $2\dfrac{1}{3}$

73. $3\dfrac{8}{15}$ **74.** $\dfrac{19}{20}$ **75.** $4\dfrac{3}{40}$ **76.** $\dfrac{7}{16}$

5 CHAPTER TEST

1. Test 116 for divisibility by 2, 3, 5, 6, 9, and 10.

2. Is the number 83 *prime* or *composite*? *Explain* your reasoning.

Write the prime factorization of the number.

3. 28   4. 96   5. 125   6. 340

Find the GCF of the numbers.

7. 8, 52   8. 5, 16   9. 7, 56   10. 16, 48, 88

11. Write two fractions that are equivalent to $\frac{5}{6}$.

Write the fraction in simplest form.

12. $\frac{4}{20}$ 13. $\frac{22}{34}$ 14. $\frac{15}{60}$ 15. $\frac{14}{42}$

Find the LCM of the numbers.

16. 6, 15   17. 10, 14   18. 5, 18   19. 4, 10, 15

20. Order the numbers $\frac{17}{5}$, $3\frac{3}{10}$, $\frac{15}{4}$, and $3\frac{1}{2}$ from least to greatest.

Rewrite the number as specified.

21. $\frac{22}{3}$ (mixed number)   22. 4.3 (improper fraction)   23. $3\frac{5}{9}$ (decimal)

24. **BREAKFAST** You are buying breakfast bagels. You buy 3 blueberry, 6 plain, 5 cinnamon raisin, and 1 honey grain. Find the fraction of the bagels that are cinnamon raisin. Write your answer in simplest form.

25. **DECORATING** You want to tile an area of wall 114 inches tall by 144 inches wide with square tiles. You don't want to have to cut any of the tiles to fit. Find the largest square tile you can use. How many of these tiles will you need?

26. **AGRICULTURE** A farmer plants a variety of crops on his land. The farmer plants $\frac{1}{12}$ of the land with corn, $\frac{1}{4}$ with soybeans, $\frac{3}{8}$ with wheat, and $\frac{3}{16}$ with potatoes. Which crop takes up the most land? the least land?

27. **WATER** About three hundredths of Earth's water is fresh water. Write this number as a decimal and as a fraction.

SHORT RESPONSE QUESTIONS

PROBLEM

The table shows the heights, in inches, of 3 brothers posing for a photo. One brother sits and the two closest in height stand. Which 2 brothers are standing? *Explain* your reasoning.

Name	Tommy	Taylor	Tate
Height (in.)	$\dfrac{197}{3}$	$65\dfrac{9}{16}$	$65\dfrac{3}{4}$

Below are sample solutions to the problem. Read each solution and the comments in blue to see why the sample represents full credit, partial credit, or no credit.

SAMPLE 1: Full Credit Solution

The process reflects correct mathematical reasoning.

Write the heights as improper fractions with a common denominator of 48 and compare the numerators to see which pair is closest.

Tommy's height: $\dfrac{197}{3} = \dfrac{197 \times 16}{3 \times 16} = \dfrac{3152}{48}$

The calculations are correct.

Taylor's height: $65\dfrac{9}{16} = \dfrac{1049}{16} = \dfrac{1049 \times 3}{16 \times 3} = \dfrac{3147}{48}$

Tate's height: $65\dfrac{3}{4} = \dfrac{263}{4} = \dfrac{263 \times 12}{4 \times 12} = \dfrac{3156}{48}$

The explanation is clear, and the question is answered correctly.

Since the numerator pair 3152 and 3156 is the closest, $\dfrac{3152}{48}$ and $\dfrac{3156}{48}$ are the closest heights. Tommy and Tate are standing.

SAMPLE 2: Partial Credit Solution

The process is correct, but the solution is incomplete. The question is not answered.

Write the heights as improper fractions with a common denominator of 48.

Tommy: $\dfrac{197 \times 16}{3 \times 16} = \dfrac{3152}{48}$ **Taylor:** $\dfrac{1049 \times 3}{16 \times 3} = \dfrac{3147}{48}$ **Tate:** $\dfrac{263 \times 12}{4 \times 12} = \dfrac{3156}{48}$

Compare: $\dfrac{3152}{48}$ and $\dfrac{3156}{48}$ are closest.

SAMPLE 3: Partial Credit Solution

The process is correct, but there is an error rewriting Tate's height as an improper fraction.

Tommy: $\dfrac{197 \times 16}{3 \times 16} = \dfrac{3152}{48}$ **Taylor:** $\dfrac{1049 \times 3}{16 \times 3} = \dfrac{3147}{48}$ **Tate:** $\dfrac{780 \times 12}{4 \times 12} = \dfrac{9360}{48}$

Because $\dfrac{3152}{48}$ and $\dfrac{3147}{48}$ are closest, Tommy and Taylor are standing.

SAMPLE 4: No Credit Solution

Both the reasoning and the answer are incorrect.

Tommy is $\dfrac{197}{3}$ inches, Taylor is $\dfrac{1049}{16}$ inches, and Tate is $65\dfrac{3}{4}$ inches. Because 197 and 1049 are the two largest numerators, Tommy and Taylor are standing.

PRACTICE   Apply the Scoring Rubric

Score the solution to the problem below as *full credit, partial credit,* or *no credit. Explain* your reasoning.

> **PROBLEM** Kayla, Hannah, and Ann compete in the long jump. At the last meet, Kayla jumped $16\dfrac{2}{5}$ feet, Hannah jumped $16\dfrac{1}{2}$ feet, and Ann jumped $16\dfrac{3}{5}$ feet. Was Ann's jump closer to Kayla's jump or to Hannah's jump? *Explain.*

1. Write each distance as an improper fraction with a common denominator of 10 and compare the numerators to compare the girls' jumps.

    Kayla: $16\dfrac{2}{5} = \dfrac{82}{5} = \dfrac{82 \times 2}{5 \times 2} = \dfrac{164}{10}$ Hannah: $16\dfrac{1}{2} = \dfrac{33}{2} = \dfrac{33 \times 5}{2 \times 5} = \dfrac{165}{10}$

    Ann: $16\dfrac{3}{5} = \dfrac{83}{5} = \dfrac{83 \times 2}{5 \times 2} = \dfrac{166}{10}$

    Because 166 is closer to 165 than it is to 164, you know that Ann's jump was closer to Hannah's jump.

2. Since the jumps were all fractions just over 16 feet, you can just compare the fractional part of each distance using a common denominator of 10.

    $\left(\dfrac{4}{10}, \dfrac{5}{10}, \text{and } \dfrac{6}{10}\right)$. So, $\dfrac{3}{5}$ foot is closer to $\dfrac{1}{2}$ foot than to $\dfrac{2}{5}$ foot.

SHORT RESPONSE

1. Judy has 126 pencil boxes stacked in piles of equal size. What are all the possible pile sizes? *Explain* how you found your answer.

2. Tom is building a deck. He has nails that are $1\frac{3}{4}$ inches long and $1\frac{1}{2}$ inches long. The deck is $\frac{13}{8}$ inches thick. He does not want the tips of the nails to come through the wood. Which size nail should Tom use? *Explain.*

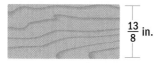

$\frac{13}{8}$ in.

3. Kaylene's score on a quiz was $\frac{23}{25}$. Roger's score was 0.92, and Devon's score was $\frac{9}{10}$. Which two students received the same score? Was Devon's score higher or lower than the other two scores? *Explain.*

4. You are waiting in line to ride a roller coaster. The roller coaster holds a total of 16 people, and the first 2 people in line get to sit in the front row. There are 193 people ahead of you in line and the roller coaster is always fully loaded. Will you get to sit in the front row? *Explain.*

5. Sandra has three boards. The length of each board is given in the table below.

Board	1	2	3
Length (inches)	60	96	120

She needs to cut all the boards into smaller pieces of the same length. What is the greatest possible length that she can use for the smaller pieces? How many pieces of this length will she have altogether after cutting the boards? *Explain* your reasoning.

6. Yesterday, Jerome spent $1\frac{3}{4}$ hours skateboarding, while Alisha played basketball for $\frac{17}{10}$ hours. Yolanda jogged for $1\frac{4}{5}$ hours, while Miguel played soccer for $\frac{3}{2}$ hours. Who devoted the most time to his or her activity? the least? *Justify* your answers.

7. Seth and Steve both work as security guards for a software company. Seth works the night shift every 6 days, and Steve works the night shift every 8 days. Seth and Steve both worked the night shift on July 1. On what date in July will Seth and Steve next work the night shift together? *Explain* your reasoning.

8. A grocery store sells oranges individually by their weight or in 5-pound bags, as shown below. Which is the better buy? *Explain* how you found your answer.

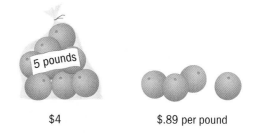

5 pounds

$4 $.89 per pound

9. You earn $4.75 per hour working $3\frac{1}{2}$ hours per day, 4 days per week. How much do you make in 4 weeks? *Explain* how you found your answer.

10. A vase holds 16 roses, 5 sunflowers, and some carnations. The fraction of the roses in the vase is $\frac{2}{3}$. How many carnations are in the vase? *Justify* your answer.

MULTIPLE CHOICE

11. A farmer is planting tomato plants and can arrange them in rows of 2, 3, 5, 6, 9, or 10, without having any left over. How many tomato plants could the farmer have?

(**A**) 120　(**B**) 150　(**C**) 180　(**D**) 600

12. Mr. Washington wants to divide his class of 30 students into groups of the same size with no students left. Which number of groups would *not* be possible?

(**A**) 3　(**B**) 4　(**C**) 5　(**D**) 6

13. An adult has 206 bones. Of these, 106 are in the feet, ankles, wrists, and hands. What fraction of the bones in an adult are *not* in the feet, ankles, wrists, and hands?

(**A**) $\frac{1}{2}$　(**B**) $\frac{53}{103}$　(**C**) $\frac{50}{53}$　(**D**) $\frac{50}{103}$

GRIDDED ANSWER

14. Val has recorded 0.4 of the school concert on a cassette tape. What fraction of the concert has she *not* recorded?

15. The weights, in pounds, of 5 pineapples at a fruit stand are $\frac{15}{4}$, 4.25, $4\frac{1}{8}$, $\frac{37}{8}$, and $4\frac{7}{16}$. What is the median weight, in pounds, of these 5 pineapples? Write your answer as a decimal rounded to the nearest hundredth.

16. Sheri ran a mile in 6.15 minutes. Previously, her best time was 6.2 minutes. By what fraction of a minute did Sheri's time improve? Write your answer as a fraction in simplest form.

17. Ethan missed 8 field goals out of 21 attempts. Write his completed field goal average as a decimal rounded to the nearest thousandth.

EXTENDED RESPONSE

18. The table shows the number of minutes of commercials on each of three channels for a certain number of minutes of viewing time.

Channel	A	B	C
Minutes of commercials	22	29	14
Viewing time (minutes)	90	120	60

  a. Which channel showed commercials for the greatest fraction of the viewing time?

  b. Show how your answer to part (a) would change if Channel A was viewed for 120 minutes with the same number of minutes of commercials.

  c. What happens to the value of a fraction when the denominator increases and the numerator stays the same? *Justify* your answer.

  d. Use decimals to answer part (a). Compare and contrast the two methods.

19. Today every eighth customer at a restaurant will get a free sandwich, and every sixth customer will get a free drink.

  a. Which customers will be the first three to get free sandwiches? Which customers will be the first three to get free drinks?

  b. Which customer will be the first to get both a free drink and a free sandwich? *Explain.*

  c. The owner of the restaurant expects to serve about 70 customers during lunch. How many free sandwiches and free drinks will the owner give out during lunch? *Justify* your answer.

6 Addition and Subtraction of Fractions

Before

In previous chapters you've ...

- Compared and ordered fractions
- Changed between mixed numbers and fractions

Now

In Chapter 6 you'll study ...

- 6.1 Fraction estimation
- 6.2 Common denominators
- 6.3 Different denominators
- 6.4 Combining mixed numbers
- 6.5 Subtraction with renaming
- 6.6 Measures of time

Why?

So you can solve real-world problems about ...

- the Appalachian Trail, p. 306
- volcanoes, p. 311
- horses, p. 317
- the Tour de France, p. 322

 **Math**

at classzone.com

- Cavern Exploration, p. 303
- Mixed Number Cooking, p. 316
- Snooze Game, p. 323

Get-Ready Games

Review Prerequisite Skills by playing *Jungle Fractions.*

> **Skill Focus:** Comparing fractions and mixed numbers

JUNGLE FRACTIONS

If you want to be amazed, take a walk through the tangled vegetation of a jungle. This matching game involves some amazing facts about jungle animals.

MATERIALS

16 jungle cards

HOW TO PLAY The 16 jungle cards consist of 8 fact cards and 8 number cards. Each fact card contains a fraction or mixed number that is equivalent to a fraction on one of the number cards. Shuffle all 16 jungle cards together. Arrange the cards face down in 4 rows.

Some toucans have bills that are about $\frac{1}{3}$ the length of their bodies.

$\frac{20}{60}$

1 **Reveal** 2 cards and read them aloud.

2 **DECIDE** whether the numbers on the 2 cards are equivalent. If they are, you may keep the cards. Otherwise, turn them back over.

3 **REMEMBER** where the cards are so you can find equivalent number pairs on future turns.

HOW TO WIN The player who collects the most cards wins.

Stop and Think

1. **WRITING** Suppose you get a number card with an improper fraction on it. What can you predict about the numerator and the denominator in the mixed number on the matching fact card? Explain.

2. **CRITICAL THINKING** As you learned in *Jungle Fractions*, a spider monkey's tail is $\frac{7}{12}$ of the monkey's total length. Sketch a visual model to illustrate this fact. Based on your model, would you say that a spider monkey is about twice as long as its tail? Explain your thinking.

Review Prerequisite Skills

REVIEW WORDS

- fraction, *p. 243*
- equivalent fractions, *p. 243*
- simplest form, *p. 244*
- least common multiple (LCM), *p. 251*
- mixed number, *p. 260*
- improper fraction, *p. 260*

VOCABULARY CHECK

Tell whether the number is an *improper fraction*, a *mixed number*, or a *whole number*.

1. $3\frac{1}{8}$ **2.** $\frac{3}{2}$ **3.** 6   **4.** $\frac{5}{4}$

SKILL CHECK

Copy and complete the statement. *(p. 754)*

5. 2 hours = $\underline{\ ?\ }$ min   **6.** 4 min = $\underline{\ ?\ }$ sec

7. 400 sec = $\underline{\ ?\ }$ min $\underline{\ ?\ }$ sec   **8.** 250 min = $\underline{\ ?\ }$ hours $\underline{\ ?\ }$ min

Find the sum or difference. *(p. 148)*

9. $7.2 + 4.9$ **10.** $2.43 + 16.7$ **11.** $10.8 - 8.9$ **12.** $51.0 - 2.57$

Copy and complete the statement. *(p. 243)*

13. $\frac{3}{6} = \frac{1}{?}$ **14.** $\frac{2}{3} = \frac{?}{12}$ **15.** $\frac{2}{5} = \frac{10}{?}$ **16.** $\frac{6}{16} = \frac{?}{8}$

Find the least common multiple of the numbers. *(p. 250)*

17. 3 and 5   **18.** 8 and 10   **19.** 4 and 12   **20.** 6 and 7

Order the fractions from least to greatest. *(p. 254)*

21. $\frac{3}{8}, \frac{1}{4}, \frac{1}{6}$ **22.** $\frac{7}{20}, \frac{2}{5}, \frac{3}{10}$ **23.** $\frac{5}{6}, \frac{13}{18}, \frac{2}{3}$

@HomeTutor   Prerequisite skills practice at classzone.com

Notetaking Skills   Writing a Summary

In each chapter you will learn a new notetaking skill. As you study Chapter 6, you may want to use an outline to summarize each lesson. Include key examples, such as Example 2 on page 303.

To summarize a chapter in your notes, first create an outline of the chapter using the headings from the lesson. Then fill in the outline with concepts and examples from the lesson.

Lesson 5.3 Equivalent Fractions

Write two fractions that are equivalent to $\frac{2}{5}$.

$$\frac{2}{5} = \frac{2 \times 3}{5 \times 3} = \frac{6}{15}$$ $$\frac{2}{5} = \frac{2 \times 4}{5 \times 4} = \frac{8}{20}$$

6.1 Fraction Estimation

Before	You estimated with whole numbers and decimals.
Now	You'll estimate with fractions and mixed numbers.
Why?	So you can estimate lengths, as in Example 4.

KEY VOCABULARY
- **fraction,** *p. 243*
- **mixed number,** *p. 260*
- **round,** *p. 739*

Geckos The world's smallest adult reptile is a dwarf gecko that is about $\frac{5}{8}$ inch in body length. From the ruler, you can tell that $\frac{5}{8}$ is closer to $\frac{1}{2}$ than to 1.

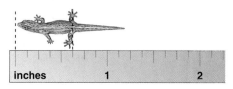

One way to round fractions is to compare the numerator and the denominator. Fractions are usually rounded to the nearest half. Mixed numbers are usually rounded to the nearest whole number.

EXAMPLE 1 Rounding Fractions

Round the fraction.

a. $\frac{1}{8} \approx 0$ Because 1 is much less than 8, round $\frac{1}{8}$ to 0.

b. $\frac{5}{9} \approx \frac{1}{2}$ Because 5 is about half of 9, round $\frac{5}{9}$ to $\frac{1}{2}$.

c. $\frac{6}{7} \approx 1$ Because 6 is almost as great as 7, round $\frac{6}{7}$ to 1.

EXAMPLE 2 Rounding Mixed Numbers

ROUNDING

If the fraction or mixed number that you are rounding is halfway between two whole numbers, round to the greater number.

Round the mixed number.

a. $4\frac{1}{3} \approx 4$ Because $\frac{1}{3}$ is less than $\frac{1}{2}$, round $4\frac{1}{3}$ down to 4.

b. $5\frac{3}{4} \approx 6$ Because $\frac{3}{4}$ is greater than $\frac{1}{2}$, round $5\frac{3}{4}$ up to 6.

✓ **GUIDED PRACTICE** for Examples 1 and 2

Round the fraction or mixed number.

1. $\frac{1}{4}$ **2.** $\frac{5}{6}$ **3.** $2\frac{9}{16}$ **4.** $5\frac{3}{7}$

5. Geckos Estimate the length of the gecko at the top of the page. Measure from its head to the tip of its tail. Round to the nearest inch.

EXAMPLE 3 Estimating a Difference

Estimate the difference $6\frac{1}{4} - 1\frac{5}{6}$.

$$6\frac{1}{4} - 1\frac{5}{6} \approx 6 - 2 \qquad \text{Round each mixed number.}$$

$$= 4 \qquad \text{Find the difference.}$$

Real-World Estimates In some situations, you may want to round the numbers so that you get an estimate that is high or low.

EXAMPLE 4 Estimating a Sum

Costumes You need $\frac{1}{5}$ yard of ribbon for one costume and $\frac{7}{8}$ yard for another costume. You want to know how much ribbon you need.

a. Should your estimate of the amount of ribbon be *high* or *low*?

b. Estimate the amount of ribbon you need.

SOLUTION

a. Your estimate of the amount of ribbon you need should be high so that you will not run out of ribbon before finishing the costumes.

b. Estimate the sum $\frac{1}{5} + \frac{7}{8}$.

$$\frac{1}{5} + \frac{7}{8} \approx \frac{1}{2} + 1 \qquad \text{Round each fraction up to get a high estimate.}$$

$$= 1\frac{1}{2} \qquad \text{Find the sum.}$$

▶ **Answer** You will need about $1\frac{1}{2}$ yards of ribbon.

✓ **GUIDED PRACTICE** for Examples 3 and 4

Estimate the sum or difference.

6. $\frac{7}{8} + \frac{4}{5}$ **7.** $\frac{9}{16} + \frac{1}{6}$ **8.** $3\frac{1}{5} + 2\frac{7}{10}$ **9.** $1\frac{5}{6} + 2\frac{1}{2}$

10. $\frac{5}{9} - \frac{2}{15}$ **11.** $\frac{11}{12} - \frac{1}{7}$ **12.** $2\frac{3}{4} - 2\frac{2}{5}$ **13.** $5\frac{2}{3} - 1\frac{11}{18}$

14. Recipes You need $\frac{3}{4}$ cup of flour for one recipe and $2\frac{1}{3}$ cups for another. You want to know how much flour you need. Should your estimate be *high* or *low*? *Explain* your reasoning. Then estimate the amount you need.

6.1 EXERCISES

HOMEWORK KEY

★ = **STANDARDIZED TEST PRACTICE**
Exs. 23, 38, 39, 40, and 52

○ = **HINTS AND HOMEWORK HELP**
for Exs. 7, 13, 15, 19, 37 at classzone.com

SKILL PRACTICE

VOCABULARY Copy and complete the statement.

1. Fractions are usually rounded to the nearest __?__.

2. __?__ numbers are usually rounded to the nearest whole number.

ROUNDING Round the fraction or mixed number.

SEE EXAMPLES
1 AND 2
on p. 291
for Exs. 3–10

3. $\dfrac{4}{9}$

4. $\dfrac{1}{6}$

5. $\dfrac{4}{5}$

6. $\dfrac{7}{10}$

7. $1\dfrac{3}{8}$

8. $3\dfrac{5}{7}$

9. $3\dfrac{1}{2}$

10. $4\dfrac{3}{8}$

ESTIMATING SUMS AND DIFFERENCES Estimate the sum or difference.

SEE EXAMPLES
3 AND 4
on p. 292
for Exs. 11–24

11. $\dfrac{1}{6} + \dfrac{1}{5}$

12. $\dfrac{9}{16} + \dfrac{7}{9}$

13. $\dfrac{8}{9} - \dfrac{3}{8}$

14. $\dfrac{9}{10} - \dfrac{1}{3}$

15. $2\dfrac{7}{8} + 4\dfrac{1}{6}$

16. $1\dfrac{5}{6} + 3\dfrac{5}{12}$

17. $2\dfrac{7}{10} + 2\dfrac{5}{14}$

18. $1\dfrac{3}{17} + 2\dfrac{1}{2}$

19. $5\dfrac{3}{10} - 1\dfrac{1}{8}$

20. $8\dfrac{11}{20} - 3\dfrac{3}{5}$

21. $7\dfrac{2}{15} - 2\dfrac{1}{18}$

22. $4\dfrac{8}{9} - 1\dfrac{1}{2}$

23. ★ **MULTIPLE CHOICE** Which sum is the best estimate of $3\dfrac{3}{4} + 2\dfrac{1}{3}$?

Ⓐ $3 + 2$ Ⓑ $4 + 2$ Ⓒ 4×2 Ⓓ $4 + 3$

24. **ERROR ANALYSIS** You need $3\dfrac{1}{2}$ cups of flour for a recipe. You have $2\dfrac{1}{2}$ cups in a canister and $\dfrac{3}{4}$ cup left in the bag. Describe and correct the error in your quantity estimate.

$$\times \quad \begin{array}{l} 2\dfrac{1}{2}c + \dfrac{3}{4}c \approx \\ 3c + 1c = 4c \end{array}$$

ESTIMATION Tell whether the answer is a *high estimate* or a *low estimate*.

25. $3\dfrac{7}{11} + 8\dfrac{6}{7} \approx 13$

26. $2\dfrac{1}{6} + 4\dfrac{2}{9} \approx 8$

27. $10\dfrac{4}{5} - 3\dfrac{1}{8} \approx 6$

28. $5\dfrac{2}{9} + 7\dfrac{3}{5} \approx 14$

29. $8\dfrac{9}{11} - 5\dfrac{4}{5} \approx 2$

30. $5\dfrac{2}{3} + 1\dfrac{1}{8} \approx 6$

COMPARING Use estimation to copy and complete the expressions using > or <.

31. $3\dfrac{1}{5} + 4\dfrac{2}{3} \; ? \; 9\dfrac{1}{2} - \dfrac{7}{8}$

32. $2\dfrac{3}{5} - 1\dfrac{9}{10} \; ? \; 6\dfrac{5}{8} - 5\dfrac{1}{2}$

33. $2\dfrac{4}{9} + 5\dfrac{1}{10} \; ? \; 3\dfrac{5}{9} + 4\dfrac{1}{8}$

ESTIMATING *Explain* how each estimate was made and why it is reasonable.

34. $4\dfrac{7}{9} + 2\dfrac{1}{8} - 3\dfrac{1}{7} \approx 4$

35. $10\dfrac{1}{4} - 6\dfrac{1}{5} + 1\dfrac{9}{10} \approx 6$

36. $12\dfrac{1}{8} - 9\dfrac{11}{12} - \dfrac{1}{6} \approx 2$

SEE EXAMPLES 3 AND 4
on p. 292
for Ex. 37–39

37. **PARK RIDERS** You wait in line for $1\frac{1}{3}$ hours for a mountain ride and $1\frac{4}{5}$ hours for a water ride. Estimate how many hours you wait in line.

38. ★ **MULTIPLE CHOICE** You have $5\frac{7}{8}$ cups of flour. You use $1\frac{2}{3}$ cups of flour to make blueberry muffins. Estimate how much flour you have left.

   A 3 cups   **B** 4 cups   **C** 5 cups   **D** 6 cups

39. ★ **SHORT RESPONSE** You need $4\frac{1}{4}$ gallons of paint for one room and $3\frac{1}{3}$ gallons for another room. Estimate how much paint you need. Is it better to have a *low* or *high* estimate of the answer? *Explain.*

40. ★ **WRITING** You have $2\frac{1}{4}$ yards of fabric and buy $3\frac{7}{8}$ yards more. You use 5 yards to decorate your room. Estimate the total amount of fabric you have left. *Explain* your steps.

41. **SCALE MODELS** Estimate the total length of the Saturn V rocket shown. Then use a ruler to measure the photograph and estimate the scale.

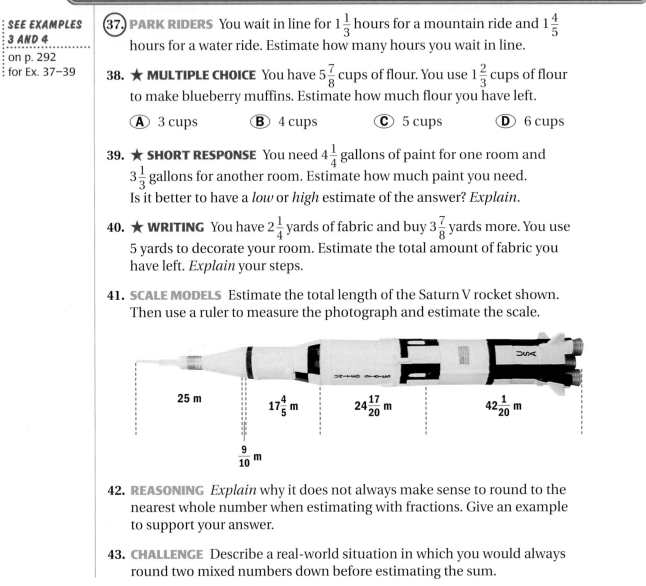

25 m $17\frac{4}{5}$ m $24\frac{17}{20}$ m $42\frac{1}{20}$ m

$\frac{9}{10}$ m

42. **REASONING** *Explain* why it does not always make sense to round to the nearest whole number when estimating with fractions. Give an example to support your answer.

43. **CHALLENGE** Describe a real-world situation in which you would always round two mixed numbers down before estimating the sum.

Get-Ready
Prepare for
Lesson 6.2
in Exs. 44–47

Write the fraction in simplest form. *(p. 243)*

44. $\frac{12}{30}$ **45.** $\frac{6}{26}$ **46.** $\frac{25}{45}$ **47.** $\frac{18}{39}$

Write the improper fraction as a mixed number. *(p. 260)*

48. $\frac{15}{2}$ **49.** $\frac{8}{3}$ **50.** $\frac{49}{10}$ **51.** $\frac{33}{4}$

52. ★ **MULTIPLE CHOICE** What is the first step in evaluating $21 + 15 \div 5 - 2$? *(p. 21)*

   A $21 + 15$ **B** $15 \div 5$ **C** $5 - 2$ **D** $21 - 2$

6.2 Fractions with Common Denominators

Before	You estimated the sums and differences of fractions.
Now	You'll find actual sums and differences of fractions.
Why?	So you can find totals, such as snowfall in Ex. 44.

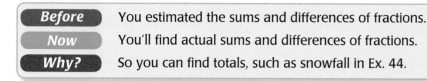

KEY VOCABULARY

• mixed number,
  p. 260

• improper fraction,
  p. 260

ACTIVITY

You can use a model to add two fractions.

STEP 1 **Draw** a rectangle divided into 5 squares of the same size. Color 1 square red and 3 squares blue.

STEP 2 **Copy** and complete the following statement with the correct numbers:

$$\frac{?\text{ red squares}}{?\text{ total squares}} + \frac{?\text{ blue squares}}{?\text{ total squares}} = \frac{?\text{ colored squares}}{?\text{ total squares}}$$

Use a model to find the sum.   **1.** $\frac{2}{9} + \frac{5}{9}$ **2.** $\frac{1}{8} + \frac{3}{8}$

The activity suggests the following rules about adding fractions with common denominators.

KEY CONCEPT   *For Your Notebook*

Adding Fractions with Common Denominators

Words   To add two fractions with a common denominator, write the sum of the numerators over the denominator.

Numbers $\frac{2}{7} + \frac{4}{7} = \frac{6}{7}$ **Algebra** $\frac{a}{c} + \frac{b}{c} = \frac{a+b}{c}$

EXAMPLE 1 **Adding Fractions**

REWRITE FRACTIONS
Need help with rewriting improper fractions as mixed numbers? See p. 244.

$$\frac{3}{5} + \frac{4}{5} = \frac{3+4}{5}$$ **Add the numerators.**

$$= \frac{7}{5}$$ **Simplify the numerator.**

$$= 1\frac{2}{5}$$ **Rewrite the improper fraction as a mixed number.**

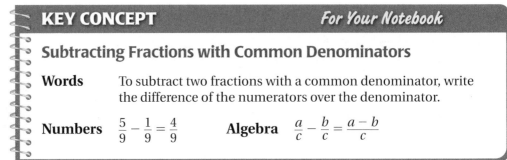

KEY CONCEPT   *For Your Notebook*

Subtracting Fractions with Common Denominators

Words   To subtract two fractions with a common denominator, write
the difference of the numerators over the denominator.

Numbers $\dfrac{5}{9} - \dfrac{1}{9} = \dfrac{4}{9}$ **Algebra** $\dfrac{a}{c} - \dfrac{b}{c} = \dfrac{a-b}{c}$

EXAMPLE 2   Subtracting Fractions

$\dfrac{7}{10} - \dfrac{3}{10} = \dfrac{7-3}{10}$ **Subtract the numerators.**

SIMPLIFY FRACTIONS
Need help with writing
fractions in simplest
form? See p. 244.

$= \dfrac{4}{10}$ **Simplify the numerator.**

$= \dfrac{2}{5}$ **Simplify the fraction.**

✓ **GUIDED PRACTICE**   for Examples 1 and 2

Find the sum or difference. Simplify if possible.

1. $\dfrac{1}{9} + \dfrac{7}{9}$ 2. $\dfrac{5}{7} + \dfrac{6}{7}$ 3. $\dfrac{5}{8} + \dfrac{1}{8}$ 4. $\dfrac{9}{10} + \dfrac{3}{10}$

5. $\dfrac{5}{6} - \dfrac{1}{6}$ 6. $\dfrac{7}{12} - \dfrac{5}{12}$ 7. $\dfrac{6}{7} - \dfrac{3}{7}$ 8. $\dfrac{8}{9} - \dfrac{2}{9}$

EXAMPLE 3   Using a Verbal Model

Recipes You and your mom are baking.
The recipe uses $\dfrac{5}{8}$ cup of raisins. You have
only $\dfrac{3}{8}$ cup of raisins. How many more cups
do you need?

SOLUTION

Amount you need	=	Amount for recipe	−	Amount you have	
	=	$\dfrac{5}{8}$	−	$\dfrac{3}{8}$	**Substitute amounts you know.**
	=	$\dfrac{2}{8}$			**Subtract the fractions.**
	=	$\dfrac{1}{4}$			**Simplify.**

▶ **Answer** You need $\dfrac{1}{4}$ cup of raisins.

★ **EXAMPLE 4** **Standardized Test Practice**

Bobsledding The bobsled track in Igls, Austria, is $\frac{19}{25}$ mile. The track in Lillehammer, Norway, is $\frac{6}{25}$ mile longer. How would you find the length of the track in Lillehammer?

A Subtract $\frac{6}{25}$ from $\frac{19}{25}$. **B** Add $\frac{19}{25}$ and $\frac{6}{25}$.

C Multiply $\frac{19}{25}$ and $\frac{6}{25}$. **D** Divide $\frac{19}{25}$ by $\frac{6}{25}$.

ELIMINATE CHOICES
There is no multiplication or division required. So, you can eliminate choices C and D.

SOLUTION

$$
\begin{array}{ccccc}
\text{Length of the} & = & \text{Length of} & + & \text{Difference in} \\
\text{Lillehammer track} & & \text{the Igls track} & & \text{their lengths} \\
& = & \dfrac{19}{25} & + & \dfrac{6}{25} \\
& = & \dfrac{25}{25}, \text{ or } 1 & &
\end{array}
$$

▶ **Answer** You need to add $\frac{19}{25}$ and $\frac{6}{25}$. The correct answer is B. Ⓐ **Ⓑ** Ⓒ Ⓓ

✓ **GUIDED PRACTICE** **for Examples 3 and 4**

9. **What If?** In Example 3, suppose the recipe uses $\frac{7}{8}$ cup of raisins. How many more cups of raisins do you need? Write a model to help you find the answer. Then find the answer.

6.2 **EXERCISES**

HOMEWORK KEY

★ = **STANDARDIZED TEST PRACTICE**
Exs. 19, 40, 42, 43, 45, 46, 47, and 58

◯ = **HINTS AND HOMEWORK HELP**
for Exs. 7, 13, 15, 21, 39 at classzone.com

SKILL PRACTICE

1. **VOCABULARY** Copy and complete: To add fractions with a common denominator, add the __?__ and write the sum over the __?__.

FINDING SUMS **Find the sum. Simplify if possible.**

SEE EXAMPLE 1
on pp. 295–296
for Exs. 2–10

2. $\frac{1}{3} + \frac{1}{3}$ 3. $\frac{4}{5} + \frac{2}{5}$ 4. $\frac{8}{9} + \frac{1}{9}$ 5. $\frac{7}{8} + \frac{1}{8}$

6. $\frac{1}{4} + \frac{1}{4}$ ⑦ $\frac{1}{9} + \frac{2}{9}$ 8. $\frac{5}{8} + \frac{1}{8}$ 9. $\frac{7}{10} + \frac{3}{10}$

10. **ERROR ANALYSIS** Describe and correct the error made in the solution.

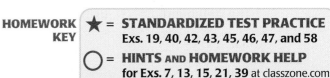

$$\times \quad \frac{6}{7} + \frac{3}{7} = \frac{9}{14}$$

FINDING DIFFERENCES Find the difference. Simplify if possible.

SEE EXAMPLE 2
on p. 296
for Exs. 11–22

11. $\dfrac{5}{7} - \dfrac{3}{7}$

12. $\dfrac{5}{6} - \dfrac{1}{6}$

13. $\dfrac{15}{16} - \dfrac{5}{16}$

14. $\dfrac{7}{9} - \dfrac{4}{9}$

15. $\dfrac{13}{14} - \dfrac{9}{14}$

16. $\dfrac{11}{12} - \dfrac{5}{12}$

17. $\dfrac{9}{10} - \dfrac{1}{10}$

18. $\dfrac{3}{4} - \dfrac{3}{4}$

19. ★ **MULTIPLE CHOICE** What is the difference represented by the model at the right?

Ⓐ $\dfrac{5}{12}$ 　Ⓑ $\dfrac{1}{2}$ 　Ⓒ $\dfrac{7}{12}$ 　Ⓓ $1\dfrac{1}{3}$

INTERPRETING MODELS Write and evaluate the expression represented by the model.

20. ⊞ + ⊞

21. ⊘ − ⊘

22. △ − △

EVALUATING EXPRESSIONS Evaluate the expression.

23. $\dfrac{7}{12} + \dfrac{11}{12} + \dfrac{5}{12}$

24. $\dfrac{9}{20} + \dfrac{17}{20} - \dfrac{9}{20}$

25. $\dfrac{13}{16} - \dfrac{5}{16} + \dfrac{3}{16}$

26. $\dfrac{1}{9} + \left(\dfrac{7}{9} - \dfrac{5}{9} \right)$

27. $\left(\dfrac{11}{14} + \dfrac{3}{14} \right) - \dfrac{5}{14}$

28. $\dfrac{36}{37} - \left(\dfrac{22}{37} - \dfrac{14}{37} \right)$

Ⓧⓥ ALGEBRA Use mental math to find x.

29. $x + \dfrac{1}{8} = \dfrac{5}{8}$

30. $x - \dfrac{2}{5} = \dfrac{1}{5}$

31. $\dfrac{3}{4} - x = \dfrac{1}{2}$

32. $\dfrac{7}{10} + x = 1\dfrac{2}{5}$

33. $x + \dfrac{2}{7} = 1$

34. $x - \dfrac{4}{9} = 0$

Ⓧⓥ CHALLENGE Describe the relationship between a and b by completing the statement $a = \underline{\ ?\ }$ using an expression involving b.

35. $\dfrac{a}{c} + \dfrac{b}{c} = \dfrac{2a}{c}$

36. $\dfrac{a}{c} - \dfrac{b}{c} = \dfrac{2b}{c}$

37. $\dfrac{a}{c} + \dfrac{b}{c} = \dfrac{2}{c}$

PROBLEM SOLVING

SEE EXAMPLES 3 AND 4
on pp. 296–297
for Ex. 38–40

38. **DRAWING** You finish $\dfrac{1}{8}$ of a drawing on Friday and $\dfrac{3}{8}$ more on Tuesday. How much of the drawing do you finish?

39. **WEIGHTS** Your sponge weighs $\dfrac{1}{16}$ ounce when dry and $\dfrac{13}{16}$ ounce when you soak part of it in water. How many ounces heavier is the wet sponge?

40. ★ **MULTIPLE CHOICE** Today you picked $\dfrac{1}{5}$ bushel of apples, $\dfrac{2}{5}$ bushel less than you picked yesterday. How many bushels did you pick yesterday?

Ⓐ $\dfrac{1}{5}$ bushel 　Ⓑ $\dfrac{2}{5}$ bushel 　Ⓒ $\dfrac{3}{5}$ bushel 　Ⓓ 2 bushels

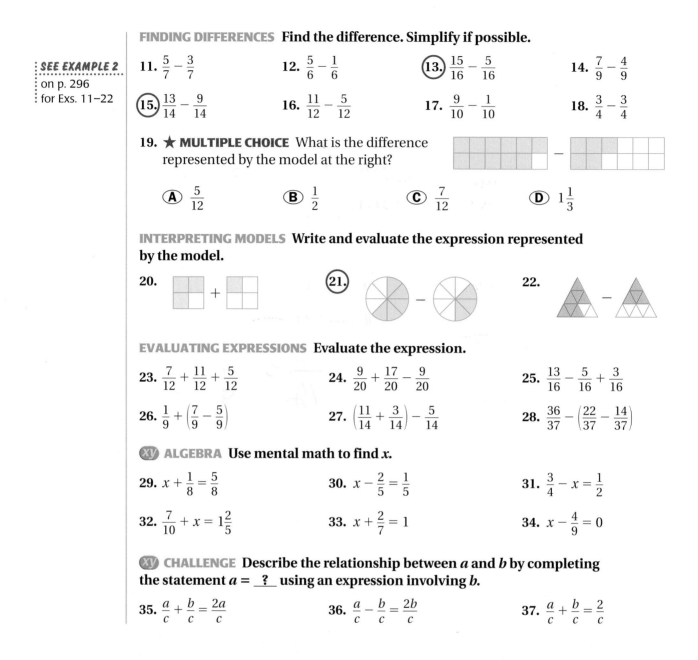

41. GUIDED PROBLEM SOLVING You and two friends are competing in a swim race. Your friends each swim $\frac{1}{5}$ of the race. You swim $\frac{3}{5}$ of the race. How much more of the race do you swim than your friends combined?

   a. What fraction of the race do you swim?

   b. How much of the race do your two friends swim altogether?

   c. Write a verbal model and evaluate an expression to find how much more of the race you swim than your friends.

42. ★ WRITING How can you tell whether the sum of two fractions with a common denominator is greater than 1? less than 1? equal to 1?

43. ★ SHORT RESPONSE At a rural airport, Runway B is $\frac{3}{25}$ mile shorter than Runway A.

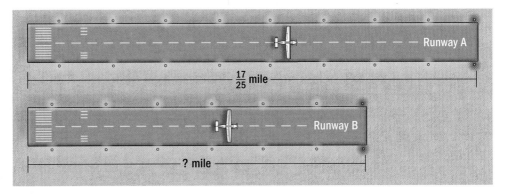

   a. Write a Verbal Model Write a verbal model you can use to find the length of Runway B.

   b. Calculate Write and evaluate a numerical expression to find the length of Runway B.

44. SNOWFALL A weather report states that $\frac{3}{4}$ foot of snow fell on Sunday and on Monday. Snowfall on Tuesday was $\frac{1}{4}$ foot less than on Monday. How many feet of snow fell in total on the three days?

45. ★ MULTIPLE CHOICE You make a home movie using $\frac{5}{6}$ hour of family trips and $\frac{5}{6}$ hour of birthday parties. If the tape is 2 hours long, how many hours are left on the tape?

   Ⓐ $1\frac{2}{3}$ hours   **Ⓑ** $1\frac{1}{6}$ hours   **Ⓒ** $\frac{1}{3}$ hour   **Ⓓ** $\frac{1}{6}$ hour

46. ★ SHORT RESPONSE A recipe calls for $\frac{7}{8}$ cup of sugar. What fraction of a cup should you remove from a full cup of sugar to measure $\frac{7}{8}$ cup? There are 16 tablespoons of sugar in one cup. How many tablespoons of sugar must you remove?

47. ★ **OPEN-ENDED MATH** Write and solve a real-world addition problem in which the sum of two fractions is 1.

48. ◆ **MULTIPLE REPRESENTATIONS** The table shows the results of a survey asking 100 students how much of their day is spent online.

Hours per day online	Fraction of students
0–1	$\frac{5}{10}$
2–3	$\frac{2}{10}$
4–5	$\frac{1}{10}$
more than 5	$\frac{?}{10}$

a. **Calculate** What fraction of the students spend from 0 to 3 hours per day online?

b. **Calculate** What fraction of the students spend more than 5 hours per day online?

c. **Make a Circle Graph** Draw a circle graph of the data to check the reasonableness of your answers to parts (a) and (b).

49. 🆇🆈 **CHALLENGE** You spend one fifth of a musical rehearsal singing and three fifths dancing. Choose the equation you can use to find how much more of the rehearsal is spent dancing than singing. Then write a related equation and solve it.

A. $\frac{1}{5} + x = \frac{3}{5}$

B. $x - \frac{1}{5} = \frac{3}{5}$

MIXED REVIEW

Get-Ready

Prepare for Lesson 6.3 in Exs. 50–53

Find the LCM of the two numbers. *(p. 250)*

50. 3 and 4   **51.** 5 and 10   **52.** 6 and 8   **53.** 12 and 18

Estimate the sum or difference. *(p. 291)*

54. $\frac{3}{8} + \frac{9}{10}$ **55.** $\frac{6}{7} - \frac{1}{12}$ **56.** $4\frac{1}{5} + 2\frac{5}{6}$ **57.** $5\frac{7}{8} - 1\frac{3}{4}$

58. ★ **SHORT RESPONSE** Write two fractions that are equivalent to 0.24. *Explain* how you found your answer. *(p. 266)*

Brain Game

Fill in the Digits

Copy and complete the equations, replacing each ? with a digit from 1 through 9. You may use each digit only once, and each fraction you write must be in simplest form.

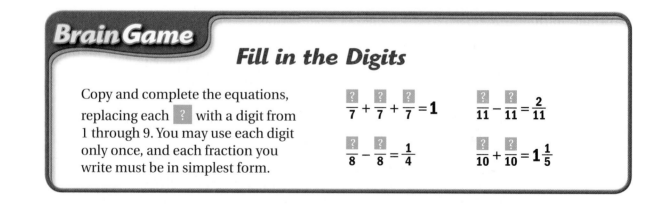

$$\frac{?}{7} + \frac{?}{7} + \frac{?}{7} = 1 \qquad \frac{?}{11} - \frac{?}{11} = \frac{2}{11}$$

$$\frac{?}{8} - \frac{?}{8} = \frac{1}{4} \qquad \frac{?}{10} + \frac{?}{10} = 1\frac{1}{5}$$

INVESTIGATION
Use before Lesson 6.3

GOAL
Model addition of fractions with different denominators.

MATERIALS
• colored pencils

6.3 Modeling Addition of Fractions

You can use models to add fractions with different denominators.

EXPLORE Use models to find $\frac{1}{2} + \frac{1}{3}$.

STEP 1 **Draw** a model of $\frac{1}{2}$ by dividing a square vertically.

STEP 2 **Draw** a model of $\frac{1}{3}$ by dividing a square horizontally.

STEP 3 **Redraw** the models so that they are divided in the same way.

STEP 4 **Combine** the models to find the sum.

$$\frac{1}{2} + \frac{1}{3} = \frac{5}{6}$$

PRACTICE Use models to find the sum. Write your answers in simplest form.

1. $\frac{1}{4} + \frac{2}{3}$

2. $\frac{3}{8} + \frac{1}{5}$

3. $\frac{2}{5} + \frac{1}{3}$

4. $\frac{3}{4} + \frac{1}{7}$

DRAW CONCLUSIONS

5. **WRITING** You add two fractions whose denominators are 4 and 5 such as $\frac{3}{4}$ and $\frac{1}{5}$. What denominator does their sum have? *Explain* how you can use models to answer this question.

6. **REASONING** Without drawing a model, tell what the denominator will be when you add two fractions whose denominators are 5 and 6. *Explain* your reasoning.

6.3 Fractions with Different Denominators

Before	You added and subtracted with common denominators.
Now	You'll add and subtract with different denominators.
Why?	So you can evaluate changes in data, as in Example 3.

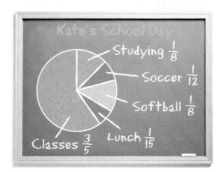

KEY VOCABULARY
• least common
  denominator
  (**LCD**), *p. 254*

Activities The circle graph shows how Kate spent her day. What fraction of her day did she spend playing sports?

As you may have observed in the Investigation on page 301, you add or subtract fractions with different denominators by first finding the least common denominator (LCD).

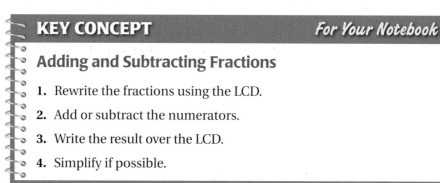

KEY CONCEPT   *For Your Notebook*

Adding and Subtracting Fractions

1. Rewrite the fractions using the LCD.

2. Add or subtract the numerators.

3. Write the result over the LCD.

4. Simplify if possible.

EXAMPLE 1 Adding Fractions

Kate spent $\frac{1}{8}$ of her day playing softball and $\frac{1}{12}$ of her day playing soccer.

To answer the real-world question above, find the sum $\frac{1}{8} + \frac{1}{12}$

$$
\begin{aligned}
\frac{1 \times 3}{8 \times 3} &= \frac{3}{24} \\
+\ \frac{1 \times 2}{12 \times 2} &= +\ \frac{2}{24} \\
\hline
&= \frac{5}{24}
\end{aligned}
$$

Rewrite both fractions using the LCD, 24.

Add the fractions.

REWRITE FRACTIONS
Need help with rewriting
fractions? See p. 254.

▶ **Answer** Kate spent $\frac{5}{24}$ of her day playing sports.

EXAMPLE 2 Rewriting Sums of Fractions

TAKE NOTES
In your summary of this chapter, you may want to include examples of adding and subtracting fractions with common and different denominators.

Find the sum $\frac{5}{8} + \frac{3}{4}$.

$$
\begin{array}{ll}
\dfrac{5}{8} & = \quad \dfrac{5}{8} \\[2mm]
+\dfrac{3 \times 2}{4 \times 2} & = \quad +\dfrac{6}{8} \qquad \text{Rewrite } \frac{3}{4} \text{ using the LCD, 8.} \\[2mm]
& \qquad\quad \dfrac{11}{8}, \text{ or } 1\dfrac{3}{8} \qquad \text{Add the fractions.}
\end{array}
$$

✓ **GUIDED PRACTICE** for Examples 1 and 2

Find the sum. Simplify if possible.

1. $\frac{1}{3} + \frac{1}{9}$ **2.** $\frac{2}{3} + \frac{1}{2}$ **3.** $\frac{4}{5} + \frac{3}{4}$ **4.** $\frac{5}{6} + \frac{7}{10}$

5. What if? Suppose you wanted to know the fraction of Kate's day that was spent in class or studying. Find the fraction.

EXAMPLE 3 Subtracting Fractions

Rainfall Last week, $\frac{2}{3}$ inch of rain fell on Monday and $\frac{4}{5}$ inch fell on Tuesday. How much more rain fell on Tuesday than on Monday?

SOLUTION

You need to find the difference of $\frac{4}{5}$ and $\frac{2}{3}$.

$$
\begin{array}{ll}
\dfrac{4 \times 3}{5 \times 3} & = \quad \dfrac{12}{15} \qquad \text{Rewrite both fractions using the LCD, 15.} \\[2mm]
-\dfrac{2 \times 5}{3 \times 5} & = \quad -\dfrac{10}{15} \\[2mm]
& \qquad\quad \dfrac{2}{15} \qquad \text{Subtract the fractions.}
\end{array}
$$

▶ **Answer** On Tuesday, $\frac{2}{15}$ inch more rain fell than on Monday.

Animated Math at classzone.com

✓ **GUIDED PRACTICE** for Example 3

Find the difference. Simplify if possible.

6. $\frac{5}{6} - \frac{3}{4}$ **7.** $\frac{7}{8} - \frac{1}{4}$ **8.** $\frac{1}{2} - \frac{4}{9}$ **9.** $\frac{5}{6} - \frac{3}{10}$

10. Racing One lap of Speedway A is $\frac{2}{5}$ mile. One lap of Speedway B is $\frac{3}{4}$ mile. How much longer is one lap of Speedway B?

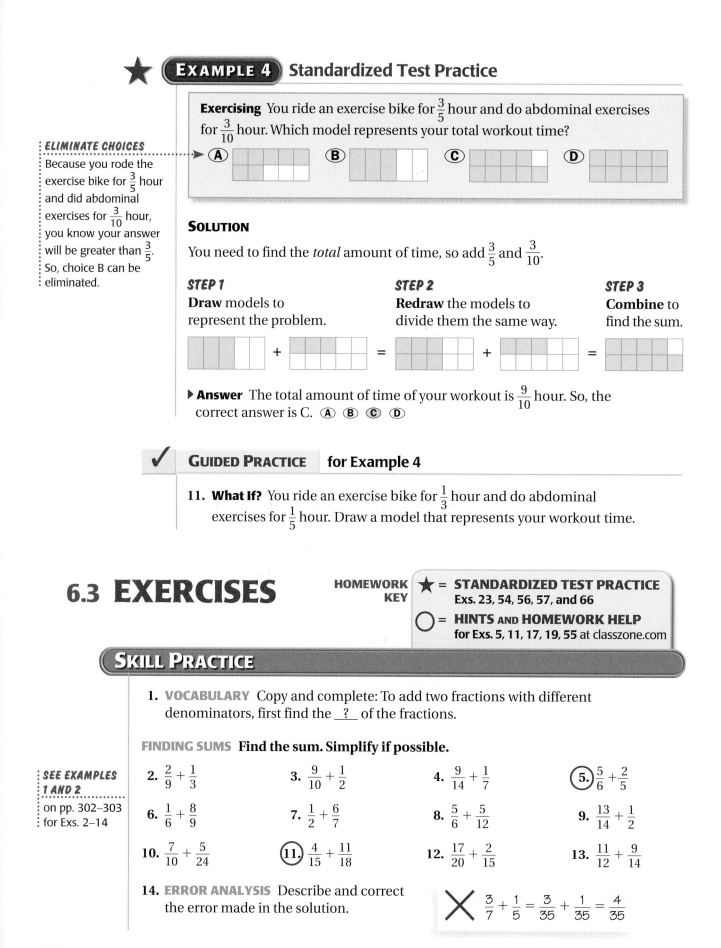

EXAMPLE 4 Standardized Test Practice

Exercising You ride an exercise bike for $\frac{3}{5}$ hour and do abdominal exercises for $\frac{3}{10}$ hour. Which model represents your total workout time?

Ⓐ Ⓑ Ⓒ Ⓓ

ELIMINATE CHOICES
Because you rode the exercise bike for $\frac{3}{5}$ hour and did abdominal exercises for $\frac{3}{10}$ hour, you know your answer will be greater than $\frac{3}{5}$. So, choice B can be eliminated.

SOLUTION

You need to find the *total* amount of time, so add $\frac{3}{5}$ and $\frac{3}{10}$.

STEP 1
Draw models to represent the problem.

STEP 2
Redraw the models to divide them the same way.

STEP 3
Combine to find the sum.

▸ **Answer** The total amount of time of your workout is $\frac{9}{10}$ hour. So, the correct answer is C. Ⓐ Ⓑ Ⓒ Ⓓ

✓ **GUIDED PRACTICE** for Example 4

11. What If? You ride an exercise bike for $\frac{1}{3}$ hour and do abdominal exercises for $\frac{1}{5}$ hour. Draw a model that represents your workout time.

6.3 EXERCISES

HOMEWORK KEY

★ = **STANDARDIZED TEST PRACTICE**
Exs. 23, 54, 56, 57, and 66

◯ = **HINTS AND HOMEWORK HELP**
for Exs. 5, 11, 17, 19, 55 at classzone.com

SKILL PRACTICE

1. VOCABULARY Copy and complete: To add two fractions with different denominators, first find the __?__ of the fractions.

FINDING SUMS Find the sum. Simplify if possible.

SEE EXAMPLES 1 AND 2
on pp. 302–303
for Exs. 2–14

2. $\frac{2}{9} + \frac{1}{3}$

3. $\frac{9}{10} + \frac{1}{2}$

4. $\frac{9}{14} + \frac{1}{7}$

5. $\frac{5}{6} + \frac{2}{5}$

6. $\frac{1}{6} + \frac{8}{9}$

7. $\frac{1}{2} + \frac{6}{7}$

8. $\frac{5}{6} + \frac{5}{12}$

9. $\frac{13}{14} + \frac{1}{2}$

10. $\frac{7}{10} + \frac{5}{24}$

11. $\frac{4}{15} + \frac{11}{18}$

12. $\frac{17}{20} + \frac{2}{15}$

13. $\frac{11}{12} + \frac{9}{14}$

14. ERROR ANALYSIS Describe and correct the error made in the solution.

✗ $\frac{3}{7} + \frac{1}{5} = \frac{3}{35} + \frac{1}{35} = \frac{4}{35}$

FINDING DIFFERENCES Find the difference. Simplify if possible.

SEE EXAMPLE 3
on p. 303
for Exs. 15–22

15. $\dfrac{7}{8} - \dfrac{2}{3}$

16. $\dfrac{3}{4} - \dfrac{1}{6}$

17. $\dfrac{7}{10} - \dfrac{1}{8}$

18. $\dfrac{5}{8} - \dfrac{1}{3}$

19. $\dfrac{3}{5} - \dfrac{1}{15}$

20. $\dfrac{11}{16} - \dfrac{1}{4}$

21. $\dfrac{3}{4} - \dfrac{2}{7}$

22. $\dfrac{6}{11} - \dfrac{1}{2}$

SEE EXAMPLE 4
on p. 304
for Ex. 23

23. ★ **MULTIPLE CHOICE** Which expression is represented by the model if an X means minus?

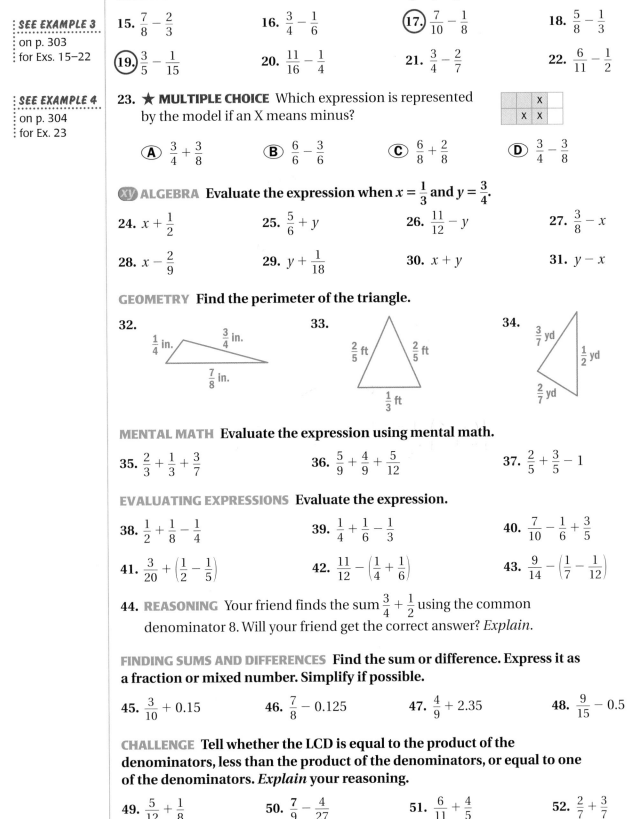

A $\dfrac{3}{4} + \dfrac{3}{8}$

B $\dfrac{6}{6} - \dfrac{3}{6}$

C $\dfrac{6}{8} + \dfrac{2}{8}$

D $\dfrac{3}{4} - \dfrac{3}{8}$

ⓧⓨ ALGEBRA Evaluate the expression when $x = \dfrac{1}{3}$ and $y = \dfrac{3}{4}$.

24. $x + \dfrac{1}{2}$

25. $\dfrac{5}{6} + y$

26. $\dfrac{11}{12} - y$

27. $\dfrac{3}{8} - x$

28. $x - \dfrac{2}{9}$

29. $y + \dfrac{1}{18}$

30. $x + y$

31. $y - x$

GEOMETRY Find the perimeter of the triangle.

32. $\dfrac{1}{4}$ in. $\dfrac{3}{4}$ in. $\dfrac{7}{8}$ in.

33. $\dfrac{2}{5}$ ft $\dfrac{2}{5}$ ft $\dfrac{1}{3}$ ft

34. $\dfrac{3}{7}$ yd $\dfrac{1}{2}$ yd $\dfrac{2}{7}$ yd

MENTAL MATH Evaluate the expression using mental math.

35. $\dfrac{2}{3} + \dfrac{1}{3} + \dfrac{3}{7}$

36. $\dfrac{5}{9} + \dfrac{4}{9} + \dfrac{5}{12}$

37. $\dfrac{2}{5} + \dfrac{3}{5} - 1$

EVALUATING EXPRESSIONS Evaluate the expression.

38. $\dfrac{1}{2} + \dfrac{1}{8} - \dfrac{1}{4}$

39. $\dfrac{1}{4} + \dfrac{1}{6} - \dfrac{1}{3}$

40. $\dfrac{7}{10} - \dfrac{1}{6} + \dfrac{3}{5}$

41. $\dfrac{3}{20} + \left(\dfrac{1}{2} - \dfrac{1}{5} \right)$

42. $\dfrac{11}{12} - \left(\dfrac{1}{4} + \dfrac{1}{6} \right)$

43. $\dfrac{9}{14} - \left(\dfrac{1}{7} - \dfrac{1}{12} \right)$

44. REASONING Your friend finds the sum $\dfrac{3}{4} + \dfrac{1}{2}$ using the common denominator 8. Will your friend get the correct answer? *Explain.*

FINDING SUMS AND DIFFERENCES Find the sum or difference. Express it as a fraction or mixed number. Simplify if possible.

45. $\dfrac{3}{10} + 0.15$

46. $\dfrac{7}{8} - 0.125$

47. $\dfrac{4}{9} + 2.35$

48. $\dfrac{9}{15} - 0.5$

CHALLENGE Tell whether the LCD is equal to the product of the denominators, less than the product of the denominators, or equal to one of the denominators. *Explain* your reasoning.

49. $\dfrac{5}{12} + \dfrac{1}{8}$

50. $\dfrac{7}{9} - \dfrac{4}{27}$

51. $\dfrac{6}{11} + \dfrac{4}{5}$

52. $\dfrac{2}{7} + \dfrac{3}{7}$

53. GUIDED PROBLEM SOLVING The monkey bars make up $\frac{1}{4}$ of an obstacle course. The tires make up $\frac{1}{3}$ of the course. The tunnel makes up $\frac{5}{12}$ of the course. How much shorter is the tunnel than the monkey bars and tires combined?

a. How much of the course do the monkey bars and tires make up?

b. Write an expression to find how much shorter the tunnel is than the monkey bars and tires combined.

c. Evaluate the expression you wrote in part (b).

SEE EXAMPLE 4
on p. 304
for Ex. 54

54. ★ MULTIPLE CHOICE Which model represents the combined thickness of two boards if one board is $\frac{1}{4}$ inch thick and the other board is $\frac{5}{8}$ inch thick?

(A) **(B)** **(C)** **(D)**

55. MULTI-STEP PROBLEM Your peppermint plant is $\frac{3}{10}$ inch tall. After one week, it is $\frac{1}{2}$ inch tall.

a. Calculate How much did the plant grow in one week?

b. Interpret If it grows at the same rate, how tall would you expect the plant to be after 2 weeks? after 3 weeks?

c. Predict If it grows at the same rate, how many weeks total will it take the plant to reach a height of $1\frac{7}{10}$ inches?

56. ★ EXTENDED RESPONSE Use the map that shows the fraction of the Appalachian Trail that is in each region.

a. Calculate What fraction of the trail is in the central and northeastern regions combined?

b. Explain What fraction of the trail is in the southern region? *Explain* how you found your answer.

c. Compare Which two regions together make up the longer path, the *northeastern and central regions* or the *central and southern regions*? *Explain* your reasoning.

Northeastern
$\frac{1}{3}$

Central
$\frac{1}{5}$

Southern
$\frac{?}{15}$

N

★ = **STANDARDIZED TEST PRACTICE**   ◯ = **HINTS AND HOMEWORK HELP** *at classzone.com*

57. ★ **OPEN-ENDED MATH** Write and solve a real-world problem in which you would add $\frac{2}{3}$ and $\frac{1}{2}$.

CHALLENGE Use the information about musical notes given at the right.

58. What is the combined value of one eighth note, one quarter note, and one half note?

59. What note do you need to add to the notes in Exercise 58 to equal one whole note?

60. A dotted quarter note, such as "♩.", has a value of $\frac{3}{8}$. What note(s) do you need to add to two eighth notes and one dotted quarter note to equal one whole note?

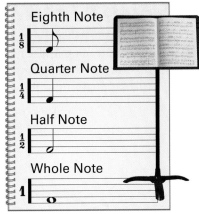

Eighth Note
$\frac{1}{8}$

Quarter Note
$\frac{1}{4}$

Half Note
$\frac{1}{2}$

Whole Note
1

MIXED REVIEW

Get-Ready

Prepare for Lesson 6.4 in Exs. 61–64

Find the sum. *(p. 295)*

61. $\frac{1}{8} + \frac{3}{8}$

62. $\frac{3}{5} + \frac{3}{5}$

63. $\frac{6}{7} + \frac{1}{7}$

64. $\frac{11}{12} + \frac{7}{12}$

CHOOSE A STRATEGY Use a strategy from the list to solve the following problem. Explain your choice of strategy.

65. Of all the pairs of whole numbers whose sum is 15, find the pair that has the greatest product.

66. ★ **MULTIPLE CHOICE** Which number rounded to the nearest thousand is 50,000? *(p. 739)*

Ⓐ 49,601   Ⓑ 50,500   Ⓒ 50,900   Ⓓ 50,999

Problem Solving Strategies

- Guess, Check, and Revise *(p. 763)*
- Work Backward *(p. 764)*
- Make a List *(p. 765)*
- Look for a Pattern *(p. 766)*

QUIZ *for Lessons 6.1–6.3*

Estimate the sum or difference. *(p. 291)*

1. $\frac{1}{6} + \frac{9}{10}$

2. $\frac{4}{7} - \frac{2}{11}$

3. $7\frac{11}{16} - 4\frac{2}{15}$

4. $3\frac{5}{8} + 1\frac{7}{9}$

Find the sum or difference. *(p. 295)*

5. $\frac{7}{8} + \frac{5}{8}$

6. $\frac{7}{10} + \frac{1}{10}$

7. $\frac{8}{13} - \frac{3}{13}$

8. $\frac{11}{15} - \frac{2}{15}$

9. $\frac{5}{18} + \frac{4}{9}$

10. $\frac{2}{3} + \frac{3}{4}$

11. $\frac{1}{2} - \frac{2}{11}$

12. $\frac{3}{4} - \frac{3}{10}$

13. **GEOMETRY** Estimate the perimeter of the figure. *(p. 66)*

35 yd

$12\frac{3}{4}$ yd $14\frac{5}{6}$ yd

$32\frac{1}{4}$ yd

MIXED REVIEW *of Problem Solving*

STATE TEST PRACTICE
classzone.com

Lessons 6.1–6.3

1. **MULTI-STEP PROBLEM** Some space in the basement of an apartment complex is used for storage. The storage space is shared among three apartment units as shown below.

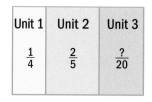

Unit 1	Unit 2	Unit 3
$\frac{1}{4}$	$\frac{2}{5}$	$\frac{?}{20}$

   a. Which storage unit occupies the biggest part of the storage space?

   b. What fraction of the storage space is allocated to Units 1 and 2?

   c. What fraction of the storage space is used by the Unit 3 occupant? *Explain* your reasoning.

   d. Which two storage units together make up the bigger portion of the space, *Unit 1 and Unit 3* or *Unit 1 and Unit 2*?

2. **OPEN-ENDED** Wood manufacturers allow plywood to be slightly less thick or slightly more thick than intended. The amount less than or greater than the intended thickness is called the tolerance. The tolerance for a piece of $\frac{3}{4}$ inch plywood is $\frac{1}{32}$ inch. Besides $\frac{3}{4}$ inch, what are three different thicknesses that the plywood could have?

3. **OPEN-ENDED** You want to add two fractions with different denominators. Explain why you do not necessarily have to use the LCD to obtain the correct answer. Give an example to support your answer.

4. **GRIDDED ANSWER** A triangular plot of land measures $25\frac{1}{3}$ feet on each side. How much fencing is needed for the perimeter of the plot?

5. **EXTENDED RESPONSE** The circle graph below shows the results of a survey asking 100 students how many hours a week they spend shopping.

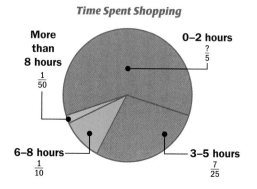

Time Spent Shopping

   a. What fraction of the students spend 6 or more hours shopping?

   b. What fraction of the students spend 3 or more hours shopping?

   c. What fraction of the students spend 0–2 hours shopping? *Explain* your reasoning.

   d. Suppose $\frac{1}{4}$ of the students spend less than 1 hour shopping. What fraction spend 1–2 hours shopping? *Explain* your reasoning.

6. **SHORT RESPONSE** You need $\frac{1}{4}$ cup of plant food for two plants and $\frac{1}{8}$ cup for two other plants. How much food is needed for all four plants? A store sells a 1 cup container of food. Is that enough to feed the plants? If so, how much is left over? If not, how much more is needed?

7. **SHORT RESPONSE** You are putting up a wallpaper border in your bedroom. The bedroom is rectangular with a width of $12\frac{1}{4}$ feet and a length of $15\frac{13}{16}$ feet. Estimate how many feet of border you will need. Would you want your estimate to be *high* or *low*? *Explain* your reasoning.

6.4 Adding and Subtracting Mixed Numbers

Before	You added and subtracted fractions.
Now	You'll add and subtract mixed numbers.
Why?	So you can find distances, as in Example 1.

KEY VOCABULARY
- **simplest form,** *p. 244*
- **mixed number,** *p. 260*

Adding and subtracting mixed numbers is similar to adding and subtracting fractions.

KEY CONCEPT *For Your Notebook*

Adding and Subtracting Mixed Numbers

1. Rewrite the fractions using the LCD if necessary.
2. Add or subtract the fractions.
3. Add or subtract the whole numbers.
4. Simplify if possible.

EXAMPLE 1 Adding Mixed Numbers

Sports Korey is training to compete in a race. What is the total distance he will run in the race?

SOLUTION

Find the sum $2\frac{1}{3} + 4\frac{1}{3}$.

$$\begin{array}{r} 2\frac{1}{3} \\ +\ 4\frac{1}{3} \\ \hline 6\frac{2}{3} \end{array}$$ Add the fractions. Then add the whole numbers.

Forest City Race
Prizes awarded to top 3 in each class!

Run $2\frac{1}{3}$ mi
Bike 2 mi
Run $4\frac{1}{3}$ mi

August 2   8:00 A.M.

▶ **Answer** Korey will run $6\frac{2}{3}$ miles in the race.

✓ **GUIDED PRACTICE** for Example 1

Find the sum.

1. $1\frac{4}{9} + 3\frac{1}{9}$ **2.** $3\frac{3}{11} + 2\frac{5}{11}$ **3.** $2\frac{1}{5} + 2\frac{3}{5}$ **4.** $2\frac{1}{7} + 1\frac{3}{7}$

EXAMPLE 2 Simplifying MIxed Number Sums

Find the sum $2\frac{1}{12} + 1\frac{3}{4}$.

<table>
<tr><td colspan="3" style="text-align:left">ANOTHER WAY</td></tr>
</table>

ANOTHER WAY
Rewrite the mixed numbers as improper fractions, then add.

$$2\frac{1}{12} \quad = \quad 2\frac{1}{12}$$
$$+\ 1\frac{3\times3}{4\times3} \quad = \quad +\ 1\frac{9}{12}$$
$$\overline{\phantom{+\ 1\frac{3\times3}{4\times3}}}$$
$$3\frac{10}{12},\text{ or } 3\frac{5}{6}$$

Rewrite $\frac{3}{4}$ using the LCD, 12.

Add the fractions, and then the whole numbers. Simplify.

▶ **Answer** The sum is $3\frac{10}{12}$, or $3\frac{5}{6}$.

✓ **GUIDED PRACTICE** for Example 2

Find the sum. Simplify if possible.

5. $1\frac{4}{9} + 3\frac{1}{3}$ **6.** $6\frac{3}{4} + 3\frac{1}{5}$ **7.** $4\frac{7}{8} + 5\frac{1}{4}$ **8.** $3\frac{3}{5} + 7\frac{9}{10}$

EXAMPLE 3 Solving Addition Problems

Sculpture The base of a sculpture is $1\frac{1}{2}$ feet tall. The sculpture is $2\frac{2}{3}$ feet tall. How tall is the sculpture with the base?

SOLUTION

You need to add $1\frac{1}{2}$ and $2\frac{2}{3}$.

$$1\frac{1\times3}{2\times3} \quad = \quad 1\frac{3}{6}$$
$$+\ 2\frac{2\times2}{3\times2} \quad = \quad +\ 2\frac{4}{6}$$
$$3\frac{7}{6}$$

Rewrite both fractions using the LCD, 6.

Add the fractions. Then add the whole numbers.

VOCABULARY
A mixed number is in *simplest form* when the fraction is a proper fraction that cannot be simplified.

Think of $3\frac{7}{6}$ as $3 + \frac{7}{6}$, or $3 + 1\frac{1}{6}$. To simplify, write the sum as $4\frac{1}{6}$.

▶ **Answer** The sculpture with the base is $4\frac{1}{6}$ feet tall.

✓ **GUIDED PRACTICE** for Example 3

9. Circus Performers A clown is $5\frac{3}{4}$ feet tall while barefoot and $1\frac{1}{3}$ feet taller while wearing stilts. How tall is the clown while wearing stilts?

10. Home Improvement You want to cover a length of $32\frac{3}{4}$ inches and a length of $5\frac{1}{2}$ inches with wood trim. How much trim do you need to buy in all?

EXAMPLE 4 **Subtracting Mixed Numbers**

Volcanoes Before it erupted in 1980, the height of the Mount St. Helens volcano was about $1\frac{17}{20}$ miles. After the eruption, the height was about $1\frac{3}{5}$ miles. What was the decrease in the height?

SOLUTION

You need to find the difference $1\frac{17}{20} - 1\frac{3}{5}$.

$$1\frac{17}{20} \qquad = \qquad 1\frac{17}{20}$$
$$-\,1\frac{3 \times 4}{5 \times 4} \quad = \quad -\,1\frac{12}{20}$$
$$\overline{\qquad\qquad\qquad\qquad \frac{5}{20}, \text{ or } \frac{1}{4}}$$

Rewrite $\frac{3}{5}$ using the LCD, 20.

Subtract the fractions, then the whole numbers. Simplify.

▶ **Answer** The decrease in the height was about $\frac{1}{4}$ mile.

✓ **GUIDED PRACTICE** for Example 4

11. $6\frac{4}{9} - 1\frac{2}{3}$ **12.** $8\frac{3}{5} - 2\frac{7}{10}$ **13.** $10\frac{5}{6} - 3\frac{1}{8}$ **14.** $2\frac{3}{4} - 1\frac{11}{12}$

15. Height You are $4\frac{11}{12}$ feet tall and your friend is $4\frac{3}{4}$ feet tall. How much taller are you than your friend?

6.4 EXERCISES

HOMEWORK KEY

★ = **STANDARDIZED TEST PRACTICE**
Exs. 14, 23, 58, 59, 61, 62, 64, 65, 80

◯ = **HINTS AND HOMEWORK HELP**
for Exs. 7, 9, 17, 19, 57 at classzone.com

SKILL PRACTICE

VOCABULARY Write the mixed number in simplest form.

1. $4\frac{6}{9}$ **2.** $5\frac{5}{4}$ **3.** $3\frac{7}{4}$ **4.** $2\frac{15}{9}$

FINDING SUMS Find the sum. Simplify if possible.

SEE EXAMPLES 1 AND 2
on pp. 309–310 for Exs. 5–13

5. $5\frac{2}{9} + 4\frac{5}{9}$ **6.** $2\frac{1}{6} + 8\frac{1}{6}$ **7.** $9\frac{3}{4} + 3\frac{1}{12}$ **8.** $4\frac{7}{10} + 3\frac{1}{5}$

9. $8\frac{3}{5} + 3\frac{1}{2}$ **10.** $3\frac{2}{3} + 6\frac{3}{4}$ **11.** $2\frac{7}{8} + 7\frac{1}{4}$ **12.** $9\frac{7}{9} + 6\frac{1}{3}$

13. ERROR ANALYSIS Describe and correct the error made in the solution.

$$\times \quad 7\frac{2}{5} + 1\frac{4}{5} = 8\frac{6}{5}$$
$$= 8\frac{1}{5}$$

SEE EXAMPLE 2
on p. 310
for Ex. 14

14. ★ **MULTIPLE CHOICE** Which simplifies to $2\frac{2}{3}$?

  (A) $\frac{8}{3}$ (B) $\frac{12}{4}$ (C) $1\frac{4}{3}$ (D) $\frac{8}{6}$

FINDING DIFFERENCES Find the difference. Simplify if possible.

SEE EXAMPLE 4
on p. 311
for Exs. 15–23

15. $2\frac{3}{5} - 1\frac{1}{5}$ 16. $10\frac{7}{8} - 4\frac{1}{8}$ (17.) $4\frac{5}{6} - 1\frac{1}{12}$ 18. $7\frac{11}{12} - 4\frac{1}{3}$

(19.) $5\frac{5}{6} - 3\frac{1}{4}$ 20. $3\frac{3}{4} - 1\frac{1}{6}$ 21. $8\frac{6}{7} - 5\frac{1}{2}$ 22. $9\frac{7}{10} - 1\frac{1}{4}$

23. ★ **MULTIPLE CHOICE** What is the value of the expression $8\frac{4}{9} - 2\frac{1}{12}$?

  (A) $6\frac{1}{3}$ (B) $6\frac{13}{36}$ (C) $6\frac{4}{9}$ (D) $6\frac{1}{2}$

CHOOSE A METHOD Find the sum or difference. Tell whether you used *mental math* or *paper and pencil* to find the answer.

**SEE EXAMPLES
1, 2, 3, AND 4**
on pp. 309–311
for Exs. 24–35

24. $2\frac{5}{8} + 4$ 25. $8\frac{1}{3} + 3\frac{3}{5}$ 26. $7\frac{2}{3} - 5\frac{1}{2}$ 27. $12\frac{5}{6} - 3$

28. $6\frac{2}{5} + \frac{3}{5}$ 29. $9\frac{4}{11} - \frac{1}{11}$ 30. $5\frac{3}{8} + \frac{7}{8}$ 31. $1\frac{5}{6} - \frac{1}{6}$

32. $7\frac{3}{4} - \frac{3}{4}$ 33. $8\frac{7}{10} - \frac{7}{10}$ 34. $4\frac{5}{7} + \frac{2}{7}$ 35. $3\frac{8}{9} + \frac{1}{9}$

ALGEBRA Evaluate the expression when $x = 2\frac{1}{3}$ and $y = 1\frac{1}{2}$.

36. $y + 5 - x$ 37. $x + 1\frac{1}{3} - y$ 38. $7 + y - 6\frac{1}{3}$

39. $x + y + 2\frac{2}{3} + x$ 40. $y - 1\frac{1}{6} + x$ 41. $3\frac{4}{5} - x + 1\frac{3}{7} + y$

GEOMETRY Find the perimeter of the triangle. Use estimation to check.

42.

$4\frac{1}{3}$ m $4\frac{1}{3}$ m

$4\frac{1}{3}$ m

43.

$1\frac{1}{5}$ cm   2 cm

$1\frac{3}{5}$ cm

44.

$5\frac{2}{3}$ ft

$2\frac{1}{2}$ ft

6 ft

FINDING PATTERNS Write the next three numbers in the pattern. Describe the rule you used.

45. $1\frac{5}{8}, 2\frac{1}{8}, 2\frac{5}{8}, 3\frac{1}{8}, \ldots$ 46. $2\frac{2}{3}, 4, 5\frac{1}{3}, 6\frac{2}{3}, \ldots$ 47. $12, 10\frac{1}{6}, 8\frac{1}{3}, 6\frac{1}{2}, \ldots$

EXAMPLE AND NONEXAMPLES Give an example of the following. Then find the sum or difference.

48. Two mixed numbers whose sum is in simplest form and two mixed numbers whose sum is *not* in simplest form.

49. Two mixed numbers whose difference is in simplest form and two mixed numbers whose difference is *not* in simplest form.

ALGEBRA Use mental math to find the value of *x*.

50. $3\frac{3}{5} + 2\frac{2}{5} + x = 7$ **51.** $1\frac{3}{4} + 7\frac{1}{4} + x = 11$ **52.** $6\frac{2}{3} - 2\frac{2}{3} + x = 8$

53. $5\frac{1}{2} + x + 4\frac{1}{4} = 13\frac{3}{4}$ **54.** $12\frac{1}{5} = 9\frac{3}{10} + x - 1\frac{1}{10}$ **55.** $4\frac{2}{3} = x + 7\frac{8}{9} - 4\frac{2}{9}$

56. CHALLENGE Use the properties of addition to show why $6\frac{1}{2} + 8\frac{1}{2} = 14 + 1$. Use this method to simplify $8\frac{1}{2} + 2\frac{1}{8} + 3\frac{3}{8}$. Tell which property you used for each step.

PROBLEM SOLVING

SEE EXAMPLES 3 AND 4
on pp. 310–311
for Exs. 57–62

57. SKIS A 6 foot tall ski jumper buys skis that are $2\frac{1}{4}$ feet longer than his height. How long are the skis?

58. ★ MULTIPLE CHOICE You play two piano pieces at a recital. One piece is $5\frac{1}{2}$ minutes long. The other lasts $4\frac{2}{3}$ minutes. How long are the two combined?

(A) $9\frac{1}{6}$ minutes   **(B)** $9\frac{2}{3}$ minutes   **(C)** $10\frac{1}{6}$ minutes   **(D)** $10\frac{1}{3}$ minutes

59. ★ MULTIPLE CHOICE A shoemaker has $1\frac{5}{8}$ yards of canvas. After some canvas is used, $1\frac{1}{6}$ yards are left over. Which method can be used to find how many yards of canvas are used?

(A) Find the sum of $1\frac{5}{8}$ and $1\frac{1}{6}$.

(B) Find the difference of $1\frac{5}{8}$ and $1\frac{1}{6}$.

(C) Find the product of $1\frac{5}{8}$ and $1\frac{1}{6}$.

(D) Find the quotient of $1\frac{5}{8}$ and $1\frac{1}{6}$.

60. HAT HEIGHTS You use two top hats for a magic show. One hat is $8\frac{3}{4}$ inches tall, and the other is $7\frac{1}{8}$ inches tall. How much taller is the first hat? Use a verbal model to help you find your answer.

61. ★ SHORT RESPONSE The width of a rectangle is $5\frac{1}{8}$ inches. Its length is $2\frac{1}{10}$ inches less than its width. Find the perimeter of the rectangle. *Explain* how you can use estimation to check whether your answer is reasonable.

62. ★ WRITING Find the sum $3\frac{1}{4} + 2\frac{5}{6}$ using the method in Example 3. Then find the sum by first rewriting both mixed numbers as improper fractions. *Compare* the methods.

6.4 Adding and Subtracting Mixed Numbers   **313**

63. ◆ **MULTIPLE REPRESENTATIONS** A scientist measures the levels of ocean tides from a cliff overlooking the ocean. The high tide is $9\frac{1}{2}$ feet below the edge of the cliff. The low tide is 20 feet below the edge of the cliff.

    a. Draw a Diagram Draw and label a diagram that shows the relationship between the high and low tides. Label the heights.

    b. Write and Solve an Equation Write an equation you can use to find how much higher the high tide is than the low tide. Solve the equation using mental math.

64. ★ **OPEN-ENDED MATH** Write and solve a real-world problem in which you would add $3\frac{2}{3}$ to $1\frac{1}{4}$ and then subtract $1\frac{1}{2}$ from the result.

65. ★ **SHORT RESPONSE** In 1838, bank notes worth 6.25 cents and $12\frac{1}{2}$ cents were issued in Pennsylvania. What was the combined value of two 6.25 cent notes and two $12\frac{1}{2}$ cent notes? *Explain* how you found your answer.

CHALLENGE In Exercises 66 and 67, use the following information.

In a frog jumping contest, your frog jumps $2\frac{3}{16}$ feet farther than 13 feet. Your friend's frog jumps $1\frac{5}{12}$ feet farther than your frog. Then it jumps $\frac{1}{3}$ foot in the opposite direction.

66. In the end, how far did your friend's frog jump forward? *Explain* how you found your answer.

67. Your cousin's frog jumps $1\frac{1}{3}$ feet farther than your frog. Did your cousin's frog jump farther than your friend's frog? *Explain* how you found your answer.

MIXED REVIEW

Get-Ready

Prepare for
Lesson 6.5 in
Exs. 68–75

Find the sum or difference. *(p. 302)*

68. $\frac{3}{4} + \frac{3}{8}$ **69.** $\frac{1}{3} + \frac{5}{12}$ **70.** $\frac{2}{5} + \frac{1}{15}$ **71.** $\frac{9}{14} + \frac{6}{7}$

72. $\frac{2}{3} - \frac{1}{2}$ **73.** $\frac{4}{5} - \frac{3}{10}$ **74.** $\frac{9}{12} - \frac{1}{4}$ **75.** $\frac{7}{8} - \frac{5}{6}$

Copy and complete the statement with <, >, or =. *(p. 254)*

76. $\frac{5}{9}$? $\frac{2}{3}$ **77.** $\frac{1}{4}$? $\frac{2}{7}$ **78.** $\frac{1}{2}$? $\frac{6}{12}$ **79.** $\frac{4}{15}$? $\frac{3}{10}$

80. ★ **MULTIPLE CHOICE** Which set of numbers is ordered from least to greatest? *(p. 738)*

    A 450, 455, 540, 504, 545   **B** 1002, 1020, 1202, 1211, 1200

    C 606, 607, 667, 670, 760   **D** 1400, 1401, 1114, 1141, 1411

EXTRA PRACTICE for Lesson 6.4, p. 781   ⟳ **ONLINE QUIZ** at classzone.com

INVESTIGATION
Use before Lesson 6.5

GOAL
Use models to subtract mixed numbers by renaming.

MATERIALS
• colored pencils

6.5 Using Models to Subtract

Sometimes you need to rename mixed numbers when you subtract.

EXPLORE Use models to find $3\frac{1}{4} - 1\frac{3}{4}$.

STEP 1 Draw a model of $3\frac{1}{4} - 1\frac{3}{4}$.

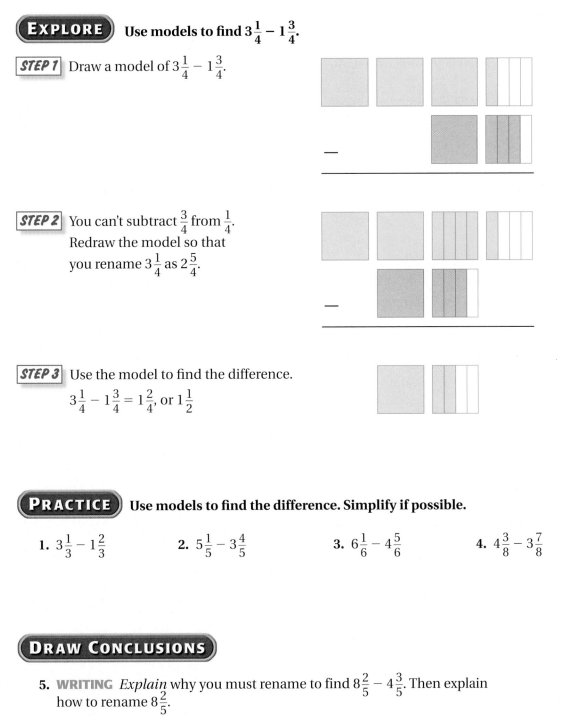

STEP 2 You can't subtract $\frac{3}{4}$ from $\frac{1}{4}$. Redraw the model so that you rename $3\frac{1}{4}$ as $2\frac{5}{4}$.

STEP 3 Use the model to find the difference.
$$3\frac{1}{4} - 1\frac{3}{4} = 1\frac{2}{4}, \text{ or } 1\frac{1}{2}$$

PRACTICE Use models to find the difference. Simplify if possible.

1. $3\frac{1}{3} - 1\frac{2}{3}$

2. $5\frac{1}{5} - 3\frac{4}{5}$

3. $6\frac{1}{6} - 4\frac{5}{6}$

4. $4\frac{3}{8} - 3\frac{7}{8}$

DRAW CONCLUSIONS

5. **WRITING** *Explain* why you must rename to find $8\frac{2}{5} - 4\frac{3}{5}$. Then explain how to rename $8\frac{2}{5}$.

6.5 Subtracting Mixed Numbers by Renaming

Before	You subtracted mixed numbers without renaming.
Now	You'll subtract mixed numbers by renaming.
Why?	So you can find differences in heights, as in Example 3.

KEY VOCABULARY

- least common denominator (LCD), *p. 254*
- mixed number, *p. 260*

When you subtract mixed numbers, as in Example 1, you may need to rename the first mixed number.

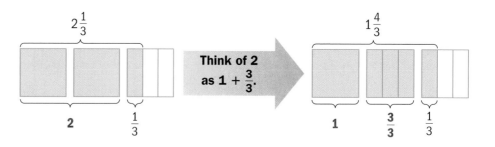

EXAMPLE 1 Subtracting Mixed Numbers

Find the difference $2\frac{1}{3} - 1\frac{2}{3}$.

You can't subtract $\frac{2}{3}$ from $\frac{1}{3}$. Think of $2\frac{1}{3}$ as $1 + \frac{3}{3} + \frac{1}{3}$.

$$2\frac{1}{3} \quad = \quad 1\frac{4}{3} \qquad \text{Rename } 2\frac{1}{3} \text{ as } 1\frac{4}{3}$$

$$\frac{-1\frac{2}{3} \quad = \quad -1\frac{2}{3}}{\qquad\qquad\quad \frac{2}{3} \qquad \text{Subtract.}}$$

Animated Math
at classzone.com

The example above shows the process of renaming in order to subtract mixed numbers.

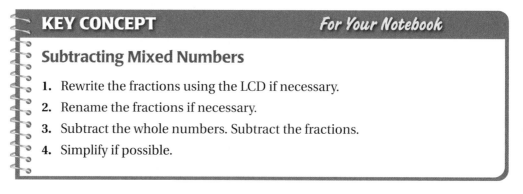

KEY CONCEPT *For Your Notebook*

Subtracting Mixed Numbers

1. Rewrite the fractions using the LCD if necessary.
2. Rename the fractions if necessary.
3. Subtract the whole numbers. Subtract the fractions.
4. Simplify if possible.

Renaming a Whole Number Sometimes you need to rename a whole number as a mixed number. To do this, rename one whole part as a fraction equal to 1.

EXAMPLE 2   Subtracting from a Whole Number

Find the difference $5 - 3\frac{1}{7}$.

Think of 5 as $4 + 1$, or $4 + \frac{7}{7}$.

$$
\begin{array}{rcl}
5 & = & 4\frac{7}{7} \qquad \text{Rename 5 as } 4\frac{7}{7}. \\
-\,3\frac{1}{7} & = & -\,3\frac{1}{7} \\
\hline
 & & 1\frac{6}{7} \qquad \text{Subtract.}
\end{array}
$$

EXAMPLE 3   Solving Subtraction Problems

Horses The height of a horse is measured from its shoulders, as shown in the figure. How much taller is the Clydesdale than the Shetland?

$5\frac{1}{3}$ ft

$3\frac{3}{4}$ ft

SOLUTION

You need to find the difference $5\frac{1}{3} - 3\frac{3}{4}$. Use the LCD, 12.

$$
\begin{array}{rclcl}
5\frac{1}{3} & = & 5\frac{4}{12} & = & 4\frac{16}{12} \qquad \text{Rename } 5\frac{4}{12} \text{ as } 4\frac{16}{12}. \\
-\,3\frac{3}{4} & = & -\,3\frac{9}{12} & = & -\,3\frac{9}{12} \\
\hline
 & & & & 1\frac{7}{12} \qquad \text{Subtract.}
\end{array}
$$

▶ **Answer** The Clydesdale is $1\frac{7}{12}$ feet taller than the Shetland.

✓ **GUIDED PRACTICE**   for Examples 1, 2, and 3

Find the difference. Simplify if possible.

1. $6\frac{2}{7} - 4\frac{3}{7}$

2. $3\frac{1}{4} - 1\frac{3}{4}$

3. $3 - 2\frac{1}{2}$

4. $8 - 5\frac{3}{8}$

5. $6\frac{1}{4} - 2\frac{3}{5}$

6. $10\frac{2}{3} - 7\frac{5}{6}$

7. **What If?** Suppose an Arabian horse is $4\frac{7}{10}$ feet tall. How much shorter is it than the Clydesdale from Example 3?

6.5 EXERCISES

HOMEWORK KEY

★ = **STANDARDIZED TEST PRACTICE**
Exs. 23, 48, 51, 54, and 61

◯ = **HINTS AND HOMEWORK HELP**
for Exs. 9, 11, 17, 19, 47 at classzone.com

SKILL PRACTICE

VOCABULARY **Copy and complete to rename the mixed number.**

SEE EXAMPLE 1
on p. 316
for Exs. 5–10

1. $2\frac{1}{6} = 1\frac{?}{6}$

2. $4\frac{3}{5} = \underline{\ ?\ }\frac{8}{5}$

3. $5\frac{1}{3} = \underline{\ ?\ }\frac{4}{3}$

4. $3\frac{4}{7} = 2\frac{?}{7}$

5. **MODELING** What renaming do the models represent?

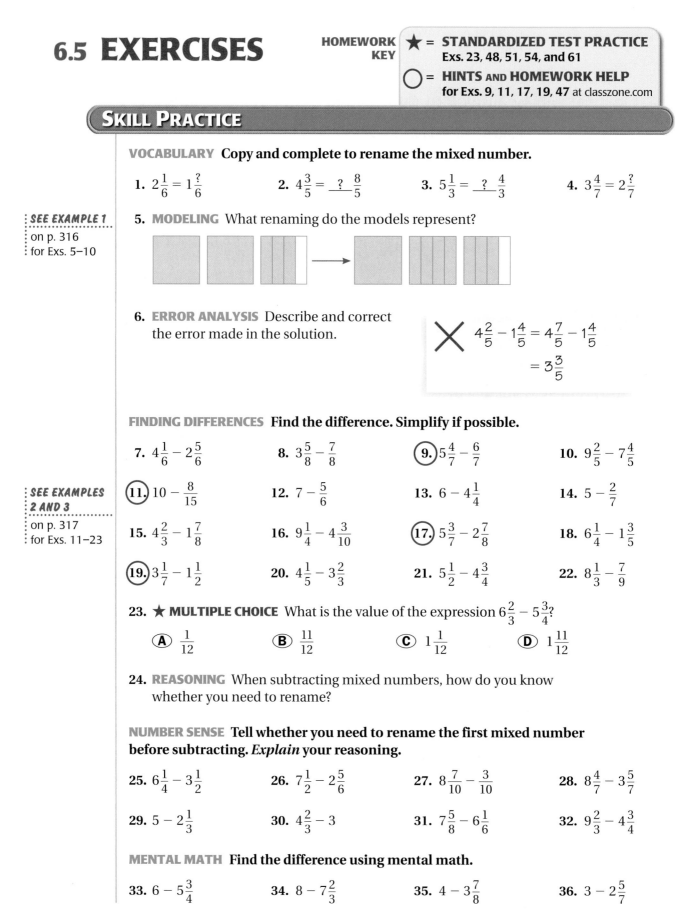

6. **ERROR ANALYSIS** Describe and correct the error made in the solution.

$$4\frac{2}{5} - 1\frac{4}{5} = 4\frac{7}{5} - 1\frac{4}{5}$$
$$= 3\frac{3}{5}$$

FINDING DIFFERENCES **Find the difference. Simplify if possible.**

7. $4\frac{1}{6} - 2\frac{5}{6}$

8. $3\frac{5}{8} - \frac{7}{8}$

9. $5\frac{4}{7} - \frac{6}{7}$

10. $9\frac{2}{5} - 7\frac{4}{5}$

*SEE EXAMPLES
2 AND 3*
on p. 317
for Exs. 11–23

11. $10 - \frac{8}{15}$

12. $7 - \frac{5}{6}$

13. $6 - 4\frac{1}{4}$

14. $5 - \frac{2}{7}$

15. $4\frac{2}{3} - 1\frac{7}{8}$

16. $9\frac{1}{4} - 4\frac{3}{10}$

17. $5\frac{3}{7} - 2\frac{7}{8}$

18. $6\frac{1}{4} - 1\frac{3}{5}$

19. $3\frac{1}{7} - 1\frac{1}{2}$

20. $4\frac{1}{5} - 3\frac{2}{3}$

21. $5\frac{1}{2} - 4\frac{3}{4}$

22. $8\frac{1}{3} - \frac{7}{9}$

23. ★ **MULTIPLE CHOICE** What is the value of the expression $6\frac{2}{3} - 5\frac{3}{4}$?

A $\frac{1}{12}$

B $\frac{11}{12}$

C $1\frac{1}{12}$

D $1\frac{11}{12}$

24. **REASONING** When subtracting mixed numbers, how do you know whether you need to rename?

NUMBER SENSE **Tell whether you need to rename the first mixed number before subtracting.** *Explain* **your reasoning.**

25. $6\frac{1}{4} - 3\frac{1}{2}$

26. $7\frac{1}{2} - 2\frac{5}{6}$

27. $8\frac{7}{10} - \frac{3}{10}$

28. $8\frac{4}{7} - 3\frac{5}{7}$

29. $5 - 2\frac{1}{3}$

30. $4\frac{2}{3} - 3$

31. $7\frac{5}{8} - 6\frac{1}{6}$

32. $9\frac{2}{3} - 4\frac{3}{4}$

MENTAL MATH **Find the difference using mental math.**

33. $6 - 5\frac{3}{4}$

34. $8 - 7\frac{2}{3}$

35. $4 - 3\frac{7}{8}$

36. $3 - 2\frac{5}{7}$

ALGEBRA Evaluate the expression when $x = 3\frac{5}{6}$ and $y = 6\frac{1}{4}$.

37. $5\frac{1}{6} - x + y$ **38.** $x + 11\frac{7}{8} - y$ **39.** $8\frac{1}{5} - y + x$ **40.** $y - 1\frac{3}{4} - x$

41. $8 - (y - x)$ **42.** $14 - (x + y)$ **43.** $7 - (y - x)$ **44.** $(10 - y) + x$

45. CHALLENGE Compare and contrast the procedure for subtracting mixed numbers with the procedure for subtracting multi-digit whole numbers.

PROBLEM SOLVING

SEE EXAMPLE 3
on p. 317
for Ex. 46

46. UNICYCLES Members of a unicycle club are taking a two day trip. The trip is a total of $16\frac{1}{4}$ miles. They travel $6\frac{1}{2}$ miles on the first day. How far will they travel on the second day?

47. BLUE CRABS A fisherman catches a blue crab that is $2\frac{1}{3}$ inches wide. Blue crabs that are less than 5 inches wide are returned to the water. How much wider must the crab be before it will be 5 inches wide?

48. ★ MULTIPLE CHOICE A jar contains $2\frac{1}{2}$ cups of honey. You pour $1\frac{2}{3}$ cups into a bowl. How many cups of honey are left in the jar?

(A) $\frac{1}{6}$ cup (B) $\frac{1}{2}$ cup (C) $\frac{2}{3}$ cup (D) $\frac{5}{6}$ cup

HOCKEY A professional ice hockey goal is 4 feet tall. You buy a hockey goal that is $3\frac{2}{3}$ feet tall.

SEE EXAMPLE 3
on p. 317
for Exs. 49–50

49. How much taller than your goal is the professional goal? Show your steps.

50. A goalie is $5\frac{3}{4}$ feet tall. How much taller is the goalie than the smaller goal? Show your steps.

51. ★ SHORT RESPONSE There are $5\frac{1}{2}$ inches from the ground to the bottom of a car's bumper. The curb is $4\frac{1}{4}$ inches high. What is the distance between the curb and the car? Another car's bumper is $\frac{1}{8}$ inch above the curb. How high is its bumper from the ground? *Explain* your reasoning.

52. CHECKING REASONABLENESS A road sign says that Exit 1 is $1\frac{3}{4}$ miles ahead and Exit 2 is $3\frac{1}{2}$ miles ahead. How far is Exit 2 from Exit 1? *Explain* how you could use estimation to check the reasonableness of your answer.

53. MULTI-STEP PROBLEM Use the table that shows the lengths of four snakes at a zoo exhibit.

  a. Range Find the range of the data in the table.

  b. Make a Graph Make a bar graph of the data.

  c. Compare Which snake is about 3 times longer than another? What is the difference in their lengths?

Snake	Length
green water snake	$35\frac{5}{8}$ in.
northern brown snake	$11\frac{5}{6}$ in.
southern ringneck snake	$13\frac{7}{8}$ in.
checkered garter snake	20 in.

54. ★ WRITING You are subtracting a mixed number from a whole number. *Describe* how to find the fraction you should use when you rename the whole number.

CHALLENGE **Some of the tallest trees in Massachusetts can be found in the Mohawk Trail State Forest.**

55. A White Pine is $47\frac{1}{6}$ feet taller than an American Basswood, which is $7\frac{7}{12}$ feet shorter than a Northern Red Oak. The Northern Red Oak is 119 feet tall. How tall is the White Pine?

56. A White Ash is $13\frac{11}{12}$ feet shorter than the White Pine in Exercise 55. Is the White Ash taller or shorter than the Northern Red Oak in Exercise 55? How much taller or shorter? *Explain* your method.

MIXED REVIEW

Get-Ready

Prepare for Lesson 6.6 in Exs. 57–60

Copy and complete the statement. *(p. 754)*

57. 8 minutes = __?__ seconds

58. 290 min = __?__ hours __?__ min

59. 343 sec = __?__ min __?__ sec

60. 11 hours = __?__ minutes

61. ★ OPEN-ENDED MATH Write two mixed number expressions whose sum is $6\frac{3}{5}$. *Explain* how you found your answers. *(p. 309)*

CHOOSE A STRATEGY Use a strategy from the list to solve the following problem. Explain your choice of strategy.

62. The perimeter of a triangle is 9.8 meters. One side of the triangle is 3.2 meters. The other two sides have the same length. Find the length of the other two sides.

Problem Solving Strategies

▪ Draw a Diagram *(p. 762)*
▪ Guess, Check, and Revise *(p. 763)*
▪ Make a Table *(p. 765)*
▪ Solve a Simpler Problem *(p. 768)*

ONLINE QUIZ at classzone.com

6.5 Subtracting Mixed Numbers by Renaming

EXAMPLE You can use an Internet search engine to find information about paper sizes. Your search engine may have special features to help make a search more precise. Read its Help section for alternative search methods.

Some common paper sizes are U.S. letter (11 in. $\times$ $8\frac{1}{2}$ in.) and European A4.

What are the dimensions of A4 paper? How does this size compare to the U.S. letter size?

SOLUTION

Choose a search engine. Type in the key words and phrases that are likely to generate a list of Web sites that give the dimensions of A4 paper, in inches. Then examine the list of sites until you find the information you need.

A4 paper is measured in metric units, so your search may give slightly different results because of rounding.

Find the difference in length and in width of the paper sizes.

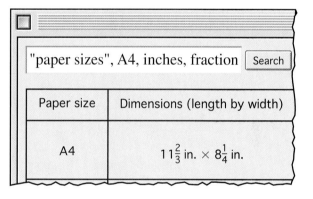

"paper sizes", A4, inches, fraction [Search]

Paper size	Dimensions (length by width)
A4	$11\frac{2}{3}$ in. $\times$ $8\frac{1}{4}$ in.

difference in length

$$
\begin{array}{ll}
11\frac{2}{3} & \text{(A4)} \\
-\ 11 & \text{(U.S. letter)} \\
\hline
\frac{2}{3} &
\end{array}
$$

difference in width

$$
\begin{array}{lll}
8\frac{1}{2} & = & 8\frac{2}{4} \quad \text{(U.S. letter)} \\
-\ 8\frac{1}{4} & = & -\ 8\frac{1}{4} \quad \text{(A4)} \\
\hline
& & \frac{1}{4}
\end{array}
$$

▶ **Answer** The A4 size is $\frac{2}{3}$ inch longer, and the U.S. letter size is $\frac{1}{4}$ inch wider.

PRACTICE Use the Internet to find information about the paper sizes. Then find the difference in length and in width.

1. A5 and A4   **2.** B5 and A5   **3.** legal and letter

6.6 Measures of Time

Before	You added and subtracted fractions and mixed numbers.
Now	You'll add and subtract measures of time.
Why?	So you can compare race times, as in Example 1.

KEY VOCABULARY
• elapsed time, *p. 323*

Tour de France Lance Armstrong won the 2003 Tour de France. His total time over the course of the three week event was 83 hours, 41 minutes, and 12 seconds. Haimar Zubeldia's time was 6 minutes and 51 seconds greater. What was Haimar Zubeldia's time?

When you add or subtract measures of time, use the information below.

1 hour (h) = 60 minutes (min)
1 minute (min) = 60 seconds (sec)

EXAMPLE 1 Adding Measures of Time

To answer the real-world question above, add 6 minutes and 51 seconds to 83 hours, 41 minutes, and 12 seconds.

```
    83 h  41 min  12 sec
 +        6 min  51 sec
    83 h  47 min  63 sec     Add the hours, the minutes, and the seconds.
```

Think of 63 sec as 1 min 3 sec. Then add 1 min to 47 min.

▶ **Answer** Haimar Zubeldia's time was 83 hours, 48 minutes, and 3 seconds.

EXAMPLE 2 Subtracting Measures of Time

```
    11 h  17 min      Think of 11 h 17 min          10 h  77 min     Rename.
 −   8 h  42 min      as 10 h 77 min.           −    8 h  42 min
                                                      2 h  35 min     Subtract.
```

✓ **GUIDED PRACTICE** for Examples 1 and 2

Add or subtract the measures of time.

1. 3 min 26 sec
    + 1 min 40 sec

2. 5 h 29 min   8 sec
    + 2 h 45 min 33 sec

3. 4 min 16 sec
    − 2 min 18 sec

4. 6 h 32 min 27 sec
    − 4 h   1 min 45 sec

Elapsed Time The amount of time between a start time and an end time is called **elapsed time**. To find elapsed time, think about the number of hours that pass, then the number of minutes that pass.

EXAMPLE 3 Solve a Multi-Step Problem

Winter Solstice The winter solstice occurs on the day with the least amount of daylight. Suppose that on this day, the sun rises at 7:15 A.M. and sets at 4:22 P.M. How long does the daylight last?

SOLUTION

Break the problem into parts.

STEP 1 **Find** the elapsed time from 7:15 A.M. to 12:00 P.M.

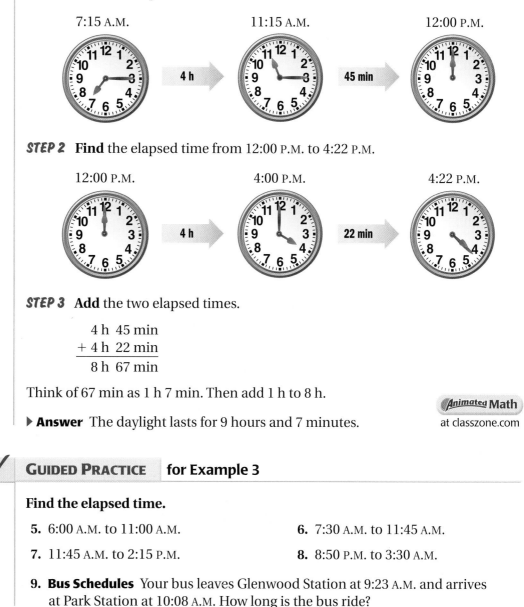

STEP 2 **Find** the elapsed time from 12:00 P.M. to 4:22 P.M.

STEP 3 **Add** the two elapsed times.

$$\begin{array}{r} 4\text{ h }\ 45\text{ min} \\ +\ 4\text{ h }\ 22\text{ min} \\ \hline 8\text{ h }\ 67\text{ min} \end{array}$$

Think of 67 min as 1 h 7 min. Then add 1 h to 8 h.

▶ **Answer** The daylight lasts for 9 hours and 7 minutes.

AVOID ERRORS
You can't always subtract two times to find elapsed time. For example, to find the elapsed time from 8:00 A.M. to 4:25 P.M., you can't compute 4 h 25 min − 8 h. You need to break the problem into parts.

Animated **Math**
at classzone.com

✓ **GUIDED PRACTICE** for Example 3

Find the elapsed time.

5. 6:00 A.M. to 11:00 A.M.

6. 7:30 A.M. to 11:45 A.M.

7. 11:45 A.M. to 2:15 P.M.

8. 8:50 P.M. to 3:30 A.M.

9. Bus Schedules Your bus leaves Glenwood Station at 9:23 A.M. and arrives at Park Station at 10:08 A.M. How long is the bus ride?

EXAMPLE 4 Standardized Test Practice

Homework On Wednesday night Sam spent 28 min on mathematics homework, 33 min on language arts homework, and 50 min on chemistry homework. About how much time in all did Sam spend on his homework?

   A 1 h 10 min   **B** 1 h 30 min   **C** 1 h 50 min   **D** 2 h 10 min

ELIMINATE CHOICES
1 h 10 min equals 70 min. Sam spent 28 min + 50 min, or 78 min, on only two subjects. So, the answer will be greater than 70, and choice A can be eliminated.

SOLUTION

You can estimate the total time by rounding.

$$28 \text{ min} \approx 30 \text{ min}$$
$$33 \text{ min} \approx 30 \text{ min}$$
$$\underline{50 \text{ min} = 50 \text{ min}}$$
$$110 \text{ min} = 1 \text{ h } 50 \text{ min}$$

▶ **Answer** The best estimate of Sam's total time spent on homework is 1 hour 50 minutes. The correct answer is C. (A) (B) **(C)** (D)

✓ **GUIDED PRACTICE** for Example 4

10. **School Day** Karen got out of bed at 6:55 A.M. and arrived home from school at 3:10 P.M. About how many hours passed from the time she rose until the time she arrived home?

6.6 EXERCISES

HOMEWORK KEY

★ = **STANDARDIZED TEST PRACTICE**
Exs. 15, 28, 29, 30, 33, 38, and 54

◯ = **HINTS AND HOMEWORK HELP**
for Exs. 3, 7, 9, 13, 27 at classzone.com

SKILL PRACTICE

1. **VOCABULARY** Copy and complete: Elapsed time is the amount of time between a(n) __?__ time and a(n) __?__ time.

SEE EXAMPLES 1 AND 2
on p. 322
for Exs. 2–8

2. **ERROR ANALYSIS** Describe and correct the error made in the solution.

$$
\begin{array}{cccc}
 & 52 \text{ h} & 54 \text{ min} & 13 \text{ sec} \\
+ & 21 \text{ h} & 51 \text{ min} & 40 \text{ sec} \\
\hline
 & 73 \text{ h} & 105 \text{ min} & 53 \text{ sec} \longrightarrow 74 \text{ h } 5 \text{ min } 53 \text{ sec}
\end{array}
$$

CALCULATING TIME Add or subtract the measures of time. Estimate to check.

3.   2 h 50 min
    +   35 min

4.   4 h 38 min
    + 3 h 22 min

5.   3 h 12 min 53 sec
    + 2 h 20 min 42 sec

6.   4 h 25 min
    − 1 h 31 min

7.   5 h 10 min
    − 2 h 55 min

8.   3 h 2 min
    −   58 min 12 sec

SEE EXAMPLE 3
on p. 323
for Exs. 9–14

FINDING ELAPSED TIME Find the elapsed time. Use estimation to check.

9. 1:00 P.M. to 3:00 P.M.

10. 7:00 A.M. to 10:00 A.M.

11. 9:30 P.M. to 2:45 A.M.

12. 6:35 A.M. to 2:30 P.M.

13. 12:22 A.M. to 1:31 P.M.

14. 5:17 A.M. to 8:52 A.M.

15. ★ **MULTIPLE CHOICE** What is the most appropriate length of time for a letter you mail at the post office to be delivered in the United States?

Ⓐ 12 hours   Ⓑ 1 week   Ⓒ 6 weeks   Ⓓ 40 weeks

SELECTING UNITS Estimate how long each activity might take using the appropriate unit of measure. Choose from seconds, minutes, or hours.

16. writing and sending an e-mail

17. building a model airplane

18. boiling a pot of water

19. running a 40-yard dash

20. constructing scenery for a school play

21. watering a plant

ESTIMATION Estimate the elapsed time in the appropriate units (weeks, days, or hours).

22. 8 A.M. July 3 to 3:55 P.M. July 7

23. 11:58 P.M. April 1 to 12:07 A.M. April 18

24. 6:32 A.M. May 1 to 10:25 P.M. May 1

25. 12:01 A.M. May 30 to 11:59 P.M. June 1

26. **CHALLENGE** Explain how adding and subtracting mixed numbers is similar to adding and subtracting measures of time.

PROBLEM SOLVING

27. **BASEBALL DOUBLE HEADER** The first game of a baseball double-header lasts 2 hours and 35 minutes. The second game lasts 3 hours and 45 minutes. How long is the double-header?

28. ★ **SHORT RESPONSE** The first part of a train ride lasts 3 hours. The second part lasts 1 hour and 8 minutes. How much longer is the first part? How long is the entire train ride? *Explain* your answers.

SEE EXAMPLE 4
on p. 324
for Ex. 29

29. ★ **MULTIPLE CHOICE** You get out of bed at 8:55 a.m. and return home from the beach at 4:10 p.m. About how many hours elapsed between the time you got out of bed and the time you returned home from the beach?

Ⓐ 4 h   Ⓑ 5 h   Ⓒ 6 h   Ⓓ 7 h

30. ★ **MULTIPLE CHOICE** You go snorkeling from 10:30 a.m. to 12:15 p.m. You take a half hour lunch break, then snorkel until 2:15 p.m. How much time do you spend snorkeling?

Ⓐ 2 h 45 min   Ⓑ 3 h 15 min

Ⓒ 3 h 40 min   Ⓓ 3 h 45 min

31. MULTI-STEP PROBLEM Your first class period starts at 8:15 A.M. and ends at 9:04 A.M. Each class period lasts the same amount of time. There are 5 minutes between classes.

    a. Calculate Write the length of one class period in minutes and fractions of an hour. *Explain* how you found your answers.

    b. Explain What is the most appropriate unit of measure of time for a class period? *Explain.*

    c. Reasoning By the end of third period, how much time have you spent in class?

32. REASONING A train schedule lists departures at 8:03 A.M., 8:34 A.M., 9:05 A.M., and 9:36 A.M. Assume the departure times continue to follow a pattern. *Predict* the departure times for the next three trains.

33. ★ OPEN-ENDED MATH You need to schedule a $1\frac{1}{2}$ hour meeting to begin no earlier than 10:00 A.M. and end no later than 4:00 P.M. It must not overlap the 12:00–1:00 P.M. lunch hour. Select 3 possible starting times.

READING *IN* MATH   **Read the information below for Exercises 34–37.**

Time Zones The map shows four standard time zones in the lower 48 states of the United States. Each time zone differs from the next by one hour.

Los Angeles (Pacific)   Denver (Mountain)   Chicago (Central)   New York (Eastern)

34. Calculate It is 12:30 P.M. in Chicago. What time is it in Los Angeles?

35. Calculate Your plane leaves New York at 9:10 A.M., Eastern Standard Time. The flight lasts 4 hours and 20 minutes. What time will it be in Denver when you land?

36. Compare When it is 4 P.M. in Los Angeles, it is 3 P.M. in Fairbanks, Alaska. What time is it in Fairbanks when it is 10 A.M. in Chicago?

37. Open-Ended Name a city not shown on this map where the time is 2 hours later than the time in Los Angeles.

---

38. ★ SHORT RESPONSE The first part of a California road trip lasts 3 hours and 49 minutes. After a 50 minute break, the second part lasts 2 hours and 14 minutes. Estimate the length of the whole trip. If the trip began at 7:35 P.M., about what time did it end? *Explain.*

39. WORKING BACKWARD You are playing a role in a school play. The play begins at 7:30 P.M. It takes 15 minutes to get into costume, 35 minutes to do your makeup, and 20 minutes to fix your hair. By what time should you start getting ready? *Explain.*

   ★ = STANDARDIZED TEST PRACTICE   ◯ = HINTS AND HOMEWORK HELP *at classzone.com*

40. CALCULATING TIME You use your cell phone from 11:57 A.M. to 1:23 P.M. Before the call, you had 941 free minutes left on your calling plan for the month. How much free calling time, in hours, do you have left after the call? Write your answer as a mixed number.

41. CHALLENGE Your flight from Seattle to Dallas takes 3 hours 48 minutes. Seattle is two time zones west of Dallas. If you left at 11:31 A.M. Pacific Time, what time would you land in Dallas, Central Time?

MIXED REVIEW

Get-Ready

Prepare for Lesson 7.1 in Exs. 42–49

Find the product. Use estimation to check your answer. *(p. 169)*

42. 4×0.7 **43.** 9×1.2 **44.** 4.8×15 **45.** 1.76×25

46. 2×3.142 **47.** 9.005×14 **48.** 0.014×6 **49.** 8×6.625

Find the difference. *(p. 316)*

50. $6\frac{5}{8} - 5\frac{7}{8}$ **51.** $8 - 3\frac{4}{7}$ **52.** $4\frac{1}{6} - 2\frac{5}{9}$ **53.** $6\frac{1}{4} - 1\frac{7}{10}$

54. ★ **MULTIPLE CHOICE** Which of the numbers is divisible by 6? *(p. 230)*

(A) 134 **(B)** 208 **(C)** 258 **(D)** 5800

QUIZ *for Lessons 6.4–6.6*

Find the sum or difference. *(p. 309)*

1. $9\frac{3}{5} + 7\frac{1}{5}$ **2.** $3\frac{9}{17} + 11$ **3.** $5\frac{3}{8} + 2\frac{1}{6}$ **4.** $2\frac{3}{10} + 8\frac{3}{4}$

5. $9\frac{5}{7} - 3\frac{2}{7}$ **6.** $10\frac{11}{12} - 4\frac{3}{4}$ **7.** $5\frac{1}{3} - 1\frac{4}{9}$ **8.** $6 - 2\frac{1}{8}$

9. DOG WEIGHTS A beagle weighs $25\frac{3}{4}$ pounds. A collie weighs $60\frac{1}{2}$ pounds. How much more does the collie weigh? *(p. 309)*

Add or subtract the measures of time. *(p. 322)*

10.   3 h 15 min
  − 1 h 40 min

11.   8 h 55 min
  +   20 min

12.   4 h 14 min 51 sec
  + 1 h 36 min 35 sec

Find the elapsed time. *(p. 322)*

13. 2:30 P.M. to 6:45 P.M.   **14.** 6:00 A.M. to 11:50 A.M.

15. 8:10 P.M. to 1:15 A.M.   **16.** 2:40 A.M. to 7:05 P.M.

17. SLEEP A baby sleeps from 10:18 A.M. to 12:05 P.M., from 4:10 P.M. to 5:25 P.M., and from 9:36 P.M. to 6:10 A.M. Find the total sleep time. *(p. 322)*

Lessons 6.4–6.6

1. **MULTI-STEP PROBLEM** The table shows the lengths of four sharks at an aquarium.

Shark	Length
Basking shark	20 ft
Hammerhead shark	$15\frac{1}{3}$ ft
Mako shark	$10\frac{7}{12}$ ft
Thresher shark	$12\frac{3}{4}$ ft

   a. How much longer is the hammerhead shark than the thresher shark?

   b. How much longer is the basking shark than the hammerhead shark?

   c. How much longer is the thresher shark than the mako shark?

   d. What is the sum of the 3 differences in (a), (b), and (c)? *Explain* why the sum is equal to the range of the shark data.

2. **GRIDDED ANSWER** Gary took an English test that had a multiple choice section and an essay section. He looked at the clock at the beginning and at the end of the test. He spent 3 times as long on the essay section as on the multiple choice section. How many minutes did he spend on the essay section?

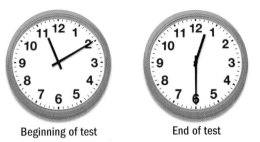

Beginning of test   End of test

3. **SHORT RESPONSE** The first part of a flight lasts 2 hours and 38 minutes. The second part lasts 3 hours and 26 minutes. Is the flight longer than 6 hours? *Explain.*

4. **OPEN-ENDED** Give possible side lengths of a rectangle with a perimeter of $10\frac{1}{2}$ feet.

5. **SHORT RESPONSE** Your dog started an obstacle course 5 seconds past 1:30 P.M. and finished 41 seconds after 1:30 P.M. Your friend's dog started 30 seconds after 1:13 P.M. and finished 8 seconds after 1:14 P.M. Whose dog won, and by how much? *Explain* your answer.

6. **GRIDDED ANSWER** You want to buy $1\frac{5}{8}$ pounds of turkey at the supermarket. An employee slices and weighs the turkey. The scale reads 1.44 pounds. How many more pounds does the employee need to add? Express your answer as a decimal.

7. **EXTENDED RESPONSE** An ice-skating rink is open from 6:30 A.M. to 4:45 P.M. every day. On Saturday, Sara teaches 45-minute ice-skating lessons at the rink.

   a. Sara starts 30 minutes after the rink opens and takes a 10 minute break between lessons. How many lessons can she teach?

   b. She makes $25 an hour for the time she spends teaching lessons. What is the greatest amount Sara can make on Saturday? *Explain* your answer.

8. **SHORT RESPONSE** You set your watch to chime every 15 minutes. Your friend sets her watch to chime every 25 minutes. Both watches chime at 1:22 P.M. What is the next time that they will both chime at the same time? *Explain* how you found your answer.

REVIEW KEY VOCABULARY

- round, *p. 739*
- fraction, *p. 243*
- equivalent fractions, *p. 243*
- simplest form, *p. 244*
- least common denominator, *p. 254*
- mixed number, *p. 260*
- improper fraction, *p. 260*
- elapsed time, *p. 323*

VOCABULARY EXERCISES

Copy and complete the statement.

1. You usually round fractions to the nearest __?__, and you round __?__ to the nearest whole number.

2. If the sum of two fractions is a(n) __?__, you rewrite it as a mixed number.

3. The LCD of $\frac{3}{8}$ and $\frac{1}{6}$ is __?__.

4. The amount of time between a start time and an end time is called __?__.

5. Explain how to round $3\frac{1}{2}$ to the nearest whole number.

6. Do you get a closer estimate if you round a mixed number to the nearest half or to the nearest whole number? *Explain.*

7. Explain why the mixed number $3\frac{1}{3}$ is equivalent to the mixed number $2\frac{4}{3}$.

REVIEW EXAMPLES AND EXERCISES

6.1 Fraction Estimation

pp. 291–294

EXAMPLE

Estimate the sum or difference.

a. $\frac{4}{5} + \frac{7}{12} \approx 1 + \frac{1}{2}$ **Round each fraction to the nearest half.**

$\quad\quad = 1\frac{1}{2}$

b. $4\frac{5}{6} - 1\frac{1}{4} \approx 5 - 1$ **Round each mixed number to the nearest whole.**

$\quad\quad\quad = 4$

EXERCISES

SEE EXAMPLES
1 AND 2
on p. 291
for Exs. 8–11

Round the fraction or mixed number.

8. $\dfrac{5}{8}$ **9.** $\dfrac{3}{7}$ **10.** $3\dfrac{3}{10}$ **11.** $7\dfrac{14}{15}$

SEE EXAMPLES
3 AND 4
on p. 292
for Exs. 12–16

Estimate the sum or difference.

12. $\dfrac{9}{20}+\dfrac{2}{9}$ **13.** $\dfrac{7}{8}-\dfrac{5}{12}$ **14.** $11\dfrac{4}{5}+8\dfrac{3}{4}$ **15.** $9\dfrac{1}{3}-2\dfrac{8}{11}$

16. Concert At a music concert one group performs for $1\dfrac{1}{4}$ hours, and a second group performs for $1\dfrac{2}{3}$ hours. Estimate the total number of hours of music at the concert.

6.2 Fractions with Common Denominators
pp. 295–300

EXAMPLE

Find the sum or difference.

a. $\dfrac{3}{10}+\dfrac{1}{10}=\dfrac{4}{10}=\dfrac{2}{5}$ **b.** $\dfrac{11}{12}-\dfrac{5}{12}=\dfrac{6}{12}=\dfrac{1}{2}$

EXERCISES

SEE EXAMPLES
1 AND 2
on pp. 295–296
for Exs. 17–20

Find the sum or difference.

17. $\dfrac{2}{9}+\dfrac{4}{9}$ **18.** $\dfrac{3}{4}+\dfrac{3}{4}$ **19.** $\dfrac{11}{16}-\dfrac{7}{16}$ **20.** $\dfrac{9}{10}-\dfrac{3}{10}$

6.3 Fractions with Different Denominators
pp. 302–307

EXAMPLE

Find the sum or difference: **a.** $\dfrac{1}{14}+\dfrac{2}{7}$ **b.** $\dfrac{3}{5}-\dfrac{1}{3}$

Rewrite the fractions using the LCD.

a.
$$
\begin{aligned}
\frac{1}{14} &= \frac{1}{14} &= \frac{1}{14}\\
+\frac{2}{7} &= +\frac{2\times 2}{7\times 2} &= +\frac{4}{14}\\
\hline
& & \frac{5}{14}
\end{aligned}
$$

b.
$$
\begin{aligned}
\frac{3}{5} &= \frac{3\times 3}{5\times 3} &= \frac{9}{15}\\
-\frac{1}{3} &= \frac{1\times 5}{3\times 5} &= -\frac{5}{15}\\
\hline
& & \frac{4}{15}
\end{aligned}
$$

EXERCISES

Find the sum or difference.

**SEE EXAMPLES
1, 2, AND 3**
on pp. 302–303
for Exs. 21–29

21. $\dfrac{1}{10} + \dfrac{4}{5}$ **22.** $\dfrac{5}{8} + \dfrac{1}{2}$ **23.** $\dfrac{3}{4} + \dfrac{2}{7}$ **24.** $\dfrac{8}{9} + \dfrac{5}{6}$

25. $\dfrac{3}{4} - \dfrac{2}{5}$ **26.** $\dfrac{2}{3} - \dfrac{1}{6}$ **27.** $\dfrac{9}{10} - \dfrac{1}{2}$ **28.** $\dfrac{11}{12} - \dfrac{3}{8}$

29. Candles You light a candle that is $\dfrac{5}{6}$ inch tall. The candle melts to $\dfrac{3}{4}$ inch tall. What is the decrease in height?

6.4 Adding and Subtracting Mixed Numbers

pp. 309–314

EXAMPLE 1

Find the sum $3\dfrac{7}{8} + 4\dfrac{3}{4}$.

$$
\begin{array}{llll}
3\dfrac{7}{8} & = & 3\dfrac{7}{8} & = & 3\dfrac{7}{8} \\
+ 4\dfrac{3}{4} & = & + 4\dfrac{3 \times 2}{4 \times 2} & = & + 4\dfrac{6}{8} \quad \text{Rewrite using the LCD, 8.} \\
& & & & 7\dfrac{13}{8}, \text{ or } 8\dfrac{5}{8} \quad \text{Add. Think of } 7\dfrac{13}{8} \text{ as } 7 + 1\dfrac{5}{8}.
\end{array}
$$

EXAMPLE 2

Find the difference $5\dfrac{11}{12} - 2\dfrac{3}{8}$.

$$
\begin{array}{llll}
5\dfrac{11}{12} & = & 5\dfrac{11 \times 2}{12 \times 2} & = & 5\dfrac{22}{24} \quad \text{Rewrite using the LCD, 24.} \\
- 2\dfrac{3}{8} & = & - 2\dfrac{3 \times 3}{8 \times 3} & = & - 2\dfrac{9}{24} \\
& & & & 3\dfrac{13}{24} \quad \text{Subtract.}
\end{array}
$$

EXERCISES

Find the sum or difference.

**SEE EXAMPLES
3 AND 4**
on pp. 310–311
for Exs. 30–38

30. $2\dfrac{5}{12} + 6\dfrac{7}{8}$ **31.** $3\dfrac{2}{3} + \dfrac{1}{7}$ **32.** $8\dfrac{17}{28} + 3\dfrac{1}{4}$ **33.** $5\dfrac{3}{5} + 1\dfrac{1}{6}$

34. $5\dfrac{2}{3} - 2\dfrac{1}{4}$ **35.** $7\dfrac{1}{2} - 3\dfrac{2}{5}$ **36.** $6\dfrac{8}{9} - 5\dfrac{1}{6}$ **37.** $2\dfrac{9}{10} - 2\dfrac{3}{4}$

38. Office Furniture Luigi is making a computer desk. He needs $2\dfrac{3}{4}$ feet of length for his printer and $1\dfrac{5}{6}$ feet for his scanner. At least how many feet long must the desk be?

6.5 Subtracting Mixed Numbers by Renaming

pp. 316–320

EXAMPLE

Find the difference.

$$
\begin{array}{rll}
9\frac{2}{9} & = & 8\frac{11}{9} \qquad \text{Rename } 9\frac{2}{9} \text{ as } 8\frac{11}{9}. \\
-4\frac{5}{9} & = & -4\frac{5}{9} \\
\hline
& & 4\frac{6}{9}, \text{ or } 4\frac{2}{3} \qquad \text{Subtract and simplify.}
\end{array}
$$

EXERCISES

Find the difference.

SEE EXAMPLES
2 AND 3
on p. 317
for Exs. 39–43

39. $5\frac{1}{4} - 2\frac{2}{3}$ **40.** $5\frac{1}{3} - 2\frac{5}{12}$ **41.** $8 - 2\frac{7}{9}$ **42.** $3 - 1\frac{3}{5}$

43. Interior Decorating Maria is putting a wood chair rail around her bedroom. She has a section of wall that is $4\frac{11}{12}$ feet long that she still has to trim. Her last piece of wood is $6\frac{2}{3}$ feet long. After she trims this section, how many feet of wood trim will remain?

6.6 Measures of Time

pp. 322–327

EXAMPLE

Find the elapsed time from 9:40 A.M. to 5:35 P.M.

$$
\begin{array}{ll}
2\text{ h } 20\text{ min} & \text{Find the elapsed time from 9:40 A.M. to 12:00 P.M.} \\
+\ 5\text{ h } 35\text{ min} & \text{Find the elapsed time from 12:00 P.M. to 5:35 P.M.} \\
\hline
7\text{ h } 55\text{ min} & \text{Add the elapsed times.}
\end{array}
$$

EXERCISES

SEE EXAMPLES
1 AND 2
on p. 322
for Exs. 44–45

Add or subtract the measures of time. Use estimation to check.

44.   1 h 50 min
     +   15 min

45.   6 h 35 min 21 sec
     − 5 h 55 min 37 sec

SEE EXAMPLE 3
on p. 323
for Exs. 46–50

Find the elapsed time. Use estimation to check.

46. 7:45 A.M. to 2:00 P.M.   **47.** 1:40 P.M. to 8:00 P.M.

48. 10:30 P.M. to 4:45 A.M.   **49.** 6:00 A.M. to 3:00 P.M.

50. Movies A movie starts at 9:45 P.M. and ends at 12:20 A.M. How long is the movie?

Round the fraction or mixed number.

1. $\frac{13}{20}$

2. $\frac{2}{13}$

3. $4\frac{3}{8}$

4. $8\frac{13}{15}$

Estimate the sum or difference.

5. $\frac{1}{8} + \frac{17}{20}$

6. $\frac{7}{12} - \frac{2}{11}$

7. $6\frac{3}{10} - 3\frac{9}{16}$

8. $3\frac{1}{6} + 5\frac{3}{8}$

Find the sum or difference.

9. $\frac{5}{7} + \frac{1}{7}$

10. $\frac{3}{5} + \frac{4}{5}$

11. $\frac{7}{10} - \frac{3}{10}$

12. $\frac{7}{12} - \frac{1}{12}$

13. $\frac{5}{6} + \frac{5}{8}$

14. $\frac{7}{16} + \frac{1}{4}$

15. $\frac{2}{3} - \frac{1}{6}$

16. $\frac{4}{5} - \frac{1}{4}$

17. $2\frac{5}{7} + 8\frac{1}{7}$

18. $4\frac{7}{10} + 5\frac{3}{10}$

19. $6\frac{7}{15} + 3\frac{4}{5}$

20. $7\frac{1}{4} + 2\frac{1}{8}$

21. $7\frac{2}{3} - 4\frac{1}{8}$

22. $12\frac{7}{10} - 8\frac{1}{2}$

23. $8\frac{1}{6} - 4\frac{5}{9}$

24. $5 - 1\frac{3}{5}$

Add or subtract the measures of time. Use estimation to check.

25.
$$
\begin{array}{r}
4 \text{ h } 35 \text{ min} \\
+ \phantom{4 \text{ h }} 45 \text{ min} \\
\hline
\end{array}
$$

26.
$$
\begin{array}{r}
9 \text{ h } 20 \text{ min } 52 \text{ sec} \\
- 2 \text{ h } 42 \text{ min } 4 \text{ sec} \\
\hline
\end{array}
$$

Find the elapsed time. Use estimation to check.

27. 1:50 P.M. to 3:35 P.M.

28. 6:38 A.M. to 10:05 A.M.

29. 4:45 A.M. to 2:15 P.M.

30. 7:25 P.M. to 12:30 A.M.

31. **BANQUET** At a banquet, chicken, vegetarian, and beef dinners are served. The chef knows that $\frac{1}{4}$ of the guests order chicken and $\frac{1}{3}$ order beef. What fraction of the guests order meat dinners?

32. **BICYCLE HELMETS** Your friend's bicycle helmet weighs $10\frac{2}{5}$ ounces. Your helmet weighs $12\frac{3}{4}$ ounces. Estimate how much more your helmet weighs. Then find the exact answer.

33. **VIDEO** You use 2 hours and 48 minutes of a 6 hour videotape to record your sister's school play. How much time is left on the tape?

EXTENDED RESPONSE QUESTIONS

PROBLEM

The diagram at the right shows the fraction of the height of Earth's atmosphere at each layer.

Ionosphere: $\frac{31}{40}$

Mesosphere: $\frac{1}{10}$

Stratosphere: $\frac{?}{25}$ Tropopause: $\frac{1}{100}$

Troposphere: $\frac{7}{200}$

a. What fraction of the height lies above the stratosphere?

b. What fraction of the height lies below the stratosphere?

c. What fraction of the height is the stratosphere? *Explain*.

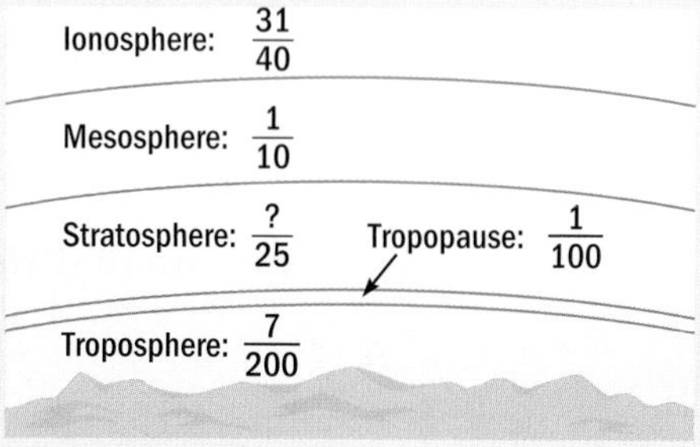

Below are sample solutions to the problem. Read each solution and the comments in blue to see why the sample represents *full credit, partial credit,* or *no credit.*

SAMPLE 1: Full Credit Solution

The steps of the solution are clearly written, and the calculations are correct.

a. **Fraction above stratosphere:**
mesosphere + ionosphere

$$\frac{1 \times 4}{10 \times 4} = \frac{4}{40}$$
$$+ \frac{31}{40} = + \frac{31}{40}$$
$$\frac{35}{40}, \text{ or } \frac{7}{8}$$

$\frac{7}{8}$ lies above the stratosphere.

b. **Fraction below stratosphere:**
tropopause + troposphere

$$\frac{1 \times 2}{100 \times 2} = \frac{2}{200}$$
$$+ \frac{7}{200} = + \frac{7}{200}$$
$$\frac{9}{200}$$

$\frac{9}{200}$ lies below the stratosphere.

The explanation is clear and reflects correct mathematical thinking. The calculations are correct.

c. To find the fraction of the height that is the stratosphere, subtract the results of parts (a) and (b) from 1, or $\frac{200}{200}$.

$$\frac{200}{200} - \frac{7 \times 25}{8 \times 25} - \frac{9}{200} = \frac{200}{200} - \frac{175}{200} - \frac{9}{200}$$
$$= \frac{25}{200} - \frac{9}{200}$$
$$= \frac{16}{200}, \text{ or } \frac{2}{25}$$

$\frac{2}{25}$ of the height is the stratosphere.

SAMPLE 2: Partial Credit Solution

The steps of the solution are not written. The answers are correct, but no work is shown.

a. **Fraction above stratosphere:**

$$\frac{1}{10} + \frac{31}{40} = \frac{35}{40}$$

$\frac{35}{40}$ lies above the stratosphere.

b. **Fraction below stratosphere:**

$$\frac{1}{100} + \frac{7}{200} = \frac{9}{200}$$

$\frac{9}{200}$ lies below the stratosphere.

The final answer is correct, but there is no explanation and no steps are shown.

c. $1 - \frac{35}{40} - \frac{9}{200} = \frac{2}{25}$

SAMPLE 3: No Credit Solution

The questions in parts (a) and (b) were not answered. All of the calculations are incorrect. No work is shown. No explanations or steps are given.

a. Ionosphere and Mesosphere

b. Tropopause and Troposphere

c. $\frac{4}{25}$

EXERCISES   Apply the Scoring Rubric

Score each of the following solutions to the problem on the previous page as *full credit, partial credit,* or *no credit. Explain* your reasoning. If you choose partial credit or no credit, explain how you would change the solution so that it earns a score of full credit.

1. Fraction of stratosphere: $1 - \left(\frac{1}{10} + \frac{31}{40}\right) - \left(\frac{1}{100} + \frac{7}{200}\right) = \frac{2}{25}$

2. a. **Fraction above stratosphere:**

$$\frac{1}{10} + \frac{31}{40} = \frac{4}{40} + \frac{31}{40}$$

$$= \frac{35}{40} \text{ or } \frac{7}{8}$$

b. **Fraction below stratosphere:**

$$\frac{1}{100} + \frac{7}{200} = \frac{2}{200} + \frac{7}{200}$$

$$= \frac{9}{200}$$

c. $1 - \frac{7}{8} - \frac{9}{200} = \frac{200}{200} - \frac{175}{200} - \frac{9}{200}$

$$= \frac{16}{200} \text{ or } \frac{2}{25}$$

I subtracted the fraction above the atmosphere and the fraction below the stratosphere from 1 to find the fraction that is the stratosphere.

EXTENDED RESPONSE

1. The circle graph shows the results of a survey asking students at your school to name their favorite hamburger topping.

   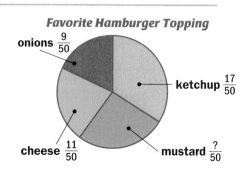

   Favorite Hamburger Topping

   a. What fraction of the students surveyed chose onions or ketchup?

   b. What fraction of the students surveyed chose mustard? *Explain* how you found your answer.

   c. Can you assume from the circle graph that 50 students were surveyed? *Explain* your reasoning.

2. A carpenter wants to cut a 12 foot board into pieces of length $1\frac{3}{4}$ feet, $2\frac{2}{3}$ feet, $3\frac{1}{6}$ feet, and $4\frac{1}{2}$ feet. Does the carpenter have enough board to cut these pieces? If so, how much board is remaining? If not, how much longer must the board be? *Justify* your answer with a diagram and calculations.

3. The courtyard of an apartment complex is shown at the right. Bushes are being planted about every 8 feet around the perimeter of the courtyard. What is the perimeter of the courtyard? Estimate the number of bushes to be planted? *Explain* your reasoning and draw a diagram to justify your answer.

   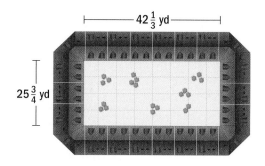

4. The first part of a play lasts 2 hours and 7 minutes. The second part lasts 1 hour and 42 minutes. There is a 15-minute intermission between parts. How much longer is the first part than the second part? How long is the whole play including the intermission? If the play started at 2:00 P.M., what times does it finish? *Explain.*

5. A friend is traveling abroad. You talk to each other several times a month. The data set shows the lengths, in minutes, of your telephone calls for one month.

   $$3\frac{2}{3}, \, 4\frac{1}{4}, \, 3\frac{3}{10}, \, 4\frac{5}{6}, \, 5$$

   a. Estimate the total number of minutes of the telephone calls.

   b. It costs $.25 per minute for each call. Estimate the total cost of the telephone calls. *Explain* your reasoning.

   c. Is the cost in part (b) *greater than* or *less than* the actual cost of the telephone calls? *Justify* your answer.

MULTIPLE CHOICE

6. What is the sum represented by the model shown?

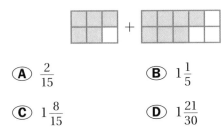

(A) $\frac{2}{15}$

(B) $1\frac{1}{5}$

(C) $1\frac{8}{15}$

(D) $1\frac{21}{30}$

7. You practice playing the guitar for $1\frac{1}{5}$ hours on Wednesday and $\frac{3}{4}$ hour on Thursday. You practice again on Friday. Overall, you practice a total of 3 hours for the three days. How long did you practice on Friday?

(A) 1 h

(B) $1\frac{1}{20}$ h

(C) $1\frac{1}{10}$ h

(D) $1\frac{2}{5}$ h

GRIDDED ANSWER

8. You are defrosting food in the microwave. The food is in the microwave for $4\frac{1}{3}$ minutes, $2\frac{5}{6}$ minutes, and $\frac{3}{4}$ minute until it is completely defrosted. Estimate the amount of time it took for the food to defrost in the microwave to the nearest minute?

9. The thicknesses, in inches, of 5 dictionaries at a library are shown below. What is the range, in inches, of the dictionaries' thicknesses? Write your answer as a fraction.

$$3, 3\frac{3}{8}, 2\frac{3}{4}, 3\frac{1}{4}, 2\frac{7}{8}$$

10. Sandy has a part-time job working three days a week from 5:30 P.M. to 9:00 P.M. She checks her watch at 7:34 P.M. How many more minutes will she be working?

SHORT RESPONSE

11. The perimeter of the triangle shown is $13\frac{7}{8}$ feet. The side with length x is $2\frac{1}{4}$ feet longer than the given side. Find x and y. *Explain* your answers.

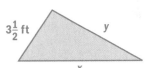

12. Two subways reach a station at 12:15 P.M. One subway returns to the station every 1 hour and 40 minutes. The other subway returns every 1 hour and 20 minutes. What is the next time that the subways will both reach the station at the same time? *Explain* how you found your answer.

13. You are making a snack mix that contains $3\frac{7}{8}$ cups of peanuts, $3\frac{2}{3}$ cups of cashews and $4\frac{1}{4}$ cups of almonds. Will the mix fit in a 12 cup container? *Explain* your reasoning.

14. On a 420 mile road trip, your family drives 336 miles and uses 12 gallons of gasoline. How many miles does the car travel per gallon? You started with $15\frac{1}{4}$ gallons of gasoline. Do you have enough left to finish the trip? If so, how much gasoline will be left in the tank? If not, how much more gasoline do you need to complete the trip? *Explain* your reasoning.

7 Multiplication and Division of Fractions

Get-Ready Games

Review Prerequisite Skills by playing *Mixed Number Race* and *Triple Jump.*

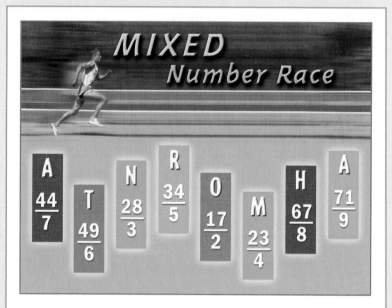

Skill Focus: Writing fractions as mixed numbers and ordering mixed numbers

- Write the improper fractions as mixed numbers. Then order the mixed numbers from least to greatest.

- The letters associated with the numbers will spell out the name of a town in ancient Greece whose name is used for a modern track and field event.

Triple jump

$\frac{1}{6}$ of a Hop $+$ $\frac{1}{4}$ of a Step $+$ $\frac{1}{3}$ of a Jump $=$ Total Distance

Skill Focus: Finding parts of whole numbers

In the triple jump, athletes perform a hop, a step, and a jump. In this game you will complete a mathematical triple jump.

• Choose one of the following numbers to be your hop, one to be your step, and one to be your jump: 24, 36, 48. Use each number once.

• Use the fractions in the formula above. Find the given parts of the hop, step, and jump numbers you chose. Then add these results to find your total distance. Your goal is to get the greatest distance possible.

Stop and Think

1. **WRITING** In *Mixed Number Race*, a student thinks that $\frac{71}{9}$ is greater than $\frac{67}{8}$ because 71 is greater than 67 and 9 is greater than 8. What is wrong with the student's reasoning?

2. **CRITICAL THINKING** What is the greatest total distance you can get in *Triple Jump*? What is the least total distance? Explain how you know.

Review Prerequisite Skills

VOCABULARY CHECK

Copy and complete using a review word from the list at the left.

1. _?_ measures the amount that a container can hold.

2. Two numbers that divide evenly using mental math are called _?_.

SKILL CHECK

Estimate the quotient. *(p. 11)*

3. $47 \div 8$ **4.** $186 \div 22$ **5.** $342 \div 48$

Copy and complete the statement. *(p. 207)*

6. $16\,\text{kg} = \underline{\ ?\ }\,\text{g}$ **7.** $25\,\text{L} = \underline{\ ?\ }\,\text{mL}$ **8.** $150\,\text{cm} = \underline{\ ?\ }\,\text{m}$

9. $5\,\text{g} = \underline{\ ?\ }\,\text{mg}$ **10.** $1800\,\text{L} = \underline{\ ?\ }\,\text{kL}$ **11.** $4\,\text{m} = \underline{\ ?\ }\,\text{mm}$

Write the mixed number as an improper fraction. *(p. 260)*

12. $4\frac{1}{6}$ **13.** $6\frac{2}{3}$ **14.** $2\frac{5}{6}$ **15.** $1\frac{3}{4}$

Round the fraction or mixed number. *(p. 291)*

16. $\frac{7}{8}$ **17.** $1\frac{2}{9}$ **18.** $7\frac{1}{4}$ **19.** $2\frac{8}{11}$

@HomeTutor Prerequisite skills practice at classzone.com

Notetaking Skills   Drawing a Model

In each chapter you will learn a new notetaking skill. In Chapter 7 you will apply the strategy of drawing a model to Example 1 on p. 348.

When you take notes, include the visual models that are used in the lesson. Seeing the models can help you to understand and remember what you have learned. Below are some fraction models.

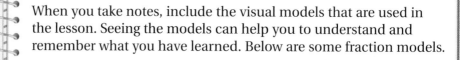

$\frac{5}{8}$ $\frac{9}{20}$ $1\frac{2}{5}$

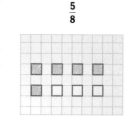   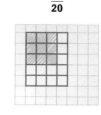   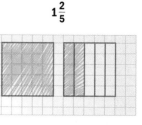

5 out of 8 objects   9 out of 20 parts   1 whole and $\frac{2}{5}$ of 1 whole

7.1 Multiplying Fractions and Whole Numbers

Before   You multiplied decimals and whole numbers.

Now   You'll multiply fractions and whole numbers.

Why?   So you can find part of a whole, as with postcards in Ex. 38.

KEY VOCABULARY
- whole number, *p. 3*
- compatible numbers, *p. 12*

ACTIVITY

You can use repeated addition to multiply a fraction by a whole number.

STEP 1   The product $6 \times \frac{2}{3}$ can be written as the sum $\frac{2}{3} + \frac{2}{3} + \frac{2}{3} + \frac{2}{3} + \frac{2}{3} + \frac{2}{3}$.

Show that the sum is equal to $\frac{6 \times 2}{3}$.

STEP 2   Write a rule for multiplying a fraction by a whole number.

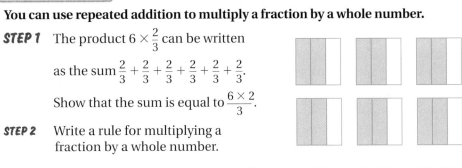

As you saw in the activity, you can think of multiplication as repeated addition.

KEY CONCEPT   *For Your Notebook*

Multiplying Fractions by Whole Numbers

Words   To multiply a fraction by a whole number, multiply the numerator by the whole number and write the product over the denominator.

Numbers $2 \times \frac{3}{7} = \frac{2 \times 3}{7} = \frac{6}{7}$ **Algebra** $a \cdot \frac{b}{c} = \frac{b}{c} \cdot a = \frac{a \cdot b}{c}$

EXAMPLE 1   Multiply Fractions by Whole Numbers

TAKE NOTES

When you write examples on multiplying fractions by whole numbers in your notebook, such as Example 1, include a model like the one in the activity.

$$6 \times \frac{3}{4} = \frac{6 \times 3}{4}$$ **Multiply the numerator by the whole number.**

$$= \frac{18}{4}$$

$$= \frac{9}{2}, \text{ or } 4\frac{1}{2}$$ **Simplify.**

EXAMPLE 2 Multiply Whole Numbers by Fractions

a. $\dfrac{3}{8} \times 2 = \dfrac{6}{8}$

   $\qquad\quad = \dfrac{3}{4}$

b. $\dfrac{4}{3} \times 2 = \dfrac{8}{3}$

   $\qquad\quad = 2\dfrac{2}{3}$

✓ **GUIDED PRACTICE**   for Examples 1 and 2

Find the product. Simplify if possible.

1. $3 \times \dfrac{3}{10}$ **2.** $9 \times \dfrac{3}{8}$ **3.** $\dfrac{6}{5} \times 7$ **4.** $\dfrac{5}{6} \times 3$

5. Look at the results in Example 2. Which product is greater than 2? Name three other fractions you can multiply by 2 to get a product greater than 2.

Using Mental Math and Models You can sometimes find the product of a whole number and a fraction using mental math or a model, as in Example 3.

❖ EXAMPLE 3 Using Mental Math or a Model

Party Music You are choosing 18 CDs to take to a party. You want $\dfrac{2}{3}$ of the CDs to have dance music. How many dance music CDs should you choose?

SOLUTION

The number of dance music CDs you should choose is $\dfrac{2}{3}$ *of* 18, or $\dfrac{2}{3} \times 18$.

The word *of* indicates multiplication. You can use a model or mental math to find this product.

METHOD 1 **Use a model.** Draw an array of 18 circles. Divide them into three equal parts. Circle two of the three parts.

METHOD 2 **Use mental math.** Think: $\dfrac{1}{3}$ of 18 is 6, because $18 \div 3 = 6$. So, $\dfrac{2}{3}$ of 18 is 12, because $2 \times 6 = 12$.

▶ **Answer** You should choose 12 dance music CDs to take to the party.

EXAMPLE 4   Estimating a Product

CD Rack You have 15 CDs. Each CD case is $\frac{3}{8}$ inch wide. Estimate how wide a space you need on a CD rack to fit all 15 CDs.

SOLUTION

$$\text{Space} = \frac{3}{8} \times 15 \qquad \text{Multiply width of a CD case by number of cases.}$$

$$= \frac{3}{8} \times 16 \qquad \text{Replace 15 with the closest number that is compatible with 8.}$$

$$= 6 \qquad \text{Think: } \frac{1}{8} \text{ of 16 is 2, so } \frac{3}{8} \text{ of 16 is 6.}$$

▶**Answer** You need a space that is about 6 inches wide.

✓ **GUIDED PRACTICE**   **for Examples 3 and 4**

Use mental math or a model.

6. Find $\frac{3}{4}$ of 28.

7. Find $36 \times \frac{2}{9}$.

8. Estimate $\frac{3}{5} \times 26$.

9. What if? In Example 4, suppose you have 38 CDs. Estimate how wide a space you need on a CD rack to fit all 38 CDs.

7.1 EXERCISES

HOMEWORK KEY

★ = **STANDARDIZED TEST PRACTICE**
Exs. 15, 38, 42, and 55

◯ = **HINTS** AND **HOMEWORK HELP**
for Exs. 3, 9, 11, 33 at classzone.com

SKILL PRACTICE

1. VOCABULARY Is 9 compatible with 36 in the product $\frac{7}{9} \times 36$? *Explain.*

FINDING PRODUCTS **Find the product.**

SEE EXAMPLES 1, 2, AND 3
on pp. 341–342
for Exs. 2–15

2. $6 \times \frac{3}{7}$

3. $3 \times \frac{3}{10}$

4. $\frac{3}{2} \times 5$

5. $\frac{4}{3} \times 4$

6. $2 \times \frac{5}{12}$

7. $6 \times \frac{2}{9}$

8. $\frac{1}{6} \times 15$

9. $\frac{5}{8} \times 6$

10. $\frac{1}{5} \times 30$

11. $\frac{5}{6} \times 12$

12. $70 \times \frac{4}{7}$

13. $40 \times \frac{9}{10}$

14. ERROR ANALYSIS Describe and correct the error made in the solution.

$$\diagup\!\!\!\!\!\times \quad 4 \times \frac{2}{5} = \frac{2}{20} = \frac{1}{10}$$

15. ★ **MULTIPLE CHOICE** Find the product $\frac{5}{6} \times 18$.

    A $\frac{5}{108}$ **B** 15   **C** $18\frac{5}{6}$ **D** $21\frac{3}{5}$

SEE EXAMPLE 4
on p. 343
for Exs. 16–23

ESTIMATION Identify the compatible whole number to use in estimating the product. Then estimate the product.

16. $\frac{1}{4}$ of 19   **17.** $\frac{1}{7}$ of 47   **18.** $\frac{2}{5}$ of 28   **19.** $\frac{5}{8}$ of 43

20. $\frac{7}{8} \times 46$ **21.** $\frac{8}{9} \times 83$ **22.** $32 \times \frac{2}{3}$ **23.** $53 \times \frac{2}{11}$

USING PROPERTIES OF MULTIPLICATION Use the commutative and associative properties to find the product.

24. $\left(4 \times \frac{5}{7}\right) \times 35$ **25.** $15 \times 8 \times \frac{2}{3}$ **26.** $\frac{2}{9} \times 11 \times 18$

27. **xy ALGEBRA** Solve the equation $\frac{3}{4}x = 15$ for x.

CHALLENGE Use the part of a set to find the size of the whole set.

28. $\frac{1}{3}$ of a set is 8.   **29.** $\frac{3}{4}$ of a set is 9.   **30.** $\frac{5}{6}$ of a set is 10.

PROBLEM SOLVING

31. GUIDED PROBLEM SOLVING Each student needs $\frac{3}{4}$ pound of sand for an experiment. About how much sand is needed for 21 students?

  a. Write an expression for what you need to find.

  b. Choose a number compatible with $\frac{3}{4}$ to substitute for 21.

  c. Use mental math to estimate the answer. About how much sand is needed for 21 students? Is the estimate *high* or *low*? *Explain.*

FINDING AMOUNTS In Exercises 32–35, use mental math or a model to find the amount for the given situation.

SEE EXAMPLE 3
on p. 342
for Exs. 32–35

32. Number of minutes in $\frac{2}{3}$ hour   **33.** Cost of $\frac{3}{4}$ pound of nuts at $8 per pound

34. Distance of 10 laps on a $\frac{1}{4}$ mile track   **35.** Distance of $\frac{1}{2}$ mile per day for a week

36. NATIONAL PARKS The total land area in the National Park system is about 78 million acres. Estimate the land area for each category shown in the circle graph.

37. PREDICT Predict whether the product of 24 and each of the following fractions is *less than* or *greater than* 24: $\frac{2}{3}, \frac{3}{2}, \frac{1}{2}, \frac{5}{3}, \frac{3}{8}$. Find the products to check your answers.

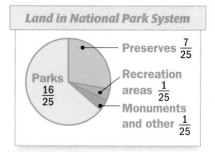

Land in National Park System

Preserves $\frac{7}{25}$

Recreation areas $\frac{1}{25}$

Parks $\frac{16}{25}$

Monuments and other $\frac{1}{25}$

38. ★ SHORT RESPONSE You and a friend exchange travel postcards. You give your friend $\frac{1}{6}$ of your 54 cards. Your friend gives you $\frac{2}{9}$ of his 63 cards. How many cards do each of you have now? *Explain.*

★ = **STANDARDIZED TEST PRACTICE**   ◯ = **HINTS AND HOMEWORK HELP** *at classzone.com*

Recipes Tomatoes are a key ingredient in many popular recipes, as for chili and guacamole.

39. **Calculate** How many cups of chopped tomatoes are needed to make 6 times the chili recipe?

40. **Calculate** How many cups of chopped tomatoes are needed to make 6 times the guacamole recipe?

Recipe: CHILI
1 tbsp vegetable oil
1 1/2 lb lean ground beef
2/3 c chopped tomatoes
1/2 c chopped onion
continued →

Recipe: GUACAMOLE
2 ripe avocados
3/4 c chopped tomatoes
1 small onion
1 clove garlic
continued →

41. **Interpret** One small chopped tomato makes about $\frac{1}{2}$ cup. Will 12 small tomatoes be enough to make 6 times a chili recipe and 6 times a guacamole recipe? *Explain* your reasoning.

42. ★ **WRITING** Is the estimate in Example 4 on page 343 *high* or *low*? Is the estimate appropriate for the situation? *Explain*.

43. **REASONING** How does the product of a whole number and an improper fraction compare with the whole number? *Explain* your reasoning.

44. **NUTRITION** Three friends share a package of crackers containing 2 servings of 192 calories each. Write and evaluate a multiplication expression to find how many calories each friend consumed.

CHALLENGE Write the temperature in degrees Celsius. Use the formula $F = \frac{9}{5}C + 32$, where F is the temperature in degrees Fahrenheit (°F) and C is the temperature in degrees Celsius (°C).

45. 32°F   46. 95°F   47. 212°F

MIXED REVIEW

Get-Ready

Prepare for
Lesson 7.2
in Exs. 48–50

Write a fraction to represent the shaded region. *(p. 753)*

48.

49.

50.

Multiply. Use estimation to check your answer. *(p.181)*

51. 18.7×4.2 52. 2.63×0.51 53. 0.034×6.8 54. 0.74×0.059

55. ★ **MULTIPLE CHOICE** Which fraction does *not* round to $\frac{1}{2}$? *(p. 291)*

Ⓐ $\frac{1}{3}$ Ⓑ $\frac{4}{7}$ Ⓒ $\frac{2}{11}$ Ⓓ $\frac{5}{12}$

GOAL
Understand how to model the product of two fractions.

MATERIALS
• tiles (plastic counters, pennies, squares of paper)
• graph paper

7.2 Modeling Products of Fractions

You can model products of fractions in two ways. To create a model for the product $\frac{1}{3} \times \frac{1}{2}$, you need to find $\frac{1}{3}$ *of* $\frac{1}{2}$ of a whole.

EXPLORE 1 Model $\frac{1}{3} \times \frac{1}{2}$ using a rectangle of tiles.

STEP 1

Make a 2 by 3 rectangle of tiles to model halves and thirds.

Each tile is $\frac{1}{6}$ of the group.

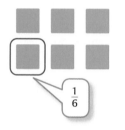

STEP 2

Each row is $\frac{1}{2}$ of the tiles.

Each column is $\frac{1}{3}$ of the tiles.

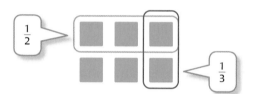

STEP 3

Select $\frac{1}{2}$ of the tiles.

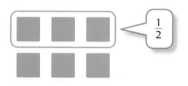

STEP 4

Find $\frac{1}{3}$ of $\frac{1}{2}$ of the tiles.

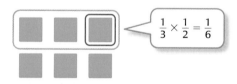

$$\frac{1}{3} \times \frac{1}{2} = \frac{1}{6}$$

PRACTICE Model the product using the given size rectangle of tiles.

1. $\frac{1}{4} \times \frac{3}{4}$, 4 by 4 rectangle   2. $\frac{1}{2} \times \frac{3}{4}$, 2 by 4 rectangle   3. $\frac{3}{5} \times \frac{4}{7}$, 5 by 7 rectangle

4. $\frac{2}{3} \times \frac{1}{5}$, 3 by 5 rectangle   5. $\frac{5}{6} \times \frac{1}{3}$, 6 by 3 rectangle   6. $\frac{5}{8} \times \frac{3}{4}$, 8 by 4 rectangle

7. **WRITING** *Explain* how you can decide what size rectangle of tiles to use to create a model for the product $\frac{1}{3} \times \frac{5}{6}$.

Animated Math at classzone.com

EXPLORE 2 Model $\frac{1}{3} \times \frac{1}{2}$ on graph paper.

STEP 1 Draw a 2 by 3 rectangle on graph paper to model halves and thirds. There are 6 small squares, so each square is $\frac{1}{6}$ of the rectangle.

STEP 2 Shade $\frac{1}{2}$ of the rectangle.

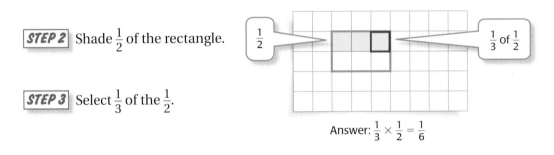

$\frac{1}{2}$

$\frac{1}{3}$ of $\frac{1}{2}$

STEP 3 Select $\frac{1}{3}$ of the $\frac{1}{2}$.

Answer: $\frac{1}{3} \times \frac{1}{2} = \frac{1}{6}$

PRACTICE Model the product on graph paper.

8. $\frac{1}{4} \times \frac{3}{4}$

9. $\frac{1}{2} \times \frac{3}{4}$

10. $\frac{3}{5} \times \frac{4}{7}$

11. Copy and complete the table. Use the model shown above and the ones you drew in Exercises 8–10.

Product	$\frac{1}{3} \times \frac{1}{2} = \frac{?}{?}$	$\frac{1}{4} \times \frac{3}{4} = \frac{?}{?}$	$\frac{1}{2} \times \frac{3}{4} = \frac{?}{?}$	$\frac{3}{5} \times \frac{4}{7} = \frac{?}{?}$
Number of squares in large rectangle you drew	6	?	?	?
Product of denominators	?	?	?	?
Number of squares in small rectangle you selected	1	?	?	?
Product of numerators	?	?	?	?

DRAW CONCLUSIONS

12. REASONING Use the information in your table to suggest a method for finding the product of two fractions without using a model.

13. NUMBER SENSE For each product in the table, compare the answer with each of the fractions being multiplied. Is the answer *greater than* or *less than* the first fraction? the second fraction? *Explain* why this happens.

7.2 Multiplying Fractions

Before	You multiplied a fraction by a whole number.
Now	You'll multiply fractions.
Why?	So you can find part of a part, as with basketball games in Ex. 63.

KEY VOCABULARY
- **factor,** *p. 15*
- **common factor,** *p. 236*
- **simplest form,** *p. 244*

Sporting Goods The table at the right shows the fraction of a sporting goods store's total sales in four categories. John, a salesperson at the store, made $\frac{2}{3}$ of the push scooter sales. What fraction of the total sales is this?

John's sales are $\frac{2}{3}$ of $\frac{1}{5}$ of the total. To find part *of* a part, you multiply two fractions.

Fraction of Total Sales	
push scooters	$\frac{1}{5}$
in-line skates	$\frac{1}{10}$
bicycles	$\frac{3}{5}$
skateboards	$\frac{1}{10}$

EXAMPLE 1 **Using a Model to Multiply Fractions**

To answer the question above about John's sales, you can use a model to find $\frac{2}{3}$ *of* $\frac{1}{5}$, or $\frac{2}{3} \times \frac{1}{5}$.

STEP 1 Draw a 3 by 5 rectangle to model thirds and fifths. Each small square is $\frac{1}{15}$ of the whole.

STEP 2 Shade $\frac{1}{5}$ of the rectangle.

STEP 3 Select $\frac{2}{3}$ of the shaded rectangle.

▶ **Answer** Two of the 15 squares are selected, so $\frac{2}{3} \times \frac{1}{5} = \frac{2}{15}$. John's push scooter sales are $\frac{2}{15}$ of the store's total sales.

✓ **GUIDED PRACTICE** for Example 1

Draw a model to find the product.

1. $\frac{1}{2} \times \frac{1}{5}$

2. $\frac{2}{3} \times \frac{2}{5}$

3. $\frac{3}{4} \times \frac{5}{7}$

Using a Rule Look back at the model of the product $\frac{2}{3} \times \frac{1}{5}$ in Example 1 to see how the model is related to the rule below.

$$\frac{\text{area of a selected rectangle}}{\text{area of a whole rectangle}} = \frac{2 \times 1}{3 \times 5} = \frac{\text{product of the numerators}}{\text{product of the denominators}}$$

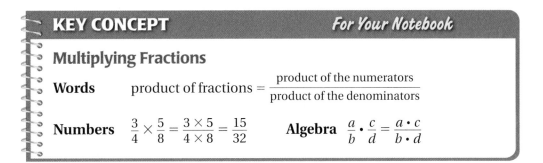

KEY CONCEPT   *For Your Notebook*

Multiplying Fractions

Words $\text{product of fractions} = \dfrac{\text{product of the numerators}}{\text{product of the denominators}}$

Numbers $\dfrac{3}{4} \times \dfrac{5}{8} = \dfrac{3 \times 5}{4 \times 8} = \dfrac{15}{32}$ **Algebra** $\dfrac{a}{b} \cdot \dfrac{c}{d} = \dfrac{a \cdot c}{b \cdot d}$

EXAMPLE 2   **Multiplying Two Fractions**

$\dfrac{2}{5} \times \dfrac{5}{3} = \dfrac{2 \times 5}{5 \times 3}$ **Use the rule for multiplying fractions.**

$= \dfrac{10}{15}$ **Multiply.**

$= \dfrac{2}{3}$ **Simplify.**

EXAMPLE 3   **Evaluating an Algebraic Expression**

Evaluate the expression $\frac{1}{3}n$ when $n = \frac{2}{7}$.

$\dfrac{1}{3}n = \dfrac{1}{3} \times \dfrac{2}{7}$ **Substitute $\frac{2}{7}$ for n.**

$= \dfrac{1 \times 2}{3 \times 7}$ **Use the rule for multiplying fractions.**

$= \dfrac{2}{21}$ **Multiply. The product is in simplest form.**

COMPARE
In Example 3, the product of $\frac{1}{3}$ and $\frac{2}{7}$ is less than either fraction.

✓   **GUIDED PRACTICE**   **for Examples 2 and 3**

4. Find the product $\frac{1}{3} \times \frac{1}{6}$.

5. Find the product $\frac{3}{7} \times \frac{1}{4}$.

6. Evaluate $\frac{3}{4}n$ when $n = \frac{3}{5}$.

7. Evaluate $\frac{2}{3}x$ when $x = \frac{4}{9}$.

8. Is the product in Example 2 less than both fractions? Why or why not?

Simplifying First When you multiply fractions, you can sometimes simplify before multiplying.

EXAMPLE 4 Simplifying Before Multiplying

Football Kyle successfully completed 8 out of his 15 passes during one football season. Kyle's friend Lou successfully completed $\frac{1}{4}$ the fraction of Kyle. What fraction of his passes did Lou complete during the season?

SOLUTION

$$\frac{1}{4} \times \frac{8}{15} = \frac{1 \times 8}{4 \times 15} \qquad \text{Use the rule for multiplying fractions.}$$

$$= \frac{1 \times \overset{2}{\cancel{8}}}{\underset{1}{\cancel{4}} \times 15} \qquad \begin{array}{l}\text{4 is a factor of 4 and 8.}\\ \text{Divide 4 and 8 by 4.}\end{array}$$

$$= \frac{1 \times 2}{1 \times 15} \qquad \text{Rewrite.}$$

$$= \frac{2}{15} \qquad \text{Multiply.}$$

DIVIDE COMMON FACTORS
To simplify in Example 4, find the greatest factor of 8 that is also a factor of 4 or 15.

▶ **Answer** Lou completed $\frac{2}{15}$ of his passes.

Multiplying Two or More Fractions You can extend the rule for multiplying fractions to find the product of three or more fractions.

EXAMPLE 5 Multiplying Three Fractions

$$\frac{1}{6} \times \frac{3}{4} \times \frac{2}{5} = \frac{1 \times 3 \times 2}{6 \times 4 \times 5} \qquad \text{Use the rule for multiplying fractions.}$$

$$= \frac{1 \times \overset{1}{\cancel{3}} \times \overset{1}{\cancel{2}}}{\underset{2}{\cancel{6}} \times \underset{2}{\cancel{4}} \times 5} \qquad \begin{array}{l}\text{3 is a factor of 3 and 6. Divide 3 and 6 by 3.}\\ \text{2 is a factor of 2 and 4. Divide 2 and 4 by 2.}\end{array}$$

$$= \frac{1 \times 1 \times 1}{2 \times 2 \times 5} \qquad \text{Rewrite.}$$

$$= \frac{1}{20} \qquad \text{Multiply.}$$

AVOID ERRORS
Rewrite the fraction after dividing out common factors. Then you will be less likely to make an error when multiplying.

✓ **GUIDED PRACTICE** for Examples 4 and 5

Find the product. Write the answer in simplest form.

9. $\frac{3}{8} \times \frac{5}{9}$ **10.** $\frac{5}{16} \times \frac{8}{15}$ **11.** $\frac{1}{2} \times \frac{3}{5} \times \frac{1}{6}$ **12.** $\frac{3}{7} \times \frac{5}{9} \times \frac{7}{10}$

13. Look at the rule for multiplying fractions on page 349. Use variables to write a rule for multiplying the fractions $\frac{a}{b}$, $\frac{c}{d}$, and $\frac{e}{f}$.

7.2 **EXERCISES**

HOMEWORK KEY

★ = **STANDARDIZED TEST PRACTICE**
Exs. 20, 55, 57, 58, 60, 61, and 80

◯ = **HINTS AND HOMEWORK HELP**
for Exs. 3, 9, 15, 23, 53 at classzone.com

SKILL PRACTICE

1. **VOCABULARY** How can you tell whether a fraction is in simplest form?

2. **VOCABULARY** Identify the common factors of 18 and 30.

SEE EXAMPLE 1
on p. 348
for Exs. 3–6

DRAWING MODELS Draw a model to find the product.

3. $\frac{1}{3} \times \frac{4}{7}$

4. $\frac{1}{3} \times \frac{1}{3}$

5. $\frac{3}{4} \times \frac{1}{4}$

6. $\frac{7}{8} \times \frac{1}{2}$

FINDING PRODUCTS Find the product.

SEE EXAMPLES 2 AND 4
on pp. 349–350
for Exs. 7–20

7. $\frac{1}{2} \times \frac{3}{10}$

8. $\frac{4}{5} \times \frac{6}{7}$

9. $\frac{2}{5} \times \frac{2}{9}$

10. $\frac{6}{5} \times \frac{3}{7}$

11. $\frac{1}{4} \times \frac{8}{15}$

12. $\frac{1}{2} \times \frac{4}{7}$

13. $\frac{2}{3} \times \frac{3}{8}$

14. $\frac{6}{1} \times \frac{1}{6}$

15. $\frac{7}{9} \times \frac{9}{14}$

16. $\frac{3}{7} \times \frac{7}{9}$

17. $\frac{5}{8} \times \frac{24}{25}$

18. $\frac{11}{10} \times \frac{5}{22}$

19. **ERROR ANALYSIS** Describe and correct the error made in the solution.

$$\frac{3}{4} \times \frac{5}{9} = \frac{\overset{1}{\cancel{3}} \times 5}{4 \times \underset{2}{\cancel{9}}} = \frac{5}{8}$$

20. ★ **MULTIPLE CHOICE** Which product is equal to $\frac{3}{5}$?

Ⓐ $\frac{1}{5} \times \frac{2}{5}$

Ⓑ $\frac{3}{7} \times \frac{7}{10}$

Ⓒ $\frac{5}{6} \times \frac{9}{25}$

Ⓓ $\frac{5}{6} \times \frac{18}{25}$

✕⁄ **ALGEBRA** Evaluate the expression when $x = \frac{3}{4}$ and $y = \frac{1}{5}$.

SEE EXAMPLE 3
on p. 349
for Exs. 21–28

21. $\frac{1}{5}x$

22. $\frac{8}{9}x$

23. $\frac{3}{4}x$

24. $\frac{1}{7}y$

25. $\frac{7}{10}y$

26. $\frac{6}{11}y$

27. $\frac{8}{9}y$

28. xy

EVALUATING EXPRESSIONS Evaluate the expression.

29. $\frac{2}{3} + \frac{1}{3} \times \frac{3}{4}$

30. $\frac{5}{6} - \frac{1}{6} \times \frac{1}{2}$

31. $\frac{4}{5} \times \frac{2^3}{7+4}$

32. $\frac{1}{2} \times \left(\frac{3}{5}\right)^2$

33. $\frac{3}{4} - \frac{6}{7} \times \frac{7}{24}$

34. $\frac{1}{4} + \frac{2}{5} \times \frac{3}{4}$

35. $\frac{1}{18} \times \left(\frac{6}{7}\right)^2$

36. $\frac{5}{8} \times \frac{3^2}{2^2+6}$

FINDING PRODUCTS Find the product.

SEE EXAMPLE 5
on p. 350
for Exs. 37–44

37. $\frac{2}{3} \times \frac{3}{5} \times \frac{7}{10}$

38. $\frac{5}{8} \times \frac{3}{10} \times \frac{16}{21}$

39. $\frac{7}{8} \times \frac{4}{15} \times \frac{3}{14}$

40. $\frac{9}{10} \times \frac{5}{12} \times \frac{4}{27}$

41. $\frac{7}{24} \times \frac{18}{13} \times \frac{16}{21}$

42. $\frac{48}{77} \times \frac{33}{52} \times \frac{7}{18}$

43. $\frac{36}{49} \times \frac{25}{54} \times \frac{21}{40}$

44. $\frac{15}{28} \times \frac{9}{55} \times \frac{4}{63}$

NUMBER SENSE Copy and complete the statement using <, >, or =.

45. $\frac{3}{8} \times \frac{4}{5}$ _?_ 1

46. $1 \times \frac{2}{3}$ _?_ $\frac{2}{3}$

47. $\frac{3}{8} \times \frac{5}{5}$ _?_ $\frac{3}{8}$

48. $\frac{1}{3} \times \frac{4}{3}$ _?_ $\frac{1}{3}$

49. $\frac{1}{2} \times \frac{5}{2}$ _?_ $\frac{5}{2}$

50. $\frac{1}{5} \times \frac{3}{4}$ _?_ $\frac{1}{5}$

51. NUMBER SENSE If $\frac{a}{b} < \frac{c}{d}$ and $\frac{c}{d} < 1$, what do you know about $\frac{a}{b} \times \frac{c}{d}$ relative to $\frac{a}{b}$? *Explain* your reasoning.

52. CHALLENGE Use number sense to order the expressions from least to greatest without finding the products. *Explain* your reasoning.

$$\frac{17}{32} \times \frac{7}{12} \qquad \frac{7}{12} \times \frac{13}{27} \qquad \frac{18}{19} \times \frac{7}{12} \qquad \frac{7}{12} \times \frac{1}{2} \qquad \frac{7}{12} \times \frac{2}{21}$$

PROBLEM SOLVING

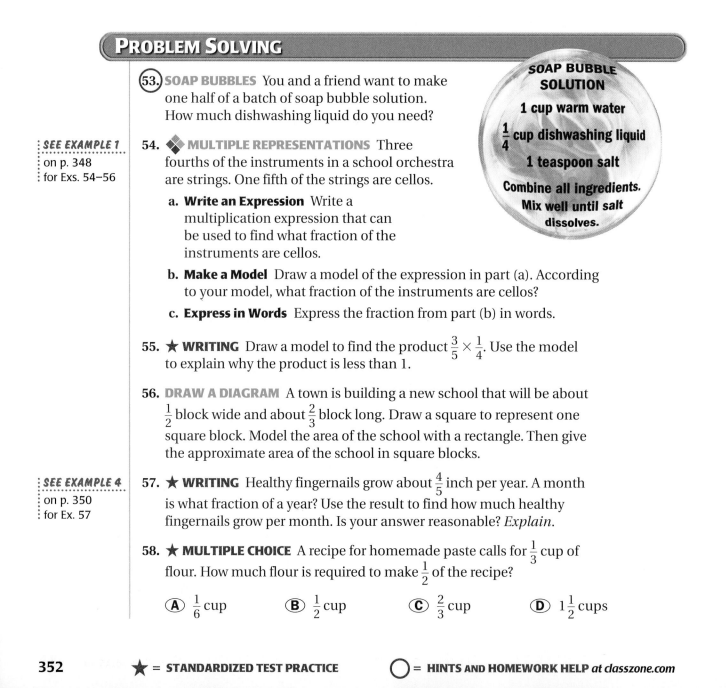

(53.) SOAP BUBBLES You and a friend want to make one half of a batch of soap bubble solution. How much dishwashing liquid do you need?

SOAP BUBBLE SOLUTION

1 cup warm water

$\frac{1}{4}$ cup dishwashing liquid

1 teaspoon salt

Combine all ingredients. Mix well until salt dissolves.

SEE EXAMPLE 1
on p. 348
for Exs. 54–56

54. ◆ MULTIPLE REPRESENTATIONS Three fourths of the instruments in a school orchestra are strings. One fifth of the strings are cellos.

  a. Write an Expression Write a multiplication expression that can be used to find what fraction of the instruments are cellos.

  b. Make a Model Draw a model of the expression in part (a). According to your model, what fraction of the instruments are cellos?

  c. Express in Words Express the fraction from part (b) in words.

55. ★ WRITING Draw a model to find the product $\frac{3}{5} \times \frac{1}{4}$. Use the model to explain why the product is less than 1.

56. DRAW A DIAGRAM A town is building a new school that will be about $\frac{1}{2}$ block wide and about $\frac{2}{3}$ block long. Draw a square to represent one square block. Model the area of the school with a rectangle. Then give the approximate area of the school in square blocks.

SEE EXAMPLE 4
on p. 350
for Ex. 57

57. ★ WRITING Healthy fingernails grow about $\frac{4}{5}$ inch per year. A month is what fraction of a year? Use the result to find how much healthy fingernails grow per month. Is your answer reasonable? *Explain*.

58. ★ MULTIPLE CHOICE A recipe for homemade paste calls for $\frac{1}{3}$ cup of flour. How much flour is required to make $\frac{1}{2}$ of the recipe?

  Ⓐ $\frac{1}{6}$ cup   **Ⓑ** $\frac{1}{2}$ cup   **Ⓒ** $\frac{2}{3}$ cup   **Ⓓ** $1\frac{1}{2}$ cups

59. MULTI-STEP PROBLEM The World Glacier Inventory contains data from more than 67,000 glaciers around the world. About $\frac{1}{50}$ of the glaciers are in North America. About $\frac{5}{8}$ of these glaciers are in the Queen Elizabeth Islands in Northern Canada.

   a. **Calculate** About what fraction of the glaciers are in the Queen Elizabeth Islands?

   b. **Estimate** Estimate the number of glaciers in the Queen Elizabeth Islands. *Explain* your steps.

60. ★ SHORT RESPONSE Two teams of students are running a relay race. The total distance of the race is $\frac{1}{2}$ mile. The teams are tied $\frac{3}{4}$ of the way through the race. At this point, how far have the teams run? How much farther do they have to run? *Explain* how you found your answer.

61. ★ OPEN-ENDED MATH Give three different pairs of fractions that have the same product.

62. REASONING *Compare* simplifying before multiplying fractions with simplifying after multiplying fractions. What are the advantages and disadvantages of each method?

63. CHALLENGE This season the school basketball team played $\frac{3}{7}$ of its games at night and $\frac{4}{7}$ of its games during the day. The team won $\frac{3}{4}$ of its night games and $\frac{7}{18}$ of its total games. What fraction of the day games did the team win? *Explain* how you found your answer.

MIXED REVIEW

Get-Ready
Prepare for Lesson 7.3 in Exs. 64–71

Write the number as an improper fraction or a mixed number. *(p. 260)*

64. $4\frac{2}{5}$ **65.** $5\frac{1}{3}$ **66.** $\frac{17}{6}$ **67.** $\frac{25}{7}$

68. $\frac{49}{9}$ **69.** $1\frac{15}{19}$ **70.** $\frac{27}{10}$ **71.** $2\frac{11}{12}$

Estimate the product. Use compatible whole numbers. *(p. 341)*

72. $\frac{2}{5} \times 31$ **73.** $\frac{5}{8} \times 18$ **74.** $40 \times \frac{5}{6}$ **75.** $28 \times \frac{2}{3}$

76. $\frac{3}{4} \times 29$ **77.** $\frac{8}{9} \times 52$ **78.** $65 \times \frac{3}{7}$ **79.** $81 \times \frac{7}{10}$

80. ★ MULTIPLE CHOICE What is the product 6.3094×0.01? *(p. 193)*

   A 0.063094   **B** 0.63094   **C** 6.3094   **D** 630.94

7.3 Multiplying Mixed Numbers

Before You multiplied fractions.

Now You'll multiply mixed numbers.

Why? So you can find the height of an object, as in Ex. 48.

KEY VOCABULARY

• mixed number, *p. 260*

• improper fraction, *p. 260*

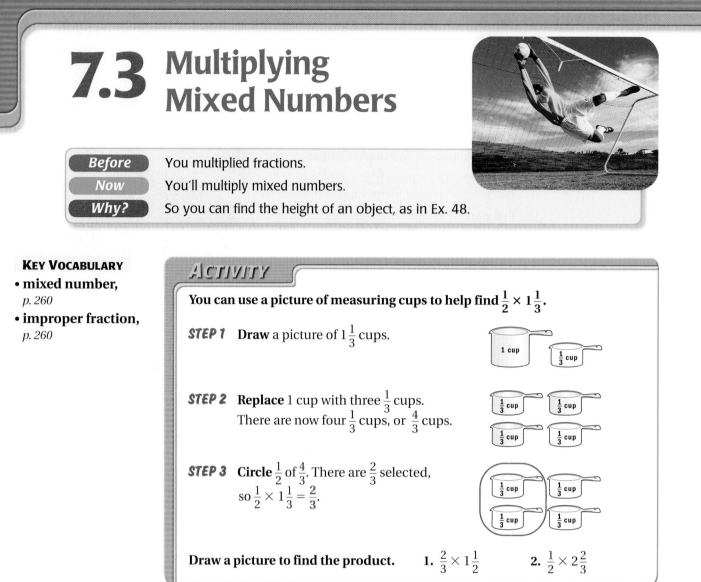

ACTIVITY

You can use a picture of measuring cups to help find $\frac{1}{2} \times 1\frac{1}{3}$.

STEP 1 Draw a picture of $1\frac{1}{3}$ cups.

STEP 2 Replace 1 cup with three $\frac{1}{3}$ cups. There are now four $\frac{1}{3}$ cups, or $\frac{4}{3}$ cups.

STEP 3 Circle $\frac{1}{2}$ of $\frac{4}{3}$. There are $\frac{2}{3}$ selected, so $\frac{1}{2} \times 1\frac{1}{3} = \frac{2}{3}$.

Draw a picture to find the product.   **1.** $\frac{2}{3} \times 1\frac{1}{2}$ **2.** $\frac{1}{2} \times 2\frac{2}{3}$

When finding a product involving a mixed number, first write all the numbers in fraction form.

EXAMPLE 1 Multiplying with Mixed Numbers

a. $\dfrac{5}{8} \times 1\dfrac{2}{3} = \dfrac{5}{8} \times \dfrac{5}{3}$ Write $1\frac{2}{3}$ as an improper fraction.

$= \dfrac{5 \times 5}{8 \times 3}$ Use the rule for multiplying fractions.

$= \dfrac{25}{24}$, or $1\dfrac{1}{24}$ Multiply. Write the answer in simplest form.

b. $1\dfrac{3}{4} \times 3 = \dfrac{7}{4} \times \dfrac{3}{1}$ Write $1\frac{3}{4}$ and 3 as improper fractions.

$= \dfrac{7 \times 3}{4 \times 1}$ Use the rule for multiplying fractions.

$= \dfrac{21}{4}$, or $5\dfrac{1}{4}$ Multiply. Write the answer in simplest form.

ANOTHER WAY

You can write 3 as $\frac{3}{1}$ (read "3 wholes") and multiply, or you can multiply as in Lesson 7.1:
$\frac{7}{4} \times 3 = \frac{21}{4} = 5\frac{1}{4}$.

EXAMPLE 2 Simplifying Before Multiplying

$2\frac{2}{9} \times 4\frac{4}{5} = \frac{20}{9} \times \frac{24}{5}$ Write $2\frac{2}{9}$ and $4\frac{4}{5}$ as improper fractions.

$= \dfrac{\overset{4}{\cancel{20}} \times \overset{8}{\cancel{24}}}{\underset{3}{\cancel{9}} \times \underset{1}{\cancel{5}}}$ Use the rule for multiplying fractions. Divide out common factors.

$= \dfrac{4 \times 8}{3 \times 1}$ Rewrite.

$= \dfrac{32}{3}$, or $10\frac{2}{3}$ Multiply. Write the answer in simplest form.

Check Round $2\frac{2}{9}$ to 2 and $4\frac{4}{5}$ to 5. Because $2 \times 5 = 10$, the product $10\frac{2}{3}$ is reasonable.

EXAMPLE 3 Multiplying to Solve Problems

Olympics Olympic trampoliners get points deducted from their scores if they land outside a rectangle called the *jump zone*. The jump zone measures $7\frac{1}{21}$ feet by $3\frac{1}{2}$ feet. What is the area of the jump zone?

SOLUTION

Write the formula for the area of a rectangle.

Area = **Length** × **Width**

$= 7\frac{1}{21} \times 3\frac{1}{2}$ Substitute for length and width.

$= \dfrac{148}{21} \times \dfrac{7}{2}$ Write $7\frac{1}{21}$ and $3\frac{1}{2}$ as improper fractions.

$= \dfrac{\overset{74}{\cancel{148}} \times \overset{1}{\cancel{7}}}{\underset{3}{\cancel{21}} \times \underset{1}{\cancel{2}}}$ Use the rule for multiplying fractions. Divide out common factors.

$= \dfrac{74}{3}$, or $24\frac{2}{3}$ Multiply. Write the answer in simplest form.

▶ **Answer** The area of the jump zone is $24\frac{2}{3}$ square feet.

✓ **GUIDED PRACTICE** for Examples 1, 2, and 3

Find the product. Write the answer in simplest form.

1. $2\frac{1}{3} \times \frac{5}{6}$ **2.** $5 \times 2\frac{2}{5}$ **3.** $3\frac{1}{3} \times 2\frac{1}{4}$ **4.** $3\frac{1}{4} \times 2\frac{3}{5}$

5. Crafts Jordan makes a banner $5\frac{1}{3}$ feet by $11\frac{1}{4}$ feet. What is the area of the banner?

7.3 EXERCISES

HOMEWORK KEY

★ = **STANDARDIZED TEST PRACTICE**
Exs. 24, 48, 51, 52, and 60

○ = **HINTS** AND **HOMEWORK HELP**
for Exs. 3, 9, 11, 19, 49 at classzone.com

SKILL PRACTICE

1. **VOCABULARY** Give an example of a mixed number.

2. **VOCABULARY** Give an example of an improper fraction.

SEE EXAMPLES 1 AND 2
on pp. 354–355
for Exs. 3–24

MODELING MULTIPLICATION Draw a picture of measuring cups to find the product.

3. $1\frac{1}{4} \times \frac{1}{5}$ **4.** $1\frac{1}{2} \times \frac{1}{3}$ **5.** $\frac{2}{3} \times 2\frac{1}{4}$ **6.** $1\frac{1}{3} \times \frac{3}{4}$

FINDING PRODUCTS Find the product.

7. $1\frac{5}{6} \times \frac{1}{2}$ **8.** $\frac{3}{4} \times 2\frac{1}{4}$ **9.** $2 \times 5\frac{2}{3}$ **10.** $1\frac{2}{5} \times 4$

11. $1\frac{1}{6} \times 2\frac{1}{2}$ **12.** $3\frac{2}{3} \times 3\frac{1}{2}$ **13.** $1\frac{2}{5} \times 2\frac{1}{3}$ **14.** $7 \times \frac{4}{9}$

15. $1\frac{1}{6} \times 8$ **16.** $2\frac{1}{3} \times \frac{3}{5}$ **17.** $1\frac{1}{2} \times 1\frac{1}{3}$ **18.** $1\frac{4}{5} \times 2\frac{1}{3}$

19. $\frac{1}{6} \times 6\frac{3}{4}$ **20.** $2\frac{2}{3} \times 5\frac{2}{5}$ **21.** $\frac{5}{8} \times 36$ **22.** $6 \times 2\frac{2}{9}$

23. **ERROR ANALYSIS** Describe and correct the error made in finding the product.

$$\times \quad 3 \times 5\frac{3}{4} = 15\frac{3}{4}$$

24. ★ **MULTIPLE CHOICE** Which product is equal to $\frac{3}{4}$?

   A $1\frac{1}{4} \times 1\frac{1}{3}$ **B** $3\frac{1}{3} \times \frac{2}{5}$ **C** $4\frac{1}{8} \times \frac{2}{11}$ **D** $\frac{1}{13} \times 8\frac{2}{3}$

SEE EXAMPLE 2
on p. 355
for Exs. 25–36

REASONING Tell whether you can simplify before multiplying. If so, tell how.

25. $\frac{7}{3} \times \frac{3}{2}$ **26.** $\frac{5}{2} \times \frac{5}{3}$ **27.** $\frac{3}{2} \times \frac{15}{13}$ **28.** $\frac{18}{25} \times \frac{10}{9}$

ESTIMATION Use rounding to estimate the product.

29. $4\frac{5}{8} \times 3\frac{1}{3}$ **30.** $6 \times 5\frac{7}{8}$ **31.** $3\frac{2}{3} \times 3\frac{4}{5}$ **32.** $2\frac{1}{8} \times 1\frac{2}{9}$

MULTIPLYING MIXED NUMBERS Find the product. Use estimation to check your answer.

33. $25\frac{3}{5} \times 2\frac{13}{16} \times 7$ **34.** $15\frac{3}{4} \times 4\frac{2}{9} \times 3$ **35.** $\frac{2}{3} \times 7\frac{1}{5} \times 45$ **36.** $\frac{7}{8} \times 4\frac{4}{9} \times 36$

SEE EXAMPLE 3
on p. 355
for Ex. 37

37. **GEOMETRY** Find the area of a rectangle with a length of $\frac{3}{4}$ yard and a width of $1\frac{3}{8}$ yards.

FINDING PRODUCTS Evaluate the expression when $x = \frac{2}{5}$ and $y = 4\frac{1}{2}$.

38. $\frac{2}{3} \cdot y$

39. $5y \cdot \frac{2}{9}$

40. $0.375 \cdot 2x$

41. $0.75xy$

NUMBER SENSE *Explain* how you can use the distributive property to evaluate the expression mentally.

42. $6 \cdot 3\frac{1}{3}$

43. $\frac{1}{2} \cdot 12\frac{2}{3}$

44. $\frac{4}{7} \cdot 7\frac{1}{4}$

45. $10\frac{10}{11} \cdot \frac{9}{10}$

46. CHALLENGE Rewrite $11a \div 4b$ as a mixed number times a fraction.

PROBLEM SOLVING

SEE EXAMPLE 3
on p. 355
for Exs. 47–50

47. RACING The diagram shows the components of a race. How many miles of the race are on the road?

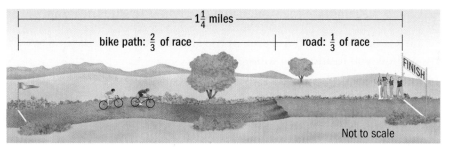

bike path: $\frac{2}{3}$ of race — road: $\frac{1}{3}$ of race

$1\frac{1}{4}$ miles

FINISH

Not to scale

48. ★ **MULTIPLE CHOICE** An outdoor soccer goal is $1\frac{3}{13}$ times as high as an indoor goal that is $6\frac{1}{2}$ feet high. How high is an outdoor goal?

A $1\frac{1}{13}$ ft

B $6\frac{1}{2}$ ft

C $7\frac{4}{13}$ ft

D 8 ft

(49.) MINIATURE BOOKS The Morgan Library in New York City owns a miniature book called *Book of Hours* that dates back to around 1535. The cover measures $2\frac{4}{5}$ inches by $1\frac{9}{10}$ inches. What is the area of the cover?

50. BAKING A recipe makes 12 muffins. Your pan will hold a total of 18 muffins. Will your pan hold $1\frac{1}{2}$ times the recipe? *Explain*.

Animated Math at classzone.com

51. ★ **WRITING** Look back at Example 4 on page 343 of Lesson 7.1. *Explain* how you can use this method to estimate the product of a fraction and a mixed number. *Describe* the steps you would use to estimate $\frac{5}{8} \times 42\frac{2}{5}$.

52. ★ **SHORT RESPONSE** Each of 20 students will give a $3\frac{1}{2}$ minute report.
  a. How much time will it take for all 20 reports to be presented?
  b. A 15 minute introduction by the teacher was recorded on a $1\frac{1}{2}$ hour videotape. Can all the student reports be recorded on that same videotape? *Explain* your reasoning.

53. REASONING Jason is estimating $5\frac{1}{2} \times 2\frac{1}{2}$. Will he get a better estimate if he calculates 6×3 or 5×3? *Explain* your answer.

54. MULTI-STEP PROBLEM In 1958, Massachusetts Institute of Technology student Oliver Reed Smoot, Jr., was used as a unit of measure to determine the length of the Harvard Bridge. One "Smoot" equals $5\frac{7}{12}$ feet. The length of the Harvard Bridge is $364\frac{2}{5}$ Smoots plus an ear.

   a. Calculate Find the number of feet in 360 Smoots.

   b. Estimate Use rounding to estimate the number of feet in $4\frac{2}{5}$ Smoots.

   c. Writing *Explain* how you can use parts (a) and (b) to estimate the length of the bridge in feet. Then estimate the length.

55. CHALLENGE Find the area of the shaded region. *Explain* how you found your answer.

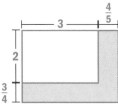

MIXED REVIEW

Get-Ready

Prepare for
Lesson 7.4
in Exs. 56–58

Use the division equation $48 \div 6 = 8$. The 48 tells you the total number of people who are being split into groups. *(p. 744)*

56. If the 6 tells you the size of each group, what does the 8 tell you?

57. If the 6 tells you the number of equal groups, what does the 8 tell you?

58. Rewrite the division equation so that it describes 48 people divided into 12 equal groups. How many people are in each group?

CHOOSE A STRATEGY Use a strategy from the list to solve the following problem. *Explain* your choice of strategy.

59. After spending $1 for bus fare and $4 for lunch and then earning $3, you have $6. How much money did you start with?

> **Problem Solving Strategies**
> - Draw a Diagram *(p. 762)*
> - Guess, Check, and Revise *(p. 763)*
> - Work Backward *(p. 764)*
> - Look for a Pattern *(p. 766)*

60. ★ **MULTIPLE CHOICE** Find the elapsed time from 6:20 P.M. to 1:35 A.M. *(p. 322)*

   A 4 h 45 min   **B** 5 h 45 min   **C** 6 h 15 min   **D** 7 h 15 min

Find the product.

1. $5 \times \frac{3}{4}$ *(p. 341)*

2. $14 \times \frac{3}{4}$ *(p. 341)*

3. $\frac{3}{5} \times \frac{7}{10}$ *(p. 348)*

4. $\frac{3}{8} \times \frac{2}{7} \times \frac{4}{5}$ *(p. 348)*

5. $2\frac{2}{3} \times \frac{3}{4}$ *(p. 354)*

6. $2\frac{6}{7} \times 4\frac{1}{12}$ *(p. 354)*

Estimate the product.

7. $19 \times \frac{2}{9}$ *(p. 341)*

8. $26 \times \frac{5}{9}$ *(p. 341)*

9. $4\frac{1}{4} \times 6\frac{7}{8}$ *(p. 354)*

10. GARDENING Teva planted 160 flower bulbs in her garden. Only $\frac{3}{5}$ of the flowers bloomed. How many flowers bloomed? *(p. 341)*

11. MODELING A sculptor creates a model of a statue with a square base. The side length of the base of the model is $5\frac{3}{4}$ inches. The actual side length of the base is $7\frac{1}{2}$ times the side length of the base of the model. What is the actual side length of the base? *(p. 354)*

12. THEATER You need to paint a piece of stage scenery that is $5\frac{5}{16}$ feet wide and 8 feet tall. A can of paint covers 50 square feet. Is there enough paint to cover the entire piece of stage scenery? *Explain* your reasoning. *(p. 354)*

Brain Game

Making Up Your Own Unit of Measure

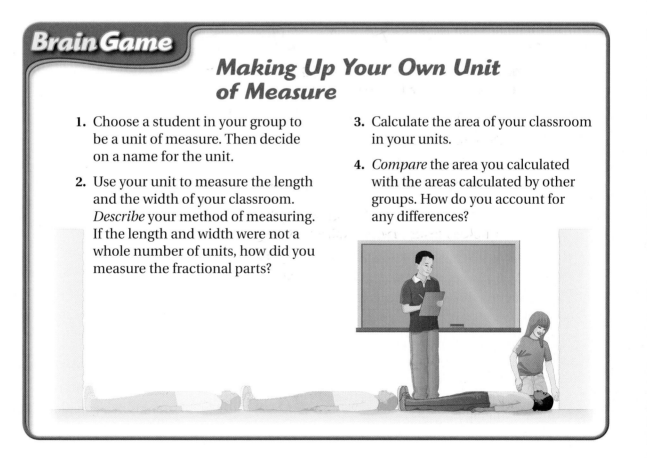

1. Choose a student in your group to be a unit of measure. Then decide on a name for the unit.

2. Use your unit to measure the length and the width of your classroom. *Describe* your method of measuring. If the length and width were not a whole number of units, how did you measure the fractional parts?

3. Calculate the area of your classroom in your units.

4. *Compare* the area you calculated with the areas calculated by other groups. How do you account for any differences?

Lessons 7.1–7.3

1. **GRIDDED ANSWER** A weather update on the news lasts $\frac{1}{15}$ hour. How many minutes does the update last?

2. **EXTENDED RESPONSE** You usually run about 5 miles every day. Today, you run $\frac{1}{4}$ the usual distance.

   a. Write a numeric expression that could be used to find the distance you ran today.

   b. Evaluate the expression you wrote in part (a). Interpret your result.

   c. It takes you about $\frac{2}{15}$ hour to run one mile. About how many minutes did it take you to finish today's run? *Explain* how you found your answer.

3. **OPEN-ENDED** *Describe* a situation that can be modeled by the expression $\frac{1}{2} \times \frac{1}{2} \times \frac{3}{4}$.

4. **SHORT RESPONSE** You burn 450 calories per hour when biking. You biked $\frac{3}{4}$ hour on Friday, $1\frac{1}{2}$ hours on Saturday, and $3\frac{1}{4}$ hours on Sunday. How many calories did you burn altogether on those days? *Explain* how you found your answer.

5. **SHORT RESPONSE** Write a rule that describes when the product of a nonzero whole number and a fraction is greater than the whole number and when it is less than the whole number.

6. **EXTENDED RESPONSE** You work at a scrapbook supply store. There are 18 inches of space on a shelf for a display of new scrapbooks and cardstock packets. Each scrapbook is about $1\frac{1}{4}$ inches wide and each packet is about $\frac{7}{8}$ inch wide.

   a. Write an expression for the amount of space needed for 11 scrapbooks and 7 packets.

   b. Using compatible whole numbers, estimate the amount of space needed. *Explain* your steps.

   c. Is your estimate *high* or *low*? *Explain* your answer.

   d. Based on the estimate from part (b), will the 11 scrapbooks and 7 packets fit on the shelf? *Explain* your reasoning.

   e. Find the actual amount of space needed. How does this value compare with your estimate? Will the 11 scrapbooks and 7 packets fit on the shelf?

7. **MULTI-STEP PROBLEM** The diagram shows a page from a magazine.

   a. Estimate the area of the page.

   b. Find the actual area of the page. How does this compare with your estimate?

   c. The width of the garden diagram is about $\frac{2}{5}$ the width of the page, and the length of the diagram is about $\frac{3}{4}$ the length of the page. Estimate the area of the diagram. *Explain* your steps.

8. **GRIDDED ANSWER** You want to make $\frac{1}{2}$ of a recipe that calls for $2\frac{1}{4}$ cups of flour. There are 16 tablespoons in a cup. How many tablespoons more than a cup of flour do you need?

INVESTIGATION
Use before Lesson 7.4

7.4 Modeling Fraction Division

In this activity, you will use a ruler and patterns to explore fraction division.

EXPLORE Model division by $\frac{3}{8}$. Use a table to look for a pattern.

STEP 1 Use a ruler to find the quotient $3 \div \frac{3}{8}$.

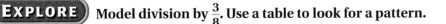

$$\frac{3}{8} \quad \frac{3}{8} \quad \frac{3}{8} \quad \frac{3}{8} \quad \frac{3}{8} \quad \frac{3}{8} \quad \frac{3}{8} \quad \frac{3}{8}$$

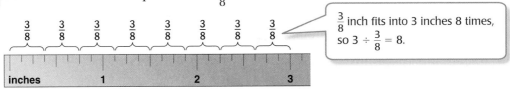

$\frac{3}{8}$ inch fits into 3 inches 8 times, so $3 \div \frac{3}{8} = 8$.

STEP 2 Copy and complete the table. Use a ruler to complete the left side.

Dividend	Divisor	Quotient	Dividend	Multiplier	Product
$3 \div$	$\frac{3}{8}$	$= 8$	$3 \times$	$\frac{8}{3}$	$= 8$
$\frac{3}{4} \div$	$\frac{3}{8}$	$= \underline{?}$	$\frac{3}{4} \times$	$\frac{8}{3}$	$= \underline{?}$
$\frac{3}{8} \div$	$\frac{3}{8}$	$= \underline{?}$	$\frac{3}{8} \times$	$\frac{8}{3}$	$= \underline{?}$

STEP 3 Compare the product to the quotient for each dividend. For example, compare $3 \div \frac{3}{8} = 8$ and $3 \times \frac{8}{3} = 8$.

PRACTICE Use a ruler to find the quotient. Then find the product.

1. $3 \div \frac{3}{4}$; $3 \times \frac{4}{3}$

2. $\frac{3}{4} \div \frac{1}{8}$; $\frac{3}{4} \times 8$

3. $\frac{3}{8} \div \frac{3}{16}$; $\frac{3}{8} \times \frac{16}{3}$

DRAW CONCLUSIONS

4. **REASONING** *Describe* how the divisor and the multiplier are related in the table shown above and in Exercises 1–3.

5. **WRITING** *Explain* how you could use multiplication to find the quotient $\frac{3}{4} \div \frac{3}{16}$. Try your method. Use a ruler to check your result.

7.4 Dividing Fractions

Before	You multiplied fractions.
Now	You'll use reciprocals to divide fractions.
Why?	So you can determine how many objects you can make, as in Ex. 55.

KEY VOCABULARY
• **reciprocal,** *p. 362*

For each pair of fractions multiplied below, the numerator and denominator of the product are equal, so the product is 1.

$$\frac{5}{3} \times \frac{3}{5} = \frac{15}{15} = 1 \qquad\qquad \frac{1}{12} \times \frac{12}{1} = \frac{12}{12} = 1$$

Two numbers, such as $\frac{5}{3}$ and $\frac{3}{5}$, whose product is 1 are **reciprocals**. Every number except 0 has a reciprocal. To find it, write the number as a fraction, and then switch the numerator and the denominator.

EXAMPLE 1 Writing Reciprocals

VOCABULARY
The *inverse property of multiplication* states that $\frac{a}{b} \times \frac{b}{a} = 1$. So, another term for *reciprocal* is *multiplicative inverse*.

	Original number	Fraction	Reciprocal	Check
a.	$\frac{4}{7}$	$\frac{4}{7}$ ⤫	$\frac{7}{4}$	$\frac{4}{7} \times \frac{7}{4} = \frac{28}{28} = 1$
b.	10	$\frac{10}{1}$ ⤫	$\frac{1}{10}$	$10 \times \frac{1}{10} = \frac{10}{10} = 1$
c.	$1\frac{3}{8}$	$\frac{11}{8}$ ⤫	$\frac{8}{11}$	$1\frac{3}{8} \times \frac{8}{11} = \frac{88}{88} = 1$

✓ **GUIDED PRACTICE** for Example 1

Write the reciprocal of the number.

1. $\frac{1}{2}$ **2.** 6 **3.** 1 **4.** $1\frac{2}{5}$

Dividing Fractions In the activity on page 361, you may have become aware of the following rule for dividing by a fraction.

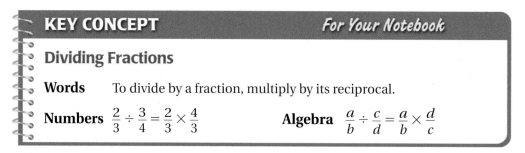

KEY CONCEPT *For Your Notebook*

Dividing Fractions

Words   To divide by a fraction, multiply by its reciprocal.

Numbers $\frac{2}{3} \div \frac{3}{4} = \frac{2}{3} \times \frac{4}{3}$ **Algebra** $\frac{a}{b} \div \frac{c}{d} = \frac{a}{b} \times \frac{d}{c}$

EXAMPLE 2 Dividing Two Fractions

Caves An underground boat ride at Howe Caverns in New York is $\frac{1}{4}$ mile long. The ride takes $\frac{1}{3}$ hour. Find the average rate of travel.

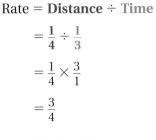

SOLUTION

Rate = **Distance** ÷ **Time**	Write the formula.
$= \frac{1}{4} \div \frac{1}{3}$	Use $\frac{1}{4}$ for the distance and $\frac{1}{3}$ for the time.
$= \frac{1}{4} \times \frac{3}{1}$	Multiply by the reciprocal of the divisor.
$= \frac{3}{4}$	Simplify.

▶ **Answer** The boat's average rate of travel is $\frac{3}{4}$ mile per hour.

Animated Math at classzone.com

AVOID ERRORS
When dividing, be sure to take the reciprocal of the divisor, *not* the dividend.

EXAMPLE 3 Dividing a Fraction and a Whole Number

a. How can you share $\frac{3}{4}$ pound of granola equally among 6 people?

b. Three fourths cup serves one person. How many people does 6 cups serve?

SOLUTION

a. Divide $\frac{3}{4}$ by 6.

$$\frac{3}{4} \div 6 = \frac{3}{4} \div \frac{6}{1}$$

Write 6 as a fraction.

$$= \frac{3}{4} \times \frac{1}{6}$$

$$= \frac{\overset{1}{\cancel{3}} \times 1}{4 \times \underset{2}{\cancel{6}}}$$

$$= \frac{1}{8}$$

▶ **Answer** Each person gets $\frac{1}{8}$ pound.

b. Divide 6 by $\frac{3}{4}$.

$$6 \div \frac{3}{4} = \frac{6}{1} \div \frac{3}{4}$$

$$= \frac{6}{1} \times \frac{4}{3}$$

$$= \frac{\overset{2}{\cancel{6}} \times 4}{1 \times \underset{1}{\cancel{3}}}$$

$$= 8$$

▶ **Answer** 6 cups serves 8 people.

CHECK ANSWERS
You can multiply to check your work. In Example 3,
$\frac{1}{8} \times 6 = \frac{3}{4}$ and
$8 \times \frac{3}{4} = 6$, so the quotients are correct.

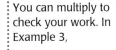 **GUIDED PRACTICE** for Examples 2 and 3

5. Find $\frac{5}{8} \div \frac{4}{3}$.

6. Find $\frac{9}{10} \div 3$.

7. Find $12 \div \frac{2}{3}$.

8. Running It takes you $\frac{1}{6}$ hour to run $\frac{4}{5}$ mile. What is your average rate?

7.4 EXERCISES

HOMEWORK KEY

★ = **STANDARDIZED TEST PRACTICE**
Exs. 21, 48, 53, 54, and 70

◯ = **HINTS** AND **HOMEWORK HELP**
for Exs. 7, 9, 13, 19, 49 at classzone.com

SKILL PRACTICE

VOCABULARY Tell whether the two numbers are reciprocals.

1. $\frac{3}{10}$ and $\frac{5}{3}$
　　2. $1\frac{1}{2}$ and $\frac{2}{3}$
　　3. 8 and $\frac{1}{8}$
　　4. 1 and 1

SEE EXAMPLE 1
on p. 362
for Exs. 5–8

FINDING RECIPROCALS Write the reciprocal of the number.

5. $\frac{4}{5}$
　　6. $\frac{9}{4}$
　　7. 10
　　8. $2\frac{1}{7}$

SEE EXAMPLES 2 AND 3
on p. 363
for Exs. 9–22

REWRITING EXPRESSIONS Rewrite the division expression as an equivalent multiplication expression. Then evaluate the expression.

9. $\frac{9}{2} \div \frac{3}{4}$
　　10. $\frac{5}{8} \div \frac{1}{3}$
　　11. $\frac{2}{3} \div 4$
　　12. $3 \div \frac{6}{5}$

FINDING QUOTIENTS Find the quotient.

13. $\frac{1}{3} \div \frac{2}{3}$
　　14. $\frac{2}{9} \div \frac{1}{4}$
　　15. $\frac{1}{12} \div \frac{5}{24}$
　　16. $\frac{2}{5} \div \frac{4}{5}$

17. $\frac{25}{9} \div 5$
　　18. $\frac{1}{8} \div 4$
　　19. $6 \div \frac{3}{10}$
　　20. $3 \div \frac{10}{9}$

21. ★ **MULTIPLE CHOICE** Which expression is equivalent to $\frac{5}{6} \div 18$?

A $\frac{5}{6} \times 18$
　　B $\frac{5}{6} \times \frac{1}{18}$
　　C $\frac{6}{5} \times 18$
　　D $\frac{6}{5} \times \frac{1}{18}$

22. **ERROR ANALYSIS** Describe and correct the error made in the solution.

$$\cancel{\quad} \quad \frac{3}{4} \div \frac{1}{8} = \frac{4}{3} \times \frac{1}{8} = \frac{4}{24} = \frac{1}{6}$$

23. **ESTIMATION** *Describe* how you could use estimation to verify that the quotient in Exercise 22 is incorrect.

MENTAL MATH Copy and complete the statement.

24. $\frac{8}{5} \times \underline{\ ?\ } = 1$
　　25. $\underline{\ ?\ } \times 7 = 1$
　　26. $4 \div \frac{1}{6} = 4 \times \underline{\ ?\ } = \underline{\ ?\ }$

27. $0.1 \times \underline{\ ?\ } = 1$
　　28. $\underline{\ ?\ } \times 0.75 = 1$
　　29. $6 \div 0.2 = 6 \times \underline{\ ?\ } = \underline{\ ?\ }$

NUMBER SENSE Copy and complete the statement using <, >, or = without actually finding the quotient. *Explain* your reasoning.

30. $\frac{4}{9} \div 1 \underline{\ ?\ } \frac{4}{9}$
　　31. $\frac{3}{5} \div 4 \underline{\ ?\ } \frac{3}{5}$
　　32. $4 \div \frac{2}{3} \underline{\ ?\ } 4$
　　33. $6 \div \frac{3}{2} \underline{\ ?\ } 6$

ALGEBRA Evaluate the expression when $p = \frac{1}{3}$, $q = \frac{5}{9}$, and $r = 3$.

34. $16 \div p$
　　35. $20 \div q$
　　36. $q \div 10$
　　37. $p \div 5$

38. $p \div q$
　　39. $q \div p$
　　40. $(p \div q) \div r$
　　41. $p \div (q \div r)$

42. REASONING Use your results from Exercises 40 and 41. Can you conclude that fraction division is commutative? associative? *Explain*.

(XY) ALGEBRA **Evaluate the expression for** $x = \frac{6}{7}$, $y = 4$, **and** $z = \frac{5}{2}$.

43. $\frac{2x}{y}$

44. $\frac{y}{2 + x}$

45. $y - \frac{x}{z}$

46. CHALLENGE Simplify the variable expression $\frac{a}{b} \div \frac{c}{b}$ for $b \neq 0$ and $c \neq 0$. Then test your answer by replacing the variables with numbers.

PROBLEM SOLVING

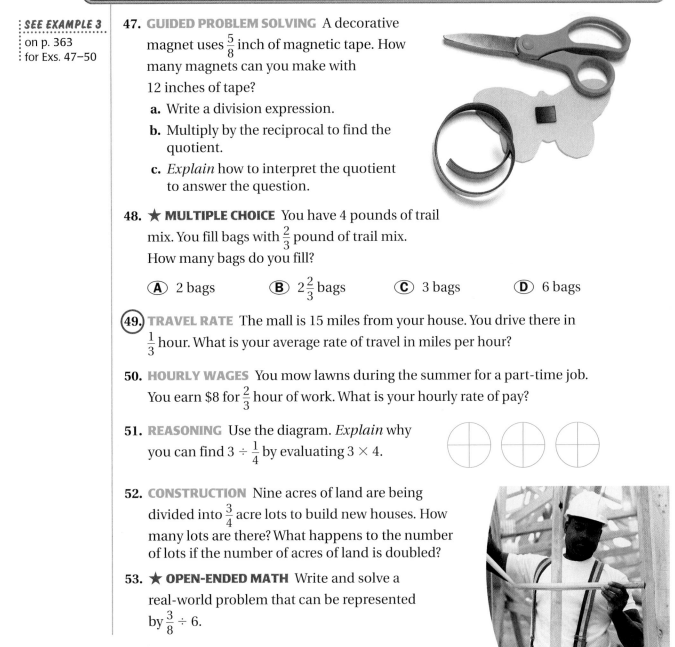

SEE EXAMPLE 3
on p. 363
for Exs. 47–50

47. GUIDED PROBLEM SOLVING A decorative magnet uses $\frac{5}{8}$ inch of magnetic tape. How many magnets can you make with 12 inches of tape?

  a. Write a division expression.

  b. Multiply by the reciprocal to find the quotient.

  c. *Explain* how to interpret the quotient to answer the question.

48. ★ MULTIPLE CHOICE You have 4 pounds of trail mix. You fill bags with $\frac{2}{3}$ pound of trail mix. How many bags do you fill?

  (A) 2 bags   **(B)** $2\frac{2}{3}$ bags   **(C)** 3 bags   **(D)** 6 bags

49. TRAVEL RATE The mall is 15 miles from your house. You drive there in $\frac{1}{3}$ hour. What is your average rate of travel in miles per hour?

50. HOURLY WAGES You mow lawns during the summer for a part-time job. You earn \$8 for $\frac{2}{3}$ hour of work. What is your hourly rate of pay?

51. REASONING Use the diagram. *Explain* why you can find $3 \div \frac{1}{4}$ by evaluating 3×4.

52. CONSTRUCTION Nine acres of land are being divided into $\frac{3}{4}$ acre lots to build new houses. How many lots are there? What happens to the number of lots if the number of acres of land is doubled?

53. ★ OPEN-ENDED MATH Write and solve a real-world problem that can be represented by $\frac{3}{8} \div 6$.

54. ★ **SHORT RESPONSE** Two paddleboat shops offer different rates for every minute of a rental. Shop A charges a rate that results in a paddleboat rental costing $27 per hour. Shop B rents out paddleboats for a a rate that results in a session costing $21 for $\frac{3}{4}$ hour.

  a. Which shop charges a lower rate per hour?

  b. The Jones family rents a paddleboat for $\frac{4}{5}$ hour at Shop A. The Gonsalves family rents a paddleboat for $\frac{3}{4}$ hour at Shop B. Which family spends less money on its rental? *Explain.*

  c. *Explain* which operations you used to solve parts (a) and (b).

55. **MULTI-STEP PROBLEM** It takes $\frac{9}{16}$ pound of clay to make a teacup and $\frac{7}{8}$ pound of clay to make a mug.

  a. **Compare** How many teacups can you make with 4 pounds of clay? How many mugs?

  b. **Calculate** With the 4 pounds of clay, you want to make 3 mugs first and then use the rest of the clay for teacups. How many teacups can you make? How much clay will be left over?

  c. **Writing** How many of each object can you make with the 4 pounds of clay so that there is no clay left over? *Explain* the strategy you used to find your answer.

56. **REASONING** Use the rule for dividing whole numbers by fractions to write rules for dividing a whole number *n* by 0.1, 0.01, and 0.001. First write the decimals as fractions.

57. **CHALLENGE** Draw a ruler that can be used to model $3 \div \frac{5}{8}$.

  a. How many whole times does $\frac{5}{8}$ go into 3? What is the remainder?

  b. What fraction of $\frac{5}{8}$ is the remainder?

  c. Evaluate $3 \div \frac{5}{8}$ using the Key Concept on page 362. How does this answer compare with the answer you found using the ruler model?

MIXED REVIEW

Get-Ready

Prepare for
Lesson 7.5
in Exs. 58–65

Find the product. *(p. 354)*

58. $4\frac{3}{5} \times \frac{1}{9}$ **59.** $1\frac{7}{8} \times 1\frac{6}{7}$ **60.** $8 \times 2\frac{1}{2}$ **61.** $2\frac{2}{3} \times 1\frac{5}{6}$

62. $\frac{1}{3} \times 5\frac{1}{4}$ **63.** $6\frac{5}{8} \times 7\frac{2}{5}$ **64.** $3\frac{1}{10} \times 10\frac{1}{3}$ **65.** $4\frac{8}{9} \times 5\frac{1}{2}$

You buy an item using a $20 bill. Find the amount of change you will receive for the given price of the item. *(p. 751)*

66. $7.50   **67.** $14.78   **68.** $.97   **69.** $12.39

70. ★ **MULTIPLE CHOICE** You pay $62 for 12 phone calls. Estimate the cost per phone call. *(p. 11)*

  Ⓐ $4   Ⓑ $5   Ⓒ $6   Ⓓ $7

7.5 Dividing Mixed Numbers

Before	You divided fractions.
Now	You'll divide mixed numbers.
Why?	So you can solve problems involving lengths, as in Ex. 53.

KEY VOCABULARY
- compatible numbers, *p. 12*
- mixed number, *p. 260*
- improper fraction, *p. 260*

You can use a model to find the quotient $3\frac{1}{3} \div \frac{2}{3}$. Begin by drawing a model for $3\frac{1}{3}$. Then divide the model into groups of $\frac{2}{3}$.

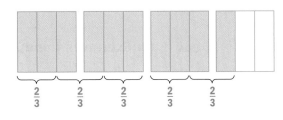

There are 5 groups of $\frac{2}{3}$. So, $3\frac{1}{3} \div \frac{2}{3} = 5$.

Animated Math at classzone.com

You can also find the quotient $3\frac{1}{3} \div \frac{2}{3}$ using paper and pencil, as in part (a) of Example 1. First rewrite the mixed number as an improper fraction.

EXAMPLE 1 Dividing a Mixed Number

a. $3\frac{1}{3} \div \frac{2}{3} = \frac{10}{3} \div \frac{2}{3}$ Write $3\frac{1}{3}$ as an improper fraction.

$= \frac{10}{3} \times \frac{3}{2}$ Multiply by the reciprocal of the divisor.

$= \frac{\overset{5}{\cancel{10}} \times \overset{1}{\cancel{3}}}{\underset{1}{\cancel{3}} \times \underset{1}{\cancel{2}}}$ Use the rule for multiplying fractions. Divide out common factors.

$= 5$ Multiply.

b. $2\frac{5}{8} \div 6 = \frac{21}{8} \div \frac{6}{1}$ Write $2\frac{5}{8}$ and 6 as improper fractions.

$= \frac{21}{8} \times \frac{1}{6}$ Multiply by the reciprocal of the divisor.

$= \frac{\overset{7}{\cancel{21}} \times 1}{8 \times \underset{2}{\cancel{6}}}$ Use the rule for multiplying fractions. Divide out common factor.

$= \frac{7}{16}$ Multiply.

EXAMPLE 2 Dividing by a Mixed Number

AVOID ERRORS
When you divide by a mixed number, first rewrite it as an improper fraction. Then multiply by the *reciprocal* of the improper fraction.

$$6\frac{3}{5} \div 2\frac{1}{4} = \frac{33}{5} \div \frac{9}{4}$$ Write $6\frac{3}{5}$ and $2\frac{1}{4}$ as improper fractions.

$$= \frac{33}{5} \times \frac{4}{9}$$ Multiply by the reciprocal of the divisor.

$$= \frac{\overset{11}{\cancel{33}} \times 4}{5 \times \underset{3}{\cancel{9}}}$$ Use the rule for multiplying fractions. Divide out common factor.

$$= \frac{44}{15}, \text{ or } 2\frac{14}{15}$$ Multiply.

Check Round $2\frac{1}{4}$ to 2 and replace $6\frac{3}{5}$ with the compatible number 6. The answer is reasonable because it is close to the estimate $6 \div 2 = 3$.

✓ **GUIDED PRACTICE** for Examples 1 and 2

Find the quotient. Use estimation to check your answer.

1. $9\frac{1}{6} \div 5$ **2.** $6\frac{2}{3} \div \frac{8}{9}$ **3.** $\frac{7}{8} \div 3\frac{1}{4}$ **4.** $12\frac{1}{2} \div 3\frac{3}{4}$

EXAMPLE 3 Choosing an Operation

Cider Forty pounds of apples make about $3\frac{1}{2}$ gallons of cider. About how many pounds of apples are needed to make 1 gallon of cider?

SOLUTION

STEP 1 **Choose** the operation by thinking about a similar whole number problem: If 40 pounds of apples made 4 gallons of cider, you would *divide* 40 by 4. So, *divide* 40 by $3\frac{1}{2}$.

STEP 2 **Divide.** $40 \div 3\frac{1}{2} = \frac{40}{1} \div \frac{7}{2}$

$$= \frac{40}{1} \times \frac{2}{7}$$

$$= \frac{80}{7}, \text{ or } 11\frac{3}{7}$$

▶ **Answer** You need about $11\frac{3}{7}$ pounds of apples to make 1 gallon of cider.

✓ **GUIDED PRACTICE** for Example 3

5. What If? Explain how to find the number of gallons of cider that can be made with 75 pounds of apples. Then solve the problem.

7.5 EXERCISES

HOMEWORK KEY	★ = **STANDARDIZED TEST PRACTICE** Exs. 19, 30, 46, 52, 55, 56, 58, 60, and 77
	◯ = **HINTS AND HOMEWORK HELP** for Exs. 3, 9, 11, 45, 49 at classzone.com

SKILL PRACTICE

1. **VOCABULARY** Write $6\frac{3}{4}$ and 8 as improper fractions.

2. **VOCABULARY** Write the reciprocal of $2\frac{3}{8}$.

FINDING QUOTIENTS Find the quotient.

SEE EXAMPLES 1 AND 2
on pp. 367–368 for Exs. 3–19

(3.) $7\frac{1}{5} \div \frac{2}{5}$ **4.** $8\frac{2}{3} \div \frac{2}{9}$ **5.** $4\frac{7}{8} \div \frac{13}{16}$ **6.** $2\frac{1}{10} \div 3$

7. $3\frac{4}{7} \div 5$ **8.** $\frac{5}{9} \div 4\frac{1}{6}$ **(9.)** $\frac{3}{8} \div 2\frac{1}{4}$ **10.** $5 \div 3\frac{1}{8}$

(11.) $11 \div 2\frac{4}{9}$ **12.** $15 \div 2\frac{1}{7}$ **13.** $4\frac{1}{4} \div 2\frac{1}{2}$ **14.** $2\frac{5}{6} \div 5\frac{1}{6}$

15. $16 \div 8\frac{3}{4}$ **16.** $5\frac{1}{10} \div 1\frac{1}{10}$ **17.** $1\frac{11}{12} \div 8$ **18.** $4\frac{3}{7} \div 6\frac{1}{3}$

19. ★ **MULTIPLE CHOICE** Which expression is equivalent to $2\frac{3}{7} \div 9$?

   A $\frac{17}{7} \div \frac{9}{1}$ **B** $\frac{7}{17} \div \frac{9}{1}$ **C** $\frac{17}{7} \div \frac{1}{9}$ **D** $\frac{7}{17} \div \frac{1}{9}$

20. **INTERPRETING A MODEL** What division problem involving a mixed number is represented by the model? What is the quotient?

21. **SKETCHING A MODEL** Sketch a model similar to the model in Exercise 20 for $2\frac{4}{5} \div \frac{2}{5}$. Find the quotient.

ESTIMATION Estimate the quotient.

22. $15\frac{1}{3} \div 2\frac{2}{3}$ **23.** $28\frac{9}{10} \div 5\frac{1}{4}$ **24.** $18\frac{3}{5} \div 1\frac{11}{12}$ **25.** $20 \div 3\frac{1}{7}$

26. $21\frac{1}{2} \div 4\frac{3}{4}$ **27.** $35\frac{5}{6} \div 4\frac{3}{8}$ **28.** $40\frac{5}{9} \div 2\frac{17}{18}$ **29.** $14\frac{3}{10} \div 5$

30. ★ **MULTIPLE CHOICE** Which statement describes how to find the next number in the pattern $\frac{1}{2}, \frac{1}{4}, \frac{1}{8}, \frac{1}{16}, \underline{\quad?\quad}, \underline{\quad?\quad}$?

   A Multiply $\frac{1}{16}$ by 2.   **B** Divide $\frac{1}{16}$ by 2.

   C Subtract $\frac{1}{4}$ from $\frac{1}{16}$.   **D** Square $\frac{1}{16}$.

ALGEBRA Solve the equation.

31. $n - 1\frac{1}{3} = 5\frac{2}{3}$

32. $a \cdot 2\frac{1}{2} = 10$

33. $b \div \frac{2}{5} = 6$

34. $2\frac{1}{3} + c = 8\frac{5}{6}$

35. $8\frac{1}{2} \cdot x = 3\frac{3}{4}$

36. $14 \div n = 2\frac{2}{3}$

Animated Math at classzone.com

EVALUATING EXPRESSIONS Evaluate the expression.

37. $\left(6\frac{3}{4} \div \frac{3}{4}\right) \times 1\frac{1}{2}$

38. $4\frac{3}{8} \div 5 + 1\frac{3}{10}$

39. $7\frac{1}{6} - 2\frac{1}{4} \div 3\frac{6}{7}$

40. $7\frac{1}{5} \div 4\frac{2}{7} + 0.7$

41. $6\frac{3}{10} \div \left(0.3 \times \frac{1}{9}\right)$

42. $(1.5 - 1.2) \div \frac{18}{25}$

43. **CHALLENGE** *Describe* the values of x for which the expression $4\frac{4}{5} \div x$ will be greater than, less than, or equal to 1. Use the symbol < or >.

PROBLEM SOLVING

CHOOSE THE OPERATION In Exercises 44–53, solve the problem. *Explain* why you chose the operation you used.

SEE EXAMPLE 3
on p. 368
for Exs. 44–53

44. **VOLUNTEER WORK** You split $5\frac{1}{2}$ hours of volunteer work equally over the next three weeks. How much time will you volunteer each week?

45. **PACKAGING** You are stacking computer games in a shipping box that is 12 inches high. Each game is $1\frac{1}{4}$ inches thick. How many games can you fit in the box in a single stack?

46. ★ **MULTIPLE CHOICE** Your cereal box recommends $\frac{1}{2}$ cup of milk per serving. How much milk does a family of four people need so that each person can have a serving of cereal?

(A) $\frac{3}{4}$ cup   **(B)** 2 cups   **(C)** $2\frac{1}{2}$ cups   **(D)** 4 cups

47. **RECIPES** You have only a $\frac{1}{4}$ cup measure. How many times must you fill the $\frac{1}{4}$ cup measure for a recipe that uses $2\frac{1}{4}$ cups of milk?

48. **STORE DISPLAYS** The hardcover edition of a bestselling book is $2\frac{11}{16}$ inches thick. The paperback edition is $1\frac{3}{8}$ inches thick. Will one of each edition of the book fit together in a display that is 4 inches wide?

49. **NEWBORN WEIGHTS** Twin babies weigh $7\frac{1}{2}$ pounds and $6\frac{5}{16}$ pounds. How much more does the heavier baby weigh than the lighter baby?

50. **PET CARE** A bag contains 40 cups of dog food. You feed $2\frac{2}{3}$ cups to your dog per day. In how many days will you need to buy more dog food?

51. INTERIOR DESIGN You want to make 3 curtains from a $2\frac{1}{3}$ yard piece of material. How much material will you have for each curtain?

52. ★ MULTIPLE CHOICE You buy $2\frac{1}{2}$ pounds of ground beef for a cookout. You want to make hamburger patties that are each $\frac{1}{4}$ pound. Which expression could you use to find how many hamburger patties you can make?

Ⓐ $2\frac{1}{2} \cdot \frac{1}{4}$ 　　Ⓑ $2\frac{1}{2} \div \frac{1}{4}$ 　　Ⓒ $\frac{1}{4} \cdot 2\frac{1}{2}$ 　　Ⓓ $\frac{1}{4} \div 2\frac{1}{2}$

53. ALLIGATORS What fraction of the alligator's total length is its tail?

54. ERROR ANALYSIS A recipe calls for $2\frac{1}{3}$ cups of broth. A cook is making $\frac{3}{4}$ of the recipe. Describe and correct the error made in finding the amount of broth needed.

$$\times \quad 2\frac{1}{3} \div \frac{3}{4} = \frac{7}{3} \div \frac{3}{4}$$
$$= \frac{7}{3} \times \frac{4}{3}$$
$$= \frac{28}{9} \text{ cups}$$
$$= 3\frac{1}{9} \text{ cups}$$

55. ★ SHORT RESPONSE How many $1\frac{1}{2}$ foot long shelves can you cut from a board that is $4\frac{3}{4}$ feet long? Is there wood left over? *Explain.*

56. ★ MULTIPLE CHOICE You read for $1\frac{1}{2}$ hours every night. You read one chapter of your book in $\frac{3}{4}$ hour. Which procedure could you use to find the number of chapters you read in one week?

Ⓐ Multiply the number of hours you read every night by 7 nights. Then multiply by the number of hours it takes you to read one chapter.

Ⓑ Multiply the number of hours you read every night by 7 nights. Then divide by the number of hours it takes you to read one chapter.

Ⓒ Divide the number of hours you read every night by 7 nights. Then multiply by the number of hours it takes you to read one chapter.

Ⓓ Divide the number of hours you read every night by 7 nights. Then divide by the number of hours it takes you to read one chapter.

57. CERAMIC TILES You want to install a row of ceramic tiles on a wall that is $21\frac{3}{8}$ inches wide. Each tile is $4\frac{1}{2}$ inches wide. How many whole tiles do you need? You want to make the row of tiles symmetrical. What fraction of a tile must you install on each end of the row?

58. ★ **EXTENDED RESPONSE** Talent show auditions are scheduled to last about $3\frac{3}{4}$ hours. There are 31 acts to be viewed.

  a. Represent Each act is allowed the same amount of time. Write an expression that represents the amount of time, in hours, for one act.

  b. Estimate Use a pair of compatible numbers to estimate the value of the expression you wrote in part (a).

  c. Interpret How many whole minutes should be allowed for each act so that the auditions don't exceed $3\frac{3}{4}$ hours? *Explain.*

59. **WEATHER** During a 5 hour snowstorm, it snows $6\frac{1}{2}$ inches in the first 2 hours and 4 inches in the last 3 hours. What is the average rate of snowfall, in inches per hour, for the entire snowstorm?

60. ★ **OPEN-ENDED MATH** Write and solve a real-world problem that involves dividing a mixed number by a whole number.

61. **FOOTBALL** Your football team gains a mean of $5\frac{1}{2}$ yards on five consecutive plays. The first four gains were $3\frac{1}{2}$ yards, 5 yards, $4\frac{1}{2}$ yards, and 8 yards. How many yards did the team gain on the fifth play?

62. **CHALLENGE** A screening room at a movie theater is open from 12:30 P.M. to 1:00 A.M. The length of each movie showing on the screen is $2\frac{1}{4}$ hours. How many movies can be shown on the screen during one day? How does your answer change if there is a 15 minute break between movies? *Explain* your answer.

MIXED REVIEW

Get-Ready

Prepare for
Lesson 7.6
in Exs. 63–66

Use a benchmark to estimate the length in the given unit. Then measure to check your estimate. *(p. 59)*

63. height of a refrigerator (feet)

64. length of a fork (inches)

65. width of a pencil's eraser (millimeters)

66. height of a cup (centimeters)

Copy and complete the statement. *(p. 754)*

67. 5 weeks 3 days = __?__ days

68. 265 min = __?__ hours __?__ min

Find the sum. *(p. 309)*

69. $6\frac{4}{7} + 2\frac{5}{7}$

70. $3\frac{2}{3} + 4\frac{3}{4}$

71. $5\frac{2}{5} + 1\frac{2}{3}$

72. $1\frac{2}{11} + 4\frac{8}{11}$

Find the difference. *(p. 316)*

73. $5 - 3\frac{1}{3}$

74. $7 - 3\frac{4}{9}$

75. $8\frac{1}{3} - 6\frac{7}{12}$

76. $5\frac{1}{4} - 2\frac{7}{10}$

77. ★ **SHORT RESPONSE** You have $\frac{7}{8}$ cup of tuna salad. Could you divide the salad into 4 equal portions using a $\frac{1}{4}$ cup scoop? *Explain.* *(p. 362)*

7.6 Weight and Capacity in Customary Units

Before	You used metric units of mass and capacity.
Now	You'll use customary units of weight and capacity.
Why?	So you can determine reasonable weights, as with hang gliders in Ex. 18.

KEY VOCABULARY
- **ounce (oz)**, *p. 373*
- **pound (lb)**, *p. 373*
- **ton (T)**, *p. 373*
- **fluid ounce (fl oz)**, *p. 374*
- **cup (c)**, *p. 374*
- **pint (pt)**, *p. 374*
- **quart (qt)**, *p. 374*
- **gallon (gal)**, *p. 374*

Bakery If a baker slices a 1 pound loaf of bread into 16 slices, each slice weighs 1 ounce. Knowing the weight of familiar objects, such as a slice of bread, can help you to choose appropriate units.

Weight Three customary units of weight are the **ounce** (oz), the **pound** (lb), and the **ton** (T). You can use the following benchmarks to estimate weight.

1 ounce
slice of bread

1 pound
soccer ball

1 ton
compact car

Ounces, pounds, and tons are related to one another.

$$1 \text{ lb} = 16 \text{ oz} \qquad 1 \text{ T} = 2000 \text{ lb}$$

EXAMPLE 1 Choosing Units of Weight

Copy and complete the statement using an appropriate customary unit.

a. An apple weighs $6\frac{1}{4}$ __?__ .

b. A laptop computer weighs $6\frac{1}{4}$ __?__ .

SOLUTION

a. An apple weighs $6\frac{1}{4}$ *ounces* because it is heavier than a slice of bread and lighter than a soccer ball.

b. A laptop computer weighs $6\frac{1}{4}$ *pounds* because it is heavier than a soccer ball and much lighter than a compact car.

✓ **GUIDED PRACTICE** for Example 1

Choose an appropriate customary unit to measure the weight.

1. golf ball   **2.** blue whale   **3.** bicycle

Capacity Five customary units of capacity are the **fluid ounce** (fl oz), the **cup** (c), the **pint** (pt), the **quart** (qt), and the **gallon** (gal).

1 fluid ounce   1 cup   1 pint   1 quart   1 gallon

The units of capacity are related to one another.

$$1 \text{ c} = 8 \text{ fl oz} \qquad 1 \text{ pt} = 2 \text{ c} \qquad 1 \text{ qt} = 2 \text{ pt} \qquad 1 \text{ gal} = 4 \text{ qt}$$

EXAMPLE 2 **Choosing Units of Capacity**

Choose an appropriate customary unit to measure the capacity.

a. large mug   **b.** water cooler

SOLUTION

a. A large mug holds about as much as a pint-sized milk carton does. You can use pints or one of the smaller units, fluid ounces or cups.

b. A water cooler holds much more than a gallon jug does. You can use gallons or quarts, but you wouldn't use the smaller units.

EXAMPLE 3 **Choosing Customary Units**

What does each measurement describe about an empty glass aquarium?

a. 55 gallons   **b.** 45 pounds

SOLUTION

a. A gallon is a measure of capacity, so 55 gallons describes the amount of water the aquarium can hold.

b. A pound is a measure of weight, so 45 pounds describes how much the empty aquarium weighs.

✓ **GUIDED PRACTICE** for Examples 2 and 3

Choose an appropriate customary unit to measure the capacity.

4. teakettle   **5.** juice glass   **6.** swimming pool

Tell whether the measurement is a *weight* or a *capacity*.

7. 3 quarts   **8.** 16 tons   **9.** $\frac{7}{8}$ pound

Animated Math

at classzone.com

EXAMPLE 4 **Standardized Test Practice**

Boat Safety Carlos and 5 other adults go to a lake. They want to take a motorboat to the other side of the lake, but the boat has a weight limit. Carlos wants to know if he and his 5 friends can safely cross the lake in one trip.

Arrange the following problem-solving steps in the correct order for Carlos to determine whether he and his friends can safely cross the lake in one trip.

STEP X Compare the 6 adults' total estimated weight with the boat's weight limit.

STEP Y Estimate the average weight of an adult.

STEP Z Multiply the estimated average weight of an adult by 6.

 Ⓐ X, Y, Z   Ⓑ X, Z, Y   Ⓒ Z, X, Y   Ⓓ Y, Z, X

SOLUTION

First Carlos must estimate the average weight of an adult. Then he must multiply his estimate by 6 to find the total estimated weight of all 6 adults. Finally, he should compare the total estimated weight of the adults with the weight limit of the boat.

▶**Answer** The correct order of the steps is Y, Z, X.
The correct answer is D. Ⓐ Ⓑ Ⓒ ⬤

✓ **GUIDED PRACTICE**   **for Example 4**

10. Birds Sue has a gallon of hummingbird syrup and wants to fill 20 feeders. Write the steps Sue could use to determine if she has enough syrup.

7.6 EXERCISES

HOMEWORK KEY

★ = **STANDARDIZED TEST PRACTICE**
 Exs. 18, 32, 33, and 46

◯ = **HINTS AND HOMEWORK HELP**
 for Exs. 5, 7, 11, 17, 31 at classzone.com

SKILL PRACTICE

VOCABULARY **Order the units from least to greatest.**

1. Units of capacity: pints, gallons, cups, quarts, fluid ounces

2. Units of weight: tons, ounces, pounds

MATCHING WEIGHTS **Match the object with its correct weight.**

SEE EXAMPLE 1
on p. 373
for Exs. 3–5

3. wrecking ball   **4.** kitten   **5.** cellular phone

A $3\frac{1}{2}$ ounces   **B** $3\frac{1}{2}$ tons   **C** $3\frac{1}{2}$ pounds

SEE EXAMPLES 1 AND 2
on pp. 373–374
for Exs. 6–13

6. weight of a gorilla

7. weight of a slipper

8. capacity of a bathtub

9. capacity of a serving spoon

CHOOSING UNITS OF CAPACITY **Copy and complete the statement using** *fluid ounces, pints,* **or** *gallons.*

10. The amount of water in a carnival dunking booth is 400 __?__.

11. The amount of water you can hold in the palm of one hand is $\frac{3}{4}$ __?__.

12. The capacity of a punch bowl is 24 __?__.

13. **ERROR ANALYSIS** Describe and correct the error made in estimating the capacity of a water bottle.

> ✗ The capacity of a water bottle is about 20 ounces.

SEE EXAMPLE 3
on p. 374
for Exs. 14–17

IDENTIFYING CUSTOMARY UNITS **Tell whether the measurement is a** *weight,* **a** *capacity,* **or a** *length.*

14. 7 quarts

15. 2 pounds

16. 15 inches

17. 4 ounces

18. ★ **MULTIPLE CHOICE** Choose the most reasonable estimate for the weight of a hang glider.

(A) 70 oz **(B)** 70 lb **(C)** 700 lb **(D)** 7 T

19. **WHICH ONE DOESN'T BELONG** Which unit doesn't belong: gallons, pints, cups, or ounces? *Justify* your answer.

ESTIMATION **Tell whether the item weighs** *less than* **or** *more than* **2 pounds.**

20. banana

21. bushel of apples

22. gallon can of paint

ESTIMATING CAPACITY **Is the capacity of the given object** *less than, about equal to,* **or** *more than* **a quart?** *Explain* your answer.

23. bathroom sink

24. bottle of cough syrup

25. ice cube tray

CHALLENGE **Estimate the capacity of the item.** *Explain* your reasoning. **Then measure the capacity. Which measuring tool did you use?**

26. cereal bowl

27. paper cup

28. kitchen sink

PROBLEM SOLVING

29. **ANIMALS** Choose an appropriate customary unit to measure the weight of each type of animal in the pictures at the right.

Bird   Zebra   Elephant

★ = **STANDARDIZED TEST PRACTICE**   ◯ = **HINTS AND HOMEWORK HELP** *at classzone.com*

30. **MEASUREMENT** Fill a 2 liter bottle with water. Then use a measuring cup to find the approximate number of cups in 2 liters.

31. **COMPARE** Order the empty containers from smallest to largest by height, by capacity, and by weight. If you can't, explain why not.

glass vase   plastic bowl   paper cup

32. ★ **OPEN-ENDED MATH** Give a different benchmark than the one pictured for each customary unit of weight and capacity on pages 373 and 374.

SEE EXAMPLE 4
on p. 375
for Ex. 33

33. ★ **MULTIPLE CHOICE** Jared must haul 30 crates to an upper floor using a building's freight elevator. The elevator has a weight limit of 3000 pounds. Arrange the problem-solving steps in the correct order for Jared to determine whether he can haul all the crates in the elevator.

STEP X Multiply the weight of a crate by 30. Then add Jared's weight.

STEP Y Compare the weight limit of the freight elevator with the combined weight of the crates and Jared.

STEP Z Estimate how much a crate weighs.

(A) X, Y, Z   **(B)** X, Z, Y   **(C)** Z, X, Y   **(D)** Y, Z, X

34. **REASONING** One pound of margarine measures 2 cups. You measure 2 cups of breakfast cereal and record its weight. Do you think the breakfast cereal also weighs one pound? *Explain* your reasoning.

35. **CHALLENGE** With a family member, estimate the weight or capacity of items in your home, such as a drinking glass, a bowl, and a stack of coins. Then use a kitchen scale and a measuring cup to find the exact weights or capacities. *Compare* your estimates with the actual measurements.

MIXED REVIEW

Get-Ready

Prepare for
Lesson 7.7
in Exs. 36–41

Copy and complete the statement. *(p. 207)*

36. 76 cm = _?_ mm

37. 8.5 kg = _?_ g

38. 175 mL = _?_ L

39. 0.25 L = _?_ kL

40. 160 km = _?_ m

41. 0.044 g = _?_ mg

Write the fraction as a decimal. *(p. 271)*

42. $\frac{5}{8}$

43. $\frac{3}{40}$

44. $\frac{5}{6}$

45. $\frac{2}{9}$

46. ★ **MULTIPLE CHOICE** Four gold prospectors equally divide $\frac{7}{8}$ ounce of gold. What is each prospector's share of the gold? *(p. 362)*

(A) $\frac{7}{32}$ ounce   **(B)** $\frac{1}{4}$ ounce   **(C)** $\frac{7}{16}$ ounce   **(D)** $3\frac{1}{2}$ ounces

7.7 Changing Customary Units

Before	You learned the customary units of measure.
Now	You'll change customary units of measure.
Why?	So you can interpret measures, as with underwater vehicles in Ex. 46.

KEY VOCABULARY
- **inch (in.),** *p. 59*
- **foot (ft),** *p. 59*
- **yard (yd),** *p. 59*
- **mile (mi),** *p. 59*

You can use the relationships below to convert among customary units.

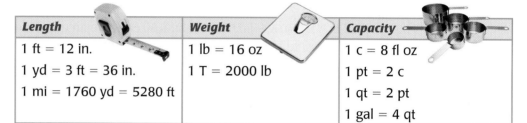

Length	Weight	Capacity
1 ft = 12 in.	1 lb = 16 oz	1 c = 8 fl oz
1 yd = 3 ft = 36 in.	1 T = 2000 lb	1 pt = 2 c
1 mi = 1760 yd = 5280 ft		1 qt = 2 pt
		1 gal = 4 qt

EXAMPLE 1 Changing Units Using Multiplication

AVOID ERRORS
When changing from a larger unit to a smaller unit, you *multiply*. When changing from a smaller unit to a larger unit, you *divide*.

Change 3 ft 7 in. to inches.

$$3 \text{ ft } 7 \text{ in.} = \mathbf{3 \text{ ft}} + 7 \text{ in.} \qquad \text{Write the measurement as a sum.}$$
$$= (\mathbf{3 \times 12}) \text{ in.} + 7 \text{ in.} \qquad \text{Change the feet to inches.}$$
$$= \mathbf{36 \text{ in.}} + 7 \text{ in.} \qquad \text{Multiply.}$$
$$= 43 \text{ in.} \qquad \text{Add.}$$

EXAMPLE 2 Changing Units Using Division

Change 35 oz to pounds. Express the answer in two ways.

There are 16 oz in a pound, so divide 35 by 16.

$$16\overline{)35} \quad \begin{array}{r} 2 \text{ R } \mathbf{3} \end{array}$$ ◄── You can interpret the remainder as **3** oz.

$$\frac{32}{\mathbf{3}}$$ ◄── You can also interpret the remainder as $\frac{3}{16}$ lb, because the remaining division 3 ÷ 16 can be written as $\frac{3}{16}$.

▶ **Answer** There are 2 lb 3 oz in 35 oz. This can also be written as $2\frac{3}{16}$ lb.

✓ GUIDED PRACTICE   for Examples 1 and 2

Copy and complete the statement.

1. 2 mi 480 yd = __?__ yd   **2.** 26 fl oz = __?__ c   **3.** $7\frac{1}{2}$ T = __?__ lb

Multiplying by a Form of 1 You can also change units without deciding whether to multiply or divide. Instead, multiply by a fraction that is equal to 1. For example, 1 gal = 4 qt, so $\dfrac{4\text{ qt}}{1\text{ gal}} = \dfrac{1\text{ gal}}{4\text{ qt}} = 1$.

EXAMPLE 3 **Multiplying by a Form of 1**

Change $2\dfrac{1}{4}$ ft to yards.

$2\dfrac{1}{4}$ ft $= \dfrac{9\text{ ft}}{4}$ **Write the measurement in fraction form.**

CHOOSE A FORM OF 1

To get the correct unit in the answer, choose the form of 1 that has the unit you are changing to in the numerator and the unit you are changing from in the denominator.

$= \dfrac{9\text{ ft}}{4} \times \dfrac{1\text{ yd}}{3\text{ ft}}$ **Multiply by a form of 1. Use $\dfrac{1\text{ yd}}{3\text{ ft}}$.**

$= \dfrac{\overset{3}{\cancel{9}}\text{ ft} \times 1\text{ yd}}{4 \times \underset{1}{\cancel{3}}\text{ ft}}$ **Divide out "ft" so you are left with "yd."**

$= \dfrac{3}{4}$ yd

★ **EXAMPLE 4** **Standardized Test Practice**

Camels A camel can drink 30 gallons of water in 10 minutes. How many cups are in 30 gallons?

(A) 16 c (B) 120 c

(C) 240 c (D) 480 c

ELIMINATE CHOICES

In Example 4, you are changing from gallons to cups. Because one cup is smaller than one gallon, your answer should have more cups than gallons. So, you can eliminate choice A.

SOLUTION

STEP 1 **Find** the relationship between gallons and cups. Use these three relationships: 1 gal = 4 qt, 1 qt = 2 pt, and 1 pt = 2 c.

$\dfrac{1\text{ gal}}{4\text{ qt}} \times \dfrac{1\text{ qt}}{2\text{ pt}} \times \dfrac{1\text{ pt}}{2\text{ c}} = \dfrac{1\text{ gal} \times 1\text{ }\cancel{qt} \times 1\text{ }\cancel{pt}}{4\text{ }\cancel{qt} \times 2\text{ }\cancel{pt} \times 2\text{ c}} = \dfrac{1\text{ gal}}{16\text{ c}}$

STEP 2 **Multiply** 30 gal by a form of 1 that relates gallons and cups.

$30\text{ gal} \times \dfrac{16\text{ c}}{1\text{ gal}} = \dfrac{30\text{ }\cancel{gal} \times 16\text{ c}}{1\text{ }\cancel{gal}} = 480\text{ c}$

▸ **Answer** A camel can drink 480 cups of water in 10 minutes. The correct answer is D. (A) (B) (C) (D)

✓ **GUIDED PRACTICE** **for Examples 3 and 4**

4. Change $2\dfrac{3}{8}$ lb to ounces.

5. Change 28 fl oz to quarts.

Solving a Related Problem To add or subtract customary units, think about how you added and subtracted units of time in Lesson 6.6. You will set up the problem and rename units in the same way.

EXAMPLE 5   Adding and Subtracting Measures

Model Trains A steam locomotive on a large model train has a length of 3 feet 2 inches. The length of a passenger car is 1 foot 11 inches.

The model locomotive shown is $26\frac{3}{8}$ in. long. it is built to a scale of 1 in. : 32 in.

a. How long is the model train with the locomotive and one passenger car?

b. What is the difference in the lengths of the locomotive and a passenger car?

SOLUTION

a. Add. Then rename the sum.

$$\begin{array}{r} 3 \text{ ft} \quad 2 \text{ in.} \\ + 1 \text{ ft} \ 11 \text{ in.} \\ \hline 4 \text{ ft } \mathbf{13 \text{ in.}} \end{array}$$

 Rename: Think of 13 in. as 1 ft 1 in.

= 4 ft + (**1 ft 1 in.**)
= (4 ft + 1 ft) + 1 in.
= 5 ft 1 in.

▸**Answer** The model train with the locomotive and one passenger car is 5 ft 1 in. long.

b. Rename. Then subtract.

$$\begin{array}{r} 3 \text{ ft} \quad 2 \text{ in.} \\ - 1 \text{ ft} \ 11 \text{ in.} \end{array}$$

 Rename: Think of 3 ft 2 in. as 2 ft 14 in.

$$\begin{array}{r} 2 \text{ ft} \ 14 \text{ in.} \\ - 1 \text{ ft} \ 11 \text{ in.} \\ \hline 1 \text{ ft} \quad 3 \text{ in.} \end{array}$$

▸**Answer** The difference in the lengths of the locomotive and a passenger car is 1 foot 3 inches.

✓ **GUIDED PRACTICE**   **for Example 5**

6. Camping You take a full backpack and a tent on a camping trip. The backpack weighs 13 pounds 10 ounces. The tent weighs 5 pounds 13 ounces.

  a. What is the difference in the weight of the backpack and the weight of the tent?

  b. You attach the tent to the outside of the backpack. What is the combined weight of the backpack and the tent?

7.7 EXERCISES

HOMEWORK KEY

★ = STANDARDIZED TEST PRACTICE
Exs. 17, 45, 51, 52, 72, and 73

◯ = HINTS AND HOMEWORK HELP
for Exs. 7, 15, 19, 21, 43 at classzone.com

SKILL PRACTICE

VOCABULARY Copy and complete the statement.

1. $1 = \dfrac{8 \text{ fl oz}}{? \text{ c}}$

2. $1 = \dfrac{? \text{ mi}}{1760 \text{ yd}}$

3. $1 = \dfrac{1 \text{ lb}}{? \text{ oz}}$

4. $1 = \dfrac{? \text{ qt}}{1 \text{ gal}}$

CHANGING UNITS Change the measurement to the specified unit.

SEE EXAMPLES 1, 2, AND 3
on pp. 378–379
for Exs. 5–17

5. 6 T to pounds

6. 2 mi to yards

7. 10 pt to quarts

8. 24 fl oz to cups

9. 45 in. to feet

10. 4500 lb to tons

11. 2 T 300 lb to pounds

12. 3 lb 7 oz to ounces

13. 4 yd 1 ft to feet

14. $\dfrac{5}{8}$ lb to ounces

15. $40\dfrac{1}{2}$ in. to yards

16. $8\dfrac{1}{2}$ c to pints

17. ★ **MULTIPLE CHOICE** Which of the following is *not* equivalent to 64 inches?

Ⓐ $1\dfrac{7}{9}$ yd

Ⓑ 5 ft 4 in.

Ⓒ $5\dfrac{1}{3}$ ft

Ⓓ $5\dfrac{1}{4}$ ft

ADDING AND SUBTRACTING MEASURES Find the sum or difference.

SEE EXAMPLE 5
on p. 380
for Exs. 18–24

18. $\begin{array}{r} 6 \text{ ft } 7 \text{ in.} \\ + 5 \text{ ft } 8 \text{ in.} \\ \hline \end{array}$

19. $\begin{array}{r} 10 \text{ lb } 9 \text{ oz} \\ + 11 \text{ lb } 8 \text{ oz} \\ \hline \end{array}$

20. $\begin{array}{r} 4 \text{ gal } 1 \text{ qt} \\ + 2 \text{ gal } 3 \text{ qt} \\ \hline \end{array}$

21. $\begin{array}{r} 17 \text{ yd } 1 \text{ ft} \\ - 14 \text{ yd } 2 \text{ ft} \\ \hline \end{array}$

22. $\begin{array}{r} 9 \text{ T } 397 \text{ lb} \\ - 2 \text{ T } 478 \text{ lb} \\ \hline \end{array}$

23. $\begin{array}{r} 7 \text{ c } 3 \text{ fl oz} \\ - 1 \text{ c } 5 \text{ fl oz} \\ \hline \end{array}$

24. **ERROR ANALYSIS** Describe and correct the error made in the solution.

$$\times \quad \begin{array}{r} 4 \text{ lb } 3 \text{ oz} \\ - 2 \text{ lb } 8 \text{ oz} \\ \hline \end{array} \longrightarrow \begin{array}{r} 3 \text{ lb } 13 \text{ oz} \\ - 2 \text{ lb } 8 \text{ oz} \\ \hline 1 \text{ lb } 5 \text{ oz} \end{array}$$

COMPLETING CONVERSION TABLES Copy and complete the table.

25.

ounces	pounds
14	?
?	2
70	?

26.

pints	cups
?	3
3	?
7	?

27.

feet	miles
?	$\dfrac{1}{2}$
?	2
18,480	?

CHANGING UNITS Copy and complete the statement. Tell which form of 1 you used.

SEE EXAMPLE 4
on p. 379
for Exs. 28–33

28. $2\dfrac{1}{2}$ gal = __?__ pt

29. 48 fl oz = __?__ qt

30. 300 c = __?__ gal

31. 3 mi = __?__ in.

32. 5 T = __?__ oz

33. 79,200 in. = __?__ yd

CHOOSE A METHOD Choose *mental math* or *paper and pencil* to copy and complete the statement with <, >, or =. *Explain* your choice.

34. 3645 lb ? $1\frac{1}{2}$ T

35. $\frac{7}{8}$ mi ? 4875 ft

36. $1\frac{2}{3}$ c ? $13\frac{1}{3}$ fl oz

37. $2\frac{1}{2}$ pt ? $1\frac{1}{4}$ qt

38. $2\frac{5}{12}$ ft ? 30 in.

39. 280 oz ? 17 lb

ORDERING MEASUREMENTS Order the measurements from least to greatest.

40. $\frac{1}{4}$ lb, 8 oz, $\frac{3}{8}$ lb, $\frac{33}{5}$ oz

41. 25 in., $1\frac{3}{4}$ ft, $\frac{2}{3}$ yd, $\frac{13}{6}$ ft

42. CHALLENGE Write rules for performing the following conversions: fluid ounces to gallons, miles to yards, and tons to ounces. Represent each rule with a one-step equation involving decimal multiplication.

PROBLEM SOLVING

43. MAPLE SYRUP One tap hole in a maple tree typically yields enough sap in a year to produce one third gallon of syrup. How many quarts of syrup are in one third gallon?

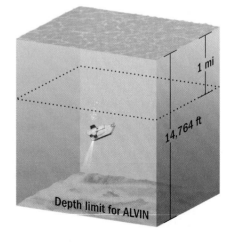

44. AMUSEMENT PARK RIDES Riders on a roller coaster must be more than 50 inches tall. You are 4 feet 3 inches tall. Are you tall enough for the ride?

SEE EXAMPLE 4
on p. 379
for Ex. 45

45. ★ MULTIPLE CHOICE You can buy drinks in three sizes: 12 fluid ounces, $\frac{1}{2}$ pint, and 2 cups. Which list shows these sizes from greatest to least?

(A) 12 fl oz, $\frac{1}{2}$ pt, 2 c

(B) 2 c, 12 fl oz, $\frac{1}{2}$ pt

(C) 12 fl oz, 2 c, $\frac{1}{2}$ pt

(D) $\frac{1}{2}$ pt, 2 c, 12 fl oz

SUBMERSIBLES ALVIN is an underwater vehicle used for research.

46. ALVIN weighs 35,200 pounds. What is its weight in tons?

47. ALVIN can carry up to 1500 pounds. How many tons can ALVIN carry?

48. CALCULATOR What is ALVIN's depth limit in miles? Round to the nearest tenth of a mile.

1 mi

14,764 ft

Depth limit for ALVIN

★ = **STANDARDIZED TEST PRACTICE**   ◯ = **HINTS AND HOMEWORK HELP** *at classzone.com*

49. REFRESHMENTS You are making fruit punch for a party. You need 14 cups of orange juice for the punch. If you buy a gallon jug of orange juice, will you have enough for the punch?

50. SPORTS Hank Aaron hit a record 755 home runs in his career. The distance around a baseball diamond is 360 feet. About how many miles did Hank Aaron run after hitting home runs?

51. ★ **SHORT RESPONSE** You are taking a seaplane to an island. There is a 24 pound weight limit for luggage on the seaplane. Your suitcase weighs 6 lb 4 oz, your clothes weigh 9 lb 2 oz, your shoes weigh 4 lb 10 oz, and your toiletries weigh 2 lb 11 oz. Is your luggage within the weight limit for the seaplane? *Explain* your reasoning.

52. ★ **EXTENDED RESPONSE** The picture below shows a recipe for veggie dip and the amount of each ingredient that you have. This recipe makes enough dip for 6 people.

   a. Writing *Explain* how to increase the recipe to make 24 servings.

   b. Calculate Do you have enough cottage cheese, yogurt, and onion soup mix to make 24 servings of veggie dip?

   c. Interpret With the ingredients shown above, how many servings of veggie dip can you make? Which ingredient(s) will be leftover? *Explain* how you found your answers.

53. GEOMETRY You walk around this city park clockwise starting at A. How many times do you need to walk around the park to walk a mile?

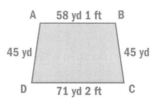

54. CONSUMERISM About 6 gallons of ice cream and related frozen desserts are eaten per person per year in the United States. About how many fluid ounces per person per day is that? Round to the nearest fluid ounce.

55. CHALLENGE A baker needs 375 cups of flour to bake a large order of sourdough bread. The baker has a one cup measure and a small bucket for scooping the flour from 100 pound sacks. *Describe* a method the baker can use to efficiently measure the right amount of flour for the bread.

Get-Ready

Prepare for
Lesson 8.1
in Exs. 56–63

Copy and complete the statement. *(p. 243)*

56. $\dfrac{4}{5} = \dfrac{20}{?}$ **57.** $\dfrac{3}{11} = \dfrac{?}{22}$ **58.** $\dfrac{42}{18} = \dfrac{?}{3}$ **59.** $\dfrac{16}{36} = \dfrac{4}{?}$

60. $\dfrac{1}{6} = \dfrac{9}{?}$ **61.** $\dfrac{56}{140} = \dfrac{4}{?}$ **62.** $\dfrac{5}{3} = \dfrac{?}{36}$ **63.** $\dfrac{3}{8} = \dfrac{?}{72}$

Find the quotient. *(p. 367)*

64. $8\dfrac{1}{3} \div \dfrac{10}{27}$ **65.** $3\dfrac{1}{9} \div 5$ **66.** $2\dfrac{3}{4} \div 2\dfrac{2}{7}$ **67.** $\dfrac{1}{10} \div 7\dfrac{3}{5}$

68. $\dfrac{15}{21} \div 12\dfrac{2}{3}$ **69.** $4\dfrac{3}{8} \div 1\dfrac{1}{6}$ **70.** $9 \div 6\dfrac{3}{4}$ **71.** $2\dfrac{9}{16} \div \dfrac{11}{12}$

72. ★ **MULTIPLE CHOICE** Find the next two numbers in the pattern:
729, 243, 81, 27, __?__, __?__. *(p. 3)*

    A $3, \dfrac{1}{3}$ **B** 3, 1 **C** 9, 3 **D** 24, 21

73. ★ **MULTIPLE CHOICE** A rectangle has a length of 14 cm and an area of
70 cm². What is the width of the rectangle? *(p. 66)*

    A 5 cm **B** 7 cm **C** 14 cm **D** 35 cm

QUIZ *for Lessons 7.4–7.7*

Find the quotient.

1. $\dfrac{2}{15} \div \dfrac{3}{10}$ *(p. 362)* **2.** $7 \div \dfrac{4}{5}$ *(p. 362)* **3.** $2\dfrac{5}{8} \div 3$ *(p. 367)* **4.** $6\dfrac{3}{5} \div 2\dfrac{4}{9}$ *(p. 367)*

Copy and complete the statement using an appropriate customary unit.
(p. 373)

  5. weight of a bulldozer = 15 __?__   **6.** capacity of a thermos = 32 __?__

Copy and complete the statement. *(p. 378)*

  7. 2 T 1500 lb = __?__ lb   **8.** $2\dfrac{2}{3}$ yd = __?__ in.   **9.** 22 c = __?__ qt

Find the sum or difference. *(p. 378)*

10.   7 ft 5 in.
     + 2 ft 8 in.

11.   13 T 9 lb
     − 10 T 8 lb

12.   5 gal 1 qt
     − 2 gal 3 qt

13. **CRAFTS** You have a length of ribbon that is $\dfrac{3}{4}$ yard long. How many
pieces that are $\dfrac{1}{8}$ yard long can you cut from the ribbon? *(p. 362)*

14. **ELECTRONICS** Your television weighs 19 pounds 8 ounces. Your stereo
weighs 20 pounds 12 ounces. Can you safely place your television and
your stereo on a shelf that holds 40 pounds? *Explain.* *(p. 378)*

EXTRA PRACTICE for Lesson 7.7, p. 782   **ONLINE QUIZ** at classzone.com

7.7 Changing Units

EXPLORE The calculator memory can help you change units.

You plan to take the Marine Drive along the coast of Nova Scotia in Canada. The distance is given as 340 kilometers. What is the distance in miles?

SOLUTION

STEP 1 To change metric units to customary units, use the relationships shown in the table.

Length	Capacity	Weight
1 mm ≈ 0.0394 in.	1 mL ≈ 0.0338 fl oz	1 g ≈ 0.0353 oz
1 m ≈ 3.28 ft	1 L ≈ 1.06 qt	1 kg ≈ 2.2 lb
1 km ≈ 0.621 mi	1 kL ≈ 264 gal	

STEP 2 To change between kilometers and miles, use the fact that 1 km ≈ 0.621 mi. You will use 0.621 any time you change between these units, so store this value in memory.

Keystrokes   **Display**

0.621 [STO ▶] [=]   **0.621**

STEP 3 To change to miles, you would evaluate $340 \text{ km} \times \dfrac{0.621 \text{ mi}}{1 \text{ km}}$, so *multiply* by the value in memory. (To change miles to kilometers, *divide* by the value in memory.)

Keystrokes   **Display**

340 [×] [2nd] [RCL] [=] [=]   **211.14**

▶ **Answer** The Marine Drive is about 211 miles long.

 PRACTICE Find each unknown value to the nearest whole number.

1.

Length	
km	**mi**
127	?
?	34
1388	?

2.

Capacity	
mL	**fl oz**
500	?
?	6
1600	?

3.

Weight	
kg	**lb**
12	?
50	?
?	77

Lessons 7.4–7.7

1. OPEN-ENDED *Describe* a real-world situation in which you would express a number as a mixed number. *Describe* a situation in which you would express a number as an improper fraction. *Explain* your reasoning.

2. EXTENDED RESPONSE Sammy makes trail mix by mixing the ingredients in the recipe below.

Recipe: TRAIL MIX
$3\frac{1}{4}$ cups granola
2 cups nuts
$1\frac{1}{2}$ cups raisins

a. How many cups of trail mix does this recipe make?

b. Sammy wants to make snack bags of the mix that are $\frac{3}{4}$ cup each. How many bags can he make?

c. The recipe makes enough trail mix for 10 servings. Do each of Sammy's bags contain *less than* or *more than* one serving? *Explain* your reasoning.

3. SHORT RESPONSE Nick is planning a party. He invites 24 guests. He wants to serve at least 2 cups of fruit punch to each guest. He plans to fill a $3\frac{1}{2}$ gallon punch bowl. Will he have enough punch? *Explain* your reasoning.

4. MULTI-STEP PROBLEM Cindy is throwing a party for her soccer team at the end of the season. She buys a sub that is 5 feet long to feed the team.

a. How many inches long is the sub?

b. How many $4\frac{1}{2}$ inch subs can be cut from the original sub? *Explain*.

c. How much of the original sub is left over after it is cut into pieces?

5. GRIDDED ANSWER The area of the rectangle below is $64\frac{1}{6}$ square feet. What is the width, in feet, of the rectangle?

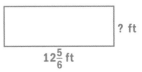

? ft
$12\frac{5}{6}$ ft

6. SHORT RESPONSE A commercial truck loaded with cargo weighs 30,128 pounds. The driver wants to cross a bridge that has a weight limit of 15 tons. Use mental math to determine whether the truck can cross the bridge. *Explain* your reasoning.

7. EXTENDED RESPONSE A movie poster is about $2\frac{1}{2}$ feet wide. The width of a wall in your bedroom is 14 feet.

a. How many movie posters can you fit across the wall without overlapping? *Explain* your reasoning.

b. Each poster costs $12. How much does it cost to put posters across your wall?

c. You decide to leave at least 4 inches of wall space on each side of the posters. How many posters can you fit across the room? If the amount of space on each side of the posters will be the same, how many inches of space will you leave on each side? *Explain*.

8. OPEN-ENDED Write a real-world problem that involves dividing a mixed number by a whole number. Then solve the problem.

REVIEW KEY VOCABULARY

- reciprocal, *p. 362*
- ounce (oz), *p. 373*
- pound (lb), *p. 373*
- ton (T), *p. 373*
- fluid ounce (fl oz), *p. 374*
- cup (c), *p. 374*
- pint (pt), *p. 374*
- quart (qt), *p. 374*
- gallon (gal), *p. 374*

VOCABULARY EXERCISES

Tell whether the statement is *true* or *false*. If false, change the statement so that it is true.

1. The number 0 has no reciprocal.

2. The reciprocal of $\frac{1}{5}$ is 5.

3. The reciprocal of $1\frac{1}{3}$ is $\frac{4}{3}$.

4. The number 1 has no reciprocal.

5. The unit *pint* is used to measure weight.

6. 1 yard = 36 inches

7. 4 quarts = 1 gallon

8. 1000 pounds = 1 ton

REVIEW EXAMPLES AND EXERCISES

7.1 Multiplying Fractions and Whole Numbers

pp. 341–345

EXAMPLE

$3 \times \frac{5}{9} = \frac{3 \times 5}{9}$ **Multiply the numerator by the whole number.**

$= \frac{15}{9}$

$= \frac{5}{3}$, or $1\frac{2}{3}$ **Simplify.**

EXERCISES

Find the product.

**SEE EXAMPLES
1, 2, 3, AND 4**
on pp. 341–343
for Exs. 9–17

9. $\frac{1}{6} \times 19$

10. $\frac{3}{4} \times 14$

11. $15 \times \frac{1}{7}$

12. $30 \times \frac{3}{8}$

Estimate the product. Use compatible whole numbers.

13. $11 \times \frac{8}{9}$

14. $\frac{1}{12} \times 22$

15. $41 \times \frac{5}{6}$

16. $\frac{2}{15} \times 77$

17. Restaurant Supplies A restaurant manager wants to put 30 boxes of pasta on a shelf in the kitchen. Each box of pasta is $\frac{7}{8}$ inch wide. Estimate the width of the shelf the manager needs to fit the boxes.

Multiplying Fractions *pp. 348–353*

EXAMPLE

Evaluate the expression $\frac{5}{7}y$ when $y = \frac{3}{8}$.

$\frac{5}{7}y = \frac{5}{7} \times \frac{3}{8}$ Substitute $\frac{3}{8}$ for y.

$= \frac{5 \times 3}{7 \times 8}$ Use the rule for multiplying fractions.

$= \frac{15}{56}$ Multiply. The product is in simplest form.

EXERCISES

Find the product.

SEE EXAMPLES 2, 3, 4, AND 5
on pp. 349–350
for Exs. 18–29

18. $\frac{1}{2} \times \frac{5}{6}$ **19.** $\frac{4}{7} \times \frac{8}{9}$ **20.** $\frac{2}{5} \times \frac{4}{5}$ **21.** $\frac{2}{3} \times \frac{1}{4}$

22. $\frac{7}{12} \times \frac{4}{5}$ **23.** $\frac{3}{22} \times \frac{11}{18}$ **24.** $\frac{2}{3} \times \frac{1}{4} \times \frac{3}{8}$ **25.** $\frac{3}{5} \times \frac{5}{6} \times \frac{5}{12}$

Evaluate the expression when $x = \frac{3}{4}$.

26. $\frac{8}{9}x$ **27.** $\frac{4}{15}x$ **28.** $\frac{7}{12}x$ **29.** $\frac{12}{23}x$

Multiplying Mixed Numbers *pp. 354–359*

EXAMPLE

$2\frac{2}{9} \times 4\frac{4}{5} = \frac{20}{9} \times \frac{24}{5}$ Write $2\frac{2}{9}$ and $4\frac{4}{5}$ as improper fractions.

$= \frac{\overset{4}{\cancel{20}} \times \overset{8}{\cancel{24}}}{\underset{3}{\cancel{9}} \times \underset{1}{\cancel{5}}}$ Use the rule for multiplying fractions. Divide out common factors.

$= \frac{32}{3}$, or $10\frac{2}{3}$ Multiply. Write the answer in simplest form.

EXERCISES

Find the product.

SEE EXAMPLES 1, 2, AND 3
on pp. 354–355
for Exs. 30–34

30. $2 \times 5\frac{1}{6}$ **31.** $6\frac{2}{5} \times \frac{3}{16}$ **32.** $2\frac{1}{4} \times 1\frac{2}{3}$ **33.** $3\frac{2}{7} \times 4\frac{2}{3}$

34. Billboards A billboard measures $4\frac{2}{3}$ yards by 16 yards. What is the area of the billboard?

7.4 Dividing Fractions

pp. 362–366

EXAMPLE

$$\frac{4}{9} \div \frac{5}{6} = \frac{4}{9} \times \frac{6}{5} \qquad \text{Multiply by the reciprocal of the divisor.}$$

$$= \frac{4 \times \overset{2}{\cancel{6}}}{\underset{3}{\cancel{9}} \times 5} \qquad \text{Use the rule for multiplying fractions.}$$
Divide out common factor.

$$= \frac{8}{15} \qquad \text{Multiply.}$$

EXERCISES

Find the quotient.

SEE EXAMPLES 2 AND 3
on p. 363
for Exs. 35–43

35. $\frac{1}{6} \div \frac{9}{10}$ **36.** $\frac{4}{7} \div \frac{1}{5}$ **37.** $\frac{7}{8} \div \frac{3}{4}$ **38.** $\frac{1}{2} \div \frac{7}{12}$

39. $8 \div \frac{1}{4}$ **40.** $\frac{5}{8} \div 15$ **41.** $\frac{2}{9} \div 6$ **42.** $14 \div \frac{4}{7}$

43. Tutoring You earn \$15 for tutoring Spanish for $\frac{3}{4}$ hour. What is your hourly rate of pay?

7.5 Dividing Mixed Numbers

pp. 367–372

EXAMPLE

$$7 \div 4\frac{2}{3} = \frac{7}{1} \div \frac{14}{3} \qquad \text{Write 7 and } 4\frac{2}{3} \text{ as improper fractions.}$$

$$= \frac{7}{1} \times \frac{3}{14} \qquad \text{Multiply by the reciprocal of the divisor.}$$

$$= \frac{\overset{1}{\cancel{7}} \times 3}{1 \times \underset{2}{\cancel{14}}} \qquad \text{Use the rule for multiplying fractions.}$$
Divide out common factor.

$$= \frac{3}{2}, \text{ or } 1\frac{1}{2} \qquad \text{Multiply.}$$

EXERCISES

Find the quotient. Use estimation to check your answer.

SEE EXAMPLES 1 AND 2
on pp. 367–368
for Exs. 44–48

44. $5\frac{5}{6} \div \frac{7}{10}$ **45.** $1\frac{4}{7} \div 5$ **46.** $\frac{3}{8} \div 2\frac{2}{5}$ **47.** $6\frac{3}{4} \div 1\frac{3}{4}$

48. Snacks A camp counselor has $4\frac{1}{3}$ cups of dried fruit to split equally among 13 campers. How much dried fruit does each camper get?

7.6 Weight and Capacity in Customary Units

pp. 373–377

EXAMPLE

Choose an appropriate customary unit to measure the item.

a. weight of a stapler

▶ **Answer** A stapler is heavier than a slice of bread and lighter than a soccer ball. So, you can use *ounces* to measure its weight.

b. capacity of a large bucket

▶ **Answer** A large bucket can hold more than a gallon of milk. So, you can use *gallons* to measure its capacity.

EXERCISES

Choose an appropriate customary unit to measure the item.

SEE EXAMPLES 1, 2, AND 3 on pp. 373–374 for Exs. 49–56

49. weight of a television set

50. capacity of a bottle of glue

51. capacity of a gasoline can

52. weight of a wallet

Tell whether the measurement is a *weight*, a *capacity*, or a *length*.

53. 9 pints

54. 10 inches

55. 7 ounces

56. 19 pounds

7.7 Changing Customary Units

pp. 378–384

EXAMPLE

Change $3\frac{1}{4}$ tons to pounds.

$$3\frac{1}{4}\,T = \frac{13\,T}{4} = \frac{13\,T}{4} \times \frac{2000\,lb}{1\,T} = \frac{13\,\cancel{T} \times \overset{500}{\cancel{2000}}\,lb}{\underset{1}{\cancel{4}} \times 1\,\cancel{T}} = 6500\,lb$$

EXERCISES

Copy and complete the statement.

SEE EXAMPLES 1, 2, 3, AND 4 on p. 378–379 for Exs. 57–67

57. 2 yd 14 in. = __?__ in.

58. 48 fl oz = __?__ qt

59. 8 gal 3 qt = __?__ qt

60. $2\frac{3}{4}$ lb = __?__ oz

61. $9\frac{1}{2}$ gal = __?__ c

62. 6600 yd = __?__ mi

63. 3 ft 7 in. = __?__ in.

64. 54 oz = __?__ lb

65. 12 pt 1 c = __?__ c

66. Reptiles A python at the zoo is 138 inches long. How many feet are in 138 inches? How many yards are in 138 inches?

67. Drinks A pitcher holds $1\frac{2}{3}$ quarts. If a glass of juice holds $\frac{2}{3}$ cup, how many glasses of juice can be poured from the pitcher?

Find the product.

1. $10 \times \frac{4}{15}$

2. $\frac{1}{5} \times \frac{2}{9}$

3. $\frac{5}{12} \times \frac{3}{7}$

4. $\frac{1}{6} \times \frac{3}{8} \times \frac{2}{5}$

5. $3\frac{1}{4} \times 2$

6. $4\frac{5}{8} \times \frac{8}{11}$

7. $1\frac{2}{9} \times 1\frac{7}{11}$

8. $6 \times 7\frac{2}{3}$

Estimate the product. Use compatible whole numbers.

9. $\frac{3}{13} \times 62$

10. $\frac{9}{11} \times 27$

11. $43 \times \frac{7}{8}$

12. $74 \times \frac{1}{5}$

Evaluate the expression when $x = \frac{2}{7}$ and $y = \frac{1}{4}$.

13. $\frac{1}{8}x$

14. $\frac{5}{6}x$

15. $\frac{5}{12}y$

16. xy

Find the quotient.

17. $\frac{5}{6} \div \frac{4}{9}$

18. $\frac{1}{7} \div \frac{7}{12}$

19. $8 \div \frac{2}{5}$

20. $\frac{3}{10} \div 9$

21. $9\frac{1}{2} \div 3\frac{1}{8}$

22. $4\frac{1}{5} \div 1\frac{1}{10}$

23. $7\frac{1}{6} \div 2\frac{1}{3}$

24. $6\frac{1}{8} \div \frac{7}{16}$

25. $2\frac{5}{8} \div 7$

26. $6\frac{3}{5} \div \frac{3}{4}$

27. $\frac{1}{12} \div 3\frac{1}{4}$

28. $10\frac{1}{2} \div 2\frac{3}{4}$

Choose an appropriate customary unit to measure the item.

29. weight of a tow truck

30. weight of an earring

31. capacity of a cereal bowl

Copy and complete the statement.

32. 8 yd = __?__ ft

33. $7\frac{1}{2}$ gal = __?__ pt

34. 2 c 3 fl oz = __?__ fl oz

35. 5000 lb = __?__ T

36. 6 ft 9 in. = __?__ in.

37. 5 lb 3 oz = __?__ oz

38. **TRAINS** A train has 50 cars. Three fifths of the cars are carrying grain. How many cars are carrying grain?

39. **ART SUPPLIES** A roll of newsprint is 100 feet long. How many pieces of newsprint that are $5\frac{1}{2}$ feet long can you cut from the roll?

MUSIC Use the instruments shown.

40. How many times as long as a flute is an English horn?

41. Change each length to inches.

42. Copy and complete the statement using *ounces*, *pounds*, or *tons*: A flute weighs about $15\frac{1}{2}$ __?__ .

English Horn

$2\frac{5}{8}$ ft

Flute

$2\frac{1}{4}$ ft

MULTIPLE CHOICE QUESTIONS

If you have difficulty solving a multiple choice problem directly, you may be able to eliminate incorrect answer choices to obtain the correct answer.

PROBLEM 1

Rectangle A is $2\frac{1}{3}$ feet long and $1\frac{1}{2}$ feet wide. The length and width of rectangle B are twice the length and width of rectangle A. How do the areas of rectangle A and rectangle B compare?

(A) The area of rectangle B is twice the area of rectangle A.

(B) The area of rectangle A is twice the area of rectangle B.

(C) The area of rectangle B is 4 times the area of rectangle A.

(D) The area of rectangle A is 4 times the area of rectangle B.

METHOD 1

SOLVE DIRECTLY Use the area formula, $A = lw$ and the information in the problem to find the relationship between the areas of rectangle A and rectangle B.

Area of A = Length of A × Width of A

$$= 2\frac{1}{3} \text{ ft} \times 1\frac{1}{2} \text{ ft}$$

$$= \frac{7}{3} \text{ ft} \times \frac{3}{2} \text{ ft}$$

$$= \frac{7}{2} \text{ ft}^2, \text{ or } 3\frac{1}{2} \text{ ft}^2$$

Area of B = Length of B × Width of B

$$= (2 \times \text{Length of A}) \times (2 \times \text{Width of A})$$

$$= \left(2 \times 2\frac{1}{3} \text{ ft}\right) \times \left(2 \times 1\frac{1}{2} \text{ ft}\right)$$

$$= \left(2 \times \frac{7}{3} \text{ ft}\right) \times \left(2 \times \frac{3}{2} \text{ ft}\right)$$

$$= \frac{14}{3} \text{ ft} \times 3 \text{ ft}$$

$$= 14 \text{ ft}^2$$

The area of rectangle B is $14 \div 3\frac{1}{2}$, or 4 times the area of rectangle A.

The correct answer is C. (A) (B) (C) (D)

METHOD 2

ELIMINATE CHOICES In some multiple choice questions, you can identify the answer choices that can be eliminated.

The area of rectangle B must be greater than the area of rectangle A. So you can eliminate choices B and D.

Then you can use estimation to determine which of the remaining choices is reasonable.

Area of A $= 2\frac{1}{3} \text{ ft} \times 1\frac{1}{2} \text{ ft}$

$$\approx 2 \text{ ft} \times 2 \text{ ft}$$

$$= 4 \text{ ft}^2$$

Area of B $= \left(2 \times 2\frac{1}{3} \text{ ft}\right) \times \left(2 \times 1\frac{1}{2} \text{ ft}\right)$

$$\approx (2 \times 2 \text{ ft}) \times (2 \times 2 \text{ ft})$$

$$= 4 \text{ ft} \times 4 \text{ ft}$$

$$= 16 \text{ ft}^2$$

The area of rectangle B is about 4 times the area of rectangle A.

The correct answer is C. (A) (B) (C) (D)

PROBLEM 2

A recipe for Key lime cake calls for $1\frac{1}{2}$ cups of flour. You have a 5 pound bag of flour. There are $3\frac{1}{2}$ cups of flour in one pound of flour. How many Key lime cakes can you make?

Ⓐ 2 cakes   **Ⓑ** 11 cakes   **Ⓒ** $11\frac{2}{3}$ cakes   **Ⓓ** $26\frac{1}{2}$ cakes

METHOD 1

SOLVE DIRECTLY The number of cakes you can make is the number of cups of flour in a 5 pound bag divided by the number of cups of flour in each cake.

STEP 1 **Find** the number of cups in a 5 pound bag.

$$5 \times 3\frac{1}{2} = \frac{5}{1} \times \frac{7}{2} = \frac{35}{2} = 17\frac{1}{2}$$

STEP 2 **Find** the number of cakes you can make.

$$17\frac{1}{2} \div 1\frac{1}{2} = \frac{35}{2} \times \frac{2}{3} = \frac{35}{3} = 11\frac{2}{3}$$

Because it is impossible to make a fraction of a cake, you can make at most 11 cakes.

The correct answer is B. Ⓐ **Ⓑ** Ⓒ Ⓓ

METHOD 2

ELIMINATE CHOICES In some multiple choice questions, you can identify the answer choices that can be eliminated.

It is impossible to make a fraction of a cake, so you can immediately eliminate choices C and D.

Then you can use estimation to determine whether any of the remaining choices are unreasonable.

There are about 5×4, or 20 cups of flour in a 5 pound bag of flour. So, you can make about $20 \div 2$, or 10 cakes. You can eliminate choice A, because an estimate of 2 cakes is too low.

The only remaining choice is B.

The correct answer is B. Ⓐ **Ⓑ** Ⓒ Ⓓ

PRACTICE

Explain why you can eliminate the highlighted answer choice.

1. What is the width of a rectangle that has a length of $6\frac{3}{4}$ meters and an area of 54 square meters?

   Ⓐ 8 m   ✗**Ⓑ 8 m²**   **Ⓒ** $364\frac{1}{2}$ m   **Ⓓ** $364\frac{1}{2}$ m²

2. Which measurement could be the weight of an apple?

   Ⓐ 4 oz   ✗**Ⓑ 4 qt**   **Ⓒ** 4 lb   **Ⓓ** 4 T

3. A recipe calls for $1\frac{3}{4}$ cups of milk. How many cups of milk are needed to double the recipe?

   ✗**Ⓐ $\frac{7}{8}$ cup**   **Ⓑ** $2\frac{3}{4}$ cups   **Ⓒ** $3\frac{1}{2}$ cups   **Ⓓ** 4 cups

MULTIPLE CHOICE

1. The weight of a hockey puck is $5\frac{1}{2}$ ounces. The weight of a soccer ball is 1 pound. The weight of 4 soccer balls is equal to the weight of about how many hockey pucks?

(A) 3 pucks   (B) 5 pucks

(C) 12 pucks   (D) 22 pucks

2. How many inches of ribbon are left over if you cut $\frac{1}{6}$ yard pieces of ribbon from $\frac{3}{4}$ yard of ribbon?

(A) $\frac{1}{2}$ inch   (B) 3 inches

(D) $4\frac{1}{2}$ inches   (D) 5 inches

3. A recipe for lemonade is shown. You need to make $1\frac{1}{2}$ times the recipe. How many more cups of water than cups of lemon juice do you need?

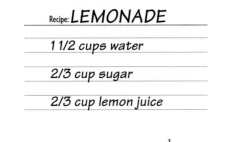

Recipe: **LEMONADE**

1 1/2 cups water

2/3 cup sugar

2/3 cup lemon juice

(A) 1 cup   (B) $1\frac{1}{4}$ cups

(C) $2\frac{1}{4}$ cups   (D) $3\frac{1}{4}$ cups

4. The capacity of an aquarium is 40 times the capacity of a fish bowl. If the capacity of the aquarium is 60 gallons, what is the capacity of the fish bowl?

(A) $1\frac{1}{2}$ quarts   (B) $2\frac{2}{3}$ quarts

(C) 6 quarts   (D) 20 quarts

5. The dimensions of a rectangular garden bed are shown below. You want to give $\frac{1}{6}$ square yard of space for each plant in the bed. How many plants will the bed contain?

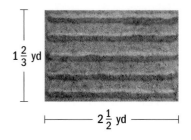

$1\frac{2}{3}$ yd

$2\frac{1}{2}$ yd

(A) $4\frac{1}{6}$ plants   (B) $8\frac{1}{3}$ plants

(C) 25 plants   (D) 50 plants

6. A magic show is scheduled to last $2\frac{3}{4}$ hours and includes five 1 minute breaks. Each of the 6 magicians in the show is given the same amount of performing time. How much time does each magician have?

(A) $\frac{7}{18}$ hour   (B) $\frac{4}{9}$ hour

(C) $\frac{1}{2}$ hour   (D) $\frac{5}{6}$ hour

7. A sparrow lands on a tree branch that is 17 feet 7 inches above the ground. A cardinal sits on a branch 11 feet 9 inches above the sparrow. How far above the ground is the cardinal?

(A) 5 ft 10 in.   (B) 28 ft 4 in.

(C) 29 ft 4 in.   (D) 29 ft 6 in.

8. You practice dribbling a basketball for $\frac{3}{4}$ hour each day for the first 3 days of the week and $\frac{2}{3}$ hour for each of the other days of the week. How many hours do you practice dribbling during the week?

(A) $1\frac{5}{12}$ hours   (B) $2\frac{1}{2}$ hours

(C) $4\frac{11}{12}$ hours   (D) 7 hours

GRIDDED ANSWER

9. You cut the maximum possible number of $2\frac{1}{3}$ foot wood segments from an 8 foot board. How many feet of wood are leftover?

10. Ralph makes $2\frac{1}{2}$ batches of oatmeal cookies. Each batch makes 24 cookies. Ralph gives away $\frac{1}{4}$ of the cookies to his class at school and $\frac{2}{5}$ of the remaining cookies to his bus driver. How many cookies does Ralph have left?

11. A rectangular cake is $12\frac{1}{2}$ inches by 15 inches. You want to cut the cake into square pieces that are $2\frac{1}{2}$ inches by $2\frac{1}{2}$ inches. How many square pieces can you cut?

SHORT RESPONSE

12. A total of 144 sixth grade students at a middle school voted on where to go for their class trip. The circle graph shows the results. How many more votes were for the science museum than for the amusement park? *Explain* how you found your answer.

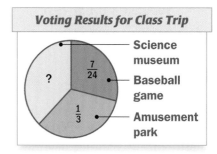

Voting Results for Class Trip

Science museum — $\frac{7}{24}$ — Baseball game

? — $\frac{1}{3}$ — Amusement park

13. A slice of bread weighs one ounce. Will two quarter pound hamburger patties placed between two slices of bread weigh *less than* or *more than* one pound? *Explain*.

EXTENDED RESPONSE

14. A quilt pattern uses squares with sides that are each $4\frac{1}{2}$ inches long, not including seams. Sue wants to reduce each side to $\frac{2}{3}$ of the length on the pattern. What are the dimensions of a reduced square? How many reduced squares does she need to sew together to make a 1 foot by 1 foot square? *Explain* how you found your answers.

15. You are planning to make a bookcase with two identical shelves using the dimensions shown. The wood that you will use to make the bookcase is $\frac{3}{4}$ inch thick. You have a set of 32 encyclopedias. Each encyclopedia is $1\frac{1}{2}$ inches thick, 9 inches wide, and 11 inches tall.

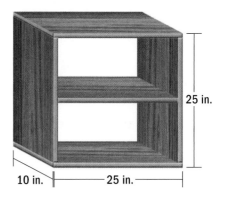

25 in.

10 in. 25 in.

   a. What are the length and height of each shelf, not including the wood?

   b. How many encyclopedias can the bookshelf hold on both shelves? *Explain* how you got your answer.

   c. *Describe* how you would change the dimensions of the bookcase so that the bookcase can hold all of the encyclopedias. *Justify* your answer.

Find the sum, difference, product, or quotient.

1. $79 - 22$ *(p. 3)*   **2.** $86 + 271$ *(p. 3)*   **3.** 21×42 *(p. 3)*

4. $244 \div 4$ *(p. 3)*   **5.** $9.6 - 3.5$ *(p. 148)*   **6.** $13.2 + 4.9$ *(p. 148)*

7. 7×4.5 *(p. 169)*   **8.** 2.3×6 *(p. 169)*   **9.** $16.2 \div 9$ *(p. 186)*

10. 1.23×0.1 *(p. 193)*   **11.** $10.12 \div 4.6$ *(p. 198)*   **12.** $\frac{3}{11} + \frac{7}{11}$ *(p. 295)*

13. $\frac{1}{3} - \frac{1}{6}$ *(p. 302)*   **14.** $2\frac{1}{4} + 11\frac{1}{8}$ *(p. 309)*   **15.** $10 - 4\frac{1}{4}$ *(p. 316)*

16. $4\frac{3}{7} - 1\frac{4}{7}$ *(p. 316)*   **17.** $\frac{4}{5} \times 8$ *(p. 341)*   **18.** $\frac{3}{5} \times \frac{7}{9}$ *(p. 348)*

19. $3\frac{5}{8} \times \frac{6}{11}$ *(p. 354)*   **20.** $\frac{15}{16} \div \frac{5}{24}$ *(p. 362)*   **21.** $10\frac{1}{2} \div 2\frac{1}{2}$ *(p. 367)*

Graph the point on the same coordinate grid. *(p. 88)*

22. $(3, 1)$ **23.** $(8, 0)$ **24.** $(5, 5)$ **25.** $(0, 1)$

Use front-end estimation to estimate the sum. *(p. 143)*

26. $2.4 + 8.1 + 6.2$ **27.** $9.4 + 6.1 + 8.7 + 10.9$

Evaluate the expression when $x = 0.35$ and $y = 35$. *(p. 148)*

28. $7 - 8x$ **29.** $8y \div 6$ **30.** $x + 2.74$ **31.** $y - 9x$

Find the GCF of the numbers. *(p. 236)*

32. 4, 12   **33.** 6, 45   **34.** 50, 75   **35.** 6, 9, 24

Order the numbers from least to greatest. *(p. 254)*

36. $\frac{7}{12}, \frac{11}{18}, \frac{2}{3}, \frac{5}{9}$ **37.** $\frac{2}{5}, \frac{4}{15}, \frac{3}{20}, \frac{2}{9}$

Find the elapsed time. *(p. 322)*

38. 1:30 P.M. to 7:15 P.M.   **39.** 5:20 A.M. to 3:45 P.M.

Find the area of the rectangle described. *(p. 354)*

40. length $= 2\frac{1}{6}$ ft, width $= \frac{1}{2}$ ft   **41.** length $= 6\frac{1}{2}$ in., width $= 7\frac{3}{4}$ in.

Copy and complete the statement.

42. $1.2 \text{ g} = \underline{\ ?\ } \text{ mg}$ *(p. 207)*   **43.** $35 \text{ km} = \underline{\ ?\ } \text{ m}$ *(p. 207)*   **44.** $200 \text{ L} = \underline{\ ?\ } \text{ mL}$ *(p. 207)*

45. $12 \text{ yd} = \underline{\ ?\ } \text{ ft}$ *(p. 378)*   **46.** $6\frac{1}{2} \text{ gal} = \underline{\ ?\ } \text{ pt}$ *(p. 378)*   **47.** $3 \text{ c } 4 \text{ fl oz} = \underline{\ ?\ } \text{ fl oz}$ *(p. 378)*

48. DELIVERY SERVICE You need to deliver 75 plants for a florist. So far, you have delivered 27 plants. Solve the equation $x + 27 = 75$ to find how many more plants you need to deliver. *(p. 34)*

49. SCALE DRAWINGS Carmela makes a scale drawing of a room. The room is 33 feet long. She uses a scale of 2 in. : 3 ft. How long is the room on her drawing? *(p. 72)*

BAGELS The circle graph shows the number of bagels sold at a bakery in one day. *(p. 94)*

Types of Bagels Sold

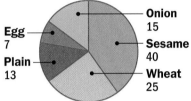

50. What type of bagel was most popular?

51. Predict the number of sesame bagels sold when the bakery sells a total of 300 bagels.

52. HOCKEY The save percentages of four goalies in a hockey league are 0.898, 0.936, 0.983, and 0.832. Write the save percentages in order from least to greatest. *(p. 130)*

53. AVERAGE RATES You bike 41.4 miles in 4.5 hours. What is the average rate in miles per hour? *(p. 198)*

54. FOOTBALL A total of 70 students signed up to play in a football league. The league coordinator is dividing the students into teams of equal size. Can the coordinator evenly divide the students into 5 teams? 6 teams? *(p. 230)*

55. HAMBURGERS Hamburgers come in boxes of 20 while hamburger rolls come in packages of 8. What is the least number of hamburgers that you can purchase so that each has a roll and there are no rolls or burgers leftover. *(p. 250)*

56. BIKE RELAY Clint, Chris, and Rebecca are competing in a three part bike relay race. Clint rode $\frac{2}{3}$ mile, Chris rode $\frac{5}{6}$ mile, and Rebecca rode the last $\frac{3}{5}$ mile. How long is the bike relay race? *(p. 302)*

57. BASS FISHING The winner of a bass fishing contest caught 14 pounds of bass. The runner-up caught $12\frac{11}{16}$ pounds of bass. How many more pounds did the winner catch than the runner-up? *(p. 316)*

58. COSTUMES You buy 10 yards of fabric to make costumes. Each costume needs $3\frac{5}{8}$ yards of fabric. Do you have enough fabric to make 3 costumes? *Explain* your reasoning. *(p. 367)*

59. BAKING You need $2\frac{1}{2}$ cups of flour, but you can find only the $\frac{1}{4}$ cup measuring cup. How many $\frac{1}{4}$ cups of flour do you need? *(p. 378)*

8 Ratio, Proportion, and Percent

Animated Math *at classzone.com*

Get-Ready Games

Review Prerequisite Skills by playing *Number Challenge.*

Skill Focus: Comparing fractions and decimals

NUMBER CHALLENGE

MATERIALS

- 1 deck of *Number Challenge* cards

HOW TO PLAY
Deal half the cards to each player. Place your cards face down in front of you in a pile. On each turn, follow the steps on the next page.

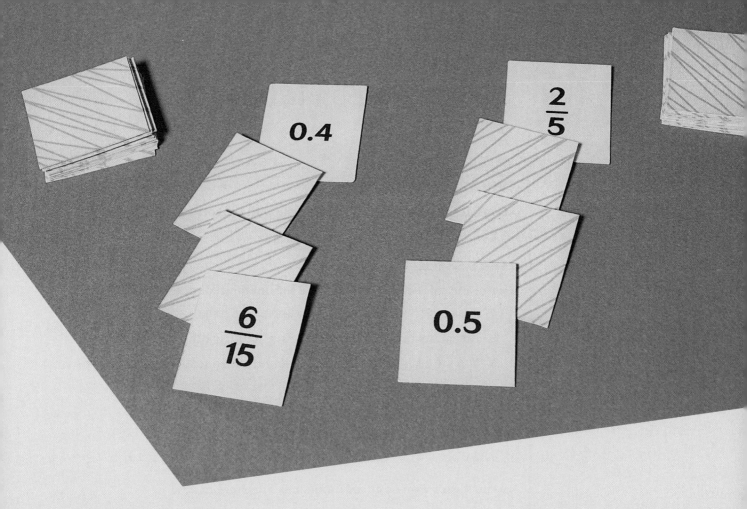

 COMPARE Turn over the top cards from your piles. The player with the greater number collects the cards and puts them on the bottom of his or her pile.

 **CHALLENGE** If the two cards have the same value, each player places two new cards face down on the cards played in Step 1. Then repeat Step 1.

HOW TO WIN Collect all the cards, or collect the greater number of cards after a set period of time.

Stop and Think

1. **CRITICAL THINKING** Which cards have the greatest value in this game? If you have all of these cards, is there any way you can lose?

2. **EXTENSION** Design six new cards to add to the deck. The cards may be either decimals or fractions, but make sure that each card has a matching card with an equivalent number on it.

Review Prerequisite Skills

REVIEW WORDS
• **variable,** *p. 29*
• **equation,** *p. 34*
• **solution,** *p. 34*
• **area,** *p. 67*
• **scale drawing,** *p. 72*
• **scale,** *p. 72*
• **decimal,** *p. 120*
• **fraction,** *p. 243*
• **simplest form,** *p. 244*

VOCABULARY CHECK

Consider $x + 3 = 5$. Match the example with the correct word at the left.

1. 2　　　　　　　　　　**2.** $x + 3 = 5$　　　　　　　**3.** x

SKILL CHECK

Write and solve an equation to find the unknown dimension. *(p. 66)*

4. Area of rectangle = 12 in.^{2}, width = 3 in., length = ___?___

5. Area of rectangle = 96 m^2, length = 12 m, width = ___?___

6. You are building a model playground with a scale of 1 in. : 2 ft. The slide in your model is 6 inches long. How long is the actual slide? *(p. 72)*

Find the product. Simplify if possible. *(pp. 169, 341)*

7. 2.61×4　　　**8.** 6.78×9　　　**9.** $\dfrac{3}{8} \times 24$　　　**10.** $9 \times \dfrac{4}{3}$

Write the fraction or mixed number as a decimal. *(p. 271)*

11. $\dfrac{3}{4}$　　　　**12.** $\dfrac{8}{9}$　　　　**13.** $3\dfrac{1}{5}$　　　　**14.** $2\dfrac{1}{8}$

@HomeTutor　Prerequisite skills practice at classzone.com

Notetaking Skills　　Drawing a Concept Map

In each chapter you will learn a new notetaking skill. In Chapter 8 you will apply the strategy of drawing a concept map to Example 2 on p. 425.

You can draw a diagram called a *concept map* to show connections among key ideas. Here is a concept map showing some forms of numbers.

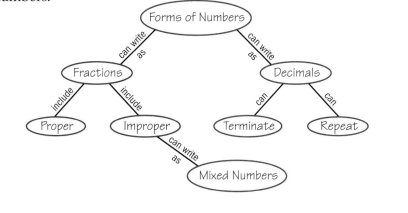

INVESTIGATION

Use before Lesson 8.1

GOAL
Compare the areas of figures on a geoboard.

MATERIALS
• geoboard
• colored rubber bands

8.1 Comparing Areas

EXPLORE **Compare areas of figures using a geoboard.**

Use a geoboard that is 5 pegs long on each side. The diagram at the right shows a *unit square*.

a unit square

STEP 1

Use a blue rubber band to make a square around the entire geoboard.

STEP 2

Use a red rubber band to make a square that is 3 pegs on each side.

STEP 3

Use the verbal model. Write a fraction that compares the number of unit squares in the two figures.

$$\frac{\text{Unit squares in red square}}{\text{Unit squares in blue square}} = \frac{?}{?}$$

PRACTICE **Add the rectangle to your geoboard from Steps 1 and 2. Use the verbal model to write a fraction comparing the number of unit squares.**

1. green rectangle: 3 pegs by 2 pegs

   $$\frac{\text{Unit squares in green rectangle}}{\text{Unit squares in red square}} = \frac{?}{?}$$

2. purple rectangle: 4 pegs by 3 pegs

   $$\frac{\text{Unit squares in purple rectangle}}{\text{Unit squares in blue square}} = \frac{?}{?}$$

DRAW CONCLUSIONS

3. **REASONING** *Compare* the number of unit squares in the blue square to the number of unit squares in the red square. How many times the area of the red square is the area of the blue square? What does this tell you about the area of the red square compared to the area of the blue square?

4. **REASONING** When you compare a smaller area to a larger area, is the ratio a fraction that is *less than* one or *greater than* one? How does your answer change if you are comparing a larger area to a smaller area? *Explain* your reasoning.

8.1 Ratios

Before You wrote fractions and equivalent fractions.

Now You'll write ratios and equivalent ratios.

Why? So you can compare numbers of instruments, as in Example 1.

KEY VOCABULARY

• **ratio**, *p. 402*

• **equivalent ratio**, *p. 403*

Music In some school orchestras, all of the instruments are stringed: violins, violas, cellos, and double basses. How can you compare the numbers of instruments in the orchestra?

One way to compare the numbers of instruments is to use a *ratio*. The **ratio** of a number *a* to a nonzero number *b* is the quotient when *a* is divided by *b*. You can write the ratio of *a* to *b* as $\frac{a}{b}$, as $a : b$, or as "*a* to *b*."

18 violins 8 violas 6 cellos 3 double basses

EXAMPLE 1 Writing a Ratio in Different Ways

In the orchestra shown above, 8 of the 35 instruments are violas. The ratio of the number of violas to the total number of instruments, $\frac{\text{Violas}}{\text{Total instruments}}$, can be written as $\frac{8}{35}$, as 8 : 35, or as 8 to 35.

EXAMPLE 2 Writing Ratios in Simplest Form

SIMPLIFY RATIOS

It is good practice to write ratios in simplest form. When rewriting a ratio such as "3 to 6" in fraction form, write $\frac{1}{2}$.

Use the diagram above. Write the ratio of the number of double basses to the number of cellos in simplest form.

$$\frac{\text{Double basses}}{\text{Cellos}} = \frac{3}{6} = \frac{1 \times \overset{1}{\cancel{3}}}{2 \times \underset{1}{\cancel{3}}} = \frac{1}{2}$$

▸**Answer** The ratio is $\frac{1}{2}$, or 1 to 2, so there is 1 double bass for every 2 cellos.

✓ **GUIDED PRACTICE** for Examples 1 and 2

In Exercises 1 and 2, write the ratio in three ways.

1. violins to total instruments   2. violas to double basses

3. Write the ratio of cellos to violins in simplest form.

EQUIVALENT FRACTIONS

Need help with equivalent fractions? See p. 243.

Writing Equivalent Ratios You can multiply or divide the numerator and denominator of a ratio by the same nonzero number to get an **equivalent ratio.**

EXAMPLE 3 Writing an Equivalent Ratio

Complete the statement $\frac{5}{15} = \frac{?}{60}$ to write equivalent ratios.

SOLUTION

Think about the denominators of the two fractions.

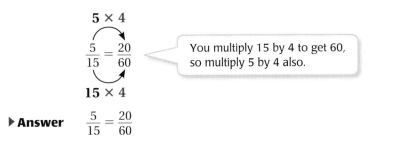

$$5 \times 4$$
$$\frac{5}{15} = \frac{20}{60}$$
$$15 \times 4$$

You multiply 15 by 4 to get 60, so multiply 5 by 4 also.

▶ **Answer** $\frac{5}{15} = \frac{20}{60}$

Animated **Math**
at classzone.com

Writing Ratios as Decimals Writing ratios as decimals may make it easier to compare the ratios.

EXAMPLE 4 Comparing Ratios Using Decimals

Football Sofia completes $\frac{3}{4}$ of her passes. Mike completes 7 out of every 10 passes. Who has the better record?

SOLUTION

Write each ratio as a decimal. Then compare the decimals.

Sofia: $\frac{3}{4} = 0.75$ **Mike:** 7 out of 10 $= \frac{7}{10} = 0.7$

▶ **Answer** Because $0.75 > 0.7$, Sofia has the better record.

ANOTHER WAY

You can also solve the problem by writing the ratios as fractions, rewriting the fractions using the LCD, and comparing the fractions.

✓ **GUIDED PRACTICE**   for Examples 3 and 4

Copy and complete the statement.

4. $\frac{2}{3} = \frac{?}{15}$ **5.** $\frac{7}{?} = \frac{35}{50}$ **6.** $\frac{20}{32} = \frac{5}{?}$

Copy and complete the statement using <, >, or =.

7. $\frac{5}{20}$? $\frac{4}{10}$ **8.** $\frac{3}{5}$? 18 out of 30   **9.** $2 : 4$? $7 : 35$

8.1 EXERCISES

SKILL PRACTICE

VOCABULARY Copy and complete the statement

1. A comparison of two numbers using division is a(n) __?__ .

2. If you multiply or divide the numerator and denominator of a ratio by the same nonzero number, you get a(n) __?__ .

SEE EXAMPLE 1
on p. 402
for Exs. 3–4

3. WRITING RATIOS Write the ratio 13 to 20 in two other ways.

4. ★ **MULTIPLE CHOICE** Which is *not* a ratio comparing 3 to 10?

    A 3 to 10   **B** $\frac{3}{10}$ **C** 3 : 10   **D** 10 to 3

SEE EXAMPLE 2
on p. 402
for Exs. 5–8

WRITING IN SIMPLEST FORM Write the ratio in simplest form.

5. $\frac{6}{15}$ **6.** $\frac{8}{20}$ **7.** $\frac{20}{75}$ **8.** $\frac{12}{3}$

SEE EXAMPLE 3
on p. 403
for Exs. 9–22

9. ★ **MULTIPLE CHOICE** Which ratio is equivalent to 2 : 5?

    A 7 : 15   **B** 3 : 6   **C** 6 : 15   **D** 12 : 45

WRITING EQUIVALENT RATIOS Copy and complete the statement.

10. $\frac{4}{5} = \frac{?}{10}$ **11.** $\frac{?}{7} = \frac{6}{21}$ **12.** $\frac{5}{6} = \frac{15}{?}$ **13.** $\frac{24}{?} = \frac{8}{9}$

14. $\frac{3}{8} = \frac{?}{24}$ **15.** $\frac{7}{10} = \frac{14}{?}$ **16.** $\frac{2}{?} = \frac{22}{33}$ **17.** $\frac{?}{2} = \frac{5}{10}$

18. $\frac{27}{?} = \frac{9}{14}$ **19.** $\frac{?}{15} = \frac{20}{75}$ **20.** $\frac{11}{12} = \frac{?}{36}$ **21.** $\frac{5}{8} = \frac{45}{?}$

22. ERROR ANALYSIS Describe and correct the error made in writing an equivalent ratio.

$$\frac{8}{9} = \frac{?}{18} \longrightarrow \frac{8}{9} = \frac{17}{18} \quad ✗$$
(+9 to numerator, +9 to denominator)

GEOMETRY Find the ratio of the perimeter of the shaded region to the perimeter of the unshaded region.

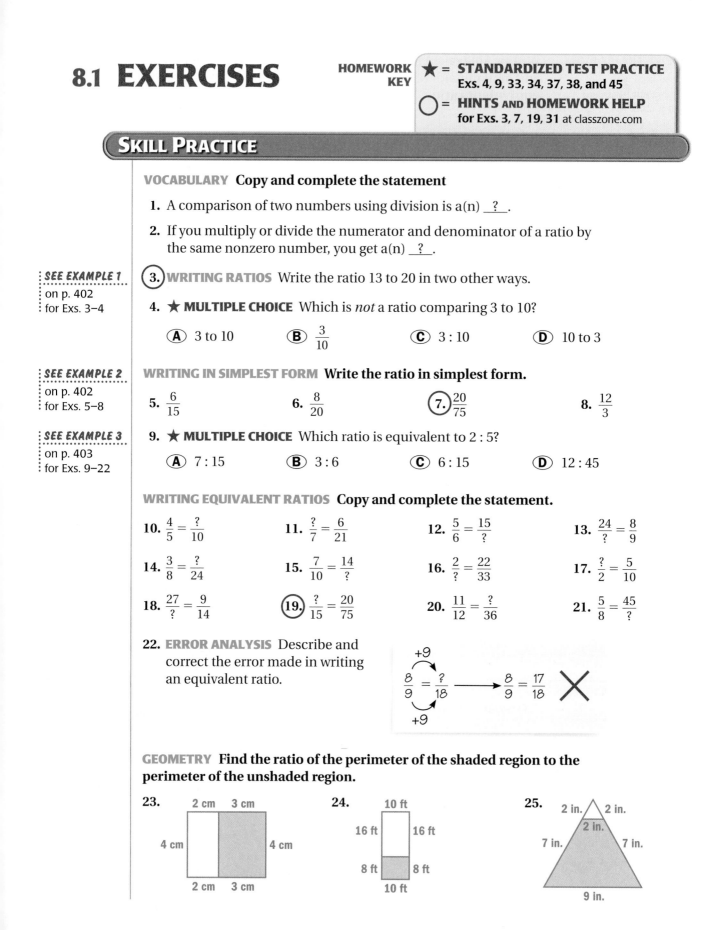

23. 2 cm 3 cm / 4 cm 4 cm / 2 cm 3 cm

24. 10 ft / 16 ft 16 ft / 8 ft 8 ft / 10 ft

25. 2 in. 2 in. / 2 in. / 7 in. 7 in. / 9 in.

SEE EXAMPLE 4
on p. 403
for Exs. 26–27

BASEBALL A batting average is the ratio of the number of hits to the number of times at bat. Who has the greater batting average?

26. Carl: 11 to 31, Joel: $\frac{7}{20}$

27. Sara: 0.258, Miranda: $\frac{19}{75}$

28. CHALLENGE Find two numbers that form a ratio equivalent to 2 : 3 and have a sum of 25.

PROBLEM SOLVING

AVERAGE TEMPERATURES Use the average December temperatures for the cities shown to write the ratio described in simplest form.

SEE EXAMPLE 2
on p. 402
for Exs. 29–31

29. $\dfrac{\text{Number of temperatures over } 68°\text{F}}{\text{Total number of temperatures}}$

30. $\dfrac{\text{Number of temperatures over } 33°\text{F}}{\text{Total number of temperatures}}$

31. $\dfrac{\text{Number of temperatures over } 33°\text{F}}{\text{Number of temperatures under } 33°\text{F}}$

City	Temperature
Washington, D.C.	39°F
Miami Beach, FL	70°F
Dallas, TX	48°F
Sacramento, CA	45°F
Helena, MT	21°F
Chicago, IL	30°F

32. KEYBOARDS On a musical keyboard, 31 of the 76 keys are black. Write this ratio in three different ways.

33. ★ MULTIPLE CHOICE A farmer plants corn on 18 acres of a 48 acre field. What ratio compares the size of the cornfield to the size of the whole field?

(A) $\frac{1}{3}$　　　　**(B)** $\frac{3}{8}$　　　　**(C)** $\frac{1}{2}$　　　　**(D)** $\frac{2}{3}$

34. ★ WRITING *Explain* how to compare two ratios by using common denominators.

SUMMER CAMP In Exercises 35 and 36, use the table. The ratio of the number of counselors to the number of campers is constant.

Counselors	2	3	4	5
Campers	16	24	?	?

35. Write the ratio of counselors to campers in simplest form.

36. Copy and complete the table. At what point is the difference between the numbers of campers and counselors greater than 100? *Explain.*

37. ★ SHORT RESPONSE A survey says that 28 out of 42 people have a pet. Write a ratio in simplest form that compares the number of people that do *not* have a pet to the number of people that do have a pet. *Explain* how you found your answer.

38. ★ **EXTENDED RESPONSE** A chorus has 68 singers. The graph shows that the chorus includes tenors, basses, altos, and sopranos.

   a. Calculate Find the number of sopranos in the chorus. *Describe* your method.

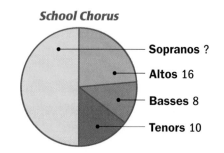

School Chorus

Sopranos ?
Altos 16
Basses 8
Tenors 10

   b. Interpret Write the ratio of the number of sopranos to the number of other singers. Then write the ratio of the number of sopranos to the total number of singers. *Compare* the two ratios.

   c. Compare Another chorus has 112 singers: 41 sopranos, 29 altos, 24 tenors, and 18 basses. *Compare* the sizes of the two choruses.

39. CHALLENGE Find the ratio of the perimeter to the area for squares with side lengths of 8, 9, 10, and 11. Is there a pattern? *Justify* your answer.

MIXED REVIEW

Get-Ready

Prepare for Lesson 8.2 in Exs. 40–43

Divide. Round to the nearest tenth if necessary. *(p. 186)*

40. $13.5 \div 4$ **41.** $22.4 \div 8$ **42.** $11.3 \div 7$ **43.** $45.12 \div 12$

CHOOSE A STRATEGY Use a strategy from the list to solve the following problem. *Explain* your choice of strategy.

44. Find the next two figures in the pattern.

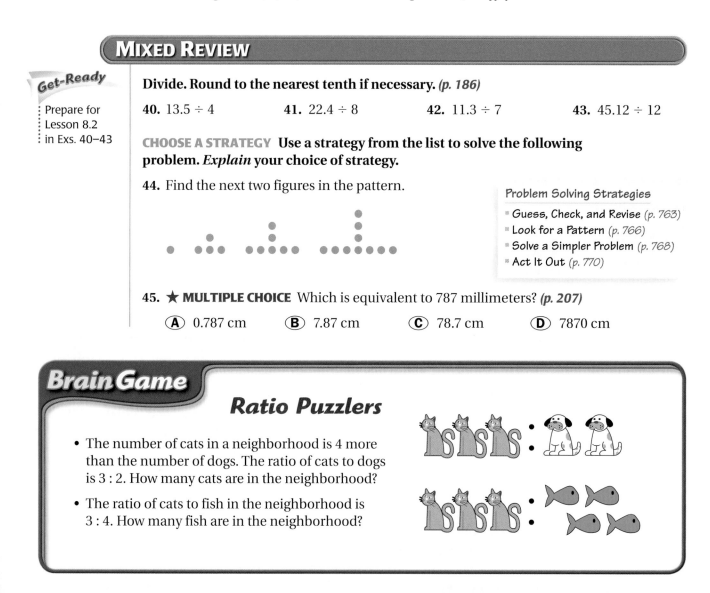

Problem Solving Strategies
- Guess, Check, and Revise *(p. 763)*
- Look for a Pattern *(p. 766)*
- Solve a Simpler Problem *(p. 768)*
- Act It Out *(p. 770)*

45. ★ **MULTIPLE CHOICE** Which is equivalent to 787 millimeters? *(p. 207)*

   (A) 0.787 cm   **(B)** 7.87 cm   **(C)** 78.7 cm   **(D)** 7870 cm

Brain Game

Ratio Puzzlers

- The number of cats in a neighborhood is 4 more than the number of dogs. The ratio of cats to dogs is 3 : 2. How many cats are in the neighborhood?

- The ratio of cats to fish in the neighborhood is 3 : 4. How many fish are in the neighborhood?

EXTRA PRACTICE for Lesson 8.1, p. 783

ONLINE QUIZ at classzone.com

8.2 Rates

Before You wrote ratios and equivalent ratios.

Now You'll write rates, equivalent rates, and unit rates.

Why? So you can relate distance and time, as in Example 1.

KEY VOCABULARY
• rate, *p. 407*
• unit rate, *p. 407*

A **rate** is a ratio of two measures that have different units, such as $\dfrac{15 \text{ mi}}{3 \text{ sec}}$.

A **unit rate** has a denominator of 1 unit, such as $\dfrac{20 \text{ words}}{1 \text{ min}}$ or $\dfrac{20 \text{ words}}{\text{min}}$.

EXAMPLE 1 Writing an Equivalent Rate

Space The International Space Station orbits Earth at an average rate of 15 miles every 3 seconds. How long will it take the space station to travel 150 miles?

SOLUTION

Write an *equivalent rate* that has 150 miles in the numerator.

$$\overset{15 \times 10}{\frown}$$
$$\frac{15 \text{ mi}}{3 \text{ sec}} = \frac{150 \text{ mi}}{30 \text{ sec}}$$
$$\underset{3 \times 10}{\smile}$$

> You multiply 15 mi by 10 to get 150 mi, so multiply 3 sec by 10 also.

▶ **Answer** It will take the space station 30 seconds to travel 150 miles.

EXAMPLE 2 Writing a Unit Rate

Write the Space Station's average rate of $\dfrac{15 \text{ mi}}{3 \text{ sec}}$ as a unit rate.

$$\overset{15 \div 3}{\frown}$$
$$\frac{15 \text{ mi}}{3 \text{ sec}} = \frac{5 \text{ mi}}{1 \text{ sec}}$$
$$\underset{3 \div 3}{\smile}$$

> Find the equivalent fraction that has a denominator of 1.

READING
You read $\frac{5 \text{ mi}}{1 \text{ sec}}$ as
"5 miles per second."

▶ **Answer** The space station's average unit rate is 5 miles per second.

✓ **GUIDED PRACTICE**   for Examples 1 and 2

Copy and complete the statement.

1. $\dfrac{5 \text{ lb}}{\$10} = \dfrac{20 \text{ lb}}{?}$

2. $\dfrac{35 \text{ mi}}{6 \text{ h}} = \dfrac{?}{12 \text{ h}}$

3. $\dfrac{32 \text{ oz}}{\$8} = \dfrac{?}{\$1}$

EXAMPLE 3 Using a Unit Rate

Measurement There are 2.54 centimeters in 1 inch. How many centimeters are in 3 inches?

SOLUTION

Write an equivalent rate that has 3 inches in the denominator.

$$\overset{2.54 \times 3}{\overbrace{\frac{2.54 \text{ cm}}{1 \text{ in.}}}} = \frac{7.62 \text{ cm}}{3 \text{ in.}}$$
$$\underset{1 \times 3}{}$$

You multiply 1 in. by 3 to get 3 in., so multiply 2.54 cm by 3 also.

▸ **Answer** There are 7.62 centimeters in 3 inches.

READING RULERS
Need help reading metric lengths? See page 125.

Check Use rulers to check: 3 in. is about 7.6 cm. The answer is reasonable.

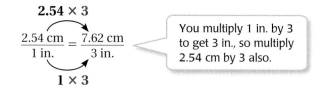

EXAMPLE 4 Comparing Unit Rates

Refreshments A 12 ounce tub of popcorn costs $3.00. A 20 ounce tub of popcorn costs $4.00. Which tub is the better buy? *Explain.*

SOLUTION

The rates for the two sizes are $\frac{\$3.00}{12 \text{ oz}}$ and $\frac{\$4.00}{20 \text{ oz}}$. Find the *unit price* for each tub of popcorn by finding the cost for 1 ounce of popcorn.

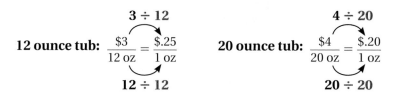

▸ **Answer** Compare the unit price: $.25 > $.20. The 12 ounce tub costs more per ounce, so the 20 ounce tub is the better buy.

Animated **Math** at classzone.com

✓ **GUIDED PRACTICE** for Examples 3 and 4

4. How many centimeters are in 2.5 inches?

5. **What If?** In Example 4, suppose a 16 ounce tub of popcorn costs $3.68. Is the 12 ounce tub or the 16 ounce tub a better buy? *Explain.*

★ **EXAMPLE 5** Standardized Test Practice

Racing A driver completes 5 laps of a race in 3 minutes and 30 seconds and continues driving at this rate. How many laps will the driver complete in 10.5 minutes?

➤ **(A)** 5 laps   **(B)** 10 laps   **(C)** 15 laps   **(D)** 20 laps

ELIMINATE CHOICES
The driver completes 5 laps in 3 minutes and 30 seconds, so choice A can be eliminated.

SOLUTION

STEP 1 **Rewrite** the time so that the units are the same.

3 min + 30 sec = 3 min + 0.5 min = 3.5 min

STEP 2 **Use** a table to find the number of laps the driver will complete.

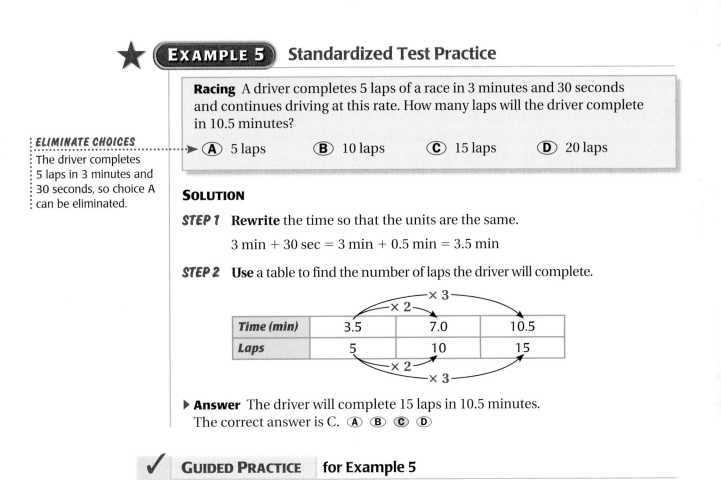

Time (min)	3.5	7.0	10.5
Laps	5	10	15

▶ **Answer** The driver will complete 15 laps in 10.5 minutes. The correct answer is C. (A) (B) **(C)** (D)

✓ **GUIDED PRACTICE** for Example 5

6. **What If?** If the driver in Example 5 completed 5 laps in 5.5 minutes, how many laps would the driver complete in 22 minutes?

8.2 EXERCISES

HOMEWORK KEY

★ = **STANDARDIZED TEST PRACTICE**
Exs. 14, 33, 35, 37, and 50

◯ = **HINTS** AND **HOMEWORK HELP**
for Exs. 5, 11, 17, 35 at classzone.com

SKILL PRACTICE

VOCABULARY Write as a ratio. Then tell whether the ratio is written as a *rate*, a *unit rate*, or *neither*.

1. 2 feet per second
2. 12 inches to 3 inches
3. 76 words in 2 minutes

WRITING EQUIVALENT RATES Copy and complete the statement.

SEE EXAMPLE 1
on p. 407
for Exs. 4–9

4. $\dfrac{\$4}{3 \text{ oz}} = \dfrac{\$16}{?}$

5. $\dfrac{40 \text{ gal}}{8 \text{ h}} = \dfrac{20 \text{ gal}}{?}$

6. $\dfrac{54.9 \text{ mi}}{9 \text{ h}} = \dfrac{?}{3 \text{ h}}$

7. $\dfrac{36 \text{ laps}}{90 \text{ m}} = \dfrac{?}{10 \text{ m}}$

8. $\dfrac{18 \text{ mi}}{45 \text{ sec}} = \dfrac{?}{15 \text{ sec}}$

9. $\dfrac{\$2}{5.8 \text{ cm}} = \dfrac{\$6}{?}$

WRITING RATES Write the rate in fraction form. Then find the unit rate.

SEE EXAMPLE 2
on p. 407
for Exs. 10–13

10. 20 words in 5 minutes
11. 48 students for 24 computers
12. 160 miles in 4 hours
13. 250 pages in 5 chapters

SEE EXAMPLE 2
on p. 407 for
Exs. 14–22

14. ★ **MULTIPLE CHOICE** Denise works for 3 hours and earns $24. How could you find the unit rate that expresses how much Denise earns in 1 hour?

(A) Divide 3 by 24.

(B) Multiply 3 by 24.

(C) Divide 24 by 3.

(D) Subtract 3 from 24.

WRITING UNIT RATES Write the unit rate.

15. $\dfrac{220 \text{ mi}}{4 \text{ h}}$

16. $\dfrac{\$15}{12 \text{ muffins}}$

17. $\dfrac{94.5 \text{ m}}{27 \text{ sec}}$

18. $\dfrac{4000 \text{ ft}}{15 \text{ sec}}$

19. $\dfrac{6.63 \text{ lb}}{3 \text{ kg}}$

20. $\dfrac{56.7 \text{ g}}{2 \text{ oz}}$

21. $\dfrac{10.16 \text{ cm}}{4 \text{ in.}}$

22. $\dfrac{8.05 \text{ km}}{5 \text{ mi}}$

SEE EXAMPLE 4
on p. 408 for
Exs. 23–26

COMPARING RATES Tell whether the rates are *equivalent* or *not equivalent*.

23. $\dfrac{32 \text{ calories}}{2 \text{ h}}$ and $\dfrac{64 \text{ calories}}{4 \text{ h}}$

24. $\dfrac{60 \text{ words}}{3 \text{ min}}$ and $\dfrac{25 \text{ words}}{1 \text{ min}}$

25. $\dfrac{8 \text{ lb}}{\$4}$ and $\dfrac{12 \text{ lb}}{\$3}$

26. $\dfrac{42 \text{ visits}}{3 \text{ h}}$ and $\dfrac{28 \text{ visits}}{2 \text{ h}}$

27. **ERROR ANALYSIS** Describe and correct the error made in finding the cost per book when paying $19.50 for 3 books.

$$\frac{19.50}{3 \text{ books}} = 6.50$$
6.50 books per $1.00

CHALLENGE Write the speed in feet per second. Round to the nearest foot if necessary.

28. 75 mi in 2 h

29. 150 mi in 3 h

30. 100 mi in 4 h

31. 425 mi in 9 h

PROBLEM SOLVING

32. **GUIDED PROBLEM SOLVING** On average, a Ruby-throated Hummingbird beats its wings about 3000 times in 60 seconds. A Giant Hummingbird beats its wings about 180 times in 15 seconds. Which bird beats its wings faster?

   a. Find the unit rate for the Ruby-throated Hummingbird.

   b. Find the unit rate for the Giant Hummingbird.

   c. *Compare* the unit rates.

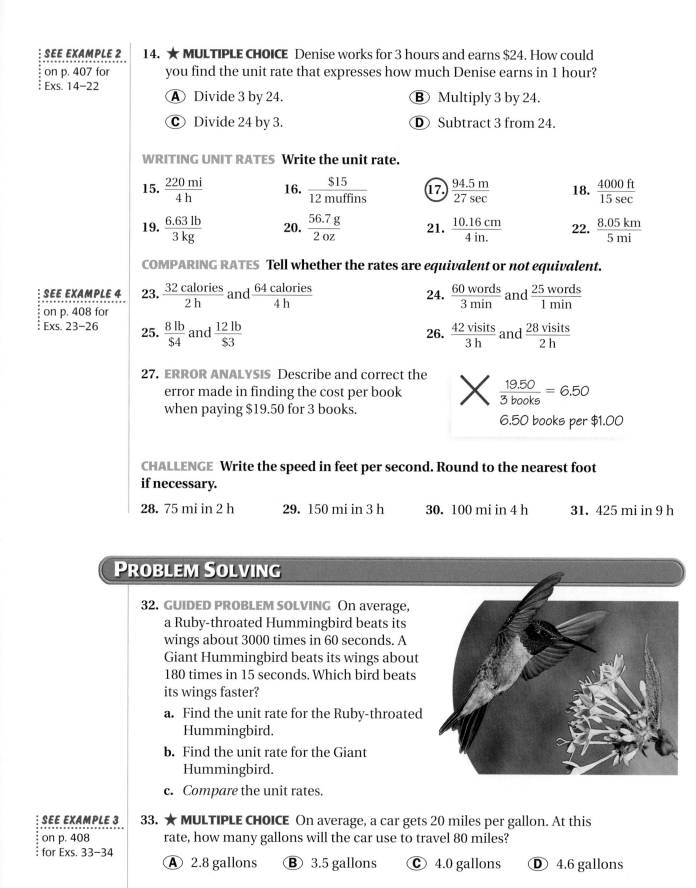

SEE EXAMPLE 3
on p. 408
for Exs. 33–34

33. ★ **MULTIPLE CHOICE** On average, a car gets 20 miles per gallon. At this rate, how many gallons will the car use to travel 80 miles?

(A) 2.8 gallons   (B) 3.5 gallons   (C) 4.0 gallons   (D) 4.6 gallons

34. **GARDENING** You work in a local park removing weeds. You earn $7.50 per hour. How much do you earn for working for 6 hours?

SEE EXAMPLE 4
on p. 408
for Ex. 35

(35.) ★ **SHORT RESPONSE** Your friend purchases 26 bagels for $10.40. You purchase 39 bagels at a price of 3 bagels for $1. Which purchase is the better buy? *Explain* your reasoning.

36. **REASONING** Would the result be different in Example 2 on page 407 by using the rate $\frac{150 \text{ mi}}{30 \text{ sec}}$ to find the unit rate? *Explain*.

37. ★ **WRITING** *Describe* the difference between a ratio and a rate. Is a ratio always a rate? Is a rate always a ratio? *Explain*.

SEE EXAMPLE 5
on p. 409
for Exs. 38–39

38. **BOTTLED WATER** A factory produces an average of 45,000 bottles of water per hour. How many bottles are produced in 75 minutes?

39. ◆ **MULTIPLE REPRESENTATIONS** Bart and Tia make fruit baskets. Bart works from 8:00 A.M. to 5:00 P.M. Tia works from 9:00 A.M. to 3:30 P.M. The diagram shows the number of baskets each of them makes in the shaded number of minutes.

Bart's Basket Production   Tia's Basket Production

a. **Write Unit Rates** Write the unit rates describing Bart and Tia's basket making speeds.

b. **Compare** *Compare* the unit rates to find who is faster.

c. **Make a Table** Use a table to find who makes more fruit baskets.

40. **CHALLENGE** An office has two paper shredders, A and B. Shredder A shreds 1100 pounds of paper in 5 hours. Shredder B shreds 4.4 pounds of paper per minute. Which shredder is faster?

41. **CHALLENGE** A car travels at 30 miles per hour. How many minutes per mile is this? A car travels at 4 minutes per mile. How many miles per hour is this?

MIXED REVIEW

Get-Ready

Prepare for
Lesson 8.3
in Exs. 42–45

Find the GCF of the numbers. *(p. 236)*

42. 16, 40   **43.** 36, 81   **44.** 18, 72   **45.** 20, 56

Solve the equation using mental math. *(p. 34)*

46. $63 \div m = 7$ **47.** $3t = 18$ **48.** $8 + y = 43$ **49.** $s - 5 = 7$

50. ★ **OPEN-ENDED MATH** Find three fractions that are greater than $\frac{1}{2}$ and less than $\frac{2}{3}$. *Describe* your method for finding the fractions. *(p. 254)*

8.3 Solving Proportions

Before	You solved equations.
Now	You'll write and solve proportions.
Why?	So you can estimate distance, as for hops in Ex. 50.

KEY VOCABULARY
- proportion, *p. 412*
- cross products, *p. 412*

A **proportion** is an equation that shows that two ratios are equivalent. The proportion below shows that the ratios in the pictures are equivalent.

Ratio: 2 of 3 rows   **Ratio: 8 of 12 dots**   **Proportion**

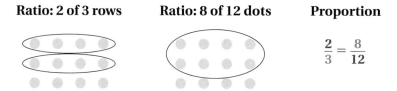

$$\frac{2}{3} = \frac{8}{12}$$

When you multiply the numerator of each ratio by the denominator of the other ratio, you find the *cross products*. For the proportion $\frac{a}{b} = \frac{c}{d}$, where b and d are nonzero, the **cross products** are ad and bc.

The cross products for the proportion above are $2 \cdot 12$ and $3 \cdot 8$.

KEY CONCEPT   *For Your Notebook*

Cross Products Property

Words   The cross products of a proportion are equal.

Numbers $\frac{3}{4} = \frac{6}{8}$ $4 \cdot 6 = 24$
                                               $3 \cdot 8 = 24$

Algebra   If $\frac{a}{b} = \frac{c}{d}$, where b and d are nonzero numbers, then $ad = bc$.

EXAMPLE 1   **Checking a Proportion**

Use cross products to decide whether the ratios form a proportion.

a. $\frac{3}{5} \stackrel{?}{=} \frac{12}{18}$

$3 \cdot 18 \stackrel{?}{=} 5 \cdot 12$

$54 \neq 60$

The cross products are *not* equal, so the ratios do *not* form a proportion.

b. $\frac{8}{10} \stackrel{?}{=} \frac{20}{25}$

$8 \cdot 25 \stackrel{?}{=} 10 \cdot 20$

$200 = 200$

The cross products are equal, so the ratios form a proportion.

Solving Proportions To solve a proportion, you find the value of any missing part. One way to solve a proportion is to use mental math.

EXAMPLE 2 Solving Using Mental Math

Solve the proportion $\frac{4}{12} = \frac{20}{x}$.

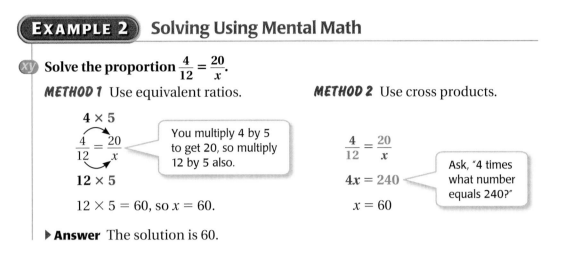

METHOD 1 Use equivalent ratios.

4×5

$\dfrac{4}{12} = \dfrac{20}{x}$

12×5

You multiply 4 by 5 to get 20, so multiply 12 by 5 also.

$12 \times 5 = 60$, so $x = 60$.

METHOD 2 Use cross products.

$\dfrac{4}{12} = \dfrac{20}{x}$

$4x = 240$

$x = 60$

Ask, "4 times what number equals 240?"

▶ **Answer** The solution is 60.

EXAMPLE 3 Solving Using a Verbal Model

Boating You are on a riverboat trip. You travel 5 miles in 3 hours. At that same rate, how long will it take you to travel 20 miles?

SOLUTION

Use a proportion. Let t represent the total time, in hours, of the 20 mile trip.

WRITING PROPORTIONS
When you write a proportion, be sure each ratio compares quantities in the same order. In Example 3, each ratio compares distance to time.

$$\dfrac{\text{Distance traveled}}{\text{Time traveled}} = \dfrac{\text{Total distance}}{\text{Total time}}$$ Write a verbal model.

$$\dfrac{5 \text{ mi}}{3 \text{ h}} = \dfrac{20 \text{ mi}}{t \text{ h}}$$ Substitute values.

$$\dfrac{5}{3} = \dfrac{20}{t}$$ Write the cross products. They are equal.

$$5t = 60$$

$$t = 12$$ Solve using mental math.

▶ **Answer** It will take you 12 hours to travel 20 miles.

Animated Math at classzone.com

✓ **GUIDED PRACTICE** for Examples 1, 2, and 3

1. Does $\frac{3}{8} \overset{?}{=} \frac{12}{32}$ form a proportion?

2. Does $\frac{5}{6} \overset{?}{=} \frac{25}{36}$ form a proportion?

Solve the proportion using mental math.

3. $\dfrac{n}{4} = \dfrac{6}{24}$

4. $\dfrac{25}{10} = \dfrac{5}{k}$

5. $\dfrac{30}{x} = \dfrac{6}{11}$

6. $\dfrac{10}{4} = \dfrac{s}{12}$

7. **What If?** In Example 3, suppose you travel 4 miles in 2 hours. At that same rate, how long will it take you to travel 20 miles?

EXAMPLE 4 Solving Using a Related Equation

Solve the proportion $\frac{2.1}{1.4} = \frac{x}{3}$.

SOLUTION

$$\frac{2.1}{1.4} = \frac{x}{3}$$ **Write the cross products.**
                             They are equal.

$$6.3 = 1.4x$$

$$6.3 \div 1.4 = x$$ **Write the related division equation.**

$$4.5 = x$$ **Divide.**

▶ **Answer** The solution is 4.5.

Need help writing a related equation? See p. 740.

✔ **GUIDED PRACTICE**   for Example 4

Write the related equation. Use it to solve the proportion.

8. $\frac{22.5}{6} = \frac{a}{6}$ **9.** $\frac{30}{y} = \frac{50}{60}$ **10.** $\frac{x}{1.5} = \frac{1}{0.6}$ **11.** $\frac{1.1}{3.5} = \frac{13.2}{m}$

8.3 EXERCISES

★ = **STANDARDIZED TEST PRACTICE**
   Exs. 23, 46, 48, 49, 51, and 61

◯ = **HINTS AND HOMEWORK HELP**
   for Exs. 13, 15, 25, 45, 47 at classzone.com

SKILL PRACTICE

VOCABULARY Copy and complete the statement.

1. The cross products for the proportion $\frac{3}{8} = \frac{9}{x}$ are __?__ and __?__.

2. A __?__ is a type of equation that shows that two ratios are equivalent.

USING CROSS PRODUCTS Use cross products to decide whether the ratios form a proportion.

SEE EXAMPLE 1
on p. 412
for Exs. 3–14

3. $\frac{3}{4} \overset{?}{=} \frac{9}{12}$ **4.** $\frac{10}{16} \overset{?}{=} \frac{5}{8}$ **5.** $\frac{6}{14} \overset{?}{=} \frac{8}{20}$ **6.** $\frac{3}{8} \overset{?}{=} \frac{15}{40}$

7. $\frac{9}{21} \overset{?}{=} \frac{3}{7}$ **8.** $\frac{30}{16} \overset{?}{=} \frac{20}{15}$ **9.** $\frac{3}{2} \overset{?}{=} \frac{12}{10}$ **10.** $\frac{4}{5} \overset{?}{=} \frac{16}{21}$

11. $\frac{24}{15} \overset{?}{=} \frac{11}{8}$ **12.** $\frac{91}{65} \overset{?}{=} \frac{7}{5}$ **⑬.** $\frac{50}{24} \overset{?}{=} \frac{12}{6}$ **14.** $\frac{3}{120} \overset{?}{=} \frac{35}{1400}$

Animated Math at classzone.com

SOLVING PROPORTIONS Solve the proportion using mental math.

SEE EXAMPLE 2
on p. 413
for Exs. 15–22

⑮. $\frac{1}{6} = \frac{5}{x}$ **16.** $\frac{2}{5} = \frac{r}{20}$ **17.** $\frac{n}{28} = \frac{2}{7}$ **18.** $\frac{45}{z} = \frac{15}{3}$

19. $\frac{12}{28} = \frac{3}{c}$ **20.** $\frac{9}{x} = \frac{27}{30}$ **21.** $\frac{a}{5} = \frac{99}{55}$ **22.** $\frac{5}{6} = \frac{n}{120}$

414   Chapter 8   Ratio, Proportion, and Percent

SEE EXAMPLE 4
on p. 413
for Exs. 23–31

23. ★ **MULTIPLE CHOICE** Which equation is related to the equation $8x = 112$?

Ⓐ $x = 112 + 8$ Ⓑ $x = 112 - 8$ Ⓒ $x = 112 \div 8$ Ⓓ $x = 112 \times 8$

SOLVING PROPORTIONS Solve the proportion using a related equation.

24. $\dfrac{1.2}{1.8} = \dfrac{2}{p}$

25. $\dfrac{12}{r} = \dfrac{8}{20}$

26. $\dfrac{m}{8} = \dfrac{1.8}{14.4}$

27. $\dfrac{t}{4} = \dfrac{45}{18}$

28. $\dfrac{9}{6} = \dfrac{h}{14}$

29. $\dfrac{24}{36} = \dfrac{10}{x}$

30. $\dfrac{12.7}{z} = \dfrac{25.4}{3}$

31. $\dfrac{22}{6.8} = \dfrac{x}{3.4}$

CHOOSE A METHOD Tell whether you would solve the proportion using *mental math* or a *related equation. Explain* your choice. Then solve.

SEE EXAMPLES 2 AND 4
on pp. 413–414
for Exs. 32–39

32. $\dfrac{26.3}{b} = \dfrac{5.26}{7}$

33. $\dfrac{10}{9.75} = \dfrac{s}{15.6}$

34. $\dfrac{40}{2.72} = \dfrac{5}{w}$

35. $\dfrac{13}{k} = \dfrac{52}{5}$

36. $\dfrac{x}{14} = \dfrac{3}{7}$

37. $\dfrac{10}{12} = \dfrac{m}{30}$

38. $\dfrac{6}{y} = \dfrac{8}{44}$

39. $\dfrac{2.4}{12} = \dfrac{5}{w}$

40. **ERROR ANALYSIS** Describe and correct the error made in solving the proportion.

$$\dfrac{8}{x} = \dfrac{3}{6} \longrightarrow 8 \cdot 3 = x \cdot 6 \longrightarrow x = 4 \quad ✗$$

USING PROPORTIONS Copy and complete the table using proportions.

41.

Games played	6	9	?	?
Total cost	$8	?	$16	?

42.

Servings	?	10	16	?
Cups	10	?	40	?

43. **CHALLENGE** For nonzero numbers a, b, c, and d, if $\dfrac{a}{b} = \dfrac{c}{d}$, is it true that $\dfrac{d}{b} = \dfrac{c}{a}$? *Explain* your reasoning.

PROBLEM SOLVING

SEE EXAMPLE 3
on p. 413
for Exs. 44–45

44. **LITERATURE** In *Gulliver's Travels,* by Jonathan Swift, Gulliver's body height and the height of a Lilliputian are "in the proportion of twelve to one."

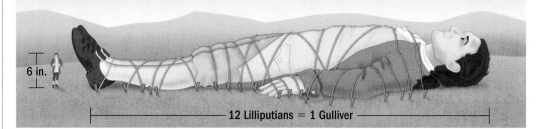

6 in.

12 Lilliputians = 1 Gulliver

A Lilliputian is 6 inches tall. Use a verbal model to write a proportion to find Gulliver's height. How tall is Gulliver?

45. **QUIZ SCORES** You and a friend got the same proportion of questions correct on your quizzes. You got 6 out of 8 questions correct. Your friend's quiz had 12 questions. How many questions did your friend get correct?

SEE EXAMPLE 4
on p. 414
for Exs. 46–47

46. ★ **MULTIPLE CHOICE** At a health food store, the cost of 8 ounces of curry powder is $8.98. At that rate, what is the cost of 12 ounces of curry powder?

Ⓐ $4.48 Ⓑ $12.98 Ⓒ $13.47 Ⓓ $20.98

47. **CURRENCY** The value of 5 U.S. dollars is 19 Malaysian ringgits. What is the value in U.S. dollars of 14 ringgits?

48. ★ **OPEN-ENDED MATH** *Describe* a real-world situation that can be modeled by one of the proportions in Exercises 36–39. Write a verbal model to show how the proportion describes the situation.

49. ★ **WRITING** In May, 8 of 10 students in your school saw a movie. Your school has 480 students. Is there enough information to find the number of students in your school who did *not* see a movie in May? *Explain.*

50. **KANGAROOS** A kangaroo travels 40 feet in 2 hops. Hannah and Juan are trying to estimate the distance *x*, in feet, the kangaroo will travel in 6 hops. Are both methods below correct? Use cross products to check.

Hannah: $\frac{2}{40} = \frac{6}{x}$ Juan: $\frac{2}{6} = \frac{40}{x}$

51. ★ **SHORT RESPONSE** A farmer has 10 hens that produce a total of 65 eggs each week. Use proportions to find the number of weeks it would take 2 hens to produce 65 eggs. *Describe* the steps you used to solve the problem.

52. **INSECTS** A flea that is 3 millimeters long can jump 33 centimeters. Suppose the jumping ability of a human were proportional to the jumping ability of a flea. How far could a human who is 180 centimeters tall jump? Is this reasonable? *Explain.*

CHALLENGE Another way to use cross products is to compare fractions. Use the following rule: $\frac{a}{b} > \frac{c}{d}$ if $ad > bc$. Tell whether the inequality is *true* or *false*.

53. $\frac{6}{5} \overset{?}{>} \frac{11}{7}$ **54.** $\frac{2}{3} \overset{?}{>} \frac{19}{31}$ **55.** $\frac{24}{7} \overset{?}{>} \frac{7}{2}$ **56.** $\frac{18}{3} \overset{?}{>} \frac{6}{1}$

MIXED REVIEW

Prepare for
Lesson 8.4
in Exs. 57–59

Find the perimeter and area of the figure described. *(p. 66)*

57. a 7 cm by 7 cm square   **58.** a 9 ft by 3 ft rectangle   **59.** a 15 m by 14 m rectangle

60. A rock weighs $8\frac{1}{2}$ tons. How many pounds does it weigh? *(p. 378)*

61. ★ **MULTIPLE CHOICE** A puppy's weight is greater than 3.5 pounds and less than 3.55 pounds. Which is a possible weight of the puppy? *(p.130)*

Ⓐ 3.05 pounds   Ⓑ 3.5 pounds   Ⓒ 3.52 pounds   Ⓓ 3.55 pounds

8.4 Proportions and Scale Drawings

Before	You used mental math to find the actual length of an object.
Now	You'll use proportions to find measures of objects.
Why?	So you can interpret scale drawings, as in Example 1.

KEY VOCABULARY
• **scale drawing,** *p. 72*
• **scale,** *p. 72*

Soap Box Racing You are building a car for a Soap Box race. In the *scale drawing* below, the car is 2.8 inches long. What is the actual length of the car?

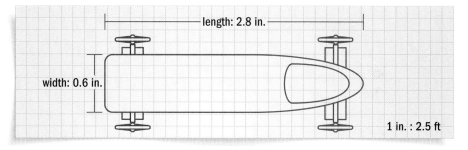

SCALE DRAWINGS
Need help with scale drawings? See p. 72.

The *scale* of 1 in. : 2.5 ft on the drawing is a ratio that means 1 inch on the drawing represents an actual distance of 2.5 feet on the car.

Measure on drawing ⟶ 1 in.
Actual measure ⟶ 2.5 ft

EXAMPLE 1 Using a Scale Drawing

To find the actual length of the car above, write and solve a proportion. Let x represent the car's actual length in feet.

$$\frac{1 \text{ in.}}{2.5 \text{ ft}} = \frac{\text{Length on drawing}}{\text{Actual length}} \qquad \textbf{Write a proportion.}$$

$$\frac{1 \text{ in.}}{2.5 \text{ ft}} = \frac{2.8 \text{ in.}}{x \text{ ft}} \qquad \textbf{Substitute values.}$$

$$1 \cdot x = (2.5)(2.8) \qquad \textbf{The cross products are equal.}$$

$$x = 7 \qquad \textbf{Multiply.}$$

▶ **Answer** The actual length of the car is 7 feet.

✓ GUIDED PRACTICE for Example 1

1. Use the scale drawing above to find the actual width of the car.

2. The actual distance from the front axle to the rear axle is 5.5 feet. Find this distance in the scale drawing above.

Perimeter and Area The ratio of the perimeter of a scale drawing to the actual perimeter is related to the scale. So is the ratio of the areas.

EXAMPLE 2 Finding Ratios of Perimeters

School Murals A finished mural is to be 20 feet by 10 feet. Your scale drawing of the mural is shown.

a. What is the perimeter of the drawing? of the mural?

b. Find the ratio of the drawing's perimeter to the mural's perimeter. How is this ratio related to the scale?

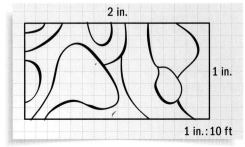

2 in.

1 in.

1 in. : 10 ft

SOLUTION

FIND MEASURES
Need help finding the perimeter and area of a rectangle? See page 66.

a. Perimeter of drawing: $P = 2l + 2w = 2(2) + 2(1) = 6$ in.

Perimeter of mural: $P = 2l + 2w = 2(20) + 2(10) = 60$ ft

b. $\dfrac{\text{Perimeter of drawing}}{\text{Perimeter of mural}} = \dfrac{6 \text{ in.}}{60 \text{ ft}} = \dfrac{1 \text{ in.}}{10 \text{ ft}}$

▸ **Answer** The ratio of the perimeters is equal to the scale ratio. One inch of perimeter in the drawing represents 10 feet of actual perimeter.

EXAMPLE 3 Finding Ratios of Areas

Use the information from Example 2. Find the ratio of the drawing's area to the mural's area. How is this ratio related to the scale?

SOLUTION

AVOID ERRORS
Don't forget:
inches × inches = inches²
feet × feet = feet²

Area of drawing: $A = lw = 2 \cdot 1 = 2$ in.^{2}

Area of mural: $A = lw = 20 \cdot 10 = 200$ ft^2

$\dfrac{\text{Area of drawing}}{\text{Area of mural}} = \dfrac{2 \text{ in.}^2}{200 \text{ ft}^2} = \dfrac{1 \text{ in.}^2}{100 \text{ ft}^2} = \dfrac{1 \cdot 1 \text{ in.}^2}{10 \cdot 10 \text{ ft}^2}$

▸ **Answer** The ratio of the areas, $1 \cdot 1$ in.$^2 : 10 \cdot 10$ ft^2, is equal to the square of the scale ratio. One square inch of area in the drawing represents $10 \times 10 = 100$ ft^2 of actual area.

✓ GUIDED PRACTICE for Examples 2 and 3

3. A scale drawing of another mural has a length of 5 cm and a width of 3 cm. The scale of the drawing is 1 cm : 2 m. What is the ratio of the perimeter of the drawing to the perimeter of the mural? What is the ratio of the area of the drawing to the area of the mural?

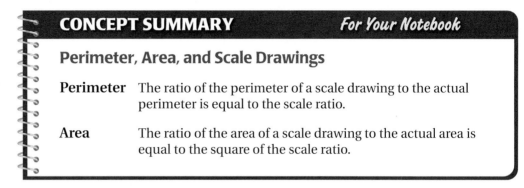

CONCEPT SUMMARY *For Your Notebook*

Perimeter, Area, and Scale Drawings

Perimeter   The ratio of the perimeter of a scale drawing to the actual perimeter is equal to the scale ratio.

Area   The ratio of the area of a scale drawing to the actual area is equal to the square of the scale ratio.

8.4 EXERCISES

HOMEWORK KEY

★ = **STANDARDIZED TEST PRACTICE**
Exs. 18, 35, 36, 40, 43, and 54

◯ = **HINTS AND HOMEWORK HELP**
for Exs. 3, 9, 15, 33 at classzone.com

SKILL PRACTICE

SEE EXAMPLE 1
on p. 417
for Exs. 3–16

1. **VOCABULARY** Copy and complete: The __?__ of a map tells how the drawing's dimensions are related to the actual dimensions of the figures displayed.

2. **VOCABULARY** Express the scale 1 in. : 5 ft as a ratio in two other ways.

3. **FINDING ACTUAL LENGTH** A scale drawing has a scale of 1 in. : 6 ft. The actual length of the object is 48 feet. Choose the proportion you can use to find the actual length of the object. Then find the length.

   A. $\dfrac{1 \text{ in.}}{6 \text{ ft}} = \dfrac{48 \text{ ft}}{\text{Length in drawing}}$

   B. $\dfrac{1 \text{ in.}}{6 \text{ ft}} = \dfrac{\text{Length in drawing}}{48 \text{ ft}}$

USING A MAP A map uses a scale of 1 in. : 50 mi. Find the actual distance for the given distance on the map.

4. 3 inches
5. 8 inches
6. 13 inches
7. 2.1 inches
8. 0.5 inch
9. 4.5 inches
10. 1 foot
11. 1.5 feet

USING SCALES The scale of a drawing is 9 mm : 2 cm. Find the unknown measure.

12. length on drawing = 27 mm;
    length of object = __?__

13. length on drawing = 45 mm;
    length of object = __?__

14. width of object = 40 cm;
    width on drawing = __?__

15. width of object = 58.5 mm;
    width on drawing = __?__

16. **FINDING SCALE** The perimeter of a scale drawing is 14 centimeters. The actual perimeter is 126 meters. What does 1 centimeter represent in the drawing?

17. FINDING SCALE The area of a figure in a scale drawing is 3 square inches. The actual area of the figure is 36 square feet. Tell how much actual area one square inch on the scale drawing represents.

18. ★ MULTIPLE CHOICE A model airplane uses the scale 2 in. : 15 ft. The model's length is 20 inches. Which proportion can be used to find the actual length x, in feet, of the airplane?

(A) $\dfrac{2}{15} = \dfrac{20}{x}$ (B) $\dfrac{2}{15} = \dfrac{x}{20}$ (C) $\dfrac{2}{20} = \dfrac{x}{15}$ (D) $\dfrac{x}{2} = \dfrac{15}{20}$

19. ERROR ANALYSIS A model of a table has a scale of 1 in. : 2 ft. The model is 6 inches long. Describe and correct the error made in finding the length x, in feet, of the table.

$$\frac{1 \text{ in.}}{2 \text{ ft}} = \frac{\text{Actual length}}{6 \text{ in.}} \longrightarrow \frac{1 \text{ in.}}{2 \text{ ft}} = \frac{x}{6 \text{ in.}}$$
$$x = 3$$
The actual length of the table is 3 feet. ✗

FINDING RATIOS A scale is given. Find the ratio of the perimeter of a figure drawn to this scale to the figure's actual perimeter. Then find the ratio of the area of a figure drawn to this scale to the figure's actual area.

SEE EXAMPLES 2 AND 3 on p. 418 for Exs. 20–29

20. 1 in. : 10 ft **21.** 15 cm : 1 km **22.** 10 mm : 1000 km **23.** 8 in. : 300 mi

24. 2 cm : 1 m **25.** 12 cm : 0.05 mm **26.** 3 in. : 15 ft **27.** 0.5 cm. : 10 km

RATIOS OF PERIMETERS The actual perimeter P of an object and the perimeter P of its scale drawing are given. Find the scale.

28. P(actual) = 42 yards
P(scale drawing) = 10.5 inches

29. P(actual) = 4.2 millimeters
P(scale drawing) = 21 centimeters

30. ✖ **ALGEBRA** A scale drawing has the scale $a : b$. Write algebraic expressions for the ratio of the perimeters and for the ratio of the areas.

CHALLENGE The actual area A of an object and its scale drawing are given. Find the scale of the drawing.

31. A(actual) = 56 square feet
A(scale drawing) = 14 square inches

32. A(actual) = 1.1 square centimeters
A(scale drawing) = 17.6 square meters

PROBLEM SOLVING

33. **STATUE OF LIBERTY** The model shown has a scale of about 1 in. : 20 ft. Use a proportion to approximate the actual height of the Statue of Liberty with its pedestal.

34. **USING A SCALE** A drawing of a garden has a scale of 1 in. : 3 ft. The perimeter of the scale drawing is 22 inches. What is the actual perimeter of the garden?

35. **★ SHORT RESPONSE** Choose a scale that relates inches to miles. *Explain* how one square inch of area in a drawing that uses this scale relates to the real-world area.

15 in.

★ = STANDARDIZED TEST PRACTICE   ◯ = HINTS AND HOMEWORK HELP *at classzone.com*

36. ★ **MULTIPLE CHOICE** Hamilton is 2 inches from Clinton on a map with a scale of 1 inch : 15 miles. How far is Clinton from Hamilton?

   Ⓐ 2 miles   Ⓑ 15 miles   Ⓒ 17 miles   Ⓓ 30 miles

LANDSCAPE DESIGN A landscape architect is designing a garden for a city park. The drawing has a scale of 1 cm : 5 m.

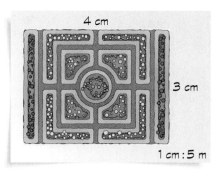

4 cm
3 cm
1 cm : 5 m

SEE EXAMPLES 2 AND 3
on p. 418
for Exs. 37–41

37. Find the actual dimensions of the garden.

38. Find the ratio of the drawing's perimeter to the garden's perimeter.

39. Find the ratio of the drawing's area to the garden's area.

40. ★ **WRITING** You want to make a poster-size scale drawing of a bug. What scale could you use? *Explain*.

41. **MULTI-STEP PROBLEM** Use the table.

   a. **Draw** Use a metric ruler to draw a rectangle with the dimensions given in the table. Copy the table and fill in the data for this rectangle.

Dimensions	Perimeter	Area
2 cm by 5 cm	?	?
?	?	?

   b. **Predict** Suppose you enlarge your rectangle so that 3 centimeters on the new rectangle represents 1 centimeter on the original rectangle. Predict the perimeter and area of the new rectangle. Record your answers in the table.

   c. **Compare** Draw the enlarged rectangle described in part (b). Find its perimeter and area. Do these results match your prediction? *Explain* your reasoning.

42. ◆ **MULTIPLE REPRESENTATIONS** The actual dimensions of a paddle are shown below.

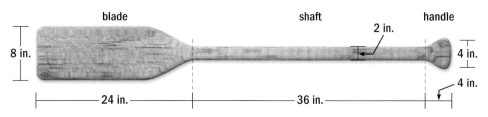

blade   shaft   handle
8 in.   2 in.   4 in.
                                       4 in.
24 in.   36 in.

   a. **Write a Proportion** The scale of the drawing you want to make of the paddle is 1 in. : 8 in. Use the scale to write a proportion involving the words "Length on drawing" and "Actual length."

   b. **Make a Table** Make a table showing the actual measure of each labeled part of the paddle and its corresponding measure in your scale drawing.

   c. **Make a Scale Drawing** Use your table to make the scale drawing of the paddle.

43. ★ **EXTENDED RESPONSE** A scale drawing or model can be *smaller* or *larger* than the figure it represents.

    a. *Describe* three situations where a scale drawing smaller than the item represented would be useful. Give the scales you would use.

    b. *Describe* three situations where a scale drawing larger than the item represented would be useful. Give the scales you would use.

    c. *Compare* your answers to parts (a) and (b). *Explain* the difference between the scales you can use in parts (a) and (b).

44. **CHALLENGE** An architect's blueprint of a house uses a scale of $\frac{1}{4}$ in. : 1 ft. The perimeter of a square window on the blueprint is 3 inches. How many square feet of fabric would be needed to make a shade to cover the actual window?

45. **CHALLENGE** The ratio of the area of a scale drawing to the actual area is 4 in.^{2} : 9 ft^2. What is the ratio of the perimeter of the scale drawing to the actual perimeter? *Explain* how you found your answer.

MIXED REVIEW

Get-Ready

Prepare for Lesson 8.5 in Exs. 46–49

Find the quotient using mental math. *(p. 193)*

46. $1.5 \div 10$ **47.** $71 \div 10$ **48.** $230 \div 100$ **49.** $68 \div 100$

Solve the proportion. *(p. 412)*

50. $\frac{5}{4} = \frac{x}{16}$ **51.** $\frac{2}{3} = \frac{22}{a}$ **52.** $\frac{6}{y} = \frac{9}{21}$ **53.** $\frac{10}{n} = \frac{25}{40}$

54. ★ **OPEN-ENDED MATH** Write the ratio 25 to 50 in two other ways. *(p. 402)*

QUIZ *for Lessons 8.1–8.4*

Match the numbered ratio with an equivalent lettered ratio. *(p. 402)*

    1. 5 to 30   **2.** 12 : 4   **3.** 24 to 18   **4.** 9 : 72

    A. 3 to 1   **B.** $\frac{1}{6}$ **C.** 1 : 8   **D.** 4 to 3

5. **SHOPPING** A 64 ounce carton of juice costs \$3.20. A 32 ounce carton of juice costs \$1.92. Which carton is the better buy? *Explain.* *(p. 407)*

Solve the proportion. *(p. 412)*

6. $\frac{4}{21} = \frac{x}{84}$ **7.** $\frac{25}{z} = \frac{100}{84}$ **8.** $\frac{36}{g} = \frac{8}{10}$ **9.** $\frac{n}{30} = \frac{8}{12}$

10. Use a metric ruler to make a scale drawing of the rectangle shown using the scale 1 cm : 5 cm. Then find the ratio of the area of the original rectangle to the area of the enlarged rectangle. *(p. 417)*

1 cm

2 cm

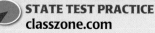
Lessons 8.1–8.4

1. **MULTI-STEP PROBLEM** Joe can run 100 yards in 12 seconds. Sarah can run 920 yards in 2 minutes.

   a. Convert Joe's speed to yards per second and explain your method.

   b. Convert Sarah's speed to yards per second and explain your method.

   c. *Compare* Joe's and Sarah's rates. Who runs faster?

2. **GRIDDED ANSWER** A car travels 3 miles in 4 minutes. At this rate, how many miles does the car travel in one hour?

3. **SHORT RESPONSE** Engineers tested two cars. Car A traveled 225 miles and used 14 gallons of gas. Car B traveled 312 miles and used 15 gallons of gas. Which car traveled more miles per gallon of gas used? *Explain* your reasoning.

4. **EXTENDED RESPONSE** A survey asked some of the students at your school which of five fruits they liked best. The results are shown in the circle graph below.

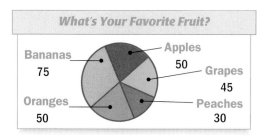

What's Your Favorite Fruit?

Bananas 75 · Apples 50 · Grapes 45 · Peaches 30 · Oranges 50

   a. Write the ratio of the number of students who chose peaches to the total number of students who took the survey. Then simplify. What does the ratio tell you about the number of students that chose peaches?

   b. There are a total of 1125 students in your school. Predict how many students would say peaches are their favorite fruit. *Explain* how you made your prediction.

5. **OPEN-ENDED** Name three ratios that form a proportion with the ratio $\frac{5}{7}$.

6. **SHORT RESPONSE** A group of 24 students go camping over the weekend. Two out of three campers go hiking. One out of four of the remaining campers goes swimming, and the rest stay at the campsite. How many campers stay at the campsite? *Explain* how you found your answer.

7. **EXTENDED RESPONSE** The sixth grade class sold three sizes of candles to raise money for a class trip. The ratio of small candles to medium candles sold was 3 to 1, and the ratio of medium candles to large candles sold was 2 to 7.

   a. Using the given information, can you determine which candle was the least popular? *Explain*.

   b. The class sold 24 medium candles. How many small candles were sold? How many large candles were sold?

   c. The class earned $1.50 for each small candle, $1.75 for each medium candle, and $2.25 for each large candle sold. How much money did the class earn?

8. **GRIDDED ANSWER** A scale drawing of a fountain has a scale of 1 in. : 2 ft. The actual width of the fountain is 8 feet. What is the width, in inches, of the fountain on the scale drawing?

GOAL
Use models to represent percents.

MATERIALS
• graph paper
• colored pencils

8.5 Modeling Percents

A *percent* is a ratio that compares a number to 100. The symbol for percent is %.

EXPLORE Model 25%.

STEP 1

On graph paper, make a border to form a 10×10 grid that contains 100 squares.

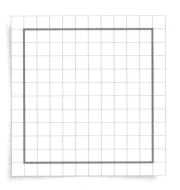

STEP 2

Each of the small squares in the grid represents $\frac{1}{100}$ of the grid.

$\frac{1}{100} = 1\%$

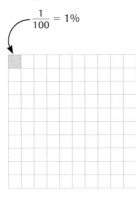

STEP 3

To model 25%, shade 25 squares. The shaded portion represents 25%, the decimal 0.25, and the fraction $\frac{25}{100} = \frac{1}{4}$.

PRACTICE Write the percent, decimal, and fraction for the model.

1.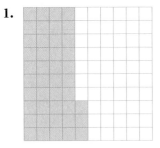

2.

3.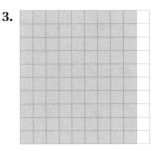

4. Use graph paper to make a model that represents 80%.

DRAW CONCLUSIONS

5. **REASONING** How could you model 100%? 150%? 200%? *Explain.*

8.5 Understanding Percent

Before	You wrote ratios and rates.
Now	You'll write percents as decimals and fractions.
Why?	So you can interpret concert survey results, as in Ex. 34.

KEY VOCABULARY
• percent, *p. 425*

A **percent** is a ratio that compares a number to 100. The word *percent* means "per hundred," or "out of 100." The symbol for percent is %.

There are 100 marbles shown at the right, and 43 out of 100 are blue. You can represent this ratio using a percent, a decimal, or a fraction.

Percent	Decimal	Fraction
43%	0.43	$\frac{43}{100}$

Each marble represents 1% of the group of 100 marbles.

EXAMPLE 1 — Writing Ratios in Different Forms

In the diagram above, 7 out of the 100 marbles are red. Write this ratio as a percent, a decimal, and a fraction.

Percent: 7%   **Decimal:** 0.07   **Fraction:** $\frac{7}{100}$

EXAMPLE 2 — Writing Percents

TAKE NOTES
In your notes, you may want to include percents in a concept map about forms of numbers, like the concept map shown on page 400.

Write the number in words, and as a percent.

a. $\frac{9}{100}$ b. 0.39   c. $\frac{32.5}{100}$ d. 3, or $\frac{300}{100}$

SOLUTION

a. nine hundredths, or 9%   b. thirty-nine hundredths, or 39%

c. thirty-two and five tenths hundredths, or 32.5%   d. three hundred hundredths, or 300%

✓ GUIDED PRACTICE — for Examples 1 and 2

Write the ratio as a percent, a decimal, and a fraction, or write the number in words and as a percent.

1. 29 to 100   **2.** 0.03   **3.** 0.325   **4.** $\frac{5}{1}$

KEY CONCEPT

For Your Notebook

Writing Percents as Decimals and Fractions

To write a percent as a *decimal:*

Divide the value by 100. $57\% = 57 \div 100 = 0.57$

To write a percent as a *fraction:*

Rewrite the percent using
a denominator of 100. $35\% = \dfrac{35}{100} = \dfrac{7}{20}$
Simplify if possible.

EXAMPLE 3   **Writing Percents in Different Forms**

a. Write 64.5% as a decimal.

$64.5\% = 64.5 \div 100 = 0.645$

b. Write 80% as a fraction.

$80\% = \dfrac{80}{100} = \dfrac{4}{5}$

Circle Graphs Circle graphs are often used to represent the results of a survey. The parts of a circle graph together represent a total of 100%.

EXAMPLE 4   **Circle Graphs with Percents**

Survey In a survey, 100 dog owners were asked where their dogs sleep. The results are shown as percents.

a. What percent of the people responded "Other"?

b. What percent of the people did *not* respond "Dog bed"?

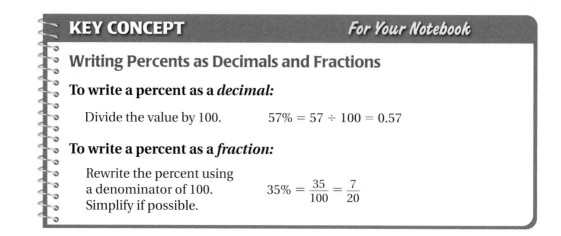

Where does your dog sleep?

- Owner's bed 42%
- Doghouse 30%
- Dog bed 18%
- Other ?

ANOTHER WAY

Another way to answer part (b) is to add the percents of people who responded with each response other than "Dog bed":

42% + 30% + 10%, which equals 82%.

SOLUTION

a. The circle graph represents 100%. The sum of the percents shown is
$42\% + 30\% + 18\% = 90\%$, so the "Other" part is $100\% - 90\% = 10\%$.

b. The percent of people who did *not* respond "Dog bed" is
$100\% - 18\% = 82\%$.

✓ **GUIDED PRACTICE**   **for Examples 3 and 4**

Write the percent as a decimal and a fraction.

5. 5%   **6.** 75%   **7.** 20%   **8.** 3.5%

9. What If? If "Dog crate" is added to the circle graph at 4% and "Other" is reduced to 6%, what percent of the people did *not* respond "Other"?

426   Chapter 8   Ratio, Proportion, and Percent

8.5 EXERCISES

SKILL PRACTICE

VOCABULARY Copy and complete the statement.

1. When you write a percent as a fraction, you rewrite the percent using a denominator of __?__ .

2. Percent means "per __?__ ."

USING MODELS Each small square in the model represents 1%. Represent the number of shaded squares as a percent, a decimal, and a fraction.

SEE EXAMPLE 1
on p. 425
for Exs. 3–5

3.

4.

5.

REWRITING NUMBERS Write the number in words and as a percent.

SEE EXAMPLE 2
on p. 425
for Exs. 6–13

6. 0.42   7. 0.06   8. 0.57   9. 0.74

10. $\frac{28}{100}$ 11. $\frac{19}{100}$ 12. $\frac{200}{100}$ 13. $\frac{52.8}{100}$

REWRITING PERCENTS Write the percent as a decimal and a fraction.

SEE EXAMPLE 3
on p. 426
for Exs. 14–23

14. 34%   15. 40%   16. 85%   17. 7%

18. 73.8%   19. $18\frac{1}{2}$%   20. 0.1%   21. 33.3%

22. **ERROR ANALYSIS** Describe and correct the error made in rewriting the percent as a decimal.

$$34.8\% = 34.8 \times 100 = 3480 \quad ✗$$

23. ★ **MULTIPLE CHOICE** Which choice shows 12.5% written as a fraction?

Ⓐ $\frac{1}{80}$ Ⓑ $\frac{1}{8}$ Ⓒ $\frac{5}{4}$ Ⓓ $\frac{4}{5}$

NUMBER SENSE Copy and complete the statement using <, >, or = .

24. 50% _?_ 0.05   25. 14% _?_ $\frac{1.4}{100}$ 26. 0.4 _?_ 40%

27. 10% _?_ 0.01   28. 99% _?_ 99.9   29. $\frac{65}{100}$ _?_ 65%

30. ★ **OPEN-ENDED MATH** Write a number between 0 and 1 as a decimal, a fraction, and a percent.

31. **CHALLENGE** Let *a* be any decimal greater than zero. For what values of *a* will the percent be less than 1%? between 10% and 20%? greater than 100%?

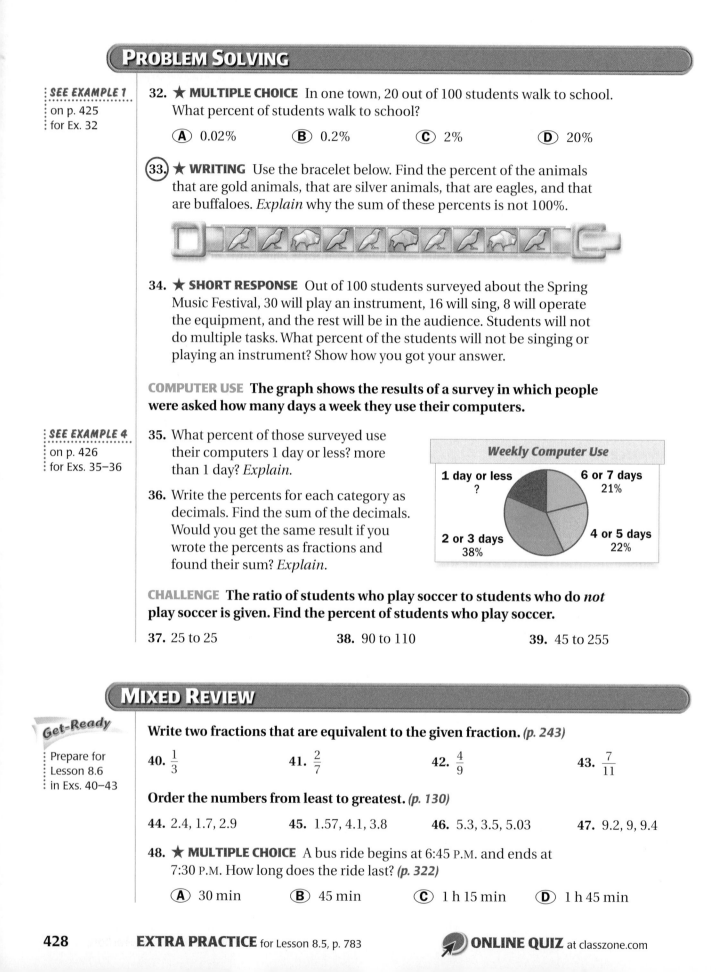

PROBLEM SOLVING

SEE EXAMPLE 1
on p. 425
for Ex. 32

32. ★ **MULTIPLE CHOICE** In one town, 20 out of 100 students walk to school. What percent of students walk to school?

(A) 0.02%   (B) 0.2%   (C) 2%   (D) 20%

33. ★ **WRITING** Use the bracelet below. Find the percent of the animals that are gold animals, that are silver animals, that are eagles, and that are buffaloes. *Explain* why the sum of these percents is not 100%.

34. ★ **SHORT RESPONSE** Out of 100 students surveyed about the Spring Music Festival, 30 will play an instrument, 16 will sing, 8 will operate the equipment, and the rest will be in the audience. Students will not do multiple tasks. What percent of the students will not be singing or playing an instrument? Show how you got your answer.

COMPUTER USE The graph shows the results of a survey in which people were asked how many days a week they use their computers.

SEE EXAMPLE 4
on p. 426
for Exs. 35–36

35. What percent of those surveyed use their computers 1 day or less? more than 1 day? *Explain.*

36. Write the percents for each category as decimals. Find the sum of the decimals. Would you get the same result if you wrote the percents as fractions and found their sum? *Explain.*

Weekly Computer Use

1 day or less ?
6 or 7 days 21%
2 or 3 days 38%
4 or 5 days 22%

CHALLENGE The ratio of students who play soccer to students who do *not* play soccer is given. Find the percent of students who play soccer.

37. 25 to 25   **38.** 90 to 110   **39.** 45 to 255

MIXED REVIEW

Get-Ready

Prepare for
Lesson 8.6
in Exs. 40–43

Write two fractions that are equivalent to the given fraction. *(p. 243)*

40. $\frac{1}{3}$ **41.** $\frac{2}{7}$ **42.** $\frac{4}{9}$ **43.** $\frac{7}{11}$

Order the numbers from least to greatest. *(p. 130)*

44. 2.4, 1.7, 2.9   **45.** 1.57, 4.1, 3.8   **46.** 5.3, 3.5, 5.03   **47.** 9.2, 9, 9.4

48. ★ **MULTIPLE CHOICE** A bus ride begins at 6:45 P.M. and ends at 7:30 P.M. How long does the ride last? *(p. 322)*

(A) 30 min   (B) 45 min   (C) 1 h 15 min   (D) 1 h 45 min

8.6 Percents, Decimals, and Fractions

Before	You wrote percents as fractions and decimals.
Now	You'll write fractions and decimals as percents.
Why?	So you can plan for a field trip, as in Example 3.

KEY VOCABULARY
- **decimal,** *p. 120*
- **fraction,** *p. 243*
- **percent,** *p. 425*

Volleyball In a volleyball game, a player's serves must land in a certain region to be playable. What percent of serves did Maria get "in" today? What percent did she get "in" so far this season?

You can use the fraction of Maria's serves that she got "in" to find the percent that she got "in." To do this, write an equivalent fraction with a denominator of 100.

Serving Record		
Maria	Serves "in"	Total serves
Today	4	10
Season	17	25

EXAMPLE 1 Writing Fractions as Percents

To answer the questions above, first write each result as a fraction. Then write an equivalent fraction with a denominator of 100 to find the percent.

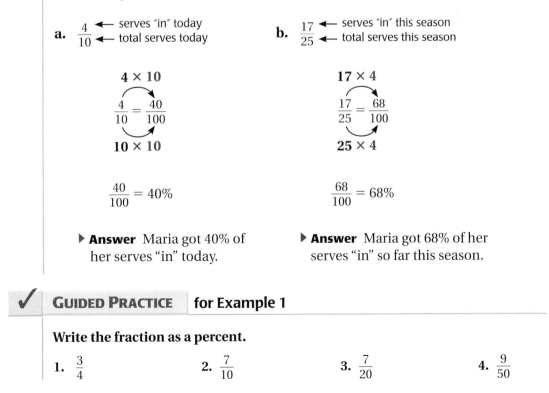

a. $\dfrac{4}{10}$ ← serves "in" today
← total serves today

$$\overset{4 \times 10}{\underset{10 \times 10}{\dfrac{4}{10} = \dfrac{40}{100}}}$$

$$\dfrac{40}{100} = 40\%$$

▶ **Answer** Maria got 40% of her serves "in" today.

b. $\dfrac{17}{25}$ ← serves "in" this season
← total serves this season

$$\overset{17 \times 4}{\underset{25 \times 4}{\dfrac{17}{25} = \dfrac{68}{100}}}$$

$$\dfrac{68}{100} = 68\%$$

▶ **Answer** Maria got 68% of her serves "in" so far this season.

✓ GUIDED PRACTICE for Example 1

Write the fraction as a percent.

1. $\dfrac{3}{4}$ **2.** $\dfrac{7}{10}$ **3.** $\dfrac{7}{20}$ **4.** $\dfrac{9}{50}$

EXAMPLE 2 Writing Decimals as Percents

Write the decimal as a percent.

a. $0.06 = \dfrac{6}{100} = 6\%$ 0.06 is six hundredths, or 6%.

b. $0.6 = \dfrac{6}{10}$ 0.6 is six tenths.

$= \dfrac{60}{100}$ **Multiply the numerator and denominator by 10 to get a denominator of 100.**

$= 60\%$

DIVIDE BY 10
To divide by 10, move the decimal point 1 place to the left. In part (c) of Example 2, $25 \div 10 = 2.5$.

c. $0.025 = \dfrac{25}{1000}$ 0.025 is twenty-five thousandths.

$= \dfrac{2.5}{100}$ **Divide the numerator and denominator by 10 to get a denominator of 100.**

$= 2.5\%$

Using Decimals When the denominator of a fraction is not a factor of 100, it may be easier to write the fraction as a decimal first.

EXAMPLE 3 Using Decimals to Write Percents

Field Trip You attend 5 out of 8 Biology Club meetings. You must attend at least 60% of the meetings to go on a field trip. Can you go?

AVOID ERRORS
In Example 3, you do not have to attend *exactly* 60% of the meetings. So check whether it is true that $\dfrac{5}{8}$ is greater than or equal to 60%.

SOLUTION

$\dfrac{5}{8} = 0.625$ **Divide 5 by 8 to write the fraction as a decimal.**

$= \dfrac{625}{1000}$ **0.625 is 625 thousandths.**

$= \dfrac{62.5}{100}$ **Divide the numerator and denominator by 10 to get a denominator of 100.**

$= 62.5\%$

▶**Answer** Because 62.5% > 60%, you can go on the field trip.

Animated Math
at classzone.com

✓ **GUIDED PRACTICE** for Examples 2 and 3

Write the decimal or fraction as a percent.

5. 0.3   **6.** 0.105   **7.** $\dfrac{3}{8}$ **8.** $\dfrac{9}{40}$

9. What If? In Example 3, can you take the trip if you go to 7 out of 12 meetings?

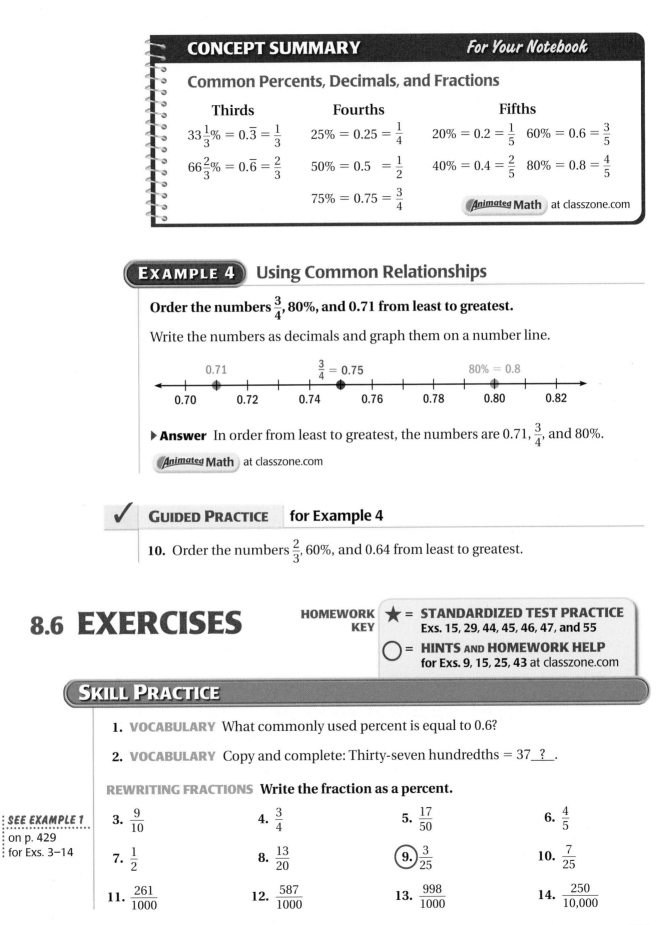

CONCEPT SUMMARY
For Your Notebook

Common Percents, Decimals, and Fractions

Thirds	**Fourths**	**Fifths**

$33\frac{1}{3}\% = 0.\overline{3} = \frac{1}{3}$ $25\% = 0.25 = \frac{1}{4}$ $20\% = 0.2 = \frac{1}{5}$ $60\% = 0.6 = \frac{3}{5}$

$66\frac{2}{3}\% = 0.\overline{6} = \frac{2}{3}$ $50\% = 0.5 = \frac{1}{2}$ $40\% = 0.4 = \frac{2}{5}$ $80\% = 0.8 = \frac{4}{5}$

$75\% = 0.75 = \frac{3}{4}$

Animated Math at classzone.com

EXAMPLE 4   **Using Common Relationships**

Order the numbers $\frac{3}{4}$, 80%, and 0.71 from least to greatest.

Write the numbers as decimals and graph them on a number line.

0.71 $\frac{3}{4}$ = 0.75   80% = 0.8

0.70   0.72   0.74   0.76   0.78   0.80   0.82

▶ **Answer** In order from least to greatest, the numbers are 0.71, $\frac{3}{4}$, and 80%.

Animated Math at classzone.com

✓ **GUIDED PRACTICE**   **for Example 4**

10. Order the numbers $\frac{2}{3}$, 60%, and 0.64 from least to greatest.

8.6 EXERCISES

★ = **STANDARDIZED TEST PRACTICE**
Exs. 15, 29, 44, 45, 46, 47, and 55

◯ = **HINTS AND HOMEWORK HELP**
for Exs. 9, 15, 25, 43 at classzone.com

SKILL PRACTICE

1. VOCABULARY What commonly used percent is equal to 0.6?

2. VOCABULARY Copy and complete: Thirty-seven hundredths = 37 _?_ .

REWRITING FRACTIONS Write the fraction as a percent.

SEE EXAMPLE 1
on p. 429
for Exs. 3–14

3. $\frac{9}{10}$ **4.** $\frac{3}{4}$ **5.** $\frac{17}{50}$ **6.** $\frac{4}{5}$

7. $\frac{1}{2}$ **8.** $\frac{13}{20}$ **9.** $\frac{3}{25}$ **10.** $\frac{7}{25}$

11. $\frac{261}{1000}$ **12.** $\frac{587}{1000}$ **13.** $\frac{998}{1000}$ **14.** $\frac{250}{10,000}$

8.6 Percents, Decimals, and Fractions   **431**

SEE EXAMPLE 1
on p. 429
for Ex. 15

(15.) ★ MULTIPLE CHOICE What is *two fifths* written as a percent?

(A) 20%   (B) 25%   (C) 40%   (D) 60%

REWRITING DECIMALS Write the decimal as a percent.

SEE EXAMPLE 2
on p. 430
for Exs. 16–28

16. 0.92   **17.** 0.2   **18.** 0.02   **19.** 0.084

20. 0.268   **21.** 0.571   **22.** 0.125   **23.** 0.037

24. 0.015   **(25.)** 0.377   **26.** 0.0995   **27.** 0.586

28. ERROR ANALYSIS Describe and correct the error made in writing the decimal as a percent.

$$\times \quad 0.046 = \frac{46}{100} = 46\%$$

29. ★ OPEN-ENDED MATH Write 3 fractions that are equivalent to 28%.

ORDERING Use a number line to order the numbers from least to greatest.

SEE EXAMPLES
3 AND 4
on pp. 430–431
for Exs. 30–35

30. 68%, $\frac{67}{100}$, 0.64   **31.** $\frac{1}{4}$, 15%, 0.16   **32.** $\frac{17}{20}$, 82%, 0.88

33. 50%, 0.77, $\frac{7}{10}$, $\frac{2}{3}$ **34.** $\frac{4}{5}$, 0.72, 79%, $\frac{3}{4}$ **35.** $\frac{1}{3}$, 33%, 34%, 0.3

36. CHOOSE A METHOD Tell whether you would use a *calculator, paper and pencil,* or *mental math* to write (a) $\frac{3}{10}$ and (b) $\frac{2}{7}$ as percents. Then write and compare the percents. Round to the nearest whole percent, if necessary.

37. MENTAL MATH Copy and complete: If $\frac{7}{20} = 35\%$, then $\frac{14}{20} = \underline{\ ?\ }\%$.

REWRITING Write the decimal as a percent or the percent as a decimal.

38. 1.25   **39.** 3.5   **40.** 200%   **41.** 570%

42. CHALLENGE Tell whether the following statement is *true* or *false*: A fraction with a denominator in the thousands will always have a decimal form with more decimal places than a fraction with a single-digit denominator. *Explain* your reasoning.

PROBLEM SOLVING

SEE EXAMPLE 1
on p. 429
for Ex. 43

(43.) DESERTS Deserts cover about $\frac{1}{5}$ of Earth's land surface. What percent of Earth's land surface is desert?

44. ★ WRITING What percent of a meter is 5 centimeters? What percent of a meter is 5 millimeters? *Explain* how you found your answers.

★ = STANDARDIZED TEST PRACTICE   ○ = **HINTS AND HOMEWORK HELP** *at classzone.com*

SEE EXAMPLE 3
on p. 430
for Ex. 45

45. ★ **MULTIPLE CHOICE** A survey at Roosevelt Middle School showed that $\frac{11}{40}$ of the sixth grade students named soccer as their favorite sport. What percent of the sixth grade students named soccer as their favorite sport?

   (A) 0.275%   (B) 11%   (C) 27.5%   (D) 40%

46. ★ **OPEN-ENDED MATH** Estimate the time in hours that you spend during a typical weekday sleeping, eating, doing homework, at school, and so on. Write each estimate as a fraction of a full day. Then write the fractions as percents. Apart from sleeping, which activity takes the most of your day?

47. ★ **SHORT RESPONSE** Consider the decimal forms of fractions such as $\frac{1}{10}$, $\frac{1}{25}$, $\frac{1}{50}$, $\frac{10}{200}$, $\frac{10}{400}$, and $\frac{1}{1000}$. *Describe* the types of fractions that can be most easily rewritten as decimals by finding equivalent fractions instead of by dividing.

POPULATION In Exercises 48 and 49, use the information below.

The map at the right shows the regions in the United States that were states or territories in 1850. Texas became a state in 1845. By 2004, its population was about 22.5 million.

48. What percent of the 1850 United States population was the population of Texas in 1850? Use that percent to predict the population of the United States in 2004.

49. **CHALLENGE** In 2004, the population of the United States was about 293.7 million. *Explain* why your prediction does not match this number.

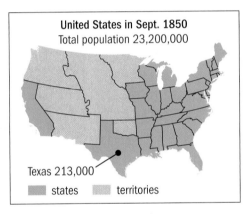

United States in Sept. 1850
Total population 23,200,000

Texas 213,000

☐ states   ☐ territories

MIXED REVIEW

Get-Ready
Prepare for
Lesson 8.7
in Exs. 50–53

Write the percent as a decimal and a fraction. *(p. 425)*

50. 2%   51. 37%   52. 75%   53. 96%

CHOOSE A STRATEGY Use a strategy from the list to solve the following problem. *Explain* your choice of strategy.

54. On a shopping trip, you spend $10.75 at one store. At another store, you spend $16.30. You have $4.35 left. How much did you start with?

55. ★ **OPEN-ENDED MATH** *Describe* how you could use both the commutative and associative properties of multiplication to rewrite and evaluate $5 \times 2.2 \times 10$. *(p. 169)*

Problem Solving Strategies
- Guess, Check, and Revise *(p. 763)*
- Work Backward *(p. 764)*
- Make a List or Table *(p. 765)*
- Solve a Simpler Problem *(p. 768)*

8.7 Finding a Percent of a Number

Before	You multiplied whole numbers by decimals and fractions.
Now	You'll multiply to find a percent of a number.
Why?	So you can calculate a tip, as in Example 4.

KEY VOCABULARY
- **interest,** *p. 436*
- **principal,** *p. 436*
- **annual interest rate,** *p. 436*
- **simple interest,** *p. 436*

ACTIVITY

You can change a percent to a fraction or a decimal to find a percent of a number.

Recall that "of" means "multiply." To find 50% of 8, find $\frac{1}{2} \times 8$ or 0.5×8.

STEP 1 **Write** the percent as a fraction and multiply to find the percent of the number.

    a. 25% of 72   **b.** 10% of 72   **c.** 62% of 72   **d.** $33\frac{1}{3}$% of 72

STEP 2 **Write** the percents in Step 1 as decimals to find the percent of the number.

STEP 3 **Compare** Steps 1 and 2. Which answers were easier to find by changing the percents to fractions? Which answers were easier to find by changing the percents to decimals? *Explain.*

The activity above suggests two ways to find a percent of a number.

- Change the percent to a fraction and multiply by the number.

- Change the percent to a decimal and multiply by the number.

EXAMPLE 1 Finding a Percent of a Number

TAKE NOTES
Include Example 1 in your notes to illustrate when a fraction is more convenient to use, as in part (a), or when a decimal is more convenient, as in part (b).

a. Find 75% of 60. Use a fraction.

$$75\% \text{ of } 60 = \frac{3}{4} \times 60$$

$$= \frac{180}{4}$$

$$= 45$$

▶**Answer** 75% of 60 is 45.

b. Find 10% of 74. Use a decimal.

$$10\% \text{ of } 74 = 0.1 \times 74$$

$$= 7.4$$

▶**Answer** 10% of 74 is 7.4.

✓ GUIDED PRACTICE for Example 1

1. Find 50% of 48.

2. Find 10% of 36.

EXAMPLE 2 Finding a Discount

AVOID ERRORS

Don't confuse the calculated discount with the sale price. You need to subtract the discount from the regular price to find the sale price.

Discounts The regular price of a pair of sneakers is $40. The sale price is 25% off the regular price. What is the sale price?

STEP 1 **Find** the discount.

$$25\% \text{ of } \$40 = \frac{1}{4} \times \$40 = \$10$$

STEP 2 **Subtract** the discount from the regular price.

$$\$40 - \$10 = \$30$$

▶ **Answer** The sale price of the sneakers is $30.

Animated Math
at classzone.com

EXAMPLE 3 Finding the Sales Tax

Sales Tax You are buying dog food that costs $8.50. There is a 6% sales tax. What is the total amount of your purchase?

STEP 1 **Find** the sales tax.

$$6\% \text{ of } \$8.50 = 0.06 \times \$8.50 = \$.51$$

STEP 2 **Add** the sales tax to the cost of the item.

$$\$8.50 + \$.51 = \$9.01$$

▶ **Answer** The total amount of your purchase is $9.01.

EXAMPLE 4 Solve a Multi-Step Problem

Tipping You take a taxi ride. The fare is $23.78. You want to give a 15% tip. Use simpler percents and mental math to estimate the amount of the tip.

STEP 1 **Round** the fare to the nearest dollar.

$$\$23.78 \approx \$24.00$$

STEP 2 **Find** 10% of the fare.

$$0.1 \times \$24 = \$2.40$$

ANOTHER WAY

In some states, the tax is 5%. So, if a 5% tax is given on a bill, you can multiply the tax by 3 to find a 15% tip.

STEP 3 **Find** 5% of the fare. It is half of 10% of the fare.

$$\frac{1}{2} \times \$2.40 = \$1.20$$

STEP 4 **Add** the partial tips.

$$\$2.40 + \$1.20 = \$3.60$$

▶ **Answer** A 15% tip for a $23.78 taxi fare is about $3.60.

✓ **GUIDED PRACTICE** for Examples 2, 3, and 4

3. **Discounts** A book's regular price is $19.95. Find the sale price with a 20% discount.

4. **Tax** The price of a cat toy is $9.50. Find the total cost with a sales tax of 8%.

5. **Tip** The price of a shoe shine is $4.75. Use mental math to estimate the total cost if you tip 15%.

EXAMPLE 5 Standardized Test Practice

> **Total Bill** The bill for breakfast is $28.60. You want to leave a 15% tip. Which equation can be used to find t, the total cost in dollars?
>
> **A** $t = 0.15(28.60)$ **B** $t = 28.60 - 0.15(28.60)$
>
> **C** $t = 28.60 + 0.15(28.60)$ **D** $t = 28.60 + 15(28.60)$

ELIMINATE CHOICES
The problem asks for the total cost rather than just the amount of the tip, so choice A can be eliminated.

SOLUTION

STEP 1 **Write** an expression to find 15% of the bill.

$$0.15(28.60)$$

STEP 2 **Add** the expression to the bill.

$$28.60 + 0.15(28.60)$$

▸ **Answer** An equation to find the total cost is $t = 28.60 + 0.15(28.60)$. The correct answer is C. Ⓐ Ⓑ ● Ⓓ

VOCABULARY
The word annual means *yearly*. So you can remember the definition of annual interest rate as a *yearly* interest rate.

Simple Interest When you save money at a bank, you *earn interest*. When you borrow money, you *pay interest*. **Interest** is the amount paid for the use of money. The amount you save or borrow is the **principal**. The percent of the principal you earn or pay per year is the **annual interest rate**.

> **KEY CONCEPT** *For Your Notebook*
>
> **Simple Interest Formula**
>
> Interest paid on only the principal is **simple interest**.
>
> **Words**   Simple interest = **Principal** · Annual interest rate · Time in years
>
> **Algebra** $I = Prt$

EXAMPLE 6 Finding Simple Interest

VOCABULARY
An interest rate is usually given as an annual percent. However, you write the interest rate as a decimal to compute interest earned.

Savings You deposit $75 in an account. The annual interest rate is 4%. How much simple interest will you earn in 2 years?

$I = Prt$ Write the simple interest formula.

$= 75(0.04)(2)$ Substitute values. Write 4% as a decimal.

$= 6$ Multiply.

▸ **Answer** You will earn $6 in simple interest in 2 years.

6. **Tips** Breakfast for you and a friend costs $12.09, and you leave a 20% tip. Which equation would you use to find t, the total amount paid in dollars: $t = 0.2(12.09)$ or $t = 0.2(12.09) + 12.09$? Find the total amount paid.

7. **Savings** You deposit $100 in a bank account. The annual interest rate is 3%. How much simple interest will you earn in 3 years?

8.7 EXERCISES

HOMEWORK KEY

★ = **STANDARDIZED TEST PRACTICE**
Exs. 40, 41, 50, 54, 57, 59, and 70

○ = **HINTS AND HOMEWORK HELP**
for Exs. 17, 23, 29, 51 at classzone.com

SKILL PRACTICE

1. **VOCABULARY** What does each variable in the formula $I = Prt$ represent?

2. **VOCABULARY** Copy and complete: Interest paid on only the principal is called __?__ .

FINDING PERCENTS OF NUMBERS Find the percent of the number.

SEE EXAMPLE 1
on p. 434
for Exs. 3–20

3. 50% of 84
4. 25% of 80
5. 10% of 100
6. 60% of 60

7. 45% of 20
8. 75% of 72
9. 85% of 12
10. 11% of 4

11. 60% of 15
12. 40% of 150
13. 18% of 45
14. 83% of 20

15. 31% of 120
16. 65% of 150
17. $33\frac{1}{3}$% of 63
18. $66\frac{2}{3}$% of 9

19. **ERROR ANALYSIS** Describe and correct the error made in finding the percent of the number.

$$1\% \text{ of } 400 = \frac{1}{10} \times 400 = \frac{400}{10} = 40 \quad \times$$

MENTAL MATH The regular price of a pair of jeans is $40. Find the sale price with the given discount.

SEE EXAMPLE 2
on p. 435
for Exs. 20–27

20. 5% discount
21. 10% discount
22. 15% discount
23. 20% discount

24. 25% discount
25. 30% discount
26. 40% discount
27. 50% discount

ALGEBRA Find the simple interest for the given principal, rate, and time.

SEE EXAMPLE 6
on p. 436
for Exs. 28–31

28. $P = \$275$, $r = 4\%$, $t = 5$ years
29. $P = \$320$, $r = 3\%$, $t = 4$ years

30. $P = \$84$, $r = 2\%$, $t = 3$ years
31. $P = \$112$, $r = 2.5\%$, $t = 2$ years

ESTIMATION Estimate the percent of the number.

32. 11% of 400
33. 75% of 804
34. 48% of 7.9
35. 15% of 8.50

36. 19% of 205
37. 6% of 62
38. 89% of 80.1
39. 33% of 80.5

40. ★ **OPEN-ENDED MATH** *Describe* how to find the total cost of a meal including sales tax and tip for you and two friends. Let the amount of the bill be between $30 and $50. Specify the tax rate and tip rate you used.

41. ★ **MULTIPLE CHOICE** A shoe store is having a 25% off sale. If a pair of shoes costs $39.99, the first step in calculating the sale price is:

(A) multiply 39.99 by 25   (B) multiply 39.99 by 0.25

(C) divide 39.99 by 25   (D) divide 39.99 by 0.25

NUMBER SENSE **Copy and complete the statement using <, >, or =.**

42. 98 _?_ 90% of 98   **43.** 0.5 _?_ 150% of 0.5   **44.** 60 _?_ 30% of 200

45. 40 _?_ 80% of 50   **46.** 0.05 _?_ 5% of 0.01   **47.** 150 _?_ 80% of 250

48. (xy) **REASONING** You know that 20% of a number *n* is 16. How can you use this information to find 40% of *n*? 30% of *n*? *Explain.*

49. **CHALLENGE** You can buy laundry soap in box A or box B. Box A weighs 100 ounces and is priced at 90% of the cost of box B. Box B costs $10 and weighs 110% of box A's weight. Which is the better buy? *Explain.*

PROBLEM SOLVING

SEE EXAMPLE 1
on p. 434
for Ex. 50

50. ★ **MULTIPLE CHOICE** You have a stamp collection with 120 stamps. The circle graph shows the percent of stamps from each country. How many of your stamps are from Canada?

(A) 6 stamps   (B) 18 stamps

(C) 24 stamps   (D) 60 stamps

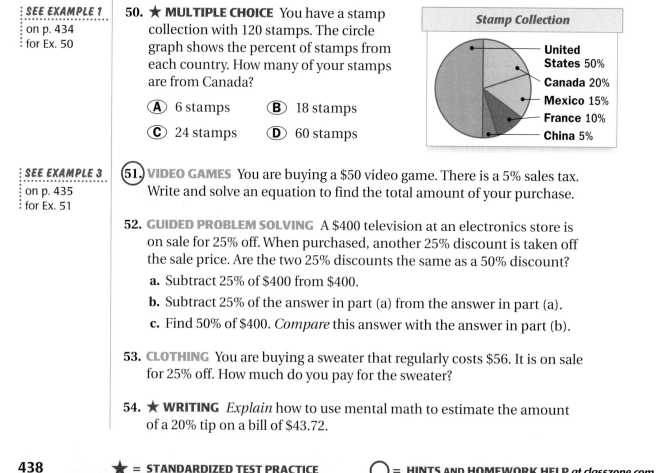

Stamp Collection

United States 50%
Canada 20%
Mexico 15%
France 10%
China 5%

SEE EXAMPLE 3
on p. 435
for Ex. 51

51. **VIDEO GAMES** You are buying a $50 video game. There is a 5% sales tax. Write and solve an equation to find the total amount of your purchase.

52. **GUIDED PROBLEM SOLVING** A $400 television at an electronics store is on sale for 25% off. When purchased, another 25% discount is taken off the sale price. Are the two 25% discounts the same as a 50% discount?

  a. Subtract 25% of $400 from $400.

  b. Subtract 25% of the answer in part (a) from the answer in part (a).

  c. Find 50% of $400. *Compare* this answer with the answer in part (b).

53. **CLOTHING** You are buying a sweater that regularly costs $56. It is on sale for 25% off. How much do you pay for the sweater?

54. ★ **WRITING** *Explain* how to use mental math to estimate the amount of a 20% tip on a bill of $43.72.

SEE EXAMPLE 4
on p. 435
for Ex. 55

55. ESTIMATION A tourist group is eating at a restaurant. The bill is $37.53. They want to leave a 15% tip. Estimate the amount of the tip.

56. ⊗ **COMPARING OPTIONS** Which principal P and interest rate r give a greater simple interest after 5 years, $P = \$120$ with $r = 3\%$, or $P = \$125$ with $r = 2\%$? *Explain* your reasoning.

SEE EXAMPLE 5
on p. 436
for Exs. 57–59

57. ★ MULTIPLE CHOICE You are selling boxes of cookies. Your cost per box is $2.50. You sell each box for 15% more than your cost. Which equation can be used to find p, the price of each box in dollars?

    Ⓐ $p = 0.15(2.50)$ **Ⓑ** $p = 2.50 + 0.15(2.50)$

    Ⓒ $p = 2.50 - 15(2.50)$ **Ⓓ** $p = 2.50 + 15(2.50)$

58. VIDEO GAMING You are playing a game where your power determines your character's capabilities. Your power grows 5% every time you pass a purple star but drops by 10% every time you jump a red barrier.

    a. Your beginning power is 100. What is it at the bridge?

    b. You cannot jump a blue barrier unless your power is at least 90. Can you jump the blue barrier without getting more power? *Explain.*

59. ★ SHORT RESPONSE You have a coupon for a 15% discount off any item in a store. You'll pay 5% sales tax on the sale price. How much will you pay for a shirt whose regular price is $16.50? *Explain* your reasoning.

READING *IN* MATH   Read the school newspaper article for Exercises 60–62.

Spanish More Popular in Grade 7

This reporter surveyed 6th and 7th graders last week about their interest in taking Spanish. Demand was clearly higher among 7th grade students, as shown in the table.

Grade	Number surveyed	Number who want to take Spanish
6	40	24
7	75	45

60. Calculate How many more seventh graders than sixth graders want to take Spanish?

61. Compare Find the percent of sixth graders surveyed and the percent of seventh graders surveyed who want to take Spanish. How do these percents compare?

62. Interpret Do your results support the reporter's claim that Spanish is more popular in grade 7 than grade 6? *Explain* your answer.

63. MULTI-STEP PROBLEM A sporting goods store offers a package of hockey equipment for 20% less than the cost of the same items sold separately. The individual cost of each item is shown in the table.

Item	Price
helmet	$ 46
shoulder pads	$ 58
shin guards	$ 46
elbow pads	$ 30
skates	$110

  a. Find the cost of the equipment without the helmet. Then add 6% sales tax.

  b. Find the cost of all the equipment. Next find the cost of this package after the 20% discount. Then add 6% sales tax.

  c. You already have a helmet. Which costs less, buying the package or buying just the equipment you do not have? *Explain.*

64. CHALLENGE You deposited $120 in an account with an annual interest rate of 4%. In how many years will the simple interest earned be $1.92? *Explain* your reasoning.

MIXED REVIEW

Get-Ready

Prepare for Lesson 9.1 in Exs. 65–67

Find the length of the line segment to the nearest millimeter. *(p. 59)*

65. —————— **66.** ———— **67.** ——————

Find the mean, median, mode(s), and range of the data. *(p. 99)*

68. 4, 7, 5, 26, 10, 8, 10

69. 3, 6, 1, 9, 10, 9, 8, 3, 16, 5

70. ★ **MULTIPLE CHOICE** An engineer looks at a blueprint of a bridge that has a scale of 1 cm : 20 m. On the blueprint, the span of the bridge is 35 centimeters. What is the actual span of the bridge? *(p. 417)*

  A 1.75 m   **B** 700 cm   **C** 35 m   **D** 700 m

QUIZ *for Lessons 8.5–8.7*

Write the percent as a decimal and a fraction. *(p. 425)*

1. 43%   **2.** 97%   **3.** 2%   **4.** 12%

Write the fraction or decimal as a percent. *(p. 429)*

5. $\frac{27}{100}$ **6.** 0.82   **7.** 0.7   **8.** $\frac{3}{5}$

9. Order the numbers 34%, $\frac{8}{25}$, and 0.37 from least to greatest. *(p. 429)*

Find the simple interest for the given principal, rate, and time. *(p. 434)*

10. $P = \$375$, $r = 7\%$, $t = 3$ years   **11.** $P = \$215$, $r = 3\%$, $t = 5$ years

12. TIPPING Your bill in a restaurant is $28.70. You want to leave a 20% tip. Estimate the amount of the tip. *(p. 434)*

EXTRA PRACTICE for Lesson 8.7, p. 783   **ONLINE QUIZ** at classzone.com

8.7 Finding a Percent of a Number

EXPLORE You deposit $100 in an account with an annual interest rate of 3.25%. How much simple interest will you earn in 7 years?

You can use the percent feature, **2nd** [%], to find a percent of a number. The percent feature can often be found above the left parenthesis key, **(**.

SOLUTION

Use the formula for simple interest $I = Prt$ with $P = \$100$, $r = 3.25\%$, and $t = 7$ years.

Keystrokes	Display
100 **×** 3.25 **2nd** [%] **×** 7 **=**	22.75

▶ **Answer** You will earn $22.75 in simple interest.

Check Round 3.25% to 3%. Because $100 \times 3\% \times 7 = 21$, the answer is reasonable.

PRACTICE Use a calculator to find the answer.

1. 8% of 90
2. 14% of 173
3. 57% of 13.7
4. 3.5% of 8
5. 24.3% of 99
6. 7.28% of 205
7. 72% of 12
8. 59% of 20
9. 93% of 65
10. 49.1% of 11
11. 26.8% of 5
12. 87.3% of 60
13. 10.25% of 80
14. 17.84% of 300
15. 9.42% of 150

16. **SIMPLE INTEREST** You deposit $75 in an account with an annual interest rate of 3.5%. How much simple interest will you earn in 4 years?

17. **SALES TAX** You are buying a CD that costs $14.95. The sales tax is 7%. What is the amount of tax that you owe? What is the total amount of your purchase?

18. **DISCOUNT** A store is having a 35% off sale on all items. An item is regularly priced at $49.50. What is the sale price, not including sales tax?

Lessons 8.5–8.7

1. **OPEN-ENDED** You want to invest $250 until the sum of this initial amount and the simple interest earned is between $400 and $500. Find a combination of a specific number of years and an interest rate between 1% and 7% that will allow you to achieve your goal.

2. **EXTENDED RESPONSE** The bar graph shows the results of a survey in which students at Hopedale Middle School were asked whether they wanted a bald eagle, a cougar, a hornet, or a buffalo as the school mascot.

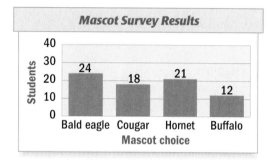

a. Find the percent of students that want each animal as the school mascot.

b. Predict how many students in a group of 500 would choose each animal as their mascot.

c. Would you use your prediction in part (b) to select the mascot, or would you have a vote between the top two selections? *Justify* your answer.

3. **OPEN-ENDED** On their math quiz papers, John's score is written as "$\frac{22}{25}$ correct" and Vince's score is written as "84.5% correct." Sam's score is written as a decimal and is between John's score and Vince's score. Write two decimals that could represent Sam's score.

4. **SHORT RESPONSE** You want to buy a $30 game and a $22 movie. You have a coupon for 20% off the price of any one item. How much more money do you save if you apply the coupon to the game instead of to the movie? *Explain* your steps.

5. **EXTENDED RESPONSE** Use the figure below.

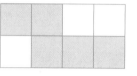

a. Write the ratio of shaded sections to all sections.

b. Is the part of the figure that is shaded greater than or less than 87.5%?

c. *Explain* how you would modify the diagram to represent 87.5%.

6. **GRIDDED ANSWER** The gas gauge in a car indicates that 25% of the gasoline has been used since the tank was last filled. Write as a decimal the percent of gasoline that is left in the tank.

7. **MULTI-STEP PROBLEM** Your street's community garden is a 10 foot by 12 foot rectangle. Neighbors plan to enlarge the garden by extending the 10 foot length by 3 feet, adding a 12 foot by 3 foot rectangular section to one end.

a. Draw a labeled diagram of the old garden with the new section added.

b. Write the ratio of the perimeter of the old garden to the perimeter of the enlarged garden in simplest form.

c. What percent of the perimeter of the enlarged garden is the perimeter of the old garden? What method of finding the percent did you use? *Explain.*

REVIEW KEY VOCABULARY

- ratio, *p. 402*
- equivalent ratio, *p. 403*
- rate, *p. 407*
- unit rate, *p. 407*

- proportion, *p. 412*
- cross products, *p. 412*
- percent, *p. 425*
- interest, *p. 436*

- principal, *p. 436*
- annual interest rate, *p. 436*
- simple interest, *p. 436*

VOCABULARY EXERCISES

In Exercises 1 and 2, tell whether the statement is *true* or *false*.

1. The ratios $\frac{4}{7}$ and $\frac{16}{21}$ are equivalent.

2. A rate is a ratio of two measures that have different units.

3. Copy and complete: A __?__ is a rate that has a denominator of 1.

4. Copy and complete: In the proportion $\frac{a}{b} = \frac{c}{d}$, *ad* is equal to __?__.

REVIEW EXAMPLES AND EXERCISES

8.1 Ratios

pp. 402–406

EXAMPLE

Amusement Parks The bar graph shows the favorite amusement park rides for a group of students. Write the ratio of bumper cars votes to roller coaster votes in simplest form. What does the ratio mean?

$$\frac{\text{Bumper car votes}}{\text{Roller coaster votes}} = \frac{15}{30} = \frac{1 \times \cancel{15}}{2 \times \cancel{15}} = \frac{1}{2}$$

The ratio is $\frac{1}{2}$, or 1 to 2. So, for every student who likes bumper cars, two students like roller coasters.

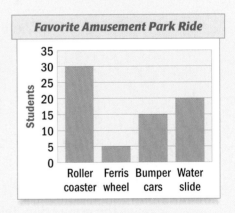

Favorite Amusement Park Ride

EXERCISES

Use the bar graph to write the given ratio in simplest form.

SEE EXAMPLE 2
on p. 402
for Exs. 5–6

5. water slide votes to total students surveyed

6. Ferris wheel votes to water slide votes

Rates

pp. 407–411

EXAMPLE

Shopping A 20 ounce jar of jelly costs $1.50. A 32 ounce jar of jelly costs $2.56. To determine which jar is the better buy, find the unit price for each size.

$$1.50 \div 20$$

20 ounce jar: $\dfrac{\$1.50}{20 \text{ oz}} = \dfrac{\$.075}{1 \text{ oz}}$

$$20 \div 20$$

$$2.56 \div 32$$

32 ounce jar: $\dfrac{\$2.56}{32 \text{ oz}} = \dfrac{\$.08}{1 \text{ oz}}$

$$32 \div 32$$

▶ **Answer** Because $\$.075 < \$.08$, the 20 ounce jar is the better buy.

EXERCISES

SEE EXAMPLE 4
on p. 408
for Ex. 7

7. A 4-pack of AAA batteries costs $2.84. An 8-pack of AAA batteries costs $5.60. Which is the better buy? *Explain.*

Solving Proportions

pp. 412–416

EXAMPLE

Solve the proportion $\dfrac{3}{4} = \dfrac{9}{x}$.

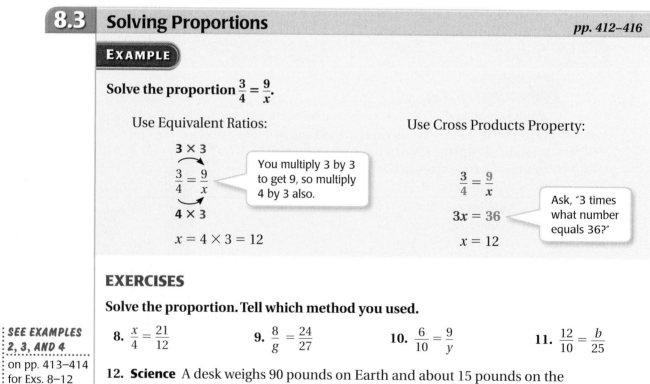

Use Equivalent Ratios:

$$3 \times 3$$
$$\dfrac{3}{4} = \dfrac{9}{x}$$
$$4 \times 3$$

You multiply 3 by 3 to get 9, so multiply 4 by 3 also.

$$x = 4 \times 3 = 12$$

Use Cross Products Property:

$$\dfrac{3}{4} = \dfrac{9}{x}$$

$$3x = 36$$

$$x = 12$$

Ask, "3 times what number equals 36?"

EXERCISES

Solve the proportion. Tell which method you used.

**SEE EXAMPLES
2, 3, AND 4**
on pp. 413–414
for Exs. 8–12

8. $\dfrac{x}{4} = \dfrac{21}{12}$

9. $\dfrac{8}{g} = \dfrac{24}{27}$

10. $\dfrac{6}{10} = \dfrac{9}{y}$

11. $\dfrac{12}{10} = \dfrac{b}{25}$

12. Science A desk weighs 90 pounds on Earth and about 15 pounds on the moon. A rock weighs 450 pounds on Earth. Approximate the weight of the rock on the moon.

8.4 Proportions and Scale Drawings

EXAMPLE

Maps A map uses a scale of 1 in. : 75 mi. On the map, two cities are 2 inches apart. What is the actual distance between the cities?

$$\frac{1 \text{ in.}}{75 \text{ mi}} = \frac{\text{Distance on a map}}{\text{Actual distance}}$$ **Write a proportion.**

$$\frac{1 \text{ in.}}{75 \text{ mi}} = \frac{2 \text{ in.}}{x \text{ mi}}$$ **Substitute values.**

$$1 \cdot x = 75 \cdot 2$$ **The cross products are equal.**

$$x = 150$$ **Multiply.**

▶ **Answer** The actual distance between the cities is 150 miles.

EXERCISES

USING A MAP A map uses a scale of 1 mm : 12 km. Find the actual distance for the given distance on the map.

SEE EXAMPLES
1 AND 3
on pp. 417–418
for Exs. 13–18

13. 4 millimeters   **14.** 7 millimeters   **15.** 8 millimeters   **16.** 1 centimeter

17. In a scale drawing, a parking lot has a length of 7 inches and a width of 3 inches. The drawing uses a scale of 1 in. : 25 ft. What are the dimensions of the actual parking lot?

18. Use the dimensions of the scale drawing in Exercise 17 to find the ratio of the scale drawing's area to the parking lot's actual area.

8.5 Understanding Percent

EXAMPLE

a. Write 82.75% as a decimal.

$$82.75\% = 82.75 \div 100 = 0.8275$$

b. Write 36% as a fraction.

$$36\% = \frac{36}{100} = \frac{9}{25}$$

EXERCISES

Write the number in words and as a percent.

SEE EXAMPLES
2 AND 3
on pp. 425–426
for Exs. 19–26

19. 0.64   **20.** 0.15   **21.** $\frac{31}{100}$ **22.** $\frac{112}{100}$

Write the percent as a decimal and a fraction.

23. 64%   **24.** 26%   **25.** 90%   **26.** 8%

Chapter Review   **445**

8.6 Percents, Decimals, and Fractions

pp. 429–433

EXAMPLE

Write the decimal or fraction as a percent.

a. $0.63 = \dfrac{63}{100} = 63\%$

b. $\dfrac{1}{8} = 0.125 = \dfrac{125}{1000} = \dfrac{12.5}{100} = 12.5\%$

EXERCISES

Write the decimal or fraction as a percent.

SEE EXAMPLES 1, 2, AND 4
on pp. 429–431
for Exs. 27–31

27. 0.4   **28.** $\dfrac{4}{5}$ **29.** $\dfrac{9}{16}$ **30.** 0.425

31. Order the numbers from least to greatest: $\dfrac{1}{3}$, 25%, 0.2, 40%, $\dfrac{3}{5}$, 0.35.

8.7 Finding a Percent of a Number

pp. 434–440

EXAMPLE

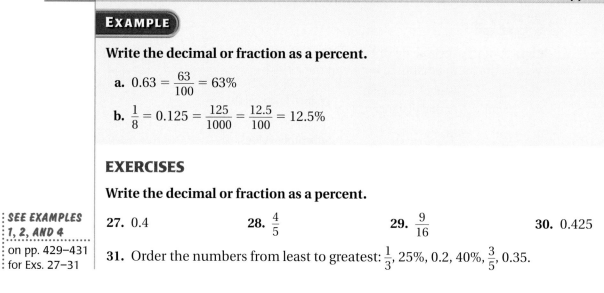

a. Find 30% of 48. Use a fraction.

$$30\% \text{ of } 48 = \dfrac{3}{10} \times 48$$
$$= \dfrac{144}{10}$$
$$= 14.4$$

▶ **Answer** 30% of 48 is 14.4.

b. Find 20% of 65. Use a decimal.

$$20\% \text{ of } 65 = 0.2 \times 65$$
$$= 13$$

▶ **Answer** 20% of 65 is 13.

EXERCISES

Find the percent of the number.

SEE EXAMPLES 1, 3, AND 6
on pp. 434–436
for Exs. 32–41

32. 25% of 400   **33.** 60% of 105   **34.** 10% of 24   **35.** 85% of 130

36. 12% of 75   **37.** 35% of 300   **38.** 92% of 100   **39.** 40% of 225

40. Groceries The cost for your grocery items is $32 and there is a 6% sales tax. How much do you pay for your grocery items?

41. Savings You deposit $150 in a savings account. The annual interest rate is 6%. How much simple interest will you earn in 6 years?

1. Write the ratio $\frac{2}{5}$ in two other ways.

Solve the proportion.

2. $\frac{x}{4} = \frac{63}{28}$

3. $\frac{18}{81} = \frac{2}{n}$

4. $\frac{r}{10} = \frac{4}{8}$

5. $\frac{6}{j} = \frac{10}{25}$

Write the decimal or fraction as a percent.

6. 0.36

7. 0.08

8. $\frac{23}{100}$

9. $\frac{2}{25}$

10. Write *fifty-five percent* as a fraction in simplest form.

Find the percent of the number.

11. 40% of 85

12. 75% of 60

13. 12% of 150

14. 88% of 1000

RESTAURANT BILL **A restaurant bill is $45.80. Use mental math to estimate the tip described.**

15. 10%

16. 20%

17. 15%

18. 25%

ONLINE SHOPPING **The graph shows the number of people in a survey who chose different reasons for using online shopping. In Exercises 19 and 20, write the ratios in simplest form.**

19. discounts responses to total number of shoppers surveyed

20. free shipping responses to discounts responses

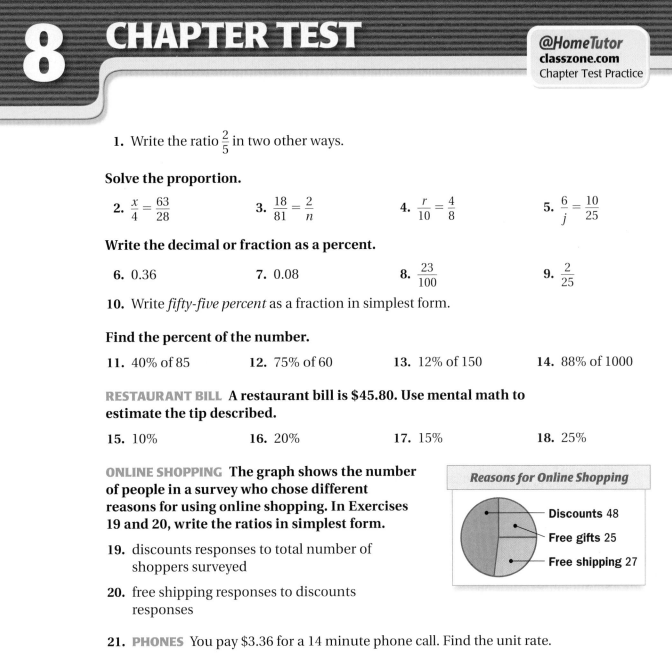

Reasons for Online Shopping

Discounts 48
Free gifts 25
Free shipping 27

21. **PHONES** You pay $3.36 for a 14 minute phone call. Find the unit rate.

22. **CURRENCY** In July 2004, six U.S. dollars were worth about 660 Japanese yen. How many Japanese yen was one U.S. dollar worth?

23. **BIKES** A model of a bike has a scale of 1 in. : 2 ft. The length of the model is 2.5 inches. What is the actual length of the bike?

24. **FLOWERS** One sixth of your flower garden contains petunias, 0.195 of your garden contains marigolds, and 18% contains pansies. Order these numbers from least to greatest.

25. **GEOGRAPHY** In the United States, 23 of the 50 states border an ocean. What percent of the states border an ocean?

26. **NIAGARA FALLS** One section of Niagara Falls is known as the Canadian Falls. About 700,000 gallons of water flow over the Canadian Falls every second. How many gallons flow over the Canadian Falls in 1 hour?

CONTEXT-BASED MULTIPLE CHOICE QUESTIONS

Some of the information you need to solve a context-based multiple choice question may appear in a table, a diagram, or a graph.

PROBLEM 1

A magazine ad for a car includes a scale drawing of the car. The actual width of the car is 200 centimeters. What is the actual length of the car?

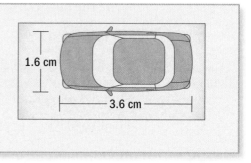

- **A** 125 cm
- **B** 203.6 cm
- **C** 450 cm
- **D** 720 cm

Plan

STEP 1
Read the problem carefully. Decide how you can use the given information to solve the problem.

INTERPRET THE DIAGRAM From the problem and the diagram, you know the following information:

width on drawing = 1.6 centimeters   actual width = 200 centimeters

length on drawing = 3.6 centimeters   actual length = ?

You can use the width on the drawing and the actual width to find the scale of the drawing. Then you can use the scale to find the actual length of the car.

Solution

STEP 2
Find the scale.

The scale of the drawing is $\frac{1.6 \text{ cm}}{200 \text{ cm}}$, or $\frac{1 \text{ cm}}{125 \text{ cm}}$.

STEP 3
Write and solve a proportion to find the actual length of the car. Use cross products.

Let x represent the actual length, in centimeters, of the car.

$$\frac{1 \text{ cm}}{125 \text{ cm}} = \frac{\text{Length on drawing}}{\text{Actual length}}$$ **Write a proportion.**

$$\frac{1 \text{ cm}}{125 \text{ cm}} = \frac{3.6 \text{ cm}}{x \text{ cm}}$$ **Substitute values.**

$$1 \cdot x = 125(3.6)$$ **The cross products are equal.**

$$x = 450$$ **Multiply.**

The actual length of the car is 450 centimeters.

The correct answer is C. Ⓐ Ⓑ ● Ⓓ

PROBLEM 2

A clothing store is having a sale in which it discounts 20% off all items. The table at the right shows the regular prices of a few items in the store. You decide to buy a sweater, a pair of pants, and a belt. What is the total amount you spend, not including sales tax?

Item	Price
shirt	$25
sweater	$40
pair of pants	$35
belt	$15
pair of socks	$8

Ⓐ $18   Ⓑ $72

Ⓒ $90   Ⓓ $108

Plan

STEP 1
Read the problem carefully. Decide how you can use the given information to solve the problem.

INTERPRET THE TABLE From the table, you know that the regular price of a sweater is $40, the regular price of a pair of pants is $35, and the regular price of a belt is $15. Find the sum of these regular prices. Then find the amount you spend by determining their cost after the discount.

Solution

STEP 2
Find the sum of the regular prices.

The sum of the regular prices of the items you want to buy is
$40 + $35 + $15 = $90.

STEP 3
Find the discount and subtract it from the sum of the regular prices.

Discount (20%):   20% of $90 = 0.2 × $90 = **$18**

Total Amount: $90 − **$18** = $72

You spend a total of $72. So, the correct answer is B. Ⓐ **Ⓑ** Ⓒ Ⓓ

PRACTICE

1. Use the table and the information above. Your friend decides to buy a pair of pants and a pair of socks. What is the total amount your friend spends, not including sales tax?

   Ⓐ $4.60   Ⓑ $9.20   Ⓒ $18.40   Ⓓ $34.40

In Exercises 2 and 3, use the figure shown.

2. What is the ratio of blue squares to white squares?

   Ⓐ 5 : 11   Ⓑ 5 : 16

   Ⓒ 11 : 5   Ⓓ 16 : 5

3. About what percent of the figure is blue? Round to the nearest whole number percent.

   Ⓐ 5%   Ⓑ 31%   Ⓒ 45%   Ⓓ 69%

MULTIPLE CHOICE

1. Hal scored $\frac{4}{5}$ on a pop quiz. What percent of the questions did Hal get incorrect?

   (A) 20%   (B) 40%

   (C) 60%   (D) 80%

2. Mr. and Mrs. Chin have 6 nephews and nieces altogether. The number of nephews is twice the number of nieces. What is the ratio of nieces to nephews?

   (A) 1 : 3   (B) 1 : 2

   (C) 2 : 1   (D) 3 : 1

3. Henry bought 3 yards of fabric for a costume. He paid $10.35. Later he bought 5 yards of the same fabric and paid with a $20 bill. What was the amount of change?

   (A) $2.75   (B) $3.45

   (C) $9.65   (D) $17.25

4. You receive a discount of $6.57 on an $18 item. What is the percent discount?

   (A) 4.9%   (B) 11.43%

   (C) 36.5%   (D) 63.5%

5. The bar graph shows the results of a survey in which several students were asked which season they liked the least. There are 210 students in your grade. About how many students in your grade would you expect to like winter the least?

   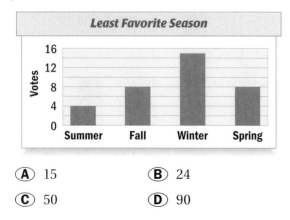

   (A) 15   (B) 24

   (C) 50   (D) 90

6. The table shows the numbers of girls and boys in each grade participating in the middle school band. The ratio of girls to boys in the entire middle school band is 3 : 2. How many 7th grade boys are in the band?

Class	Girls	Boys
6th grade	10	10
7th grade	20	?
8th grade	12	15

   (A) 2   (B) 3

   (C) 14   (D) 17

7. You deposit $250 into an account with an annual interest rate of 4%. How much simple interest will you earn on the money in 3 years?

   (A) $10   (B) $20

   (C) $25   (D) $30

8. A school raises a total of $24,478 at a fair. Twenty-five percent of the amount raised goes to a charity. How much money will the school keep?

   (A) $6119.50   (B) $18,987.50

   (C) $18,358.50   (D) $30,597.50

9. Based on the scale provided, about how much farther from Franklin is Washington than is Lincoln?

   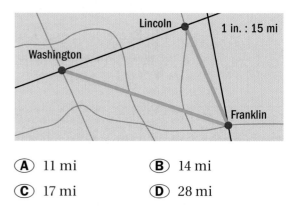

   (A) 11 mi   (B) 14 mi

   (C) 17 mi   (D) 28 mi

GRIDDED ANSWER

10. A car travels 3 miles in 4 minutes. At this rate, how many miles, in decimal form, will the car travel in one minute?

11. Michelle owns jazz, rap, and rock CDs. The ratio of jazz CDs to rap CDs is equal to the ratio of rap CDs to rock CDs. Michelle owns 4 jazz CDs and 16 rock CDs. How many rap CDs does she own?

12. Doreen has a collection of 80 baseball caps. Twenty percent of the baseball caps are blue. How many baseball caps are *not* blue?

13. The market value of a house is $180,000. Property taxes are based on the assessed value of the property. The assessment is 40% of the market value of the house, and the property tax is 3.5% of the assessment. How much, in dollars, is the property tax on the house?

SHORT RESPONSE

14. A store sells two different sizes of contact lens solution. Which size is a better buy, the larger or the smaller? *Explain* your reasoning.

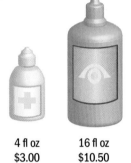

4 fl oz   16 fl oz
$3.00 $10.50

15. Bart wants to buy a shirt that regularly costs $15 and a hat that regularly costs $10. He has a coupon for 20% off the price of any one item. To save more money, should Bart use the coupon for the hat or the shirt? *Justify* your choice.

EXTENDED RESPONSE

16. An unfinished furniture company sells a coffee table, an end table, and a snack table as a set. The tabletops are all rectangles. It takes Yoanna 36 minutes to sand the top of the coffee table.

  a. How does the area of the snack tabletop compare to the area of the coffee tabletop? of the end tabletop?

  b. Yoanna works at the same rate on all three tables. How long does it take her to sand the top of the snack table? of the end table? *Justify* your answer.

  c. Suppose a 14 inch by 30 inch rectangle is cut out of the coffee tabletop and replaced by glass. How long does it take Yoanna to sand the top of the coffee table if she works at the same rate as before? *Explain*.

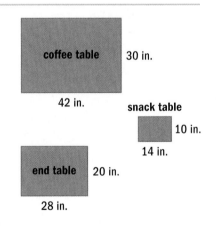

coffee table   30 in.

42 in.   snack table

10 in.

14 in.

end table   20 in.

28 in.

17. The owners of Bird World observe that more people prefer parakeets than canaries. So they stock 6 parakeets for every canary.

  a. The total number of parakeets and canaries in the store is 28. How many parakeets are in stock? *Explain* your method.

  b. After a week of sales, the store is left with 10 parakeets and 3 canaries. The owners decide to restock only one type of bird. How many of which type of bird should the owners order to restore the ratio of 6 parakeets stocked for every canary? *Explain* your reasoning.

9 Geometric Figures

***Animated* Math**
at classzone.com

Review Prerequisite Skills by playing *Mix and Match* and *Computer Graphics.*

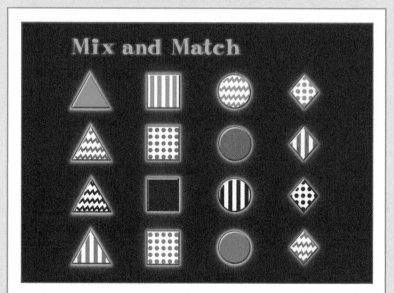

Skill Focus: Classifying objects

Materials: 16 small squares of paper

Computers classify objects by their characteristics. The objects above can be classified based on shape, color, and pattern.

- On your turn, name a characteristic. Use a paper square to cover each object that has that characteristic. For example, you might cover all the green objects, or all the squares, or all the striped objects.

- Take turns, always covering at least one uncovered object. The player who covers the last object wins. Play the game a few times.

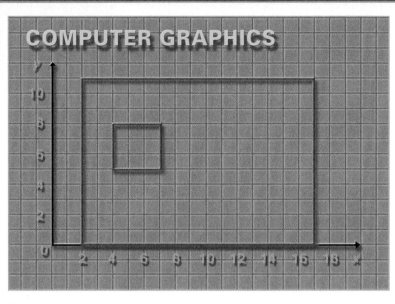

COMPUTER GRAPHICS

Skill Focus: Plotting points on a coordinate grid

Materials: graph paper

Computer drawing programs rely on precise instructions. In this game, you'll write instructions for drawing a house on a coordinate grid.

- Follow these instructions to draw a window and the outline of a house:

  Draw a square connecting (4, 5), (4, 8), (7, 8), and (7, 5).

  Draw a rectangle connecting (2, 0), (2, 11), (17, 11), and (17, 0).

- Then write instructions for drawing a door and a roof for the house. Have your partner test your instructions.

Stop and Think

1. **CRITICAL THINKING** Suppose it is your turn in a game of *Mix and Match*. The uncovered shapes are a solid green triangle, a dotted orange square, and a solid purple square. In order to win on your next turn, which characteristic should you name? Explain your thinking.

2. **WRITING** Points (8, 8) and (8, 16) are the corners of a square drawn on a coordinate grid. Name two points that could form the other corners of the square. Are these the only points you could use? Explain your thinking.

Review Prerequisite Skills

VOCABULARY CHECK

Copy and complete using a review word from the list to the left.

1. The first coordinate in an __?__ tells you how many units to move to the right.

2. The __?__ of a square can be found using the formula $P = 4s$ where s is the length of each side.

SKILL CHECK

In Exercises 3 and 4, find the perimeter of the rectangle. (p. 66)

3. length = 6 in., width = 5 in.

4. length = 10 m, width = 7 m

5. Write and solve an equation to find the length of a side of a square that has a perimeter of 48 centimeters. (p. 66)

Find the length of the segment to the nearest tenth of a centimeter. (p. 125)

6. ────────────

7. ──────

Find the length of the segment to the nearest eighth of an inch. (p. 260)

8. ──────────

9. ──────

Solve the equation. (p. 35)

10. $140 + x = 180$

11. $x + 145 = 180$

12. $x + 90 = 180$

@HomeTutor Prerequisite skills practice at classzone.com

Notetaking Skills   Drawing a Venn Diagram

In each chapter you will learn a new notetaking skill. In Chapter 9 you will apply the strategy of drawing a Venn diagram to Example 1 on p. 480.

Each oval in the Venn diagram represents a group with something in common. The region or regions where the ovals overlap represents the things that both groups have in common. The Venn diagram below shows that the number 2 is both even and prime.

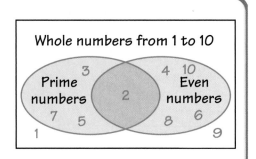

Whole numbers from 1 to 10

Prime numbers: 3, 7, 5, 1

2

Even numbers: 4, 10, 8, 6, 9

9.1 Introduction to Geometry

Before	You used points and lines to draw diagrams.
Now	You'll identify lines, rays, and segments.
Why?	So you can describe real world objects, as in Exs. 37–40.

KEY VOCABULARY
- point, endpoint, line, ray, segment, *p. 455*
- plane, *p. 456*
- parallel lines, *p. 456*
- intersecting lines, *p. 456*

In geometry, a **point** is usually represented by a dot and labeled with a letter such as *A* or *B*. Points are used to name *lines, rays,* and *segments.*

Words	Diagram	Symbols
A **line** extends without end in two *opposite* directions.	A ← • ————— • → B	$\overleftrightarrow{AB}$ or $\overleftrightarrow{BA}$
A **ray** has one **endpoint** and extends without end in *one* direction.	A • ————— • → B	$\overrightarrow{AB}$
A **segment** has two endpoints.	A • ————— • B	$\overline{AB}$ or $\overline{BA}$

EXAMPLE 1 Identifying Lines, Rays, and Segments

READING IN MATH
You may name a line using any two points on the line in any order. You must use the endpoints to name a segment, but they may be listed in either order.

From the diagram, identify the *line, ray,* or *segment* using words. Then name it using symbols.

a. M • —— • N →

b. Q • ————— • P

c. ← • R —— • S →

SOLUTION

a. The figure is a ray and is represented by $\overrightarrow{MN}$.

b. The figure is a segment and is represented by $\overline{QP}$ or $\overline{PQ}$.

c. The figure is a line and is represented by $\overleftrightarrow{RS}$ or $\overleftrightarrow{SR}$.

✓ **GUIDED PRACTICE** for Example 1

Identify the *line, ray,* or *segment* using words and using symbols.

1. ← • F —— • G

2. ← • H —— • J →

3. • K —————— • L

EXAMPLE 2 Naming Lines, Rays, and Segments

Use the aerial photo at the right.

a. Name two rays.

b. Name two segments that have *G* as an endpoint.

c. Name a line.

SOLUTION

a. Two possible rays are $\vec{HG}$ and $\vec{HL}$. The ray $\vec{HL}$ can also be called $\vec{HJ}$.

b. Two segments that have *G* as an endpoint are $\overline{GJ}$ and $\overline{GH}$.

c. One line is $\overleftrightarrow{GH}$. This line can also be called $\overleftrightarrow{HG}$.

Planes and Lines A **plane** is a flat surface that extends without end. You can represent a plane by a figure that looks like a floor or a wall. Two different lines in a plane will either be *parallel* or *intersect*. **Parallel lines** never meet. **Intersecting lines** meet at a point.

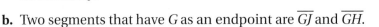

EXAMPLE 3 Intersecting and Parallel Lines

a. Which lines are intersecting?

b. Which lines are parallel?

SOLUTION

a. $\overleftrightarrow{AB}$ and $\overleftrightarrow{BC}$ intersect at point *B*. $\overleftrightarrow{AD}$ and $\overleftrightarrow{AB}$ intersect at point *A*.

b. $\overleftrightarrow{AD}$ and $\overleftrightarrow{BC}$ are parallel.

✓ **GUIDED PRACTICE** for Examples 2 and 3

Use the diagram at the right.

4. What is another way to write $\vec{AD}$? $\overleftrightarrow{EA}$?

5. Which lines are intersecting? parallel?

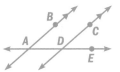

9.1 EXERCISES

HOMEWORK KEY

★ = **STANDARDIZED TEST PRACTICE**
Exs. 8, 30, 41, 42, 43, 44, and 50

◯ = **HINTS** AND **HOMEWORK HELP**
for Exs. 5, 15, 17, 37 at classzone.com

SKILL PRACTICE

VOCABULARY Match the name with the correct figure.

1. $\overleftrightarrow{XY}$

2. $\overrightarrow{XY}$

3. $\overline{XY}$

A.

B.

C.

SEE EXAMPLE 1
on p. 455
for Exs. 4–11

NAMING FIGURES Identify the symbol using words.

4. $\overrightarrow{MN}$

(5.) $\overleftrightarrow{AB}$

6. endpoints of $\overline{RS}$

7. endpoint of $\overrightarrow{HG}$

8. ★ **MULTIPLE CHOICE** Which extends without end in two opposite directions?

(A) line   (B) ray   (C) segment   (D) plane

IDENTIFYING FIGURES Identify and name the *line, ray,* or *segment.*

9.

10.

11.

NAMING FIGURES In Exercises 12–17, use the diagram.

SEE EXAMPLE 2
on p. 456
for Exs. 12–15

12. Name three points.

13. Name two rays.

14. Name a segment that has *B* as an endpoint.

(15.) Name $\overline{AE}$ in another way.

SEE EXAMPLE 3
on p. 456
for Exs. 16–17

16. Name a pair of parallel lines.

(17.) Name two pairs of intersecting lines.

18. **ERROR ANALYSIS** Describe and correct the error made in naming the figure.

The figure is a ray named $\overrightarrow{LM}$.

IDENTIFYING OBJECTS Tell whether the object is best modeled by a *point,* a *ray,* a *segment,* or a *line.*

19. a speck of dust

20. a laser beam

21. a ruler

REASONING Is the statement *true* or *false*? *Explain* your reasoning.

22. $\overrightarrow{AB}$ can be written as $\overrightarrow{BA}$.

23. $\overrightarrow{AB}$ can be written as $\overleftrightarrow{AB}$.

24. $\overline{QP}$ can be written as $\overline{PQ}$.

25. $\overleftrightarrow{PQ}$ can be written as $\overleftrightarrow{QP}$.

26. $\overrightarrow{WR}$ can be written as $\overline{WR}$.

27. $\overline{DE}$ can be written as $\overleftrightarrow{DE}$.

28. parallel lines $\overleftrightarrow{PR}$ and $\overleftrightarrow{JK}$.

29. intersecting lines $\overleftrightarrow{AB}$ and $\overleftrightarrow{BC}$.

30. ★ **OPEN-ENDED MATH** Draw a diagram. Make $\overleftrightarrow{LM}$ parallel to $\overleftrightarrow{NO}$. Make $\overleftrightarrow{PQ}$ intersect $\overleftrightarrow{NO}$ at *P* and $\overleftrightarrow{LM}$ at *Q*. Then make $\overline{QR}$ intersect $\overleftrightarrow{NO}$ at a point *R* between *P* and *O*.

IDENTIFYING FIGURES **In Exercises 31–33, imagine 12 lines containing the edges of the cube.**

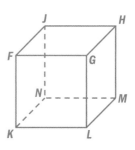

31. Which lines are parallel to $\overleftrightarrow{KL}$?

32. Which lines intersect $\overleftrightarrow{LM}$?

33. Two lines lying in different planes that do not intersect are *skew lines*, such as $\overleftrightarrow{HM}$ and $\overleftrightarrow{FJ}$. Which other lines are skew to $\overleftrightarrow{HM}$? Which lines are not skew to $\overleftrightarrow{HM}$?

34. **CHALLENGE** Lines $\overleftrightarrow{AB}$ and $\overleftrightarrow{CD}$ are parallel. If $\overleftrightarrow{PQ}$ intersects $\overleftrightarrow{CD}$, will $\overleftrightarrow{PQ}$ also intersect $\overleftrightarrow{AB}$ where all three lines lie on the same plane? *Explain* your reasoning.

PROBLEM SOLVING

IDENTIFYING LINES **Tell whether the lines pictured are *parallel* or *intersecting*.**

SEE EXAMPLE 3
on p. 456
for Exs. 35–40

35.

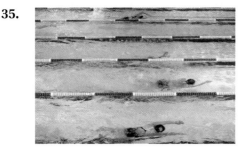

36.

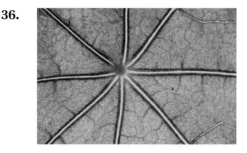

TALL SHIPS **In Exercises 37–40, use the figure.**

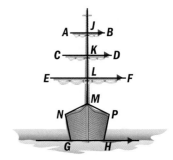

37. Name a segment parallel to $\overline{AB}$.

38. Are $\overline{NG}$ and $\overline{PH}$ parallel, intersecting, or neither? *Explain* your reasoning.

39. Name the point of intersection of $\overline{CD}$ and $\overline{JM}$.

40. Name the line in the same plane as the water.

41. ★ **SHORT RESPONSE** In the figure at the right, if you drew a line through points *M* and *P*, could $\overleftrightarrow{MP}$ be parallel to $\overleftrightarrow{LM}$? to $\overleftrightarrow{LN}$? *Explain* your reasoning.

42. ★ **WRITING** *Explain* how $\overrightarrow{EF}$ and $\overrightarrow{EG}$ could both be names of the same ray.

43. ★ OPEN-ENDED MATH Sketch a map of an imaginary town, park, amusement park, or space colony. Show and label lines, rays, segments, points, and a plane on your map. Show and label figures that are parallel and others that are intersecting.

44. ★ EXTENDED RESPONSE The map shows several locations in a town.

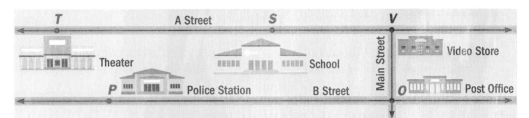

a. Which point represents the School? The Police Station?

b. Does the street the Police Station is on intersect with other streets? If so, name the street(s) and the point(s) of intersection.

c. The Town Hall is located between the Police Station and the Post Office, but closer to the Post Office. Copy the map and add the Town Hall, point *H*, to your map.

d. C street is built to connect the Town Hall and the School. What is the shortest route between the Theater and the Post Office? *Explain*.

45. DRAW A DIAGRAM You and Emily live 3 blocks apart on a street with your school and a library. The street resembles a ray, with one of your houses at its endpoint. The library is 2 blocks from Emily's house. You live 4 blocks from school. Emily walks past the library to get to school. Who lives at the endpoint of the ray? *Justify* your answer with a diagram.

46. CHALLENGE Point *C* lies on $\overleftrightarrow{AB}$ and on $\overleftrightarrow{DE}$. Must $\overleftrightarrow{AB}$ and $\overleftrightarrow{DE}$ name the same line? $\overleftrightarrow{DE}$ intersects $\overrightarrow{AF}$ at point *C*. Can $\overrightarrow{AF}$ be called by another name? If so, list the name(s) and *justify* your answer with a diagram.

MIXED REVIEW

Get-Ready

Prepare for
Lesson 9.2
in Exs. 47–48

MEASUREMENT **Find the length of the segment to the nearest millimeter and to the nearest centimeter.** *(p. 59)*

47.

| cm | 1 | 2 | 3 | 4 | 5 |

48.

| cm | 1 | 2 | 3 | 4 | 5 |

49. Sketch a segment that is 65 millimeters long without using a ruler. Then use a ruler to check your estimate. How close was your estimate? *(p. 125)*

50. ★ SHORT RESPONSE The regular price of a computer is $1100. The sale price is 25% off the regular price. Another store offers the same computer for a regular price of $1200 and a sale price of 30% off the regular price. Which is the better buy? *Explain* your reasoning. *(p. 434)*

9.2 Angles

Before You named lines, rays, and segments.

Now You'll name, measure, and draw angles.

Why? So you can classify angles in activities, as in Example 1.

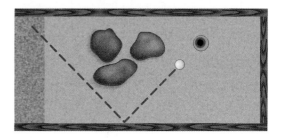

KEY VOCABULARY
- **angle,** *p. 460*
- **vertex,** *p. 460*
- **degrees (°),** *p. 461*

Miniature Golf A miniature golf course has a hole similar to the one shown. You can get a hole-in-one if you hit the ball off the wall as shown. How can you describe the path of the ball?

The path of the golf ball forms an *angle.* An **angle** is formed by two rays with the same endpoint. The endpoint is called the **vertex**. The symbol ∠ is used to represent an angle.

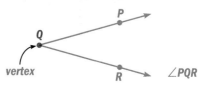

EXAMPLE 1 Naming Angles

The path of the golf ball is shown at the right. You can name the angle formed by the path of the golf ball in three ways.

> Name the angle by its vertex alone: ∠B.
>
> Name the angle by its vertex and two points, with the vertex as the middle point: ∠ABC.
>
> Name the angle by its vertex and two points, but switch the order of the two points: ∠CBA.

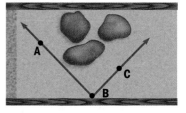

READING
The notation ∠ABC is read "angle *ABC*."

✓ **GUIDED PRACTICE** for Example 1

Name the angle in three ways.

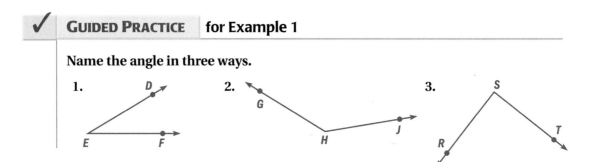

1.   **2.**   **3.**

Using a Protractor A protractor is a tool you can use to draw and measure angles. Angles are measured in units called **degrees** (°).

EXAMPLE 2 Standardized Test Practice

ELIMINATE CHOICES
The measure of the angle is greater than 90°. So choices A and B can be eliminated.

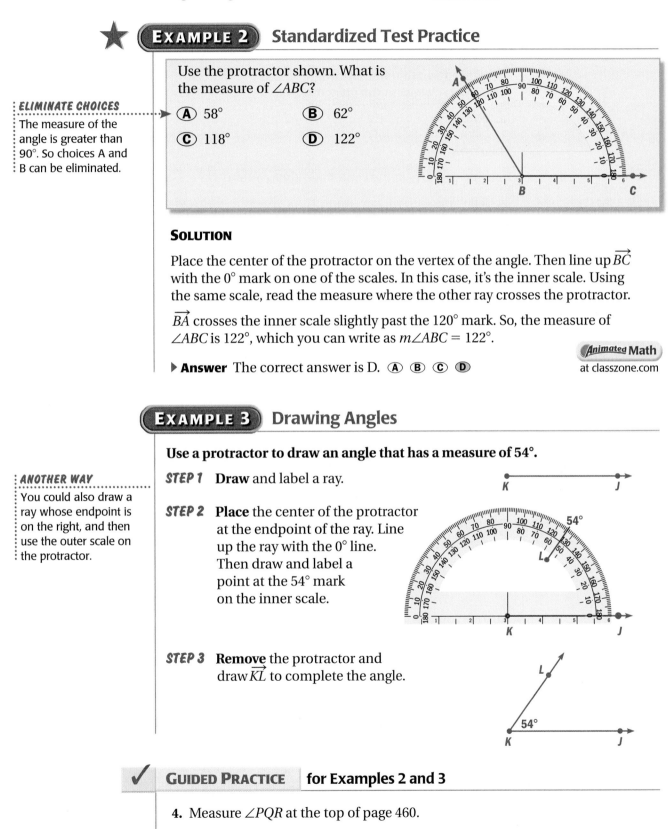

Use the protractor shown. What is the measure of ∠ABC?

A 58°   **B** 62°

C 118°   **D** 122°

SOLUTION

Place the center of the protractor on the vertex of the angle. Then line up $\overrightarrow{BC}$ with the 0° mark on one of the scales. In this case, it's the inner scale. Using the same scale, read the measure where the other ray crosses the protractor.

$\overrightarrow{BA}$ crosses the inner scale slightly past the 120° mark. So, the measure of ∠ABC is 122°, which you can write as m∠ABC = 122°.

▶ **Answer** The correct answer is D. Ⓐ Ⓑ Ⓒ ⦿

Animated **Math**
at classzone.com

EXAMPLE 3 Drawing Angles

Use a protractor to draw an angle that has a measure of 54°.

STEP 1 **Draw** and label a ray.

ANOTHER WAY
You could also draw a ray whose endpoint is on the right, and then use the outer scale on the protractor.

STEP 2 **Place** the center of the protractor at the endpoint of the ray. Line up the ray with the 0° line. Then draw and label a point at the 54° mark on the inner scale.

STEP 3 **Remove** the protractor and draw $\overrightarrow{KL}$ to complete the angle.

✓ **GUIDED PRACTICE** for Examples 2 and 3

4. Measure ∠PQR at the top of page 460.

5. Draw a 145° angle.

Estimating Angle Measures You can estimate angle measures by mentally comparing them to the benchmarks of 0°, 90°, and 180° on a protractor.

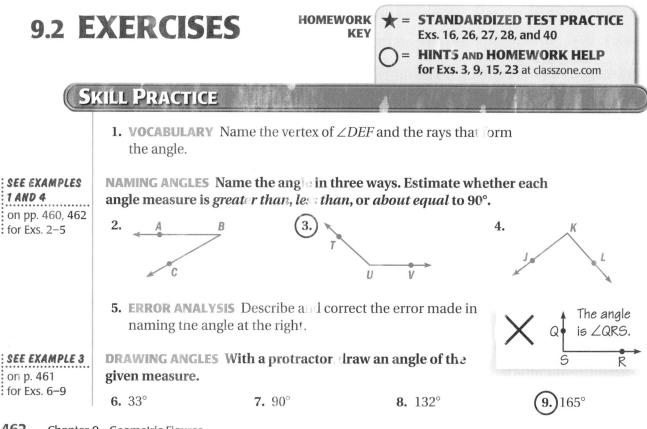

EXAMPLE 4 Estimating Angle Measures

Use estimation to name the angle whose measure is closest to the given measure.

a. 90° **b.** 15° **c.** 135°

SOLUTION

Imagine that D is at the center and that $\overrightarrow{DC}$ and $\overrightarrow{DB}$ are on the 0° line

AVOID ERRORS
When two or more angles share a vertex, each angle must be named using three points.

a. A 90° angle is halfway around a protractor, so ∠*BDA* and ∠*CDA* have measures that are equally close to 90°.

b. A 15° angle is close to 0° and less than halfway to 90°, so ∠*CDF* has the measure that is closest to 15°.

c. A 135° angle is halfway between 90° and 180°, so ∠*CDE* has the measure that is closest to 135°.

✓ **GUIDED PRACTICE** for Example 4

6. Name the angle in Example 4 whose measure is closest to 165°.

9.2 EXERCISES

HOMEWORK KEY

★ = **STANDARDIZED TEST PRACTICE**
Exs. 16, 26, 27, 28, and 40

◯ = **HINTS AND HOMEWORK HELP**
for Exs. 3, 9, 15, 23 at classzone.com

SKILL PRACTICE

1. VOCABULARY Name the vertex of ∠*DEF* and the rays that form the angle.

SEE EXAMPLES 1 AND 4
on pp. 460, 462
for Exs. 2–5

NAMING ANGLES Name the angle in three ways. Estimate whether each angle measure is *greater than*, *less than*, or *about equal* to 90°.

2.

3.

4.

5. ERROR ANALYSIS Describe and correct the error made in naming the angle at the right.

The angle is ∠*QRS*.

SEE EXAMPLE 3
on p. 461
for Exs. 6–9

DRAWING ANGLES With a protractor, draw an angle of the given measure.

6. 33° **7.** 90° **8.** 132° **9.** 165°

MEASUREMENT Use a protractor to measure the angle in the diagram.

SEE EXAMPLE 2
on p. 461
for Exs. 10–15

10. ∠PTS   **11.** ∠QTR

12. ∠QTS   **13.** ∠RTS

14. ∠PTQ   **15.** ∠PTR

16. ★ **MULTIPLE CHOICE** Find the measure of ∠W in the figure at the right to the nearest degree.

A 24°   **B** 36°

C 156°   **D** 164°

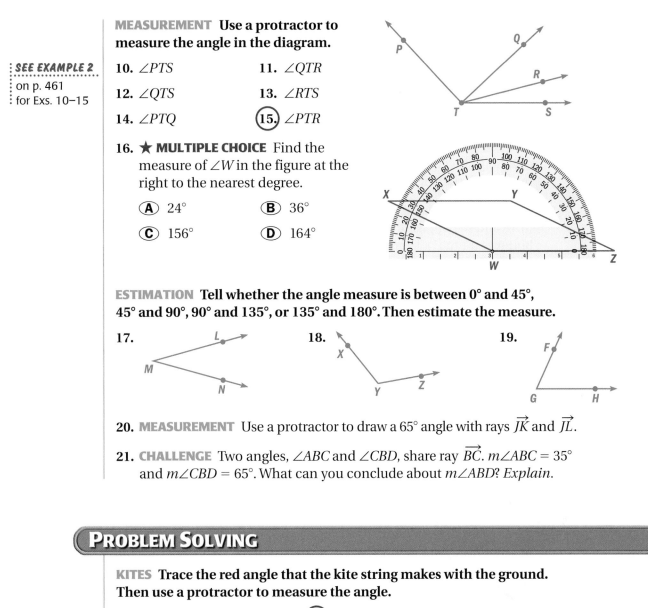

ESTIMATION Tell whether the angle measure is between 0° and 45°, 45° and 90°, 90° and 135°, or 135° and 180°. Then estimate the measure.

17.   **18.**   **19.**

20. MEASUREMENT Use a protractor to draw a 65° angle with rays $\overrightarrow{JK}$ and $\overrightarrow{JL}$.

21. CHALLENGE Two angles, ∠ABC and ∠CBD, share ray $\overrightarrow{BC}$. m∠ABC = 35° and m∠CBD = 65°. What can you conclude about m∠ABD? *Explain.*

PROBLEM SOLVING

KITES Trace the red angle that the kite string makes with the ground. Then use a protractor to measure the angle.

SEE EXAMPLE 2
on p. 461
for Exs. 22–24

22.   **23.**   **24.**

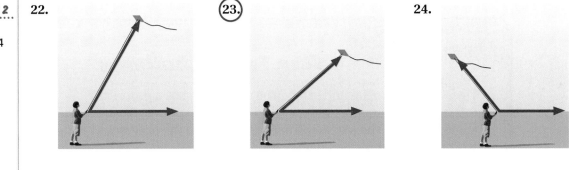

25. LETTERS Using only straight lines, print the word MANTLE in capital letters on a piece of paper. Circle each point that represents a vertex of an angle. How many points did you circle? How many angles are there?

26. ★ **WRITING** A photograph shows a ladder leaning against a wall. *Explain* where and how to place a protractor to measure the angle the ladder makes with the wall. Include a diagram.

27. ★ **SHORT RESPONSE** The photo shows a parasailer being pulled behind a boat. *Estimate* the measure of the angle the rope makes with the water. When the boat reaches top speed, the parasail rope's angle is 35° greater than the angle shown in the photo. *Estimate* the angle measure of the rope at top speed.

28. ★ **OPEN-ENDED MATH** Sketch a diagram of an everyday object that contains an angle. *Estimate* the measure of the angle in your sketch.

29. **BILLIARDS** Imagine a coordinate grid over a pool table. One corner is at (0, 0) and the opposite corner is at (30, 15). A ball starts at point (16, 9), bounces off the rail at point (10, 0), and then rolls into a pocket at point (0, 15). Graph the path of the ball and measure its angle.

CHALLENGE Name three times of day when you could estimate that the hands on a clock form the given angle.

30. 15°   31. 75°   32. 150°

MIXED REVIEW

Get-Ready

Prepare for Lesson 9.3 in Exs. 33–35

Tell whether the given number is a solution of the equation. *(p. 34)*

33. $x + 9 = 35$; 26   34. $67 - y = 11$; 58   35. $8 + m = 120$; 112

Find the sum or difference. Simplify if possible. *(p. 295)*

36. $\dfrac{4}{11} + \dfrac{9}{11}$ 37. $\dfrac{1}{6} + \dfrac{4}{6}$ 38. $\dfrac{13}{25} - \dfrac{8}{25}$ 39. $\dfrac{7}{10} - \dfrac{5}{10}$

40. ★ **MULTIPLE CHOICE** Solve the proportion $\dfrac{m}{8} = \dfrac{10}{5}$. *(p. 412)*

(A) $m = 4$ (B) $m = 12$ (C) $m = 13$ (D) $m = 16$

Brain Game

Flag Team Challenge

Trace the blue angles and extend the rays. Then use a protractor to measure the angles. Find the letter that corresponds to each angle measure. The letters will spell the name of the only state whose flag is not rectangular.

A = 50°

U = 35°

T = 150°

W = 85°

I = 75°

O = 115°

H = 105°

9.3 Classifying Angles

Before You named and measured angles.

Now You'll classify angles and find angle measures.

Why? So you can find angles in architecture, as in Example 4.

KEY VOCABULARY
- **right, acute, obtuse, and straight angles,** *p. 465*
- **vertical angles,** *p. 466*
- **complementary angles,** *p. 466*
- **supplementary angles,** *p. 466*

If you take a look around you, you can probably see many types of angles. Angles are classified by their measures.

Classifying Angles

A **right angle** is an angle whose measure is exactly 90°.

Indicates a right angle

An **acute angle** is an angle whose measure is less than 90°.

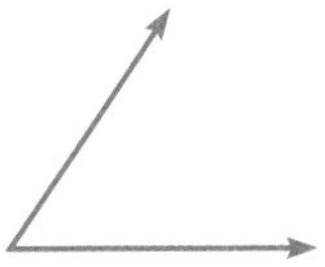

An **obtuse angle** is an angle whose measure is between 90° and 180°.

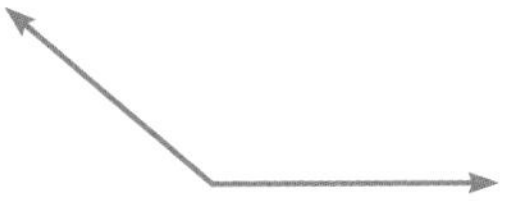

A **straight angle** is an angle whose measure is exactly 180°.

EXAMPLE 1 Classifying Angles

Classify the angles in the figure as *acute, right,* or *obtuse.*

∠*A* is marked as a right angle.

∠*B* is an acute angle because *m*∠*B* is less than 90°.

∠*C* and ∠*D* are obtuse angles because *m*∠*C* and *m*∠*D* are between 90° and 180°.

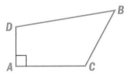
Animated Math
at classzone.com

VOCABULARY
When you are standing "upright," you make a 90° angle, or *right* angle, with the floor.

✓ **GUIDED PRACTICE** **for Example 1**

Classify the angle as *acute, right, obtuse,* or *straight.*

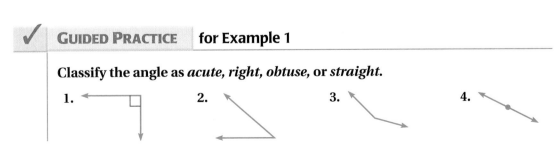

1.

2.

3.

4.

Vertical Angles When two lines intersect, the angles opposite each other are called **vertical angles**. In the diagram, ∠1 and ∠3 are vertical angles, and ∠2 and ∠4 are vertical angles. Vertical angles have equal measures.

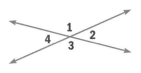

EXAMPLE 2 Using Vertical Angles

Find the measure of ∠QRS.

Because ∠QRS and ∠TRU are vertical angles, $m\angle QRS = m\angle TRU = 40°$.

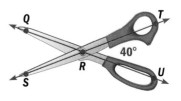

▶**Answer** The measure of ∠QRS is 40°.

KEY CONCEPT   *For Your Notebook*

Complementary and Supplementary Angles

Complementary angles Two angles are complementary if the sum of their measures is 90°.

$$m\angle 1 + m\angle 2 = 90°$$

Supplementary angles Two angles are supplementary if the sum of their measures is 180°.

$$m\angle 3 + m\angle 4 = 180°$$

EXAMPLE 3 Classifying Pairs of Angles

VOCABULARY
To associate complementary angles with 90° and supplementary angles with 180°, remember that "c" is before "s" in the alphabet and 90 is before 180 on a number line.

Decide whether the angles are *complementary*, *supplementary*, or *neither*.

a.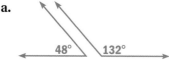
48°   132°

b.
50°
40°

SOLUTION

a. The angles are supplementary because $48° + 132° = 180°$.

b. The angles are complementary because $40° + 50° = 90°$.

at classzone.com

✓ **GUIDED PRACTICE** for Examples 2 and 3

TAKE NOTES
Copy the seven types of angles in your notebook. Draw a diagram of each, and describe the angles in your own words.

Find the measure of the given angle.

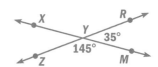

5. ∠XYZ   **6.** ∠XYR

Decide whether ∠A and ∠B are *complementary*, *supplementary*, or *neither*.

7. $m\angle A = 23°$, $m\angle B = 157°$ **8.** $m\angle A = 8°$, $m\angle B = 82°$

❖ **EXAMPLE 4** Solving for an Unknown Measure

Architecture Before efforts to make the Tower of Pisa more upright began in 1990, the angle between the side of the tower and the ground was about 84.5°. About how many degrees from vertical did the tower lean?

SOLUTION

STEP 1 **Draw** a diagram. Label the angle 84.5°. Then label its complementary angle as $x°$.

STEP 2 **Write** and solve an equation to find the value of x.

$$84.5° + x° = 90°$$
$$x = 90 - 84.5$$
$$x = 5.5$$

▶ **Answer** The Tower of Pisa leaned about 5.5° from vertical.

✓ **GUIDED PRACTICE** for Example 4

9. Find the angle supplementary to 84.5°.

9.3 EXERCISES

HOMEWORK KEY
★ = **STANDARDIZED TEST PRACTICE**
Exs. 5, 39, 40, 41, and 50

○ = **HINTS AND HOMEWORK HELP**
for Exs. 7, 11, 15, 19, 33 at classzone.com

SKILL PRACTICE

VOCABULARY Match the type of angle with an appropriate measure.

1. acute
2. obtuse
3. right
4. straight

A. 180°
B. 34°
C. 90°
D. 112°

SEE EXAMPLE 1
on p. 465
for Exs. 5–9

5. ★ **MULTIPLE CHOICE** What type of angle is *not* shown in the diagram?

Ⓐ acute
Ⓑ right
Ⓒ obtuse
Ⓓ straight

CLASSIFYING ANGLES Classify the angles.

6. ∠E
7. ∠F
8. ∠G
9. ∠H

SEE EXAMPLE 3
on p. 466
for Exs. 10

10. **EXAMPLES AND NONEXAMPLES** Using angle measures, give three examples of a pair of complementary angles. Then give three examples of a pair of angles that are *not* complementary.

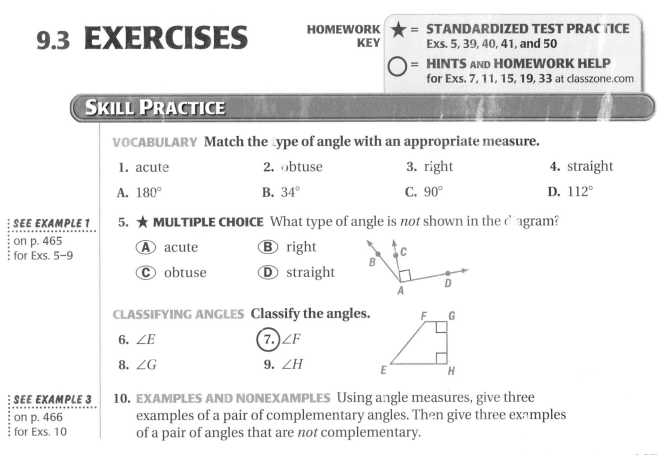

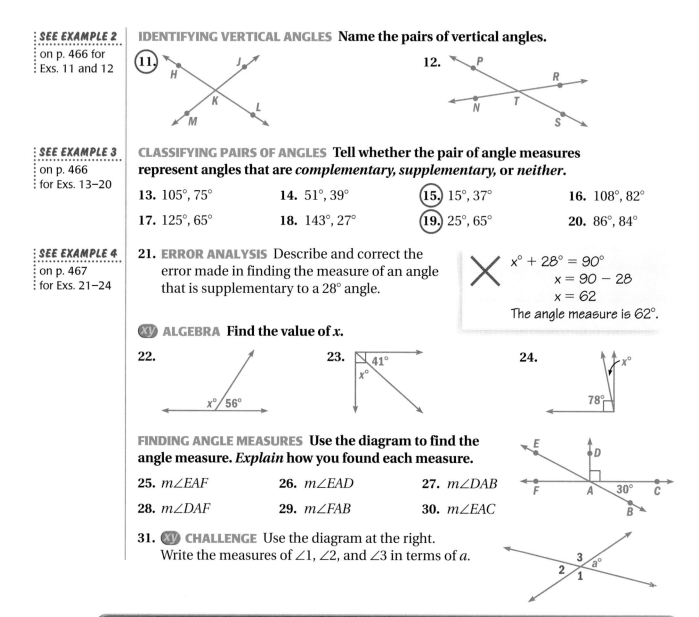

SEE EXAMPLE 2
on p. 466 for
Exs. 11 and 12

IDENTIFYING VERTICAL ANGLES **Name the pairs of vertical angles.**

11.

12.

SEE EXAMPLE 3
on p. 466
for Exs. 13–20

CLASSIFYING PAIRS OF ANGLES **Tell whether the pair of angle measures represent angles that are *complementary*, *supplementary*, or *neither*.**

13. 105°, 75°   **14.** 51°, 39°   **15.** 15°, 37°   **16.** 108°, 82°

17. 125°, 65°   **18.** 143°, 27°   **19.** 25°, 65°   **20.** 86°, 84°

SEE EXAMPLE 4
on p. 467
for Exs. 21–24

21. **ERROR ANALYSIS** Describe and correct the error made in finding the measure of an angle that is supplementary to a 28° angle.

$$x° + 28° = 90°$$
$$x = 90 - 28$$
$$x = 62$$
The angle measure is 62°.

ALGEBRA **Find the value of *x*.**

22.   **23.**   **24.**

FINDING ANGLE MEASURES **Use the diagram to find the angle measure. *Explain* how you found each measure.**

25. $m\angle EAF$ **26.** $m\angle EAD$ **27.** $m\angle DAB$

28. $m\angle DAF$ **29.** $m\angle FAB$ **30.** $m\angle EAC$

31. **CHALLENGE** Use the diagram at the right. Write the measures of $\angle 1$, $\angle 2$, and $\angle 3$ in terms of *a*.

PROBLEM SOLVING

CLOCKS **Classify the angle formed by the hands of the clock.**

32.   **33.**   **34.**   **35.**

Cairo   Prague   Mexico City   Denver

SEE EXAMPLE 4
on p. 467
for Exs. 36–37

36. **GARDEN WALL** A garden wall is leaning at an angle. The angle between a leaning wall and the ground is 81.5°. How many degrees from vertical is the wall leaning?

37. **REASONING** For greatest strength, a branch of a fruit tree should make a 30° to 45° angle with the ground. What is the greatest angle measure the complement of this angle can have? *Explain* your reasoning.

38. MULTI-STEP PROBLEM Draw a diagram of the building and the hill on which it sits. On your diagram, draw a horizontal line through the vertex of the 74° angle shown. To find the angle the hillside makes with the horizontal line, would you use complementary angles or supplementary angles? Find the angle of the hillside.

74°

39. ★ SHORT RESPONSE ∠*ABC* and ∠*DBE* are obtuse angles. ∠*ABE* is a straight angle. What type of angles are ∠*ABD* and ∠*DBE*? *Explain* your reasoning.

40. ★ WRITING Suppose that two lines intersect to form ∠1, ∠2, ∠3, and ∠4. If ∠1 is a right angle, *explain* why ∠2, ∠3, and ∠4 must be right angles.

41. ★ EXTENDED RESPONSE The light from a tree reflected in a pond bounces off the water to reach your eyes as shown below. The measure of the angle that is formed by the ray of light and the water is the same before and after the light bounces off the water.

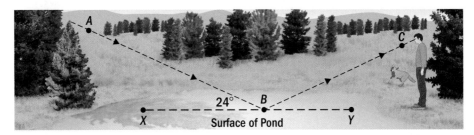
A
C
24°
B
X
Surface of Pond
Y

a. Calculate Find the measure of ∠*YBC*.

b. Calculate Find the measure of ∠*ABC*.

c. Conjecture How could you see your face in the pond?

d. Reasoning When you see your face in the pond, what is the measure of ∠*ABC*? *Justify* your answer.

42. CHALLENGE Use the information from Exercise 41. Is there a maximum or minimum angle measure of ∠*YBC* for seeing something reflected in a pond? *Explain*.

MIXED REVIEW

Get-Ready

Prepare for Lesson 9.4 in Exs. 43–46

Use estimation to name an angle whose measure is closest to the given measure. *(p. 460)*

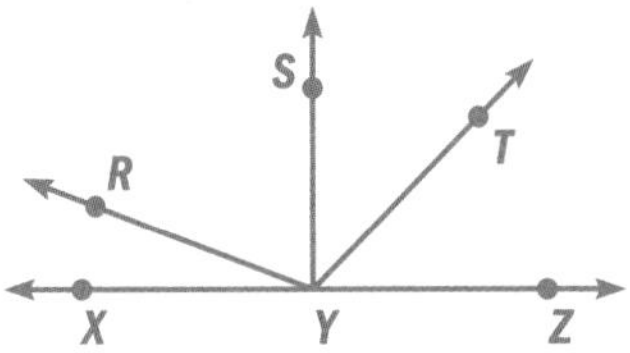

43. 115°   **44.** 20°

45. 45°   **46.** 90°

S
R
T
X
Y
Z

Find the sum or difference. *(p. 148)*

47. $54.2 + 6.12$ **48.** $9.49 + 37.8$ **49.** $18.02 - 0.45$

50. ★ MULTIPLE CHOICE Which figure is *not* shown in the diagram at the right? *(p. 455)*

P   Q

A $\overleftrightarrow{PQ}$ **B** $\overrightarrow{PQ}$ **C** $\overline{QP}$ **D** $\overrightarrow{QP}$

INVESTIGATION
Use before Lesson 9.4

GOAL
Investigate the sum of the angle measures of a triangle.

MATERIALS
• ruler
• scissors
• protractor

9.4 Investigating Angles of a Triangle

You can use models to find the sum of the angle measures of a triangle.

EXPLORE Find the sum of the angle measures of a triangle.

STEP 1 **Draw** a triangle on a piece of paper. Make each side at least 3 inches long.

STEP 2 **Cut** out your triangle, and tear off the three corners as shown.

STEP 3 **Arrange** the three corners as shown. What type of angle do they appear to form?

STEP 4 **Repeat** steps 1–3 with a different triangle. Compare your results with the results for the first triangle.

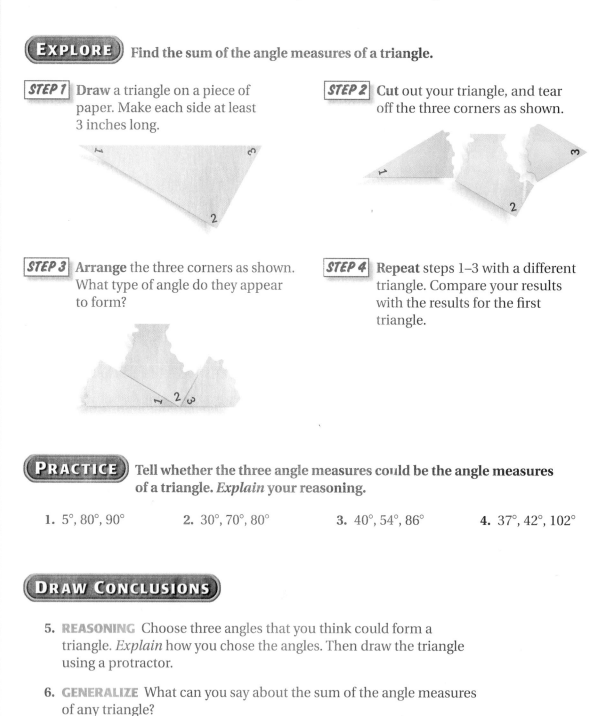

PRACTICE Tell whether the three angle measures could be the angle measures of a triangle. *Explain* your reasoning.

1. 5°, 80°, 90°
2. 30°, 70°, 80°
3. 40°, 54°, 86°
4. 37°, 42°, 102°

DRAW CONCLUSIONS

5. **REASONING** Choose three angles that you think could form a triangle. *Explain* how you chose the angles. Then draw the triangle using a protractor.

6. **GENERALIZE** What can you say about the sum of the angle measures of any triangle?

9.4 Classifying Triangles

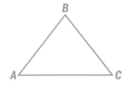

Before	You classified angles as acute, right, obtuse, or straight.
Now	You'll classify triangles by their angles and by their sides.
Why?	So you can identify types of real-world triangles, as in Ex. 36.

KEY VOCABULARY
- triangle, *p. 471*
- acute triangle,
  right triangle,
  obtuse triangle,
  p. 471
- equilateral triangle,
  isosceles triangle,
  scalene triangle,
  p. 472

Carpentry The carpentry work in the photo has many *triangles*. A **triangle** is a closed plane figure with three straight sides that connect three points, such as *A*, *B*, and *C*. You read △*ABC* as "triangle *ABC*." △*ABC* has sides $\overline{AB}$, $\overline{BC}$, and $\overline{AC}$, and vertices *A*, *B*, and *C*. You can classify triangles by their angles or their sides.

Classifying Triangles by Angles		
An **acute triangle** has three acute angles. 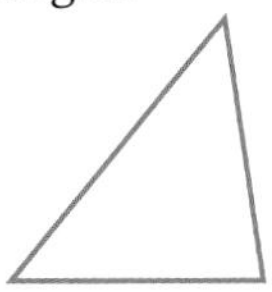	A **right triangle** has one right angle. 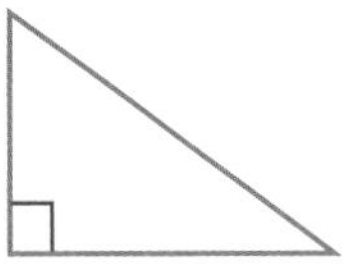	An **obtuse triangle** has one obtuse angle. 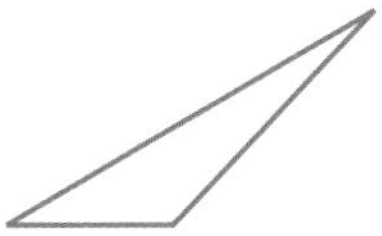

EXAMPLE 1   Classifying Triangles by Angles

Classify the triangle by its angles.

a. 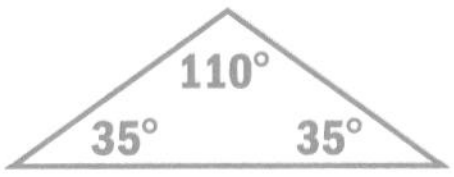 110°, 35°, 35°

b. 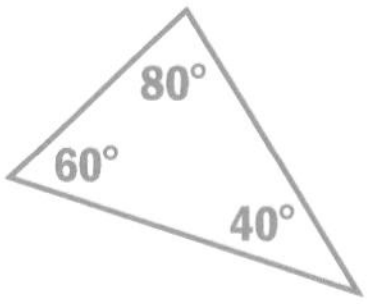 80°, 60°, 40°

c. 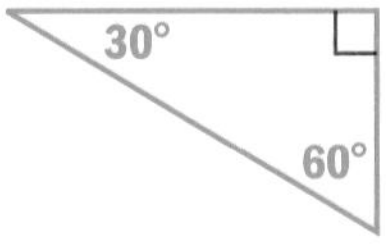 30°, 60°

SOLUTION

a. The triangle is obtuse because it has 1 obtuse angle.

b. The triangle is acute because it has 3 acute angles.

c. The triangle is right because it has 1 right angle.

✔ **GUIDED PRACTICE**   for Example 1

Classify the triangle by its angles.

1. 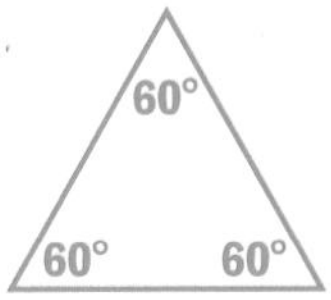 60°, 60°, 60°

2. 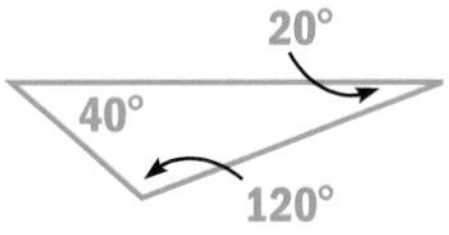 20°, 40°, 120°

3. 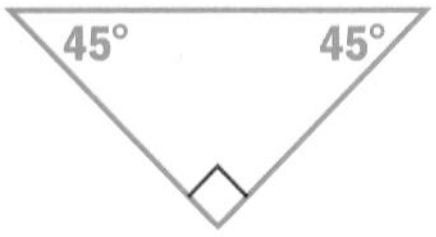 45°, 45°

Sides of a Triangle You can use special marks on a drawing to indicate that two sides have the same length as shown at the right.

Classifying Triangles by Sides		
An **equilateral triangle** has three sides of the same length.	An **isosceles triangle** has at least two sides of the same length.	A **scalene triangle** has three sides of different lengths.

EXAMPLE 2 Classifying Triangles by Sides

Classify the triangle by its sides.

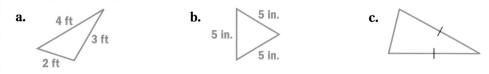

a. 4 ft, 3 ft, 2 ft **b.** 5 in., 5 in., 5 in. **c.**

SOLUTION

a. The triangle is scalene because all of its sides have different lengths.

b. The triangle is equilateral because all of its sides have the same length.

c. The triangle is isosceles because two of its sides have the same length.

✓ **GUIDED PRACTICE** for Example 2

4. Measure the sides of the triangles in Exercises 1–3 of the Guided Practice for Example 1. Classify each triangle by its sides.

Angles of a Triangle As you may have noticed in the investigation on page 470, the measures of the angles of any triangle add up to 180°.

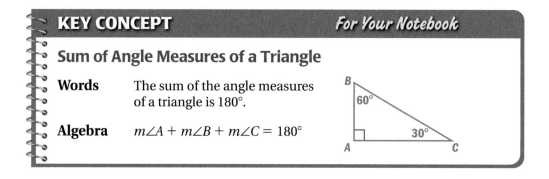

KEY CONCEPT *For Your Notebook*

Sum of Angle Measures of a Triangle

Words The sum of the angle measures of a triangle is 180°.

Algebra $m\angle A + m\angle B + m\angle C = 180°$

Stained Glass Use the stained glass to the right to determine which number represents the value of x.

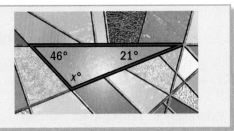

(A) 23 **(B)** 33

(C) 113 **(D)** 293

ELIMINATE CHOICES
The angle with the unknown measure is obtuse. So choices A and B can be eliminated.

SOLUTION

Use the fact that the measures of the angles of a triangle add up to 180°.

$46° + 21° + x° = 180°$	The angle measures add up to 180°.
$67 + x = 180$	Simplify.
$x = 180 - 67$	Write a related equation.
$x = 113$	Simplify.

▶ **Answer** The value of x is 113. The correct answer is C. **(A)** **(B)** **(C)** **(D)**

✓ **GUIDED PRACTICE** for Example 3

Tell whether the angle measures can be those of a triangle.

5. 15°, 160°, 15° **6.** 22°, 92°, 66° **7.** 102°, 12°, 65°

8. **XY Algebra** Find the value of x if the angles of a triangle measure $x°$, 70°, and 80°.

9.4 EXERCISES

HOMEWORK KEY

★ = **STANDARDIZED TEST PRACTICE**
Exs. 14, 21, 35, and 55

○ = **HINTS AND HOMEWORK HELP**
for Exs. 9, 11, 15, 37 at classzone.com

SKILL PRACTICE

VOCABULARY Match each description with exactly one triangle.

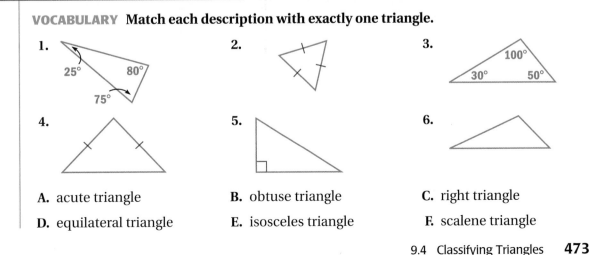

1. 25° 80° 75°

2.

3. 100° 30° 50°

4.

5.

6.

A. acute triangle   **B.** obtuse triangle   **C.** right triangle

D. equilateral triangle   **E.** isosceles triangle   **F.** scalene triangle

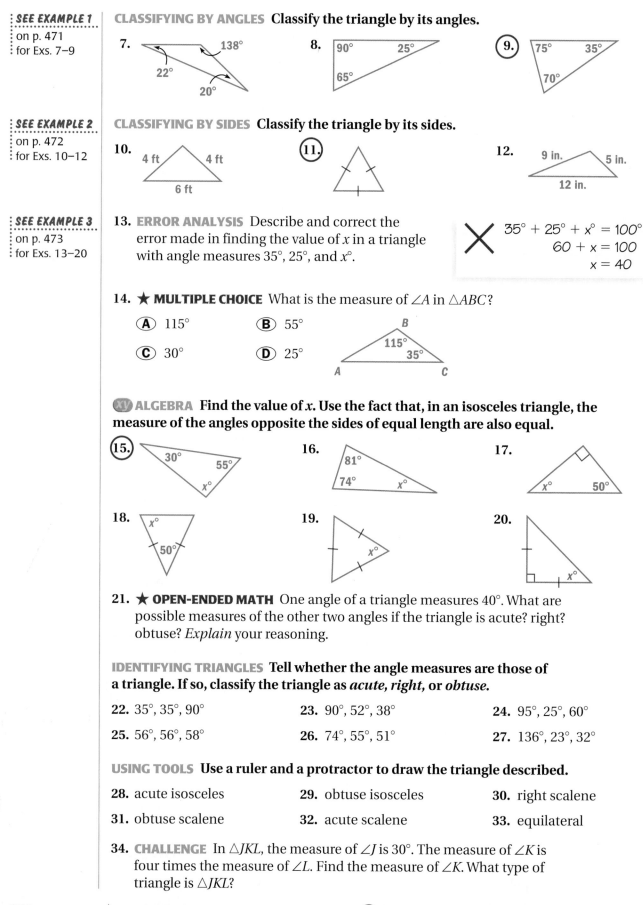

SEE EXAMPLE 1
on p. 471
for Exs. 7–9

CLASSIFYING BY ANGLES Classify the triangle by its angles.

7.

138°
22°
20°

8.

90°   25°
65°

9.

75°   35°
70°

SEE EXAMPLE 2
on p. 472
for Exs. 10–12

CLASSIFYING BY SIDES Classify the triangle by its sides.

10.

4 ft   4 ft
6 ft

11.

12.

9 in.   5 in.
12 in.

SEE EXAMPLE 3
on p. 473
for Exs. 13–20

13. **ERROR ANALYSIS** Describe and correct the error made in finding the value of x in a triangle with angle measures 35°, 25°, and $x°$.

$$35° + 25° + x° = 100°$$
$$60 + x = 100$$
$$x = 40$$

14. ★ **MULTIPLE CHOICE** What is the measure of $\angle A$ in $\triangle ABC$?

(A) 115°   (B) 55°

(C) 30°   (D) 25°

B
115°
35°
A   C

ALGEBRA Find the value of x. Use the fact that, in an isosceles triangle, the measure of the angles opposite the sides of equal length are also equal.

15.

30°   55°
$x°$

16.

81°
74° $x°$

17.

$x°$ 50°

18.

$x°$
50°

19.

$x°$

20.

$x°$

21. ★ **OPEN-ENDED MATH** One angle of a triangle measures 40°. What are possible measures of the other two angles if the triangle is acute? right? obtuse? *Explain* your reasoning.

IDENTIFYING TRIANGLES Tell whether the angle measures are those of a triangle. If so, classify the triangle as *acute, right,* or *obtuse.*

22. 35°, 35°, 90°   23. 90°, 52°, 38°   24. 95°, 25°, 60°

25. 56°, 56°, 58°   26. 74°, 55°, 51°   27. 136°, 23°, 32°

USING TOOLS Use a ruler and a protractor to draw the triangle described.

28. acute isosceles   29. obtuse isosceles   30. right scalene

31. obtuse scalene   32. acute scalene   33. equilateral

34. **CHALLENGE** In $\triangle JKL$, the measure of $\angle J$ is 30°. The measure of $\angle K$ is four times the measure of $\angle L$. Find the measure of $\angle K$. What type of triangle is $\triangle JKL$?

35. ★ **MULTIPLE CHOICE** What type of triangle is the stamp shown at the right?

    A right, isosceles   **B** acute, isosceles

    C right, scalene   **D** acute, equilateral

SEE EXAMPLE 3
on p. 473 for
Exs. 36 and 37

36. **CONSTRUCTION** The end of a roof is in the shape of an isosceles triangle. The measure of the angle at the peak, between the two equal sides, is 120°. The other two angle measures are equal. What is their measure?

GREAT PYRAMID **The triangle below shows a view of one of the sides of the Great Pyramid.**

37. What is the value of x in the triangle?

38. Classify the triangle by its sides and angles.

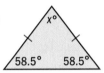

READING *IN* MATH Read the information below for Exercises 39–41.

Crystals Crystals occur when the smallest particles of a mineral are arranged in a pattern. The mineral calcite has hundreds of crystalline forms, two of which are shown. For each given crystal, their triangular surfaces, or faces, are all the same shape.

scalenohedron
(skay-LEE-nuh-HEE-druhn)

trigonal dipyramid
(tri-GO-nuhl DY-PIR-uh-mihd)

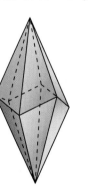

39. **Identify** From the name *scalenohedron*, what type of triangle do you think forms each face of the crystal?

40. **Calculate** The surface of the trigonal dipyramid is made up of how many triangles?

41. **Classify** The triangle where the top and bottom sections of the trigonal dipyramid meet is an equilateral triangle. What type of triangles make up its surface?

REASONING Tell whether the statement is *always, sometimes,* or *never* true. *Justify* your reasoning and include examples.

42. A right triangle is isosceles.

43. In a right triangle, the two acute angles are complementary.

44. The sum of any two angle measures in an acute triangle is greater than 90°.

45. The sum of the two acute angle measures in an obtuse triangle is less than 90°.

46. In an isosceles triangle, the angles opposite the sides of equal measure are equal in measure.

47. CHALLENGE In the figure, △DBE is a right scalene triangle. Is △ABC also a right scalene triangle? *Explain.*

48. CHALLENGE Draw an angle and label it *ABC*. Draw line $\overleftrightarrow{AC}$. Choose point *D* on $\overrightarrow{BA}$ and point *E* on $\overrightarrow{BC}$ so that $\overleftrightarrow{DE}$ is parallel to $\overleftrightarrow{AC}$. Do △ABC and △DBE *always* have the same classification when classified by their angles? by their sides? *Explain* your reasoning.

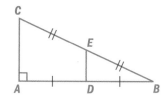

MIXED REVIEW

Get-Ready

Prepare for
Lesson 9.5
in Exs. 49–50

Use the figure shown. *(p. 465)*

49. Name two pairs of supplementary angles.

50. Find $m\angle1$, $m\angle2$, and $m\angle3$.

Write the decimal as a fraction or mixed number in simplest form. *(p. 266)*

51. 0.35   **52.** 0.68   **53.** 6.42   **54.** 12.37

55. ★ SHORT RESPONSE A baseball player pitches $\frac{4}{9}$ of a game. The remaining fraction of the game is evenly divided among three relief pitchers. What fraction of the game did each relief pitcher play? *Explain* how you found your answer. *(pp. 316, 362)*

QUIZ *for Lessons 9.1–9.4*

Use the figure to name the following. *(p. 455)*

1. a point   **2.** two rays

3. parallel lines   **4.** a segment

5. Rays $\overrightarrow{AB}$ and $\overrightarrow{AD}$ form an angle. Name the angle three different ways. *(p. 460)*

Tell whether the angle is *acute, obtuse, right,* or *straight.* *(p. 465)*

6. $m\angle A = 180°$ **7.** $m\angle B = 92°$ **8.** $m\angle C = 18°$ **9.** $m\angle D = 90°$

Tell whether the angles are *complementary, supplementary,* or *neither.* *(p. 465)*

10. 25°, 75°   **11.** 148°, 32°   **12.** 100°, 90°   **13.** 85°, 5°

Find the value of *x.* *(p. 471)*

14. 35° 25° *x*°   **15.** 49° 45° *x*°   **16.** 62° *x*° 62°

Tell whether the angle measures are those of a triangle. *(p. 471)*

17. 30°, 60°, 90°   **18.** 45°, 90°, 45°   **19.** 35°, 45°, 110°   **20.** 59°, 43°, 68°

9.4 Angle Measures of Triangles

EXAMPLE **You can enter formulas in a spreadsheet to add or subtract numbers.**

A school's Student Association logo is a triangle that has one 78° angle and one 57° angle. What is the measure of the third angle?

SOLUTION

Create a spreadsheet with the format shown. To calculate the measure of the third angle, you must subtract the sum of the first two angle measures (entered in cells B1 and B2) from 180°. This can be done by entering this formula in cell B3: = 180 − SUM(B1 : B2).

	A	B
1	1st angle measure (degrees)	78
2	2nd angle measure (degrees)	57
3	3rd angle measure (degrees)	45

▶ **Answer** The measure of the third angle is 45°.

= 180 − SUM(B1 : B2) gives the result 180 − (78 + 57), or 45.

PRACTICE **Use a spreadsheet to find the value of *x*.**

1.
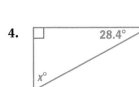
70°
60°   *x*°

2.
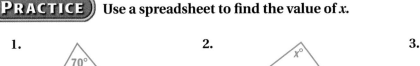
x°
37°   53°

3.
34°
x°   112°

4.
28.4°
x°

5.
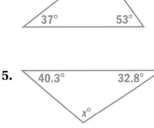
40.3°   32.8°
x°

6.
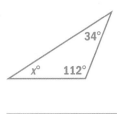
x°   60°
83.7°

7. **WEATHER** The logo for the National Tsunami Hazard Mitigation Program is a triangle with two 57.5° angles. What is the measure of the third angle?

8. **SCIENCE** The Nauru99 Triangle is an oceanic and atmospheric research area formed by two research vessels and the island of Nauru. The angle measures at the two research vessels are 80° and 63°. What is the angle measure at the island of Nauru?

Lessons 9.1–9.4

1. **MULTI-STEP PROBLEM** The side of a cliff has the angle measure shown below.

75°

a. Find the complement of the angle to determine how many degrees the cliff leans from vertical.

b. Find the supplement of the angle shown. What does this angle represent?

c. How many more degrees is the supplement than the complement?

2. **EXTENDED RESPONSE** The table shows several measures for an angle.

Angle	90°	75°	55°	35°	$x°$
Supplement	?	?	?	?	?

a. Copy and complete the table.

b. Based on your table write expressions for the measures of $\angle POQ$ and $\angle SOR$ in terms of x.

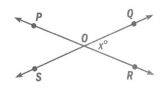

c. *Explain* why the measures of $\angle POQ$ and $\angle SOR$ are equal. Give two reasons in your explanation.

3. **GRIDDED ANSWER** Use a protractor to measure $\angle POQ$ in Exercise 2. Round your answer to the nearest degree.

4. **GRIDDED ANSWER** A stained glass window is made of small equilateral triangles, as shown below. How many equilateral triangles of all sizes can be found in the window?

5. **GRIDDED ANSWER** The complement of $\angle ABC$ is equal to the supplement of an angle measuring 150°. Find $m\angle ABC$.

6. **OPEN-ENDED** Find values of w, x, y, and z that make the figure possible. *Explain* your reasoning.

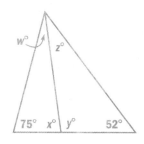

7. **SHORT RESPONSE** Cecelia measured angles in a drawing for an art project. She needed a 3° angle, a 92° angle, and a 175° angle. *Explain* how she could use the benchmarks 0°, 90°, and 180° to check to see if her measurements were reasonable.

8. **SHORT RESPONSE** Use what you know about triangles and angles to find the measures of $\angle 2$, $\angle 3$, $\angle 4$, $\angle 6$, and $\angle 7$. *Explain* how you found your answers.

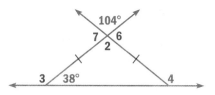

GOAL
Investigate relationships among angles of four-sided figures.

MATERIALS
• protractor

9.5 Angles of Quadrilaterals

You can use a protractor to investigate angles of four-sided figures.

EXPLORE Investigate the angles of the figures below.

STEP 1 **Trace** the figures below on a piece of paper.

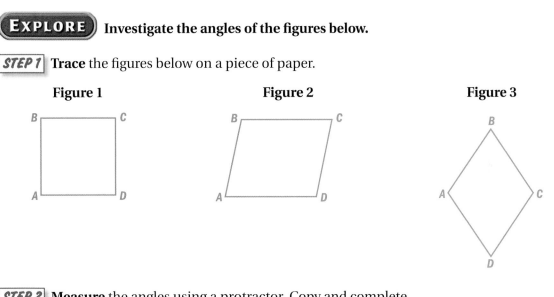

Figure 1   **Figure 2**   **Figure 3**

STEP 2 **Measure** the angles using a protractor. Copy and complete the table.

	m∠A	m∠B	m∠C	m∠D	m∠A + m∠B + m∠C + m∠D
Figure 1	?	?	?	?	?
Figure 2	?	?	?	?	?
Figure 3	?	?	?	?	?

PRACTICE

1. Sketch and label a four-sided figure with straight sides. Copy and extend the table in Step 2 for your figure.

DRAW CONCLUSIONS

2. **WRITING** Based on the table you completed, write a rule for the sum of the angle measures of a four-sided figure.

3. **REASONING** What other angle relationships do you notice in your table? *Describe* these relationships in words.

Before	You classified triangles by their angles and sides.
Now	You'll classify quadrilaterals by their angles and sides.
Why?	So you can classify figures such as quilt patches in Exs. 26–28.

KEY VOCABULARY
- quadrilateral, *p. 480*
- parallelogram, *p. 480*
- rectangle, *p. 480*
- rhombus, *p. 480*
- square, *p. 480*

A **quadrilateral** is a plane figure formed by four segments called *sides*. Each side intersects exactly two other sides, one at each endpoint, and no two sides are part of the same line. The chart below shows some types of quadrilaterals.

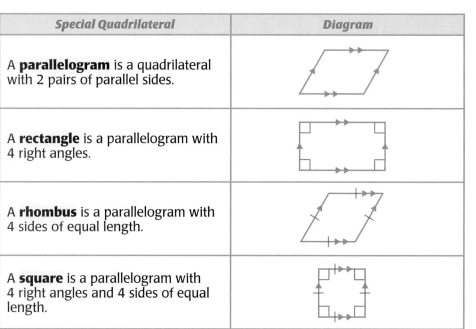

Special Quadrilateral	Diagram
A **parallelogram** is a quadrilateral with 2 pairs of parallel sides.	
A **rectangle** is a parallelogram with 4 right angles.	
A **rhombus** is a parallelogram with 4 sides of equal length.	
A **square** is a parallelogram with 4 right angles and 4 sides of equal length.	

EXAMPLE 1 **Classifying Quadrilaterals**

Tell whether the statement is *true* or *false*. *Explain* your reasoning.

a. All squares are rectangles.

b. Some rhombuses do not have 2 pairs of parallel sides.

SOLUTION

a. True: All squares are parallelograms with 4 right angles, so all squares are rectangles.

b. False: All rhombuses are parallelograms, so all rhombuses have 2 pairs of parallel sides.

TAKE NOTES
Make a Venn diagram in your notebook to help you organize the different types of quadrilaterals. For help with Venn diagrams, see p. 756.

Classify Quadrilaterals You need to look at all the marks and labels on a quadrilateral to decide how to classify it. Some quadrilaterals can be classified in more than one way.

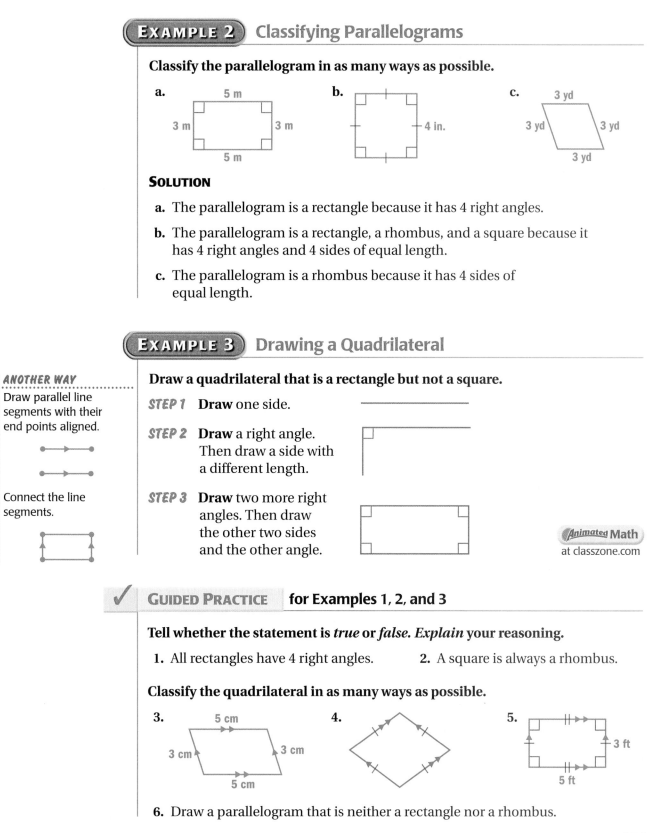

EXAMPLE 2 Classifying Parallelograms

Classify the parallelogram in as many ways as possible.

a. 5 m / 3 m / 3 m / 5 m

b. 4 in.

c. 3 yd / 3 yd / 3 yd / 3 yd

SOLUTION

a. The parallelogram is a rectangle because it has 4 right angles.

b. The parallelogram is a rectangle, a rhombus, and a square because it has 4 right angles and 4 sides of equal length.

c. The parallelogram is a rhombus because it has 4 sides of equal length.

EXAMPLE 3 Drawing a Quadrilateral

ANOTHER WAY
Draw parallel line segments with their end points aligned.

Connect the line segments.

Draw a quadrilateral that is a rectangle but not a square.

STEP 1 **Draw** one side.

STEP 2 **Draw** a right angle. Then draw a side with a different length.

STEP 3 **Draw** two more right angles. Then draw the other two sides and the other angle.

Animated Math
at classzone.com

✓ **GUIDED PRACTICE** **for Examples 1, 2, and 3**

Tell whether the statement is *true* or *false*. *Explain* your reasoning.

1. All rectangles have 4 right angles.

2. A square is always a rhombus.

Classify the quadrilateral in as many ways as possible.

3. 5 cm / 3 cm / 3 cm / 5 cm

4.

5. 3 ft / 5 ft

6. Draw a parallelogram that is neither a rectangle nor a rhombus.

Angles of a Quadrilateral As you may have noticed in the Investigation on page 479, the sum of the measures of the angles of any quadrilateral is 360°.

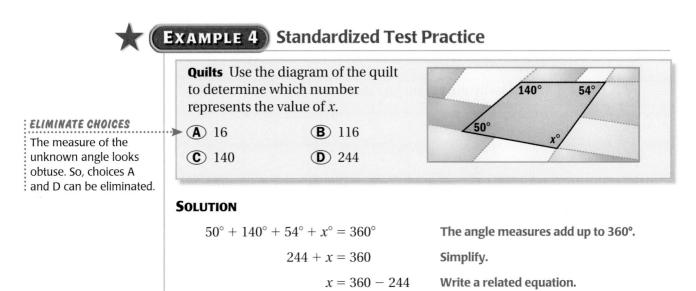

⭐ **EXAMPLE 4** **Standardized Test Practice**

Quilts Use the diagram of the quilt to determine which number represents the value of *x*.

(**A**) 16   (**B**) 116

(**C**) 140   (**D**) 244

ELIMINATE CHOICES
The measure of the unknown angle looks obtuse. So, choices A and D can be eliminated.

SOLUTION

$$50° + 140° + 54° + x° = 360°$$ **The angle measures add up to 360°.**

$$244 + x = 360$$ **Simplify.**

$$x = 360 − 244$$ **Write a related equation.**

$$x = 116$$ **Simplify.**

▶ **Answer** The value of *x* is 116. The correct answer is B. (**A**) (**B**) (**C**) (**D**)

✓ **GUIDED PRACTICE** **for Example 4**

7. What If? Suppose the quadrilateral in the figure in Example 4 had angle measures of 120°, 53°, 19°, and *x*°. Find the value of *x*.

9.5 **EXERCISES**

HOMEWORK KEY

⭐ = **STANDARDIZED TEST PRACTICE**
Exs. 13, 23, 31, 32, 33, 34, and 43

◯ = **HINTS AND HOMEWORK HELP**
for Exs. 7, 11, 15, 27, 29 at classzone.com

SKILL PRACTICE

VOCABULARY Copy and complete the statement using *all* or *some*.

SEE EXAMPLE 1
on p. 480
for Exs. 1–8, 12

1. _?_ rectangles are squares.

2. _?_ rhombuses are parallelograms.

3. _?_ squares are rhombuses.

4. _?_ parallelograms are squares.

5. _?_ squares are rectangles.

6. _?_ rhombuses are squares.

(**7.**) _?_ rectangles are rhombuses.

8. _?_ rhombuses are rectangles.

SEE EXAMPLE 2
on p. 481
for Exs. 9–11

CLASSIFYING Classify the parallelogram in as many ways as possible.

9.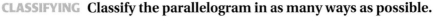

10.
7 m
7 m   7 m
7 m

(**11.**)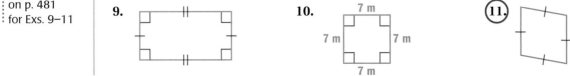

12. ERROR ANALYSIS Chloe said, "Because all squares are rhombuses, all rhombuses are squares." Describe and correct her error.

SEE EXAMPLE 3
on p. 481 for
Exs. 13, 20–22

13. ★ **OPEN-ENDED MATH** Draw a rectangle that is also a rhombus.

RECOGNIZING QUADRILATERALS Tell whether the angle measures are those of a quadrilateral.

SEE EXAMPLE 4
on p. 482
for Exs. 14–19

14. 110°, 60°, 40°, 50°   **15.** 88°, 90°, 90°, 92°   **16.** 68°, 152°, 19°, 121°

ALGEBRA Find the value of x.

17.

112°   96°

$x°$ 86°

18.

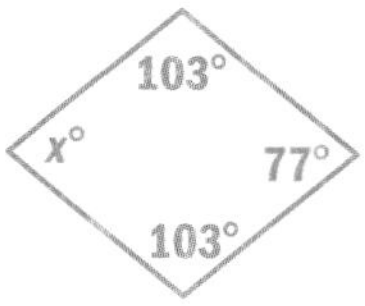

103°

$x°$ 77°

103°

19.

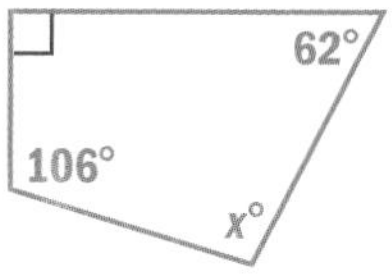

62°

106°

$x°$

REASONING Draw an example of each type of quadrilateral that always fits the description.

20. 4 equal sides   **21.** 4 right angles   **22.** 2 pairs of parallel sides

23. ★ **MULTIPLE CHOICE** The acute angle in the quadrilateral is labeled incorrectly. What is the correct angle measure?

138°

52°

(A) 32°   (B) 42°   (C) 48°   (D) 142°

24. CHALLENGE Is it reasonable that three angles of a quadrilateral can each have a measure greater than 90°? *Explain* your reasoning.

25. EXAMPLES AND NON-EXAMPLES The figure shows several trapezoids, and several quadrilaterals that are *not* trapezoids. *Describe* what makes a quadrilateral a trapezoid.

Trapezoids   Not trapezoids

PROBLEM SOLVING

QUILTS Classify the quadrilateral patches from a quilt in as many ways as possible.

26.   **27.** 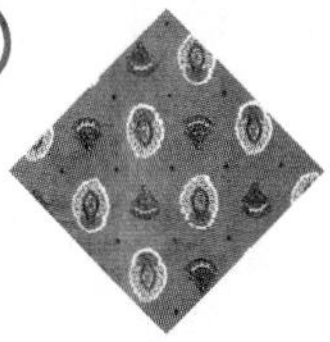   **28.**

29. PARKING LOT A parking lot has the shape of a quadrilateral. One side of the parking lot borders the road. The two angles bordering the road measure 90°. The measure of another corner is 75°. Find the angle measure of the fourth corner.

30. WOODWORKING Classify the numbered quadrilaterals in the woodwork at the right. What type of quadrilateral is the entire woodwork? How many rhombuses that are not squares are shown in the woodwork?

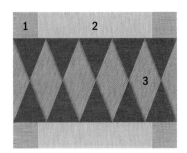

31. ★ MULTIPLE CHOICE Your uncle is designing a patio in the shape of a quadrilateral. Its opposite sides are parallel, its adjacent sides are of equal length, and at least one of its angles is obtuse. Which term best describes the shape of the patio?

   (A) parallelogram   **(B)** rectangle   **(C)** rhombus   **(D)** square

32. ★ WRITING *Explain* how a rhombus may also be a rectangle.

33. ★ SHORT RESPONSE Is a square always a rectangle, a rhombus, a parallelogram, and a quadrilateral? *Explain* your answer.

34. ★ EXTENDED RESPONSE A kaleidoscope makes geometric patterns using mirrors. Use the diagram of the pattern formed by the kaleidoscope.

   a. Properties If *ABCD* is a rhombus, what can you say about the other quadrilaterals in the figure outlined in yellow? *Explain.*

   b. Conjecture If you know the area of *ABCD*, how can you find the area of the figure outlined in yellow? *Explain* your reasoning.

   c. Apply Use part (a) to name all the segments parallel to $\overline{AB}$. *Justify* your answer.

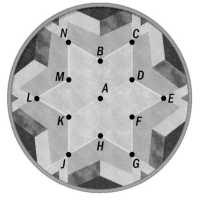

35. CHALLENGE Is it possible to draw a quadrilateral that has two right angles but is not a rectangle? Is this possible with three right angles? *Explain.*

36. CHALLENGE An angle of a rhombus measures 60°. Find the other angle measures. *Explain* your reasoning.

MIXED REVIEW

Get-Ready

Prepare for
Lesson 9.6
for Exs. 37–40

Tell whether the angle measures are those of a triangle. If so, classify the triangle as *acute, right,* or *obtuse*. (p. 471)

37. 28°, 38°, 124°   **38.** 20°, 80°, 80°   **39.** 23°, 55°, 102°   **40.** 45°, 45°, 90°

Find the total amount spent. (p. 169)

41. 7 light bulbs for $1.50 each   **42.** 4 bags of pretzels for $2.75 each

43. ★ MULTIPLE CHOICE Order the numbers 42%, 0.45, and $\frac{2}{5}$ from least to greatest. (p. 429)

   (A) 42%, 0.45, $\frac{2}{5}$ **(B)** 42%, $\frac{2}{5}$, 0.45   **(C)** $\frac{2}{5}$, 42%, 0.45   **(D)** 0.45, $\frac{2}{5}$, 42%

9.6 Polygons

Before	You classified figures by their angles and sides.
Now	You'll classify polygons by their sides.
Why?	So you can describe objects, as in Example 1.

KEY VOCABULARY
- **polygon,** *p. 485*
- **vertex,** *p. 485*
- **pentagon,** *p. 485*
- **hexagon,** *p. 485*
- **octagon,** *p. 485*
- **regular polygon,** *p. 486*
- **diagonal,** *p. 486*

Soccer Many soccer balls are made so that the cover shows two different figures. How can you describe these figures?

A **polygon** is a closed plane figure that is formed by three or more segments called *sides*. Each side intersects exactly two other sides at a **vertex.**

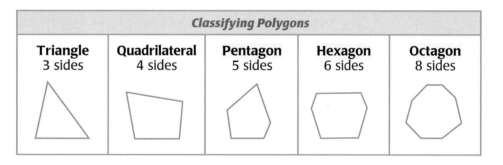

Classifying Polygons				
Triangle 3 sides	**Quadrilateral** 4 sides	**Pentagon** 5 sides	**Hexagon** 6 sides	**Octagon** 8 sides

---

EXAMPLE 1 Classifying Polygons

VOCABULARY

To help remember how many sides a polygon has, think of the meaning of the prefixes.

"tri" means 3.

"quad" means 4.

"penta" means 5.

"hexa" means 6.

"octa" means 8.

To describe the figures found on the soccer ball shown above, count the number of sides of each figure.

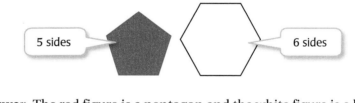

▶ **Answer** The red figure is a pentagon and the white figure is a hexagon.

Animated Math at classzone.com

✓ **GUIDED PRACTICE** for Example 1

Classify the polygon.

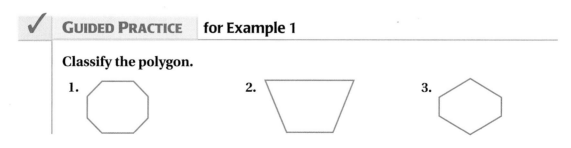

1.
2.
3.

Regular Polygons A **regular polygon** is a polygon with equal side lengths and equal angle measures. A stop sign is an example of a regular octagon.

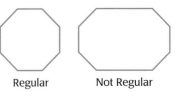

Regular   Not Regular

EXAMPLE 2 Classifying Regular Polygons

Classify the polygon and tell whether it is regular.

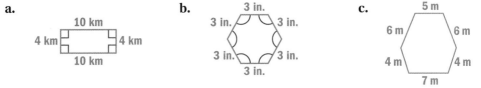

a.

10 km
4 km   4 km
10 km

b.

3 in.
3 in.   3 in.
3 in.   3 in.
3 in.

c.

5 m
6 m   6 m
4 m   4 m
7 m

SOLUTION

a. The side lengths of the quadrilateral are not equal, so it is not regular.

b. The side lengths of the hexagon are equal and the angle measures are equal, so it is a regular hexagon.

c. The side lengths of the hexagon are not equal, so it is not regular.

Diagonals A **diagonal** of a polygon is a segment, other than a side, that connects two vertices of the polygon.

EXAMPLE 3 Diagonals of a Regular Polygon

How many diagonals can be drawn from one vertex of a regular pentagon? How many triangles do the diagonals form?

SOLUTION

Sketch a regular pentagon and draw all the possible diagonals from one vertex.

▶ **Answer** There are 2 diagonals and 3 triangles.

✓ **GUIDED PRACTICE** for Examples 2 and 3

Classify the polygon and tell whether it is regular.

4.

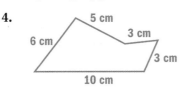

5 cm
6 cm   3 cm
3 cm
10 cm

5.

6. Tell how many triangles are formed by the diagonals from one vertex of a regular hexagon.

9.6 EXERCISES

SKILL PRACTICE

VOCABULARY Match the polygon with its correct classification.

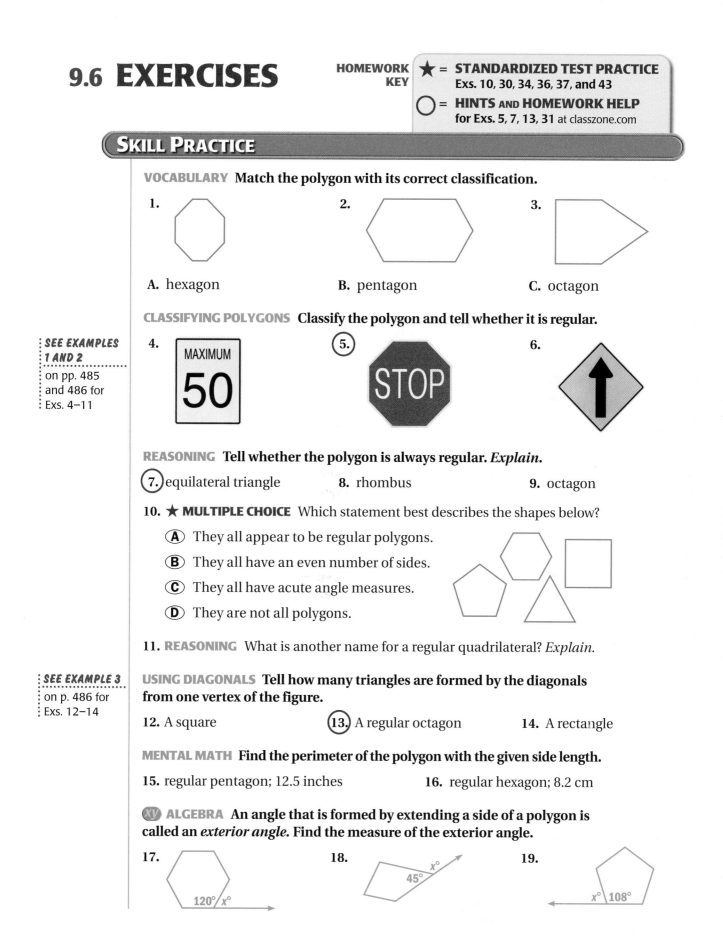

1.

2.

3.

A. hexagon

B. pentagon

C. octagon

CLASSIFYING POLYGONS Classify the polygon and tell whether it is regular.

SEE EXAMPLES 1 AND 2
on pp. 485 and 486 for Exs. 4–11

4.
MAXIMUM
50

(5.)
STOP

6.

REASONING Tell whether the polygon is always regular. *Explain.*

(7.) equilateral triangle

8. rhombus

9. octagon

10. ★ MULTIPLE CHOICE Which statement best describes the shapes below?

Ⓐ They all appear to be regular polygons.

Ⓑ They all have an even number of sides.

Ⓒ They all have acute angle measures.

Ⓓ They are not all polygons.

11. REASONING What is another name for a regular quadrilateral? *Explain.*

SEE EXAMPLE 3
on p. 486 for Exs. 12–14

USING DIAGONALS Tell how many triangles are formed by the diagonals from one vertex of the figure.

12. A square

(13.) A regular octagon

14. A rectangle

MENTAL MATH Find the perimeter of the polygon with the given side length.

15. regular pentagon; 12.5 inches

16. regular hexagon; 8.2 cm

ⓧⓥ ALGEBRA An angle that is formed by extending a side of a polygon is called an *exterior angle*. Find the measure of the exterior angle.

17.
$120°$ $x°$

18.
$45°$ $x°$

19.
$x°$ $108°$

GEOMETRY Graph the points on a coordinate grid and connect them to form a polygon. Then classify the polygon.

20. $A(7, 3)$, $B(3, 3)$, $C(3, 9)$, $D(7, 8)$

21. $A(2, 8)$, $B(2, 2)$, $C(8, 2)$, $D(10, 5)$, $E(8, 8)$

22. PREDICT Sketch a regular polygon with n sides for $n = 6, 7, 8, 9,$ and 10. As n increases, what happens to the shape? *Predict* what the polygon will look like for $n = 50$.

23. CHALLENGE Find the *total* number of diagonals of a regular hexagon.

In Exercises 24–27, find the sum of the measures of the interior angles of the polygon.

EXTENSION Sums of Interior Angle Measures of a Polygon

In an n-sided polygon in which the measure of each interior angle is less than $180°$, the sum of the measures of the interior angles is $(n - 2) \cdot 180°$. Find the sum of the measures of the interior angles of a hexagon.

SOLUTION

$(n - 2) \cdot 180° = (6 - 2) \cdot 180°$ A hexagon has 6 sides. Substitute 6 for n.

$\quad\quad\quad\quad\quad\quad = 4 \cdot 180°$ Simplify.

$\quad\quad\quad\quad\quad\quad = 720°$ Multiply.

▶ **Answer** The sum of the measures of the interior angles of a hexagon is $720°$.

---

24. quadrilateral   **25.** octagon   **26.** 10-sided polygon   **27.** pentagon

PROBLEM SOLVING

28. MEASUREMENT The cross section of a wooden pencil is a regular hexagon. One side of the hexagon is 4 millimeters. Find the distance around the pencil, in centimeters.

29. MEASUREMENT The perimeter of a regular octagonal lighthouse is 40 yards. Find the length of one outer wall, in feet.

30. ★ **WRITING** *Explain* why a triangle has no diagonals.

SEE EXAMPLES 1 AND 2 on pp. 485–486 for Exs. 31–33

CLASSIFYING POLYGONS Classify the polygon and tell whether it is regular.

31.

32.

33.

★ = STANDARDIZED TEST PRACTICE   ◯ = HINTS AND HOMEWORK HELP *at classzone.com*

34. ★ **OPEN-ENDED MATH** Draw a hexagon. Make the sides of equal length, but do not make the angle measures equal.

35. **MULTI-STEP PROBLEM** The points on the quadrilateral are equally spaced.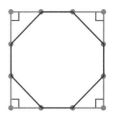

   a. *Explain* why the quadrilateral is regular.

   b. Are the triangles regular? Why or why not?

   c. Classify the red polygon. Is it regular? *Justify* your reasoning.

36. ★ **WRITING** *Explain* how you could help a classmate remember that an octagon has 8 sides.

37. ★ **EXTENDED RESPONSE** Use the table below to answer the questions.

   a. **Calculate** Copy and complete the table. You may want to draw the polygon described.

   b. **Look for a Pattern** How does the number of diagonals from one vertex change as the number of sides of the polygon increases?

Number of sides of regular polygon	4	5	6
Number of diagonals from one vertex	?	?	?

   c. **Model** Find a general expression for the number of diagonals from one vertex for an *n*-sided polygon.

   d. **Extend a Pattern** Use the expression you wrote in part (c) to predict the number of diagonals from one vertex of a regular polygon with 9 sides. Then sketch the polygon to check your answer.

38. **CHALLENGE** Draw a regular hexagon. Draw two diagonals from different vertices so that you form two triangles and one quadrilateral. Classify the triangles and the quadrilateral formed by the diagonals.

MIXED REVIEW

Get-Ready

Prepare for
Lesson 9.7 in
Exs. 39–41

Draw a quadrilateral that fits the description. *(p. 480)*

39. at least 3 right angles   **40.** 2 pairs of parallel sides   **41.** 4 sides of equal length

CHOOSE A STRATEGY Use a strategy from the list to solve the following problem. *Explain* your choice of strategy.

42. A diagram of a set of concrete steps is shown below. How many concrete blocks are needed to build the steps?

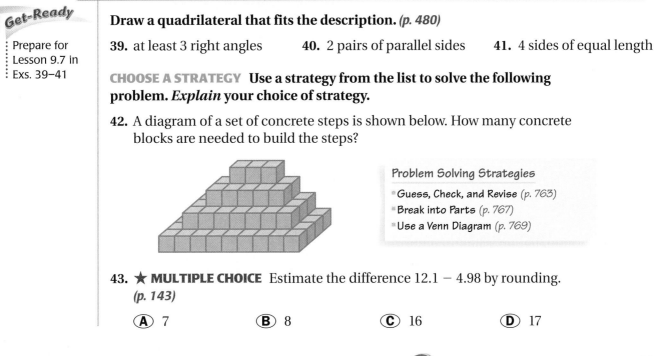

Problem Solving Strategies

▪ Guess, Check, and Revise *(p. 763)*
▪ Break into Parts *(p. 767)*
▪ Use a Venn Diagram *(p. 769)*

43. ★ **MULTIPLE CHOICE** Estimate the difference $12.1 - 4.98$ by rounding. *(p. 143)*

   (A) 7   **(B)** 8   **(C)** 16   **(D)** 17

9.7 Congruent and Similar Figures

Before	You classified polygons by their angles and sides.
Now	You'll identify congruent and similar figures.
Why?	So you can find unknown measures, as in Example 3.

KEY VOCABULARY
- **congruent,** *p. 490*
- **similar,** *p. 490*
- **corresponding parts,** *p. 491*

ACTIVITY

Investigate the size and shape of the triangles below.

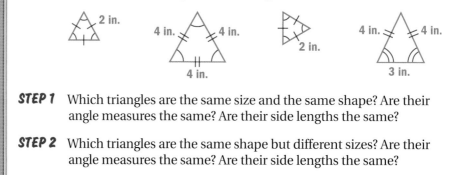

STEP 1 Which triangles are the same size and the same shape? Are their angle measures the same? Are their side lengths the same?

STEP 2 Which triangles are the same shape but different sizes? Are their angle measures the same? Are their side lengths the same?

Two figures are **congruent** if they have the same size and shape. Two figures are **similar** if they have the same shape, but not necessarily the same size.

EXAMPLE 1 Congruent and Similar Triangles

Tell whether the triangles are *similar*, *congruent*, or *neither*.

MATCHING FIGURES
You can tell △*ABC* and △*KLM* are congruent, because if △*KLM* is flipped over, it will fit exactly on △*ABC*.

SOLUTION

△*ABC*, △*FGH*, and △*KLM* are similar because they have the same shape. △*ABC* and △*KLM* are congruent because they have the same size and shape.

✓ **GUIDED PRACTICE** for Example 1

Tell whether the triangles are *similar*, *congruent*, or *neither*.

1.

2.

Corresponding Parts **Corresponding parts** are the matching sides and angles of two figures. When two figures are similar, their *corresponding angles* have the same measure. When two figures are congruent, their *corresponding parts* have the same measure. In other words, congruent figures have congruent corresponding angles and congruent corresponding sides.

EXAMPLE 2 Listing Corresponding Parts

△*ABC* and △*DEF* **are congruent. List the corresponding parts.**

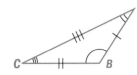

When listing corresponding parts, list corresponding vertices in the same order.

Corresponding angles: ∠*A* and ∠*D*, ∠*B* and ∠*E*, ∠*C* and ∠*F*

Corresponding sides: $\overline{AB}$ and $\overline{DE}$, $\overline{BC}$ and $\overline{EF}$, $\overline{AC}$ and $\overline{DF}$

EXAMPLE 3 Using Corresponding Parts

Bridges In the photograph, △*ABC* and △*DBC* are congruent.

a. $\overline{AC}$ is about 51 meters long. How long is $\overline{DC}$? *Explain.*

b. $m∠A ≈ 50°$. Find $m∠D$. *Explain.*

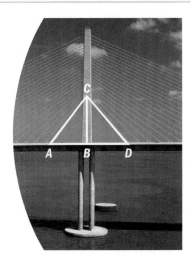

SOLUTION

a. Corresponding sides of congruent triangles have the same length. So, $\overline{DC}$ has a length of about 51 meters.

b. Corresponding angles of congruent triangles have the same measure. So, $m∠D ≈ 50°$.

✓ **GUIDED PRACTICE** for Examples 2 and 3

3. △*GHJ* and △*KML* are similar. Use the fact that corresponding angles of similar figures have the same measure to list the corresponding parts. Then find $m∠G$ and $m∠L$.

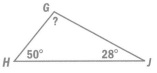 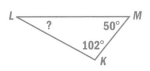

9.7 EXERCISES

HOMEWORK KEY

★ = **STANDARDIZED TEST PRACTICE**
Exs. 9, 19, 20, 21, and 31

◯ = **HINTS** AND **HOMEWORK HELP**
for Exs. 3, 5, 7, 17 at classzone.com

SKILL PRACTICE

VOCABULARY Tell whether the statement is *true* or *false*. *Explain.*

1. $\triangle VUW$ is similar to $\triangle YXZ$.

2. In the figures, $\overline{UV}$ corresponds to $\overline{XZ}$.

SEE EXAMPLE 1
on p. 490
for Exs. 3–5

CLASSIFYING FIGURES Tell whether the triangles are *similar, congruent,* or *neither.*

3.

4.

5.

SEE EXAMPLE 2
on p. 491
for Exs. 6–8

FINDING CORRESPONDING PARTS List the corresponding parts of the figures.

6.

7.

8.

SEE EXAMPLES 2 AND 3
on p. 491
for Exs. 9 and 11–13

9. ★ **MULTIPLE CHOICE** The triangles shown are congruent. What is the measure of $\angle J$?

Ⓐ 25°   Ⓑ 40°

Ⓒ 65°   Ⓓ 70°

10. **ERROR ANALYSIS** A classmate claims that if $\triangle ABC$ is similar to $\triangle TSR$, then $\angle A$ corresponds to $\angle R$. Describe and correct the classmate's error.

ALGEBRA The two figures are congruent. Find the values of x and y.

11.

12.

13.

14. **CHALLENGE** The two quadrilaterals shown are similar. Corresponding side lengths of two similar figures are proportional. Find the values of the variables. *Explain* how you found your answers.

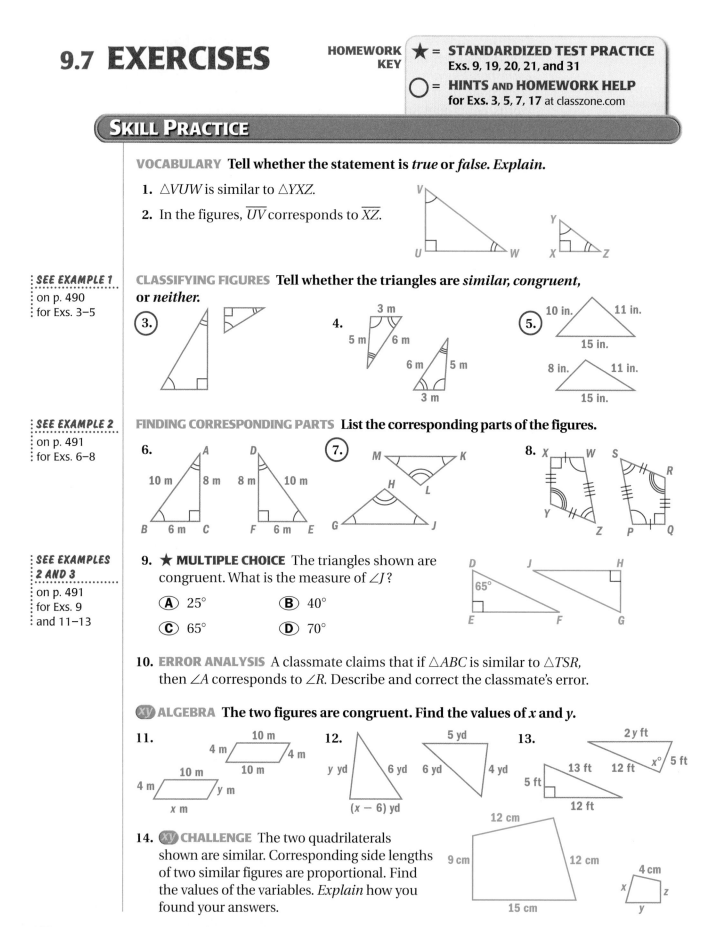

CLASSIFYING FIGURES Decide if the objects are usually *similar, congruent,* or *neither. Explain* your reasoning.

SEE EXAMPLES 1 AND 3
on pp. 490–491
for Exs. 15–21

15. buttons on a shirt

16. a C battery and a AA battery

17. a tennis ball and a basketball

18. a pair of earrings

19. ★ **SHORT RESPONSE** You are viewing photographs on a computer screen at a scale of 2 in. : 1 in. Are the images on the screen and the actual photographs similar? congruent? *Explain* your reasoning.

20. ★ **OPEN-ENDED MATH** Draw any triangle. Then draw a triangle with the same angle measures but different side lengths. Are the triangles *similar, congruent,* or *neither? Explain* your reasoning.

21. ★ **WRITING** If two figures are congruent, are they also similar? If two figures are similar, are they also congruent? *Explain.*

22. **AUTOMOBILES** The front view and top view of an automobile are shown at the right. A toy manufacturer is designing a scale model of the automobile. The model is 7.5 inches tall, 8.5 inches wide, and 19.25 inches long. Are the two vehicles similar? If not, how can the dimensions of the model be changed to make it similar to the actual automobile? *Explain* your reasoning.

Automobile

60 in.

├─ 68 in. ─┤ ├──── 155 in. ────┤

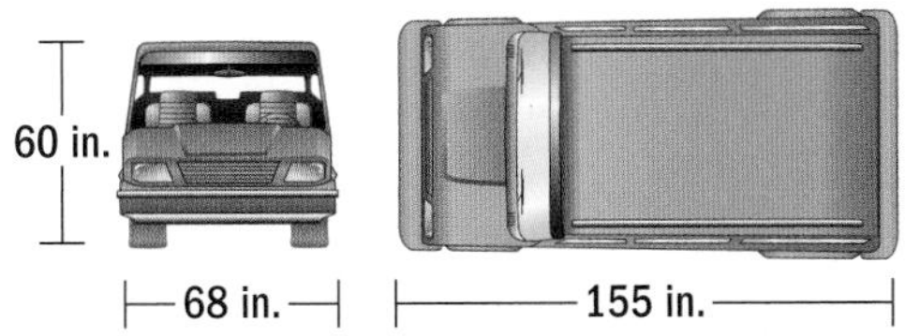

REASONING Tell whether a diagonal *always, sometimes,* or *never* divides the given polygon into two congruent figures. *Justify* your reasoning.

23. square

24. rectangle

25. pentagon

26. **CHALLENGE** Draw a rectangle of length 4 cm and width 7 cm. Draw a second rectangle, so that the measure of each side is increased by 2 cm. Draw a third rectangle, so that the measure of each side is twice the length of the first rectangle. Determine whether the rectangles are *similar, congruent,* or *neither.* List the corresponding parts of the rectangles.

Get-Ready

Prepare for
Lesson 4.2
in Exs. 27–29

Use the distributive property to evaluate the expression for $x = 7$. *(p. 485)*

27. $x(9 + 11.2)$

28. $3(1.2 + x)$

29. $x(x - 4)$

30. Draw an angle with a measure of $55°$. *(p 460)*

31. ★ **MULTIPLE CHOICE** A Spanish language CD set costs $28.75. There is a 6% sales tax. What is the total amount of your purchase? *(p. 434)*

A $17.25 **B** $28.81 **C** $30.45 **D** $30.48

9.8 Line Symmetry

Before	You learned about congruent and similar figures.
Now	You'll identify lines of symmetry.
Why?	So you can find symmetry in real objects, as in Example 1.

KEY VOCABULARY
- line symmetry, p. 494
- line of symmetry, p. 494

ACTIVITY

Create a figure with symmetry.

STEP 1
Fold a sheet of paper in half.

STEP 2
Cut a design out of the folded edge as shown. Unfold the design.

STEP 3
Compare the figures on opposite sides of the fold. Are they the same size? the same shape?

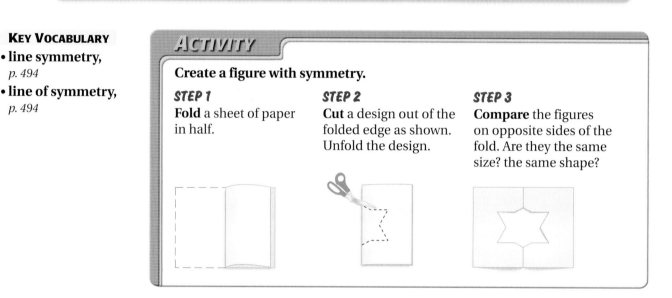

A figure has **line symmetry** if a line can be drawn that divides the figure into two congruent parts that are mirror images of each other. The line is called the **line of symmetry**.

EXAMPLE 1 Identifying Lines of Symmetry

Tell whether the object has line symmetry. If so, draw the line of symmetry.

a.

Yes, this guitar has line symmetry.

b.

No, this guitar does not have line symmetry.

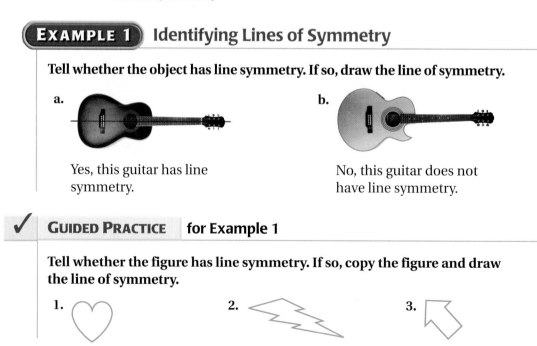

✓ **GUIDED PRACTICE** for Example 1

Tell whether the figure has line symmetry. If so, copy the figure and draw the line of symmetry.

1.

2.

3.

KEY CONCEPT

For Your Notebook

Lines of Symmetry

A figure can have zero, one, or multiple lines of symmetry.

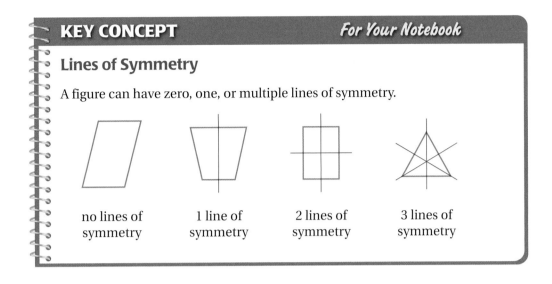

| no lines of symmetry | 1 line of symmetry | 2 lines of symmetry | 3 lines of symmetry |

Properties of Line Symmetry Because a line of symmetry divides a figure into two congruent parts, if you fold a figure along its line of symmetry its two parts match exactly.

EXAMPLE 2 **Multiple Lines of Symmetry**

AVOID ERRORS

Make sure when you draw a line of symmetry that it divides the figure into mirror images.

Incorrect Correct

Find the number of lines of symmetry in a square.

Think about how many different ways you can fold a square in half so that the two halves match up perfectly.

vertical fold   horizontal fold   diagonal fold   diagonal fold

▶ **Answer** A square has 4 lines of symmetry.

Animated Math at classzone.com

✓ **GUIDED PRACTICE** for Example 2

Find the number of lines of symmetry in the object.

4.   5.   6.

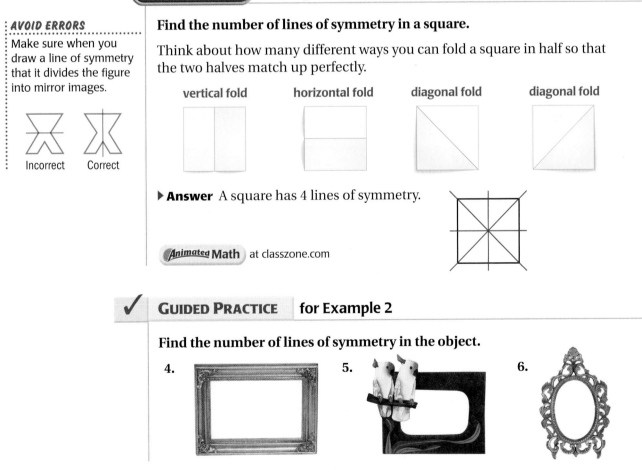

EXAMPLE 3 Completing Symmetrical Figures

Complete the polygon so that it has the line of symmetry shown.

DRAW A MIRROR IMAGE
A point and its mirror image are the same distance from the line of symmetry. Use this to help you draw a mirror image.

STEP 1
Draw the mirror image of each vertex that is not on the line of symmetry.

STEP 2
Connect the points to complete the mirror image so that the two halves are congruent.

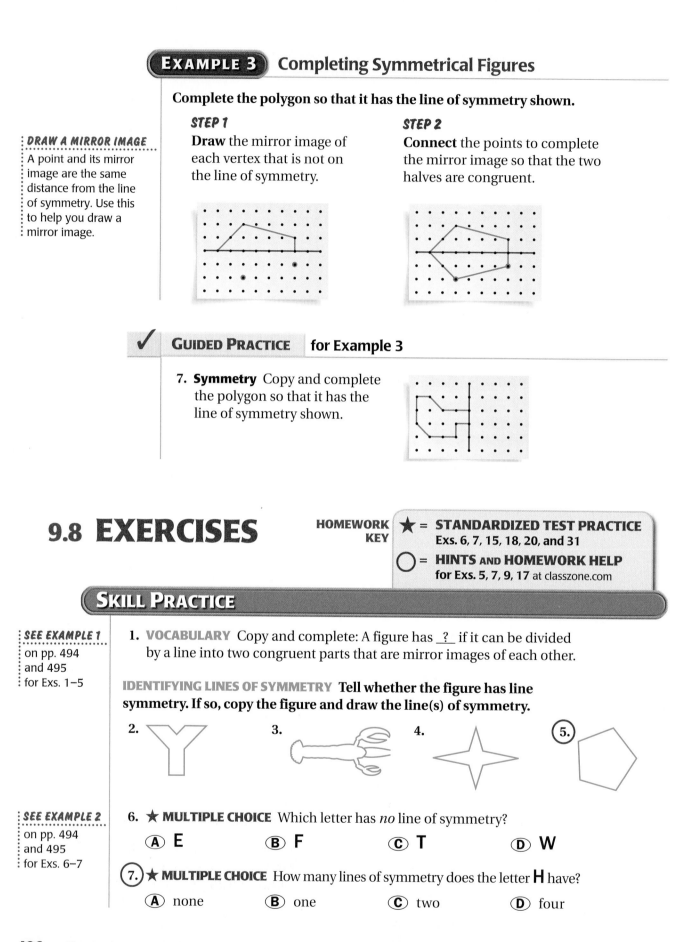

✓ **GUIDED PRACTICE**   for Example 3

7. **Symmetry** Copy and complete the polygon so that it has the line of symmetry shown.

9.8 EXERCISES

HOMEWORK KEY
★ = **STANDARDIZED TEST PRACTICE**
   Exs. 6, 7, 15, 18, 20, and 31
○ = **HINTS** AND **HOMEWORK HELP**
   for Exs. 5, 7, 9, 17 at classzone.com

SKILL PRACTICE

SEE EXAMPLE 1
on pp. 494 and 495
for Exs. 1–5

1. **VOCABULARY** Copy and complete: A figure has ? if it can be divided by a line into two congruent parts that are mirror images of each other.

IDENTIFYING LINES OF SYMMETRY Tell whether the figure has line symmetry. If so, copy the figure and draw the line(s) of symmetry.

2.   3.   4.   5.

SEE EXAMPLE 2
on pp. 494 and 495
for Exs. 6–7

6. ★ **MULTIPLE CHOICE** Which letter has *no* line of symmetry?

Ⓐ E   Ⓑ F   Ⓒ T   Ⓓ W

7. ★ **MULTIPLE CHOICE** How many lines of symmetry does the letter **H** have?

Ⓐ none   Ⓑ one   Ⓒ two   Ⓓ four

COMPLETING SYMMETRICAL FIGURES Copy and complete the figure so that it has the line of symmetry shown.

SEE EXAMPLE 3
on p. 496
for Exs. 8–10

8.

9.

10.

11. MAKE A MODEL Copy the figure at the right. Cut out your copy and use it to find the number of lines of symmetry in the figure.

12. ERROR ANALYSIS Courtney says that the rectangle has line symmetry about its diagonal because the diagonal divides it into two congruent halves. Describe and correct her error.

13. CHALLENGE Which quadrilaterals have exactly two lines of symmetry? Sketch the quadrilaterals and show the lines of symmetry.

14. CHALLENGE Draw a quadrilateral that has exactly one line of symmetry.

PROBLEM SOLVING

15. ★ MULTIPLE CHOICE Which object has *no* line of symmetry?

Ⓐ   Ⓑ   Ⓒ   Ⓓ

SYMMETRY IN SPORTS Find the number of lines of symmetry in the diagram.

16.

17.

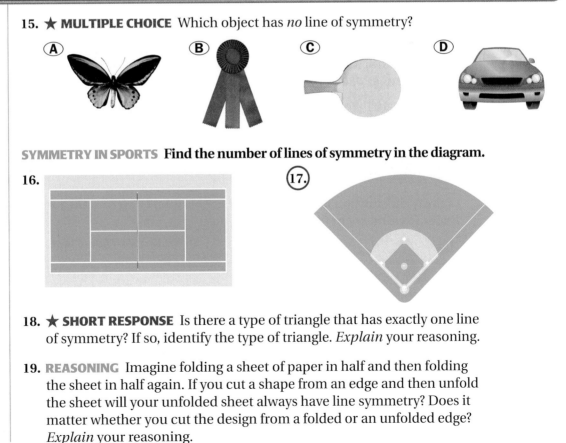

18. ★ SHORT RESPONSE Is there a type of triangle that has exactly one line of symmetry? If so, identify the type of triangle. *Explain* your reasoning.

19. REASONING Imagine folding a sheet of paper in half and then folding the sheet in half again. If you cut a shape from an edge and then unfold the sheet will your unfolded sheet always have line symmetry? Does it matter whether you cut the design from a folded or an unfolded edge? *Explain* your reasoning.

20. ★ WRITING *Explain* why some regular polygons have diagonals that are lines of symmetry and some regular polygons do not.

21. SYMMETRY One of the photographs below is the actual photo of a flower. The others show half of the photo next to its mirror image. Which photograph is the original image? *Explain* how you can tell.

22. CHALLENGE Which of the fifty state names, when written in capital letters, has a horizontal line of symmetry?

MIXED REVIEW

Get-Ready

Prepare for
Lesson 10.1
in Exs. 23–26

Find the area of the rectangle with the given dimensions. *(p. 348)*

23. 12 cm by 8 cm   **24.** 5 ft by 7 ft   **25.** 21 in. by 4 in.   **26.** 6 ft by 11 ft

Use mental math to solve the equation. *(p. 34)*

27. $12 + x = 24$ **28.** $x - 8 = 22$ **29.** $3x = 27$ **30.** $x \div 5 = 4$

31. ★ MULTIPLE CHOICE A polygon has four sides. Its opposite sides are parallel and it has four right angles. Which term best represents the polygon? *(p. 480)*

Ⓐ quadrilateral   Ⓑ rectangle   Ⓒ rhombus   Ⓓ parallelogram

QUIZ *for Lessons 9.5–9.8*

Classify the polygon in as many ways as possible. Then find the number of lines of symmetry in the polygon.

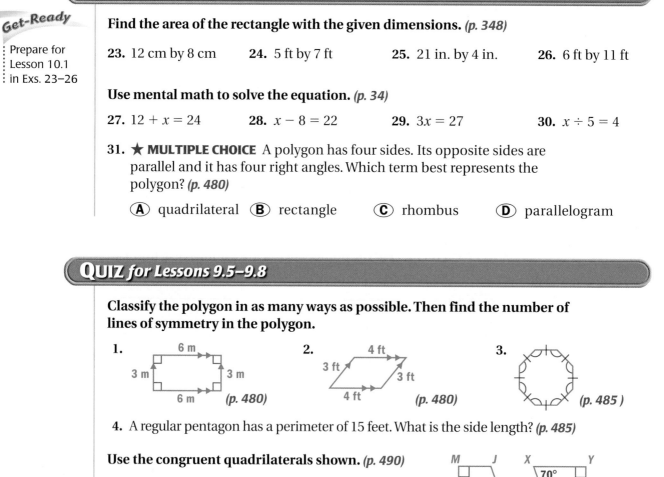

1. 6 m 3 m 3 m 6 m *(p. 480)*

2. 4 ft 3 ft 3 ft 4 ft *(p. 480)*

3. *(p. 485)*

4. A regular pentagon has a perimeter of 15 feet. What is the side length? *(p. 485)*

Use the congruent quadrilaterals shown. *(p. 490)*

5. List the corresponding parts.

6. Find the value of *a*.

7. What is $m\angle J$?

M J X Y 70°
12 cm a
L 11 cm K W Z

EXTRA PRACTICE for Lesson 9.8, p. 784   ⟐ **ONLINE QUIZ** at classzone.com

Lessons 9.5–9.8

1. **MULTI-STEP PROBLEM** You are designing a lampshade that is similar to the lampshade below, but half the size. Use the fact that $\overleftrightarrow{AC}$ is a line of symmetry in the figure below.

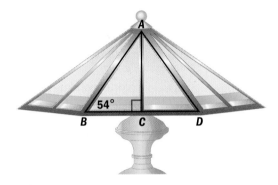

a. What can you conclude about △ABC and △ADC? *Explain.*

b. Name the corresponding parts of △ABC and △ADC.

c. Find the unknown angle measurements in the two triangles.

d. Classify △ABD by its sides and by its angles.

2. **GRIDDED ANSWER** What is the value of *x* in the parallelogram?

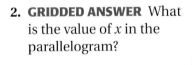

3. **SHORT RESPONSE** Figure *ABCDEF* is a regular hexagon. The area of △AHB is 5 square meters. If you draw all of the lines of symmetry of *ABCDEF,* how many congruent right triangles do you form? What is the area of each right triangle? *Explain.*

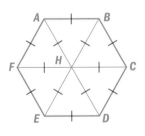

4. **OPEN-ENDED** Draw a design that has exactly two lines of symmetry and that uses at least three polygons. *Explain* how you created your design.

5. **GRIDDED ANSWER** Your yard has the shape of a quadrilateral. Two corners of the yard form right angles with a road. Another corner measures 94°. Find the angle measure of the fourth corner in degrees.

6. **SHORT RESPONSE** *Describe* how to fold a rectangular piece of paper and make a single straight cut to form an octagon when the paper is unfolded. What shape of paper would you need to form a regular octagon?

7. **EXTENDED RESPONSE** In a community garden, three friends have garden patches as shown below. The gardens are all similar rectangles. It takes Jack 126 minutes to weed his garden.

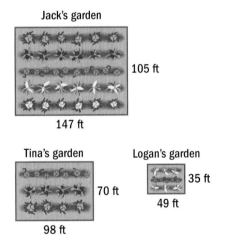

Jack's garden
105 ft
147 ft

Tina's garden
70 ft
98 ft

Logan's garden
35 ft
49 ft

a. How does the area of Logan's garden compare to the area of Jack's garden?

b. Assuming all three friends weed at the same rate, how long does it take Logan to weed her garden?

c. How long does it take Tina to weed her garden? *Explain* how you found your answer.

9 CHAPTER REVIEW

@HomeTutor
classzone.com
Vocabulary Practice

REVIEW KEY VOCABULARY

- point, endpoint, *p. 455*
- line, ray, segment, *p. 455*
- plane, *p. 456*
- intersecting lines, *p. 456*
- parallel lines, *p. 456*
- angle, *p. 460*
- vertex, *p. 460*
- degrees(°), *p. 461*
- angles: right, acute, obtuse, straight, *p. 465*
- vertical angles, *p. 466*
- complementary angles, *p. 466*
- supplementary angles, *p. 466*
- triangles: acute, right, obtuse, equilateral, isosceles, scalene, *pp. 471, 472*
- quadrilaterals: parallelogram, rectangle, rhombus, square, *p. 480*
- polygons: pentagon, hexagon, octagon, *p. 485*
- vertex, *p. 485*
- regular polygon, *p. 486*
- diagonal, *p. 486*
- congruent and similar figures, *p. 490*
- corresponding parts, *p. 491*
- line symmetry, *p. 494*
- line of symmetry, *p. 494*

VOCABULARY EXERCISES

1. What are vertical angles?
2. How many obtuse angles does an obtuse triangle have?
3. Are all rhombuses regular polygons? Why or why not?

Copy and complete the statement.

4. An __?__ is formed by two rays with the same endpoint.
5. Two angles are __?__ angles if the sum of their measures is 180°.
6. A __?__ is a quadrilateral with two pairs of parallel sides.
7. A regular polygon has __?__ side lengths and __?__ angle measures.
8. Two figures are __?__ if they have the same size and shape.

REVIEW EXAMPLES AND EXERCISES

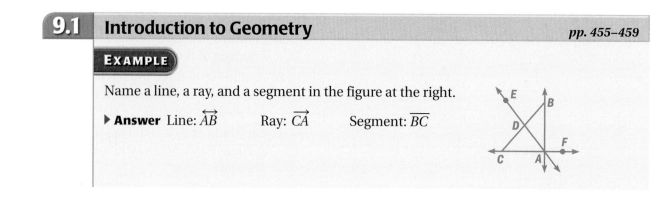

9.1 Introduction to Geometry *pp. 455–459*

EXAMPLE

Name a line, a ray, and a segment in the figure at the right.

▸ **Answer** Line: $\overleftrightarrow{AB}$ Ray: $\overrightarrow{CA}$ Segment: $\overline{BC}$

EXERCISES

Use the figure in the example on page 500.

SEE EXAMPLE 2
on p. 456
for Exs. 9–14

9. Name another ray. **10.** Name another segment. **11.** Name another line.

12. Name a third segment. **13.** Name a third line. **14.** Name a third ray.

9.2 Angles
pp. 460–464

EXAMPLE

Use a protractor to measure ∠XYZ.

Place the center of the protractor on the vertex of the angle and line up $\overrightarrow{YZ}$ with the 0° line.

▶ **Answer** The measure of ∠XYZ is 139°.

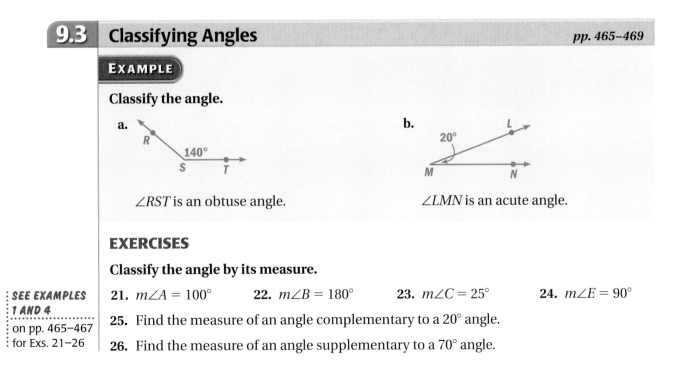

EXERCISES

Use a protractor to draw ∠ABC with the given measure.

SEE EXAMPLE 3
on p. 461
for Exs. 15–20

15. $m\angle ABC = 13°$ **16.** $m\angle ABC = 85°$ **17.** $m\angle ABC = 127°$

18. $m\angle ABC = 170°$ **19.** $m\angle ABC = 90°$ **20.** $m\angle ABC = 58°$

9.3 Classifying Angles
pp. 465–469

EXAMPLE

Classify the angle.

a.

∠RST is an obtuse angle.

b.

∠LMN is an acute angle.

EXERCISES

Classify the angle by its measure.

SEE EXAMPLES
1 AND 4
on pp. 465–467
for Exs. 21–26

21. $m\angle A = 100°$ **22.** $m\angle B = 180°$ **23.** $m\angle C = 25°$ **24.** $m\angle E = 90°$

25. Find the measure of an angle complementary to a 20° angle.

26. Find the measure of an angle supplementary to a 70° angle.

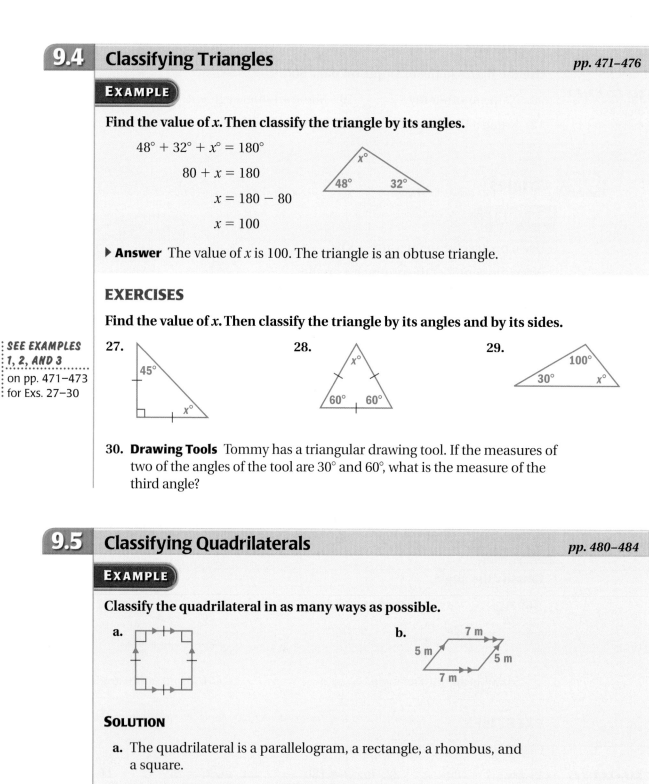

9.4 Classifying Triangles

pp. 471–476

EXAMPLE

Find the value of *x.* Then classify the triangle by its angles.

$$48° + 32° + x° = 180°$$

$$80 + x = 180$$

$$x = 180 - 80$$

$$x = 100$$

▶ **Answer** The value of *x* is 100. The triangle is an obtuse triangle.

EXERCISES

Find the value of *x.* Then classify the triangle by its angles and by its sides.

SEE EXAMPLES 1, 2, AND 3 on pp. 471–473 for Exs. 27–30

27.

45°

x°

28.

x°

60° 60°

29.

100°

30°   *x*°

30. Drawing Tools Tommy has a triangular drawing tool. If the measures of two of the angles of the tool are 30° and 60°, what is the measure of the third angle?

9.5 Classifying Quadrilaterals

pp. 480–484

EXAMPLE

Classify the quadrilateral in as many ways as possible.

a.

b.

7 m

5 m   5 m

7 m

SOLUTION

a. The quadrilateral is a parallelogram, a rectangle, a rhombus, and a square.

b. The quadrilateral is a parallelogram.

EXERCISES

Classify the figure in as many ways as possible.

SEE EXAMPLES 2 AND 4
on pp. 481–482
for Exs. 31–34

31.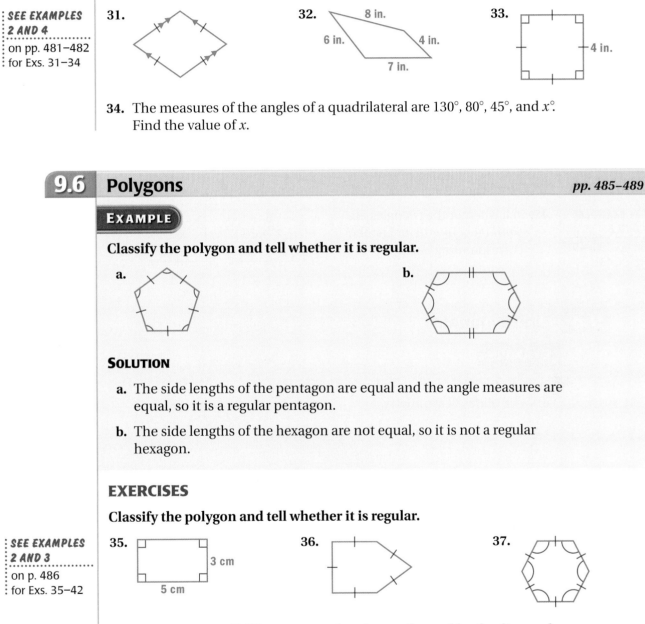

32. 8 in. 6 in. 4 in. 7 in.

33. 4 in.

34. The measures of the angles of a quadrilateral are 130°, 80°, 45°, and $x°$. Find the value of x.

9.6 Polygons

pp. 485–489

EXAMPLE

Classify the polygon and tell whether it is regular.

a.

b.

SOLUTION

a. The side lengths of the pentagon are equal and the angle measures are equal, so it is a regular pentagon.

b. The side lengths of the hexagon are not equal, so it is not a regular hexagon.

EXERCISES

Classify the polygon and tell whether it is regular.

SEE EXAMPLES 2 AND 3
on p. 486
for Exs. 35–42

35. 3 cm 5 cm

36.

37.

USING DIAGONALS Tell how many triangles are formed by the diagonals from one vertex of the figure.

38. a rectangle

39. a regular pentagon

40. a regular hexagon

41. How many sides does an octagon have?

42. Is a quadrilateral with four equal sides always a regular polygon? *Explain* your reasoning.

9.7 Congruent and Similar Figures

pp. 490–493

EXAMPLE

The triangles at the right are similar. List the corresponding parts.

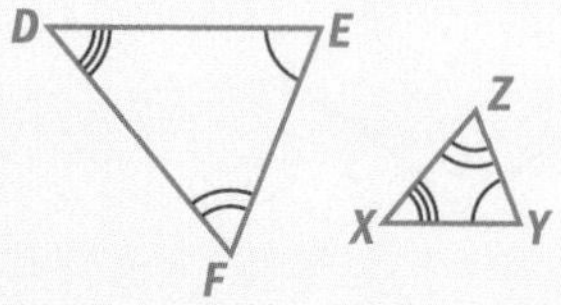

▶ **Answer** Corresponding angles: ∠D and ∠X, ∠E and ∠Y, ∠F and ∠Z

Corresponding sides: $\overline{DE}$ and $\overline{XY}$, $\overline{EF}$ and $\overline{YZ}$, $\overline{FD}$ and $\overline{ZX}$

EXERCISES

SEE EXAMPLES
1 AND 2
on pp. 490–491
for Ex. 43

43. Tell whether the triangles are *similar* or *congruent*. List the corresponding parts.

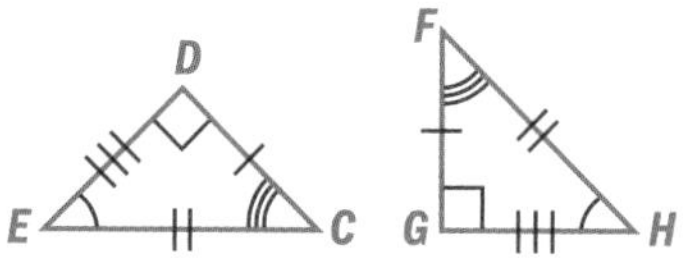

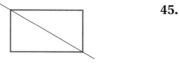

9.8 Line Symmetry

pp. 494–498

EXAMPLE

Tell whether the figure has line symmetry. If so, draw any lines of symmetry.

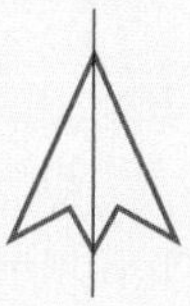

▶ **Answer** The figure has one line of symmetry.

EXERCISES

Tell whether the line shown is a line of symmetry.

SEE EXAMPLES
1 AND 2
on pp. 494–495
for Exs. 44–49

44.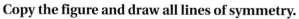

45.

46.

Copy the figure and draw all lines of symmetry.

47.

48.

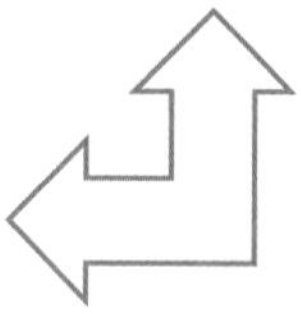

49.

1. Use the figure at the right to name a line, a ray, and a segment.

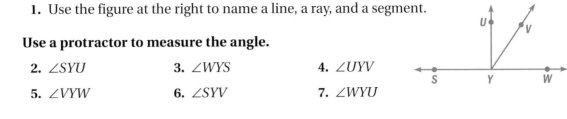

Use a protractor to measure the angle.

2. ∠SYU   3. ∠WYS   4. ∠UYV

5. ∠VYW   6. ∠SYV   7. ∠WYU

Classify the angle by its measure.

8. $m\angle A = 105°$ 9. $m\angle B = 180°$

10. $m\angle C = 35°$ 11. $m\angle D = 95°$

Find the value of *x*. Then classify the triangle by its angles.

12.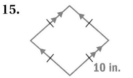

13.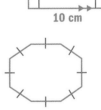

14.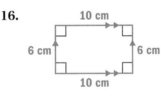

Classify the quadrilateral in as many ways as possible.

15.

16.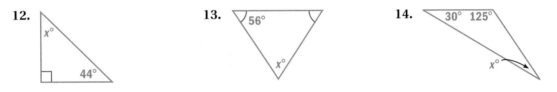

17.

18. Classify the polygon and tell whether it is regular.

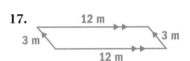

19. **TELEVISION** You are adjusting the volume on the television shown. Are the lines that represent the volume *parallel* or *intersecting*? *Explain*.

20. △JKL and △XYZ are congruent. List the corresponding parts.

21. **BASKETBALL** How many lines of symmetry does the basketball court at the right have?

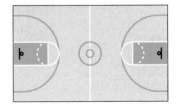

SHORT RESPONSE QUESTIONS

PROBLEM

A window in the shape of a rhombus is made of two panes that are congruent isosceles triangles. The two congruent angles of each triangle have measures of 35°. Find the measures of all four angles of the window. *Justify* your answer.

Below are sample solutions to the problem. Read each solution and the comments in blue to see why the sample represents full credit, partial credit, or no credit.

SAMPLE 1: Full Credit Solution

> Drawing a diagram is the key to solving this problem correctly.

The diagram shows different ways that the sides of two isosceles triangles can be matched together. Because a rhombus is a parallelogram with four sides of equal length, you can eliminate Figures 2 and 3.

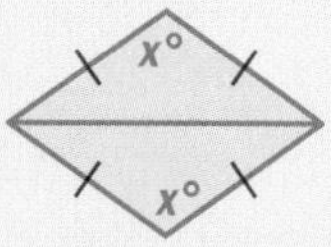

> The reasoning and calculations are correct.

To find $x°$ in Figure 1, use the fact that the sum of the angle measures of a triangle is 180°.

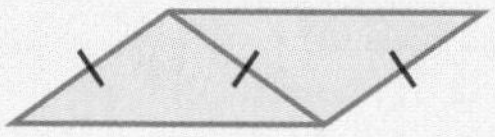

$$35° + 35° + x° = 180°$$
$$70 + x = 180$$
$$x = 180 - 70$$
$$x = 110$$

Two window angles have measures of 110°. The other two angles are each made of two 35° angles. Their measures are $35° + 35° = 70°$.

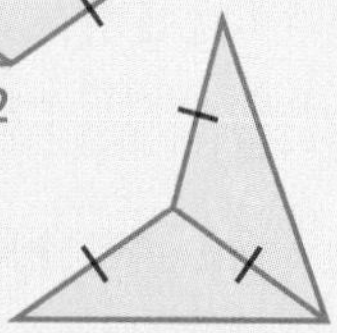

> The answer is correct.

The measures of the four angles of the window are 110°, 110°, 70°, and 70°.

SAMPLE 2: Partial Credit Solution

The two known angle measures of the window are $35° + 35° = 70°$.

> The reasoning and process are correct.

The angle measures of a triangle add up to 180°.

$$35° + 35° + x° = 180°$$

> The operation in this step is incorrect.

$$x = 180 + 70$$
$$x = 250$$

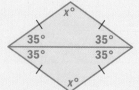

> The answer is incorrect.

The measures of the window angles are 250°, 250°, 70°, and 70°.

SAMPLE 3: Partial Credit Solution

The reasoning and calculations are correct.

Find the unknown angle measure $x°$ of each triangle.

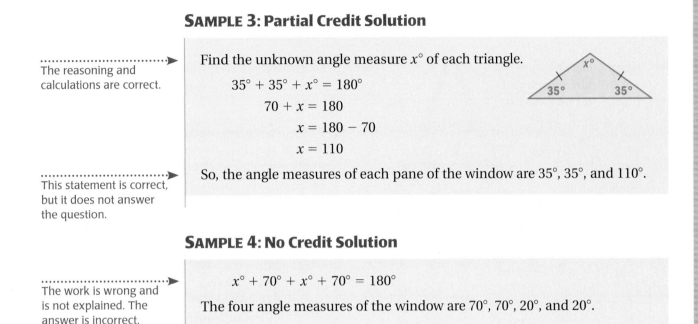

$$35° + 35° + x° = 180°$$
$$70 + x = 180$$
$$x = 180 - 70$$
$$x = 110$$

This statement is correct, but it does not answer the question.

So, the angle measures of each pane of the window are 35°, 35°, and 110°.

SAMPLE 4: No Credit Solution

The work is wrong and is not explained. The answer is incorrect.

$$x° + 70° + x° + 70° = 180°$$

The four angle measures of the window are 70°, 70°, 20°, and 20°.

PRACTICE Apply the Scoring Rubric

Score the solution to the problem below as *full credit*, *partial credit*, or *no credit*. *Explain* your reasoning.

PROBLEM The rectangular flag of the Philippines is made of a white equilateral triangle and two congruent red and blue quadrilaterals, as shown. Find the value of x in the diagram. *Justify* your answer.

1. $x° + 60° + 90° + 90° = 360°$
   $$x = 120$$

2. Draw a diagram and label the angles that you know, as shown. Let $y°$ represent the measure of the other unknown angle of the blue quadrilateral.

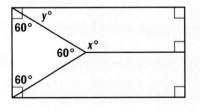

Because $y°$ and 60° form a right angle, they are complementary. So, you know that $y + 60 = 90$, and $y = 30$.

The angle measures of the blue quadrilateral add up to 360°. So, you can write the equation $x + 30 + 90 + 90 = 360$. So, $x = 150$.

SHORT RESPONSE

1. In the house of cards at the right, △LMN and △LPQ are similar isosceles triangles. The measure of ∠M is 64°. Find the measures of ∠MLN, ∠LPQ, and ∠LQP. *Explain* how you found your answers.

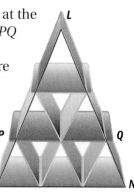

2. You play the triangle in your school's concert band. The range of sounds produced by the instrument is higher in pitch for smaller triangles than for larger triangles. You have two brass triangles that are similar but not congruent. Do both of these triangles produce the same range of sounds? *Explain.*

3. The quilt design below is made of two kinds of rhombuses. Each orange rhombus has a side length of $2\frac{1}{2}$ inches. *Explain* how to find the perimeter of a red rhombus.

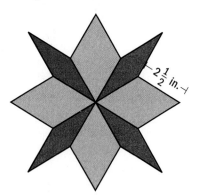

$2\frac{1}{2}$ in.

4. A carpenter's square like the one at the right can be used to check for right angles in everyday objects. *Explain* how you could use a carpenter's square to distinguish between a diamond-shaped kite and a square kite.

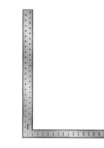

5. *Describe* how an octagonal stop sign can be divided into two congruent pentagons. Are the pentagons regular? *Explain* your reasoning.

6. You fold a square piece of paper in half to form a smaller rectangle. You make a single straight cut along a diagonal of the rectangle, and then unfold the triangle that remains. Classify the unfolded triangle. Classify the triangles that are cut off. *Justify* your answer.

7. A *palindrome* is a word or number that reads the same forward and backward. For example, the word "wow" and the number "3003" are palindromes. Do all palindromes have a line of symmetry? *Explain.*

8. Each student in your art class has a rectangular piece of paper. Your art teacher instructs everyone to draw two diagonals and then draw a third line that intersects both diagonal lines. Will all the drawings look the same? *Explain* your reasoning.

9. Sketch a large coordinate grid on a piece of graph paper. Graph the points A(1, 5), B(4, 1), C(1, 1), D(1, 9), and E(7, 1). Connect the points to form △ABC and △DEC. Measure ∠CAB, ∠ABC, ∠CDE, and ∠DEC to the nearest degree. What can you conclude about △ABC and △DEC? *Explain* your reasoning.

In Exercises 10 and 11, the ironing board in the photo has hinged legs so it can be adjusted to various heights.

10. Is the height of the ironing board greater when △UVW is acute or obtuse? *Explain* your reasoning.

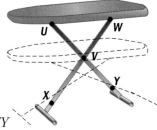

11. *Explain* why m∠UVW decreases when m∠XVY decreases.

MULTIPLE CHOICE

12. Which name does *not* apply to the figure shown?

    Ⓐ equilateral triangle

    Ⓑ scalene triangle

    Ⓒ regular triangle

    Ⓓ polygon

13. A wading pool in a community park is shaped like a regular hexagon. One edge of the pool is 50 feet wide. Which statement is true about the wading pool?

    Ⓐ The perimeter of the pool is 300 feet.

    Ⓑ The pool is a parallelogram with obtuse angles.

    Ⓒ A stripe along the diagonal of the bottom of the pool divides the pool into two parallelograms.

    Ⓓ The pool has 7 corners.

GRIDDED ANSWER

14. $\triangle ABC$ and $\triangle DEF$ are similar triangles and $m\angle A = m\angle C$. The measure of $\angle B$ is 104°. Find $m\angle F$, in degrees.

15. Use a protractor to find $m\angle K$, in degrees, in the picture. Round your answer to the nearest degree.

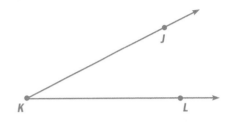

16. You are covering a path with flat rocks that are shaped like quadrilaterals. One rock has two complementary angles and a third angle that is 128°. What is the measure of the fourth angle, in degrees?

EXTENDED RESPONSE

17. Use graph paper to graph the points $A(3, 8)$, $B(8, 8)$, $C(11, 4)$, $D(8, 0)$, $E(3, 0)$, and $F(0, 4)$ on a coordinate grid. Then connect them to form a polygon.

  a. Use a ruler and a protractor to determine whether polygon $ABCDEF$ is a regular hexagon. *Justify* your answer.

  b. Draw all the diagonals from point F. How many triangles are formed?

  c. *Explain* how you can use line symmetry to determine which pairs of triangles might be congruent.

  d. *Confirm* your answer from part (c) using a ruler and a protractor.

18. The design for a pillow cover is shown.

  a. Ignoring color, how many lines of symmetry does the entire design have? *Explain* your reasoning.

  b. The measure of $\angle 1$ is 30°. Use the symmetry of the design to find measures of the rest of the numbered angles. *Explain* your method.

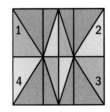

10 Geometry and Measurement

Before

In previous chapters you've ...

- Solved measurement problems
- Identified and classified polygons

Now

In Chapter 10 you'll study ...

- 10.1 Area of parallelograms
- 10.2 Area of triangles
- 10.3 Circumference
- 10.4 Area of circles
- 10.5 Solid figures
- 10.6 Surface area of prisms
- 10.7 Volume of prisms

Why?

So you can solve real-world problems about ...

- hang gliders, p. 522
- basketball, p. 532
- skateboarding, p. 544
- aquariums, p. 551

 **Math**
at classzone.com

- Area of a Circle, p. 531
- Solid Figures, p. 544
- Volume of a Prism, p. 551

Get-Ready Games

Review Prerequisite Skills by playing *Polygon Count.*

Skill Focus: Identifying and classifying polygons

POLYGON COUNT

HOW TO PLAY

In this game, you'll hunt for polygons in the kite design shown on page 511. In the design, angles that appear to be right angles are right angles. Line segments that appear to be parallel are parallel.

 MAKE a polygon tally sheet like the one shown. Use a separate piece of paper.

 COUNT how many of each type of polygon you find in the kite design. You may count each polygon only once. For example, if you count a polygon as a rectangle, you may not count it as a parallelogram.

Polygon Tally Sheet

Triangle	?
Quadrilateral	?
Parallelogram	?
Rectangle	?
Pentagon	?
Hexagon	?

COMPARE your count with your partner's. Be prepared to justify your thinking.

Stop and Think

1. **WRITING** Suppose that the words *rectangle* and *parallelogram* were removed from the tally sheet. How would your polygon count change? Explain your thinking.

2. **CRITICAL THINKING** In the game *Polygon Count*, some of the polygons you found in the kite design are part of other, larger polygons. Describe some examples.

Review Prerequisite Skills

REVIEW WORDS

- **area,** *p. 67*
- **circle graph,** *p. 94*
- **right triangle,** *p. 471*
- **parallelogram,** *p. 480*

VOCABULARY CHECK

Copy and complete using a review word from the list at the left.

1. A __?__ is a quadrilateral with two pairs of parallel sides.

2. A __?__ is a triangle that has one right angle.

SKILL CHECK

Evaluate the expression when $x = 10$ and $y = 4$. *(p. 15)*

3. x^2 **4.** y^2 **5.** $3x^2$ **6.** $2x^2 - y^2$

Find the area of a rectangle with the given dimensions. *(p. 66)*

7. length = 8 feet
width = 4 feet

8. length = 12 inches
width = 6 inches

The circle graph at the right shows the ages of the first 43 presidents at the time they took office. *(p. 94)*

9. How many presidents were 61 years old or older?

10. How many presidents were 51 years old or older?

Ages of U.S. Presidents

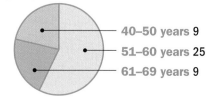

40–50 years 9
51–60 years 25
61–69 years 9

 Prerequisite skills practice at classzone.com

---

Notetaking Skills   Learning to Use Formulas

In each chapter you will learn a new notetaking skill. In Chapter 10 you will apply the strategy of using formulas to Example 1 on p. 514.

You may want to create a special section in your notebook for formulas. Be sure to write down each formula completely. Tell what each variable represents, and include an example. You learned the formula for the area of a rectangle in Lesson 2.2.

Area of a Rectangle

A is the area, l is the length, and w is the width.

$A = lw$

$= 18 \cdot 9$

$= 162$ square yards

9 yd

18 yd

GOAL
Compare the area of a parallelogram and the area of a rectangle.

MATERIALS
• graph paper
• scissors

10.1 Investigating Area

In this activity, you will find the area of a parallelogram.

EXPLORE You can find the area of a parallelogram by finding the area of a related rectangle.

STEP 1
Draw a parallelogram like the one shown below on graph paper. Cut out the parallelogram.

STEP 2
Draw a line to make a right triangle as shown.

STEP 3
Cut out the triangle. Move the triangle to the other side of the parallelogram to form a rectangle.

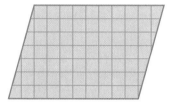

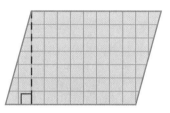

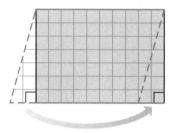

STEP 4

Find the area of the rectangle. Use the grid lines and the area formula for rectangles.

$$A = lw = 10 \times 7 = 70$$

The area of the parallelogram is 70 square units.

PRACTICE Follow the steps above to find the area of the parallelogram.

1.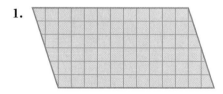

2.

DRAW CONCLUSIONS

3. **REASONING** *Explain* how the area of a rectangle compares to the area of a parallelogram with the same length and height.

4. **WRITING** *Describe* in words how to find the area of any parallelogram.

10.1 Area of a Parallelogram

Before	You found the area of a rectangle.
Now	You'll find the area of a parallelogram.
Why?	So you can estimate the area of a lake, as in Example 3.

KEY VOCABULARY
- base of a parallelogram, p. 514
- height of a parallelogram, p. 514
- perpendicular, p. 514

The **base of a parallelogram** is the length of any of its sides. The **height of a parallelogram** is the *perpendicular distance* between the side whose length is the base and the opposite side. Two lines are **perpendicular** if they meet at a right angle.

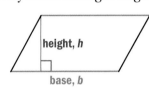

The area of a parallelogram is the product of the base and the height.

KEY CONCEPT   *For Your Notebook*

Area of a Parallelogram

Words   Area = **base** · **height**

Algebra $A = bh$

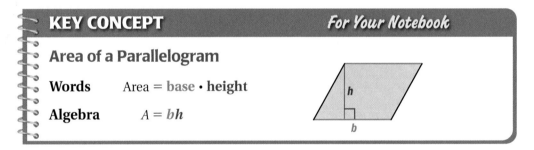

EXAMPLE 1   Finding the Area of a Parallelogram

TAKE NOTES
Include the formula for the area of a parallelogram in your notebook. Also include an example like Example 1.

Find the area of the parallelogram shown.

SOLUTION

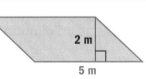

$A = bh$ **Write the formula for the area of a parallelogram.**

$= 5 \cdot 2$ **Substitute 5 for *b* and 2 for *h*.**

$= 10$ **Simplify.**

▶ **Answer** The area of the parallelogram is 10 square meters.

✓ **GUIDED PRACTICE**   for Example 1

Find the area of the described parallelogram.

1. base = 6 in., height = 10 in.   **2.** base = 7 cm, height = 4 cm

EXAMPLE 2 Finding an Unknown Dimension

The area of a parallelogram is 45 square centimeters and the height is 9 centimeters. What is the base?

SOLUTION

$A = bh$	Write the formula for the area of a parallelogram.
$45 = b \cdot 9$	Substitute 45 for *A* and 9 for *h*.
$b = 45 \div 9$	Write a related division equation.
$b = 5$	Simplify.

▶ **Answer** The base is 5 centimeters.

EXAMPLE 3 Estimating Area

Geography A parallelogram can be used to approximate the shape of Lake Erie. Use the map and scale to estimate the area of Lake Erie.

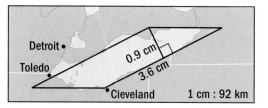

SOLUTION

STEP 1 **Use** the scale to find the base *b* and the height *h* in kilometers.

WRITING PROPORTIONS

Need help using scales and writing proportions? See p. 417.

Base

$$\frac{1 \text{ cm}}{92 \text{ km}} = \frac{3.6 \text{ cm}}{b \text{ km}}$$

$$1 \cdot b = 92(3.6)$$

$$b = 331.2$$

Height

$$\frac{1 \text{ cm}}{92 \text{ km}} = \frac{0.9 \text{ cm}}{h \text{ km}}$$

$$1 \cdot h = 92(0.9)$$

$$h = 82.8$$

STEP 2 **Estimate** the area of Lake Erie.

$A = bh$	Write the formula for the area of a parallelogram.
$= 330(80)$	Round the base and the height to the nearest tens.
$= 26{,}400$	Simplify.

▶ **Answer** The area of Lake Erie is about 26,400 square kilometers.

✓ GUIDED PRACTICE for Examples 2 and 3

In Exercises 3 and 4, find the unknown dimension.

3. Area of parallelogram = 72 in.^{2}, base = 12 in., height = __?__

4. Area of parallelogram = 125 mm^2, height = 5 mm, base = __?__

5. What If? In Example 3, suppose the area is approximated using a different parallelogram with a base of 3.3 centimeters and a height of 0.9 centimeter. Estimate the area of Lake Erie using this parallelogram.

10.1 EXERCISES

★ = **STANDARDIZED TEST PRACTICE**
Exs. 7, 13, 17, 18, 19, 20, 24, and 34

○ = **HINTS** AND **HOMEWORK HELP**
for Exs. 3, 5, 17, 19 at classzone.com

SKILL PRACTICE

1. **VOCABULARY** Copy and complete: To find the area of a parallelogram, you multiply the __?__ by the __?__ .

2. **VOCABULARY** What is the height of a parallelogram?

FINDING AREAS Find the area of the parallelogram. Estimate to check.

SEE EXAMPLE 1
on p. 514
for Exs. 3–8

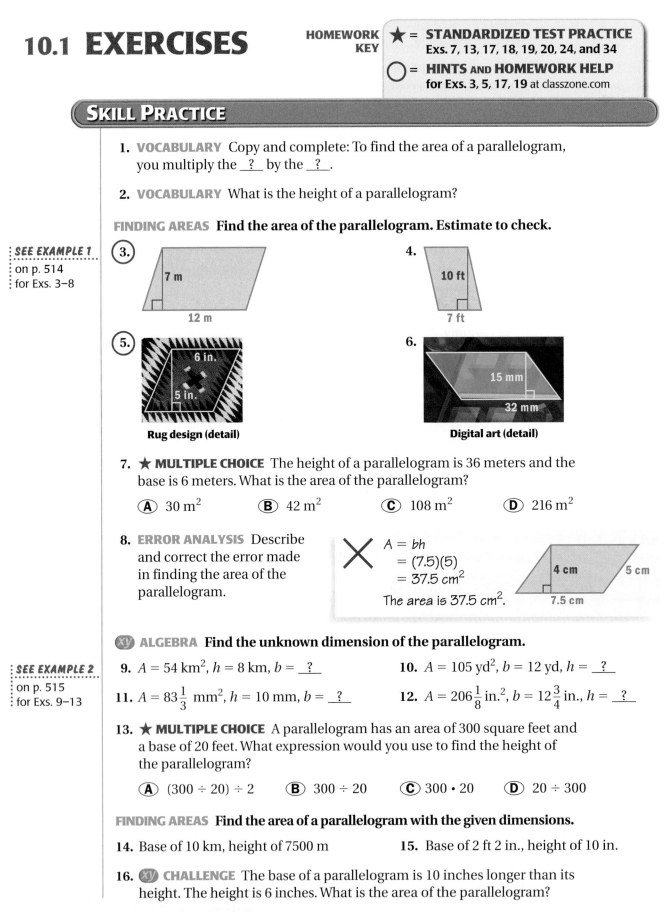

3. 7 m, 12 m

4. 10 ft, 7 ft

5. 6 in., 5 in.
Rug design (detail)

6. 15 mm, 32 mm
Digital art (detail)

7. ★ **MULTIPLE CHOICE** The height of a parallelogram is 36 meters and the base is 6 meters. What is the area of the parallelogram?

Ⓐ 30 m^2 Ⓑ 42 m^2 Ⓒ 108 m^2 Ⓓ 216 m^2

8. **ERROR ANALYSIS** Describe and correct the error made in finding the area of the parallelogram.

$A = bh$
$= (7.5)(5)$
$= 37.5 \text{ cm}^2$
The area is 37.5 cm^2.

4 cm, 5 cm, 7.5 cm

ALGEBRA Find the unknown dimension of the parallelogram.

SEE EXAMPLE 2
on p. 515
for Exs. 9–13

9. $A = 54 \text{ km}^2$, $h = 8$ km, $b = $ __?__

10. $A = 105 \text{ yd}^2$, $b = 12$ yd, $h = $ __?__

11. $A = 83\frac{1}{3} \text{ mm}^2$, $h = 10$ mm, $b = $ __?__

12. $A = 206\frac{1}{8} \text{ in.}^2$, $b = 12\frac{3}{4}$ in., $h = $ __?__

13. ★ **MULTIPLE CHOICE** A parallelogram has an area of 300 square feet and a base of 20 feet. What expression would you use to find the height of the parallelogram?

Ⓐ $(300 \div 20) \div 2$ Ⓑ $300 \div 20$ Ⓒ $300 \cdot 20$ Ⓓ $20 \div 300$

FINDING AREAS Find the area of a parallelogram with the given dimensions.

14. Base of 10 km, height of 7500 m

15. Base of 2 ft 2 in., height of 10 in.

16. **CHALLENGE** The base of a parallelogram is 10 inches longer than its height. The height is 6 inches. What is the area of the parallelogram?

516 Chapter 10 Geometry and Measurement

17. ★ **MULTIPLE CHOICE** What is the area of a parallelogram with base 7.3 inches and height 4.6 inches?

   Ⓐ 33.58 in.²   Ⓑ 23.8 in.²   Ⓒ 16.79 in.²   Ⓓ 11.9 in.²

18. ★ **WRITING** *Explain* how you can find the base of a parallelogram if you know the height and the area.

19. ★ **OPEN-ENDED MATH** Draw two different parallelograms that each have an area of 12 square centimeters.

20. ★ **SHORT RESPONSE** The base of one parallelogram in a quilt is 6 inches. Its height is 3 inches. About how many of these parallelograms do you need to cover an area of 7500 square inches? *Explain.*

ESTIMATION **Measure the parallelogram. Then estimate the given land area of the state or commonwealth. Tell which tool you used and whether your estimate is *high* or *low*. *Explain* your reasoning.**

SEE EXAMPLE 3
on p. 515
for Exs. 21–22

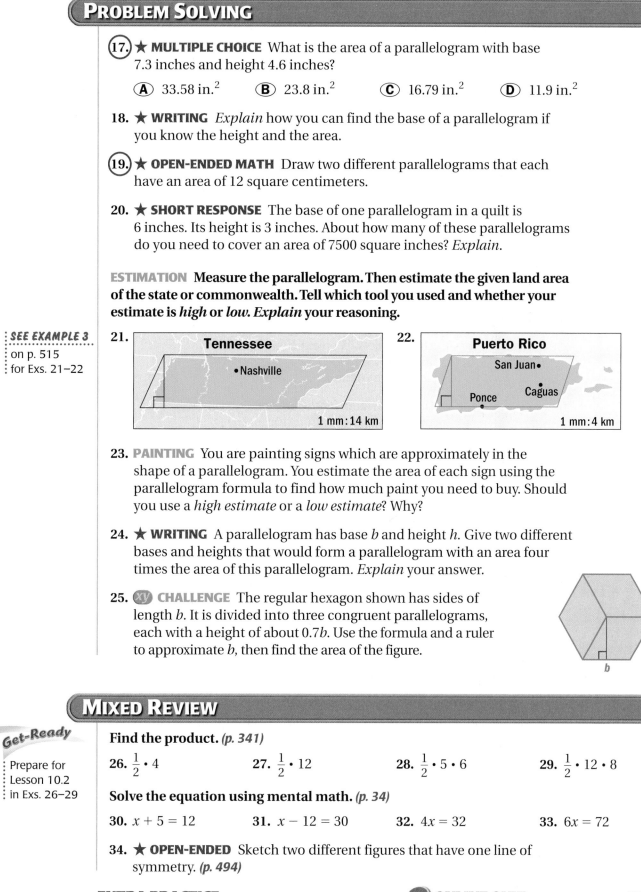

21.

Tennessee

• Nashville

1 mm : 14 km

22.

Puerto Rico

San Juan •

Caguas

Ponce

1 mm : 4 km

23. **PAINTING** You are painting signs which are approximately in the shape of a parallelogram. You estimate the area of each sign using the parallelogram formula to find how much paint you need to buy. Should you use a *high estimate* or a *low estimate*? Why?

24. ★ **WRITING** A parallelogram has base b and height h. Give two different bases and heights that would form a parallelogram with an area four times the area of this parallelogram. *Explain* your answer.

25. *xy* **CHALLENGE** The regular hexagon shown has sides of length b. It is divided into three congruent parallelograms, each with a height of about $0.7b$. Use the formula and a ruler to approximate b, then find the area of the figure.

b

b

MIXED REVIEW

Get-Ready

Prepare for
Lesson 10.2
in Exs. 26–29

Find the product. *(p. 341)*

26. $\frac{1}{2} \cdot 4$ 27. $\frac{1}{2} \cdot 12$ 28. $\frac{1}{2} \cdot 5 \cdot 6$ 29. $\frac{1}{2} \cdot 12 \cdot 8$

Solve the equation using mental math. *(p. 34)*

30. $x + 5 = 12$ 31. $x - 12 = 30$ 32. $4x = 32$ 33. $6x = 72$

34. ★ **OPEN-ENDED** Sketch two different figures that have one line of symmetry. *(p. 494)*

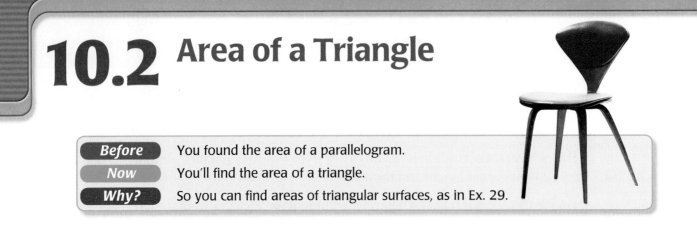

10.2 Area of a Triangle

Before You found the area of a parallelogram.

Now You'll find the area of a triangle.

Why? So you can find areas of triangular surfaces, as in Ex. 29.

KEY VOCABULARY
- base of a triangle, *p. 518*
- height of a triangle, *p. 518*

ACTIVITY

You can use a parallelogram to find the area of a triangle.

STEP 1 **Draw** the parallelogram at the right on graph paper and cut it out. Find its area.

STEP 2 **Draw** a diagonal, *d*, like the one shown below. Then cut along the diagonal to form two congruent triangles.

STEP 3 **Use** the formula for the area of a parallelogram to write a rule for the area of a triangle.

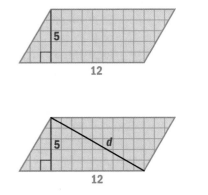

The **base of a triangle** is the length of any of its sides. The **height of a triangle** is the perpendicular distance between the side whose length is the base and the vertex opposite that side.

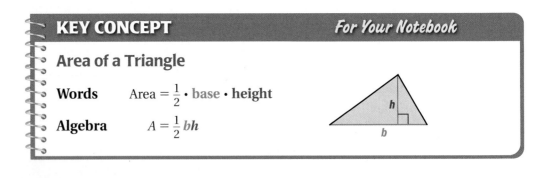

KEY CONCEPT *For Your Notebook*

Area of a Triangle

Words Area $= \frac{1}{2} \cdot$ base $\cdot$ height

Algebra $A = \frac{1}{2} bh$

EXAMPLE 1 Finding the Area of a Triangle

Find the area of the triangle.

READ DIAGRAM

As you see in Example 1, the height of an obtuse triangle can be drawn outside the figure.

$A = \frac{1}{2} bh$ Write the formula for the area of a triangle.

$= \frac{1}{2} \cdot 4 \cdot 11$ Substitute 4 for *b* and 11 for *h*.

$= 22 \text{ ft}^2$ Simplify.

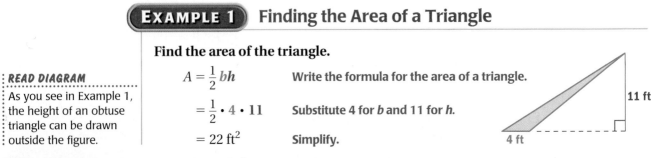

EXAMPLE 2 Standardized Test Practice

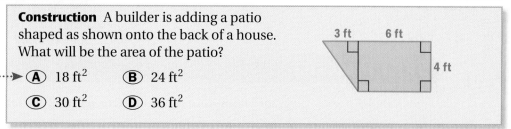

Construction A builder is adding a patio shaped as shown onto the back of a house. What will be the area of the patio?

(A) 18 ft^2 (B) 24 ft^2

(C) 30 ft^2 (D) 36 ft^2

ELIMINATE CHOICES
Because the area of the rectangle is 24 square feet, the area of the patio is greater than 24 square feet. So, choices A and B can be eliminated.

SOLUTION

STEP 1 **Find** the area of each shape.

Area of the triangle = $\frac{1}{2}bh$ Area of the rectangle = lw

$$A = \frac{1}{2} \cdot 3 \cdot 4 \qquad\qquad A = 6 \cdot 4$$
$$= 6 \qquad\qquad\qquad = 24$$

STEP 2 **Add** the areas to find the total area.

$$6 + 24 = 30$$

▶ **Answer** The patio will be 30 square feet in area.

The correct answer is C. (A) (B) (C) (D)

at classzone.com

EXAMPLE 3 Finding the Height of a Triangle

xy The area of a triangle is 36 square inches and the base is 8 inches. What is the height of the triangle?

$A = \frac{1}{2}bh$	Write the formula for the area of a triangle.
$36 = \frac{1}{2} \cdot 8 \cdot h$	Substitute 36 for A and 8 for b.
$36 = 4 \cdot h$	Simplify.
$h = 36 \div 4$	Write a related division equation.
$h = 9$	Simplify.

▶ **Answer** The height of the triangle is 9 inches.

✓ **GUIDED PRACTICE** for Examples 1, 2, and 3

In Exercises 1 and 2, find the area of the described triangle.

1. base = 12 kilometers, height = 5 kilometers

2. base = 6 inches, height = 4 inches

3. Find the area of the figure at the right.

4. The area of a triangle is 45 square feet and the base is 10 feet. Find the height.

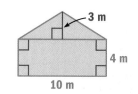

10.2 EXERCISES

HOMEWORK KEY

★ = **STANDARDIZED TEST PRACTICE**
Exs. 20, 26, 30, 31, 32, 33, and 48

◯ = **HINTS AND HOMEWORK HELP**
for Exs. 3, 5, 7, 11, 27 at classzone.com

SKILL PRACTICE

VOCABULARY Copy and complete the statement using the triangle at the right.

1. The __?__ of the triangle is 5 yards and the __?__ of the triangle is 6 yards.

2. The __?__ of the triangle is 15 square yards.

3. The height of a right triangle is also a __?__ of the triangle.

FINDING AREAS Find the area of the figure.

SEE EXAMPLE 1
on p. 518
for Exs. 4–9

4.

5.

6.

7.

8.

9.

SEE EXAMPLE 2
on p. 519
for Exs. 10–12

10.

11.

12.

FINDING DIMENSIONS Find the missing base or height of the described triangle.

SEE EXAMPLE 3
on p. 519
for Exs. 13–18

13. Area: 20 in.^{2}
base: 8 in.

14. Area: 32 ft^2
height: 4 ft

15. Area: 30.6 cm^2
height: 6 cm

16. Area: 19.25 mm^2
height: 7 mm

17. Area: $34\frac{1}{2}$ mi^2
base: $11\frac{1}{2}$ mi

18. Area: $422\frac{5}{8}$ m^2
base: $10\frac{1}{2}$ m

19. **ERROR ANALYSIS** Describe and correct the error made in drawing the height of the obtuse triangle.

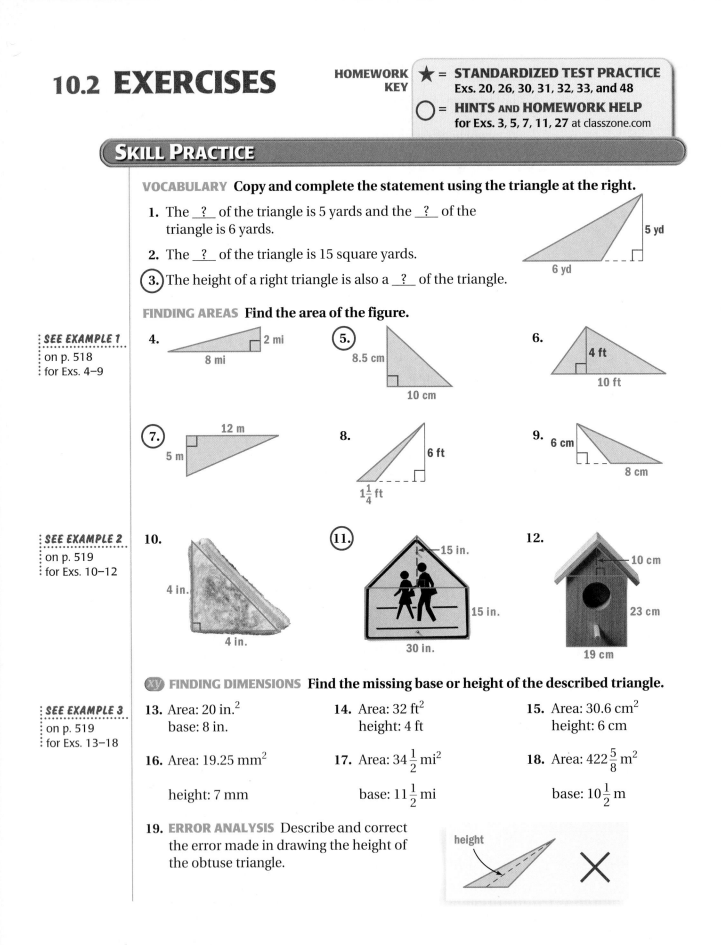

20. ★ **MULTIPLE CHOICE** The table shows the area of a triangle as the base stays the same but the height changes. Which expression gives the area when the height is *h* centimeters?

Base (cm)	8	8	8	8
Height (cm)	3	5	7	h
Area (cm²)	12	20	28	?

    A $4h$ cm²   **B** $8h$ cm²   **C** $\frac{4}{h}$ cm²   **D** $\frac{h}{4}$ cm²

COMPARING AREA Find the area of the figure when the given lengths (in meters) are $a = 4$, $b = 2$, and $c = 3$. What would the area be if all three lengths were doubled? What pattern do you notice?

21.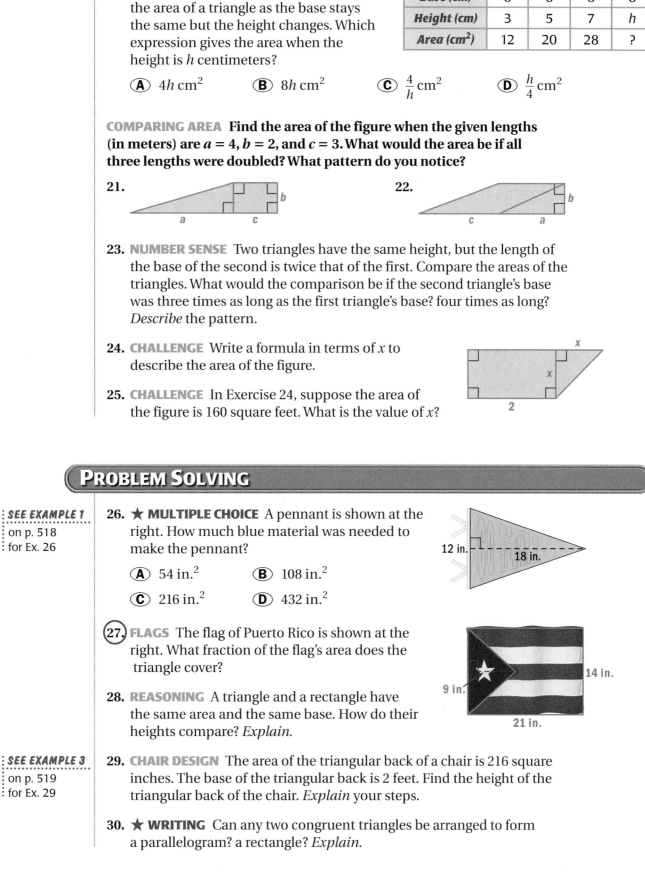

22.

23. **NUMBER SENSE** Two triangles have the same height, but the length of the base of the second is twice that of the first. Compare the areas of the triangles. What would the comparison be if the second triangle's base was three times as long as the first triangle's base? four times as long? *Describe* the pattern.

24. **CHALLENGE** Write a formula in terms of *x* to describe the area of the figure.

25. **CHALLENGE** In Exercise 24, suppose the area of the figure is 160 square feet. What is the value of *x*?

PROBLEM SOLVING

SEE EXAMPLE 1
on p. 518
for Ex. 26

26. ★ **MULTIPLE CHOICE** A pennant is shown at the right. How much blue material was needed to make the pennant?

    A 54 in.²   **B** 108 in.²

    C 216 in.²   **D** 432 in.²

12 in.
18 in.

27. **FLAGS** The flag of Puerto Rico is shown at the right. What fraction of the flag's area does the triangle cover?

14 in.
9 in.
21 in.

28. **REASONING** A triangle and a rectangle have the same area and the same base. How do their heights compare? *Explain.*

SEE EXAMPLE 3
on p. 519
for Ex. 29

29. **CHAIR DESIGN** The area of the triangular back of a chair is 216 square inches. The base of the triangular back is 2 feet. Find the height of the triangular back of the chair. *Explain* your steps.

30. ★ **WRITING** Can any two congruent triangles be arranged to form a parallelogram? a rectangle? *Explain.*

31. ★ **OPEN-ENDED MATH** The area of a triangle is quadrupled to get a new triangle. *Describe* how the height or base of the original triangle might have changed.

32. ★ **SHORT RESPONSE** Use the obtuse triangle at the right.

   a. Use $\overline{AB}$ as the base. Use a metric ruler to measure the base and the approximate height of the triangle. Find the area of the triangle.

   b. Repeat the process using $\overline{AC}$ and then $\overline{BC}$ as bases.

   c. Describe what you observed in parts (a) and (b). Is this true for every triangle? *Explain.*

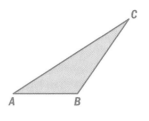

33. ★ **EXTENDED RESPONSE** Some hang glider wings are in the shape of a triangle.

   a. **Calculate** The base of a wing is 208 inches and the area of the wing is 16,848 square inches. Find the height of the wing.

   b. **Calculate** What is the new area if the base of the wing is doubled and the height stays the same?

   c. **Compare** The base and the height of the original wing are both doubled. How many times larger is the area?

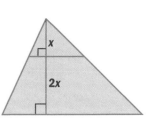

34. **CHALLENGE** Three non-congruent triangles can be created with a side of length 3.5 centimeters and angles of 35° and 80°. Use a ruler and a protractor to draw the three triangles and find the area of each.

35. **CHALLENGE** The area of the smaller triangle in the figure at the right is 0.75 square centimeter. The small and large triangles are similar. Find the area of the larger triangle.

MIXED REVIEW

Get-Ready

Prepare for Lesson 10.3 in Exs. 36–44

Find the product. *(p. 169)*

36. $(5)(4.5)$

37. $(3.25)(5)$

38. $(7.05)(6)$

39. $(3)(8.21)(4)$

40. $(5)(2.8)(3)$

41. $(18)(2.5)$

42. $(6.7)(5)(3)$

43. $(12)(2.24)(9)$

44. $(7.77)(3)(8)$

Tell whether the measure is *mass*, *capacity*, or *length*.

45. 4 kg *(p. 203)*

46. 917 mL *(p. 125)*

47. 14 L *(p. 203)*

48. ★ **MULTIPLE CHOICE** What is the base of a parallelogram that has an area of 135 square centimeters and a height of 15 centimeters? *(p. 514)*

   (A) $\frac{1}{9}$ cm

   (B) 8 cm

   (C) 9 cm

   (D) 18 cm

INVESTIGATION
Use before Lesson 10.3

GOAL
Investigate the circumference of a circle.

MATERIALS
• metric ruler
• compass
• string
• scissors

10.3 Investigating Circumference

In this activity, you will construct circles with a given *radius,* the distance from the center to any point on the circle. Then you will use the constructions to investigate the relationship between the *diameter,* the distance across the circle through its center, and the *circumference,* the distance around the circle.

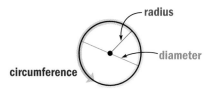

EXPLORE 1 Use a compass to draw a circle with a radius of 2 cm.

STEP 1 **Open** the compass so that the distance between the point and the pencil is 2 centimeters on a metric ruler.

STEP 2 **Place** the point on a piece of paper and rotate the pencil around the point to draw a circle.

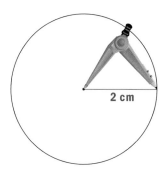

2 cm

PRACTICE Use a compass to draw a circle with the given radius.

1. 2.5 centimeters   **2.** 3 centimeters   **3.** 5 centimeters

DRAW CONCLUSIONS

4. **WRITING** *Explain* how you can use a compass to draw a circle when you are given only its diameter. Then draw a circle with a diameter of 7 centimeters.

Continued on next page

EXPLORE 2 Find the ratio of the circumference of a circle to the diameter of the circle.

STEP 1 **Use** a compass to draw a circle with a diameter of 8 centimeters. You will need to set the opening of your compass to 4 centimeters.

STEP 2 **Cut** a piece of string so that the length equals the circumference of the circle. Then measure the string to the nearest tenth of a centimeter.

STEP 3 **Find** the ratio of the circumference to the diameter by dividing the circumference in Step 2 by the diameter given in Step 1. Round your answer to the nearest hundredth.

$$\frac{\text{Circumference in Step 2}}{\text{Diameter in Step 1}} \approx \frac{25.1}{8} \approx 3.14$$

PRACTICE Repeat Steps 1–3 above to find the ratio of the circumference to the diameter for a circle with the given diameter. Round your answer to the nearest hundredth.

5. 2 cm   **6.** 2.5 cm   **7.** 3 cm

8. 1.5 in.   **9.** 2 in.   **10.** 2.5 in.

DRAW CONCLUSIONS

11. **WRITING** Compare the ratios in Exercises 5–10. What does this tell you about the relationship between the circumference and the diameter of a circle?

10.3 Circumference of a Circle

Before	You found the perimeter of a rectangle.
Now	You'll find the circumference of a circle.
Why?	So you can estimate distances, as in Ex. 27.

KEY VOCABULARY
- circle, *p. 525*
- center, *p. 525*
- radius, *p. 525*
- diameter, *p. 525*
- circumference,
  pi (π), *p. 525*

A **circle** is the set of all points in a plane that are the same distance from a point called the **center**. The **radius**, *r*, is the distance from the center to any point on the circle. The distance across the circle through its center is the **diameter**, *d*. The diameter of a circle is twice the radius.

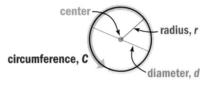

The distance around a circle is called the **circumference**, *C*.

The ratio of any circle's circumference to its diameter is always the same. This ratio is 3.14159. . . . It is represented by the Greek letter π, or **pi**. You can use 3.14 or $\frac{22}{7}$ to approximate π.

VOCABULARY

The word circumference comes from the Latin words *"circum"* meaning *"around"* and *"ferre"* meaning *"to carry."*

> **KEY CONCEPT** *For Your Notebook*
>
> **Circumference of a Circle**
>
> **Words** **Algebra**
>
> Circumference = pi · **diameter** $C = \pi d$
>
> Circumference = 2 · pi · **radius** $C = 2\pi r$

EXAMPLE 1 Finding the Circumference of a Circle

Find the circumference of a circle with diameter 8 feet.

$C = \pi d$ — **Write the formula for the circumference of a circle.**

$\approx (3.14)(8)$ — **Substitute 3.14 for π and 8 for *d*.**

$= 25.12$ — **Simplify.**

▶ **Answer** The circumference of the circle is about 25.12 feet.

ESTIMATE TO CHECK

When estimating, 3 is a reasonable approximation of pi.

Check Estimate to check whether the answer is reasonable.

$$(3.14)(8) \approx 3 \cdot 8 = 24$$

So, the circumference 25.12 feet is reasonable.

EXAMPLE 2 **Standardized Test Practice**

> **What expression approximates the circumference of the circle shown?**
>
> **(A)** 2(6) mm   **(B)** 3.14(6) mm
>
> **(C)** $\frac{1}{2}$(3.14)(6) mm   **(D)** 2(3.14)(6) mm
>
> 6 mm

ELIMINATE CHOICES

An expression for the circumference of a circle must have pi or an approximation of pi in it. Choice A does not, so it can be eliminated.

SOLUTION

When you know the radius of a circle, use $C = 2\pi r$ to find the circumference.

$C = 2\pi r$ **Write the formula for the circumference of a circle.**

$\approx 2(3.14)(6)$ **Substitute 3.14 for π and 6 for r.**

▸ **Answer** The expression for the circumference is 2(3.14)(6). The correct answer is D. (A) (B) (C) **(D)**

EXAMPLE 3 **Choosing an Approximation of Pi**

Find the circumference of a circle with a diameter of 14 centimeters.

SOLUTION

Because the diameter is a multiple of 7, use $\frac{22}{7}$ for π.

$C = \pi d$ **Write the formula for the circumference of a circle.**

$\approx \frac{22}{7} \cdot 14$ **Substitute $\frac{22}{7}$ for π and 14 for d.**

$= \frac{22 \cdot \overset{2}{\cancel{14}}}{\underset{1}{\cancel{7}}}$ **Multiply. Divide out the common factor.**

$= 44$ **Simplify.**

APPROXIMATE PI

When the diameter or the radius of a circle is a multiple of 7, use $\frac{22}{7}$ for pi.

▸ **Answer** The circumference of the circle is about 44 centimeters.

✓ **GUIDED PRACTICE**   **for Examples 1, 2, and 3**

Find the circumference of the circle.

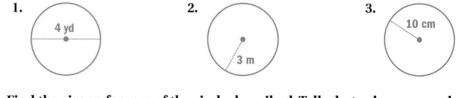

1. 4 yd   **2.** 3 m   **3.** 10 cm

Find the circumference of the circle described. Tell what value you used for π. *Explain* your choice.

4. $d = 10$ ft   **5.** $d = 35$ km   **6.** $r = 42$ cm

EXAMPLE 4 Applying Circumference

Geology The Barringer Meteor Crater has a diameter of about 1186 meters. Find the circumference of the crater to the nearest meter.

SOLUTION

$C = \pi d$ Write the formula for the circumference of a circle.

$\approx (3.14)(1186)$ Substitute 3.14 for π and 1186 for d.

$= 3724.04$ Simplify.

▶ **Answer** The circumference of the crater is about 3724 meters.

Check Estimate: $(3.14)(1186) \approx 3 \cdot 1200 = 3600$. So, the circumference of 3724 meters is reasonable.

✓ **GUIDED PRACTICE**   **for Example 4**

7. **Ice Rink** A circular ice rink has a diameter of about 35 meters. Find the circumference to the nearest meter.

8. **Automobile Tires** The diameter of a tire is 26 inches. What is the circumference of the tire to the nearest inch?

10.3 EXERCISES

HOMEWORK KEY

★ = **STANDARDIZED TEST PRACTICE**
Exs. 9, 27, 29, 31, and 38

◯ = **HINTS AND HOMEWORK HELP**
for Exs. 5, 7, 9, 27 at classzone.com

SKILL PRACTICE

VOCABULARY Copy and complete the statement.

1. The distance across a circle through its center is the __?__.

2. The product of a circle's radius and 2π is the __?__.

3. The diameter of a circle is twice the __?__.

4. The ratio of the circumference of a circle to its diameter is __?__.

FINDING CIRCUMFERENCE Find the circumference of the circular object. Round your answer to the nearest whole number. Estimate to check.

SEE EXAMPLES 1 AND 2
on pp. 525–526
for Exs. 5–7

5.
23 ft

6.
3 in.

7.
1.5 m

8. ERROR ANALYSIS Describe and correct the error made in finding the circumference of a circle with a radius of 3 millimeters.

$C = \pi d$
$\approx (3.14)(3)$
$= 9.42$ mm

9. ★ **MULTIPLE CHOICE** Which expression can be used to approximate the circumference of a circle with a diameter of 25 centimeters?

Ⓐ 2(25)   Ⓑ 3.14(25)   Ⓒ $\frac{1}{2}$(3.14)(25)   Ⓓ 2(3.14)(25)

CHOOSING AN APPROXIMATION OF PI Find the circumference of the circle described. Tell what value you used for π. *Explain* your choice.

10. $d = 28$ m   **11.** $d = 12$ yd   **12.** $r = 2$ in.   **13.** $r = 21$ km

14. $r = 17$ mm   **15.** $d = 70$ yd   **16.** $d = 49$ mi   **17.** $r = 6$ in.

FINDING PERIMETERS Find the distance around the outside of the figure.

18.   **19.**   **20.**   **21.**

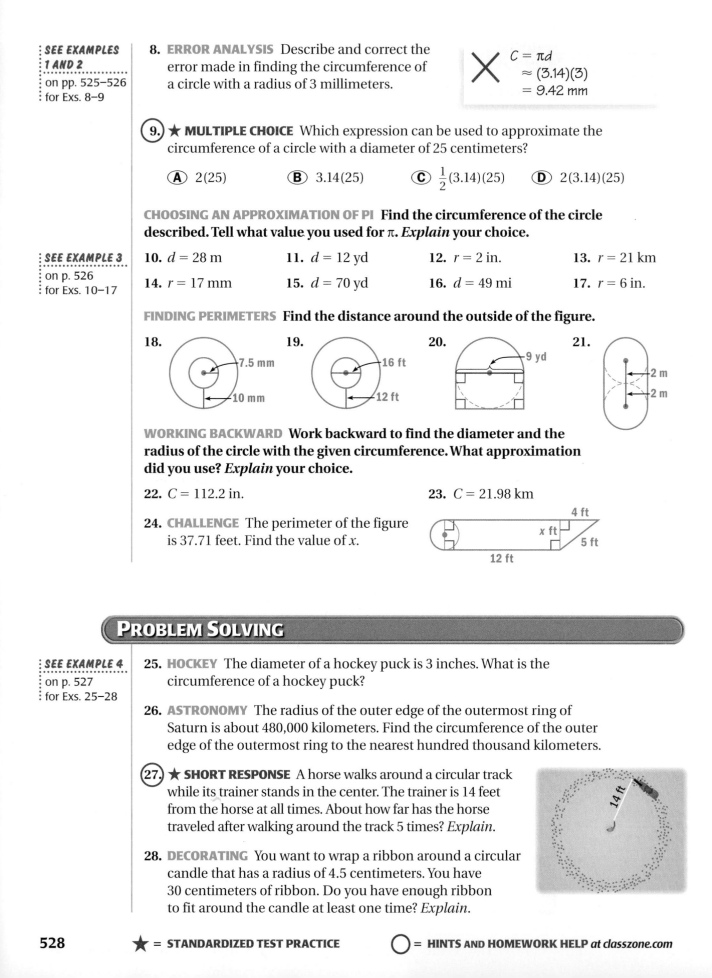

7.5 mm
10 mm
16 ft
12 ft
9 yd
2 m
2 m

WORKING BACKWARD Work backward to find the diameter and the radius of the circle with the given circumference. What approximation did you use? *Explain* your choice.

22. $C = 112.2$ in.   **23.** $C = 21.98$ km

24. CHALLENGE The perimeter of the figure is 37.71 feet. Find the value of x.

4 ft
x ft
5 ft
12 ft

PROBLEM SOLVING

25. HOCKEY The diameter of a hockey puck is 3 inches. What is the circumference of a hockey puck?

26. ASTRONOMY The radius of the outer edge of the outermost ring of Saturn is about 480,000 kilometers. Find the circumference of the outer edge of the outermost ring to the nearest hundred thousand kilometers.

27. ★ **SHORT RESPONSE** A horse walks around a circular track while its trainer stands in the center. The trainer is 14 feet from the horse at all times. About how far has the horse traveled after walking around the track 5 times? *Explain.*

14 ft

28. DECORATING You want to wrap a ribbon around a circular candle that has a radius of 4.5 centimeters. You have 30 centimeters of ribbon. Do you have enough ribbon to fit around the candle at least one time? *Explain.*

29. ★ **MULTIPLE CHOICE** You know the circumference *C* of a log. Which expression could you use to find the diameter of the log?

   (A) $(2 \cdot C) \div \pi$ **(B)** $(C \div 2) \cdot \pi$ **(C)** $C \cdot \pi$ **(D)** $C \div \pi$

30. **MULTI-STEP PROBLEM** A gym wheel is a piece of gymnastics equipment operated by the gymnast shifting his or her weight. Use the diagram below to complete the following.

  a. The scale of the diagram is 1 cm : 1.2 m. What is the diameter of the wheel?

  b. What is the circumference of the gym wheel?

  c. The gymnast causes the wheel to rotate forward 2 times. How far does it travel?

31. ★ **WRITING** Which is a better estimate for pi: 3.14 or $\frac{22}{7}$? *Explain.*

32. **CHALLENGE** The circumference of Earth at the equator is about 24,900 miles. Find the diameter and the radius of Earth to the nearest mile. *Explain* how you found your answers.

MIXED REVIEW

Get-Ready

Prepare for
Lesson 10.4
in Exs. 33–35

Evaluate the expression.

33. $6.1(4)^2$ *(p. 169)*   **34.** $(2.5)(5)^2$ *(p. 169)*   **35.** $(2.4)(3.1)^2$ *(p. 181)*

36. Make a frequency table and a line plot of the data. *(p. 76)*
   2, 5, 6, 3, 2, 1, 1, 0, 5, 1, 7, 6, 6, 4, 5, 3, 2, 1, 1, 6

CHOOSE A STRATEGY Use a strategy from the list to solve the following problem. *Explain* your choice of strategy.

37. You fold a piece of paper in half. Then you fold it in half again in the other direction and draw a figure at the folded corner like the one shown. Describe the shape that will be cut out when you unfold the paper.

   Problem Solving Strategies
   ▪ Make a Model *(p. 761)*
   ▪ Draw a Diagram *(p. 762)*
   ▪ Make a List *(p. 765)*
   ▪ Solve a Simpler Problem *(p. 768)*

38. ★ **MULTIPLE CHOICE** A square has a perimeter of 100 meters. What is the side length of the square? *(p. 66)*

   (A) 10 m   **(B)** 25 m   **(C)** 50 m   **(D)** 100 m

10.3 Circumference of a Circle

EXAMPLE You can find the circumference of a circle using the pi key on a calculator.

The *Place Charles de Gaulle,* a traffic circle which surrounds the Arc de Triomphe in Paris, has a diameter of about 137 meters. What is the circumference of the *Place Charles de Gaulle?*

SOLUTION

Use the formula $C = \pi d$ to find the circumference of a circle. To enter π on a calculator, you can use the approximation 3.14 or you can use the pi key, . Although both methods give approximately the same answer, using the pi key gives a slightly more accurate answer.

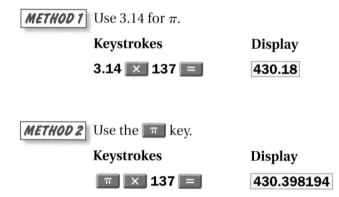

METHOD 1 Use 3.14 for π.

Keystrokes	Display
3.14 × 137 =	430.18

METHOD 2 Use the [π] key.

Keystrokes	Display
π × 137 =	430.398194

▶ **Answer** The circumference of the *Place Charles de Gaulle* is about 430 meters.

PRACTICE Use a calculator to find the circumference of the circle described. Round your answer to the nearest whole number.

1. $d = 12$ ft
2. $d = 86$ in.
3. $d = 341$ cm
4. $d = 7.95$ m
5. $r = 15$ km
6. $r = 550$ in.
7. $r = 0.8$ m
8. $r = 30.57$ mi

9. **ARCTIC CIRCLE** The Arctic Circle, located at 66.5°N latitude, has a radius of about 2543 kilometers. What is the circumference of the Arctic Circle to the nearest kilometer?

10.4 Area of a Circle

Before	You found the areas of triangles and parallelograms.
Now	You'll find the area of a circle.
Why?	So you can find areas of circular objects, as in Example 1.

KEY VOCABULARY
- **area,** *p. 67*
- **radius,** *p. 525*
- **pi,** *p. 525*

Button Designs You are making a design for a circular button. Your design fits on a circle with a radius of 3 centimeters. How much area will be covered by your design?

The area of a circle is the amount of surface covered by the circle.

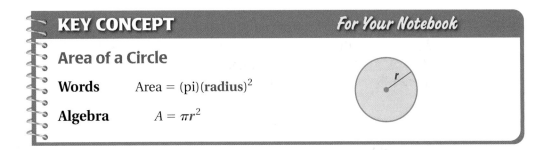

KEY CONCEPT   *For Your Notebook*

Area of a Circle

Words   Area = (pi)(radius)^2

Algebra $A = \pi r^2$

EXAMPLE 1   Finding the Area of a Circle

To answer the question above, find the area of a circle with a radius of 3 centimeters. Round to the nearest square centimeter.

$A = \pi r^2$ **Write the formula for the area of a circle.**

$\approx (3.14)(3)^2$ **Substitute 3.14 for π and 3 for *r*.**

$= 28.26$ **Simplify.**

▶ **Answer** The area covered by your design is about 28 square centimeters.

Check A good estimate of πr^2 is $3 \cdot 3^2 = 27$. An area of 28 cm^2 is reasonable.

Animated Math at classzone.com

✓ **GUIDED PRACTICE**   for Example 1

Find the area of the circle.

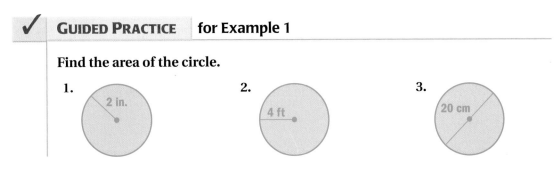

1. 2 in.

2. 4 ft

3. 20 cm

EXAMPLE 2 Finding the Area of Combined Figures

Basketball Find the area of the free throw area to the nearest square foot.

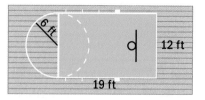

SOLUTION

STEP 1 Find the area of each shape.

Rectangle

$A = lw$

$= 19 \cdot 12$

$= 228$

Half circle

$A = \frac{1}{2}\pi r^2$

$\approx \frac{1}{2}(3.14)(6)^2$

$= 56.52$

STEP 2 Add the areas to find the total area: $228 + 56.52 = 284.52$.

▸ **Answer** The area of the free throw area is about 285 square feet.

✓ **GUIDED PRACTICE** for Example 2

Find the area of the figure to the nearest square unit.

4.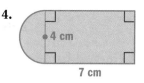
4 cm
7 cm

5.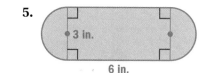
3 in.
6 in.

EXAMPLE 3 Solve a Multi-Step Problem

Pizza How many times as great as the area of an 8 inch pizza is the area of a 16 inch pizza?

8 in.

16 in.

SOLUTION

STEP 1 Find the area of each pizza.

8 inch pizza

$A = \pi r^2$

$\approx (3.14)(4)^2$

$= 50.24 \text{ in.}^2$

16 inch pizza

$A = \pi r^2$

$\approx (3.14)(8)^2$

$= 200.96 \text{ in.}^2$

STEP 2 Divide the area of the 16 inch pizza by the area of the 8 inch pizza.

$\frac{200.96}{50.24} = 4$

▸ **Answer** The area of a 16 inch pizza is 4 times the area of an 8 inch pizza.

Making Circle Graphs A circle graph is made of *sectors* that represent portions of a data set. Each sector is formed by an angle whose vertex is the center of the circle. In a circle graph, the sum of the measures of all these angles is 360°.

The ratio of a sector's area to the total circle's area is equal to the ratio of the sector's data to the total circle graph's data.

EXAMPLE 4 Making a Circle Graph

Ski Trails The table shows what fraction of the trails at a ski resort are beginner, intermediate, and expert. Make a circle graph to represent the data.

Types of Ski Trails			
Trail Type	*Beginner*	*Intermediate*	**Expert**
Fraction of Trails	$\frac{3}{10}$	$\frac{1}{2}$	$\frac{1}{5}$

SOLUTION

ANOTHER WAY
Change all fractions to tenths. Because 36° is one tenth of 360°, you can find the angle measures as follows
$3 \cdot 36° = 108°$,
$5 \cdot 36° = 180°$, and
$2 \cdot 36° = 72°$.

STEP 1 **Find** the angle measure of each sector. Each sector's angle measure is a fraction of 360°. Multiply each fraction in the table by 360° to get the angle measure for each sector.

Beginner

$\frac{3}{10}(360)° = 108°$

Intermediate

$\frac{1}{2}(360)° = 180°$

Expert

$\frac{1}{5}(360)° = 72°$

STEP 2 **Draw** the circle graph.

Use a compass to draw a circle.

Use a protractor to draw the angle for each sector.

Label each sector and give your graph a title.

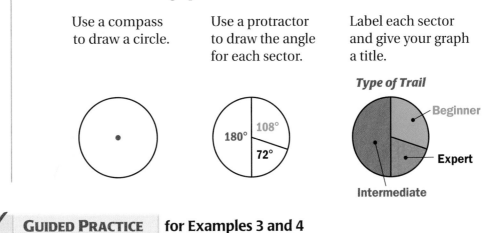

✓ GUIDED PRACTICE for Examples 3 and 4

6. What is the ratio of the area of a circle with radius 2 feet to the area of a circle with radius 6 feet?

7. What If? In Example 4, suppose $\frac{2}{5}$ of the trails at the ski resort are beginner, $\frac{1}{10}$ are intermediate, and $\frac{1}{5}$ are expert. Make a circle graph to represent the data.

10.4 EXERCISES

HOMEWORK KEY

★ = **STANDARDIZED TEST PRACTICE**
  Exs. 13, 33, 35, 36, and 50

◯ = **HINTS** AND **HOMEWORK HELP**
  for Exs. 3, 5, 7, 15, 31 at classzone.com

SKILL PRACTICE

VOCABULARY Copy and complete the statement.

1. You can use the expression πr^2 to find the __?__ of a circle.

2. A commonly used decimal approximation of π is __?__.

FINDING AREAS OF CIRCLES In Exercises 3–11, find the area of the circle with the given radius or diameter. Round to the nearest square unit.

SEE EXAMPLE 1
on p. 531
for Exs. 3–13

3. 12 ft

4. 30 mi

5. 18 m

6. $r = 3$ mm

7. $d = 17$ ft

8. $d = 24$ yd

9. $d = \frac{7}{2}$ ft

10. $r = 3.4$ m

11. $r = 4.2$ yd

12. ERROR ANALYSIS Describe and correct the error made in finding the area of a circle with a radius of 2.1 feet.

$$A \approx 2(3.14)(2.1)$$
$$= 13.2$$
The area is about 13.2 square feet.

13. ★ **MULTIPLE CHOICE** What is the best estimate of the area of a circle that has a diameter of 10 feet?

Ⓐ 30 ft^2 Ⓑ 75 ft^2 Ⓒ 225 ft^2 Ⓓ 300 ft^2

ADDING AREAS Find the area of the figure to the nearest tenth of a unit.

SEE EXAMPLE 2
on p. 532
for Exs. 14–16

14. 5 ft / 4 ft

15. 1 m

16. 13 cm / 12 cm / 5 cm

SUBTRACTING AREAS Find the area of the shaded portion of the figure to the nearest square unit.

17. 5 in. / 8 in.

18. 14 m

19. 9 yd / 6 yd

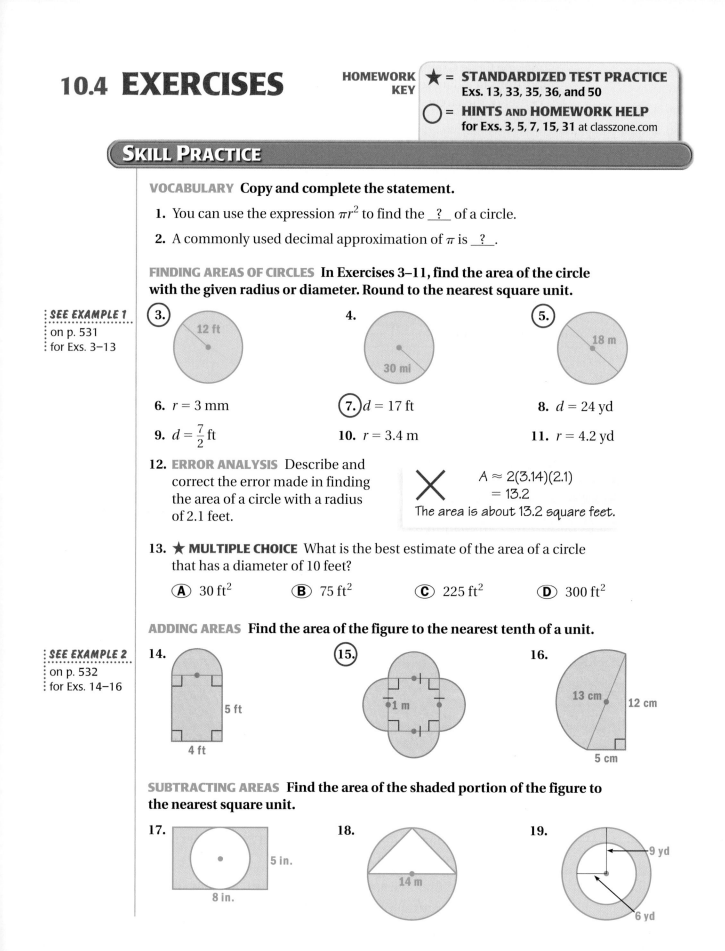

SEE EXAMPLE 4
on p. 533
for Ex. 20

20. SCHOOL ORCHESTRA Make a circle graph to represent the data in the table. Use the circle graph to determine which grade has the most students in the orchestra. *Explain.*

Students in the School Orchestra			
Grade	6th	7th	8th
Students	$\frac{7}{20}$	$\frac{2}{5}$	$\frac{1}{4}$

COMPARING AREAS You multiply the radius of a circle by the given number. What is the ratio of the area of the new circle to the area of the first circle?

21. 2   **22.** 3   **23.** 10   **24.** 100

25. $\frac{1}{2}$ **26.** $\frac{1}{5}$ **27.** $\frac{1}{8}$ **28.** $\frac{1}{10}$

29. CHALLENGE Use the expression πr^2 to write an expression for the area of a circle when the radius r is doubled.

30. CHALLENGE The given figure is made up of a right triangle and three half circles. Find the area of the shaded region.

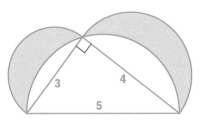

PROBLEM SOLVING

31. LIGHTHOUSES A lighthouse beam makes a circle that reaches 18 miles from the lighthouse. Find the area that is lit by the lighthouse beam to the nearest square mile.

32. FOOTBALL A circular team logo on a football field has a radius of 12 feet. What is the area of the logo?

33. ★ WRITING A circular flower garden has an area of about 314 square feet. A sprinkler at the center of the garden covers an area that has a radius of 12 feet. Will the sprinkler water the entire garden? *Explain.*

34. JAPANESE COINS A 50 yen coin is circular with a circular hole in its center. The diameters of the two circles are 21 millimeters and 4 millimeters. Find the area of the coin.

SEE EXAMPLE 3
on p. 532
for Ex. 35

35. ★ SHORT RESPONSE In a dark room, the iris of your eye opens until the pupil is about 8 millimeters in diameter. In a lit room, the pupil has a diameter of about 2 millimeters. How many times as great is the area of the pupil in the lit room as the area of the pupil in the dark room? *Explain* your reasoning.

36. ★ EXTENDED RESPONSE The dimensions of a rectangular wall are 12 feet by 8 feet. The diameter of a circular window in the wall is 4 feet.

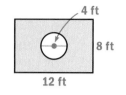

a. Make a Scale Drawing Make a scale drawing of wall and window on graph paper.

b. Estimate Count squares to estimate the area of the wall around the window. Then estimate the area using formulas.

c. Compare Which estimate in part (b) is a better estimate? *Explain.*

d. Apply Estimates Will a can of paint that covers 140 square feet be enough to cover the wall with one coat of paint? with two coats? *Explain.*

READING *IN* MATH Read the passage below for Exercises 37–40.

Animal Shelters The Jefferson County Humane Association comes to the aid of animals in need after disasters, accidents, or abandonment. The Association provides these animals with shelter, food, and medical attention, and then places them in humane environments. Last year the Association placed over 2000 animals, including 54 rabbits, in new homes.

Animal Placements Last Year	
Animal	**Number**
Dogs	732
Cats	1206
Other	222

37. Interpret What was the total number of animals placed in new homes?

38. Rewrite Write the fraction of all animals that are in each category. Use simplest form.

39. Make a Circle Graph Find the angle measures for the sectors of a circle graph. Then make a circle graph of the data. What percent of the graph's area represents cats placed in new homes?

40. Extend Suppose the rabbits, which are included in the Other category, are to be broken out into their own category. What will be the size (in degree measure) of the new Other category? *Explain* your reasoning.

41. WEATHER Weather radar information is displayed on a screen with a scale of 1 inch : 2 miles. The circle on the screen has a radius of 4 inches. About how many square miles does the radar cover?

42. ◆ MULTIPLE REPRESENTATIONS At a car dealership, there are 80 cars for sale. Of the 80 cars, 22.5% are black, 25% are red, 12.5% are blue, and 40% are "other" colors.

a. Make a Table Make a table of the colors and percents.

b. Draw a Graph Make a circle graph of the data in the table.

c. Draw a Graph Make a bar graph showing the number of each color car. Discuss a few advantages of each type of display.

43. GEOMETRY The hour hand of a clock is 3 inches long. What is the area that the hour hand passes through between 2:00 P.M. and 6:00 P.M. on the same day?

44. CHALLENGE A pool is enclosed in a circular area by a fence. The length of fence used is 160 feet. What is the area of the space enclosed by the fence? *Explain* how you found your answer.

45. CHALLENGE A circle has an area of 10 square yards. What is the area of the smallest square that can enclose the circle? *Explain*.

MIXED REVIEW

Get-Ready

Prepare for
Lesson 10.5
in Exs. 46–49

Classify the polygon with the given number of sides. *(p. 485)*

46. 3   **47.** 4   **48.** 5   **49.** 6

50. ★ MULTIPLE CHOICE What is 0.064 written as a percent? *(p. 429)*

     (A) 0.00064%   **(B)** 0.64%   **(C)** 6.4%   **(D)** 64%

Find the circumference of the described circle. *(p. 525)*

51. $d = 7$ yd   **52.** $d = \frac{5}{8}$ in.   **53.** $r = 3.7$ m   **54.** $r = 6$ ft

55. $d = 3$ cm   **56.** $r = \frac{2}{3}$ km   **57.** $r = 55$ mm   **58.** $d = 2.5$ mi

QUIZ *for Lessons 10.1–10.4*

Find the area of the figure to the nearest square unit.

1. *(p. 514)*   6 in.   3 in.   **2.** *(p. 518)*   10 m   12 m   **3.** *(p. 531)*   7 yd

4. A parallelogram has an area of 32 square feet and a height of 4 feet. What is the length of the base? *(p. 514)*

5. A triangle has a height of 6 meters and an area of 12 square meters. What is the length of the base? *(p. 518)*

6. Find the circumference of a circle with a diameter of 22 feet. *(p. 525)*

7. GYM CLASS Make a circle graph to represent the data in the table. *(p. 531)*

8. COMMUNICATION Cellular telephones send messages within a circular area called a *cell*. A cell has a radius of about 2 miles. Find the area of the cell to the nearest square mile. *(p. 531)*

Students in Gym Class			
Grade	7th	8th	9th
Students	$\frac{11}{20}$	$\frac{1}{4}$	$\frac{1}{5}$

Extension

Use after Lesson 10.4

Constructions

GOAL Construct geometric figures.

You can use a compass and a straightedge to construct geometric figures. Use a compass to draw **arcs**, which are parts of circles. Use a straightedge to draw lines, rays, and segments.

EXAMPLE 1 Copying a Segment

Use a compass and a straightedge to copy a segment.

STEP 1 **Draw** any segment $\overline{AB}$. Then draw a ray with endpoint *C*.

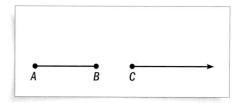

STEP 2 **Draw** an arc with center *A* that passes through *B*. Using the same compass setting, draw an arc with center *C* as shown. Label *D*. $\overline{CD}$ and $\overline{AB}$ have the same length.

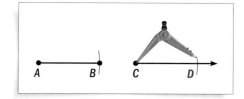

EXAMPLE 2 Copying an Angle

Use a compass and a straightedge to copy an angle.

STEP 1 **Draw** any ∠*A*. Then draw a ray with endpoint *D*. Draw an arc with center *A* that intersects the sides of ∠*A*. Label *B* and *C*. Using the same compass setting, draw an arc with center *D*. Label *E*.

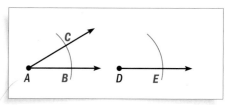

STEP 2 **Draw** an arc with center *B* that passes through *C*. Using the same compass setting, draw an arc with center *E*. Label *F*. Draw a ray from *D* through *F* as shown. ∠*D* and ∠*A* have the same measure.

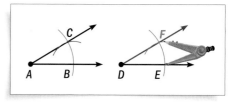

Bisecting Figures The **perpendicular bisector** of a segment is the line that divides the segment into two segments of equal length and forms four right angles. The **bisector of an angle** is the ray that divides the angle into two angles with the same measure.

EXAMPLE 3 Constructing a Perpendicular Bisector

Construct the perpendicular bisector of a segment.

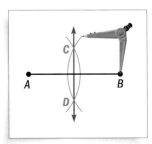

STEP 1 **Draw** any $\overline{AB}$. Using any compass setting greater than half the length of $\overline{AB}$, draw an arc with center A.

STEP 2 **Use** the same compass setting. Draw an arc with center B that intersects the first arc. Label the intersections C and D.

STEP 3 **Draw** $\overleftrightarrow{CD}$, the perpendicular bisector of $\overline{AB}$.

EXAMPLE 4 Constructing an Angle Bisector

Construct the bisector of an angle.

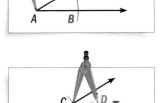

STEP 1 **Draw** any $\angle A$. Using any compass setting, draw an arc with center A that intersects the sides of $\angle A$ as shown. Label B and C.

STEP 2 **Use** any compass setting to draw an arc with center B. Using the same compass setting, draw an arc with center C that intersects the first arc as shown. Label the intersection D.

STEP 3 **Draw** $\overrightarrow{AD}$, the bisector of $\angle A$.

EXERCISES

In Exercises 1–3, use a compass and straightedge.

1. Draw any segment and copy it. Then construct the perpendicular bisector of the segment you constructed.

2. Draw any angle and copy it. Then construct the bisector of the angle you constructed.

3. Draw any segment and label a point A on it. Then construct the line through A perpendicular to the segment by putting your compass point on A and making congruent arcs on the segment on each side of A. Open your compass wider and strike congruent arcs from both points. Draw the line through the intersection of these arcs and A.

Lessons 10.1–10.4

1. SHORT RESPONSE You buy a measuring wheel that you roll on the ground to measure distances. The circular wheel travels 1 yard in a full rotation. What is its diameter? *Explain* how you found your answer.

2. GRIDDED ANSWER The figure shows a map of Molokai, Hawaii, which is approximately in the shape of a parallelogram.

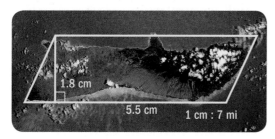

1.8 cm
5.5 cm
1 cm : 7 mi

a. Find the approximate area of Molokai in square centimeters. Round your answer to the nearest square centimeter.

b. Find the approximate area of Molokai in square miles.

c. Molokai's actual area is about 261 square miles. Is your estimate close to the actual area? If not, how could you improve your estimate?

3. EXTENDED RESPONSE Use the diagram of a Palau flag shown below.

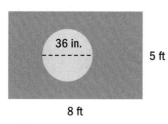

36 in.
5 ft
8 ft

a. Find the area of the rectangle in square feet.

b. Find the area of the yellow circle in square feet.

c. Find the ratio of the area of the circle to the area of the blue region. *Explain* how you found your answer.

4. OPEN-ENDED The area of a parallelogram was reduced by 75% by changing both the height and the base. What changes could have been made to the height and the base?

5. SHORT RESPONSE A kite has the shape and dimensions shown. Show two methods for finding the area. Which is easier? *Justify* your choice.

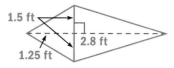

1.5 ft
2.8 ft
1.25 ft

6. MULTI-STEP PROBLEM A multiple lane road circles a landmark. The diameter of the circle is 450 feet. How far is the walk around half of the circle? How much farther is this distance than walking to that point in a straight line across the circle? *Explain.*

7. EXTENDED RESPONSE Use the table below showing the flight status of departing flights from an airport in one year.

Departure Status		
Canceled	*Delayed*	*On Time*
3%	18%	79%

a. Make a circle graph of the data.

b. If there were 18,500 departures, how many were on time?

c. The next year the airport handled 23,400 departures. Only 491 were cancelled, and 710 fewer were delayed than in the previous year. What percent were on time?

8. GRIDDED ANSWER A stage has the dimensions shown. How many square feet is the area of the stage?

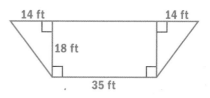

14 ft   14 ft
18 ft
35 ft

10.5 Solid Figures

Before	You classified polygons by their sides.
Now	You'll classify solids.
Why?	So you can analyze shapes such as ramps, as in Ex. 23.

KEY VOCABULARY
- **solid,** *p. 541*
- **prism,** *p. 541*
- **cylinder,** *p. 541*
- **pyramid,** *p. 541*
- **cone,** *p. 541*
- **sphere,** *p. 541*
- **face, edge, vertex,** *p. 542*

A **solid** is a three-dimensional figure that encloses a part of space. Some solids can be classified by the number and shape of their *bases*. The bases of some common solids are shaded in the table below.

Classifying Solids

Rectangular prism   **Triangular prism**

A **prism** is a solid with two parallel bases that are congruent polygons.

A **cylinder** is a solid with two parallel bases that are congruent circles.

A **pyramid** is a solid made of polygons. The base can be any polygon, and the other polygons are triangles that share a common vertex.

A **cone** is a solid that has one circular base and a vertex that is not in the same plane.

A **sphere** is the set of all points that are the same distance from a point called the center.

EXAMPLE 1 Classifying Solids

VOCABULARY

A pyramid is named according to the shape of its base. For example, a pyramid with a rectangular base is called a rectangular pyramid.

Classify the solid.

a.

Cone

b.

Triangular pyramid

c.

Pentagonal prism

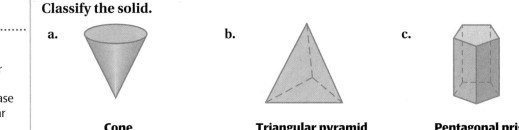

Faces, Edges, and Vertices Some solids are formed by polygons called **faces**. The segments where the faces meet are **edges**. Each point where the edges meet is called a **vertex**. The plural of vertex is *vertices*.

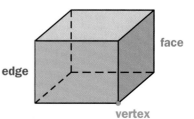

face

edge

vertex

EXAMPLE 2 Counting Faces, Edges, and Vertices

Count the number of faces, edges, and vertices of the square pyramid shown.

SOLUTION

There are 4 triangular faces and 1 square base for a total of 5 faces. There are 8 edges. There are 5 vertices.

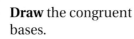

AVOID ERRORS
Do not forget about the bottom of the solid. The square base is also a face of the square pyramid.

EXAMPLE 3 Drawing a Solid

Draw a triangular prism.

SOLUTION

CONGRUENT FIGURES
Need help with congruent figures? See p. 490.

STEP 1	STEP 2	STEP 3
Draw the congruent bases.	**Connect** the corresponding vertices.	**Make** hidden lines by partially erasing lines.

 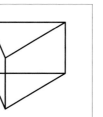 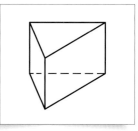

✓ **GUIDED PRACTICE** for Examples 1, 2, and 3

Classify the solid and count the number of faces, edges, and vertices.

1.   2.   3.

4. A *cube* is a rectangular prism with square faces. Draw a cube.

5. Draw a sphere.

10.5 EXERCISES

HOMEWORK KEY

★ = **STANDARDIZED TEST PRACTICE**
Exs. 10, 22, 24, 25, and 40

◯ = **HINTS** AND **HOMEWORK HELP**
for Exs. 3, 5, 7, 9, 23 at classzone.com

SKILL PRACTICE

1. VOCABULARY What is a solid?

2. VOCABULARY Copy and complete: Cylinders and __?__ have two bases.

CLASSIFYING SOLIDS Tell whether the solid has a base. Then classify the solid.

SEE EXAMPLE 1
on p. 541
for Exs. 3–6

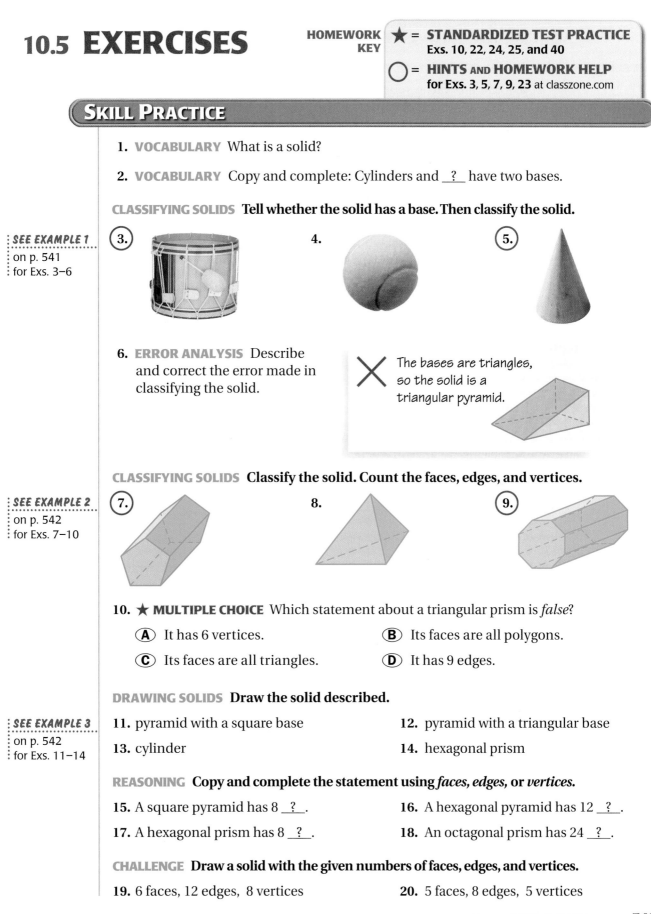

3.

4.

5.

6. ERROR ANALYSIS Describe and correct the error made in classifying the solid.

✗ The bases are triangles, so the solid is a triangular pyramid.

CLASSIFYING SOLIDS Classify the solid. Count the faces, edges, and vertices.

SEE EXAMPLE 2
on p. 542
for Exs. 7–10

7.

8.

9.

10. ★ MULTIPLE CHOICE Which statement about a triangular prism is *false*?

(A) It has 6 vertices.

(B) Its faces are all polygons.

(C) Its faces are all triangles.

(D) It has 9 edges.

DRAWING SOLIDS Draw the solid described.

SEE EXAMPLE 3
on p. 542
for Exs. 11–14

11. pyramid with a square base

12. pyramid with a triangular base

13. cylinder

14. hexagonal prism

REASONING Copy and complete the statement using *faces, edges,* or *vertices.*

15. A square pyramid has 8 __?__.

16. A hexagonal pyramid has 12 __?__.

17. A hexagonal prism has 8 __?__.

18. An octagonal prism has 24 __?__.

CHALLENGE Draw a solid with the given numbers of faces, edges, and vertices.

19. 6 faces, 12 edges, 8 vertices

20. 5 faces, 8 edges, 5 vertices

SEE EXAMPLE 3
on p. 542
for Ex. 21

21. GUIDED PROBLEM SOLVING Follow the steps to sketch a party hat.

 a. Draw an oval on your paper to represent a circle. Draw a point outside the oval. The point should be directly above the center of the oval.

 b. Draw segments from the right side and the left side of the oval to the point you drew. The segments will look like two sides of a triangle.

 c. Classify the solid you drew.

22. ★ WRITING *Describe* all the differences between a rectangular pyramid and a triangular pyramid.

SEE EXAMPLES
1 AND 2
on pp. 541–542
for Ex. 23

(23.) SKATEBOARDING A skateboard ramp is shown at the right. What type of solid does it resemble? How many faces, edges, and vertices does this solid have?

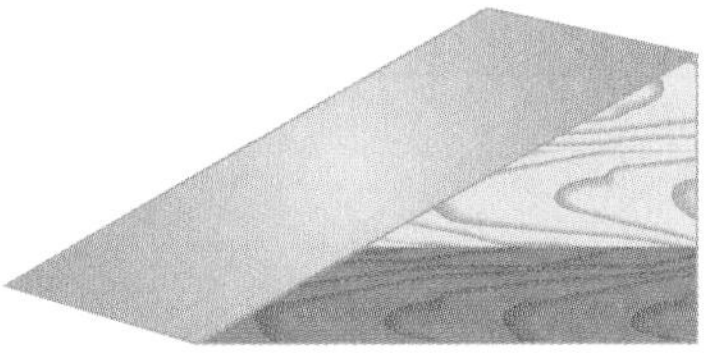

Animated **Math** at classzone.com

24. ★ OPEN-ENDED MATH Give a real-world example of a prism and a real-world example of a pyramid. Then classify each solid by its base.

25. ★ SHORT RESPONSE What is the minimum number of edges that a pyramid can have? that a prism can have? *Explain* your reasoning.

REASONING Tell whether the statement is *true* or *false*. *Justify* your answer.

26. A cone has two circles as bases.

27. A cylinder can have two triangles as bases.

28. A triangular prism has two congruent bases.

29. Any face of a prism has an opposite face that is parallel to it.

30. CHALLENGE *Explain* how to find the number of edges of any pyramid whose base is a polygon with n sides.

Get-Ready

Prepare for
Lesson 10.6 in
Exs. 31–36

Evaluate using the order of operations. *(p. 21)*

31. $2(4) + 2(5) + 2(6)$ **32.** $2(4 \times 3) + 2(4 \times 2)$ **33.** $4(6) + 3(4 + 5)$

34. $3 + 8 \div 2$ **35.** $(5 + 9) \div 7 \times 9$ **36.** $3 \times (10 \div 2)$

Copy and complete the statement. *(p. 207)*

37. $5 \text{ cm} = \underline{\ ?\ } \text{ mm}$ **38.** $10 \text{ kg} = \underline{\ ?\ } \text{ g}$ **39.** $35 \text{ m} = \underline{\ ?\ } \text{ km}$

40. ★ MULTIPLE CHOICE What is the approximate area of a circle with a diameter of 10 centimeters? *(p. 531)*

 (A) 15.7 cm^2 **(B)** 31.4 cm^2 **(C)** 78.5 cm^2 **(D)** 314 cm^2

10.6 Surface Area of a Prism

Before	You found areas of polygons.
Now	You'll find the surface area of a prism.
Why?	So you can cover a surface, as in Ex. 26.

KEY VOCABULARY
• surface area, *p. 545*

ACTIVITY

You can break a prism into parts to find the total area.

STEP 1 **Imagine** unfolding a box into a *net*, a flat view of the faces of the box.

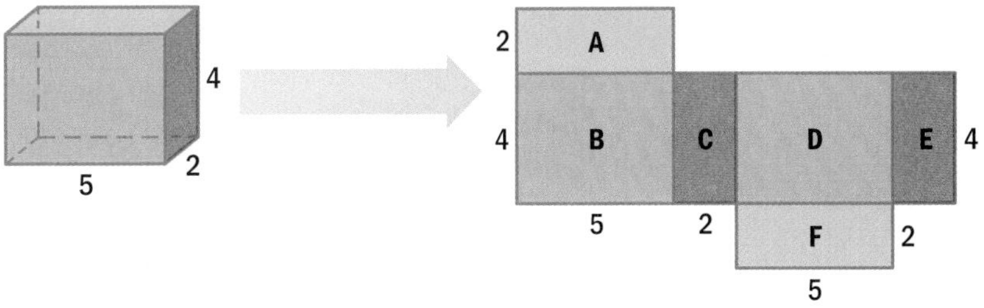

STEP 2 **Find** the area of each rectangular face of the net. Record your results in a table.

STEP 3 **Add** the areas of the six faces to find the total area.

In the activity, you found the *surface area* of a rectangular prism. The **surface area** S of a prism is the sum of the areas of its faces.

EXAMPLE 1 Finding the Surface Area of a Prism

Find the surface area of the rectangular prism.

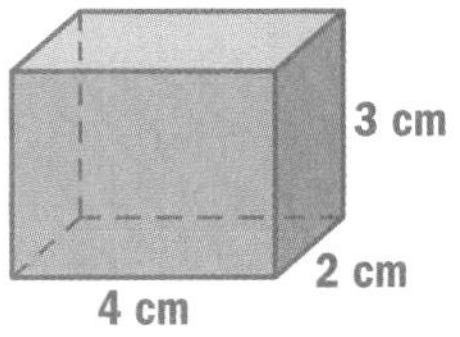

STEP 1 **Find** the area of each face.

Area of the top or bottom face: $4 \times 2 = 8$ cm^2

Area of the front or back face: $4 \times 3 = 12$ cm^2

Area of the left or right face: $3 \times 2 = 6$ cm^2

STEP 2 **Add** the areas of all six faces to find the surface area.

$S = 8 + 8 + 12 + 12 + 6 + 6$

$\quad = 52$

▶ **Answer** The surface area is 52 square centimeters.

EXAMPLE 2 Drawing a Diagram

Find the surface area of a rectangular prism that is 8 inches by 2 inches by 5 inches.

SOLUTION

STEP 1 **Draw** a diagram of the prism and label the dimensions.

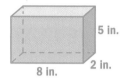
5 in.
2 in.
8 in.

STEP 2 **Find** the area of each face. Then add these areas to find the surface area.

$$S = (8 \times 2) + (8 \times 2) + (8 \times 5) + (8 \times 5) + (5 \times 2) + (5 \times 2)$$

$$= 16 + 16 + 40 + 40 + 10 + 10$$

$$= 132$$

▶ **Answer** The prism has a surface area of 132 square inches.

EXAMPLE 3 Using Surface Area

Painting You want to paint a jewelry box that is 8 inches by $7\frac{1}{2}$ inches by 3 inches with a clear polish. The label on the bottle of polish says it covers a total area of 250 square inches. Do you have enough to cover the entire box?

SOLUTION

Find the surface area of the box and compare it to the area the polish will cover.

$$S = 60 + 60 + 36 + 36 + 22\frac{1}{2} + 22\frac{1}{2}$$

$$= 237$$

▶ **Answer** The surface area of the box is 237 square inches. Your bottle of polish covers 250 square inches. You do have enough polish to cover the entire box.

✓ **GUIDED PRACTICE** **for Examples 1, 2, and 3**

1. Find the surface area of the rectangular prism shown at the right.

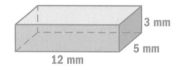
3 mm
5 mm
12 mm

2. A rectangular prism is 3 feet by 4 feet by 6 feet. Find its surface area.

3. You have 60 square stickers. Each sticker has an area of 1 square inch. Do you have enough stickers to cover a rectangular box that is 2 inches by 4 inches by 6 inches? *Explain* your answer.

10.6 EXERCISES

HOMEWORK KEY

★ = **STANDARDIZED TEST PRACTICE**
Exs. 18, 24, 26, 27, 28, 30, and 45

◯ = **HINTS AND HOMEWORK HELP**
for Exs. 3, 5, 7, 25 at classzone.com

SKILL PRACTICE

VOCABULARY Copy and complete the statement.

1. The ___?___ of a prism is the sum of the areas of its faces.

2. A flat view of the faces of a box is called a ___?___.

FINDING SURFACE AREA Find the surface area of the rectangular prism.

SEE EXAMPLE 1
on p. 545
for Exs. 3–8

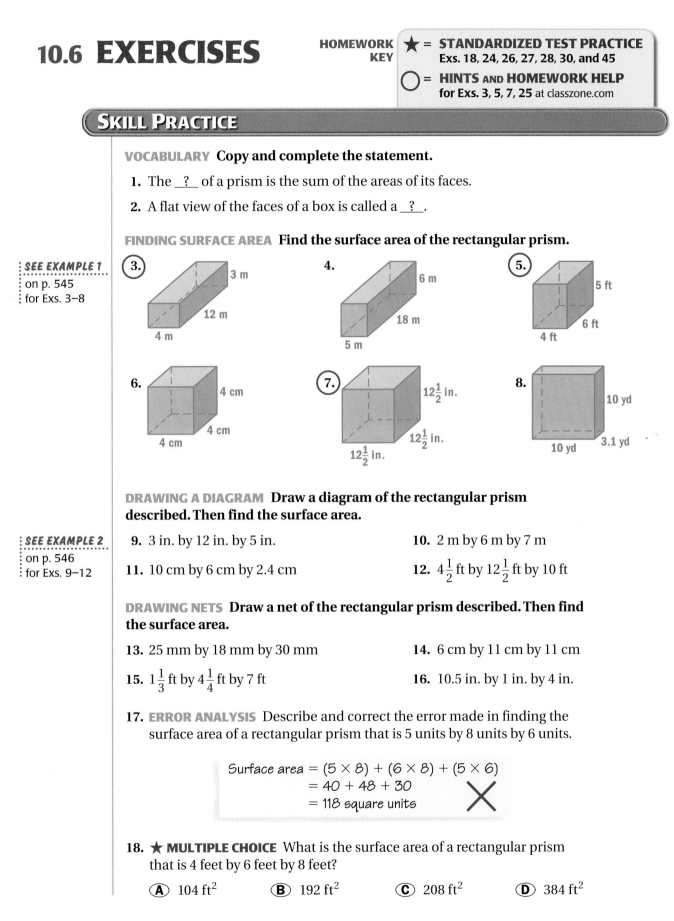

3. 3 m, 12 m, 4 m

4. 6 m, 18 m, 5 m

5. 5 ft, 6 ft, 4 ft

6. 4 cm, 4 cm, 4 cm

7. $12\frac{1}{2}$ in., $12\frac{1}{2}$ in., $12\frac{1}{2}$ in.

8. 10 yd, 10 yd, 3.1 yd

DRAWING A DIAGRAM Draw a diagram of the rectangular prism described. Then find the surface area.

SEE EXAMPLE 2
on p. 546
for Exs. 9–12

9. 3 in. by 12 in. by 5 in.

10. 2 m by 6 m by 7 m

11. 10 cm by 6 cm by 2.4 cm

12. $4\frac{1}{2}$ ft by $12\frac{1}{2}$ ft by 10 ft

DRAWING NETS Draw a net of the rectangular prism described. Then find the surface area.

13. 25 mm by 18 mm by 30 mm

14. 6 cm by 11 cm by 11 cm

15. $1\frac{1}{3}$ ft by $4\frac{1}{4}$ ft by 7 ft

16. 10.5 in. by 1 in. by 4 in.

17. **ERROR ANALYSIS** Describe and correct the error made in finding the surface area of a rectangular prism that is 5 units by 8 units by 6 units.

Surface area = (5 × 8) + (6 × 8) + (5 × 6)
= 40 + 48 + 30
= 118 square units ✕

18. ★ **MULTIPLE CHOICE** What is the surface area of a rectangular prism that is 4 feet by 6 feet by 8 feet?

　Ⓐ 104 ft² 　Ⓑ 192 ft² 　Ⓒ 208 ft² 　Ⓓ 384 ft²

FINDING SURFACE AREA The solid is made up of two rectangular prisms.
Find the surface area of the solid.

19.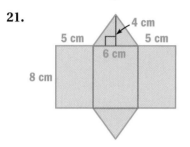
    3 ft
    6 ft   2 ft
    4 ft
    7 ft

20.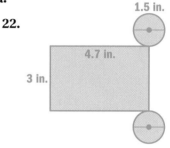
    5 m
    10 m   2 m
    7 m
    15 m

CHALLENGE Use the net shown to draw the solid figure it represents.
Name the solid figure and find its surface area.

21.
    4 cm
    5 cm   5 cm
    6 cm
    8 cm

22.
    1.5 in.
    4.7 in.
    3 in.

PROBLEM SOLVING

23. **GUIDED PROBLEM SOLVING** You make a rectangular cake that is
    9 inches wide, 13 inches long, and 2 inches high. You remove it from
    the pan to frost it. How many square inches of frosting do you need?

    a. Find the area of each of the faces.

    b. Tell which face(s) do not need to be frosted.

    c. Find the surface area of the part of the cake that needs to be frosted.

SEE EXAMPLE 3
on p. 546
for Exs. 24–26

24. ★ **SHORT RESPONSE** You are creating a rectangular
    paper lantern that is 28 centimeters by 15 centimeters
    by 12 centimeters. The paper you plan to use comes in
    sheets that have an area of 9 square centimeters and
    costs $0.08 a sheet. You buy just enough paper to cover
    the sides of the lantern. How much do you spend?

25. **CARPENTRY** You want to paint a rectangular toolbox
    that is 20 inches by 10 inches by 8 inches. A tube of paint
    covers 300 square inches. How many tubes of paint
    should you buy? *Explain* your answer.

26. ★ **SHORT RESPONSE** A marketing company commissions the design
    of a parade float. The base of the float is to be 14 feet long, 4 feet wide,
    and 2 feet tall. Violet flowers will be used to cover the sides of the base
    so that 42 flowers cover 1 square foot of the float. How many dozen
    flowers will the designer need? *Explain* your answer.

27. ★ **WRITING** *Explain* how the surface area of a rectangular prism
    changes when its length, width, and height are doubled.

548   ★ = **STANDARDIZED TEST PRACTICE**   ◯ = **HINTS AND HOMEWORK HELP** *at classzone.com*

28. ★ **OPEN-ENDED MATH** Can the net shown be folded to form a closed rectangular prism? If not, redraw the net so that it can be folded to form a closed rectangular prism.

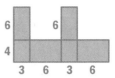

29. 🆇 **ALGEBRA** Draw a cube with side length x and make a net for the figure. Write a formula for the surface area S of the cube in terms of its side length.

30. ★ **MULTIPLE CHOICE** Which figure could represent the solid whose top, side, and front views are shown?

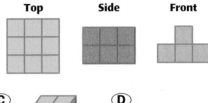

31. **SPATIAL REASONING** Draw the front, side, and top view for each incorrect answer choice in Exercise 30. Which of these figures has a different surface area from the other two? *Explain.*

32. **CHALLENGE** You need to cover the outside of a 1 foot by 1 foot by 1 foot box with paper. The paper comes in 8 inch by 11 inch sheets. How many sheets of paper will you need to cover the box without any overlapping? *Explain* your reasoning.

MIXED REVIEW

Get-Ready

Prepare for
Lesson 10.7
in Exs. 33–40

Solve the equation using mental math. *(p. 34)*

33. $15x = 45$
34. $60x = 180$
35. $25x = 250$
36. $120x = 600$

37. $8x = 246$
38. $12x = 72$
39. $105x = 840$
40. $63x = 441$

41. Find the least common multiple of 4 and 6. *(p. 250)*

Classify the solid. *(p. 541)*

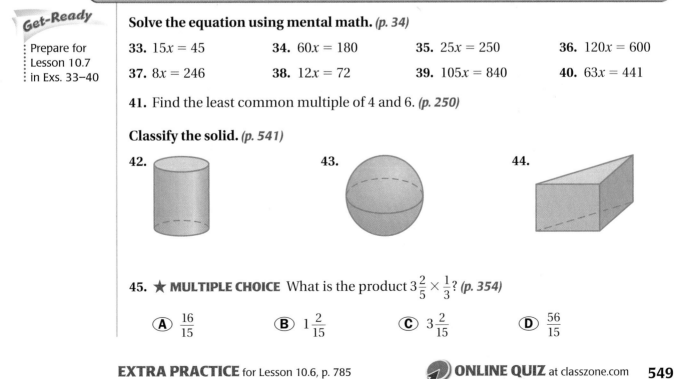

42. **43.** **44.**

45. ★ **MULTIPLE CHOICE** What is the product $3\frac{2}{5} \times \frac{1}{3}$? *(p. 354)*

Ⓐ $\frac{16}{15}$ Ⓑ $1\frac{2}{15}$ Ⓒ $3\frac{2}{15}$ Ⓓ $\frac{56}{15}$

10.7 Volume of a Prism

Before You found the surface area of a rectangular prism.

Now You'll find the volume of a rectangular prism.

Why? So you can find the volume of a solid, as in Ex. 27.

KEY VOCABULARY
• volume, *p. 550*

Notepads A manufacturer stacks cube-shaped notepads and wraps them in plastic as shown in Example 1. The manufacturer then puts them into a rectangular box for shipping. How many notepads will fit into each box?

❖ **EXAMPLE 1** Counting Cubes in a Stack

To find the total number of notepads that will fit in one box, multiply the number of notepads in one layer by the number of layers. The notepads are stacked in 2 layers. Each layer is a rectangle that is 4 notepads long and 3 notepads wide.

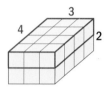

Notepads in one layer × Number of layers = **Number of notepads**

$$4 \times 3 \times 2 = 24$$

▶ **Answer** The manufacturer can fit 24 notepads in one box.

Check You can count the number of notepads in the *front* layer, then multiply that number by the number of layers going front to back.

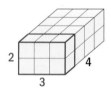

Notepads in front layer × Number of layers = **Number of notepads**

$$3 \times 2 \times 4 = 24$$

Volume The **volume** of a solid is the amount of space the solid occupies. Volume is measured in cubic units. One way to find the volume of a rectangular prism is to use the formula below.

KEY CONCEPT *For Your Notebook*

Volume of a Rectangular Prism

Words Volume = **length** · **width** · **height**

Algebra $V = lwh$

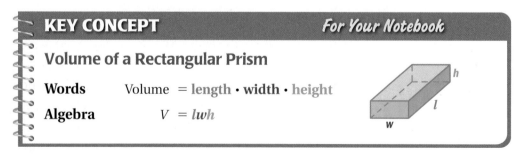

EXAMPLE 2 Finding the Volume of a Prism

Find the volume of the rectangular prism.

$V = lwh$ Write the volume formula.

$\quad = 8(6.2)(3.9)$ Substitute for *l*, *w*, and *h*.

$\quad = 193.44$ Simplify.

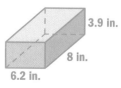

3.9 in.

8 in.

6.2 in.

▶ **Answer** The volume is 193.44 cubic inches.

Check You can check your answer by rounding the decimals, and then multiplying.

$\quad 8 \cdot 6 \cdot 4 = 192$ The answer is reasonable.   **Animated Math** at classzone.com

---

✓ **GUIDED PRACTICE**   for Examples 1 and 2

1. **What If?** In Example 1, suppose a box can hold one more horizontal layer of notepads. How many notepads would fit in a box?

Find the volume of the rectangular prism with the given dimensions.

2. 5 m by 2 m by 4 m

3. 12.5 ft by 6 ft by 6 ft

EXAMPLE 3 Using the Formula for Volume

 Aquariums A pool at an aquarium is a rectangular prism that is 30 meters wide and 12 meters deep. Its volume is 21,600 cubic meters. How long is the pool?

SOLUTION

$V = lwh$ Write the volume formula.

$21{,}600 = l \cdot 30 \cdot 12$ Substitute for *V*, *w*, and *h*.

$21{,}600 = l \cdot 360$ Simplify.

$l = 21{,}600 \div 360$ Write a related division equation.

$l = 60$ Simplify.

▶ **Answer** The length of the pool is 60 meters.

✓ **GUIDED PRACTICE**   for Example 3

In Exercises 4 and 5, the solids are rectangular prisms.

4. The volume of a swimming pool is 3750 cubic meters. The pool is 25 meters wide and 3 meters deep. How long is the pool?

5. The volume of a bathtub is 16 cubic feet. The bathtub is 4 feet long and 2 feet wide. How deep is the bathtub?

10.7 EXERCISES

SKILL PRACTICE

1. **VOCABULARY** Copy and complete: When you find the product of the length, width, and height of a rectangular prism, you are finding its __?__.

2. **VOCABULARY** What units do you use to measure volume?

FINDING VOLUME Find the volume of the rectangular prism with the given dimensions. Use estimation to check.

SEE EXAMPLES 1 AND 2
on pp. 550–551
for Exs. 3–10

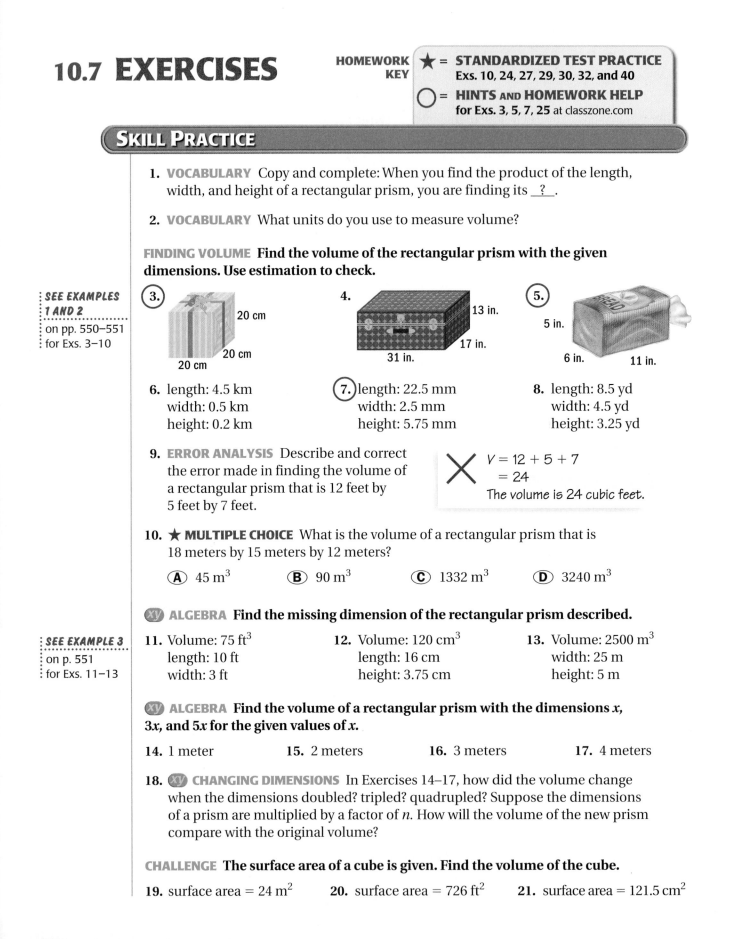

3. 20 cm, 20 cm, 20 cm

4. 13 in., 17 in., 31 in.

5. BREAD 5 in., 6 in., 11 in.

6. length: 4.5 km
   width: 0.5 km
   height: 0.2 km

7. length: 22.5 mm
   width: 2.5 mm
   height: 5.75 mm

8. length: 8.5 yd
   width: 4.5 yd
   height: 3.25 yd

9. **ERROR ANALYSIS** Describe and correct the error made in finding the volume of a rectangular prism that is 12 feet by 5 feet by 7 feet.

$$V = 12 + 5 + 7$$
$$= 24$$
The volume is 24 cubic feet.

10. ★ **MULTIPLE CHOICE** What is the volume of a rectangular prism that is 18 meters by 15 meters by 12 meters?

   Ⓐ 45 m^3 Ⓑ 90 m^3 Ⓒ 1332 m^3 Ⓓ 3240 m^3

SEE EXAMPLE 3
on p. 551
for Exs. 11–13

XY ALGEBRA Find the missing dimension of the rectangular prism described.

11. Volume: 75 ft^3
    length: 10 ft
    width: 3 ft

12. Volume: 120 cm^3
    length: 16 cm
    height: 3.75 cm

13. Volume: 2500 m^3
    width: 25 m
    height: 5 m

XY ALGEBRA Find the volume of a rectangular prism with the dimensions x, $3x$, and $5x$ for the given values of x.

14. 1 meter   15. 2 meters   16. 3 meters   17. 4 meters

18. **XY CHANGING DIMENSIONS** In Exercises 14–17, how did the volume change when the dimensions doubled? tripled? quadrupled? Suppose the dimensions of a prism are multiplied by a factor of n. How will the volume of the new prism compare with the original volume?

CHALLENGE The surface area of a cube is given. Find the volume of the cube.

19. surface area = 24 m^2 20. surface area = 726 ft^2 21. surface area = 121.5 cm^2

**SEE EXAMPLES
1 AND 2**
on pp. 550–551
for Exs. 22–23

22. VOLUME A planter in the shape of a rectangular prism is 24 inches by 4 inches by 5 inches. How much dirt is needed to fill the planter?

23. GUIDED PROBLEM SOLVING Use the pasta box shown to find the volume of the part of the pasta box that is *not* filled with pasta.

  a. Find the volume of the pasta box shown.

  b. Find the volume of the pasta in the box.

  c. Subtract the volume of the pasta from the volume of the pasta box.

SEE EXAMPLE 3
on p. 551
for Ex. 24

24. ★ MULTIPLE CHOICE The volume of a fish tank is 864 cubic inches. The fish tank is a rectangular prism. Its length is 12 inches, and its height is 9 inches. What is the width of the fish tank?

  A 4 inches   **B** 8 inches   **C** 648 inches   **D** 843 inches

25. ALGEBRA A rectangular prism has a length of 3 feet and a width of 5 feet. The table at the right gives the volume of the prism for several heights. Write an expression for the volume of the prism when the height is *h* feet.

Height (ft)	Volume (ft³)
1	15
2	30
3	45
h	?

26. MEASUREMENT Measure the length, width, and the height of a box of cereal. Tell which unit and tool you used. Then find the volume of the box of cereal. Would you use the same unit and tool to measure the volume of a pool? *Explain.*

27. ★ SHORT RESPONSE An ice sculptor begins a sculpture with one 300 pound frozen rectangular prism of ice 40 inches high by 20 inches wide by 10 inches long. The ice sculptor uses a chain saw to carve away 42% of the block of ice. What is the volume of the remaining ice? *Explain.*

28. MULTI-STEP PROBLEM The manager of a gymnastics center wants to buy foam cubes for a landing pit that is a rectangular prism 120 inches long by 96 inches wide by 72 inches deep.

  a. Calculate Find the volume of the landing pit. Estimate to check.

  b. Estimate A company recommends buying only enough cubes to fill 70% of the landing pit. What volume is 70% of the landing pit?

  c. Interpret and Apply Each foam cube has a side length of 6 inches. About how many foam cubes should the center buy? *Explain.*

29. ★ **MULTIPLE CHOICE** Which value is a reasonable estimate for the volume of a kitchen sink?

   (A) 40 in.³   **(B)** 400 in.³   **(C)** 4000 in.³   **(D)** 40,000 in.³

30. ★ **WRITING** *Explain* why the formula $V = s^3$ can be used to find the volume of a cube with a side length of *s*.

31. **REASONING** You find the volume of a rectangular prism using the formula $V = lwh$. Your friend finds the volume of the same prism by multiplying the area of the base by the height. Are the methods the same or are they different? *Explain* your reasoning.

32. ★ **EXTENDED RESPONSE** A movie theater sells three sizes of popcorn. Find the volume of each popcorn container. About how many times greater is the volume of the large container than the volume of the small container? the medium container? Which container gives you the most popcorn for your money? *Explain* your reasoning.

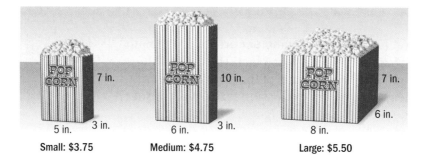

Small: $3.75   Medium: $4.75   Large: $5.50

33. **CHALLENGE** The volume of a rectangular prism is 375 cubic centimeters. Find all the possible whole number lengths, widths, and heights the prism can have. *Explain* the method you used to find your answer.

34. **CHALLENGE** The sum of the length, width, and height of a rectangular prism is 18 meters. What whole number dimensions produce the greatest volume? *Explain* how you found your answer.

MIXED REVIEW

Get-Ready

Prepare for
Lesson 11.1
in Exs. 35–38

Copy and complete the statement with <, >, or =. *(p. 254)*

35. $\frac{7}{10}$? $\frac{3}{10}$ **36.** $\frac{1}{8}$? $\frac{7}{8}$ **37.** $\frac{5}{12}$? $\frac{4}{9}$ **38.** $\frac{2}{3}$? $\frac{10}{15}$

39. **RACING** Your time in a road race is 40 minutes and 32 seconds. Your friend finishes 3 minutes and 43 seconds later. What is your friend's time? *(p. 322)*

40. ★ **SHORT RESPONSE** You are wrapping two gifts. One gift is a rectangular prism that is 22 inches by 4 inches by 15 inches. The other gift is a rectangular prism that is 14 inches by 14 inches by 8 inches. You have 2500 square inches of wrapping paper. Do you have enough to wrap both gifts? *Explain* your reasoning. *(p. 545)*

Classify the solid. *(p. 541)*

1.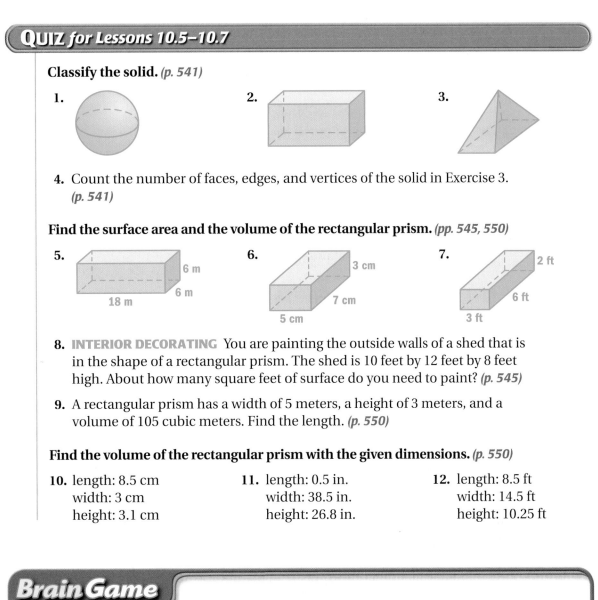

2.

3.

4. Count the number of faces, edges, and vertices of the solid in Exercise 3. *(p. 541)*

Find the surface area and the volume of the rectangular prism. *(pp. 545, 550)*

5. 6 m
6 m
18 m

6. 3 cm
7 cm
5 cm

7. 2 ft
6 ft
3 ft

8. **INTERIOR DECORATING** You are painting the outside walls of a shed that is in the shape of a rectangular prism. The shed is 10 feet by 12 feet by 8 feet high. About how many square feet of surface do you need to paint? *(p. 545)*

9. A rectangular prism has a width of 5 meters, a height of 3 meters, and a volume of 105 cubic meters. Find the length. *(p. 550)*

Find the volume of the rectangular prism with the given dimensions. *(p. 550)*

10. length: 8.5 cm
    width: 3 cm
    height: 3.1 cm

11. length: 0.5 in.
    width: 38.5 in.
    height: 26.8 in.

12. length: 8.5 ft
    width: 14.5 ft
    height: 10.25 ft

Brain Game

Counting Blocks

Two views of a tower of blocks are shown. Each block is a cube that measures 1 inch by 1 inch by 1 inch. Find the volume of the tower. Then find the area of the outer surface, including the base.

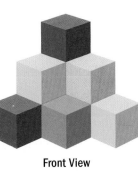

Front View

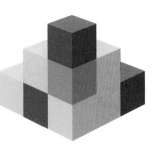

Back View

Extension: Mass, Weight, and Capacity

KEY VOCABULARY

• **mass,** *p. 203*
• **capacity,** *p. 204*
• **metric units,** *pp. 203, 204*
• **customary units,** *pp. 373, 374*

Metric Measuring Metric units of mass include grams (g), milligrams (mg), and kilograms (kg). Metric units of capacity include liters (L), milliliters (mL), and kiloliters (kL).

EXAMPLE 1 Measuring Mass in Metric Units

Use the spring balance to find the mass of the meteorite.

Recall that 1 kilogram equals 1000 grams. Each 1000 grams on the scale is divided into 10 equal parts, so each mark represents $\frac{1000}{10}$, or 100 grams. The pointer on the scale is at the sixth mark.

$$\text{Mass} = 6(100)$$
$$= 600$$

▶ **Answer** The mass of the meteorite is 600 grams.

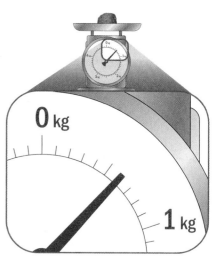

EXAMPLE 2 Measuring Capacity in Metric Units

Find the amount of liquid in the measuring cup.

Each 100 milliliters on the measuring cup is divided into 4 intervals, so each interval represents $\frac{100}{4}$, or 25 milliliters. The liquid is 3 intervals past 200 milliliters.

$$\text{Capacity} = 200 + 3(25)$$
$$= 275$$

▶ **Answer** There are 275 milliliters of liquid in the measuring cup.

Customary Measuring Customary units of weight include ounces (oz), pounds (lb), and tons (T). Customary units of capacity include fluid ounces (fl oz), cups (c), pints (pt), quarts (qt), and gallons (gal).

EXAMPLE 3   Measuring Weight in Customary Units

CHOOSING TOOLS

You can use a kitchen scale to measure weights in ounces or in small numbers of pounds. Bathroom scales can be used to measure weights up to about 250 lb. Truck scales measure weights in the tons.

Use the spring balance to find the weight of the watermelon.

Each pound on the scale is divided into 16 equal parts, so each mark represents $\frac{1}{16}$ pound. The pointer on the scale is 8 marks past 7 lb.

▶ **Answer** The weight of the watermelon is $7\frac{8}{16}$ lb, or $7\frac{1}{2}$ pounds.

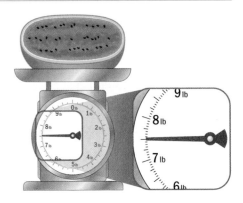

EXAMPLE 4   Measuring Customary Capacity

Find the amount of liquid in the measuring cup.

Each cup on the measuring cup is divided into 4 intervals, so each interval represents $\frac{1}{4}$ cup. The liquid is 3 intervals past 1 cup.

▶ **Answer** The amount of liquid is $1\frac{3}{4}$ cup.

EXERCISES

1. Find the mass of the oranges.

2. Find the amount of liquid in the measuring cup.

3. Estimate the total weight in pounds of the books you carried home from school today. Then find the actual weight. Tell what tool and unit you used. Then compare your estimate to the actual weight.

4. Use a bathroom scale to measure your weight. How does your weight in pounds compare to your weight in kilograms? (There are about 2.2 pounds in 1 kilogram.) About how much do you weigh in kilograms?

5. Would you use a *kitchen scale*, a *bathroom scale*, or a *truck scale* to measure the weight of an elephant? of a letter? of a suitcase? *Explain* your reasoning.

MIXED REVIEW *of Problem Solving*

STATE TEST PRACTICE
classzone.com

Lessons 10.5–10.7

1. **EXTENDED RESPONSE** A 600 pound fire safe is shaped like a rectangular prism. Its volume is 45,000 cubic inches.

   a. The safe is 30 inches wide by 25 inches long. What is the height of the safe?

   b. What is the surface area of the safe in square inches? *Explain* how you found your answer.

   c. *Explain* how to find the surface area of the safe in square feet.

2. **SHORT RESPONSE** You fold the shape on the dashed lines until the edges of the triangles touch. What solid does the net form? *Explain.* How many faces, edges, and vertices does the solid have?

3. **EXTENDED RESPONSE** A restaurant has an aquarium with an unusual shape. The tank's bottom and top each are parallel regular hexagons. Six heavy panes of unbreakable glass, each perpendicular to both hexagons, make up the sides.

   a. What kind of solid is the aquarium?

   b. How many faces, edges, and vertices does the aquarium have?

   c. The aquarium is $5\frac{1}{2}$ feet tall, and the longest diagonal of one of the hexagons measures 18 inches. Will the aquarium fit inside a rectangular prism $5\frac{1}{2}$ feet tall that has an 18 inch by 18 inch base? *Justify* your answer.

4. **OPEN-ENDED** Measure the length, width, and thickness of a book. Find its volume. What is the volume of a book that is twice as thick as the book you measured?

5. **MULTI-STEP PROBLEM** The scale model of a new office building is shown below. It uses a scale of 2 in. : 5 ft.

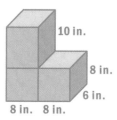

   10 in.

   8 in.

   6 in.

   8 in.   8 in.

   a. Find the volume of the model.

   b. The company wants to shorten the taller tower, reducing the volume of the model to 1152 cubic inches. How much height needs to be removed from the taller tower?

   c. By how much will this reduce the volume of the actual building?

6. **GRIDDED ANSWER** The dimensions of a storage shed, not including the rafters, are 14 feet by 9 feet by $6\frac{1}{3}$ feet. What is the volume of the storage shed in cubic feet? Round your answer to the nearest cubic foot.

7. **OPEN-ENDED** Describe a real life situation in which you would need to find the volume of a prism.

10 CHAPTER REVIEW

REVIEW KEY VOCABULARY

- base of a parallelogram, *p. 514*
- height of a parallelogram, *p. 514*
- perpendicular, *p. 514*
- base of a triangle, *p. 518*
- height of a triangle, *p. 518*
- circle, *p. 525*
- center, *p. 525*

- radius, *p. 525*
- diameter, *p. 525*
- circumference, *p. 525*
- pi (π), *p. 525*
- solid, *p. 541*
- prism, *p. 541*
- cylinder, *p. 541*

- pyramid, *p. 541*
- cone, *p. 541*
- sphere, *p. 541*
- face, edge, vertex, *p. 542*
- surface area, *p. 545*
- volume, *p. 550*

VOCABULARY EXERCISES

Tell whether the statement is *true* or *false*. Justify your reasoning.

1. The circumference of a circle is measured in square units.

2. The surface area of a prism is measured in square units.

3. The distance from the center of a circle to any point on the circle is called the diameter.

Copy and complete the statement.

4. Two intersecting lines that meet at a right angle are __?__.

5. The base of a cone is a(n) __?__.

6. The __?__ of a prism is the sum of the areas of its faces.

7. The __?__ of a prism is the amount of space that it occupies.

REVIEW EXAMPLES AND EXERCISES

10.1 Area of a Parallelogram

pp. 514–517

EXAMPLE

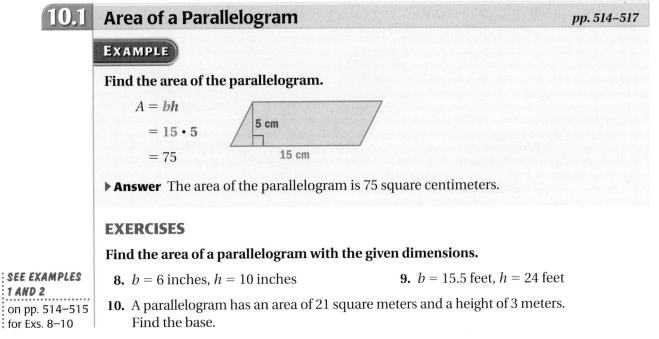

Find the area of the parallelogram.

$A = bh$

$= 15 \cdot 5$

$= 75$

▶ **Answer** The area of the parallelogram is 75 square centimeters.

EXERCISES

Find the area of a parallelogram with the given dimensions.

SEE EXAMPLES 1 AND 2
on pp. 514–515
for Exs. 8–10

8. $b = 6$ inches, $h = 10$ inches

9. $b = 15.5$ feet, $h = 24$ feet

10. A parallelogram has an area of 21 square meters and a height of 3 meters. Find the base.

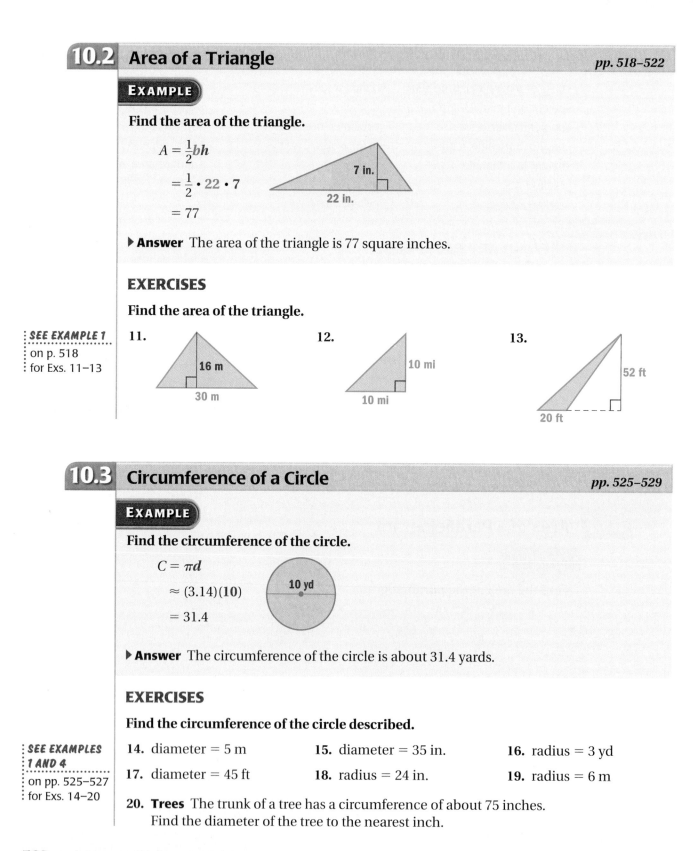

10.2 Area of a Triangle

pp. 518–522

EXAMPLE

Find the area of the triangle.

$A = \frac{1}{2}bh$

$= \frac{1}{2} \cdot 22 \cdot 7$

$= 77$

7 in.

22 in.

▶ **Answer** The area of the triangle is 77 square inches.

EXERCISES

Find the area of the triangle.

SEE EXAMPLE 1
on p. 518
for Exs. 11–13

11.

16 m

30 m

12.

10 mi

10 mi

13.

52 ft

20 ft

10.3 Circumference of a Circle

pp. 525–529

EXAMPLE

Find the circumference of the circle.

$C = \pi d$

$\approx (3.14)(10)$

$= 31.4$

10 yd

▶ **Answer** The circumference of the circle is about 31.4 yards.

EXERCISES

Find the circumference of the circle described.

**SEE EXAMPLES
1 AND 4**
on pp. 525–527
for Exs. 14–20

14. diameter = 5 m

15. diameter = 35 in.

16. radius = 3 yd

17. diameter = 45 ft

18. radius = 24 in.

19. radius = 6 m

20. Trees The trunk of a tree has a circumference of about 75 inches. Find the diameter of the tree to the nearest inch.

10.4 Area of a Circle

pp. 531–537

EXAMPLE

Find the area of the circle.

$A = \pi r^2$

$\approx (3.14)(4)^2$

$= 50.24$

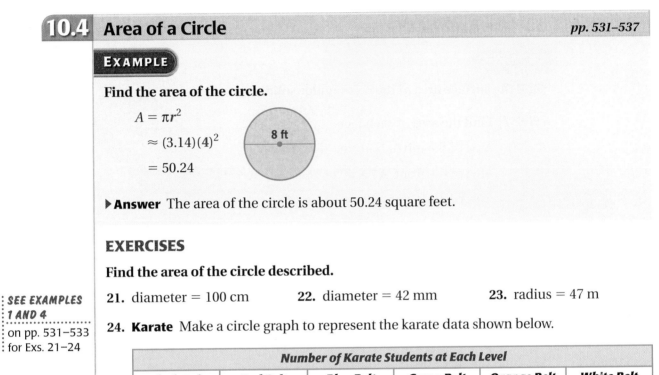

8 ft

▶ **Answer** The area of the circle is about 50.24 square feet.

EXERCISES

Find the area of the circle described.

SEE EXAMPLES 1 AND 4
on pp. 531–533
for Exs. 21–24

21. diameter = 100 cm **22.** diameter = 42 mm **23.** radius = 47 m

24. Karate Make a circle graph to represent the karate data shown below.

Number of Karate Students at Each Level					
Black Belt	*Red Belt*	*Blue Belt*	*Green Belt*	*Orange Belt*	*White Belt*
3	5	13	20	12	7

10.5 Solid Figures

pp. 541–544

EXAMPLE

Classify the solid. Then count the number of faces, edges, and vertices.

▶ **Answer** The solid is a pentagonal prism because it has 2 parallel pentagonal bases. It has 7 faces, 15 edges, and 10 vertices.

EXERCISES

SEE EXAMPLES 1 AND 2
on pp. 541–542
for Ex. 25

25. Classify the solid. Then count the number of faces, edges, and vertices.

10.6 Surface Area of a Prism

pp. 545–549

EXAMPLE

Find the surface area of the rectangular solid.

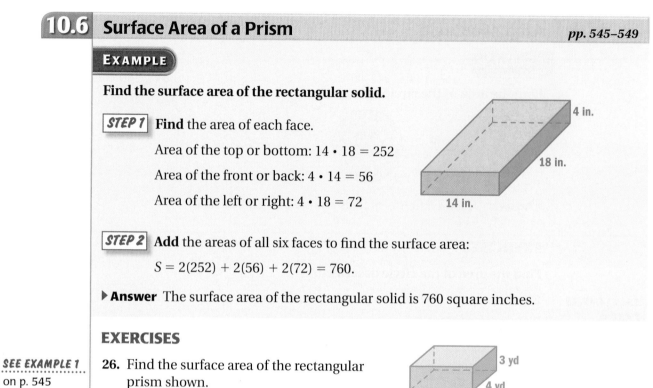

STEP 1 **Find** the area of each face.

Area of the top or bottom: $14 \cdot 18 = 252$

Area of the front or back: $4 \cdot 14 = 56$

Area of the left or right: $4 \cdot 18 = 72$

STEP 2 **Add** the areas of all six faces to find the surface area:

$S = 2(252) + 2(56) + 2(72) = 760.$

▶ **Answer** The surface area of the rectangular solid is 760 square inches.

EXERCISES

SEE EXAMPLE 1
on p. 545
for Ex. 26

26. Find the surface area of the rectangular prism shown.

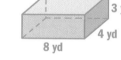

10.7 Volume of a Prism

pp. 550–554

EXAMPLE

Find the volume of the rectangular solid.

$V = lwh$

$= 5 \cdot 8 \cdot 10$

$= 400$

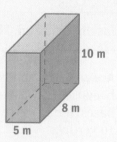

▶ **Answer** The volume of the rectangular prism is 400 cubic meters.

EXERCISES

**SEE EXAMPLES
1, 2, AND 3**
on pp. 550–551
for Exs. 27–28

27. A rectangular prism has a length of 7 meters, a width of 5 meters, and a height of 3 meters. Find the volume of the prism.

28. **Juice Boxes** A juice box is a rectangular prism with a volume of 8.75 cubic inches. The juice box is 2.5 inches wide and 1 inch deep. How tall is the juice box?

1. The base of a parallelogram is 6 inches and the height is 4 inches. Find the area of the parallelogram.

2. The base of a triangle is 10 centimeters and the height is 18 centimeters. Find the area of the triangle.

3. A parallelogram has an area of 60 square feet and a height of 5 feet. Find the base.

Find the area of the figure.

4.
5 m

5.
4 in.
10 in.   3 in.

6.
20 mm
35 mm

7. Classify the solid shown at the right.

8. Draw a triangular prism.

Find the surface area and the volume of the rectangular prism.

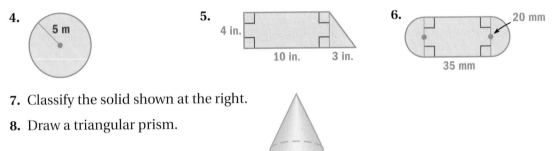

9.
5 in.
30 in.   5 in.

10.
8 ft
6 ft
6 ft

11.
22 cm
30 cm   18 cm

12. Count the faces, edges, and vertices of the solid in Exercise 11.

13. **CRATERS** Tycho is a circular crater located on the moon. Tycho has a radius of about 43.5 kilometers. Find the circumference of Tycho to the nearest kilometer.

14. **PAINTING** You are painting a rectangular box that is 5 feet by 4 feet by 2 feet. The paint can says that the paint will cover 100 square feet. Do you have enough paint to cover the entire box? *Explain.*

15. **TISSUE BOX** A tissue box measures 9 inches by 5 inches by 3 inches. Find the volume of the tissue box.

16. **PLANT SALE** The number of plants sold at a plant sale is shown. Make a circle graph to represent the data.

Types of Plants Sold	
Type of plant	**Plants sold**
Potted palm	70
Geranium	30
African violet	50

EXTENDED RESPONSE QUESTIONS

Scoring Rubric

Full Credit
• solution is complete and correct

Partial Credit
• solution is complete but errors are made, *or*
• solution is without error, but incomplete

No Credit
• no solution is given, *or*
• solution makes no sense

PROBLEM

WOODWORKING You are building a wooden storage chest using the dimensions shown. How many square feet of wood do you need? The wood you are using costs $1.80 per square foot. You have $50. Do you have enough money to make the storage chest? *Justify* your answer.

1.5 ft

3 ft   2 ft

Below are sample solutions to the problem. Read each solution and the comments in blue to see why the sample represents full credit, partial credit, or no credit.

SAMPLE 1: Full Credit Solution

The steps of the solution are clearly written and reflect correct mathematical reasoning.

You must construct the top, the bottom, and the sides of the chest. So, you must find the surface area to find out how much wood you need.

$$S = (3 \times 2) + (3 \times 2) + (3 \times 1.5) + (3 \times 1.5) + (1.5 \times 2) + (1.5 \times 2)$$

$$= 6 + 6 + 4.5 + 4.5 + 3 + 3$$

The calculations are correct.

$$= 27 \qquad \text{You need 27 square feet of wood.}$$

You know that the wood costs $1.80 per square foot. To find the total cost of the wood, multiply the surface area by the cost per square foot.

Each question is correctly answered.

$$\text{Total cost} = 27 \times 1.8 = 48.6$$

The wood will cost $48.60, so $50 is enough money.

SAMPLE 2: Partial Credit Solution

The mathematical reasoning is correct, but the surface area is calculated incorrectly.

You must find the surface area to find out how much wood you need.

$$S = 6 + 4.5 + 3$$

$$= 13.5 \qquad \text{The surface area is 13.5 square feet.}$$

To find the total cost of the wood, multiply the surface area by $1.80.

The answers are incorrect.

$$\text{Total cost} = 13.5 \times 1.8 = 24.3$$

The wood will cost $24.30. You do have enough money.

SAMPLE 3: Partial Credit Solution

> The solution is correct but incomplete and not clearly explained.

Surface area = 6 + 6 + 4.5 + 4.5 + 3 + 3 = 27 square feet

Total cost = 27 × 1.8 = 48.60

SAMPLE 4: No Credit Solution

> The solution does not reflect correct mathematical reasoning. The answers are not clearly stated, and they are incorrect.

Volume: 3 × 2 × 1.5 = 9

Total cost: 9 ÷ 1.8 = 5

PRACTICE Apply the Scoring Rubric

Score each solution to the problem on the previous page as *full credit*, *partial credit*, or *no credit*. Explain your reasoning. If you choose *partial credit* or *no credit*, explain how to change the solution so that it earns a score of full credit.

1. Surface area: 6 + 6 + 4.5 + 4.5 + 3 + 3 = 27

    To find the total cost of the wood, multiply the surface area by the cost per square foot.

    $$27 \times \frac{\$1.8}{ft^2} = \$48.60, \text{ which is less than } \$50$$

2. The top, the bottom, and the sides of the storage chest are being made out of wood. So find the surface area to find out how much wood you need.

    Area of the top or bottom: 3 × 2 = 6

    Area of each of the four sides: 3 × 1.5 = 4.5

    Find the sum of the areas of all six sides of the storage chest.

    $$S = (6 \times 2) + (4.5 \times 4)$$
    $$= 12 + 18$$
    $$= 30 \qquad \text{You need 30 square feet of wood.}$$

    To find the total cost of the wood, multiply the surface area by the cost per square foot.

    $$\text{Total cost} = 30 \times 1.8$$
    $$= 54$$

    The wood will cost $54 so there is not enough money.

EXTENDED RESPONSE

1. Create a new parallelogram by multiplying the sides and height of the parallelogram shown by 3. Keep the angle measures the same. Is the new parallelogram similar to the old one? Is it congruent to the old one? *Explain* why or why not. Then find the perimeters and the areas of the old and new parallelograms. Is the ratio of the areas the same as the ratio of the perimeters? *Explain*.

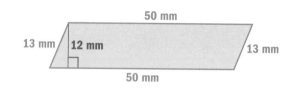

2. Use a ruler to sketch the three triangles described below.

   Triangle 1: same height as the triangle at the right, but double its base

   Triangle 2: same base as the triangle at the right, but double its height

   Triangle 3: double both the base and the height of the triangle at the right

   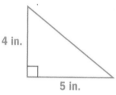

   Find the area of each triangle. What happens to the area of the triangle when you double only its base? when you double only its height? when you double both its base and height? What do you think happens to the area of a triangle when you *triple* both its base and height? *Explain* your reasoning.

3. A popcorn box is shaped like a rectangular prism. It has length 10 cm, width 4.5 cm, and height 16 cm. Sketch the popcorn box. How much cardboard would be needed to make the box, assuming there are no overlaps? How much popcorn would the box hold? *Justify* your answers.

4. A circular rug is shown. How many square feet of floor are covered by this rug? Binding ribbon is sold by the foot. How much binding ribbon is needed to bind off the blue outer edge of the rug? *Explain* how you found your answers.

5. You want to make a cushion shaped like a rectangular prism for your couch. The cushion will be 16 inches by 18 inches by 4 inches.

   a. How much fabric do you need to cover the cushion? Did you use surface area or volume to find your answer? *Explain* your choice.

   b. How much filling do you need to stuff the cushion? Did you use surface area or volume to find your answer? *Explain* your choice.

   c. You buy 1 square yard of fabric. Do you have enough fabric to cover the cushion? *Justify* your answer.

MULTIPLE CHOICE

6. The area of a parallelogram is 110 square inches. The height is 10 inches. What is the length of the base?

(A) 11 in. **(B)** 22 in.

(C) 100 in. **(D)** 110 in.

7. Classify the solid.

(A) cone

(B) sphere

(C) triangular pyramid

(D) triangular prism

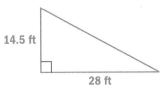

8. Which of the following is *true* about the solid in Exercise 7?

(A) It has 12 faces.

(B) It has 6 edges.

(C) It has 8 vertices.

(D) It has 2 bases.

GRIDDED ANSWER

9. A triangular area has been roped off for a booth at a convention center. The dimensions of the roped off area are shown. How many square feet is the roped off area?

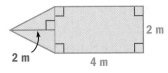

14.5 ft

28 ft

10. What is the total area of the figure below in square meters?

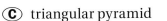

2 m

2 m   4 m

11. A wading pool is 6 feet by 4 feet by 1.5 feet. A container holds 1.8 cubic feet of water. How many containers of water are needed to fill the wading pool?

SHORT RESPONSE

12. A circle has a radius of 6 centimeters. A square has a side length of 12 centimeters. Without doing any calculations, determine whether the circle or the square has the greater perimeter. *Explain* your reasoning.

13. The table shows the number of wins, losses, and ties a soccer team had during one season. Make a circle graph of the data. *Explain* your steps.

Soccer Season		
Wins	**Losses**	**Ties**
12	6	2

14. Deborah's bicycle wheel has a diameter of 26 inches. Deborah rides her bicycle so that the front wheel makes 120 complete rotations. To the nearest ten feet, how many feet has she traveled? *Explain* how you found your answer.

15. A diagram of a set of concrete steps is shown at the right. Each cube in the diagram represents a volume of $\frac{1}{8}$ cubic foot. What volume of concrete is needed for the set of steps? *Justify* your answer.

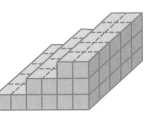

10 CUMULATIVE REVIEW Lessons 1–10

Find the value of the power. *(p. 15)*

1. 7^3 2. 12 squared 3. 8 cubed 4. 6^4

Find the mean, median, mode(s), and range of the data. *(p. 99)*

5. 1, 8, 5, 3, 7, 5, 4, 2, 9, 7 6. 25, 30, 20, 15, 45, 100, 50, 30

Find the sum, difference, product, or quotient.

7. $22.6 - 13.9$ *(p. 148)* 8. $24.1 + 5.6$ *(p. 148)* 9. 9×2.3 *(p. 169)*

10. 6.8×5.2 *(p. 181)* 11. $0.108 \div 0.001$ *(p. 198)* 12. $11.83 \div 9.1$ *(p. 198)*

13. $\frac{10}{11} + \frac{11}{12}$ *(p. 302)* 14. $9\frac{1}{3} - 2\frac{4}{9}$ *(p. 316)* 15. $\frac{5}{6} \times \frac{8}{9}$ *(p. 348)*

16. $3\frac{1}{5} \times \frac{3}{8}$ *(p. 354)* 17. $6\frac{7}{10} \div 4$ *(p. 367)* 18. $8\frac{3}{4} \div 3\frac{1}{2}$ *(p. 367)*

Solve the proportion. *(p. 412)*

19. $\frac{x}{8} = \frac{21}{24}$ 20. $\frac{45}{85} = \frac{9}{n}$ 21. $\frac{r}{10} = \frac{14}{8}$ 22. $\frac{14}{j} = \frac{2.4}{15}$

In Exercises 23–26, write the decimal or fraction as a percent. *(p. 429)*

23. 0.38 24. 0.06 25. $\frac{27}{100}$ 26. $\frac{7}{20}$

27. Find 75% of 80. *(p. 434)* 28. Find 16% of 150. *(p. 434)*

In Exercises 29 and 30, use the diagram at the right. *(p. 465)*

29. Are $\angle 1$ and $\angle 2$ vertical angles? *Explain.*

30. Find the measures of $\angle 1$, $\angle 2$, and $\angle 3$.

1
28°
2
3

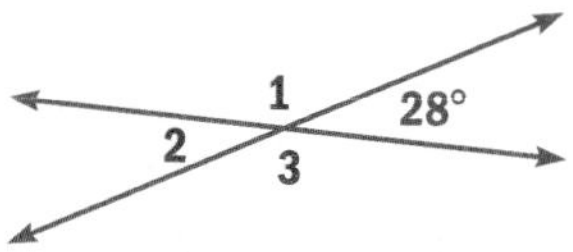

Find the area of each of the figures below.

31.

8 in.
6 in.

(p. 514)

32.

15 cm
9 cm
12 cm

(p. 518)

33.

10 yd

(p. 531)

34. Find the circumference of the circle in Exercise 33. *(p. 525)*

35. Classify the solid at the right. Then count the number of faces, edges, and vertices. *(p. 541)*

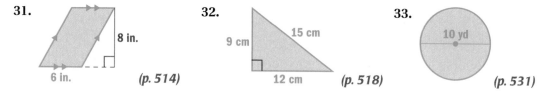

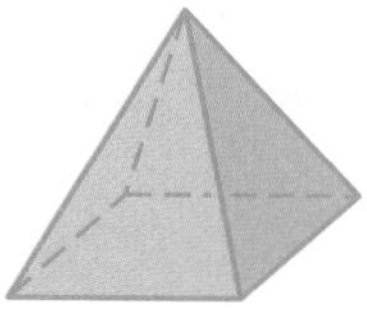

36. **RUNNING** The table shows the distance a runner traveled after various lengths of time. Make a line graph of the data given in the table. Use it to estimate how far the runner traveled in 25 seconds. *(p. 88)*

Time (seconds)	0	10	20	30	40
Distance (meters)	0	60	130	200	260

37. **CATS** The normal body temperature for a cat is between 100°F and 102.5°F. Is a temperature of 102.45°F normal? *Explain. (p. 130)*

38. **GEOMETRY** Use the diagram shown at the right. What fraction of the large rectangle's area is shaded red? *(p. 243)*

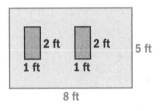

39. **HIKING** You went on a hike with a group of friends from 8:15 A.M. to 4:30 P.M. How long were you hiking? *(p. 322)*

SCALE DRAWINGS In Exercises 40 and 41, use the following information. A scale drawing of a room has a scale of 1 in. : 8 ft. In the drawing, the floor of the room is 2.5 inches long and 2 inches wide. *(p. 417)*

40. What are the actual dimensions of the room?

41. What is the ratio of the floor area of the room in the drawing to the floor area of the actual room?

42. **BANKING** A bank account pays 4% annual interest. How much simple interest will $2000 earn in 6 years? *(p. 434)*

FLAGS In Exercises 43–45, use the flag of the Bahamas at the right.

43. Use a centimeter ruler to measure the sides of the black triangle. Then classify it by its sides. *(p. 466)*

44. How many pairs of congruent figures are in the flag? *(p. 490)*

45. How many lines of symmetry does the flag have? *(p. 494)*

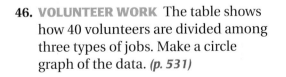

46. **VOLUNTEER WORK** The table shows how 40 volunteers are divided among three types of jobs. Make a circle graph of the data. *(p. 531)*

Spring Fundraiser Volunteers			
Job	tickets	snacks	booths
Number of volunteers	8	6	26

47. **GEOMETRY** A box measures 10 inches by 5 inches by 6 inches. Find the surface area and the volume of the box. *(pp. 545, 550)*

11 Integers

Before

In previous chapters you've ...

• Plotted points
• Studied line symmetry

Now

In Chapter 11 you'll study ...

• 11.1 Comparing integers
• 11.2 Adding integers
• 11.3 Subtracting integers
• 11.4 Multiplying integers
• 11.5 Dividing integers
• 11.6 Translations
• 11.7 Reflections

Why?

So you can solve real-world problems about ...

• scuba divers, p. 576
• Mauna Loa, p. 587
• black bears, p. 595
• photography, p. 608

Animated Math
at classzone.com

• Subtracting Integers, p. 586
• Multiplying Integers, p. 593
• Translations, Reflections, and Rotations, p. 604

Get-Ready Games

Review Prerequisite Skills by playing *Constellation Mapping* and *Unidentified Symmetrical Object*.

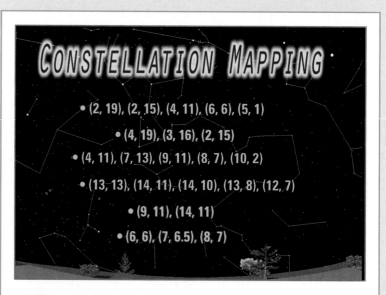

CONSTELLATION MAPPING

• (2, 19), (2, 15), (4, 11), (6, 6), (5, 1)

• (4, 19), (3, 16), (2, 15)

• (4, 11), (7, 13), (9, 11), (8, 7), (10, 2)

• (13, 13), (14, 11), (14, 10), (13, 8), (12, 7)

• (9, 11), (14, 11)

• (6, 6), (7, 6.5), (8, 7)

Skill Focus: Plotting points

Materials: graph paper

Plot each group of points in the same coordinate plane. Then connect the points in each group in the order they are given. The resulting diagram will be a map of a famous constellation.

Skill Focus: Line symmetry

Materials: graph paper

• Some of the data beamed to Earth from a distant spaceship's computer have been lost in transmission. Your goal is to reconstruct a picture sent by the ship.

• The picture sent by the ship has line symmetry. Copy the drawing and the line of symmetry shown above onto graph paper. Then reconstruct the picture.

Stop and Think

1. **EXTENSION** The constellation you plotted on page 570 is Orion. Draw a picture of another star grouping, such as the Big Dipper. Then write directions for graphing the star grouping in a coordinate plane.

2. **WRITING** Describe the procedure you used to reconstruct the *Unidentified Symmetrical Object*.

11

Review Prerequisite Skills

- ordered pair, *p. 88*
- coordinates, *p. 88*
- mean, *p. 99*
- congruent, *p. 490*

VOCABULARY CHECK

1. *Explain* what it means for two figures to be congruent.
2. *Explain* how an ordered pair is related to the coordinates on a graph.
3. *Explain* how to find a mean.

SKILL CHECK

Graph the numbers on a number line. Then order the numbers from least to greatest. *(p. 738)*

4. 4, 3, 7, 8, 6   **5.** 12, 2, 14, 19, 9   **6.** 16, 5, 21, 18, 23

Find the sum, difference, product, or quotient. *(p. 3)*

7. $189 + 12$ **8.** $420 + 297$ **9.** $316 - 29$ **10.** $587 - 219$

11. 16×43 **12.** 45×34 **13.** $140 \div 28$ **14.** $210 \div 15$

Graph and connect the points. Then identify the resulting figure. *(pp. 88, 471, 480)*

15. $A(2, 1)$, $B(3, 4)$, $C(0, 4)$ **16.** $D(6, 2)$, $E(8, 2)$, $F(6, 5)$, $G(8, 5)$

@HomeTutor Prerequisite skills practice at classzone.com

Notetaking Skills   Multiple Representations

In each chapter you will learn a new notetaking skill. In Chapter 11 you will apply the strategy of using multiple representations to Example 1 on p. 579.

You can often record a number in different ways in your notes. In earlier chapters, you saw decimals represented in several ways as shown below.

Expanded form	1 one + 7 tenths + 3 hundredths 1.0 + 0.7 + 0.03
Decimal form	1.73
Word form	one and seventy-three hundredths
Visual form	

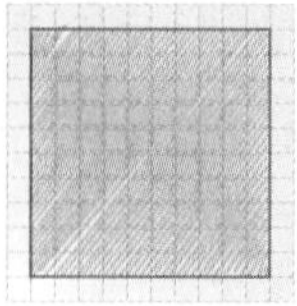

1 one (1 whole) 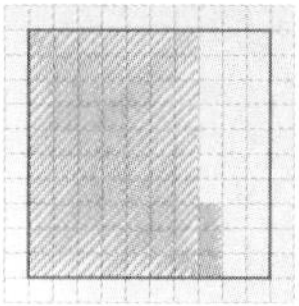   73 hundredths

11.1 Comparing Integers

Before You compared and ordered fractions and decimals.

Now You'll compare and order integers.

Why? So you can represent times in seconds, as in Example 1.

KEY VOCABULARY
- integers, *p. 573*
- negative integers, *p. 573*
- positive integers, *p. 573*
- opposites, *p. 574*

Integers are often used to represent real-world quantities. The following numbers are **integers**.

$$\ldots, -5, -4, -3, -2, -1, 0, 1, 2, 3, 4, 5, \ldots$$

Negative integers are integers that are less than 0.

Positive integers are integers that are greater than 0.

Zero is neither negative nor positive.

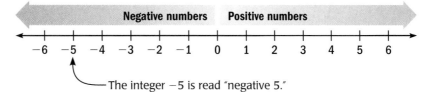

The integer −5 is read "negative 5."

Words like *profit, increase,* and *above* often indicate a positive integer. Words like *loss, decrease,* and *below* indicate a negative integer.

★ EXAMPLE 1 Standardized Test Practice

Space Shuttles During a shuttle launch, the solid rocket boosters separate from the shuttle at "T + 150 seconds" or 150 seconds after liftoff. Other events include the shuttle reaching a height of 1 mile at T + 30 seconds, the shuttle's computers taking over the countdown at T − 31 seconds, and the computers checking that the engines are ready at T − 60 seconds. What integer represents when the shuttle's computers take over the countdown?

(A) −60   **(B)** −31   **(C)** 30   **(D)** 150

ELIMINATE CHOICES
The shuttle's computers take over countdown *before* liftoff, so the answer is negative. Choices C and D can be eliminated.

SOLUTION

The shuttle's computers take over at T − 31 seconds. The correct answer is B.   (A) **B** (C) (D)

✓ GUIDED PRACTICE for Example 1

Write the integer that represents the situation.

1. a $15 profit   **2.** a 9 point decrease   **3.** a loss of 5 yards

Opposites Numbers increase as you move from left to right on a number line. Two numbers are **opposites** if they are the same distance from 0 on a number line but are on opposite sides of 0.

EXAMPLE 2 Identifying Opposites

READING
The integer −3 is read "negative 3" or "the opposite of 3."

Find the opposite of −3.

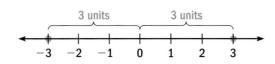

▶ **Answer** The opposite of −3 is 3.

EXAMPLE 3 Comparing Integers

Compare −8 and −5.

▶ **Answer** Because −8 is to the left of −5 on the number line, −8 < −5.

EXAMPLE 4 Ordering Integers

Sports In a golf tournament, the player with the lowest score wins. The table shows the scores of several golfers (including the winner) in a recent Masters Tournament. Who won?

Golfer	Score
Ernie Els	−8
Tiger Woods	2
Sergio Garcia	−3
Retief Goosen	0
Phil Mickelson	−9

SOLUTION

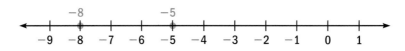

▶ **Answer** Phil Mickelson won with the lowest score of −9.

Animated **Math**
at classzone.com

✓ **GUIDED PRACTICE** for Examples 2, 3, and 4

Find the opposite of the integer.

4. 8　　　　　　**5.** −7　　　　　　**6.** 0　　　　　　**7.** −1

Copy and complete the statement using < or >.

8. −2 _?_ 2　　　　**9.** 0 _?_ −1　　　　**10.** −8 _?_ −9　　　　**11.** −5 _?_ −4

12. What If? Suppose the scores in another golf tournament are −14, 4, −5, 0, and −16. Which score is the lowest?

11.1 EXERCISES

HOMEWORK KEY

★ = **STANDARDIZED TEST PRACTICE**
Exs. 34, 38, 44, 46, 53, and 63

◯ = **HINTS** AND **HOMEWORK HELP**
for Exs. 3, 5, 9, 19, 25, 43 at classzone.com

SKILL PRACTICE

VOCABULARY Copy and complete the statement.

1. Numbers that are the same distance from 0 on a number line but are on opposite sides of 0 are called __?__.

2. Integers that are less than 0 are __?__.

SEE EXAMPLE 1
on p. 573
for Exs. 3–8

USING INTEGERS Write the integer that represents the situation.

3. 6 degrees below 0   **4.** an increase of 20 cm   **5.** 5 people join the Math Club

6. a loss of $3   **7.** 2 feet under water   **8.** a deposit of 35 dollars

SEE EXAMPLE 2
on p. 574
for Exs. 9–13

IDENTIFYING OPPOSITES Find the opposite of the integer.

9. 4   **10.** -8 **11.** -11 **12.** -20 **13.** 13

SEE EXAMPLE 3
on p. 574
for Exs. 14–22

COMPARING INTEGERS Copy and complete the statement using < or >.

14. -3 __?__ 7   **15.** -6 __?__ 0   **16.** 0 __?__ -4

17. 5 __?__ -7 **18.** -9 __?__ 9   **19.** 1 __?__ -5

20. -11 __?__ -12 **21.** -10 __?__ -8 **22.** -15 __?__ -16

SEE EXAMPLE 4
on p. 574
for Exs. 23–32

ORDERING INTEGERS Order the integers from least to greatest.

23. $-2, -5, 6, 10, -8$ **24.** $-9, 0, -2, -3, -5$ **25.** $8, -2, 6, 7, -3$

26. $-1, 4, -4, 9, -6$ **27.** $-8, 0, 5, -1, 1$ **28.** $11, 14, -13, 12, -15$

29. $-67, 40, 2, -4, -24$ **30.** $-98, 45, -32, 91, -61$ **31.** $59, -39, 25, -16, 47$

32. **ERROR ANALYSIS** Describe and correct the error made in ordering the integers from least to greatest.

✗ $-2, -3, -8, -11, -20$

33. **WHICH ONE DOESN'T BELONG?** Which pair of integers doesn't belong? Why?

   A. 5 and -5 **B.** -2 and 1   **C.** -3 and 3   **D.** 12 and -12

34. ★ **MULTIPLE CHOICE** Find the median of $-4, 11, -12, 11,$ and -7.

   A -12 **B** -7 **C** -4 **D** 11

REASONING Tell whether the statement is *always*, *sometimes*, or *never* true. *Explain* your reasoning.

35. Zero is greater than a negative number.

36. A negative number is greater than its opposite.

37. The opposite of a negative number is less than 10.

38. ★ **OPEN-ENDED MATH** Write a list of six integers and order them from greatest to least. Then list the opposites of the integers in order from greatest to least.

39. **CHALLENGE** Two integers are opposites of each other. One integer is 7 units to the right of −5 on a number line. What are the two integers?

ORDERING NEGATIVE FRACTIONS In Exercises 40–42, order the numbers from least to greatest.

EXTENSION Ordering Negative Fractions

To order $-2\frac{1}{3}$, $-3\frac{1}{2}$, and $-3\frac{1}{4}$ from least to greatest, graph the numbers on a number line.

Remember that numbers increase from left to right on a number line. So $-3\frac{1}{2}$ is to the left of $-3\frac{1}{4}$.

▶ **Answer** The numbers from least to greatest are $-3\frac{1}{2}$, $-3\frac{1}{4}$, and $-2\frac{1}{3}$.

---

40. $-1\frac{1}{2}$, $-2\frac{1}{2}$, $-4\frac{1}{3}$

41. $-3\frac{1}{3}$, $-\frac{1}{3}$, $-2\frac{1}{3}$

42. $-\frac{1}{4}$, $-1\frac{1}{5}$, $-\frac{1}{2}$

PROBLEM SOLVING

SEE EXAMPLE 1
on p. 573
for Exs. 43–45

43. **SCUBA DIVERS** A scuba diver is 12 feet below sea level. A second scuba diver is 25 feet below sea level. Write integers to represent the divers' positions relative to sea level. Which diver is farther from sea level?

44. ★ **MULTIPLE CHOICE** A 2 degree decrease in temperature is represented by which of the following?

A −20 **B** −2 **C** 2 **D** 20

45. **IN-LINE SKATING** In-line skates are on sale for $10 off, helmets are $5 off, and knee pads are $4 off. Use an integer to represent the change in price for each item.

46. ★ **WRITING** Two numbers a and b are opposites, and c is between b and 0. *Explain* where the opposite of c is located on the number line.

47. **MULTI-STEP PROBLEM** Use a number line to answer the questions.

a. Graph and label the following points on a number line: A = −2, P = 0, T = −7, and R = −4. What word do the letters spell?

b. Draw another number line. Graph and label the opposite of each value in part (a). What do the letters spell now?

Wind Chill Weather forecasters use wind chill to determine how much colder unprotected skin feels due to varying wind speeds. These equivalent temperatures are based on research begun in the 1940s. The table shows the wind chill temperatures that we feel under certain conditions.

Wind (mi/h)	Temperature (°F) 15	10	5
5	7	1	−5
10	3	−4	−10
15	0	−7	−13
20	−2	−9	−15
25	−4	−11	−17
30	−5	−12	−19

48. **Analyze** What is the wind chill temperature if the temperature outside is 10°F and the wind speed is 25 mi/h?

49. **Compare** Which feels colder, a temperature of 5°F with a wind speed of 10 mi/h or a temperature of 10°F with a wind speed of 25 mi/h?

50. **Extend** A weather forecaster reports that temperatures will range from 8°F to 12°F and the wind speed will be 30 mi/h. Is this information misleading? *Explain.*

51. ◆ **MULTIPLE REPRESENTATIONS** Use the pattern at the right.

    11, 7, 3, −1, ?, ?

    a. **Graph the Numbers** Graph each integer on a number line.

    b. **Describe the Pattern** *Describe* the pattern in words.

    c. **Complete the Pattern** Use your number line to find the missing integers.

52. **ALGEBRA** Solve the equation $-x = 4$. *Explain* your solution method.

53. ★ **WRITING** *Explain* why a number is sometimes less than its opposite.

54. **CHALLENGE** Use the following clues to order the integers represented by the letters a, b, c, d, and e from least to greatest on a number line.

    • a lies halfway between e and d.   • e lies halfway between c and a.
    • d is a positive integer.   • a is a negative integer.
    • b lies 3 units to the right of d.

MIXED REVIEW

Get-Ready

Prepare for
Lesson 11.2
in Exs. 55–58

Use a number line to add the numbers. *(p. 741)*

55. $5 + 4$ **56.** $12 + 3$ **57.** $8 + 2$ **58.** $2 + 11$

Evaluate the expression when $x = 4.5$ and $y = 1.23$. *(p.148)*

59. $6.07 - x$ **60.** $x + 2.58$ **61.** $y + 10.9$ **62.** $5.2 - y$

63. ★ **MULTIPLE CHOICE** Classify the solid at the right. *(p.541)*

    (A) triangular prism   (B) triangular pyramid

    (C) square pyramid   (D) cone

INVESTIGATION
Use before Lesson 11.2

GOAL
Use integer chips to add integers.

MATERIALS
• integer chips

11.2 Modeling Integer Addition

In this activity, you will use integer chips to model integer addition.

 = positive 1   = negative 1

EXPLORE Model $3 + (-5)$ using integer chips.

When you combine a positive integer chip and a negative integer chip, the result is zero. This pair of integer chips is called a *zero pair*.

STEP 1

Represent the expression using integer chips.

$3 + (-5)$

STEP 2

Group the zero pairs, if any.

STEP 3

Remove the zero pairs and write the result.

$3 + (-5) = -2$

PRACTICE Use the model to evaluate the expression.

1.
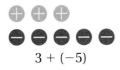
$2 + (-4)$

2.
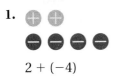
$-2 + 5$

3.
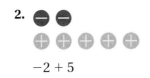
$4 + (-4)$

DRAW CONCLUSIONS

4. **REASONING** Use integer chips to show that the expressions $4 + (-3)$ and $-3 + 4$ are equivalent. Does the commutative property of addition appear to be true for integers?

5. **MAKE A CONCLUSION** Use your answers to Exercises 1–3. Suggest a method for finding the sum of two integers with different signs without using integer chips.

11.2 Adding Integers

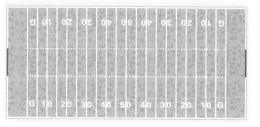

Before	You added whole numbers, fractions, and decimals.
Now	You'll add integers.
Why?	So you can find total yardage, as in Example 1.

KEY VOCABULARY
• absolute value, *p. 580*

Football During a high school football game, your team gained 6 yards on the first play, lost 8 yards on the second play, and gained 11 yards on the third play. Did your team gain the 10 yards needed for a first down?

 EXAMPLE 1 Modeling Integer Addition

TAKE NOTES
In your notebook, you may want to record the different ways you can represent the problem.

To understand the problem above, read and organize the information.

First play: 6 means a gain of 6 yards.

Second play: -8 means a loss of 8 yards.

Third play: 11 means a gain of 11 yards.

Start at 0 on a number line. Use arrows to represent gains and losses. Move right to add a positive number and left to add a negative number.

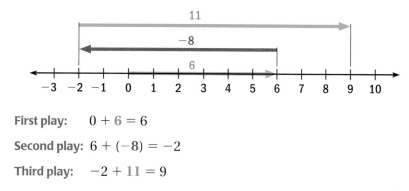

First play: $0 + 6 = 6$

Second play: $6 + (-8) = -2$

Third play: $-2 + 11 = 9$

▶ **Answer** Your team gained only 9 yards during the three plays. It did not gain the 10 yards needed for a first down.

✓ **GUIDED PRACTICE**   for Example 1

Find the sum using a number line.

1. $-4 + (-4)$ **2.** $-6 + 6$ **3.** $-8 + 10$ **4.** $5 + (-9)$

11.2 Adding Integers   **579**

Absolute Value The **absolute value** of a number is its distance from 0 on a number line. The absolute value of a number a is written $|a|$.

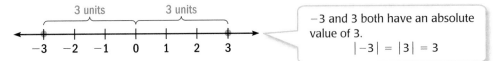

3 units   3 units

−3 and 3 both have an absolute value of 3.
$$|-3| = |3| = 3$$

You can use absolute value to add integers.

KEY CONCEPT   *For Your Notebook*

Adding Integers

Words

Same Signs Add the absolute values and use the common sign.

Different Signs Subtract the lesser absolute value from the greater absolute value. Then use the sign of the number with the greater absolute value.

Opposites The sum of an integer and its opposite is 0. This property, written as $a + (-a) = 0$, is called the *inverse property of addition*.

Numbers

$3 + 5 = 8$
$-3 + (-5) = -8$

$-7 + 10 = 3$
$7 + (-10) = -3$

$-2 + 2 = 0$

EXAMPLE 2 **Adding Integers**

Find the sum.

  a. $-4 + (-7)$ **b.** $-8 + 3$ **c.** $-6 + 9$

SOLUTION

  a. Both numbers have the same sign.

$$-4 + (-7) = -11 \longleftarrow \text{Add } |-4| \text{ and } |-7|.$$
Use the common sign.

  b. The numbers have different signs, and -8 has the greater absolute value.

$$-8 + 3 = -5 \longleftarrow \text{Subtract } |3| \text{ from } |-8|.$$
Use the sign of -8.

  c. The numbers have different signs, and 9 has the greater absolute value.

$$-6 + 9 = 3 \longleftarrow \text{Subtract } |-6| \text{ from } |9|.$$
Use the sign of 9.

AVOID ERRORS
When you find the sum of two numbers with different signs, be sure to use the sign of the number with the greater absolute value.

✓ **GUIDED PRACTICE** **for Example 2**

Find the absolute value of each number. Then find the sum.

  5. $-10 + (-5)$ **6.** $-6 + 19$ **7.** $8 + (-15)$ **8.** $25 + (-25)$

11.2 EXERCISES

SKILL PRACTICE

VOCABULARY Find the absolute value of the number.

1. -5 **2.** -28 **3.** 35 **4.** 0

5. VOCABULARY Copy and complete: To find the value of $-4 + 3$, subtract ___?___ from ___?___. Then write the sign of the number with the ___?___, 4.

SEE EXAMPLE 1
on p. 579
for Exs. 6–14

6. ERROR ANALYSIS Describe and correct the error made in the solution.

$\times$ $-1 + 5 = 5$

MODELING INTEGER ADDITION Find the sum using a number line.

7. $3 + (-6)$ **8.** $5 + (-4)$ **9.** $-7 + (-1)$ **10.** $-2 + (-8)$

11. $-1 + 6$ **12.** $8 + (-9)$ **13.** $-3 + (-3)$ **14.** $5 + (-5)$

SEE EXAMPLE 2
on p. 580
for Exs. 15–27

15. ★ MULTIPLE CHOICE Which expression does *not* have a sum of -7?

(A) $-4 + (-3)$ **(B)** $10 + (-17)$ **(C)** $-13 + 6$ **(D)** $-5 + 2$

ADDING INTEGERS Find the sum.

16. $0 + (-4)$ **17.** $-3 + (-7)$ **18.** $-1 + (-9)$ **19.** $-14 + 8$

20. $7 + (-1)$ **21.** $13 + (-13)$ **22.** $-10 + 10$ **23.** $-1 + 17$

24. $5 + (-15)$ **25.** $15 + (-8)$ **26.** $-19 + (-1)$ **27.** $-21 + (-2)$

28. $-1 + 16 + |-4|$ **29.** $11 + (-13) + |-2|$

30. $3 + (-9) + |8| + (-7)$ **31.** $-15 + 6 + (-2) + 10$

32. $4 + (-9) + 12 + (-6) + 15$ **33.** $|21| + 11 + (-7) + (-5) + (-14)$

ESTIMATION Tell whether the sum is *positive* or *negative*. Then estimate the sum.

34. $443 + (-976) + 769$ **35.** $-552 + (-922) + 812$

36. $-905 + (-107) + (-621)$ **37.** $651 + 199 + (-584)$

38. $-374 + 773 + (-245)$ **39.** $-860 + 517 + (-435)$

REASONING Tell whether the statement is *always, sometimes,* or *never* true. *Explain* your reasoning.

40. The sum of two negative integers is negative.

41. The sum of a positive integer and a negative integer is negative.

42. The sum of two positive integers is 0.

ALGEBRA Use mental math to solve.

43. $-3 + x = 0$ **44.** $x + 2 = 13$ **45.** $-4 + x = 4$

46. $x + (-2) = 9$ **47.** $x + (-2) = -2$ **48.** $7 + x = -5$

49. CHALLENGE The sum of $\frac{1}{2}$ and another fraction is $-\frac{1}{4}$. What is the other fraction?

50. CHALLENGE Let a and b be two integers. *Describe* the values of b that will make the sum $a + b$ less than a. What value of b will make the sum equal to zero? What values of b will make the sum greater than a?

PROBLEM SOLVING

51. LANDSCAPING A landscape architect uses a new process that puts him 3 days ahead of schedule. Then he loses 2 days due to rain and 2 days due to illness. Is he now *ahead of* schedule, *on* schedule, or *behind* schedule?

SEE EXAMPLE 1
on p. 579
for Ex. 52

52. SPORTS A football team lost 3 yards on the first play, lost 5 yards on the second play, and gained 12 yards on the third play. Did the team gain the 10 yards needed for a first down? *Explain* how you found your answer.

53. ★ MULTIPLE CHOICE You write a term paper worth 100 points. The teacher deducts 15 points for grammar. You earn 8 bonus points for creativity. Which expression could *not* represent your final total score?

(A) $100 + (-15) + 8$ **(B)** $100 - 15 + 8$

(C) $|100| + |-15| + |8|$ **(D)** $|100| - |-15| + |8|$

54. ★ SHORT RESPONSE Golf scores are measured by the number of strokes over or under par, as shown in the table. You score 2 birdies, 3 pars, 3 bogeys, and 1 double bogey. How does your total score compare with par? *Explain* how you found your answer.

Score	Compared with par
Birdie	1 under
Par	even
Bogey	1 over
Double bogey	2 over

55. TOTAL SCORE In a contest, you can gain or lose points. You have 25 points, lose 40 points, and then gain 10 points. Write an addition expression to find your score.

56. STOCK PRICES The table shows the changes in value of a $58 stock in one week. Write an addition expression that describes the situation. Then find the value of the stock at the end of the week.

Change in Stock Value				
Day of the week	Monday	Tuesday	Wednesday	Thursday	Friday
Change in value	up $8	down $12	down $20	up $3	up $4

57. MULTI-STEP PROBLEM Ethan runs a 4 mile race. In the table below, his time for each mile is compared with his previous best time.

	1st mile	2nd mile	3rd mile	4th mile
Previous best	6 min 44 sec	7 min 5 sec	7 min 18 sec	7 min
Current time	6 min 48 sec	7 min 2 sec	7 min 18 sec	6 min 58 sec
Comparison	4 sec more	3 sec less	same time	2 sec less

    a. Write each comparison using an integer.

    b. How did his time for the whole race compare with his previous best time?

58. ★ **WRITING** The inverse property of addition states that for all integers, $a + (-a) = 0$. *Explain* how you would show this on a number line.

59. ★ **SHORT RESPONSE** In a game of tug of war, the first team to pull the ribbon past the puddle wins. The ribbon starts in the middle of the puddle. Team B pulls 2 feet, then Team A pulls 3 feet. This pattern repeats until one team wins. Which team wins, and after how many tugs? *Explain* your answer.

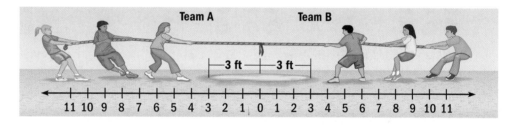

60. SPORTS A football team lost 6 yards on the first play, lost 3 yards on the second play, and gained 5 yards on the third play. How many yards does the team need to gain in the fourth play to gain the 10 yards needed overall for a first down? *Explain* your reasoning.

61. CHALLENGE The temperature in Ashville at 10 P.M. was $-4°$F. The temperature had dropped 3 degrees per hour since noon. What was the temperature at 2 P.M.?

MIXED REVIEW

Get-Ready

Prepare for
Lesson 11.3
in Exs. 62–65

Find the difference. *(p. 3)*

62. $38 - 19$ **63.** $52 - 26$ **64.** $123 - 48$ **65.** $301 - 99$

Copy and complete the statement using < or >. *(p. 573)*

66. $-5 \underline{?} 5$ **67.** $4 \underline{?} -1$ **68.** $-13 \underline{?} -19$ **69.** $-24 \underline{?} 0$

70. ★ **OPEN-ENDED MATH** Draw an obtuse angle. Use a protractor to find the measure of your angle. *(p. 465)*

GOAL
Use integer chips to subtract integers.

MATERIALS
• integer chips

11.3 Modeling Integer Subtraction

In this activity, you will use integer chips to model integer subtraction.

 = 1   = −1   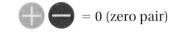 = 0 (zero pair)

EXPLORE 1 Model −6 − (−2) using integer chips.

STEP 1	STEP 2	STEP 3
Start with 6 negative integer chips.	**Remove** 2 negative integer chips to subtract −2.	**Count** the remaining integer chips and write the result.
		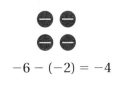
−6	−6 − (−2)	−6 − (−2) = −4

PRACTICE Use an integer chip model to evaluate the expression.

1. −5 − (−1)   **2.** −7 − (−4)   **3.** −8 − (−6)

EXPLORE 2 Model −3 − 1 using integer chips.

STEP 1	STEP 2
Start with 3 negative integer chips.	**Add** a zero pair because there are no positive integer chips.
−3	−3 = −3 + 0

STEP 3	STEP 4
Remove 1 positive integer chip to subtract 1.	**Count** the remaining integer chips and write the result.
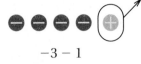	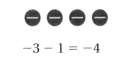
−3 − 1	−3 − 1 = −4

PRACTICE Use an integer chip model to evaluate the expression.

4. $-5 - 2$ **5.** $-6 - 3$ **6.** $-7 - 4$

EXPLORE 3 Model $-2 - (-4)$ using integer chips.

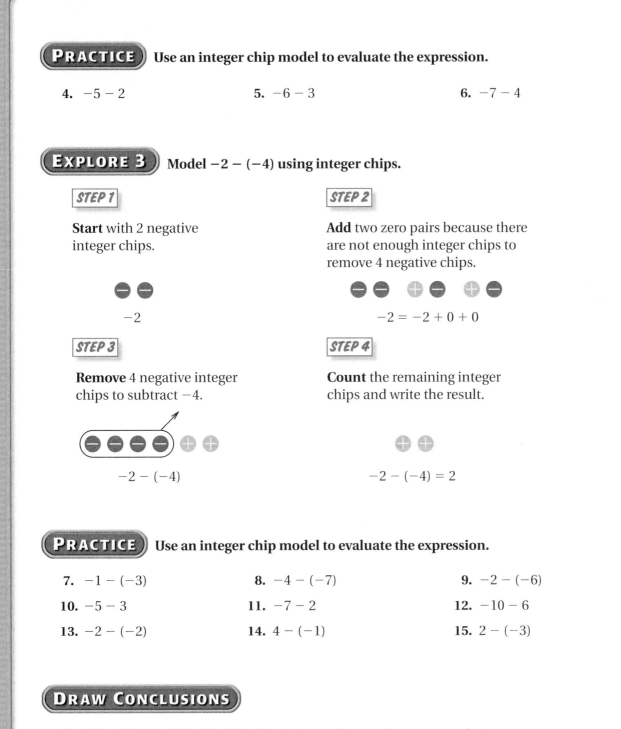

STEP 1

Start with 2 negative integer chips.

-2

STEP 2

Add two zero pairs because there are not enough integer chips to remove 4 negative chips.

$-2 = -2 + 0 + 0$

STEP 3

Remove 4 negative integer chips to subtract -4.

$-2 - (-4)$

STEP 4

Count the remaining integer chips and write the result.

$-2 - (-4) = 2$

PRACTICE Use an integer chip model to evaluate the expression.

7. $-1 - (-3)$ **8.** $-4 - (-7)$ **9.** $-2 - (-6)$

10. $-5 - 3$ **11.** $-7 - 2$ **12.** $-10 - 6$

13. $-2 - (-2)$ **14.** $4 - (-1)$ **15.** $2 - (-3)$

DRAW CONCLUSIONS

16. EVALUATING EXPRESSIONS Use integer chips to demonstrate that the expressions $-5 - (-8)$ and $-8 - (-5)$ are *not* equivalent.

17. REASONING When you subtract a positive integer from a negative integer, will you get a *negative* or a *positive* integer? Use examples to support your answer.

11.3 Subtracting Integers

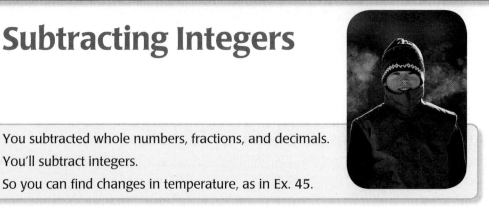

Before	You subtracted whole numbers, fractions, and decimals.
Now	You'll subtract integers.
Why?	So you can find changes in temperature, as in Ex. 45.

KEY VOCABULARY
• **opposites,** *p. 574*

When subtracting whole numbers, subtraction is the opposite of addition. This can help you subtract integers on a number line. The direction you move to subtract an integer is the opposite of the direction you move to add the integer.

EXAMPLE 1 Modeling Integer Subtraction

a. Find the difference 3 − 5.

When you add a positive integer, you move to the right on a number line. When you *subtract* a positive integer, you move to the left.

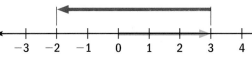

To find 3 − 5, move right
3 units then left 5 units.

TAKE NOTES
In your notes on subtracting integers, you may want to include a number line model and a numerical example, as in Examples 1 and 2.

▶ **Answer** The final position is −2. So, 3 − 5 = −2.

b. Find the difference 2 − (−4).

When you add a negative integer, you move to the left on a number line. So to *subtract* a negative integer, you move to the right.

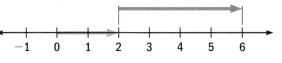

To find 2 − (−4), move right
2 units then right 4 units.

Animated **Math**
at classzone.com

▶ **Answer** The final position is 6. So, 2 − (−4) = 6.

You can use opposites and rules for adding integers to subtract integers.

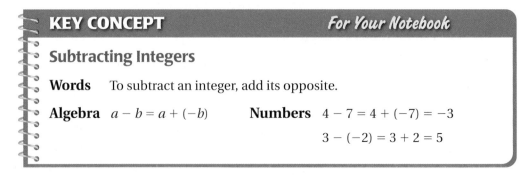

KEY CONCEPT   *For Your Notebook*

Subtracting Integers

Words   To subtract an integer, add its opposite.

Algebra $a - b = a + (-b)$ **Numbers** $4 - 7 = 4 + (-7) = -3$

$3 - (-2) = 3 + 2 = 5$

EXAMPLE 2 Subtracting Integers

Find the difference.

a. $-2 - (-9) = -2 + 9$ To subtract -9, add its opposite.

$\qquad\qquad\quad = 7$ Find $|9| - |-2|$. Use the sign of 9.

b. $-5 - 7 = -5 + (-7)$ To subtract 7, add its opposite.

$\qquad\qquad = -12$ Find $|-5| + |-7|$. Use the common sign.

EXAMPLE 3 Using Integers to Solve Problems

Mauna Loa The base of the Hawaiian volcano Mauna Loa is about 13,000 meters below sea level. Its summit is 4170 meters above sea level. Find the difference between the elevations of Mauna Loa's summit and its base.

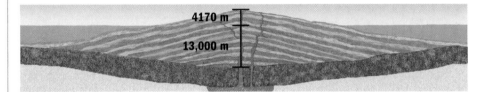

4170 m

13,000 m

SOLUTION

STEP 1 **Use** integers to represent the two elevations.

    summit: 4170 meters   **base:** $-13,000$ meters

STEP 2 **Subtract** the lesser elevation from the greater elevation.

$\qquad 4170 - (-13,000) = 4170 + 13,000$ To subtract $-13,000$, add its opposite.

$\qquad\qquad\qquad\qquad\quad = 17,170$

▶ **Answer** The difference between the elevations is 17,170 meters.

✓ **GUIDED PRACTICE**   for Examples 1, 2, and 3

Find the difference using a number line.

1. $4 - 6$ **2.** $7 - 10$ **3.** $3 - (-4)$ **4.** $0 - (-4)$

Find the difference.

5. $3 - 7$ **6.** $-5 - 6$ **7.** $4 - (-8)$ **8.** $-2 - (-9)$

9. $6 - 10$ **10.** $-4 - 9$ **11.** $5 - (-5)$ **12.** $-3 - (-1)$

13. Aoba The base of the volcano Aoba on Vanuatu in the South Pacific is about 3000 meters below sea level. Its summit is 1496 meters above sea level. Find the difference between the elevations of Aoba's summit and its base.

11.3 EXERCISES

HOMEWORK KEY

★ = **STANDARDIZED TEST PRACTICE**
Exs. 24, 39, 47, 48, 50, 51, and 62

○ = **HINTS AND HOMEWORK HELP**
for Exs. 5, 7, 17, 23, 47 at classzone.com

SKILL PRACTICE

VOCABULARY Copy and complete the statement.

1. To subtract 5 from 2, add the __?__ of 5 to 2.

2. To subtract a negative integer, move to the __?__ on a number line.

MODELING INTEGER SUBTRACTION Find the difference using a number line.

SEE EXAMPLE 1
on p. 586
for Exs. 3–11

3. $4 - 7$

4. $-5 - 6$

5. $-2 - (-3)$

6. $8 - 1$

7. $8 - 12$

8. $6 - (-6)$

9. $-9 - (-9)$

10. $9 - (-8)$

11. **ERROR ANALYSIS** Describe and correct the error made in the solution.

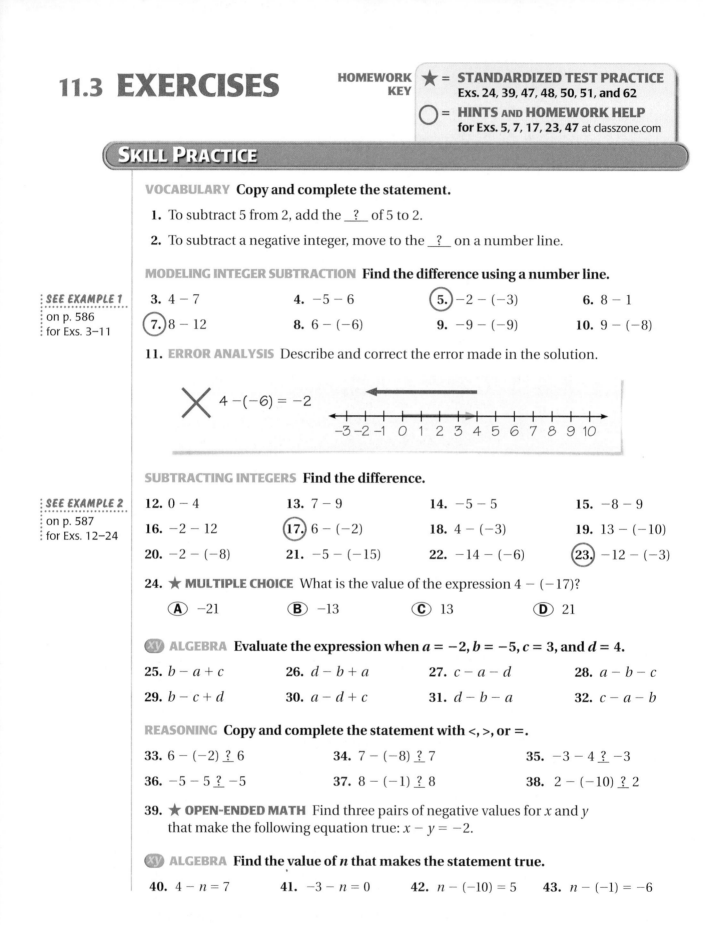

$4 - (-6) = -2$

−3 −2 −1 0 1 2 3 4 5 6 7 8 9 10

SUBTRACTING INTEGERS Find the difference.

SEE EXAMPLE 2
on p. 587
for Exs. 12–24

12. $0 - 4$

13. $7 - 9$

14. $-5 - 5$

15. $-8 - 9$

16. $-2 - 12$

17. $6 - (-2)$

18. $4 - (-3)$

19. $13 - (-10)$

20. $-2 - (-8)$

21. $-5 - (-15)$

22. $-14 - (-6)$

23. $-12 - (-3)$

24. ★ **MULTIPLE CHOICE** What is the value of the expression $4 - (-17)$?

   A -21

   B -13

   C 13

   D 21

ALGEBRA Evaluate the expression when $a = -2$, $b = -5$, $c = 3$, and $d = 4$.

25. $b - a + c$

26. $d - b + a$

27. $c - a - d$

28. $a - b - c$

29. $b - c + d$

30. $a - d + c$

31. $d - b - a$

32. $c - a - b$

REASONING Copy and complete the statement with <, >, or =.

33. $6 - (-2)$ __?__ 6

34. $7 - (-8)$ __?__ 7

35. $-3 - 4$ __?__ -3

36. $-5 - 5$ __?__ -5

37. $8 - (-1)$ __?__ 8

38. $2 - (-10)$ __?__ 2

39. ★ **OPEN-ENDED MATH** Find three pairs of negative values for x and y that make the following equation true: $x - y = -2$.

ALGEBRA Find the value of n that makes the statement true.

40. $4 - n = 7$

41. $-3 - n = 0$

42. $n - (-10) = 5$

43. $n - (-1) = -6$

44. CHALLENGE Evaluate the expressions $-9 - 12$ and $12 - (-9)$. Use the results to predict how the expressions $a - b$ and $b - a$ are related. Test your prediction with several values of a and b.

PROBLEM SOLVING

SEE EXAMPLE 3
on p. 587
for Exs. 45–48

45. GUIDED PROBLEM SOLVING When the actual temperature is 5°F and the wind speed is 15 miles per hour, the wind chill temperature is -13°F. What is the difference between the actual temperature and the wind chill temperature?

    a. Write a subtraction expression for the difference between the actual temperature and the wind chill temperature.

    b. Rewrite the expression in part (a) as an addition expression.

    c. What is the difference between the two temperatures?

46. ELEVATION The elevations of the highest and lowest points in California are shown below. Find the range of elevations in California. Show the subtraction expression you used.

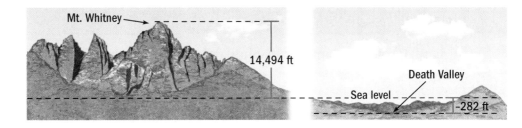

Mt. Whitney 14,494 ft
Sea level — Death Valley — -282 ft

47. ★ **MULTIPLE CHOICE** You pour juice that has a temperature of 10°C into cups and freeze the juice to -2°C. What is the *change* in temperature?

    (A) -12°C   **(B)** -8°C   **(C)** 8°C   **(D)** 12°C

48. ★ **WRITING** The bow of a sunken ship relative to the water's surface is at -44 feet. The position of the stern is -53 feet. Write and solve a subtraction problem about the ship using these integers.

49. ◆ **MULTIPLE REPRESENTATIONS** An elevator is 50 feet below ground. It descends to a point 125 feet below ground. Draw a diagram of the situation. Then write and evaluate a subtraction expression to find the *change* in elevation.

50. ★ **SHORT RESPONSE** At noon the temperature was 8°F. By 6 P.M. the temperature had dropped 12°. What was the temperature at 6 P.M.? Demonstrate how to solve the problem using a number line and then using the rules for subtracting integers.

51. ★ **WRITING** Is the statement $a - (b - c) = (a - b) - c$ true for all integers? *Explain* your reasoning using examples.

CHALLENGE Tell whether the statement is *always, sometimes,* or *never* true. *Explain* your reasoning.

52. A negative integer minus a negative integer is negative.

53. A positive integer minus a positive integer is positive.

54. A positive integer minus a negative integer is positive.

55. Any number minus a positive number is greater than the original number.

MIXED REVIEW

Get-Ready

Prepare for
Lesson 11.4
in Exs. 56–61

Find the product.

56. 1.8×1.1 *(p. 181)*

57. 7.1×0.3 *(p. 181)*

58. 0.63×0.2 *(p. 181)*

59. $2\frac{3}{5} \cdot 3\frac{8}{9}$ *(p. 354)*

60. $1\frac{1}{3} \cdot 4\frac{5}{6}$ *(p. 354)*

61. $3\frac{1}{8} \cdot \frac{7}{5}$ *(p. 354)*

62. ★ **MULTIPLE CHOICE** What is the value of $4 + (-7)$? *(p. 579)*

    A -11 **B** -3 **C** 3 **D** 11

QUIZ *for Lessons 11.1 – 11.3*

Find the opposite and the absolute value of the number. *(pp. 573, 579)*

1. 6 **2.** -4 **3.** -10 **4.** 0

Order the integers from least to greatest. *(p. 573)*

5. $-1, 8, 0, -4, 1$ **6.** $-5, 3, -7, -3, 5$ **7.** $-2, 1, 10, -11, -14$

Find the difference. *(p. 586)*

8. $-3 - 6$ **9.** $-5 - 15$ **10.** $-14 - 4$ **11.** $-8 - (-10)$

12. **TEMPERATURES** In one state, the coldest recorded average temperature in January was about 35°F. In another state, the coldest average temperature was 2°F below zero. Find the difference between these average temperatures. *(p. 586)*

Brain Game

Magic Square

In the magic square at the right, the sum of each row, column, and diagonal is the same. Copy and complete the magic square.

-5	?	?
?	-2	?
-1	?	1

EXTRA PRACTICE for Lesson 11.3, p. 786

ONLINE QUIZ at classzone.com

Lessons 11.1–11.3

1. MULTI-STEP PROBLEM Weather stations use buoys in the ocean to monitor wave height. In a hurricane, a buoy takes these readings of several waves: -9, -5, 3, 17, 10, -3, -17, -12, 13, 18, and 5. Each integer gives the buoy's height, in feet, above or below the still-water level.

   a. What is the lowest point that the buoy reached?

   b. What is the highest point that the buoy reached?

   c. What is the range of these hurricane waves?

2. EXTENDED RESPONSE You live in a high-rise apartment building. Your best friend lives 5 floors above you. Your cousin lives 7 floors below your best friend.

   a. Draw a Diagram Draw a vertical number line of the situation. Let 0 represent the location of your apartment.

   b. Write an Expression Write and evaluate a subtraction expression to find the number of floors between you and your cousin.

   c. Apply A laundromat is located 3 floors above your cousin's apartment. How many floors is this above or below your apartment? *Justify* your answer with an integer expression.

3. OPEN-ENDED Find a negative value of x and a negative value of y so that the difference $x - y$ is positive.

4. GRIDDED ANSWER Darren's scores on the first five holes of a golf game, relative to par, are 4, -2, -1, 3, and -1. What is Darren's total score so far?

5. SHORT RESPONSE Use the table below of the lowest temperatures in degrees Fahrenheit recorded in five states. Order the states from coldest to warmest low temperature. Then find the median temperature.

State	Low temperature (°F)
Alaska	-80
Georgia	-17
Idaho	-60
Illinois	-36
Maine	-48

6. EXTENDED RESPONSE Use the bar graph of the daily high temperatures in a city in Alaska during one week in January.

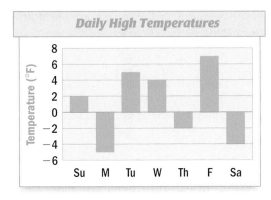

   a. Find the difference in temperature for the two consecutive days with the least difference in temperature. *Explain* your method.

   b. Find the difference in temperature for the two consecutive days with the greatest difference in temperature. *Explain* your method.

   c. Is your answer to part (b) the range for the data? Why or why not?

11.4 Multiplying Integers

Before	You multiplied whole numbers, fractions, and decimals.
Now	You'll multiply integers.
Why?	So you can find changes in water levels, as in Example 2.

KEY VOCABULARY
• **negative integers,** p. 573
• **positive integers,** p. 573

ACTIVITY

You can use addition to understand integer multiplication.

STEP 1 Copy and complete the table.

Product	Repeated addition	Result
4 · 2	= 2 + 2 + 2 + 2	= ?
4 · 1	= 1 + 1 + 1 + 1	= ?
4 · 0	= 0 + 0 + 0 + 0	= ?
4 · (−1)	= (−1) + (−1) + (−1) + (−1)	= ?
4 · (−2)	= (−2) + (−2) + (−2) + (−2)	= ?

STEP 2 Describe the pattern of the results. Use the pattern to find 4 · (−3).

STEP 3 Copy the table at the right. Then look for a pattern to complete it.

Product	Result
2 · (−4)	= ?
1 · (−4)	= ?
0 · (−4)	= ?
(−1) · (−4)	= ?
(−2) · (−4)	= ?

STEP 4 Tell what you observe about the product of two integers with the same sign; with different signs.

In the activity, you may have observed the following rules about multiplying integers.

KEY CONCEPT   For Your Notebook

Multiplying Integers

Words	Numbers
The product of two positive integers is positive.	$3(5) = 15$
The product of two negative integers is positive.	$-4(-6) = 24$
The product of a positive integer and a negative integer is negative.	$2(-8) = -16$

EXAMPLE 1 Multiplying Integers

a. $-7(-4) = 28$ The product of two negative integers is positive.

b. $8(-6) = -48$ The product of a positive integer and a negative integer is negative.

EXAMPLE 2 Applying Integers

High and Low Tide In the Bay of Fundy there are about 6 hours between each high and low tide. Suppose that the water level decreases at a rate of about 4 feet per hour during this time. What is the change in the water level?

SOLUTION

$$\text{Change in water level} = \text{Rate of change} \times \text{Number of hours}$$
$$= \quad -4 \quad \times \quad 6$$
$$= \quad -24$$

▶ **Answer** The water level decreases by about 24 feet between tides.

EXAMPLE 3 Evaluating Expressions

Evaluate the expression when $m = 5$ and $n = -8$.

READING
The expression "$-mn$" means "$-1mn$." It is read "the opposite of mn."

a. $-mn = (-1)(5)(-8)$ Substitute 5 for m and -8 for n.

$= 40$ The product of two negative integers is positive.

b. $n^3 = (-8)^3$ Substitute -8 for n.

$= (-8)(-8)(-8)$ Write the power as a product.

$= -512$ The product of three negative integers is negative.

Animated Math at classzone.com

✓ GUIDED PRACTICE   for Examples 1, 2, and 3

Find the product.

1. $9(8)$ **2.** $-2(-11)$ **3.** $7(-7)$ **4.** $-8(4)$

5. What If? In Example 2, what integer represents the change in the water level 2 hours after high tide?

Evaluate the expression when $x = 3$ and $y = -2$.

6. $6y$ **7.** y^2 **8.** y^3 **9.** $-xy$

11.4 EXERCISES

HOMEWORK KEY

★ = **STANDARDIZED TEST PRACTICE**
Exs. 20, 52, 53, 56, 57, 58, and 75

◯ = **HINTS AND HOMEWORK HELP**
for Exs. 5, 7, 17, 23, 53 at classzone.com

SKILL PRACTICE

VOCABULARY Copy and complete the statement.

1. The product of two negative integers is a _?_ integer.

2. The product of a negative integer and a positive integer is a _?_ integer.

MULTIPLYING INTEGERS Find the product.

SEE EXAMPLE 1
on p. 593
for Exs. 3–20

3. $6(4)$

4. $3(8)$

5. $5(-7)$

6. $-7(6)$

7. $-2(-9)$

8. $15(-3)$

9. $-12(-8)$

10. $-7(0)$

11. $20(11)$

12. $18(-10)$

13. $-30(30)$

14. $-12(-50)$

15. $-2(4)(-3)$

16. $-5(-2)(-10)$

17. $3(-5)(-2)(-2)$

18. $-4(-2)(-6)(-10)$

19. **ERROR ANALYSIS** Describe and correct the error made in the solution.

$$\times \quad (-2)(-6) = -12$$

20. ★ **MULTIPLE CHOICE** Which expression represents the sum $(-5) + (-5) + (-5)$?

Ⓐ $-3 \cdot (-5)$

Ⓑ $(-5)^3$

Ⓒ $3 + (-5)$

Ⓓ $3 \cdot (-5)$

Ⓧⓥ **ALGEBRA** Evaluate the expression when $n = -6$, $p = 5$, and $t = -10$.

SEE EXAMPLE 3
on p. 593
for Exs. 21–28

21. $7n$

22. $-8p$

23. $-n$

24. $-p^3$

25. t^2

26. nt

27. $-2nt$

28. $-4pt$

LOOK FOR A PATTERN Find the missing numbers in the pattern. Then describe the rule for the pattern.

29. $-5, -10, \underline{\ ?\ }, -40, -80, \underline{\ ?\ }$

30. $3, \underline{\ ?\ }, 3, -3, \underline{\ ?\ }, -3$

31. $-12, \underline{\ ?\ }, -36, -48, \underline{\ ?\ }, -72$

32. $-4, \underline{\ ?\ }, -16, 32, \underline{\ ?\ }, \underline{\ ?\ }$

NUMBER SENSE Tell whether the statement is *always*, *sometimes*, or *never* true.

33. A negative integer times a negative integer is positive.

34. A negative integer times a positive integer is negative.

35. A positive integer times a negative integer is positive.

Ⓧⓥ **MENTAL MATH Find the value of x that makes the statement true.**

36. $4(-x) = -40$

37. $-8x = 48$

38. $-x(-3) = -6$

39. $7(-x) = 21$

40. $-7x = 35$

41. $3(-x) = -12$

42. $-x(-5) = -15$

43. $6(-x) = -54$

44. REASONING Evaluate $3(-5)$ and $(-5)3$. What do you notice about the results? What property for multiplication of integers do your results illustrate?

XY ALGEBRA **Find the values of x that make the statement true.**

45. $x^2 = 49$

46. $x^2 = 121$

47. $x^2 = 400$

48. $3x^2 = 300$

49. $10x^2 = 640$

50. $5x^2 = 405$

51. CHALLENGE Copy and complete the pattern: $\dfrac{3}{2}, -\dfrac{3}{4}, \underline{\ ?\ }, -\dfrac{3}{16}, \underline{\ ?\ }, \underline{\ ?\ }$.

PROBLEM SOLVING

SEE EXAMPLE 2
on p. 593
for Exs. 52–55

52. ★ **SHORT RESPONSE** A female Asiatic black bear loses about 7 pounds per month during its 6 months of hibernation. What is its *change* in weight during hibernation? The bear weighs 210 pounds before hibernation. What does it weigh after hibernation? *Explain* your reasoning.

53. ★ **MULTIPLE CHOICE** You have $90 in your savings account. Each week you withdraw $5. What integer represents the *change* in the number of dollars in your account over 6 weeks?

A -60 **B** -30 **C** 60 **D** 120

54. DIVING Think of the surface of the ocean as 0 on a number line. A sea otter can dive to a depth of -30 meters. A dolphin can dive to a depth that is 10 times as great as the sea otter's depth. At that depth, what is the dolphin's position relative to sea level?

55. EXAMPLES AND NONEXAMPLES Your math teacher writes the passwords shown on the board. No one may leave class without giving a different valid password. Name two valid passwords you could give. *Explain* your reasoning.

Valid Passwords	Invalid Passwords
$-4(-5)$	$11(-2)$
$12(7)$	$-3(5)$
$-1(-3)$	$9(0)$

56. ★ **WRITING** Edward burns 8 calories per minute when he runs for 20 minutes. *Explain* how to use integer multiplication to represent the change in Edward's calories.

57. ★ **SHORT RESPONSE** Your aunt drives 50 miles every day. Her car uses 1 gallon of gasoline every 25 miles. Write a product of two integers that represents the change in gallons of gasoline in the tank after 5 days. *Explain* how you found your answer.

58. ★ **OPEN-ENDED MATH** *Describe* a situation that can be modeled by the product (7 days)(−2 units per day). Then find and interpret the product.

59. ◆ **MULTIPLE REPRESENTATIONS** You deposit $60 into a school lunch account at the beginning of each month. Then you charge $3 to the account every weekday to pay for your lunch.

   a. **Write a Product** Write a multiplication expression to represent the *change* in the account balance after 5 days.

   b. **Write a Sum** Rewrite your answer to part (a) as a sum.

   c. **Make a Model** Model the sum in part (b) using a number line model. *Explain* why the model also represents the product in part (a).

60. **LOOK FOR A PATTERN** Give a rule for the pattern in the table. Then find y when $x = -1, -2,$ and -3.

61. **REASONING** Let a and b represent any integers. When is the product $-ab$ positive? *Explain* your reasoning.

62. **CHALLENGE** What 2-digit negative integer and 3-digit positive integer created by using the digits 2, 3, 5, 6, and 9 each exactly once will have the greatest possible product? the least possible product? What are the products?

x	y
0	0
1	−4
2	−8
3	−12

MIXED REVIEW

Get-Ready

Prepare for Lesson 11.5 in Exs. 63–68

Find the quotient. *(p. 198)*

63. $4.8 \div 6$ **64.** $5.4 \div 6$ **65.** $10.9 \div 0.5$

66. $21 \div 1.2$ **67.** $8.52 \div 0.16$ **68.** $28.4 \div 0.04$

Find the sum. *(p. 579)*

69. $-4 + 12$ **70.** $5 + (-8)$ **71.** $-7 + (-7)$

Find the difference. *(p. 586)*

72. $16 - 20$ **73.** $-31 - 9$ **74.** $18 - (-25)$

75. ★ **MULTIPLE CHOICE** What is the surface area of the rectangular prism? *(p. 545)*

   Ⓐ 770 cm^2 Ⓑ 1085 cm^2

   Ⓒ 1260 cm^2 Ⓓ 2170 cm^2

7 cm
20 cm
35 cm

11.5 Dividing Integers

Before   You divided whole numbers, fractions, and decimals.

Now   You'll divide integers.

Why?   So you can find mean temperatures, as in Example 3.

KEY VOCABULARY
• **mean,** *p. 99*

ACTIVITY

You can use multiplication to understand integer division.

One way to find the quotient of two integers, such as $-32 \div 4$, is to rewrite the division problem as a multiplication problem.

STEP 1 **Rewrite** the problem using multiplication.

$$-32 \div 4 = \underline{\ ?\ } \qquad \longrightarrow \qquad \underline{\ ?\ } \times 4 = -32$$

STEP 2 **Use** mental math to solve the multiplication problem.

$$\underline{\ ?\ } \times 4 = -32 \qquad \longrightarrow \qquad -8 \times 4 = -32$$

In Exercises 1–3, rewrite the problem using multiplication to find the quotient. Then use your results in Exercises 4–6.

1. $40 \div (-8) = \underline{\ ?\ }$ **2.** $-45 \div (-9) = \underline{\ ?\ }$ **3.** $-20 \div 5 = \underline{\ ?\ }$

4. Is a positive integer divided by a negative integer *positive* or *negative*?

5. Is a negative integer divided by a negative integer *positive* or *negative*?

6. Is a negative integer divided by a positive integer *positive* or *negative*?

EXAMPLE 1   Dividing Integers Using Mental Math

Divide by solving a related multiplication equation.

    a. $-36 \div (-6) = 6$ Ask, "what number times -6 equals -36?"

    b. $27 \div (-9) = -3$ Ask, "what number times -9 equals 27?"

    c. $-42 \div 7 = -6$ Ask, "what number times 7 equals -42?"

✓   **GUIDED PRACTICE**   for Example 1

Write and solve a related multiplication equation.

    1. $-30 \div 5$ **2.** $18 \div (-2)$ **3.** $-27 \div (-9)$ **4.** $0 \div (-5)$

KEY CONCEPT

For Your Notebook

Dividing Integers

Words	**Numbers**
Same Sign The quotient of two integers with the same sign is positive.	$15 \div 3 = 5$ $-14 \div (-7) = 2$
Different Signs The quotient of two integers with different signs is negative.	$12 \div (-4) = -3$ $-10 \div 2 = -5$
Zero The quotient of 0 and any nonzero integer is 0.	$0 \div 13 = 0$

AVOID ERRORS
You cannot divide a number by 0. Any number divided by 0 is *undefined*.

EXAMPLE 2 **Dividing Integers**

a. $-54 \div (-6) = 9$ The quotient of two integers with the same sign is positive.

b. $14 \div (-2) = -7$ The quotient of two integers with different signs is negative.

★ **EXAMPLE 3** **Standardized Test Practice**

Antarctica A scientist in Antarctica records the maximum temperature three days in a row. What integer represents the mean of the temperatures shown on the thermometers?

Ⓐ -6 Ⓑ -4

Ⓒ -2 Ⓓ 4

ELIMINATE CHOICES
Because the temperatures are all negative, the mean will be negative. So, choice D can be eliminated.

SOLUTION

$$\text{Mean} = \frac{-6 + (-4) + (-2)}{3} = \frac{-12}{3} = -4$$

▶ **Answer** The mean of the temperatures is $-4°C$. The correct answer is B. Ⓐ **Ⓑ** Ⓒ Ⓓ

✓ **GUIDED PRACTICE** for Examples 2 and 3

Find the quotient.

5. $-63 \div 7$ **6.** $40 \div (-5)$ **7.** $0 \div (-5)$ **8.** $-22 \div (-2)$

9. What If? In Example 3, suppose a scientist records a maximum temperature of $-8°C$ on the fourth day. Find the mean now.

11.5 EXERCISES

HOMEWORK KEY

★ = **STANDARDIZED TEST PRACTICE**
Exs. 19, 20, 55, 57, 58, 59, and 64

○ = **HINTS AND HOMEWORK HELP**
for Exs. 3, 5, 13, 21, 55 at classzone.com

SKILL PRACTICE

VOCABULARY Copy and complete the statement.

1. The quotient of two negative integers is __?__.

2. To find the mean of a group of integers, you add the integers and __?__ by the number of integers.

WRITING RELATED EQUATIONS Write and solve a related multiplication equation.

SEE EXAMPLE 1
on p. 597
for Exs. 3–9

3. $6 \div (-2)$ **4.** $0 \div (-12)$ **5.** $-21 \div (-3)$

6. $-45 \div (-5)$ **7.** $-30 \div 6$ **8.** $-14 \div 7$

9. ERROR ANALYSIS Describe and correct the error made in the solution.

$$\times \quad -18 \div (-3) = -6$$

DIVIDING INTEGERS Find the quotient.

SEE EXAMPLE 2
on p. 598
for Exs. 10–19

10. $15 \div (-3)$ **11.** $0 \div 5$ **12.** $-12 \div (-3)$

13. $-24 \div 8$ **14.** $28 \div (-7)$ **15.** $-90 \div 15$

16. $750 \div (-50)$ **17.** $-128 \div (-32)$ **18.** $-195 \div (-15)$

19. ★ **MULTIPLE CHOICE** Which expression has a value of -8?

(A) $-96 \div (-12)$ **(B)** $56 \div (-7)$ **(C)** $-32 \div (-4)$ **(D)** $56 \div (-8)$

SEE EXAMPLE 3
on p. 598
for Exs. 20–23

20. ★ **MULTIPLE CHOICE** What is the mean of $-19, -10, -10, -4, 4,$ and 9?

(A) -10 **(B)** -7 **(C)** -5 **(D)** -4

FINDING THE MEAN Find the mean of the data.

21. $-8, -3, 2, -7$ **22.** $-11, -15, 12, -6$ **23.** $-9, -2, -8, 19$

ORDER OF OPERATIONS Simplify the expression.

24. $8 + 3 - 10$ **25.** $7 + 3 \times 2$ **26.** $9 - (-5) \times 2$

27. $-10 \div 2 \times (-3)$ **28.** $6 - 8 + 2 \times (-4)$ **29.** $20 \div 5 + 8 \times 3$

30. $(3 \times 4 + 2) + (-8)$ **31.** $-5(6 + 3 \times 2) - 1$ **32.** $12 \div (-6) + 2 \times (-4)$

ALGEBRA Recall that you can use a fraction bar to express division. Evaluate the expression when $a = -9$, $b = 6$, and $c = -1$.

33. $\dfrac{36}{a}$ **34.** $\dfrac{b}{-6}$ **35.** $\dfrac{a}{3}$ **36.** $\dfrac{-54}{a}$

37. $\dfrac{-81}{c - 2}$ **38.** $\dfrac{84}{a + 3}$ **39.** $\dfrac{66}{-b}$ **40.** $\dfrac{-72}{-c}$

CHALLENGE Determine whether the value of $\frac{m}{n}$ is *positive*, *negative*, or *zero*. *Explain* your reasoning.

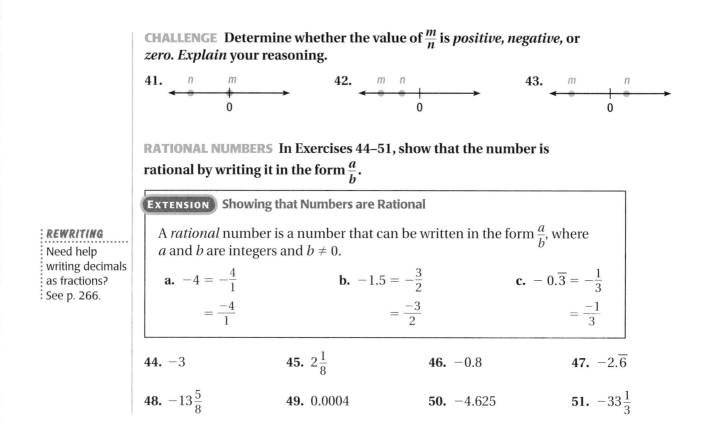

41.
n   m
0

42.
m   n
0

43.
m   n
0

RATIONAL NUMBERS In Exercises 44–51, show that the number is rational by writing it in the form $\frac{a}{b}$.

REWRITING
Need help writing decimals as fractions? See p. 266.

> **EXTENSION** Showing that Numbers are Rational
>
> A *rational* number is a number that can be written in the form $\frac{a}{b}$, where a and b are integers and $b \neq 0$.
>
> **a.** $-4 = -\frac{4}{1}$ **b.** $-1.5 = -\frac{3}{2}$ **c.** $-0.\overline{3} = -\frac{1}{3}$
>
> $= \frac{-4}{1}$ $= \frac{-3}{2}$ $= \frac{-1}{3}$

44. -3 **45.** $2\frac{1}{8}$ **46.** -0.8 **47.** $-2.\overline{6}$

48. $-13\frac{5}{8}$ **49.** 0.0004 **50.** -4.625 **51.** $-33\frac{1}{3}$

PROBLEM SOLVING

SEE EXAMPLE 3
on p. 598
for Exs. 52–53

In Exercises 52–53, use the table below. The table shows the highest and lowest recorded temperatures for each continent.

Global Temperatures							
Continent	**Africa**	**Antarctica**	**Asia**	**Australia**	**Europe**	**North America**	**South America**
High (°F)	136	59	129	128	122	134	120
Low (°F)	−11	−129	−90	−9	−67	−81	−27

52. MEAN TEMPERATURES Find the mean of the high temperatures and the mean of the low temperatures to the nearest degree.

53. TEMPERATURE RANGES Find the range of the high temperatures and the range of the low temperatures. Which set of data has the greater range?

54. REASONING Is a nonzero integer divided by its opposite always equal to -1? *Explain* and include examples.

55. ★ **MULTIPLE CHOICE** During a storm, there is a total change in temperature of $-28°F$ in 4 hours. What is the mean change in temperature per hour?

   A $-24°F$ **B** $-14°F$ **C** $-7°F$ **D** $-4°F$

56. GOLF Find the mean of the golf scores.

Golfer	Sara	Lauren	Matt	Audrey	Isaias
Score	4	5	−2	−4	−3

57. ★ WRITING The equation $4 \div 0 = \underline{\ ?\ }$ can be rewritten as $\underline{\ ?\ } \cdot 0 = 4$. Use the rewritten equation to explain why an integer divided by 0 is undefined.

58. ★ EXTENDED RESPONSE The table shows how much money a student earned or spent each day.

Day	Amount	Activity
Sunday	$20	Earned money weeding gardens
Monday	$15	Earned money running errands
Tuesday	$3	Bought ice cream
Wednesday	$9	Earned money mowing the lawn
Friday	$21	Bought new jeans

   a. Use positive and negative integers to show which amounts represent earnings and which amounts represent money spent.

   b. Find the mean of the data.

   c. *Explain* what the mean tells you about the student's spending habits.

59. ★ SHORT RESPONSE Evaluate $-\dfrac{6}{2}$, $\dfrac{-6}{2}$, and $\dfrac{6}{-2}$. Compare the results. Then make and test a conjecture about the relationship between $-\dfrac{a}{b}$, $\dfrac{-a}{b}$, and $\dfrac{a}{-b}$. *Explain* your reasoning.

60. WORK BACKWARD The mean of seven temperatures is −2°C. Six of the temperatures are shown at the right. Find the seventh temperature.

      −4°C −2°C 0°C
      −3°C −1°C 2°C

61. CHALLENGE Give 6 integers, four negative and two positive, that have a mean of −5. *Explain* how you found your answer.

MIXED REVIEW

Get-Ready
Prepare for
Lesson 11.6
in Exs. 62–63

Graph the points on a coordinate grid and connect them to form a polygon. Then classify the polygon. *(pp. 88, 480)*

62. $A(3, 5)$, $B(8, 5)$, $C(8, 1)$, $D(3, 1)$ **63.** $A(1, 2)$, $B(1, 4)$, $C(7, 4)$

64. ★ MULTIPLE CHOICE A dictionary is seven and nine hundredths centimeters thick. What is the thickness in decimal form? *(p. 119)*

  (A) 7.009 cm   **(B)** 7.09 cm   **(C)** 7.9 cm   **(D)** 7900 cm

CHOOSE A STRATEGY Use a strategy from the list to solve the following problem. *Explain* your choice of strategy.

65. How many square inches of carpet are needed to cover the platform shown?

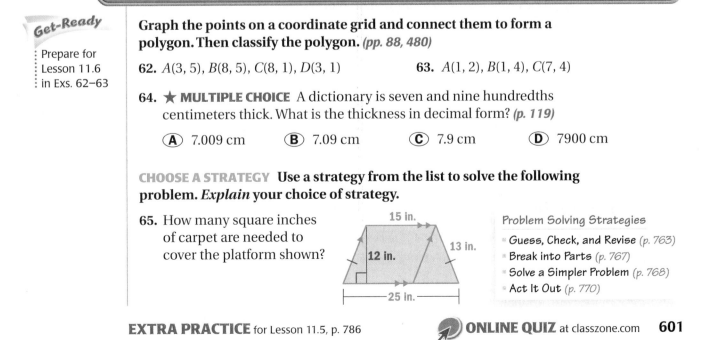

Problem Solving Strategies
• Guess, Check, and Revise *(p. 763)*
• Break into Parts *(p. 767)*
• Solve a Simpler Problem *(p. 768)*
• Act It Out *(p. 770)*

GOAL
Use a calculator to perform operations with integers.

11.5 Integer Operations

EXAMPLE You can use the ⊙ key to enter negative numbers.

The average monthly temperatures during the months of December through March in Caribou, Maine, are listed below, to the nearest degree. Find the mean of the temperatures.

$$-10°C \qquad -13°C \qquad -11°C \qquad -4°C$$

SOLUTION

To find the mean of the temperatures, first find the sum of the temperatures. To enter a negative number, use the negation key, ⊙, *not* the subtraction key, ⊟.

Keystrokes   **Display**

⊙ 10 ⊞ ⊙ 13 ⊞ ⊙ 11 ⊞ ⊙ 4 = | −38 |

Then divide the sum by the number of temperatures.

Keystrokes   **Display**

⊙ 38 ÷ 4 = | −9.5 |

▶ **Answer** The mean of the temperatures is −9.5°C.

PRACTICE Use a calculator to evaluate the expression.

1. $28 - (-937)$ **2.** $402 \times (-59)$ **3.** $-45 + 63 - (-30)$

4. $-33 \times (-74)$ **5.** $810 \div (-45)$ **6.** $-72 \div (-6) + (-93)$

7. VOLCANOES New Zealand has three volcanoes beneath the surface of the water. Their elevations are −700 meters, −450 meters, and −140 meters. Find the mean of the elevations.

8. MONEY You have a savings account. During the week you withdraw $75, withdraw $115, deposit $100, and withdraw $55. At the end of the week, do you have *more* or *less* money in the account than you had at the beginning of the week? *Describe* the change in the amount of money.

9. TIME A student noticed that the classroom clock lost 2 minutes every day. How many minutes did the clock lose over 5 days?

11.6 Translations in a Coordinate Plane

Before	You graphed points with positive coordinates.
Now	You'll graph points with negative coordinates.
Why?	So you can describe the path of a tornado, as in Ex. 34.

KEY VOCABULARY
- **coordinate plane,** *p. 603*
- **quadrants,** *p. 603*
- **translation,** *p. 604*
- **image,** *p. 604*

In Chapter 2, you graphed points whose coordinates were positive or zero on a coordinate grid. Now you'll graph points whose coordinates are integers on a **coordinate plane** as shown below. The axes divide a coordinate plane into four areas, called **quadrants**, as shown.

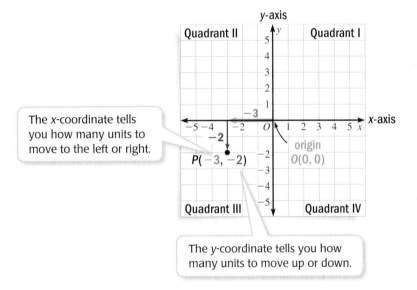

The *x*-coordinate tells you how many units to move to the left or right.

The *y*-coordinate tells you how many units to move up or down.

EXAMPLE 1 Graphing Points

Graph the point and describe its location.

VOCABULARY
Quad- means "4."
A quadrilateral has 4 sides. A quadrant is one of 4 sections of a coordinate plane.

a. To graph point $A(-2, 0)$, start at $(0, 0)$. Move 2 units to the left and 0 units up. Point A is on the x-axis.

b. To graph point $B(4, -2)$, start at $(0, 0)$. Move 4 units to the right and 2 units down. Point B is in Quadrant IV.

✓ **GUIDED PRACTICE** **for Example 1**

Graph the point and describe its location.

1. $A(0, -3)$ **2.** $B(-2, -1)$ **3.** $C(-1, 2)$ **4.** $D(1, -4)$

Translations In a **translation**, each point of a figure slides the same distance in the same direction. The new figure is the **image** of the original figure.

For example, each point on △*DEF* has moved 6 units to the right and 3 units up from each point on △*ABC*. △*DEF* is the image of △*ABC*.

Notice that in a translation, the image is congruent to the original figure.

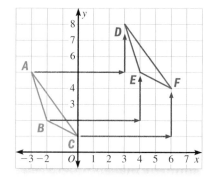

EXAMPLE 2 Translating a Figure

Animation In an animation, a kite will be translated 4 units to the right and 5 units down. The images of points *A*, *B*, *C*, and *D* will be points *P*, *Q*, *R*, and *S*. Draw the image and give the coordinates of points *P*, *Q*, *R*, and *S*.

SOLUTION

ANOTHER WAY

You can also slide the original figure 5 units down and then 4 units to the right. You will still get the same image.

To draw the image, think of sliding the original figure 4 units to the right and 5 units down.

You'll get the same image if you add 4 to the *x*-coordinates and subtract 5 from the *y*-coordinates.

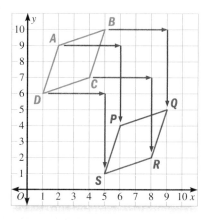

$A(2, 9) \longrightarrow (2 + 4, 9 - 5) \longrightarrow P(6, 4)$

$B(5, 10) \longrightarrow (5 + 4, 10 - 5) \longrightarrow Q(9, 5)$

$C(4, 7) \longrightarrow (4 + 4, 7 - 5) \longrightarrow R(8, 2)$

$D(1, 6) \longrightarrow (1 + 4, 6 - 5) \longrightarrow S(5, 1)$

▶ **Answer** The coordinates are *P*(6, 4), *Q*(9, 5), *R*(8, 2), and *S*(5, 1).

Animated **Math** at classzone.com

✓ **GUIDED PRACTICE** for Example 2

GRAPH POINTS

Need help graphing ordered pairs with positive coordinates? See p. 88.

Graph the points and connect them to form △*ABC*. Then translate the triangle 3 units to the left and 2 units down to form △*DEF*. Give the coordinates of the vertices of △*DEF*.

5. *A*(−4, 1), *B*(−1, −1), *C*(2, 1)

6. *A*(2, −1), *B*(−4, 2), *C*(0, −2)

7. *A*(3, 0), *B*(5, −3), *C*(1, −4)

8. *A*(1, 3), *B*(5, 2), *C*(2, 1)

11.6 **EXERCISES**

HOMEWORK KEY

★ = **STANDARDIZED TEST PRACTICE**
Exs. 17, 18, 23, 24, 29, 30, 32, 33, and 46

◯ = **HINTS AND HOMEWORK HELP**
for Exs. 5, 7, 15, 29 at classzone.com

SKILL PRACTICE

VOCABULARY Tell whether the statement is *true* or *false*.

1. The *y*-axis is the horizontal axis on a coordinate plane.

2. A quadrant is one of three sections that make up the coordinate plane.

GRAPHING POINTS Graph the point and describe its location.

SEE EXAMPLE 1
on p. 603
for Exs. 3–17

3. $A(5, -1)$ 4. $B(0, 3)$ **5.** $C(-1, 3)$ 6. $D(5, 0)$

7. $E(3, 4)$ 8. $F(-7, -5)$ 9. $G(0, -7)$ 10. $H(3, -2)$

USING MAPS Use the map to give the coordinates of the location.

11. school   12. library

13. post office   14. statue

15. city hall   16. store

17. ★ **MULTIPLE CHOICE** In which quadrant is the point $(-9, 4)$?

(A) I   **(B)** II   **(C)** III   **(D)** IV

SEE EXAMPLE 2
on p. 604
for Exs. 18–20

18. ★ **MULTIPLE CHOICE** You translate a point at the origin 6 units to the left and then 5 units down. Which ordered pair describes the point's new location?

(A) $(-6, -5)$ **(B)** $(0, 5)$ **(C)** $(-5, -6)$ **(D)** $(5, -6)$

19. **ERROR ANALYSIS** Use the coordinate plane to describe and correct the error made in translating the point $A(2, 1)$ four units to the right and one unit down to point B.

20. **TRANSLATING A SEGMENT** Graph the points $P(-5, 4)$ and $Q(-2, -2)$. Connect the points to form a segment. Then translate the segment 1 unit to the left and 2 units down to form $\overline{RS}$. Give the coordinates of R and S.

21. **GRAPHING A TRIANGLE** Graph right triangle QRS with vertices $Q(-2, 5)$, $R(-2, -1)$, and $S(6, -1)$. Then translate $\triangle QRS$ 3 units to the right and 5 units down. Graph the image and give its coordinates.

22. **GRAPHING A RECTANGLE** Graph rectangle $JKLM$ with points $J(8, 4)$, $K(3, 4)$, and $L(3, 6)$. Label point M with its coordinates. Then translate $JKLM$ 1 unit to the left and 3 units up. Graph the image and give its coordinates.

FINDING COORDINATES In Exercises 23 and 24, use the rectangle shown.

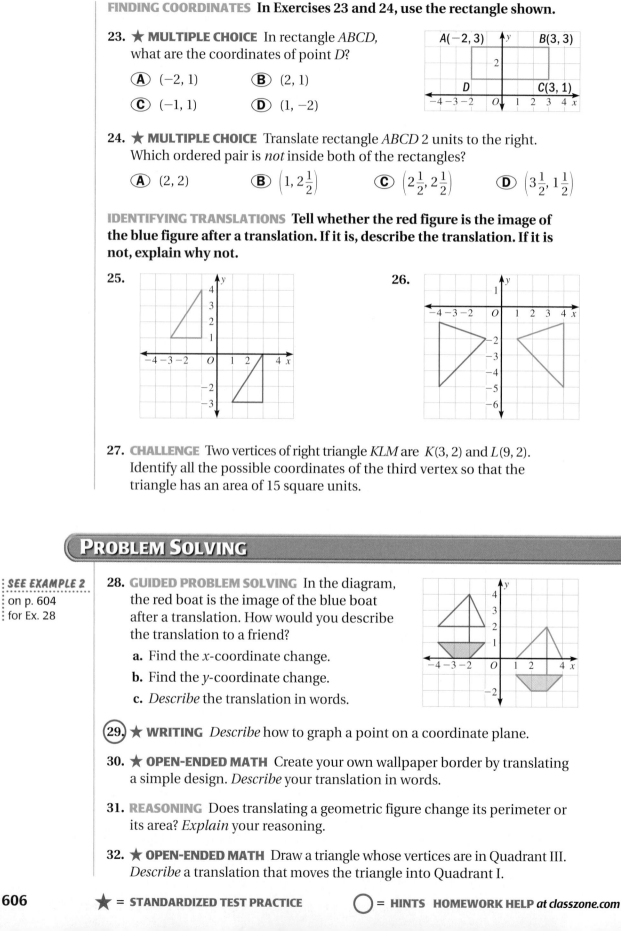

23. ★ **MULTIPLE CHOICE** In rectangle *ABCD*, what are the coordinates of point *D*?

   Ⓐ (−2, 1)   Ⓑ (2, 1)

   Ⓒ (−1, 1)   Ⓓ (1, −2)

24. ★ **MULTIPLE CHOICE** Translate rectangle *ABCD* 2 units to the right. Which ordered pair is *not* inside both of the rectangles?

   Ⓐ (2, 2)   Ⓑ $\left(1, 2\frac{1}{2}\right)$ Ⓒ $\left(2\frac{1}{2}, 2\frac{1}{2}\right)$ Ⓓ $\left(3\frac{1}{2}, 1\frac{1}{2}\right)$

IDENTIFYING TRANSLATIONS Tell whether the red figure is the image of the blue figure after a translation. If it is, describe the translation. If it is not, explain why not.

25.

26.

27. **CHALLENGE** Two vertices of right triangle *KLM* are *K*(3, 2) and *L*(9, 2). Identify all the possible coordinates of the third vertex so that the triangle has an area of 15 square units.

PROBLEM SOLVING

SEE EXAMPLE 2
on p. 604
for Ex. 28

28. **GUIDED PROBLEM SOLVING** In the diagram, the red boat is the image of the blue boat after a translation. How would you describe the translation to a friend?

   a. Find the *x*-coordinate change.

   b. Find the *y*-coordinate change.

   c. *Describe* the translation in words.

29. ★ **WRITING** *Describe* how to graph a point on a coordinate plane.

30. ★ **OPEN-ENDED MATH** Create your own wallpaper border by translating a simple design. *Describe* your translation in words.

31. **REASONING** Does translating a geometric figure change its perimeter or its area? *Explain* your reasoning.

32. ★ **OPEN-ENDED MATH** Draw a triangle whose vertices are in Quadrant III. *Describe* a translation that moves the triangle into Quadrant I.

33. ★ **SHORT RESPONSE** A figure is translated 7 units up and 4 units to the right. Will you get the same image if the figure is translated 4 units to the right first and then 7 units up? Is there another pair of horizontal and vertical movements that will produce the same image? *Explain.*

34. **TORNADOS** The graph shows the approximate points where a tornado touched down in South Dakota. *Describe* the translation between points *A* and *B*, between points *B* and *C*, and between points *C* and *D*. Is the tornado traveling in a straight line? *Explain.*

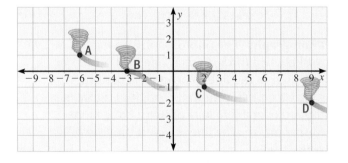

35. **XY ALGEBRA** Write the coordinates of the image of the point (x, y) after a translation of *a* units to the right and *b* units down.

36. **REASONING** Multiply each *x*- and *y*-coordinate of the vertices of the figure by 1.5. Graph the new figure and give the coordinates of its vertices. Is the new figure a translation? *Explain* why or why not. *Describe* the relationship between the new and the original figures.

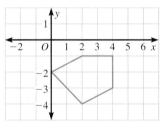

CHALLENGE The points $A(-5, -1)$, $B(-1, -1)$, $C(-1, -4)$ and $D(-5, -4)$ form a rectangle. Use these points for the given translation.

37. *Describe* a translation for which the image will have two vertices in Quadrant II and two vertices in Quadrant I.

38. *Describe* a translation for which the image will have one vertex in each quadrant.

MIXED REVIEW

Get-Ready

⋮ Prepare for
⋮ Lesson 11.7
⋮ in Exs. 39–41

Copy the figure and draw all lines of symmetry. *(p. 494)*

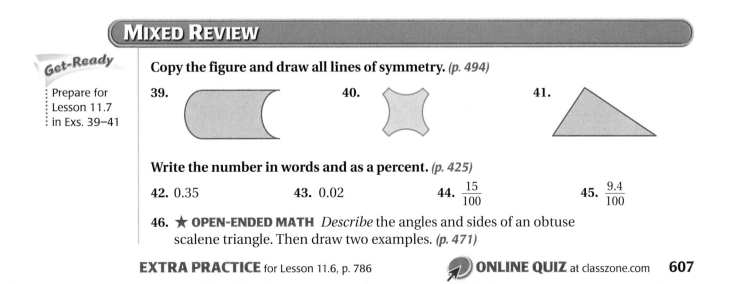

39. 40. 41.

Write the number in words and as a percent. *(p. 425)*

42. 0.35   43. 0.02   44. $\frac{15}{100}$ 45. $\frac{9.4}{100}$

46. ★ **OPEN-ENDED MATH** *Describe* the angles and sides of an obtuse scalene triangle. Then draw two examples. *(p. 471)*

EXTRA PRACTICE for Lesson 11.6, p. 786   🌐 **ONLINE QUIZ** at classzone.com   **607**

11.7 Reflections and Rotations

Before	You learned how to recognize translations.
Now	You'll learn how to recognize reflections and rotations.
Why?	So you can identify transformations in weaving designs, as in Exs. 28–31.

KEY VOCABULARY

- **reflection, line of reflection,** *p. 608*
- **rotation, center of rotation, angle of rotation,** *p. 608*
- **transformation,** *p. 609*

Photography The photograph appears to show two birds. In fact, one bird is reflected in the line to produce a congruent image. In a **reflection**, the original figure is flipped over a line to produce a congruent mirror image. The line is called the **line of reflection**.

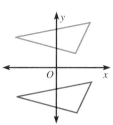

line of reflection

EXAMPLE 1 Identifying Reflections

Tell whether the red figure is a reflection of the blue figure. If it is a reflection, identify the line of reflection.

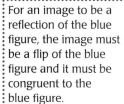

RECOGNIZE REFLECTIONS

For an image to be a reflection of the blue figure, the image must be a flip of the blue figure and it must be congruent to the blue figure.

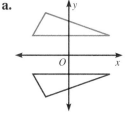

a.

Yes. The line of reflection is the *x*-axis.

b.

Yes. The line of reflection is the *y*-axis.

c.

No. The figure is not flipped.

Rotations The blue figure below was turned 90° clockwise about the origin to produce the congruent red image. The diagram illustrates a *rotation*. In a **rotation**, a figure is rotated through a given angle about a fixed point called the **center of rotation**. The angle is called the **angle of rotation**. In this book, all rotations are clockwise rotations about the origin.

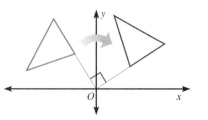

EXAMPLE 2 Identifying Rotations

Tell whether the red figure is a rotation of the blue figure about the origin. If it is a rotation, state the angle of rotation.

a.

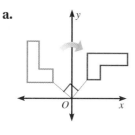

Yes. The figure is rotated 90°.

b.

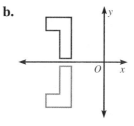

No. This is a flip, not a turn.

c.

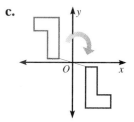

Yes. The figure is rotated 180°.

Transformations A **transformation**, such as a translation, reflection, or rotation, is a movement of a figure on a plane. To distinguish one transformation from another, decide whether the movement is a slide, a flip, or a turn.

EXAMPLE 3 Identifying Transformations

Tell whether the transformation is a *translation*, a *reflection*, or a *rotation*.

USE TOOLS

You can use tracing paper to help you identify transformations. Trace the original figure, then try to slide, flip, or turn it to produce the image.

a.

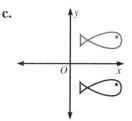

This is a reflection. The figure is flipped over the *x*-axis.

b.

This is a rotation. The figure is rotated 90° clockwise.

c.

This is a translation. The figure is slid straight down.

Animated Math at classzone.com

✓ GUIDED PRACTICE for Examples 1, 2, and 3

Tell whether the transformation is a *translation*, a *reflection*, or a *rotation*. Identify any line(s) of reflection or angle(s) of rotation.

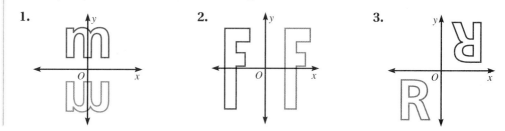

1.

2.

3.

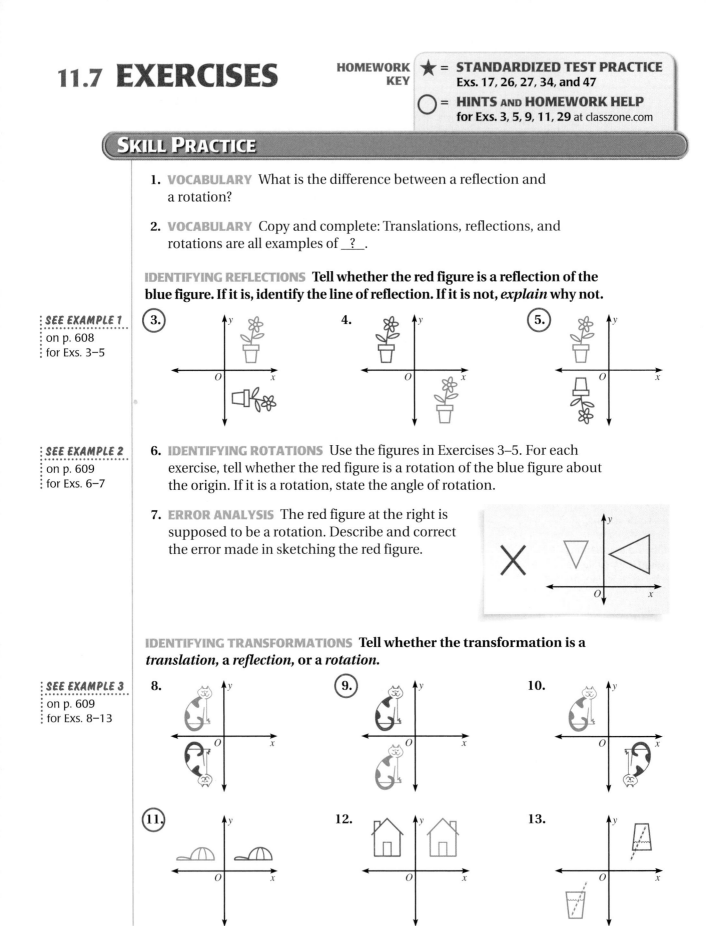

11.7 EXERCISES

SKILL PRACTICE

1. **VOCABULARY** What is the difference between a reflection and a rotation?

2. **VOCABULARY** Copy and complete: Translations, reflections, and rotations are all examples of _?_.

IDENTIFYING REFLECTIONS **Tell whether the red figure is a reflection of the blue figure. If it is, identify the line of reflection. If it is not, *explain* why not.**

SEE EXAMPLE 1
on p. 608
for Exs. 3–5

3.

4.

5.

SEE EXAMPLE 2
on p. 609
for Exs. 6–7

6. **IDENTIFYING ROTATIONS** Use the figures in Exercises 3–5. For each exercise, tell whether the red figure is a rotation of the blue figure about the origin. If it is a rotation, state the angle of rotation.

7. **ERROR ANALYSIS** The red figure at the right is supposed to be a rotation. Describe and correct the error made in sketching the red figure.

IDENTIFYING TRANSFORMATIONS **Tell whether the transformation is a *translation*, a *reflection*, or a *rotation*.**

SEE EXAMPLE 3
on p. 609
for Exs. 8–13

8.

9.

10.

11.

12.

13.

DRAWING REFLECTIONS Copy and reflect the figure in the indicated axis.

14. *y*-axis

15. *x*-axis

16. *x*-axis

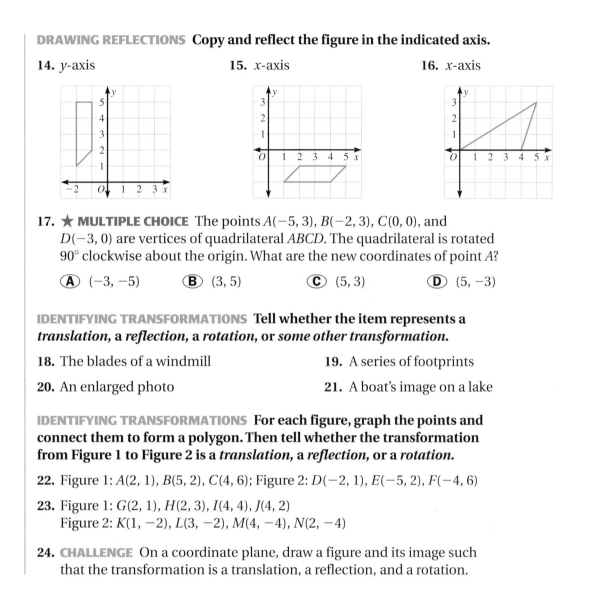

17. ★ **MULTIPLE CHOICE** The points $A(-5, 3)$, $B(-2, 3)$, $C(0, 0)$, and $D(-3, 0)$ are vertices of quadrilateral *ABCD*. The quadrilateral is rotated $90°$ clockwise about the origin. What are the new coordinates of point *A*?

(A) $(-3, -5)$ **(B)** $(3, 5)$ **(C)** $(5, 3)$ **(D)** $(5, -3)$

IDENTIFYING TRANSFORMATIONS Tell whether the item represents a *translation,* a *reflection,* a *rotation,* or *some other transformation.*

18. The blades of a windmill

19. A series of footprints

20. An enlarged photo

21. A boat's image on a lake

IDENTIFYING TRANSFORMATIONS For each figure, graph the points and connect them to form a polygon. Then tell whether the transformation from Figure 1 to Figure 2 is a *translation,* a *reflection,* or a *rotation.*

22. Figure 1: $A(2, 1)$, $B(5, 2)$, $C(4, 6)$; Figure 2: $D(-2, 1)$, $E(-5, 2)$, $F(-4, 6)$

23. Figure 1: $G(2, 1)$, $H(2, 3)$, $I(4, 4)$, $J(4, 2)$
Figure 2: $K(1, -2)$, $L(3, -2)$, $M(4, -4)$, $N(2, -4)$

24. **CHALLENGE** On a coordinate plane, draw a figure and its image such that the transformation is a translation, a reflection, and a rotation.

PROBLEM SOLVING

SEE EXAMPLES 2 AND 3
on pp. 608–609
for Ex. 25

25. **JEWELRY** Which piece of jewelry has a design that appears to be based on a reflection? Which appears based on a series of rotations about its center?

A.

B.

26. ★ **OPEN-ENDED MATH** Create a jewelry design based on rotations.

27. ★ **SHORT RESPONSE** When you look at yourself in the mirror, your right side appears to be on the left side. Is this also true when you look at a photo of yourself? *Explain* your answer.

WEAVING Ignoring color, tell whether the design can be formed by a *reflection*, a *series of translations*, or a *series of rotations*. *Describe* all transformations that apply.

28.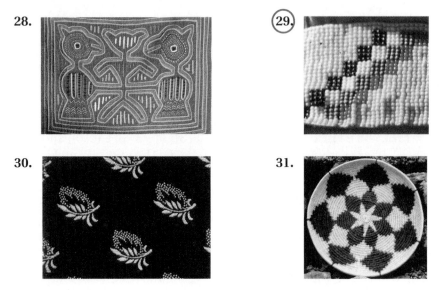

29.

30.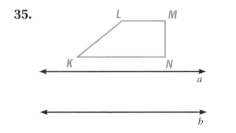

31.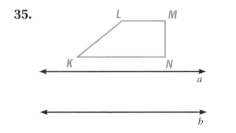

32. **GEOMETRY** Draw a rectangle that is not a square. Then draw a diagonal. Are the two triangles formed by the diagonal *reflections, rotations,* or *translations*?

33. **GEOMETRY** A regular hexagon is drawn in a coordinate plane with its center at the origin. The hexagon is rotated 120°. What is the result?

34. ★ **EXTENDED RESPONSE** Each step in the spiral staircase at the right is a rotation of the previous step.

　　a. What part of the staircase represents the center of rotation?

　　b. As you ascend the staircase, are the rotations *clockwise* or *counterclockwise*?

　　c. Estimate the angle of rotation for each step. *Explain* your reasoning.

REASONING In Exercises 35 and 36, trace the quadrilateral and the two lines. Sketch the reflection of *KLMN* in line *a*. Call it *PQRS*. Sketch the reflection of *PQRS* in line *b*. Call it *VWXY*. Is the transformation from *KLMN* to *VWXY* a *translation* or a *reflection*? *Explain* your reasoning.

35.

36.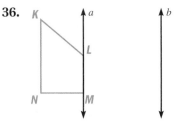

★ = **STANDARDIZED TEST PRACTICE**　　　◯ = **HINTS AND HOMEWORK HELP** *at classzone.com*

CHALLENGE A figure has *point symmetry* if a line through its center divides it into two congruent parts that are related by a rotation of 180°. Tell whether the figure has *line symmetry, point symmetry,* or *both*.

37.

38.

39.

MIXED REVIEW

Get-Ready

Prepare for Lesson 12.1 in Exs. 40–45

Evaluate the expression. *(p. 29)*

40. $9 + x$, when $x = 35$

41. $m \div 9$, when $m = 81$

42. $6b$, when $b = 12$

Is the given number a solution of the equation? *(p. 34)*

43. $7 + p = 24$; 14

44. $56 \div n = 7$; 8

45. $120c = 20$; 5

CHOOSE A STRATEGY Use a strategy from the list to solve the following problem. *Explain* your choice of strategy.

46. Your friend treated you to lunch and left a tip of $3. The tip was 20% of the bill. How much was the bill?

> **Problem Solving Strategies**
> ▪ Draw a Diagram *(p. 762)*
> ▪ Guess, Check, and Revise *(p. 763)*
> ▪ Work Backward *(p. 764)*
> ▪ Break into Parts *(p. 767)*

47. ★ **MULTIPLE CHOICE** Which quotient is equal to -9? *(p. 597)*

Ⓐ $-54 \div (-6)$ Ⓑ $45 \div 5$ Ⓒ $27 \div (-3)$ Ⓓ $-108 \div (-12)$

QUIZ *for Lessons 11.4–11.7*

Find the product or quotient.

1. $7(-7)$ *(p. 592)*

2. $-5(-8)$ *(p. 592)*

3. $-6(0)$ *(p. 592)*

4. $-140 \div 7$ *(p. 597)*

5. $-30 \div (-6)$ *(p. 597)*

6. $-25 \div (-5)$ *(p. 597)*

7. The vertices of $\triangle ABC$ are $A(-2, -3)$, $B(1, -1)$, and $C(0, 4)$. Draw $\triangle ABC$ in a coordinate plane. Then translate it 5 units to the right and 4 units up to form $\triangle DEF$. Give the coordinates of points D, E, and F. *(p. 603)*

Tell whether the transformation is a *translation*, a *reflection*, or a *rotation*. *(p. 608)*

8.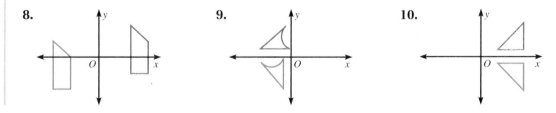

9.

10.

Tessellations

GOAL Identify and construct tessellations.

KEY VOCABULARY
- **tessellation,** *p. 614*
- **regular tessellation,** *p. 614*

A **tessellation** is a repeating pattern of figures that fill a plane with no gaps or overlaps. The coat at the right has a repeating pattern of triangles.

A **regular tessellation** is made from only one type of regular polygon. For example, the kitchen floor tiles below suggest a regular tessellation.

Not all regular polygons can form regular tessellations.

EXAMPLE 1 Forming Regular Tessellations

Tell whether the polygon can form a regular tessellation.

a. regular pentagon

b. regular hexagon

SOLUTION

a. Start with a regular pentagon. Make two copies and fit the pentagons together as shown. The gap around their common vertex cannot be filled by a fourth regular pentagon. So, regular pentagons cannot form a regular tessellation.

b. Start with a regular hexagon. Make six copies and fit the hexagons together as shown. The resulting pattern will fill a plane with no gaps or overlaps. So, regular hexagons can form a regular tessellation.

Other Tessellations The only regular polygons that form regular tessellations are equilateral triangles, squares, and regular hexagons. Tessellations can also be formed using more than one regular polygon, or one or more nonregular polygons. The polygons may be translated, reflected, or rotated to fill the plane.

EXAMPLE 2 Forming Tessellations

Draw a tessellation of the scalene triangle shown.

SOLUTION

STEP 1 **Locate** and mark a point at the middle of one side of the triangle. Rotate the triangle 180° about the point to form a parallelogram.

STEP 2 **Translate** the parallelogram as shown so that the pattern fills the plane with no gaps or overlaps.

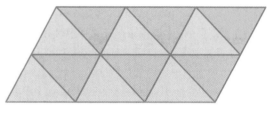

EXERCISES

1. Draw a regular tessellation of equilateral triangles. *Describe* any transformations you use.

In Exercises 2–4, use the given triangle and the method in Example 2 to draw a tessellation.

2.    3.    4.

5. You can use any quadrilateral to create a tessellation. Draw any quadrilateral and follow the steps below to create a tessellation.

STEP 1
Locate and mark a point in the middle of one side.

STEP 2
Rotate the quadrilateral 180° about the point to form a hexagon.

STEP 3
Translate the hexagons to draw a tessellation.

Lessons 11.4–11.7

1. **MULTI-STEP PROBLEM** You are fishing on a boat anchored on a lake. You drop a line with a sinker into the water. The sinker descends at a rate of 2 feet per second.

   a. Using the surface as level 0, write an integer to describe the sinker's rate of change in water level, in feet per second.

   b. Write a multiplication expression for the sinker's position relative to the surface after 8 seconds.

   c. Evaluate your expression from part (b) to find the sinker's position relative to the surface after 8 seconds.

2. **SHORT RESPONSE** *Describe* the next figure in the pattern below. *Explain* your reasoning.

3. **EXTENDED RESPONSE** A computer animator graphs the points $A(-2, 4)$, $B(-3, 1)$, and $C(-1, 1)$ and connects them. Translate $\triangle ABC$ 4 units to the right to form $\triangle XYZ$. Give the coordinates of each vertex. *Describe* a different transformation of $\triangle ABC$ to $\triangle XZY$.

4. **SHORT RESPONSE** Does the photo show a *reflection* or a *rotation*? How is the image the same as the original? How is the image different from the original?

5. **GRIDDED ANSWER** A temperature change was $-3°F$ per hour. How many hours did it take to change $-15°F$?

6. **OPEN-ENDED** *Describe* a series of transformations that will transform pentagon *ABCDE* to pentagon *RSTUV*. Make a sketch of each transformation. *Explain* how you decided what transformations to use.

   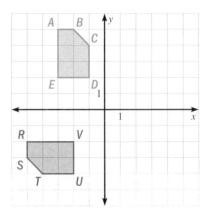

7. **EXTENDED RESPONSE** On a coordinate plane, draw a triangle with vertices $A(-5, -5)$, $B(-5, -2)$, and $C(-3, -2)$.

   a. Translate $\triangle ABC$ 5 units up and then reflect it in the *y*-axis. Draw the new triangle.

   b. Reflect original $\triangle ABC$ in the *y*-axis and then translate it 5 units up. Draw the new triangle.

   c. Did it matter in what order you performed the transformations in parts (a) and (b)? Is your answer true for *any* reflection and translation? *Explain* your reasoning.

8. **SHORT RESPONSE** Use the pattern below. What are the next two numbers? What is the rule for finding the next number?

   $$-3, 6, -12, \underline{\ ?\ }, \underline{\ ?\ }$$

9. **OPEN-ENDED** *Explain* how the rules for multiplying integers and dividing integers are similar. *Describe* a situation that can be represented by multiplying integers. *Describe* a situation that can be represented by dividing integers.

REVIEW KEY VOCABULARY

- integers, *p. 573*
- negative integers, *p. 573*
- positive integers, *p. 573*
- opposites, *p. 574*
- absolute value, *p. 580*

- coordinate plane, *p. 603*
- quadrants, *p. 603*
- translations, *p. 604*
- image, *p. 604*
- reflection, *p. 608*

- line of reflection, *p. 608*
- rotation, *p. 608*
- center of rotation, *p. 608*
- angle of rotation, *p. 608*
- transformation, *p. 609*

VOCABULARY EXERCISES

1. *Explain* how to tell if one figure is a translation of another.

Copy and complete the statement.

2. The numbers 9 and −9 are called __?__ .

3. The __?__ of −4 is written $|-4|$ and it equals 4.

4. The __?__ is divided into four quadrants by the two axes.

5. In a __?__ , an original figure is flipped over a line to produce a congruent mirror image.

6. In a __?__ , a figure is turned about a fixed point called the __?__ .

REVIEW EXAMPLES AND EXERCISES

11.1 Comparing Integers

pp. 573–577

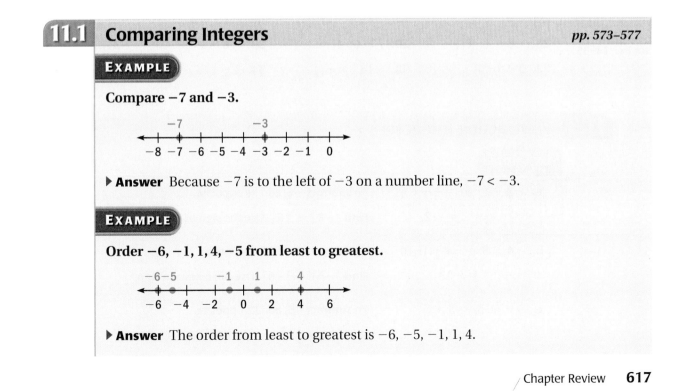

EXAMPLE

Compare −7 and −3.

▶ **Answer** Because −7 is to the left of −3 on a number line, −7 < −3.

EXAMPLE

Order −6, −1, 1, 4, −5 from least to greatest.

▶ **Answer** The order from least to greatest is −6, −5, −1, 1, 4.

EXERCISES

Write the integer that represents the situation.

SEE EXAMPLES
1, 3, AND 4
on pp. 573–574
for Exs. 7–23

7. a profit of $25   **8.** 15 degrees below zero   **9.** a decrease of 3 feet

Copy and complete the statement using < or >.

10. 5 <u>?</u> −5   **11.** −3 <u>?</u> −2   **12.** 1 <u>?</u> −4   **13.** 0 <u>?</u> −1

14. −9 <u>?</u> −10   **15.** −8 <u>?</u> 5   **16.** −5 <u>?</u> −1   **17.** 6 <u>?</u> −7

Order the integers from least to greatest.

18. 3, −4, 10, 2, −9   **19.** −8, 0, −13, 6, −6   **20.** 5, −15, 7, −5, −7

21. −12, −3, −11, 3, 5   **22.** 1, 0, −1, −2, −39   **23.** −4, −8, 6, −3, −14

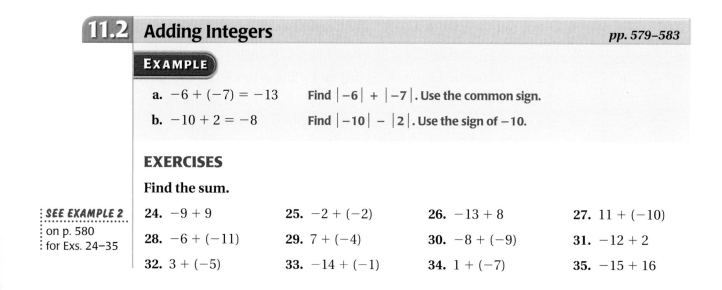

11.2 Adding Integers

pp. 579–583

EXAMPLE

a. $-6 + (-7) = -13$ Find $\left| -6 \right| + \left| -7 \right|$. Use the common sign.

b. $-10 + 2 = -8$ Find $\left| -10 \right| - \left| 2 \right|$. Use the sign of -10.

EXERCISES

Find the sum.

SEE EXAMPLE 2
on p. 580
for Exs. 24–35

24. $-9 + 9$ **25.** $-2 + (-2)$ **26.** $-13 + 8$ **27.** $11 + (-10)$

28. $-6 + (-11)$ **29.** $7 + (-4)$ **30.** $-8 + (-9)$ **31.** $-12 + 2$

32. $3 + (-5)$ **33.** $-14 + (-1)$ **34.** $1 + (-7)$ **35.** $-15 + 16$

11.3 Subtracting Integers

pp. 586–590

EXAMPLE

a. $-8 - (-6) = -8 + 6$ To subtract -6, add its opposite.

$= -2$ Find $\left| -8 \right| - \left| 6 \right|$. Use the sign of -8.

b. $-4 - 9 = -4 + (-9)$ To subtract 9, add its opposite.

$= -13$ Find $\left| -4 \right| + \left| -9 \right|$. Use the common sign.

c. $3 - (-5) = 3 + 5$ To subtract -5, add its opposite.

$= 8$ Find $\left| 3 \right| + \left| 5 \right|$. Use the common sign.

EXERCISES

Find the difference.

SEE EXAMPLE 2
on p. 587
for Exs. 36–47

36. $2 - 6$ **37.** $10 - 15$ **38.** $-8 - 3$ **39.** $-14 - 4$

40. $15 - (-9)$ **41.** $18 - (-6)$ **42.** $-13 - (-7)$ **43.** $-5 - (-25)$

44. $-7 - (-5)$ **45.** $-9 - (-1)$ **46.** $11 - (-3)$ **47.** $12 - (-8)$

11.4 Multiplying Integers

pp. 592–596

EXAMPLE

a. $-4(-8) = 32$ **The product of two negative integers is positive.**

b. $7(-3) = -21$ **The product of a positive integer and a negative integer is negative.**

EXERCISES

Find the product.

SEE EXAMPLE 1
on p. 593
for Exs. 48–59

48. $2(-2)$ **49.** $-7(8)$ **50.** $-10(4)$ **51.** $-9(7)$

52. $5(-6)$ **53.** $3(-11)$ **54.** $-3(-90)$ **55.** $-2(-12)$

56. $-4(-9)$ **57.** $-5(-10)$ **58.** $6(-6)$ **59.** $8(-40)$

11.5 Dividing Integers

pp. 597–601

EXAMPLE

a. $72 \div (-8) = -9$ **The quotient of two integers with different signs is negative.**

b. $-18 \div (-3) = 6$ **The quotient of two integers with the same sign is positive.**

EXERCISES

Find the quotient.

SEE EXAMPLE 2
on p. 598
for Exs. 60–71

60. $-20 \div 2$ **61.** $-35 \div 5$ **62.** $42 \div (-7)$ **63.** $24 \div (-6)$

64. $81 \div (-9)$ **65.** $-20 \div (-5)$ **66.** $-48 \div (-8)$ **67.** $-50 \div (-10)$

68. $-36 \div (-4)$ **69.** $-50 \div 25$ **70.** $-72 \div 9$ **71.** $44 \div (-11)$

11.6 Translations in a Coordinate Plane

pp. 603–607

EXAMPLE

Translate △*ABC* 3 units to the left and 4 units up to form △*XYZ*. Give the coordinates of points *X*, *Y*, and *Z*.

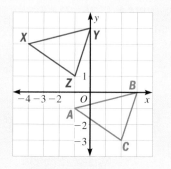

▶ **Answer** $A(-1, -1) \longrightarrow X(-4, 3)$

$B(3, 0) \longrightarrow Y(0, 4)$

$C(2, -3) \longrightarrow Z(-1, 1)$

EXERCISES

Draw the figure in a coordinate plane. Then translate the figure as described. Give the coordinates of the vertices of the image.

SEE EXAMPLE 2
on p. 604
for Exs. 72–73

72. △*ABC*: $A(-3, 6)$, $B(-1, 4)$, $C(-4, 2)$
Translation: 5 units right and 3 units down to form △*DEF*

73. △*HJK*: $H(-2, 3)$, $J(2, 2)$, $K(-1, -1)$
Translation: 4 units left and 3 units up to form △*RST*

11.7 Reflections and Rotations

pp. 608–613

EXAMPLE

Tell whether the transformation is a *translation*, a *reflection*, or a *rotation*.

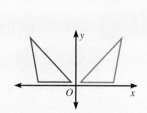

▶ **Answer**   The transformation is a reflection in the *y*-axis.

EXERCISES

Tell whether the transformation is a *translation*, a *reflection*, or a *rotation*. If it is a reflection, identify the line of reflection. If it is a rotation, state the angle and direction of rotation.

SEE EXAMPLE 3
on p. 609
for Exs. 74–76

74.   **75.**   **76.**

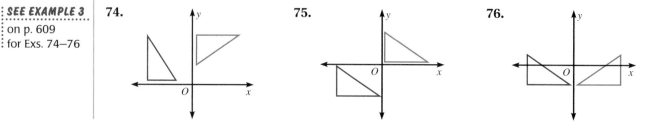

Order the integers from least to greatest.

1. $-1, 9, -6, 3, 0$ **2.** $21, -22, 13, -14, 4$ **3.** $-1, 10, -11, -111, 110$

Find the sum.

4. $3 + (-4)$ **5.** $9 + (-9)$ **6.** $15 + (-5)$ **7.** $-7 + 2$

8. $-6 + 11$ **9.** $-1 + (-1)$ **10.** $-8 + (-10)$ **11.** $-12 + (-12)$

Find the difference.

12. $8 - 9$ **13.** $2 - 12$ **14.** $-6 - 10$ **15.** $-15 - 15$

16. $8 - (-18)$ **17.** $5 - (-13)$ **18.** $-14 - (-7)$ **19.** $-10 - (-20)$

Find the product or quotient.

20. $5(-5)$ **21.** $8(-9)$ **22.** $-7(4)$ **23.** $-3(6)$

24. $44 \div (-2)$ **25.** $-54 \div 9$ **26.** $-42 \div (-6)$ **27.** $-10 \div (-10)$

28. Graph the points $A(3, 2)$, $B(4, -4)$, and $C(-2, -3)$. Then translate $\triangle ABC$ 4 units to the right and 5 units up to form $\triangle XYZ$. Give the coordinates of points X, Y, and Z.

Tell whether the transformation is a *translation*, a *reflection*, or a *rotation*. If it is a reflection, identify the line of reflection. If it is a rotation, state the angle of rotation.

29.   **30.**   **31.**

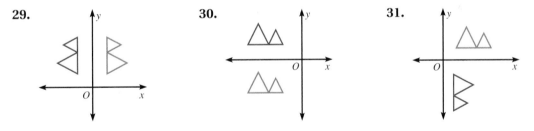

32. **BANK BALANCE** You had a balance of $77 in your savings account before you withdrew $50 and then $20. What is your balance now?

Write the integer that represents the situation.

33. an increase of $20   **34.** a profit of $5   **35.** a decrease of $8

36. a loss of 10 meters   **37.** 15 degrees below 0   **38.** 35 feet above sea level

39. **TEMPERATURE** On Monday at noon, the temperature was 23°F. By 9 P.M. the temperature was -4°F. On Tuesday at noon, the temperature was 18°F. By 9 P.M. the temperature was -11°F. On which day did the greater change in temperature occur? *Explain.*

MULTIPLE CHOICE QUESTIONS

If you have difficulty solving a multiple choice problem directly, you may be able to eliminate incorrect answer choices and obtain the correct answer.

PROBLEM 1

A scout is taking a land navigation test using a map with a coordinate plane. On the map, north is pointing up, and each unit on the plane represents 1 kilometer. The scout begins at point $(-2, -1)$. The scout first hikes 3 kilometers east and 2 kilometers north. The scout then hikes 2 kilometers east. What are the coordinates of the scout's final position?

Ⓐ $(3, -3)$ **Ⓑ** $(1, 1)$ **Ⓒ** $(3, 1)$ **Ⓓ** $(-7, 1)$

METHOD 1

SOLVE DIRECTLY Use the distances and directions to find the scout's translation from point to point.

STEP 1 The scout begins at $(-2, -1)$ and hikes 3 kilometers east and 2 kilometers north. This is a translation of 3 units to the right and 2 units up on the coordinate plane. The scout is now at $(-2 + 3, -1 + 2) = (1, 1)$.

STEP 2 From $(1, 1)$, the scout hikes 2 kilometers east. This is a translation of 2 units to the right on the coordinate plane. The scout is now at $(1 + 2, 1 + 0) = (3, 1)$.

STEP 3 Graph the points to check your answer.

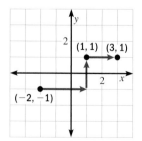

So, the coordinates of the scout's final position are $(3, 1)$.

The correct answer is C. Ⓐ Ⓑ Ⓒ Ⓓ

METHOD 2

ELIMINATE CHOICES In some multiple choice questions, you can identify answer choices that can be eliminated.

The scout hikes east and north, and then east. On the map, the directions of these translations are to the right and up, then to the right. This means that both coordinates of the final position must be greater than those of the starting point. So, you can eliminate choices A and D.

Of the remaining choices, only the x-coordinates are different:

Choice B is 3 units to the right of the starting point: $-2 + 3 = 1$.

Choice C is 5 units to the right of the starting point: $-2 + 5 = 3$.

From the problem statement, you know that the total distance hiked east is $3 + 2 = 5$ kilometers. So, you can eliminate choice B.

The correct answer is C. Ⓐ Ⓑ Ⓒ Ⓓ

PROBLEM 2

A mine shaft is being drilled from the surface using a method that progresses downward through the rock the same amount each day. In a 6 day period, the drill went from -16 feet to -64 feet. What integer represents the drill's position relative to the surface after 26 days?

(**A**) -256 feet (**B**) -208 feet (**C**) 208 feet (**D**) 256 feet

METHOD 1

SOLVE DIRECTLY Find the amount drilled each day. Multiply the drill's position relative to the surface after one day by 26 to find its position after 26 days.

STEP 1 **Subtract** to find the amount drilled in 6 days.

$$-64 - (-16) = -48 \text{ feet}$$

STEP 2 **Divide** by 6 days to find the drill's position relative to the surface after one day.

$$-48 \div 6 = -8 \text{ feet}$$

STEP 3 **Multiply** by 26 to find its position after 26 days.

$$-8 \times 26 = -208 \text{ feet}$$

The correct answer is B. (**A**) (**B**) (**C**) (**D**)

METHOD 2

ELIMINATE CHOICES The drill's position relative to the surface must be a negative number because each day it progresses farther *below* the surface. So, you can eliminate choices C and D.

You can use estimation to determine which of the remaining choices is reasonable. Less than 50 feet is drilled in 6 days, or about 8 feet per day, which can be represented as a position relative to the surface of -8. The product -8×30 represents the position after 30 days. Because $-8 \times 30 = -240$, you know the drill must be closer to the surface than -240 feet after 26 days. So, you can eliminate choice A.

The correct answer is B. (**A**) (**B**) (**C**) (**D**)

PRACTICE

Explain why you can eliminate the highlighted answer choice.

1. You have 45 video game tokens. You use 6 tokens at the arcade every week for 3 weeks in a row. What integer represents the change in your number of tokens over 3 weeks?

   (**A**) -18 (**B**) -9 ✗(**C**) **27**   (**D**) 36

2. The table shows the scores, in points, of five game show contestants. What is the range of the scores?

Contestant	A	B	C	D	E
Score	250	-40	225	130	-45

   (**A**) -45 points   (**B**) 104 points   ✗(**C**) **205 points**   (**D**) 295 points

3. Points $L(4, 1)$ and $M(2, 4)$ form $\overrightarrow{ML}$. The ray is translated 5 units to the left and 1 unit down. What is the location of the endpoint of the translated ray?

   ✗(**A**) $(-1, 0)$ (**B**) $(9, 2)$ (**C**) $(-3, 3)$ (**D**) $(7, 5)$

MULTIPLE CHOICE

1. If $a < 0$ and $b > 0$, which statement is true?

   (A) $a(-b) < 0$ **(B)** $-a(b) < 0$

   (C) $-a(-b) < 0$ **(D)** $-a(-b) > 0$

2. The peak of a mountain is 5016 feet above sea level. A nearby lake has a depth of 120 feet below sea level. Which expression could you use to represent the distance (in feet) between the mountain peak and the bottom of the lake?

   (A) $-5016 - 120$ **(B)** $-5016 + 120$

   (C) $5016 - 120$ **(D)** $5016 + 120$

3. What kind of transformation is shown?

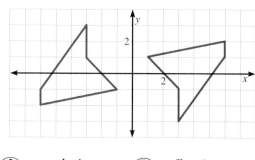

   (A) translation   **(B)** reflection

   (C) rotation   **(D)** other

4. You are a contestant on a game show with a score of $-\$250$. Remaining in the game are questions worth \$100, \$150, and \$200. If you answer all three questions correctly, your score will be twice your opponent's current score. What is your opponent's score?

   (A) \$100   **(B)** \$200

   (C) \$225   **(D)** \$400

5. Which expression does *not* have the same value as the other three expressions?

   (A) the absolute value of 7

   (B) the absolute value of -7

   (C) the opposite of 7

   (D) the opposite of -7

6. For the first 3 days of a 4 day tournament, a golfer's mean score is, relative to par, -1. If the golfer's total score for the tournament is -6, what does the golfer score on the fourth day?

   (A) -5 **(B)** -3 **(C)** -1 **(D)** 3

7. A store buys used CDs for \$3 each and sells them for \$7 each. The store bought 50 used CDs last month and sold 30. How much money did the store make from used CDs?

   (A) \$60   **(B)** \$80   **(C)** \$120   **(D)** \$200

8. Point $A(-2, -3)$ is translated 2 units left and 5 units up to point B. Where is point B located?

   (A) Quadrant I   **(B)** Quadrant II

   (C) Quadrant III   **(D)** Quadrant IV

9. A test has 20 questions that are each worth 5 points. The teacher marked -2 next to four of the questions on Maura's test. How many points did Maura receive on the test?

   (A) -8 **(B)** 8   **(C)** 90   **(D)** 92

10. The high and low temperatures for four cities are given. Which pair of temperatures has the greatest range of temperatures?

   (A) $102°F, -8°F$ **(B)** $105°F, -3°F$

   (C) $113°F, 2°F$ **(D)** $115°F, 8°F$

11. Use the figure shown. You translate the figure 1 unit to the right and 2 units down. Which point is *not* a vertex of the translated figure?

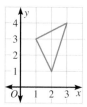

   (A) $(2, 1)$ **(B)** $(3, -1)$

   (C) $(4, 2)$ **(D)** $(5, 3)$

12. Scores on two tests have a mean of 87 and a range of 12. What was the low score?

   (A) 80   **(B)** 81   **(C)** 82   **(D)** 87

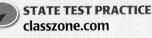
GRIDDED ANSWER

13. You work at a movie theater. You make 2 batches of popcorn every half hour. One batch can fill 10 bags of popcorn. Every hour you sell about 35 bags of popcorn. About how many bags of popcorn are left after 2 hours?

14. A point is translated 6 units to the left and 4 units down. The x-coordinate of the translated point is the opposite of the x-coordinate of the original point. What was the original x-coordinate?

15. Over 10 plays, a football team gained 63 yards. On 4 of the plays the team gained 0 yards, on 1 play the team lost 3 yards, and on 1 play the team lost 6 yards. What was the team's mean gain, in yards, per play for the remaining plays?

16. Every week you earn $8. Every other week you spend $5. What is the total number of dollars you have after 8 weeks?

SHORT RESPONSE

17. One evening, the temperature decreased by the same amount each hour. Use the data in the table to find the number of degrees the temperature decreased each hour. *Justify* your answer.

4:00 P.M.	17°F
10:00 P.M.	−7°F

18. A triangle in Quadrant III is reflected in the x-axis and then rotated 90° clockwise about the origin. In what quadrant does the new triangle lie? *Explain* your reasoning.

19. Your teacher writes "-2" at the top of a quiz paper to indicate that a student lost 2 points on a quiz worth 20 points. The marks for all the students in your class were as follows: $-2, -3, 0, 0, -5, -2, -6,$ $0, -1, 0, -2,$ and -3. Find the mean of the marks. Then determine the mean score out of 20. *Describe* another method for finding the students' mean score.

EXTENDED RESPONSE

20. One quadrant of a quilt pattern is shown. What transformation does it show? Copy the pattern on the other 3 quadrants using a series of 3 reflections. Then copy the pattern a second time on the other 3 quadrants using a series of 3 rotations. *Compare* and describe the results.

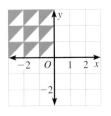

21. The first ten letters of the Braille alphabet are shown below. These ten letters are formed by arranging 1 to 4 dots in a 2 by 2 grid, as shown.

A	B	C	D	E	F	G	H	I	J

a. Which of these Braille letters are reflections of each other? *Explain.*

b. Which are rotations of each other? *Explain.*

c. Can any of these letters be considered reflections *or* rotations? *Explain* your answers.

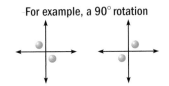

For example, a 90° rotation

12 Equations and Functions

Animated Math
at classzone.com

Get-Ready Games

Review Prerequisite Skills by playing *Expression Race.*

Skill Focus: Evaluating expressions

EXPRESSION RACE

MATERIALS

- *Expression Race* game board
- 1 number cube
- 1 place marker for each player

PREPARE Each player puts a place marker on the START space. Take turns. On your turn, follow the steps on page 627.

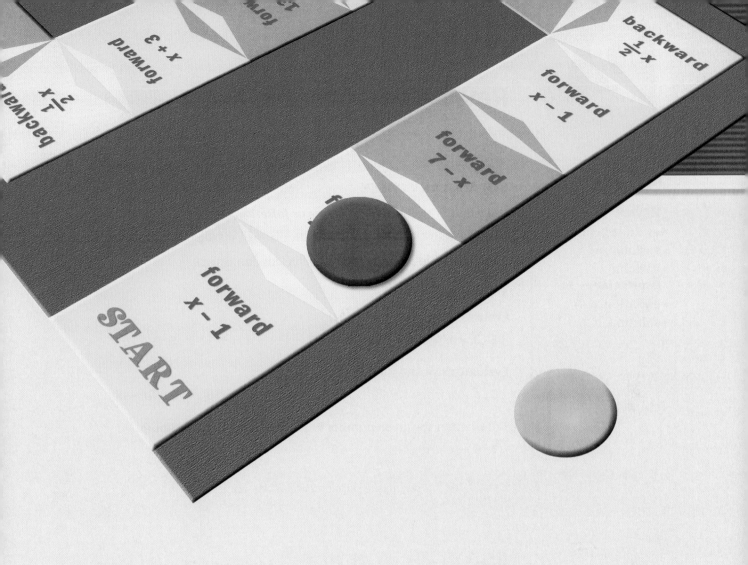

backward
$\frac{1}{2}x$

forward
$x - 1$

forward
$7 - x$

forward
$x + 3$

backward
$\frac{1}{2}x$

forward
$x - 1$

START

 ROLL the number cube. The number you roll is the *x*-value for the expression on the space your marker is on.

 EVALUATE the expression on your space for the *x*-value you rolled. If the result is a fraction, round to the nearest whole number.

3 MOVE your marker forward or backward the same number of spaces as your result from Step 2.

HOW TO WIN

Be the first player to land on the FINISH space, or be closest to the FINISH space after a set period of time.

Stop and Think

1. **WRITING** If you are on the space labeled "Forward $13 - 2x$," what is the best number to roll? Explain your thinking.

2. **CRITICAL THINKING** If you rolled a 2 on every turn, would you ever get to the FINISH space? Explain why or why not. What if you rolled a 3 on every turn?

Review Prerequisite Skills

REVIEW WORDS

- **evaluate,** *p. 21*
- **variable,** *p. 29*
- **variable expression,** *p. 29*
- **equation,** *p. 34*
- **solution,** *p. 34*

VOCABULARY CHECK

Tell whether the statement is *true* or *false*.

1. The letter a in the equation $2a + 5 = 15$ is called a variable.

2. A variable expression always has an equal sign.

SKILL CHECK

Evaluate the expression. *(p. 21)*

3. $3 + 9 \times 10$

4. $15 \div (14 - 11) + 42$

5. $\dfrac{12 \times 5}{30 \div 3}$

Evaluate the expression. *(p. 29)*

6. $t + 4$, when $t = 20$

7. $z \div 4$, when $z = 16$

8. $7p$, when $p = 8$

Tell whether the given number is a solution of the equation. *(p. 34)*

9. $6 + x = 19$; 11

10. $24 - m = 17$; 6

11. $5n = 60$; 12

@HomeTutor Prerequisite skills practice at classzone.com

Notetaking Skills   Making a Flow Chart

In each chapter you will learn a new notetaking skill. In Chapter 12 you can use a flowchart to remember the steps for identifying linear functions in Example 2 on p. 661.

You can show a mathematical process in your notes using a flow chart like the one below for the order of operations.

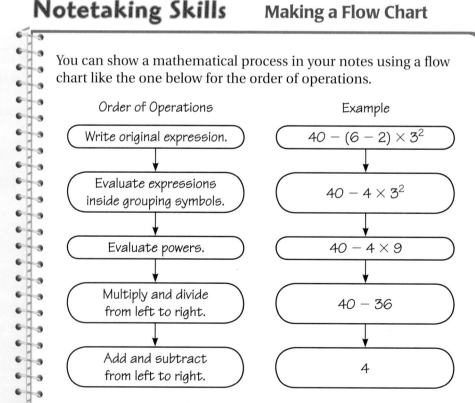

Order of Operations

Write original expression.
↓
Evaluate expressions inside grouping symbols.
↓
Evaluate powers.
↓
Multiply and divide from left to right.
↓
Add and subtract from left to right.

Example

$40 - (6 - 2) \times 3^2$
↓
$40 - 4 \times 3^2$
↓
$40 - 4 \times 9$
↓
$40 - 36$
↓
4

12.1 Writing Expressions and Equations

Before	You evaluated numerical and variable expressions.
Now	You'll write variable expressions and equations.
Why?	So you can model real world situations, as in Example 1.

KEY VOCABULARY
- **variable expression,** *p. 29*
- **equation,** *p. 34*

Art Show Your school's art show has x pieces in it. You expect to add 3 pieces. What will be the total number of pieces in the show? You will see a way to express the total in Example 1.

To write phrases and sentences as variable expressions or equations, look for key words that indicate addition, subtraction, multiplication, or division.

Addition	*Subtraction*	*Multiplication*	*Division*
plus	minus	times	divided by
the sum of	the difference of	the product of	the quotient of
increased by	decreased by	multiplied by	separate into
total	fewer than	of	equal parts
added to	less than	twice	
more than	subtracted from		

EXAMPLE 1 Expressions: Adding and Subtracting

Write the phrase as a variable expression.

Phrase	Expression
3 pieces **added to** x pieces in the art show	$3 + x$
The sum of 4 and a number n	$4 + n$
The difference of 12 and a number x	$12 - x$
9 **fewer than** the number of boys b	$b - 9$

AVOID ERRORS
Order is important with subtraction. "The difference of 12 and a number x" means $12 - x$, not $x - 12$.

✓ **GUIDED PRACTICE** for Example 1

Write the phrase as a variable expression.

1. 16 decreased by a number d

2. The total of 10 and a number n

3. A number h increased by 15

4. 10 subtracted from a number m

5. Four fewer than a number g

6. Seven more than a number k

EXAMPLE 2 **Expressions: Multiplying and Dividing**

Write the phrase as an expression. Let _y_ represent the number.

Phrase	Expression
The product of 5 and the number of girls	$5 \cdot y$, or $5y$
8 **multiplied by** a number	$y \cdot 8$, or $8y$
The quotient of a number and 6	$\dfrac{y}{6}$
24 **divided by** the number of hours	$\dfrac{24}{y}$

AVOID ERRORS

Order is important with division. "The quotient of a number and 6" means $\dfrac{y}{6}$, not $\dfrac{6}{y}$.

Writing Equations To translate a sentence into an equation, look for key words such as *equals* or *is* to find the place for the equal sign.

EXAMPLE 3 **Writing Simple Equations**

Write the sentence as an equation.

Sentence	Equation
A number _x_ minus 5 **equals** 12.	$x - 5 = 12$
15 times a number _y_ **is** 75.	$15y = 75$

EXAMPLE 4 **Modeling a Situation**

Restaurant Three friends share the cost of a dinner equally. The total cost of the dinner is $27. Write a multiplication equation that you could use to find the amount _a_ that each friend pays.

SOLUTION

Number of friends · **Amount each pays** = Total cost

$$3a = 27$$

✓ **GUIDED PRACTICE** for Examples 2, 3, and 4

Write the phrase as an expression. Let _x_ represent the number.

7. 25 divided by the number of inches   **8.** Twice the number of people

Write the sentence as an equation.

9. A number _n_ added to 4 is 11.   **10.** The quotient of _x_ and 96 is 8.

11. A number _p_ times 3 is 36.   **12.** Twelve minus a number _q_ is 2.

13. Temperatures Today's high temperature of 59°F is 3°F less than yesterday's high temperature _t_. Write a subtraction equation you could use to find _t_.

12.1 EXERCISES

SKILL PRACTICE

VOCABULARY Copy and complete the statement.

1. The phrase *decreased by* represents the operation of __?__.

2. A mathematical statement that contains an equal sign is a(n) __?__.

WRITING EXPRESSIONS Write the phrase as an expression.

SEE EXAMPLES 1 AND 2 on pp. 629–630 for Exs. 3–9

3. A number divided by 9

4. The difference of a number and 32

5. 16 subtracted from a number

6. The total of 17 and a number

7. 20 multiplied by a number

8. A number separated into 2 equal parts

9. ★ **MULTIPLE CHOICE** Which expression represents "12 more than x"?

A $12 - x$ **B** $x + 12$ **C** $12 > x$ **D** $12 < x$

WRITING EQUATIONS Write the sentence as an equation.

SEE EXAMPLE 3 on p. 630 for Exs. 10–17

10. 27 less than a number s is 6.

11. 6 times a number t is 42.

12. A number n plus 6 is 30.

13. A number t decreased by 4 is 26.

14. 32 divided by a number r is 2.

15. The sum of 9 and q is 15.

16. The product of x and 3 is 123.

17. The quotient of 50 and w is 10.

18. **WHICH ONE DOESN'T BELONG?** Which description below *cannot* be represented by an equation?

A. A number y added to 4 is 7.

B. 21 is 8 more than a number x.

C. A number m divided by 16

D. A number h times 6 is 24.

19. **ERROR ANALYSIS** Miguel has x cookies to divide among 6 friends. He says that each friend gets $6x$ cookies. Describe and correct his error.

★ **OPEN-ENDED MATH** Write a phrase for the variable expression.

20. $n + 4$ **21.** $y - 7$ **22.** $8r$ **23.** $\dfrac{d}{3}$

WRITING EXPRESSIONS Write the phrase as an expression.

24. The quotient of 2 and the sum of a number and 5

25. The sum of 2 and the quotient of a number and 5

26. The difference of 12 and the sum of 6 and a number

27. The product of 2 plus a number divided by 3 and a number minus 4

28. **CHALLENGE** Write a sentence for the equation to convert temperature: $C = \dfrac{5}{9}(F - 32)$.

ALGEBRA In Exercises 29–32, match the situation with its equation.

A. $x - 8 = 24$ **B.** $8x = 24$ **C.** $8 + x = 24$ **D.** $\dfrac{x}{8} = 24$

SEE EXAMPLE 4
on p. 630
for Exs. 29–33

29. You have $8. How much more do you need to make a $24 purchase?

30. You pay $24 for shoes after an $8 discount. What was the original price?

31. The total cost of tickets for a concert is split equally among 8 friends, with each paying $24. What is the total cost of the tickets?

32. You earn $24 for eight hours of work. How much do you earn per hour?

33. **TEST SCORES** You have 38 correct answers on a test and score 95 points. Write an equation to find p, the value of each correct answer.

34. ★ **SHORT RESPONSE** You plan to practice 10 hours this week for your piano recital. You want to split the time equally over 5 days. Write a multiplication *and* division sentence to find t, the amount of time you practice each day. Write both sentences as equations. *Describe* how they are related.

35. ★ **WRITING** In Grand Canyon National Park, the North Kaibab trailhead has an elevation of 8241 feet. The elevation of Bright Angel Camp is 2400 feet. Write and compare two equations you could use to find c, the difference in elevation between the two locations.

★ **OPEN-ENDED MATH** *Describe* a real-world situation that could be represented by the equation.

36. $6 + y = 20$ **37.** $k - 25 = 60$

38. $4m = 32$ **39.** $\dfrac{r}{5} = 25$

40. **CHALLENGE** Lauren has 10 more CD's than Kevin. Together they have 26 CD's. Write an equation that you could use to find the number of CD's Kevin has. Using mental math, find how many CD's Kevin has.

Get-Ready

Prepare for
Lesson 12.2
in Exs. 41–44

Solve the equation using mental math. *(p. 34)*

41. $d + 6 = 15$ **42.** $45 - f = 10$ **43.** $8g = 88$ **44.** $48 \div x = 6$

Use the distributive property to evaluate the expression. *(p. 175)*

45. $5(20 + 7)$ **46.** $2(9 + 0.1)$ **47.** $6(30 - 4)$ **48.** $10(7 + 0.3)$

49. ★ **EXTENDED RESPONSE** Graph and connect the points $A(0, -1)$, $B(-3, 0)$, $C(-3, 4)$. Reflect $\triangle ABC$ about the y-axis and translate the new triangle 1 unit left to form $\triangle XYZ$. Give the coordinates of each vertex. *Describe* a different series of transformations of $\triangle ABC$ to $\triangle XYZ$. *(p. 608)*

Simplifying Expressions

GOAL Simplify variable expressions.

KEY VOCABULARY
• **terms,** *p. 633*
• **like terms,** *p. 633*
• **constant term,** *p. 633*

In the variable expression at the right, the parts being added together, x, 5, and $3x$ are called **terms**. When terms have identical variable parts, they are called **like terms**. In the expression, x and $3x$ are like terms. A term such as 5, that has a number but no variable, is called a **constant term**.

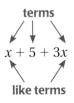

terms

$x + 5 + 3x$

like terms

You can represent and simplify variable expressions using the two types of algebra tiles shown.

 x-tile

Represents the variable x.

 1-tile

Represents positive 1.

EXAMPLE 1 Adding Like Terms

Use algebra tiles to simplify the expression $2x + 5 + 4x + 2$.

SOLUTION

STEP 1 **Represent** each term in the expression using x-tiles and 1-tiles.

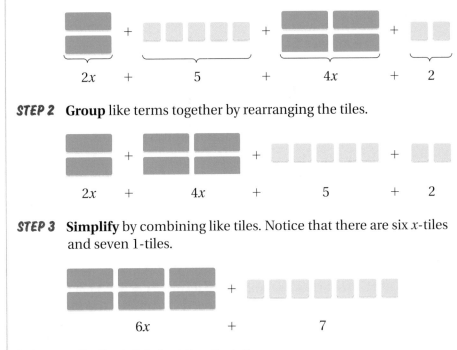

STEP 2 **Group** like terms together by rearranging the tiles.

STEP 3 **Simplify** by combining like tiles. Notice that there are six x-tiles and seven 1-tiles.

▶ **Answer** So, $2x + 5 + 4x + 2 = 6x + 7$.

EXAMPLE 2 · Subtracting Like Terms

Use algebra tiles to simplify the expression $5x + 3 - 2x - 1$.

SOLUTION

STEP 1 **Represent** the terms being added in the expression using x-tiles and 1-tiles.

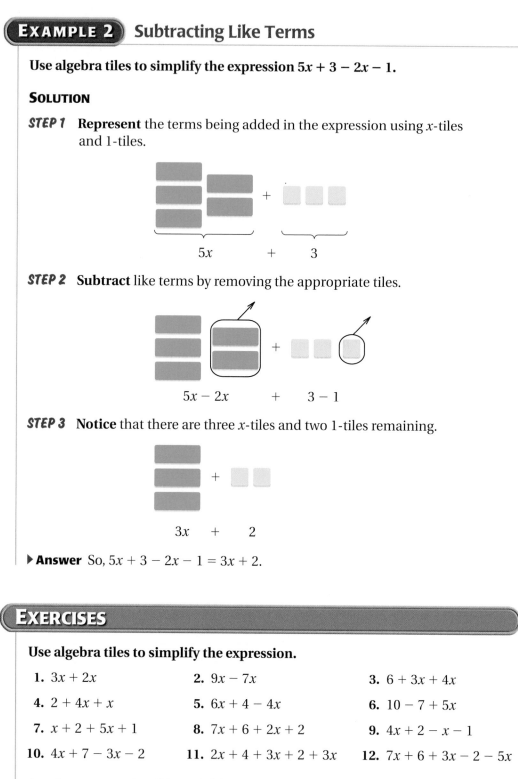

STEP 2 **Subtract** like terms by removing the appropriate tiles.

$$5x - 2x \quad + \quad 3 - 1$$

STEP 3 **Notice** that there are three x-tiles and two 1-tiles remaining.

$$3x \quad + \quad 2$$

▶**Answer** So, $5x + 3 - 2x - 1 = 3x + 2$.

EXERCISES

Use algebra tiles to simplify the expression.

1. $3x + 2x$　　　　**2.** $9x - 7x$　　　　**3.** $6 + 3x + 4x$

4. $2 + 4x + x$　　　**5.** $6x + 4 - 4x$　　　**6.** $10 - 7 + 5x$

7. $x + 2 + 5x + 1$　**8.** $7x + 6 + 2x + 2$　**9.** $4x + 2 - x - 1$

10. $4x + 7 - 3x - 2$　**11.** $2x + 4 + 3x + 2 + 3x$　**12.** $7x + 6 + 3x - 2 - 5x$

Another way to simplify variable expressions is to use the distributive property to combine like terms: $2x + 5 + 4x = (2 + 4)x + 5 = 6x + 5$. Use the distributive property to simplify the expression. Check your result using algebra tiles.

13. $13x + 2x$　　　　**14.** $7x - 5x$　　　　**15.** $4x + 9 + 2x$

16. $9x + 3 - x$　　　**17.** $7x + 6 - x - 5$　　**18.** $8x + 6 - 3x + 1$

12.2 Algebra Tiles

You can solve some simple equations using these two types of algebra tiles.

x-tile

Represents the variable *x*.

1-tile

Represents positive 1.

EXPLORE Use algebra tiles to solve the equation $x + 3 = 7$.

STEP 1 **Represent** the equation using an *x*-tile and ten 1-tiles.

STEP 2 **Solve** the equation by getting the *x*-tile by itself on one side. You can take away three 1-tiles from each side. By taking away the same amount from each side, you keep the two sides equal.

STEP 3 **Notice** that one *x*-tile remains on the left side and four 1-tiles remain on the right side. So, $x = 4$.

PRACTICE Use algebra tiles to solve the equation.

1. $x + 2 = 3$ **2.** $x + 3 = 6$ **3.** $x + 1 = 4$ **4.** $x + 4 = 8$

5. $1 + x = 7$ **6.** $4 + x = 7$ **7.** $2 + x = 9$ **8.** $3 + x = 5$

DRAW CONCLUSIONS

9. **WRITING** *Describe* how you could solve equations like those in Exercises 1–8 without using algebra tiles.

12.2 Solving Addition Equations

Before	You solved equations using mental math.
Now	You'll solve one-step addition equations.
Why?	So you can find distances, as in Ex. 49.

KEY VOCABULARY
• **variable,** *p. 29*
• **solution,** *p. 34*
• **solve,** *p. 35*

One way to solve addition equations is to use algebra tiles.

An *x*-tile represents the variable *x*.   A 1-tile represents positive 1.

You can model an equation by imagining that tiles are placed on a balance scale.

$$x + 2 \quad = \quad 4$$

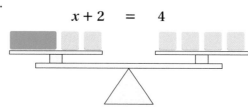

VOCABULARY
An equation is like a balanced scale because it has two sides that are equal.

You can solve the equation by removing tiles until the *x*-tile is by itself on one side. If you remove tiles from one side, you must remove the same number of tiles from the other side to keep the scale balanced.

◆ **EXAMPLE 1** **Solving Equations Using Algebra Tiles**

Use algebra tiles to solve $x + 2 = 4$.

STEP 1 Represent the equation using algebra tiles.

$$x + 2 \quad = \quad 4$$

STEP 2 Take away two 1-tiles from each side.

$$x + 2 - 2 \quad = \quad 4 - 2$$

STEP 3 The remaining tiles show that the value of *x* is 2.

$$x \quad = \quad 2$$

▶ **Answer** The solution is 2.

Animated Math at classzone.com

✓ **GUIDED PRACTICE** for Example 1

Use algebra tiles to solve the equation.

1. $x + 1 = 5$ **2.** $x + 3 = 9$ **3.** $4 + x = 4$ **4.** $8 = 7 + x$

The idea behind the algebra tile method can be used to solve equations with numbers that are hard to model with tiles.

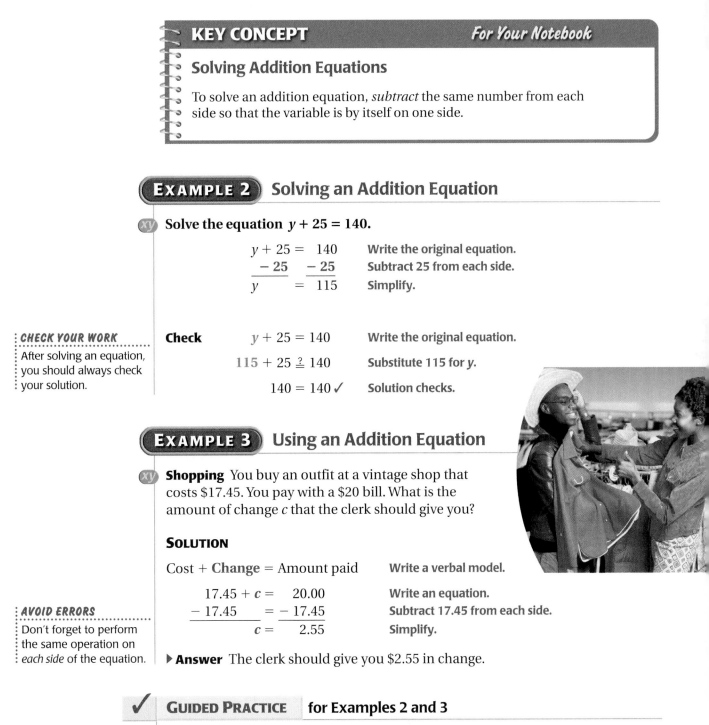

KEY CONCEPT *For Your Notebook*

Solving Addition Equations

To solve an addition equation, *subtract* the same number from each side so that the variable is by itself on one side.

EXAMPLE 2 Solving an Addition Equation

Solve the equation $y + 25 = 140$.

$$
\begin{array}{ll}
y + 25 = 140 & \text{Write the original equation.} \\
\underline{-25 \quad -25} & \text{Subtract 25 from each side.} \\
y \quad = 115 & \text{Simplify.}
\end{array}
$$

CHECK YOUR WORK
After solving an equation, you should always check your solution.

Check

$$
\begin{array}{ll}
y + 25 = 140 & \text{Write the original equation.} \\
115 + 25 \overset{?}{=} 140 & \text{Substitute 115 for } y. \\
140 = 140 \checkmark & \text{Solution checks.}
\end{array}
$$

EXAMPLE 3 Using an Addition Equation

Shopping You buy an outfit at a vintage shop that costs $17.45. You pay with a $20 bill. What is the amount of change c that the clerk should give you?

SOLUTION

Cost + **Change** = Amount paid   Write a verbal model.

$$
\begin{array}{ll}
17.45 + c = 20.00 & \text{Write an equation.} \\
\underline{-17.45 \quad = -17.45} & \text{Subtract 17.45 from each side.} \\
c = 2.55 & \text{Simplify.}
\end{array}
$$

AVOID ERRORS
Don't forget to perform the same operation on *each side* of the equation.

▶ **Answer** The clerk should give you $2.55 in change.

✓ **GUIDED PRACTICE** for Examples 2 and 3

Solve the equation. Then check the solution.

5. $p + 24 = 88$ **6.** $15 + q = 105$ **7.** $76 = r + 39$

8. $s + 2.5 = 10.7$ **9.** $8.35 + t = 10.55$ **10.** $u + 1.85 = 50$

11. What If? Suppose the total cost in Example 3 is $23.65, and you give the clerk $25. How much change should you receive?

12.2 EXERCISES

HOMEWORK KEY

★ = **STANDARDIZED TEST PRACTICE**
Exs. 4, 21, 46, 47, 49, and 56

◯ = **HINTS AND HOMEWORK HELP**
or Exs. 5, 11, 13, 19, 45 at classzone.com

SKILL PRACTICE

VOCABULARY Tell whether the given number is a solution of the equation.

1. $x + 3 = 8; 5$

2. $x + 1.1 = 3.7; 2.6$

3. $3.5 + x = 3.5; 3.5$

SEE EXAMPLE 1
on p. 636
for Ex. 4

4. ★ **MULTIPLE CHOICE** Which set of algebra tiles represents $x + 2 = 3$?

Ⓐ ▢ ▬ ▬ ▬ = ▢ ▢ ▢

Ⓑ ▬ ▬ ▢ ▢ = ▬ ▬ ▬

Ⓒ ▬ ▢ ▢ = ▢ ▢ ▢

Ⓓ ▬ = ▢ ▢ ▢ ▢ ▢

SOLVING ADDITION EQUATIONS Solve the equation. Then check the solution.

SEE EXAMPLE 2
on p. 637
for Exs. 5–22

5. $x + 5 = 7$

6. $m + 9 = 15$

7. $6 = 6 + y$

8. $6 + x = 13$

9. $x + 1 = 8$

10. $x + 5 = 11$

11. $x + 2 = 2$

12. $9 = 4 + x$

13. $15 = 10 + x$

14. $15 + p = 50$

15. $4 + x = 20$

16. $x + 3 = 18$

17. $a + 13 = 26$

18. $27 = d + 27$

19. $42 + g = 70$

20. $17 + h = 66$

21. ★ **MULTIPLE CHOICE** What is the solution of $12 + x = 21$?

Ⓐ 6

Ⓑ 9

Ⓒ 11

Ⓓ 33

22. **ERROR ANALYSIS** Describe and correct the error made in solving the equation $b + 6 = 18$.

$$\times \quad \begin{array}{c} b + 6 = 18 \\ \underline{\quad 6 \quad\quad 6} \\ b \quad = 24 \end{array} \text{ The solution is 24.}$$

CHOOSE A METHOD Solve the equation. Tell whether you used *algebra tiles, mental math,* or *paper and pencil.*

23. $x + 3 = 9$

24. $y + 25 = 80$

25. $z + 5.6 = 8.3$

26. $0.08 + r = 1.28$

27. $m + 3.7 = 9.9$

28. $n + 0.8 = 1.5$

29. $9.5 + d = 14.3$

30. $j + 3 = 5\frac{2}{3}$

31. $k + 3\frac{1}{2} = 8\frac{1}{3}$

ESTIMATION Estimate the solution of the equation.

32. $x + 3\frac{6}{7} = 27\frac{24}{25}$

33. $y + 10\frac{1}{12} = 24\frac{13}{15}$

34. $z + 5\frac{7}{8} = 30\frac{1}{9}$

SOLVING EQUATIONS Simplify and then solve the equation.

35. $k + 14.8 - 3.2 = 20$

36. $a + 3 = 22 - 4^2$

37. $2.6 + m + 3.1 = 18.7$

38. $n + 0.1 = 1.5 + 3^2$

39. $34 + p - 5^2 = 8$

40. $8.7 + t - 2^3 = 0.7$

CHALLENGE Solve the equation.

41. $x + (-4) = 8$

42. $a + (-7) = -2$

43. $-n + 4 = 12$

44. $-c + 2 = -8$

PROBLEM SOLVING

SEE EXAMPLE 3
on p. 637
for Exs. 45–47

45. **PARKING RATES** You have 10 minutes left at a parking meter. After you put in a quarter, you have 25 minutes left. Write and solve an addition equation to find q, the number of minutes a quarter is worth.

46. ★ **MULTIPLE CHOICE** A video game has 16 levels. You are on level 5. Which equation does *not* have a solution equal to the number of levels left, n?

(A) $n + 5 = 16$ **(B)** $n = 16 - 5$ **(C)** $5 + n = 16$ **(D)** $n - 5 = 16$

47. ★ **SHORT RESPONSE** You spend 39 minutes walking and brushing your dog. Brushing takes 15 minutes. Write and solve an addition equation to find the number of minutes you spend walking your dog. *Explain* another method you could use to find your walking time.

48. **GEOMETRY** The perimeter of the triangle shown is 11.1 kilometers. Write and solve an addition equation to find the length of the third side.

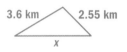

49. ★ **EXTENDED RESPONSE** Lois is training for a race. Her goal is to travel 28 miles this week. So far this week she has traveled the distances shown.

Monday (6 miles)
Wednesday (8 miles)
Thursday (6 miles)

  a. **Mental Math** How many miles has Lois traveled so far?

  b. **Model** Write and solve an addition equation to find the number of miles m Lois has left to travel to meet her goal.

  c. **Reasoning** Lois wants to split the remaining miles equally over the next two days. How does this value compare with the mean distance per day that Lois traveled? *Justify* your answer.

50. **CHALLENGE** Kyle has read x books on hiking and wants to learn more. He goes to the library and borrows 1 book. Each week he returns what he borrowed and takes out 1 more than the number he returns. After 4 weeks he has read 13 books about hiking. Write and solve an addition equation to find x. *Explain* how you found your answer.

MIXED REVIEW

Get-Ready

Prepare for
Lesson 12.3
in Exs. 51–54

Find the sum. *(p. 148)*

51. $1.4 + 3.16$ **52.** $3.2 + 0.06$ **53.** $0.71 + 8.3$ **54.** $61.1 + 27.45$

55. Write the equation: The sum of 6 and a number c is 19. *(p. 629)*

56. ★ **SHORT RESPONSE** Tell whether 97 is *prime* or *composite*. *Explain* your reasoning. *(p. 230)*

EXTRA PRACTICE for Lesson 12.2, p. 787   **ONLINE QUIZ** at classzone.com   **639**

12.3 Solving Subtraction Equations

Before	You solved one-step addition equations.
Now	You'll solve one-step subtraction equations.
Why?	So you can find starting values, as in Example 1.

KEY VOCABULARY
- **variable,** *p. 29*
- **solution,** *p. 34*
- **solve,** *p. 35*

Collecting You gave away 2 conch shells from your collection and now you have 5 conch shells left. How many conch shells did you have at the start?

An equation that represents this situation is $x - 2 = 5$, where x is the number of conch shells you had in your collection at the start.

EXAMPLE 1 Working Backward

One way to solve the equation above to find the number of conch shells you had in your collection at the start is to work backward.

After giving away 2 conch shells, you have 5 conch shells. $\qquad x - 2 = 5$

To find the value x you had before subtracting 2, you can add 2 to *undo* the subtraction. $\qquad 5 + 2 = x$

▶ **Answer** You had 7 conch shells in your collection at the start.

Check	$x - 2 = 5$	Write the original equation.
	$7 - 2 \stackrel{?}{=} 5$	Substitute 7 for *x*.
	$5 = 5 \checkmark$	Solution checks.

✓ **GUIDED PRACTICE** for Example 1

1. **Postcards** You mailed 5 postcards and now you have 9 postcards left. How many postcards did you have at the start?

Isolating the Variable You can also solve the equation in Example 1 by getting the variable by itself as you did in Lesson 12.2. Use the steps below.

$$
\begin{array}{r}
x - 2 = 5 \\
\underline{+2 \quad +2} \\
x = 7
\end{array}
$$

By adding 2 to each side of the equation, you undo the subtraction while keeping the two sides of the equation equal to each other.

For Your Notebook

Solving Subtraction Equations

To solve a subtraction equation, *add* the same number to each side so that the variable is by itself on one side.

EXAMPLE 2 Solving Subtraction Equations

Solve the equation.

  a. $14 = n - 6$ **b.** $m - 3.1 = 11.95$

SOLUTION

  a. In this equation, the variable is on the right side of the equation.

$$
\begin{aligned}
14 &= n - 6 \qquad &&\text{Write the original equation.}\\
\underline{+\,6} \quad &\underline{+\,6} \qquad &&\text{Add 6 to each side.}\\
20 &= n \qquad &&\text{Simplify.}
\end{aligned}
$$

AVOID ERRORS
Line up decimal points correctly before adding decimals.

WRONG	RIGHT
11.95	11.95
+ 3.1	+ 3.1
12.26	15.05

  b.

$$
\begin{aligned}
m - 3.1 &= 11.95 \qquad &&\text{Write the original equation.}\\
\underline{+\,3.1} \quad &\underline{+\,3.1} \qquad &&\text{Add 3.1 to each side.}\\
m &= 15.05 \qquad &&\text{Simplify.}
\end{aligned}
$$

Check Estimate. Substitute using rounded values: $15 - 3 \stackrel{?}{=} 12$

$$12 = 12 \checkmark$$

EXAMPLE 3 Using a Subtraction Equation

Elevator You are riding an elevator. You go down 14 floors and exit on the 23rd floor. On what floor did you enter the elevator?

SOLUTION

Let f represent the number of the floor on which you entered the elevator.

$$
\begin{aligned}
f - 14 &= 23 \qquad &&\text{Write an equation.}\\
\underline{+\,14} \quad &\underline{+\,14} \qquad &&\text{Add 14 to each side.}\\
f &= 37 \qquad &&\text{Simplify.}
\end{aligned}
$$

▶ **Answer** You entered the elevator on the 37th floor.

Animated **Math**
at classzone.com

✓ **GUIDED PRACTICE** for Examples 2 and 3

Solve the equation. Then check the solution.

  2. $q - 7 = 2$ **3.** $25 = s - 17$ **4.** $3.2 = r - 2.1$

  5. What If? In Example 3, suppose you went down 15 floors and exited on the 29th floor. On what floor did you enter the elevator?

12.3 EXERCISES

SKILL PRACTICE

VOCABULARY Copy and complete the statement.

1. When solving an equation, you should get the __?__ by itself on one side.

2. The number 17.5 is the __?__ of the equation $x - 7.1 = 10.4$.

WORKING BACKWARD Find the number of items you had at the start.

SEE EXAMPLE 1
on p. 640
for Exs. 3–4

3. You gave away 3 baseball cards and now you have 12 baseball cards left.

4. You ate 5 carrot sticks and now you have 3 carrot sticks left.

SOLVING EQUATIONS Solve the equation. Then check the solution.

SEE EXAMPLE 2
on p. 641
for Exs. 5–20

5. $p - 2 = 7$ **6.** $z - 1 = 4$ **7.** $m - 6 = 16$

8. $11 = c - 0$ **9.** $3 = m - 15$ **10.** $7 = n - 8$

11. $22 = p - 12$ **12.** $25 = h - 19$ **13.** $39 = j - 14$

14. $x - 2.8 = 6.5$ **15.** $13.4 = x - 1.8$ **16.** $6.02 = x - 9.3$

17. $a - 1\frac{1}{3} = 2\frac{1}{6}$ **18.** $b - \frac{5}{8} = 3\frac{1}{4}$ **19.** $c - 2\frac{2}{3} = 3\frac{3}{4}$

20. ★ **MULTIPLE CHOICE** Which equation does *not* have 8 as a solution?

(A) $t - 1 = 7$ **(B)** $t - 5 = 3$ **(C)** $t - 6 = 14$ **(D)** $0 = t - 8$

21. ★ **OPEN-ENDED MATH** Give three examples of an equation where the variable is *isolated*, and three examples of an equation where the variable is *not isolated*.

22. **ERROR ANALYSIS** Anya used 3 cups of flour and has 4 cups left. Describe and correct Anya's error in finding c, the number of cups of flour she had at the start.

$$\begin{array}{r} c + 3 = 4 \\ -3 = -3 \\ \hline c = 1 \end{array}$$

WRITING EQUATIONS Write the sentence as an equation. Then solve.

23. Five less than a number x is 25.

24. 14 is a number c minus 2.

25. Eleven from a number b is 24.

26. 16 subtracted from a number f is 2.

NUMBER SENSE Without solving the equations, tell which equation has the greater solution. *Explain* your reasoning.

27. $x - 50 = 3271$; $x - 500 = 3271$ **28.** $x - 0.5 = 8.6$; $x - 0.05 = 8.6$

29. $x - 368 = 532$; $x - 368 = 475$ **30.** $x - 7.2 = 9.3$; $x - 7.2 = 0.93$

CHALLENGE Solve the equation.

31. $x - (-5) = -2$ **32.** $2 - x = -5$ **33.** $-3 - x = 8$

PROBLEM SOLVING

SEE EXAMPLE 3
on p. 641
for Exs. 34–37

34. GUIDED PROBLEM SOLVING Your class is planting trees. After planting 17 trees, the class has 14 trees left. How many trees did the class have at the start?

a. What is the unknown value? Choose a variable to represent it.

b. Write a subtraction equation using the information in the problem.

c. Solve the equation. How many trees did your class have at the start? Check your solution.

35. ★ **MULTIPLE CHOICE** You eat 9 strawberries from a carton. There are 12 strawberries left. Which equation can be used to find *s*, the number of strawberries in the full carton?

(A) $9 + s = 12$ **(B)** $12 - 9 = s$ **(C)** $12 - s = 9$ **(D)** $s - 9 = 12$

36. ★ **SHORT RESPONSE** Your team has won 12 games so far this season. Your friend says that your team has lost 9 games. No games were tied. Write and solve two different subtraction equations to find the number of games your team has played. *Compare* the solutions. What information do you need to find the number of games you have left?

37. EXTRANEOUS INFORMATION Your cousin made 10 of the bookmarks you are selling at a craft show. You sell 3 bookmarks in the first 2 hours, and 11 more in the next 3 hours. You have 21 bookmarks left. Write and solve a subtraction equation to find the number of bookmarks you started with. What information is *not* needed to solve the problem?

38. WORK BACKWARD You remove four 1.5 inch wide encyclopedias from a full bookshelf as shown. How wide is the bookshelf? *Justify* your answer.

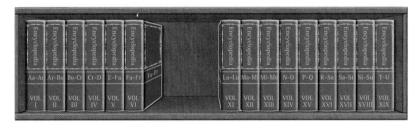

39. ★ **WRITING** Compare solving a subtraction equation to solving an addition equation. How are the steps alike? How are they different?

40. REASONING You received 92 points on a test. Your classmate says that the difference between your test scores is 5 points. Write a subtraction equation to model this situation. *Explain* why there is more than one possible answer.

41. CHALLENGE On Saturday Marcus spent $9.99, received $8 from his neighbor for mowing her lawn, then lent money to his sister. He started with $15 and has $5.24 left. Write and solve an equation to find how much money Marcus lent his sister.

Get-Ready

Prepare for
Lesson 12.4
in Exs. 42–47

Find the product. *(p. 181)*

42. 36×0.5 **43.** 2.2×50 **44.** 6.1×3.1

Find the quotient. *(p. 198)*

45. $44 \div 0.5$ **46.** $12.3 \div 3$ **47.** $64.6 \div 9.5$

Graph the point. Name the quadrant that contains the point. *(p. 603)*

48. $A(4, -5)$ **49.** $B(-3, 2)$ **50.** $C(-6, -1)$ **51.** $D(1, 4)$

52. ★ **MULTIPLE CHOICE** Which equation has a solution of 12? *(p. 636)*

(A) $5 + p = 17$ **(B)** $x + 6 = 6$ **(C)** $b + 5 = 8$ **(D)** $3 + p = 4$

QUIZ *for Lessons 12.1–12.3*

Write the phrase as an expression. Let x represent the number. *(p. 629)*

1. A number decreased by 5 **2.** The total of 14 and a number

3. A number multiplied by 9 **4.** The quotient of a number and 10

Write the sentence as an equation. Let y represent the number. *(p. 629)*

5. 8 more than a number is 35. **6.** 3 times a number is 0.

7. 48 divided by a number is 6. **8.** 10 less than a number is 10.

Solve the equation.

9. $x + 15 = 29$ *(p. 636)* **10.** $3 + y = 14$ *(p. 636)* **11.** $24 = f + 17$ *(p. 636)*

12. $d - 5 = 9$ *(p. 640)* **13.** $z - 14 = 2$ *(p. 640)* **14.** $12 = a - 12$ *(p. 640)*

15. **LIZARDS** A Komodo dragon can grow to be 120 inches long. One Komodo dragon is 92 inches long. Write and solve an addition equation to find x, the number of inches it still needs to grow to be 120 inches long. *(p. 636)*

Brain Game

Symbologic

Use the first two symbol equations to complete the third equation.

EXTRA PRACTICE for Lesson 12.3, p. 787 **ONLINE QUIZ** at classzone.com

Lessons 12.1–12.3

1. **MULTI-STEP PROBLEM** There were 2492 dogs entered in a dog show. The table shows the number of dogs in each category.

Category	Number of Dogs
Sporting	478
Hound	351
Working	388
Terrier	308
Toy	400
Non-Sporting	293
Herding	?

   a. How many dogs were *not* in the herding group?

   b. Write an addition equation that can be used to find h, the number of dogs entered in the herding group.

   c. Solve your equation from part (b). How many dogs were in the herding group?

2. **GRIDDED ANSWER** Today's low temperature of 12°F is 4 degrees higher than the record low for this location. An addition equation that you could use to find the record low temperature t is $12 = t + 4$. Find the record low temperature.

3. **SHORT RESPONSE** Four friends share the cost of a movie rental. Each friend pays $1.06. Write a division equation that you could use to find the cost m of the movie rental. *Explain* another method you could use to solve the problem.

4. **GRIDDED ANSWER** After you give your friend $3.59, you have $4.82 left. A subtraction equation you can use to find the amount of money m that you started with is $m - 3.59 = 4.82$. Find the value of m.

5. **OPEN-ENDED** *Describe* a situation that can be modeled by the equation, $12x = 3.60$. *Explain* what the value of x represents.

6. **EXTENDED RESPONSE** You are using a coin-operated car wash. You put enough quarters in the meter to start with 3 minutes and 45 seconds.

   a. When the meter has 1 minute remaining, the machine starts beeping. Write an addition equation that you could use to find t, the amount of time (in seconds) you used before the machine started beeping.

   b. Solve your equation from part (a). Express your answer in minutes and seconds.

   c. When the meter has 42 seconds left, you add a quarter, and the meter increases your time to 1 minute 7 seconds. Write and solve an addition equation to find q, the number of seconds a quarter buys. *Explain* your reasoning.

7. **SHORT RESPONSE** Your class of 21 students pays $52.50 for admission to a planetarium. Your teacher hands the clerk $60.00. Write and solve an addition equation that you could use to find the amount of change due c. Write a multiplication equation that you could use to find the admission price per student p.

12.4 Solving Multiplication and Division Equations

Before	You solved one-step addition and subtraction equations.
Now	You'll solve multiplication and division equations.
Why?	So you can find individual costs, as in Ex. 55.

KEY VOCABULARY
- **variable,** *p. 29*
- **solution,** *p. 34*
- **solve,** *p. 35*

ACTIVITY

You can use algebra tiles to solve a multiplication equation.

STEP 1 **Use** algebra tiles to represent the equation $2x = 6$.

STEP 2 **Divide** the x-tiles into two equal groups. Divide the 1-tiles into the same number of equal groups.

STEP 3 **Match** a group on the left with a group on the right. *Explain* how this tells you the solution of the equation.

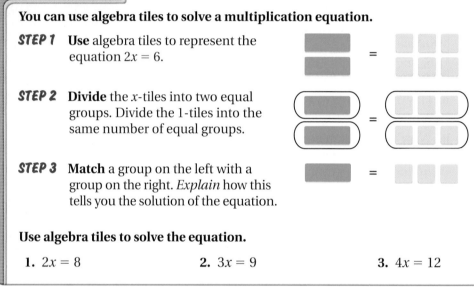

Use algebra tiles to solve the equation.

1. $2x = 8$ **2.** $3x = 9$ **3.** $4x = 12$

The activity shows how you can solve a multiplication equation using algebra tiles. You can also use division to solve a multiplication equation.

EXAMPLE 1   Solving a Multiplication Equation

Solve the equation $5x = 20$.

USE FRACTIONS
The fraction bar is a way to express division. You will use a fraction bar in multiplication and division equations.

$$5x = 20 \quad \text{Write the original equation.}$$

$$\frac{5x}{5} = \frac{20}{5} \quad \text{Divide each side by 5.}$$

$$x = 4 \quad \text{Simplify.}$$

✓ **GUIDED PRACTICE**   **for Example 1**

Solve the equation. Then check the solution.

1. $4n = 20$ **2.** $3m = 15$ **3.** $24 = 2p$ **4.** $65 = 5q$

Solving Multiplication and Division Equations

To solve an equation, try to get the variable by itself on one side of the equation. You can use multiplication and division to undo each other.

Multiplication Equations To solve a multiplication equation, *divide* each side by the number that the variable is multiplied by.

Division Equations To solve a division equation, *multiply* each side by the divisor.

EXAMPLE 2 **Solving a Division Equation**

Solve the equation $\frac{x}{7} = 3$.

$$\frac{x}{7} = 3 \qquad \text{Write the original equation.}$$

$$7 \cdot \frac{x}{7} = 7 \cdot 3 \qquad \text{Multiply each side by 7.}$$

$$x = 21 \qquad \text{Simplify.}$$

EXAMPLE 3 **Using an Equation**

Cheerleading In a local cheerleading competition, a team is awarded points in 3 categories. The mean of the team's scores for the 3 categories is 19.2. Write and solve a division equation to find t, the total number of points the team earns.

ANOTHER WAY

You could also model this situation with the equation $\frac{t}{19.2} = 3$.

$$\frac{t}{3} = 19.2 \qquad \text{Write an equation.}$$

$$3 \cdot \frac{t}{3} = 3 \cdot 19.2 \qquad \text{Multiply each side by 3.}$$

$$t = 57.6 \qquad \text{Simplify.}$$

▶ **Answer** The team earns a total of 57.6 points.

Check Estimate: $3 \cdot 19.2 \approx 3 \cdot 20 = 60$.
So, the answer 57.6 is reasonable. ✓

✓ **GUIDED PRACTICE** for Examples 2 and 3

Solve the equation. Then check the solution.

5. $\frac{a}{2} = 7$ **6.** $\frac{b}{5} = 6$ **7.** $45 = \frac{c}{3}$ **8.** $12 = \frac{d}{8}$

9. What If? Suppose the total in Example 3 is 58.5 points. Write and solve an equation to find the mean.

12.4 EXERCISES

HOMEWORK KEY

★ = **STANDARDIZED TEST PRACTICE**
Exs. 23, 48, 49, 51, and 64

◯ = **HINTS AND HOMEWORK HELP**
for Exs. 5, 7, 9, 15, 45 at classzone.com

SKILL PRACTICE

VOCABULARY Copy and complete the statement.

1. Solve a multiplication equation by _?_.　**2.** Solve a division equation by _?_.

COMPLETING STEPS Copy and complete the solution.

SEE EXAMPLES 1 AND 2
on pp. 646–647
for Exs. 3–23

3. $5x = 10$

$\dfrac{5x}{?} = \dfrac{10}{?}$

$x = \underline{?}$

4. $27 = 9x$

$\dfrac{27}{?} = \dfrac{9x}{?}$

$\underline{?} = x$

⑤. $\dfrac{x}{9} = 4$

$\underline{?} \cdot \dfrac{x}{9} = \underline{?} \cdot 4$

$x = \underline{?}$

6. $\dfrac{x}{6} = 12$

$\underline{?} \cdot \dfrac{x}{6} = \underline{?} \cdot 12$

$x = \underline{?}$

SOLVING EQUATIONS Solve the equation.

⑦. $4m = 32$

8. $3n = 60$

⑨. $5p = 0$

10. $7q = 63$

11. $5m = 28$

12. $40 = 9p$

13. $7.2 = 5j$

14. $17.6 = 2k$

⑮. $\dfrac{t}{10} = 12$

16. $\dfrac{u}{5} = 10$

17. $\dfrac{w}{6} = 15$

18. $\dfrac{x}{21} = 4$

19. $5 = \dfrac{a}{4}$

20. $12 = \dfrac{b}{7}$

21. $\dfrac{x}{4} = 2.7$

22. $1.6 = \dfrac{d}{8}$

23. ★ **MULTIPLE CHOICE** Solve the equation $\dfrac{z}{8} = 7$.

　Ⓐ $\dfrac{7}{8}$　　**Ⓑ** 8　　**Ⓒ** 15　　**Ⓓ** 56

24. ERROR ANALYSIS Describe and correct the error made in finding a number x given that the quotient of x and 7 is 21.

$$x = \dfrac{21}{7}$$
$$= 3$$

WRITING EQUATIONS Write the sentence as an equation. Then solve.

25. Five times a number x is 105.

26. 24 is a number c divided by 2.

27. Eleven times a number b is 44.

28. A number f divided by 6 is 9.

CHOOSE A METHOD Tell whether you need to *add, subtract, multiply,* or *divide* to solve the equation.

29. $n - 13 = 3$

30. $\dfrac{m}{15} = 5$

31. $2w = 12.5$

32. $-56q = 8$

33. $y + (-13) = -7$

34. $14 = p - (-6)$

35. $2x + 4 = 26$

36. $-3 = \dfrac{t}{2} + 1$

37. $8 - \dfrac{y}{3} = -1$

38. CHALLENGE *Describe* how you could use the rules for solving multiplication and division equations to solve $\dfrac{4}{x} = \dfrac{2}{5}$. Then solve the equation.

In Exercises 39–44, solve the equation.

SEE EXAMPLE 3
on p. 647
for Exs. 45–48

EXTENSION Solving after Combining Like Terms

Solve the equation $5x + 2x = 35$.

SOLUTION

VOCABULARY
The parts of an expression that are added together are called *terms*. The distributive property allows you to combine *like terms*.

Terms added together that have identical variable parts are *like terms*. In order to solve this equation, you need to combine like terms.

$5x + 2x = 35$	Write the original equation.
$(5 + 2)x = 35$	Use the distributive property to combine like terms.
$7x = 35$	Simplify.
$\dfrac{7x}{7} = \dfrac{35}{7}$	Divide each side by 7.
$x = 5$	Simplify.

39. $2x + 7x = 18$ **40.** $20 = x + 4x$ **41.** $13x - 7x = 24$

42. $28 = 21x - 7x$ **43.** $1.9x + 0.2x = 6.3$ **44.** $0.8x - 0.6x = 6$

PROBLEM SOLVING

45. **COST PER ITEM** You purchase 8 soft pretzels for $14. Write a multiplication equation you can use to find the cost of a pretzel. Then solve the equation.

46. **SCHOOL SUPPLIES** Four friends share a box of pens. Each receives 3 pens. Write and solve a division equation to find the number of pens in the box.

47. **JETS** NASA's unmanned Hyper-X aircraft set a new world speed record for jets on November 16, 2004. It flew about 33 km with an average speed of about 3300 m/s (more than 9.5 times the speed of sound). About how long did it fly?

48. ★ **SHORT RESPONSE** A basketball team won 45% of its games this year. The team won 9 games. Write and solve a multiplication equation to find the number of games the team played. *Explain* how to use estimation to check your answer.

NASA research jet

49. ★ **OPEN-ENDED MATH** *Describe* a classroom situation that can be modeled by a division equation.

50. **EXAMPLES AND NONEXAMPLES** Give two examples of equations that can be solved using multiplication or division and two that cannot. What operations would you use to solve the second pair of equations?

51. ★ **WRITING** *Explain* why you can multiply each side of the equation $\frac{1}{4}x = 20$ by the reciprocal of $\frac{1}{4}$ to solve the equation.

New York Subways The New York City subway system carries the greatest number of passengers per year of any subway system in the United States. In 2002, it ranked fifth in the world for its number of riders. Approximately 4.5 million people ride the New York City subway every weekday, and it has a total of about 1.4 billion riders per year.

52. Calculate Using the total number of riders per year, write and solve a multiplication equation to find n, the mean number of riders per day.

53. Compare *Compare* the mean number of riders per day with the mean number of riders on a weekday.

54. Number Sense Is the mean number of riders on a weekend day greater than or less than the mean number of riders on a weekday? *Explain* your reasoning.

55. BIKE PARTS At a bike shop, Ronnie gives the clerk $40.00 and receives $.20 in change. Including tax, he bought a chain for $19.95, pedals for $9.95, and 2 tire tubes. Write and solve a multiplication equation to find the cost of a tire tube.

56. FINDING COSTS A pound contains 3 apples or 4 oranges. Write and solve two multiplication equations to find the cost of one apple and one orange. Which one is more expensive? How much more?

Apples $1.20/lb
Oranges $1.80/lb

57. CHALLENGE An *acre* covers 43,560 square feet. The unit is based on early farmers' rectangular fields that were 10 times as long as they were wide. Find $10x$ and x, the length and width, in feet, of such a field.

MIXED REVIEW

Get-Ready

Prepare for Lesson 12.5 in Exs. 58–60

Evaluate the expression when $x = 3$ and $y = 6$. *(p. 29)*

58. $5x + 4 - y$

59. $8 + 7y - 9x$

60. $30 - 3x - 3y$

Solve the equation. *(p. 640)*

61. $b - 8 = 17$

62. $x - 12 = 5$

63. $41 = m - 19$

64. ★ MULTIPLE CHOICE Which is the name of a ray in the diagram at the right? *(p. 455)*

(A) $\overleftrightarrow{AC}$

(B) $\overrightarrow{MB}$

(C) $\overline{BA}$

(D) $\overrightarrow{BN}$

Solving Inequalities

GOAL Solve one-step inequalities.

KEY VOCABULARY
• **inequality,** *p. 651*
• **solve an inequality,** *p. 651*
• **solution of an inequality,** *p. 651*
• **graph of an inequality,** *p. 652*

An **inequality** is a statement formed by placing an inequality symbol between two expressions. To translate sentences into inequalities, look for the following phrases.

Phrase	Symbol
is less than	$<$
is less than or equal to	$\leq$
is greater than	$>$
is greater than or equal to	$\geq$

EXAMPLE 1 Writing Simple Inequalities

Write the sentence as an inequality. Let x represent the number.

Sentence	Inequality
A number **is less than** 5.	$x < 5$
Twice a number **is greater than or equal to** 8.	$2x \geq 8$
A number minus 7 **is less than or equal to** 5.	$x - 7 \leq 5$
6 more than a number **is greater than** 10	$x + 6 > 10$

WRITE EXPRESSIONS
Need help writing expressions? See pages 629–630.

EXAMPLE 2 Modeling a Situation

Restaurant A restaurant can seat 54 people. A party of 12 joins the number of people already seated and the restaurant is not full. Write an inequality you could use to find the number of people, n, who are already seated in the restaurant.

SOLUTION

Number already seated		Number who join		Number restaurant can seat
	$+$		$<$	
n	$+$	12	$<$	54

Solving Inequalities You **solve** an inequality by finding the *solution*. The **solution** of an inequality is the set of all values of the variable that make the inequality true. Solving an inequality is similar to solving an equation. You perform the same operation on each side of the inequality in order to get the variable by itself.

EXAMPLE 3 **Solving an Inequality**

Solve the inequality $x + 2 \geq 3$.

$x + 2 \geq 3$	Write the original inequality.
$x + 2 - 2 \geq 3 - 2$	Subtract 2 from each side.
$x \geq 1$	Simplify.

Graphing Solutions The **graph** of an inequality is all the points on a number line that represent the solution of the inequality. An open dot on a graph indicates a number that is *not* part of the solution. A closed dot on a graph indicates a number that *is* part of the solution.

EXAMPLE 4 **Graphing Solutions of an Inequality**

Solve the inequality. Then graph the solution.

a. $3x < 21$

$\dfrac{3x}{3} < \dfrac{21}{3}$	Divide each side by 3.
$x < 7$	Simplify.

7 is not part of the solution, so use an open dot at 7 on the graph.

AVOID ERRORS
The graph starts at 7, not 6, because all of the numbers between 6 and 7 are also included.

b. $x + 2 \geq 4$

$x + 2 - 2 \geq 4 - 2$	Subtract 2 from each side.
$x \geq 2$	Simplify.

2 is part of the solution, so use a closed dot at 2 on the graph.

Animated **Math**
at classzone.com

EXERCISES

1. **Saving** If you double the amount of money you've saved, you will have more than $275. Write an inequality to find how much you have saved.

Solve the inequality. Then graph the solution.

2. $x + 1 > 3$ 3. $x - 2 \leq 5$ 4. $3x \geq 9$ 5. $\dfrac{x}{3} < 4$

6. $x - 4 < 0$ 7. $\dfrac{x}{2} \leq 1$ 8. $x + 2 \geq 2$ 9. $2x > 12$

10. **Modeling Inequalities** Label 11 cards with the integers -5 through 5. Arrange the cards face up in order from least to greatest. If the integer on a card is a solution of the inequality $3x \leq 6$, leave the card face up. If not, turn the card over. Use your results to solve the inequality $3x \leq 6$.

INVESTIGATION
Use before Lesson 12.5

GOAL
Find an expression for an input-output table.

MATERIALS
• paper
• pencil

12.5 Input-Output Tables

Imagine a machine that evaluates expressions. The value of the variable is the *input* and the value of the evaluated expression is the *output*.

EXPLORE Find an expression for an input-output table.

STEP 1 **Look** for a relationship between the first input and the first output. Write an expression that gives the value of the output when the input is x. The first output is twice the first input, so try $2x$.

Input	Output
2	4
3	5
4	6
5	7

STEP 2 **Check** whether the expression works for the next input-output pair.

$3 \rightarrow 2x \rightarrow 6$ — The output should be 5.

STEP 3 **Try** another expression using a different operation if the first expression doesn't work. The first output is 2 more than the first input, so try $x + 2$.

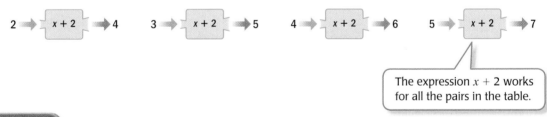

The expression $x + 2$ works for all the pairs in the table.

PRACTICE Find an expression for the input-output table.

1.

Input	12	11	10	9
Output	10	9	8	7

2.

Input	3	7	10	12
Output	9	21	30	36

DRAW CONCLUSIONS

3. **REASONING** A machine performs one of the four basic operations. Can a given input value produce more than one output value?

12.5 Functions

Before	You evaluated variable expressions.	
Now	You'll evaluate functions and write function rules.	
Why?	So you can solve problems involving time, as in Example 1.	

KEY VOCABULARY
- **function,** *p. 654*
- **input,** *p. 654*
- **output,** *p. 654*

Giant Pandas Giant pandas eat about 30 pounds of bamboo every day. About how many pounds of bamboo will a giant panda eat in 2 days? in 5 days?

The *function rule* below relates the pounds of bamboo eaten to the number of days.

$$\text{Pounds of bamboo} = 30 \times \text{Number of days}$$

A **function** is a pairing of each number in one set with a number in a second set. Starting with a number in the first set, called an **input**, the function pairs it with exactly one number in the second set, called an **output**.

EXAMPLE 1   Evaluating a Function

READING

A function rule tells you what to do to the input to get the output. The rule $p = 30d$ tells you to multiply the input by 30 to get the output.

To solve the problem above about giant pandas, you can make an *input-output table*. Use the function rule $p = 30d$, where d is the number of days (input) and p is the pounds of bamboo eaten (output).

Input Days, d	Substitute in the function $p = 30d$	Output Pounds eaten, p
1	$p = 30(1)$	30
2	$p = 30(2)$	60
3	$p = 30(3)$	90
4	$p = 30(4)$	120
5	$p = 30(5)$	150

▶ **Answer** A giant panda will eat about 60 pounds of bamboo in 2 days, and about 150 pounds in 5 days.

✓ **GUIDED PRACTICE**   for Example 1

Make an input-output table using the function rule and the input values $x = 5, 6, 7, 8,$ and 9.

1. $y = x - 1$ **2.** $y = 10 - x$ **3.** $y = 5x$ **4.** $y = 2x + 3$

EXAMPLE 2   Standardized Test Practice

The table shows Payton's age x and Carl's age y over 4 years. Which function rule relates the input x and the output y?

Payton's age, x (years)	9	10	11	12
Carl's age, y (years)	3	4	5	6

(A) $x = 3y$ **(B)** $y = 3x$ **(C)** $x = y - 6$ **(D)** $y = x - 6$

ELIMINATE CHOICES
Only two of the columns in the table show x as a multiple of y. So, choice A can be eliminated.

SOLUTION

Each output y is 6 less than the input x. So, a function rule is $y = x - 6$.

▸ **Answer** The rule that relates Payton's age x and Carl's age y is $y = x - 6$. The correct answer is D. Ⓐ Ⓑ Ⓒ ●

Animated Math
at classzone.com

EXAMPLE 3   Making a Table to Write a Rule

Geometric Pattern Use the pattern below.

a. Make an input-output table using the number of squares, s, as the input and the number of triangles, t, as the output.

b. Describe how the number of triangles relates to the number of squares.

c. Write a function rule that relates s and t.

USE MEANINGFUL LETTERS
It can be helpful to choose letters that remind you of what the variables stand for. The letters s and t represent *squares* and *triangles*.

SOLUTION

a.

Squares, s	1	2	3	4
Triangles, t	2	4	6	8

b. The number of triangles is twice the number of squares.

c. Each output t is 2 times the input s. A function rule is $t = 2s$.

✓ GUIDED PRACTICE   for Examples 2 and 3

5. **Writing a Rule** Write a function rule for the relationship shown in the table at the right.

Input, x	9	18	27	36
Output, y	1	2	3	4

6. **Geometric Patterns** Make an input-output table for the pattern below. Use the number of dots in the bottom row n as the input and the total number of dots t as the output. Write a function rule relating n and t.

12.5 EXERCISES

HOMEWORK KEY

★ = STANDARDIZED TEST PRACTICE
Exs. 22, 28, 29, 30, 31, 32, and 43

◯ = HINTS AND HOMEWORK HELP
for Exs. 3, 9, 11, 15, 27 at classzone.com

SKILL PRACTICE

1. **VOCABULARY** Copy and complete: In a function, each __?__ has exactly one __?__ .

MAKING AN INPUT-OUTPUT TABLE Make an input-output table using the function rule and the input values $x = 3, 6, 9, 12,$ and 15.

SEE EXAMPLE 1
on p. 654
for Exs. 2–9

2. $y = 6x$
3. $y = x + 10$
4. $y = 15 - x$
5. $y = \frac{x}{3}$
6. $y = 4x + 1$
7. $y = 8x - 5$
8. $y = 2x - 4$
9. $y = 20 - x$

WRITING A RULE Write a function rule for the input-output table.

SEE EXAMPLE 2
on p. 655
for Exs. 10–13

10.

Original price, p	Sale price, s
$50	$45
$60	$55
$70	$65
$80	$75

11.

Age now, n	Age in 15 years, t
10	25
11	26
12	27
13	28

12.

Boxes, b	1	2	3	4
Muffins, m	12	24	36	48

13.

Guests, g	80	100	120	140
Tables, t	8	10	12	14

GEOMETRY Make an input-output table. Then write a function rule that relates the input n and the output p.

SEE EXAMPLE 3
on p. 655
for Exs. 14–15

14. Each figure is made up of triangles with sides of 1 unit. Let n represent the number of triangles and let p represent the perimeter of the figure.

1   2   3   4   5

15. Each figure is made up of 5-pointed stars. Let n represent the number of stars and let p represent the number of points.

1   2   3   4

16. **ERROR ANALYSIS** A student said that the function rule for the input-output table at the right is $n = 1.5m$. Describe and correct the error made.

Input, m	10	20	30	40
Output, n	15	25	35	45

FUNCTION RULES Make an input-output table. Then write a function rule.

17. input: cats, output: paws
18. input: hours, output: days
19. input: feet, output: yards

WORKING BACKWARD **Copy and complete the table.**

20. $k = j + 25$

j	0	3	8	?	?
k	?	?	?	40	100

21. $q = 1.6p$

p	10	15	?	?	?
q	?	?	32	40	56

22. ★ **MULTIPLE CHOICE** Which function rule relates the number of squares s and the perimeter p?

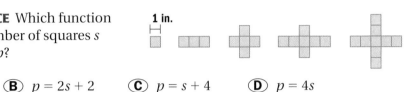

1 in.

A $p = s + 2$ **B** $p = 2s + 2$ **C** $p = s + 4$ **D** $p = 4s$

23. **CHALLENGE** Make an input-output table using $x = y^2$ and the values $y = -4, -2, 0, 2,$ and 4. Does the equation represent a function if y is considered the input? If x is considered the input? *Explain.*

In Exercises 24 and 25, make a table and write a function rule that relates the given input and output for the pattern.

EXTENSION **Writing Two-Step Functions Rule**

Let n represent the figure number and let A represent the area of the figure. Assume that the area of Figure 1 is 1 square unit. Write a function rule relating the input n and the output A.

1   2   3   4

SOLUTION

Begin by making an input-output table.

Figure number, n	1	2	3	4
Area in square units, A	1	4	7	10

Notice that for each consecutive figure, the area increases by 3. The simplest of this kind of pattern is 3, 6, 9, 12, . . ., $3n$. Subtracting 2 from each of these values gives you the output values in the table.

▸ **Answer** A function rule that relates n and A is $A = 3n - 2$.

---

24. input: figure number
output: perimeter

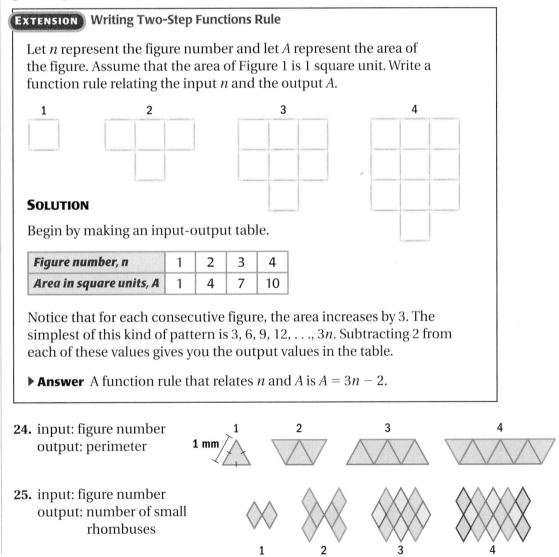

1 mm

1   2   3   4

25. input: figure number
output: number of small rhombuses

1   2   3   4

SEE EXAMPLE 1
on p. 654
for Exs. 26–27

26. MEASUREMENT A function rule to convert inches to centimeters is $c = 2.54i$, where i is the number of inches and c is the number of centimeters. Make an input-output table using the input values of 3 inches, 6 inches, 9 inches, 12 inches, and 36 inches. Round to the nearest tenth of a centimeter.

27. TEMPERATURE To convert degrees Celsius C to degrees Fahrenheit F you can use the function rule $F = 1.8C + 32$. Make an input-output table using the input values of 0°C, 5°C, 10°C, 15°C, 20°C, and 25°C.

28. ★ MULTIPLE CHOICE Each number in the following list has the same relationship to the previous number: 16, 8, 4, 2, 1, . . .
How can the next number be found?

(A) Subtract 8 from the previous number.

(B) Add 2 to the previous number.

(C) Multiply the previous number by 2.

(D) Divide the previous number by 2.

29. ★ WRITING The table shows the cost c for t tickets to the school dance. *Explain* in words how to find the cost of t tickets. Write a function rule that relates the input t and the output c. How much would it cost to buy 12 tickets?

Tickets, t	2	3	4	5
Cost, c	$12	$18	$24	$30

30. ★ SHORT RESPONSE Make input-output tables for converting dollars to quarters and quarters to nickels. Write function rules for the conversions. Then write a function rule to convert from dollars directly to nickels. How many nickels are in $2.35? *Explain* how to check your answer.

31. ★ EXTENDED RESPONSE The *Tyrannosaurus rex* in the photo stands 65 feet tall. Scientists estimate that an actual *Tyrannosaurus rex* was between 15 and 20 feet tall.

a. Find the scale using an actual height of 15 feet. Use this to write a function rule relating lengths on an actual dinosaur to lengths on the model.

b. Now find the scale using an actual height of 20 feet. Use this to write a function rule relating lengths on an actual dinosaur to lengths on the model.

c. The toes on the model are about 6 feet long. Use your function rules to find both a high and a low estimate of the length of an actual *Tyrannosaurus rex's* toe. Which function rule gave the high estimate?

32. ★ OPEN-ENDED MATH Create your own visual pattern that can be represented with a function rule. Make an input-output table and write the function rule.

33. ROAD TRIP While on a road trip, you record the following times and miles driven. Assume you travel at a constant rate. Find the missing values. Then write a function rule that relates *t* (in minutes) and *d*.

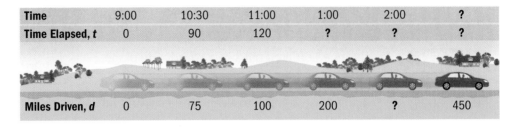

Time	9:00	10:30	11:00	1:00	2:00	?
Time Elapsed, *t*	0	90	120	?	?	?
Miles Driven, *d*	0	75	100	200	?	450

34. GEOMETRY *Explain* in words how to find the area of a square given its perimeter. Make an input-output table for using the perimeter of a square to find its area. Write a function rule for the conversion. What is the area of a square with perimeter 32 centimeters? What is the perimeter of a square with area 144 square inches? *Explain* how to check your answers.

35. SALES TAX You went shopping at four stores. The table shows the totals at each store, before tax and after tax. Write a function rule that relates the cost before tax *c* and the amount of tax *t* on the item. *Explain* how you found your answer.

Before tax	After tax
$10.60	$11.13
$25.00	$26.25
$12.99	$13.64
$2.80	$2.94

36. GARDENS The circumference of a circular garden is 11π feet. Use the function rule for circumference to find the radius, *r*. Then find the area of the garden, rounded to the nearest square foot.

37. CHALLENGE All employees at your aunt's company receive a 3% annual raise. They also receive a 5% increase after obtaining a master's degree. Write function rules for each increase. Your aunt obtained her master's degree this year. She made $30,000 last year. What is her salary now?

MIXED REVIEW

Get-Ready

Prepare for
Lesson 12.6
in Exs. 38–41

Graph the points on the same coordinate grid. *(p. 603)*

38. $(0, -5)$ **39.** $(2, 0)$ **40.** $(-1, 3)$ **41.** $(-4, -2)$

CHOOSE A STRATEGY Use a strategy from the list to solve the following problem. *Explain* your choice of strategy.

Problem Solving Strategies
- Draw a Diagram *(p. 762)*
- Make a List or Table *(p. 765)*
- Act It Out *(p. 770)*

42. In a city, you walk 3 blocks north, 5 blocks east, 2 blocks north, 6 blocks west, and 6 blocks south. *Describe* the shortest walking route to get back to your starting point.

43. ★ MULTIPLE CHOICE About how much time has elapsed from 11:59 A.M. to 4:43 P.M.? *(p. 322)*

(A) 3 hours **(B)** 4 hours **(C)** 5 hours **(D)** 6 hours

12.6 Graphing Functions

Before	You graphed ordered pairs in a coordinate plane.
Now	You'll graph linear functions in a coordinate plane.
Why?	So you can use a graph to evaluate real world functions, as in Ex. 35.

KEY VOCABULARY
• **linear function,**
  p. 661

Walking You are training for a long distance walking race. In your practice walks, you maintain a steady rate of about 15 minutes per mile. How can you use a graph to represent this relationship?

The number of miles you walk x and the number of minutes it takes y are related by the rule $y = 15x$. So, the distances and times for practice walks are represented by points on the graph of the function $y = 15x$.

◆ EXAMPLE 1   Graphing a Function

To graph the function $y = 15x$ mentioned above, follow the steps below.

ANOTHER WAY
....
Whole numbers are
usually convenient input
values, but you can also
use decimals.

STEP 1 **Make** an input-output table for the function $y = 15x$.

STEP 2 **Write** the input and output values as ordered pairs: (input, output).
(0, 0), (1, 15), (2, 30), (3, 45)

Input, x	Output, y
0	0
1	15
2	30
3	45

STEP 3 **Graph** the ordered pairs. Notice that the points all lie along a straight line. If you chose other input values for your table, the points you would graph would also lie along that same line.

STEP 4 **Draw** a line through the points. That line represents the complete graph of the function $y = 15x$.

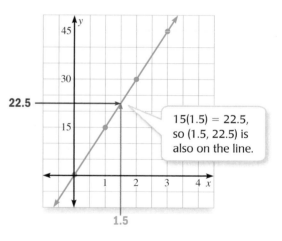

15(1.5) = 22.5,
so (1.5, 22.5) is
also on the line.

✓ GUIDED PRACTICE   for Example 1

1. Copy and complete the input-output table for the function $y = x + 0.5$. Then graph the function. Check whether the point (0.5, 1) is on the line.

Input, x	1	1.5	2	2.5
Output, y	?	?	?	?

Animated **Math** at classzone.com

KEY CONCEPT

For Your Notebook

Representing Functions

There are many ways to represent the same function.

Words   A number is the sum of another number and one.

Algebra $y = x + 1$

Ordered Pairs $(-2, -1), (-1, 0), (0, 1), (1, 2), (2, 3)$

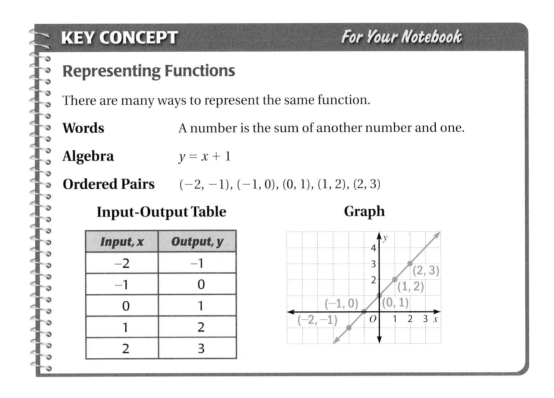

Input-Output Table

Input, x	Output, y
−2	−1
−1	0
0	1
1	2
2	3

Graph

Types of Functions A **linear function** is a function whose graph is a straight line. You can remember the shape of a linear function's graph by noticing that "linear" contains the word "line." Not all functions are linear functions.

EXAMPLE 2   Identifying Linear Functions

Tell whether the function is *linear* or *not linear*. Explain.

a.

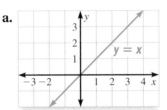

The function is linear, because the graph is a straight line.

b.

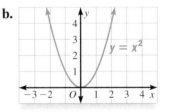

The function is not linear, because the graph is not a straight line.

✓ GUIDED PRACTICE   for Example 2

Graph the function using the input values $x = 1, 2, 3, 4,$ and 5. Tell whether the function is *linear* or *not linear*. Explain.

  2. $y = x - 1$ **3.** $y = 3 - x$ **4.** $y = 2x + 1$

  5. Can a graph in the shape of a V represent a linear function? *Explain.*

Predictions You can use the graph of a function to help make predictions.

⭐ **EXAMPLE 3** Standardized Test Practice

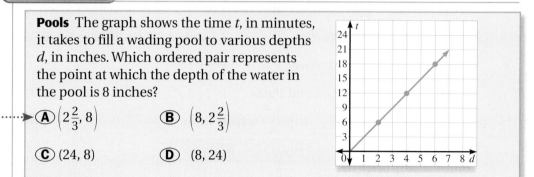

Pools The graph shows the time *t*, in minutes, it takes to fill a wading pool to various depths *d*, in inches. Which ordered pair represents the point at which the depth of the water in the pool is 8 inches?

(A) $\left(2\frac{2}{3}, 8\right)$ **(B)** $\left(8, 2\frac{2}{3}\right)$

(C) $(24, 8)$ **(D)** $(8, 24)$

ELIMINATE CHOICES
The *x*-axis represents the depth. Because the depth is 8 inches, the first coordinate is 8. So, choices A and C can be eliminated.

SOLUTION

STEP 1 **Write** some ordered pairs from the graph: $(2, 6)$, $(4, 12)$, $(6, 18)$.

STEP 2 **Write** a function rule: $t = 3d$.

STEP 3 **Evaluate** the function when $d = 8$: $t = 3(8) = 24$.

▸ **Answer** The water will be 8 inches deep in about 24 minutes. The correct answer is D, ordered pair $(8, 24)$. Ⓐ Ⓑ Ⓒ ⬤

THINK ABOUT CONTEXT
Often it does not make sense to have values less than 0. In Example 3, it also does not make sense for *d*-values to be greater than the height of the pool.

Check Visually extend the line on the graph. When $d = 8$, $t = 24$.

✓ **GUIDED PRACTICE** for Example 3

6. What If? In Example 3, predict how deep the water is in 20 minutes.

12.6 EXERCISES

HOMEWORK KEY
⭐ = **STANDARDIZED TEST PRACTICE**
8, 32, 33, 35, 36, and 54

◯ = **HINTS** AND **HOMEWORK HELP**
for Exs. 3, 9, 11, 15, 29 at classzone.com

SKILL PRACTICE

1. **VOCABULARY** Copy and complete: A function whose graph is a straight line is a(n) __?__ function.

2. **VOCABULARY** Name three ways, other than words, to represent a function.

GRAPHING Graph the ordered pairs. Draw a line through the points.

SEE EXAMPLE 1
on p. 660
for Exs. 3–6

3. $(-3, -1)$, $(0, 0)$, $(3, 1)$, $(6, 2)$

4. $(-1, 2)$, $(1, 2)$, $(3, 2)$, $(5, 2)$

5. $\left(2\frac{1}{2}, 5\right)$, $(2, 3)$, $\left(1\frac{3}{4}, 2\right)$, $\left(3\frac{1}{3}, 8\frac{1}{3}\right)$

6. $(0, 6)$, $(1.5, 4.5)$, $(3, 3)$ $(4.5, 1.5)$

SEE EXAMPLE 1
on p. 660
for Exs. 7–17

7. ERROR ANALYSIS Describe and correct the error made in graphing the line from the table of values.

Input, x	0	1	2	3	4
Output, y	0	2	4	6	8

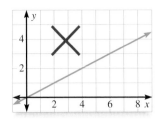

8. ★ **MULTIPLE CHOICE** Which ordered pairs are part of the graph of the function $y = 5x + 7$?

Ⓐ $(5, 7), (10, 14), (15, 21)$ Ⓑ $(0, 7), (1, 2), (2, -3)$

Ⓒ $(0, 5), (1, 12), (2, 19)$ Ⓓ $(1, 12), (2, 17), (4, 27)$

GRAPHING FUNCTIONS Make an input-output table using the function rule and the input values $x = 0, 1, 2, 3,$ and 4. Graph the function.

9. $y = x + 4$ **10.** $y = 3x$ **11.** $y = 7 - x$

12. $y = 5x + 1$ **13.** $y = x + 2.5$ **14.** $y = x - 3$

15. $y = 10 - 3x$ **16.** $y = \frac{1}{2}x$ **17.** $y = \frac{1}{2}x + 2$

IDENTIFYING FUNCTIONS Tell whether the function is *linear* or *not linear*.

SEE EXAMPLE 2
on p. 661
for Exs. 18–20

18. $y = 2x - 3$ **19.** $y = 5 - x$ **20.** $y = x^2 - 1$

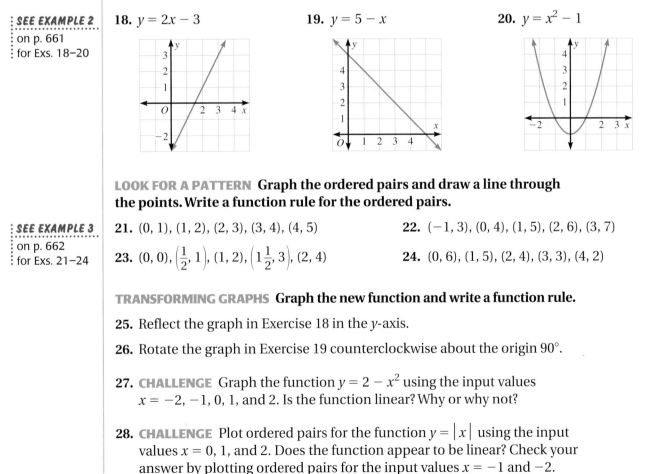

LOOK FOR A PATTERN Graph the ordered pairs and draw a line through the points. Write a function rule for the ordered pairs.

SEE EXAMPLE 3
on p. 662
for Exs. 21–24

21. $(0, 1), (1, 2), (2, 3), (3, 4), (4, 5)$ **22.** $(-1, 3), (0, 4), (1, 5), (2, 6), (3, 7)$

23. $(0, 0), \left(\frac{1}{2}, 1\right), (1, 2), \left(1\frac{1}{2}, 3\right), (2, 4)$ **24.** $(0, 6), (1, 5), (2, 4), (3, 3), (4, 2)$

TRANSFORMING GRAPHS Graph the new function and write a function rule.

25. Reflect the graph in Exercise 18 in the y-axis.

26. Rotate the graph in Exercise 19 counterclockwise about the origin 90°.

27. CHALLENGE Graph the function $y = 2 - x^2$ using the input values $x = -2, -1, 0, 1,$ and 2. Is the function linear? Why or why not?

28. CHALLENGE Plot ordered pairs for the function $y = |x|$ using the input values $x = 0, 1,$ and 2. Does the function appear to be linear? Check your answer by plotting ordered pairs for the input values $x = -1$ and -2.

**SEE EXAMPLES
1 AND 2**
on pp. 660–661
for Ex. 29

29. **SCIENCE** A baby rhinoceros drinks about 12 gallons of milk every day. The number of days d and the number of gallons of milk g are related by the function rule $g = 12d$. Make an input-output table for the values $d = 1, 2, 3, 4,$ and 5. Graph the function. Is the function linear?

**SEE EXAMPLES
2 AND 3**
on p. 662
for Exs. 30–32

30. **MULTI-STEP PROBLEM** The table shows the cost of a salad with a cup of soup for lunch.

   a. Write the values in the table as ordered pairs (ounces, total cost).

   b. Use your ordered pairs from part (a) to graph the function. Is the function linear?

   c. Use your graph from part (b) to find the cost of a 7 ounce salad with a cup of soup.

Ounces of salad, s	Total cost of lunch, t
2	$2.50
4	$3.00
6	$3.50
8	$4.00

31. **EROSION** A beach erodes 8 feet every year. Write a function rule that relates the amount of erosion e and the number of years n. Graph the function. Is the function linear? Estimate how many feet will erode after $9\frac{1}{2}$ years.

32. ★ **MULTIPLE CHOICE** You are cutting out paper stars for a bulletin board display. The graph at the right shows the total number of stars you have cut out after various amounts of time. If you continue at this pace, how many stars will you have cut out in 11 minutes?

   Ⓐ 27 stars   **Ⓑ** 30 stars

   Ⓒ 32 stars   **Ⓓ** 33 stars

33. ★ **SHORT RESPONSE** On the same coordinate plane, graph the functions $y = 3x + 4$, $y = 3x$, and $y = 3x - 4$. Use the input values $x = 0, 1, 2, 3,$ and 4. What do you notice about the graphs? Predict another function that has this property. Graph the function to check.

34. ◆ **MULTIPLE REPRESENTATIONS** Use the table.

   a. **Write a Function** Write a function rule that relates the number of correct answers and the test score.

Correct answers, n	5	10	20
Test score, s	20	40	80

   b. **Make a Graph** Graph the data from the table.

   c. **Describe a Solution** *Describe* how to find the test score for 15 correct answers using your function rule and your graph.

35. ★ **WRITING** The number of riders carried on the Duquesne Incline in Pittsburgh, Pennsylvania, is given by the function rule $y = 25x$, where x is the number of trips and y is the number of riders. *Explain* how to find the number of riders for 11 trips by using a graph and without using a graph.

36. ★ **EXTENDED RESPONSE** The function $V = s^3$ gives the volume V of a cube, where s is the side length of the cube.

   a. **Calculate** Make an input-output table using the input values 1, 2, 4, 8, and 16.

   b. **Graph** Graph the ordered pairs from the table. Is the function linear? *Justify* your answer.

   c. **Compare and Contrast** How does the volume of a cube change when its side length doubles? *Explain* your reasoning.

37. **CHALLENGE** Make an input-output table for the function for the area of a circle using the radius r as the input. Graph the function. How does the area change if the input value is doubled? tripled? quadrupled? *Explain.*

In Exercises 38–41, the figures in the patterns are similar. Write a function rule that relates the given input and output. Then graph the function. Classify the function as *linear* or *nonlinear*.

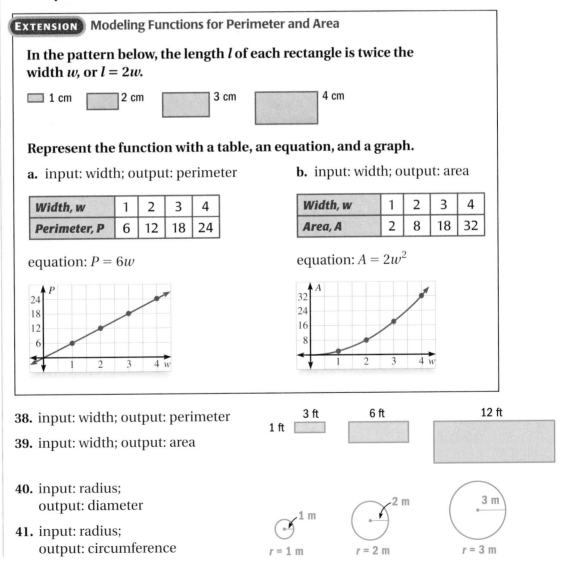

EXTENSION Modeling Functions for Perimeter and Area

In the pattern below, the length l of each rectangle is twice the width w, or $l = 2w$.

1 cm   2 cm   3 cm   4 cm

Represent the function with a table, an equation, and a graph.

a. input: width; output: perimeter

Width, w	1	2	3	4
Perimeter, P	6	12	18	24

equation: $P = 6w$

b. input: width; output: area

Width, w	1	2	3	4
Area, A	2	8	18	32

equation: $A = 2w^2$

38. input: width; output: perimeter

39. input: width; output: area

1 ft   3 ft   6 ft   12 ft

40. input: radius; output: diameter

41. input: radius; output: circumference

1 m   2 m   3 m

$r = 1$ m $r = 2$ m $r = 3$ m

Get-Ready

Prepare for
Lesson 13.1
in Exs. 42–49

Write the fraction or mixed number as a decimal. Use bar notation to show a repeating decimal. *(p. 271)*

42. $\dfrac{3}{10}$　　　　**43.** $\dfrac{11}{6}$　　　　**44.** $1\dfrac{4}{11}$　　　　**45.** $6\dfrac{3}{8}$

46. $\dfrac{13}{4}$　　　　**47.** $8\dfrac{2}{3}$　　　　**48.** $4\dfrac{2}{5}$　　　　**49.** $\dfrac{8}{9}$

You have \$21. Determine how many packs of trading cards you can buy for the given price. *(p. 198)*

50. \$1.25 per pack　　　　**51.** \$1.50 per pack　　　　**52.** \$1.75 per pack

53. Write a function rule for the input-output table. *(p. 654)*

Input, x	7	8	9	10
Output, y	15	16	17	18

54. ★ **MULTIPLE CHOICE** Which equation has a solution of 9? *(p. 402)*

(A) $\dfrac{2}{3} = \dfrac{8}{x}$　　　　(B) $\dfrac{x}{36} = \dfrac{4}{12}$　　　　(C) $\dfrac{3}{9} = \dfrac{x}{36}$　　　　(D) $\dfrac{x}{11} = \dfrac{18}{22}$

QUIZ *for Lessons 12.4–12.6*

Solve the equation. *(p. 646)*

1. $10w = 20$　　　**2.** $13x = 78$　　　**3.** $72 = 2z$　　　**4.** $77 = 7y$

5. $\dfrac{a}{5} = 8$　　　**6.** $\dfrac{b}{13} = 4$　　　**7.** $24 = \dfrac{c}{2}$　　　**8.** $6 = \dfrac{d}{30}$

Write the sentence as an equation. Then solve the equation. *(p. 646)*

9. Five times a number r is 75.　　　**10.** A number d divided by 7 is 8.

11. **WAGES** You earn \$5 per hour raking leaves. Write and solve a multiplication equation to find t, the number of hours you must work to earn \$35. *(p. 646)*

Write a function rule for the input-output table. *(p. 654)*

12.

Tickets, t	Cost, c
2	\$8
4	\$16
6	\$24
8	\$32

13.

Sale price, s	Original price, p
\$70	\$80
\$63	\$73
\$85	\$95
\$56	\$66

Make an input-output table using the function rule and the input values $x = 3, 6, 9,$ and 12. Then graph the function. *(p. 660)*

14. $y = x$　　　**15.** $y = 5x - 10$　　　**16.** $y = 14 - x$　　　**17.** $y = \dfrac{1}{3}x + 3$

12.6 Graphing Linear Functions

EXAMPLE You can graph linear functions using a graphing calculator.

At a local bank, a money order costs the amount of the money order plus a $1 fee. A function rule for the money order is $y = x + 1$, where x is the amount of the money order and y is the total cost. Graph this function.

SOLUTION

STEP 1 Press ⟨Y=⟩ to enter the function rule into a calculator. With the cursor next to $Y_1 =$, enter the function rule by pressing ⟨x⟩ ⟨+⟩ 1.

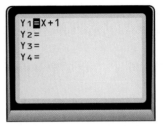

STEP 2 Press ⟨GRAPH⟩ to display the graph. If you use the standard viewing window, the graph shows values from -10 through 10 along the x- and y-axes.

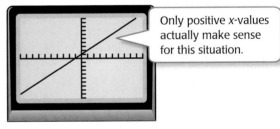

Only positive x-values actually make sense for this situation.

PRACTICE Use a graphing calculator to graph the function. In Exercises 13 and 14, also tell what x-values make sense.

1. $y = x + 2$ **2.** $y = x - 4$ **3.** $y = 3x$ **4.** $y = \dfrac{x}{3}$

5. $y = 0.2x$ **6.** $y = 3 - x$ **7.** $y = 3x - 5$ **8.** $y = 2x + 1$

9. $y = 1 - 4x$ **10.** $y = -x$ **11.** $y = 2x - 5$ **12.** $y = 0.75x$

13. GEOMETRY The function rule $y = 3.14x$ can be used to estimate the circumference of a circle, where x is the diameter of the circle.

14. SNOW Under certain weather conditions, the function rule $y = 0.1x$ can be used to estimate the number of inches of water y contained in x inches of snow.

Lessons 12.4–12.6

1. MULTI-STEP PROBLEM An online electronics store is offering 25% off all purchases for a limited time. You are ordering a portable stereo whose regular price is $49.96.

   a. Write a function that relates the discount d to the regular price p.

   b. Find the discount for the stereo.

   c. The tax on this stereo is 5%. Find the total cost of the stereo after discount and tax.

2. GRIDDED ANSWER Every year, you and your family drive to your cousin's house 253 miles away. The trip usually takes about $5\frac{1}{2}$ hours. Use the *distance = rate • time* formula to find the average speed, in miles per hour, that you travel.

3. SHORT RESPONSE A shoe store is having a clearance sale. The table below gives the original price x and the sale price y for several different pairs of shoes. Write a function rule that relates x and y. By what percent are the shoes marked down? *Explain.*

Original price, x	$20	$25	$30	$35
Sale price, y	$16	$20	$24	$28

4. EXTENDED RESPONSE The figures below form a pattern. Let the input x be the number below the figure, and let the output y be the number of squares in the figure.

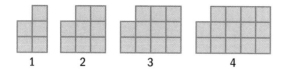

1   2   3   4

   a. Make an input-output table for x and y.

   b. Write a function rule that relates x and y.

   c. Graph the function.

   d. Find the number of squares in the fourteenth figure. *Explain* how you found your answer.

5. OPEN-ENDED Zoe is trying to earn money by knitting and selling scarves. She pays $120 for supplies to make 20 scarves. Assuming that Zoe can sell all 20 scarves, the function rule $p = 20c - 120$ relates the amount Zoe charges per scarf c and her profit p. A friend suggests Zoe charge $4 per scarf. Is this reasonable? *Explain.* How much must Zoe charge per scarf in order to make a profit of $50? *Explain.*

6. EXTENDED RESPONSE A triangle has a base of 10 centimeters. Choose various heights h as inputs. For each input, find the area A of the triangle as the output. Record your results in an input-output table. Graph the ordered pairs (h, A). Write a function rule relating h and A.

7. MULTI-STEP PROBLEM You are traveling to Europe as a foreign exchange student. You plan to take some cash for souvenirs. Your teacher says that when he went to Europe, one American dollar equaled about 0.8 euros. Assuming the exchange rate is about the same, you write the rule $e = 0.8a$ to convert a American dollars to e euros.

   a. Make an input-output table using the input values of $50, $60, $70, and $80.

   b. Graph the function.

   c. Use your graph from part (b) to estimate how much money you should take if you want to have about 70 euros.

REVIEW KEY VOCABULARY

- function, *p. 654*
- input, *p. 654*
- output, *p. 654*
- linear function, *p. 661*

VOCABULARY EXERCISES

1. Explain the difference between a variable expression and an equation.

2. In the function $y = 3x + 1$, what variable represents the input? the output?

3. How can you tell from its graph whether a function is linear?

4. Sketch an example of a linear function and a function that is not linear.

5. In a function, what is special about the relationship of inputs and outputs?

6. Explain what it means to isolate a variable.

REVIEW EXAMPLES AND EXERCISES

12.1 Writing Expressions and Equations
pp. 629–632

EXAMPLE

Words	Algebra
A number y **increased by** 8	$y + 8$
The difference of 2 and a number y	$2 - y$
The product of 10 and a number y is 30.	$10 \cdot y = 30$

EXERCISES

Write the phrase as an expression. Let x represent the number.

SEE EXAMPLES 1, 2, AND 3
on pp. 629–630
for Exs. 7–18

7. A number divided by 7

8. A number times 6

9. 80 less than a number

10. 25 plus a number

11. The difference of 7 and a number

12. The quotient of a number and 2

Write the sentence as an equation.

13. 100 is 40 increased by a number r.

14. Five fewer than a number p is 7.

15. The product of 2 and a number q is 10.

16. A number n divided by 3 is 15.

17. Fifty more than a number k is 61.

18. A number d added to 21 is 30.

12.2 Solving Addition Equations

pp. 636–639

EXAMPLE

a. $13 = f + 8$
$\underline{-8 \quad\; -8}$ Subtract 8 from
$\;\;\; 5 = f$ each side.

b. $c + 7 = 11$
$\underline{-7 \quad\; -7}$ Subtract 7 from
$\;\; c \;\; = \;\; 4$ each side.

EXERCISES

Solve the equation.

SEE EXAMPLES 2 AND 3 on p. 637 for Exs. 19–28

19. $a + 8 = 12$ **20.** $3 + b = 21$ **21.** $32 = 12 + c$ **22.** $22 = d + 18$

23. $69 = f + 17$ **24.** $41 = h + 17$ **25.** $g + 2.7 = 4.6$ **26.** $23.2 + c = 40$

27. Golf Distances Your friend hits a golf ball 250 yards. Your ball lands 35 yards short of it. Write and solve an addition equation to find the distance your ball traveled.

28. Supplies You need 144 pine cones for an art project. So far, you have picked up 87. Write and solve an addition equation to find how many more you need.

12.3 Solving Subtraction Equations

pp. 640–644

EXAMPLE

a. $16 = k - 9$
$\underline{+9 \quad\; +9}$ Add 9 to each side.
$\;\; 25 = k$

b. $g - 4 = 11$
$\underline{+4 \quad\; +4}$ Add 4 to each side.
$\; g \;\; = \;\; 15$

EXERCISES

Solve the equation.

SEE EXAMPLES 2 AND 3 on p. 641 for Exs. 29–38

29. $x - 7 = 9$ **30.** $15 = q - 5$ **31.** $p - 8 = 21$ **32.** $19 = r - 19$

33. $s - 25 = 18$ **34.** $2 = r - 29$ **35.** $18 = w - 3.8$ **36.** $z - 4.02 = 1.86$

37. Employee Attendance Eleven employees of a company are out of the office. There are 98 employees currently in the office. Write and solve a subtraction equation to find the total number of employees.

38. Shopping You spent $3 less than a friend at the bookstore. You spent $28. Write and solve a subtraction equation to find the amount of money your friend spent at the bookstore.

Solving Multiplication and Division Equations *pp. 646–650*

EXAMPLE

a. $2x = 10$

$$\frac{2x}{2} = \frac{10}{2} \quad \text{Divide each side by 2.}$$

$$x = 5$$

b. $7 = \frac{z}{3}$

$$3 \cdot 7 = 3 \cdot \frac{z}{3} \quad \text{Multiply each side by 3.}$$

$$21 = z$$

EXERCISES

Solve the equation.

*SEE EXAMPLES
1, 2, AND 3*
on pp. 646–647
for Exs. 39–47

39. $4p = 36$

40. $3t = 132$

41. $58 = 2r$

42. $135 = 9w$

43. $\frac{h}{7} = 5$

44. $\frac{m}{20} = 4$

45. $10 = \frac{c}{3}$

46. $12 = \frac{d}{10}$

47. Geometry A rectangle has a width of 3 feet and an area of 57 square feet. Write and solve a multiplication equation to find the length of the rectangle.

12.5 **Functions** *pp. 654–659*

EXAMPLE 1

Make an input-output table for the function $y = 4x - 2$.

Input, x	y = 4x − 2	Output, y
1	y = 4(1) − 2	2
2	y = 4(2) − 2	6
3	y = 4(3) − 2	10
4	y = 4(4) − 2	14

EXAMPLE 2

Write a function rule for the input-output table.

▶ **Answer** Each output is 6 less than the input x. A function rule is $y = x - 6$.

Input, x	Output, y
8	2
9	3
10	4
11	5

EXERCISES

Make an input-output table using the function rule and the input values
$x = 0, 5, 10, 15,$ and 20.

SEE EXAMPLES
1 AND 2
on pp. 654–655
for Exs. 48–53

48. $y = 10x$ **49.** $y = 2x + 15$ **50.** $y = 100 - x$ **51.** $y = \dfrac{x}{5}$

52. Write a function rule for the input-output table.

Gallons, g	1	2	3	4
Cups, c	16	32	48	64

53. Make an input-output table that has feet as the input and inches as the output. Then write a function rule for the relationship.

12.6 Graphing Functions

pp. 660–666

EXAMPLE

Graph the function $y = x - 2$.

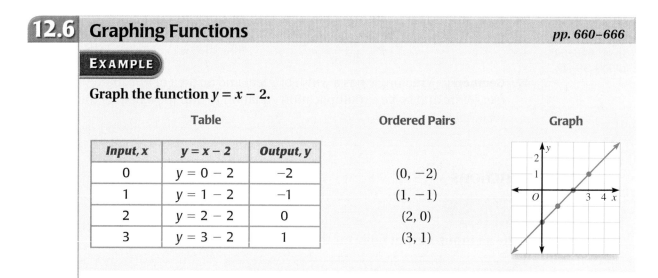

Input, x	y = x − 2	Output, y
0	y = 0 − 2	−2
1	y = 1 − 2	−1
2	y = 2 − 2	0
3	y = 3 − 2	1

Ordered Pairs

(0, −2)
(1, −1)
(2, 0)
(3, 1)

Graph

EXERCISES

Make an input-output table using the function rule and the input values
$x = 0, 2, 4, 6,$ and 8. Graph the function.

SEE EXAMPLES
1 AND 2
on pp. 660–661
for Exs. 54–59

54. $y = 12 - x$ **55.** $y = 3x - 4$ **56.** $y = \dfrac{1}{2}x + 3$

Graph the ordered pairs and draw a line through the points. Write a function rule for the ordered pairs.

57. (0, 0), (2, 1), (4, 2), (6, 3), (8, 4)

58. (1, 8), (2, 7), (3, 6), (4, 5), (5, 4)

59. Tell whether the graph of the function $y = \dfrac{1}{2}x - 1$ at the right is *linear* or *not linear*. *Explain*.

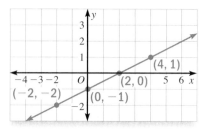

Write the sentence as an equation.

1. Five times a number b is 30.

2. 15 is a number c divided by 3.

3. A number d decreased by 5 is 22.

4. The sum of e and 25 is 100.

Solve the equation.

5. $x + 4 = 15$

6. $7 + y = 13$

7. $z + 9 = 18$

8. $25 = w + 3$

9. $a - 8 = 24$

10. $b - 17 = 15$

11. $44 = c - 12$

12. $d - 52 = 9$

13. $15p = 60$

14. $9q = 99$

15. $198 = 6r$

16. $52 = 2s$

17. $\dfrac{m}{7} = 7$

18. $\dfrac{n}{13} = 4$

19. $9 = \dfrac{w}{20}$

20. $16 = \dfrac{x}{3}$

Make an input-output table using the function rule and the input values $x = 0, 3, 6, 9,$ and 12.

21. $y = 5x$

22. $y = 4x + 6$

23. $y = 60 - 2x$

24. $y = \dfrac{x}{3}$

Make an input-output table. Then write a function rule for the relationship.

25. input: kilometers
output: meters

26. input: days
output: weeks

27. input: side length
output: area of square

Make an input-output table using the function rule and the input values $x = 2, 4, 6, 8,$ and 10. Graph the function.

28. $y = 10 - x$

29. $y = 2x - 5$

30. $y = \dfrac{1}{2}x + 1$

31. Graph the ordered pairs (w, b). Write a function rule for the ordered pairs.

Week w	7	8	9	10	11
Books read b	3	4	5	6	7

32. POTTERY A pottery class has 26 students. Seventeen of the students are girls. Write and solve an addition equation to find the number of boys in the class.

33. EGGS You use 3 eggs from a carton. There are 9 eggs remaining in the carton. Write and solve a subtraction equation to find the number of eggs in the full carton.

34. MUSIC Jorge practiced his trumpet three times as long as Randy did. Jorge practiced for 105 minutes. Write and solve a multiplication equation to find how long Randy practiced.

35. PETS Don's 16 ducks share a bowl of cracked corn. Each duck eats half a cup. Write and solve a division equation to find how much corn Don put in the bowl.

CONTEXT-BASED MULTIPLE CHOICE QUESTIONS

Some of the information you need to solve a context-based multiple choice question may appear in a table, a diagram, or a graph.

PROBLEM 1

The table shows your scores for the past 5 quizzes in history class. After the next quiz, you want your mean score for the 6 quizzes to be at least 93. What is the lowest score that you can get and still reach your goal?

Quiz 1	95
Quiz 2	90
Quiz 3	92
Quiz 4	87
Quiz 5	98

(A) 90 (B) 93

(C) 94 (D) 96

Plan

STEP 1
Decide how to use the information in the table to solve the problem.

INTERPRET THE TABLE The table gives your first 5 scores. You can use this information after working backward to find the sum of the 6 scores.

Solution

STEP 2
Write an expression for the mean of the 6 scores, and set this equal to 93.

Let s represent the sum of the 6 scores. The mean of the 6 scores is $\frac{s}{6}$.

The mean score must be at least 93.

$$\frac{s}{6} = 93$$

$$6 \cdot \frac{s}{6} = 6 \cdot 93$$

$$s = 558$$

So, the sum of the 6 scores must be at least 558.

STEP 3
Use the information in the table to find the score for Quiz 6.

If x represents the score for your sixth quiz, then:

$$95 + 90 + 92 + 87 + 98 + x = 558$$

$$462 + x = 558$$

$$x = 96$$

So, 96 is the lowest score you can get and still reach your goal.
The correct answer is D. (A) (B) (C) (D)

PROBLEM 2

A leaky faucet has a steady drip. The graph shows the amount of water that drips after various numbers of hours. *Predict* how much water drips after 15 hours.

(A) $7\frac{1}{2}$ cups   **(B)** $9\frac{1}{2}$ cups

(C) 10 cups   **(D)** 12 cups

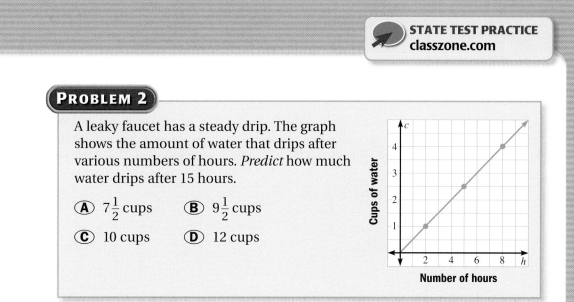

Plan

STEP 1
Interpret the graph and decide how to use the information to solve the problem.

INTERPRET THE GRAPH The graph shows the numbers of cups *c* that have dripped after *h* hours. Three points are plotted. You can write these as ordered pairs, and then use them to write a function rule.

Solution

STEP 2
Write the points as ordered pairs. Then write a function rule.

The ordered pairs for the points are (2, 1), (5, $2\frac{1}{2}$), and (8, 4). Each *c*-coordinate is half the value of the *h*-coordinate. So, a function rule is $c = \frac{1}{2}h$.

STEP 3
Evaluate the function when $h = 15$.

When $h = 15$, $c = \frac{1}{2}(15) = \frac{15}{2} = 7\frac{1}{2}$. So, $7\frac{1}{2}$ cups drip after 15 hours.

The correct answer is A.   (A) (B) (C) (D)

EXERCISES

In Exercises 1 and 2, use the pattern of isosceles triangles.

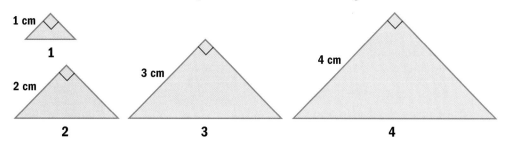

1. Which function rule relates the triangle number *n* and the triangle's area *a*?

(A) $a = n^2$ **(B)** $a = \frac{1}{2}n^2$ **(C)** $a = \frac{1}{2}n$ **(D)** $a = 2n$

2. What is the area of the 12th triangle in the pattern?

(A) 6 cm^2 **(B)** 24 cm^2 **(C)** 72 cm^2 **(D)** 144 cm^2

CONTEXT-BASED MULTIPLE CHOICE

1. A store is offering a special savings on every pair of jeans in the store. The table shows the original price and the sale price for various pairs of jeans. What is the sale price for a pair of jeans originally marked $95?

Original Price	Sale Price
$20	$15
$32	$24
$36	$27
$45	$33.75

(A) $47.50   (B) $71.25

(C) $83.75   (D) $90

2. Which function rule has the graph shown?

(A) $y = x + 2$

(B) $y = 2x + 2$

(C) $y = \frac{1}{2}x + 2$

(D) $y = 2x - 2$

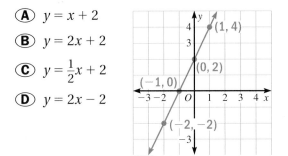

3. The forecast below shows the high and low temperatures for the next five days. Which function rule relates the day number d and the high temperature h?

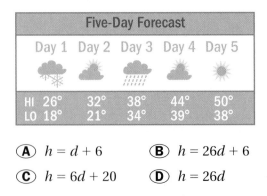

(A) $h = d + 6$ (B) $h = 26d + 6$

(C) $h = 6d + 20$ (D) $h = 26d$

4. The graph shows the amounts of water you need in an aquarium for various numbers of angelfish. Find the number of angelfish that you can put in a 30-gallon aquarium.

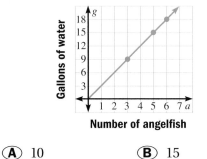

(A) 10   (B) 15

(C) 30   (D) 90

5. In the pattern below, which expression represents the number of dots in each figure number n?

1   2   3   4

(A) $n + 1$ (B) n^2

(C) $2n + 1$ (D) $n^2 + 1$

6. You are pumping gas into a tank that has a capacity of 15 gallons. You fill the tank completely, and the gas pump displays the amounts shown below. Which equation can you use to find how many gallons were in the tank before you started pumping?

(A) $x - 18.87 = 15$ (B) $15 - x = 18.87$

(C) $x - 6.53 = 15$ (D) $15 - x = 6.53$

GRIDDED ANSWER

7. The function rule $n = 0.69p$ relates the population p of the United States in 2004 and the number n of these people who used the Internet. The number of people who used the Internet that year was about 202 million. What was the population? Round your answer to the nearest million.

8. How many squares are in the 22nd figure of the pattern below?

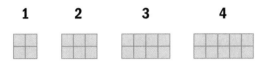

9. Every weekday you practice your flute for the same length of time. By the end of the 15th week, you have practiced a total of $37\frac{1}{2}$ weekday hours. How many hours do you practice every weekday?

SHORT RESPONSE

10. The graph shows the relationship between time traveled t and distance D for a car driven at a constant rate. Write a rule for the function. Predict the number of hours it takes to drive 240 miles as this rate. *Explain.*

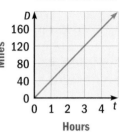

11. Each day, the average dog or cat requires at least 6 teaspoons of water for every pound of body weight. Write and solve a multiplication equation to find the minimum number of teaspoons that a 12 pound cat needs each day. There are 48 teaspoons in one cup. How many cups of water does the cat need? *Explain.*

EXTENDED RESPONSE

12. In the pattern below, the height of each triangle is 3 centimeters. The base of each triangle is 1 centimeter greater than the base of the previous triangle. Make an input-output table with each triangle's base b as the input and its area A as the output. Graph the ordered pairs. Write a function rule that relates b and A. How much greater is the area of each triangle than the area of the previous triangle? *Explain.*

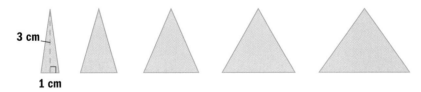

13. In the last 6 gym classes you ran a mile around the track. Your mean time so far is 7 minutes and 10 seconds per mile. Today you run the mile in 6 minutes and 56 seconds. What is your new mean time? You hope to run your next mile in 7 minutes and 6 seconds. Will this increase or decrease your mean time? *Explain* your answers.

14. You make 15 paperweights for a craft show. You charge x dollars for each paperweight. You sell all the paperweights and collect $45. Write and solve an equation to find x. Suppose you spent $10 on supplies. Write and solve another equation to find how much of a *profit* you make.

13 Probability and Statistics

Animated Math
at classzone.com

- Simple Probability, p. 684
- Finding Outcomes, p. 691
- Independent Events, p. 696

Get-Ready Games

Review Prerequisite Skills by playing *Spider Web Maze* and *Butterfly Challenge.*

Spider Web Maze

Skill Focus: Comparing percents, decimals, and fractions

- Copy the spider web maze. Start at 1% near the center of the web. Your goal is to escape to 100% at the top of the web.

- Move along the threads of the web. You may only move to a number that is greater than the number you are on. You may not pass through the spider at the center of the web.

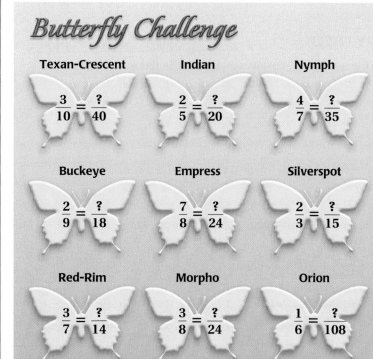

Butterfly Challenge

Texan-Crescent	Indian	Nymph
$\dfrac{3}{10} = \dfrac{?}{40}$	$\dfrac{2}{5} = \dfrac{?}{20}$	$\dfrac{4}{7} = \dfrac{?}{35}$

Buckeye	Empress	Silverspot
$\dfrac{2}{9} = \dfrac{?}{18}$	$\dfrac{7}{8} = \dfrac{?}{24}$	$\dfrac{2}{3} = \dfrac{?}{15}$

Red-Rim	Morpho	Orion
$\dfrac{3}{7} = \dfrac{?}{14}$	$\dfrac{3}{8} = \dfrac{?}{24}$	$\dfrac{1}{6} = \dfrac{?}{108}$

Skill Focus: Solving proportions

• Copy and solve the proportions. Order your answers from least to greatest. Write the butterfly names associated with your answers in the same order.

• The first letters of the names will spell out the name of a butterfly whose name is also a word that means "sulfur."

Stop and Think

1. **CRITICAL THINKING** Give an example from *Spider Web Maze* in which simplifying helped you compare two fractions. Give an example in which you changed a fraction to a decimal in order to compare two numbers.

2. **EXTENSION** For each proportion in *Butterfly Challenge*, find one of the cross products. Order these products from least to greatest. Write the butterfly names associated with the products in the same order. The last letters of the names will spell out the lifespan of the butterfly whose name you spelled in the puzzle.

Review Prerequisite Skills

VOCABULARY CHECK

Copy and complete using a review word from the list at the left.

1. If a value occurs the most often in a data set, it is the __?__ .

2. The __?__ is the sum of the data values divided by the number of values.

SKILL CHECK

Find the mean, median, mode(s), and range of the data. *(p. 99)*

3. 13, 2, 23, 12, 2, 3, 8

4. 8, 9, 3, 4, 8, 6, 9, 8, 9, 6

Write the fraction as a decimal and as a percent. *(p. 429)*

5. $\frac{1}{4}$ **6.** $\frac{5}{5}$ **7.** $\frac{2}{3}$ **8.** $\frac{1}{8}$

The table shows the results of a survey asking 100 students their favorite after-school activity. *(p. 94)*

9. Make a circle graph of the data.

10. Which activity is preferred by slightly less than one fourth of the students?

Activity	Students
sports	28
music lessons	24
clubs	35
other	13

@HomeTutor   Prerequisite skills practice at classzone.com

Notetaking Skills   Summarizing Material

In each chapter you will learn a new notetaking skill. In Chapter 13 you will apply the strategy of summarizing material to Example 3 on p. 720.

At the end of the year, write a summary of key ideas from different lessons that are related to each other. Include definitions and examples of the key ideas.

Simplify Fractions

$$\frac{10}{80} = \frac{1 \times 10}{8 \times 10}$$

$$= \frac{1 \times \overset{1}{\cancel{10}}}{8 \times \underset{1}{\cancel{10}}}$$

$$= \frac{1}{8}$$

Fractions to Decimals

$$\frac{1}{8} \longrightarrow \begin{array}{r} 0.125 \\ 8\overline{)1.000} \\ \underline{8} \\ 20 \\ 16 \\ \underline{} \\ 40 \\ \underline{40} \\ 0 \end{array}$$

Decimals to Percents

$$0.125 = \frac{125}{1000}$$

$$= \frac{12.5}{100}$$

$$= 12.5\%$$

13.1 Conducting an Experiment

You can predict the results of rolling a number cube and use an experiment to test your predictions.

EXPLORE **Make and test predictions about rolling a number cube.**

STEP 1 **Predict** whether a number *less than 2, equal to 2,* or *greater than 2* will occur most often when you roll a number cube 30 times. *Explain* your answer.

STEP 2 **Make** a frequency table like the one at the right. Then roll a number cube 30 times and record your results in the frequency table.

Number on cube	Tally	Frequency
1	?	?
2	?	?
3	?	?
4	?	?
5	?	?
6	?	?

STEP 3 **Summarize** your results. What fraction of the results is less than 2? equal to 2? greater than 2? Do your results match your predictions?

PRACTICE

1. Predict whether a number *less than 4, equal to 4,* or *greater than 4* will occur most often when you roll a number cube 30 times. Then repeat the experiment above to test your prediction.

DRAW CONCLUSIONS

2. **REASONING** When you roll a number cube, do you think that any one of the numbers is more likely to occur than each of the other numbers? Use the data in the two frequency tables you made above to support your answer.

13.1 Introduction to Probability

Before	You wrote ratios.
Now	You'll write probabilities.
Why?	So you can find likelihoods of events, as in Example 1.

KEY VOCABULARY
- outcome, *p. 682*
- event, *p. 682*
- favorable outcomes, *p. 682*
- probability, *p. 682*
- complementary events, *p. 684*

Tossing a coin is an example of an *experiment*. An **outcome**, such as "heads," is a possible result of an experiment.

An **event** is a collection of outcomes. Once you specify an event, the outcomes for that event are called **favorable outcomes**. You can find *probabilities* by counting favorable outcomes.

KEY CONCEPT *For Your Notebook*

Finding Probabilities

The **probability** of an event is a measure of the likelihood that the event will occur. When all outcomes are equally likely, the probability is found as follows.

$$\text{Probability of an event} = \frac{\text{Number of favorable outcomes}}{\text{Number of possible outcomes}}$$

EXAMPLE 1 Finding a Probability

Football A coin toss determines which team gets to kick the football first. A team captain calls "heads." How likely is it that the captain's team will win the toss?

SOLUTION

There is 1 favorable outcome, which is "heads." The 2 possible outcomes are "heads" and "tails."

Probability of winning the toss

$$= \frac{\text{Number of favorable outcomes}}{\text{Number of possible outcomes}}$$

$$= \frac{1}{2}$$

▶ **Answer** The captain's team is as likely to win the toss as to lose it.

Probabilities As shown in Example 1, an event that has a probability of $\frac{1}{2}$ is likely to occur half the time. You can write a probability P as a fraction, a decimal, or a percent.

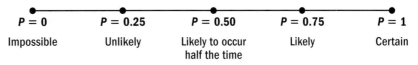

$P = 0$	$P = 0.25$	$P = 0.50$	$P = 0.75$	$P = 1$
Impossible	Unlikely	Likely to occur half the time	Likely	Certain

EXAMPLE 2 Describing Probabilities

READING
When you flip a coin, roll a number cube, or randomly choose objects from a bag, you are assuming that all the outcomes are equally likely to occur.

You roll a number cube. Find and describe the probability of the event.

a. You roll an odd number.

Because there are 3 odd outcomes, $P = \frac{3}{6} = 0.5 = 50\%$.

▶ **Answer** You are likely to roll an odd number half the time.

b. You roll a whole number.

Because all 6 outcomes are whole numbers, $P = \frac{6}{6} = 1 = 100\%$.

▶ **Answer** You are certain to roll a whole number.

c. You roll a 7.

Because 7 is not one of the outcomes, $P = \frac{0}{6} = 0 = 0\%$.

▶ **Answer** It is impossible to roll a 7.

AVOID ERRORS
Be sure you don't count rolling a 3 as a favorable outcome, just count outcomes less than 3.

d. You roll a number less than 3.

Because there are 2 outcomes less than 3, $P = \frac{2}{6} = 0.\overline{3} = 33\frac{1}{3}\%$.

▶ **Answer** You are unlikely to roll a number less than 3.

Animated Math at classzone.com

✓ **GUIDED PRACTICE** for Examples 1 and 2

1. **Coins** You have 3 quarters in your pocket. Only one is a state quarter. If you randomly choose a quarter from your pocket, what is the probability that it will be a state quarter?

Find and describe the probability of the event.

2. You roll a number greater than 3 on a number cube.

3. You randomly choose a pair of white socks from a drawer containing 4 pairs of black socks, 2 pairs of brown socks, and 7 pairs of white socks.

Complementary Events Two events are **complementary events**, or *complements* of each other, if they have no outcomes in common and if together they contain all the outcomes of the experiment. The probability of an event plus the probability of its complement equals 1.

EXAMPLE 3 Complementary Events

The outcomes on the spinner are equally likely. You spin the spinner.

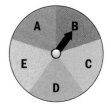

a. Find the probability of spinning a vowel.

b. *Describe* the complement of the event in part (a) and find its probability.

c. *Predict* the number of spins out of 50 that will be consonants.

SOLUTION

a. Because 2 of the 5 letters are vowels, $P = \frac{2}{5} = 0.4 = 40\%$.

b. The complement of spinning a vowel is spinning a consonant. Because 3 of the 5 letters are consonants, $P = \frac{3}{5} = 0.6 = 60\%$.

c. The probability of spinning a consonant is $\frac{3}{5}$, so in 50 spins, you can predict $50\left(\frac{3}{5}\right) = 30$ spins to be consonants.

Animated Math at classzone.com

EXAMPLE 4 Standardized Test Practice

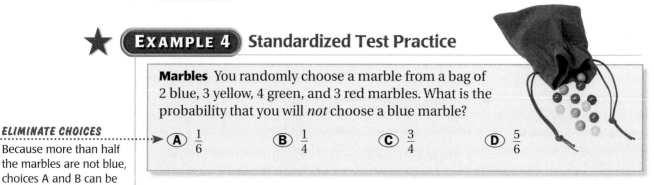

Marbles You randomly choose a marble from a bag of 2 blue, 3 yellow, 4 green, and 3 red marbles. What is the probability that you will *not* choose a blue marble?

(A) $\frac{1}{6}$ (B) $\frac{1}{4}$ (C) $\frac{3}{4}$ (D) $\frac{5}{6}$

SOLUTION

Choosing a blue marble and not choosing a blue marble are complements, so the sum of their probabilities is 1. The probability of choosing a blue marble is $\frac{2}{12}$, or $\frac{1}{6}$, so the probability of *not* choosing a blue marble is $1 - \frac{1}{6} = \frac{5}{6}$.

▶ **Answer** The probability of *not* choosing a blue marble is $\frac{5}{6}$. The correct answer is D. (A) (B) (C) (D)

✓ **GUIDED PRACTICE** for Examples 3 and 4

4. In Example 3, *predict* the number of spins out of 50 that will be vowels.

5. In Example 4, what is the probability that you will *not* choose a red marble?

13.1 **EXERCISES**

HOMEWORK KEY

★ = **STANDARDIZED TEST PRACTICE**
Exs. 19, 31, 34, 35, 36, 37, and 47

○ = **HINTS** AND **HOMEWORK HELP**
for Exs. 5, 13, 17, 29 at classzone.com

SKILL PRACTICE

VOCABULARY List all the favorable outcomes for the event.

1. Spinning a vowel on the spinner

2. Rolling an integer on a number cube

3. Randomly choosing a red marble

SEE EXAMPLE 1
on p. 682
for Exs. 4–8

FINDING PROBABILITIES You roll a number cube. Find the probability of the event.

4. You roll a 1.

5. You roll an 8.

6. You roll a multiple of 3.

7. You roll a prime number.

8. ERROR ANALYSIS Describe and correct the error made in finding the probability of rolling a 5 on a number cube.

$$\text{Probability of rolling } 5 = \frac{1}{5} \quad \times$$

SEE EXAMPLE 2
on p. 683
for Exs. 9–16

DESCRIBING PROBABILITIES Tell whether the event is *impossible, unlikely, likely,* or *certain.*

9. A randomly chosen person is right-handed.

10. It will be July in at least one of the next 15 months.

11. June will have 31 days this year.

12. A person bowls a perfect score.

USING A SPINNER You spin the spinner, which is divided into equal parts. Find the probability of the event. Then tell whether the event is *impossible, unlikely, likely,* or *certain.*

13. You spin a 5.

14. You spin a 0.

15. You spin an integer.

16. You spin a factor of 12.

PREDICTING OUTCOMES Use the spinner from Exercises 13–16.

SEE EXAMPLE 3
on p. 684
for Exs. 17–18

17. Predict the number of spins out of 40 that will be an odd number.

18. Predict the number of spins out of 64 that will be a factor of 10.

19. ★ MULTIPLE CHOICE A bag holds 26 tiles, each marked with a different letter. What is the probability that one tile chosen at random is *not* a vowel?

A $\frac{5}{26}$ **B** $\frac{21}{26}$ **C** $\frac{3}{13}$ **D** $\frac{1}{21}$

DESCRIBING COMPLEMENTS **Find the probability of the event. Then describe and find the probability of the complement of the event.**

SEE EXAMPLES 3 AND 4
on p. 684
for Exs. 20–22

20. You roll a number cube and the result is *not* a multiple of 3.

21. You randomly choose a consonant from the letters in MATH.

22. You randomly choose a marble that is *not* red from a bag of 3 black, 8 white, 2 red, and 5 yellow marbles.

FINDING ODDS **The *odds in favor* of an event are the ratio of favorable outcomes to unfavorable outcomes. You roll a number cube. Find the odds in favor of the event.**

23. Rolling a 6.

24. Rolling a 5 or higher.

25. Rolling a 1 *or* 2.

26. Rolling an odd number.

27. CHALLENGE The probability of spinning an even number on the spinner at the right is $\frac{1}{2}$. The probability of spinning a prime number is $\frac{2}{3}$. Find the missing number on the spinner.

PROBLEM SOLVING

SEE EXAMPLE 1
on p. 682
for Exs. 28–32

28. VIDEO GAMES You randomly choose a level from 12 different levels in a video game. You don't know which 4 levels have secret warp zones. Find the probability that you choose a level that has a secret warp zone.

29. GROUNDHOGS The groundhog Punxsutawney Phil is said to predict six more weeks of winter if he sees his shadow on February 2. From 1946 to 2005, Phil saw his shadow 50 of the 60 years. You randomly choose one year from 1946 to 2005. Find the probability that you choose a year in which Phil saw his shadow.

30. CD CHANGER A CD changer holds 3 CDs. Each CD has 12 songs. You let the CD changer randomly select which song to play first. Find the probability that your favorite song is played first.

31. ★ MULTIPLE CHOICE There are 12 fruit juice bars in a box: 4 cherry, 4 orange, and 4 grape. If you randomly choose a bar, what is the probability it will be cherry?

(A) $\frac{1}{4}$ **(B)** $\frac{1}{3}$ **(C)** $\frac{2}{3}$ **(D)** 4

32. LANGUAGE STUDY In a middle school, 320 students take French, 576 students take Spanish, and the remaining 384 students do not take a language. No student can take both languages. What is the probability that a student chosen at random is taking French? What is the probability that a language student chosen at random is taking French?

33. PIANO KEYS The eight keys labeled on the piano below produce a tone of C. There are a total of 52 white keys and 36 black keys. You randomly play one key. Use the diagram to find the probability that it produces a C tone.

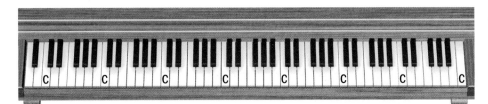

SEE EXAMPLE 2
on p. 683
for Ex. 34

34. ★ SHORT RESPONSE Can the probability of an event be greater than 1? Can the probability of an event be less than 0? *Explain.*

35. ★ WRITING The probability of losing a raffle is 98%. *Describe* the complement of losing a raffle and find its probability.

36. ★ EXTENDED RESPONSE Your school's band is holding a raffle to raise money. The raffle tickets are $1 each and the winner will receive a cash prize. The band is selling 100 tickets.

   a. If you buy one ticket, what is your probability of winning?

   b. You and 9 other people plan to put in a dollar each for raffle tickets as a group. Then, if one person wins, the cash prize will be equally split among the group. If you go in on this plan, what is the probability that you will win something?

   c. Should you enter the raffle by yourself or with the group? If the band was selling 1000 tickets, would that change your answer? *Explain.*

37. ★ OPEN-ENDED MATH An experiment is *fair* if each outcome is equally likely to occur. You roll a number cube to find out which of two players goes first in a game. *Describe* two ways that you can use the number cube to fairly decide who goes first.

38. CHALLENGE You have a number cube that has a 1 on three of its faces, a 2 on one face, and a 3 on two faces. Draw a spinner with 3 sections such that the probability of spinning each number is the same as that of rolling the number on the number cube. *Explain* how you solved the problem.

MIXED REVIEW

Get-Ready

Prepare for
Lesson 13.2
in Exs. 39–42

Find the GCF of the numbers using factor trees. *(p. 236)*

39. 15, 55   **40.** 24, 96   **41.** 28, 42   **42.** 36, 120

Graph the function using the input values $x = 0, 3, 6,$ and 9. *(p. 660)*

43. $y = x + 7$ **44.** $y = x - 4$ **45.** $y = 2x$ **46.** $y = 3x - 6$

47. ★ SHORT RESPONSE Find the volume of a rectangular prism that is 12 inches by 3 inches by 6 inches. What happens to the volume of this prism if the dimensions are doubled? *Explain.* *(p. 550)*

GOAL

Use a calculator to generate a set of random data so you can test probabilities.

13.1 Testing Probabilities

EXPLORE You can use the random integer feature RANDI to generate a set of random integers.

Generate a set of random data to show the results of 10 rolls on a number cube. Then compare your results with the probability of rolling an odd number.

SOLUTION

To simulate rolling a number cube, use the random integer feature RANDI.

Keystrokes   **Display**

   PRB ◄ ≡ 1 2nd [,] 6)   RANDI(1, 6)

Press ≡ 10 times to generate the results of rolling a number cube 10 times. Record your results as you generate them. Suppose you generate the following numbers:

2, 4, 5, 6, 3, 1, 3, 4, 3, and 5.

In the simulation, 6 of the 10 results are odd numbers.

▶ **Answer** You generated an odd number $\frac{6}{10}$, or $\frac{3}{5}$, of the time. This is slightly greater than the probability of rolling an odd number, $\frac{1}{2}$.

PRACTICE Use a calculator to solve the problems below.

1. Let 1 represent heads and 2 represent tails. Generate a set of random data to show the results of 15 coin tosses. How do the results of the simulation compare to the probability of getting heads?

2. A spinner is divided into three equal sections. Let 1 and 2 represent red and 3 represent green. Generate a set of random data to show the results of 24 spins. How do the results of the simulation compare to the probability of spinning green?

3. Generate a set of random data to show the results of rolling a number cube 18 times. How do the results of the simulation compare to the probability of rolling a 1?

Number Sets and Probability

GOAL Apply set theory to numbers and probability.

KEY VOCABULARY

• **set,** *p. 689*
• **element,** *p. 689*
• **empty set,** *p. 689*
• **universal set,** *p. 689*
• **union,** *p. 689*
• **intersection,** *p. 689*

A **set** is a collection of distinct objects. Each object in a set is an **element** or *member* of the set. You can define a particular set by using braces { }. For example, the set *A* of whole numbers between 4 and 11 can be written as

$A = \{5, 6, 7, 8, 9, 10\}$.

Two special sets are the *empty set* and the *universal set*. The **empty set** is the set with no elements and is written as $\varnothing$. The **universal set** is the set of all elements under consideration and is written as *U*.

KEY CONCEPT *For Your Notebook*

Union and Intersection of Two Sets

The **union** of two sets *A* and *B* is the set of all elements in *either* *A* or *B* and is written as $A \cup B$.

The **intersection** of two sets *A* and *B* is the set of all elements in *both A* and *B* and is written as $A \cap B$.

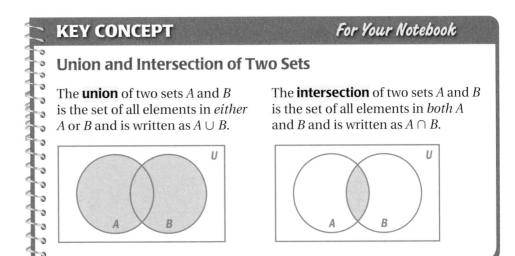

EXAMPLE 1 **Finding the Union and Intersection of Two Sets**

Let *U* be the set of integers from 1 to 9. Let $A = \{1, 2, 3, 4\}$ and $B = \{2, 3, 5, 7\}$.

a. Find $A \cup B$.

b. Find $A \cap B$.

DRAW VENN DIAGRAMS

When drawing diagrams for unions shade all parts in either set, but when drawing diagrams for intersections shade only the parts of the two sets that overlap.

SOLUTION

a. The union of *A* and *B* consists of elements that are in either set.

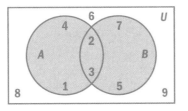

▶ **Answer** $A \cup B = \{1, 2, 3, 4, 5, 7\}$

b. The intersection of *A* and *B* consists of the elements that are in both sets.

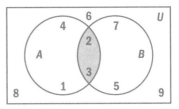

▶ **Answer** $A \cap B = \{2, 3\}$

**WRITE
PROBABILITIES
OF EVENTS**
....
The probability
of an event can
be written
as P(event).

Probability and Sets You can find the probability that an element is in
a set as you did for other probabilities.

$$P(\text{event}) = \frac{\text{Number of favorable outcomes}}{\text{Total number of outcomes}} = \frac{\text{Number of elements in a set}}{\text{Number of elements in } U}$$

EXAMPLE 2 Finding Probabilities for Intersection and Union

You choose a number randomly from a universal set U, the whole numbers
less than 12: $\{0, 1, 2, 3, , , , 11\}$. Set A is the set of even numbers, and set B is
the set of prime numbers. Find $P(A \cap B)$ and $P(A \cup B)$.

SOLUTION

STEP 1 **List** the elements of A and B.

$A = \{0, 2, 4, 6, 8, 10\}$ $\qquad\qquad$ $B = \{2, 3, 5, 7, 11\}$

STEP 2 **Find** $A \cap B$ and $A \cup B$.

$A \cap B = \{2\}$ $\qquad\qquad\qquad\qquad$ **The elements in both sets.**

$A \cup B = \{0, 2, 3, 4, 5, 6, 7, 8, 10, 11\}$ $\qquad$ **All elements in either set.**

STEP 3 **Calculate** the probabilities.

$$P(A \cap B) = \frac{\text{Number of elements in } A \cap B}{\text{Number of elements in } U} = \frac{1}{12}$$

$$P(A \cup B) = \frac{\text{Number of elements in } A \cup B}{\text{Number of elements in } U} = \frac{10}{12} = \frac{5}{6}$$

EXERCISES

Let **U** be the set of whole numbers from 0 to 10. Find $A \cup B$ and $A \cap B$ for
the specified sets **A** and **B**.

SEE EXAMPLE 1
....
on p. 689
for Exs. 1–4

1. $A = \{1, 2, 3, 4, 5\}$ and $B = \{4, 6, 8\}$

2. $A = \{1, 3, 5, 7\}$ and $B = \{4, 5, 6, 7, 8\}$

3. $A = \{6, 8, 10\}$ and $B = \{7, 9\}$

4. $A = \{0, 6\}$ and $B = \{0, 4, 8\}$

Find the probabilities $P(A)$, $P(B)$, $P(A \cup B)$, and $P(A \cap B)$ of the given sets
U, A, and **B**.

SEE EXAMPLE 2
....
on p. 690
for Exs. 5–7

5. Let U be the set of whole numbers from 0 to 24, let A be the set of even
numbers, and let B be the set of multiples of three.

6. Let U be the set of whole numbers from 1 to 40, let A be the set of
multiples of 4, and let B be the set of multiples of 5.

7. Let U be the set of whole numbers from 0 to 15, let A be the set of odd
numbers, and let B be the set of prime numbers.

13.2 Finding Outcomes

Before	You identified outcomes.
Now	You'll use diagrams, tables, and lists to find outcomes.
Why?	So you can count your choices, as in Example 1.

KEY VOCABULARY
- **tree diagram,** *p. 691*
- **combination,** *p. 692*
- **permutation,** *p. 692*

Pottery Your art class is painting pottery for an art fair. You can choose a small or a large size, and you can paint a vase, a jar, or a plate. What are the different kinds of pottery you can paint?

A **tree diagram** can help you organize a list of possible outcomes by placing different choices on different branches of the "tree."

EXAMPLE 1 Solve a Multi-Step Problem

To find all possible outcomes in the problem above, use a tree diagram.

STEP 1 **List** the sizes.   *STEP 2* **List** the items for each size.   *STEP 3* **Find** the outcomes.

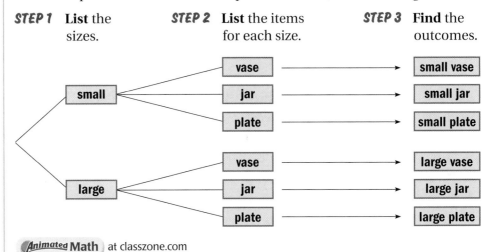

Animated Math at classzone.com

✓ **GUIDED PRACTICE** for Example 1

Use a tree diagram to list all the possible outcomes.

1. You can order a tuna, ham, roast beef, or egg sandwich. You can choose rye, white, wheat, or oatmeal bread. List all possible sandwiches.

2. A roller hockey team is choosing jerseys. The body can be red, white, purple, green, or blue. The sleeves can be black, red, or blue. List all possible jerseys that the team can choose.

Combinations and Permutations To choose outcomes, you need to decide whether the order of the objects matters. A **combination** is a grouping of objects in which order is not important. A **permutation** is an arrangement of objects in which order is important.

EXAMPLE 2 Finding Combinations

Sundaes You can choose 2 toppings for a sundae from nuts, sprinkles, caramel, and marshmallows. Find all possible pairs of toppings.

SOLUTION

Each outcome is a combination because it doesn't matter which topping you choose first. Use a table to show all possible pairs of toppings.

Nuts	Sprinkles	Caramel	Marshmallows	Outcomes
X	X			nuts, sprinkles
X		X		nuts, caramel
X			X	nuts, marshmallows
	X	X		sprinkles, caramel
	X		X	sprinkles, marshmallows
		X	X	caramel, marshmallows

EXAMPLE 3 Finding Permutations

List all two digit numbers that can be formed using two different digits from 1, 4, 7, and 9.

SOLUTION

ANOTHER WAY
You could also find all the possible two-digit numbers by drawing a tree diagram.

Each outcome is a permutation because the order of the digits matters. You can use an organized list to arrange all the possible outcomes.

Starts with 1:	Starts with 4:	Starts with 7:	Starts with 9:
14 17 19	41 47 49	71 74 79	91 94 97

✓ **GUIDED PRACTICE** for Examples 2 and 3

READING
Read each problem carefully to determine whether the situation involves a combination or a permutation.

3. Stir-fry You can choose two vegetables for a stir-fry from green peppers, pea pods, onions, and broccoli. List all possible pairs of vegetables.

4. Books You are placing a math book, a novel, and a dictionary on a shelf. List all possible ways you can order the books on the shelf.

13.2 EXERCISES

HOMEWORK KEY

★ = **STANDARDIZED TEST PRACTICE**
Exs. 10, 22, 23, 25, 26, 27, and 35

○ = **HINTS AND HOMEWORK HELP**
for Exs. 5, 7, 11, 21 at classzone.com

SKILL PRACTICE

VOCABULARY **Copy and complete the statement.**

1. Choosing any 2 DVDs from 5 DVDs describes a __?__ .

2. Arranging 4 letters to make a word describes a __?__ .

SEE EXAMPLE 1
on p. 691
for Exs. 3–5

3. **FINDING POSSIBILITIES** Three people are taking a car ride. Person A and Person B can drive, but Person C cannot. Copy and complete the tree diagram. Then find all possible ways that two people can sit in front.

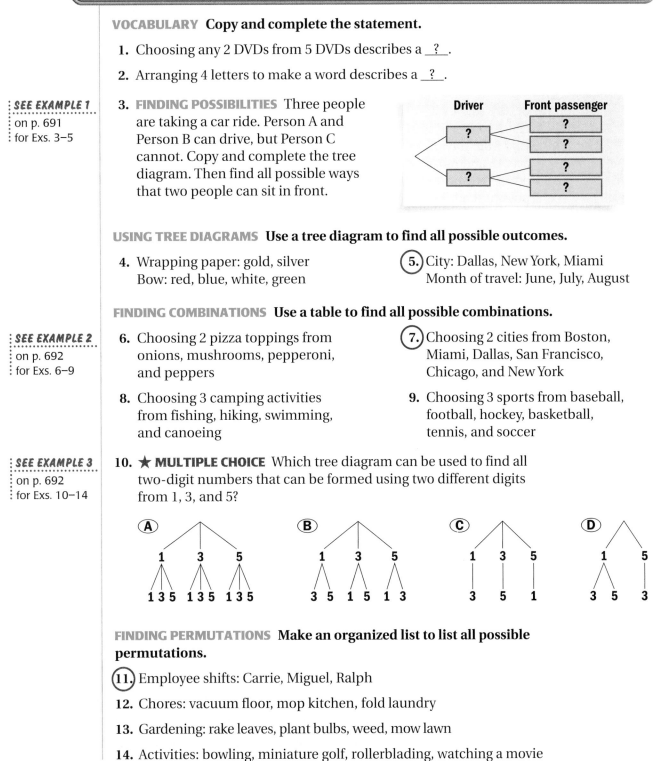

Driver   Front passenger

USING TREE DIAGRAMS **Use a tree diagram to find all possible outcomes.**

4. Wrapping paper: gold, silver
Bow: red, blue, white, green

5. City: Dallas, New York, Miami
Month of travel: June, July, August

FINDING COMBINATIONS **Use a table to find all possible combinations.**

SEE EXAMPLE 2
on p. 692
for Exs. 6–9

6. Choosing 2 pizza toppings from onions, mushrooms, pepperoni, and peppers

7. Choosing 2 cities from Boston, Miami, Dallas, San Francisco, Chicago, and New York

8. Choosing 3 camping activities from fishing, hiking, swimming, and canoeing

9. Choosing 3 sports from baseball, football, hockey, basketball, tennis, and soccer

SEE EXAMPLE 3
on p. 692
for Exs. 10–14

10. ★ **MULTIPLE CHOICE** Which tree diagram can be used to find all two-digit numbers that can be formed using two different digits from 1, 3, and 5?

A
1   3   5
1 3 5   1 3 5   1 3 5

B
1   3   5
3 5   1 5   1 3

C
1   3   5
3   5   1

D
1   5
3 5   3

FINDING PERMUTATIONS **Make an organized list to list all possible permutations.**

11. Employee shifts: Carrie, Miguel, Ralph

12. Chores: vacuum floor, mop kitchen, fold laundry

13. Gardening: rake leaves, plant bulbs, weed, mow lawn

14. Activities: bowling, miniature golf, rollerblading, watching a movie

CHOOSE A METHOD In Exercises 15–17, use a tree diagram, a table, or an
organized list to find all possible outcomes. *Explain* your choice.

**SEE EXAMPLES
1, 2, AND 3**
on pp. 691–692
for Exs. 15–17

15. On a trip, you may choose two of the following six activities for the first
day: golf, horseback riding, snorkeling, tennis, hiking, or sailing. How
many different activity pairs are available to you?

16. A phone company offers 5 phone plan options: call waiting, call
forwarding, voice mail, three-way calling, and caller ID. You can choose
3 options. List all possible sets of 3 options.

17. Bill, Justin, Camille, Katie, and Joey are running in a race. List all
possible ways they can finish in first and second place.

18. ERROR ANALYSIS A student must
choose 2 electives for the next school
year from the following: Spanish (S),
art (A), and music (M). Describe and
correct the error made in listing all
possible choices.

Starts with 'S':   SA   SM
Starts with 'A':   AS   AM
Starts with 'M':   MS   MA

She has 6 different choices
of 2 electives.

19. CHALLENGE How many different two-digit numbers can you make
using the digits 1, 4, 7, 8, and 9 if the numbers are odd and no digit
appears more than once in a number?

PROBLEM SOLVING

In Exercises 20–21, decide whether the situation is a *permutation* or
combination. Then solve the problem.

20. MOVIES You rent 4 movies for a party: a comedy, a drama, a science
fiction movie, and an adventure movie. List all possible orders you can
show two of the movies.

21. SCULPTURES You have 5 colors of clay: blue, green, yellow, red, and
purple. Each clay sculpture you can make uses exactly 2 colors. List all
possible pairs of different colors you can use.

22. ★ SHORT RESPONSE Juggling balls come in blue, green, red, orange,
and purple. How many ways can a juggler choose exactly 3 balls that are
different colors? *Explain* how you found your answer.

23. ★ OPEN-ENDED MATH
Write a problem that
can be solved using the
tree diagram.

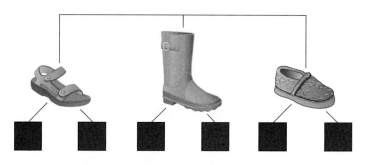

24. ICE SKATING Jenna, Karen, Angela, and Terry draw numbers from a hat to determine their order in an ice skating competition. Find all the ways that the skaters can be arranged if Jenna skates first.

25. ★ WRITING *Explain* why there are more permutations than combinations of the numbers 2, 7, and 9.

26. ★ WRITING The sixth-grade class is electing 4 class officers: president, vice-president, secretary, and treasurer. The class is also choosing a 5-person fundraising committee. Tell which situation is a *combination* and which is a *permutation. Explain* your reasoning.

27. ★ EXTENDED RESPONSE For the first course of a meal, you can order soup or salad. For the main course, you can order pasta, seafood, or beef. For dessert, you can order pie or cake.

  a. You order one of each course, and one dessert. List all possible meals.

  b. You learn you can also have your dessert with or without ice cream. How many meals are possible now?

  c. You can also choose between French dressing, Italian dressing, or no dressing when you order the salad. How many meals are possible now? *Explain* how you found your answer.

28. CHALLENGE A sub shop offers 2 sizes of subs, 3 types of bread, and 4 types of filling as shown.

  a. Draw a tree diagram showing all possible outcomes. How many possible outcomes are there?

  b. Use the numbers of items in each category. How could you find the number of outcomes without using a tree diagram, chart, or list? *Explain* your reasoning.

> **Sub sandwiches**
>
> Size: whole, half
> Bread: white, wheat, rye
> Filling: meatball, turkey, ham, veggie

MIXED REVIEW

Get-Ready

Prepare for
Lesson 13.3
in Exs. 29–31

A bag has 6 tiles labeled A, B, E, L, R, and U. You randomly choose one tile. Find the probability of the event. *(p. 682)*

29. You choose an R.   **30.** You choose a vowel.   **31.** You choose an S.

Solve the equation. *(p. 636)*

32. $z + 5 = 9.7$ **33.** $13.4 + n = 20$ **34.** $x + 0.25 = 4.5$

35. ★ MULTIPLE CHOICE What is the best estimate for the area of a circular garden with a 6 meter radius? *(p. 531)*

  A 19 m^2 **B** 38 m^2 **C** 113 m^2 **D** 452 m^2

13.3 Probability of Independent Events

Before	You found the probability of a single event.
Now	You'll find the probability of two independent events.
Why?	So you can find a probability in sports, as in Example 1.

KEY VOCABULARY
• **independent events,** *p. 696*

Two events are **independent** if the occurrence of one event does not affect the likelihood that the other event will occur.

EXAMPLE 1 Two Independent Events

VOCABULARY
In Example 1, your choice does not affect your friend's choice, so the events are independent.

Recreation You and your friend each randomly choose to go swimming or play basketball on Saturday. What is the probability that both of you choose basketball?

SOLUTION

To find the probability, first make a tree diagram of the possible outcomes.

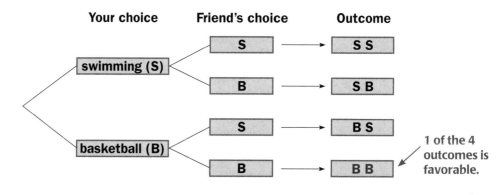

▶**Answer** The probability that both you and your friend choose basketball is $\frac{1}{4}$.

Animated **Math** at classzone.com

✓ GUIDED PRACTICE   for Example 1

In Exercises 1 and 2, use the situation in Example 1.

1. Find the probability that both of you choose the same activity.

2. Find the probability that at least one of you chooses swimming.

3. At school, an equal number of students are randomly placed in either the morning or the afternoon gym class. Use a tree diagram to find the probability that you and your friend will be in the same gym class.

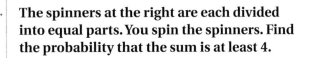 **Probability of a Sum**

ANOTHER WAY

A tree diagram could also be used to solve Example 2:

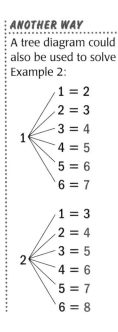

The spinners at the right are each divided into equal parts. You spin the spinners. Find the probability that the sum is at least 4.

SOLUTION You can use a table of sums to list all the possible outcomes.

	1	2	3	4	5	6
1	2	3	4	5	6	7
2	3	4	5	6	7	8

← 9 of the 12 sums are at least 4.

▶ **Answer** The probability that the sum is at least 4 is $\frac{9}{12} = \frac{3}{4}$.

EXAMPLE 3 **Three Independent Events**

Games You are playing a game in which 3 canes are tossed. One side of each cane is flat, and the other side is round. Find the probability that all 3 canes land the same side up.

SOLUTION

You can use a tree diagram to find all the possible outcomes.

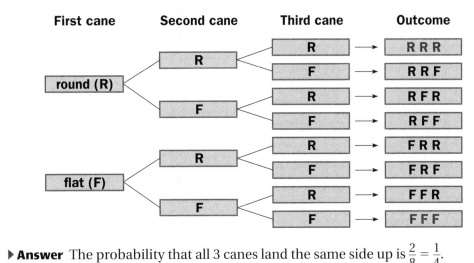

▶ **Answer** The probability that all 3 canes land the same side up is $\frac{2}{8} = \frac{1}{4}$.

✓ **GUIDED PRACTICE** for Examples 2 and 3

Find the probability of the event.

4. The sum in Example 2 is at most 4.

5. Exactly one cane in Example 3 lands flat side up.

13.3 EXERCISES

HOMEWORK KEY

★ = **STANDARDIZED TEST PRACTICE**
Exs. 8, 13, 20, 22, 24, and 35

◯ = **HINTS** AND **HOMEWORK HELP**
for Exs. 3, 9, 15, 21 at classzone.com

SKILL PRACTICE

VOCABULARY You randomly choose two marbles from a bag of 6 red and 4 blue marbles. Tell whether the two events are independent. *Explain.*

1. Choose a red marble and put it back in the bag. Then choose a blue marble.

2. Choose a blue marble but don't put it back in the bag. Then choose a red marble.

FINDING PROBABILITIES WITH SPINNERS Each spinner is divided into equal parts. You spin the spinners. Find the probability of the event.

SEE EXAMPLE 1
on p. 696
for Exs. 3–8

3. You spin green on both spinners.

4. You spin red on both spinners.

5. You spin red on one spinner and green on the other spinner.

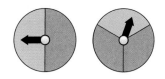

6. You spin red on at least 1 spinner.

7. **ERROR ANALYSIS** Use the spinners from Exercises 3–6. Describe and correct the error made in finding the probability of spinning green on at least one of the spinners.

> There are 5 sections on the spinners and 2 of them are green. So, the probability of spinning green on at least one of them is $\frac{2}{5}$.

8. ★ **MULTIPLE CHOICE** What is the probability of spinning red exactly once on the spinners from Exercises 3–6?

Ⓐ $\frac{1}{6}$ Ⓑ $\frac{3}{5}$ Ⓒ $\frac{1}{2}$ Ⓓ $\frac{2}{3}$

FINDING PROBABILITIES OF SUMS A bag contains three tiles numbered 1, 2, and 3. Another bag contains four tiles numbered 1, 3, 5, and 7. You randomly draw one tile from each bag. Find the probability of the event.

SEE EXAMPLE 2
on p. 697
for Exs. 9–12

9. The sum of the numbers is 8.

10. The sum of the numbers is 9.

11. The sum of the numbers is odd.

12. The sum of the numbers is prime.

13. ★ **MULTIPLE CHOICE** A number cube is rolled two times. Find the probability that you roll a 1 and a 4.

Ⓐ $\frac{1}{6}$ Ⓑ $\frac{1}{3}$ Ⓒ $\frac{1}{18}$ Ⓓ $\frac{1}{36}$

PROBABILITY OF THREE INDEPENDENT EVENTS You toss a coin three times. Find the probability of the event.

SEE EXAMPLE 3
on p. 697
for Exs. 14–17

14. You get heads 0 times.

15. You get tails exactly 1 time.

16. You get tails at least 2 times.

17. You get heads at most 2 times.

18. REASONING A license plate has 2 letters followed by 3 digits. Is it more likely that a person could correctly guess the first letter on the license plate, or correctly guess the last digit on it? *Explain* your reasoning.

19. CHALLENGE You roll a number cube two times. What is the probability that the sum of the numbers is 12? *Justify* your reasoning.

PROBLEM SOLVING

SEE EXAMPLE 1
on p. 696
for Exs. 20–22

20. ★ SHORT RESPONSE You and a friend each randomly choose among the dunk tank, face painting, and the balloon throw for your first carnival activity. What is the probability that you both choose the same activity? *Explain.*

21. HIDDEN COIN You are guessing which of 2 hands is holding a coin. Find all the possible results of playing the game twice. Then find the probability that you guess correctly both times.

22. ★ MULTIPLE CHOICE You are guessing on 2 multiple-choice questions. Each question has answer choices A, B, and C. Find the probability that you answer both questions correctly.

(A) $\frac{1}{9}$ **(B)** $\frac{1}{6}$ **(C)** $\frac{1}{2}$ **(D)** $\frac{2}{3}$

SEE EXAMPLE 3
on p. 697
for Ex. 23

23. CHOOSING CLOTHES Your friend decides to wear a solid shirt with a green sweater and plaid shorts. What is the probability you'll wear the same outfit if you randomly choose a shirt, a pair of shorts, and a sweater from the items of clothing below?

24. ★ WRITING A bag contains only blue and red tiles. You draw a blue tile but do not put it back in the bag. Does this *increase, decrease,* or *not change* the probability that the next tile chosen is red? *Explain.*

25. COMPUTER SECURITY You forgot the last 2 digits of your user ID for a games website. You know that both digits are odd. Find the probability that you type the correct last digits by randomly typing 2 odd digits.

26. CHALLENGE You roll a number cube and toss a coin.

  a. Are the two events *independent? Explain* your reasoning.

  b. Find the probability that you roll a 2. Find the probability that you get heads. Find the probability that you roll a 2 and get heads. Label the three probabilities $P(2)$, $P(H)$, and $P(2 \text{ and } H)$.

  c. How are the probabilities $P(2)$, $P(H)$, and $P(2 \text{ and } H)$ related? Write an equation showing this relationship.

13.3 Probability of Independent Events **699**

Get-Ready

Prepare for
Lesson 13.4
in Exs. 27–30

Find the mean, median, mode(s), and range of the data. *(p. 99)*

27. 1, 3, 8, 7, 1, 5, 2, 5

28. 14, 16, 12, 11, 14, 15, 13, 20

29. 15, 28, 21, 17, 28, 20, 21

30. 6, 2, 3, 4, 8, 3, 7

Solve the proportion. *(p. 412)*

31. $\dfrac{4}{3} = \dfrac{x}{12}$

32. $\dfrac{5}{25} = \dfrac{s}{15}$

33. $\dfrac{10}{30} = \dfrac{6}{c}$

34. $\dfrac{24}{9} = \dfrac{8}{n}$

35. ★ **OPEN-ENDED MATH** Write three fractions that are equivalent to 0.25.
Explain how you found your answer. *(p. 266)*

QUIZ *for Lessons 13.1–13.3*

**A bag contains twelve tiles numbered 1 through 12. You randomly choose
one tile from the bag. Find the probability of the event.** *(p. 682)*

1. You choose a 7.

2. You choose an even number.

3. You choose a multiple of 3.

4. You choose a 15.

5. **POSTERS** A poster comes in 3 sizes: 1 foot by 2 feet, 2 feet by 4 feet, and
3 feet by 6 feet. You can choose a black-and-white or a colored poster.
List all the different kinds of posters you can choose. *(p. 691)*

6. Find all the two-digit numbers that can be formed using two different
digits from 1, 2, 4, and 6. *(p. 691)*

7. **PHONE NUMBERS** You forgot the first two digits of your friend's phone
number. You know that each of the digits is 7 or 8. Find the probability that
you get the correct first two digits by randomly choosing 7 or 8. *(p. 696)*

Brain Game

Create a Spinner

Create a spinner that has 6 equal parts. Use the clues
below to find out which numbers to put on the spinner.

- The probability of spinning a 4 is $\dfrac{1}{3}$.

- The probability of spinning a 2 is $\dfrac{1}{6}$.

- The probability of spinning a factor of 15 is $\dfrac{1}{2}$.

- The sum of the odd numbers on the spinner is 13.

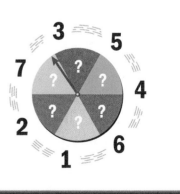

MIXED REVIEW *of Problem Solving*

STATE TEST PRACTICE
classzone.com

Lessons 13.1–13.3

1. **MULTI-STEP PROBLEM** A box contains seven tiles numbered 1 through 7. You randomly choose a tile.

   a. What is the probability that you choose a number greater than 3?

   b. *Describe* the complement of the event in part (a). Then find its probability.

2. **MULTI-STEP PROBLEM** You have 2 quarters, a nickel, and a dime in your pocket. You randomly pull two coins out of your pocket.

   a. Draw a tree diagram showing all the possible outcomes.

   b. What is the probability that you pull $.30 from your pocket?

3. **OPEN-ENDED** Give an example of a real-life situation that is a *permutation.* Give an example of a real-life situation that is a *combination.*

4. **GRIDDED ANSWER** Lauren, Luis, Carol, and Debbie are a team playing tug-of-war. How many different ways can you arrange them so that Luis is *not* the person in front?

5. **SHORT RESPONSE** Based on last year's record, the probability that the boy's soccer team will win a game is $\frac{3}{4}$. The probability that they will tie a game is $\frac{1}{6}$. What is the probability that they will lose a game? *Explain* how you found your answer.

6. **GRIDDED ANSWER** The probability that it will rain tomorrow is 80%. What is the probability that it will *not* rain tomorrow? Express your answer as a decimal.

7. **EXTENDED RESPONSE** The spinner below is divided into four equal sections.

   a. Make a tree diagram to show all the possible outcomes when you spin the spinner two times.

   b. Find the probability that the sum of the two numbers that you spin is 5.

   c. Find the probability that you get an even number at least one time.

   d. Consider the events in parts (b) and (c). Which event is less likely to occur? *Explain* your reasoning.

8. **OPEN-ENDED** *Describe* a real-life event that is (a) *impossible,* (b) *likely,* and (c) *certain.*

9. **SHORT RESPONSE** A teacher needs to choose a pair of students from the list below.

Alexa	Harold
Beth	Ilene
Duke	Sara

   a. How many pairs of students are possible?

   b. In each pair, one student will be the recorder and the other will be the presenter for a class project. How many ways can a recorder and a presenter be selected? *Explain* how you found your answer.

Experimental Probability

GOAL Find experimental probabilities.

Games *Rock, Paper, Scissors* is a popular hand game involving two players. To play, each player taps his or her fist in the palm of his or her hand two times. Then, both players simultaneously extend a hand in the shape of a rock, a piece of paper, or a pair of scissors.

The winner is decided as follows: a rock beats scissors, scissors beats paper, and paper beats a rock. What is the probability that there is a tie?

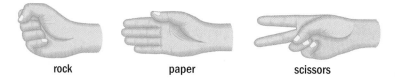

| rock | paper | scissors |

Theoretical and Experimental Probability In the previous lessons, you have found the *theoretical probability* of an event occurring. The **theoretical probability** is based on knowing all of the equally likely outcomes of an event.

Probability that is based on repeated *trials* of an experiment is called an **experimental probability**. Each trial in which the event occurs is a *success*. The experimental probability of an event is defined as:

$$\text{Experimental probability} = \frac{\text{Number of successes}}{\text{Number of trials}}.$$

EXAMPLE 1 Finding Experimental Probability

Find the experimental probability of a tie in the game *Rock, Paper, Scissors* after 8 trials and after 20 trials.

SOLUTION

The first table shows the results of 8 trials. Two ties occurred in 8 trials, so a tie has an experimental probability of

$$\frac{\text{Number of successes}}{\text{Number of trials}} = \frac{2}{8} = \frac{1}{4}, \text{ or } 25\%.$$

Frequency Table	
Player 1 wins	IIII
Player 2 wins	II
Tie	II

The second table shows the results of 20 trials. Six ties occurred in 20 trials, so a tie has an experimental probability of $\frac{6}{20} = \frac{3}{10}$, or 30%.

Frequency Table	
Player 1 wins	JHT I
Player 2 wins	JHT III
Tie	JHT I

EXAMPLE 2 Comparing Probabilities

Compare the experimental probability from Example 1 with the theoretical probability of a tie in the game *Rock, Paper, Scissors*.

EXTEND THE RESULTS

The experimental probability usually becomes closer to the theoretical probability as the number of trials increases.

SOLUTION

There are 9 possible outcomes in the game and three of those outcomes are ties. So, the theoretical probability of a tie is $\frac{3}{9} = \frac{1}{3} \approx 33\%$.

The experimental probabilities were 25% and 30%, which are close to, but not equal to, the theoretical probability.

EXAMPLE 3 Performing a Simulation

You can perform the following steps by yourself to *simulate* playing *Rock, Paper,* and *Scissors* with another person. You can use this simulation to calculate the experimental probability of a tie.

STEP 1 Make two sets of three index cards labeled R, P, and S for *Rock, Paper, Scissors*.

STEP 2 Shuffle each set of cards separately. Randomly draw a card from each set and record the results. Then replace the cards and repeat the process for a total of 25 trials.

STEP 3 Find the experimental probability of a tie.

Probability $= \frac{9}{25}$, or 36%

| | R | P | S |

| | R | P | S |

TIE	NO TIE
⊬⊬⊦ ‖‖	⊬⊬⊦ ⊬⊬⊦ ⊬⊬⊦ ‖

EXERCISES

SEE EXAMPLES 1 AND 2
on pp. 702–703
for Exs. 1–3

1. Play *Rock, Paper, Scissors* 25 times with a partner and record the results. Find the experimental probability that one person throws rock and the other throws paper and compare it with the theoretical probability.

2. Combine all the class results. Based on these results, what is the experimental probability that one person throws a rock and the other throws paper? How does this compare to the theoretical probability?

3. Roll two number cubes 30 times and record the sum of each roll. Find the experimental probability of rolling a sum of 3 and compare it with the theoretical probability.

SEE EXAMPLE 3
on p. 703
for Ex. 4

4. **Marine Biology** During one observation period, a marine mammal research group spotted 99 whales in the waters of Canada's Saguenay St. Lawrence Marine Park. Sixty-three of the whales were Fin Whales. What was the experimental probability that a whale spotted by researchers was a Fin Whale?

13.4 Misleading Statistics

Before	You made conclusions based on graphs of data.
Now	You'll recognize how statistics can be misleading.
Why?	So you can identify misleading statistics, as in Example 2.

KEY VOCABULARY
- **scale,** *p. 72*
- **bar graph,** *p. 83*
- **line graph,** *p. 89*
- **mean,** *p. 99*
- **median,** *p. 99*
- **mode,** *p. 99*

ACTIVITY

You can use graphs to influence the way people interpret data.

The table shows the results of a survey asking 100 students their favorite drink.

Drink	Students
Milk	25
Juice	21
Soda	31
Water	23

STEP 1 Draw a bar graph of the data with a scale from 0 to 35 in increments of 5.

STEP 2 Draw a bar graph of the data with a scale from 0 to 50 in increments of 10.

STEP 3 Which graph is more likely to persuade someone that students drink too much soda? *Explain* your choice.

Misleading Graphs As you saw in the activity, graphs can be misleading if the scale appears to distort the data in some way.

EXAMPLE 1 Potentially Misleading Graphs

AVOID ERRORS
Make sure you read the scale on the vertical axis carefully. Notice the break in the scale in Example 1.

Movie Theaters The bar graph shows the total sales of movie tickets in the United States for five different years. Without using the scale, compare the sales in 1999 and 2003. Then compare the sales using the scale.

Movie Ticket Sales

Sales (billions of dollars) vertical axis: 0, 7.0, 7.5, 8.0, 8.5, 9.0, 9.5, 10.0; horizontal axis years: 1999, 2000, 2001, 2002, 2003

SOLUTION

The total sales in 1999 appear to be about a third of that in 2003, because the 1999 bar is only a third of the height of the 2003 bar.

The total sales in 1999 were actually about 79% of the sales in 2003, because $7.5 \div 9.5 \approx 79\%$. The break in the scale distorts the relative heights of the bars.

704 Chapter 13 Probability and Statistics

1. Tell which line graph makes the average price of a movie ticket in the United States appear to increase more dramatically. *Explain.*

REVIEW AVERAGES

Need help with mean, median, and mode? See page 99.

Misleading Averages   An *average* can be represented by the mean, the median, or the mode. You may get a misleading impression of a data set if the average that is used does not represent the data well.

EXAMPLE 2   **Misleading Averages**

Cameras   A store owner says that the average price of a digital camera at the store is $65. The prices of the 10 digital cameras sold at the store are:

$65, $65, $80, $90, $95, $100, $112, $120, $168, and $215.

Does $65 describe the prices well? Why might a store owner use this number?

SOLUTION

The mode, $65, does not describe the data well because it is less than most of the prices. A store owner might use $65 as the average price to convince people that the store sells very inexpensive digital cameras.

RECOGNIZE MISLEADING AVERAGES

If one data value is very small or very large compared to the other data, then the mean could be distorted.

The following data shows the numbers of books donated to a library in each of 12 months. Use these data in Exercises 2–4.

23, 28, 36, 45, 25, 31, 39, 47, 28, 32, 40, 226

2. Find the mean of the data.

3. Does the mean describe the monthly donations well? *Explain* why or why not.

4. Why might a library use the mean as the average number of donated books?

13.4 EXERCISES

HOMEWORK KEY

★ = STANDARDIZED TEST PRACTICE
Exs. 5, 16, 17, 18, 22, and 30

◯ = HINTS AND HOMEWORK HELP
for Exs. 3, 5, 11, 15 at classzone.com

SKILL PRACTICE

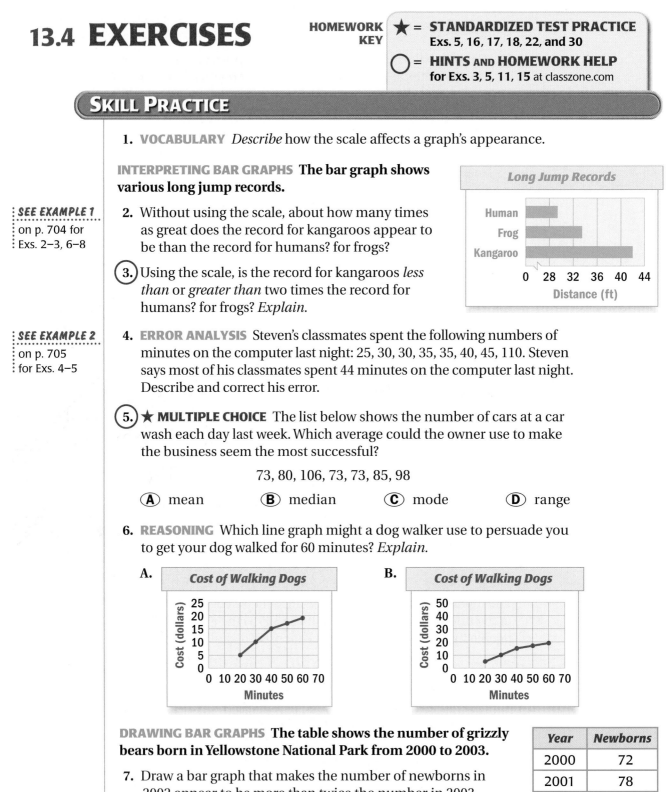

1. **VOCABULARY** *Describe* how the scale affects a graph's appearance.

INTERPRETING BAR GRAPHS **The bar graph shows various long jump records.**

SEE EXAMPLE 1
on p. 704 for
Exs. 2–3, 6–8

2. Without using the scale, about how many times as great does the record for kangaroos appear to be than the record for humans? for frogs?

3. Using the scale, is the record for kangaroos *less than* or *greater than* two times the record for humans? for frogs? *Explain.*

Long Jump Records

Distance (ft)

SEE EXAMPLE 2
on p. 705
for Exs. 4–5

4. **ERROR ANALYSIS** Steven's classmates spent the following numbers of minutes on the computer last night: 25, 30, 30, 35, 35, 40, 45, 110. Steven says most of his classmates spent 44 minutes on the computer last night. Describe and correct his error.

5. ★ **MULTIPLE CHOICE** The list below shows the number of cars at a car wash each day last week. Which average could the owner use to make the business seem the most successful?

73, 80, 106, 73, 73, 85, 98

Ⓐ mean   Ⓑ median   Ⓒ mode   Ⓓ range

6. **REASONING** Which line graph might a dog walker use to persuade you to get your dog walked for 60 minutes? *Explain.*

A. **Cost of Walking Dogs**

B. **Cost of Walking Dogs**

DRAWING BAR GRAPHS **The table shows the number of grizzly bears born in Yellowstone National Park from 2000 to 2003.**

7. Draw a bar graph that makes the number of newborns in 2002 appear to be more than twice the number in 2003.

8. Draw a bar graph of the grizzly bear data whose scale is labeled at every increment of 10, starting at 0.

9. **CHALLENGE** Find a potentially misleading graph in a newspaper or magazine. *Explain* why the graph might be misleading.

Year	Newborns
2000	72
2001	78
2002	102
2003	75

SEE EXAMPLE 2
on p. 705
for Exs. 10,
14–16, 18

10. GUIDED PROBLEM SOLVING Jill says that her average score on a video game is 500. Do the scores below support this? Why might Jill say this?

350, 305, 300, 200, 500, 325, 375, 225, 275, 500

   a. Find the mean, median, and mode(s) of the scores.

   b. Does 500 describe Jill's scores well? Why or why not?

   c. Why might Jill use 500 as her average score?

STORMS **The bar graph shows how many hurricanes and tropical storms started in various months from 1995 to 2001 in the Eastern Pacific.**

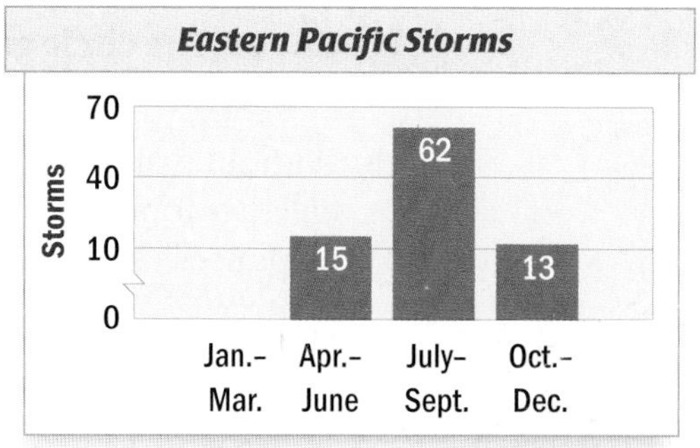

11. ESTIMATE Without using the scale or the data values, about how many times more storms appeared to start from July to September than from April to June?

Eastern Pacific Storms

	Jan.–Mar.	Apr.–June	July–Sept.	Oct.–Dec.
Storms		15	62	13

70
40
10
0

12. CALCULATE Use the data values. About how many times more storms actually started from July to September than from April to June?

13. REASONING Would a travel agent use the *data values* or the *bars on the graph* to convince someone *not* to travel to the Eastern Pacific in the summer? *Explain* your answer.

BASEBALL **In Exercises 14–16, the numbers of games won by a baseball team in 10 seasons are: 82, 94, 97, 88, 88, 71, 69, 55, 59, 72.**

14. CALCULATE Find the mean, median, and mode(s) of the data set.

15. ANALYZE A sports report states that the average number of wins by the team is 88. Does 88 describe the numbers of wins well? Why or why not?

16. ★ WRITING *Explain* why a report might use 88 as the average number of wins.

17. ★ SHORT RESPONSE The bar graph shows the heights of two buildings. Without using the scale, tell how many times taller Building B appears than Building A. Does your answer represent the actual relationship? *Explain* your reasoning.

Heights of Buildings

Height (m)	Building A	Building B
300		
225		
150		
0		

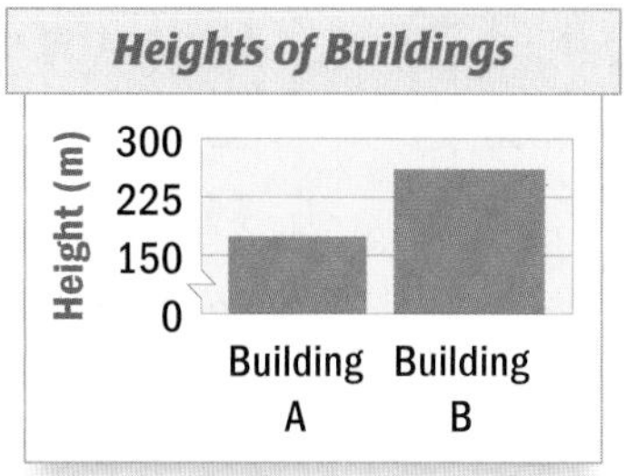

18. ★ EXTENDED RESPONSE The ages of athletes in a skateboarding competition are 15, 17, 29, 17, 15, 16, 15, and 20. Which average or averages represent the data well? *Explain* your reasoning. Later, two 13 year olds qualify for the competition. Does the same average(s) still represent the data well?

19. MULTI-STEP PROBLEM The list below shows the prices of several houses in one area.

$145,000, $115,000, $150,000, $115,000, $198,000,
$215,000, $130,000, $140,000, $152,000, $190,000

a. A real estate agent says that the average cost of a home in the area is $115,000. Does $115,000 describe the prices well? Why or why not?

b. Why might a real estate agent use $115,000 as the average price?

c. Which average provides you with the information you would most want to know when buying a house? *Explain*.

ELECTIVES The circle graph shows the results of a survey asking students their favorite elective.

20. Without using the percents, which elective appears to have the most responses? *Explain*.

21. Draw a circle graph that more accurately shows the actual percent for each elective.

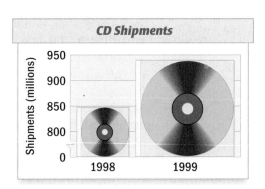

Favorite Electives

Music 35%
Languages 20%
Other 10%
Art 35%

22. ★ **OPEN-ENDED MATH** Create a data set for which the mean does *not* represent the data well. Repeat this exercise for the median and the mode(s).

CHALLENGE The graph shows the numbers, in millions, of CD shipments in the United States in 1998 and 1999.

23. About how many times as great in area is the picture for 1999 than the picture for 1998? *Explain* how this may distort the data.

24. Was the actual number of shipments in 1999 *less than* or *greater than* twice the number of shipments in 1998? *Explain*.

MIXED REVIEW

Get-Ready

Prepare for Lesson 13.5 in Exs. 25–28

Order the numbers from least to greatest. *(p. 130)*

25. 19.96, 1.54, 2.2, 7.3, 19.5, 11.2, 17.73

26. 11.9, 14.25, 13.2, 12.69, 112.2, 16.3

27. 1.97, 12.82, 8.8, 19.19, 7.3, 19.56, 14.9

28. 1.188, 15.57, 13.5, 11.18, 3.44, 13.47

29. You toss a coin twice. Find the probability that you get heads at least one time. *(p. 696)*

30. ★ **MULTIPLE CHOICE** Which variable expression represents *6 more than a number*? *(p. 629)*

(A) $n + 6$ (B) $6 - n$ (C) $n - 6$ (D) $6 > n$

13.5 Stem-and-Leaf Plots

	Before	You organized data using line plots and frequency tables.
	Now	You'll organize data using stem-and-leaf plots.
	Why?	So you can organize data, as with ages of patrons in Example 2.

KEY VOCABULARY
- **stem-and-leaf plot,** *p. 709*
- **leaf,** *p. 709*
- **stem,** *p. 709*

Internet The table below lists how long, in minutes, you were online each day for three weeks. How can you display the data in an organized manner?

			Daily Internet Use (minutes)			
Sunday	**Monday**	**Tuesday**	**Wednesday**	**Thursday**	**Friday**	**Saturday**
22	41	15	28	50	19	44
27	23	35	54	70	40	37
42	19	29	53	31	31	35

You can use a *stem-and-leaf* plot to organize a large set of data. In a **stem-and-leaf plot**, each data value has two parts, a *stem* and a *leaf*. The **leaf** is the last digit in the data value. The **stem** is the remaining digits. For example, the leaf of the data value 37 is 7. The stem is 3.

EXAMPLE 1 Making a Stem-and-Leaf Plot

To organize the minutes online in the table above, you can make a stem-and-leaf plot. The numbers range from 15 to 70. So, the least stem is 1 and the greatest stem is 7.

AVOID ERRORS
Be sure to include all the stems between the least and the greatest data values. In Example 1, 6 is a stem even though none of the data have a 6 in the tens' place.

STEP 1
Order stems from least to greatest.

```
1 |
2 |
3 |
4 |
5 |
6 |
7 |
```

STEP 2
Write the leaves next to their stems.

```
1 | 9 5 9
2 | 2 7 3 9 8
3 | 5 1 1 7 5
4 | 2 1 0 4
5 | 4 3 0
6 |
7 | 0
```
↙ This stands for 53.

  Math at classzone.com

STEP 3
Order the leaves from least to greatest.

```
1 | 5 9 9
2 | 2 3 7 8 9
3 | 1 1 5 5 7
4 | 0 1 2 4
5 | 0 3 4
6 |
7 | 0     Key: 5 | 3 = 53
```
↖ Be sure to include a key.

✓ **GUIDED PRACTICE** for Example 1

1. Make a stem-and-leaf plot of the data 31, 14, 22, 51, 33, 16, 21, 24, 22, 15, 30, 28, and 39.

EXAMPLE 2 Interpreting Stem-and-Leaf Plots

Diners The stem-and-leaf plot shows the ages of people at a diner.

a. What is the range of the ages?

b. Describe the age group with the most people.

```
0 | 4 6 7 9
1 | 0 1 1 2 2 2 4 9
2 | 2 5 8
3 | 0 1 4      Key: 3 | 1 = 31
```

SOLUTION

a. The youngest person at the diner is 4 years old, because the least data value is 0 | 4. The oldest is 34 years old, because the greatest data value is 3 | 4. The range is 30 years, because 34 − 4 = 30.

b. The stem of 1 has more leaves than any other, so the age group with the most people is 10–19 years.

EXAMPLE 3 Finding the Mean, Median, and Mode

Use the stem-and-leaf plot shown below.

a. Find the mean.

b. Find the median.

c. Find the mode.

```
5 | 7 7
6 | 1 2 7
7 | 0 4      Key: 5 | 7 = 5.7
```

SOLUTION

Make an ordered list of the 7 values in the stem-and-leaf plot.

5.7, 5.7, 6.1, 6.2, 6.7, 7.0, 7.4

a. $\text{Mean} = \dfrac{5.7 + 5.7 + 6.1 + 6.2 + 6.7 + 7.0 + 7.4}{7} = \dfrac{44.8}{7} = 6.4$

b. $\text{Median} = 6.2$, because the middle value is 6.2.

c. $\text{Mode} = 5.7$, because it is the only value that occurs more than once.

✓ **GUIDED PRACTICE** for Examples 2 and 3

2. Use the stem-and-leaf plot in Example 2. How many people at the diner are over 20 years old? What are their ages?

Find the mean, median, and mode(s) of the data.

3.
```
3 | 1 7 9
4 | 2 2 3 6
5 | 0 4 7 7 7
6 | 2 5 8
   Key: 3 | 1 = 31
```

4.
```
7 | 3 3 4 5 9 9
8 | 0 1 2 6 6 6
9 | 2 4 4 7 9
   Key: 7 | 3 = 7.3
```

5.
```
1 | 2 3 5 9
2 | 3 6 7 8 9
3 |
4 | 1 1 2 4 6
   Key: 1 | 2 = 12
```

13.5 EXERCISES

HOMEWORK KEY

★ = **STANDARDIZED TEST PRACTICE**
8, 9, 19, 21, 22, 24, and 36

◯ = **HINTS AND HOMEWORK HELP**
for Exs. 3, 5, 15, 17 at classzone.com

SKILL PRACTICE

SEE EXAMPLE 1
on p. 709
for Exs. 3–7

1. **VOCABULARY** Identify the stems and the leaves in the stem-and-leaf plot.

2. **VOCABULARY** What number does the red entry represent?

```
1 | 2 4 7
2 | 1 9
3 | 5 6 8 9
4 | 1 2 2 3
5 | 3 4 4 4 4 5 5    Key: 1|4 = 14
```

MAKING STEM-AND-LEAF PLOTS Make a stem-and-leaf plot of the data.

3. 15, 18, 24, 32, 28, 18, 21, 16, 32, 41, 25, 31, 18, 25

4. 67, 55, 61, 69, 50, 51, 67, 62, 39, 50, 35, 62, 58, 60

5. 15, 38, 9, 33, 16, 7, 5, 35, 30, 35, 55, 49, 41, 52, 51

6. 5.6, 5.8, 6.2, 3.1, 5.2, 3.5, 2.9, 3.8, 5.2, 6.0, 5.3, 5.2, 3.9

7. **ERROR ANALYSIS** Describe and correct the error in making the stem-and-leaf plot.

```
1 | 5 9
2 | 0 2
4 | 3 3 7    Key: 4|3 = 43    ✗
```

In Exercises 8 and 9, use the stem-and-leaf plot below.

SEE EXAMPLE 2
on p. 710
for Ex. 8

8. ★ **MULTIPLE CHOICE** What is the greatest number in the stem-and-leaf plot?

   (A) 2.2   (B) 9

   (C) 22   (D) 29

```
0 | 9 9
1 | 5 5 6 7 9
2 | 0 0 0 1 2    Key: 2|0 = 20
```

SEE EXAMPLE 3
on p. 710
for Exs. 9–11

9. ★ **MULTIPLE CHOICE** What is the mode of the data?

   (A) 13   (B) 16.9   (C) 18   (D) 20

FINDING MEAN, MEDIAN, AND MODE Find the mean, median, and mode(s) of the data in the stem-and-leaf plot.

10.
```
4 | 0 0
5 | 3 3 5 5 5 6 9
6 | 4              Key: 5|3 = 53
```

11.
```
0 | 5 5 8 9
1 | 1 1
2 |
3 | 6 7 9 9    Key: 1|1 = 1.1
```

12. **MAKING A GRAPH** Use the stem-and-leaf plot to make a bar graph of the data.

```
1 | 7 9
2 | 4 4 8
3 | 1          Key: 2|4 = 24
```

13. **CHALLENGE** Make a stem-and-leaf plot of the data below. *Explain* how you chose a key for the stem-and-leaf plot.

   13.8, 12.5, 12.62, 13.55, 13, 12.75, 12.8, 12.75, 13.12

**SEE EXAMPLES
1 AND 2**
on pp. 709–710
for Ex. 14

14. GUIDED PROBLEM SOLVING The list below shows
the weights, in pounds, of pets owned by students.
Describe where the weights of most of the pets fall.

25, 7, 8, 10, 13, 22, 10, 15, 12,
13, 9, 40, 15, 21, 14

a. Find the least stem and the greatest stem
for the data.

b. Make a stem-and-leaf plot of the data.

c. Which stem has the most leaves? *Explain*
what this means.

TENNIS In Exercises 15–19, the stem-and-leaf plot shows the lengths,
in minutes, of mixed doubles finals matches in Wimbledon tournaments
for a period of years.

SEE EXAMPLE 3
on p. 710
for Ex. 15

15. Find the mean, median, mode(s), and range.

16. Which average from Exercise 15 best
describes the data? *Explain*.

17. Which stem has the most leaves? *Explain*
what this means.

18. What is the length of the shortest match?
the longest?

```
 5 | 9
 6 | 6 9
 7 | 1 1 3 3 3 5
 8 | 5 5
 9 | 3 7
10 | 0
11 |
12 | 1     Key: 12 | 1 = 121
```

19. ★ **WRITING** *Describe* two ways you can
compare the shortest and longest matches.

20. BOWLING The table shows your bowling
scores in several games. Make a stem-and-leaf
plot of the scores. Use the key 19 | 6 = 196.
Your goal was to score at least 230 in 10 of the
games. By how many games did you miss
your goal?

Bowling Scores				
181	222	196	210	217
195	199	204	215	190
202	251	222	230	235

21. ★ **MULTIPLE CHOICE** The numbers of miles you walked per day over
a two week period of time are listed below. Which stem-and-leaf plot
correctly displays the data?

2.2, 1.1, 3.5, 2.0, 3.2, 3.0, 0.5, 0.8, 1.0, 2.2, 1.5, 3.5, 2.2, 2.0

A
```
0 | 5 8
1 | 0 1 5
2 | 0 2
3 | 0 2 5     Key: 1 | 0 = 1.0
```

B
```
0 | 5 8
1 | 0 1 5
2 | 0 2
3 | 0 2 5     Key: 1 | 0 = 10
```

C
```
0 | 5 8
1 | 0 1 5
2 | 0 0 2 2 2
3 | 0 2 5 5     Key: 1 | 0 = 1.0
```

D
```
0 | 5 8
1 | 0 1 5
2 | 0 0 2 2 2
3 | 0 2 5 5     Key: 1 | 0 = 10
```

22. ★ **EXTENDED RESPONSE** The table below shows the average weights, in ounces, of several species of Amazon parrots.

Species	Weight (in oz)	Species	Weight (in oz)
Blue-fronted	11.0	Tucuman	11.3
Double Yellow-headed	15.9	Red Lored	12.3
Lilac crowned	11.5	Yellow-fronted	13.4
Orange-winged	12.7	Vinaceous	13.1

a. Make a stem-and-leaf plot of the data.

b. Use the stem-and-leaf plot to select an appropriate average by visually analyzing the data. *Explain* how you chose the average.

c. Find the mean, median, and mode(s) of the data. Which of the three is closest to the average you chose in part (b)?

CELL PHONES In Exercises 23 and 24, the stem-and-leaf plot shows the weights, in ounces, of 15 cell phones at a store.

23. Find the mean, median, and mode(s).

24. ★ **WRITING** Which average from Exercise 23 describes the data well? *Explain.*

```
4 | 0 3 8 8
5 | 0 4 9
6 | 0 1 2
7 | 1 2 9
8 | 2 6      Key: 8 | 6 = 8.6
```

25. **U.S. PRESIDENTS** Find the ages of the twentieth-century United States presidents at the times they first took office. Make a stem-and-leaf plot of the data. What can you conclude from the plot?

26. **CHALLENGE** The least value of a data set is 12.3. The greatest value is 90.7. Is it appropriate to make a stem-and-leaf plot of the data? *Explain* why or why not.

MIXED REVIEW

Get-Ready

Prepare for Lesson 13.6 in Exs. 27–29

Graph the integer on a number line. *(p. 573)*

27. -6

28. 5

29. 0

Find the sum or difference. *(p. 302)*

30. $\frac{1}{2} + \frac{4}{5}$

31. $\frac{3}{11} + \frac{2}{3}$

32. $\frac{8}{9} - \frac{1}{18}$

33. $\frac{9}{10} - \frac{6}{7}$

34. $\frac{3}{4} + \frac{5}{6} + \frac{1}{2}$

35. $\frac{7}{12} - \frac{1}{4} - \frac{1}{3}$

36. ★ **SHORT RESPONSE** The scores of 10 contestants at a cooking contest are given below. Your score at the contest is 7. Which average can you use to state that your score is above average? *Explain.* *(p. 704)*

7, 10, 10, 6, 9, 5, 8, 7, 5, 5

13.6 Box-and-Whisker Plots

Before	You represented data using stem-and-leaf plots.
Now	You'll represent data using box-and-whisker plots.
Why?	So you can analyze work done, as with recycling in Ex. 14.

KEY VOCABULARY
- box-and-whisker plot, *p. 714*
- lower quartile, *p. 714*
- upper quartile, *p. 714*
- lower extreme, *p. 714*
- upper extreme, *p. 714*

A **box-and-whisker plot** divides a data set into four parts, two below the median and two above it. The **lower quartile** is the median of the lower half of the data. The **upper quartile** is the median of the upper half. The **lower extreme** is the least data value. The **upper extreme** is the greatest data value.

EXAMPLE 1 Making a Box-and-Whisker Plot

Ticket Prices The notebook shows the ticket prices for 11 concerts you attended. How can you display the data to see how the prices are spread out?

Ticket Prices
$14 $36 $9 $12
$24 $27 $22 $42
$25 $19 $18

SOLUTION

To display the concert ticket prices, make a box-and-whisker plot.

STEP 1 **Order** the data to find the median, the quartiles, and the extremes.

	Lower half					Upper half			
9	12	14	18	19	22	24	25	27	36	42

Lower extreme: 9
Lower quartile: 14
Median: 22
Upper quartile: 27
Upper extreme: 42

ORDER DATA
If a data set has an odd number of data values, then the median is not included in either half of the data, as shown in Example 1.

STEP 2 **Plot** the five values below a number line.

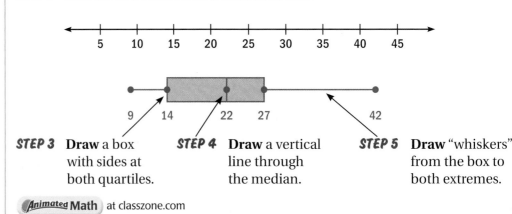

STEP 3 **Draw** a box with sides at both quartiles. **STEP 4** **Draw** a vertical line through the median. **STEP 5** **Draw** "whiskers" from the box to both extremes.

Animated Math at classzone.com

EXAMPLE 2 Reading a Box-and-Whisker Plot

Identify the median, the lower and upper quartiles, and the lower and upper extremes in the box-and-whisker plot below.

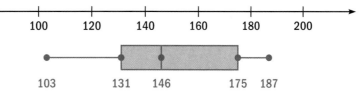

▶ **Answer** The median is 146. The lower quartile is 131. The upper quartile is 175. The lower extreme is 103. The upper extreme is 187.

EXAMPLE 3 Interpreting Box-and-Whisker Plots

Jellyfish The box-and-whisker plots below represent the body widths (in inches) of a sample of jellyfish from two different species.

a. Find the range of the body widths.

b. Compare the body widths in the two samples.

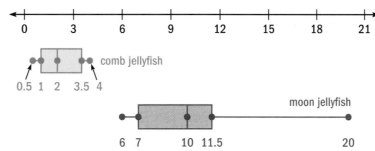

SOLUTION

AVOID ERRORS
When finding ranges of data in a double box-and-whisker plot, do not confuse values from separate plots.

a. The range is the difference between the extremes.
The range for comb jellyfish is 3.5 inches, because $4 - 0.5 = 3.5$.
The range for moon jellyfish is 14 inches, because $20 - 6 = 14$.

b. All of the moon jellyfish in the sample have a greater body width than all of the comb jellyfish.

✓ **GUIDED PRACTICE** for Examples 1, 2, and 3

1. Make a box-and-whisker plot of the data: 5, 9, 16, 8, 6, 15, 14, 5, 15, 12.

Use the box-and-whisker plots above.

2. Identify the median, the lower and upper quartiles, and the lower and upper extremes for the body widths of the moon jellyfish in Example 3.

3. Find the range of the data in Example 2.

13.6 EXERCISES

HOMEWORK KEY

★ = **STANDARDIZED TEST PRACTICE**
Exs. 7, 12, 16, and 27

◯ = **HINTS** AND **HOMEWORK HELP**
for Exs. 3, 5, 9, 15 at classzone.com

SKILL PRACTICE

1. **VOCABULARY** Identify the median, lower quartile, upper quartile, lower extreme, and upper extreme in the box-and-whisker plot.

BOX-AND-WHISKER PLOTS Make a box-and-whisker plot of the data.

SEE EXAMPLE 1
on p. 714
for Exs. 2–6, 11

2. 9, 11, 15, 8, 6, 18, 13, 14, 10

3. 22, 7, 4, 29, 15, 30, 8, 9, 11

4. 37, 14, 30, 24, 32, 16, 20, 13

5. 17, 3, 42, 39, 10, 12, 33, 25

6. **ERROR ANALYSIS** Describe and correct the error made in finding the upper quartile.

✗ 12 15 15 17 19 20 20 21 25
                      | |
                   Median   Upper quartile

SEE EXAMPLE 3
on p. 715
for Ex. 7

7. ★ **MULTIPLE CHOICE** The box-and-whisker plot shows the prices (in dollars) of the DVD players at a store. Find the range of the data.

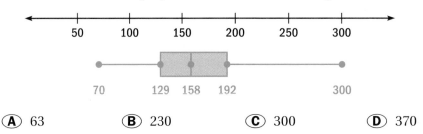

(A) 63 **(B)** 230 **(C)** 300 **(D)** 370

SEE EXAMPLES 2 AND 3
on p. 715
for Exs. 8–10

READING BOX-AND-WHISKER PLOTS Use the box-and-whisker plot from Exercise 7. Find and interpret the value.

8. lower extreme 9. upper quartile 10. median

11. This stem-and-leaf plot shows the number of stair steps in 15 houses. Make a box-and-whisker plot of this data.

```
0 | 0 2 3 3 6 9
1 | 2 4 5 7
2 | 0 1 1 3 8     Key: 2 | 1 = 21
```

12. ★ **OPEN-ENDED MATH** Create a data set of 10 values that meets the conditions given below.

median = 123, lower quartile = 92, range = 87, upper extreme = 170

13. **CHALLENGE** In a box-and-whisker plot, is the difference of the lower quartile and lower extreme and the difference of the upper extreme and upper quartile always the same? *Explain.*

SEE EXAMPLE 1
on p. 714
for Ex. 14

14. RECYCLING The list shows the numbers of recyclable cans collected by students. Make a box-and-whisker plot of the data.

36, 42, 12, 39, 34, 71, 33, 32, 40, 32

*SEE EXAMPLES
1, 2, AND 3*
on p. 714–715
for Ex. 15

15. MULTI-STEP PROBLEM The table shows the running times (in minutes) of the movies that won the award for Best Picture from 1970 to 1999.

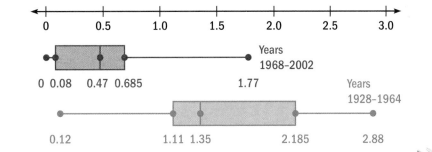

RUNNING TIMES OF BEST PICTURES (MINUTES)									
1970s 170	104	175	129	200	133	119	93	183	105
1980s 124	123	188	132	158	150	120	160	133	99
1990s 183	118	131	197	142	177	160	194	122	121

a. Graph Make a box-and-whisker plot of each decade using the same number line.

b. Interpret Identify the median and the range of the running times for each decade.

c. Compare Compare and contrast the running times of the Best Pictures in the 1970s, the 1980s, and the 1990s.

16. ★ WRITING *Explain* why the medians of the lower half and the upper half of a set of data are called quartiles.

BOBSLEDS **The box-and-whisker plots show the differences (in seconds) between the gold and silver medalists' times in men's Olympic bobsled events from 1928 to 2002.**

0	0.5	1.0	1.5	2.0	2.5	3.0

Years 1968–2002

0   0.08   0.47   0.685   1.77

Years 1928–1964

0.12   1.11   1.35   2.185   2.88

SEE EXAMPLE 3
on p. 715
for Exs. 17–19

17. Which time period generally had a lesser time difference? *Explain.*

18. Which time period had a wider range of time differences? *Explain.*

19. In a box-and-whisker plot, the box represents about 50% of the data. The whiskers each represent about 25% of the data. About what percent of the time differences from 1928 to 1964 were between 1.11 and 2.88 seconds?

Total Solar Eclipse   In a solar eclipse, the Moon is between Earth and the Sun. During a *total* solar eclipse, the view of the Sun from Earth is completely blocked by the Moon. Scientists, amateur astronomers, and others travel from all over the world to the best viewing locations.

At the last total solar eclipse, one eclipse enthusiast said "Most total eclipses last about $4\frac{1}{2}$ minutes." From 1981 to 2003, sixteen total eclipses occurred. The data below list the longest duration, in seconds, of each eclipse.

122, 311, 120, 119, 226, 153, 413, 321, 263, 130, 170, 249, 143, 297, 124, 117

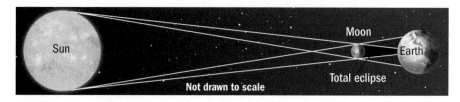

20. **Organize**   Make a box-and-whisker plot of the data.

21. **Analyze**   How many seconds separate the eclipse with the longest duration and the eclipse with the shortest duration?

22. **Interpret**   Why do you think the eclipse enthusiast said that most total solar eclipses last about $4\frac{1}{2}$ minutes? *Explain* why that is not accurate. Summarize the data in another way using your box-and-whisker plot.

23. **CHALLENGE**   A science teacher makes a box-and-whisker plot of 16 test scores. The upper quartile is 83 and the upper extreme is 98. No students have the same score. Is it possible to determine how many students scored an 83 or better? *Explain.*

MIXED REVIEW

Prepare for
Lesson 13.7
in Exs. 24–25

Make a stem-and-leaf plot of the data. *(p. 709)*

24. 14, 33, 31, 22, 18, 19, 26, 34, 24, 24, 39, 10, 35, 37

25. 62, 57, 68, 73, 58, 67, 73, 60, 71, 66, 84, 78, 50, 71

CHOOSE A STRATEGY   **Use a strategy from the list to solve the following problem. *Explain* your choice.**

26. Ferries arrive at 11:07 A.M., 11:21 A.M., 11:35 A.M., and 11:49 A.M. Predict when the next two ferries will arrive.

Problem Solving Strategies

- Draw a Diagram *(p. 762)*
- Guess, Check, and Revise *(p. 763)*
- Make a Table *(p. 765)*
- Look for a Pattern *(p. 766)*

27. ★ **OPEN-ENDED MATH**   Write a data set of 9 numbers. Find the mean, median, mode(s), and range. *(p. 99)*

13.7 Choosing an Appropriate Data Display

Before	You created different data displays.
Now	You'll choose appropriate data displays.
Why?	So you can compare survey responses, as in Ex. 15.

KEY VOCABULARY
- **line plot,** *p. 77*
- **bar graph,** *p. 83*
- **line graph,** *p. 89*
- **circle graph,** *p. 94*
- **stem-and-leaf plot,** *p. 709*
- **box-and-whisker plot,** *p. 714*

Data Displays Below is a summary of the different ways you can display data and how to use each display.

KEY CONCEPT   *For Your Notebook*

Using Appropriate Data Displays

Use a **line plot** to show how often each number occurs.

Use a **bar graph** to display data in distinct categories.

Use a **line graph** to display data over time.

Use a **circle graph** to represent data as parts of a whole.

Use a **stem-and-leaf plot** to order a data set.

Use a **box-and-whisker plot** to show the data's distribution in quarters, using the median, quartiles, and extremes.

❖ **EXAMPLE 1** Choosing an Effective Display

Stamps Which graph is more effective in comparing the percent of people who prefer sports stamps to the total number of people?

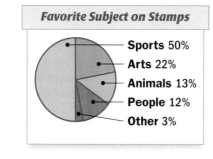

Favorite Subject on Stamps

- **Sports** 50%
- **Arts** 22%
- **Animals** 13%
- **People** 12%
- **Other** 3%

Favorite Subject on Stamps

▶ **Answer** The circle graph shows the whole, so it is more effective in showing that 50% of the people chose sports as their favorite stamp subject.

EXAMPLE 2 Making an Appropriate Display

Sunglasses You ask 20 people at a beach how many pairs of sunglasses they own. The list below shows their responses. Make a data display that shows the spread of data.

0, 1, 1, 1, 2, 2, 2, 2, 2, 3, 3, 3, 3, 3, 4, 4, 4, 6, 6, 10

SOLUTION

You can use a box-and-whisker plot to show the spread of data. The box tells you that about half of the people own 2 to 4 pairs of sunglasses.

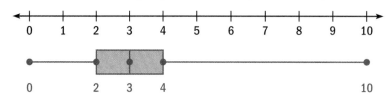

EXAMPLE 3 Choosing an Appropriate Display

Weather The data displays organize the daily high temperatures during a recent month in Boston, Massachusetts. Which display can you use to find the median high temperature?

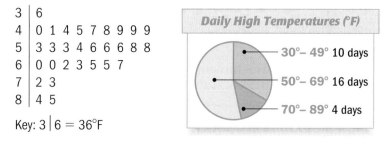

```
3 | 6
4 | 0 1 4 5 7 8 9 9 9
5 | 3 3 3 4 6 6 6 8 8
6 | 0 0 2 3 5 5 7
7 | 2 3
8 | 4 5
```
Key: 3 | 6 = 36°F

SOLUTION

You can use the stem-and-leaf plot to find the median high temperature, 56°F, because it displays the data in order. The circle graph does not display the individual temperatures.

TAKING NOTES
Include an example in your notebook for each type of data display you have studied. Also include a summary of the information that you can read from the display.

✓ **GUIDED PRACTICE**   for Examples 1, 2, and 3

1. **What If?** In Example 1 on page 719, suppose you want to compare people preferring art stamps to people preferring animal stamps. Which graph is more effective? *Explain.*

2. You record the temperature (in degrees Fahrenheit) at noon for seven days in a row. The data are listed below. Which data display would you use to show how the temperature changed during that time? Make the display.

50°F   42°F   30°F   32°F   45°F   55°F   50°F

13.7 EXERCISES

HOMEWORK KEY

★ = **STANDARDIZED TEST PRACTICE**
Exs. 9, 14, 19, 20, and 26

◯ = **HINTS AND HOMEWORK HELP**
for Exs. 7, 11, 13, 15 at classzone.com

SKILL PRACTICE

VOCABULARY Match the data display with its description.

1. line plot   **A.** shows all values and orders data

2. circle graph   **B.** displays data changing over time

3. line graph   **C.** uses X's to show how often a number occurs

4. stem-and-leaf plot   **D.** shows how data in various categories compare

5. bar graph   **E.** represents data as parts of a whole

SEE EXAMPLE 1
on p. 719
for Ex. 6

6. ◆ **MULTIPLE REPRESENTATIONS** Tell which of the data displays below is more effective in the given situation.

    a. To find the number of students who read 5 books last month

    b. To see that half of the students read 3 or 4 books

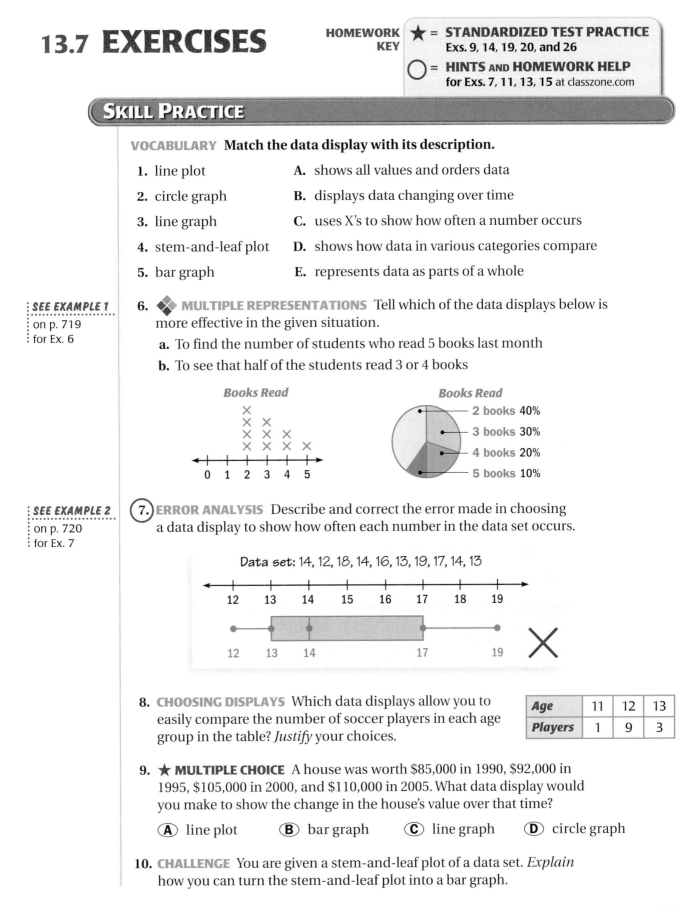

SEE EXAMPLE 2
on p. 720
for Ex. 7

7. **ERROR ANALYSIS** Describe and correct the error made in choosing a data display to show how often each number in the data set occurs.

Data set: 14, 12, 18, 14, 16, 13, 19, 17, 14, 13

8. **CHOOSING DISPLAYS** Which data displays allow you to easily compare the number of soccer players in each age group in the table? *Justify* your choices.

Age	11	12	13
Players	1	9	3

9. ★ **MULTIPLE CHOICE** A house was worth $85,000 in 1990, $92,000 in 1995, $105,000 in 2000, and $110,000 in 2005. What data display would you make to show the change in the house's value over that time?

    Ⓐ line plot   **Ⓑ** bar graph   **Ⓒ** line graph   **Ⓓ** circle graph

10. **CHALLENGE** You are given a stem-and-leaf plot of a data set. *Explain* how you can turn the stem-and-leaf plot into a bar graph.

11. **STOCKS** The closing prices of a company stock on Monday through Friday are listed in order. Make a data display that shows the change in price over the week.

$26.20, $25.50, $25.00, $24.80, $24.65

SEE EXAMPLE 2
on p. 720
for Exs. 12–14

12. **BICYCLE STUNTS** The table at the right shows the scores of 10 athletes at a bicycle stunt competition. Make a data display that shows the median and the spread of the scores.

Bicycle Stunt Scores	
91.4	91.0
90.3	90.0
89.7	89.4
87.5	86.7
84.3	84.1

13. **CONCERTS** The list below shows the ages of the first twelve people who enter a concert hall. Make a data display that orders the ages from least to greatest. Then use the display to find the median of the ages.

34, 19, 60, 45, 42, 38, 49, 58, 70, 41, 39, 31

14. ★ **MULTIPLE CHOICE** A survey at a restaurant asked customers how much they spent on their lunches. Which data display could be used to find the mean amount spent on lunch?

(**A**) box-and-whisker plot   (**B**) bar graph

(**C**) stem-and-leaf plot   (**D**) circle graph

15. **MULTI-STEP PROBLEM** After playing 3 new songs, a disc jockey records that 186 callers prefer the first song, 79 callers prefer the second song, and 310 callers prefer the third song.

  a. Which data display would you use to compare the responses for the first song to all responses?

  b. Make the display.

◆ **MULTIPLE REPRESENTATIONS** **The table below shows the results of a survey asking 100 students their favorite way to get in touch with friends.**

SEE EXAMPLE 3
on p. 720
for Exs. 16–18

16. *Explain* whether a *line graph* or a *bar graph* is more appropriate for displaying the data. Then make the display.

17. *Explain* which data display is most appropriate for comparing the results for each category to the overall results of the survey. Then make the display.

18. This survey is repeated every year for 5 years. Which data display would be most appropriate to show the changes in the results of the survey over the 5 years?

Form of communication	Responses
instant messaging	33
email	20
telephone	28
letter writing	11
other	8

19. ★ **WRITING** Name two data displays that you can use to find the mode of a set of data. *Explain* your reasoning.

★ = **STANDARDIZED TEST PRACTICE**   ◯ = **HINTS AND HOMEWORK HELP** *at classzone.com*

20. ★ **SHORT RESPONSE** The stamps below show the cost to mail a letter in the given years. Choose and make a display of the data. *Explain* your choice.

1960   1970   1980   1990   2000

21. **CHALLENGE** Which data displays would you use to show where the bulk of the data in a data set fall? *Explain* your choices.

MIXED REVIEW

Evaluate the expression. *(p. 21)*

22. $24 - 3^3 \div 9$ **23.** $61 - 5 \times 2^3$ **24.** $7 \times 6 + 68 \div 4$

25. Make a box-and-whisker plot of the data. *(p. 714)*

23, 62, 32, 32, 10, 24, 35, 27, 22, 21, 19, 16

26. ★ **MULTIPLE CHOICE** What is the name for a polygon that has 6 sides? *(p. 485)*

(A) quadrilateral **(B)** octagon   **(C)** hexagon   **(D)** pentagon

QUIZ *for Lessons 13.4–13.7*

1. Which line graph might a travel agent use to convince people that train travel is becoming too expensive? *Explain* your choice. *(p. 704)*

2. Make a stem-and-leaf plot of the data: 36, 33, 21, 8, 39, 24, 26, 50, 4, 16. *(p. 709)*

3. Make a box-and-whisker plot of the data: 80, 81, 90, 83, 74, 73, 91, 84, 86. *(p. 714)*

4. **SURVEY** In a survey of 100 people, 64 people liked a new movie, 20 people didn't like the movie, and the rest had not seen it. Make a data display that compares the results for each response to all responses. *(p. 719)*

Lessons 13.4–13.7

1. EXTENDED RESPONSE A school has two academic trivia teams that compete in local competitions in which the highest score wins. The scores for each team in the last six competitions are given below.

Competition Number	1	2	3	4	5	6
Team A	91	120	102	130	139	138
Team B	118	115	126	124	126	125

a. What type of data display would you use to convince the school to send Team A? Team B? *Explain.*

b. Decide which team should go. *Justify* your reasoning using a data display.

2. EXTENDED RESPONSE A model train club says that the average age of its members is 15. The ages of all the members are listed below.

27, 40, 14, 59, 28, 29, 15, 13,
29, 37, 53, 15, 67, 36, 15

a. Make a stem-and-leaf plot of the ages. Which age group has the most people?

b. Make a box-and-whisker plot.

c. From which of your displays might someone choose 15 as an average for the data? From which might someone choose 29? Which average is a better description of the data? *Explain.*

3. GRIDDED ANSWER What is the lower quartile of the data set?

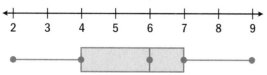

4. OPEN-ENDED *Describe* a real-world data set that you could effectively display with a line graph. *Describe* a real-world data set that you could effectively display with a circle graph.

5. GRIDDED ANSWER The stem-and-leaf plot below shows the number of miles that each track team member ran last month. How many miles is the mode of the data?

```
4 | 3 5 8
5 | 2 5 5 9
6 | 0 0 0 6
7 | 2          Key: 5|9 = 59
```

6. MULTI-STEP PROBLEM The table below shows how many female grizzly bears with cubs were sighted each year from 1988 to 2003 in Yellowstone National Park. Make box-and-whisker plots showing the number of bears with cubs from 1988–1995 and from 1996–2003. *Compare* the displays. What do you notice?

Year	Females	Year	Females
1988	19	1996	33
1989	16	1997	31
1990	25	1998	35
1991	24	1999	33
1992	25	2000	37
1993	20	2001	42
1994	20	2002	52
1995	17	2003	38

7. SHORT RESPONSE The bar graph below shows the number of boxes of two types of cereal sold in one day. *Explain* how the bar graph could be misleading. Redraw the bar graph so that it is not misleading.

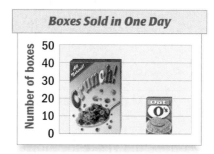

REVIEW KEY VOCABULARY

- outcome, *p. 682*
- event, *p. 682*
- favorable outcomes, *p. 682*
- probability, *p. 682*
- complementary events, *p. 684*
- tree diagram, *p. 691*

- combination, *p. 692*
- permutation, *p. 692*
- independent events, *p. 696*
- stem-and-leaf plot, *p. 709*
- leaf, *p. 709*
- stem, *p. 709*

- box-and-whisker plot, *p. 714*
- lower quartile, *p.714*
- upper quartile, *p. 714*
- lower extreme, *p. 714*
- upper extreme, *p. 714*

VOCABULARY EXERCISES

Copy and complete the statement.

1. Two events are __?__ if they have no outcomes in common and if together they contain all the outcomes of the experiment.

2. Two events are __?__ if the occurrence of one event does not affect the likelihood that the other event will occur.

3. An arrangement of objects in which order is important is a __?__.

4. In a stem-and-leaf plot, the __?__ is the first digit on the left of a row, and the __?__ are the remaining digits.

5. In a box-and-whisker plot, the __?__ is the least data value, and the __?__ is the greatest data value.

6. Outcomes for which a desired event occurs are __?__.

REVIEW EXAMPLES AND EXERCISES

13.1 Introduction to Probability

pp. 682–687

EXAMPLE

Find the probability of rolling an even number on a number cube.

$$\frac{\text{Number of favorable outcomes}}{\text{Number of possible outcomes}} = \frac{3}{6} = \frac{1}{2}$$

▶ **Answer** The probability of rolling an even number on a number cube is $\frac{1}{2}$.

EXERCISES

SEE EXAMPLE 1
on p. 682
for Exs. 7–9

You roll a number cube. Find the probability of the event. Then describe and find the probability of the complement of the event.

7. You roll a 10.

8. You roll a factor of 60.

9. You roll a multiple of 20.

13.2 Finding Outcomes

pp. 691–695

EXAMPLE

Find all the two-digit numbers that can be formed using two different digits from 3, 6, 8, and 9.

You can use an organized list to arrange all the possible outcomes.

Starts with 3:	Starts with 6:	Starts with 8:	Starts with 9:
36 38 39	63 68 69	83 86 89	93 96 98

EXERCISES

SEE EXAMPLES 2 AND 3
on p. 692
for Exs. 10–11

10. **Computers** You can choose 2 free accessories from among a printer, a camera, and a scanner when you buy a computer. Find all the possible pairs of accessories from which you can choose.

11. **Competitive Diving** Leah, Sarah, Jenny, and Michelle are competing in a diving competition. How many ways can 1st, 2nd, and 3rd place be awarded?

13.3 Probability of Independent Events

pp. 696–700

EXAMPLE

You toss a coin twice. Find the probability that you get tails both times.

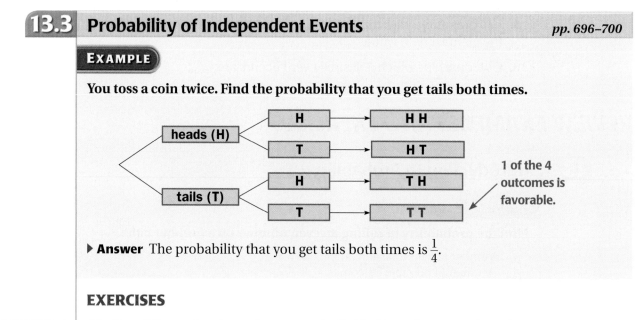

1 of the 4 outcomes is favorable.

▶ **Answer** The probability that you get tails both times is $\frac{1}{4}$.

EXERCISES

SEE EXAMPLE 1
on p. 696
for Exs. 12–13

12. **Board Game** A spinner for a game is divided into three equal sections of red, yellow, and blue. What is the probability of spinning yellow and then blue?

13. Your friend is thinking of a two-digit number. You know that the first digit is 6 or 7, and the second digit is 1 or 2. Find the probability that you randomly choose the correct number.

13.4 Misleading Statistics
pp. 704–708

EXAMPLE

Explain why the bar graph could be misleading.

Value A appears to be one fourth of Value B. However, using the scale, Value A is about 63% of Value B, because $100 \div 160 \approx 63\%$.

The break in the scale distorts the relative heights of the bars.

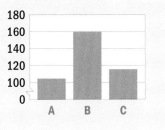

EXERCISE

SEE EXAMPLE 1
on p. 704
for Ex. 14

14. What fraction of Value A does Value B appear to be without using the scale? Using the scale, what fraction of Value A is Value B? What would you change about the graph to make it more accurate?

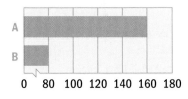

13.5 Stem-and-Leaf Plots
pp. 709–713

EXAMPLE

Make a stem-and-leaf plot of the data.

15, 11, 9, 7, 32, 21, 16, 9, 13, 17, 15, 8, 30, 20, 23

STEP 1 **Order** the stems from least to greatest.

```
0 |
1 |
2 |
3 |
```

STEP 2 **Write** the leaves next to their stems. Include a key.

```
0 | 9 7 9 8
1 | 5 1 6 3 7 5
2 | 1 0 3
3 | 2 0
```
Key: 2 | 3 = 23

STEP 3 **Order** the leaves from least to greatest.

```
0 | 7 8 9 9
1 | 1 3 5 5 6 7
2 | 0 1 3
3 | 0 2
```
Key: 2 | 3 = 23

EXERCISES

SEE EXAMPLES 1 AND 3
on pp. 709–710
for Exs. 15–16

15. What are the mean, median, and mode(s) of the data in the stem-and-leaf plot to the right?

16. Make a stem-and-leaf plot of the data: 45, 52, 59, 32, 48, 55, 41, 60.

```
3 | 4 6 7 7
4 |
5 | 0 0 0 1 6
6 | 2 5        Key: 3 | 7 = 37
```

13.6 Box-and-Whisker Plots

pp. 714–718

EXAMPLE

Make a box-and-whisker plot of the data.

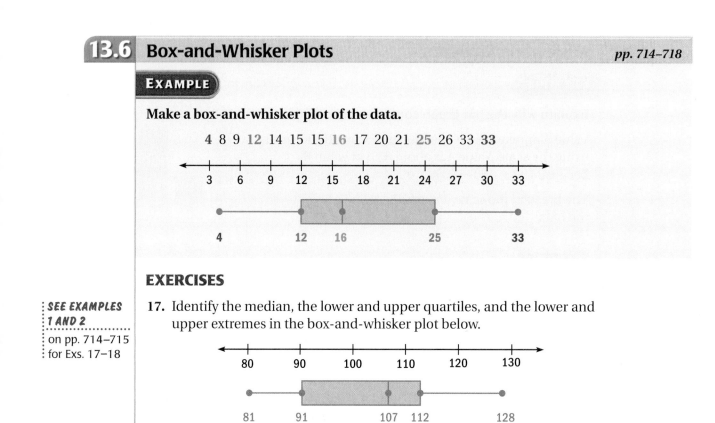

4 8 9 **12** 14 15 15 **16** 17 20 21 **25** 26 33 **33**

EXERCISES

SEE EXAMPLES
1 AND 2
on pp. 714–715
for Exs. 17–18

17. Identify the median, the lower and upper quartiles, and the lower and upper extremes in the box-and-whisker plot below.

18. Make a box-and-whisker plot of the data: 13, 5, 10, 6, 17, 8, 5, 7, 13, 9, 11.

13.7 Choosing an Appropriate Data Display

pp. 719–723

EXAMPLE

Temperature The low temperature in a city was 37°F on Sunday, 25°F on Monday, 19°F on Tuesday, and 29°F on Wednesday. Make a data display that shows the change in temperature over the four days.

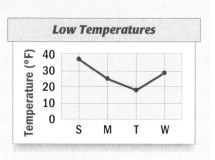

SOLUTION

Make a line graph of the data to show the change in temperature over the four days.

EXERCISE

SEE EXAMPLE 2
on p. 720
for Ex. 19

19. Studying In a survey, 10 people said they studied 31–60 minutes, 30 people said they studied 61–90 minutes, and 20 people said they studied 91–120 minutes. Draw a display that shows 50% of the people surveyed said they studied 61–90 minutes.

A bag contains 10 tiles labeled 1, 4, 7, 8, L, T, M, A, U, and Z. You randomly choose one tile. Find the probability of the event.

1. You choose a letter.

2. You choose an odd number.

3. You choose a factor of 16.

4. You don't choose a consonant.

Use the spinners at the right. Each spinner is divided into equal parts. You spin the spinners. Find the probability of the event.

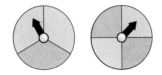

5. You spin green on both spinners.

6. You spin blue on at least 1 spinner.

7. You spin yellow on exactly 1 spinner.

8. You don't spin orange on either spinner.

Make a stem-and-leaf plot and a box-and-whisker plot of the data.

9. 90, 81, 93, 95, 68, 63, 97, 88, 59, 39, 54

10. 98, 117, 129, 154, 160, 145, 120, 135, 172

11. **CLOTHING** You have 4 shirts: solid, striped, checkered, and plaid. You have 2 pairs of pants: overalls and jeans. Use a tree diagram to find all the possible outfits you can wear.

12. **VACATION** You want to go to a museum, an aquarium, a circus, and an amusement park during your vacation. You have time for only 2 places. Find all the combinations of 2 places that you can choose from.

13. **PHOTOS** You are arranging your brother, sister, and cousin for a photo. Find all the possible ways you can arrange them in a row.

14. **FUEL PRICES** Which line graph would someone use to convince people that the price per gallon of gasoline in a state was nearly stable over seven months? *Explain.*

15. **IN-LINE SKATES** An advertiser says that the average price of inline skates at a store is $130. The list below shows the prices of inline skates offered at the store. Why do you think this average was used?

$150, $250, $200, $190, $150, $100, $130, $130, $130, $190

16. **LICENSE PLATES** You record the states of the first 200 license plates of vehicles you see enter a highway. You find 134 Oklahoma plates, 35 Texas plates, and 31 Louisiana plates. Which data display would you use to compare the number of Texas plates to total plates?

SHORT RESPONSE QUESTIONS

PROBLEM

Your social studies teacher is giving your class a surprise quiz. You are unsure of two of the questions on the quiz. One is a true-or-false question and the other is a multiple-choice question with the answer choices A, B, C, and D. You randomly choose the answers to these questions. What is the probability that you answer both questions correctly? *Justify* your answer.

Below are sample solutions to the problem. Read each solution and the comments in blue to see why the sample represents full credit, partial credit, or no credit.

SAMPLE 1: Full Credit Solution

The plan reflects correct mathematical thinking.

The steps of the solution are clearly written and justified.

The probability of answering both questions correctly is found by dividing the number of favorable outcomes by the number of possible outcomes.

First, make a tree diagram showing all the possible outcomes.

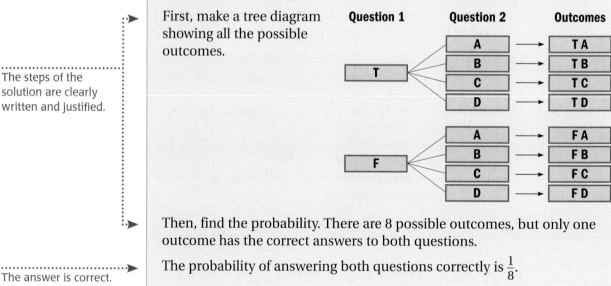

Then, find the probability. There are 8 possible outcomes, but only one outcome has the correct answers to both questions.

The answer is correct.

The probability of answering both questions correctly is $\frac{1}{8}$.

SAMPLE 2: Partial Credit Solution

The answer is correct, but no justification is given.

$$2 \times 4 = 8$$

The probability of answering both questions correctly is $\frac{1}{8}$.

SAMPLE 3: Partial Credit Solution

The reasoning and process are correct.

The tree diagram does not correctly show all the possible outcomes.

The answer is incorrect.

The tree diagram shows all the possible outcomes. Divide the number of favorable outcomes by the number of possible outcomes.

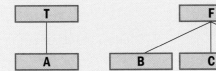

There are 4 possible outcomes.

Only one combination of the answer choices can be correct. So, the probability of answering both questions correctly is $\frac{1}{4}$.

SAMPLE 4: No Credit Solution

No explanation is given, and the answer is incorrect.

$$\frac{1}{2} + \frac{1}{4} = \frac{2+1}{4} = \frac{3}{4}$$

PRACTICE   Apply the Scoring Rubric

Score the solution to the problem below as *full credit*, *partial credit*, or *no credit*. *Explain* your reasoning.

PROBLEM You toss a coin twice. What is the probability of getting tails at least one time? Show your work.

1.   Possible outcomes: HH   HT   TH   TT

There are 4 possible outcomes. The last three outcomes have at least one tail. So, the probability of getting tails at least one time is $\frac{3}{4}$.

2.

H	→	H H
	→	H T

T → H → T H
T → T → T T

Two of the four outcomes are favorable.

The probability of getting tails one time is $\frac{2}{4} = \frac{1}{2}$.

SHORT RESPONSE

1. Burrito choices at Casa Burrito are: vegetarian, chicken, or beef; regular size or large; with mild salsa or hot salsa. Find all the different burrito orders possible. *Explain* how you found your answer.

2. Gwen wants to buy two of the items below as party favors. Make a table showing all the possible combinations of two different items and their total cost. How many combinations of two different items can Gwen buy for $5.00? *Explain*.

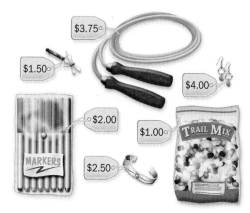

3. Alberto, Chris, Edgar, and Manny are running in a relay race. How many ways can you order the first two runners? *Explain* your reasoning.

4. Each spinner below is divided into equal parts. You spin the two spinners. Is the sum of the 2 numbers more likely to be odd or more likely to be even? *Explain*.

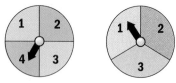

5. Based on last year's record, the probability that the girls' hockey team will win a game is $\frac{2}{3}$. The probability that the girls' hockey team will tie a game is 0.25. What is the probability that the team will lose a game? *Justify* your answer.

6. You record the cost of parking fees in the city for the last 10 years. Which data display would best show the changes in parking fees over time? *Explain* your reasoning.

7. Make a bar graph of the company profit data shown below. Make it appear that the profits have increased much more steeply than they actually have. *Explain* why your graph gives this impression.

Year	2001	2002	2003	2004
Profit	$28,000	$32,000	$39,000	$48,000

8. The probability that it will snow tomorrow is 60%. What is the probability that it will *not* snow tomorrow? *Explain*.

9. The owners of a business are trying to figure out how to increase their sales. They record the ages of customers in their store on a typical afternoon. The results are given below. Make a stem-and-leaf plot of the data. What age group should the business target when advertising? *Explain* your reasoning.

Ages: 10, 34, 3, 9, 51, 22, 10, 15, 12, 62, 55, 25, 4, 11, 19, 54, 63, 17, 29, 55

10. The stem-and-leaf plot shows Cassie's scores for the past 6 tests in her science class. After the next test, she wants her mean test score for the 7 tests to be at least 87. What is the lowest score that Cassie can get and still reach her goal? *Explain* your reasoning.

```
6 | 5
7 |
8 | 0 8
9 | 1 5 9     Key: 6 | 5 = 65
```

11. You toss a coin three times. What is the probability of getting tails at least one time? *Explain* how you found your answer.

MULTIPLE CHOICE

12. Use the box-and-whisker plot shown below. What is the difference between the upper quartile and the lower quartile?

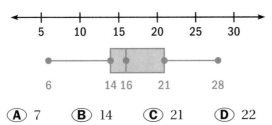

Ⓐ 7   Ⓑ 14   Ⓒ 21   Ⓓ 22

13. There are seven cards in a bag, numbered 1 through 7. You randomly choose one card. What is the probability that it is an even number?

Ⓐ $\frac{3}{7}$ Ⓑ $\frac{1}{2}$ Ⓒ $\frac{4}{7}$ Ⓓ 1

GRIDDED ANSWER

14. Today's menu items and their costs are given in the table below. You have $3.50. How many different lunches of one sandwich and one drink can you order?

Sandwiches	Cost	Drinks	Cost
tuna	$2.50	milk	$.80
ham	$1.75	juice	$.75
chicken	$2.95	lemonade	$1.00

15. You choose 2 flowers from a lily, a daisy, a rose, a carnation, and an iris. How many pairs of flowers are possible?

16. You choose one marble from a bag that has 4 red marbles, 5 blue marbles, and 1 white marble. What is the probability that you choose a blue marble? Write your answer as a fraction in simplest form.

EXTENDED RESPONSE

17. You roll a number cube once. What is the probability that you roll a 3? *not* a 3? a number greater than 3? a number less than 3? *Explain* how you found each answer.

18. The data below show the sizes of classes at North Junior High School. Make a stem-and-leaf plot of the data. Then make a box-and-whisker plot of the data. North Junior High's principal wants to know the median class size. Which of your data displays should you show to the principal? *Explain* your reasoning.

> 15, 23, 38, 12, 24, 26, 14, 23, 34, 34, 23, 17, 30,
> 23, 24, 28, 32, 26, 28, 17, 21, 29, 31, 26, 21

19. Two golfers from a youth golf club compete in local tournaments. In each tournament, the lowest score wins. The scores for two golfers in the last six tournaments are given in the table. Only one golfer can represent the club in a championship tournament. Which golfer should represent the club? *Explain* your reasoning. Include one average and one data display in your explanation.

Tournament number	Golfer A's score	Golfer B's score
1	142	150
2	150	145
3	146	146
4	153	148
5	150	152
6	146	144

Find the sum, difference, product, or quotient.

1. $56 + 134$ *(p. 3)*
2. 42×30 *(p. 3)*
3. $279 \div 9$ *(p. 3)*
4. $14.3 - 8.7$ *(p. 148)*
5. 6×2.4 *(p. 169)*
6. 9.1×5.6 *(p. 181)*
7. $11.2 \div 7$ *(p. 186)*
8. 14.65×0.01 *(p. 193)*
9. $1.275 \div 0.25$ *(p. 198)*
10. $13 - (-21)$ *(p. 586)*
11. $6(-15)$ *(p. 592)*
12. $-132 \div (-11)$ *(p. 597)*

13. Tell which property is being illustrated: $4.8 + 6.2 = 6.2 + 4.8$. *(p. 148)*

Choose the appropriate metric unit and customary unit to measure the item.

14. distance between towns *(p. 59)*
15. width of a ruler *(p. 59)*
16. mass (or weight) of a marble *(pp. 203, 373)*
17. capacity of a soup spoon *(pp. 203, 373)*

In Exercises 18–21, use the diagram at the right.

18. Name two rays and two parallel lines. *(p. 455)*

19. Name three angles with vertex B. *(p. 460)*

20. Name a pair of supplementary angles. *(p. 465)*

21. Find the measure of $\angle CAE$. Then classify $\triangle CAE$ by its angles. *(p. 471)*

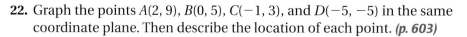

22. Graph the points $A(2, 9)$, $B(0, 5)$, $C(-1, 3)$, and $D(-5, -5)$ in the same coordinate plane. Then describe the location of each point. *(p. 603)*

Write the sentence as an equation. Then solve it.

23. Eight times a number is 40. *(pp. 629, 646)*
24. The sum of 14 and a number is 30. *(pp. 629, 636)*

25. Seven less than a number is 4. *(pp. 629, 640)*
26. The quotient of a number and 7 is 5. *(pp. 629, 646)*

The spinners below are each divided into equal parts. You spin the spinners. Find the probability of the event.

27. You spin two sixes. *(p. 696)*

28. You spin an odd sum. *(p. 696)*

29. You spin two prime numbers. *(p. 696)*

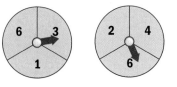

In Exercises 30 and 31, use the stem-and-leaf plot below.

30. Find the mean, median, mode, and range of the data. *(p. 709)*

31. Use the stem-and-leaf plot to make a box-and-whisker plot of the data. *(p. 714)*

```
3 | 4 6 7 7
4 |
5 | 0 0 0 1 6
6 | 2 5      Key: 3 | 7 = 37
```

SURVEY In Exercises 32–35, use the circle graph. The circle graph shows the results of a survey asking students how they travel to school each morning.

32. What is the most popular form of transportation? *(p. 94)*

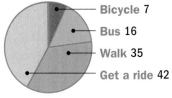

Transportation to School
- Bicycle 7
- Bus 16
- Walk 35
- Get a ride 42

33. Write each category in the graph as a fraction of all the students surveyed. Write each fraction in simplest form. *(p. 243)*

34. What fraction of the students ride a bicycle or walk to school each morning? Write this result as a percent and as a decimal. *(pp. 271, 295, 425)*

35. Predict how many students walk to school out of a group of 300 students. *(p. 94)*

36. **GEOMETRY** Draw a triangle that has zero lines of symmetry. Then classify the triangle by its sides. *(pp. 471, 484)*

TEMPERATURE In Exercises 37 and 38, use the table below. The table shows the high and low temperatures for one week.

Day	Mon.	Tues.	Wed.	Thurs.	Fri.	Sat.	Sun.
High	30°F	15°F	8°F	25°F	20°F	36°F	32°F
Low	10°F	−2°F	−10°F	0°F	−4°F	2°F	20°F

37. Order the low temperatures from least to greatest. Which day had the lowest low temperature? *(p. 573)*

38. Find the difference between the high temperature and the low temperature for each day. Which day had the greatest range in temperatures? *(p. 586)*

39. **GEOMETRY** The perimeter of the triangle shown is 16.82 meters. Write and solve an addition equation to find the length of the third side. *(p. 636)*

6.13 m   2.8 m

40. **SHOVELING SNOW** You earn $12 for each sidewalk you shovel. Write and solve a multiplication equation to find s, the number of sidewalks you must shovel to earn $84. *(p. 646)*

41. **SWIMMING** Alex, Chris, Pat, and Sandy are competing in a swimming meet. Find all the possible top three placements. *(p. 691)*

42. **BASKETBALL** The total points earned by a basketball team during each finals game are: 98, 78, 100, 98, 82, 79, 88. A local sports reporter states that the team's average number of points per game is 98. Does 98 describe the team's average well? Why or why not? *(p. 704)*

Contents of Student Resources

Skills Review Handbook

Whole Number Place Value

The **whole numbers** are the numbers 0, 1, 2, 3, ... A **digit** is any of the numbers 0, 1, 2, 3, 4, 5, 6, 7, 8, or 9. The value of each digit in a whole number depends on its position within the number. For example, in the whole number 127,891, the 8 has a value of 800 because it is in the hundreds' place and $8 \times 100 = 800$.

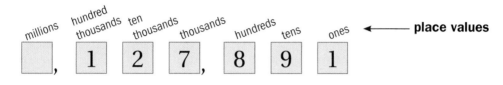

← **place values**

millions, hundred thousands, ten thousands, thousands, hundreds, tens, ones

, 1 2 7, 8 9 1

EXAMPLE 1

Write the number 4062 in expanded form and in words.

Expanded form: $4062 = 4000 + 60 + 2$

The zero in the hundreds' place is a placeholder.

$$= (4 \times 1000) + (6 \times 10) + (2 \times 1)$$

Words: four thousand, sixty-two

EXAMPLE 2

Write the number in standard form.

a. $(6 \times 100,000) + (4 \times 1000) + (2 \times 100) + (3 \times 1) = 600,000 + 4000 + 200 + 3$

$$= 604,203$$

b. seventy-three thousand, five hundred six

Write 7 in the ten thousands' place, 3 in the thousands' place, 5 in the hundreds' place, and 6 in the ones' place. Write a zero as a placeholder in the tens' place. The answer is 73,506.

PRACTICE

Identify the place value of the red digit. Then write the number in expanded form and in words.

1. 5890 **2.** 50,208 **3.** 906,201 **4.** 1,350,601

Write the number in standard form.

5. $(1 \times 100,000) + (5 \times 1000) + (3 \times 100)$ **6.** $(7 \times 10,000) + (9 \times 10) + (3 \times 1)$

7. forty-two thousand, six hundred **8.** six hundred fifty-one thousand, forty-one

Ordering Whole Numbers

A **number line** is a line whose points are associated with numbers. The numbers from left to right are in order from least to greatest. You can graph whole numbers on a number line to compare and order them. You can also compare the digits in each place from left to right.

The symbol < means *is less than* and the symbol > means *is greater than*.

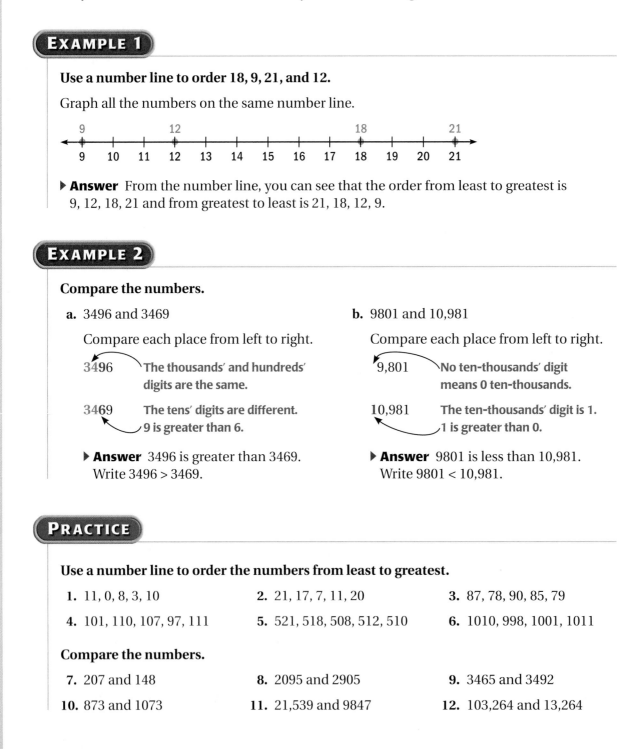

EXAMPLE 1

Use a number line to order 18, 9, 21, and 12.

Graph all the numbers on the same number line.

▶ **Answer** From the number line, you can see that the order from least to greatest is 9, 12, 18, 21 and from greatest to least is 21, 18, 12, 9.

EXAMPLE 2

Compare the numbers.

a. 3496 and 3469

Compare each place from left to right.

3496   The thousands' and hundreds' digits are the same.

3469   The tens' digits are different. 9 is greater than 6.

▶ **Answer** 3496 is greater than 3469. Write 3496 > 3469.

b. 9801 and 10,981

Compare each place from left to right.

9,801   No ten-thousands' digit means 0 ten-thousands.

10,981   The ten-thousands' digit is 1. 1 is greater than 0.

▶ **Answer** 9801 is less than 10,981. Write 9801 < 10,981.

PRACTICE

Use a number line to order the numbers from least to greatest.

1. 11, 0, 8, 3, 10

2. 21, 17, 7, 11, 20

3. 87, 78, 90, 85, 79

4. 101, 110, 107, 97, 111

5. 521, 518, 508, 512, 510

6. 1010, 998, 1001, 1011

Compare the numbers.

7. 207 and 148

8. 2095 and 2905

9. 3465 and 3492

10. 873 and 1073

11. 21,539 and 9847

12. 103,264 and 13,264

Rounding Whole Numbers

To **round** a whole number means to approximate the number to a given place value. For example, 84 rounded to the nearest ten is 80, because 84 is closer to 80 than to 90. When rounding to a specified place value, look at the digit to the right of that place value.

If the digit to the right is less than 5 (0, 1, 2, 3, or 4), round down.

If the digit to the right is 5 or greater (5, 6, 7, 8, or 9), round up.

EXAMPLE 1

Round the number to the place value of the red digit.

a. 479

b. 35,174

SOLUTION

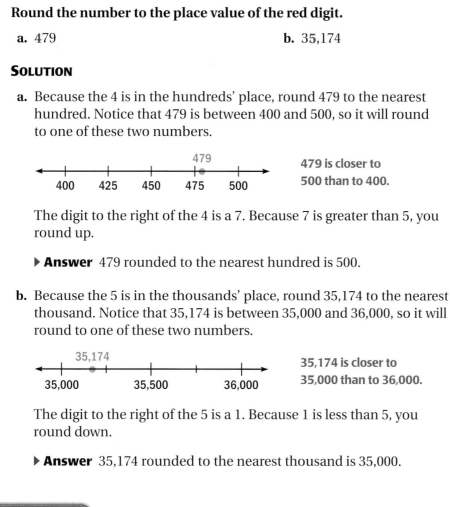

a. Because the 4 is in the hundreds' place, round 479 to the nearest hundred. Notice that 479 is between 400 and 500, so it will round to one of these two numbers.

479 is closer to 500 than to 400.

The digit to the right of the 4 is a 7. Because 7 is greater than 5, you round up.

▸ **Answer** 479 rounded to the nearest hundred is 500.

b. Because the 5 is in the thousands' place, round 35,174 to the nearest thousand. Notice that 35,174 is between 35,000 and 36,000, so it will round to one of these two numbers.

35,174 is closer to 35,000 than to 36,000.

The digit to the right of the 5 is a 1. Because 1 is less than 5, you round down.

▸ **Answer** 35,174 rounded to the nearest thousand is 35,000.

PRACTICE

Round the number to the place value of the red digit.

1. 86
2. 21
3. 247
4. 558
5. 4283
6. 9561
7. 10,954
8. 36,982
9. 143,543
10. 593,121

Number Fact Families

Inverse operations are operations that "undo" each other, such as addition and subtraction or multiplication and division. A **number fact family** consists of three numbers related by inverse operations. For example, the facts $6 \times 2 = 12$, $2 \times 6 = 12$, $12 \div 6 = 2$, and $12 \div 2 = 6$ are in the same fact family.

EXAMPLE 1

Copy and complete the number fact family.

$$4 + 2 = 6 \qquad 2 + \underline{\ ?\ } = 6 \qquad 6 - \underline{\ ?\ } = 2 \qquad 6 - \underline{\ ?\ } = 4$$

SOLUTION

The numbers in this fact family are 4, 2, and 6. Identify which of the three numbers is missing in each of the last three equations.

The 4 is missing in $2 + \underline{\ ?\ } = 6$ and in $6 - \underline{\ ?\ } = 2$.
The 2 is missing in $6 - \underline{\ ?\ } = 4$.

▶ **Answer** The complete number fact family is:
$4 + 2 = 6$; $2 + 4 = 6$; $6 - 4 = 2$; $6 - 2 = 4$.

EXAMPLE 2

Write a related division equation for $4 \times 7 = 28$.

Think of the number fact family that contains the multiplication fact $4 \times 7 = 28$. The three numbers in this fact family are 4, 7, and 28, so the two related division equations are $28 \div 4 = 7$ and $28 \div 7 = 4$.

You can also think about "undoing" the multiplication. You multiply 4 and 7 to get 28, so divide 28 by 4 to get 7 or divide 28 by 7 to get 4.

PRACTICE

In Exercises 1–4, copy and complete the number fact family.

1. $14 - 9 = 5$ $14 - \underline{\ ?\ } = 9$ $\underline{\ ?\ } + 9 = 14$ $9 + \underline{\ ?\ } = \underline{\ ?\ }$

2. $2 \times 8 = 16$ $8 \times \underline{\ ?\ } = 16$ $16 \div \underline{\ ?\ } = 8$ $\underline{\ ?\ } \div \underline{\ ?\ } = 2$

3. $32 \div \underline{\ ?\ } = 4$ $32 \div \underline{\ ?\ } = 8$ $8 \times \underline{\ ?\ } = 32$ $\underline{\ ?\ } \times \underline{\ ?\ } = 32$

4. $\underline{\ ?\ } + 5 = 11$ $\underline{\ ?\ } + 6 = 11$ $11 - \underline{\ ?\ } = 5$ $\underline{\ ?\ } - \underline{\ ?\ } = 6$

5. Write a related subtraction equation for $7 + 8 = 15$.

6. Write a related multiplication equation for $54 \div 6 = 9$.

Addition and Subtraction on a Number Line

To **add** two whole numbers on a number line:

1) Start at 0. Move to the *right* as far as the first number.

2) To add the second number, continue from the location of the first number and move to the *right* the number of units indicated by the second number. The final location is the answer.

SKILLS REVIEW HANDBOOK

EXAMPLE 1

Use a number line to add 4 + 5.

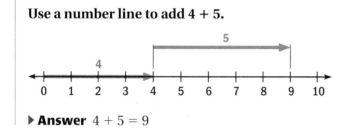

Start at 0.
Move 4 units to the *right*.
Then move 5 more units to the *right*.

▶ **Answer** $4 + 5 = 9$

To **subtract** two whole numbers on a number line:

1) Start at 0. Move to the *right* as far as the first number.

2) To subtract the second number, continue from the location of the first number and move to the *left* the number of units indicated by the second number. The final location is the answer.

EXAMPLE 2

Use a number line to subtract 11 − 7.

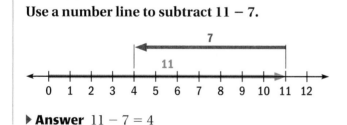

Start at 0.
Move 11 units to the *right*.
Then move 7 units to the *left*.

▶ **Answer** $11 - 7 = 4$

PRACTICE

Use a number line to add or subtract the numbers.

1. $8 + 5$ **2.** $7 + 8$ **3.** $4 + 7$ **4.** $3 + 9$

5. $10 + 3$ **6.** $12 + 12$ **7.** $8 + 12$ **8.** $15 + 8$

9. $10 - 4$ **10.** $12 - 6$ **11.** $14 - 6$ **12.** $15 - 7$

13. $17 - 9$ **14.** $22 - 8$ **15.** $19 - 3$ **16.** $18 - 5$

Addition and Subtraction of Whole Numbers

A **sum** is the result when you add two or more numbers. A **difference** is the result when you subtract two numbers. To add and subtract whole numbers, write the numbers in columns by place value. Start computing with the digits in the ones' place. Moving to the left, add or subtract the digits one place value at a time, regrouping as needed.

EXAMPLE 1

Find the sum 287 + 36.

STEP 1 **Add** the ones. Then regroup the 13 ones as **1** ten and **3** ones.

$$
\begin{array}{r}
1 \\
287 \\
+36 \\
\hline
3
\end{array}
$$

STEP 2 **Add** the tens. Then regroup the 12 tens as **1** hundred and **2** tens.

$$
\begin{array}{r}
1\,1 \\
287 \\
+36 \\
\hline
23
\end{array}
$$

STEP 3 **Add** the hundreds.

$$
\begin{array}{r}
1\,1 \\
287 \\
+36 \\
\hline
323
\end{array}
$$

EXAMPLE 2

Find the difference 305 − 86.

STEP 1 **Start** with the ones. There are not enough ones in 305 to subtract 6. You will need to regroup. There are no tens, so go to the hundreds' place.

$$
\begin{array}{r}
305 \\
-86 \\
\hline
\end{array}
$$

STEP 2 **Regroup** the 3 hundreds as 2 hundreds and 10 tens. Then regroup the 10 tens as **9** tens and **10** ones. Now subtract one place value at a time.

$$
\begin{array}{r}
9 \\
2\ \cancel{10}15 \\
\cancel{3}\ \cancel{0}\ \cancel{5} \\
-8\ 6 \\
\hline
2\ 1\ 9
\end{array}
$$

← 5 ones plus **10** ones from regrouping makes 15 ones.

Check Because addition and subtraction are *inverse operations*, you can check your answer by adding: 219 + 86 = 305.

PRACTICE

Find the sum or difference.

1. 43 + 28   **2.** 81 + 59   **3.** 192 + 48   **4.** 85 + 357

5. 235 + 165   **6.** 586 + 287   **7.** 283 + 1129   **8.** 3547 + 385

9. 75 − 58   **10.** 62 − 17   **11.** 245 − 26   **12.** 574 − 67

13. 326 − 177   **14.** 402 − 258   **15.** 1461 − 282   **16.** 4340 − 173

Multiplication of Whole Numbers

A **product** is the result when you multiply two or more numbers. To **multiply** two whole numbers, multiply the entire top number by the digit in each place value of the bottom number to obtain partial products. Then add the partial products.

SKILLS REVIEW HANDBOOK

EXAMPLE 1

Find the product 263 × 54.

STEP 1 **Multiply** 263 by the ones' digit in 54.

$$
\begin{array}{r}
{\scriptstyle 2\,1} \\
263 \\
\times \quad 54 \\
\hline
1052
\end{array}
$$

STEP 2 **Multiply** by the tens' digit. Start the partial product in the tens' place.

$$
\begin{array}{r}
{\scriptstyle 3\,1} \\
263 \\
\times \quad 54 \\
\hline
1052 \\
1315
\end{array}
$$

STEP 3 **Add** the partial products.

$$
\begin{array}{r}
263 \\
\times \quad 54 \\
\hline
1052 \\
1\,315 \\
\hline
14{,}202
\end{array}
$$

To multiply a whole number by a *power of 10*, such as 10, 100, or 1000, write the number followed by the number of zeros in the power. Because multiplying by such powers of 10 shifts each digit of the number to a higher place value, the zeros are needed as placeholders.

EXAMPLE 2

Find the product.

a. 74×100

b. 234×1000

SOLUTION

a. 100 is a power of 10 with 2 zeros, so write 2 zeros after 74.

▶ **Answer** $74 \times 100 = 7400$

b. 1000 is a power of 10 with 3 zeros, so write 3 zeros after 234.

▶ **Answer** $234 \times 1000 = 234{,}000$ ⟵ Place commas as neccessary.

PRACTICE

Find the product.

1. 41×80

2. 73×34

3. 26×37

4. 68×42

5. 217×28

6. 483×53

7. 975×62

8. 371×88

9. 1987×74

10. 6581×25

11. 4657×10

12. 9876×100

13. 123×100

14. 2568×1000

15. $2319 \times 10{,}000$

16. $7923 \times 100{,}000$

Division of Whole Numbers

In a division problem, the number being divided is called the **dividend** and the number it is being divided by is called the **divisor**. The result of the division is called the **quotient**. To **divide** two whole numbers, you use the following pattern: divide, multiply, subtract, bring down. Continue this pattern until there are no more digits to bring down. If the divisor does not divide the dividend evenly, then there is a **remainder**.

EXAMPLE 1

Find the quotient 236 ÷ 4.

STEP 1 Decide where to write the first digit of the quotient. Because 4 is between 2 and 23, place the first digit above the 3.

divisor ⟶ 4)236 ⟵ first digit of quotient
⟵ dividend

STEP 2 Because 23 ÷ 4 is between 5 and 6, multiply 4 by **5**. Then subtract **20** from 23. Be sure the difference is less than the divisor.

$$\begin{array}{r} 5 \\ 4\overline{)236} \\ 20 \\ \hline 3 \end{array}$$

STEP 3 Bring down the next digit, **6**. Divide 36 by 4. Because 36 ÷ 4 = **9**, multiply 4 by **9**. Subtract **36**. The remainder is 0.

$$\begin{array}{r} 59 \\ 4\overline{)236} \\ 20 \\ \hline 36 \\ 36 \\ \hline 0 \end{array}$$

EXAMPLE 2

Find the quotient 7346 ÷ 24.

STEP 1

24)7346 ⟵ first digit of quotient

STEP 2

$$\begin{array}{r} 30 \\ 24\overline{)7346} \\ 72 \\ \hline 14 \end{array}$$ ⟵ Bring down the **4**. But 24 < 14, so write a **0**.

STEP 3

$$\begin{array}{r} 306 \text{ R2} \\ 24\overline{)7346} \\ 72 \\ \hline 146 \\ 144 \\ \hline 2 \end{array}$$ ⟵ remainder

146 ⟵ Then bring down the **6** to continue dividing.

Check (24 × 306) + 2 = 7346, so the answer 306 R2 is correct.

PRACTICE

Find the quotient.

1. 6)852

2. 5)650

3. 7)378

4. 7)126

5. 3645 ÷ 9

6. 2388 ÷ 4

7. 580 ÷ 10

8. 783 ÷ 12

9. 436 ÷ 33

10. 2100 ÷ 100

11. 1617 ÷ 65

12. 1488 ÷ 72

Estimating Sums

To **estimate** the solution of a problem means to find an approximate answer. One way to estimate a sum when all the numbers have the same number of digits is to use **front-end estimation**. First add the digits in the *greatest* place to get a low estimate. Then use the remaining digits to adjust the sum and get a closer estimate.

EXAMPLE 1

Estimate the sum 465 + 342 + 198.

STEP 1
Add the digits in the greatest place: the hundreds' place.

$$\begin{array}{r} 465 \\ 342 \\ + 198 \\ \hline 800 \end{array}$$

STEP 2
Estimate the sum of the remaining digits. Look for more hundreds.

$$\begin{array}{r} 465 \searrow \\ 342 \rightarrow \text{about } 100 \\ + 198 \rightarrow \text{about } 100 \\ \hline \text{about } 200 \text{ more} \end{array}$$

STEP 3
Add the two sums.

$$\begin{array}{r} 800 \\ + \ 200 \\ \hline 1000 \end{array}$$

▶ **Answer** The sum 465 + 342 + 198 is *about* 1000.

When numbers being added have about the same value, you can use *clustering* to estimate their sum.

EXAMPLE 2

Estimate the sum 72 + 68 + 65.

The numbers all cluster around the value 70.

$$\begin{array}{r} 72 \\ 68 \\ + 65 \\ \hline \end{array} \longrightarrow \begin{array}{r} 70 \\ 70 \\ + 70 \\ \hline \end{array} \qquad 3 \times 70 = 210$$

▶ **Answer** The sum 72 + 68 + 65 is *about* 210.

PRACTICE

Estimate the sum.

1. 290 + 419 + 578

2. 549 + 127 + 328

3. 643 + 294 + 861

4. 328 + 560 + 781 + 533

5. 1289 + 2716 + 5952

6. 6429 + 5381 + 7232

7. 42 + 43 + 36 + 37

8. 99 + 100 + 95 + 107

9. 274 + 292 + 307 + 315

Estimating Differences

One way to estimate a difference is to find a low estimate and
a high estimate.

EXAMPLE 1

Find a low and high estimate for the difference 534 − 278.

STEP 1 For the **low estimate**, round
the greater number down
and the lesser number up
to decrease the difference.

STEP 2 For the **high estimate**, round
the greater number up and the
lesser number down to
increase the difference.

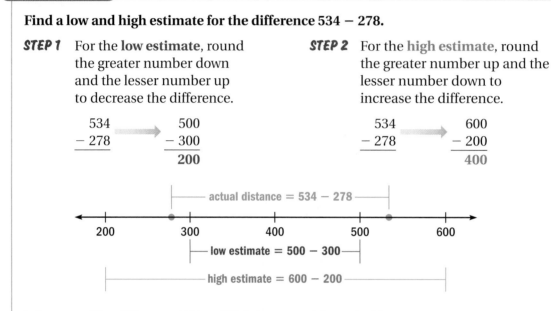

▶ **Answer** The difference 534 − 278 is between 200 and 400.

PRACTICE

Find a low and high estimate for the difference.

1. 924
    − 105

2. 876
    − 328

3. 724
    − 286

4. 639
    − 427

5. 642
    − 268

6. 745
    − 197

7. 839
    − 381

8. 593
    − 402

9. 2768
    − 1319

10. 2913
    − 1245

11. 7943
    − 3872

12. 5639
    − 2088

13. 6543
    − 1739

14. 7561
    − 2972

15. 8421
    − 6384

Estimating Products

One way to estimate a product is to find a low estimate and a high estimate.

EXAMPLE 1

Find a low and high estimate for the product 253 × 15.

For the **low estimate**, round both factors *down*.

$$
\begin{array}{r}
200 \\
\times\ \ 10 \\
\hline
2000
\end{array}
$$

For the **high estimate**, round both factors *up*.

$$
\begin{array}{r}
300 \\
\times\ \ 20 \\
\hline
6000
\end{array}
$$

▶ **Answer** The product 253 × 15 is between 2000 and 6000.

Another way is to use compatible numbers. **Compatible numbers** are numbers that are easy to use in computations.

EXAMPLE 2

Use compatible numbers to estimate the product 147 × 12.

Replace 147 and 12 with two numbers that are easy to multiply.

$$
\begin{array}{r}
147 \\
\times\ \ 12
\end{array}
\longrightarrow
\begin{array}{r}
150 \\
\times\ \ 10 \\
\hline
1500
\end{array}
$$

▶ **Answer** The product 147 × 12 is *about* 1500.

PRACTICE

Find a low and high estimate for the product.

1. 42 × 21	**2.** 63 × 59	**3.** 74 × 38	**4.** 92 × 29
5. 129 × 34	**6.** 563 × 48	**7.** 67 × 215	**8.** 26 × 749
9. 4786 × 73	**10.** 1793 × 41	**11.** 13 × 6721	**12.** 64 × 8516

Use compatible numbers to estimate the product.

13. 213 × 53	**14.** 395 × 43	**15.** 528 × 98	**16.** 821 × 78
17. 22 × 742	**18.** 14 × 683	**19.** 52 × 932	**20.** 62 × 287
21. 865 × 712	**22.** 912 × 233	**23.** 268 × 543	**24.** 387 × 603
25. 2751 × 32	**26.** 8613 × 44	**27.** 98 × 7361	**28.** 67 × 1322

Estimating Quotients

One way to estimate a quotient is to find a low estimate and a high estimate by using numbers that divide with no remainder.

EXAMPLE 1

Find a low and high estimate for the quotient 2692 ÷ 8.

Replace 2692 with numbers that are easily divisible by 8.

For the **low estimate**, use a number less than 2692.

$$\overset{300}{8)\overline{2400}}$$

For the **high estimate**, use a number greater than 2692.

$$\overset{400}{8)\overline{3200}}$$

▶ **Answer** The quotient 2692 ÷ 8 is between 300 and 400.

Another way to estimate a quotient is to use compatible numbers.

EXAMPLE 2

Use compatible numbers to estimate the quotient 99 ÷ 23.

Look for numbers close to 99 and 23 that divide evenly.

$$23)\overline{99} \longrightarrow \overset{4}{25)\overline{100}}$$

▶ **Answer** The quotient 99 ÷ 23 is *about* 4.

PRACTICE

Find a low and high estimate for the quotient.

1. 211 ÷ 4   **2.** 423 ÷ 5   **3.** 394 ÷ 6   **4.** 449 ÷ 8

5. 198 ÷ 6   **6.** 347 ÷ 9   **7.** 1946 ÷ 7   **8.** 2124 ÷ 4

9. 2198 ÷ 6   **10.** 2476 ÷ 9   **11.** 3601 ÷ 8   **12.** 1396 ÷ 3

13. 5989 ÷ 5   **14.** 7431 ÷ 4   **15.** 6172 ÷ 7   **16.** 4382 ÷ 9

Use compatible numbers to estimate the quotient.

17. 125 ÷ 62   **18.** 239 ÷ 38   **19.** 489 ÷ 48   **20.** 342 ÷ 81

21. 973 ÷ 87   **22.** 391 ÷ 42   **23.** 632 ÷ 87   **24.** 439 ÷ 58

25. 4201 ÷ 43   **26.** 2702 ÷ 73   **27.** 7378 ÷ 92   **28.** 1024 ÷ 28

Solving Problems Using Addition and Subtraction

You can use the following guidelines to tell whether to use addition or subtraction to solve a word problem.

Use *addition* when you need to combine, add on, or find a total.

Use *subtraction* when you need to compare, take away, find how many are left, or find how many more you need.

SKILLS REVIEW HANDBOOK

EXAMPLE 1

You paid $15 for a T-shirt and $35 for a pair of jeans. How much did you pay in all?

You need to find a total, so you need to add.

$15 + $35 = $50

▶ **Answer** You paid $50 in all.

EXAMPLE 2

You need to make 40 muffins for a bake sale. You already made 24 muffins. How many more do you need to make?

You need to find how many more you need, so you need to subtract.

$40 - 24 = 16$

▶ **Answer** You need to make 16 more muffins.

PRACTICE

1. You have $13 to spend. You buy a poster for $4. How much money do you have left?

2. You spend $19 for a movie on DVD and $8 for a movie on video tape. How much more did you spend for the DVD movie?

3. You buy 18 pencils and 8 pens. How many items did you buy in all?

4. You have 27 stamps in your stamp collection. Your friend gives you 8 stamps. How many stamps do you have in your collection now?

5. You need $25 for school supplies. You have $18. How much more money do you need for school supplies?

6. You have to sell 31 tickets for the dance. You have already sold 14 of them. How many more do you have to sell?

Solving Problems Using Multiplication and Division

You can use the following guidelines to tell whether to use multiplication or division to solve a word problem.

Use *multiplication* when you need to combine or join together the total number of objects in groups of equal size.

Use *division* when you need to find the number of equal groups or find the number in each equal group.

EXAMPLE 1

You buy 4 packages of markers. Each package contains 8 markers. How many markers did you buy?

You need to combine groups of equal size, so you need to multiply.

$$4 \times 8 = 32$$

▶ **Answer** You bought 32 markers.

EXAMPLE 2

You have 20 beads. You put an equal number of beads on 5 bracelets. How many beads do you put on each bracelet?

You need to find the number in each equal group, so you need to divide.

$$20 \div 5 = 4$$

▶ **Answer** You put 4 beads on each bracelet.

PRACTICE

1. You order 6 packages of folders for the school store. Each package contains 10 folders. How many folders do you get?

2. You have 30 plants. You split the plants evenly among 5 pots. How many plants do you put in each pot?

3. You buy 32 bottles of water in boxes of 8. How many boxes did you buy?

4. You have 4 boxes of straws. Each box contains 12 straws. How many straws do you have?

5. You buy 5 CDs at a yard sale for $4 each. How much did you spend?

6. You need to make 96 cookies. One batch of cookies makes 24. How many batches do you need to make?

Operations with Money

You can use the following guidelines to tell whether to use subtraction or addition to solve a money problem.

Use *addition* when finding the total cost of several items.

Use *subtraction* when finding how much change you should receive.

EXAMPLE 1

You buy a book for $4.89. You give the clerk $10.00. How much change do you receive?

You are finding the amount of change, so you need to subtract.

Subtract as you would with whole numbers.

$$
\begin{array}{r}
9 \\
9 \;\; \cancel{10}\;10 \\
\cancel{1}\cancel{0} \,.\, \cancel{0}\;\cancel{0} \\
-\;\;\;\; 4\,.\,8\;9 \\
\hline
5\,.\,1\;1
\end{array}
$$

> Place the decimal point in the answer so that it lines up with the other decimal points.

▶ **Answer** Your change is $5.11.

EXAMPLE 2

You buy shoes for $28.99, a backpack for $32.50, and jeans for $29.95. How much do you spend in all?

You are finding the total cost of several items, so you need to add.

Add as you would with whole numbers.

$$
\begin{array}{r}
2\,2\;\;1 \\
28.99 \\
32.50 \\
+\;29.95 \\
\hline
91.44
\end{array}
$$

> Place the decimal point in the answer so that it lines up with the other decimal points.

▶ **Answer** You spent $91.44 in all.

PRACTICE

1. You buy a carton of juice for $2.98. You give the clerk $5. How much change do you receive?

2. You buy a calendar for $12.48. You give the clerk $13.03. How much change do you receive?

3. You buy a package of CDs for $18.98, a printer cartridge for $21.35, and a box of printer paper for $17.75. How much do you spend in all?

Adding and Subtracting Decimals

You add and subtract decimals one place value at a time from right to left in the same way you add and subtract whole numbers. Line up the decimal points in your calculation and place a decimal point in your answer.

EXAMPLE 1

Find the sum 16.8 + 29.5.

STEP 1 **Line up** the decimal points. Add the tenths. Regroup the 13 tenths as **1** one and **3** tenths.

```
    1
  1 6 . 8
+ 2 9 . 5
        3
```

STEP 2 **Add** the ones. Regroup the 16 ones as **1** ten and **6** ones. Then add the tens. Write the decimal point.

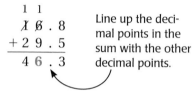

Line up the decimal points in the sum with the other decimal points.

EXAMPLE 2

Find the difference 18.25 − 6.79.

STEP 1 **Line up** the decimal points. Regroup to be able to subtract the hundredths. The 2 tenths become **1** tenth and **10** hundredths. Then subtract hundredths.

```
        1 15
  1 8 . 2 5
−   6 . 7 9
          6
```

5 hundredths plus 10 hundredths from regrouping makes 15 hundredths.

STEP 2 **Regroup** to be able to subtract the tenths. The 8 ones become **7** ones and **10** tenths. Now subtract the tenths. Then subtract the ones and the tens. Write the decimal point.

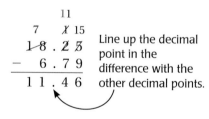

Line up the decimal point in the difference with the other decimal points.

PRACTICE

Find the sum or difference.

1. 17.9 + 23.5

2. 25.8 + 17.3

3. 56.3 + 86.7

4. 2.76 + 8.54

5. 6.91 + 4.38

6. 7.35 + 8.96

7. 10.65 + 9.48

8. 24.76 + 8.08

9. 48.55 + 8.67

10. 18.2 − 10.8

11. 36.4 − 19.9

12. 64.3 − 25.6

13. 9.75 − 2.87

14. 7.14 − 2.94

15. 8.75 − 2.99

16. 45.78 − 6.89

17. 28.93 − 9.06

18. 72.17 − 8.28

Modeling Fractions

A **fraction** is used to describe one or more parts of a whole or a set. The top part of a fraction is called the **numerator**. It tells how many parts of the whole or how many objects from the set to consider. The bottom part of a fraction is called the **denominator**. It tells how many equal sized parts make up the whole or how many objects make up the set.

EXAMPLE 1

Write a fraction to represent the shaded region or part of a set.

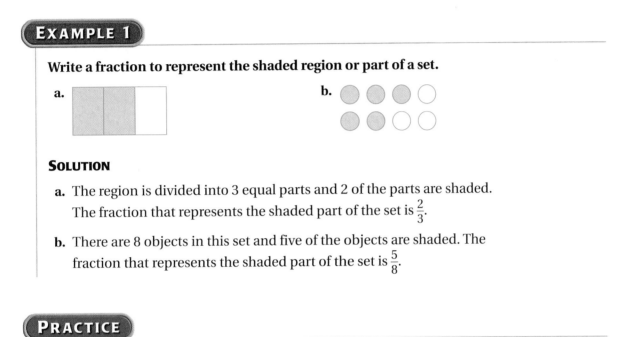

a.

b.

SOLUTION

a. The region is divided into 3 equal parts and 2 of the parts are shaded. The fraction that represents the shaded part of the set is $\frac{2}{3}$.

b. There are 8 objects in this set and five of the objects are shaded. The fraction that represents the shaded part of the set is $\frac{5}{8}$.

PRACTICE

Write a fraction to represent the shaded region or part of a set.

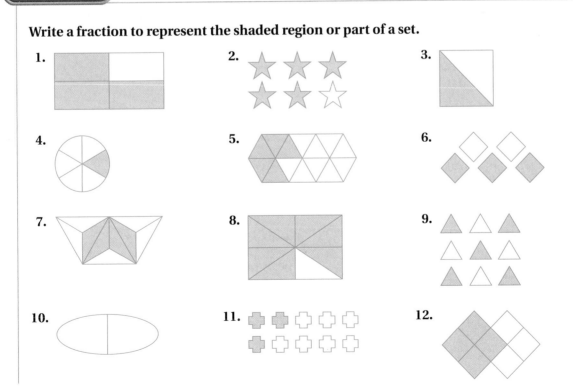

1.

2.

3.

4.

5.

6.

7.

8.

9.

10.

11.

12.

Units of Time

Use the equivalent units of time given at the right to change one unit of time to another.

Divide to change from a smaller unit to a larger unit.

Multiply to change from a larger unit to a smaller unit.

> 1 week = 7 days
> 1 day = 24 hours
> 1 hour = 60 minutes
> 1 minute = 60 seconds

EXAMPLE 1

Copy and complete.

 a. 28 days = __?__ weeks

 b. 3 hours 15 minutes = __?__ minutes

 c. 67 seconds = __?__ minutes __?__ seconds

SOLUTION

 a. You are changing days to weeks, a smaller unit to a larger unit. There are 7 days in one week, so divide by 7.

$$28 \text{ days} = (28 \div 7) \text{ weeks}$$
$$= 4 \text{ weeks}$$

 b. You are changing hours to minutes, a larger unit to a smaller unit. There are 60 minutes in one hour, so multiply by 60. Then add the extra minutes.

$$3 \text{ hours } 15 \text{ minutes} = [(3 \times 60) + 15] \text{ minutes}$$
$$= (180 + 15) \text{ minutes}$$
$$= 195 \text{ minutes}$$

 c. You are changing seconds to minutes, a smaller unit to a larger unit. There are 60 seconds in one minute, so divide by 60. If there is a remainder, write it as seconds.

$$
\begin{array}{r}
1 \leftarrow \text{ minutes} \\
60\overline{)67} \\
\underline{60} \\
7 \leftarrow \text{ extra seconds}
\end{array}
$$

1 minute 7 seconds

PRACTICE

Copy and complete.

 1. 4 hours = __?__ minutes

 2. 3 weeks = __?__ days

 3. 96 hours = __?__ days

 4. 420 seconds = __?__ minutes

 5. 1 week 5 days = __?__ days

 6. 2 hours 25 minutes = __?__ minutes

 7. 2 days 4 hours = __?__ hours

 8. 3 minutes 10 seconds = __?__ seconds

 9. 16 days = __?__ weeks __?__ days

 10. 90 minutes = __?__ hours __?__ minutes

 11. 40 hours = __?__ days __?__ hours

 12. 200 seconds = __?__ minutes __?__ seconds

Perimeter and Area

Perimeter is the distance around a figure measured in linear units.

Area is the amount of surface covered by a figure measured in square units.

EXAMPLE 1

Find the perimeter of the rectangle below.

To find the perimeter, add the side lengths.
3 in. + 6 in. + 3 in. + 6 in. = 18 in.

▶ **Answer** The perimeter is 18 inches.

EXAMPLE 2

Find the area.

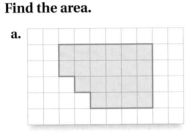
a.

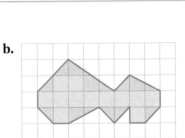
b.

Find the area by counting the number of squares inside the figure. There are 21 squares. So the area is 21 square units.

Count the **whole squares**. Estimate how many more whole squares can be made by the **partial squares**. The total area is about **12 + 8** = 20 square units.

PRACTICE

Find the perimeter.

1.
3 in.
2 in. ▢ 2 in.
3 in.

2.
8 ft
4 ft ▭ 4 ft
8 ft

3.
6 cm ◸ 4 cm
5 cm

Find the area.

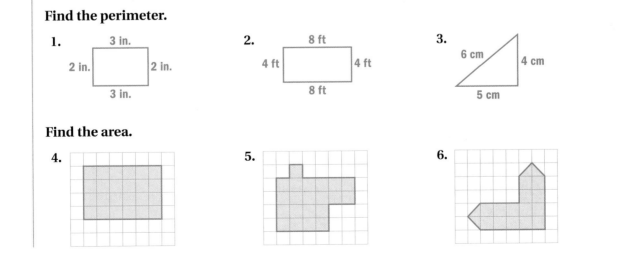

4.

5.

6.

Venn Diagrams and Logical Reasoning

A **Venn diagram** uses shapes to show how sets are related.

EXAMPLE 1

Draw and use a Venn diagram.

a. Draw a Venn diagram of the whole numbers between 0 and 10 where set *A* consists of even whole numbers and set *B* consists of multiples of 3.

b. If an even whole number is between 0 and 10, then is it *always, sometimes,* or *never* a multiple of 3?

c. If a number is in set *B*, then is it *always, sometimes,* or *never* in set *A*?

SOLUTION

a.

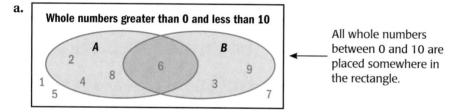

All whole numbers between 0 and 10 are placed somewhere in the rectangle.

b. This statement is *sometimes* true because 6 is an even whole number that is a multiple of 3, but 2, 4, and 8, the other even whole numbers between 0 and 10, are not multiples of 3.

c. This statement is *sometimes* true because 3 and 9 are in set *B* only, but 6 is in sets *B* and *A*.

PRACTICE

Draw a Venn diagram of the sets described.

1. Use the set of whole numbers less than 15. Set *A* consists of multiples of 3 and set *B* consists of multiples of 4.

2. Use the set of whole numbers between 10 and 20. Set *C* consists of numbers less than 15 and set *D* consists of numbers greater than 12.

Use the Venn diagrams from Exercises 1 and 2 to tell whether the statement is *always, sometimes,* or *never* true. Explain your reasoning.

3. If a number is in set *A*, then it is in set *B*.

4. If a number is between 12 and 15, then it is in both set *C* and set *D*.

5. If a number is greater than 15, then it is in set *C*.

Reading Bar Graphs

Data are numbers or facts. One way to display data is in **bar graphs**, which use bars to show how quantities compare.

EXAMPLE 1

A group of students collected data on the number of students in each sixth grade math period at their school. The bar graph below displays the data they collected.

  a. Which class has the most students?

  b. Which class has 15 students?

SOLUTION

  a. The longest bar in the bar graph represents period 3, which shows a class with 25 students. So period 3 has the most students.

  b. Look at the vertical scale and locate 15. Then find the bar that ends at 15. The bar that shows students represents period 5.

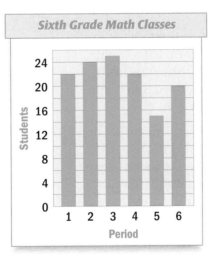

Sixth Grade Math Classes

PRACTICE

Use the bar graph above.

  1. How many students are in period 6?

  2. Which two periods have the same number of students?

  3. Which period has 24 students?

  4. Which period has the fewest students?

  5. How many more students are in period 1 than in period 5?

  6. Which period has two more students than period 4?

  7. Which two periods have a difference of 1 in the number of students they have?

Reading Line Graphs

You can use a line graph to display data. A **line graph** uses line segments to show how quantities change over time.

EXAMPLE 1

The line graph below shows the data you collected on the depth of a creek behind your house each day for one week.

a. Did the depth of the creek *increase* or *decrease* from Monday to Tuesday?

b. On which day was the creek 6 inches deep when you measured it?

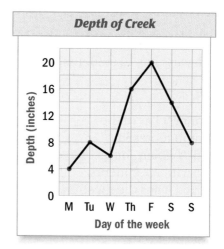

SOLUTION

a. If the line rises from left to right, the data increase. If the line falls from left to right, the data decrease. Because the line from Monday to Tuesday rises, the depth of the creek increased.

b. Look at the vertical scale and locate 6. Then find the bullet on the horizontal line with the value of 6. The creek was 6 inches deep when you measured it on Wednesday.

PRACTICE

Use the line graph above.

1. On which day was the creek 16 inches deep when you measured it?

2. Between which two days did the depth of the creek decrease by 2 inches?

3. How deep was the creek on Sunday?

4. On which day was the creek the deepest?

5. Did the depth of the creek *increase* or *decrease* from Friday to Saturday?

6. On which two days was the depth of the creek the same when you measured it?

7. On which day was the creek the shallowest?

8. Between which two days did the depth of the creek increase the most? How much was the increase?

Reading a Pictograph

A **pictograph** is a way to display data using pictures. To read a pictograph, find the key and read the amount that each symbol represents. Multiply that amount by the number of whole symbols shown for the category. Then find and add on the value of any partial symbols.

SKILLS REVIEW HANDBOOK

EXAMPLE 1

The pictograph shows data on the eye colors of students in a history class. How many students have green eyes?

SOLUTION

Each symbol represents 2 students.

The 3 whole symbols represent $3 \times 2 = 6$ students.

Because $\frac{1}{2}$ of 2 is 1, the half symbol represents 1 student.

▶ **Answer** $6 + 1 = 7$, so there are 7 students with green eyes.

Color of Eyes

Brown	👤👤👤👤👤👤👤
Blue	👤👤👤
Green	👤👤👤◗

👤 = 2 students

PRACTICE

Use the pictograph above.

1. Which eye color do most students have? How many students have this eye color?

2. Which eye color do the fewest students have? How many students have this eye color?

Use the pictograph at the right.

3. How many pictures were taken on Tuesday?

4. On which day were the most pictures taken? How many pictures were taken?

5. About how many fewer pictures were taken on Thursday than on Monday?

6. How many pictures were taken on Wednesday?

7. On which day was the number of pictures taken twice the number taken on Tuesday?

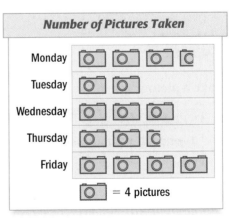

Number of Pictures Taken

Monday	📷 📷 📷 📷
Tuesday	📷 📷
Wednesday	📷 📷 📷
Thursday	📷 📷 📷
Friday	📷 📷 📷 📷

📷 = 4 pictures

Making a Pictograph

To make a pictograph, first choose a symbol and find an appropriate amount for that symbol to represent. Then draw the graph.

EXAMPLE 1

You collected data on the types of bagels sold in one hour at a bagel shop. Make a pictograph of the data.

Bagels Sold in One Hour	
Type of Bagel	**Number sold**
plain	12
sesame	7
rye	4
cinnamon raisin	10
egg	11

SOLUTION

Choose a symbol to represent 2 bagels. Half of a symbol represents 1 bagel. Write the types of bagels along the left hand side of the graph. Then draw symbols to represent the number of bagels of each type sold that hour.

PRACTICE

Make a pictograph of the data.

1.

CDs Sold in One Day	
Type of CD	**Number sold**
country	15
rock	25
pop	35

2.

Pets Owned by Students	
Pet	**Number of students**
dog	24
cat	18
turtle	6
rabbit	3
hamster	21

Make a Model

Problem You are making a quilted pillow using scrap pieces of cloth from other projects. You have a rectangular piece of cloth that measures 9 inches by 4 inches. Using as few cuts as possible, how can you cut and then sew the cloth so that it forms a square?

Make a Model
Draw a Diagram
Guess, Check, and Revise
Work Backward
Make a List or Table
Look for a Pattern
Break into Parts
Solve a Simpler Problem
Use a Venn Diagram
Act It Out

 Read and Understand

Using the least number of cuts as possible, you need to turn a 9 inch by 4 inch rectangle into a square that has the same area.

 Make a Plan

It is hard to tell how the cloth should be cut without actually seeing the shape of the cloth and trying out different cuts. Making a model of the cloth can help.

3 Solve the Problem

Make a model to represent the piece of cloth. Draw and cut out a 9 unit by 4 unit rectangle on a piece of graph paper. Count the number of grid squares in the rectangle. There are 36 squares, so the rectangle has an area of 36 square units.

To form a square, the grid squares would have to be arranged in 6 rows of 6 grid squares. Cut 3 units off the length of the original rectangle so that the remaining length is 6 units. Then cut the new rectangle in half as shown.

The three pieces can now be arranged as shown to form a square. The 9 inch by 4 inch piece of cloth can be cut and sewn in a similar fashion to from a square.

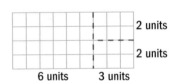

4 Look Back

Make sure that it is impossible to form a square using fewer then two cuts. The first cut results in a 6 unit by 4 unit rectangle and a 4 unit by 3 unit rectangle. Since these rectangles cannot be put together to form a square, there must be more than one cut.

Practice the Strategy

A builder wants to fit a piece of plywood through a window opening that is 35 inches by 30 inches. If the piece of plywood is a square with a side length of 40 inches, will the builder be able to fit the plywood through the opening?
(See p. 771 for more practice.)

Draw a Diagram

Make a Model
Draw a Diagram
Guess, Check, and Revise
Work Backward
Make a List or Table
Look for a Pattern
Break into Parts
Solve a Simpler Problem
Use a Venn Diagram
Act It Out

Problem In the town of Springfield, the library is 3 miles north of the grocery store. The video store is 9 miles south of the library. How far and in what direction would you have to travel to get from the video store to the grocery store?

1 Read and Understand

You need to find the distance between the video store and the grocery store. You also need to find what direction the grocery store is from the video store.

2 Make a Plan

The given information involves both distances and directions. Drawing a diagram would make it easier to see how to use this information to find the answer to the problem.

3 Solve the Problem

The library is 3 miles north of the grocery store. First draw a point to represent the grocery store. Since the library is north of the grocery store, draw a point for the library directly above the point for the grocery store. Label the distance between the grocery store and the library as 3 miles.

The video store is 9 miles south of the library. Notice that the grocery store is 3 miles south of the library. Draw a point for the video store directly below the point for grocery store. Label the distance between the library and video store as 9 miles.

From the diagram you can see that the distance between the video store and the grocery store is $9 - 3 = 6$ miles. You would have to travel 6 miles north to get from the video store to the grocery store.

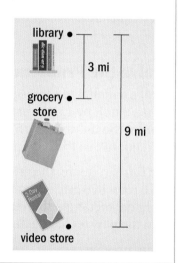

4 Look Back

Reread the problem and check that your diagram is consistent with each piece of the given information.

Practice the Strategy

From left to right, the order in which four friends stand for a photo is Jan, Henry, Pete, and Sri. Jan switches places with Pete. Then the first and last people switch places. Finally, the first and second people switch places. What is the final order, from left to right, of the four friends?

(See p. 771 for more practice.)

Guess, Check, and Revise

Problem The 24 players on the Dale High School football team voted for next year's team captain. Players could vote for one of the seniors on the team: John or Bill. John received three times as many votes as Bill. How many more votes did John receive than Bill?

Make a Model
Draw a Diagram
Guess, Check, and Revise
Work Backward
Make a List or Table
Look for a Pattern
Break into Parts
Solve a Simpler Problem
Use a Venn Diagram
Act It Out

 Read and Understand

You need to find the difference in the number of votes received by John and by Bill. To find the difference, you first need to find the number of votes each senior received.

2 Make a Plan

You are given two pieces of information: there are a total of 24 votes, and John received three times as many votes as Bill. Each piece of information says something about both numbers of votes, but not the individual numbers of votes. This suggests the strategy of guessing, checking, and then revising an answer.

3 Solve the Problem

Because there are 24 players on the team, there are a total of 24 votes. The number of votes received by each of the two seniors must be between 0 and 24.

Try guessing 20 votes for John. That leaves 4 votes for Bill. But since 20 is 5 times 4, this guess is incorrect.

Try guessing 18 votes for John. That leaves 6 votes for Bill. Since 18 is 3 times 6, this guess is correct. John received 18 votes and Bill received 6 votes. Since $18 - 6 = 12$, John received 12 more votes than Bill.

4 Look Back

Reread the problem to make sure that you answered the question being asked. Notice that the question asks for the difference in the numbers of votes, not the number of votes received by each senior.

Practice the Strategy

The sum of two numbers is 56. The difference of the same two numbers is 14. What is the product of the two numbers?

(See p. 772 for more practice.)

PROBLEM SOLVING HANDBOOK

Work Backward

Problem Liz is filling 14 backpacks with school supplies for kids in an after-school program. There are 86 pencils and 21 rulers available. Liz wants to place the same number of pencils in each backpack. If there are 16 pencils left over, how many pencils did Liz put in each of the backpacks?

Make a Model
Draw a Diagram
Guess, Check, and Revise
Work Backward
Make a List or Table
Look for a Pattern
Break into Parts
Solve a Simpler Problem
Use a Venn Diagram
Act It Out

1 Read and Understand

You need to find the number of pencils in each of the backpacks.

2 Make a Plan

You know that when the number of pencils in each backpack is multiplied by 14 and then 16 pencils are added to the result, you have 86 pencils. You can work backward from 86 pencils, undoing each operation, to find the number of pencils in each backpack.

3 Solve the Problem

The total number of pencils placed in the backpacks plus 16 pencils equals 86 pencils. To find the total number of pencils placed in the backpacks, work backward by subtracting 16 from 86:

86 pencils − 16 pencils = 70 pencils

Since the number of pencils in each backpack times 14 equals 70 pencils, work backward by dividing 70 by 14 to find the number of pencils in each backpack:

70 pencils ÷ 14 = 5 pencils

Liz put 5 pencils in each of the backpacks.

4 Look Back

Work forward to check that your answer is correct. Liz put a total of 5 × 14 = 70 pencils in the backpacks. There are 16 pencils left over, so the total number of available pencils is 70 + 16 = 86 pencils. The answer is correct.

Practice the Strategy

A youth group is selling rolls of wrapping paper. This year, the youth group sold 55 more rolls than they did last year. Last year, the youth group sold twice as many rolls as they did the year before. If the youth group sold 295 rolls this year, how many rolls did they sell two years ago?
(See p. 772–773 for more practice.)

Make a List or Table

Make a Model
Draw a Diagram
Guess, Check, and Revise
Work Backward
Make a List or Table
Look for a Pattern
Break into Parts
Solve a Simpler Problem
Use a Venn Diagram
Act It Out

Problem Kylie is baking oatmeal cookies which take 12 minutes to bake, and sugar cookies which take 9 minutes to bake. Kylie puts one tray of each kind of cookie dough in the oven at 1:20 P.M. As soon as a tray of cookies is baked, Kylie replaces it with a tray of the same kind of cookie dough. At what time will both a tray of oatmeal cookies and a tray of sugar cookies finish baking simultaneously? Show your work.

1 Read and Understand

You need to find the time at which both a tray of oatmeal cookies and a tray of sugar cookies finish baking. To do this, you first need to find the number of minutes since the first trays were put in the oven.

2 Make a Plan

You need to keep track of the elapsed time as trays of each type of cookie finish baking. Then you can identify when the elapsed time is the same for a tray of each type of cookie. A table is a good way to organize this information.

3 Solve the Problem

Record the elapsed time as trays of each type of cookie finish baking.

Tray number	Oatmeal cookies	Sugar cookies
1	12 min	9 min
2	24 min	18 min
3	**36 min**	27 min
4	48 min	**36 min**

You can see from the table that after 36 minutes, the third tray of oatmeal cookies and the fourth tray of sugar cookies finish baking. To find the time that this happens, find 36 minutes past 1:20 P.M., which is 1:56 P.M.

4 Look Back

Make sure that your answer is reasonable. Since sugar cookies bake faster than oatmeal cookies, it makes sense that 4 trays of sugar cookies are baked in the same time that 3 trays of oatmeal cookies are baked.

Practice the Strategy

Dan is placing four books in a row on a shelf: a dictionary, a thesaurus, a biography, and a novel. Dan wants the dictionary to be on one end of the row. In how many ways can Dan place the books upright on the shelf?
(See p. 773 for more practice.)

PROBLEM SOLVING HANDBOOK

Look for a Pattern

Make a Model
Draw a Diagram
Guess, Check, and Revise
Work Backward
Make a List or Table
Look for a Pattern
Break into Parts
Solve a Simpler Problem
Use a Venn Diagram
Act It Out

Problem A Web site sells jump ropes in packages of six ropes. The costs of packages of six ropes of different lengths are given in the table. How much would you expect a package of six 12-foot ropes to cost?

JUMP ROPE PRICES

Jump rope length	Cost for six
7 ft	$10.80
8 ft	$11.70
9 ft	$12.60
10 ft	$13.50

1 Read and Understand

You need to predict the cost of a package of six 12-foot jump ropes, based on the given costs of the ropes in the table.

2 Make a Plan

Since you are not given any information about the cost of a package of 12-foot ropes, you need to look for a pattern in the costs of the ropes that you are given.

3 Solve the Problem

Notice that as the length of a jump rope increases, the cost of a package of six ropes also increases. Find the amount by which the cost of each package increases.

For each additional 1 foot of length, the cost of a package of jump ropes increases by $.90. So, it can be expected that a package of 11-foot ropes costs $14.40 and a package of 12-foot ropes costs $15.30.

Jump rope length	Cost for 6	
7 ft	$10.80	) + $.90
8 ft	$11.70	) + $.90
9 ft	$12.60	) + $.90
10 ft	$13.50	

4 Look Back

Make sure that you performed your calculations correctly. To find the cost of a rope 2 feet longer than 10 feet, you add $1.80 to $13.50: $13.50 + $1.80 = $15.30

Practice the Strategy

A soccer coach has her team sprint a certain distance and then gives the team time to rest. The first four sprinting distances are 10 yards, 20 yards, 40 yards, and 80 yards. If the coach continues to have her team run in this manner, what is the total distance that the team will have run after the fifth sprint?
(See p. 773–774 for more practice.)

Break into Parts

Problem Darren wants his birthday party to be held at the local bowling alley. The costs associated with a bowling birthday party are given at the right. How much will a birthday party for 6 people, including Darren, cost?

Bowling
Birthday Party
Costs
Party room rental..$20
Cake $15
Cost of lunch............$4
(per person)
Cost of bowling $5
(per person)

Make a Model
Draw a Diagram
Guess, Check, and Revise
Work Backward
Make a List or Table
Look for a Pattern
Break into Parts
Solve a Simpler Problem
Use a Venn Diagram
Act It Out

1 Read and Understand

You need to find cost of a party for 6 people.

2 Make a Plan

Some of the given costs are group costs and apply just one time. Some of the given costs are individual costs and apply to each person at the party. You can break the problem into parts according to the type of cost.

3 Solve the Problem

The cost of the party room rental and the cost of the cake are group costs. The sum of these costs is $20 + $15 = $35.

The cost of lunch and the cost of bowling are individual costs. The sum of these costs is $4 + $5 = $9. For 6 people, this cost is $9 \times 6 = $54.

The total cost is $35 + $54 = $89.

4 Look Back

Estimate to check the reasonableness of your answer. The sum of the individual costs is about $10. Since $10 \times 6 = $60 and $60 + $35 = $95, an answer of $89 is reasonable.

Practice the Strategy

How many different triangles are in the figure shown?

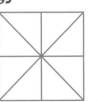

(See p. 774 for more practice.)

Solve a Simpler Problem

Problem An auditorium has seats numbered from 100 through 899. New seat numbers were just placed on each arm rest. By mistake, the letter O was used instead of a zero in the seat numbers. How many of the seats have at least one letter O used in the seat number?

Make a Model
Draw a Diagram
Guess, Check, and Revise
Work Backward
Make a List or Table
Look for a Pattern
Break into Parts
Solve a Simpler Problem
Use a Venn Diagram
Act It Out

1 Read and Understand

You need to find how many numbers from 100 through 899 contain at least one zero.

2 Make a Plan

You could write out every single number from 100 through 899 that contains at least one zero, but this would take a long time. Instead, you could look for a simpler problem whose solution can help you find an answer.

3 Solve the Problem

Think of the numbers from 100 through 899 as being in 8 groups. The first group is 100 through 199, the second is 200 through 299, and so on. Solve the simpler problem of finding how many numbers from 100 through 199 contain at least one zero. The numbers are:

There are 19 numbers that contain at least one zero in the group of numbers from 100 through 199. Since the only digit that differs from group to group is the digit in the hundreds' place, every group has 19 numbers with at least one zero. There are $19 \times 8 = 152$ numbers from 100 through 899 with at least one zero. So, 152 seats have at least one letter O used in the seat number.

4 Look Back

Make sure that you answered the question being asked. Notice that the question does not ask for the total number of zeros contained in the numbers from 100 through 899.

Practice the Strategy

You are collecting rubber bands to make a rubber band ball. The first day you collect 1 rubber band. Each day you collect one more rubber band than the previous day. How many rubber bands will you have collected after 30 days?
(See p. 774–775 for more practice.)

Use a Venn Diagram

Problem Your town has organized a trip to a mountain where participants may ski, snowboard, and snowshoe. There are 3 people who have skis, a snowboard, and snowshoes. There are 5 people who have skis and a snowboard, but no snowshoes. There are 2 people who have skis and snowshoes, but no snowboard. If 19 people have skis, how many people have only skis?

| Make a Model |
| Draw a Diagram |
| Guess, Check, and Revise |
| Work Backward |
| Make a List or Table |
| Look for a Pattern |
| Break into Parts |
| Solve a Simpler Problem |
| **Use a Venn Diagram** |
| Act It Out |

1 Read and Understand

You need to find the number of people who have skis but who do not also have snowshoes or a snowboard.

2 Make a Plan

It is not immediately apparent how many people have only skis because some of the people with skis also have snowshoes or a snowboard. A Venn diagram can help organize this type of overlapping information.

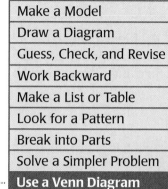

3 Solve the Problem

Draw a Venn diagram to represent the given information. You can see that there are $5 + 3 + 2 = 10$ people who have skis and either a snowboard or snowshoes, or both. Since you know that 19 people have skis, you can subtract to find the number of people who have only skis. $19 - 10 = 9$, so 9 people have only skis.

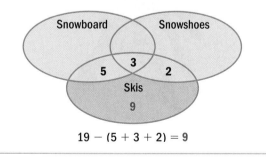

$19 - (5 + 3 + 2) = 9$

4 Look Back

Make sure that you placed the numbers in the correct places in the Venn diagram.

Practice the Strategy

A display case has 15 rings with diamonds, 12 rings with rubies, and 10 rings with pearls. 2 rings have all three gems, 3 have only rubies and diamonds, 4 have only pearls and rubies, and 3 have only pearls. How many rings have only diamonds?
(See p. 775 for more practice.)

PROBLEM SOLVING HANDBOOK

Act It Out

Problem Holly, Paul, Anne, and Jim are rehearsing a dance routine. How many different ways can you arrange the 4 dancers in a line if Anne must be first or second?

Make a Model
Draw a Diagram
Guess, Check, and Revise
Work Backward
Make a List or Table
Look for a Pattern
Break into Parts
Solve a Simpler Problem
Use a Venn Diagram
Act It Out

 Read and Understand

You need to place 4 people in a line. Anne must be either first or second in line.

 Make a Plan

You can solve the problem by acting. You need 4 people to act out the roles of Holly, Paul, Anne, and Jim.

3 Solve the Problem

Work in a group of four students playing the roles of Holly, Paul, Anne, and Jim. Arrange yourselves in as many ways as possible. List the arrangements.

If Anne is first, then the possible arrangements are as follows.

Anne, Holly, Paul, Jim   **Anne**, Holly, Jim, Paul
Anne, Paul, Holly, Jim   **Anne**, Paul, Jim, Holly
Anne, Jim, Paul, Holly   **Anne**, Jim, Holly, Paul

If Anne is second, then the possible arrangements are as follows.

Holly, **Anne**, Paul, Jim   Holly, **Anne**, Jim, Paul
Paul, **Anne**, Holly, Jim   Paul, **Anne**, Jim, Holly
Jim, **Anne**, Paul, Holly   Jim, **Anne**, Holly, Paul

There are 12 ways to arrange the dancers in a line if Anne is the first or second person in line.

4 Look Back

You can solve the problem a different way. Draw a diagram to find all the possible ways to arrange the four dancers. Then count all the outcomes in which Anne is either first or second.

Practice the Strategy

A bag has 4 socks of different colors: blue, red, white, and black. Find all the ways you can choose two socks.
(See p. 775 for more practice.)

Problem Solving Strategy Practice

Solve the problem and show your work.

Make a Model

1. A rectangular tablecloth is folded in half lengthwise and then in half widthwise, as shown below. The tablecloth is folded in half lengthwise and widthwise again, to make a rectangle that is 18 inches by 12 inches. What are the original dimensions of the tablecloth? *(Problem Solving Strategy Review, p. 761)*

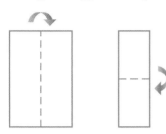

2. Chris has three railroad ties that measure 10 feet, 18 feet, and 7 feet. She wants to use the railroad ties to enclose a triangular garden. Is this possible without cutting the ties? *(Problem Solving Strategy Review, p. 761)*

3. A rectangular raft is 5 feet long and 2 feet wide. How many rafts can fit (without gaps or overlaps) in a rectangular pool that is 20 feet long and 8 feet wide? *(Problem Solving Strategy Review, p. 761)*

Draw a Diagram

4. On rainy days, a custodian at a school rolls out mats to prevent students from slipping on wet floors. Each mat is the same length. The main hallway in the school is 39 feet long. If a mat is unrolled at either end of the hall and there is 3 feet of overlap where the two mats meet, how long is each mat? *(Problem Solving Strategy Review, p. 762)*

5. You have a 12 inch by 16 inch rectangular piece of fabric that you want to cut into fabric swatches that are 2 inches by 2 inches. How many swatches can you cut? *(Problem Solving Strategy Review, p. 762)*

6. Mike and Sal are canoeing in opposite directions on a river. Every hour, Mike canoes 2 miles north, and Sal canoes 1 mile south. Mike and Sal start canoeing at the same time and leave from the same place. In how many hours will they be 12 miles apart? *(Problem Solving Strategy Review, p. 762)*

7. Your little brother thought it would be fun to hide your birthday present outside. He wrote instructions for finding the present, using your front door as the starting point. How far from the front door is your birthday present? *(Problem Solving Strategy Review, p. 762)*

Go 15 steps north.

Go 8 steps east.

Go 10 steps north.

Go 17 steps west.

Go 25 steps south. You will see your present.

8. In lacrosse, one type of passing drill has 5 groups of players standing in a circle, as shown below. Group A always passes to group C, group B always passes to group D, group C always passes to group E, group D always passes to group A, and group E always passes to group B. The drill is named after the shape that the path of the ball forms. What is the shape? *(Problem Solving Strategy Review, p. 762)*

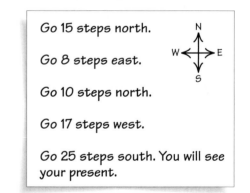

Solve the problem and show your work.

Guess, Check, and Revise

9. The sum of two numbers is 21. The difference of the two numbers is 3. What are the numbers? *(Problem Solving Strategy Review, p. 763)*

10. A store sells $1, $2, and $3 birthday cards. Rick spent $11 buying 5 cards. If Rick bought at least one of each kind of card, how many of each kind of card did he buy? *(Problem Solving Strategy Review, p. 763)*

11. In track and field, the triple jump involves taking a hop, a step, and a jump. Kylie always hops 2 more feet than she jumps, and jumps 2 more feet than she steps. If Kylie does a triple jump of 42 feet, how far did she hop, step, and jump? *(Problem Solving Strategy Review, p. 763)*

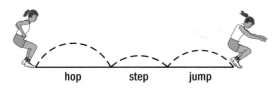

12. Shandi has $1.20 worth of nickels and dimes in her pocket. If Shandi knows that she has twice as many nickels as dimes, how many of each does she have? *(Problem Solving Strategy Review, p. 763)*

13. Two positive numbers have a product of 168. One number is 2 more than the other number. What are the numbers? *(Problem Solving Strategy Review, p. 763)*

14. Serge is trying to guess his grandfather's age. Serge's grandfather gives him the following clues about his age:

    • It is greater than 65.
    • It is an even number.
    • It is less than 80.
    • It is divisible by 4, but not 6.
    • If the digits are switched, the resulting number is an odd number.

    How old is Serge's grandfather? *(Problem Solving Strategy Review, p. 763)*

15. How can each circle in the triangle below be filled with one of the digits 1, 2, 3, 4, 5, and 6 so that the sum of the numbers on each side of the triangle is 12? Each digit must be used exactly once. *(Problem Solving Strategy Review, p. 763)*

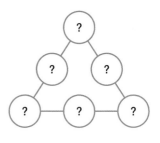

Work Backward

16. Henry ran twice as far on Tuesday as he did on Monday. He ran three times as far on Wednesday as he did on Tuesday. If Henry ran 18 miles on Wednesday, how far did he run on Monday? *(Problem Solving Strategy Review, p. 764)*

17. You keep only $1 bills and $5 bills in your wallet. At the end of one day, you have triple the number of $1 bills and double the number of $5 bills that you had in your wallet at the start of the day. If you have nine $1 bills and four $5 bills in your wallet, how much money did you have at the start of the day? *(Problem Solving Strategy Review, p. 764)*

18. Kathleen wants to watch her favorite TV show at 8:00 P.M. Before she can watch the show, she has to do 50 minutes of homework, take 15 minutes to clean her room, and allow 12 minutes for taking a shower. What is the latest time that Kathleen can start these activities and still finish in time to watch her favorite TV show? *(Problem Solving Strategy Review, p. 764)*

19. Colin is 4 times as old as Fiona. Fiona is 5 years younger than Brad. If Colin is 20 years old, how many years older is he than Brad? *(Problem Solving Strategy Review, p. 764)*

Solve the problem and show your work.

20. Today is Tuesday. You had a track meet 3 days ago. Your friend's party was 8 days before the track meet. On which day of the week was the party? *(Problem Solving Strategy Review, p. 764)*

Make a List or Table

21. You have sixteen 1 foot by 1 foot square patio bricks. If the bricks are arranged to form a rectangle, what is the greatest the perimeter of the rectangle can be? What is the least the perimeter of the rectangle can be? *(Problem Solving Strategy Review, p. 765)*

22. Binary code is a system in which data is represented using only 0's and 1's. How many different three-digit codes can be formed using 0 or 1 for each digit? For example, 001 is one possible code. *(Problem Solving Strategy Review, p. 765)*

23. Roberto, Amy, and Paul go to a movie. How many different ways can the three friends sit together in a row? *(Problem Solving Strategy Review, p. 765)*

24. You and a group of your friends are putting on a puppet show to raise money for the town library. Tickets cost $3 for children and $5 for adults. You are responsible for selling 6 tickets. What are all the possible dollar amounts that your ticket sales could total? *(Problem Solving Strategy Review, p. 765)*

Look for a Pattern

25. Describe the pattern shown below. Then draw the next figure in the pattern. *(Problem Solving Strategy Review, p. 766)*

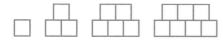

26. A radio station plays the number one pop song according to the schedule shown. When is the next time that you would expect the radio station to play the number one pop song? *(Problem Solving Strategy Review, p. 766)*

Number one song	12:10 P.M.
Commercial break	12:15 P.M.
Commercial break	12:35 P.M.
Number one song	12:50 P.M.
Commercial break	12:55 P.M.
Commercial break	1:15 P.M.
Number one song	1:30 P.M.
Commercial break	1:35 P.M.
Commercial break	1:55 P.M.
Number one song	2:10 P.M.

27. The bar graph shows the prices for 3 sizes of the same drink at a movie theater. The manager of the movie theater is thinking about adding a 22 fluid ounce drink size. What would you expect the price to be for a 22 fluid ounce drink? *(Problem Solving Strategy Review, p. 766)*

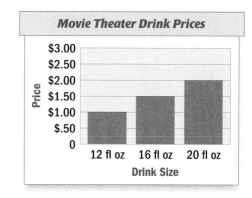

28. Rehan plants a square garden that has a side length of 1 yard. Each year, he plans to increase the length of each side of the square by 1 yard. In the tenth year of his garden how many yards of fencing will Rehan need to enclose the garden? *(Problem Solving Strategy Review, p. 766)*

Solve the problem and show your work.

29. Mara teaches swimming. The cost of one lesson for various numbers of students is given in the table below. How much would each student have to pay for a swimming lesson in a group of 6 students? *(Problem Solving Strategy Review, p. 766)*

Number of students	1	2	3	4
Total cost	$40	$50	$60	$70

Break Into Parts

30. Mrs. Smith's class is taking a field trip to a science museum. The costs are shown below. If 35 people are going on the field trip, using one bus, what is the total cost? What should each person pay to go on the field trip? *(Problem Solving Strategy Review, p. 767)*

Bus rental	$70
Museum admission	$6 per person
Lunch	$4 per person

31. Paul works in a school cafeteria. He earns $12 per hour for working 40 hours a week. For every hour over 40 hours that Paul works in one week, he earns $18 per hour. One week Paul works 46 hours. What is the total amount he earns that week? *(Problem Solving Strategy Review, p. 767)*

32. Coach Roberts is running a summer basketball league. The costs are shown below. The basketball league will have 80 players and will run for 8 weeks. How much will running the league cost? *(Problem Solving Strategy Review, p. 767)*

T-shirts	$6 per player
Referees	$200 per week
Court time	$80 per week

33. A state park offers canoeing and tubing on a river. A two-person canoe rents for $30 and a single-person tube rents for $14. Parking is $5 per car. A family of four arrives at the park in one car. Each person plans to go canoeing and tubing. How much will the family spend in total? *(Problem Solving Strategy Review, p. 767)*

34. You want to line all sides of the inside of a box that is 8 inches tall, 10 inches wide, and 6 inches deep. How many square inches of liner do you need? *(Problem Solving Strategy Review, p. 767)*

Solve a Simpler Problem

35. A *palindromic number* is a number that is the same when written forward or backward. For example, 101 is a palindromic number. How many 3-digit palindromic numbers are there? *(Problem Solving Strategy Review, p. 768)*

36. A manager at a banquet hall has a total of 8 small rectangular tables that can be pushed together to make one large table. Individually, each small table can seat 6 people, as shown below. What is the maximum number of people that can be seated at one large table? *(Problem Solving Strategy Review, p. 768)*

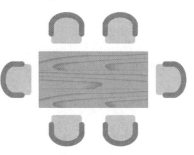

37. A proof coin set for a single year has one half-dollar, one quarter, one dime, one nickel, and one penny from that year. Mr. Leland has a proof set for each of the last 5 years. What is the total value of the coins in all his proof sets? *(Problem Solving Strategy Review, p. 768)*

Solve the problem and show your work.

38. The lockers at a city pool are numbered from 1 to 150. How many lockers from 1 to 50 have a 2 in the number? How many lockers from 1 to 150 have a 2 in the number? *(Problem Solving Strategy Review, p. 768)*

39. Your school is collecting money for a local charity. The first day, 1 one dollar bill is placed in a jar. The second day, 2 one dollar bills are added to the jar. The third day, 3 one dollar bills are added to the jar. Suppose this pattern continues. How much money will have been collected after 100 days? *(Problem Solving Strategy Review, p. 768)*

Use a Venn Diagram

40. On a beach there are 13 people wearing hats, but not sunglasses. There are 17 people wearing sunglasses, but not hats. There are 19 people wearing both a hat and sunglasses. How many people are wearing sunglasses? *(Problem Solving Strategy Review, p. 769)*

41. A group of 12 people is having dinner at a restaurant. Two people order both a salad and a dessert. Four people order a salad, but not a dessert. Five people order a dessert. How many people ordered neither a salad nor a dessert? *(Problem Solving Strategy Review, p. 769)*

42. Seven households on Maple Street have a VCR but not a DVD player. Eight households have both a VCR and a DVD player. Ten households have a DVD player but not a VCR. How many households on Maple Street have a DVD player? *(Problem Solving Strategy Review, p. 769)*

43. Your class participates in a survey about pets. Ten students have a dog, but no cat or fish. Seven students have a cat and fish, but no dog. Four students have a dog and cat, but no fish. Five students have fish, but no dog or cat. One student has a dog, a cat, and fish. How many students do not have fish? *(Problem Solving Strategy Review, p. 769)*

44. At a small school, 17 students play volleyball, 12 students play basketball, and 42 students run track. Of the 100 students at the school, 3 play volleyball and basketball, 10 play volleyball and run track, and 2 play all three sports. How many students play none of these three sports? *(Problem Solving Strategy Review, p. 769)*

Act It Out

45. You just won three tickets to a concert. Six of your friends would like to go with you. How many different ways could you pick two out of these six friends? *(Problem Solving Strategy Review, p. 770)*

46. Betty, Louis, Carl, Mary, Phil, and Kate are seated in seats 1 to 6 as shown below. Phil is sitting in seat 3. Betty is sitting across from Phil. Carl is sitting between Betty and Kate. Mary is sitting across from Carl. In which seat is Louis sitting? *(Problem Solving Strategy Review, p. 770)*

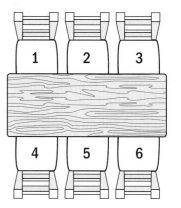

47. You have $4. You sell a trading card for $1, then buy two more trading cards for $2 each. Then you sell both those cards for $3 each. How much money do you have now? *(Problem Solving Strategy Review, p. 770)*

48. A game starts with 6 tokens on a table. Two players take turns removing 1, 2, or 3 tokens. The player who takes the last token on his or her turn wins. If you go first, how many tokens should you remove to make sure that you win the game? *(Problem Solving Strategy Review, p. 770)*

Extra Practice

Chapter 1

1.1 **Find the sum, difference, product, or quotient.**

    1. $262 - 59$ **2.** $47 + 158$ **3.** $306 \div 6$ **4.** 34×21

    5. 34×5 **6.** $348 - 72$ **7.** $156 \div 4$ **8.** $13 + 19$

    Describe the pattern. Then find the next two numbers.

    9. 5, 9, 13, 17, ? , ?   **10.** 50, 43, 36, 29, ? , ?   **11.** 1600, 800, 400, 200, ? , ?

1.2 **Estimate the sum, difference, product, or quotient.**

    12. $257 + 91$ **13.** $435 - 69$ **14.** 173×29 **15.** $381 \div 52$

    16. $680 + 134$ **17.** $805 - 37$ **18.** $583 \div 61$ **19.** 48×32

    20. You are buying spring water for use by runners at a road race. The water comes in cases of 36 bottles each. You buy 12 cases. Estimate the number of bottles you buy.

1.3 **Find the value of the power.**

    21. 7^3 **22.** 6^4 **23.** 2 cubed   **24.** 12 squared

1.4 **Evaluate the expression.**

    25. $27 - 17 + 4$ **26.** $5 \times 12 \div 20$ **27.** $18 + 9 \div 3$ **28.** $4 + 3^3$

    29. $9 \times (2 + 6) \div 12$ **30.** $100 \div 5^2 + 5$ **31.** $10 - 2 \times 3 + 7$ **32.** $\dfrac{8^2}{9 - 5}$

1.5 **Evaluate the expression when $x = 9$ and $y = 4$.**

    33. $3x$ **34.** $4x + y$ **35.** $92 - x^2$ **36.** $2x \div 3 + 5$

    37. $y + x + 1$ **38.** $6 - y$ **39.** $x - y \div 2$ **40.** $x + y^2$

    41. Let a represent your age in years. Your cousin is 9 years older. You can use the expression $a + 9$ to represent your cousin's age. Use the expression to find how old your cousin is if you are 13 years old.

1.6 **Solve the equation using mental math.**

    42. $2b = 8$ **43.** $8 + z = 11$ **44.** $x - 2 = 21$ **45.** $18 \div x = 9$

    46. $1 + x = 4$ **47.** $13 - q = 9$ **48.** $70 \div t = 10$ **49.** $4 \cdot c = 0$

1.7   **50.** The product of two whole numbers is 56. Their difference is 10. Find the two numbers. Begin by making a list of all the pairs of numbers whose product is 56.

Chapter 2

2.1 1. Find the length of the line segment to the nearest centimeter.

_____

Choose an appropriate customary unit and metric unit for the length.

  2. your height   3. distance between towns   4. thickness of a ruler

2.2 **Find the perimeter and the area of the rectangle or square.**

  5. a rectangle that is 6 in. by 3 in.   6. a square that is 12 mi by 12 mi

2.3 **The scale on a map is 1 cm : 120 km. Find the actual distance, in kilometers, for the given length on the map.**

  7. 2 cm   8. 5 cm   9. 7 cm   10. 18 cm

2.4 **The following data show the heights, in inches, of flowers in a flower box.**

  4, 6, 5, 5, 5, 6, 8, 4, 6, 5, 5, 6, 5

  11. Make a frequency table of the data.   12. Make a line plot of the data.

2.5 13. Make a bar graph of the fish swimming speed data at the right.

Fish	Carp	Cod	Mackerel	Pike
Speed (km/h)	6	8	11	6

2.6 **Graph the points on the same coordinate grid.**

  14. (0, 0)   15. (7, 1)   16. (2, 3)   17. (5, 4)   18. (1, 0)

  19. Make a line graph of the running data at the right.

Time spent running (seconds)	0	10	20	30	40
Distance from start (meters)	0	25	40	45	45

2.7 **The circle graph shows the number of bagels sold at a bakery in one day.**

  20. What type of bagel was most popular?

  21. Suppose 300 bagels were sold at the bakery. Predict how many sesame bagels would be sold.

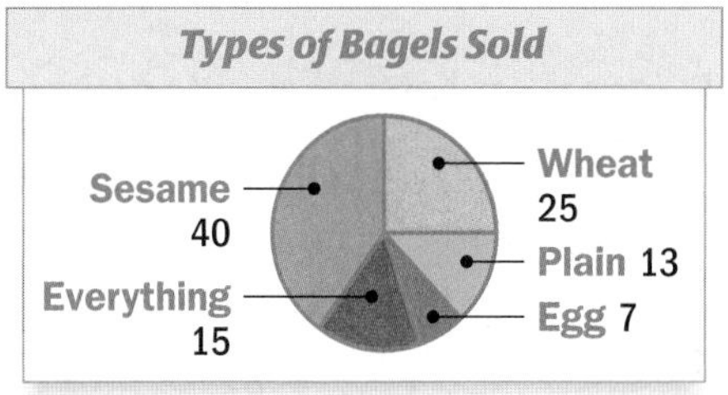

Types of Bagels Sold

Sesame 40
Everything 15
Wheat 25
Plain 13
Egg 7

2.8 **Find the mean, median, mode(s), and range. Then choose the best average(s) to represent a typical data value. Explain your choice.**

  22. Number of telephones in students' homes: 3, 4, 3, 4, 1, 2, 4, 2, 3, 4

  23. Temperatures at 6 A.M. (°F): 22, 25, 30, 31, 34, 40, 49

Chapter 3

3.1 **Write the number as a decimal.**

1. fifty and forty-two hundredths
2. seventy-two thousandths

Write the decimal in words.

3. 0.008   4. 2.09   5. 1.11   6. 12.721   7. 7.0275

3.2 8. Find the length of the word *mathematics* to the nearest tenth of a centimeter.

9. A pencil is 15 centimeters long. Write the length of the pencil to the nearest hundredth of a meter.

3.3 **Copy and complete the statement with <, >, or =.**

10. 5.7 ? 7.5   11. 13.76 ? 13.81

12. 6.05 ? 6.50   13. 17.98 ? 17.89

14. 0.03 ? 0.003   15. 0.84 ? 0.840

Order the numbers from least to greatest.

16. 0.90, 0.09, 0.99   17. 2.3, 2.12, 2.01   18. 4.5, 4.05, 4.55

3.4 **Round the decimal as specified.**

19. 13.2709 (nearest tenth)   20. 0.090909 (nearest hundredth)

Round the decimal to the place value of the leading digit.

21. 0.7004   22. 0.06111   23. 0.0089   24. 0.000192

3.5 **Use rounding to estimate the sum or difference.**

25. $3.9 - 2.1$ 26. $4.7 + 5.2$ 27. $6.7 + 12.4$ 28. $19.73 - 5.82$

Use front-end estimation to estimate the sum.

29. $13.89 + 8.72 + 9.45$ 30. $6.25 + 8.33 + 9.40$ 31. $7.30 + 2.50 + 3.80$

3.6 **Find the sum or difference.**

32. $3.8 + 9.2$ 33. $2.11 + 8.7$ 34. $13.2 - 4.7$ 35. $8.24 - 6.1$

Evaluate the expression when $x = 0.35$ and $y = 2.19$.

36. $x + 0.062$ 37. $2.1 + x$ 38. $8.5 - y$ 39. $y - x$

40. Tell which property is being illustrated: $1.8 + 6.3 = 6.3 + 1.8$.

Chapter 4

4.1 **Find the product. Use estimation to check your answer.**

1. 4×8.13 **2.** 27.5×6 **3.** 22×5.69 **4.** 3.897×14

4.2 **Use the distributive property to find the product.**

5. $6(8.2 + 3)$ **6.** $6(20 - 3)$ **7.** $7(29)$ **8.** $8(4.8)$

4.3 **Multiply. Use estimation to check that the product is reasonable.**

9. 0.8×2.6 **10.** 9.2×0.36 **11.** 4.09×1.23 **12.** 0.005×2.1

4.4 **Copy the answer and place the decimal point in the correct location.**

13. $35.2 \div 11 = \mathbf{32}$ **14.** $492.17 \div 7 = \mathbf{7031}$ **15.** $29 \div 8 = \mathbf{3625}$

Divide. Round to the nearest tenth if necessary.

16. $9.9 \div 11$ **17.** $13.5 \div 9$ **18.** $21 \div 8$ **19.** $4.2 \div 4$

4.5 **Find the product or quotient using mental math.**

20. 16.9×1000 **21.** 2.05×100 **22.** 40×0.01 **23.** 17.98×0.1

24. $0.008 \div 10$ **25.** $935 \div 1000$ **26.** $8.3 \div 0.01$ **27.** $9.38 \div 0.1$

4.6 **Divide. Round to the nearest tenth if necessary.**

28. $0.9 \div 0.3$ **29.** $4.2 \div 3.5$ **30.** $50 \div 1.5$ **31.** $39 \div 7.8$

32. $9.25 \div 0.4$ **33.** $9.9 \div 0.03$ **34.** $8.3 \div 0.41$ **35.** $6.32 \div 7.4$

4.7 **Choose an appropriate metric unit to measure the item.**

36. mass of a marble

37. mass of a cat

38. capacity of a soup spoon

39. capacity of a water tank

40. mass of a facial tissue

41. capacity of a large can of paint

4.8 **Copy and complete the statement.**

42. $188 \text{ mg} = \underline{\ ?\ } \text{ g}$ **43.** $480 \text{ L} = \underline{\ ?\ } \text{ mL}$ **44.** $3.8 \text{ km} = \underline{\ ?\ } \text{ m}$

45. $67.4 \text{ kg} = \underline{\ ?\ } \text{ g}$ **46.** $25 \text{ mL} = \underline{\ ?\ } \text{ L}$ **47.** $100 \text{ cm} = \underline{\ ?\ } \text{ mm}$

Copy and complete the statement with <, >, or =.

48. $212 \text{ m } \underline{\ ?\ } 0.1 \text{ km}$ **49.** $4.9 \text{ mm } \underline{\ ?\ } 5 \text{ cm}$ **50.** $0.025 \text{ L } \underline{\ ?\ } 249 \text{ mL}$

51. $1.6 \text{ kL } \underline{\ ?\ } 160,000 \text{ mL}$ **52.** $980 \text{ g } \underline{\ ?\ } 0.98 \text{ kg}$ **53.** $3800 \text{ mg } \underline{\ ?\ } 4.9 \text{ g}$

Chapter 5

5.1 **Test the number for divisibility by 2, 3, 5, 6, 9, and 10.**

1. 406   **2.** 721   **3.** 534   **4.** 1557   **5.** 510

Tell whether the number is *prime*, *composite*, **or** *neither*.

6. 13   **7.** 8   **8.** 25   **9.** 1   **10.** 71

Write the prime factorization of the number.

11. 95   **12.** 330   **13.** 76   **14.** 400   **15.** 175

5.2 **Find the GCF of the numbers.**

16. 15, 21   **17.** 8, 20   **18.** 16, 24   **19.** 25, 50, 70

5.3 **Write two fractions that are equivalent to the given fraction.**

20. $\frac{1}{4}$ **21.** $\frac{2}{5}$ **22.** $\frac{5}{6}$ **23.** $\frac{3}{10}$ **24.** $\frac{4}{7}$

Tell whether the fraction is in simplest form. If not, simplify it.

25. $\frac{5}{9}$ **26.** $\frac{18}{27}$ **27.** $\frac{3}{42}$ **28.** $\frac{17}{20}$ **29.** $\frac{12}{15}$

5.4 **Find the LCM of the numbers.**

30. 3, 9   **31.** 8, 12   **32.** 20, 30   **33.** 4, 8, 10

5.5 **Order the fractions from least to greatest.**

34. $\frac{1}{2}, \frac{2}{5}, \frac{3}{8}$ **35.** $\frac{13}{15}, \frac{9}{10}, \frac{4}{5}$ **36.** $\frac{7}{12}, \frac{2}{3}, \frac{5}{9}, \frac{11}{18}$ **37.** $\frac{2}{5}, \frac{4}{15}, \frac{3}{20}, \frac{2}{9}$

5.6 **Rewrite the number as an improper fraction or mixed number.**

38. $1\frac{3}{4}$ **39.** $3\frac{8}{9}$ **40.** $5\frac{3}{10}$ **41.** $2\frac{3}{7}$ **42.** $1\frac{6}{11}$

43. $\frac{13}{6}$ **44.** $\frac{21}{4}$ **45.** $\frac{17}{5}$ **46.** $\frac{20}{3}$ **47.** $\frac{19}{12}$

Order the numbers from least to greatest.

48. $2\frac{1}{2}, \frac{19}{16}, \frac{35}{12}$ **49.** $2\frac{1}{4}, \frac{17}{8}, 2\frac{1}{3}, \frac{55}{24}$ **50.** $\frac{13}{8}, 1\frac{2}{5}, \frac{7}{4}, 2$

5.7 **Write the decimal as a fraction or mixed number in simplest form.**

51. 0.95   **52.** 3.8   **53.** 2.08   **54.** 6.09   **55.** 0.645

5.8 **Write the fraction or mixed number as a decimal.**

56. $\frac{5}{8}$ **57.** $\frac{7}{4}$ **58.** $\frac{8}{15}$ **59.** $5\frac{1}{6}$ **60.** $\frac{57}{40}$

Chapter 6

6.1 **Estimate the sum or difference.**

1. $\dfrac{15}{16} - \dfrac{5}{8}$ **2.** $\dfrac{1}{8} + \dfrac{5}{6}$ **3.** $\dfrac{7}{12} - \dfrac{8}{15}$ **4.** $\dfrac{5}{12} + \dfrac{3}{5}$

5. $7\dfrac{1}{8} - 2\dfrac{5}{6}$ **6.** $1\dfrac{2}{3} + 2\dfrac{7}{9}$ **7.** $5\dfrac{8}{15} + 3\dfrac{5}{12}$ **8.** $6\dfrac{2}{9} - 1\dfrac{6}{7}$

6.2 **Find the sum or difference.**

9. $\dfrac{5}{8} + \dfrac{1}{8}$ **10.** $\dfrac{7}{12} + \dfrac{5}{12}$ **11.** $\dfrac{8}{15} - \dfrac{4}{15}$ **12.** $\dfrac{5}{9} - \dfrac{4}{9}$

13. $\dfrac{17}{20} - \dfrac{9}{20}$ **14.** $\dfrac{2}{11} + \dfrac{7}{11}$ **15.** $\dfrac{7}{10} - \dfrac{3}{10}$ **16.** $\dfrac{5}{14} + \dfrac{3}{14}$

6.3 **Find the sum or difference.**

17. $\dfrac{5}{9} - \dfrac{1}{6}$ **18.** $\dfrac{2}{3} - \dfrac{1}{2}$ **19.** $\dfrac{11}{16} + \dfrac{1}{4}$ **20.** $\dfrac{2}{7} + \dfrac{2}{3}$

21. $\dfrac{11}{15} - \dfrac{1}{10}$ **22.** $\dfrac{6}{12} + \dfrac{1}{3}$ **23.** $\dfrac{7}{20} + \dfrac{3}{5}$ **24.** $\dfrac{9}{16} - \dfrac{1}{8}$

6.4 **Find the sum or difference.**

25. $6\dfrac{5}{6} - 4\dfrac{1}{6}$ **26.** $2\dfrac{5}{12} + 4\dfrac{2}{3}$ **27.** $3\dfrac{1}{2} + 12\dfrac{3}{4}$ **28.** $9\dfrac{2}{3} - 1\dfrac{3}{8}$

29. $1\dfrac{5}{14} + 6\dfrac{3}{14}$ **30.** $12\dfrac{1}{2} - 3\dfrac{1}{5}$ **31.** $3\dfrac{7}{8} - 3\dfrac{3}{4}$ **32.** $2\dfrac{5}{9} + 4\dfrac{1}{6}$

6.5 **Find the difference.**

33. $3\dfrac{2}{13} - 1\dfrac{9}{13}$ **34.** $8\dfrac{3}{4} - 6\dfrac{4}{5}$ **35.** $2\dfrac{3}{8} - \dfrac{5}{8}$ **36.** $4 - 2\dfrac{3}{4}$

37. $4\dfrac{1}{10} - 3\dfrac{1}{2}$ **38.** $4\dfrac{1}{6} - 1\dfrac{2}{3}$ **39.** $9 - 6\dfrac{4}{5}$ **40.** $5\dfrac{2}{3} - 4\dfrac{3}{4}$

6.6 **Add or subtract the measures of time.**

41. 6 h 15 min
− 2 h 40 min

42. 45 min
+ 4 h 25 min

43. 1 h 24 min 38 sec
+   56 min 12 sec

44. 4 h 17 min
−   38 min

45. 5 h 28 min
+ 1 h 47 min

46. 3 h 4 min 12 sec
+ 2 h 17 min 35 sec

Find the elapsed time.

47. 6:00 A.M. to 8:30 A.M. **48.** 9:00 A.M. to 3:15 P.M.

49. 6:30 P.M. to 12:15 A.M. **50.** 7:30 A.M. to 9:10 P.M.

51. 3:40 P.M. to 5:15 P.M. **52.** 11:40 P.M. to 2:30 A.M.

53. You went on a hike with a group of friends from 8:15 A.M. to 4:30 P.M. How long were you hiking?

Chapter 7

7.1 **Use compatible numbers to estimate the product.**

    1. $25 \times \frac{3}{8}$ **2.** $10 \times \frac{1}{3}$ **3.** $\frac{9}{10} \times 32$ **4.** $\frac{5}{7} \times 34$

    Find the product.

    5. $8 \times \frac{3}{4}$ **6.** $6 \times \frac{5}{8}$ **7.** $\frac{4}{7} \times 28$ **8.** $\frac{2}{3} \times 7$

7.2 **Find the product.**

    9. $\frac{5}{3} \times \frac{3}{4}$ **10.** $\frac{7}{12} \times \frac{8}{9}$ **11.** $\frac{1}{3} \times \frac{2}{9}$ **12.** $\frac{4}{9} \times \frac{3}{8} \times \frac{2}{3}$

7.3 **Find the product.**

    13. $4 \times 1\frac{5}{6}$ **14.** $\frac{2}{5} \times 3\frac{2}{5}$ **15.** $1\frac{3}{4} \times \frac{2}{3}$ **16.** $2\frac{1}{4} \times 1\frac{1}{3}$

7.4 **Find the quotient.**

    17. $\frac{5}{6} \div 4$ **18.** $1 \div \frac{5}{12}$ **19.** $\frac{1}{5} \div \frac{5}{4}$ **20.** $\frac{2}{3} \div \frac{1}{9}$

7.5 **Find the quotient.**

    21. $2\frac{1}{4} \div \frac{3}{4}$ **22.** $\frac{7}{8} \div 1\frac{1}{2}$ **23.** $1\frac{4}{5} \div 4$ **24.** $12 \div 1\frac{1}{2}$

    25. $3\frac{1}{2} \div 1\frac{1}{5}$ **26.** $5\frac{2}{5} \div 1\frac{1}{8}$ **27.** $6 \div 2\frac{2}{5}$ **28.** $3\frac{3}{4} \div 6\frac{1}{2}$

    Solve the problem. Explain why you chose the operation you used.

    29. You buy 10 yards of fabric to make some costumes. If each costume needs $3\frac{5}{8}$ yards of fabric, do you have enough fabric to make 3 costumes?

    30. Amy is $1\frac{1}{3}$ feet taller than Frank. Frank is $4\frac{1}{4}$ feet tall. How tall is Amy?

7.6 **Copy and complete the statement using an appropriate customary unit.**

    31. weight of a horse = 850 _?_   **32.** capacity of a washing machine = 19 _?_

    33. weight of a jar of jam = 10 _?_   **34.** capacity of a can of soup = 12 _?_

7.7 **Copy and complete the statement.**

    35. 3 gal 2 qt = _?_ qt   **36.** 2 yd 6 in. = _?_ in.   **37.** 25 oz = _?_ lb _?_ oz, or _?_ lb

    Change the measurement to the specified unit.

    38. $3\frac{1}{4}$ cups to fluid ounces   **39.** $1\frac{1}{8}$ tons to pounds   **40.** 9 pints to gallons

    Find the sum or difference.

    41. 3 lb 6 oz + 2 lb 10 oz   **42.** 3 ft 5 in. − 1 ft 9 in.   **43.** 1 yd 2 ft + 2 yd 2 ft

Chapter 8

8.1 **Write the ratio in simplest form.**

1. $12 : 18$ 2. 6 to 3 3. $2 : 10$ 4. 5 to 20 5. $16 : 12$

Copy and complete the statement.

6. $\dfrac{3}{8} = \dfrac{9}{?}$ 7. $\dfrac{10}{?} = \dfrac{1}{2}$ 8. $\dfrac{?}{12} = \dfrac{7}{6}$ 9. $\dfrac{3}{5} = \dfrac{?}{15}$

8.2 **Copy and complete the statement.**

10. $\dfrac{\$5}{2 \text{ items}} = \dfrac{?}{12 \text{ items}}$ 11. $\dfrac{38 \text{ cm}}{30 \text{ min}} = \dfrac{?}{15 \text{ min}}$ 12. $\dfrac{?}{3 \text{ classes}} = \dfrac{25 \text{ students}}{1 \text{ class}}$

Write the unit rate.

13. $\dfrac{2750 \text{ visitors}}{10 \text{ hours}}$ 14. $\dfrac{90 \text{ meters}}{18 \text{ seconds}}$ 15. $\dfrac{5000 \text{ words}}{25 \text{ pages}}$ 16. $\dfrac{40{,}000 \text{ bits}}{5 \text{ minutes}}$

8.3 **Solve the proportion.**

17. $\dfrac{81}{6} = \dfrac{27}{r}$ 18. $\dfrac{16}{x} = \dfrac{40}{25}$ 19. $\dfrac{8}{20} = \dfrac{b}{28}$ 20. $\dfrac{a}{51} = \dfrac{10}{15}$

8.4 **A scale drawing of a room has a scale of 1 in. : 8 ft. In the drawing, the floor of the room is 2.5 inches long by 2 inches wide.**

21. What are the actual dimensions of the floor of the room?

22. What is the ratio of the floor area of the room in the drawing to the floor area of the actual room?

8.5 **Write the percent as a decimal and a fraction.**

23. 18% 24. 69% 25. 2.5% 26. 45%

8.6 **Write the fraction or decimal as a percent.**

27. $\dfrac{17}{20}$ 28. $\dfrac{3}{8}$ 29. 0.83 30. 0.9 31. 0.005

Order the numbers from least to greatest.

32. $0.24, \dfrac{7}{25}, \dfrac{1}{4}, 23\%$ 33. $67\%, \dfrac{5}{6}, 0.76, \dfrac{2}{3}$ 34. $0.2, \dfrac{3}{20}, 14\%, 0.018$

8.7 **Find the percent of the number.**

35. 20% of 90 36. 8% of 4 37. 16% of 350 38. $33\dfrac{1}{3}\%$ of 150

39. A bank account pays 4% annual interest. How much simple interest will $2000 earn 6 years?

40. You want to buy a sweater that costs $18.50. The sales tax is 5%. You realize that you have only $20 with you. Can you buy the sweater?

Chapter 9

Use the diagram at the right.

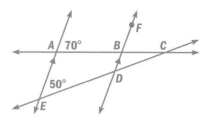

9.1   **1.** Name two rays and two segments with endpoint *B*.

     2. Name two parallel lines.

     3. Name two lines that intersect at *D*.

9.2   **4.** Name three angles with vertex *B*.

     5. Name an angle in the diagram whose measure is 50°.

     6. Use a protractor to draw an angle that has a measure of 180°.

Use the diagram at the right.

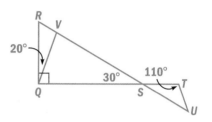

9.3   **7.** Classify each angle as *acute, right, obtuse,* or *straight*: ∠RQS, ∠QSU, ∠QSR, ∠QST.

     8. Find the measures of ∠TSU, ∠VQS, and ∠RST.

9.4   **9.** Find the measures of ∠QRS, ∠QVR, and ∠QVS.

     10. Classify each triangle by its angles as *acute, right,* or *obtuse*: △STU, △SVQ, △QRV, △QRS.

9.5   **Copy and complete the statement using *All, Some,* or *No*.**

     11. __?__ squares are parallelograms.   **12.** __?__ rhombuses are squares.

     13. __?__ rectangles are rhombuses.   **14.** __?__ quadrilaterals have four right angles.

9.6   **Classify the polygon and tell whether it is regular.**

     15.   **16.**   **17.**   **18.**

9.7   **△XYZ and △DEF are congruent.**

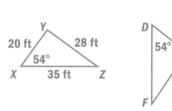

     19. List the corresponding parts.

     20. How long is $\overline{EF}$? Explain.

9.8   **Tell whether the figure has line symmetry. If so, copy the figure and draw all lines of symmetry.**

     21.   **22.**   **23.**   **24.**

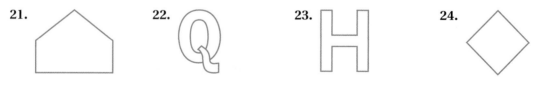

Chapter 10

10.1 **Find the unknown measure of the parallelogram described.**

    1. base = 12 ft, height = 30 ft, Area = _?_

    2. base = 5 m, Area = 20 m^2, height = _?_

10.2 **Find the area of the triangle.**

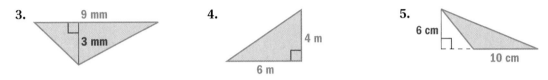

    3. 9 mm, 3 mm   **4.** 4 m, 6 m   **5.** 6 cm, 10 cm

10.3 **Find the circumference of the circle described. Tell what value you used for π. Explain your choice.**

    6. $r = 80$ m   **7.** $d = 35$ cm   **8.** $d = 9$ mm   **9.** $r = 7$ in.

10.4 **Find the area of the circle described. Round to the nearest tenth of a unit.**

    10. $r = 42$ m   **11.** $d = 8$ cm   **12.** $d = 200$ mm   **13.** $r = 15$ ft

    Find the area of the figure to the nearest whole unit.

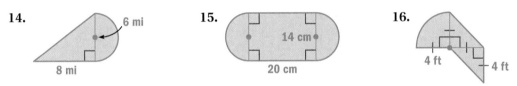

    14. 6 mi, 8 mi   **15.** 14 cm, 20 cm   **16.** 4 ft, 4 ft

    17. The table shows how many of the 40 volunteers will be assigned to each of the three types of jobs. Make a circle graph of the data.

Spring Fundraiser Volunteers			
Job	tickets	snacks	booths
Number of volunteers	8	6	26

10.5 **Draw the solid described.**

    18. cone   **19.** pyramid with a rectangular base

    20. Count the number of faces, edges, and vertices of the solid you drew in Exercise 19.

10.6 **Draw a diagram of the rectangular prism described. Then find the surface area.**

    21. 5 cm by 5 cm by 3 cm   **22.** 6 in. by 4 in. by 10 in.

10.7   **23.** Find the volumes of the prisms described in Exercises 21 and 22.

Chapter 11

11.1   **1.** Find the opposites of the integers 4, −18, and 0.

Copy and complete the statement using < or >.

2. −4 ? 0   **3.** 2 ? −5   **4.** −10 ? −11   **5.** −4 ? 13

Order the integers from least to greatest.

6. 3, −4, 7, 2, −1   **7.** −5, 6, −1, 4, −3   **8.** −7, 9, −9, 8, −6   **9.** 0, 2, −3, 5, 3

11.2 **Find the sum.**

10. 8 + (−22)   **11.** −6 + 10   **12.** 6 + (−12)   **13.** −5 + (−5)

14. 2 + (−15)   **15.** −14 + 14   **16.** −20 + 16   **17.** −9 + (−5)

11.3 **Find the difference.**

18. 2 − 7   **19.** 13 − (−3)   **20.** −7 − 9   **21.** −24 − (−7)

22. 16 − (−17)   **23.** −10 − 18   **24.** −9 − (−11)   **25.** 8 − 17

11.4 **Find the product.**

26. 13(4)   **27.** −8(5)   **28.** −6(10)   **29.** −7(−20)

30. 0(−12)   **31.** −4(−8)   **32.** 14(−5)   **33.** −11(−9)

11.5 **Find the quotient.**

34. −9 ÷ (−1)   **35.** −200 ÷ 25   **36.** 42 ÷ (− 6)   **37.** −70 ÷ (−14)

38. 110 ÷ (−5)   **39.** −45 ÷ 15   **40.** −51 ÷ (−17)   **41.** 300 ÷ (−12)

11.6 **Graph the point and describe its location.**

42. $P(3, −7)$ **43.** $Q(4, 4)$ **44.** $R(−2, −6)$ **45.** $S(−8, 4)$ **46.** $T(−5, 0)$

Draw the figure on a coordinate plane. Then translate the figure as described. Give the coordinates of the vertices of the image.

47. $\triangle ABC$: $A(0, 4)$, $B(−2, 2)$, $C(1, −1)$

Translation: 3 units to the left and 4 units up to form $\triangle DEF$

48. $\triangle ABC$: $A(−5, 3)$, $B(1, 4)$, $C(−2, −3)$

Translation: 5 units to the right and 2 units down to form $\triangle DEF$

11.7 **Tell whether the transformation is a *translation*, a *reflection*, or a *rotation*.**

49.

50.

51.

52.

Chapter 12

12.1 **Write the phrase as an expression. Let n represent the number.**

1. A number increased by 7

2. 30 multiplied by a number

3. A number subtracted from 20

4. The quotient of a number and 50

Write the sentence as an equation.

5. The product of 8 and a number n is 32.

6. The sum of 7 and a number x is 19.

7. A number y divided by 6 is 5.

8. 15 less than a number k is 6.

12.2 **Solve the equation.**

9. $9 + p = 38$

10. $x + 17 = 50$

11. $16 + z = 30$

12. $q + 2.8 = 4.7$

12.3 **Solve the equation.**

13. $8 = z - 8$

14. $x - 31 = 41$

15. $1 = n - 24$

16. $w - 4.8 = 2.5$

12.4 **Solve the equation.**

17. $30 = 3n$

18. $20c = 100$

19. $8n = 72$

20. $68 = 4x$

21. $\dfrac{x}{12} = 5$

22. $10 = \dfrac{b}{8}$

23. $\dfrac{x}{7} = 3$

24. $\dfrac{n}{5} = 13$

12.5 **Make an input-output table using the function rule and the input values $x = 4, 8, 12, 16,$ and 20.**

25. $y = x - 3$

26. $y = 5x$

27. $y = 2x + 5$

28. $y = \dfrac{x}{4}$

29. Write a function rule for the input-output table.

Price of each item, p	$10	$20	$30	$40	$50
Total cost of items, c	$60	$120	$180	$240	$300

Make an input-output table. Then write a function rule for the relationship.

30. input: dollars
    output: cents

31. input: quarts
    output: gallons

Make an input-output table using the function rule and the input values $x = 0, 1, 2, 3,$ and 4. Graph the function.

32. $y = 10 - x$

33. $y = x - 2$

34. $y = 2x - 1$

35. $y = \dfrac{1}{2}x + 3$

12.6 **Graph the ordered pairs and draw a line through the points. Write a function rule for the ordered pairs.**

36. $(-2, 1), (-1, 2), (0, 3), (1, 4), (2, 5)$

37. $(-6, -2), (-3, -1), (0, 0), (3, 1), (6, 2)$

Chapter 13

13.1 **A box contains seven tiles numbered 1 through 7. You randomly choose a tile. Find the probability of the event.**

1. You choose an odd number.

2. You choose a multiple of 3.

3. You choose a number less than 10.

4. You choose the number 18.

5. Describe the complement of the event in Exercise 2. Then find its probability.

13.2 6. The cover of a yearbook can be white, red, or gold. The printing on the cover can be black or blue. Use a tree diagram to find all the possible covers.

7. An electronic lock has four buttons, labeled 1, 2, 3, and 4. List all possible two-digit numbers that can be formed using these four buttons. Include repeated digits, such as 11.

13.3 **You toss a coin and then you roll a number cube. Find the probability of the event.**

8. You get tails and then roll a 2.

9. You get heads and then roll an even number.

13.4 10. A family, using the data below, claims that the average water bill on their street is $147. Does $147 describe the average water bill well? Why or why not?

$98, $105, $105, $106, $110, $118, $125, $125, $130, $448

In Exercises 11–13, use the list of data below. The data show the number of students using the library's study room each day.

9, 4, 8, 11, 24, 8, 20, 15, 29, 7, 6, 7, 8, 16, 20, 19, 24, 21, 12, 18

13.5 11. Make a stem-and-leaf plot of the data.

12. Find the mean, median, and mode(s).

13.6 13. Make a box-and-whisker plot of the data. Find the range.

13.7 **Choose an appropriate data display for the given situation. Explain your choice.**

14. Each student in a math class gives the number of pets in his or her family. You want to find the most common number of pets.

15. You have data on the average rainfall in your town each year for the past 50 years and want to see how the average has changed over time.

16. You want to compare the number of votes each candidate for class president received to the total number of votes cast.

Table of Symbols

Symbol	Meaning	Page
+	Plus	**3**
=	equals, is equal to	**3, 34**
−	Minus	**4**
×	Times	**4**
÷	Divided by	**4**
R	Remainder	**4**
≈	is about equal to	**12**
4^3	4 to the 3rd power	**16**
( )	parentheses—a grouping symbol	**21**
$\frac{14}{2}$	14 divided by 2	**22**
$3 \cdot x$ $3(x)$ $3x$	3 times x	**29**
$\overset{?}{=}$	is equal to?	**34**
≠	is not equal to	**34**
(4, 3)	ordered pair of numbers	**88**
28.6	decimal point	**120**
<	is less than	**130, 651**
>	is greater than	**130, 651**
. . .	continues on	**250**
$1.1\overline{6}$	repeating decimal 1.1666 . . .	**272**
$a : b, \frac{a}{b}$	ratio of a to b	**402**

Symbol	Meaning	Page
%	Percent	**425**
$\overleftrightarrow{AB}$	line AB	**455**
$\overrightarrow{AB}$	ray AB	**455**
$\overline{AB}$	segment AB	**455**
⇉	parallel lines	**456**
∠PQR	angle PQR	**460**
°	degrees(s)	**461**
$m\angle B$	measure of angle B	**461**
⌐	right angle	**465**
△ABC	triangle with vertices A, B, and C	**471**
π	pi—a number approximately equal to 3.14	**525**
−3	negative 3	**573**
−3	the opposite of 3	**574**
$|a|$	the absolute value of a number a	**580**
≤	is less than or equal to	**651**
≥	is greater than or equal to	**651**

Table of Measures

Time

60 seconds (sec) = 1 minute (min)	365 days ⎤
60 minutes = 1 hour (h)	52 weeks (approx.) ⎬ = 1 year
24 hours = 1 day	12 months ⎦
7 days = 1 week	10 years = 1 decade
4 weeks (approx.) = 1 month	100 years = 1 century

Metric

Length

10 millimeters (mm) = 1 centimeter (cm)

$\left.\begin{array}{l}100 \text{ cm} \\ 1000 \text{ mm}\end{array}\right]$ = 1 meter (m)

10,000 m = 1 kilometer (km)

Area

100 square millimeters = 1 square centimeter
(mm^2)   (cm^2)

10,000 cm^2 = 1 square meter (m^2)

10,000 m^2 = 1 hectare (ha)

Volume

100 cubic millimeters = 1 cubic centimeter
(mm^3)   (cm^3)

1,000,000 cm^3 = 1 cubic meter (m^3)

Liquid capacity

$\left.\begin{array}{l}1000 \text{ millimeters (mL)} \\ 1000 \text{ cubic centimeters (cm}^3) \end{array}\right]$ = 1 liter (L)

1000 L = 1 kiloliter (kL)

Mass

1000 milligrams = 1 gram (g)

1000 g = 1 kilogram (kg)

1000 kg = 1 metric ton (t)

Temperature Degrees Celcius (°C)

0°C = freezing point of water

37°C = normal body temperature

100°C = boiling point of water

United States Customary

Length

12 inches (in.) = 1 foot (ft)

$\left.\begin{array}{l}36 \text{ in.} \\ 3 \text{ ft}\end{array}\right]$ = 1 yard (yd)

$\left.\begin{array}{l}5280 \text{ ft} \\ 1760 \text{ yd}\end{array}\right]$ = 1 mile (mi)

Area

144 square inches (in.^{2}) = 1 square foot (ft^2)

9 ft^2 = 1 square foot (d^2)

$\left.\begin{array}{l}43, 560 \text{ ft}^2 \\ 4840 \text{ yd}^2\end{array}\right]$ = 1 acre (A)

Volume

1728 cubic inches (in.^{3}) = 1 cubic foot (ft^3)

27 ft^3 = 1 cubic foot (yd^3)

Liquid Capacity

8 fluid ounces (fl oz) = 1 cup (c)

2 c = 1 pint (pt)

2 pt = 1 quart (qt)

4 qt = 1 gallon (gal)

Weight

16 ounces (oz) = 1 pound (lb)

2000 lb = 1 ton

Temperature Degrees Fahrenheit (°F)

32°F = freezing point of water

98.6°F = normal body temperature

212°F = boiling point of water

Table of Formulas

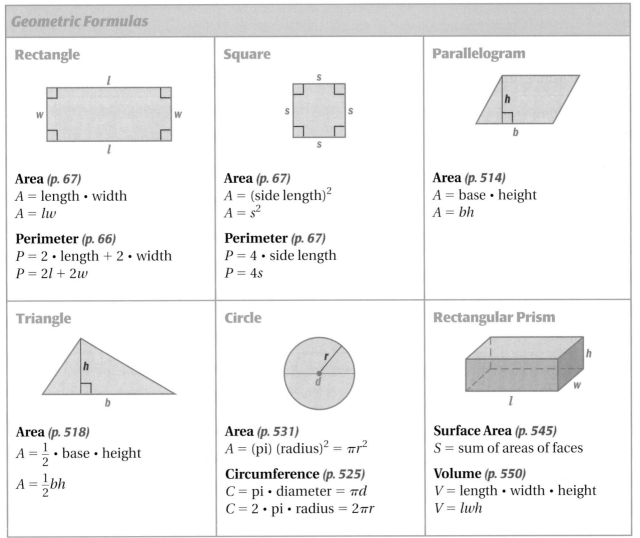

Geometric Formulas

Rectangle

Area *(p. 67)*
A = length • width
$A = lw$

Perimeter *(p. 66)*
$P = 2$ • length + 2 • width
$P = 2l + 2w$

Square

Area *(p. 67)*
A = (side length)^2
$A = s^2$

Perimeter *(p. 67)*
$P = 4$ • side length
$P = 4s$

Parallelogram

Area *(p. 514)*
A = base • height
$A = bh$

Triangle

Area *(p. 518)*
$A = \frac{1}{2}$ • base • height
$A = \frac{1}{2}bh$

Circle

Area *(p. 531)*
A = (pi) (radius)$^2 = \pi r^2$

Circumference *(p. 525)*
C = pi • diameter = πd
$C = 2$ • pi • radius = $2\pi r$

Rectangular Prism

Surface Area *(p. 545)*
S = sum of areas of faces

Volume *(p. 550)*
V = length • width • height
$V = lwh$

Other Formulas

Distance traveled *(p. 170)*	$d = rt$ where d = distance, r = rate, and t = time
Simple interest *(p. 436)*	$I = Prt$ where I = simple interest, P = principal, r = annual interest rate, and t = time in years
Temperature *(p. 345)*	$F = \frac{9}{5}C + 32$ and $C = \frac{5}{9}(F - 32)$ where F = degrees Fahrenheit and C = degrees Celsius

Table of Properties

Number Properties

Identity Property of Addition *(p. 35)* The sum of any number and 0 is that number.	**Numbers** **Algebra**	$7 + 0 = 7$ $a + 0 = a$
Multiplication Property of 0 *(p. 35)* The product of any number and 0 is 0.	**Numbers** **Algebra**	$4 \times 0 = 0$ $a \times 0 = 0$
Identity Property of Multiplication *(p. 35)* The product of any number and 1 is that number.	**Numbers** **Algebra**	$3 \times 1 = 3$ $a \times 1 = a$
Commutative Property of Addition *(p. 149)* You can add numbers in any order.	**Numbers** **Algebra**	$2 + 5 = 5 + 2$ $a + b = b + a$
Associative Property of Addition *(p. 149)* The value of a sum does not depend on how the numbers are grouped.	**Numbers** **Algebra**	$(2 + 4) + 6 = 2 + (4 + 6)$ $(a + b) + c = a + (b + c)$
Commutative Property of Multiplication *(p. 171)* You can multiply numbers in any order.	**Numbers** **Algebra**	$2 \times 6.5 = 6.5 \times 2$ $a \cdot b = b \cdot a$
Associative Property of Multiplication *(p. 171)* The value of a product does not depend on how the numbers are grouped.	**Numbers** **Algebra**	$(6 \times 2.5) \times 4 = 6 \times (2.5 \times 4)$ $(a \cdot b) \cdot c = a \cdot (b \cdot c)$
Distributive Property *(p. 176)* You can multiply a number and a sum by multiplying the number by each part of the sum and then adding these products. The same property applies with subtraction.	**Numbers** **Algebra**	$3(4 + 6) = 3(4) + 3(6)$ $2(8 - 5) = 2(8) - 2(5)$ $a(b + c) = ab + ac$ $a(b - c) = ab - ac$
Inverse Property of Multiplication *(p. 362)* The product of a nonzero number and its multiplicative inverse, or reciprocal, is 1.	**Numbers** **Algebra**	$\frac{2}{3} \cdot \frac{3}{2} = 1$ For any nonzero integers a and b, $\frac{a}{b} \cdot \frac{b}{a} = 1$.
Cross Products Property *(p. 412)* In a proportion, the cross products are equal.	**Numbers** **Algebra**	If $\frac{3}{4} = \frac{6}{8}$, then $3 \cdot 8 = 4 \cdot 6$. If $\frac{a}{b} = \frac{c}{d}$ and b and d do not equal 0, then $ad = bc$.
Inverse Property of Addition *(p. 580)* The sum of a number and its additive inverse, or opposite, is zero.	**Numbers** **Algebra**	$4 + (-4) = 0$ $a + (-a) = 0$

English-Spanish Glossary

A

absolute value (p. 580) The absolute value of a number is its distance from 0 on a number line. The absolute value of a is written $|a|$.

valor absoluto (pág. 580) El valor absoluto de un número es la distancia a la que se encuentra del cero en una recta numérica. El valor absoluto de a se escribe $|a|$.

$$|2| = |-2| = 2$$

2 units/2 unidades 2 units/2 unidades

acute angle (p. 465) An angle whose measure is less than 90°.

ángulo agudo (pág. 465) Un ángulo que mide menos de 90°.

acute triangle (p. 471) A triangle with three acute angles.

triángulo acutángulo (pág. 471) Un triángulo que tiene tres ángulos agudos.

angle (p. 460) A figure formed by two rays with the same endpoint.

ángulo (pág. 460) Figura formada por dos semirrectas que comparten un mismo extremo.

∠DEF, or ∠E, or ∠FED
∠DEF, o ∠E, o ∠FED

angle of rotation (p. 608) *See* rotation.

ángulo de rotación (pág. 608) *Véase* rotación.

annual interest rate (p. 436) The percent of the principal you earn or pay per year.

tasa de interés anual (pág. 436) El porcentaje sobre el capital que ganas o pagas por año.

If you deposit $100 in a bank account that pays 4% per year, then 4% is the *annual interest rate.*

Si depositas $100 dólares en una cuenta bancaria que paga 4% al año, entonces la *tasa de interés anual* es de 4%.

arc (p. 538) Part of a circle.

arco (pág. 538) Parte de un círculo.

area (p. 67) The amount of surface covered by a figure. Area is measured in square units such as square feet (ft^2) or square meters (m^2).

área (pág. 67) La cantidad de superficie que cubre una figura. El área se mide en unidades cuadradas, como pies cuadrados ($pies^2$) o metros cuadrados (m^2).

3 units/
3 unidades

4 units/
4 unidades

Area = 12 square units

Área = 12 unidades cuadradas

---

associative property of addition (p. 149) The value of a sum does not depend on how the numbers are grouped.

propiedad asociativa de la suma (pág. 149) El valor de una suma no depende de cómo se agrupan los números.

$$(a + b) + c = a + (b + c)$$
$$(2 + 5) + 4 = 2 + (5 + 4)$$

---

associative property of multiplication (p. 171) The value of a product does not depend on how the numbers are grouped.

propiedad asociativa de la multiplicación (pág. 171) El valor de un producto no depende de cómo se agrupan los números.

$$(a \cdot b) \cdot c = a \cdot (b \cdot c)$$
$$(2 \times 6.5) \times 4 = 2 \times (6.5 \times 4)$$

---

average (p. 99) A single number used to describe what is typical of a set of data.

promedio (pág. 99) Un único número que se usa para describir lo que es típico de un conjunto de datos.

See **mean, median,** *and* **mode.**

Véase **media, mediana** *y* **moda.**

---

axes (p. 88) A horizontal number line, the *horizontal axis*, and a vertical number line, the *vertical axis*, that meet at (0, 0).

ejes (pág. 88) Una recta numérica horizontal, el *eje horizontal*, y una recta numérica vertical, el *eje vertical*, que se encuentran en (0, 0).

See **coordinate plane.**

Véase **plano de coordenadas.**

B

bar graph (p. 83) A graph in which the lengths of bars are used to represent and compare data.

gráfica de barras (pág. 83) Una gráfica en la que la longitud de las barras se usa para representar y comparar datos.

**Favorite Place to Swim/
Lugar favorito para nadar**

---

base of a parallelogram (p. 514) The base of a parallelogram is the length of any of its sides.

base de un paralelogramo (pág. 514) La base de un paralelogramo es la longitud de cualquiera de sus lados.

height/altura, *h*

base/base, *b*

base of a power (p. 15) The base of a power is the repeated factor. **base de una potencia** (pág. 15) La base de una potencia es el factor de repetición.	The *base* of the power 2^3 is 2. La *base* de la potencia 2^3 es 2.
base of a solid (p. 541) *See* prism, cylinder, pyramid, *and* cone. **base de un cuerpo geométrico** (pág. 541) *Véase* prisma, cilindro, pirámide *y* cono.	
base of a triangle (p. 518) The length of any of its sides. **base de un triángulo** (pág. 518) La longitud de cualquiera de sus lados.	 height/altura, *h* base/base, *b*
benchmark (p. 61) A familiar object that can be used to approximate the size of a unit. **medida de referencia** (pág. 61) Un objeto conocido que puede usarse para determinar aproximadamente el tamaño de una unidad.	The length of a small paper clip is about one inch. La longitud de un sujetapapeles pequeño es de alrededor de una pulgada.
bisector of an angle (p. 539) The ray that divides an angle into two angles with the same measure. **bisector de un ángulo** (pág. 539) La semirrecta que divide un ángulo en dos ángulos de la misma medida.	 angle bisector/ bisector de un ángulo
box-and-whisker plot (p. 714) A display that divides a data set into four parts, two below the median and two above it. **diagrama de líneas y bloques** (pág. 714) Diagrama que divide un conjunto de datos en cuatro partes, dos por debajo y dos por encima de la mediana.	 10 20 30 40 50 60 11 20 36 44 57

C

capacity (p. 204) Capacity measures the amount that a container can hold. **capacidad** (pág. 204) La capacidad mide la cantidad que un recipiente puede contener.	
center of a circle (p. 525) The point inside a circle that is the same distance from all points on the circle. **centro de un círculo** (pág. 525) El punto interior del círculo que está a la misma distancia de todos los puntos del círculo.	*See* circle. *Véase* círculo.
center of rotation (p. 608) *See* rotation. **centro de rotación** (pág. 608) *Véase* rotación.	

circle (p. 525) The set of all points in a plane that are the same distance from a point called the *center*.

círculo (pág. 525) El conjunto de todos los puntos en un plano que están a la misma distancia de un punto llamado *centro*.

center/centro

circle/círculo

circle graph (p. 94) A graph that represents data as part of a circle. The entire circle represents all of the data.

gráfica circular (pág. 94) Una gráfica que representa datos como parte de un círculo. El círculo completo representa todos los datos.

Opinions of Roller Coasters/
Opinión sobre montañas rusas

Not fun/
No son divertidas 7

OK/OK 15

Great/
Estupendas 78

circumference (p. 525) The distance around a circle.

circunferencia (pág. 525) La distancia alrededor de un círculo.

center/centro   radius/radio

circumference/
circunferencia

diameter/
diámetro

clustering (p. 745) A method of estimating a sum when numbers being added have about the same value.

agrupación (pág. 745) Un método para estimar una suma cuando los números a sumarse tienen valores similares.

You can estimate the sum $72 + 69 + 65$ as $3(70) = 210$.

Puedes estimar la suma de $72 + 69 + 65$ como $3(70) = 210$.

combination (p. 692) A grouping of objects in which order is not important.

combinación (pág. 692) Una agrupación de objetos en la que el orden no es importante.

Counting the ways to choose two essays to write from eight possibilities involves a *combination*.

Contar las maneras de escoger dos ensayos para escribir entre ocho posibilidades implica una *combinación*.

common factor (p. 236) A whole number that is a factor of two or more nonzero whole numbers.

factor común (pág. 236) Un número natural que es factor de dos o más números naturales distintos de cero.

The *common factors* of 64 and 120 are 1, 2, 4, and 8.

Los *factores comunes* de 64 y 120 son 1, 2, 4 y 8.

common multiple (p. 250) A whole number that is a multiple of two or more nonzero whole numbers.

múltiplo común (pág. 250) Un número natural que es múltiplo de dos o más números naturales distintos de cero.

The *common multiples* of 6 and 8 are 24, 48, 72, 96, ...

Los *múltiplos comunes* de 6 y 8 son 24, 48, 72, 96, ...

commutative property of addition (p. 149) In a sum, you can add numbers in any order. **propiedad conmutativa de la suma** (pág. 149) En una suma, puedes sumar números en cualquier orden.	$a + b = b + a$ $2 + 5 = 5 + 2$
commutative property of multiplication (p. 171) In a product, you can multiply numbers in any order. **propiedad conmutativa de la multiplicación** (pág. 171) En un producto, puedes multiplicar los números en cualquier orden.	$a \cdot b = b \cdot a$ $2 \times 6.5 = 6.5 \times 2$
compatible numbers (p. 12) Numbers that are easy to use in computations. **números compatibles** (pág. 12) Números fáciles de usar al hacer cálculos.	You can estimate the quotient $2605 \div 7$ by using the *compatible numbers* 2800 and 7. Because $2800 \div 7 = 400, 2605 \div 7 \approx 400$. Puedes estimar el cociente de $2605 \div 7$ usando los *números compatibles* 2800 y 7, ya que $2800 \div 7 = 400, 2605 \div 7 \approx 400$.
complementary angles (p. 466) Two angles whose measures have a sum of 90°. **ángulos complementarios** (pág. 466) Dos ángulos cuyas medidas suman 90°.	
complementary events (p. 684) Events that have no outcomes in common and that together contain all the outcomes of the experiment. **eventos complementarios** (pág. 684) Eventos que no tienen resultados en común y que juntos contienen todos los resultados del experimento.	Rolling an odd number on a number cube and rolling an even number on a number cube are *complementary events*, or *complements*. Al arrojar un cubo numerado, obtener un número par y obtener un número impar son *eventos complementarios* o *complementos*.
composite number (p. 231) A whole number greater than 1 that has factors other than itself and 1. **número compuesto** (pág. 231) Un número natural mayor que 1 que tiene factores distintos a sí mismo y a 1.	6 is a *composite number* because its factors are 1, 2, 3, and 6. 6 es un *número compuesto* porque sus factores son 1, 2, 3 y 6.
cone (p. 541) A solid that has one circular base and a vertex that is not in the same plane. **cono** (pág. 541) Un cuerpo geométrico que tiene una base circular y un vértice que no está en el mismo plano.	
congruent figures (p. 490) Figures with the same size and shape. **figuras congruentes** (pág. 490) Figuras que tienen el mismo tamaño y forma.	

constant term (p. 632) A term that has a number but no variable.

término constante (pág. 632) Un término que tiene un número pero no una variable.

In the expression $5y + 9$, the term 9 is a *constant term*.

En la expresión $5y + 9$, el término 9 es un *término constante*.

---

coordinate grid (p. 88, 603) *See* coordinate plane.

cuadrícula de coordenadas (pág. 88, 603) *Véase* plano de coordenadas.

---

coordinate plane (p. 603) A plane divided into four *quadrants* by a horizontal number line called the x-axis and a vertical line called the y-axis.

plano de coordenadas (pág. 603) Un plano dividido en cuatro *cuadrantes* por una recta numérica horizontal llamada eje x y una recta numérica vertical llamada eje y.

---

coordinates (p. 88) The numbers in an ordered pair that locate a point on a coordinate grid. *See also* x-coordinate and y-coordinate.

coordenadas (pág. 88) Los números en un par ordenado que ubican un punto en una cuadrícula de coordenadas. *Véase también* coordenada x y coordenada y.

The numbers 4 and 3 in the *ordered pair* (4, 3) are the *coordinates* of the graph of (4, 3), which is located 4 units to the right and 3 units up from (0, 0).

Los números 4 y 3, en el *par ordenado* (4, 3) son las *coordenadas* de la gráfica de (4, 3), que está ubicada 4 unidades hacia la derecha y 3 unidades hacia arriba a partir de (0, 0).

---

corresponding parts (p. 491) The matching sides and angles of two figures.

elementos correspondientes (pág. 491) Los lados y ángulos correspondientes de dos figuras.

Corresponding parts:
$\angle U$ and $\angle X$, $\angle V$ and $\angle Y$, $\angle W$ and $\angle Z$, $\overline{UV}$ and $\overline{XY}$, $\overline{VW}$ and $\overline{YZ}$, $\overline{UW}$ and $\overline{XZ}$.

Elementos correspondientes:
$\angle U$ y $\angle X$, $\angle V$ y $\angle Y$, $\angle W$ y $\angle Z$, $\overline{UV}$ y $\overline{XY}$, $\overline{VW}$ y $\overline{YZ}$, $\overline{UW}$ y $\overline{XZ}$.

---

cross products (p. 412) For the proportion $\frac{a}{b} = \frac{c}{d}$, where $b \neq 0$ and $d \neq 0$, the cross product are ad and bc.

productos cruzados (pág. 412) Para la proporción $\frac{a}{b} = \frac{c}{d}$, donde $b \neq 0$ y $d \neq 0$, los productos cruzados son ad y bc.

In the proportion $\frac{2}{3} = \frac{8}{12}$, the *cross products* are $2 \cdot 12$ and $3 \cdot 8$.

Los *productos cruzados* de la proporción $\frac{2}{3} = \frac{8}{12}$, son $2 \cdot 12$ y $3 \cdot 8$.

cube (p. 541) A rectangular prism with 6 congruent square faces.

cubo (pág. 541) Un prisma rectangular que tiene 6 caras cuadradas congruentes.

See solid.

Véase cuerpo geométrico.

---

cubed (p. 16) A number cubed is the third power of the number.

elevado al cubo (pág. 16) Un número elevado al cubo es la tercera potencia del número.

4 *cubed* indicates 4^3, or 64.

4 *elevado al cubo* indica 4^3 ó 64.

---

cylinder (p. 541) A solid with two parallel bases that are congruent circles.

cilindro (pág. 541) Un cuerpo geométrico que tiene dos bases paralelas que son círculos congruentes.

bases/bases

D

data (p. 76) Information, often given in the form of numbers or facts.

datos (pág. 76) Información, dada frecuentemente en forma de números o hechos.

---

decimal (p. 120) A number that is written using the base-ten place value system. Each place value is ten times the place value to the right.

decimal (pág. 120) Un número que se escribe usando el sistema de valor posicional de base diez. Cada valor posicional es diez veces el valor posicional a la derecha.

The *decimal* 3.12 represents 3 ones plus 1 tenth plus 2 hundredths, or three and twelve hundredths.

El *decimal* 3.12 representa 3 unidades más 1 décima más 2 centésimas, o tres y doce centésimas.

---

degree (°) (p. 461) A unit used to measure angles. There are 180° on a *protractor*, a semicircular tool used to measure degrees.

grado (°) (pág. 461) Unidad de medida para ángulos. Hay 180° en un *transportador*, una herramienta usada para medir grados.

The measure of the angle is 90°.
La medida del ángulo es 90°.

---

denominator (p. 753) The number below the fraction bar in a fraction. It represents the number of equal parts into which the whole is divided or the number of objects that make up the set.

denominador (pág. 753) El número debajo de la barra de fracción. Representa el número de partes iguales en las que un todo es dividido o el número de objetos que hacen el todo.

In the fraction $\frac{3}{4}$, the *denominator* is 4.

En la fracción $\frac{3}{4}$, el *denominador* es 4.

diagonal (p. 486) A segment, other than a side, that connects two vertices of a polygon.

diagonal (pág. 486) Un segmento, distinto de un lado, que conecta dos vértices de un polígono.

diagonals/
diagonales

---

diameter of a circle (p. 525) The distance across the circle through its center.

diámetro de un círculo (pág. 525) La distancia que atraviesa el círculo por el centro.

See **circumference.**

Véase **circunferencia.**

---

difference (p. 4, 742) The result when two numbers are subtracted.

diferencia (pág. 4, 742) El resultado cuando un número se resta de otro número.

The *difference* of 7 and 3 is 7 − 3, or 4.

La *diferencia* de 7 y 3 es 7 − 3, ó 4.

---

digit (p. 737) Any of the numbers 0, 1, 2, 3, 4, 5, 6, 7, 8, or 9.

dígito (pág. 737) Cualquiera de los números 0, 1, 2, 3, 4, 5, 6, 7, 8 ó 9.

In the whole number 127,891, the *digit* 8 has a value of 800, or 8 × 100, because it is in the hundreds' place.

En el número natural 127,891, el *dígito* 8 tiene un valor de 800, u 8 × 100, porque está en la posición de las centenas.

---

discount (p. 435) An amount subtracted from the regular price of an item to get the sale price.

descuento (pág. 435) Una cantidad restada del precio habitual de un artículo para obtener el precio de oferta.

When $40 sneakers are on sale at 25% off, the *discount* is 25% of $40, or $10.

Cuando los zapatos de tenis de $40 están en oferta con un 25% menos de descuento, el *descuento* es 25% de $40, ó $10.

---

distributive property (p. 175) You can multiply a number and a sum by multiplying the number by each part of the sum and then adding these products. The same property applies to subtraction.

propiedad distributiva (pág. 175) Para multiplicar un número y una suma puedes multiplicar el número por cada parte de la suma y luego sumar estos productos. La misma propiedad se aplica a la resta.

$$a(b + c) = ab + ac$$
$$3(4 + 6) = 3(4) + 3(6)$$

$$a(b - c) = ab - ac$$
$$2(8 - 5) = 2(8) - 2(5)$$

---

dividend (p. 4) A number that is divided by another number.

dividendo (pág. 4) Un número que es dividido por otro número.

In 18 ÷ 6 = 3, the *dividend* is 18.

En 18 ÷ 6 = 3, el *dividendo* es 18.

---

divisible (p. 230) A number is divisible by another number if that other number is a factor of the first.

divisible (pág. 230) Un número es divisible por otro número si ese otro número es un factor del primero.

Because 3 × 4 = 12, 12 is *divisible* by 3 and by 4.

Como 3 × 4 = 12, 12 es *divisible* por 3 y por 4.

divisor (p. 4) The number by which another number is divided.

divisor (pág. 4) El número por el que otro número es dividido.

In $18 \div 6 = 3$, the *divisor* is 6.

En $18 \div 6 = 3$, el *divisor* es 6.

---

double bar graph (p. 84) A bar graph that shows two sets of data on the same graph.

gráfica de doble barra (pág. 84) Una gráfica de barras que muestra dos conjuntos de datos en la misma gráfica.

**Favorite Zoo Animal/
Animal favorito del zoológico**

Sixth grade/
Sexto grado

Seventh grade/
Séptimo grado

---

edges of a solid (p. 542) The segments where the faces meet.

aristas de un cuerpo geométrico (pág. 542) Los segmentos de recta donde se encuentran dos caras del cuerpo geométrico.

See vertex of a solid.

Véase vértice de un cuerpo geométrico.

---

elapsed time (p. 323) The amount of time between a start time and an end time.

tiempo transcurrido (pág. 323) La cantidad de tiempo entre una hora inicial y una hora final.

The *elapsed time* from 7:15 A.M. to 12 P.M. is 4 hours and 45 minutes.

El *tiempo transcurrido* entre las 7:15 A.M. y las 12:00 P.M. es de 4 horas y 45 minutos.

---

element (p. 689) An object in a set.

elemento (pág. 689) Un objeto en un conjunto.

5 is an *element* of the set of whole numbers, $W = \{0, 1, 2, 3, 4, 5, \ldots\}$.

5 es un *elemento* en el conjunto de los números naturales $N = \{0, 1, 2, 3, 4, 5, \ldots\}$.

---

empty set (p. 689) A set with no elements written as $\varnothing$.

conjunto vacío (pág. 689) Un conjunto que no tiene elementos y se expresa como $\varnothing$.

The set of fraction whole numbers = $\varnothing$.

El conjunto de números naturales que son fracciones = $\varnothing$.

---

endpoint (p. 455) *See* segment *and* ray.

extremo (pág. 455) *Véase* segmento *y* semirrecta.

---

equation (p. 34) A mathematical sentence formed by placing an equal sign (=) between two expressions.

ecuación (pág. 34) Un enunciado matemático que se forma colocando un signo de igualdad (=) entre dos expresiones.

$3y = 21$ and $x - 3 = 7$ are *equations*.

$3y = 21$ y $x - 3 = 7$ son *ecuaciones*.

equilateral triangle (p. 472) A triangle with three sides of the same length. **triángulo equilátero** (pág. 472) Un triángulo que tiene tres lados de la misma longitud.	
equivalent fractions (p. 243) Fractions that represent the same number. **fracciones equivalentes** (pág. 243) Fracciones que representan el mismo número.	$\frac{5}{15}$ and $\frac{20}{60}$ are *equivalent fractions* that both represent $\frac{1}{3}$. $\frac{5}{15}$ y $\frac{20}{60}$ son *fracciones equivalentes* porque ambas representan $\frac{1}{3}$.
equivalent ratios (p. 403) Ratios that can be written as equivalent fractions. **razones equivalentes** (pág. 403) Razones que pueden escribirse como fracciones equivalentes.	*See* equivalent fractions. *Véase* fracciones equivalentes.
estimate (p. 745) To find an approximate solution to the problem. **estimar** (pág. 745) Hallar una solución aproximada a un problema.	You can *estimate* the sum $88 + 51$ as $90 + 50$, or 140. Puedes *estimar* la suma de $88 + 51$ como $90 + 50$, ó 140.
evaluate (p. 21) To find the value of an expression. **hallar el valor** (pág. 21) Encontrar el valor de una expresión.	To *evaluate* $2t - 1$ when $t = 3$, substitute 3 for t and find the value of $2 \times 3 - 1$. So, $2t - 1 = 5$ when $t = 3$. Para *hallar el valor* de $2t - 1$ cuando $t = 3$, substituye 3 por t para hallar el valor de $2 \times 3 - 1$. Así que, $2t - 1 = 5$ cuando $t = 3$.
event (p. 682) A collection of outcomes of an experiment. **evento** (pág. 682) Un conjunto de resultados de un experimento.	The *event* "getting an odd number" on a number cube consists of the outcomes 1, 3, and 5. El *evento* "obtener un número impar" en un cubo numerado consiste en los resultados 1, 3 y 5.
experimental probability (p. 702) A probability based on repeated trials of an experiment. The experimental probability of an event is given by: $P(\text{event}) = \dfrac{\text{Number of successes}}{\text{Number of trials}}$ **probabilidad experimental** (pág. 702) Una probabilidad basada en el número de ensayos de un experimento. La probabilidad experimental de un evento se expresa: $P(\text{evento}) = \dfrac{\text{Números de éxitos}}{\text{Número de ensayos}}$	During one month, your school bus is on time 17 out of 22 school days. The *experimental probability* that the bus is on time is: $P(\text{bus is on time}) = \frac{17}{22} \approx 0.773$ Durante un mes, tu autobús llega a tiempo 17 de 22 días escolares. La *probabilidad experimental* de que el autobús llegue a tiempo es: $P(\text{autobús a tiempo}) = \frac{17}{22} \approx 0.773$

exponent (p. 15) The exponent of a power is the number of times the factor is repeated.

exponente (pág. 15) El exponente de una potencia es el número de veces que se repite el factor.

The *exponent* of the power 2^3 is 3.

El *exponente* de la potencia 2^3 es 3.

F

faces of a solid (p. 542) The polygons that form the solid figure.

caras de un cuerpo geométrico (pág. 542) Los polígonos que forman el cuerpo geométrico.

See vertex of a solid.

Véase vértice de un cuerpo geométrico.

factor (p. 15) When whole numbers other than zero are multiplied together, each number is a factor of the product.

factor (pág. 15) Cuando los números naturales distintos de cero se multiplican entre sí, cada número es un factor del producto.

Because $2 \times 3 \times 7 = 42$, 2, 3, and 7 are *factors* of 42.

Como $2 \times 3 \times 7 = 42$, 2, 3 y 7 son *factores* de 42.

factor tree (p. 232) A diagram that can be used to write the prime factorization of a number.

árbol de factores (pág. 232) Un diagrama que puede usarse para escribir la descomposición de un número en factores primos.

```
        90
      /    \
     9  ×  10
    / \    / \
   3 × 3 × 2 × 5
```

favorable outcomes (p. 682) Once you specify an event, the outcomes for that event are *favorable outcomes*.

resultados favorables (pág. 682) Una vez que un evento se especifica, los resultados de ese evento son *resultados favorables*.

If you toss a number cube, the *favorable outcomes* for getting an odd number are 1, 3, and 5.

Al lanzar un cubo numerado, los *resultados favorables* para el evento "obtener un número impar" son 1, 3 y 5.

fraction (p. 243) A number of the form $\frac{a}{b}$ ($b \neq 0$) used to describe parts of a whole or a set.

fracción (pág. 243) Un número de la forma $\frac{a}{b}$ ($b \neq 0$) usado para describir partes de un todo o de un conjunto.

$\frac{3}{8}$

frequency table (p. 76) A table that displays the number of times each item or category occurs in a data set.

tabla de frecuencias (pág. 76) Una tabla que muestra cuántas veces aparecen determinados elementos o categorías en un conjunto de datos.

Art Project/ Proyecto de arte	Tally/ Marca	Frequency/ Frecuencia
painting/pintura	卌 l	6
sculpture/escultura	llll	4
drawing/dibujo	ll	2

front-end estimation (p. 144) A method of estimating a sum by adding the front-end digits and using the remaining digits to adjust the sum.

estimación por la izquierda (pág. 144) Un método para estimar una suma sumando los dígitos de la izquierda y usando los dígitos restantes para ajustar la suma.

To estimate the sum 3.75 + 1.28 + 6.93, first add the ones: 3 + 1 + 6 = 10. Then estimate the sum of the remaining digits: $0.75 + 0.28 + 0.93 \approx 2$.
The sum is about 10 + 2, or 12.

Para estimar la suma de 3.75 + 1.28 + 6.93, suma primero las unidades: 3 + 1 + 6 = 10. Luego estima la suma de los dígitos restantes: $0.75 + 0.28 + 0.93 \approx 2$.
La suma es aproximadamente 10 + 2 ó 12.

function (p. 654) A pairing of two values, called an *input* and an *output*. In a function, each input has exactly one output.

función (pág. 654) La asociación de dos valores, llamados *entrada* y *salida*. En una función, cada entrada tiene exactamente una salida.

Input/ Entrada, x	Output/ Salida, y
-2	-1
-1	0
0	1
1	2
2	3

G

graph of an inequality (p. 652) All the points on a number line that represent the solution of the inequality.

gráfica de una desigualdad (pág. 652) Todos los puntos de una recta numérica que representan la solución de la desigualdad.

The number line shows the solution of $x < 2$. The open dot at 2 shows that 2 is not part of the solution.

La recta numérica muestra la solución de $x < 2$. El punto hueco en 2 muestra que 2 no es parte de la solución.

greatest common factor (GCF) (p. 236) The largest of the common factors of two or more nonzero whole numbers.

máximo común divisor (MCD) (pág. 236) El mayor de los factores comunes de dos o más números naturales distintos de cero.

The *greatest common factor* of 64 and 120 is the greatest of the common factors 1, 2, 4, and 8, which is 8.

El *máximo común divisor* de 64 y 120 es el mayor de los factores comunes 1, 2, 4 y 8, que es 8.

grouping symbols (p. 21) Symbols such as parentheses, brackets, or fraction bars that group parts of an expression.

signos de agrupación (pág. 21) Signos tales como paréntesis, corchetes o barras de fracción que agrupan partes de una expresión.

The parentheses in $12 \div (4 - 1)$ are *grouping symbols* that indicate that the subtraction is done first.

Los paréntesis en $12 \div (4 - 1)$ son *signos de agrupación* que indican que la resta se hace primero.

height of a parallelogram (p. 514) The perpendicular distance between the side whose length is the base and the opposite side.

altura de un paralelogramo (pág. 514) La distancia perpendicular entre el lado cuya longitud es la base y el lado opuesto.

height/altura, *h*

base/base, *b*

height of a triangle (p. 518) The perpendicular distance between the side whose length is the base and the vertex opposite that side.

altura de un triángulo (pág. 518) La distancia perpendicular entre el lado cuya longitud es la base y el vértice opuesto a ese lado.

height/altura, *h*

base/base, *b*

height/altura, *h*

base/base, *b*

height/altura, *h*

base/base, *b*

hexagon (p. 485) A polygon with six sides.

hexágono (pág. 485) Polígono que tiene seis lados.

image (p. 604) The new figure that results from the translation, reflection, or rotation of a figure in a coordinate plane.

imagen (pág. 604) La figura nueva formada por la traslación, reflexión o rotación de una figura en un plano de coordenadas.

See translation, rotation, *and* reflection.

Véase traslación, rotación *y* reflexión.

improper fraction (p. 260) Any fraction in which the numerator is greater than or equal to the denominator.

fracción impropia (pág. 260) Una fracción en la cual el numerador es mayor que el denominador o igual a él.

$\frac{21}{8}$ and $\frac{6}{6}$ are *improper fractions.*

$\frac{21}{8}$ y $\frac{6}{6}$ son *fracciones impropias.*

independent events (p. 696) Events for which the occurrence of one event does not affect the likelihood that the other event will occur.

eventos independientes (pág. 696) Dos eventos tales que la ocurrencia de uno no afecta la probabilidad de que ocurra el otro.

Rolling a number cube and then flipping a coin are *independent events.*

Lanzar un cubo numerado y después lanzar una moneda son *eventos independientes.*

inequality (p. 651) A statement formed by placing an inequality symbol such as < (is less than) or > (is greater than) between two expressions.

$2 > x$, $n + 12 < 54$, and $x - 7 \leq 5$ are *inequalities*.

desigualdad (pág. 651) Un enunciado matemático formado colocando un signo de desigualdad, como < (es menor que) o > (es mayor que), entre dos expresiones.

$2 > x$, $n + 12 < 54$ y $x - 7 \leq 5$ son *desigualdades*.

---

input (p. 654) *See* function.

entrada (pág. 654) *Véase* función.

---

input-output table (p. 653) A table used to represent a function by listing the *output* for each of the several different *inputs*.

See **function.**

tabla de entrada-salida (pág. 653) Una tabla usada para representar una función enumerando la *salida* para cada una de las diferentes *entradas*.

Véase **función.**

---

integers (p. 573) The numbers . . . , –5, –4, –3, –2, –1, 0, 1, 2, 3, 4, 5 . . . .

See **number line.**

números enteros (pág. 573) Los números ..., –5, –4, –3, –2, –1, 0, 1, 2, 3, 4, 5...

Véase **recta numérica.**

---

interest (p. 436) An amount of money paid for the use of money.

See **simple interest.**

interés (pág. 436) Una cantidad de dinero pagada por el uso de dinero.

Véase **interés simple.**

---

intersecting lines (p. 456) Lines in a plane that meet at a point.

rectas secantes (pág. 456) Rectas en un plano que se encuentran en un punto.

---

intersection of a set (p. 689) The set of all elements in *both* of two given sets.

intersección de conjuntos (pág. 689) El conjunto de todos los elementos *comunes* en dos conjuntos dados.

---

inverse operations (p. 740) Operations that "undo" each other, such as addition and subtraction or multiplication and division.

operaciones inversas (pág. 740) Operaciones que se "deshacen" mutuamente, como la suma y la resta, y la multiplicación y la división.

---

isosceles triangle (p. 472) A triangle with at least two sides of the same length.

triángulo isósceles (pág. 472) Un triángulo que tiene al menos dos lados de la misma longitud.

L

leading digit (p. 12) The leading digit of a whole number is the first digit at the left.

dígito dominante (pág. 12) El dígito dominante de un número natural es el primer dígito a la izquierda.

The *leading digit* of 59 is 5.

El *dígito dominante* de 59 es 5.

---

leaf (p. 709) The last digit on the right of a number displayed in the stem-and-leaf plot.

hoja (pág. 709) El último dígito a la derecha de un número representado en un diagrama de tallo y hojas.

See stem-and-leaf plot.

Véase diagrama de tallo y hojas.

---

least common denominator (LCD) (p. 254) The least common multiple of the denominators of two or more fractions.

mínimo común denominador (m.c.d.) (pág. 254) El mínimo común múltiplo de los denominadores de dos o más fracciones.

The *least common denominator* of $\frac{5}{6}$ and $\frac{7}{9}$ is the least common multiple of 6 and 9, or 18.

El *mínimo común denominador* de $\frac{5}{6}$ y $\frac{7}{9}$ es el mínimo común múltiplo de 6 y 9, ó 18.

---

least common multiple (LCM) (p. 251) The smallest of the common multiples of two or more nonzero whole numbers.

mínimo común múltiplo (m.c.m.) (pág. 251) El menor de los múltiplos comunes de dos o más números naturales distintos de cero.

The *least common multiple* of 9 and 12 is the smallest of the common multiples 36, 72, 108, . . . , or 36.

El *mínimo común múltiplo* de 9 y 12 es el menor de los múltiplos comunes 36, 72, 108, ... ó 36.

---

like terms (p. 633) Terms that have identical variable parts. (Two or more constant terms are considered like terms.)

términos semejantes (pág. 633) Términos que tienen partes variables idénticas. (Dos o más términos constantes se consideran términos semejantes.)

In the expression $x + 4 - 2x + 1$, x and $-2x$ are *like terms*, and 4 and 1 are *like terms*.

En la expresión $x + 4 - 2x + 1$, x y $-2x$ son *términos semejantes*, y 4 y 1 son *términos semejantes*.

---

line (p. 455) A set of points the extends without end in two opposite directions.

recta (pág. 455) Una secuencia de puntos que se extiende infinitamente en dos direcciones opuestas.

$\overleftrightarrow{RS}$ or $\overleftrightarrow{SR}$
$\overleftrightarrow{RS}$ o $\overleftrightarrow{SR}$

line graph (p. 89) A graph that represents data using points connected by line segments to show how quantities change over time.

gráfica lineal (pág. 89) Un tipo de gráfica que representa datos usando puntos conectados por segmentos de recta para mostrar cómo las cantidades cambian en el tiempo.

**Growth of Puppy/
Crecimiento del cachorro**

line of reflection (p. 608) *See* reflection.

línea de reflexión (pág. 608) *Véase* reflexión.

line of symmetry (p. 494) *See* line symmetry.

línea de simetría (pág. 494) *Véase* simetría lineal.

line plot (p. 77) A number line diagram that uses X marks to show the frequencies of items or categories being tallied.

diagrama lineal (pág. 77) Un diagrama de recta numérica que usa marcas X para mostrar las frecuencias con las que se marcan artículos o categorías.

line symmetry (p. 494) A figure has line symmetry if a line can be drawn that divides the figure into two congruent parts that are mirror images of each other. The line is the *line of symmetry*.

simetría lineal (pág. 494) Una figura tiene simetría lineal si se puede pasar una recta que divida la figura en dos partes congruentes que sean imágenes reflejas entre sí. La recta es la *línea de simetría*.

lines of symmetry/
líneas de simetría

linear function (p. 661) A function whose graph is a straight line.

función lineal (pág. 661) Una función cuya gráfica es una recta.

lower extreme (p. 714) The least value of a data set.

extremo inferior (pág. 714) El menor valor en un conjunto de datos.

See **box-and-whisker plot.**

Véase **diagrama de líneas y bloques.**

lower quartile (p. 714) The median of the lower half of a data set.	*See* box-and-whisker plot.
cuartil inferior (pág. 714) La mediana de la mitad inferior de un conjunto de datos.	*Véase* diagrama de líneas y bloques.

M

mean (p. 99) The sum of the data values divided by the number of values.	The *mean* of the values 7, 10, 9, and 6 is $$\frac{7 + 10 + 9 + 6}{4} = \frac{32}{4} = 8.$$
media (pág. 99) La suma de los valores en un conjunto de datos dividida por el número de valores.	La *media* de los valores 7, 10, 9 y 6 es $$\frac{7 + 10 + 9 + 6}{4} = \frac{32}{4} = 8.$$
median (p. 99) The middle data value when the values are written in numerical order. If a data set has an even number of values, the median is the mean of the two middle values.	The *median* of the ages 36, 36, 37, 37, 39, 40, 41 is 37, because 37 is the middle number.
mediana (pág. 99) El valor que está en el medio de un conjunto de datos cuando los valores están escritos en orden numérico. Si un conjunto de datos tiene un número par de valores, la mediana es la media de los dos valores que están en el medio.	La *mediana* de las edades 36, 36, 37, 37, 39, 40, 41 es 37 porque 37 es el número que está en el medio.
mixed number (p. 260) The sum of a whole number and a fraction less than 1.	$2\frac{5}{8}$ is a *mixed number*.
número mixto (pág. 260) La suma de un número natural y de una fracción menor que 1.	$2\frac{5}{8}$ es un *número mixto*.
mode (p. 99) The data value that occurs most often. A data set can have one mode, more that one mode, or no mode.	In the data set 36, 36, 37, 37, 39, 40, 41, both 36 and 37 occur twice, so there are two *modes*, 36 and 37.
moda (pág. 99) El valor que ocurre con mayor frecuencia en un conjunto de datos. Un conjunto de datos puede tener una moda, más de una moda o ninguna moda.	En el conjunto de datos 36, 36, 37, 37, 39, 40, 41, tanto 36 como 37 aparecen dos veces, por lo tanto hay dos *modas*: 36 y 37.
multiple (p. 250) A multiple of a whole number is the product of the number and any nonzero whole number.	The *multiples* of 2 are 2, 4, 6, 8, 10, ...
múltiplo (pág. 250) Un múltiplo de un número natural es el producto de ese número y cualquier número natural distinto de cero.	Los *múltiplos* de 2 son 2, 4, 6, 8, 10, ...

N

negative integers (p. 573) Integers that are less than 0.	The *negative integers* are $-1, -2, -3, -4, \ldots$.
números enteros negativos (pág. 573) Números enteros menores que cero.	Los *números enteros negativos* son $-1, -2, -3, -4, \ldots$

net (p. 545) A two-dimensional figure that can be folded to form a solid.

red (pág. 545) Una figura bidimensional que forma un cuerpo geométrico cuando se dobla.

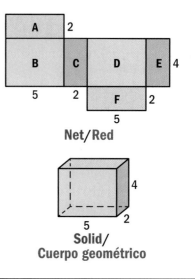

Net/Red

Solid/
Cuerpo geométrico

---

number fact family (p. 738) Four number facts consisting of three numbers related by inverse operations.

familia de operaciones numéricas (pág. 738) Cuatro operaciones numéricas que consisten en tres números relacionados por operaciones inversas.

The facts $8 + 2 = 10, 10 - 2 = 8, 2 + 8 = 10$, and $10 - 8 = 2$ are in the same *number fact family*.

Las operaciones $8 + 2 = 10, 10 - 2 = 8, 2 + 8 = 10$ y $10 - 8 = 2$ están en la misma *familia de operaciones numéricas.*

---

number line (p. 573, 741) A line whose points are associated with numbers. You can use a number line to compare and order numbers. The numbers on a number line increase from left to right.

recta numérica (pág. 573, 741) Una recta cuyos puntos se asocian con números. Se puede usar una recta numérica para comparar y ordenar números. En una recta numérica los números aumentan de izquierda a derecha.

$-2 \quad -1 \quad 0 \quad 1 \quad 2$

---

numerator (p. 753) The number above the fraction bar in a fraction. It represents the number of equal parts out of the whole or the number of objects from the set that are being considered.

numerador (pág. 753) El número encima de la barra de fracción, que representa el número de partes iguales del total o el número de objetos del conjunto al que se refiere.

In the fraction $\frac{3}{4}$, the *numerator* is 3.

En la fracción $\frac{3}{4}$, el *numerador* es 3.

---

numerical expression (p. 21) An expression, consisting of numbers and operations to be performed, that represents a particular value.

expresión numérica (pág. 21) Una expresión que consiste en números y operaciones a realizar y representa un valor particular.

The *numerical expression* $2 \times 3 - 1$ represents 5.

La *expresión numérica* $2 \times 3 - 1$ representa 5.

obtuse angle (p. 465) An angle whose measure is between 90° and 180°.

ángulo obtuso (pág. 465) Ángulo cuya medida es mayor de 90° y menor de 180°.

obtuse triangle (p. 471) A triangle with one obtuse angle.

triángulo obtusángulo (pág. 471) Triángulo que tiene un ángulo obtuso.

octagon (p. 485) A polygon with eight sides.

octágono (pág. 485) Polígono que tiene ocho lados.

opposites (p. 574) Numbers that are the same distance from 0 on a number line, but are on opposite sides of 0.

opuestos (pág. 574) Dos números que están a la misma distancia de 0 en una recta numérica pero en lados opuestos de 0.

3 and −3 are *opposites*.

3 y −3 son *opuestos*.

order of operations (p. 21) The order in which to perform operations when evaluating expressions with more than one operation.

orden de las operaciones (pág. 21) Orden en que se realizan las operaciones para hallar el valor de una expresión que tiene más de una operación.

$$1 + 3^2(5 - 1) = 1 + 3^2(4) =$$
$$1 + 9(4) = 1 + 36 = 37$$

ordered pair (p. 88) *See* coordinates.

par ordenado (pág. 88) *Véase* coordenadas.

See coordinate plane.

Véase plano de coordenadas.

origin (p. 88) The point (0, 0) on a coordinate plane.

origen (pág. 88) El punto (0, 0) de un plano de coordenadas.

See coordinate plane.

Véase plano de coordenadas.

outcome (p. 682) A possible result of an experiment.

resultado (pág. 682) Un resultado posible de un experimento.

When you toss a coin, the *outcomes* are heads and tails.

Cuando lanzas una moneda, los *resultados* son cara y cruz.

output (p. 654) *See* function.

salida (pág. 654) *Véase* función.

ENGLISH-SPANISH GLOSSARY

parallel lines (p. 456) Lines in the same plane that never meet.

rectas paralelas (pág. 456) Rectas en el mismo plano que nunca se encuentran.

parallelogram (p. 480) A quadrilateral with two pairs of parallel sides.

paralelogramo (pág. 480) Cuadrilátero que tiene dos pares de lados paralelos.

pentagon (p. 485) A polygon with five sides.

pentágono (pág. 485) Polígono que tiene cinco lados.

percent (p. 425) A ratio that compares a number to 100. *Percent* means "per hundred."

porcentaje (pág. 425) Razón que compara un número con 100. *Porcentaje* significa "por cada cien".

$$43\% = \frac{43}{100} = 0.43$$

perimeter (p. 66) The distance around a figure, measured in linear units such as feet, inches, or meters.

perímetro (pág. 66) La distancia alrededor de una figura, que se mide en unidades lineales, tales como pies, pulgadas o metros.

7 cm 5 cm 8 cm

Perimeter = 5 + 7 + 8, or 20 cm

Perímetro = 5 + 7 + 8, ó 20 cm

permutation (p. 692) An arrangement of objects in which order is important.

permutación (pág. 692) Disposición de objetos en la cual el orden es importante.

Counting the ways to list the members of the student council in a program involves a *permutation*.

Contar las maneras de hacer una lista de los miembros del consejo estudiantil en un programa implica una *permutación*.

perpendicular bisector (p. 539) A line that divides a segment into two segments of equal length and forms four right angles.

bisector perpendicular (pág. 539) Una recta que divide un segmento en dos segmentos de igual longitud y forma cuatro ángulos.

perpendicular lines (p. 514) Two lines are perpendicular if they meet at a right angle.

rectas perpendiculares (pág. 514) Dos rectas son perpendiculares si se intersecan formando un ángulo recto.

pi (π) (p. 525) The ratio of the circumference of a circle to its diameter.

pi (π) (pág. 525) La razón entre la circunferencia de un círculo y su diámetro.

You can use 3.14 or $\frac{22}{7}$ to approximate π.

Puedes usar 3.14 ó $\frac{22}{7}$ para calcular la aproximación de π.

---

pictograph (p. 759) A graph that uses pictures or symbols to display data.

pictograma (pág. 759) Gráfica que utiliza imágenes o símbolos para representar datos.

Color of Eyes/
Color de ojos

Brown/Marrón
Blue/Azul
Green/Verde

= 2 students/2 estudiantes

---

place value (p. 737) The place value of each digit in a number depends on its position within the number.

valor posicional (pág. 737) El valor posicional de cada uno de los dígitos de un número depende de la posición que ocupa dentro del número.

In 723, the 2 is in the tens' place and it has a value of 20.

En 723, el 2 está en la posición de las decenas y tiene un valor de 20.

---

plane (p. 456) A flat surface that extends without end in all directions.

plano (pág. 456) Una superficie plana que se extiende infinitamente en todas direcciones.

---

point (p. 455) A position in space represented with a dot.

punto (pág. 455) Posición en el espacio representada por un punto.

P

---

polygon (p. 485) A closed plane figure that is formed by three or more segments called sides. Each side intersects exactly two other sides at a *vertex*.

polígono (pág. 485) Una figura plana que está formada por tres o más segmentos llamados lados. Cada lado interseca exactamente otros dos lados en un *vértice*.

vertex/vértice

---

positive integers (p. 573) Integers that are greater than 0.

números enteros positivos (pág. 573) Números enteros mayores que 0.

The *positive integers* are 1, 2, 3, 4, ...

Los *números enteros positivos* son 1, 2, 3, 4, ...

---

power (p. 15) An expression, such as 2^3, that represents a product formed by a repeated factor.

potencia (pág. 15) Una expresión, como 2^3, que representa un producto formado por un factor repetido.

The third *power* of 2 is $2^3 = 2 \times 2 \times 2$, which represents the product of three factors of 2.

La tercera *potencia* de 2 es $2^3 = 2 \times 2 \times 2$, que representa el producto de tres factores de 2.

prime factorization (p. 232) A whole number written as the product of prime factors.	The *prime factorization* of 20 is $2^2 \times 5$.
descomposición en factores primos (pág. 232) Número natural escrito como producto de factores primos.	La *descomposición en factores primos* de 20 es $2^2 \times 5$.
prime number (p. 231) A whole number greater than 1 whose only factors are 1 and itself.	59 is a *prime number*, because its only factors are 1 and itself.
número primo (pág. 231) Número natural mayor que 1 cuyos únicos factores son 1 y él mismo.	59 es un *número primo*, porque sus únicos factores son 1 y el mismo número.
principal (p. 436) An amount of money that is saved or borrowed.	If you deposit $100 in a bank account that pays 4% annual interest, then the *principal* is $100.
capital (pág. 436) Una cantidad de dinero que se ahorra o se pide prestada.	Si depositas $100 en una cuenta bancaria que paga un interés de 4% anual, entonces el *capital* es $100.
prism (p. 541) A solid with two parallel bases that are congruent polygons.	
prisma (pág. 541) Cuerpo geométrico que tiene dos bases paralelas que son polígonos congruentes.	bases/bases **Rectangular Prism/** **Triangular Prism/** **Prisma rectangular** **Prisma triangular**
probability of an event (p. 682) A measure of the likelihood that the event will occur, computed as $\frac{\text{number of favorable outcomes}}{\text{number of possible outcomes}}$ when all the outcomes are equally likely.	If you toss a number cube, the *probability* that you roll an odd number is $\frac{3}{6} = 0.5 = 50\%$.
probabilidad de un evento (pág. 682) Medida de la posibilidad de que un evento ocurra, calculada como $\frac{\text{número de resultados favorables}}{\text{número de resultados posibles}}$ cuando todos los resultados tienen las mismas posibilidades.	Si lanzas un cubo numerado, la *probabilidad* de que obtengas un número impar es $\frac{3}{6} = 0.5 = 50\%$.
product (p. 4, 743) The result when two or more numbers are multiplied.	The *product* of 3 and 4 is 3×4, or 12.
producto (pág. 4, 743) Resultado cuando se multiplican dos o más números.	El *producto* de 3 y 4 es 3×4, ó 12.
proper fraction (p. 261) A fraction in which the numerator is less than the denominator.	$\frac{2}{3}$ is a *proper fraction*.
fracción propia (pág. 261) Una fracción cuyo numerador es menor que el denominador.	$\frac{2}{3}$ es una *fracción propia*.
proportion (p. 412) An equation you write to show that two ratios are equivalent.	The equation $\frac{2}{3} = \frac{8}{12}$ is a *proportion*.
proporción (pág. 412) Una ecuación que se escribe para demostrar que dos razones son equivalentes.	La ecuación $\frac{2}{3} = \frac{8}{12}$ es una *proporción*.

pyramid (p. 541) A solid made up of polygons. The base can be any polygon, and the other polygons are triangles that share a common vertex.

pirámide (pág. 541) Cuerpo geométrico formado por polígonos. La base puede ser cualquier polígono y los otros polígonos son triángulos que comparten un vértice común.

base/base

Q

quadrants (p. 603) The four regions into which a coordinate plane is divided by the x-axis and the y-axis. *See also* coordinate plane.

cuadrantes (pág. 603) Las cuatro regiones en las que el eje x y el eje y dividen un plano de coordenadas. *Véase también* plano de coordenadas.

See coordinate plane.

Véase plano de coordenadas.

quadrilateral (p. 480) A plane figure formed by four segments called sides. Each side intersects exactly two other sides, one at each endpoint, and no two sides are part of the same line.

cuadrilátero (pág. 480) Una figura plana formada por cuatro segmentos llamados lados. Cada lado interseca exactamente otros dos lados, uno en cada extremo, y ninguno de ellos forma parte de la misma recta.

quotient (p. 4, 744) The result of a division.

cociente (pág. 4, 744) Resultado de una división.

The *quotient* of 18 and 6 is 18 ÷ 6, or 3.

El *cociente* de 18 y 6 es 18 ÷ 6 ó 3.

R

radius of a circle (p. 525) The distance from the center to any point on the circle. The plural of radius is *radii*.

radio de un círculo (pág. 525) Distancia del centro a cualquier punto del círculo.

See circumference.

Véase circunferencia.

range (p. 100) The difference between the greatest data value and the least data value.

rango (pág. 100) La diferencia entre el valor máximo y el valor mínimo en un conjunto de datos.

In the data set
36, 36, 37, 37, 39, 40, 41,
the *range* is 41 − 36 = 5.

En el conjunto de datos
36, 36, 37, 37, 39, 40, 41
el *rango* es 41 − 36 = 5.

rate (p. 407) A ratio of two measures that have different units.

tasa (pág. 407) Razón de dos medidas que tienen distintas unidades.

The International Space Station orbits Earth at an average *rate* of 15 miles every 3 seconds, or 5 miles per second.

La Estación Espacial Internacional orbita la Tierra a una *tasa* promedio de 15 millas cada 3 segundos o 5 millas por segundo.

ratio (p. 402) A ratio of a number *a* to a nonzero number *b* is the quotient when *a* is divided by *b*.

razón (pág. 402) La razón de un número *a* con un número *b* distinto de cero es el cociente que resulta de dividir *a* por *b*.

The *ratio* of *a* to *b* can be written as $\frac{a}{b}$, as *a* : *b*, or as "*a* to *b*."

La *razón* de *a* a *b* puede escribirse como $\frac{a}{b}$, como *a* : *b* o como "*a* a *b*".

---

ray (p. 455) A part of a line that has one *endpoint* and extends without end in one direction.

semirrecta (pág. 455) Parte de una recta que tiene un *extremo* y se extiende infinitamente en una dirección.

$\overrightarrow{AB}$ with *endpoint A.*

$\overrightarrow{AB}$ con *extremo* en A.

---

reciprocals (p. 362) Two numbers whose product is 1.

recíprocos (pág. 362) Dos números cuyo producto es 1.

Because $\frac{3}{5} \times \frac{5}{3} = 1$, $\frac{3}{5}$ and $\frac{5}{3}$ are *reciprocals.*

Como $\frac{3}{5} \times \frac{5}{3} = 1$, $\frac{3}{5}$ y $\frac{5}{3}$ son *recíprocos.*

---

rectangle (p. 480) A parallelogram with four right angles.

rectángulo (pág. 480) Paralelogramo que tiene cuatro ángulos rectos.

---

rectangular prism (p. 541) A prism with rectangular bases.

prisma rectangular (pág. 541) Un prisma que tiene bases rectangulares.

See prism.

Véase prisma.

---

reflection (p. 608) An operation that flips a figure over a line called the *line of reflection* to produce a congruent mirror image.

reflexión (pág. 608) Operación que invierte una figura sobre un recta llamada *línea de reflexión* para producir una imagen refleja congruente.

The *x*-axis is the *line of reflection.*

El eje *x* es la *línea de reflexión.*

---

regular polygon (p. 486) A polygon with equal side lengths and equal angle measures.

polígono regular (pág. 486) Un polígono cuyos lados tienen igual longitud y cuyos ángulos tienen la misma medida.

Regular/Regular   Not Regular/No regular

---

regular tessellation (p. 614) A tessellation made from only one type of regular polygon.

teselado regular (pág. 614) Teselado hecho con un solo tipo de polígono regular.

remainder (p. 4, 744) If a divider does not divide a dividend evenly, the remainder is the whole number left over after the division.

residuo (pág. 4, 744) Si un divisor no divide un dividendo exactamente, el residuo es el número natural que queda después de la división.

$$\begin{array}{r} 8\ \text{R4} \\ 7\overline{)60} \\ 56 \\ \hline 4 \end{array}$$ ⟵ remainder/residuo

---

repeating decimal (p. 272) A decimal that has one or more digits that repeat forever.

decimal periódico (pág. 272) Decimal que tiene uno o más dígitos que se repiten infinitamente.

0.3333... and $2.0\overline{1}$ are *repeating decimals.*

0.3333... y $2.0\overline{1}$ son *decimales periódicos.*

---

rhombus (p. 480) A parallelogram with four sides of equal length.

rombo (pág. 480) Paralelogramo que tiene cuatro lados de la misma longitud.

---

right angle (p. 465) An angle whose measure is exactly 90°.

ángulo recto (pág. 465) Un ángulo que mide exactamente 90°.

---

right triangle (p. 471) A triangle with one right angle.

triángulo rectángulo (pág. 471) Un triángulo que tiene un ángulo recto.

---

rotation (p. 608) An operation that rotates a figure through a given *angle of rotation* about a fixed point, the *center of rotation*, to produce a congruent image.

rotación (pág. 608) Operación que hace girar una figura por un *ángulo de rotación* dado, sobre un punto fijo, el *centro de rotación*, para producir una imagen congruente.

The origin is the center of *rotation* and the angle of rotation is 90°.

El origen es el centro de *rotación* y el ángulo de rotación es 90°.

---

round (p. 739) To approximate a number to a given place value.

redondear (pág. 739) Aproximar un número a un valor posicional dado.

518 *rounded* to the nearest ten is 520, and 518 *rounded* to the nearest hundred is 500.

518 *redondeado* a la decena más próxima es 520, y 518 *redondeado* a la centena más próxima es 500.

scale (p. 72) In a scale drawing, a key that tells how the drawing's dimensions and the actual dimensions are related.

escala (pág. 72) En un dibujo a escala, una leyenda que indica la relación entre las dimensiones del dibujo y las dimensiones reales.

If the *scale* on a scale drawing is 1 in. : 10 ft, then each inch on the drawing represents 10 feet on the scale drawing.

Si la escala de un dibujo a *escala* es 1 pulg. : 10 pies, entonces cada pulgada en el dibujo representa 10 pies en el dibujo a escala.

---

scale drawing (p. 72) A drawing of an object with the same shape as the original object, but not the same size.

dibujo a escala (pág. 72) Dibujo de un objeto que tiene la misma forma del objeto original, pero no el mismo tamaño.

---

scalene triangle (p. 472) A triangle with three sides of different lengths.

triángulo escaleno (pág. 472) Triángulo que tiene tres lados de diferentes tamaños.

4 ft/4 pies

3 ft/3 pies

2 ft/2 pies

---

segment (p. 455) A part of a line that consists of two *endpoints* and all the points between them.

segmento (pág. 455) Parte de una recta que consta de dos *extremos* y todos los puntos entre éstos.

A   B

$\overline{AB}$ or $\overline{BA}$ with endpoints A and B.

$\overline{AB}$ o $\overline{BA}$ con los extremos A y B.

---

set (p. 689) A collection of distinct objects.

conjunto (pág. 689) Una agrupación de objetos distintos.

The *set* of whole numbers is $W = \{0, 1, 2, 3, 4, 5, \ldots\}$.

El *conjunto* de los números naturales es $N = \{0, 2, 3, 4, 5, \ldots\}$.

---

similar figures (p. 490) Figures with the same shape but not necessarily the same size.

figuras semejantes (pág. 490) Figuras que tienen la misma forma pero no necesariamente el mismo tamaño.

2 in./ 2 pulg.

4 in./ 4 pulg.

---

simple interest (p. 436) Interest paid only on the principal.

interés simple (pág. 436) Interés que se paga sólo sobre el capital.

If you deposit $100 in a bank account that pays 4% annual interest, you will earn $100(0.04), or $4, *simple interest* in one year.

Si depositas 100 dólares en una cuenta bancaria que paga 4% de interés anual, ganarás $100(0.04), o $4 de *interés simple* en un año.

---

simplest form of a fraction (p. 244) A fraction is in simplest form if its numerator and denominator have a greatest common factor of 1.

mínima expresión de una fracción (pág. 244) Una fracción está en su mínima expresión si el máximo común divisor del numerador y del denominador es 1.

The *simplest form* of the fraction $\frac{4}{12}$ is $\frac{1}{3}$.

La *mínima expresión* de la fracción $\frac{4}{12}$ es $\frac{1}{3}$.

skew lines (p. 458) Two lines in different planes that do not intersect.

rectas alabeadas (pág. 458) Dos rectas que no están en un mismo plano y que no se intersecan.

Lines *n* and *p* are *skew lines*.
Las rectas *n* y *p* son *rectas alabeadas*.

---

solid (p. 541) A three-dimensional figure that encloses a part of space.

cuerpo geométrico (pág. 541) Figura tridimensional que encierra una parte del espacio.

---

solution of an equation (p. 34) A number that, when substituted for a variable, makes the equation true.

solución de una ecuación (pág. 34) Número que, cuando sustituye la variable en una ecuación, hace verdadera la ecuación.

10 is the *solution of the equation* $x - 3 = 7$.

La *solución de la ecuación* $x - 3 = 7$.

---

solution of an inequality (p. 651) The group of all values of the variable that make the inequality true.

solución de una desigualdad (pág. 651) Grupo de todos los valores de la variable que hacen verdadera la desigualdad.

The *solution of the inequality* $x + 2 \geq 3$ is $x \geq 1$, or all numbers that are greater than or equal to 1.

La *solución de la desigualdad* $x + 2 \geq 3$ es $x \geq 1$, o todos los números que son mayores que o iguales a 1.

---

solve an equation (p. 35) To find all the solutions of an equation by finding all the values of the variable that make the equation true.

resolver una ecuación (pág. 35) Hallar todas las soluciones de una ecuación al encontrar todos los valores de la variable que hacen verdadera la ecuación.

To *solve the equation* $n \div 4 = 7$, find the number that can be divided by 4 to equal 7; $28 \div 4 = 7$, so the solution is 28.

Para *resolver la ecuación* $n \div 4 = 7$, halla el número que dividido por 4 sea igual a 7; $28 \div 4 = 7$, por lo tanto la solución es 28.

---

solve an inequality (p. 651) Find all values of the variable that make the inequality true.

resolver una desigualdad (pág. 651) Hallar todos los valores de la variable que hacen verdadera la desigualdad.

To *solve the inequality* $x + 2 \geq 3$, subtract 2 from each side to get $x \geq 1$.

Para *resolver la desigualdad* $x + 2 \geq 3$, resta 2 de cada lado para obtener $x \geq 1$.

---

sphere (p. 541) The set of points in space that are a given distance from a given point.

esfera (pág. 541) Un conjunto de puntos en el espacio que están a la misma distancia de un punto determinado.

square (p. 480) A parallelogram with four right angles and four sides of equal length.

cuadrado (pág. 480) Paralelogramo que tiene cuatro ángulos rectos y cuatro lados de igual longitud.

---

squared (p. 16) A number squared is the second power of the number.

elevado al cuadrado (pág. 16) Un número elevado al cuadrado es la segunda potencia del número.

3 *squared* indicates 3^2, or 9.

3 *elevado al cuadrado* indica 3^2 ó 9.

---

stem (p. 709) All the digits except the last digit on the right of a number displayed in a stem-and-leaf plot.

tallo (pág. 709) Todos los dígitos excepto el último de la derecha de un número representado en un diagrama de tallo y hojas.

See stem-and-leaf plot.

Véase diagrama de tallo y hojas.

---

stem-and-leaf plot (p. 709) A data display that can be used to organize a large set of data.

diagrama de tallo y hojas (pág. 709) Diagrama que se usa para organizar un conjunto grande de datos.

0	7 8 9 9
1	1 3 5 5 6 7
2	0 1 3
3	0 2

Key/Clave: 2 | 3 = 23

stem/   leaf/
tallo   hoja

---

straight angle (p. 465) An angle whose measure is exactly 180°.

ángulo llano (pág. 465) Un ángulo que mide exactamente 180°.

---

success (p. 702) In experimental probability, any trial where the desired outcome occurs.

éxito (pág. 702) En la probabilidad experimental, cualquier ensayo en el que ocurren los resultados deseados.

If you want to pick a blue marble out of a bag of 20 marbles where only 7 are blue marbles, then *success* is picking a blue marble.

Si quieres sacar una canica azul de una bolsa de 20 canicas en la que sólo 7 son azules, sacar una canica azul es un *éxito*.

---

sum (p. 3, 742) The result when two or more numbers are added.

suma (pág. 3, 742) El resultado cuando se suman dos o más números.

The *sum* of 2 and 5 is 2 + 5, or 7.

La *suma* de 2 y 5 es 2 + 5, ó 7.

---

supplementary angles (p. 466) Two angles whose measures have a sum of 180°.

ángulos suplementarios (pág. 466) Dos ángulos cuyas medidas suman 180°.

48° 132°

surface area of a prism (p. 545) The sum of the areas of the faces of the prism. Surface area is measured in square units.

área de la superficie de un prisma (pág. 545) Suma de las áreas de las caras del prisma. El área de la superficie se mide en unidades cuadradas.

Surface Area = $2(8 \times 6) + 2(8 \times 4) + 2(6 \times 4) =$ 208 square inches

Área de la superficie = $2(8 \times 6) + 2(8 \times 4) + 2(6 \times 4) =$ 208 pulgadas cuadradas

---

T

terminating decimal (p. 272) A decimal that has a final digit.

decimal exacto (pág. 272) Decimal que tiene un dígito final.

0.084 and 0.6 are *terminating decimals*.

0.084 y 0.6 son *decimales exactos*.

---

terms (p. 633) The parts of an expression that are added together.

términos (pág. 633) Las partes de una expresión que se suman entre sí.

The *terms* of $2x + 3$ are $2x$ and 3.

Los *términos* de $2x + 3$ son $2x$ y 3.

---

tessellation (p. 614) A covering of a plane with congruent copies of the same pattern so that there are no gaps or overlaps.

teselado (pág. 614) La cobertura de un plano con copias congruentes del mismo patrón de modo que no haya huecos o superposiciones.

---

theoretical probability (p. 702) A probability based on all of the equally likely outcomes of an experiment. The theoretical probability of an event is given by:

$$P(\text{event}) = \frac{\text{Number of favorable outcomes}}{\text{Total number of outcomes}}$$

probabilidad teórica (pág. 702) Probabilidad basada en que todos los resultados de un experimento son igualmente probables; la probabilidad de un evento se expresa como :

$$P(\text{evento}) = \frac{\text{Número de resultados favorables}}{\text{Número total de resultados}}$$

A bag of 20 marbles contains 7 red marbles. The *theoretical probability* of randomly choosing a red marble is:

$$P(\text{red}) = \frac{7}{20} = 0.35$$

Una bolsa de 20 canicas contiene 7 canicas rojas. La *probabilidad teórica* de tomar al azar una canica roja es:

$$P(\text{roja}) = \frac{7}{20} = 0.35$$

---

transformation (p. 609) A movement of a figure in a coordinate plane. Three types of transformations are *translations*, *reflections* and *rotations*.

transformación (pág. 609) Movimiento de una figura en un plano de coordenadas. Hay tres tipos de transformaciones: *traslación*, *reflexión* y *rotación*.

See translation, rotation, *and* reflection.

Véase traslación, reflexión y rotación.

translation (p. 604) An operation that slides each point of a figure the same distance in the same direction to produce a figure that is congruent to the original figure.

traslación (pág. 604) Operación que mueve cada punto de una figura la misma distancia en la misma dirección produciendo una figura que es congruente con la figura original.

trapezoid (p. 483) A quadrilateral with exactly one pair of parallel sides.

trapecio (pág. 483) Cuadrilátero que tiene exactamente un par de lados paralelos.

tree diagram (p. 691) A diagram that shows all the possible outcomes as choices on different branches of the "tree."

diagrama de árbol (pág. 691) Diagrama que muestra como elecciones todos los resultados posibles en diferentes "ramas del árbol".

triangle (p. 471) A closed plane figure with three straight sides that connect three points.

triángulo (pág. 471) Figura plana cerrada que tiene tres lados rectos que conectan tres puntos.

triangular prism (p. 541) A prism with triangular bases.

prisma triangular (pág. 541) Prisma que tiene bases triangulares.

See prism.

Véase prisma.

U

union (p. 689) The set of all elements in *either* of two given sets.

unión de conjuntos (pág. 689) Un conjunto que incluye todos los elementos de dos conjuntos dados.

unit rate (p. 407) A rate that has a denominator of 1 unit.

tasa unitaria (pág. 407) Una tasa cuyo denominador es 1 unidad.

$9 per hour is a *unit rate*.

$9 por hora es una *tasa unitaria*.

universal set (p. 689) A set of all elements under consideration and written as U.

conjunto universal (p. 689) Un conjunto de todos los elementos bajo consideración que se expresa como U.

If the *universal set* is the set of positive integers, then $U = \{1, 2, 3, \ldots\}$.

Si el *conjunto universal* es el conjunto de los números enteros positivos, entonces $U = \{1, 2, 3, \ldots\}$.

---

upper extreme (p. 714) The greatest value of a data set.

extremo superior (pág. 714) El valor mayor en un conjunto de datos.

See box-and-whisker plot.

Véase diagrama de líneas y bloques.

---

upper quartile (p. 714) The median of the upper half of a data set.

cuartil superior (pág. 714) La mediana de la mitad superior de un conjunto de datos.

See box-and-whisker plot.

Véase diagrama de líneas y bloques.

V

variable (p. 29) A symbol, usually a letter, that represents one or more numbers.

variable (pág. 29) Símbolo, usualmente una letra, que representa uno o más números.

x is a *variable* in $4x - 3$ and in $x + 3 = 5$.

x es una *variable* en $4x - 3$ y en $x + 3 = 5$.

---

variable expression (p. 29) An expression consisting of one or more numbers, variables, and operations to be performed.

expresión variable (pág. 29) Una expresión que consiste en uno o más números, variables y operaciones a realizar.

$4x - 3$ and $2t^2$ are *variable expressions*.

$4x - 3$ y $2t^2$ son *expresiones variables*.

Venn diagram (p. 769) A diagram that uses shapes to show how sets are related.

diagrama de Venn (pág. 769) Un diagrama que usa formas para mostrar cómo se relacionan los conjuntos.

Whole numbers from 1 to 10
Números naturales de 1 a 10
Prime numbers / Números primos: 3, 7, 5
2, 4
Even numbers / Números pares: 10, 8, 6
1, 9

---

verbal model (p. 39) Words that describe how real-life values are related. Verbal models can be expressed using math symbols.

modelo verbal (pág. 39) Palabras que describen cómo se relacionan los valores en la realidad. Los modelos verbales pueden ser expresados usando signos matemáticos.

You pay $50 for a gym membership and $3 per visit. Find your total cost for 20 visits.
Verbal model:
Total cost = Membership cost + Visits cost

Pagas $50 por una cuota de socio en un gimnasio y $3 dólares por visita. Halla el costo total de 20 visitas.
Modelo verbal:
Costo total = Costo de la cuota de socio + Costo de las visitas

vertex of a polygon (p. 485) A point at which two sides of a polygon meet. The plural of vertex is *vertices*.

vértice de un polígono (pág. 485) Un punto en el que se encuentran dos lados de un polígono.

See polygon.

Véase polígono.

---

vertex of a solid (p. 542) A point where the edges meet. The plural of vertex is *vertices*.

vértice de un cuerpo geométrico (pág. 542) Punto donde se encuentran aristas.

face/cara

edge/arista

vertex/vértice

---

vertex of an angle (p. 460) The endpoint of the rays that form the angle. The plural of vertex is *vertices*.

vértice de un ángulo (pág. 460) Extremo de las semirrectas que forman el ángulo.

P

Q

vertex/vértice

R

---

vertical angles (p. 466) When two lines intersect, the angles opposite each other are vertical angles.

ángulos opuestos por el vértice (pág. 466) Cuando dos rectas se intersecan, los ángulos opuestos entre sí son ángulos opuestos por el vértice.

∠1 and ∠3 are vertical angles;
∠2 and ∠4 are also vertical angles
∠1 y ∠3 son ángulos opuestos por el vértice;
∠2 y ∠4 también son ángulos opuestos por el vértice.

---

volume of a solid (p. 550) The amount of space that the solid occupies. Volume is measured in cubic units.

volumen de un cuerpo geométrico (pág. 550) Cantidad de espacio que ocupa un cuerpo geométrico. El volumen se mide en unidades cúbicas.

4 in./4 pulg.

8 in./8 pulg.

6 in./6 pulg.

Volume = *lwh* = 6 · 8 · 4 = 192 cubic inches

Volumen = *lwh* = 6 · 8 · 4 = 192 pulgadas cúbicas

W

whole numbers (p. 737) The numbers 0, 1, 2, 3 . . . .

números naturales (pág. 737) Los números 0, 1, 2, 3...

X

x-axis (p. 603) The horizontal axis in a coordinate plane. *See also* coordinate plane.

eje x (pág. 603) Eje horizontal en un plano de coordenadas. *Véase también* plano de coordenadas.

See coordinate plane.

Véase plano de coordenadas.

x-coordinate (p. 603) The first coordinate in an ordered pair, which tells you how many units to move to the left or right.

coordenada *x* (pág. 603) Primera coordenada de un par ordenado, que dice cuántas unidades hay que moverse a la derecha o a la izquierda.

In the ordered pair $(-3, -2)$, the x-coordinate, -3, tells you to move 3 units to the left. *See also* coordinate plane.

En el par ordenado $(-3, -2)$, la coordenada *x*, -3, indica que hay que moverse 3 unidades a la izquierda. *Véase también* plano de coordenadas.

Y

y-axis (p. 603) The vertical axis in a coordinate plane. *See also* coordinate plane.

eje *y* (pág. 603) Eje vertical en un plano de coordenadas. *Véase también* plano de coordenadas.

See coordinate plane.

Véase plano de coordenadas.

y-coordinate (p. 603) The second coordinate in an ordered pair, which tells you how many units to move up or down.

coordenada *y* (pág. 603) Segunda coordenada de un par ordenado, que dice cuántas unidades hay que moverse hacia arriba o hacia abajo.

In the ordered pair $(-3, -2)$, the y-coordinate, -2, tells you to move 2 units down. *See also* coordinate plane.

En el par ordenado $(-3, -2)$, la coordenada *y*, -2, indica que hay que moverse 2 unidades hacia abajo. *Véase también* plano de coordenadas.

Index

A

Absolute value, 580, 590
Accuracy of scale, 83
Act it out, problem solving strategy, 770, 775
Activities, *See also* Games; Investigations; Technology activities
  addition
    of fractions, 295
    magic squares, 3
    repeated, in multiplication, 341
    in understanding integer multiplication, 592
  geometry
    area of a prism, 545
    area of a triangle, 518
    creating figure with symmetry, 494
    sizes and shapes of triangles, 490
  graphs
    circle, 302
    interpreting, 704
  maps, in finding distances, 72
  mass, measuring, 203
  models
    in comparing fractions, 254
    in modeling numbers, 119, 148
    in solving multiplication equation, 646
    in writing decimals as fractions, 266
  multiplication
    with base-ten pieces, 169
    pictures in, 354
    by powers of ten, 193
    repeated addition in, 341
    to understand integer division, 597
  percents, changing to fractions or decimals, 434
Acute angles, 465
Acute triangle, 471
Addition
  of areas in geometric figures, 534
  associative property of, 742
  in checking subtraction, 4
  in completing magic square, 3, 8, 590
  of customary units, 380, 381, 384
  of decimals, 147, 148–150, 151, 154, 155, 160, 161, 168, 197, 224, 290, 469, 568, 639, 752
    calculator in, 155

    estimating sums in, 143, 144, 145, 154, 160, 161, 168, 275, 745
    mental math in, 149
  fact families, 1, 740
  in finding perimeter, 66
  of fractions, 297, 302, 304, 305, 307, 314, 331, 333, 464, 568, 713
    with common denominators, 295, 301, 330
    with different denominators, 302–303, 330–331
    estimating, 292, 293, 300, 307, 329, 330, 333
    using mental math, 298
    using models, 295, 301
  of integers, 579–580, 581, 602, 618, 621
    absolute value, 580
    using models, 578, 579, 581
    using a number line, 579, 581
  inverse operation for, 740
  of like terms, 633
  lining up decimal points, 641
  of measures of time, 322, 323, 324, 325, 327, 332, 333
  of mixed numbers, 309–310, 310, 311, 312, 327, 331, 333, 372, 568
    estimating sums in, 329, 330, 333
  order of operations, 21, 22
  repeated, in multiplying fraction by whole number, 341
  rounding and, 11
  in understanding integer multiplication, 592
  of variable expressions, 629, 631
  of whole numbers, 2, 3, 6, 14, 19, 26, 47, 51, 92, 224, 384, 572, 596, 734, 740–742
    using a calculator, 24
    estimating, 11, 13, 23, 26, 48, 51, 118, 141, 275, 292, 293, 581
    using mental math, 6
  zeros, 148
Addition equations, solving, 636–637, 638, 639, 644, 649, 670, 673, 695
Additive identity, 35, 792
Additive inverse, 580, 792
Algebra
  describing patterns, 6, 7, 8
  evaluating expressions, 29, 30, 31, 32, 33, 34, 38, 45, 49, 51, 58, 65, 97, 132, 134, 147, 149, 151,

    172, 173, 179, 188, 195, 200, 206, 224, 246, 265, 298, 305, 312, 319, 349, 351, 357, 364, 365, 370, 388, 391, 420, 577, 588, 593, 594, 599, 613, 628, 650, 723
  distributive property, 175, 176, 177, 178, 191, 215, 224, 235, 493, 632
    using mental math, 176, 177, 240, 298, 313
    with two variables, 30
  finding simple interest, 437
  using fraction bar, 599
  representing quantities, 28
  simplifying expressions, 633–634, 635
  solving equations, 35, 36, 45, 50, 68, 69, 184, 268, 344, 370, 412–415, 436, 437, 454, 464, 467, 577, 613, 628, 632, 638, 644, 650, 666, 673, 695
    addition, 636–637, 638, 644, 649, 670, 673, 695
    division, 646–647, 648, 649, 671, 673
    using mental math, 35, 36, 37, 45, 50, 87, 191, 411, 498, 517, 582, 632
    multiplication, 646–647, 648, 649, 671, 673
    order of operations, 21–24, 49
    subtraction, 640–641, 643, 644, 649, 670, 673
  solving for value of x, 58, 66, 67, 68, 69, 75, 107, 132, 246, 468, 473, 474, 476, 482, 483, 505, 515, 516, 552, 553, 588, 594, 595
  writing coordinates of image, 607
  writing equations, 37, 632
  writing expressions for ratios, 420
  writing related multiplication sentence, 184
  writing statements, 209
Algebra tiles, *See also* Modeling
  in simplifying expressions, 633–636
  in solving equations, 635, 636, 646
Algorithm
  for adding and subtracting
    decimals, 752
    fractions, 295, 296, 302
    integers, 580, 587
    mixed numbers, 309, 316
    whole numbers, 742

B

Chapter Test, *See* Assessment
Checking answers with estimation,
    13, 128, 170, 172, 182, 184,
    191, 212, 219, 228, 345, 356,
    364, 368, 389, 525
Checking reasonableness, 13, 23, 36,
    128, 150, 152, 170, 178, 182,
    183, 199, 212, 319, 355, 368,
    527, 531, 647
Choosing appropriate units
    customary
        for capacity, 204, 374, 376
        for length, 61, 63, 80, 202
        for weight, 373, 374, 376
    metric
        for capacity, 204, 205
        for length, 61, 63, 80, 202
        for mass, 204, 205
    of time, 325
Choosing operation, 201, 368, 370
**Choosing problem-solving
    strategies,** 33, 65, 104, 123,
    129, 173, 248, 270, 307, 320,
    358, 370, 406, 433, 489, 501,
    529, 601, 613, 659, 718
Circle
    arc, 538
    area of, 531–533, 534, 561
    center of, 525
    choosing approximation of pi,
        526, 528
    circumference of, 523–524, 525–
        527, 530, 537, 560
    diameter of, 523, 525
    finding ratio of circumference to
        diameter, 524
    radius of, 523, 525
Circle graphs, 94–95
    comparing, 96
    examples of, 104, 110, 111, 300,
        302, 533
    interpreting, 94, 96, 708
    making predictions with, 96
    with percents, 426
    reading, 95, 96
Clustering, 745
Combinations, 692
    finding, 692, 693
Common decimals, 266
Common denominators, 405
    addition of fractions with, 295,
        301, 330
    subtraction of fractions with,
        296, 330
Common factors, 236, 237, 238,
    251, 350
Common multiple, 250, 251
Communication
    describing in words, 6, 44, 79, 86,
        97, 105, 114, 121, 128, 132,

136, 140, 145, 151, 171, 177,
179, 180, 188, 189, 192, 195,
202, 209, 233, 239, 241, 242,
246, 252, 256, 263, 268, 270,
273, 275, 293, 294, 297, 304,
311, 313, 318, 324, 352, 357,
359, 361, 364, 383, 386, 395,
406, 411, 416, 422, 433, 438,
479, 483, 499, 508, 516, 520,
521, 528, 534, 543, 544, 547,
552, 577, 599, 605, 606, 607,
610, 612, 631, 632, 635, 645,
648, 649, 656, 663, 664, 684,
685, 686, 687, 698, 701, 706,
710, 711, 712, 717, 721, 724
    reading, *See* Reading in Math;
        Reading math
    writing, *See* Writing
Commutative property
    of addition, 149, 150, 152
    of multiplication, 171, 172, 215,
        344
Compare, exercises, 78, 87, 97, 102,
    103, 133, 134, 153, 197, 202,
    209, 211, 256, 263, 273, 293,
    306, 326, 349, 359, 361, 366,
    377, 401, 406, 410, 411, 421,
    422, 423, 434, 439, 521, 522,
    535, 536, 575, 650, 665, 717
Comparing
    area, 401, 521, 535
    data, 102
    decimals, 131, 132
    fractions, 256
        cross products in, 416
        with models, 254
    graphs, 90, 97
    measurements, 208, 209
    numbers, 262, 263, 273
    percents, 427, 432
    powers, 17
    probabilities, 703
    unit rates, 408, 410
    whole numbers, 738
Compass
    in constructing geometric figures,
        538–539
    in drawing circles, 523
Compatible numbers, 12, 48
Complementary angles, 466, 476
Complementary events, 684, 686
Composite numbers, 231, 233
Concept maps, 400, 425
Concept Summary, 419, 431
Concepts, *See* Concept Summary;
    Key Concept
Conclusions, validating, *See* Drawing
    conclusions; Reasoning
Cones, 541

Congruent figures, 490–491, 504, 542
Conjecture, *See* Drawing conclusions
Connections, *See* Applications
Constructions, 538–539
    angle bisector, 539
    copying an angle, 538
    copying a segment, 538
    perpendicular bisector, 539
Conversions, *See* Customary units,
    changing; Metric units,
    changing
Coordinate plane, 88, 109, 111
    axes of, 88
    graphing points, 185, 224, 488,
        601, 603, 604, 605, 644, 659
    ordered pair, 88–89, 90, 91, 603,
        605, 606, 607
    origin, 88, 603
    points, 88, 90, 91
    quadrants, 603
    translations, 603–604, 620
**Copying and completing
    statements,** *Throughout. See
    for example* 119, 132, 212,
        238, 244, 246, 258, 290, 320,
        340, 372, 373, 377, 378, 381,
        384, 390, 391, 403, 407, 544
Corresponding parts, 491
    finding, 491, 492
Counterexample, *See* Examples and
    Nonexamples; Which One
    Doesn't Belong? questions
Counters, *See also* Models
    in finding data values, 98
Critical thinking, *See* Reasoning
Cross products, 412, 414
    in comparing fractions, 416
    in deciding whether ratios form a
        proportion, 414
    in solving proportions, 444
Cubes, 542
    surface area of, 552
Cumulative Review, 224–225, 396–
    397, 568–569, 734–735
Cups, 374, 556
Customary units
    addition of, 380, 381, 384
    of capacity, 374, 376, 384, 390, 556,
        557
    changing
        using division, 378–381, 390
        using multiplication, 378–381,
            390
    of length, 59, 61, 65, 80, 111, 202,
        376
    subtraction of, 380, 381, 384
    of weight, 373, 376, 384, 390, 556,
        557
Cylinder, 541

Data, *See also* Statistics
  analyzing
    choosing a display, 95, 719–723, 724, 732
    comparing data displays, 87, 90, 97, 715, 721, 723, 724, 733
    experimental probability, 681, 702–703
    extremes, 714–716, 728
    interpreting data displays, 78–80, 86–92, 94–97, 105, 110, 426, 428–429, 710–713, 714–718, 428–429, 733, 735, 757–759
    measures of central tendency, 99–104, 105, 110, 700, 710–713, 720, 722, 724, 728, 733
    measures of dispersion, 100–103, 105, 110, 710–711, 715–717, 735
    misleading statistics, 704–708, 724, 727
    quartile, 714–716, 724, 728, 732
    range, 100–103, 105, 110, 440, 680, 710–711, 715–717, 733
  collecting
    from an experiment, 681, 702–703
    from a simulation, 688, 703
    from a survey, 82
    generating random numbers, 688
    random sample, 700–701
  displaying
    in a bar graph, 83–87, 93, 105, 109, 719, 724, 732
    in a box-and-whisker plot, 714–718, 719–720, 723, 724, 733, 734
    in a circle graph, 533, 535–537, 719
    in a line graph, 89–92, 105, 109, 719, 723, 728
    in a pictograph, 760
    in a scatter plot, 93
  organizing
    in a frequency table, 76–80, 108, 681
    in a line plot, 76–80, 103, 108
    in a list or table, 82, 654–659, 726, 732
    in a stem-and-leaf plot, 709–715, 719, 723, 724, 727, 732, 734
    in a tree diagram, 91, 695, 696–700, 726
    in a Venn diagram, 80, 769

Data displays, *See also* Bar graphs; Box-and-whisker plots; Circle graphs; Line graphs; Line plots; Stem-and-leaf plots
  making, 78, 93, 728
Decimal(s), 120
  adding, 147, 148–150, 151, 154, 155, 160, 161, 168, 197, 224, 290, 297, 469, 568, 639, 752
    using a calculator, 155
    estimation, 143, 144, 145, 154, 160, 161, 275
    using mental math, 149
  bar notation, 272, 273, 666
  changing fractions to, 271–272, 282
  common, 266
  comparing, 131, 132
    on a number line, 130, 132
    using place value, 120, 121, 157
  dividing, 168, 182, 186–187, 188, 198–199, 200, 202, 217, 224, 406, 568, 644, 734
    using mental math, 193, 194, 195, 219, 422
    placing decimal point, 182, 183, 188
    rounding answer, 187, 188, 191, 199, 200, 202, 212, 217, 219
    by whole numbers, 186–187, 188, 197, 216, 258, 270
  expanded forms of, 121, 135
  as input values, 660
  for large numbers, 139
  modeling, 122
  multiplying, 168, 169, 181–183, 184, 191, 202, 212, 214–215, 224, 327, 345, 484, 522, 568, 590, 644, 734
    using mental math, 193, 194, 195, 212, 219
    models in, 180, 181, 183
    by whole numbers, 169, 170, 171, 172, 174, 179, 214–215, 219
  ordering, 130–131, 131, 132, 135, 159, 161
    on number line, 228
  place value, 119–120, 157
  reading, 120, 121, 199
  repeating, 272, 273
  rounding, 137–139, 140, 154, 159, 168, 182, 187, 191, 199, 200, 202, 206, 212, 216, 217, 219, 224, 270, 275, 406
  subtracting, 147, 148–150, 151, 154, 155, 160, 161, 168, 197, 224, 290, 469, 734, 752
    estimation, 143, 145, 154, 160, 161, 489

    terminating, 272, 273
  writing, 120, 121, 122, 125, 135, 147, 157, 265, 275
    as fractions, 266, 476
    as mixed numbers, 267, 476
    as percents, 430, 432, 446
  writing fractions as, 377, 400, 666, 680
  writing mixed numbers as, 400, 666
  writing percents as, 426, 427, 433
  writing ratios as, 403
  with zeros, 267
Decimal places, counting, 198
Decimal points
  lining up
    in addition, 641
    in decimal operations, 148
  placing in a product, 182, 183, 188
Degrees, measuring angles, 461
Denominators
  common, 405
    adding fractions with, 295, 301, 330
    subtracting fractions with, 296
  different
    addition of fractions with, 302
    subtraction of fractions with, 302, 303, 330–331
Diagonals of regular polygon, 486, 487, 493
Diagrams
  drawing, 18, 36, 41, 42, 43, 75, 258, 264, 314, 352, 458, 459, 466, 489, 547, 769, 771
  in multiple representations, 314, 589
  reading, 518, 532
  tree, 691, 692, 693, 697
  Venn, 44, 80, 240, 454, 480, 689, 756
Diameter of circle, 523, 524, 525
Differences, *See* Subtraction
Dimensions
  measuring, 210
  effect of change on
    area, 401, 418–422, 451, 499, 521, 535
    perimeter, 418–422, 442
Discrete mathematics
  combinations, 692–695, 701, 726, 732–733
  greatest common factor (GCF), 236, 237, 238, 252
  least common denominator (LCD), 254
  least common multiple, (LCM), 251, 252
  permutations, 692 695, 701, 702, 732, 735

INDEX

modeling, 424
sales tax, 668
tips and, 435–438
wages, 659
writing, 425
    as decimals, 426, 427, 430, 433
    as fractions, 426, 427, 433
    writing decimals as, 430, 432, 446
    writing fractions as, 429, 446, 680
Perimeter, 31, 66
    addition in finding, 66
    finding ratio of, 404, 418, 420
    formula for, 178
    modeling functions for, 665
    ratios of, 420
    of a rectangle, 66, 75, 80, 106, 111,
        145, 383, 416, 454, 755
    of a square, 67, 106, 416
    of a triangle, 31, 58, 145, 152, 305,
        312, 320, 755
Permutations, 692
    finding, 692, 693
Perpendicular bisector, 539
Perpendicular lines, 514
Pi, 525
    choosing approximation of, 526,
        528
Pictographs, 197, 759, 760
Pie chart, *See* Circle graph
Pints, 374, 556
Place value
    decimals and, 119–120, 157
    identifying, 2, 737
    reviewing, 3
    in rounding numbers, 2, 8, 11, 45,
        118, 134, 140
Placeholder, zeros as, 169, 170, 182,
        187, 193
Plane, 456
    coordinate, 603, 604, 605, 606
Points, 455
    coordinates of, 88
    graphing on coordinate plane, 88,
        90, 91, 185, 224, 488, 601, 603,
        604, 605, 644, 659
Polygon(s), 485–486, *See also*
        Quadrilaterals; Triangles
    classifying, 485–486, 487, 488, 498,
        601
    congruent, 490–493, 504
    regular, 486, 503
    similar, 490–493, 504
    sums of measures of interior
        angles, 488
    vertex of a, 485
Positive integers, 573
Pound, 373, 556
Power(s), 15
    base of, 15
    comparing, 17

evaluation of, 184, 189
exponents of, 15
finding value of, 16, 17, 20, 48, 51,
    191, 212
grouping symbols and, 22
order of operations in, 21, 22
reading, 16
writing, 15, 17, 45, 48
writing products as, 15, 17, 25, 228
Powers of ten
    in changing metric units, 207, 209
    division by, 193–194, 216–217
    multiplication by, 193–194, 216–
        217
Precision in measuring, 64
Predictions, making, 96, 144, 344,
        488, 681, 685
Prefixes
    in geometry, 485
    in metric system, 60
Prerequisite skills, review of, 2, 58,
        118, 168, 228, 290, 340, 400,
        454, 512, 572, 628, 680
Prime factorization, 230–232, 232,
        233, 248, 251, 252, 278–279,
        283
Prime numbers, 231, 233
Principal, 436
Prism, 541
    rectangular, 541
    surface area of, 545–546, 547, 548,
        562
    triangular, 541, 542
    volume of, 550–551, 562
Probability, 682
    comparing, 703
    describing, 683, 685
    experimental, 702–703
    finding, 682–684, 685, 686, 698,
        708, 725
    for intersection and union, 690
    of independent events, 696–697,
        698, 726
    performing simulations, 703
    success, 702
    testing, 688
    theoretical, 702
Problem solving, *Throughout. See for
        example* 7–8, 13–14, 18–19,
        24–25, 32–33, 37–38, 43–44,
        64–65, 70–71, 75, 79–80,
        86–87, 91–92, 96–97, 102–103,
        122–123, 128–129, 133–134,
        140–141, 146–147, 152–153,
        See also Choosing problem-
        solving strategies; Eliminate
        choices; Guided Problem
        Solving exercises
Problem-solving plan, 39–41, 42,
        44, 50

Problem-solving strategies, *See also*
        Choosing problem-solving
        strategies
    act it out, 770
    break a problem into parts, 767
    draw a diagram, 18, 36, 41, 42, 43,
        75, 258, 264, 314, 352, 458,
        459, 466, 547, 591, 762, 769
    using estimation, 9–10
    using graphs, 91
    guess, check, and revise, 33, 34,
        38, 763
    look for a pattern, 5, 6, 7, 8, 43, 44,
        66, 489, 663, 766
    make a list or table, 18, 43, 44, 80,
        237, 411, 421, 655, 722, 765
    make a model, 122, 497, 761
    solve a simpler problem, 380, 768
    using a Venn diagram, 454, 480,
        689, 769
    verbal models in, 40, 152, 296, 299,
        637, 651
    work backward, 40, 296, 299, 326,
        528, 601, 640, 642, 643, 657, 764
    writing down key facts in, 95
Products, *See also* Multiplication
    cross, 412, 414, 416, 444
    factors of, 15
    placing decimal point in, 182, 183,
        188
    writing as a power, 15, 17, 228
    writing powers as, 25, 45
Proper fractions, 261
Properties
    of addition
        associative, 149, 150, 152
        commutative, 149, 150, 152
        identity, 35
        inverse, 580
    cross products, 412
    distributive, 175, 176, 177, 178,
        191, 215, 224, 235, 357, 493,
        632, 634, 649
    of equality
        addition, 637
        division, 647
        multiplication, 647
        subtraction, 641
    of multiplication
        associative, 171, 172, 215, 344
        commutative, 171, 172, 215, 344
        identity, 35
        inverse, 362
        zero, 35
    table of, 792
Proportional reasoning
    percents, 434–440, 441
    rates, 407–411
    ratios, 402–406, 412–416, 646–650
    scale drawings, 72–75, 417–422

in place value, 2, 8, 11, 45, 118, 134

small numbers, 138

whole numbers, 8, 11, 45, 118, 134, 739

Rulers

using to find quotients, 361

reading, 408

Rules

for divisibility, 229, 230, 231, 232, 233

function, 654, 655, 656, 657, 658, 659, 663, 666, 671, 672

in multiplication, 349, 350

Sample space

use combinations to find, 692

use a list to find, 692

use a tree diagram to find, 691

Scale, 72, 417

accuracy of, 83

finding, 419, 420

interpreting, 74

on a map, 92, 419, 445

of a model, 73, 74, 80, 108

reading and writing, 72

using, 419, 420

Scale drawings, 72, 74, 107–108, 417–418, 419, 445, 517

finding actual length, 419

interpreting, 72

using metric ruler in making, 422

Scale model, 73, 74, 75, 417–422, 445, 448, 450, 658

Scalene triangle, 472

drawing a tessellation of, 615

Science, See Applications

Scientific notation, 196

Segments, 455, 500

copying, 538

drawing, 63, 258

identifying, 455

length of, 106, 118, 123, 158, 440, 454, 459

estimating, 80

naming, 456

Sequence, See Function(s)

Set(s), 689

elements of, 689

empty, 689

finding size of whole, 344

intersection of two, 689–690

union of two, 689–690

universal, 689

in Venn diagrams, 689

Short response questions, 284–286, 506–508, 730–732

practice, *Throughout. See for example* 7, 14, 19, 27, 32, 37, 38, 44, 46, 52–53, 54, 64, 70, 71, 79, 81, 86, 92, 97, 102, 105, 115, 123, 129, 136, 141, 147

Sides

classifying triangles by, 472, 475

corresponding, 491

Similar figures, 490–491, 504

corresponding sides in, 491

Simple interest, 436

finding, 440

formula for, 436, 437

Simulations, performing, 703

Skew lines, 458

Skill Check, *See* Assessment

Skill Practice, *See* Assessment

Skills Review Handbook, 737–760

estimation,

differences, 746

products, 747

quotients, 748

sums, 745

fractions, 753

graphs

bar, 757

line, 758

pictograph, 759–760

logical reasoning, Venn diagrams, 756, 756

measurement

area, 755

perimeter, 755

time, 754

number sense

comparing and ordering whole numbers, 738

fact families, 740

rounding whole numbers, 739

whole number place value, 737

operations

addition, 741, 742, 751, 752

division, 744

multiplication, 743

subtraction, 741, 742, 751, 752

problem solving, 749, 750

Solid figures, 541–542

classifying, 541–542, 543, 549, 561

drawing, 542, 543

edges of, 542

faces of, 542

vertices of, 542

volume of, 550

Solution, 34

of an equation, 34, 35, 45

of an inequality, 651

Solve a simpler problem, 768, 774

Spatial reasoning, 458, 475, 541–544, 545–549, 555

Spheres, 541

Spinners

creating, 700

in predicting outcomes, 684, 685, 697, 698

Spreadsheets

creating data displays, 93

finding angle measures of triangles, 477

multiplying decimals by whole numbers, 174

program for, 93

Spring balance, 556, 557

Squares, 480

area of, 67, 69, 106, 211, 416

lines of symmetry in, 495

perimeter of, 67, 106, 416

Stacked bar graphs, 87

Standard form, writing numbers in, 196

Standardized Test Practice, 54–55, 114–115, 164–165, 222–223, 286–287, 336–337, 394–395, 450–451, 508–509, 566–567, 624–625, 676–677, 732–733

exercises, *Throughout. See* Extended response questions; Gridded answer questions; Mixed Review of Problem Solving; Multi-Step Problems; Multiple choice questions; Open-ended questions; Short response questions

Standardized Test Preparation, 52–53, 112–113, 162–163, 220–221, 284–285, 334–335, 392–393, 448–449, 506–507, 564–565, 622–623, 674–675, 730–731

examples, 12, 22, 73, 130, 150, 175, 207, 232, 237, 262, 297, 304, 324, 375, 379, 409, 436, 461, 473, 482, 519, 526, 573, 598, 655, 662, 684

State Test Practice, *Throughout. See for example* 27, 46, 54–55, 75, 81, 105, 114–115, 136, 156, 164–165, 192, 213, 222–223, 249, 277, 286–287, 336–337, 394–395, 450–451, 508–509

Statistics

bar graph, 83–87

box-and-whisker plot, 714–715

line graph, 89

line plot, 77

mean, 99

median, 99

misleading, 704–705, 727

mode, 99

range, 100

stem-and-leaf plot, 709–710

INDEX

Credits

Cover Photography

1 Jeff Cadge/Photographer's Choice/Getty Images;
2 Premium Collection/Getty Images

Photography

xiv Charles W. Melton; **xv** Raymond Gehman/Corbis; **xvi** Index Stock; **xvii** Jose Azel/Aurora & Quanta Productions; **xviii** © Royalty-Free/Corbis; Steve Skjold/Skjold Stock Photography; **xxii** Kelly/Mooney Photography/Corbis; **1** *top left* Joe McBride/Getty Images, *center right* Nick Koudis/PhotoDisc #10; **3** © Joseph Sohm; ChromoSohm Inc./Corbis; **4** © LWA-Dann Tardif/Corbis; **5** Adam Pretty/Getty Images; **7** Anup Shah/Getty Images; **11** © Karl Weatherly/Corbis; **12** © Jeff Greenberg/PhotoEdit; **14** BG Photography Inc.; **15** Adam Block/NOAO/AURA/NSF; **16** © John Foxx/Alamy; **18** © John Gress/Reuters/Corbis; **21** © Tom Carter/PhotoEdit; **22** © Konrad Wothe/Look; **24** School Division/Houghton Mifflin; **25** Paul A. Soulders/Corbis; **27** Getty Images; **29** © Park Street/PhotoEdit; **30** © Thinkstock/Alamy; **32** Corbis: Storm Chaser (vol. 107); **33** Matthais Breiter/Accent Alaska; **34** David Young-Wolff/PhotoEdit; **36** Matthais Breiter/Accent Alaska; **39** *top* David Young-Wolff/PhotoEdit, *center* PhotoDisc; **43** John Lund/Getty Images; **46** Stanley Brown/Getty Images; **56–57** John Shaw/Panoramic Images; **59** *top* © Royalty-Free/Corbis, *bottom* Kendra Knight/AGE; **60** PhotoDisc; **61** Mark E. Gibson at CLM/Corbis Outline; **62** *left* © David A. Northcott/Corbis, *right* Burke/Triolo/Artville: Bugs and Insects; **63** *top* School Division/Houghton Mifflin, *bottom* PhotoDisc; **64** Galen Rowell/Corbis; **66** © Bob Daemmrich/The Image Works; **70** *top* Associated Press, AP Photographer Vincent Yu, *bottom* Courtesy of National Geographic Television & Film; **72** Raymond Gehman/Getty Images; **73** Melcher Media, Inc./photo by McDougal Littell School Division. Bark canoe boat from "Amazing Book of Paper Boats" © 2001 by Melcher Media, Inc.; **74** *top left* Jamie Harron/Papilio/Corbis, *top center* Peggy Heard/Frank Lane Picture Agency/Corbis, *top right* Getty Images; **75** Dr. Dennis Kunkel/Visuals Unlimited/Getty Images; **76** *top* Gilles Mingasson/Getty Images, *bottom* PhotoDisc; **79** © David Young-Wolff/PhotoEdit; **81** © Royalty-Free/Corbis; **83** PhotoDisc: Nature, Wildlife, Environment CD#44; **84** Nigel J. Dennis, Gallo Images/Corbis; **86** Tony Freeman/PhotoEdit; **88** Michael Newman/PhotoEdit; **89** Getty Images; **94** Kwame Zikomo/SuperStock; **99** Franz Walther/Artville: Air and Space; **100** NASA Johnson Space *Center*; **103** Ralph Clevenger/Corbis; **116** PhotoDisc: Backgrounds & Objects CD#8; **117** *top left* PhotoDisc: Backgrounds & Objects CD#8, *center right* Eyewire; PhotoDisc: Family & Friends CD#121; **119** Sportschrome; **120** F. Peirce Williams/FPW Photo; **122** *left, center* PhotoDisc, Inc., *right* Vaughan Fleming/Science Photo Library/Photo Researchers, Inc; **123** F. Peirce Williams/FPW Photo; **125** *top* Richard Bucich, *center* Michael S. Yamashita/Corbis; **127** *center* Joseph T. Collins/Photo Researchers, Inc., *bottom left* Ken O'Donoghue, *bottom right* Ken O'Donoghue; **128** Valerie Giles/Photo Researchers, Inc.; **130** © Michael T. Sedam/Corbis; **133** Science Source/Photo Researchers, Inc.; **134** SportsChrome; **136** © Gary Meszaros/Visuals Unlimited; **137** Peter Menzel/Stock Boston; **138** Dustin W. Carr/Harold G. Craighead/Cornell University; **140** © Royalty-Free/Corbis; **143** A. Ramey/Stock Boston; **144** © Bob Daemmrich/PhotoEdit; **146** © Joe McDonald/Corbis; **148** Joel Thomson; **150** © Jose Luis Pelaez, Inc./Corbis; **152** © Cosmo Condina/Getty Images; **166–167** Ken O'Donoghue; **169** Bob Krist/Corbis; **170** Jeff Schultz/Alaska Stock Images; **175** Bettmann/Corbis; **176** NASA; **178** Robert Frerck/Woodfin Camp and Associates; **181** Kevin Schafer/Getty Images; **183** Bureau of Reclamation; **184** Getty Images; **186** *top* John Terence Turner/Getty Images, *bottom* Stephen Simpson/Getty Images; **187** Getty Images; **189** Reuters/Corbis; **190** Dennis MacDonald/PhotoEdit; **191** Gunter Marx/Corbis; **192** Getty Images; **193** Age fotostock; **194** Tom Paiva/Getty Images; **196** © Adam Pretty/Getty Images; **198** Stephen Rose; **199** © Geri Engberg/The Image Works; **202** Bob Krist/eStock Photography/Picturequest; **203** *top center* Frank Siteman, *top right* © Tony Freeman/PhotoEdit, *bottom center* Frank Siteman; **204** School Division/Houghton Mifflin; **206** Paul Souders/Getty Images; **207** Ryan McVay/PhotoDisc; **208** US Mint Press Room; **210** FoodPix/Getty Images; **211** © Patrick Bennett/Corbis; **213** *top right* Elaine Lanmon, *bottom left* Mark Smith/Photo Researchers, Inc.; **226** PhotoSpin/Powerphotos, C Squared Studios/Photodisc; **227** Joshua Ets-Hokin/PhotoDisc Object Series–In Character CD#20; **230** © France Keyser/In Visu/Corbis; **231** © Justin Pumfrey/Getty Images; **234** Stockbyte: Education; **236** Joe Atlas/Brand X Pictures: Summer Fun; **237** Michael S. Yamshita/Corbis; **239** courtesy of Taymark; **240** Richard Nowitz/Photo Researchers, Inc.; **243** © Iain Masterton/Alamy; **244** © RNT Productions/Corbis; **247** © Tony Freeman/PhotoEdit; **249** Michael Newman/PhotoEdit; **250** Michael Newman/PhotoEdit; **254** Steve Skjold/Skjold Stock Photography; **257** Steve Gorton © Dorling Kindersley; **260** David Young-Wolff/PhotoEdit; **261** © David Young-Wolff/PhotoEdit; **262** William Strode/SuperStock; **263** *both* Ken O'Donoghue; **265** © Dennis MacDonald/PhotoEdit; **266** Powerphotos/PhotoSpin; **269** © Michael Newman/PhotoEdit; **270** PhotoSpin; **271** Mark Tomalty/Masterfile; **274** Blair Seitz/Stock Connection/Picturequest; **277** Frank Siteman/Stock Boston Inc./Picturequest; **288–289** Stuart Westmorland/Getty Images; **291** *top* © Robert Brenner/PhotoEdit, *bottom* © S. Blair Hedges; **294** © 2002 Action Products International, Inc.; **295** Bob Krist/Getty Images; **296** © Bluestone Productions/SuperStock; **299** Tony Freeman/PhotoEdit; **302** Gail Shumway/Getty Images; **306** Steve Skjold/Skjold Stock Photography; **309** © Richard Hutchings/Corbis; **310** Dave G. Houser/Post-Houserstock/Corbis; **311** John Marshall; **313** Jeff Kowalsky/Corbis; **314** Index Stock; **316** Domenico Ruzza/Envision; **319** Andrew J. Martinez/Photo Researchers, Inc.; **320** Jim McElholm/Single Source Inc.; **322** Tim De Waele/Corbis; **325** Jeff Rotman/Getty Images; **328** Kevin R. Morris/Corbis; **338** Brett/Cartwright/Getty; **339** *top left* Jake Martin/Allsport/Getty Images, *center right* Jean-Yves Ruszniewski/Corbis; **341** Royalty-Free/Corbis; **342** Ken O'Donoghue; **348** © Royalty-Free/Corbis; **350** © Duomo/Corbis; **353** Richard During/Getty Images; **354** Getty Images;

Selected Answers

Chapter 1

1.1 Skill Practice (pp. 6 – 7) **1.** C **3.** A **5.** 81 **7.** 402 **9.** 16 **11.** 209 **13.** 401 **15.** 128 **17.** 15 R 3 **19.** 1904 **21.** 2010 **23.** 120 R 5 **25.** 2432 **27.** 15,750 **29.** multiply by 2; 80, 160 **31.** subtract 2; 22, 20 **33.** add 8; 36, 44 **35.** true **37.** false; difference **39.** The partial product "27" is in the wrong place; add a placeholder 0 and move 27 so that the 2 falls under the 1, and the 3 falls under the 3; $27 \times 15 = 135 + 270 = 405$. **41.** 1 **43.** 6 **45.** skipping two letters; M, P **47.** going backwards skipping four letters with a continuous loop from A to Z and back to A again; M, H

1.1 Problem Solving (pp. 7 – 8) **49.** 47 **51.** $156 **53.** 7; 25 goes into 192 seven times with 17 inches of ribbon left.

57.

4	14	15	1
9	7	6	12
5	11	10	8
16	2	3	13

1.2 Skill Practice (p. 13) **1.** leading digits **3–25.** *Estimates may vary.* **3.** 70 **5.** 600 **7.** 1000 **9.** 410 **11.** 970 **13.** 1600 **15.** 5 **17.** 180 **19.** 600 **21.** 3 **23.** 50 **25.** 3000 **27.** yes **29.** no **31.** no **33.** 509 rounds to 500 and 86 rounds to 90; $500 \times 90 = 45,000$

1.2 Problem Solving (pp. 13 – 14) **39. a.** multiplication **b.** 50, 10 **c.** 500 **41.** 1000

1.3 Skill Practice (p. 17) **1.** base; 27 **3.** exponent; 1 **5.** 12^3 **7.** 4^5 **9.** 3^4 **11.** $5 \times 5 \times 5 \times 5 = 5^4$, not 4^5; 625 **13.** B **15.** 144 **17.** 10,000 **19.** 32 **21.** 1 **23.** 64 **25.** 1000 **27.** 10 **29.** 4^3 **31.** 10^3 **33.** 5^3 **35.** 2^{10} **37.** 7^5 **39.** 847^{12}

1.3 Problem Solving (pp. 18 – 19) **45.** 12^2; 144 **49. a.** 10^2; 100 **b.** 500 minutes **c.** no; 8 hours is 480 minutes **51.** 8^3; 512

1.3 Technology Activity (p. 20) **1.** 390,625 **3.** 1,048,576 **5.** 2,825,761 **7.** 191,102,976 **9.** 42,144,192 **11.** 442,050,625 **13.** 19,683 **15.** 2,476,099 **17.** 1,048,576

1.4 Skill Practice (pp. 23 – 24) **1.** Grouping symbols **3.** 6 **5.** 3 **7.** 10 **9.** 8 **11.** 2 **13.** 10 **15.** 24 **17.** 2 **19.** 2 **21.** 4 **23.** 32 **27.** false; 13 **29.** true **31.** true **33.** A **35.** B **37.** 123 **39.** 76 **41.** 167

1.4 Problem Solving (pp. 24 – 25) **55.** $53 **57.** No; The order of operations would evaluate the expression in that order.

1.5 Skill Practice (pp. 31 – 32) **1.** a **3.** 16 **5.** 11 **7.** 9 **9.** 6 **11.** 60 **13.** 7 **15.** 7 **17.** 3 **19.** 3(2) means 3×2; 6 **21.** 9 **23.** 2 **25.** 21 **27.** 39 **29.** 36 **31.** 4 **33.** 12 ft **35.** 14 ft **37.** 9 **39.** 20 **41.** 33 **43.** 28

1.5 Problem Solving (pp. 32 – 33) **49.** 4 mi **51.** $12

1.6 Skill Practice (pp. 36 – 37) **1.** solution **3.** yes **5.** no **7.** no **9.** no **11.** yes **13.** 9 **15.** 14 **17.** 8 **19.** 3 **21.** 7 **23.** 5 **25.** 1 **27.** 0 **29.** 5(0) = 0, not 5. 5(1) = 5, so 1 is the solution. **31–35.** *Methods may vary.* **31.** yes; mental math **33.** no; calculator **35.** no; calculator **37.** $8x = 24$; 3 **39.** $21 - x = 12$; 9 **41.** $x + 39 = 51$; 12

1.6 Problem Solving (pp. 37 – 38) **51.** When 2 times a number equals 48 and then 3 is subtracted, 45 is the result.

1.7 Skill Practice (pp. 42 – 43) **1.** (1) Read and Understand: Read the problem carefully. Identify the question and any important information. (2) Make a Plan: Decide on a problem solving strategy. (3) Solve the Problem: Use the problem solving strategy to answer the question. (4) Look Back: Check that your answer is reasonable. **3.** know: have $100, save $20 a month, need $160; Find out how many months to get to $160. **5.** D

7.

9. *Sample answer:* You have 12 inches of rope. After using some, you have 3 inches remaining. How many inches did you use?

1.7 Problem Solving (pp. 43 – 45) **13.**

; You need 7 posts.

15. There are 8 ways to pay the toll exactly if you use quarters, dimes, and nickels.

Quarters	Dimes	Nickels
1	2	0
1	1	2
1	0	4
0	4	1
0	3	3
0	2	5
0	1	7
0	0	9

17. Alice, Omar, Celine; Alice, Celine, Omar; Celine, Alice, Omar; Celine, Omar, Alice; Omar, Alice, Celine; Omar, Celine, Alice **19.** 56, 70, 84 will solve the puzzle, 21, 35, 49 will not; *Sample answer:* Even multiples of 7 solve the puzzle.

21. a.

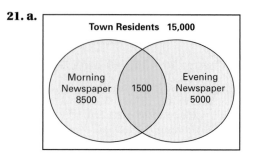

Town Residents 15,000

Morning Newspaper 8500 | 1500 | Evening Newspaper 5000

b. 5000; 15,000 have subscriptions, 15,000 do not. $\frac{1}{3}$ of 15,000 is 5000.   **23.** *Sample answer:* 4 two point baskets

Chapter Review (pp. 47 – 50)   1. order of operations
3. variable   **5.** solution   **7.** 454   **9.** 64 R3
11–15. *Estimates will vary.*   **11.** 190   **13.** 900   **15.** 9000
17. 25   **19.** 1   **21.** 13   **23.** 2500   **25.** 125   **27.** 8   **29.** 3
31. 8   **33.** 8   **35.** 115 lb   **37.** 66   **39.** 22   **41.** 27
43. 66 in.   **45.** 1   **47.** 5   **49.** $3.20

Chapter 2

2.1 Skill Practice (pp. 62 – 64)   1. ft   **3.** cm   **5.** 2 in.
7. 38 mm; 4 cm   *Sample answers for 11 – 23.*   **11.** tape measure; My friends are taller than 1 yd and taller than 1 m.   **13.** centimeter ruler; The diameter of a quarter is less than 1 ft and less than 30 cm.   **15.** tape measure; The length of a diving board is more than 1 yd and more than 1 m.   **17.** miles, kilometers; Marathons are much longer than 1 yd or 1 m.   **19.** inches, centimeters; The length of a clarinet is less than 1 yd and less than 1 m.
21. inches, centimeters; The length of a bike is a little more than 1 yd and a little more than 1 m, but inches and centimeters would be better so there wouldn't be as much rounding.   **23.** feet, meters; A flagpole is very tall, but not 1 mi or 1 km tall.   *Sample answers for 29–33.*
29. elbow to knuckle; 3 ft   **31.** small paper clip; 34 in.
33. width of little finger; 50 cm   **35.** yes   **37.** kilometers; Bike paths are very long.   *Sample answers for 41–43.*
41. 40.4 cm, 39.5 cm   **43.** 12 ft 1 in., 11 ft 10 in.

2.1 Problem Solving (pp. 64 – 65)   47. about 40 ft
51. no; If the game is just over 15 cm and has been rounded down, it will not fit in the bookcase.

2.2 Skill Practice (pp. 68 – 69)   1. perimeter
3. perimeter; linear units   **5.** area; square units
7. 18 ft, 14 ft²   **9.** 20 in., 21 in.²   **11.** 40 in., 100 in.²
13. 236 in., 3120 in.²   **15.** Perimeter is not measured in square feet. Perimeter = 20 ft.   **17.** perimeter; feet
19. area; square feet   **21.** $4l = 100$; 25 ft   **23.** $132 = 12w$; $w = 11$ m   **25.** tape measure; A parking lot has length and width much longer than 1 yd or 1m.

2.2 Problem Solving (pp. 70 – 71)   35. a. 64 feet is the perimeter. Area would be measured in ft².   **b.** $4l = 64$
c. 16 yd   **37.** 160 ft   **45. a.** 3750 ft²   **b.** 2250 ft²
c. 580 ft

2.3 Skill Practice (p. 74)   1. shape, size   **3.** 15 cm
5. 300 mi   **7.** 750 mi   **9.** 2 in.   **11.** 7 in.   **13.** 20 was used as inches instead of feet; 8 in.

2.3 Problem Solving (p. 75)   17. 800 mi

2.4 Skill Practice (p. 78)   1. frequency
3. most often: 2 points; least often: 3 points

Point value	Tally	Frequency
1	ЖII	7
2	ЖЖI	11
3	III	3

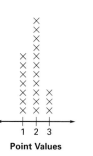

Point Values

5. most often: 10; least often: 9, 11, 13, and 14;

Age	Tally	Frequency
5	IIII	4
6	III	3
7	I	1
8	IIII	4
9		0
10	Ж I	6
11		0
12	II	2
13		0
14		0
15	II	2
16	I	1

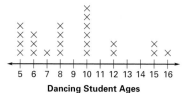

Dancing Student Ages

2.4 Problem Solving (pp. 79 – 80)   11. other fires; rescues
13. The strings section is the largest section;

Section	Tally	Frequency
woodwinds	Ж IIII	9
percussion	II	2
brass	Ж ЖI	11
strings	Ж Ж Ж Ж IIII	24

19. 4   **21.** No; The items being tallied are not numbers.

2.5 Skill Practice (pp. 85 – 86) **1.** 1. Decide how far to extend the scale. 2. Choose the increments for the scale. Use 3 to 10 equal increments. 3. Choose an increment that is easy to work with.

3.

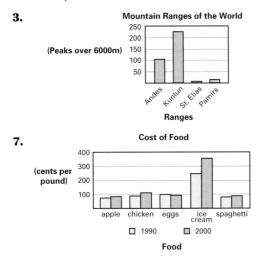

7.

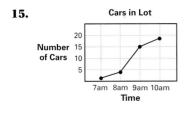

9. ice cream

2.5 Problem Solving (pp. 86 – 87) **13.** The bars would look very small but would still show which country has the highest and lowest prices.

2.6 Skill Practice (pp. 90 – 91) **1.** C **3.** E **5.** D

7–14.

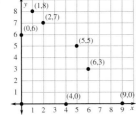

15.

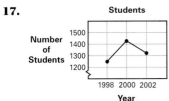

17.

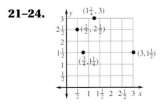

21–24.

2.6 Problem Solving (pp. 91 – 92)

27. about 120;

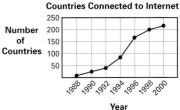

29. low value is 169, high is 190; broken scale of 160 – 200, increments of 10;

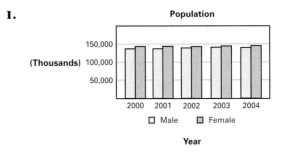

2.6 Technology Activity (p. 93)

1.

2.7 Skill Practice (pp. 95 – 96) **1.** C **3.** B **5.** A **9.** The population under 35 takes up about half the circle.
11. Pacific **13.** 10 million km^2

2.7 Problem Solving (pp. 96 – 97) **17.** 496 **19.** 28 **23.** $2500

25.

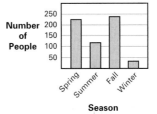

2.8 Skill Practice (pp. 101 – 102) **1.** range **3.** 2, 2, 1 and 3, 2 **5.** 4, 4, 1 and 7, 6 **7.** 9, 9, 12, 7 **9.** 12, 14, 14, 9 **11.** 19, 19, no mode, 18 **13.** The median is wrong because the data was not ordered; 35 **15.** 155, 175, 180, median or mode; One low score makes the mean too low.
17. 720, 647.5, 575, median; The score 1550 makes the mean too high. **19.** 832 **21.** 5180 **23.** left and right **25.** not reasonable; 20; midway between high and low score **27.** yes, reasonable **29.** false; There could be no mode. **31.** false; If there is an even number of terms and the two middle terms are not the same, the median is the average of the two middle terms.

2.8 Problem Solving (pp. 102 – 103) **37.** range stays the same; mean increases by 1, median increases by 3, mode stays the same **41.** 45, 39, 30 **43.** about 37.7 in.; 96 is a lot higher than the other lengths. **45.** Median is the closest to the center of the data.

Chapter Review (pp. 106 – 110) **1.** false; Change perimeter to area. **3.** coordinate **5.** mode **7.** 3 "little fingers"; 30 mm; 3 cm **9.** 32 m, 48 m² **11.** 60 yd **13.** 96 m **15.** 192 m **17.** 256 in.

19.

Scores	Tally	Frequency
71	IIII	4
72	IIII	4
73	I	1
74		0
75	II	2
76	I	1
77		0
78	III	3
79	II	2
80	IIII	4
81	IIII	4

```
 X X                   X X
 X X           X       X X
 X X      X    X X X   X X
 X X X    X X  X X X X X X
 ───────────────────────────
 71 72 73 74 75 76 77 78 79 80 81
      Band Competition Scores
```

21.

```
            Shots Made
        16
        14
Number  12
  of    10
Shots    8
         6
         4
         2
           Kaye  Teva  Olivia
                 Player
```

23.

```
8 ● (0, 8)
7
6
5
4
3
2
1                    ● (7, 1)
   1 2 3 4 5 6 7  x
```

25. Lake Ontario **27.** Lake Huron; graph **29.** 29, 25, 20 and 28, 43

Chapter 3

3.1 Skill Practice (pp. 121 – 122) **1.** hundredths **3.** hundred-thousandths **5.** 40 **7.** 15; 150 **9.** 6.009 **11.** 58.027 **13.** 0.0278 **15.** forty-five hundredths **17.** four and sixteen hundredths **19.** seventeen and

twenty-two thousandths **21.** five ten-thousandths **23.** eight and fourteen ten-thousandths **25.** ten and two hundred fifty-five ten-thousandths **29.** 0.09, 0.002 **31.** 0.007, 0.0002 **33.** $.20 **35.** $.70 **37.** $1.60 **39.** $1.40

41. 1.76;

43. 2.07;

45. 3.30;

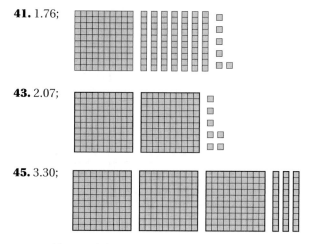

3.1 Problem Solving (pp. 122 – 123) **47.** one and ninety-eight hundredths carats

49.

51. a.

b. 1 + 0.9 + 0.09 **c.** 1.99 km **55.** 0.025; The unit will be thousandths, and twenty-five thousandths is the smallest value to be made using the digits 0, 2, and 5. **59.** United States; The United States score is only 0.017 below 229, while Japan is the next closest but is 0.857 above 229.

3.2 Skill Practice (pp. 127 – 128) **1.** 0.01 **3.** 100 **5.** 3.8 **7.** 6.7 **9.** 9.1 **11.** 1.4 **13.** A. 1.3 cm, B. 3.9 cm, C. 4.5 cm, D. 7.4 cm, E. 9.0 cm **15.** 3.4 cm **17.** The length of the segment is 2.2 cm. **19.** 0.85 m **21.** 0.98 m **23.** no; A kilometer is 1000 meters.

3.3 Skill Practice (pp. 132 – 133) **1.** < **3.** *Sample answer:* 7.34 **5.** < **7.** < **9.** > **11.** > **13.** 5 **15.** < **17.** 5 **19.** < **21.** 9.06, 9.07, 9.1 **23.** 0.1, 0.9, 1.1, 1.5 **25.** 0.98, 1.05, 1.15, 1.2 **27.** 2.99, 2.97, 2.94, 2.93, 2.90 **29.** 1.009, 1.008, 1.003, 1.002 **31.** 8.101, 8.011, 8.010, 8.001 **33.** Four and three hundred twenty thousandths is the same as four and thirty-two hundredths. *Sample answers for 35 – 39.* **35.** 0.7 **37.** 0.4515 **39.** 5.0095 **41.** <

3.3 Problem Solving (pp. 133 – 134) **45.** $2.08, $2.61, $2.62, $2.84, $3.07, $8.40

3.4 Skill Practice (pp. 139 – 140) **1.** hundredth **3.** thousandth **5.** 5 **7.** 3.8 **9.** 0 **11.** 2 **13.** 10.0 **15.** 9 **17.** 8.1 **19.** 1.16 **21.** 2.563 **23.** 0.3558

25. 0.03 **27.** 0.009 **29.** 0.0002 **31.** 0.00010 **33.** To round 9.95 to the nearest tenth, you must include the tenth unit in the final answer; 10.0 **35.** 6,500,000; 6.5 million **37.** 15,000,000; 15.0 million **43.** 350.499999, 345.000000 **45.** 0.004499, 0.003500

3.4 Problem Solving (pp. 140 – 141) **51. a.** 25,300,000; 43,600,000; 56,900,000; 57,200,000; 36,600,000

b.

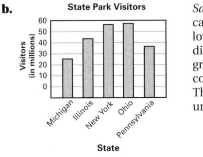

Sample answer: You can tell high and low values in both displays. The bar graph makes visual comparison easier. The table displays unrounded values.

c. millions or ten millions

3.5 Skill Practice (pp. 145 – 146) **1.** 1 **3.** 5 **5.** 12 **7.** 4 **9.** 2 **11.** 18 **13.** 3 **15.** 8 **17.** 25 **19.** 0 **21.** $6.00; too low; We rounded up and then subtracted, making the estimate too low. **25.** 15 **27.** 12 **29.** 11 **33.** 26 km **35.** either **37.** rounding

3.5 Problem Solving (pp. 146 – 147)
41. a.

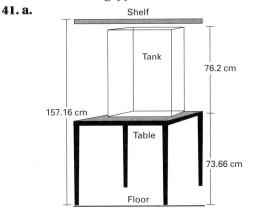

b. 150 cm **c.** yes **45.** yes, $1, low

3.6 Skill Practice (pp. 151 – 152) **1.** associative **3.** 5.49 **5.** 1.84 **7.** 9.26 **9.** 24.54 **11.** 9.961 **13.** 3.26 **15.** 4.449 **17.** 3.358 **19.** 8.4 is the same as 8.40. 0 was subtracted from 6 instead of 6 from 10; 8.4 − 3.06 = 5.34 **21.** 16.25 **23.** 4.08 **25.** 6.35 **27.** 4.6 **29.** associative; 18.95 **31.** commutative; 18.9 **35.** 19.77 **37.** 5.34 **39.** 24.835 **41.** 5.3 + (4.6 + 1.9) **43.** 21.45 mm **45.** > **47.** <

3.6 Problem Solving (pp. 152 – 153) **51.** $4.76; Rounding gives an estimate of $5.00. **53.** Karin Schmalfeld and Sara Gemperle; 0.27 min **57.** 0.369 pounds

3.6 Technology Activity (p. 155) **1.** 7.385 **3.** 8.653 **5.** 15.8 **7.** 2 **9.** 14.59 **11.** 37°C **13.** $63.79

Chapter Review (pp. 157 – 160) **1.** front-end estimation **3.** true **5.** commutative **7.** 0.0207 **9.** fifty-five and twenty-three hundredths **11.** three hundred and one hundred six thousandths **13.** 3.5 cm **15.** 2.1 **17.** 4.09 **19.** 5.005 **25.** 0.8 cm, 0.008 m **27.** < **29.** 0.283, 0.298, 0.332, 0.336 **31.** 0.007 **33.** 1.61 **35.** 0.004 in. **37.** 12 **39.** 3 **41.** 12 **43.** 24 **45.** 5.625 **47.** 9.242 **49.** 6.159 **51.** 2.92

Chapter 4

4.1 Skill Practice (pp. 171 – 172) **1.** associative property of multiplication **3.** 5.4; five and four tenths **5.** 7.32; seven and thirty-two hundredths **7.** 21.5; twenty-one and five tenths **9.** 125.1; one hundred twenty-five and one tenth **13.** 17.6; $0.3 \times 60 = 18$ **15.** 24.576; $3 \times 8 = 24$ **17.** 31.875; $2 \times 15 = 30$ **19.** 0.09; $20 \times 0.005 = 0.1$ **21.** 83; associative **23.** 15 **25.** 8.14 **27.** 64.118

4.1 Problem Solving (pp. 172 – 173) **31.** $338.45 **35.** Dog: 25.1968 in.; Child: 42.9133 in.; Adult: 72.8345 in. **41.** 60

4.1 Technology Activity (p. 174) For 1–3, follow steps 1–4 on p. 174. **1.** $1474.48; $76,672.96 **3.** $2528.40; $131,476.80

4.2 Skill Practice (pp. 177 – 178) **1.** 2(3.1) + 2(7.4) **3.** 332 **5.** 58 **7.** 67.2 **9.** 75 **11.** 271.8 **13.** 90.86 **17.** 222 **19.** 369 **21.** 46 **23.** 8.8 **25.** B **27.** D **29.** A **31.** 50 ft² **33.** $3x + 21$ **35.** $24 - 6x$

4.2 Problem Solving (pp. 178 – 179) **43.** $420 **49.** 50(3.8 − 3.0); $.40 **53.** 6.75 **57.** 8.72

4.3 Skill Practice (pp. 183 – 184) **1.** 2

3. 0.2;

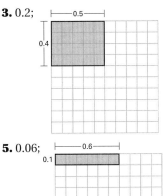

5. 0.06;

7. 60.532 **9.** 1.62 **11.** 0.00522 **13–19.** *Estimates will vary.* **13.** 0.18; $0.6 \times 0.3 = 0.18$ **15.** 14.3444; $3 \times 5 = 15$ **17.** 0.486; $1 \times 0.5 = 0.5$ **19.** 84.4262; $10 \times 9 = 90$ **21.** 17.325 ft² **23.** > **25.** < **27.** Not reasonable; 3.78 **29.** The product is reasonable. **31.** 0.000001 **33.** 0.125 **35.** $x = 80.4 \times 7.25$; 582.9 **37.** $x = 0.13 \times 26.125$; 3.39625

4.3 Problem Solving (pp. 184 − 185)   39. 34 m
45. 0.4096, 0.32768   **47.** less than; Multiplying a number greater than 1 by a fraction or decimal between 0 and 1 gives a product that is less than the original number.
51. 335   **53.** 105
55–57.

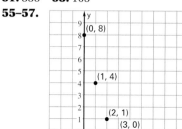

4.4 Skill Practice (pp. 188 − 189)   1. quotient   **3.** divisor
5. 0.745   **7.** 1.75   **9.** 1.125   **11.** 63.27   **15.** 4.4   **17.** 1.2
19. 3.5   **21.** 4.8   **23.** 4.0   **25.** 6.7   **27.** 9.5   **29.** 1.9
31. 0.4   **33.** 3.6   **35.** =   **37.** Two zeros were brought down instead of one after subtracting 48 from 49; 4.08   **39.** 2.000   **41.** 5.165

4.4 Problem Solving (pp. 189 − 191)   43. $7.85
45. $12.75   **47.** 0.289   **49.** 0.306   **55.** 5

4.5 Skill Practice (pp. 195 − 196)   1. 10, 100   **3.** 75.8
5. 0.1635   **7.** 5020   **9.** 31.08   **11.** 8.293   **13.** 9.813
17. A   **19.** B   **21.** <   **23.** >   **25.** 8300   **27.** 0.25
29. 1800   **31.** true; Dividing by a whole number n separates the dividend into n equal groups.   **37.** 4.92×10^4
39. 9.3×10^7 **41.** 2,100,000,000,000,000,000
43. 17,000,000,000

4.5 Problem Solving (pp. 196 − 197)   45. 5670 in.^{2}
49. Draw just less than half of a puck.   **51. a.** 14,000,000
b. 1,400,000   **c.** 12,600,000; 14,000,000 − 1,400,000 = 12,600,000   **53.** 1,609,000; *Sample answer:* 1 mi. is about 1.609 km, multiply 1.609 by 1,000,000 to get 1,609,000 mm, since 1 km = 1,000,000 mm.   **55.** 0.017 nm   **57.** 0.4 nm
59. 0.97   **61.** 0.02   **63.** 10.3   **65.** 2.6

4.6 Skill Practice (pp. 200 − 201)   1. 8.49   **3.** $128 \div 31$
5. $1488 \div 93$ **7.** $8100 \div 614$ **9.** The decimal of the divisor was moved two places, but the decimal of the dividend was only moved one place, adding only one zero; correct way to write it is $38\overline{)1700}$.   **11.** 2.1   **13.** 80
15. 3.1   **17.** 108   **19.** 2937.5   **21.** 58.4   **23.** D
25. 13.89   **27.** 13.18   **29.** 1   **31.** 1.86   **33.** $\frac{1000}{31}$; 32.26
35. $\frac{10,000}{49}$; 204.08   **37.** =   **39.** <   **41.** <   **43.** always;
When the divisor is larger than the dividend, less than one of the divisors will go into the dividend.

4.6 Problem Solving (pp. 201 − 202)   45. a. divide; To find out how many of any item are within a group, use division.   **b.** $0.09\overline{)1.35}$ **c.** 15   **47.** 365.76 cm; Multiply the length of 1 picture by 24, the total number of pictures. You can add, but that would take much longer.
49. 4.6 cm   **57.** 4.2   **59.** 6.7   **61.** inches, centimeters

4.7 Skill Practice (p. 205)   1. capacity   **3.** chair
5. water pitcher   **7.** milliliters   **9.** liters   **11.** milliliters
13. mass   **15.** capacity   **17.** length   **19.** liters

21. kiloliters   **23.** milligrams   **25.** kilograms
29. bathroom scale
4.7 Problem Solving (p. 206)   33. kilograms; A book is about one kilogram. A climber is much larger than a book.   **39.** 0.057   **41.** 0.374   **43–45.** *Estimates will vary.*   **43.** 5   **45.** 100

4.8 Skill Practice (pp. 209 − 210)   1. meter, gram, liter   **3.** 10   **5.** 1000   **7.** 3.6   **9.** 0.8   **11.** 0.468   **13.** 74
15. <   **17.** =   **19.** >   **21.** >   **23.** >   **27.** 5 centigrams, 1.19 decigrams, 0.119 dekagrams, 5000 grams
29. false; x meters = $x \div 1000$ kilometers
31. false; x meters = x kilometers $\div 1000$

4.8 Problem Solving (pp. 210 − 212)   35. 275
37. 48 mm   **39.** wingspan   **43.** 1.7 km   **47.** 1200 m; 1,440,000 m^2 **49.** 10,000; 1 m^2 is 100 cm by 100 cm. $100 \times 100 = 10,000$.   **53.** 27   **55.** 100   **57.** 2.52; $3 \times 1 = 3$
59. 3492; $1000 \times 3 = 3000$

Chapter Review (pp. 214 − 218)   1. commutative property of multiplication   **3.** distributive   *Sample answers for 5–7.*   **5.** grams, kilograms, milligrams
7. 1000   **9.** capacity   **11.** 0.6   **13.** 0.092
15. commutative   **17.** 184   **19.** 153   **21.** 639   **23.** 473
25.–27. *Check will vary.*   **25.** 40.392; $6 \times 7 = 42$; reasonable   **27.** 0.1055; $20 \times 0.005 = 0.1$; reasonable
29. 202.6654; $25 \times 8 = 200$; reasonable   **31.** 0.001995; $0.002 \times 1 = 0.002$; reasonable   **33.** 6.5   **35.** 0.2   **37.** 65.3
39. 1.0   **41.** $8.05   **43.** 4.591   **45.** 97,800   **47.** 12,340
49. 1570   **51.** 1069.0   **53.** 23.8   **55.** 355.9   **57.** 3.0
59. 1506.3   **61.** 19.4   **63.** $3.95   **65.** grams
67. aquarium; a silo has a much greater capacity, and a scuba tank has much less capacity   **69.** 0.0245
71. 2   **73.** 12,300   **75.** 7.62 meters

Chapter 5

5.1 Skill Practice (pp. 232 − 233)   1. Even numbers are divisible by 2.   **3.** Numbers that end with 0 or 5 are divisible by 5.   **5.** neither   **7.** 1, 2, 4   **9.** 1, 11   **11.** 1, 3, 9, 27   **13.** 1, 2, 3, 4, 6, 9, 12, 18, 36   **15.** 1, 2, 3, 4, 6, 9, 12, 18, 27, 36, 54, 108   **17.** 1, 5, 25, 125   **19.** 2, 3, 6, 9
21. 3, 5, 9   **23.** 2, 3, 5, 6, 9, 10   **25.** 2, 3, 5, 6, 9, 10
27. prime   **29.** composite   **31.** prime   **33.** prime
35. prime   **37.** composite

39. $2 \times 3 \times 7$

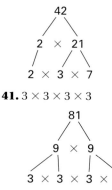

41. $3 \times 3 \times 3 \times 3$

43. 5×11 **45.** $2^4 \times 3$ **47.** 11^2 **49.** $3 \times 5 \times 11$
51. true; The rule for divisibility by 6 requires that the

number be divisible by 2. **53.** false; 2 is a prime number that is not odd. **55.** 18 **57.** 70 **59.** 90

5.1 Problem Solving (pp. 233 – 235) **63.** no; 80 is not divisible by 6 because it is not divisible by 3. **65.** A and B; 5 and 3 are factors of 75, but 6 is not a factor of 75, so C is not possible. **69.** 1, 2, 3, 6, 9, 18 **71.** 1, 2, 3, 4, 5, 6, 10, 12, 15, 20, 30, 60 **73.** 53 × 67

5.2 Skill Practice (pp. 238 – 239) **1.** 1, 2 **3.** factors for 10: 1, 2, 5, 10; factors for 28: 1, 2, 4, 7, 14, 28; common factors: 1, 2; GCF: 2 **5.** factors for 16: 1, 2, 4, 8, 16; factors for 48: 1, 2, 3, 4, 6, 8, 12, 16, 24, 48; common factors: 1, 2, 4, 8, 16; GCF: 16

7. 6

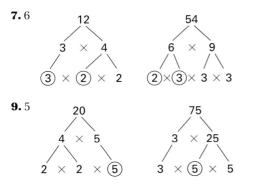

9. 5

11. 3 **13.** 3 **17.** The factor tree for 28 used 1 as a factor and did not finish because 4 can be factored into 2 × 2; GCF = 14

5.2 Problem Solving (pp. 239 – 240) *Sample answers for 29 a–b.* **29. a.** 2 rows of 15 because the GCF of 30 and 45 is 15 and 30 clowns ÷ 15 = 2 rows **b.** 3 rows of 15 because the GCF of 30 and 45 is 15 and 45 singers ÷ 15 = 3 rows

35. a.

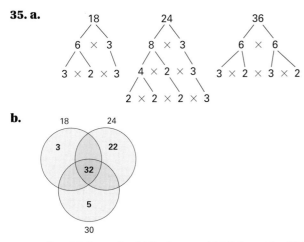

b.

c. yes; Cut 6 ft from the 24 ft piece and 12 ft from the 30 ft piece. Combine these pieces to make an 18 ft piece. There will be 4 pieces 18 ft each.

5.3 Skill Practice (p. 245 – 246) **1.** no; 2 is a common factor of 4 and 10. $\frac{4}{10}$ can be simplified to $\frac{2}{5}$. **3.** $\frac{2}{5}, \frac{4}{10}$ *Sample answers for 5 – 11.* **5.** $\frac{2}{20}, \frac{3}{30}$ **7.** $\frac{6}{10}, \frac{9}{15}$ **9.** $\frac{18}{40}, \frac{27}{60}$ **11.** $\frac{6}{200}, \frac{9}{300}$ **13.** A **15.** 45 **17.** 4

19. 54 **21.** 7 **23.** $\frac{1}{2}$ **25.** simplest form **27.** $\frac{5}{16}$ **29.** simplest form **31.** $\frac{19}{26}$ **33.** $\frac{19}{49}$ **35.** 5 **37.** 54 **39.** $\frac{1}{16}$ **41.** sometimes; The fraction $\frac{5}{10}$ has equivalent fractions $\frac{1}{2}$ and $\frac{20}{40}$. **43.** 3 **45.** 4

5.3 Problem Solving (pp. 246 – 248) **51.** $\frac{61}{121}; \frac{1}{2}$ **55.** *Sample answer:* Play baseball two hours per day; $\frac{1}{12}$; 30

5.4 Skill Practice (p. 252) **1.** *Sample answer:* 6, 12, 18 **3.** 56 **5.** 24, 48, 72, 96 **7.** 18, 36, 54, 72, 90 **9.** 60 **11.** 21 **13.** 30 **15.** 18 **17.** 30 **19.** 84 **21.** 396 **23.** 135 **25.** 360 **33.** 3, 17 **35.** 4, 16

5.5 Skill Practice (pp. 256 – 257) **1.** the least common multiple of the denominators **3.** < **5.** = **7.** > **9.** < **11.** > **13.** > **17.** D **19.** $\frac{5}{8}, \frac{2}{3}, \frac{3}{4}$ **21.** $\frac{4}{5}, \frac{17}{20}, \frac{9}{10}$ **23.** $\frac{5}{9}, \frac{7}{12}, \frac{3}{4}$ **25.** $\frac{3}{8}, \frac{4}{9}, \frac{11}{24}$ **27.** $\frac{17}{150}, \frac{13}{100}, \frac{4}{30}$ **29.** $\frac{22}{50}, \frac{105}{225}, \frac{71}{150}$

5.5 Problem Solving (pp. 257 – 258) **47.** $\frac{3}{8}, \frac{1}{2}, \frac{3}{4}$ **55.** Asia **57.** South America

5.6 Skill Practice (pp. 263 – 264) **1.** a fraction with the numerator bigger than or equal to the denominator; $\frac{7}{3}$ **3.** $1\frac{3}{4}$ in. $\frac{7}{4}$ in. **7.** $\frac{13}{4}$ **9.** $\frac{11}{4}$ **11.** $\frac{23}{4}$ **13.** $\frac{49}{4}$ **15.** $4\frac{1}{6}$ **17.** $7\frac{1}{3}$ **21.** > **23.** < **25.** $2\frac{3}{4}, 3, \frac{7}{2}$ **27.** $5, \frac{41}{8}, 5\frac{1}{6}, \frac{17}{3}$ **29.** $\frac{13}{2}, \frac{33}{5}, 6\frac{2}{3}, 6\frac{5}{6}$ **31.** $8\frac{1}{4}, \frac{25}{3}, 8\frac{3}{8}, \frac{76}{9}$ **33.** $\frac{43}{6}, \frac{36}{5}, 7\frac{3}{8}, 7\frac{4}{9}$

5.6 Problem Solving (pp. 264 – 265) **47. a.** $\frac{177}{60}, \frac{192}{60}, \frac{224}{60}$ **b.** $2\frac{19}{20}$ sec; $3\frac{1}{5}$ sec; $3\frac{11}{15}$ sec **49.** $\frac{9}{8}$; no; $\frac{9}{8} < \frac{10}{8}$ **51.** Perry

5.7 Skill Practice (pp. 268 – 269) **1.** A fraction is in simplest form when the only common factor of the numerator and the denominator is one (1). **3.** $\frac{1}{2}$ **5.** $\frac{7}{10}$ **7.** $\frac{1}{50}$ **9.** $\frac{1}{200}$ **13.** 3 **15.** 2 **17.** $5\frac{9}{10}$ **19.** $1\frac{6}{25}$ **21.** $4\frac{3}{50}$ **23.** $9\frac{1}{50}$ **25.** $\frac{39}{1000}$ **27.** $6\frac{153}{500}$ **29.** 3 **31.** 3 **33.** 30 **35.** 34 **37.** $\frac{237}{100}$ **39.** $\frac{493}{50}$ **41.** $\frac{4}{16}, \frac{10}{40}$ **43.** $\frac{12}{16}, \frac{30}{40}$

5.7 Problem Solving (pp. 269 – 270) **47.** $398\frac{2}{5}$ **53. a.** $\frac{1177}{2500}$ in. **b.** 0.5 in. **c.** $\frac{1}{2}$ **d.** $\frac{1}{2}$; 0.5 > 0.4708

5.8 Skill Practice (pp. 273 – 274) **1.** terminating **3.** repeating **5.** 0.3 **7.** 0.6 **9.** 1.125 **11.** 3.25 **15.** $3.\overline{72}$ **17.** $0.4\overline{6}$ **19.** $4.2\overline{27}$ **21.** $0.2\overline{7}$ **23.** $5.\overline{8}$ **25.** $0.58\overline{3}$ **27.** < **29.** = **31.** > **33.** > **35.** = **37.** < **43.** $0.\overline{5}, 0.56, \frac{7}{11}, \frac{11}{16}$ **45.** $2\frac{17}{25}, 2.6\overline{81}, 2\frac{13}{19}, 2.\overline{68}$

5.8 Problem Solving (pp. 274 – 275) **49.** 5.8125, 4.25, 7.125 **51.** $\frac{23}{8}$ **53.** 13.1, $13\frac{3}{16}$, 13.25, $13\frac{3}{8}$, $\frac{55}{4}$

5.8 Technology Activity (p. 276) **1.** 0.83 **3.** 0.31 **5.** 5.38 **7.** 13.39 **9.** 28.19 **11.** 50.82 **13.** 36.35 **15.** 48.58

Chapter Review (pp. 278 – 282) **1.** a multiple shared by two or more numbers **3.** *Sample answer:* 2, 3, 5; A prime number has exactly two factors, 1 and itself. **5.** equivalent **7.** proper fraction **9.** 2, 3, 6, 9 **11.** 2 **13.** 3, 5 **15.** 5 **17.** $2 \times 5 \times 7$ **19.** $3^2 \times 7^2$ **21.** $2^3 \times 3 \times 5$ **23.** $2^5 \times 3$ **25.** 12 **27.** 5 **29.** 16 **31.** 12 **33.** $6 **35.** $\frac{1}{7}$ **37.** $\frac{1}{7}$ **39.** $\frac{5}{8}$ **41.** $\frac{2}{3}$ **43.** $\frac{3}{4}$ **45.** 315 **47.** 72 **49.** $\frac{1}{8}$, $\frac{1}{7}$, $\frac{9}{56}$ **51.** $\frac{7}{25}$, $\frac{3}{10}$, $\frac{2}{5}$ **53.** $\frac{21}{5}$ **55.** $2\frac{5}{9}$ **57.** $4\frac{4}{5}$ **59.** $\frac{121}{200}$ **61.** $\frac{1}{8}$ **63.** $3\frac{16}{25}$ **65.** 0.875 **67.** $5.\overline{4}$ **69.** 6.25 **71.** $0.91\overline{6}$ **73.** $3.5\overline{3}$ **75.** 4.075

Chapter 6

6.1 Skill Practice (p. 293) **1.** half **3.** $\frac{1}{2}$ **5.** 1 **7.** 1 **9.** 4 **11.** 0 **13.** $\frac{1}{2}$ **15.** 7 **17.** 5 **19.** 4 **21.** 5 **25.** high estimate **27.** low estimate **29.** low estimate **31.** < **33.** < **35.** $10 - 6 + 2 = 6$; Answer is reasonable because it's very close to actual answer of $5\frac{19}{20}$.

6.1 Problem Solving (p. 294) **37.** 3 **41.** 111 m; *Sample answer:* The photograph is about 5 in., so a scale could be 1 in. = 22 m.

6.2 Skill Practice (pp. 297 – 298) **1.** numerators, denominators **3.** $1\frac{1}{5}$ **5.** 1 **7.** $\frac{1}{3}$ **9.** 1 **11.** $\frac{2}{7}$ **13.** $\frac{5}{8}$ **15.** $\frac{2}{7}$ **17.** $\frac{4}{5}$ **21.** $\frac{5}{8} - \frac{3}{8}$; $\frac{1}{4}$ **23.** $1\frac{11}{12}$ **25.** $\frac{11}{16}$ **27.** $\frac{9}{14}$ **29.** $\frac{1}{2}$ **31.** $\frac{1}{4}$ **33.** $\frac{5}{7}$

6.2 Problem Solving (pp. 298 – 300) **39.** $\frac{3}{4}$ **41. a.** $\frac{3}{5}$ **b.** $\frac{2}{5}$ **c.** Amount more I swam = Amount I swam – Amount my friends swam; $\frac{1}{5}$

6.3 Skill Practice (pp. 304 – 305) **1.** least common denominator **3.** $1\frac{2}{5}$ **5.** $1\frac{7}{30}$ **7.** $1\frac{5}{14}$ **9.** $1\frac{3}{7}$ **11.** $\frac{79}{90}$ **13.** $1\frac{47}{84}$ **15.** $\frac{5}{24}$ **17.** $\frac{23}{40}$ **19.** $\frac{8}{15}$ **21.** $\frac{13}{28}$ **25.** $1\frac{7}{12}$ **27.** $\frac{1}{24}$ **29.** $\frac{29}{36}$ **31.** $\frac{5}{12}$ **33.** $1\frac{2}{15}$ ft **35.** $1\frac{3}{7}$ **37.** 0 **39.** $\frac{1}{12}$ **41.** $\frac{9}{20}$ **43.** $\frac{7}{12}$ **45.** $\frac{9}{20}$ **47.** $2\frac{143}{180}$

6.3 Problem Solving (pp. 306 – 307) **53. a.** $\frac{7}{12}$ **b.** $\frac{7}{12} - \frac{5}{12}$ **c.** $\frac{1}{6}$ **55. a.** $\frac{1}{5}$ in. **b.** $\frac{7}{10}$ in.; $\frac{9}{10}$ in. **c.** 7

6.4 Skill Practice (pp. 311 – 313) **1.** $4\frac{2}{3}$ **3.** $4\frac{3}{4}$ **5.** $9\frac{7}{9}$ **7.** $12\frac{5}{6}$ **9.** $12\frac{1}{10}$ **11.** $10\frac{1}{8}$ **13.** When

simplifying $8\frac{6}{5}$, I should have added 1 to 8 and changed $\frac{6}{5}$ to $\frac{1}{5}$; $7\frac{2}{5} + 1\frac{4}{5} = 9\frac{1}{5}$ **15.** $1\frac{2}{5}$ **17.** $3\frac{3}{4}$ **19.** $2\frac{7}{12}$ **21.** $3\frac{5}{14}$ **25–35.** *Methods may vary.* **25.** $11\frac{14}{15}$; paper and pencil **27.** $9\frac{5}{6}$; mental math **29.** $9\frac{3}{11}$; mental math **31.** $1\frac{2}{3}$; mental math **33.** 8; mental math **35.** 4; mental math **37.** $2\frac{1}{6}$ **39.** $8\frac{5}{6}$ **41.** $4\frac{83}{210}$ **43.** $4\frac{4}{5}$ cm **45.** $3\frac{5}{8}$, $4\frac{1}{8}$, $4\frac{5}{8}$; Add $\frac{4}{8}$. **47.** $4\frac{2}{3}$, $2\frac{5}{6}$, 1; Subtract $1\frac{5}{6}$. **49.** *Sample answer:* $3\frac{1}{2} - 1\frac{1}{4} = 2\frac{1}{4}$; *Sample answer:* $5\frac{1}{10} - 3\frac{5}{6} = 1\frac{8}{30}$ **51.** 2 **53.** 4 **55.** 1

6.4 Problem Solving (pp. 313 – 314) **57.** $8\frac{1}{4}$ ft

63. a.

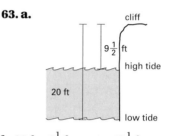

b. 20 ft – $9\frac{1}{2}$ ft = x; $x = 10\frac{1}{2}$ ft

6.5 Skill Practice (pp. 318 – 319) **1.** 7 **3.** 4 **5.** $2\frac{3}{4} = 1\frac{7}{4}$ **7.** $1\frac{1}{3}$ **9.** $4\frac{5}{7}$ **11.** $9\frac{7}{15}$ **13.** $1\frac{3}{4}$ **15.** $2\frac{19}{24}$ **17.** $2\frac{31}{56}$ **19.** $1\frac{9}{14}$ **21.** $\frac{3}{4}$ **25.** yes; $\frac{1}{4} < \frac{1}{2}$ **27.** no; $\frac{7}{10} > \frac{3}{10}$ **29.** yes; You always have to borrow to subtract a fraction from a whole. **31.** no; $\frac{5}{8} > \frac{1}{6}$ **33.** $\frac{1}{4}$ **35.** $\frac{1}{8}$ **37.** $7\frac{7}{12}$ **39.** $5\frac{47}{60}$ **41.** $5\frac{7}{12}$ **43.** $4\frac{7}{12}$

6.5 Problem Solving (pp. 319 – 320) **47.** $2\frac{2}{3}$ in. **49.** $\frac{1}{3}$ ft; $4 - 3\frac{2}{3} = 3\frac{3}{3} - 3\frac{2}{3} = \frac{1}{3}$ **53. a.** $23\frac{19}{24}$

b.

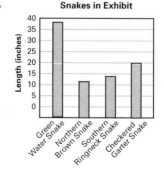

c. The green water snake is about 3 times longer than the northern brown snake; $23\frac{19}{24}$ in.

6.5 Technology Activity (p. 321) *Internet findings for European measurements are given primarily in centimeters, so measurements in inches may vary. Sample answers for 1–3:* **1.** A4 has length and width $11\frac{2}{3}$ in. $\times 8\frac{1}{4}$ in.; A5 has length and width $8\frac{1}{4}$ in. $\times 5\frac{3}{4}$ in.; The difference in length is $3\frac{5}{12}$ in. The difference in width is $2\frac{1}{2}$ in. **3.** Legal has length and width 14 in. $\times 8\frac{1}{2}$ in.; Letter has length and width 11 in. $\times 8\frac{1}{2}$ in.; The difference in length is 3 in.; The difference in width is 0 in.

6.6 Skill Practice (pp. 324 – 325) **1.** start, end **3.** 3 h 25 min **5.** 5 h 33 min 35 sec **7.** 2 h 15 min **9.** 2 h **11.** 5 h 15 min **13.** 13 h 9 min **17–21.** *Answers will vary.* **17.** 4 h **19.** 70 sec **21.** 4 sec **23.** 2 weeks 2 days **25.** 2 days 23 h 59 min

6.6 Problem Solving (pp. 325 – 327) **27.** 6 h 20 min **31. a.** 49 min; $\frac{49}{60}$ h; 9 h 4 min – 8 h 15 min = 49 min **b.** minutes; Most people will say a class is 49 minutes long instead of $\frac{49}{60}$ of an hour. **c.** 2 h 27 min **35.** 11:30 A.M. **37.** *Sample answer:* Dallas **39.** 6:20 P.M.

Chapter Review (pp. 328 – 332) **1.** half, mixed numbers **3.** 24 **5.** Any fraction that is $\frac{1}{2}$ or higher gets rounded up. $3\frac{1}{2}$ rounds to 4. **7.** *Sample answer:* 3 can be rewritten as $2\frac{3}{3}$, so $3\frac{1}{3} = 2\frac{3}{3} + \frac{1}{3} = 2\frac{4}{3}$. **9.** $\frac{1}{2}$ **11.** 8 **13.** $\frac{1}{2}$ **15.** 6 **17.** $\frac{2}{3}$ **19.** $\frac{1}{4}$ **21.** $\frac{9}{10}$ **23.** $1\frac{1}{28}$ **25.** $\frac{7}{20}$ **27.** $\frac{2}{5}$ **29.** $\frac{1}{12}$ in. **31.** $3\frac{17}{21}$ **33.** $6\frac{23}{30}$ **35.** $4\frac{1}{10}$ **37.** $\frac{3}{20}$ **39.** $2\frac{7}{12}$ **41.** $5\frac{2}{9}$ **43.** $1\frac{3}{4}$ ft **45.** 39 min 44 sec **47.** 6 h 20 min **49.** 9 h

Chapter 7

7.1 Skill Practice (pp. 343 – 344) **1.** yes; 36 is divisible by 9. **3.** $\frac{9}{10}$ **5.** $5\frac{1}{3}$ **7.** $1\frac{1}{3}$ **9.** $3\frac{3}{4}$ **11.** 10 **13.** 36 **17.** 49; 7 **19.** 40; 25 **21.** 81; 72 **23.** 55; 10 **25.** 80 **27.** 20

7.1 Problem Solving (pp. 344 – 345) **31. a.** $\frac{3}{4} \cdot 21$ **b.** 20 **c.** 15 lb; low; 21 was rounded down to 20. **33.** $6 **35.** $3\frac{1}{2}$ mi **37.** less, greater, less, greater, less; 16, 36, 12, 40, 9 **39.** 4 **41.** no; 12 small tomatoes will make 6 cups, but $\frac{2}{3} \cdot 6 + \frac{3}{4} \cdot 6 = 8\frac{1}{2}$ **43.** The product of a whole number and an improper fraction is greater than the whole number; An improper fraction is greater than 1, and when you multiply a whole number by a number greater than 1, the product is greater than the whole number.

7.2 Skill Practice (pp. 351 – 352) **1.** The numerator and denominator have no common factors except 1.

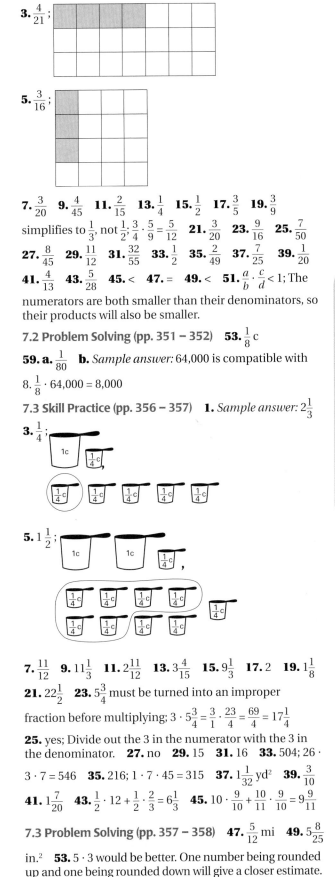

3. $\frac{4}{21}$;

5. $\frac{3}{16}$;

7. $\frac{3}{20}$ **9.** $\frac{4}{45}$ **11.** $\frac{2}{15}$ **13.** $\frac{1}{4}$ **15.** $\frac{1}{2}$ **17.** $\frac{3}{5}$ **19.** $\frac{3}{9}$ simplifies to $\frac{1}{3}$, not $\frac{1}{2}$; $\frac{3}{4} \cdot \frac{5}{9} = \frac{5}{12}$ **21.** $\frac{3}{20}$ **23.** $\frac{9}{16}$ **25.** $\frac{7}{50}$ **27.** $\frac{8}{45}$ **29.** $\frac{11}{12}$ **31.** $\frac{32}{55}$ **33.** $\frac{1}{2}$ **35.** $\frac{2}{49}$ **37.** $\frac{7}{25}$ **39.** $\frac{1}{20}$ **41.** $\frac{4}{13}$ **43.** $\frac{5}{28}$ **45.** < **47.** = **49.** < **51.** $\frac{a}{b} \cdot \frac{c}{d} < 1$; The numerators are both smaller than their denominators, so their products will also be smaller.

7.2 Problem Solving (pp. 351 – 352) **53.** $\frac{1}{8}$ c **59. a.** $\frac{1}{80}$ **b.** *Sample answer:* 64,000 is compatible with 8. $\frac{1}{8} \cdot 64,000 = 8,000$

7.3 Skill Practice (pp. 356 – 357) **1.** *Sample answer:* $2\frac{1}{3}$

3. $\frac{1}{4}$;

5. $1\frac{1}{2}$;

7. $\frac{11}{12}$ **9.** $11\frac{1}{3}$ **11.** $2\frac{11}{12}$ **13.** $3\frac{4}{15}$ **15.** $9\frac{1}{3}$ **17.** 2 **19.** $1\frac{1}{8}$ **21.** $22\frac{1}{2}$ **23.** $5\frac{3}{4}$ must be turned into an improper fraction before multiplying; $3 \cdot 5\frac{3}{4} = \frac{3}{1} \cdot \frac{23}{4} = \frac{69}{4} = 17\frac{1}{4}$ **25.** yes; Divide out the 3 in the numerator with the 3 in the denominator. **27.** no **29.** 15 **31.** 16 **33.** 504; 26 · 3 · 7 = 546 **35.** 216; 1 · 7 · 45 = 315 **37.** $1\frac{1}{32}$ yd² **39.** $\frac{3}{10}$ **41.** $1\frac{7}{20}$ **43.** $\frac{1}{2} \cdot 12 + \frac{1}{2} \cdot \frac{2}{3} = 6\frac{1}{3}$ **45.** $10 \cdot \frac{9}{10} + \frac{10}{11} \cdot \frac{9}{10} = 9\frac{9}{11}$

7.3 Problem Solving (pp. 357 – 358) **47.** $\frac{5}{12}$ mi **49.** $5\frac{8}{25}$ in.² **53.** 5 · 3 would be better. One number being rounded up and one being rounded down will give a closer estimate.

7.4 Skill Practice (pp. 364 – 365)   **1.** no   **3.** yes   **5.** $\frac{5}{4}$
7. $\frac{1}{10}$ **9.** $\frac{9}{2} \cdot \frac{4}{3}$; 6   **11.** $\frac{2}{3} \cdot \frac{1}{4}$; $\frac{1}{6}$ **13.** $\frac{1}{2}$ **15.** $\frac{2}{5}$ **17.** $\frac{5}{9}$
19. 20   **23.** $1 \div \frac{1}{8} = 8$, which is not close to $\frac{1}{6}$.
25. $\frac{1}{7}$ **27.** 1   **29.** 5, 30   **31.** <; Dividing by a number larger than 1 makes the quotient smaller.   **33.** <; Dividing by a number larger than 1 makes the quotient smaller.   **35.** 36   **37.** $\frac{1}{15}$ **39.** $\frac{5}{3}$ **41.** $\frac{9}{5}$ **43.** $\frac{3}{7}$ **45.** $3\frac{23}{35}$

7.4 Problem Solving (pp. 365 – 366)   **47. a.** $12 \div \frac{5}{8}$
b. $19\frac{1}{5}$ **c.** You can make 19 magnets.   **49.** 45   **51.** 12; 3 circles divide into 12 pieces when 3 is divided by $\frac{1}{4}$.
55. a. 7; 4   **b.** 2; $\frac{1}{4}$ lb   **c.** 4 teacups, 2 mugs; Guess and check

7.5 Skill Practice (pp. 369 – 370)   **1.** $\frac{27}{4}, \frac{8}{1}$ **3.** 18
5. 6   **7.** $\frac{5}{7}$ **9.** $\frac{1}{6}$ **11.** $4\frac{1}{2}$ **13.** $1\frac{7}{10}$ **15.** $1\frac{29}{35}$ **17.** $\frac{23}{96}$
21. 7;

├─2─┼─2─┼─2─┼─2─┼─2─┤ ├─2─┼─2─┤

23. 6   **25.** 7   **27.** 9   **29.** 3   **31.** 7   **33.** $2\frac{2}{5}$
35. $\frac{15}{34}$ **37.** $13\frac{1}{2}$ **39.** $6\frac{7}{12}$ **41.** 189

7.5 Problem Solving (pp. 370 – 372)   **45.** 9; I chose division because I found the number of CDs that fit into the box.   **47.** 9; I chose division because I wanted to know how many times to fill the cup.
49. $1\frac{3}{16}$ lb; I subtracted to find the difference in weight.   **51.** $\frac{7}{9}$ yd; I divided so I could find the amount of material I will have.   **53.** $\frac{1}{2}$; I divided to find the fraction of the total length. **57.** 5; $\frac{3}{8}$ **59.** $2\frac{1}{10}$ in./h   **61.** $6\frac{1}{2}$

7.6 Skill Practice (pp. 375 – 376)   **1.** fluid ounces, cups, pints, quarts, gallons   **3.** B   **5.** A   **7.** ounces   **9.** fluid ounces   **11.** fluid ounces   **13.** Capacity is measured in fluid ounces. The capacity of the water bottle is about 20 fluid ounces.   **15.** weight   **17.** weight   **19.** ounces; All of the other units were measures of capacity.
21. more   **23.** more than a quart; A bathroom sink will hold a couple of gallons.   **25.** less than a quart; A quart would fill up a few ice cube trays.

7.6 Problem Solving (pp. 376 – 377)   **29.** bird – ounces; zebra – pounds; elephant – tons   **31.** height: plastic bowl, glass vase, paper cup; capacity: glass vase, paper cup, plastic bowl; weight: paper cup, plastic bowl, glass vase

7.7 Skill Practice (pp. 381 – 382)   **1.** 1   **3.** 16   **5.** 12,000 lb
7. 5 qt   **9.** $3\frac{3}{4}$ ft   **11.** 4300 lb   **13.** 13 ft   **15.** $1\frac{1}{8}$ yd
19. 22 lb 1 oz   **21.** 2 yd 2 ft   **23.** 5 c 6 fl oz

25.

ounces	pounds
14	$\frac{7}{8}$
32	2
70	$4\frac{3}{8}$

27.

feet	miles
2640	$\frac{1}{2}$
10,560	2
18,480	$3\frac{1}{2}$

29. $1\frac{1}{2}$ **31.** 190,080   **33.** 2200   **35.** <; paper and pencil; $\frac{7}{8}$ mi = 4620 ft   **37.** =; paper and pencil; $13\frac{1}{3}$ fl oz converts to $1\frac{2}{3}$ c   **39.** >; paper and pencil; 17 lb = 272 oz
41. $1\frac{3}{4}$ ft, $\frac{2}{3}$ yd, 25 in., $\frac{13}{6}$ ft

7.7 Problem Solving (pp. 382 – 384)   **43.** $1\frac{1}{3}$ **47.** $\frac{3}{4}$
49. yes   **53.** 8

7.7 Technology Activity (p. 385)

1. Length

km	mi
127	79
55	34
1388	862

3. Weight

kg	lbs
12	26
50	110
35	77

Chapter Review (pp. 387 – 390)   **1.** true   **3.** false; The reciprocal of $1\frac{1}{3}$ is $\frac{3}{4}$.   **5.** false; The unit pint is used to measure capacity.   **7.** true   **9.** $3\frac{1}{6}$ **11.** $2\frac{1}{7}$ **13.** $12 \cdot \frac{8}{9} = 10\frac{2}{3}$ **15.** $42 \cdot \frac{5}{6} = 35$ **17.** 30 in.   **19.** $\frac{32}{63}$ **21.** $\frac{1}{6}$ **23.** $\frac{1}{12}$
25. $\frac{5}{24}$ **27.** $\frac{1}{5}$ **29.** $\frac{9}{23}$ **31.** $1\frac{1}{5}$ **33.** $15\frac{1}{3}$ **35.** $\frac{5}{27}$
37. $1\frac{1}{6}$ **39.** 32   **41.** $\frac{1}{27}$ **43.** $20   **45.** $\frac{11}{35}$ **47.** $3\frac{6}{7}$
49. pounds   **51.** gallons   **53.** capacity   **55.** weight
57. 86   **59.** 35   **61.** 152   **63.** 43   **65.** 25   **67.** 10 glasses

Chapter 8

8.1 Skill Practice (pp. 404 – 405) **1.** ratio **3.** $\frac{13}{20}$, 13 : 20
5. $\frac{2}{5}$ **7.** $\frac{4}{15}$ **11.** 2 **13.** 27 **15.** 20 **17.** 1 **19.** 4 **21.** 72
23. $\frac{14}{12}$ or $\frac{7}{6}$ **25.** $\frac{25}{6}$ **27.** Sara

8.1 Problem Solving (pp. 405 – 406) **29.** $\frac{1}{6}$ **31.** $\frac{2}{1}$
35. $\frac{1}{8}$

8.2 Skill Practice (pp. 409 – 410) **1.** 2 ft/s, unit rate
3. 76 words/2 min, rate or 38 words/min, unit rate **5.** 4 h
7. 4 laps **9.** 17.4 cm **11.** 48 students/24 computers,
2 students/computer **13.** 250 pages/5 chapters,
50 pages/chapter **15.** 55 mi/h **17.** 3.5 m/sec
19. 2.21 lb/kg **21.** 2.54 cm/in. **23.** equivalent **25.** not
equivalent **27.** The calculation to find the rate was done
correctly, but dollars is the unit in the numerator and
books is the unit in the denominator. The answer should
be $6.50 per book.

8.2 Problem Solving (pp. 410 – 411)
39. a. Bart: 4 baskets/h, Tia: 4.8 baskets/h
b. Since 4.8 > 4, Tia is faster.

c. Bart

Time	Number of baskets completed
8:00	0
8:45	3
9:30	6
10:15	9
11:00	12
11:45	15
12:30	18
1:15	21
2:00	24
2:45	27
3:30	30
4:15	33
5:00	36

Tia

Time	Number of baskets completed
9:00	0
9:50	4
10:40	8
11:30	12
12:20	16
1:10	20
2:00	24
2:50	28
3:30	almost 32

Bart makes the most in a day.

8.3 Skill Practice and (pp. 414 – 415) **1.** 72; 3x
3. yes **5.** no **7.** yes **9.** no **11.** no **13.** no

15. 30 **17.** 8 **19.** 7 **21.** 9 **25.** $r = \frac{240}{8}$; 30
27. $t = \frac{180}{18}$; 10 **29.** $x = \frac{360}{24}$; 15 **31.** $x = \frac{74.8}{6.8}$; 11
33–39. *Choices may vary.* **33.** related equation; $s = \frac{156}{9.75}$;
16 **35.** mental math; Divide 5 by 4; 1.25 **37.** related
equation; $m = \frac{300}{12}$; 25 **39.** related equation; $w = \frac{60}{2.4}$; 25

41.

Games Played	6	9	12	15
Total Cost	8	12	16	20

8.3 Problem Solving (pp. 415 – 416) 45. 9 **47.** $3.68

8.4 Skill Practice (pp. 419 – 420) **1.** scale **3.** $\frac{1 \text{ in.}}{6 \text{ ft}} =$
$\frac{\text{length in drawing}}{48 \text{ ft}}$; 8 in. **5.** 400 mi **7.** 105 mi
9. 225 mi **11.** 900 mi **13.** 10 cm **15.** 26.325 mm
17. 1 in.^{2} = 12 ft^2 **19.** Both rates must be of the form
$\frac{\text{in.}}{\text{ft}}$, $\frac{1 \text{ in.}}{2 \text{ ft}} = \frac{6 \text{ in.}}{x \text{ ft}}$; 12 ft **21.** 15 cm : 1 km; 225 cm^2 : 1 km^2
23. 2 in. : 75 mi; 4 in.^{2} : 5625 mi^2 **25.** 12 cm : 0.05 mm;
144 cm^2 : 0.0025 mm^2 **27.** 1 cm = 20 km; 1 cm^2 : 400 km^2
29. 1 cm : 0.2 mm

8.4 Problem Solving (pp. 420 – 422)
33. 300 ft **37.** 15 m · 20 m **39.** 1 cm^2 : 25 m^2

41. a. *Sample answer:*

Dimensions	Perimeter	Area
2 cm by 5 cm	14 cm	10 cm^2
6 cm by 15 cm	42 cm	90 cm^2

b. See table above. **c.** yes; The perimeter was multiplied
by 3, and the area was multiplied by 3^2.

8.5 Skill Practice (p. 427) **1.** 100 **3.** 15%, 0.15, $\frac{3}{20}$
5. 56%, 0.56, $\frac{14}{25}$ **7.** six hundredths, 6% **9.** seventy-four
hundredths, 74% **11.** nineteen hundredths, 19%
13. five hundred twenty-eight thousandths; 52.8%
15. 0.40, $\frac{2}{5}$ **17.** 0.07, $\frac{7}{100}$ **19.** 0.185, $\frac{37}{200}$ **21.** 0.333, $\frac{333}{1000}$
25. > **27.** > **29.** =

8.5 Problem Solving (p. 428) **35.** 19%, 81%; The entire
circle is 100%. The other categories add up to 81%.
100% − 81% = 19%. 81% represents all the categories of
more than 1 day.

8.6 Skill Practice (pp. 431 – 432) **1.** 60% **3.** 90%
5. 34% **7.** 50% **9.** 12% **11.** 26.1% **13.** 99.8%
17. 20% **19.** 8.4% **21.** 57.1% **23.** 3.7% **25.** 37.7%
27. 58.6% **31.** 15%, 0.16, $\frac{1}{4}$ **33.** 50%, $\frac{2}{3}$, $\frac{7}{10}$, 0.77
35. 0.3, 33%, $\frac{1}{3}$, 34% **37.** 70% **39.** 350% **41.** 5.7

8.6 Problem Solving (pp. 432 – 433) 43. 20%

8.7 Skill Practice (pp. 437 – 438) **1.** interest = principal · annual interest rate · time **3.** 42 **5.** 10 **7.** 9 **9.** 10.2 **11.** 9 **13.** 8.1 **15.** 37.2 **17.** 21

19. 1% is $\frac{1}{100}$, not $\frac{1}{10}$; 1% of 400 = $\frac{1}{100}$ · 400 = 4

21. $36 **23.** $32 **25.** $28 **27.** $20 **29.** $38.40 **31.** $5.60 *Sample estimates for 33 – 39.* **33.** 600 **35.** 1.5 **37.** 3.6 **39.** 27 **43.** < **45.** = **47.** <

8.7 Problem Solving (pp. 438 – 440) **51.** cost = 50 × 0.05 + 50; $52.50 **53.** $42 **55.** $6.00 **61.** 60%; 60%; The percentages are the same. **63. a.** $244; $258.64 **b.** $290; $232; $245.92 **c.** package; $245.92 < $258.64

8.7 Technology Activity (p. 441) **1.** 7.2 **3.** 7.809 **5.** 24.057 **7.** 8.64 **9.** 60.45 **11.** 1.34 **13.** 8.2 **15.** 14.13 **17.** $1.05; $16.00

Chapter Review (pp. 443 – 446) **1.** false **3.** unit rate **5.** 2 : 7 **7.** 8-pack; $5.60 ÷ 8 < 2.84 ÷ 4 **9.** 9; equivalent ratios **11.** 30; cross product **13.** 48 km **15.** 96 km **17.** 75 ft by 175 ft **19.** sixty-four hundredths, 64% **21.** thirty-one hundredths, 31% **23.** 0.64, $\frac{16}{25}$

25. 0.90, $\frac{9}{10}$ **27.** 40% **29.** 56.25% **31.** 0.2, 25%, $\frac{1}{3}$, 0.35, 40%, $\frac{3}{5}$ **33.** 63 **35.** 110.5 **37.** 105 **39.** 90 **41.** $9

Chapter 9

9.1 Skill Practice (pp. 457 – 458) **1.** C **3.** A **5.** line that extends through points A and B **7.** ray that starts at endpoint H and extends through point G **9.** ray; $\overrightarrow{HG}$ **11.** line; $\overleftrightarrow{YZ}$ *Sample Answers for 13–17.* **13.** $\overrightarrow{ED}$, $\overrightarrow{EA}$ **15.** $\overline{EA}$ **17.** $\overleftrightarrow{AC}$ and $\overleftrightarrow{BC}$, $\overleftrightarrow{AE}$ and $\overleftrightarrow{DE}$ **19.** point **21.** segment **23.** false; $\overline{AB}$ has an endpoint, but $\overleftrightarrow{AB}$ doesn't. **25.** true; $\overleftrightarrow{QP}$ and $\overleftrightarrow{PQ}$ go forever in both directions through P and Q. **27.** false; $\overline{DE}$ has two endpoints, but $\overleftrightarrow{DE}$ has none. *Sample answers for 28–29.* **29.**

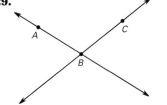

31. $\overleftrightarrow{MN}$, $\overleftrightarrow{FG}$, and $\overleftrightarrow{JH}$ **33.** $\overleftrightarrow{KN}$, $\overleftrightarrow{FG}$, $\overleftrightarrow{KL}$; $\overleftrightarrow{JH}$, $\overleftrightarrow{GH}$, $\overleftrightarrow{LM}$, $\overleftrightarrow{NM}$, $\overleftrightarrow{GL}$, $\overleftrightarrow{FK}$ and $\overleftrightarrow{JN}$

9.1 Problem Solving (pp. 458 – 459)

35. parallel **37.** $\overline{CD}$ or $\overline{EF}$ **39.** K
45.

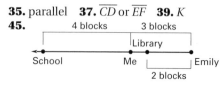

9.2 Skill Practice (pp. 462–463) **1.** E; $\overrightarrow{ED}$ and $\overrightarrow{EF}$ **3.** $\angle TUV$, $\angle VUT$, $\angle U$; greater than 90° **5.** $\angle QRS$ names R as the vertex, but in the diagram, S is the vertex. $\angle QSR$ **7.**

9.

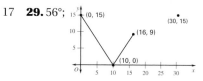

11. 30° **13.** 15° **15.** 120° **17.** between 0° and 45°; 35° **19.** between 45° and 90°; 65°

9.2 Problem Solving (pp. 463 – 464) **23.** 40° **25.** 13; 17 **29.** 56°;

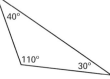

9.3 Skill Practice (pp. 467 – 468) **1.** B **3.** C **7.** obtuse **9.** right **11.** $\angle HKJ$ and $\angle MKL$, $\angle HKM$ and $\angle JKL$ **13.** supplementary **15.** neither **17.** neither **19.** complementary **21.** Supplementary angles have a sum of 180°. The equation shows a sum of 90°, which is used for complementary angles. $x° + 28° = 180°$; $x = 152$ **23.** 49° **25.** 30°; *Sample answer:* Vertical angles have the same measure. **27.** 120°; *Sample answer:* $\angle DAB$ is supplementary with $\angle EAD$ **29.** 150°; *Sample answer:* $\angle FAB$ is supplementary with $\angle CAB$

9.3 Problem Solving (pp. 468 – 469) **33.** acute **35.** straight **37.** 60°; If the fruit tree branch makes a 30° angle with the ground, then the measure of its complementary angle is 60°. If you add 1° to the 30° angle, you get 31° and 59°. As you keep increasing the 30° angle, the complementary angle keeps decreasing, so the greatest measure for this angle is 60°.

9.4 Skill Practice (pp. 473 – 474) **1.** A **3.** B **5.** C **7.** obtuse **9.** acute **11.** equilateral **13.** The sum should be equal to 180°. $35° + 25° + x° = 180°$; 120° **15.** 95° **17.** 40° **19.** 60° **23.** yes; right **25.** no **27.** no **29–33.** Check work.

9.4 Problem Solving (pp. 475 – 476) **37.** 63° **39.** scalene **41.** isosceles **43.** always; Since the sum of the angle measures is 180° and one angle measures 90°, the other two must be complementary.

45. always; Since one angle is more than 90° and the sum of the three angles must be 180°, the sum of the other two must be less than 90°.

9.4 Technology Activity (p. 477) **1.** 50° **3.** 34° **5.** 106.9° **7.** 65°

9.5 Skill Practice (pp. 482 – 483) **1.** some **3.** all **5.** all **7.** some **9.** rectangle **11.** rhombus

15. yes   **17.** 66°   **19.** 102°   **21.** The drawing could be a rectangle or a square.   **25.** A trapezoid is a quadrilateral with exactly two sides parallel.

9.5 Problem Solving (pp. 483–484)   27. parallelogram, rectangle, rhombus, square   **29.** 105°

9.6 Skill Practice (pp. 487–488)   1. C   **3.** B   **5.** octagon; yes   **7.** yes; An equilateral triangle has sides that are all equal and angle measures that are all equal.   **9.** no; An octagon can sometimes have sides that are not all equal and angle measure that are not all equal.   **11.** square; A square is a quadrilateral with all sides equal and all angles equal.   **13.** 6   **15.** 62.5 in.   **17.** 60°   **19.** 72°
21. pentagon;

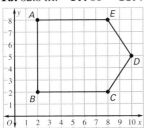

25. 1080°   **27.** 540°

9.6 Problem Solving (pp. 488–489)   29. 15 ft
31. octagon; no; 1080°   **33.** hexagon; yes; 720°
35. a. Each angle is 90°, so they all have the same measure. Because the points are equally spaced and each side has the same number of points, each side is the same length.   **b.** no; In a regular triangle, each angle measure is 60°, but each triangle has one 90° angle.   **c.** octagon; no; A right triangle cannot be an equilateral triangle. So, the sides of the octagon that do not lie on the quadrilateral are not the same length of the sides that do lie on the quadrilateral.

9.7 Skill Practice (p. 492)   1. true; Their angle measures correspond, but they are different sizes.   **3.** similar

5. neither   **7.** ∠H and ∠L, ∠G and ∠M, ∠J and ∠K, $\overline{HG}$ and $\overline{LM}$, $\overline{HJ}$ and $\overline{LK}$, $\overline{GJ}$ and $\overline{MK}$ **11.** 10, 4   **13.** 90, 6.5

9.7 Problem Solving (p. 493)   15. congruent; They are the same shape and size.   **17.** similar; They are the same shape but have different sizes.   **23.** always; The corresponding sides are the same length, and the corresponding angles have the same measure.
25. never; The figures have different numbers of sides.

9.8 Skill Practice (pp. 496–497)   1. a line of symmetry   **3.** no   **5.** yes;

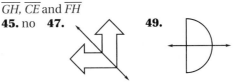

9.

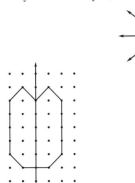

11. There are 2 lines of symmetry;

9.8 Problem Solving (pp. 497–498)   17. 1   **19.** yes; no; The fold lines are the lines of symmetry.   **21.** The image on the far left is the actual photo. *Sample answer:* I can tell by looking at the top of the flower. It curves to the left in the first photo, curves outward with symmetry in the second photo, and curves inward to a point with symmetry in the third photo.

Chapter Review (pp. 500–504)   1. angles opposite each other when two lines intersect   **3.** no; The angles do not have to be equal.   **5.** supplementary   **7.** equal;

equal   *Sample answers for 9–13.*   **9.** $\overrightarrow{AB}$ **11.** $\overleftrightarrow{CF}$

13. $\overleftrightarrow{EA}$ **15.**

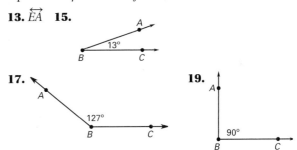

21. obtuse   **23.** acute   **25.** 70°
27. 45°; right isosceles   **29.** 50°; obtuse scalene
31. parallelogram, rhombus   **33.** parallelogram, rhombus, rectangle, square   **35.** The quadrilateral has equal angle measures but not side lengths. The quadrilateral is a rectangle but is not regular.   **37.** The sides of the hexagon and the angle measures are equal, so the hexagon is regular.   **39.** 3   **41.** 8   **43.** congruent; ∠C and ∠F, ∠D and ∠G, ∠E and ∠H, $\overline{CD}$ and $\overline{FG}$, $\overline{DE}$ and $\overline{GH}$, $\overline{CE}$ and $\overline{FH}$
45. no   **47.**   **49.**

Chapter 10

10.1 Skill Practice (p. 516)   1. base; height   **3.** 84 m²
5. 30 in.²   **9.** $6\frac{3}{4}$ km   **11.** $8\frac{1}{3}$ mm   **15.** 260 in.²

10.1 Problem Solving (p. 517)   21. 150,920 km²; high estimate; metric ruler; The entire state is within the outlined parallelogram.   **23.** high estimate; You do not want to run out of paint.

10.2 Skill Practice (pp. 520–521)   1. height; base
3. side   **5.** 42.5 cm²   **7.** 30 m²   **9.** 24 cm²   **11.** 675 in.²
13. $h = 5$ in.   **15.** $b = 10.2$ cm   **17.** $h = 6$ mi

19. The height must be perpendicular to the base;

21. 10 m²; 40 m²; The area quadrupled. **23.** The second triangle has twice the area. The second triangle has three times the area. The second triangle has four times the area. The area of the second triangle will increase as many times as the length of the base does.

10.2 Problem Solving (pp. 521 – 522) 27. $\frac{3}{14}$ **29.** 18 in.; The base of the triangle is 24 in., $\frac{1}{2} \cdot 24 \cdot h = 216$. $12 \cdot h = 216$. $h = 18$ in.

10.3 Skill Practice (pp. 527 – 528) 1. diameter **3.** radius **5.** 72 ft **7.** 9 m **11.** 37.68 yd; 3.14; 12 is not compatible with $\frac{22}{7}$. **13.** 132 km; $\frac{22}{7}$; 21 is compatible with $\frac{22}{7}$. **15.** 220 yd; $\frac{22}{7}$; 70 is compatible with $\frac{22}{7}$. **17.** 37.68 in.; 3.14; 12 is not compatible with $\frac{22}{7}$. **19.** 125.6 ft

21. 20.56 m **23.** Radius: 3.5 km, Diameter: 7 km; 3.14; 3.14 divides into 21.98 evenly.

10.3 Problem Solving (pp. 528 – 529) 25. 9.42 in.

10.3 Technology Activity (p. 530) 1. 38 ft **3.** 1071 cm **5.** 94 km **7.** 5 m **9.** 15,978 km

10.4 Skill Practice (pp. 534 – 535) 1. area **3.** 452 ft² **5.** 254 m² **7.** 227 ft² **9.** 10 ft² **11.** 55 yd² **15.** 2.6 m² **17.** 20 in.² **19.** 141 yd² **21.** 4 : 1 **23.** 100 : 1 **25.** 1 : 4 **27.** 1 : 64

10.4 Problem Solving (pp. 535 – 537) 31. 1017 mi²

37. 2160 **39.** $55\frac{5}{6}$%;

Animal Placements

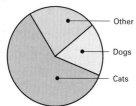

41. 200.96 mi² **43.** 9.42 in.²

10.4 Extension (p. 539) 1. A good drawing will include all necessary arcs and labels shown in Examples 1 and 3.
3.

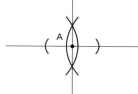

10.5 Skill Practice (p. 543) 1. A solid is a 3-dimensional figure that encloses part of space. **3.** yes; cylinder **5.** yes; cone **7.** pentagonal prism; 7, 15, 10 **9.** octagonal prism; 10, 24, 16 **15.** edges **17.** faces

10.5 Problem Solving (p. 544) 21. c. cone **23.** triangular prism; 5, 9, 6 **27.** false; A cylinder must have circles for bases. **29.** false; Opposite faces in a pentagonal prism are not parallel.

10.6 Skill Practice (pp. 547 – 548) 1. surface area **3.** 192 m² **5.** 148 ft² **7.** 937.5 in.² **9.** 222 in.² **11.** 196.8 cm² **13.** 3480 in.²;

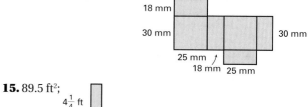

15. 89.5 ft²;

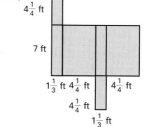

17. Only 3 faces had areas found; 236 square units **19.** 156 ft²

10.6 Problem Solving (pp. 548 – 549) 23. a. Two faces have area 26 in.², two have area 18 in.², and two have area 117 in.² **b.** bottom of the cake **c.** 205 in.²

29. $S = 6s^2$;

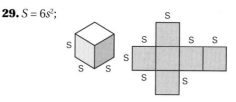

31. The figures in C and D have different surface areas: C is 40 units² and D is 30 units². A and B are both 38 units²;

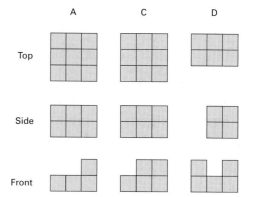

10.7 Skill Practice (p. 552) 1. volume **3.** 8000 cm³ **5.** 330 in³ **7.** 323.4375 mm³ **9.** Volume is the product of the dimensions, not the sum; 420 ft³ **11.** $h = 2.5$ ft **13.** $l = 20$ m **15.** 120 m³ **17.** 960 m³

10.7 Problem Solving (pp. 553 – 554) 23. a. 1040 cm³ **b.** 455 cm³ **c.** 585 cm³ **25.** $15h$ **31.** They are the same. The base is a rectangle, and the area of a rectangle is length times width.

10.7 Extension (p. 557) **1.** 2100 g or 2.1 kg **5.** elephant: truck scale, because the weight is in the tons; letter: kitchen scale, because the weight is in ounces; suitcase: bathroom scale, because the weight is in the tens of pounds.

Chapter Review (pp. 559 – 562) **1.** false; The circumference of a circle is measured in units. **3.** false; The distance from the center of a circle to any point on the circle is called the radius. **5.** circle **7.** volume **9.** 372 ft² **11.** 240 m² **13.** 520 ft² **15.** 109.9 in. **17.** 141.3 ft **19.** 37.68 m **21.** 7850 cm² **23.** 6936.26 m² **25.** hexagonal prism; 8, 18, 12 **27.** 105 m³

Chapter 11

11.1 Skill Practice (pp. 575 – 576) **1.** opposites **3.** −6 **5.** 5 **7.** −2 **9.** −4 **11.** 11 **13.** −13 **15.** < **17.** > **19.** > **21.** < **23.** −8, −5, −2, 6, 10 **25.** −3, −2, 6, 7, 8 **27.** −8, −1, 0, 1, 5 **29.** −67, −24, −4, 2, 40 **31.** −39, −16, 25, 47, 59 **33.** B; −2 and 1 are not opposites. **35.** always; All negatives are less than zero. **37.** sometimes; The opposite of −7 is 7, but the opposite of −12 is 12. **41.** $-3\frac{1}{3}$, $-2\frac{1}{3}$, $-\frac{1}{3}$

11.1 Problem Solving (pp. 576 – 577) **43.** −12, −25; the second diver **45.** In-Line Skates: −10, Helmets: −5, Knee Pads: −4 **47. a.** TRAP;

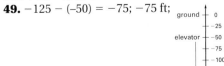

b. PART; **49.** 10°F with a 25 mi/h wind **51. a.**

b. *Sample answer:* The integers decrease by 4. **c.** −5, −9

11.2 Skill Practice (pp. 581 – 582) **1.** 5 **3.** 35 **5.** 3, 4, greater absolute value **7.** −3 **9.** −8 **11.** 5 **13.** −6 **17.** −10 **19.** −6 **21.** 0 **23.** 16 **25.** 7 **27.** −23 **29.** 0 **31.** −1 **33.** 6 **35.** negative; −700 **37.** positive; 300 **39.** negative; −800 **41.** sometimes; If the negative has the larger absolute value, the sum is negative. If the negative has a smaller absolute value, the sum is positive. **43.** 3 **45.** 8 **47.** 0

11.2 Problem Solving (pp. 582 – 583) **51.** behind **55.** 25 − 40 + 10; −5 **57. a.** 4, −3, 0, −2 **b.** 1 second less

11.3 Skill Practice (pp. 588 – 589) **1.** opposite **3.** −3 **5.** 1 **7.** −4 **9.** 0 **11.** The arrow moves 6 points to the left instead of 6 points to the right to subtract (−6). If you start at 4 on the number line and move 6 units to the right, you end up on 10. **13.** −2 **15.** −17 **17.** 8 **19.** 23 **21.** 10 **23.** −9 **25.** 0 **27.** 1 **29.** −4 **31.** 11 **33.** > **35.** < **37.** > **41.** −3 **43.** −7

11.3 Problem Solving (pp. 589 – 590) **45. a.** 5 − (−13) **b.** 5 + 13 **c.** 18°F **49.** −125 − (−50) = −75; −75 ft;

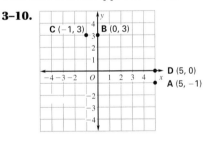

11.4 Skill Practice (pp. 594 – 595) **1.** positive **3.** 24 **5.** −35 **7.** 18 **9.** 96 **11.** 220 **13.** −900 **15.** 24 **17.** −60 **19.** The product of two negatives is always positive; 12 **21.** −42 **23.** 6 **25.** 100 **27.** −120 **29.** −20; −160; multiply by 2 **31.** −24; −60; subtract 12 or add −12 **33.** always **35.** never **37.** −6 **39.** −3 **41.** 4 **43.** 9 **45.** 7, −7 **47.** 20, −20 **49.** 8, −8

11.4 Problem Solving (pp. 595 – 596) **55.** *Sample answer:* 3(8) and −5(−3) have a positive product. **59. a.** 5(−3); −15 **b.** (−3) + (−3) + (−3) + (−3) + (−3) **c.** −3 is being added;

5 times. **61.** when either *a* or *b* is negative and the other is positive; A positive times a negative is negative. The opposite of a negative is positive.

11.5 Skill Practice (pp. 599 – 600) **1.** positive **3.** ? × (−2) = 6; −3 **5.** ? × (−3) = −21; 7 **7.** ? × 6 = −30; −5 **9.** The quotient of two negatives is positive; 6 **11.** 0 **13.** −3 **15.** −6 **17.** 4 **21.** −4 **23.** 0 **25.** 13 **27.** 15 **29.** 28 **31.** −61 **33.** −4 **35.** −3 **37.** 27 **39.** −11 **41.** 0; 0 divided by a negative is 0. **43.** negative; A negative divided by a positive is negative. **45.** $\frac{17}{8}$ **47.** $\frac{-8}{3}$ **49.** $\frac{1}{2500}$ **51.** $\frac{-100}{3}$

11.5 Problem Solving (pp. 600 – 601) **53.** 77°; 120°; low **55.** C **61.** *Sample answer:* −25, −20, −15, −5, 20, 15; The sum of the integers must be −30.

11.5 Technology Activity (p. 602) **1.** 965 **3.** 48 **5.** −18 **7.** −430 m **9.** 10 min

11.6 Skill Practice (pp. 605 – 606) **1.** false

3–10.

3. Quadrant IV **5.** Quadrant II **7.** Quadrant I **9.** negative *y*-axis **11.** (−3, 2) **13.** (2, 0) **15.** (4, −3) **19.** *A* was translated 4 units to the right and up 1 instead of down 1. *B* should be at (6,0). **21.** *Q*(1, 0), *R*(1, −6), *S*(11, −6);

25. yes; 4 right and 4 down

11.6 Problem Solving (pp. 606 – 607) **31.** no; The figures are congruent. **35.** $(x + a, y - b)$

11.7 Skill Practice (pp. 610 – 611) **1.** A reflection is flipped and a rotation is turned. **3.** no; The image has been rotated, not flipped. **5.** yes; x-axis **7.** The triangles are not congruent;

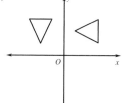

9. translation **11.** translation **13.** rotation **15.** **19.** translation

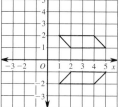

21. reflection

23. rotation;

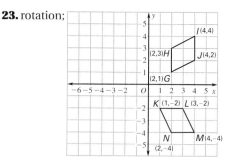

11.7 Problem Solving (pp. 611 – 613) **25.** B is a reflection, A is a rotation. **29.** reflection and rotation **31.** reflection, rotation **33.** The image and the original figure are the same. **35.** translation; Two reflections about parallel lines result in a translation;

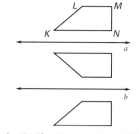

11.7 Extension (p. 615) **1.** Rotation of 180° of the midpoint of 1 side and translate the parallelogram; **3.**

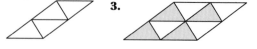

Chapter Review (pp. 617 – 620) **1.** The figures must still be congruent and have the same orientation. **3.** absolute value **5.** reflection **7.** 25 **9.** −3

11. < **13.** > **15.** < **17.** > **19.** −13, −8, −6, 0, 6 **21.** −12, −11, −3, 3, 5 **23.** −14, −8, −4, −3, 6 **25.** −4 **27.** 1 **29.** 3 **31.** −10 **33.** −15 **35.** 1 **37.** −5 **39.** −18 **41.** 24 **43.** 20 **45.** −8 **47.** 20 **49.** −56 **51.** −63 **53.** −33 **55.** 24 **57.** 50 **59.** −320 **61.** −7 **63.** −4 **65.** 4 **67.** 5 **69.** −2 **71.** −4 **73.** $R(−6, 6)$, $S(−2, 5)$, $T(−5, 2)$; **75.** translation

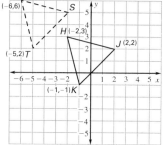

Chapter 12

12.1 Skill Practice (p. 631) **1.** subtraction **3.** $x \div 9$ **5.** $x − 16$ **7.** $20x$ **11.** $6t = 42$ **13.** $t − 4 = 26$ **15.** $9 + q = 15$ **17.** $50 \div w = 10$ **19.** Miguel used multiplication instead of division; $x \div 6$. *Sample answers for 20–23.*

25. $2 + \dfrac{x}{5}$ **27.** *Sample answer:* $\left(2 + \dfrac{x}{3}\right)(y − 4)$

12.1 Problem Solving (p. 632) **29.** C **31.** D **33.** $38p = 95$

12.1 Extension (pp. 633 – 634) **1.** $5x$ **3.** $7x + 6$ **5.** $2x + 4$ **7.** $6x + 3$ **9.** $3x + 1$ **11.** $8x + 6$ **13.** $15x$ **15.** $6x + 9$ **17.** $6x + 1$

12.2 Skill Practice (p. 638) **1.** yes **3.** no **5.** 2 **7.** 0 **9.** 7 **11.** 0 **13.** 5 **15.** 16 **17.** 13 **19.** 28 *23–31. Methods may vary.* **23.** 6 **25.** 2.7 **27.** 6.2 **29.** 4.8 **31.** $4\dfrac{5}{6}$ **33.** 15 **35.** 8.4 **37.** 13 **39.** −1

12.2 Problem Solving (p. 639) **45.** $10 + q = 25$; 15

12.3 Skill Practice (p. 642) **1.** variable **3.** 15 **5.** 9 **7.** 22 **9.** 18 **11.** 34 **13.** 53 **15.** 15.2 **17.** $3\dfrac{1}{2}$ **19.** $6\dfrac{5}{12}$ **23.** $x − 5 = 25$; 30 **25.** $b − 11 = 24$; 35 **27.** $x − 500 = 3271$; 500 will be added to both sides and $500 > 50$. **29.** $x − 368 = 532$; 368 will be added to both sides in both equations; $532 > 475$.

12.3 Problem Solving (p. 643) **37.** $b − 3 − 11 = 21$; 35; your cousin made ten bookmarks and the amount of time it took to sell them

12.4 Skill Practice (pp. 648 – 649) **1.** division **3.** 5; 5; 2 **5.** 9; 9; 36 **7.** 8 **9.** 0 **11.** 5.6 **13.** 1.44 **15.** 120 **17.** 90 **19.** 20 **21.** 10.8 **25.** $5x = 105$; 21 **27.** $11b = 44$; 4 **29.** add **31.** divide **33.** subtract **35.** subtract then divide **37.** subtract then multiply **39.** 2 **41.** 4 **43.** 3

12.4 Problem Solving (pp. 649 – 650) **45.** $8x = 14$; $1.75 **47.** 10 sec **53.** About 3.8 million people ride every day compared to 4.5 million every weekday. This is about 0.7 million less. **55.** $2x + 19.95 + 9.95 = 40 − 0.2$; $4.95

12.4 Extension (pp. 651 – 652) **1.** $2x > 275$

3. $x \le 7$;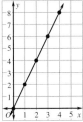
(number line: −1 0 1 2 3 4 5 6 7 8, closed dot at 7)

5. $x < 12$;
(number line: 0 2 4 6 8 10 12 14, open dot at 12)

7. $x \le 2$;
(number line: −2 −1 0 1 2 3 4, closed dot at 2)

9. $x > 6$;
(number line: −1 0 1 2 3 4 5 6 7 8, open dot at 6)

12.5 Skill Practice (pp. 656 – 657) **1.** input; output

3.

Input, x	3	6	9	12	15
Output, y	13	16	19	22	25

5.

Input, x	3	6	9	12	15
Output, y	1	2	3	4	5

7.

Input, x	3	6	9	12	15
Output, y	19	43	67	91	115

9.

Input, x	3	6	9	12	15
Output, y	17	14	11	8	5

11. $t = n + 15$ **13.** $t = \dfrac{g}{10}$

15. $p = 5n$

n	1	2	3	4
p	5	10	15	20

Sample tables for 17–19.

17. $p = 4c$

c	1	2	3	4
p	4	8	12	16

19. $y = \dfrac{f}{3}$

f	3	6	9	12
y	1	2	3	4

21.

p	10	15	20	25	35
q	16	24	32	40	56

25. $r = 4n - 2$

n	1	2	3	4
r	2	6	10	14

12.5 Problem Solving (pp. 658 – 659)

27.

C	0	5	10	15	20	25
F	32	41	50	59	68	77

33.

Time	9:00	10:30	11:00	1:00	2:00	6:00
Time Elapsed, t	0	90	120	240	300	540
Miles Driven, d	0	75	100	200	250	450

$d = \dfrac{5}{6}t$

35. $t = 0.05c$; Divide the difference between after taxes and before taxes by before taxes to find the percent of tax as a decimal.

12.6 Skill Practice (pp. 662 – 663) **1.** linear

3. 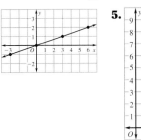   **5.**

7. The x values were graphed as y values, and the y values were graphed as x values.
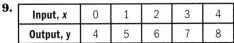

9.

Input, x	0	1	2	3	4
Output, y	4	5	6	7	8

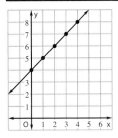

11.

Input, x	0	1	2	3	4
Output, y	7	6	5	4	3

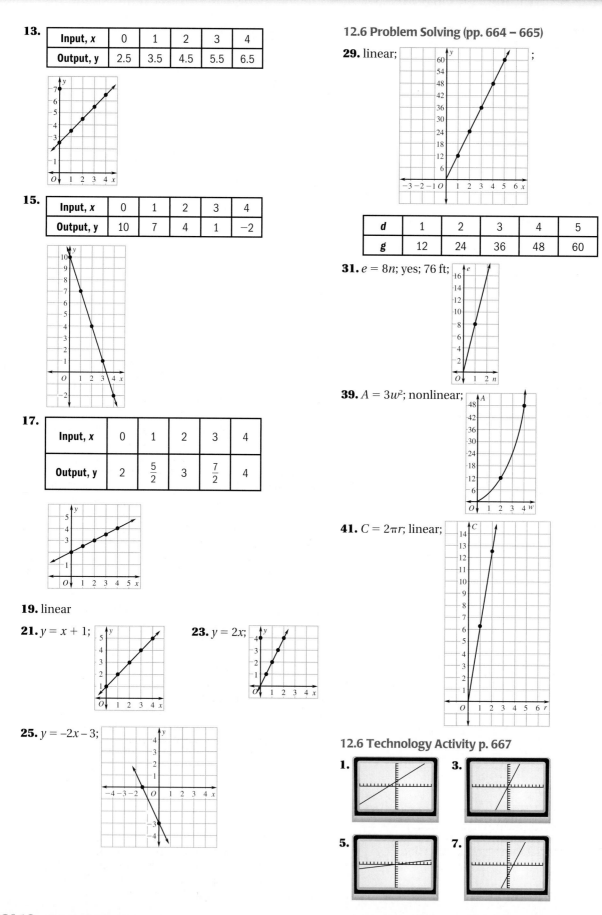

13.

Input, x	0	1	2	3	4
Output, y	2.5	3.5	4.5	5.5	6.5

15.

Input, x	0	1	2	3	4
Output, y	10	7	4	1	−2

17.

Input, x	0	1	2	3	4
Output, y	2	$\frac{5}{2}$	3	$\frac{7}{2}$	4

19. linear

21. $y = x + 1$;

23. $y = 2x$;

25. $y = -2x - 3$;

12.6 Problem Solving (pp. 664 – 665)

29. linear; ;

d	1	2	3	4	5
g	12	24	36	48	60

31. $e = 8n$; yes; 76 ft;

39. $A = 3w^2$; nonlinear;

41. $C = 2\pi r$; linear;

12.6 Technology Activity p. 667

1.   **3.**

5.   **7.**

9. **11.**

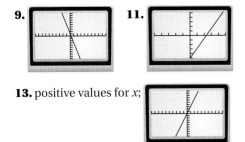

13. positive values for x;

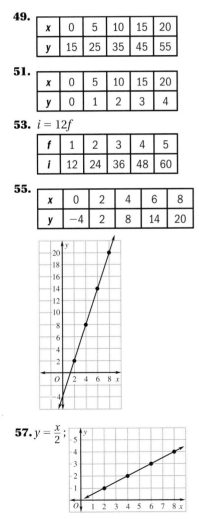

Chapter Review (pp. 669 – 672) **1.** A variable expression does not have an equal sign, while an equation does. **3.** if all of the points are on the same line **5.** In a function there can be only one output for every input value. **7.** $\frac{x}{7}$ **9.** $x - 80$ **11.** $7 - x$
13. $40 + r = 100$ **15.** $2q = 10$ **17.** $50 + k = 61$
19. 4 **21.** 20 **23.** 52 **25.** 1.9 **27.** $x + 35 = 250$; 215 yd
29. 16 **31.** 29 **33.** 43 **35.** 21.8 **37.** $x - 11 = 98$;
109 **39.** 9 **41.** 29 **43.** 35 **45.** 30 **47.** $3x = 57$; 19 ft

49.

x	0	5	10	15	20
y	15	25	35	45	55

51.

x	0	5	10	15	20
y	0	1	2	3	4

53. $i = 12f$

f	1	2	3	4	5
i	12	24	36	48	60

55.

x	0	2	4	6	8
y	−4	2	8	14	20

57. $y = \frac{x}{2}$;

59. linear; All of the points are on the same line.

Chapter 13

13.1 Skill Practice (pp. 685 – 686) **1.** A, U, E **3.** 1, 2, 3, 6 **5.** 0 **7.** $\frac{1}{2}$ **9.** likely **11.** impossible
13. $\frac{1}{8}$; unlikely **15.** 1, certain **17** 20 **21.** $\frac{3}{4}$; Randomly choose a vowel; $\frac{1}{4}$ **23.** $1 : 5$ **25.** $1 : 2$

13.1 Problem Solving (pp. 686 – 687) **29.** $\frac{5}{6}$

13.1 Technology Activity (p. 688) **1.** A good answer should be close to $\frac{1}{2}$. **3.** A good answer should be close to $\frac{1}{6}$.

13.1 Extension (p. 690) **1.** {1, 2, 3, 4, 5, 6, 8}; {4} **3.** {6, 7, 8, 9, 10}; empty set **5.** $\frac{13}{25}, \frac{9}{25}, \frac{17}{25}, \frac{1}{5}$ **7.** $\frac{1}{2}, \frac{3}{8}, \frac{9}{16}, \frac{5}{16}$

13.2 Skill Practice (pp. 693 – 694) **1.** combination **3.** 4 ways are AB, AC, BA, BC;

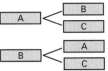

5. Dallas in June, Dallas in July, Dallas in August, New York in June, New York in July, New York in August, Miami in June, Miami in July, Miami in August **7.** Boston and Miami, Boston and Dallas, Boston and San Francisco, Boston and Chicago, Boston and New York, Miami and Dallas, Miami and San Francisco, Miami and Chicago, Miami and New York, Dallas and San Francisco, Dallas and Chicago, Dallas and New York, San Francisco and Chicago, San Francisco and New York, Chicago and New York **9.** baseball, football and hockey; baseball, football and basketball; baseball, football and tennis; baseball, football and soccer; baseball, hockey and basketball; baseball, hockey and tennis; baseball, hockey and soccer; baseball, basketball and tennis; baseball, basketball and soccer; baseball, tennis and soccer; football, hockey and basketball; football, hockey and tennis; football, hockey and soccer; football, basketball and tennis; football, basketball and soccer; football, tennis and soccer; hockey, basketball and tennis; hockey, basketball and soccer; hockey, tennis and soccer; basketball, tennis and soccer **11.** Carrie, Miguel and Ralph; Carrie, Ralph and Miguel; Miguel, Carrie and Ralph; Miguel, Ralph and Carrie; Ralph, Carrie and Miguel, Ralph, Miguel and Carrie **13.** rake, plant, weed, mow; rake, plant, mow, weed; rake, weed, plant, mow; rake, weed, mow, plant; rake, mow, plant, weed; rake, mow, weed, plant; plant, rake, weed, mow; plant, rake, mow, weed; plant, weed, rake, mow; plant, weed, mow, rake; plant, mow, rake, weed; plant, mow, weed, rake; mow, plant, weed, rake; mow, plant, rake weed; mow, weed, plant, rake; mow, weed, rake, plant; mow, rake, weed, plant; mow, rake, plant, weed; weed, plant, mow, rake; weed, plant, rake, mow; weed, mow, plant, rake; weed, mow, rake, plant; weed, rake, plant, mow; weed, rake, mow, plant **15.** golf and horseback riding; golf and snorkeling; golf and tennis, golf and hiking, golf and sailing, horseback

riding and snorkeling, horseback riding and tennis, horseback riding and hiking, horseback riding and sailing, snorkeling and tennis, snorkeling and hiking, snorkeling and sailing, tennis and hiking, tennis and sailing, hiking and sailing; organized list; It is easy to list the possibilities. **17.** Bill and Justin; Bill and Camille; Bill and Katie; Bill and Joey; Justin and Bill, Justin and Camille, Justin and Katie; Justin and Joey; Camille and Bill; Camille and Justin; Camille and Katie; Camille and Joey; Katie and Bill; Katie and Justin; Katie and Camille; Katie and Joey; Joey and Bill, Joey and Justin; Joey and Camille; Joey and Katie; organized list; The list of first and second place is easy to make.

13.2 Problem Solving (pp. 694 – 695)
21. combination; blue and green, blue and yellow, blue and red, blue and purple, green and yellow, green and red, green and purple, yellow and red, yellow and purple, red and purple

13.3 Skill Practice (pp. 698 – 699)
1. yes; Since the marble is returned, the probability of the events does not change. **3.** $\frac{1}{6}$ **5.** $\frac{1}{2}$ **7.** The sections are not all the same size; $\frac{2}{3}$ **9.** $\frac{1}{6}$ **11.** $\frac{1}{3}$ **15.** $\frac{3}{8}$ **17.** $\frac{7}{8}$

13.3 Problem Solving (pp. 699 – 700)
21. right, right; right, wrong; wrong, right; wrong, wrong; $\frac{1}{4}$ **23.** $\frac{1}{18}$ **25.** $\frac{1}{25}$

13.3 Extension (p. 703)
1. The experimental probability should be close to the theoretical probability of $\frac{2}{9}$.
3. The experimental probability should be close to the theoretical probability of $\frac{1}{18}$.

13.4 Skill Practice (p. 706)
1. The scale makes a graph more or less dramatic. **3.** less; less; The broken graph makes the graph appear different.

7.
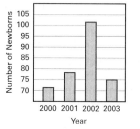
Grizzly Bears Born in Yellowstone

13.4 Problem Solving (pp. 707 – 708)
11. twice as many **13.** data values; Data values show more storms, which means more risk. **15.** no; 88 does not take into account that there were 6 seasons with wins below 88, including two in the 50s. **19. a.** no; Most are over $115,000. **b.** $115,000 makes homes seem more affordable. **c.** median; You know half are higher and half are lower. **21.**

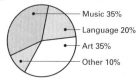
Favorite Electives
Music 35%
Language 20%
Art 35%
Other 10%

13.5 Skill Practice (p. 711)
1. stems: 1, 2, 3, 4, 5; leaves: 2, 4, 7, 1, 9, 5, 6, 8, 9, 1, 2, 2, 3, 3, 4, 4, 4, 4, 5, 5

3.

1	5 6 8 8 8
2	1 4 5 5 8
3	1 2 2
4	1

Key: 1 | 5 = 15

5.

0	5 7 9
1	5 6
2	
3	0 3 5 5 8
4	1 9
5	1 2 5

Key: 0 | 5 = 5

7. The stem 3 was omitted;

1	5 9
2	0 2
3	
4	3 3 7

11. 2, 1.1, 0.5 and 1.1 and 3.9

13.5 Problem Solving (pp. 712 – 713)
15. 80.7$\overline{3}$, 73, 73, 62 **17.** 7; The greatest number of Wimbledon doubles finals was in the interval 70–79 minutes. **23.** 6.1, 6.0, 4.8 **25.** Most presidents were in their 50s when they took office;

4	2 3 6
5	1 1 1 2 4 5 5 6 6
6	0 1 2 4 9

Key: 4 | 2 = 42

13.6 Skill Practice (p. 716)
1. 13, 10, 18, 2, 24
3.

0 5 10 15 20 25 30 35
4 7.5 11 25.5 30

5.

0 5 10 15 20 25 30 35 40 45
3 11 21 36 42

9. 192

11.
0, 2, 3, 3, 6, 9, 12, 14, 15, 17, 20, 21, 21, 23, 28

2 4 6 8 10 12 14 16 18 20 22 24 26 28
0 3 14 21 28

13.6 Problem Solving (pp. 717 – 718)
15. a.

90 110 130 150 170 190
93 105 131 175 200   1970s
99 123 132.5 158 188   1980s
118 122 151 183 197   1990s

b. 70s: 131, 107; 80s: 132.5, 89; 90s: 151, 79 **c.** The 70s and 80s have close medians, but the data is more spread out in the 70s. The median is highest in the 90s, and the data also has the smallest range, showing the most consistency. The range was progressively decreasing from the 70s to the 90s. **17.** 1968–2002; The plot for 1968–2002 is more to the left on the number line and is more condensed than the other plot. **19.** 75% **21.** 296

13.7 Skill Practice (p. 721) **1.** C **3.** B **5.** D **7.** The data should be displayed as a line plot to show frequency;

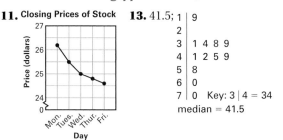

13.7 Problem Solving (pp. 722 – 723)

11. Closing Prices of Stock

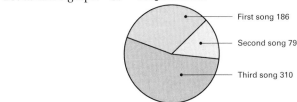

13. 41.5;

1	9
2	
3	1 4 8 9
4	1 2 5 9
5	8
6	0
7	0

Key: 3 | 4 = 34
median = 41.5

15. a. circle graph **b.**

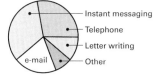

Song Preference

First song 186
Second song 79
Third song 310

17. circle graph because you need to visualize the whole;

Favorite Form of Communication

Instant messaging
Telephone
Letter writing
e-mail
Other

Chapter Review (pp. 725 – 728) **1.** complementary **3.** permutation **5.** lower extreme; upper extreme **7.** 0; you do not roll a 10; 1 **9.** 0; you do not roll a number that is not a multiple of 20; 1

11. 24 **13.** $\frac{1}{4}$ **15.** 48; 50; 50

17. 107; 91; 112; 81; 128

19.

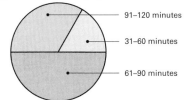

Time Spent Studying

91–120 minutes
31–60 minutes
61–90 minutes

Skills Review Handbook

Whole Number Place Value (p. 737) **1.** tens' place; $(5 \times 1000) + (8 \times 100) + (9 \times 10)$; five thousand eight hundred ninety **3.** ones' place $(9 \times 100,000) + (6 \times 1000) + (2 \times 100) + (1 \times 1)$; nine hundred six thousand, two hundred one **5.** 105,300 **7.** 42,600

Ordering Whole Numbers (p. 738) **1.** 0, 3, 8, 10, 11 **3.** 78, 79, 85, 87, 90 **5.** 508, 510, 512, 518, 521 **7.** 207 > 148 **9.** 3465 < 3492 **11.** 21,539 > 9847

Rounding Whole Numbers (p. 739) **1.** 90 **3.** 200 **5.** 4280 **7.** 11,000 **9.** 144,000

Number Fact Families (p. 740) **1.** 5; 5; 5; 14 **3.** 8; 4; 4; 8 **5.** $15 - 8 = 7$ or $15 - 7 = 8$

Addition and Subtraction on a Number Line (p. 741) **1.** 13 **3.** 11 **5.** 13 **7.** 20 **9.** 6 **11.** 8 **13.** 8 **15.** 16

Addition and Subtraction of Whole Numbers (p. 742) **1.** 71 **3.** 240 **5.** 400 **7.** 1412 **9.** 17 **11.** 219 **13.** 149 **15.** 1179

Multiplication of Whole Numbers (p. 743) **1.** 3280 **3.** 962 **5.** 6076 **7.** 60,450 **9.** 147,038 **11.** 46,570 **13.** 12,300 **15.** 23,190,000

Division of Whole Numbers (p. 744) **1.** 142 **3.** 54 **5.** 405 **7.** 58 **9.** 13 R7 **11.** 24 R57

Estimating Sums (p. 745) *1–9. Estimates may vary.* **1.** 1300 **3.** 1800 **5.** 10,000 **7.** 160 **9.** 1200

Estimating Differences (p. 746) **1.** 700; 900 **3.** 400; 600 **5.** 300; 500 **7.** 400; 600 **9.** 0; 2000 **11.** 3000; 5000 **13.** 4000; 6000 **15.** 1000; 3000

Estimating Products (p. 747) **1.** 800; 1500 **3.** 2100; 3200 **5.** 3000; 8000 **7.** 12,000; 21,000 **9.** 280,000; 400,000 **11.** 60,000; 140,000 **13.** 10,500 **15.** 52,800 **17.** 14,000 **19.** 45,000 **21.** 630,000 **23.** 150,000 **25.** 90,000 **27.** 736,100

Estimating Quotients (p. 748) **1.** 50; 60 **3.** 60; 70 **5.** 30; 40 **7.** 200; 300 **9.** 300; 400 **11.** 400; 500 **13.** 1100; 1200 **15.** 800; 900 **17.** 2 **19.** 10 **21.** 11 **23.** 7 **25.** 100 **27.** 80

Solving Problems Using Addition and Subtraction (p. 749) **1.** $9 **3.** 26 items **5.** $7

Solving Problems Using Multiplication and Division (p. 750) **1.** 60 folders **3.** 4 boxes **5.** $20

Operations with Money (p. 751) **1.** $2.02 **3.** $58.08

Adding and Subtracting Decimals (p. 752) **1.** 41.4 **3.** 143 **5.** 11.29 **7.** 20.13 **9.** 57.22 **11.** 16.5 **13.** 6.88 **15.** 5.76 **17.** 19.87

Modeling Fractions (p. 753) **1.** $\frac{3}{4}$ **3.** $\frac{1}{2}$ **5.** $\frac{5}{14}$ **7.** $\frac{4}{9}$ **9.** $\frac{5}{9}$ **11.** $\frac{3}{10}$

Units of Time (p. 754) **1.** 240 **3.** 4 **5.** 12 **7.** 52 **9.** 2; 2 **11.** 1; 16

Perimeter and Area (p. 755) **1.** 10 in. **3.** 15 cm **5.** 21 square units

Venn Diagrams and Logical Reasoning (p. 756)

1.

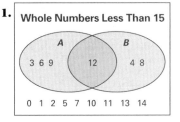

3–5. Explanations may vary. **3.** Sometimes; 12 is in both set *A* and set *B*, but 6, for example, is only in set *A*. **5.** Never; set *C* consists of numbers less than 15.

Reading Bar Graphs (p. 757) **1.** 20 students **3.** period 2
5. 7 more students **7.** periods 2 and 3

Reading Line Graphs (p. 758) **1.** Thursday **3.** 8 in.
5. decrease **7.** Monday

Reading a Pictograph (p. 759) **1.** brown; 14 students
3. 8 pictures **5.** about 4 pictures **7.** Friday

Making a Pictograph (p. 760)

1.
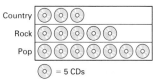
CDs Sold in One Day
Country
Rock
Pop
= 5 CDs

Problem Solving Handbook

Make a Model (p. 771) **1.** 72 in. by 48 in. **3.** 16

Draw a Diagram (p. 771) **5.** 48 **7.** 9 steps

Guess, Check, and Revise (p. 772) **9.** 12 and 9
11. hopped 16 ft, stepped 12 ft, jumped 14 ft **13.** 12 and 14
15. Starting at any corner and moving clockwise, the
numbers are: 4, 2, 6, 1, 5, and 3.

Work Backward (p. 772) **17.** $13 **19.** 10 years

Make a List or Table (p. 773) **21.** 34 ft; 16 ft **23.** 6

Look for a Pattern (pp. 773 – 774) **25.** the number of
squares increases by 2;

27. $2.25 **29.** $15

Break Into Parts (p. 774) **31.** $588 **33.** $121

Solve a Simpler Problem (pp. 774 – 775) **35.** 90
37. $4.55 **39.** $5050

Use a Venn Diagram (p. 775) **41.** 3 **43.** 14

Act It Out (p. 775) **45.** 30 **47.** $7

Extra Practice

Chapter 1 (p. 776) **1.** 203 **3.** 51 **5.** 170 **7.** 39 **9.** add
4 to the previous number; 21, 25 **11.** divide the previous
number by 2; 100, 50 *13–19. Estimates may vary.* **13.** 370
15. 8 **17.** 760 **19.** 1500 **21.** 343 **23.** 8 **25.** 14
27. 21 **29.** 6 **31.** 11 **33.** 27 **35.** 11 **37.** 14 **39.** 7
41. 22 years old **43.** 3 **45.** 2 **47.** 4 **49.** 0

Chapter 2 (p. 777) **1.** 6 cm **3.** miles, kilometers **5.** 18
in.; 18 in.^{2} **7.** 240 km **9.** 840 km

11.

Heights	Tally	Frequency
4	II	2
5	IIII I	6
6	IIII	4
7		0
8	I	1

13.
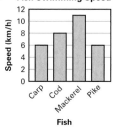
Fish Swimming Speed

14–18.
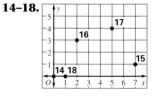

19.
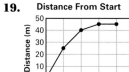
Distance From Start

21. 120 sesame bagels **23.** 33, 31, no mode, 27; mean; it
is in the middle of the data.

Chapter 3 (p. 778) **1.** 50.42 **3.** eight thousandths
5. one and eleven hundredths **7.** seven and two
hundred seventy-five ten-thousandths **9.** 0.15 meter
11. < **13.** > **15.** = **17.** 2.01, 2.12, 2.3 **19.** 13.3
21. 0.7 **23.** 0.009 **25.** 2 **27.** 19 **29.** 32 **31.** 14
33. 10.81 **35.** 2.14 **37.** 2.45 **39.** 1.84

Chapter 4 (p. 779) **1.** 32.52 **3.** 125.18 **5.** 67.2 **7.** 203
9. 2.08 **11.** 5.0307 **13.** 3.2 **15.** 3.625 **17.** 1.5 **19.** 1.1
21. 205 **23.** 1.798 **25.** 0.935 **27.** 93.8 **29.** 1.2
31. 5 **33.** 330 **35.** 0.9 **37.** kilograms **39.** kiloliters
41. liters **43.** 480,000 **45.** 67,400 **47.** 1000 **49.** <
51. > **53.** <

Chapter 5 (p. 780) **1.** 406 is divisible by 2, but not by 3,
5, 6, 9, or 10. **3.** 534 is divisible by 2, 3, and 6, but not by
5, 9, or 10. **5.** 510 is divisible by 2, 3, 5, 6, and 10, but not
by 9. **7.** composite **9.** neither **11.** 5×19 **13.** $2^2 \times 19$
15. $5^2 \times 7$ **17.** 4 **19.** 5 **21.** $\frac{4}{10}, \frac{6}{15}$ **23.** $\frac{6}{20}, \frac{9}{30}$ **25.** yes
27. no; $\frac{1}{14}$ **29.** no; $\frac{4}{5}$ **31.** 24 **33.** 40 **35.** $\frac{4}{5}, \frac{13}{15}, \frac{9}{10}$
37. $\frac{3}{20}, \frac{2}{9}, \frac{4}{15}, \frac{2}{5}$ **39.** $\frac{35}{9}$ **41.** $\frac{17}{7}$ **43.** $2\frac{1}{6}$ **45.** $3\frac{2}{5}$ **47.** $1\frac{7}{12}$
49. $\frac{17}{8}, 2\frac{1}{4}, \frac{55}{24}, 2\frac{1}{3}$ **51.** $\frac{19}{20}$ **53.** $2\frac{2}{25}$ **55.** $\frac{129}{200}$ **57.** 1.75
59. $5.1\overline{6}$

Chapter 6 (p. 781) **1.** $\frac{1}{2}$ **3.** 0 **5.** 4 **7.** 9 **9.** $\frac{3}{4}$ **11.** $\frac{4}{15}$
13. $\frac{2}{5}$ **15.** $\frac{2}{5}$ **17.** $\frac{7}{18}$ **19.** $\frac{15}{16}$ **21.** $\frac{19}{30}$ **23.** $\frac{19}{20}$ **25.** $2\frac{2}{3}$

27. $16\frac{1}{4}$ **29.** $7\frac{4}{7}$ **31.** $\frac{1}{8}$ **33.** $1\frac{6}{13}$ **35.** $1\frac{3}{4}$ **37.** $\frac{3}{5}$ **39.** $2\frac{1}{5}$

41. 3 h 35 min **43.** 2 h 20 min 50 sec **45.** 7 h 15 min
47. 2 h 30 min **49.** 5 h 45 min **51.** 1 h 35 min
53. 8 h 15 min

Chapter 7 (p. 782) **1.** 9 **3.** 27 **5.** 6 **7.** 16 **9.** $1\frac{1}{4}$

11. $\frac{2}{27}$ **13.** $7\frac{1}{3}$ **15.** $1\frac{1}{6}$ **17.** $\frac{5}{24}$ **19.** $4\frac{2}{5}$ **21.** 3 **23.** $\frac{9}{20}$

25. $2\frac{11}{12}$ **27.** $2\frac{1}{2}$ **29.** no; *Sample answer:* Use

multiplication to find the total amount of fabric needed.

31. pounds **33.** ounces **35.** 14 **37.** 1; 9; $1\frac{9}{16}$

39. 2250 lb **41.** 6 lb **43.** 4 yd 1 ft

Chapter 8 (p. 783) **1.** 2 : 3 **3.** 1 : 5 **5.** 4 : 3 **7.** 20

9. 9 **11.** 19 cm **13.** $\frac{275 \text{ visitors}}{1 \text{ hour}}$ **15.** $\frac{200 \text{ words}}{1 \text{ page}}$ **17.** 2

19. $11\frac{1}{5}$ **21.** 20 ft by 16 ft **23.** 0.18; $\frac{9}{50}$ **25.** 0.025, $\frac{1}{40}$

27. 85% **29.** 83% **31.** 0.5% **33.** $\frac{2}{3}$, 67%, 0.76, $\frac{5}{6}$ **35.** 18

37. 56 **39.** $480

Chapter 9 (p. 784) **1.** *Sample answer:* $\overrightarrow{BC}$ and $\overrightarrow{BF}$; $\overline{BD}$

and $\overline{BA}$ **3.** $\overleftrightarrow{ED}$ and $\overleftrightarrow{DF}$ **5.** ∠AED **7.** right; obtuse;
acute; straight **9.** 60°; 100°, 80° **11.** All **13.** Some

15. triangle; no **17.** hexagon; no **19.** $\overline{XY}$ and $\overline{DE}$, $\overline{YZ}$

and $\overline{EF}$, $\overline{ZX}$ and $\overline{FD}$; ∠X and ∠D, ∠Y and ∠E, ∠Z and ∠F

21. yes; **23.** yes;

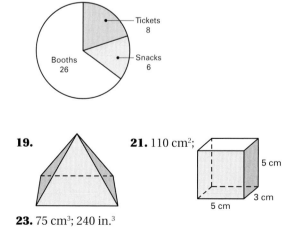

Chapter 10 (p. 785) **1.** 360 ft² **3.** 13.5 mm² **5.** 30 cm²

7. 110 cm; $\frac{22}{7}$; 35 is a multiple of 7. **9.** 44 in.; $\frac{22}{7}$; 7 is a

multiple of 7. **11.** 50.2 cm² **13.** 706.5 ft² **15.** 434 cm²

17. Spring Fundraiser Volunteers

19.

21. 110 cm²;

23. 75 cm³; 240 in.³

Chapter 11 (p. 786) **1.** −4, 18, 0 **3.** > **5.** < **7.** −3, 0,
2, 3, 5 **9.** −9, −7, −6, 8, 9 **11.** 4 **13.** −10 **15.** 0
17. −14 **19.** 16 **21.** −17 **23.** −28 **25.** −9 **27.** −40
29. 140 **31.** 32 **33.** 99 **35.** −8 **37.** 5 **39.** −3
41. −25 **43.** Quadrant I;

45. Quadrant II;

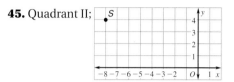

47. $D(-3, 8)$, $E(-5, 6)$, $F(-2, 3)$;

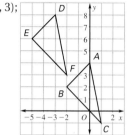

49. reflection **51.** translation

Chapter 12 (p. 787) **1.** $n + 7$ **3.** $20 - n$ **5.** $8n = 32$

7. $\frac{y}{6} = 5$ **9.** 29 **11.** 14 **13.** 16 **15.** 25 **17.** 10 **19.** 9

21. 60 **23.** 21

25.

Input, x	Output, y
4	1
8	5
12	9
16	13
20	17

27.

Input, x	Output, y
4	13
8	21
12	29
16	37
20	45

29. $c = 6p$

31. $g = \dfrac{q}{4}$;

Quarts, q	Gallons, g
2	$\dfrac{1}{2}$
4	1
6	$1\dfrac{1}{2}$
8	2

33.

Input, x	Output, y
0	-2
1	-1
2	0
3	1
4	2

35.

Input, x	Output, y
0	3
1	$3\dfrac{1}{2}$
2	4
3	$4\dfrac{1}{2}$
4	5

37. $y = \dfrac{x}{3}$;

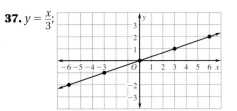

Chapter 13 (p. 788) **1.** $\dfrac{4}{7}$ **3.** 1 **5.** You do not choose a multiple of 3; $\dfrac{5}{7}$ **7.** 11, 12, 13, 14, 21, 22, 23, 24, 31, 32, 33, 34, 41, 42, 43, 44 **9.** $\dfrac{1}{4}$ **11.**

```
0 | 4 6 7 7 8 8 8 9
1 | 1 2 5 6 8 9
2 | 0 0 1 4 4 9
```
Key: 1 | 5 = 15

13. 25;

15. line graph; It shows change over time.